ÍNDICE		CONTENTS	

general editor/dirección general
Michela Clari

contributors/colaboradores
José Martín Galera, Wendy Lee, José María Ruiz Vaca

editorial coordination/coordinación editorial
Joyce Littlejohn, Marianne Davidson, Maree Airlie

series editor/colección dirigida por
Lorna Sinclair Knight

Marcas Registradas
Las marcas que creemos que constituyen marcas registradas las denominamos como tales. Sin embargo, no debe considerarse que la presencia o la ausencia de esta designación tenga que ver con la situación legal de ninguna marca.

Note on trademarks
Words which we have reason to believe constitute trademarks have been designated as such. However, neither the presence nor the absence of such designation should be regarded as affecting the legal status of any trademark.

Introducción

Estamos muy satisfechos de que hayas decidido comprar este diccionario y esperamos que lo disfrutes y que te sirva de gran ayuda ya sea en el colegio, en el trabajo, en tus vacaciones o en casa.

Esta introducción pretende darte algunas indicaciones para ayudarte a sacar el mayor provecho de este diccionario; no sólo de su extenso vocabulario, sino de toda la información que te proporciona cada entrada. Esta te ayudará a leer y comprender – y también a comunicarte y a expresarte – en inglés moderno. Este diccionario comienza con una lista de abreviaturas utilizadas en el texto y con una ilustración de los sonidos representados por los símbolos fonéticos. Al final del diccionario encontrarás una tabla de los verbos irregulares del inglés, y para terminar, una sección sobre el uso de los números y de las expresiones de tiempo.

El manejo de tu diccionario

La amplia información que te ofrece este diccionario aparece presentada en distintas tipografías, con caracteres de diversos tamaños y con distintos símbolos, abreviaturas y paréntesis. Los apartados siguientes explican las reglas y símbolos utilizados.

Entradas

Las palabras que consultas en el diccionario – las "entradas" – aparecen ordenadas alfabéticamente y en **caracteres gruesos** para una identificación más rápida. Las dos palabras que ocupan el margen superior de cada página indican la primera y la última entrada de la página en cuestión.

La información sobre el uso o la forma de determinadas entradas aparece entre paréntesis, detrás de la transcripción fonética, y generalmente en forma abreviada y en cursiva (p. ej.: *(fam)*, *(COM)*). En algunos casos se ha considerado oportuno agrupar palabras de una misma familia (**nación,** ❏ **nacionalismo; accept,** ❏ **acceptance**) bajo una misma entrada en caracteres gruesos.

Las expresiones de uso corriente en las que aparece una entrada se dan en negrita (p. ej.: **hurry:** [...] **to be in a ~**).

Símbolos fonéticos

La transcripción fonética de cada entrada inglesa (que indica su pronunciación) aparece entre corchetes, inmediatamente después de la entrada (p. ej. **knead** [ni:d]). En la página xiii encontrarás una lista de los símbolos fonéticos utilizados en este diccionario.

Traducciones

Las traducciones de las entradas aparecen en caracteres normales, y en los casos en los que existen significados o usos diferentes, éstos aparecen separados mediante un punto y coma. A menudo encontrarás también otras palabras en cursiva y entre paréntesis antes de las traducciones. Estas sugieren contextos en los que la entrada podría aparecer (p. ej.: **rough** (*voice*) o (*weather*)) o proporcionan sinónimos (p. ej.: **rough** (*violent*)).

Palabras clave

Particular relevancia reciben ciertas palabras inglesas y españolas que han sido consideradas palabras "clave" en cada lengua. Estas pueden, por ejemplo, ser de utilización muy corriente o tener distintos usos (**de, haber; get, that**). La combinación de rombos y números te permitirá distinguir las diferentes categorías gramaticales y los diferentes significados. Las indicaciones en cursiva y entre paréntesis proporcionan además importante información adicional.

Información gramatical

Las categorías gramaticales aparecen en forma abreviada y en cursiva después de la transcripción fonética de cada entrada (*vt, adv, conj*). También se indican la forma femenina y los plurales irregulares de los sustantivos del inglés (**child, -ren**).

Introduction

We are delighted that you have decided to buy this dictionary and hope you will enjoy and benefit from using it at school, at home, on holiday or at work.

This introduction gives you a few tips on how to get the most out of your dictionary – not simply from its comprehensive wordlist but also from the information provided in each entry. This will help you to read and understand modern Spanish, as well as communicate and express yourself in the language.

This dictionary begins by listing the abbreviations used in the text and illustrating the sounds shown by the phonetic symbols. You will also find Spanish verb tables, followed by a final section on numbers and time expressions.

Using your dictionary

A wealth of information is presented in the dictionary, using various typefaces, sizes of type, symbols, abbreviations and brackets. The various conventions and symbols used are explained in the following sections.

Headwords

The words you look up in a dictionary – "headwords" – are listed alphabetically. They are printed in **bold type** for rapid identification. The two headwords appearing at the top of each page indicate the first and last word dealt with on the page in question.

Information about the usage or form of certain headwords is given in brackets after the phonetic spelling. This usually appears in abbreviated form and in italics (e.g. (fam), (COMM)).

Where appropriate, words related to headwords are grouped in the same entry (**nación**, ☐ **nacionalismo**; **accept**, ☐ **acceptance**) and preceded by a white box. Common expressions in which the headword appears are shown in a different bold roman type (e.g. **cola**: [...] **hacer ~**).

Phonetic spellings

The phonetic spelling of each headword (indicating its pronunciation) is given in square brackets immediately after the headword (e.g. **cohete** [ko'ete]). A list of these symbols is given on page xi.

Translations

Headword translations are given in ordinary type and, where more than one meaning or usage exists, these are separated by a semi-colon. You will often find other words in italics in brackets before the translations. These offer suggested contexts in which the headword might appear (e.g. **grande** (*de tamaño*) or provide synonyms (e.g. **grande** (*alto*) o (*distinguido*)).

The gender of the translation also appears in *italics* immediately following the key element of the translation, except where this is a regular masculine singular noun ending in "o", or a regular feminine noun ending in "a".

"Key" words

Special status is given to certain Spanish and English words which are considered as "key" words in each language. They may, for example, occur very frequently or have several types of usage (e.g. **de, haber**; **get, that**). A combination of lozenges and numbers helps you to distinguish different parts of speech and different meanings. Further helpful information is provided in brackets and italics.

Grammatical information

Parts of speech are given in abbreviated form in italics after the phonetic spellings of headwords (e.g. *vt, adv, conj*).

Genders of Spanish nouns are indicated as follows: *nm* for a masculine and *nf* for a feminine noun. Feminine and irregular plural forms of nouns are also shown (**irlandés, esa; luz**, (*pl* **luces**)).

Abreviaturas		Abbreviations
abreviatura	*ab(b)r*	abbreviation
adjetivo, locución adjetiva	*adj*	adjective, adjectival phrase
administración	*ADMIN*	administration
adverbio, locución adverbial	*adv*	adverb, adverbial phrase
agricultura	*AGR*	agriculture
anatomía	*ANAT*	anatomy
Argentina	*ARG*	Argentina
arquitectura	*ARQ, ARCH*	architecture
el automóvil	*AUT(O)*	the motor car and motoring
aviación, viajes aéreos	*AVIAC, AVIAT*	flying, air travel
biología	*BIO(L)*	biology
botánica, flores	*BOT*	botany
inglés británico	*BRIT*	British English
Centroamérica	*CAm*	Central America
química	*CHEM*	chemistry
comercio, finanzas, banca	*COM(M)*	commerce, finance, banking
informática	*COMPUT*	computing
conjunción	*conj*	conjunction
construcción	*CONSTR*	building
compuesto	*cpd*	compound element
Cono Sur	*CS*	Southern Cone
cocina	*CULIN*	cookery
economía	*ECON*	economics
eletricidad, electrónica	*ELEC*	electricity, electronics
enseñanza, sistema escolar y universitario	*ESCOL*	schooling, schools and universities
España	*ESP*	Spain
especialmente	*esp*	especially
exclamación, interjección	*excl*	exclamation, interjection
femenino	*f*	feminine
lengua familiar (! vulgar)	*fam(!)*	colloquial usage (! particularly offensive)
ferrocarril	*FERRO*	railways
uso figurado	*fig*	figurative use

fotografía	*FOTO*	photography
(verbo inglés) del cual la	*fus*	(phrasal verb) where
partícula es inseparable		the particle is inseparable
generalmente	*gen*	generally
geografía, geología	*GEO*	geography, geology
geometría	*GEOM*	geometry
historia	*HIST*	history
uso familiar (! vulgar)	*inf(!)*	colloquial usage
		(! particularly offensive)
infinitivo	*infin*	infinitive
informática	*INFORM*	computing
invariable	*inv*	invariable
irregular	*irreg*	irregular
lo jurídico	*JUR*	law
América Latina	*LAm*	Latin America
gramática, lingüística	*LING*	grammar, linguistics
masculino	*m*	masculine
matemáticas	*MAT(H)*	mathematics
masculino/femenino	*m/f*	masculine/feminine
medicina	*MED*	medicine
México	*MÉX, MEX*	Mexico
lo militar, ejército	*MIL*	military matters
música	*MÚS, MUS*	music
substantivo, nombre	*n*	noun
navegación, náutica	*NÁUT, NAUT*	sailing, navigation
sustantivo numérico	*num*	numeral noun
complemento	*obj*	(grammatical) object
	o.s.	oneself
peyorativo	*pey, pej*	derogatory, pejorative
fotografía	*PHOT*	photography
fisiología	*PHYSIOL*	physiology
plural	*pl*	plural
política	*POL*	politics
participio de pasado	*pp*	past participle
preposición	*prep*	preposition
pronombre	*pron*	pronoun
psicología, psiquiatría	*PSICO, PSYCH*	psychology, psychiatry
tiempo pasado	*pt*	past tense

ix

química	*QUÍM*	chemistry
ferrocarril	*RAIL*	railways
religión	*REL*	religion
Río de la Plata	*RPl*	River Plate
	sb	somebody
Cono Sur	*SC*	Southern Cone
enseñanza, sistema escolar y universitario	*SCOL*	schooling, schools and universities
singular	*sg*	singular
España	*SP*	Spain
	sth	something
sujeto	*su(b)j*	(grammatical) subject
subjuntivo	*subjun*	subjunctive
tauromaquia	*TAUR*	bullfighting
también	*tb*	also
técnica, tecnología	*TEC(H)*	technical term, technology
telecomunicaciones	*TELEC,TEL*	telecommunications
imprenta, tipografía	*TIP,TYP*	typography, printing
televisión	*TV*	television
universidad	*UNIV*	university
inglés norteamericano	*US*	American English
verbo	*vb*	verb
verbo intransitivo	*vi*	intransitive verb
verbo pronominal	*vr*	reflexive verb
verbo transitivo	*vt*	transitive verb
zoología	*ZOOL*	zoology
marca registrada	®	registered trademark
indica un equivalente cultural	≈	introduces a cultural equivalent

Spanish Pronunciation

VOWELS

a	[a]	pata	not as long as *a* in far. When followed by a consonant in the same syllable (i.e. in a closed syllable), as in am**a**nte, the *a* is short, as in b**a**t
e	[e]	me	like *e* in th**ey**. In a closed syllable, as in g**e**nte, the *e* is short as in p**e**t
i	[i]	pino	as in m**ea**n or mach**i**ne
o	[o]	lo	as in l**o**cal. In a closed syllable, as in c**o**ntrol, the *o* is short as in c**o**t
u	[u]	lunes	as in r**u**le. It is silent after *q*, and in g**ue**, g**ui**, unless marked g**üe**, g**üi** e.g. antig**üe**dad, when it is pronounced like *w* in w**o**lf

SEMIVOWELS

i, y	[j]	bien hielo yunta	pronounced like *y* in y**e**s
u	[w]	huevo fuento antigüedad	unstressed *u* between consonant and vowel is pronounced like *w* in w**e**ll. See notes on *u* above.

DIPHTHONGS

ai, ay	[ai]	baile	as *i* in r**i**de
au	[au]	auto	as **ou** in sh**ou**t
ei, ey	[ei]	buey	as **ey** in gr**ey**
eu	[eu]	deuda	both elements pronounced independently [e] + [u]
oi, oy	[oi]	hoy	as **oy** in t**oy**

CONSONANTS

b	[b, β]	boda bomba labor	see notes on *v* below.
c	[ˈk]	caja	*c* before *a*, *o* or *u* is pronounced as in c**a**t
ce, ci	[θi, θe]	cero cielo	*c* before *e* or *i* is pronounced as in **th**in

xi

ch	[tʃ]	**chiste**	**ch** is pronounced as **ch** in **ch**air
d	[d, ð]	**danés**	at the beginning of a phrase or after **l** or **n**,
		ciudad	**d** is pronounced as in English. In any other position it is pronounced like **th** in **th**e
g	[g, ɤ]	**gafas**	**g** before **a**, **o** or **u** is pronounced as in **g**ap,
		paga	if at the beginning of a phrase or after **n**. In other positions the sound is softened
ge, gi	[xe, xi]	**gente**	**g** before **e** or **i** is pronounced similar to **ch**
		girar	in Scottish lo**ch**
h		**haber**	**h** is always silent in Spanish
j	[x]	**jugar**	**j** is pronounced similar to **ch** in Scottish lo**ch**
ll	[ʎ]	**talle**	**ll** is pronounced like the **lli** in mi**lli**on
ñ	[ɲ]	**niño**	**ñ** is pronounced like the **ni** in o**ni**on
q	[k]	**que**	**q** is pronounced as **k** in **k**ing
r, rr	[r, rr]	**quitar**	**r** is always pronounced in Spanish, unlike
		garra	the silent **r** in dancer. **rr** is trilled, like a Scottish **r**
s	[s]	**quizás**	**s** is usually pronounced as in pa**ss**, but
		isla	before **b**, **d**, **g**, **l**, **m** or **n** it is pronounced as in ro**s**e
v	[b, β]	**vía**	**v** is pronounced something like **b**. At the beginning of a phrase or after **m** or **n** it is pronounced as **b** in **b**oy. In any other position the sound is softened
z	[θ]	**tenaz**	**z** is pronounced as **th** in **th**in

f, k, l, m, n, p, t and x are pronounced as in English.

STRESS

The rules of stress in Spanish are as follows:

(a) when a word ends in a vowel or in **n** or **s**, the second last syllable is stressed: pa**ta**ta, pa**ta**tas, **co**me, **co**men

(b) when a word ends in a consonant other than **n** or **s**, the stress falls on the last syllable: pa**red**, ha**blar**

(c) when the rules set out in (a) and (b) are not applied, an acute accent appears over the stressed vowel: co**mún**, geogra**fía**, in**glés**

In the phonetic transcription, the symbol ['] precedes the syllable on which the stress falls.

La pronunciación inglesa

VOCALES

	Ejemplo inglés	Explicación
[ɑ:]	father	Entre *a* de p**a**dre y *o* de n**o**che
[ʌ]	but, come	*a* muy breve
[æ]	man, cat	Con los labios en la posición de *e* en p**e**na y luego se pronuncia el sonido *a* parecido a la *a* de c**a**rro
[ə]	father, ago	Vocal neutra parecida a una *e* u *o* casi muda
[ə:]	bird, heard	Entre *e* abierta, y *o* cerrada, sonido alargado
[ε]	get, bed	Como en p**e**rro
[ɪ]	it, big	Más breve que en s**i**
[i:]	tea, see	Como en f**i**no
[ɔ]	hot, wash	Como en t**o**rre
[ɔ:]	saw, all	Como en p**o**r
[u]	put, book	Sonido breve, más cerrado que b**u**rro
[u:]	too, you	Sonido largo, como en **u**no

DIPTONGOS

	Ejemplo inglés	Explicación
[aɪ]	fly, high	Como en fr**ai**le
[au]	how, house	Como en p**au**sa
[εə]	there, bear	Casi como en v**ea**, pero el sonido *a* se mezcla con el indistinto [ə]
[eɪ]	day, obey	*e* cerrada seguida por una *i* débil
[ɪə]	here, hear	Como en man**ía**, mezclándose el sonido *a* con el indistinto [ə]
[əu]	go, note	[ə] seguido por una breve *u*
[ɔɪ]	boy, oil	Como en v**oy**
[uə]	poor, sure	*u* bastante larga más el sonido indistinto [ə]

CONSONANTES

	Ejemplo inglés	*Explicación*
[b]	**b**ig, lo**bb**y	Como en tum**b**an
[d]	men**d**e**d**	Como en con**d**e, an**d**ar
[g]	**g**o, **g**et, bi**g**	Como en **g**rande, **g**ol
[dʒ]	**g**in, **j**udge	Como en la **ll** andaluza y en **G**eneralitat (*catalán*)
[ŋ]	si**ng**	Como en ví**n**culo
[h]	**h**ouse, **h**e	Como en la jota hispanoamericana
[j]	**y**oung, **y**es	Como en **y**a
[k]	**c**ome, mo**ck**	Como en **c**aña, Es**c**ocia
[r]	**r**ed, t**r**ead	Se pronuncia con la punta de la lengua hacia atrás y sin hacerla vibrar
[s]	**s**and, ye**s**	Como en ca**s**a, **s**esión
[z]	ro**s**e, **z**ebra	Como en de**s**de, mi**s**mo
[ʃ]	**sh**e, ma**ch**ine	Como en **ch**ambre (*francés*), ro**x**o (*portugués*)
[tʃ]	**ch**in, ri**ch**	Como en **ch**ocolate
[v]	**v**alley	Como en **f**, pero se retiran los dientes superiores vibrándolos contra el labio inferior
[w]	**w**ater, **wh**ich	Como en la **u** de h**u**evo, p**u**ede
[ʒ]	vi**s**ion	Como en **j**ournal (*francés*)
[θ]	**th**ink, my**th**	Como en re**c**eta, **z**apato
[ð]	**th**is, **th**e	Como en habla**d**o, verda**d**

f, l, m, n, p, t iguales que en español

El signo [*] indica que la r final escrita apenas se pronuncia en inglés británico cuando la palabra siguiente empieza con vocal. El signo ['] indica la sílaba acentuada.

Spanish Verb Tables

1 Gerund 2 Imperative 3 Present 4 Preterite 5 Future 6 Present
subjunctive 7 Imperfect subjunctive 8 Past participle 9 Imperfect
Etc indicates that the irregular root is used for all persons of the tense, *e.g.*
oír: 6 oiga, oigas, oigamos, oigáis, oigan

agradecer 3 agradezco 6 agradezca etc

aprobar 2 aprueba, aprueba, aprueba, aprueban
6 apruebe, apruebes, apruebe, aprueben

atravesar 2 atraviesa 3 atravieso, atraviesas, atraviesa, atraviesan
6 atraviese, atravieses, atraviese, atraviesen

caber 3 quepo 4 cupe, cupiste, cupo, cupimos, cupisteis, cupieron 5 cabré
etc 6 quepa etc 7 cupiera etc

caer 1 cayendo 3 caigo 4 cayó, cayeron 6 caiga etc 7 cayera etc

cerrar 2 cierra 3 cierro, cierras, cierra, cierran 6 cierre, cierres, cierre, cierren

COMER 1 comiendo 2 come, comed 3 como, comes, come,
comemos, coméis, comen 4 comí, comiste, comió, comimos, comisteis,
comieron 5 comeré, comerás, comerá, comeremos, comeréis, comerán 6
coma, comas, coma, comamos, comáis, coman 7 comiera, comieras,
comiera, comiéramos, comierais, comieran 8 comido 9 comía, comías,
comía, comíamos, comíais, comían

conocer 3 conozco 6 conozca etc

contar 2 cuenta 3 cuento, cuentas, cuenta, cuentan 6 cuente, cuentes,
cuente, cuenten

dar 3 doy 4 di, diste, dio, dimos, disteis, dieron 7 diera etc

decir 2 di 3 digo 4 dije, dijiste, dijo, dijimos, dijisteis, dijeron 5 diré etc 6
diga etc 7 dijera etc 8 dicho

despertar 2 despierta 3 despierto, despiertas, despierta, despiertan
6 despierte, despiertes, despierte, despierten

divertir 1 divirtiendo 2 divierte 3 divierto, diviertes, divierte, divierten 4
divirtió, divirtieron 6 divierta, diviertas, divierta,
divirtamos, divirtáis, diviertan 7 divirtiera etc

dormir 1 durmiendo 2 duerme 3 duermo, duermes, duerme,
duermen 4 durmió, durmieron 6 duerma, duermas, duerma,
durmamos, durmáis, duerman 7 durmiera etc

empezar 2 empieza 3 empiezo, empiezas, empieza, empiezan
4 empecé 6 empiece, empieces, empiece, empecemos, empecéis,
empiecen

entender 2 entiende 3 entiendo, entiendes, entiende, entienden
6 entienda, entiendas, entienda, entiendan

ESTAR 2 está 3 estoy, estás, está, están 4 estuve, estuviste, estuvo,
estuvimos, estuvisteis, estuvieron 6 esté, estés, esté, estén 7 estuviera etc

HABER 3 he, has, ha, hemos, han hube, hubiste, hubo, hubimos, hubisteis, hubieron 5 habré etc 7 haya etc 7 hubiera etc

HABLAR 1 hablando 2 habla, hablad 3 hablo, hablas, habla, hablamos, habláis, hablan 4 hablé, hablaste, habló, hablamos, hablasteis, hablaron 5 hablaré, hablarás, hablará, hablaremos, hablaréis, hablarán 6 hable, hables, hable, hablemos, habléis, hablen 7 hablara, hablaras, hablara, habláramos, hablarais, hablaran 8 hablado 9 hablaba, hablabas, hablaba, hablábamos, hablabais, hablaban

hacer 2 haz 3 hago 4 hice, hiciste, hizo, hicimos, hicisteis, hicieron 5 haré etc 6 haga etc 7 hiciera etc 8 hecho

instruir 1 instruyendo 2 instruye 3 instruyo, instruyes, instruye, instruyen 4 instruyó, instruyeron 6 instruya etc 7 instruyera etc

ir 1 yendo 2 ve 3 voy, vas, va, vamos, vais, van 4 fui, fuiste, fue, fuimos, fuisteis, fueron 6 vaya, vayas, vaya, vayamos, vayáis, vayan 7 fuera etc 9 iba, ibas, iba, íbamos, ibais, iban

jugar 2 juega 3 juego, juegas, juega, juegan 4 jugué 6 juegue etc

leer 1 leyendo 4 leyó, leyeron 7 leyera etc

morir 1 muriendo 2 muere 3 muero, mueres, muere, mueren 4 murió, murieron 6 muera, mueras, muera, muramos, muráis, mueran 7 muriera etc 8 muerto

mover 2 mueve 3 muevo, mueves, mueve, mueven 6 mueva, muevas, mueva, muevan

negar 2 niega 3 niego, niegas, niega, niegan 4 negué 6 niegue, niegues, niegue, neguemos, neguéis, nieguen

ofrecer 3 ofrezco 6 ofrezca etc

oír 1 oyendo 2 oye 3 oigo, oyes, oye, oyen 4 oyó, oyeron 6 oiga etc 7 oyera etc

oler 2 huele 3 huelo, hueles, huele, huelen 6 huela, huelas, huela, huelan

parecer 3 parezco 6 parezca etc

pedir 1 pidiendo 2 pide 3 pido, pides, pide, piden 4 pidió, pidieron 6 pida etc 7 pidiera etc

pensar 2 piensa 3 pienso, piensas, piensa, piensan 6 piense, pienses, piense, piensen

perder 2 pierde 3 pierdo, pierdes, pierde, pierden 6 pierda, pierdas, pierda, pierdan

poder 1 pudiendo 2 puede 3 puedo, puedes, puede, pueden 4 pude, pudiste, pudo, pudimos, pudisteis, pudieron 5 podré etc 6 pueda, puedas, pueda, puedan 7 pudiera etc

poner 2 pon 3 pongo 4 puse, pusiste, puso, pusimos, pusisteis, pusieron 5 pondré etc 6 ponga etc 7 pusiera etc 8 puesto

preferir 1 prefiriendo 2 prefiere 3 prefiero, prefieres, prefiere, prefieren 4 prefirió, prefirieron 6 prefiera, prefieras, prefiera, prefiramos, prefiráis, prefieran 7 prefiriera etc

querer 2 quiere 3 quiero, quieres, quiere, quieren 4 quise, quisiste, quiso, quisimos, quisisteis, quisieron 5 querré etc 6 quiera, quieras, quiera, quieran 7 quisiera etc

reír 2 ríe 3 río, ríes, ríe, ríen 4 reí, rieron 6 ría, rías, ría, riamos, riáis, rían 7 riera etc

repetir 1 repitiendo 2 repite 3 repito, repites, repite, repiten 4 repitió, repitieron 6 repita etc 7 repitiera etc

rogar 2 ruega 3 ruego, ruegas, ruega, ruegan 4 rogué 6 ruegue, ruegues, ruegue, roguemos, roguéis, rueguen

saber 3 sé 4 supe, supiste, supo, supimos, supisteis, supieron 5 sabré etc 6 sepa etc 7 supiera etc

salir 2 sal 3 salgo 5 saldré etc 6 salga etc

seguir 1 siguiendo 2 sigue 3 sigo, sigues, sigue, siguen 4 siguió, siguieron 6 siga etc 7 siguiera etc

sentar 3 sienta 3 siento, sientas, sienta, sientan 6 siente, sientes, siente, sienten

sentir 1 sintiendo 2 siente 3 siento, sientes, siente, sienten 4 sintió, sintieron 6 sienta, sientas, sienta, sintamos, sintáis, sientan 7 sintiera etc

SER 2 sé 3 soy, eres, es, somos, sois, son 4 fui, fuiste, fue, fuimos, fuisteis, fueron 6 sea etc 7 fuera etc 9 era, eras, era, éramos, erais, eran

servir 1 sirviendo 2 sirve 3 sirvo, sirves, sirve, sirven 4 sirvió, sirvieron 6 sirva etc 7 sirviera etc

soñar 2 sueña 3 sueño, sueñas, sueña, sueñan 6 sueñe, sueñes, sueñe, sueñen

tener 2 ten 3 tengo, tienes, tiene, tienen 4 tuve, tuviste, tuvo, tuvimos, tuvisteis, tuvieron 5 tendré etc 6 tenga etc 7 tuviera etc

traer 1 trayendo 3 traigo 4 traje, trajiste, trajo, trajimos, trajisteis, trajeron 6 traiga etc 7 trajera etc

valer 2 val 3 valgo 5 valdré etc 6 valga etc

venir 2 ven 3 vengo, vienes, viene, vienen 4 vine, viniste, vino, vinimos, vinisteis, vinieron 5 vendré etc 6 venga etc 7 viniera etc

ver 3 veo 6 vea etc 8 visto 9 veía etc

vestir 1 vistiendo 2 viste 3 visto, vistes, viste, visten 4 vistió, vistieron 6 vista etc 7 vistiera etc

VIVIR 1 viviendo 2 vive, vivid 3 vivo, vives, vive, vivimos, vivís, viven 4 viví, viviste, vivió, vivimos, vivisteis, vivieron 5 viviré, vivirás, vivirá, viviremos, viviréis, vivirán 6 viva, vivas, viva, vivamos, viváis, vivan 7 viviera, vivieras, viviera, viviéramos, vivierais, vivieran 8 vivido 9 vivía, vivías, vivía, vivíamos, vivías, vivían

volver 2 vuelve 3 vuelvo, vuelves, vuelve, vuelven 6 vuelva, vuelvas, vuelva, vuelvan 8 vuelto

Verbos irregulares en inglés

presente	pasado	participio de pasado	presente	pasado	participio de pasado
arise	arose	arisen	**creep**	crept	crept
awake	awoke	awoken	**cut**	cut	cut
be (am, is, are; being)	was, were	been	**deal**	dealt	dealt
			dig	dug	dug
			do (does)	did	done
bear	bore	born(e)	**draw**	drew	drawn
beat	beat	beaten	**dream**	dreamed, dreamt	dreamed, dreamt
become	became	become			
begin	began	begun	**drink**	drank	drunk
bend	bent	bent	**drive**	drove	driven
bet	bet, betted	bet, betted	**dwell**	dwelt	dwelt
bid (at auction, cards)	bid	bid	**eat**	ate	eaten
			fall	fell	fallen
bid (say)	bade	bidden	**feed**	fed	fed
bind	bound	bound	**feel**	felt	felt
bite	bit	bitten	**fight**	fought	fought
bleed	bled	bled	**find**	found	found
blow	blew	blown	**flee**	fled	fled
break	broke	broken	**fling**	flung	flung
breed	bred	bred	**fly**	flew	flown
bring	brought	brought	**forbid**	forbad(e)	forbidden
build	built	built	**forecast**	forecast	forecast
burn	burnt, burned	burnt, burned	**forget**	forgot	forgotten
burst	burst	burst	**forgive**	forgave	forgiven
buy	bought	bought	**forsake**	forsook	forsaken
can	could	(been able)	**freeze**	froze	frozen
			get	got	got, (US) gotten
cast	cast	cast	**give**	gave	given
catch	caught	caught	**go (goes)**	went	gone
choose	chose	chosen	**grind**	ground	ground
cling	clung	clung	**grow**	grew	grown
come	came	come	**hang**	hung	hung
cost	cost	cost	**hang** (execute)	hanged	hanged
cost (work out price of)	costed	costed	**have**	had	had
			hear	heard	heard
			hide	hid	hidden

presente	pasado	participio de pasado	presente	pasado	participio de pasado
hit	hit	hit	**say**	said	said
hold	held	held	**see**	saw	seen
hurt	hurt	hurt	**seek**	sought	sought
keep	kept	kept	**sell**	sold	sold
kneel	knelt,	knelt,	**send**	sent	sent
	kneeled	kneeled	**set**	set	set
know	knew	known	**sew**	sewed	sewn
lay	laid	laid	**shake**	shook	shaken
lead	led	led	**shear**	sheared	shorn,
lean	leant,	leant,			sheared
	leaned	leaned	**shed**	shed	shed
leap	leapt,	leapt,	**shine**	shone	shone
	leaped	leaped	**shoot**	shot	shot
learn	learnt,	learnt,	**show**	showed	shown
	learned	learned	**shrink**	shrank	shrunk
leave	left	left	**shut**	shut	shut
lend	lent	lent	**sing**	sang	sung
let	let	let	**sink**	sank	sunk
lie (lying)	lay	lain	**sit**	sat	sat
light	lit,	lit,	**slay**	slew	slain
	lighted	lighted	**sleep**	slept	slept
lose	lost	lost	**slide**	slid	slid
make	made	made	**sling**	slung	slung
may	might	—	**slit**	slit	slit
mean	meant	meant	**smell**	smelt,	smelt,
meet	met	met		smelled	smelled
mistake	mistook	mistaken	**sow**	sowed	sown,
mow	mowed	mown,			sowed
		mowed	**speak**	spoke	spoken
must	(had to)	(had to)	**speed**	sped,	sped,
pay	paid	paid			speeded
put	put	put	**spell**	spelt,	spelt,
quit	quit,	quit,		spelled	spelled
	quitted	quitted	**spend**	spent	spent
read	read	read	**spill**	spilt,	spilt,
rid	rid	rid			spilled
ride	rode	ridden		spilled	
ring	rang	rung	**spin**	spun	spun
rise	rose	risen	**spit**	spat	spat
run	ran	run	**spoil**	spoiled,	spoiled,
saw	sawed	sawed,		spoilt	spoilt
		sawn	**spread**	spread	spread
			spring	sprang	sprung

presente	pasado	participio de pasado	presente	pasado	participio de pasado
stand	stood	stood	**think**	thought	thought
steal	stole	stolen	**throw**	threw	thrown
stick	stuck	stuck	**thrust**	thrust	thrust
sting	stung	stung	**tread**	trod	trodden
stink	stank	stunk	**wake**	woke,	woken,
stride	strode	stridden		waked	waked
strike	struck	struck	**wear**	wore	worn
strive	strove	striven	**weave**	wove	woven
swear	swore	sworn	**weave**	weaved	weaved
sweep	swept	swept	*(wind)*		
swell	swelled	swollen,	**wed**	wedded,	wedded,
		swelled		wed	wed
swim	swam	swum			
swing	swung	swung	**weep**	wept	wept
take	took	taken	**win**	won	won
teach	taught	taught	**wind**	wound	wound
tear	tore	torn	**wring**	wrung	wrung
tell	told	told	**write**	wrote	written

ESPAÑOL - INGLÉS
SPANISH - ENGLISH

A, a

a

PALABRA CLAVE

[a] (*a + el = al*) *prep*

1 (*dirección*) to; **fueron a Madrid/ Grecia** they went to Madrid/Greece; **me voy a casa** I'm going home

2 (*distancia*): **está a 15 km de aquí** it's 15 kms from here

3 (*posición*): **estar a la mesa** to be at table; **al lado de** next to, beside; *ver tb* **puerta**

4 (*tiempo*): **a las 10/a medianoche** at 10/midnight; **a la mañana siguiente** the following morning; **a los pocos días** after a few days; **estamos a 9 de julio** it's the ninth of July; **a los 24 años** at the age of 24; **al año/a la semana** a year/week later

5 (*manera*): **a la francesa** the French way; **a caballo** on horseback; **a oscuras** in the dark

6 (*medio, instrumento*): **a lápiz** in pencil; **a mano** by hand; **cocina a gas** gas stove

7 (*razón*): **a 30 céntimos el kilo** at 30 cents a kilo; **a más de 50 km/h** at more than 50 kms per hour

8 (*dativo*): **se lo di a él** I gave it to him; **vi al policía** I saw the policeman; **se lo compré a él** I bought it from him

9 (*tras ciertos verbos*): **voy a verle** I'm going to see him; **empezó a trabajar** he started working *o* to work

10 (+ *infin*): **al verlo, lo reconocí inmediatamente** when I saw him I recognized him at once; **el camino a recorrer** the distance we *etc* have to travel; **¡a callar!** keep quiet!; **¡a comer!** let's eat!

abad, esa [aˈβað, ˈðesa] *nm/f* abbot/ abbess ▢ **abadía** *nf* abbey

abajo [aˈβaxo] *adv* (*situación*) (down) below, underneath; (*en edificio*) downstairs; (*dirección*) down, downwards; **el piso de ~** the downstairs flat; **la parte de ~** the lower part; **¡~ el gobierno!** down with the government!; **cuesta/río ~** downhill/ downstream; **de arriba ~** from top to bottom; **el ~ firmante** the undersigned; **más ~** lower *o* further down

abalanzarse [aβalanˈθarse] *vr*: **~ sobre** *o* **contra** to throw o.s. at

abanderado, -a [aβandeˈraðo] *nm/f* (*portaestandarte*) standard bearer; (*de un movimiento*) champion, leader; (MÉX: *linier*) linesman, assistant referee

abandonado, -a [aβandoˈnaðo, a] *adj* derelict; (*desatendido*) abandoned; (*desierto*) deserted; (*descuidado*) neglected

abandonar [aβandoˈnar] *vt* to leave; (*persona*) to abandon, desert; (*cosa*) to abandon, leave behind; (*descuidar*) to neglect; (*renunciar a*) to give up; (INFORM) to quit; **abandonarse** *vr*: **abandonarse a** to abandon o.s. to ▢ **abandono** *nm* (*acto*) desertion, abandonment; (*estado*) abandon, neglect; (*renuncia*) withdrawal, retirement; **ganar por abandono** to win by default

abanico [aβaˈniko] *nm* fan; (NÁUT) derrick

abarcar [aβar'kar] vt to include, embrace; (LAm: acaparar) to monopolize

abarrotado, -a [aβarro'taðo, a] adj packed

abarrotar [aβarro'tar] vt (local, estadio, teatro) to fill, pack

abarrotero, -a [aβarro'tero, a] (MÉX) nm/f grocer □ **abarrotes** (MÉX) nmpl groceries; **tienda de abarrotes** (MÉX, CAm) grocery store

abastecer [aβaste'θer] vt: ~ **(de)** to supply (with) □ **abastecimiento** nm supply

abasto [a'βasto] nm supply; **no dar ~ a** to be unable to cope with

abatible [aβa'tiβle] adj: **asiento ~** tip-up seat; (AUTO) reclining seat

abatido, -a [aβa'tiðo, a] adj dejected, downcast

abatir [aβa'tir] vt (muro) to demolish; (pdjaro) to shoot o bring down; (fig) to depress

abdicar [aβði'kar] vi to abdicate

abdomen [aβ'ðomen] nm abdomen □ **abdominales** nmpl (tb: **ejercicios abdominales**) sit-ups

abecedario [aβeθe'ðarjo] nm alphabet

abedul [aβe'ðul] nm birch

abeja [a'βexa] nf bee

abejorro [aβe'xorro] nm bumblebee

abertura [aβer'tura] nf = **apertura**

abeto [a'βeto] nm fir

abierto, -a [a'βjerto, a] pp de **abrir** ♦ adj open

abismal [aβis'mal] adj (fig) vast, enormous

abismo [a'βismo] nm abyss

ablandar [aβlan'dar] vt to soften; **ablandarse** vr to get softer

abocado, -a [aβo'kaðo, a] adj (vino) smooth, pleasant

abochornar [aβotʃor'nar] vt to embarrass

abofetear [aβofete'ar] vt to slap (in the face)

abogado, -a [aβo'ɣaðo, a] nm/f lawyer; (notario) solicitor; (de tribunal) barrister (BRIT), attorney (US) ► **abogado defensor** defence lawyer o (US) attorney

abogar [aβo'ɣar] vi: ~ **por** to plead for; (fig) to advocate

abolir [aβo'lir] vt to abolish; (cancelar) to cancel

abolladura [aβoʎa'ðura] nf dent

abollar [aβo'ʎar] vt to dent

abombarse (LAm) vr to go bad

abominable [aβomi'naβle] adj abominable

abonado, -a [aβo'naðo, a] adj (deuda) paid(-up) ♦ nm/f subscriber

abonar [aβo'nar] vt (deuda) to settle; (terreno) to fertilize; (idea) to endorse; **abonarse** vr to subscribe □ **abono** nm payment; fertilizer; subscription

abordar [aβor'ðar] vt (barco) to board; (asunto) to broach

aborigen [aβo'rixen] nmf aborigine

aborrecer [aβorre'θer] vt to hate, loathe

abortar [aβor'tar] vi (malparir) to have a miscarriage; (deliberadamente) to have an abortion □ **aborto** nm miscarriage; abortion

abovedado, -a [aβoβe'ðaðo, a] adj vaulted, domed

abrasar [aβra'sar] vt to burn (up); (AGR) to dry up, parch

abrazar [aβra'θar] vt to embrace, hug

abrazo [a'βraθo] nm embrace, hug; **un ~ (en carta)** with best wishes

abrebotellas [aβreβo'teʎas] nm inv bottle opener

abrecartas [aβre'kartas] nm inv letter opener

abrelatas [aβre'latas] nm inv tin (BRIT) o can opener

abreviatura [aβreβja'tura] nf abbreviation

abridor [aβri'ðor] nm bottle opener; (de latas) tin (BRIT) o can opener

abrigador, a [aβriɣa'ðor] adj (MÉX) warm

abrigar [aβri'ɣar] vt (proteger) to shelter; (ropa) to keep warm; (fig) to cherish

abrigo [a'βriɣo] nm (prenda) coat, overcoat; (lugar protegido) shelter

abril [a'βril] nm April

abrillantador nm polish

abrillantar [aβriʎan'tar] vt to polish

abrir [a'βrir] vt to open (up) ♦ vi to open; **abrirse** vr to open (up); (extenderse) to open out; (cielo) to clear; **abrirse paso** to find o force a way through

abrochar [aβro'tʃar] vt (con botones) to button (up); (zapato, con broche) to do up

abrupto, -a [a'βrupto, a] adj abrupt; (empinado) steep

absoluto, -a [aβso'luto, a] adj absolute; **en ~** adv not at all

absolver [aβsol'βer] vt to absolve; (JUR) to pardon; (: acusado) to acquit

absorbente [aβsor'βente] adj absorbent; (interesante) absorbing

absorber [aβsor'βer] vt to absorb; (embeber) to soak up

absorción [aβsor'θjon] nf absorption; (COM) takeover

abstemio, -a [aβs'temjo, a] adj teetotal

abstención [aβsten'θjon] nf abstention

abstenerse [aβste'nerse] vr: ~ (de) to abstain o refrain (from)

abstinencia [aβsti'nenθja] nf abstinence; (ayuno) fasting

abstracto, -a [aβs'trakto, a] adj abstract

abstraer [aβstra'er] vt to abstract; **abstraerse** vr to be o become absorbed

abstraído, -a [aβstra'iðo, a] adj absent-minded

absuelto [aβ'swelto] pp de **absolver**

absurdo, -a [aβ'surðo, a] adj absurd

abuchear [aβutʃe'ar] vt to boo

abuelo, -a [a'βwelo, a] nm/f grandfather(-mother); **abuelos** nmpl grandparents

abultado, -a [aβul'taðo, a] adj bulky

abultar [aβul'tar] vi to be bulky

abundancia [aβun'danθja] nf: **una ~ de** plenty of ❏ **abundante** adj abundant, plentiful

abundar [aβun'dar] vi to abound, be plentiful

aburrido, -a [aβu'rriðo, a] adj (hastiado) bored; (que aburre) boring ❏ **aburrimiento** nm boredom, tedium

aburrir [aβu'rrir] vt to bore; **aburrirse** vr to be bored, get bored

abusado, -a [MÉX: fam] [aβu'saðo, a] adj (astuto) sharp, cunning ♦ excl: **¡~!** (inv) look out!, careful!

abusar [aβu'sar] vi to go too far; **~ de** to abuse

abusivo, -a [aβu'siβo, a] adj (precio) exorbitant

abuso [a'βuso] nm abuse

acá [a'ka] adv (lugar) here

acabado, -a [aka'βaðo, a] adj finished, complete; (perfecto) perfect; (agotado) worn out; (fig) masterly ♦ nm finish

acabar [aka'βar] vt (llevar a su fin) to finish, complete; (consumir) to use up; (rematar) to finish off ♦ vi to finish, end; **acabarse** vr to finish, stop; (terminarse) to be over; (agotarse) to run out; **~ con** to put an end to; **~ de llegar** to have just arrived; **~ por hacer** to end up by doing; **¡se acabó!** it's all over!; (¡basta!) that's enough!

acabóse [aka'βose] nm: **esto es el ~** this is the last straw

academia [aka'ðemja] nf academy ❏ **académico, -a** adj academic

acalorado, -a [akalo'raðo, a] adj (discusión) heated

acampar [akam'par] *vi* to camp

acantilado [akanti'laðo] *nm* cliff

acaparar [akapa'rar] *vt* to monopolize; *(acumular)* to hoard

acariciar [akari'θjar] *vt* to caress; *(esperanza)* to cherish

acarrear [akarre'ar] *vt* to transport; *(fig)* to cause, result in

acaso [a'kaso] *adv* perhaps, maybe; **(por) si ~** just in case

acatar [aka'tar] *vt* to respect; *(ley)* obey

acatarrarse [akata'rrarse] *vr* to catch a cold

acceder [akθe'ðer] *vi*: **~ a** *(petición etc)* to agree to; *(tener acceso a)* to have access to; *(INFORM)* to access

accesible [akθe'siβle] *adj* accessible

acceso [ak'θeso] *nm* access, entry; *(camino)* access, approach; *(MED)* attack, fit

accesorio, -a [akθe'sorjo, a] *adj, nm* accessory

accidentado, -a [akθiðen'taðo, a] *adj* uneven; *(montañoso)* hilly; *(azaroso)* eventful ♦ *nm/f* accident victim

accidental [akθiðen'tal] *adj* accidental

accidente [akθi'ðente] *nm* accident; **accidentes** *nmpl (de terreno)* unevenness *sg* ► **accidente laboral/ de trabajo o de tráfico** industrial/ road o traffic accident

acción [ak'θjon] *nf* action; *(acto)* action, act; *(COM)* share; *(JUR)* action, lawsuit □ **accionar** *vt* to work, operate; *(INFORM)* to drive

accionista [akθjo'nista] *nmf* shareholder, stockholder

acebo [a'θeβo] *nm* holly; *(árbol)* holly tree

acechar [aθe'tʃar] *vt* to spy on; *(aguardar)* to lie in wait for □ **acecho** *nm*: **estar al acecho (de)** to lie in wait (for)

aceite [a'θeite] *nm* oil ► **aceite de girasol/oliva** olive/sunflower oil

□ **aceitera** *nf* oilcan □ **aceitoso, -a** *adj* oily

aceituna [aθei'tuna] *nf* olive ► **aceituna rellena** stuffed olive

acelerador [aθelera'ðor] *nm* accelerator

acelerar [aθele'rar] *vt* to accelerate

acelga [a'θelɣa] *nf* chard, beet

acento [a'θento] *nm* accent; *(acentuación)* stress

acentuar [aθen'twar] *vt* to accent; to stress; *(fig)* to accentuate

acepción [aθep'θjon] *nf* meaning

aceptable [aθep'taβle] *adj* acceptable

aceptación [aθepta'θjon] *nf* acceptance; *(aprobación)* approval

aceptar [aθep'tar] *vt* to accept; *(aprobar)* to approve; **~ hacer algo** to agree to do sth

acequia [a'θekja] *nf* irrigation ditch

acera [a'θera] *nf* pavement *(BRIT)*, sidewalk *(US)*

acerca [a'θerka]: **~ de** *prep* about, concerning

acercar [aθer'kar] *vt* to bring o move nearer o closer; **acercarse** *vr* to approach, come near

acero [a'θero] *nm* steel

acérrimo, -a [a'θerrimo, a] *adj (partidario)* staunch; *(enemigo)* bitter

acertado, -a [aθer'taðo, a] *adj* correct; *(apropiado)* apt; *(sensato)* sensible

acertar [aθer'tar] *vt (blanco)* to hit; *(solución)* to get right; *(adivinar)* to guess ♦ *vi* to get it right, be right; **~ a** to manage to; **~ con** to happen o hit on

acertijo [aθer'tixo] *nm* riddle, puzzle

achacar [atʃa'kar] *vt* to attribute

achacoso, -a [atʃa'koso, a] *adj* sickly

achicar [atʃi'kar] *vt* to reduce; *(NÁUT)* to bale out

achicharrar [atʃitʃa'rrar] *vt* to scorch, burn

achichincle *(MÉX: fam) nmf* minion

achicoria [atʃi'korja] *nf* chicory

achuras (RPl) nfpl offal sg

acicate [aθi'kate] nm spur

acidez [aθi'ðeθ] nf acidity

ácido, -a ['aθiðo, a] adj sour, acid ♦ nm acid

acierto etc [a'θjerto] vb ver **acertar** ♦ nm success; (buen paso) wise move; (solución) solution; (habilidad) skill, ability

acitronar (MÉX: fam) vt to brown

aclamar [akla'mar] vt to acclaim; (aplaudir) to applaud

aclaración [aklara'θjon] nf clarification, explanation

aclarar [akla'rar] vt to clarify, explain; (ropa) to rinse ♦ vi to clear up; **aclararse** vr (explicarse) to understand; **aclararse la garganta** to clear one's throat

aclimatación [aklimata'θjon] nf acclimatization

aclimatar [aklima'tar] vt to acclimatize; **aclimatarse** vr to become acclimatized

acné [ak'ne] nm acne

acobardar [akoβar'ðar] vt to intimidate

acogedor, a [akoxe'ðor, a] adj welcoming; (hospitalario) hospitable

acoger [ako'xer] vt to welcome; (abrigar) to shelter

acogida [ako'xiða] nf reception; refuge

acomedido, -a (MÉX) adj helpful, obliging

acometer [akome'ter] vt to attack; (emprender) to undertake ❏ **acometida** nf attack, assault

acomodado, -a [akomo'ðaðo, a] adj (persona) well-to-do

acomodador, a [akomoða'ðor, a] nm/f usher(ette)

acomodar [akomo'ðar] vt to adjust; (alojar) to accommodate; **acomodarse** vr to conform; (instalarse) to install o.s.; (adaptarse): **acomodarse (a)** to adapt (to)

acompañar [akompa'ɲar] vt to accompany; (documentos) to enclose

acondicionar [akondiθjo'nar] vt to arrange, prepare; (pelo) to condition

aconsejar [akonse'xar] vt to advise, counsel; ~ **a algn hacer** o **que haga algo** to advise sb to do sth

acontecer [akonte'θer] vi to happen, occur ❏ **acontecimiento** nm event

acopio [a'kopjo] nm store, stock

acoplar [ako'plar] vt to fit; (ELEC) to connect; (vagones) to couple

acorazado, -a [akora'θaðo, a] adj armour-plated, armoured ♦ nm battleship

acordar [akor'ðar] vt (resolver) to agree, resolve; (recordar) to remind; **acordarse** vr to agree; ~ **hacer algo** to agree to do sth; **acordarse (de algo)** to remember (sth) ❏ **acorde** adj (MÚS) harmonious; **acorde con** (medidas etc) in keeping with ♦ nm chord

acordeón [akorðe'on] nm accordion

acordonado, -a [akorðo'naðo, a] adj (calle) cordoned-off

acorralar [akorra'lar] vt to round up, corral

acortar [akor'tar] vt to shorten; (duración) to cut short; (cantidad) to reduce; **acortarse** vr to become shorter

acosar [ako'sar] vt to pursue relentlessly; (fig) to hound, pester ❏ **acoso** nm harassment ▶ **acoso sexual** sexual harassment

acostar [akos'tar] vt (en cama) to put to bed; (en suelo) to lay down; **acostarse** vr to go to bed; to lie down; **acostarse con algn** to sleep with sb

acostumbrado, -a [akostum'braðo, a] adj usual; ~ **a** used to

acostumbrar [akostum'brar] vt: ~ **a algn a algo** to get sb used to sth ♦ vi: ~ **(a) hacer** to be in the habit of doing; **acostumbrarse** vr: **acostumbrarse a** to get used to

acotación [akotaˈθjon] nf marginal note; (GEO) elevation mark; (de límite) boundary mark; (TEATRO) stage direction

acotamiento [(MÉX)] nm hard shoulder (BRIT), berm (US)

acre ['akre] adj (olor) acrid; (fig) biting ♦ nm acre

acreditar [akreðiˈtar] vt (garantizar) to vouch for, guarantee; (autorizar) to authorize; (dar prueba de) to prove; (COM: abonar) to credit; (embajador) to accredit

acreedor, a [akreeˈðor, a] nm/f creditor

acribillar [akriβiˈʎar] vt: ~ a balazos to riddle with bullets

acróbata [aˈkroβata] nmf acrobat

acta ['akta] nf certificate; (de comisión) minutes pl, record ▶ **acta de matrimonio/nacimiento** [(MÉX)] marriage/birth certificate ▶ **acta notarial** affidavit

actitud [aktiˈtuð] nf attitude; (postura) posture

activar [aktiˈβar] vt to activate; (acelerar) to speed up

actividad [aktiβiˈðað] nf activity

activo, -a [akˈtiβo, a] adj active; (vivo) lively ♦ nm (COM) assets pl

acto ['akto] nm act, action; (ceremonia) ceremony; (TEATRO) act; **en el ~** immediately

actor [akˈtor] nm actor; (JUR) plaintiff ♦ adj: **parte actora** prosecution

actriz [akˈtriθ] nf actress

actuación [aktwaˈθjon] nf action; (comportamiento) conduct, behaviour; (JUR) proceedings pl; (desempeño) performance

actual [akˈtwal] adj present(-day), current ☐ **actualidad** nf present; **actualidades** nfpl (noticias) news sg; **en la actualidad** at present; (hoy día) nowadays ☐ **actualizar** [aktwaliˈθar] vt to update, modernize

☐ **actualmente** [aktwalˈmente] adv at present; (hoy día) nowadays

⚠ No confundir **actual** con la palabra inglesa actual.

⚠ No confundir **actualmente** con la palabra inglesa actually.

actuar [akˈtwar] vi (obrar) to work, operate; (actor) to act, perform ♦ vt to work, operate; ~ **de** to act as

acuarela [akwaˈrela] nf watercolour

acuario [aˈkwarjo] nm aquarium; (ASTROLOGÍA): **A~** Aquarius

acuático, -a [aˈkwatiko, a] adj aquatic

acudir [akuˈðir] vi (asistir) to attend; (ir) to go; ~ **a** (fig) to turn to; ~ **a una cita** to keep an appointment; ~ **en ayuda de** to go to the aid of

acuerdo etc [aˈkwerðo] vb ver **acordar** ♦ nm agreement; **¡de ~!** I agreed!; **de ~ con** (persona) in agreement with; (acción, documento) in accordance with; **estar de ~** to be agreed, agree

acumular [akumuˈlar] vt to accumulate, collect

acuñar [akuˈɲar] vt (moneda) to mint; (frase) to coin

acupuntura [akupunˈtura] nf acupuncture

acurrucarse [akurruˈkarse] vr to crouch; (ovillarse) to curl up

acusación [akusaˈθjon] nf accusation

acusar [akuˈsar] vt to accuse; (revelar) to reveal; (denunciar) to denounce

acuse [aˈkuse] nm: ~ **de recibo** acknowledgement of receipt

acústica [aˈkustika] nf acoustics pl

acústico, -a [aˈkustiko, a] adj acoustic

adaptación [aðaptaˈθjon] nf adaptation

adaptador [aðaptaˈðor] nm (ELEC) adapter, adaptor ▶ **adaptador universal** universal adapter o adaptor

adaptar [aðapˈtar] vt to adapt; (acomodar) to fit

adecuado, -a [aðe'kwaðo, a] *adj* (*apto*) suitable; (*oportuno*) appropriate

a. de J.C. *abr* (= *antes de Jesucristo*) B.C.

adelantado, -a [aðelan'taðo, a] *adj* advanced; (*reloj*) fast; **pagar por ~** to pay in advance

adelantamiento [aðelanta'mjento] *nm* (AUTO) overtaking

adelantar [aðelan'tar] *vt* to move forward; (*avanzar*) to advance; (*acelerar*) to speed up; (AUTO) to overtake ♦ *vi* to go forward, advance; **adelantarse** *vr* to go forward, advance

adelante [aðe'lante] *adv* forward(s), ahead ♦ *excl* come in!; **de hoy en ~** from now on; **más ~** later on; (*más allá*) further on

adelanto [aðe'lanto] *nm* advance; (*mejora*) improvement; (*progreso*) progress

adelgazar [aðelɣa'θar] *vt* to thin (down) ♦ *vi* to get thin; (*con régimen*) to slim down, lose weight

ademán [aðe'man] *nm* gesture; **ademanes** *nmpl* manners

además [aðe'mas] *adv* besides; (*por otra parte*) moreover; (*también*) also; **~ de** besides, in addition to

adentrarse [aðen'trarse] *vr*: **~ en** to go into, get inside; (*penetrar*) to penetrate (into)

adentro [a'ðentro] *adv* inside, in; **mar ~** out at sea; **tierra ~** inland

adepto, -a [a'ðepto, a] *nm/f* supporter

aderezar [aðere'θar] *vt* (*ensalada*) to dress; (*comida*) to season ❏ **aderezo** *nm* dressing; seasoning

adeudar [aðeu'ðar] *vt* to owe

adherirse [aðe'rirse] *vr*: **~ a** to adhere to; (*partido*) to join

adhesión [aðe'sjon] *nf* adhesion; (*fig*) adherence

adicción [aðik'θjon] *nf* addiction

adición [aði'θjon] *nf* addition

adicto, -a [a'ðikto, a] *adj*: **~ a** addicted to; (*dedicado*) devoted to ♦ *nm/f*

supporter, follower; (*toxicómano*) addict

adiestrar [aðjes'trar] *vt* to train, teach; (*conducir*) to guide, lead

adinerado, -a [aðine'raðo, a] *adj* wealthy

adiós [a'ðjos] *excl* (*para despedirse*) goodbye!, cheerio!; (*al pasar*) hello!

aditivo [aði'tiβo] *nm* additive

adivinanza [aðiβi'nanθa] *nf* riddle

adivinar [aðiβi'nar] *vt* to prophesy; (*conjeturar*) to guess ❏ **adivino, -a** *nm/f* fortune-teller

adj *abr* (= *adjunto*) encl

adjetivo [aðxe'tiβo] *nm* adjective

adjudicar [aðxuði'kar] *vt* to award; **adjudicarse** *vr*: **adjudicarse algo** to appropriate sth

adjuntar [aðxun'tar] *vt* to attach, enclose ❏ **adjunto, -a** *adj* attached, enclosed ♦ *nm/f* assistant

administración [aðministra'θjon] *nf* administration; (*dirección*) management ❏ **administrador, a** *nm/f* administrator, manager(ess)

administrar [aðminis'trar] *vt* to administer ❏ **administrativo, -a** *adj* administrative

admirable [aðmi'raβle] *adj* admirable

admiración [aðmira'θjon] *nf* admiration; (*asombro*) wonder; (LING) exclamation mark

admirar [aðmi'rar] *vt* to admire; (*extrañar*) to surprise

admisible [aðmi'siβle] *adj* admissible

admisión [aðmi'sjon] *nf* admission; (*reconocimiento*) acceptance

admitir [aðmi'tir] *vt* to admit; (*aceptar*) to accept

adobar [aðo'βar] *vt* (CULIN) to season

adobe [a'ðoβe] *nm* adobe, sun-dried brick

adolecer [aðole'θer] *vi*: **~ de** to suffer from

adolescente [aðoles'θente] nmf adolescent, teenager

adonde [a'ðonde] conj (to) where

adónde [a'ðonde] adv = **dónde**

adopción [aðop'θjon] nf adoption

adoptar [aðop'tar] vt to adopt

adoptivo, -a [aðop'tiβo, a] adj (padres) adoptive; (hijo) adopted

adoquín [aðo'kin] nm paving stone

adorar [aðo'rar] vt to adore

adornar [aðor'nar] vt to adorn

adorno [a'ðorno] nm ornament; (decoración) decoration

adosado, -a [aðo'saðo, a] adj: **casa adosada** semi-detached house

adosar (MÉX) [aðo'sar] vt (adjuntar) to attach, enclose (with a letter)

adquiero etc vb ver **adquirir**

adquirir [aðki'rir] vt to acquire, obtain

adquisición [aðkisi'θjon] nf acquisition

adrede [a'ðreðe] adv on purpose

aduana [a'ðwana] nf customs pl

aduanero, -a [aðwa'nero, a] adj customs cpd ♦ nm/f customs officer

adueñarse [aðwe'narse] vr: **~ de** to take possession of

adular [aðu'lar] vt to flatter

adulterar [aðulte'rar] vt to adulterate

adulterio [aðul'terjo] nm adultery

adúltero, -a [a'ðultero, a] adj adulterous ♦ nm/f adulterer/ adulteress

adulto, -a [a'ðulto, a] adj, nm/f adult

adverbio [að'βerβjo] nm adverb

adversario, -a [aðβer'sarjo, a] nm/f adversary

adversidad [aðβersi'ðað] nf adversity; (contratiempo) setback

adverso, -a [að'βerso, a] adj adverse

advertencia [aðβer'tenθja] nf warning; (prefacio) preface, foreword

advertir [aðβer'tir] vt to notice; (avisar): **~ a algn de** to warn sb about o of

Adviento [að'βjento] nm Advent

advierto etc vb ver **advertir**

aéreo, -a [a'ereo, a] adj aerial

aerobic [ae'roβik] nm aerobics sg
❑ **aerobics** (MÉX) nmpl aerobics sg

aeromozo, -a [aero'moθo, a] (LAm) nm/f air steward(ess)

aeronáutica [aero'nautika] nf aeronautics sg

aeronave [aero'naβe] nm spaceship

aeroplano [aero'plano] nm aeroplane

aeropuerto [aero'pwerto] nm airport

aerosol [aero'sol] nm aerosol

afamado, -a [afa'maðo, a] adj famous

afán [a'fan] nm hard work; (deseo) desire

afanador, a (MÉX) nm/f (de limpieza) cleaner

afanar [afa'nar] vt to harass; (fam) to pinch

afear [afe'ar] vt to disfigure

afección [afek'θjon] nf (MED) disease

afectado, -a [afek'taðo, a] adj affected

afectar [afek'tar] vt to affect

afectísimo, -a [afek'tisimo, a] adj affectionate; **suyo ~** yours truly

afectivo, -a [afek'tiβo, a] adj (problema etc) emotional

afecto [a'fekto] nm affection; **tenerle ~ a algn** to be fond of sb

afectuoso, -a [afek'twoso, a] adj affectionate

afeitar [afei'tar] vt to shave; **afeitarse** vr to shave

afeminado, -a [afemi'naðo, a] adj effeminate

Afganistán [afyanis'tan] nm Afghanistan

afianzar [afjan'θar] vt to strengthen; to secure; **afianzarse** vr to become established

afiche [a'fitfe] (RPI) nm poster

afición [afi'θjon] nf fondness, liking; **la ~** the fans pl; **pinto por ~** I paint as a hobby ❑ **aficionado, -a** adj keen, enthusiastic; (no profesional) amateur

aficionar ♦ nm/f enthusiast, fan; amateur; **ser aficionado a algo** to be very keen on o fond of sth

aficionar [afiθjo'nar] vt: ~ **a algn a algo** to make sb like sth; **aficionarse** vr: **aficionarse a algo** to grow fond of sth

afilado, -a [afi'laðo, a] adj sharp

afilar [afi'lar] vt to sharpen

afiliarse [afi'ljarse] vr to affiliate

afín [a'fin] adj (parecido) similar; (conexo) related

afinar [afi'nar] vt (TEC) to refine; (MÚS) to tune ♦ vi (tocar) to play in tune; (cantar) to sing in tune

afincarse [afin'karse] vr to settle

afinidad [afini'ðað] nf affinity; (parentesco) relationship; **por** ~ by marriage

afirmación [afirma'θjon] nf affirmation

afirmar [afir'mar] vt to affirm, state ❑ **afirmativo, -a** adj affirmative

afligir [afli'xir] vt to afflict; (apenar) to distress

aflojar [aflo'xar] vt to slacken; (desatar) to loosen, undo; (relajar) to relax ♦ vi to drop; (bajar) to go down; **aflojarse** vr to relax

afluente [aflu'ente] adj flowing ♦ nm tributary

afmo, -a abr (= afectísimo(a) suyo(a)) Yours

afónico, -a [a'foniko, a] adj: **estar ~** to have a sore throat; to have lost one's voice

aforo [a'foro] nm (de teatro etc) capacity

afortunado, -a [afortu'naðo, a] adj fortunate, lucky

África ['afrika] nf Africa ► **África del Sur** South Africa ❑ **africano, -a** adj, nm/f African

afrontar [afron'tar] vt to confront; (poner cara a cara) to bring face to face

afrutado, -a adj fruity

after (PL afters) nm after-hours club ❑ **afterhours** [after'aurs] nm inv = **after**

afuera [a'fwera] adv out, outside; **afueras** nfpl outskirts

agachar [aɣa'tʃar] vt to bend, bow; **agacharse** vr to stoop, bend

agalla [a'ɣaʎa] nf (ZOOL) gill; **tener agallas** (fam) to have guts

agarradera [aɣarra'ðera] (MÉX) nf handle

agarrado, -a [aɣa'rraðo, a] adj mean, stingy

agarrar [aɣa'rrar] vt to grasp, grab; (LAm: tomar) to take, catch; (recoger) to pick up ♦ vi (planta) to take root; **agarrarse** vr to hold on (tightly)

agencia [a'xenθja] nf agency ► **agencia de viajes** travel agency ► **agencia inmobiliaria** estate (BRIT) o real estate (US) agent's (office)

agenciarse [axen'θjarse] vr to obtain, procure

agenda [a'xenda] nf diary; ~ **electronica** PDA

⚠ No confundir **agenda** con la palabra inglesa agenda.

agente [a'xente] nmf agent; (tb: ~ **de policía**) policeman/policewoman ► **agente de seguros** insurance agent ► **agente de tráfico** (MÉX) traffic cop ► **agente inmobiliario** estate agent (BRIT), realtor (US)

ágil ['axil] adj agile, nimble ❑ **agilidad** nf agility, nimbleness

agilizar [axili'θar] vt (trámites) to speed up

agiotista (MÉX) nmf (usurero) usurer

agitación [axita'θjon] nf (de mano etc) shaking, waving; (de líquido etc) stirring; (fig) agitation

agitado, -a [axi'taðo, a] adj hectic; (viaje) bumpy

agitar [axi'tar] vt to wave, shake; (líquido) to stir; (fig) to stir up, excite;

agitarse vr to get excited; (inquietarse) to get worried o upset

aglomeración [aɣlomera'θjon] nf agglomeration ▶ **aglomeración de gente/tráfico** mass of people/traffic jam

agnóstico, -a [aɣ'nostiko, a] adj, nm/f agnostic

agobiar [aɣo'βjar] vt to weigh down; (oprimir) to oppress; (cargar) to burden

agolparse [aɣol'parse] vr to crowd together

agonía [aɣo'nia] nf death throes pl; (fig) agony, anguish

agonizante [aɣoni'θante] adj dying

agonizar [aɣoni'θar] vi to be dying

agosto [a'ɣosto] nm August

agotado, -a [aɣo'taðo, a] adj (persona) exhausted; (libros) out of print; (acabado) finished; (COM) sold out ❑ **agotador, a** [aɣota'ðor, a] adj exhausting

agotamiento [aɣota'mjento] nm exhaustion

agotar [aɣo'tar] vt to exhaust; (consumir) to drain; (recursos) to use up, deplete; **agotarse** vr to be exhausted; (acabarse) to run out; (libro) to go out of print

agraciado, -a [aɣra'θjaðo, a] adj (atractivo) attractive; (en sorteo etc) lucky

agradable [aɣra'ðaβle] adj pleasant, nice

agradar [aɣra'ðar] vt: **él me agrada** I like him

agradecer [aɣraðe'θer] vt to thank; (favor etc) to be grateful for ❑ **agradecido, -a** adj grateful; **¡muy agradecido!** thanks a lot! ❑ **agradecimiento** nm thanks pl; gratitude

agradezco etc vb ver **agradecer**

agrado [a'ɣraðo] nm: **ser de tu** etc ~ to be to your etc liking

agrandar [aɣran'dar] vt to enlarge; (fig) to exaggerate; **agrandarse** vr to get bigger

agrario, -a [a'ɣrarjo, a] adj agrarian, land cpd; (política) agricultural, farming

agravante [aɣra'βante] adj aggravating ♦ nm: **con el ~ de que ...** with the further difficulty that ...

agravar [aɣra'βar] vt (pesar sobre) to make heavier; (irritar) to aggravate; **agravarse** vr to worsen, get worse

agraviar [aɣra'βjar] vt to offend; (ser injusto con) to wrong

agredir [aɣre'ðir] vt to attack

agregado, -a [aɣre'ɣaðo, a] nm/f: A~ ≈ teacher (who is not head of department) ♦ nm aggregate; (persona) attaché

agregar [aɣre'ɣar] vt to gather; (añadir) to add; (persona) to appoint

agresión [aɣre'sjon] nf aggression

agresivo, -a [aɣre'siβo, a] adj aggressive

agriar [a'ɣrjar] vt to (turn) sour

agrícola [a'ɣrikola] adj farming cpd, agricultural

agricultor, a [aɣrikul'tor, a] nm/f farmer

agricultura [aɣrikul'tura] nf agriculture, farming

agridulce [aɣri'ðulθe] adj bittersweet; (CULIN) sweet and sour

agrietarse [aɣrje'tarse] vr to crack; (piel) to chap

agrio, -a [a'ɣrjo, a] adj bitter

agrupación [aɣrupa'θjon] nf group; (acto) grouping

agrupar [aɣru'par] vt to group

agua ['aɣwa] nf water; (NÁUT) wake; (ARQ) slope of a roof; **aguas** nfpl (de piedra) water sg, sparkle sg; (MED) water sg, urine sg; (NÁUT) waters ▶ **agua bendita/destilada/potable** holy/distilled/drinking water ▶ **agua caliente** hot water ▶ **agua corriente**

running water ▸ **agua de colonia** eau de cologne ▸ **agua mineral (con/sin gas)** (sparkling/still) mineral water ▸ **agua oxigenada** hydrogen peroxide ▸ **aguas abajo/arriba** downstream/upstream ▸ **aguas jurisdiccionales** territorial waters

aguacate [aɣwaˈkate] *nm* avocado (pear)

aguacero [aɣwaˈθero] *nm* (heavy) shower, downpour

aguado, -a [aˈɣwaðo, a] *adj* watery, watered down

aguafiestas [aɣwaˈfjestas] *nmf inv* spoilsport, killjoy

aguamiel (*MÉX*) [aɣwaˈmjel] *nf* fermented maguey *o* agave juice

aguanieve [aɣwaˈnjeβe] *nf* sleet

aguantar [aɣwanˈtar] *vt* to bear, put up with; (*sostener*) to hold up ♦ *vi* to last; **aguantarse** *vr* to restrain o.s. ❑ **aguante** *nm* (*paciencia*) patience; (*resistencia*) endurance

aguar [aˈɣwar] *vt* to water down

aguardar [aɣwarˈðar] *vt* to wait for

aguardiente [aɣwarˈðjente] *nm* brandy, liquor

aguarrás [aɣwaˈrras] *nm* turpentine

aguaviva (*RPl*) *nf* jellyfish

agudeza [aɣuˈðeθa] *nf* sharpness; (*ingenio*) wit

agudo, -a [aˈɣuðo, a] *adj* sharp; (*voz*) high-pitched, piercing; (*dolor, enfermedad*) acute

agüero [aˈɣwero] *nm*: **buen/mal ~** good/bad omen

aguijón [aɣiˈxon] *nm* sting; (*fig*) spur

águila [ˈaɣila] *nf* eagle; (*fig*) genius

aguileño, -a [aɣiˈleɲo, a] *adj* (*nariz*) aquiline; (*rostro*) sharp-featured

aguinaldo [aɣiˈnaldo] *nm* Christmas box

aguja [aˈɣuxa] *nf* needle; (*de reloj*) hand; (*ARQ*) spire; (*TEC*) firing-pin; **agujas** *nfpl* (*ZOOL*) ribs; (*FERRO*) points

agujerear [aɣuxereˈar] *vt* to make holes in

agujero [aɣuˈxero] *nm* hole

agujetas [aɣuˈxetas] *nfpl* stitch *sg*; (*rigidez*) stiffness *sg*

ahí [aˈi] *adv* there; **de ahí que** so that, with the result that; **ahí llega** here he comes; **por ahí** that way; (*allá*) over there; **200 o por ahí** 200 or so

ahijado, -a [aiˈxaðo, a] *nm/f* godson/daughter

ahogar [aoˈɣar] *vt* to drown; (*asfixiar*) to suffocate, smother; (*fuego*) to put out; **ahogarse** *vr* (*en el agua*) to drown; (*por asfixia*) to suffocate

ahogo [aˈoɣo] *nm* breathlessness; (*fig*) financial difficulty

ahondar [aonˈdar] *vt* to deepen, make deeper; (*fig*) to study thoroughly ♦ *vi*: **~ en** to study thoroughly

ahora [aˈora] *adv* now; (*hace poco*) a moment ago, just now; (*dentro de poco*) in a moment; **~ voy** I'm coming; **~ mismo** right now; **~ bien** now then; **por ~** for the present

ahorcar [aorˈkar] *vt* to hang

ahorita [aoˈrita] (*fam*) *adv* (*LAm: en este momento*) right now; (*MÉX: hace poco*) just now; (: *dentro de poco*) in a minute

ahorrar [aoˈrrar] *vt* (*dinero*) to save; (*esfuerzos*) to save, avoid ❑ **ahorro** (*acto*) saving; **ahorros** *nmpl* (*dinero*) savings

ahuecar [awekar] *vt* to hollow (out); (*voz*) to deepen; **ahuecarse** *vr* to give o.s. airs

ahumar [auˈmar] *vt* to smoke, cure; (*llenar de humo*) to fill with smoke ♦ *vi* to smoke; **ahumarse** *vr* to fill with smoke

ahuyentar [aujenˈtar] *vt* to drive off, frighten off; (*fig*) to dispel

aire [ˈaire] *nm* air; (*viento*) wind; (*corriente*) draught; (*MÚS*) tune; **al ~ libre** in the open air ▸ **aire acondicionado** air conditioning

❏ **airear** vt to air; **airearse** vr (persona) to go out for a breath of fresh air
❏ **airoso, -a** adj windy; draughty; (fig) graceful

aislado, -a [ais'laðo, a] adj isolated; (incomunicado) cut-off; (ELEC) insulated

aislar [ais'lar] vt to isolate; (ELEC) to insulate

ajardinado, -a [axarði'naðo, a] adj landscaped

ajedrez [axe'ðreθ] nm chess

ajeno, -a [a'xeno, a] adj (que pertenece a otro) somebody else's; ~ a foreign to

ajetreado, -a [axetre'aðo, a] adj busy

ajetreo [axe'treo] nm bustle

ají [a'xi] (CS) nm chil(l)i, red pepper; (salsa) chil(l)i sauce

ajillo [a'xiʎo] nm: **gambas al ~** garlic prawns

ajo ['axo] nm garlic

ajuar [a'xwar] nm household furnishings pl; (de novia) trousseau; (de niño) layette

ajustado, -a [axus'taðo, a] adj (tornillo) tight; (cálculo) right; (ropa) tight(-fitting); (resultado) close

ajustar [axus'tar] vt (adaptar) to adjust; (encajar) to fit; (TEC) to engage; (IMPRENTA) to make up; (apretar) to tighten; (concertar) to agree (on); (reconciliar) to reconcile; (cuentas, deudas) to settle ♦ vi to fit; **ajustarse** vr: **ajustarse a** (precio etc) to be in keeping with, fit in with; ~ **las cuentas a algn** to get even with sb

ajuste [a'xuste] nm adjustment; (COSTURA) fitting; (acuerdo) compromise; (de cuenta) settlement

al [al] (= a + el); ver **a**

ala ['ala] nf wing; (de sombrero) brim; winger ❏ **ala delta** nf hang-glider

alabanza [ala'βanθa] nf praise

alabar [ala'βar] vt to praise

alacena [ala'θena] nf kitchen cupboard (BRIT) o closet (US)

alacrán [ala'kran] nm scorpion

alambrada [alam'braða] nf wire fence; (red) wire netting

alambre [a'lambre] nm wire
▶ **alambre de púas** barbed wire

alameda [ala'meða] nf (plantío) poplar grove; (lugar de paseo) avenue, boulevard

álamo ['alamo] nm poplar

alarde [a'larðe] nm show, display; **hacer ~ de** to boast of

alargador [alarɣa'ðor] nm (ELEC) extension lead

alargar [alar'ɣar] vt to lengthen, extend; (paso) to hasten; (brazo) to stretch out; (cuerda) to pay out; (conversación) to spin out; **alargarse** vr to get longer

alarma [a'larma] nf alarm ▶ **alarma de incendios** fire alarm ❏ **alarmar** vt to alarm; **alarmarse** to get alarmed ❏ **alarmante** [alar'mante] adj alarming

alba ['alβa] nf dawn

albahaca [al'βaka] nf basil

Albania [al'βanja] nf Albania

albañil [alβa'ɲil] nm bricklayer; (cantero) mason

albarán [alβa'ran] nm (COM) delivery note, invoice

albaricoque [alβari'koke] nm apricot

albedrío [alβe'ðrio] nm: **libre ~** free will

alberca [al'βerka] nf reservoir; (MÉX: piscina) swimming pool

albergar [alβer'ɣar] vt to shelter

albergue etc [al'βerɣe] vb ver **albergar**
♦ nm shelter, refuge ▶ **albergue juvenil** youth hostel

albóndiga [al'βondiɣa] nf meatball

albornoz [alβor'noθ] nm (de los árabes) burnous; (para el baño) bathrobe

alborotar [alβoro'tar] vi to make a row
♦ vt to agitate, stir up; **alborotarse** vr to get excited; (mar) to get rough ❏ **alboroto** [alβo'roto] nm row, uproar

álbum [ˈalβum] (pl **álbums, álbumes**) nm album ▸ **álbum de recortes** scrapbook

albur (MÉX) nm (juego de palabras) pun; (doble sentido) double entendre

alcachofa [alkaˈtʃofa] nf artichoke

alcalde, -esa [alˈkalde, esa] nm/f mayor(ess)

alcaldía [alkalˈdia] nf mayoralty; (lugar) mayor's office

alcance etc [alˈkanθe] vb ver **alcanzar** ♦ nm reach; (COM) adverse balance; **al ~ de algn** available to sb

alcancía [alkanˈθia] nf (para ahorrar) money box; (para colectas) collection box

alcantarilla [alkantaˈriʎa] nf (de aguas cloacales) sewer; (en la calle) gutter

alcanzar [alkanˈθar] vt (algo: con la mano, el pie) to reach; (alguien: en el camino etc) to catch up with; (autobús) to catch; (bala) to hit, strike ♦ vi (ser suficiente) to be enough; **~ a hacer** to manage to do

alcaparra [alkaˈparra] nf caper

alcayata [alkaˈjata] nf hook

alcázar [alˈkaθar] nm fortress; (NÁUT) quarter-deck

alcoba [alˈkoβa] nf bedroom

alcohol [alˈkol] nm alcohol ▸ **alcohol metílico** methylated spirits pl (BRIT), wood alcohol (US) ❑ **alcohólico, -a** adj, nm/f alcoholic ❑ **alcoholímetro** [alko'limetro] nm Breathalyser® (BRIT), drunkometer (US) ❑ **alcoholismo** [alko'lismo] nm alcoholism

alcornoque [alkorˈnoke] nm cork tree; (fam) idiot

aldea [alˈdea] nf village ❑ **aldeano, -a** adj village cpd ♦ nm/f villager

aleación [aleaˈθjon] nf alloy

aleatorio, -a [aleaˈtorjo, a] adj random

aleccionar [alekθjoˈnar] vt to instruct; (adiestrar) to train

alegar [aleˈɣar] vt to claim; (JUR) to plead ♦ vi (LAm: discutir) to argue

alegoría [aleɣoˈria] nf allegory

alegrar [aleˈɣrar] vt (causar alegría) to cheer up; (fuego) to liven up; (fiesta) to liven up; **alegrarse** vr (fam) to get merry o tight; **alegrarse de** to be glad about

alegre [aˈleɣre] adj happy, cheerful; (fam) merry, tight; (chiste) risqué, blue ❑ **alegría** nf happiness; merriment

alejar [aleˈxar] vt to remove; (fig) to estrange; **alejarse** vr to move away

alemán, -ana [aleˈman, ana] adj, nm/f German ♦ nm (LING) German

Alemania [aleˈmanja] nf Germany

alentador, a [alentaˈðor, a] adj encouraging

alentar [alenˈtar] vt to encourage

alergia [aˈlerxja] nf allergy

alero [aˈlero] nm (de tejado) eaves pl; (guardabarros) mudguard

alerta [aˈlerta] adj, nm alert

aleta [aˈleta] nf (de pez) fin; (ala) wing; (de foca, DEPORTE) flipper; (AUTO) mudguard

aletear [aleteˈar] vi to flutter

alevín [aleˈβin] nm fry, young fish

alevosía [aleβoˈsia] nf treachery

alfabeto [alfaˈβeto] nm alphabet

alfalfa [alˈfalfa] nf alfalfa, lucerne

alfarería [alfareˈria] nf pottery; (tienda) pottery shop ❑ **alfarero, -a** nm/f potter

alféizar [alˈfeiθar] nm window-sill

alférez [alˈfereθ] nm (MIL) second lieutenant; (NÁUT) ensign

alfil [alˈfil] nm (AJEDREZ) bishop

alfiler [alfiˈler] nm pin; (broche) clip

alfombra [alˈfombra] nf carpet; (más pequeña) rug ❑ **alfombrilla** nf rug, mat; (INFORM) mouse mat o pad

alforja [alˈforxa] nf saddlebag

algas [ˈalɣas] nfpl seaweed

álgebra [ˈalxeβra] nf algebra

algo [ˈalɣo] pron something; anything ♦ adv somewhat, rather; **¿~ más?**

anything else?; (en tienda) is that all?; **por ~ será** there must be some reason for it

algodón [alɣo'ðon] nm cotton; (planta) cotton plant ▶ **algodón de azúcar** candy floss (BRIT), cotton candy (US) ▶ **algodón hidrófilo** cotton wool (BRIT), absorbent cotton (US)

alguien ['alɣjen] pron someone, somebody; (en frases interrogativas) anyone, anybody

alguno, -a [al'ɣuno, a] adj (delante de nm): **algún** some; (después de n): **no tiene talento ~** he has no talent, he doesn't have any talent ♦ pron (alguien) someone, somebody; **algún que otro libro** some book or other; **algún día iré** I'll go one o some day; **sin interés** ~ without the slightest interest; **~ que otro** an occasional one; **algunos piensan** some (people) think

alhaja [a'laxa] nf jewel; (tesoro) precious object, treasure

alhelí [ale'li] nm wallflower, stock

aliado, -a [a'ljaðo, a] adj allied

alianza [a'ljanθa] nf alliance; (anillo) wedding ring

aliar [a'ljar] vt to ally; **aliarse** vr to form an alliance

alias ['aljas] adv alias

alicatado (ESP) nm tiling

alicates [ali'kates] nmpl pliers

aliciente [ali'θjente] nm incentive; (atracción) attraction

alienación [aljena'θjon] nf alienation

aliento [a'ljento] nm breath; (respiración) breathing; **sin ~** breathless

aligerar [alixe'rar] vt to lighten; (reducir) to shorten; (aliviar) to alleviate; (mitigar) to ease; (paso) to quicken

alijo [a'lixo] nm consignment

alimaña [ali'maɲa] nf pest

alimentación [alimenta'θjon] nf (comida) food; (acción) feeding; (tienda) grocer's shop

alimentar [alimen'tar] vt to feed; (nutrir) to nourish; **alimentarse** vr to feed

alimenticio, -a [alimen'tiθjo, a] adj food cpd; (nutritivo) nourishing, nutritious

alimento [ali'mento] nm food; (nutrición) nourishment

alineación [alinea'θjon] nf alignment; (DEPORTE) line-up

alinear [aline'ar] vt to align; (DEPORTE) to select, pick

aliñar [ali'ɲar] vt (CULIN) to season ◻ **aliño** nm (CULIN) dressing

alioli [ali'oli] nm garlic mayonnaise

alisar [ali'sar] vt to smooth

alistarse [alis'tarse] vr to enlist; (inscribirse) to enroll

aliviar [ali'βjar] vt (carga) to lighten; (persona) to relieve; (dolor) to relieve, alleviate

alivio [a'liβjo] nm alleviation, relief

aljibe [al'xiβe] nm cistern

allá [a'ʎa] adv (lugar) there; (por ahí) over there; (tiempo) then; **allá abajo** down there; **más allá** further on; **más allá de** beyond; **¡allá tú!** that's your problem!; **¡allá voy!** I'm coming!

allanamiento [aʎana'mjento] nm (LAm: de policía) raid ▶ **allanamiento de morada** burglary

allanar [aʎa'nar] vt to flatten, level (out); (igualar) to smooth (out); (fig) to subdue; (JUR) to burgle, break into

allegado, -a [aʎe'ɣaðo, a] adj near, close ♦ nm/f relation

allí [a'ʎi] adv there; **allí mismo** right there; **por allí** over there; (por ese camino) that way

alma ['alma] nf soul; (persona) person

almacén [alma'θen] nm (depósito) warehouse, store; (MIL) magazine; (CS: de comestibles) grocer's (shop) grandes almacenes department store sg □ **almacenaje** nm storage

almacenar [alma'θe'nar] vt to store, put in storage; (proveerse) to stock up with

almanaque [alma'nake] nm almanac

almeja [al'mexa] nf clam

almendra [al'mendra] nf almond □ **almendro** nm almond tree

almíbar [al'miβar] nm syrup

almidón [almi'ðon] nm starch

almirante [almi'rante] nm admiral

almohada [almo'aða] nf pillow; (funda) pillowcase □ **almohadilla** nf cushion; (para alfileres) pincushion; (TEC) pad

almohadón [almoa'ðon] nm large pillow; bolster

almorranas [almo'rranas] nfpl piles, haemorrhoids

almorzar [almor'θar] vt: ~ **una tortilla** to have an omelette for lunch ♦ vi to (have) lunch

almuerzo etc [al'mwerθo] vb ver **almorzar** ♦ nm lunch

alocado, -a [alo'kaðo, a] adj crazy

alojamiento [aloxa'mjento] nm lodging(s) pl; (viviendas) housing

alojar [alo'xar] vt to lodge; **alojarse** vr to lodge, stay

alondra [a'londra] nf lark, skylark

alpargata [alpar'γata] nf rope-soled sandal, espadrille

Alpes [alpes] nmpl: los ~ the Alps

alpinismo [alpi'nismo] nm mountaineering, climbing □ **alpinista** nmf mountaineer, climber

alpiste [al'piste] nm birdseed

alquilar [alki'lar] vt (propietario: inmuebles) to let, rent (out); (: coche) to hire out; (: TV) to rent (out); (alquilador: inmuebles, TV) to rent; (: coche) to hire; **"se alquila casa"** "house to let" or for rent (US)

alquiler [alki'ler] nm renting; letting; hiring; (arriendo) rent; hire charge; de ~

for hire ► **alquiler de automóviles** o **coches** car hire

alquimia [al'kimja] nf alchemy

alquitrán [alki'tran] nm tar

alrededor [alreðe'ðor] adv around, about; ~ **de** around, about; **mirar a su** ~ to look (round) about one □ **alrededores** nmpl surroundings

alta ['alta] nf (certificate of) discharge

altar [al'tar] nm altar

altavoz [alta'βoθ] nm loudspeaker; (amplificador) amplifier

alteración [altera'θjon] nf alteration; (alboroto) disturbance

alterar [alte'rar] vt to alter; to disturb; **alterarse** vr (persona) to get upset

altercado [alter'kaðo] nm argument

alternar [alter'nar] vt to alternate ♦ vi to alternate; (turnar) to take turns; **alternarse** vr to alternate; to take turns; ~ **con** to mix with □ **alternativa** nf alternative; (elección) choice □ **alternativo, -a** adj alternative; (alterno) alternating □ **alterno, -a** adj alternate; (ELEC) alternating

Alteza [al'teθa] nf (tratamiento) Highness

altibajos [alti'βaxos] nmpl ups and downs

altiplanicie [altipla'niθje] nf, **altiplano** [alti'plano] nm high plateau

altisonante [altiso'nante] adj high-flown, high-sounding

altitud [alti'tuð] nf height; (AVIAC, GEO) altitude

altivo, -a [al'tiβo, a] adj haughty, arrogant

alto, -a ['alto, a] adj high; (persona) tall; (sonido) high, sharp; (noble) high, lofty ♦ nm halt; (MÚS) alto; (GEO) hill ♦ adv (de sitio) high; (de sonido) loud, loudly ♦ excl halt!; **la pared tiene 2 metros de** ~ the wall is 2 metres high; **en alta mar** on the high seas; **en voz alta** in a loud voice; **las altas horas de la noche**

small o wee hours; **en lo ~ de** at the top of; **pasar por ~** to overlook
❑ **altoparlante** [altopar'lante] (LAm) nm loudspeaker

altura [al'tura] nf height; (NAUT) depth; (GEO) latitude; **la pared tiene 1.80 de ~** the wall is 1 metre 80cm high; **a estas alturas** at this stage; **a estas alturas del año** at this time of the year

alubia [a'luβja] nf bean

alucinación [aluθina'θjon] nf hallucination

alucinar [aluθi'nar] vi to hallucinate ♦ vt to deceive; (fascinar) to fascinate

alud [a'luð] nm avalanche; (fig) flood

aludir [alu'ðir] vi: **~ a** to allude to; **darse por aludido** to take the hint

alumbrado [alum'braðo] nm lighting

alumbrar [alum'brar] vt to light (up) ♦ vi (MED) to give birth

aluminio [alu'minjo] nm aluminium (BRIT), aluminum (US)

alumno, -a [a'lumno, a] nm/f pupil, student

alusión [alu'sjon] nf allusion

alusivo, -a [alu'siβo, a] adj allusive

aluvión [aluβjon] nm alluvium; (fig) flood

alverja [al'βerxa] (LAm) nf pea

alza ['alθa] nf rise; (MIL) sight

alzamiento [alθa'mjento] nm (rebelión) rising

alzar [al'θar] vt to lift (up); (precio, muro) to raise; (cuello de abrigo) to turn up; (AGR) to gather in; (IMPRENTA) to gather; **alzarse** vr to get up, rise; (rebelarse) to revolt; (COM) to go fraudulently bankrupt; (JUR) to appeal

ama ['ama] nf lady of the house; (dueña) owner; (institutriz) governess; (madre adoptiva) foster mother ▶ **ama de casa** housewife ▶ **ama de llaves** housekeeper

amabilidad [amaβili'ðað] nf kindness; (simpatía) niceness ❑ **amable** adj

kind; nice; **es usted muy amable** that's very kind of you

amaestrado, -a [amaes'traðo, a] adj (animal: en circo etc) performing

amaestrar [amaes'trar] vt to train

amago [a'mayo] nm threat; (gesto) threatening gesture; (MED) symptom

amainar [amai'nar] vi (viento) to die down

amamantar [amaman'tar] vt to suckle, nurse

amanecer [amane'θer] vi to dawn ♦ nm dawn; **~ afiebrado** to wake up with a fever

amanerado, -a [amane'raðo, a] adj affected

amante [a'mante] adj: **~ de** fond of ♦ nmf lover

amapola [ama'pola] nf poppy

amar [a'mar] vt to love

amargado, -a [amar'yaðo, a] adj bitter

amargar [amar'yar] vt to make bitter; (fig) to embitter; **amargarse** vr to become embittered

amargo, -a [a'maryo, a] adj bitter

amarillento, -a [amari'λento, a] adj yellowish; (tez) sallow □ **amarillo, -a** adj, nm yellow

amarrado, -a [ama'rraðo, a] (MÉX: fam) adj mean, stingy

amarrar [ama'rrar] vt to moor; (sujetar) to tie up

amarras [a'marras] nfpl: **soltar ~** to set sail

amasar [ama'sar] vt (masa) to knead; (mezclar) to mix, prepare; (confeccionar) to concoct

amateur [ama'ter] nmf amateur

amazona [ama'θona] nf horsewoman □ **Amazonas** nm: **el Amazonas** the Amazon

ámbar ['ambar] nm amber

ambición [ambi'θjon] nf ambition □ **ambicionar** vt to aspire to □ **ambicioso, -a** adj ambitious

ambidextro, -a [ambi'ðekstro, a] *adj* ambidextrous

ambientación [ambjenta'θjon] *nf* (CINE, TEATRO etc) setting; (RADIO) sound effects

ambiente [am'bjente] *nm* atmosphere; (medio) environment

ambigüedad [ambigwe'ðað] *nf* ambiguity □ **ambiguo, -a** *adj* ambiguous

ámbito ['ambito] *nm* (campo) field; (fig) scope

ambos, -as ['ambos, as] *adj pl, pron pl* both

ambulancia [ambu'lanθja] *nf* ambulance

ambulante [ambu'lante] *adj* travelling cpd, itinerant

ambulatorio [ambula'torjo] *nm* state health-service clinic

amén [a'men] *excl* amen; **~ de** besides

amenaza [ame'naθa] *nf* menace, threat □ **amenazar** [amena'θar] *vt* to threaten ♦ *vi*: **amenazar con hacer** to threaten to do

ameno, -a [a'meno, a] *adj* pleasant

América [a'merika] *nf* America ► **América Central/Latina** Central/ Latin America ► **América del Norte/ del Sur** North/South America □ **americana** *nf* coat, jacket; *ver tb* **americano** □ **americano, -a** *adj, nm/ f* American

ametralladora [ametraʎa'ðora] *nf* machine gun

amigable [ami'ɣaβle] *adj* friendly

amígdala [a'miɣðala] *nf* tonsil □ **amigdalitis** *nf* tonsillitis

amigo, -a [a'miɣo, a] *adj* friendly ♦ *nm/ f* friend; (amante) lover; **ser ~ de algo** to be fond of sth; **ser muy amigos** to be close friends

aminorar [amino'rar] *vt* to diminish; (reducir) to reduce; **~ la marcha** to slow down

amistad [amis'tað] *nf* friendship; **amistades** *nfpl* (amigos) friends □ **amistoso, -a** *adj* friendly

amnesia [am'nesja] *nf* amnesia

amnistía [amnis'tia] *nf* amnesty

amo ['amo] *nm* owner; (jefe) boss

amolar [amo'lar] (MÉX: fam) *vt* to ruin, damage

amoldar [amol'dar] *vt* to mould; (adaptar) to adapt

amonestación [amonesta'θjon] *nf* warning; **amonestaciones** *nfpl* (REL) marriage banns

amonestar [amones'tar] *vt* to warn; (REL) to publish the banns

amontonar [amonto'nar] *vt* to collect, pile up; **amontonarse** *vr* to crowd together; (acumularse) to pile up

amor [a'mor] *nm* love; (amante) lover; **hacer el ~** to make love ► **amor propio** self-respect

amoratado, -a [a'mora'taðo, a] *adj* purple

amordazar [amorða'θar] *vt* to muzzle; (fig) to gag

amorfo, -a [a'morfo, a] *adj* amorphous, shapeless

amoroso, -a [amo'roso, a] *adj* affectionate, loving

amortiguador [amortigwa'ðor] *nm* shock absorber; (parachoques) bumper; **amortiguadores** *nmpl* (AUTO) suspension sg

amortiguar [amorti'ɣwar] *vt* to deaden; (ruido) to muffle; (color) to soften

amotinar [amoti'nar] *vt* to stir up, incite (to riot); **amotinarse** *vr* to mutiny

amparar [ampa'rar] *vt* to protect; **ampararse** *vr* to seek protection; (de la lluvia etc) to shelter □ **amparo** *nm* help, protection; **al amparo de** under the protection of

amperio [am'perjo] *nm* ampère, amp

ampliación [amplja'θjon] *nf* enlargement; (extensión) extension

ampliar [am'pljar] vt to enlarge; to extend

amplificador [amplifika'ðor] nm amplifier

amplificar [amplifi'kar] vt to amplify

amplio, -a [am'pljo, a] adj spacious; (de falda etc) full; (extenso) extensive; (ancho) wide ▢ **amplitud** nf spaciousness; extent; (fig) amplitude

ampolla [am'poʎa] nf blister; (MED) ampoule

amputar [ampu'tar] vt to cut off, amputate

amueblar [amwe'βlar] vt to furnish

anales [a'nales] nmpl annals

analfabetismo [analfaβe'tismo] nm illiteracy ▢ **analfabeto, -a** adj, nm/f illiterate

analgésico [anal'xesiko] nm painkiller, analgesic

análisis [a'nalisis] nm inv analysis

analista [ana'lista] nmf (gen) analyst

analizar [anali'θar] vt to analyse

analógico, -a [ana'loxiko, a] adj (INFORM) digital; (reloj) analogue (BRIT), analog (US)

análogo, -a [a'naloɣo, a] adj analogous, similar

ananá [ana'na] (RPl) nm pineapple

anarquía [anar'kia] nf anarchy ▢ **anarquista** nmf anarchist

anatomía [anato'mia] nf anatomy

anca ['anka] nf rump, haunch; **ancas** nfpl (fam) behind sg

ancho, -a ['antʃo, a] adj wide; (falda) full; (fig) liberal ♦ nm width; (FERRO) gauge; **ponerse ~** to get conceited; **estar a sus anchas** to be at one's ease

anchoa [an'tʃoa] nf anchovy

anchura [an'tʃura] nf width; (extensión) wideness

anciano, -a [an'θjano, a] adj old, aged ♦ nm/f old man/woman; elder

ancla ['ankla] nf anchor

Andalucía [andalu'θia] nf Andalusia ▢ **andaluz, -a** adj, nm/f Andalusian

andamio [an'damjo] nm scaffold(ing)

andar [an'dar] vt to go, cover, travel ♦ vi to go, walk, travel; (funcionar) to go, work; (estar) to be ♦ nm walk, gait, pace; **andarse** vr to go away; **~ a pie/a caballo/en bicicleta** to go on foot/on horseback/by bicycle; **~ haciendo algo** to be doing sth; **¡anda!** come on!; **anda por o en los 40** he's about 40

andén [an'den] nm (FERRO) platform; (NÁUT) quayside; (CAm: de la calle) pavement (BRIT), sidewalk (US)

Andes ['andes] nmpl: **los ~** the Andes

andinismo [andi'nismo] (LAm) nm mountaineering, climbing

Andorra [an'dorra] nf Andorra

andrajoso, -a [andra'xoso, a] adj ragged

anduve etc [an'duβe] vb ver **andar**

anécdota [a'nekðota] nf anecdote, story

anegar [ane'ɣar] vt to flood; (ahogar) to drown

anemia [a'nemja] nf anaemia

anestesia [anes'tesja] nf (sustancia) anaesthetic; (proceso) anaesthesia ▶ **anestesia general/local** general/local anaesthetic

anexar [anek'sar] vt to annex; (documento) to attach ▢ **anexión** nf annexation ▢ **anexo, -a** adj attached ♦ nm annexe

anfibio, -a [an'fiβjo, a] adj amphibious ♦ nm amphibian

anfiteatro [anfite'atro] nm amphitheatre; (TEATRO) dress circle

anfitrión, -ona [anfi'trjon, ona] nm/f host(ess)

ánfora nf (cántaro) amphora; (MÉX POL) ballot box

ángel ['anxel] nm angel ▶ **ángel de la guarda** guardian angel

angina [an'xina] nf (MED) inflammation of the throat; **tener anginas** to have tonsillitis ▸ **angina de pecho** angina

anglicano, -a [angli'kano, a] adj, nm/f Anglican

anglosajón, -ona [anglosa'xon, ona] adj Anglo-Saxon

anguila [an'gila] nf eel

angula [an'gula] nf elver, baby eel

ángulo ['angulo] nm angle; (esquina) corner; (curva) bend

angustia [an'gustja] nf anguish

anhelar [ane'lar] vt to be eager for; (desear) to long for, desire ▸ vi to pant, gasp □ **anhelo** nm eagerness; desire

anidar [ani'ðar] vi to nest

anillo [a'niʎo] nm ring ▸ **anillo de boda/compromiso** wedding/ engagement ring

animación [anima'θjon] nf liveliness; (vitalidad) life; (actividad) activity; bustle

animado, -a [ani'maðo, a] adj lively; (vivaz) animated □ **animador, a** nm/f (TV) host(ess), compère; (DEPORTE) cheerleader

animal [ani'mal] adj animal; (fig) stupid ▸ nm animal; (fig) fool; (bestia) brute

animar [ani'mar] vt (BIO) to animate, give life to; (estimular) to liven up, brighten up, cheer up; (estimular) to stimulate; **animarse** vr to cheer up; to feel encouraged; (decidirse) to make up one's mind

ánimo ['animo] nm (alma) soul; (mente) mind; (valentía) courage ▸ excl cheer up!

animoso, -a [ani'moso, a] adj brave; (vivo) lively

aniquilar [aniki'lar] vt to annihilate, destroy

anís [a'nis] nm aniseed; (licor) anisette

aniversario [aniβer'sarjo] nm anniversary

anoche [a'notʃe] adv last night; **antes de ~** the night before last

anochecer [anotʃe'θer] vi to get dark ▸ nm nightfall, dark; **al ~** at nightfall

anodino, -a [ano'ðino, a] adj dull, anodyne

anomalía [anoma'lia] nf anomaly

anonadado, -a [anona'ðaðo, a] adj: **estar ~** to be overwhelmed o amazed

anonimato [anoni'mato] nm anonymity

anónimo, -a [a'nonimo, a] adj anonymous; (COM) limited ▸ nm (carta anónima) anonymous letter; (: maliciosa) poison-pen letter

anormal [anor'mal] adj abnormal

anotación [anota'θjon] nf note; annotation

anotar [ano'tar] vt to note down; (comentar) to annotate

ansia ['ansja] nf anxiety; (añoranza) yearning □ **ansiar** vt to long for

ansiedad [ansje'ðað] nf anxiety

ansioso, -a [an'sjoso, a] adj anxious; (anhelante) eager; **~ de o por algo** greedy for sth

antaño [an'taɲo] adv long ago, formerly

Antártico [an'tartiko] nm: **el ~** the Antarctic

ante ['ante] prep before, in the presence of; (problema etc) faced with ▸ nm (piel) suede; **~ todo** above all

anteanoche [antea'notʃe] adv the night before last

anteayer [antea'jer] adv the day before yesterday

antebrazo [ante'βraθo] nm forearm

antecedente [anteθe'ðente] adj previous ▸ nm antecedent; **antecedentes** nmpl (historial) record sg ▸ **antecedentes penales** criminal record

anteceder [anteθe'ðer] vt to precede, go before

antecesor, a [anteθe'sor, a] nm/f predecessor

antelación [antela'θjon] *nf*: **con ~** in advance

antemano [ante'mano]: **de ~** *adv* beforehand, in advance

antena [an'tena] *nf* antenna; (*de televisión etc*) aerial ▶ **antena parabólica** satellite dish

antenoche (*LAm*) *adv* the night before last

anteojo [ante'oxo] *nm* eyeglass; **anteojos** *nmpl* (*LAm*: *gafas*) glasses, spectacles

antepasados [antepa'saðos] *nmpl* ancestors

anteponer [antepo'ner] *vt* to place in front; (*fig*) to prefer

anterior [ante'rjor] *adj* preceding, previous ▢ **anterioridad** *nf*: **con anterioridad a** prior to, before

antes ['antes] *adv* (*con prioridad*) before ♦ *prep*: **~ de** before ♦ *conj*: **~ de ir/de que te vayas** before going/before you go; **~ bien** (but) rather; **dos días ~** two days before o earlier; **no quiso venir ~** she didn't want to come any earlier; **tomo el avión ~ que el barco** I take the plane rather than the boat; **~ de o que nada** (*en el tiempo*) first of all; (*indicando preferencia*) above all; **~ que yo** before me; **lo ~ posible** as soon as possible; **cuanto ~ mejor** the sooner the better

antibalas [anti'βalas] *adj inv*: **chaleco ~** bullet-proof jacket

antibiótico [anti'βjotiko] *nm* antibiotic

anticipación [antiθipa'θjon] *nf* anticipation; **con 10 minutos de ~** 10 minutes early

anticipado, -a [antiθi'paðo, a] *adj* (*pago*) advance; **por ~** in advance

anticipar [antiθi'par] *vt* to anticipate; (*adelantar*) to bring forward; (*COM*) to advance; **anticiparse** *vr*: **anticiparse a su época** to be ahead of one's time

anticipo [anti'θipo] *nm* (*COM*) advance

anticonceptivo, -a [antikonθep'tiβo, a] *adj*, *nm* contraceptive

anticongelante [antikonxe'lante] *nm* antifreeze

anticuado, -a [anti'kwaðo, a] *adj* out-of-date, old-fashioned; (*desusado*) obsolete

anticuario [anti'kwarjo] *nm* antique dealer

anticuerpo [anti'kwerpo] *nm* (*MED*) antibody

antidepresivo [antiðepre'siβo] *nm* antidepressant

antídoto [an'tiðoto] *nm* antidote

antiestético, -a [anties'tetiko, a] *adj* unsightly

antifaz [anti'faθ] *nm* mask; (*velo*) veil

antiglobalización *nf* anti-globalization ▢ **antiglobalizador, a** *adj* anti-globalization *cpd*

antiguamente [antiɣwa'mente] *adv* formerly; (*hace mucho tiempo*) long ago

antigüedad [antiɣwe'ðað] *nf* antiquity; (*artículo*) antique; (*rango*) seniority

antiguo, -a [an'tiɣwo, a] *adj* old, ancient; (*que fue*) former

Antillas [an'tiʎas] *nfpl*: **las ~** the West Indies

antílope [an'tilope] *nm* antelope

antinatural [antinatu'ral] *adj* unnatural

antipatía [antipa'tia] *nf* antipathy, dislike ▢ **antipático, -a** *adj* disagreeable, unpleasant

antirrobo [anti'rroβo] *adj inv* (*alarma etc*) anti-theft

antisemita [antise'mita] *adj* anti-Semitic ♦ *nmf* anti-Semite

antiséptico, -a [anti'septiko, a] *adj* antiseptic ♦ *nm* antiseptic

antojarse [anto'xarse] *vr* (*desear*): **se me antoja comprarlo** I have a mind to buy it; (*pensar*): **se me antoja que ...** I have a feeling that ...

antojitos *(MÉX)* nmpl snacks, nibbles

antojo [an'toxo] nm caprice, whim; *(rosa)* birthmark; *(lunar)* mole

antología [antolo'xia] nf anthology

antorcha [an'tortʃa] nf torch

antro ['antro] nm cavern

antropología [antropolo'xia] nf anthropology

anual [a'nwal] adj annual

anuario [a'nwarjo] nm yearbook

anulación [anula'θjon] nf annulment; *(cancelación)* cancellation

anular [anu'lar] vt *(contrato)* to annul, cancel; *(ley)* to revoke, repeal; *(suscripción)* to cancel ♦ nm ring finger

anunciar [anun'θjar] vt to announce; *(proclamar)* to proclaim; *(COM)* to advertise

anuncio [a'nunθjo] nm announcement; *(señal)* sign; *(COM)* advertisement; *(cartel)* poster

anzuelo [an'θwelo] nm hook; *(para pescar)* fish hook

añadidura [aɲaði'ðura] nf addition, extra; **por ~** besides, in addition

añadir [aɲa'ðir] vt to add

añejo, -a [a'ɲexo, a] adj old; *(vino)* mellow

añicos [a'ɲikos] nmpl: **hacer ~** to smash, shatter

año ['aɲo] nm year; **¡Feliz A~ Nuevo!** Happy New Year!; **tener 15 años** to be 15 (years old); **los años 90** the nineties; **el ~ que viene** next year ♦ **año bisiesto/escolar/fiscal/sabático** leap/school/tax/sabbatical year

añoranza [aɲo'ranθa] nf nostalgia; *(anhelo)* longing

apa *(MÉX)* excl goodness me!, good gracious!

apabullar [apaβu'ʎar] vt to crush, squash

apacible [apa'θiβle] adj gentle, mild

apaciguar [apaθi'ɣwar] vt to pacify, calm (down)

apadrinar [apaðri'nar] vt to sponsor, support; *(REL)* to be godfather to

apagado, -a [apa'ɣaðo, a] adj *(volcán)* extinct; *(color)* dull; *(voz)* quiet; *(sonido)* muted, muffled; *(persona: apático)* listless; **estar ~** *(fuego, luz)* to be out; *(RADIO, TV etc)* to be off

apagar [apa'ɣar] vt to put out; *(ELEC, RADIO, TV)* to turn off; *(sonido)* to silence, muffle; *(sed)* to quench

apagón [apa'ɣon] nm blackout; power cut

apalabrar [apala'βrar] vt to agree to; *(contratar)* to engage

apalear [apale'ar] vt to beat, thrash

apantallar *(MÉX)* vt to impress

apañar [apa'ɲar] vt to pick up; *(asir)* to take hold of, grasp; *(reparar)* to mend, patch up; **apañarse** vr to manage, get along

apapachar *(MÉX: fam)* [apapa'tʃar] vt to cuddle, hug

aparador [apara'ðor] nm sideboard; *(MÉX: escaparate)* shop window

aparato [apa'rato] nm apparatus; *(máquina)* machine; *(doméstico)* appliance; *(boato)* ostentation
▶ **aparato digestivo** *(ANAT)* digestive system ❑ **aparatoso, -a** adj showy, ostentatious

aparcamiento [aparka'mjento] nm car park *(BRIT)*, parking lot *(US)*

aparcar [apar'kar] vt, vi to park

aparear [apare'ar] vt *(objetos)* to pair, match; *(animales)* to mate; **aparearse** vr to make a pair; to mate

aparecer [apare'θer] vi to appear; **aparecerse** vr to appear

aparejador, a [aparexa'ðor, a] nm/f *(ARQ)* master builder

aparejo [apa'rexo] nm harness; rigging; *(de poleas)* block and tackle

aparentar [aparen'tar] vt *(edad)* to look; *(fingir)*: **~ tristeza** to pretend to be sad

aparente [apaˈrente] *adj* apparent; *(adecuado)* suitable

aparezco *etc vb ver* **aparecer**

aparición [apariˈθjon] *nf* appearance; *(de libro)* publication; *(espectro)* apparition

apariencia [apaˈrjenθja] *nf* (outward) appearance; **en ~** outwardly, seemingly

apartado, -a [aparˈtaðo, a] *adj* separate; *(lejano)* remote ♦ *nm* *(tipográfico)* paragraph ▶ **apartado de correos** *(ESP)* post office box ▶ **apartado postal** *(LAm)* post office box

apartamento [apartaˈmento] *nm* apartment, flat *(BRIT)*

apartar [aparˈtar] *vt* to separate; *(quitar)* to remove; **apartarse** *vr* to separate, part; *(irse)* to move away; to keep away

aparte [aˈparte] *adv* (separadamente) separately; (además) besides ♦ *nm* aside; *(tipográfico)* new paragraph

apasionado, -a [apasjoˈnaðo, a] *adj* passionate

apasionar [apasjoˈnar] *vt* to excite; **le apasiona el fútbol** she's crazy about football; **apasionarse** *vr* to get excited

apatía [apaˈtia] *nf* apathy

apático, -a [aˈpatiko, a] *adj* apathetic

Apdo *abr* (= Apartado (de Correos)) PO Box

apeadero [apeaˈðero] *nm* halt, stop, stopping place

apearse [apeˈarse] *vr* (jinete) to dismount; *(bajarse)* to get down *o* out; *(AUTO, FERRO)* to get off *o* out

apechugar [apetʃuˈɣar] *vi*: **~ con algo** to face up to sth

apegarse [apeˈɣarse] *vr*: **~ a** to become attached to ❑ **apego** *nm* attachment, devotion

apelar [apeˈlar] *vi* to appeal; **~ a** *(fig)* to resort to

apellidar [apeʎiˈðar] *vt* to call, name; **apellidarse** *vr*: **se apellida Pérez** her (sur)name's Pérez

apellido [apeˈʎiðo] *nm* surname

apenar [apeˈnar] *vt* to grieve, trouble; *(LAm: avergonzar)* to embarrass; **apenarse** *vr* to grieve; *(LAm: avergonzarse)* to be embarrassed

apenas [aˈpenas] *adv* scarcely, hardly ♦ *conj* as soon as, no sooner

apéndice [aˈpendiθe] *nm* appendix ❑ **apendicitis** *nf* appendicitis

aperitivo [periˈtiβo] *nm* (bebida) aperitif; *(comida)* appetizer

apertura [aperˈtura] *nf* opening; *(POL)* liberalization

apestar [apesˈtar] *vt* to infect ♦ *vi*: **~ (a)** to stink (of)

apetecer [apeteˈθer] *vt*: **¿te apetece un café?** do you fancy a (cup of) coffee? ❑ **apetecible** *adj* desirable; *(comida)* appetizing

apetito [apeˈtito] *nm* appetite ❑ **apetitoso, -a** *adj* appetizing; *(fig)* tempting

apiadarse [apjaˈðarse] *vr*: **~ de** to take pity on

ápice [ˈapiθe] *nm* whit, iota

apilar [apiˈlar] *vt* to pile *o* heap up

apiñarse [apiˈɲarse] *vr* to crowd *o* press together

apio [ˈapjo] *nm* celery

apisonadora [apisonaˈðora] *nf* steamroller

aplacar [aplaˈkar] *vt* to placate

aplastante [aplasˈtante] *adj* overwhelming; *(lógica)* compelling

aplastar [aplasˈtar] *vt* to squash (flat); *(fig)* to crush

aplaudir [aplauˈðir] *vt* to applaud

aplauso [aˈplauso] *nm* applause; *(fig)* approval, acclaim

aplazamiento [aplaθa'mjento] nm postponement

aplazar [apla'θar] vt to postpone, defer

aplicación [aplika'θjon] nf application; (esfuerzo) effort

aplicado, -a [apli'kaðo, a] adj diligent, hard-working

aplicar [apli'kar] vt (ejecutar) to apply; **aplicarse** vr to apply o.s.

aplique etc [a'plike] vb ver **aplicar**
♦ nm wall light

aplomo [a'plomo] nm aplomb, self-assurance

apodar [apo'ðar] vt to nickname

apoderado [apoðe'raðo] nm agent, representative

apoderarse [apoðe'rarse] vr: ~ de to take possession of

apodo [a'poðo] nm nickname

apogeo [apo'xeo] nm peak, summit

apoquinar [apoki'nar] (fam) vt to fork out, cough up

aporrear [aporre'ar] vt to beat (up)

aportar [apor'tar] vt to contribute ♦ vi to reach port; **aportarse** vr (LAm: llegar) to arrive, come

aposta [a'posta] adv deliberately, on purpose

apostar [apos'tar] vt to bet, stake; (tropas etc) to station, post ♦ vi to bet

apóstol [a'postol] nm apostle

apóstrofo [a'postrofo] nm apostrophe

apoyar [apo'jar] vt to lean, rest; (fig) to support, back; **apoyarse** vr: **apoyarse en** to lean on ♦ **apoyo** nm (gen) support; backing, help

apreciable [apre'θjaβle] adj considerable, (fig) esteemed

apreciar [apre'θjar] vt to evaluate, assess; (COM) to appreciate, value; (persona) to respect; (tamaño) to gauge, assess; (detalles) to notice

aprecio [a'preθjo] nm valuation, estimate; (fig) appreciation

aprehender [apreen'der] vt to apprehend, detain

apremio [a'premjo] nm urgency

aprender [apren'der] vt to learn; ~ **algo de memoria** to learn sth (off) by heart

aprendiz, a [apren'diθ, a] nm/f apprentice; (principiante) learner ❑ **aprendizaje** nm apprenticeship

aprensión [apren'sjon] nm apprehension, fear ♦ **aprensivo, -a** adj apprehensive

apresar [apre'sar] vt to seize; (capturar) to capture

apresurado, -a [apresu'raðo, a] adj hurried, hasty

apresurar [apresu'rar] vt to hurry, accelerate; **apresurarse** vr to hurry, make haste

apretado, -a [apre'taðo, a] adj tight; (escritura) cramped

apretar [apre'tar] vt to squeeze; (TEC) to tighten; (presionar) to press together, pack ♦ vi to be too tight

apretón [apre'ton] nm squeeze
▶ **apretón de manos** handshake

aprieto [a'prjeto] nm squeeze; (dificultad) difficulty; **estar en un ~** to be in a fix

aprisa [a'prisa] adv quickly, hurriedly

aprisionar [aprisjo'nar] vt to imprison

aprobación [aproβa'θjon] nf approval

aprobar [apro'βar] vt to approve (of); (examen, materia) to pass ♦ vi to pass

apropiado, -a [apro'pjaðo, a] adj suitable

apropiarse [apro'pjarse] vr: ~ **de** to appropriate

aprovechado, -a [aproβe'tʃaðo, a] adj industrious, hard-working; (económico) thrifty; (pey) unscrupulous

aprovechar [aproβe'tʃar] vt to use; (explotar) to exploit; (experiencia) to profit from; (oferta, oportunidad) to take advantage of ♦ vi to progress, improve; **aprovecharse** vr:

aprovecharse de to make use of; to take advantage of; **¡que aproveche!** enjoy your meal!

aproximación [aproksima'θjon] nf approximation; (de lotería) consolation prize

aproximar [aproksi'mar] vt to bring nearer; **aproximarse** vr to come near, approach

apruebo etc vb ver **aprobar**

aptitud [apti'tuð] nf aptitude

apto, -a ['apto, a] adj suitable

apuesta [a'pwesta] nf bet, wager

apuesto, -a [a'pwesto, a] adj neat, elegant

apuntar [apun'tar] vt (con arma) to aim at; (con dedo) to point at o to; (anotar) to note (down); (TEATRO) to prompt; **apuntarse** vr (DEPORTE: tanto, victoria) to score; (ESCOL) to enrol

⚠ No confundir **apuntar** con la palabra inglesa **appoint**.

apunte [a'punte] nm note

apuñalar [apuɲa'lar] vt to stab

apurado, -a [apu'raðo, a] adj needy; (difícil) difficult; (peligroso) dangerous; (LAm: con prisa) hurried, rushed

apurar [apu'rar] vt (agotar) to drain; (recursos) to use up; (molestar) to annoy; **apurarse** vr (preocuparse) to worry; (LAm: darse prisa) to hurry

apuro [a'puro] nm (aprieto) fix, jam; (escasez) want, hardship; (vergüenza) embarrassment; (LAm: prisa) haste, urgency

aquejado, -a [ake'xaðo, a] adj: ~ **de** (MED) afflicted by

aquél, aquélla [a'kel, a'keʎa] pron that (one); **aquéllos(as)** those (ones)

aquel, aquella [a'kel, a'keʎa] adj that; **aquellos(as)** those

aquello [a'keʎo] pron that, that business

aquí [a'ki] adv (lugar) here; (tiempo) now; **aquí arriba** up here; **aquí mismo** right here; **aquí yace** here lies; **de aquí a siete días** a week from now

ara ['ara] nf: **en aras de** for the sake of

árabe ['araβe] adj, nmf Arab ♦ nm (LING) Arabic

Arabia [a'raβja] nf Arabia ▶ **Arabia Saudí** o **Saudita** Saudi Arabia

arado [a'raðo] nm plough

Aragón [ara'ɣon] nm Aragon
❑ **aragonés, -esa** adj, nm/f Aragonese

arancel [aran'θel] nm tariff, duty

arandela [aran'dela] nf (TEC) washer

araña [a'raɲa] nf (ZOOL) spider; (lámpara) chandelier

arañar [ara'ɲar] vt to scratch

arañazo [ara'ɲaθo] nm scratch

arbitrar [arβi'trar] vt to arbitrate in; (DEPORTE) to referee ♦ vi to arbitrate

arbitrario, -a [arβi'trarjo, a] adj arbitrary

árbitro ['arβitro] nm arbitrator; (DEPORTE) referee; (TENIS) umpire

árbol ['arβol] nm (BOT) tree; (NÁUT) mast; (TEC) axle, shaft ▶ **árbol de Navidad** Christmas tree

arboleda [arβo'leða] nf grove, plantation

arbusto [ar'βusto] nm bush, shrub

arca ['arka] nf chest, box

arcada [ar'kaða] nf arcade; (de puente) arch, span; **arcadas** nfpl (náuseas) retching sg

arcaico, -a [ar'kaiko, a] adj archaic

arce ['arθe] nm maple tree

arcén [ar'θen] nm (de autopista) hard shoulder; (de carretera) verge

archipiélago [artʃi'pjelaɣo] nm archipelago

archivador [artʃiβa'ðor] nm filing cabinet

archivar [artʃi'βar] vt to file (away)
❑ **archivo** nm file, archive(s) pl
▶ **archivo adjunto** (INFORM)

attachment ► **archivo de seguridad** (INFORM) backup file

arcilla [ar'θiʎa] nf clay

arco ['arko] nm arch; (MAT) arc; (MIL, MÚS) bow ► **arco iris** rainbow

arder [ar'ðer] vi to burn; **estar que arde** (persona) to fume

ardid [ar'ðið] nm ploy, trick

ardiente [ar'ðjente] adj burning, ardent

ardilla [ar'ðiʎa] nf squirrel

ardor [ar'ðor] nm (calor) heat; (fig) ardour ► **ardor de estómago** heartburn

arduo, -a ['arðwo, a] adj arduous

área ['area] nf area; (DEPORTE) penalty area

arena [a'rena] nf sand; (de una lucha) arena ► **arenas movedizas** quicksand sg □ **arenal** [are'nal] nm (terreno arenoso) sandy spot

arenisca [are'niska] nf sandstone; (cascajo) grit

arenoso, -a [are'noso, a] adj sandy

arenque [a'renke] nm herring

arete (MÉX) [a'rete] nm earring

Argel [ar'xel] n Algiers □ **Argelia** nf Algeria □ **argelino, -a** adj, nm/f Algerian

Argentina [arxen'tina] nf (tb: **la ~**) Argentina

argentino, -a [arxen'tino, a] adj Argentinian; (de plata) silvery ♦ nm/f Argentinian

argolla [ar'ɣoʎa] nf (large) ring

argot [ar'ɣo] (pl **argots**) nm slang

argucia [ar'ɣuθja] nf subtlety, sophistry

argumentar [arɣumen'tar] vt, vi to argue

argumento [arɣu'mento] nm argument; (razonamiento) reasoning; (de novela etc) plot; (CINE, TV) storyline

aria ['arja] nf aria

aridez [ari'ðeθ] nf aridity, dryness

árido, -a ['ariðo, a] adj arid, dry

Aries ['arjes] nm Aries

arisco, -a [a'risko, a] adj surly; (insociable) unsociable

aristócrata [aris'tokrata] nmf aristocrat

arma ['arma] nf arm; **armas** nfpl arms ► **arma blanca** blade, knife ► **arma de doble filo** double-edged sword ► **arma de fuego** firearm

armada [ar'maða] nf armada; (flota) fleet

armadillo [arma'ðiʎo] nm armadillo

armado, -a [ar'maðo, a] adj armed; (TEC) reinforced

armadura [arma'ðura] nf (MIL) armour; (TEC) framework; (ZOOL) skeleton; (FÍSICA) armature

armamento [arma'mento] nm armament; (NÁUT) fitting-out

armar [ar'mar] vt (soldado) to arm; (máquina) to assemble; (navío) to fit out; **armarla, ~ un lío** to start a row, kick up a fuss

armario [ar'marjo] nm wardrobe; (de cocina, baño) cupboard ► **armario empotrado** built-in cupboard

armatoste [arma'toste] nm (mueble) monstrosity; (máquina) contraption

armazón [arma'θon] nf o m body, chassis; (de mueble etc) frame; (ARQ) skeleton

armiño [ar'miɲo] nm stoat; (piel) ermine

armisticio [armis'tiθjo] nm armistice

armonía [armo'nia] nf harmony

armónica [ar'monika] nf harmonica

armonizar [armoni'θar] vt to harmonize; (diferencias) to reconcile

aro ['aro] nm ring; (tejo) quoit; (CS: pendiente) earring

aroma [a'roma] nm aroma, scent □ **aromaterapia** n aromatherapy □ **aromático, -a** [aro'matiko, a] adj aromatic

arpa ['arpa] nf harp

arpía [ar'pia] nf shrew

arpón [ar'pon] nm harpoon

arqueología [arkeolo'xia] nf archaeology ❑ **arqueólogo, -a** nm/f archaeologist

arquetipo [arke'tipo] nm archetype

arquitecto [arki'tekto] nm architect ❑ **arquitectura** nf architecture

arrabal [arra'βal] nm poor suburb, slum; **arrabales** nmpl (afueras) outskirts

arraigar [arrai'ɣar] vt to establish ♦ vi to take root

arrancar [arran'kar] vt (sacar) to extract, pull out; (arrebatar) to snatch (away); (INFORM) to boot; (fig) to extract ♦ vi (AUTO, máquina) to start; (ponerse en marcha) to get going; **~ de** to stem from

arranque etc [a'rranke] vb ver **arrancar** ♦ nm sudden start; (AUTO) start; (fig) fit, outburst

arrasar [arra'sar] vt (aplanar) to level, flatten; (destruir) to demolish

arrastrar [arras'trar] vt to drag (along); (fig) to drag down, degrade; (agua, viento) to carry away ♦ vi to drag, trail on the ground; **arrastrarse** vr to crawl; (fig) to grovel; **llevar algo arrastrado** to drag sth along

arrear [arre'ar] vt to drive on, urge on ♦ vi to hurry along

arrebatar [arreβa'tar] vt to snatch (away), seize; (fig) to captivate

arrebato [arre'βato] nm fit of rage, fury; (éxtasis) rapture

arrecife [arre'θife] nm reef

arreglado, -a [arre'ɣlaðo, a] adj (ordenado) neat, orderly; (moderado) moderate, reasonable

arreglar [arre'ɣlar] vt (poner orden) to tidy up; (algo roto) to fix, repair; (problema) to solve; **arreglarse** vr to reach an understanding; **arreglárselas** (fam) to get by, manage

arreglo [a'rreɣlo] nm settlement; (orden) order; (acuerdo) agreement; (MÚS) arrangement, setting

arremangar [arreman'gar] vt to roll up, turn up; **arremangarse** vr to roll up one's sleeves

arremeter [arreme'ter] vi: **~ contra** to attack, rush at

arrendamiento [arrenda'mjento] nm letting; (alquilar) hiring; (contrato) lease; (alquiler) rent ❑ **arrendar** vt to let, lease; to rent ❑ **arrendatario, -a** nm/f tenant

arreos [a'rreos] nmpl (de caballo) harness sg, trappings

arrepentimiento [arrepenti'mjento] nm regret, repentance

arrepentirse [arrepen'tirse] vr to repent; **~ de** to regret

arresto [a'rresto] nm arrest; (MIL) detention; (audacia) boldness, daring ▶ **arresto domiciliario** house arrest

arriar [a'rrjar] vt (velas) to haul down; (bandera) to lower, strike; (cable) to pay out

arriba

PALABRA CLAVE

[a'rriβa] adv

1 (posición) above; **desde arriba** from above; **arriba de todo** at the very top, right on top; **Juan está arriba** Juan is upstairs; **lo arriba mencionado** the aforementioned

2 (dirección): **calle arriba** up the street

3: **de arriba abajo** from top to bottom; **mirar a algn de arriba abajo** to look sb up and down

4: **para arriba: de 50 euros para arriba** from 50 euros up(wards)

♦ adj: **de arriba: el piso de arriba** the upstairs (BRIT) flat o apartment; **la parte de arriba** the top o upper part

♦ prep: **arriba de** (LAm: por encima de)

above; **arriba de 200 dólares** more than 200 dollars
♦ *excl:* **¡arriba!** up!; **¡manos arriba!** hands up!; **¡arriba España!** long live Spain!

arribar [arri'βar] *vi* to put into port; (*llegar*) to arrive

arriendo *etc* [a'rrjendo] *vb ver* **arrendar** ♦ *nm* = **arrendamiento**

arriesgado, -a [arrjes'ɣaðo, a] *adj* (*peligroso*) risky; (*audaz*) bold, daring

arriesgar [arrjes'ɣar] *vt* (*poner en peligro*) to endanger; **arriesgarse** *vr* to take a risk

arrimar [arri'mar] *vt* (*acercar*) to bring close; (*poner de lado*) to set aside; **arrimarse** *vr* to come close *o* closer; **arrimarse a** to lean on

arrinconar [arrinko'nar] *vt* (*colocar*) to put in a corner; (*enemigo*) to corner; (*fig*) to put on one side; (*abandonar*) to push aside

arrodillarse [arroði'ʎarse] *vr* to kneel (down)

arrogante [arro'ɣante] *adj* arrogant

arrojar [arro'xar] *vt* to throw, hurl; (*humo*) to emit, give out; (*COM*) to yield, produce; **arrojarse** *vr* to throw *o* hurl o.s.

arrojo [a'rroxo] *nm* daring

arrollador, a [arroʎa'ðor, a] *adj* overwhelming

arrollar [arro'ʎar] *vt* (*AUTO etc*) to run over, knock down; (*DEPORTE*) to crush

arropar [arro'par] *vt* to cover, wrap up; **arroparse** *vr* to wrap o.s. up

arroyo [a'rroʝo] *nm* stream; (*de la calle*) gutter

arroz [a'rroθ] *nm* rice ► **arroz con leche** rice pudding

arruga [a'rruɣa] *nf* (*de cara*) wrinkle; (*de vestido*) crease ❑ **arrugar** [arru'ɣar] *vt* to wrinkle; to crease; **arrugarse** *vr* to get creased

arruinar [arrwi'nar] *vt* to ruin, wreck; **arruinarse** *vr* to be ruined, go bankrupt

arsenal [arse'nal] *nm* naval dockyard; (*MIL*) arsenal

arte ['arte] (*gen m en sg y siempre f en pl*) *nm* art; (*maña*) skill, guile; **artes** *nfpl* (*bellas artes*) arts

artefacto [arte'fakto] *nm* appliance

arteria [ar'terja] *nf* artery

artesanía [artesa'nia] *nf* craftsmanship; (*artículos*) handicrafts *pl* ❑ **artesano, -a** *nm/f* artisan, craftsman(-woman)

ártico, -a ['artiko, a] *adj* Arctic ♦ *nm:* **el Ártico** the Arctic

articulación [artikula'θjon] *nf* articulation; (*MED, TEC*) joint

artículo [ar'tikulo] *nm* article; (*cosa*) thing, article; **artículos** *nmpl* (*COM*) goods ► **artículos de escritorio** stationery

artífice [ar'tifiθe] *nmf* (*fig*) architect

artificial [artifi'θjal] *adj* artificial

artillería [artiʎe'ria] *nf* artillery

artilugio [arti'luxjo] *nm* gadget

artimaña [arti'maɲa] *nf* trap, snare; (*astucia*) cunning

artista [ar'tista] *nmf* (*pintor*) artist, painter; (*TEATRO*) artist, artiste ► **artista de cine** film actor/actress ❑ **artístico, -a** *adj* artistic

artritis [ar'tritis] *nf* arthritis

arveja [ar'βexa] (*LAm*) *nf* pea

arzobispo [arθo'βispo] *nm* archbishop

as [as] *nm* ace

asa ['asa] *nf* handle; (*fig*) lever

asado [a'saðo] *nm* roast (meat); (*LAm: barbacoa*) barbecue

ASADO

Traditional Latin American barbecues, especially in the River Plate area, are celebrated in the open air around a large grill which is used to grill mainly beef and various kinds of spicy pork sausage. They are usually very common during the summer and can go on for several days. The head cook is nearly always a man.

asador [asa'ðor] *nm* spit

asadura [asa'ðura] *nf* entrails *pl*, offal

asalariado, -a [asala'rjaðo, a] *adj* paid, salaried ♦ *nm/f* wage earner

asaltar [asal'tar] *vt* to attack, assault; *(fig)* to assail ❑ **asalto** *nm* attack, assault; *(DEPORTE)* round

asamblea [asam'blea] *nf* assembly; *(reunión)* meeting

asar [a'sar] *vt* to roast

ascendencia [asθen'denθja] *nf* ancestry; *(LAm: influencia)* ascendancy; **de ~ francesa** of French origin

ascender [asθen'der] *vi (subir)* to ascend, rise; *(ser promovido)* to gain promotion ♦ *vt* to promote; **~ a** to amount to ❑ **ascendiente** *nm* influence ♦ *nmf* ancestor

ascensión [asθen'sjon] *nf* ascent; *(REL)*: **la A~** the Ascension

ascenso [as'θenso] *nm* ascent; *(promoción)* promotion

ascensor [asθen'sor] *nm* lift *(BRIT)*, elevator *(US)*

asco [asko] *nm*: **¡qué ~!** how revolting *o* disgusting; **el ajo me da ~** I hate *o* loathe garlic; **estar hecho un ~** to be filthy

ascua ['askwa] *nf* ember

aseado, -a [ase'aðo, a] *adj* clean; *(arreglado)* tidy; *(pulcro)* smart

asear [ase'ar] *vt* to clean, wash; to tidy (up)

asediar [ase'ðjar] *vt (MIL)* to besiege, lay siege to; *(fig)* to chase, pester ❑ **asedio** *nm* siege; *(COM)* run

asegurado, -a [aseɣu'raðo, a] *adj* insured

asegurador, a [aseɣura'ðor, a] *nm/f* insurer

asegurar [aseɣu'rar] *vt (consolidar)* to secure, fasten; *(dar garantía de)* to guarantee; *(preservar)* to safeguard; *(afirmar, dar por cierto)* to assure, affirm; *(tranquilizar)* to reassure; *(tomar un seguro)* to insure; **asegurarse** *vr* to assure o.s., make sure

asemejarse [aseme'xarse] *vr* to be alike; **~ a** to be like, resemble

asentado, -a [asen'taðo, a] *adj* established, settled

asentar [asen'tar] *vt (sentar)* to seat, sit down; *(poner)* to place, establish; *(alisar)* to level, smooth down *o* out; *(anotar)* to note down ♦ *vi* to be suitable, suit

asentir [asen'tir] *vi* to assent, agree; **~ con la cabeza** to nod (one's head)

aseo [a'seo] *nm* cleanliness; **aseos** *nmpl* *(servicios)* toilet *sg (BRIT)*, cloakroom *sg (BRIT)*, restroom *sg (US)*

aséptico, -a [a'septiko, a] *adj* germ-free, free from infection

asequible [ase'kiβle] *adj (precio)* reasonable; *(meta)* attainable; *(persona)* approachable

asesinar [asesi'nar] *vt* to murder; *(POL)* to assassinate ❑ **asesinato** *nm* murder; assassination

asesino, -a [ase'sino, a] *nm/f* murderer, killer; *(POL)* assassin

asesor, a [ase'sor, a] *nm/f* adviser, consultant ❑ **asesorar** [aseso'rar] *vt (JUR)* to advise, give legal advice to; *(COM)* to act as consultant to; **asesorarse** *vr*: **asesorarse con** *o* **de** to take advice from, consult ❑ **asesoría** *nf (cargo)* consultancy; *(oficina)* consultant's office

asestar [ases'tar] vt (golpe) to deal, strike

asfalto [as'falto] nm asphalt

asfixia [as'fiksja] nf asphyxia, suffocation ❏ **asfixiar** [asfik'sjar] vt to asphyxiate, suffocate; **asfixiarse** vr to be asphyxiated, suffocate

así [a'si] adv (de esta manera) in this way, like this, thus; (aunque) although; (tan pronto como) as soon as; **así que** so; **así como** as well as; **así y todo** even so; **¿no es así?** isn't it?, didn't you? etc; **así de grande** this big

Asia ['asja] nf Asia ❏ **asiático, -a** adj, nm/f Asian, Asiatic

asiduo, -a [a'siðwo, a] adj assiduous; (frecuente) frequent ♦ nm/f regular (customer)

asiento [a'sjento] nm (mueble) seat, chair; (de coche, en tribunal etc) seat; (localidad) seat, place; (fundamento) site ▸ **asiento delantero/trasero** front/back seat

asignación [asiɣna'θjon] nf (atribución) assignment; (reparto) allocation; (sueldo) salary ▸ **asignación (semanal)** pocket money

asignar [asiɣ'nar] vt to assign, allocate

asignatura [asiɣna'tura] nf subject; course

asilo [a'silo] nm (refugio) asylum, refuge; (establecimiento) home, institution ▸ **asilo político** political asylum

asimilar [asimi'lar] vt to assimilate

asimismo [asi'mismo] adv in the same way, likewise

asistencia [asis'tenθja] nf audience; (MED) attendance; (ayuda) assistance ▸ **asistencia en carretera** roadside assistance ❏ **asistente** nmf assistant; **los asistentes** those present ▸ **asistente social** social worker

asistido, -a [asis'tiðo, a] adj: ~ **por ordenador** computer-assisted

asistir [asis'tir] vt to assist, help ♦ vi: ~ **a** to attend, be present at

asma ['asma] nf asthma

asno ['asno] nm donkey; (fig) ass

asociación [asoθja'θjon] nf association; (COM) partnership ❏ **asociado, -a** adj associate ♦ nm/f associate; (COM) partner

asociar [aso'θjar] vt to associate

asomar [aso'mar] vt to show, stick out ♦ vi to appear; **asomarse** vr to appear, show up; ~ **la cabeza por la ventana** to put one's head out of the window

asombrar [asom'brar] vt to amaze, astonish; **asombrarse** vr (sorprenderse) to be amazed; (asustarse) to get a fright ❏ **asombro** nm amazement, astonishment; (susto) fright ❏ **asombroso, -a** adj astonishing, amazing

asomo [a'somo] nm hint, sign

aspa ['aspa] nf (cruz) cross; (de molino) sail; **en ~** X-shaped

aspaviento [aspa'βjento] nm exaggerated display of feeling; (fam) fuss

aspecto [as'pekto] nm (apariencia) look, appearance; (fig) aspect

áspero, -a ['aspero, a] adj rough; bitter; sour; harsh

aspersión [asper'sjon] nf sprinkling

aspiración [aspira'θjon] nf breath, inhalation; (MUS) short pause; **aspiraciones** nfpl (ambiciones) aspirations

aspirador [aspira'ðor] nm = **aspiradora**

aspiradora [aspira'ðora] nf vacuum cleaner, Hoover®

aspirante [aspi'rante] nmf (candidato) candidate; (DEPORTE) contender

aspirar [aspi'rar] vt to breathe in ♦ vi: ~ **a** to aspire to

aspirina [aspi'rina] nf aspirin

asqueroso, -a [aske'roso, a] adj disgusting, sickening

asta ['asta] nf lance; (arpón) spear; (mango) shaft, handle; (ZOOL) horn; **a media ~** at half mast

asterisco [aste'risko] nm asterisk

astilla [as'tiʎa] nf splinter; (pedacito) chip; **astillas** nfpl (leña) firewood sg

astillero [asti'ʎero] nm shipyard

astro ['astro] nm star

astrología [astrolo'xia] nf astrology ❑ **astrólogo, -a** nm/f astrologer

astronauta [astro'nauta] nmf astronaut

astronomía [astrono'mia] nf astronomy

astucia [as'tuθja] nf astuteness; (ardid) clever trick

asturiano, -a [astu'rjano, a] adj, nm/f Asturian

astuto, -a [as'tuto, a] adj astute; (taimado) cunning

asumir [asu'mir] vt to assume

asunción [asun'θjon] nf assumption; (REL): **A~** Assumption

asunto [a'sunto] nm (tema) matter, subject; (negocio) business

asustar [asus'tar] vt to frighten; **asustarse** vr to be (o become) frightened

atacar [ata'kar] vt to attack

atadura [ata'ðura] nf bond, tie

atajar [ata'xar] vt (enfermedad, mal) to stop ♦ vi (persona) to take a short cut

atajo [a'taxo] nm short cut

atañer [ata'ɲer] vi: **~ a** to concern

ataque etc [a'take] vb ver **atacar** ♦ nm attack ▶ **ataque cardíaco** heart attack

atar [a'tar] vt to tie, tie up

atarantado, -a [MEX] adj (aturdido) dazed

atardecer [ataɾðe'θer] vi to get dark ♦ nm evening; (crepúsculo) dusk

atareado, -a [atare'aðo, a] adj busy

atascar [atas'kar] vt to clog up; (obstruir) to jam; (fig) to hinder;

atascarse vr to stall; (cañería) to get blocked up ❑ **atasco** nm obstruction; (AUTO) traffic jam

ataúd [ata'uð] nm coffin

ataviar [ata'βjar] vt to deck, array

atemorizar [atemori'θar] vt to frighten, scare

Atenas [a'tenas] n Athens

atención [aten'θjon] nf attention; (bondad) kindness ♦ excl (be) careful!, look out!

atender [aten'der] vt to attend to, look after; (TEL) to answer ♦ vi to pay attention

atenerse [ate'nerse] vr: **~ a** to abide by, adhere to

atentado [aten'taðo] nm crime, illegal act; (asalto) assault; **~ contra la vida de algn** attempt on sb's life

atentamente [atenta'mente] adv: **Le saluda ~** Yours faithfully

atentar [aten'tar] vi: **~ a** o **contra** to commit an outrage against

atento, -a [a'tento, a] adj attentive, observant; (cortés) polite, thoughtful; **estar ~ a** (explicación) to pay attention to

atenuar [ate'nwar] vt (disminuir) to lessen, minimize

ateo, -a [a'teo, a] adj atheistic ♦ nm/f atheist

aterrador, a [aterra'ðor, a] adj frightening

aterrizaje [aterri'θaxe] nm landing ▶ **aterrizaje forzoso** emergency o forced landing

aterrizar [aterri'θar] vi to land

aterrorizar [aterrori'θar] vt to terrify

atesorar [ateso'rar] vt to hoard

atestar [ates'tar] vt to pack, stuff; (JUR) to attest, testify to

atestiguar [atesti'ɣwar] vt to testify to, bear witness to

atiborrar [atiβo'rrar] vt to fill, stuff; **atiborrarse** vr to stuff o.s.

ático [ˈatiko] nm (desván) attic; (apartamento) penthouse

atinado, -a [atiˈnaðo, a] adj (sensato) wise; (correcto) right, correct

atinar [atiˈnar] vi (al disparar): ~ al blanco to hit the target; (fig) to be right

atizar [atiˈθar] vt to poke; (horno etc) to stoke; (fig) to stir up, rouse

atlántico, -a [atˈlantiko, a] adj Atlantic ♦ nm: **el (océano) A~** the Atlantic (Ocean)

atlas [ˈatlas] nm atlas

atleta [atˈleta] nm athlete □ **atlético, -a** adj athletic □ **atletismo** nm athletics sg

atmósfera [atˈmosfera] nf atmosphere

atolladero [atoʎaˈðero] nm (fig) jam, fix

atómico, -a [aˈtomiko, a] adj atomic

átomo [ˈatomo] nm atom

atónito, -a [aˈtonito, a] adj astonished, amazed

atontado, -a [atonˈtaðo, a] adj stunned; (bobo) silly, daft

atormentar [atormenˈtar] vt to torture; (molestar) to torment; (acosar) to plague, harass

atornillar [atorniˈʎar] vt to screw o on o down

atosigar [atosiˈɣar] vt to harass, pester

atracador, a [atrakaˈðor, a] nm/f robber

atracar [atraˈkar] vt (NÁUT) to moor; (robar) to hold up, rob ♦ vi to moor; **atracarse** vr: **atracarse (de)** to stuff o.s. (with)

atracción [atrakˈθjon] nf attraction

atraco [atˈrako] nm holdup, robbery

atracón [atraˈkon] nm: **darse o pegarse un ~ (de)** (fam) to stuff o.s. (with)

atractivo, -a [atrakˈtiβo, a] adj attractive ♦ nm appeal

atraer [atraˈer] vt to attract

atragantarse [atraɣanˈtarse] vr: ~ (con) to choke (on); **se me ha**

atragantado el chico I can't stand the boy

atrancar [atranˈkar] vt (puerta) to bar, bolt

atrapar [atraˈpar] vt to trap; (resfriado etc) to catch

atrás [aˈtras] adv (movimiento) back(-wards); (lugar) behind; (tiempo) previously; **ir hacia ~** to go back(wards), to go to the rear; **estar ~** to be behind o at the back

atrasado, -a [atraˈsaðo, a] adj slow; (pago) overdue, late; (país) backward

atrasar [atraˈsar] vi to be slow; **atrasarse** vr to remain behind; (tren) to be o run late □ **atraso** nm slowness, lateness, delay; (de país) backwardness; **atrasos** nmpl (COM) arrears

atravesar [atraβeˈsar] vt (cruzar) to cross (over); (traspasar) to pierce; to go through; (poner al través) to lay o put across; **atravesarse** vr to come in between; (intervenir) to interfere

atravieso etc vb ver **atravesar**

atreverse [atreˈβerse] vr to dare; (insolentarse) to be insolent □ **atrevido, -a** adj daring; insolent □ **atrevimiento** nm daring; insolence

atribución [atriβuˈθjon] nf attribution; **atribuciones** nfpl (POL) powers; (ADMIN) responsibilities

atribuir [atriβuˈir] vt to attribute; (funciones) to confer

atributo [atriˈβuto] nm attribute

atril [atˈril] nm (para libro) lectern; (MÚS) music stand

atropellar [atropeˈʎar] vt (derribar) to knock over o down; (empujar) to push (aside); (AUTO) to run over, run down; (agraviar) to insult □ **atropello** nm (AUTO) accident; (empujón) push; (agravio) wrong; (atrocidad) outrage

atroz [aˈtroθ] adj atrocious, awful

ATS nmf abr (= Ayudante Técnico Sanitario) nurse

atuendo [a'twendo] nm attire

atún [a'tun] nm tuna

aturdir [atur'ðir] vt to stun; (de ruido) to deafen; (fig) to dumbfound, bewilder

audacia [au'ðaθja] nf boldness, audacity ❑ **audaz** adj bold, audacious

audición [auði'θjon] nf hearing; (TEATRO) audition

audiencia [au'ðjenθja] nf audience; (JUR: tribunal) court

audífono [au'ðifono] nm (para sordos) hearing aid

auditor [auði'tor] nm (JUR) judge advocate; (COM) auditor

auditorio [auði'torjo] nm audience; (sala) auditorium

auge ['auxe] nm boom; (clímax) climax

augurar [auɣu'rar] vt to predict; (presagiar) to portend

augurio [au'ɣurjo] nm omen

aula ['aula] nf classroom; (en universidad etc) lecture room

aullar [au'ʎar] vi to howl, yell

aullido [au'ʎiðo] nm howl, yell

aumentar [aumen'tar] vt to increase; (precios) to put up; (producción) to step up; (con microscopio, anteojos) to magnify ♦ vi to increase, be on the increase; **aumentarse** vr to increase, be on the increase ❑ **aumento** nm increase; rise

aun [a'un] adv even; **~ así** even so; **~ más** even o yet more

aún [a'un] adv: **~ está aquí** he's still here; **~ no lo sabemos** we don't know yet; **¿no ha venido ~?** hasn't she come yet?

aunque [a'unke] conj though, although, even though

aúpa [a'upa] excl come on!

auricular [auriku'lar] nm (TEL) receiver; **auriculares** nmpl (cascos) headphones

aurora [au'rora] nf dawn

ausencia [au'senθja] nf absence

ausentarse [ausen'tarse] vr to go away; (por poco tiempo) to go out

ausente [au'sente] adj absent

austero, -a [aus'tero, a] adj austere

austral [aus'tral] adj southern ♦ nm monetary unit of Argentina

Australia [aus'tralja] nf Australia ❑ **australiano, -a** adj, nm/f Australian

Austria ['austrja] nf Austria ❑ **austríaco, -a** adj, nm/f Austrian

auténtico, -a [au'tentiko, a] adj authentic

auto ['auto] nm (JUR) edict, decree; (: orden) writ; (AUTO) car; **autos** nmpl (JUR) proceedings; (: acta) court record sg

autoadhesivo [autoaðe'siβo] adj self-adhesive; (sobre) self-sealing

autobiografía [autoβjoɣra'fia] nf autobiography

autobomba (RPI) nm fire engine

autobronceador [autoβronθea'ðor] adj self-tanning

autobús [auto'βus] nm bus ♦ **autobús de línea** long-distance coach

autocar [auto'kar] nm coach (BRIT), (passenger) bus (US)

autóctono, -a [au'toktono, a] adj native, indigenous

autodefensa [autoðe'fensa] nf self-defence

autodidacta [autoði'ðakta] adj self-taught

autoescuela [autoes'kwela] (ESP) nf driving school

autógrafo [au'toɣrafo] nm autograph

autómata [au'tomata] nm automaton

automático, -a [auto'matiko, a] adj automatic ♦ nm press stud

automóvil [auto'moβil] nm (motor) car (BRIT), automobile (US) ❑ **automovilismo** nm (actividad) motoring; (DEPORTE) motor racing ❑ **automovilista** nmf motorist, driver

autonomía [autono'mia] nf
autonomy ❑ **autónomo, -a** (ESP
autonómico, a) adj (POL) autonomous

autopista [auto'pista] nf motorway
(BRIT), freeway (US) ▸ **autopista de
cuota** (ESP) o **peaje** (MÉX) toll (BRIT) o
turnpike (US) road

autopsia [au'topsja] nf autopsy,
postmortem

autor, a [au'tor, a] nm/f author

autoridad [autori'ðað] nf authority
❑ **autoritario, -a** adj authoritarian

autorización [autoriθa'θjon] nf
authorization ❑ **autorizado, -a** adj
authorized; (aprobado) approved

autorizar [autori'θar] vt to authorize;
(aprobar) to approve

autoservicio [autoser'βiθjo] nm
(tienda) self-service shop (BRIT) o store
(US); (restaurante) self-service
restaurant

autostop [auto'stop] nm hitch-hiking;
hacer ~ to hitch-hike ❑ **autostopista**
nmf hitch-hiker

autovía [auto'βia] nf ≈ A-road (BRIT),
dual carriageway (BRIT), ≈ state
highway (US)

auxiliar [auksi'ljar] vt to help ♦ nmf
assistant ♦ nm **auxilio** assistance,
help; **primeros auxilios** first aid sg

Av abr (= Avenida) Av(e)

aval [a'βal] nm guarantee; (persona)
guarantor

avalancha [aβa'lantʃa] nf avalanche

avance [a'βanθe] nm advance; (pago)
advance payment; (CINE) trailer

avanzar [aβan'θar] vt, vi to advance

avaricia [aβa'riθja] nf avarice, greed
❑ **avaricioso, -a** adj avaricious,
greedy

avaro, -a [a'βaro, a] adj miserly, mean
♦ nm/f miser

Avda abr (= Avenida) Av(e)

AVE [a'βe] nm abr (= Alta Velocidad
Española) ≈ bullet train

ave [a'βe] nf bird ▸ **ave de rapiña** bird
of prey

avecinarse [aβeθi'narse] vr (tormenta:
fig) to be on the way

avellana [aβe'ʎana] nf hazelnut
❑ **avellano** nm hazel tree

avemaría [aβema'ria] nm Hail Mary,
Ave Maria

avena [a'βena] nf oats pl

avenida [aβe'niða] nf (calle) avenue

aventajar [aβenta'xar] vt (sobrepasar)
to surpass, outstrip

aventón [aβen'ton] nm (MÉX: fam) ride;
dar ~ a algn to give sb a ride

aventura [aβen'tura] nf adventure
❑ **aventurero, -a** adj adventurous

avergonzar [aβerɣon'θar] vt to shame;
(desconcertar) to embarrass;
avergonzarse vr to be ashamed; to be
embarrassed

avería [aβe'ria] nf (TEC) breakdown,
fault

averiado, -a [aβe'rjaðo, a] adj broken
down; "~" "out of order"

averiguar [aβeri'ɣwar] vt to
investigate; (descubrir) to find out,
ascertain

avestruz [aβes'truθ] nm ostrich

aviación [aβja'θjon] nf aviation;
(fuerzas aéreas) air force

aviador, a [aβja'ðor, a] nm/f aviator,
airman(-woman)

ávido, -a [a'βiðo, a] adj avid, eager

avinagrado, -a [aβina'ɣraðo, a] adj
sour, acid

avión [a'βjon] nm aeroplane; (ave)
martín ▸ **avión de reacción** jet
(plane)

avioneta [aβjo'neta] nf light aircraft

avisar [aβi'sar] vt (advertir) to warn,
notify; (informar) to tell; (aconsejar) to
advise, counsel ❑ **aviso** nm warning;
(noticia) notice

avispa [a'βispa] nf wasp

avispado, -a [aβis'paðo, a] *adj* sharp, clever

avivar [aβi'βar] *vt* to strengthen, intensify

axila [ak'sila] *nf* armpit

ay [ai] *excl* (*dolor*) owl, ouch!; (*aflicción*) oh!, oh dear!; **¡ay de mí!** poor me!

ayer [a'jer] *adv, nm* yesterday; **antes de ~** the day before yesterday; **~ mismo** only yesterday

ayote [a'jote] (*CAm*) *nm* pumpkin

ayuda [a'juða] *nf* help, assistance ♦ *nm* page ▫ **ayudante** *nmf* assistant, helper; (*ESCOL*) assistant; (*MIL*) adjutant ▫ **ayudar** *vt* to help, assist

ayunar [aju'nar] *vi* to fast ▫ **ayunas** *nfpl*: **estar en ayunas** to be fasting ▫ **ayuno** *nm* fast; fasting

ayuntamiento [ajunta'mjento] *nm* (*consejo*) town (*o* city) council; (*edificio*) town (*o* city) hall

azafata [aθa'fata] *nf* air stewardess

azafrán [aθa'fran] *nm* saffron

azahar [aθa'ar] *nm* orange/lemon blossom

azar [a'θar] *nm* (*casualidad*) chance, fate; (*desgracia*) misfortune, accident; **por ~** by chance; **al ~** at random

Azores [a'θores] *nfpl*: **las ~** the Azores

azotar [aθo'tar] *vt* to whip, beat; (*pegar*) to spank ▫ **azote** *nm* (*látigo*) whip; (*latigazo*) lash, stroke; (*en las nalgas*) spank; (*calamidad*) calamity

azotea [aθo'tea] *nf* (flat) roof

azteca [aθ'teka] *adj, nmf* Aztec

azúcar [a'θukar] *nm* sugar ▫ **azucarado, -a** *adj* sugary, sweet

azucarero, -a [aθuka'rero, a] *adj* sugar *cpd* ♦ *nm* sugar bowl

azucena [aθu'θena] *nf* white lily

azufre [a'θufre] *nm* sulphur

azul [a'θul] *adj, nm* blue ▫ **azul celeste/ marino** sky/navy blue

azulejo [aθu'lexo] *nm* tile

azuzar [aθu'θar] *vt* to incite, urge on

B, b

B.A. *abr* (= Buenos Aires) B.A.

baba ['baβa] *nf* spittle, saliva ▫ **babear** *vi* to drool, slaver

babero [ba'βero] *nm* bib

babor [ba'βor] *nm* port (side)

babosada (*MÉX, CAm: fam*) *nf* drivel ▫ **baboso, -a** [ba'βoso, a] (*LAm: fam*) *adj* silly

baca ['baka] *nf* (*AUTO*) luggage *o* roof rack

bacalao [baka'lao] *nm* cod(fish)

bache ['batʃe] *nm* pothole, rut; (*fig*) bad patch

bachillerato [batʃiʎe'rato] *nm* higher secondary school course

bacinica (*LAm*) *nf* potty

bacteria [bak'terja] *nf* bacterium, germ

Bahama [ba'ama]: **las (Islas)** *nfpl* the Bahamas

bahía [ba'ia] *nf* bay

bailar [bai'lar] *vt, vi* to dance ▫ **bailarín, -ina** *nm/f* (*ballet*) dancer ▫ **baile** *nm* dance; (*formal*) ball

baja ['baxa] *nf* drop, fall; (*MIL*) casualty; **dar de ~** (*soldado*) to discharge; (*empleado*) to dismiss

bajada [ba'xaða] *nf* descent; (*camino*) slope; (*de aguas*) ebb

bajar [ba'xar] *vi* to go down, come down; (*temperatura, precios*) to drop, fall ♦ *vt* (*cabeza*) to bow; (*escalera*) to go down, come down; (*precio, voz*) to lower; (*llevar abajo*) to take down; **bajarse** *vr* (*de coche*) to get out; (*de autobús, tren*) to get off; **bajarse algo de Internet** to download sth from the Internet; **~ de** (*coche*) to get out of; (*autobús, tren*) to get off

bajo, -a ['baxo] (*LAm*) *nm* lowlands *pl*

bajo, -a ['baxo] *adj* (*mueble, número, precio*) low; (*piso*) ground; (*de estatura*) small, short; (*color*) pale; (*sonido*) faint, soft, low; (*voz: en tono*) deep; (*metal*) base; (*humilde*) low, humble ♦ *adv* (*hablar*) softly, quietly; (*volar*) low ♦ *prep* under, below, underneath ♦ *nm* (*MÚS*) bass; **~ la lluvia** in the rain

bajón [ba'xon] *nm* fall, drop

bakalao [baka'lao] (*ESP: fam*) *nm* rave (music)

bala ['bala] *nf* bullet

balacear [MÉX, CAm] *vt* to shoot

balance [ba'lanθe] *nm* (*COM*) balance; (: *libro*) balance sheet; (: *cuenta general*) stocktaking

balancear [balanθe'ar] *vt* to balance ♦ *vi* to swing (to and fro); (*vacilar*) to hesitate; **balancearse** *vr* to swing (to and fro), to hesitate

balanza [ba'lanθa] *nf* scales *pl*, balance ▶ **balanza comercial** balance of trade ▶ **balanza de pagos** balance of payments

balaustrada [balaus'traða] *nf* balustrade; (*pasamanos*) banisters *pl*

balazo [ba'laθo] *nm* (*golpe*) shot; (*herida*) bullet wound

balbucear [balβuθe'ar] *vi*, *vt* to stammer, stutter

balcón [bal'kon] *nm* balcony

balde ['balde] *nm* bucket, pail; **de ~** (for) free, for nothing; **en ~** in vain

baldosa [bal'dosa] *nf* (*azulejo*) floor tile; (*grande*) flagstone ▶ **baldosín** *nm* (small) tile

Baleares [bale'ares] *nfpl*: **las (Islas) ~** the Balearic Islands

balero (*LAm*) *nm* (*juguete*) cup-and-ball toy

baliza [ba'liθa] *nf* (*AVIAC*) beacon; (*NÁUT*) buoy

ballena [ba'ʎena] *nf* whale

ballet [ba'le] (*pl* **ballets**) *nm* ballet

balneario [balne'arjo] *nm* spa; (*CS: en la costa*) seaside resort

balón [ba'lon] *nm* ball

baloncesto [balon'θesto] *nm* basketball

balonmano [balon'mano] *nm* handball

balsa ['balsa] *nf* raft; (*BOT*) balsa wood

bálsamo ['balsamo] *nm* balsam, balm

baluarte [ba'lwarte] *nm* bastion, bulwark

bambú [bam'bu] *nm* bamboo

banana [ba'nana] (*LAm*) *nf* banana ❑ **banano** (*LAm: árbol*) banana tree; (*CAm: fruta*) banana

banca ['banka] *nf* (*COM*) banking

bancario, -a [ban'karjo, a] *adj* banking *cpd*, bank *cpd*

bancarrota [banka'rrota] *nf* bankruptcy; **hacer ~** to go bankrupt

banco ['banko] *nm* bench; (*ESCOL*) desk; (*COM*) bank; (*GEO*) stratum ▶ **banco de arena** sandbank ▶ **banco de crédito** credit bank ▶ **banco de datos** databank

banda ['banda] *nf* band; (*pandilla*) gang; (*NÁUT*) side, edge ▶ **banda sonora** soundtrack

bandada [ban'daða] *nf* (*de pájaros*) flock; (*de peces*) shoal

bandazo [ban'daθo] *nm*: **dar bandazos** to sway from side to side

bandeja [ban'dexa] *nf* tray

bandera [ban'dera] *nf* flag

banderilla [bande'riʎa] *nf* banderilla

bandido [ban'diðo] *nm* bandit

bando ['bando] *nm* (*edicto*) edict, proclamation; (*facción*) faction; **bandos** *nmpl* (*REL*) banns

bandolera [bando'lera] *nf*: **llevar en ~** to wear across one's chest

banquero [ban'kero] *nm* banker

banqueta [ban'keta] *nf* stool; (*MÉX: en calle*) pavement (*BRIT*), sidewalk (*US*)

banquete [ban'kete] *nm* banquet; (*para convidados*) formal dinner ▶ **banquete de boda(s)** wedding reception

banquillo [ban'kiʎo] nm (JUR) dock, prisoner's bench; (banco) bench; (para los pies) footstool

banquina (RPl) nf hard shoulder (BRIT), berm (US)

bañadera (RPl) nf bathtub

bañador [baɲa'ðor] (ESP) nm swimming costume (BRIT), bathing suit (US)

bañar [ba'ɲar] vt to bath, bathe; (objeto) to dip; (de barniz) to coat; **bañarse** vr (en el mar) to bathe, swim; (en la bañera) to have a bath

bañera [ba'ɲera] (ESP) nf bath(tub)

bañero [ba'ɲero, a] (CS) nm/f lifeguard

bañista [ba'ɲista] nmf bather

baño ['baɲo] nm (en bañera) bath; (en río) dip, swim; (cuarto) bathroom; (bañera) bath(tub); (capa) coating; **darse** o **tomar un ~** (en bañera) to have a bath; (en mar, piscina) to have a swim ▶ **baño María** bain-marie

bar [bar] nm bar

barahúnda [bara'unda] nf uproar, hubbub

baraja [ba'raxa] nf pack (of cards) ❏ **barajar** vt (naipes) to shuffle; (fig) to jumble up

baranda [ba'randa] nf = barandilla

barandilla [baran'diʎa] nf rail, railing

barata (MÉX) [ba'rata] nf (bargain) sale

baratillo [bara'tiʎo] nm (tienda) junkshop; (subasta) bargain sale; (conjunto de cosas) secondhand goods pl

barato, -a [ba'rato, a] adj cheap ♦ adv cheap, cheaply

barba ['barβa] nf (mentón) chin; (pelo) beard

barbacoa [barβa'koa] nf (parrilla) barbecue; (carne) barbecued meat

barbaridad [barβari'ðað] nf (acto) barbarism; (atrocidad) outrage; **una ~** (fam) loads; **¡qué ~!** (fam) how awful!

barbarie [bar'βarje] nf barbarism, savagery; (crueldad) barbarity

bárbaro, -a ['barβaro, a] adj barbarous, cruel; (grosero) rough, uncouth ♦ nm/f barbarian ♦ adv: **lo pasamos** ~ (fam) we had a great time; **¡qué ~!** (fam) how marvellous!; **un éxito** ~ (fam) a terrific success; **es un tipo** ~ (fam) he's a great bloke

barbero [bar'βero] nm barber, hairdresser

barbilla [bar'βiʎa] nf chin, tip of the chin

barbudo, a [bar'βuðo, a] adj bearded

barca ['barka] nf (small) boat ❏ **barcaza** nf barge

Barcelona [barθe'lona] n Barcelona

barco ['barko] nm boat; (grande) ship ▶ **barco de carga/pesca** cargo/ fishing boat ▶ **barco de vela** sailing ship

barda (MÉX) nf (de madera) fence

baremo [ba'remo] nm (MAT: fig) scale

barítono [ba'ritono] nm baritone

barman ['barman] nm barman

barniz [bar'niθ] nm varnish; (en loza) glaze; (fig) veneer ❏ **barnizar** vt to varnish; (loza) to glaze

barómetro [ba'rometro] nm barometer

barquillo [bar'kiʎo] nm cone, cornet

barra ['barra] nf bar, rod; (de un bar, café) bar; (de pan) French stick; (palanca) lever ▶ **barra de labios** lipstick ▶ **barra libre** free bar

barraca [ba'rraka] nf hut, cabin

barranco [ba'rranko] nm ravine; (fig) difficulty

barrena [ba'rrena] nf drill

barrer [ba'rrer] vt to sweep; (quitar) to sweep away

barrera [ba'rrera] nf barrier

barriada [ba'rrjaða] nf quarter, district

barricada [barri'kaða] nf barricade

barrida [ba'rriða] nf sweep, sweeping

barriga [ba'rriɣa] nf belly; (panza) paunch ◻ **barrigón, -ona** adj potbellied ◻ **barrigudo, -a** adj potbellied

barril [ba'rril] nm barrel, cask

barrio ['barrjo] nm (vecindad) area, neighborhood (US); (en afueras) suburb ▶ **barrio chino** (ESP) red-light district

barro ['barro] nm (lodo) mud; (objetos) earthenware; (MED) pimple

barroco, -a [ba'rroko, a] adj, nm baroque

barrote [ba'rrote] nm (de ventana) bar

bartola [bar'tola] nf: **tirarse o tumbarse a la** ~ to take it easy, be lazy

bártulos ['bartulos] nmpl things, belongings

barullo [ba'ruʎo] nm row, uproar

basar [ba'sar] vt to base; **basarse** vr: **basarse en** to be based on

báscula ['baskula] nf (platform) scales

base ['base] nf base; **a ~ de** on the basis of; (mediante) by means of ▶ **base de datos** (INFORM) database

básico, -a ['basiko, a] adj basic

basílica [ba'silika] nf basilica

básquetbol [LAm] nm basketball

bastante

PALABRA CLAVE

[bas'tante] adj

1 (suficiente) enough; **bastante dinero** enough o sufficient money; **bastantes libros** enough books

2 (valor intensivo): **bastante gente** quite a lot of people; **tener bastante calor** to be rather hot

♦ adv: **bastante bueno/malo** quite good/rather bad; **bastante rico** pretty rich; **(lo) bastante inteligente (como) para hacer algo** clever enough o sufficiently clever to do sth

bastar [bas'tar] vi to be enough o sufficient; **bastarse** vr to be self-sufficient; ~ **para** to be enough to; **¡basta!** (that's) enough!

bastardo, -a [bas'tarðo, a] adj, nm/f bastard

bastidor [basti'ðor] nm frame; (de coche) chassis; (TEATRO) wing; **entre bastidores** (fig) behind the scenes

basto, -a ['basto, a] adj coarse, rough ◻ **bastos** nmpl (NAIPES) ~ clubs

bastón [bas'ton] nm stick, staff; (para pasear) walking stick

bastoncillo [baston'θiʎo] nm cotton bud

basura [ba'sura] nf rubbish (BRIT), garbage (US) ♦ adj: **comida/televisión** ~ junk food/TV

basurero [basu'rero] nm (persona) dustman (BRIT), garbage man (US); (lugar) dump; (cubo) (rubbish) bin (BRIT), trash can (US)

bata ['bata] nf (gen) dressing gown; (cubretodo) smock, overall; (MED, TEATRO etc) lab(oratory) coat

batalla [ba'taʎa] nf battle; **de ~** (fig) for everyday use ▶ **batalla campal** pitched battle

batallón [bata'ʎon] nm battalion

batata [ba'tata] nf sweet potato

batería [bate'ria] nf battery; (MÚS) drums ▶ **batería de cocina** kitchen utensils

batido, -a [ba'tiðo, a] adj (camino) beaten, well-trodden ♦ nm (CULIN: de leche) milk shake

batidora [bati'ðora] nf beater, mixer ▶ **batidora eléctrica** food mixer, blender

batir [ba'tir] vt to beat, strike; (vencer) to beat, defeat; (revolver) to beat, mix; **batirse** vr to fight; ~ **palmas** to applaud

batuta [ba'tuta] nf baton; **llevar la** ~ (fig) to be the boss, be in charge

baúl [ba'ul] nm trunk; (AUTO) boot (BRIT), trunk (US)

bautismo [bau'tismo] nm baptism, christening

bautizar [bauti'θar] vt to baptize, christen; (fam: diluir) to water down ❏ **bautizo** nm baptism, christening

bayeta [ba'jeta] nf floorcloth

baza ['baθa] nf trick; **meter ~** to butt in

bazar [ba'θar] nm bazaar

bazofia [ba'θofja] nf trash

be nf name of the letter B ► **be chica/grande** (MÉX) V/B ► **be larga** (LAm) B

beato, -a [be'ato, a] adj blessed; (piadoso) pious

bebé [be'βe] (pl ~s) nm baby

bebedero (MÉX, CS) [beβe'ðero, a] nm drinking fountain

bebedor, a [beβe'ðor, a] adj hard-drinking

beber [be'βer] vt, vi to drink

bebida [be'βiða] nf drink ❏ **bebido, -a** adj drunk

beca ['beka] nf grant, scholarship ❏ **becario, -a** [be'karjo, a] nm/f scholarship holder, grant holder

bedel [be'ðel] nm (ESCOL) janitor; (UNIV) porter

béisbol ['beisβol] nm baseball

Belén [be'len] nm Bethlehem ❏ **belén** nm (de Navidad) nativity scene, crib

belga ['belɣa] adj, nmf Belgian

Bélgica ['belxika] nf Belgium

bélico, -a ['beliko, a] adj (actitud) warlike

belleza [be'ʎeθa] nf beauty

bello, -a ['beʎo, a] adj beautiful, lovely; **Bellas Artes** Fine Art

bellota [be'ʎota] nf acorn

bemol [be'mol] nm (MÚS) flat; **esto tiene bemoles** (fam) this is a tough one

bencina [ben'θina] nf (QUÍM) benzine

bendecir [bende'θir] vt to bless

bendición [bendi'θjon] nf blessing

bendito, -a [ben'dito, a] pp of **bendecir** ♦ adj holy; (afortunado) lucky; (feliz) happy; (sencillo) simple ♦ nm/f simple soul

beneficencia [benefi'θenθja] nf charity

beneficiario, -a [benefi'θjarjo, a] nm/f beneficiary

beneficio [bene'fiθjo] nm (bien) benefit, advantage; (ganancia) profit, gain; **a ~ de algn** in aid of sb ❏ **beneficioso, -a** adj beneficial

benéfico, -a [be'nefiko, a] adj charitable

beneplácito [bene'plaθito] nm approval, consent

benévolo, -a [be'neβolo, a] adj benevolent, kind

benigno, -a [be'niɣno, a] adj kind; (suave) mild; (MED: tumor) benign, non-malignant

berberecho [berβe'retʃo] nm (ZOOL, CULIN) cockle

berenjena [beren'xena] nf aubergine (BRIT), eggplant (US)

Berlín [ber'lin] n Berlin

berlinesa (RPl) nf doughnut, donut (US)

bermudas [ber'muðas] nfpl Bermuda shorts

berrido [be'rriðo] nm bellow(ing)

berrinche [be'rrintʃe] (fam) nm temper, tantrum

berro ['berro] nm watercress

berza ['berθa] nf cabbage

besamel [besa'mel] nf (CULIN) white sauce, bechamel sauce

besar [be'sar] vt to kiss; (fig: tocar) to graze; **besarse** vr to kiss (one another) ❏ **beso** nm kiss

bestia ['bestja] nf beast, animal; (fig) idiot ► **bestia de carga** beast of burden ► **bestial** [bes'tjal] adj bestial; (fam) terrific ❏ **bestialidad** nf bestiality; (fam) stupidity

besugo [be'suɣo] *nm* sea bream; (*fam*) idiot

besuquear [besuke'ar] *vt* to cover with kisses; **besuquearse** *vr* to kiss and cuddle

betabel (*MÉX*) *nm* beetroot (*BRIT*), beet (*US*)

betún [be'tun] *nm* shoe polish; (*QUÍM*) bitumen

biberón [biβe'ron] *nm* feeding bottle

Biblia ['biβlja] *nf* Bible

bibliografía [biβljoɣra'fia] *nf* bibliography

biblioteca [biβljo'teka] *nf* library; (*mueble*) bookshelves ▶ **biblioteca de consulta** reference library
□ **bibliotecario, -a** *nm/f* librarian

bicarbonato [bikarβo'nato] *nm* bicarbonate

bicho ['bitʃo] *nm* (*animal*) small animal; (*sabandija*) bug, insect; (*TAUR*) bull

bici [biθi] (*fam*) *nf* bike ▶ **bicicleta** [biθi'kleta] *nf* bicycle, cycle; **ir en bicicleta** to cycle

bidé [bi'ðe] (*pl* **~s**) *nm* bidet

bidón [bi'ðon] *nm* (*de aceite*) drum; (*de gasolina*) can

bien

PALABRA CLAVE

[bjen] *nm*

1 (*bienestar*) good; **te lo digo por tu bien** I'm telling you for your own good; **el bien y el mal** good and evil

2 (*posesión*): **bienes** *nmpl* goods; **bienes de consumo** consumer goods; **bienes inmuebles** o **raíces/bienes muebles** real estate *sg*/personal property *sg*

♦ *adv*

1 (*de manera satisfactoria, correcta etc*) well; **trabaja/come bien** she works/eats well; **contestó bien** he answered correctly; **me siento bien** I feel fine; **no me siento bien** I don't

feel very well; **se está bien aquí** it's nice here

2 (*frases*): **hiciste bien en llamarme** you were right to call me

3 (*valor intensivo*) very; **un cuarto bien caliente** a nice warm room; **bien se ve que ...** it's quite clear that ...

4: **estar bien: estoy muy bien aquí** I feel very happy here; **está bien que vengan** it's all right for them to come; **¡está bien!** lo haré oh all right, I'll do it

5 (*de buena gana*): **yo bien que iría pero ...** I'd gladly go but ...

♦ *excl*: **¡bien!** (*aprobación*) O.K.!; **¡muy bien!** well done!

♦ *adj inv* (*matiz despectivo*): **gente bien** posh people

♦ *conj*

1: **bien ... bien: bien en coche bien en tren** either by car or by train

2 (*LAm*): **no bien: no bien llegue te llamaré** as soon as I arrive I'll call you

3: **si bien** even though; *ver tb* **más**

bienal [bje'nal] *adj* biennial

bienestar [bjenes'tar] *nm* well-being, welfare

bienvenida [bjembe'niða] *nf* welcome; **dar la ~ a algn** to welcome sb

bienvenido [bjembe'niðo] *excl* welcome!

bife ['bife] (*CS*) *nm* steak

bifurcación [bifurka'θjon] *nf* fork

bígamo, -a ['biɣamo, a] *adj* bigamous ♦ *nm/f* bigamist

bigote [bi'ɣote] *nm* moustache
□ **bigotudo, -a** *adj* with a big moustache

bikini [bi'kini] *nm* bikini; (*CULIN*) toasted ham and cheese sandwich

bilingüe [bi'lingwe] *adj* bilingual

billar [bi'ʎar] *nm* billiards *sg*; **billares** *nmpl* (*lugar*) billiard hall; (*sala de* *juegos)* amusement arcade ► **billar americano** pool

billete [bi'ʎete] *nm* ticket; *(de banco)* (bank)note *(BRIT)*, bill *(US)*; *(carta)* note; ~ **de 20 libras** £20 note ► **billete de ida y vuelta** return *(BRIT)* o round-trip *(US)* ticket ► **billete sencillo** o **de ida** single *(BRIT)* o one-way *(US)* ticket

billetera [biʎe'tera] *nf* wallet

billón [bi'ʎon] *nm* billion

bimensual [bimen'swal] *adj* twice monthly

bingo ['bingo] *nm* bingo

biodegradable [bioðeɣra'ðaβle] *adj* biodegradable

biografía [bjoɣra'fia] *nf* biography

biología [bjolo'xia] *nf* biology ❏ **biológico, -a** *adj* biological; *(cultivo, producto)* organic ❏ **biólogo, -a** *nm/f* biologist

biombo ['bjombo] *nm* (folding) screen

bioterrorismo *nm* bioterrorism

biquini [bi'kini] *nm* o *(RPI)* f bikini

birlar [bir'lar] *(fam)* vt to pinch

Birmania [bir'manja] *nf* Burma

birome *(RPI)* ballpoint (pen)

birria ['birrja] *nf*: **ser una ~** *(película, libro)* to be rubbish

bis [bis] *excl* encore!

bisabuelo, -a [bisa'βwelo, a] *nm/f* great-grandfather/-mother)

bisagra [bi'saɣra] *nf* hinge

bisiesto [bi'sjesto] *adj*: **año ~** leap year

bisnieto, -a [bis'njeto, a] *nm/f* great-grandson/daughter

bisonte [bi'sonte] *nm* bison

bisté [bis'te] *nm* = **bistec**

bistec [bis'tek] *nm* steak

bisturí [bistu'ri] *nm* scalpel

bisutería [bisute'ria] *nf* imitation o costume jewellery

bit [bit] *nm* (INFORM) bit

bizco, -a ['biθko, a] *adj* cross-eyed

bizcocho [biθ'kotʃo] *nm* (CULIN) sponge cake

blanca ['blanka] *nf* (MÚS) minim; **estar sin ~** *(ESP: fam)* to be broke; *ver tb* **blanco**

blanco, -a ['blanko, a] *adj* white ♦ *nm/f* white man/woman, white ♦ *nm* (color) white; *(en texto)* blank; (MIL, *fig)* target; **en ~** blank; **noche en ~** sleepless night

blandir [blan'dir] vt to brandish

blando, -a ['blando, a] *adj* soft; *(tierno)* tender, gentle; *(carácter)* mild; *(fam)* cowardly

blanqueador (MÉX) *nm* bleach

blanquear [blanke'ar] vt to whiten; *(fachada)* to whitewash; *(paño)* to bleach ♦ vi to turn white

blanquillo (MÉX, CAm) *nm* egg

blasfemar [blasfe'mar] vi to blaspheme, curse

bledo ['bleðo] *nm*: **me importa un ~** I couldn't care less

blindado, -a [blin'daðo, a] *adj* (MIL) armour-plated; *(antibala)* bullet-proof; **coche** (LAM) o **carro** (ESP) ~ armoured car

bloc [blok] *(pl* **blocs)** *nm* writing pad

blof (MÉX) *nm* bluff ❏ **blofear** (MÉX) vi to bluff

bloque ['bloke] *nm* block; (POL) bloc

bloquear [bloke'ar] vt to blockade ❏ **bloqueo** *nm* blockade; (COM) freezing, blocking ► **bloqueo mental** mental block

blusa ['blusa] *nf* blouse

bobada [bo'βaða] *nf* foolish action; foolish statement; **decir bobadas** to talk nonsense

bobina [bo'βina] *nf* (TEC) bobbin; (FOTO) spool; (ELEC) coil

bobo, -a ['boβo, a] *adj (tonto)* daft, silly; *(cándido)* naïve ♦ *nm/f* fool, idiot ♦ *nm* (TEATRO) clown, funny man

boca ['boka] *nf* mouth; *(de crustáceo)* pincer; *(de cañón)* muzzle; *(entrada)* mouth, entrance; **bocas** *nfpl* *(de río)* mouth *sg*; ~ **abajo/arriba** face down/ up; **se me hace la ~ agua** my mouth is watering ► **boca de incendios** hydrant ► **boca del estómago** pit of the stomach ► **boca de metro** underground (BRIT) o subway (US) entrance

bocacalle [boka'kaʎe] nf (entrance to a) street; **la primera ~** the first turning o street

bocadillo [boka'ðiʎo] nm sandwich

bocado [bo'kaðo] nm mouthful, bite; (de caballo) bridle

bocajarro [boka'xarro]: **a ~** adv (disparar) point-blank

bocanada [boka'naða] nf (de vino) mouthful, swallow; (de aire) gust, puff

bocata [bo'kata] (fam) nm sandwich

bocazas [bo'kaθas] (fam) nm inv bigmouth

boceto [bo'θeto] nm sketch, outline

bochorno [bo'tforno] nm (vergüenza) embarrassment; (calor): **hace** ~ it's very muggy

bocina [bo'θina] nf (MÚS) trumpet; (AUTO) horn; (para hablar) megaphone

boda ['boða] nf (tb: **bodas**) wedding, marriage; (fiesta) wedding reception ► **bodas de oro/plata** golden/silver wedding sg

bodega [bo'ðeɣa] nf (de vino) (wine) cellar; (depósito) storeroom; (de barco) hold

bodegón [boðe'ɣon] nm (ARTE) still life

bofetada [bofe'taða] nf slap (in the face)

boga ['boɣa] nf: **en ~** (fig) in vogue

Bogotá [boɣo'ta] n Bogotá

bohemio, -a [bo'emjo, a] adj, nm/f Bohemian

bohío (CAm) nm shack, hut

boicot [boi'kot] (pl **boicots**) nm boycott ❏ **boicotear** vt to boycott

bóiler (MÉX) nm boiler

boina ['boina] nf beret

bola ['bola] nf ball; (canica) marble; (NAIPES) (grand) slam; (betún) shoe

polish; (mentira) tale, story; **bolas** nfpl (LAm: caza) bolas sg ► **bola de billar** billiard ball ► **bola de nieve** snowball

boleadoras [bolea'ðoras] nfpl bolas sg

bolear (MÉX) vt (zapatos) to polish, shine

bolera [bo'lera] nf skittle o bowling alley

bolero, -a (MÉX) [bo'lero] nm/f (limpiabotas) shoeshine boy/girl

boleta [bo'leta] (LAm) nf (de rifa) ticket; (CS: recibo) receipt ► **boleta de calificaciones** (MÉX) report card

boletería [bolete'ria] (LAm) nf ticket office

boletín [bole'tin] nm bulletin; (periódico) journal, review ► **boletín de noticias** news bulletin

boleto [bo'leto] nm (LAm) ticket ► **boleto de ida y vuelta** (LAm) round trip ticket ► **boleto redondo** (MÉX) round trip ticket

boli ['boli] (fam) nm Biro®

bolígrafo [bo'liɣrafo] nm ball-point pen, Biro®

bolilla (RPl) nf topic

bolillo (MÉX) [bo'liʎo] nm (bread) roll

bolita (CS) nf marble

bolívar [bo'liβar] nm monetary unit of Venezuela

Bolivia [bo'liβja] nf Bolivia ❏ **boliviano, -a** adj, nm/f Bolivian

bollería [boʎe'ria] nf cakes pl and pastries pl

bollo ['boʎo] nm (pan) roll; (bulto) bump, lump; (abolladura) dent

bolo ['bolo] nm skittle; (píldora) (large) pill; **(juego de) bolos** nmpl skittles sg

bolsa ['bolsa] nf (para llevar algo) bag; (MÉX, CAm: bolsillo) pocket; (MÉX: de mujer) handbag; (ANAT) cavity, sac; (COM) stock exchange; (MINERÍA) pocket; **de** ~ pocket cpd ► **bolsa de agua caliente** hot water bottle ► **bolsa de aire** air pocket ► **bolsa de dormir** (MÉX, RPl) sleeping bag

► **bolsa de la compra** shopping bag
► **bolsa de papel/plástico** paper/
plastic bag

bolsear (MÉX, CAm) vt: **~ a algn** to pick sb's pocket

bolsillo [bol'siʎo] nm pocket; (cartera) purse; **de ~** pocket(-size)

bolso ['bolso] nm (bolsa) bag; (de mujer) handbag

bomba ['bomba] nf (MIL) bomb; (TEC) pump ♦ adj (fam): **noticia ~** bombshell ♦ adv (fam): **pasarlo ~** to have a great time ► **bomba atómica/de efecto retardado/de humo** atomic/time/ smoke bomb

bombacha (RPI) nf panties pl

bombardear [bombarðe'ar] vt to bombard; (MIL) to bomb ❑ **bombardeo** nm bombardment; bombing

bombazo (MÉX) nm (explosión) explosion; (fam: noticia) bombshell; (: éxito) smash hit

bombear [bombe'ar] vt (agua) to pump (out o up)

bombero [bom'bero] nm fireman

bombilla [bom'biʎa] (ESP) nf (light) bulb

bombita (RPI) nf (light) bulb

bombo ['bombo] nm (MÚS) bass drum; (TEC) drum

bombón [bom'bon] nm chocolate; (MÉX: de caramelo) marshmallow

bombona [bom'bona] (ESP) nf (de butano, oxigeno) cylinder

bonachón, -ona [bona'tʃon, ona] adj good-natured, easy-going

bonanza [bo'nanθa] nf (NÁUT) fair weather; (fig) bonanza; (MINERÍA) rich pocket o vein

bondad [bon'dað] nf goodness, kindness; **tenga la ~ de** (please) be good enough to

bonito, -a [bo'nito, a] adj pretty; (agradable) nice ♦ nm (atún) tuna (fish)

bono ['bono] nm voucher; (FINANZAS) bond

bonobús [bono'βus] (ESP) nm bus pass

bonoloto [bono'loto] nf state-run weekly lottery

boquerón [boke'ron] nm (pez) (kind of) anchovy; (agujero) large hole

boquete [bo'kete] nm gap, hole

boquiabierto, a [bokia'βjerto, a] adj: **quedarse ~** to be amazed o flabbergasted

boquilla [bo'kiʎa] nf (para riego) nozzle; (para cigarro) cigarette holder; (MÚS) mouthpiece

borbotón [borβo'ton] nm: **salir a borbotones** to gush out

borda ['borða] nf (NÁUT) (ship's) rail; **tirar algo/caerse por la ~** to throw sth/ fall overboard

bordado [bor'ðaðo] nm embroidery

bordar [bor'ðar] vt to embroider

borde ['borðe] nm edge, border; (de camino etc) side; (en la costura) hem; **al ~ de** (fig) on the verge o brink of; **ser ~** (ESP: fam) to be rude ► **bordear** vt to border

bordillo [bor'ðiʎo] nm kerb (BRIT), curb (US)

bordo ['borðo] nm (NÁUT) side; **a ~** on board

borlote (MÉX) nm row, uproar

borrachera [borra'tʃera] nf (ebriedad) drunkenness; (orgía) spree, binge

borracho, -a [bo'rratʃo, a] adj drunk ♦ nm/f (habitual) drunkard, drunk; (temporal) drunk, drunk man/woman

borrador [borra'ðor] nm (escritura) first draft, rough sketch; (goma) rubber (BRIT), eraser

borrar [bo'rrar] vt to erase, rub out

borrasca [bo'rraska] nf storm

borrego, -a [bo'rreɣo, a] nm/f (ZOOL: joven) (yearling) lamb; (adulto) sheep ♦ nm (MÉX: fam) false rumour

borrico, -a [bo'rriko, a] nm/f donkey; she-donkey; (fig) stupid man/woman

borrón [bo'rron] nm (mancha) stain

borroso, -a [bo'rroso, a] adj vague, unclear; (escritura) illegible

bosque ['boske] nm wood; (grande) forest

bostezar [boste'θar] vi to yawn
□ **bostezo** nm yawn

bota ['bota] nf (calzado) boot; (para vino) leather wine bottle ▶ **botas de agua** o **goma** Wellingtons

botana (MÉX) nf snack, appetizer

botánica [bo'tanika] nf (ciencia) botany; ver tb **botánico**

botánico, -a [bo'taniko, a] adj botanical ♦ nm/f botanist

botar [bo'tar] vt to throw, hurl; (NAUT) to launch; (LAm: echar) to throw out ♦ vi (ESP: saltar) to bounce

bote ['bote] nm (salto) bounce; (golpe) thrust; (ESP: envase) tin, can; (embarcación) boat; (MÉX, CAm: pey: cárcel) jail; **de ~ en ~** packed, jammed full ▶ **bote de la basura** (MÉX) dustbin (BRIT), trashcan (US) ▶ **bote salvavidas** lifeboat

botella [bo'teʎa] nf bottle □ **botellín** nm small bottle □ **botellón** nm (ESP: fam) outdoor drinking session

botijo [bo'tixo] nm (earthenware) jug

botín [bo'tin] nm (calzado) half boot; (polaina) spat; (MIL) booty

botiquín [boti'kin] nm (armario) medicine cabinet; (portátil) first-aid kit

botón [bo'ton] nm button; (BOT) bud

botones [bo'tones] nm inv bellboy (BRIT), bellhop (US)

bóveda ['boβeða] nf (ARQ) vault

boxeador [boksea'ðor] nm boxer

boxeo [bok'seo] nm boxing

boya ['boja] nf (NAUT) buoy; (de caña) float

boyante [bo'jante] adj prosperous

bozal [bo'θal] nm (para caballos) halter; (de perro) muzzle

bragas ['braɣas] nfpl (de mujer) panties, knickers (BRIT)

bragueta [bra'ɣeta] nf fly, flies pl

braille [breil] nm braille

brasa ['brasa] nf live o hot coal

brasero [bra'sero] nm brazier

brasier (MÉX) nm bra

Brasil [bra'sil] nm (tb: **el ~**) Brazil □ **brasileño, -a** adj, nm/f Brazilian

brassier (MÉX) nm ver **brasier**

bravo, -a ['braβo, a] adj (valiente) brave; (feroz) ferocious; (salvaje) wild; (mar etc) rough, stormy ♦ excl bravo! □ **bravura** nf bravery; ferocity

braza ['braθa] nf fathom; **nadar a ~** to swim breast-stroke

brazalete [braθa'lete] nm (pulsera) bracelet; (banda) armband

brazo ['braθo] nm arm; (ZOOL) foreleg; (BOT) limb, branch; **luchar a ~ partido** to fight hand-to-hand; **ir cogidos del ~** to walk arm in arm

brebaje [bre'βaxe] nm potion

brecha ['bretʃa] nf (hoyo, vacío) gap, opening; (MIL: fig) breach

brega ['breɣa] nf (lucha) struggle; (trabajo) hard work

breva ['breβa] nf early fig

breve ['breβe] adj short, brief ♦ nf (MÚS) breve; **en ~** (pronto) shortly, before long □ **brevedad** nf brevity, shortness

bribón, -ona [bri'βon, ona] adj idle, lazy ♦ nm/f (pícaro) rascal, rogue

bricolaje [briko'laxe] nm do-it-yourself, DIY

brida ['briða] nf bridle, rein; (TEC) clamp

bridge [britʃ] nm bridge

brigada [bri'ɣaða] nf (unidad) brigade; (de trabajadores) squad, gang ♦ nm = staff-sergeant, sergeant-major

brillante [bri'ʎante] adj brilliant ♦ nm diamond

brillar [bri'ʎar] vi to shine; (joyas) to sparkle

brillo ['briʎo] nm shine; (brillantez) brilliance; (fig) splendour; **sacar ~ a** to polish

brincar [brin'kar] vi to skip about, hop about, jump about

brinco ['brinko] nm jump, leap

brindar [brin'dar] vi: **~ a o por** to drink (a toast) to ♦ vt to offer, present

brindis ['brindis] nm inv toast

brío ['brio] nm spirit, dash

brisa ['brisa] nf breeze

británico, -a [bri'taniko, a] adj British ♦ nm/f Briton, British person

brizna ['briθna] nf (de hierba, paja) blade; (de tabaco) leaf

broca ['broka] nf (TEC) drill, bit

brocha ['brotʃa] nf (large) paintbrush ▶ **brocha de afeitar** shaving brush

broche ['brotʃe] nm brooch

broma ['broma] nf joke; **de o en ~** in fun, as a joke ▶ **broma pesada** practical joke ▶ **bromear** vi to joke

bromista [bro'mista] adj fond of joking ♦ nmf joker, wag

bronca ['bronka] nf row; **echar una ~ a algn** to tick sb off

bronce ['bronθe] nm bronze □ **bronceado, -a** adj bronze; (por el sol) tanned ♦ nm (sun)tan; (TEC) bronzing

bronceador [bronθea'ðor] nm suntan lotion

broncearse [bronθe'arse] vr to get a suntan

bronquio ['bronkjo] nm (ANAT) bronchial tube

bronquitis [bron'kitis] nf inv bronchitis

brotar [bro'tar] vi (BOT) to sprout; (aguas) to gush (forth); (MED) to break out

brote ['brote] nm (BOT) shoot; (MED, fig) outbreak

bruces ['bruθes]: **de ~** adv: **caer o dar de ~** to fall headlong, fall flat

bruja ['bruxa] nf witch □ **brujería** nf witchcraft

brujo ['bruxo] nm wizard, magician

brújula ['bruxula] nf compass

bruma ['bruma] nf mist

brusco, -a ['brusko, a] adj (súbito) sudden; (áspero) brusque

Bruselas [bru'selas] n Brussels

brutal [bru'tal] adj brutal □ **brutalidad** [brutali'ðað] nf brutality

bruto, -a ['bruto, a] adj (idiota) stupid; (bestial) brutish; (peso) gross; **en ~** raw, unworked

Bs.As. abr (= Buenos Aires) B.A.

bucal [bu'kal] adj oral; **por vía ~** orally

bucear [buθe'ar] vi to dive ♦ vt to explore □ **buceo** nm diving

bucle ['bukle] nm curl

budismo [bu'ðismo] nm Buddhism

buen [bwen] adj m ver **bueno**

buenamente [bwena'mente] adv (fácilmente) easily; (voluntariamente) willingly

buenaventura [bwenaβen'tura] nf (suerte) good luck; (adivinación) fortune

buenmozo (MÉX) adj handsome

---

bueno, -a

PALABRA CLAVE

['bweno, a] (antes de nmsg: **buen**) □

1 (excelente etc) good; **es un libro bueno, es un buen libro** it's a good book; **hace bueno, hace buen tiempo** the weather is fine, it is fine; **el pan de Paco** good old Paco; **fue muy bueno conmigo** he was very nice o kind to me

2 (apropiado): **ser bueno para** to be good for; **creo que vamos por buen camino** I think we're on the right track

3 (irónico): **le di un buen rapapolvo** I gave him a good o real ticking off;

¡buen conductor estás hecho! some
o a fine driver you are!; **¡estaría
bueno que ...!** a fine thing it would be
if ...!
4 (*atractivo, sabroso*): **está bueno
este bizcocho** this sponge is
delicious; **Carmen está muy buena**
Carmen is gorgeous
5 (*saludos*): **¡buen día!, ¡buenos días!**
(good) morning!; **¡buenas (tardes)!**
(good) afternoon!; (*más tarde*) (good)
evening!; **¡buenas noches!** good
night!
6 (*otras locuciones*): **estar de buenas**
to be in a good mood; **por las buenas**
o por las malas by hook or by crook;
de buenas a primeras all of a sudden
♦ *excl:* **¡bueno!** all right!; **bueno, ¿y
qué?** well, so what?

Buenos Aires [bweno'saires] *nm*
Buenos Aires
buey [bwei] *nm* ox
búfalo ['bufalo] *nm* buffalo
bufanda [bu'fanda] *nf* scarf
bufete [bu'fete] *nm* (*despacho de
abogado*) lawyer's office
bufón [bu'fon] *nm* clown
buhardilla [buar'ðiʎa] *nf* attic
búho ['buo] *nm* owl; (*fig*) hermit, recluse
buitre ['bwitre] *nm* vulture
bujía [bu'xia] *nf* (*vela*) candle; (*ELEC*)
candle (power); (*AUTO*) spark plug
bula ['bula] *nf* (*papal*) bull
bulbo ['bulβo] *nm* bulb
bulevar [bule'βar] *nm* boulevard
Bulgaria [bul'yarja] *nf* Bulgaria
□ **búlgaro, -a** *adj, nm/f* Bulgarian
bulla ['buʎa] *nf* (*ruido*) uproar; (*de gente*)
crowd
bullicio [bu'ʎiθjo] *nm* (*ruido*) uproar;
(*movimiento*) bustle
bulto ['bulto] *nm* (*paquete*) package;
(*fardo*) bundle; (*tamaño*) size,

bulkiness; (*MED*) swelling, lump;
(*silueta*) vague shape
buñuelo [bu'ɲwelo] *nm* ≈ doughnut
(*BRIT*), ≈ donut (*US*); (*fruta de sartén*)
fritter
buque [buke] *nm* ship, vessel ► **buque
de guerra** warship
burbuja [bur'βuxa] *nf* bubble
burdel [bur'ðel] *nm* brothel
burgués, -esa [bur'yes, esa] *adj*
middle-class, bourgeois □ **burguesía**
nf middle class, bourgeoisie
burla ['burla] *nf* (*mofa*) joke; (*broma*)
joke; (*engaño*) trick ♦ **burlar** [bur'lar]
vt (*engañar*) to deceive ♦ *vi* to joke;
burlarse *vr* to joke; **burlarse de** to
make fun of
burlón, -ona [bur'lon, ona] *adj*
mocking
buró (*MÉX*) [bu'ro] *nm* bedside table
burocracia [buro'kraθja] *nf* civil
service
burrada [bu'rraða] *nf:* **decir o soltar
burradas** to talk nonsense; **hacer
burradas** to act stupid; **una ~** (*ESP:
mucho*) a (hell of a) lot
burro, -a ['burro, a] *nm/f* donkey/she-
donkey; (*fig*) ass, idiot
bursátil [bur'satil] *adj* stock-exchange
cpd
bus [bus] *nm* bus
busca ['buska] *nf* search, hunt ♦ *nm*
(*TEL*) bleeper; **en ~ de** in search of
buscador [buska'ðor] *nm* (*INTERNET*)
search engine
buscar [bus'kar] *vt* to look for, search
for, seek ♦ *vi* to look, search, seek; **se
busca secretaria** secretary wanted
busque *etc* ['buske] *vb ver* **buscar**
búsqueda ['buskeða] *nf* = **busca**
busto ['busto] *nm* (*ANAT, ARTE*) bust
butaca [bu'taka] *nf* armchair; (*de cine,
teatro*) stall, seat
butano [bu'tano] *nm* butane (gas)
buzo ['buθo] *nm* diver

buzón [bu'θon] *nm* (*en puerta*) letter box; (*en calle*) pillar box

C, c

C. *abr* = **centígrado**; (= *compañía*) Co.
C/ *abr* (= *calle*) St
cabal [ka'βal] *adj* (*exacto*) exact; (*correcto*) right, proper; (*acabado*) finished, complete ☐ **cabales** *nmpl*: **no está en sus cabales** she isn't in her right mind
cábalas ['kaβalas] *nfpl*: **hacer ~** to guess
cabalgar [kaβal'ɣar] *vt, vi* to ride
cabalgata [kaβal'ɣata] *nf* procession
caballa [ka'βaʎa] *nf* mackerel
caballería [kaβaʎe'ria] *nf* mount; (*MIL*) cavalry
caballero [kaβa'ʎero] *nm* gentleman; (*de la orden de caballería*) knight; (*trato directo*) sir
caballete [kaβa'ʎete] *nm* (*ARTE*) easel; (*TEC*) trestle
caballito [kaβa'ʎito] *nm* (*caballo pequeño*) small horse, pony; **caballitos** *nmpl* (*en verbena*) roundabout, merry-go-round
caballo [ka'βaʎo] *nm* horse; (*AJEDREZ*) knight; (*NAIPES*) queen; **ir en ~** to ride ▶ **caballo de carreras** racehorse ▶ **caballo de fuerza** *o* **vapor** horsepower
cabaña [ka'βaɲa] *nf* (*casita*) hut, cabin
cabecear [kaβeθe'ar] *vt, vi* to nod
cabecera [kaβe'θera] *nf* head; (*IMPRENTA*) headline
cabecilla [kaβe'θiʎa] *nm* ringleader
cabellera [kaβe'ʎera] *nf* (*head of*) hair; (*de cometa*) tail
cabello [ka'βeʎo] *nm* (*tb*: **cabellos**) hair ▶ **cabello de ángel** confectionery and pastry filling made of pumpkin and syrup
caber [ka'βer] *vi* (*entrar*) to fit, go; **caben 3 más** there's room for 3 more
cabestrillo [kaβes'triʎo] *nm* sling

cabeza [ka'βeθa] *nf* head; (*POL*) chief, leader ▶ **cabeza de ajo** bulb of garlic ▶ **cabeza de familia** head of the household ▶ **cabeza rapada** skinhead ☐ **cabezada** *nf* (*golpe*) butt; **dar cabezadas** to nod off ☐ **cabezón, -ona** *adj* (*vino*) heady; (*fam*: *persona*) pig-headed
cabida [ka'βiða] *nf* space
cabina [ka'βina] *nf* cabin; (*de avión*) cockpit; (*de camión*) cab ▶ **cabina telefónica** telephone (*BRIT*) box *o* booth
cabizbajo, -a [kaβiθ'βaxo, a] *adj* crestfallen, dejected
cable ['kaβle] *nm* cable
cabo [kaβo] *nm* (*de objeto*) end, extremity; (*MIL*) corporal; (*NAUT*) rope, cable; (*GEO*) cape; **al ~ de 3 días** after 3 days; **llevar a ~** to carry out
cabra ['kaβra] *nf* goat
cabré *etc* [ka'βre] *vb ver* **caber**
cabrear [kaβre'ar] (*fam*) *vt* to bug; **cabrearse** *vr* (*enfadarse*) to fly off the handle
cabrito [ka'βrito] *nm* kid
cabrón [ka'βron] *nm* cuckold; (*fam!*) bastard (*!*)
caca ['kaka] (*fam*) *nf* pooh
cacahuete [kaka'wete] (*ESP*) *nm* peanut
cacao [ka'kao] *nm* cocoa; (*BOT*) cacao
cacarear [kakare'ar] *vi* (*persona*) to boast; (*gallina*) to crow
cacería [kaθe'ria] *nf* hunt
cacarizo, -a [kaka'riθo, a] (*MÉX*) *adj* pockmarked
cacerola [kaθe'rola] *nf* pan, saucepan
cachalote [katʃa'lote] *nm* (*ZOOL*) sperm whale
cacharro [ka'tʃarro] *nm* earthenware pot; **cacharros** *nmpl* pots and pans
cachear [katʃe'ar] *vt* to search, frisk
cachemir [katʃe'mir] *nm* cashmere
cachetada (*LAm*: *fam*) *nf* (*bofetada*) slap

cachete [ka'tʃete] nm (ANAT) cheek; (ESP: *bofetada*) slap (in the face)

cachivache [katʃi'βatʃe] nm (*trasto*) piece of junk; **cachivaches** nmpl junk sg

cacho ['katʃo] nm (small) bit; (LAm: *cuerno*) horn

cachondeo [katʃon'deo] (ESP: fam) nm farce, joke

cachondo, -a [ka'tʃondo, a] adj (ZOOL) on heat; (fam: *sexualmente*) randy; (: *gracioso*) funny

cachorro, -a [ka'tʃoro, a] nm/f (*perro*) pup, puppy; (*león*) cub

cachucha (MÉX: fam) nf cap

cacique [ka'θike] nm chief, local ruler; (POL) local party boss

cactus ['kaktus] nm inv cactus

cada ['kaða] adj inv each; (*antes de número*) every; ~ **día** each day, every day; ~ **dos días** every other day; ~ **uno/a** each one, every one; ~ **vez más/menos** more and more/less and less; ~ **vez que** ... whenever, every time (that) ...; **uno de** ~ **diez** one out of every ten

cadáver [ka'ðaβer] nm (dead) body, corpse

cadena [ka'ðena] nf chain; (TV) channel; **trabajo en** ~ assembly line work ► **cadena montañosa** mountain range ► **cadena perpetua** (JUR) life imprisonment

cadera [ka'ðera] nf hip

cadete [ka'ðete] nm cadet

caducar [kaðu'kar] vi to expire
❏ **caduco, -a** adj expired; (*persona*) very old

caer [ka'er] vi to fall (down); **caerse** vr to fall (down); **me cae bien/mal** I can't get on well with him/I can't stand him; ~ **en la cuenta** to realize; **dejar** ~ to drop; **su cumpleaños cae en viernes** his birthday falls on a Friday

café [ka'fe] (pl ~s) nm (*bebida, planta*) coffee; (*lugar*) café ♦ adj (MÉX: *color*) brown, tan ► **café con leche** white

coffee ► **café negro** (LAm) black coffee ► **café solo** (ESP) black coffee

cafetera [kafe'tera] nf coffee pot

cafetería [kafete'ria] nf (gen) café

cafetero, -a [kafe'tero, a] adj coffee cpd; **ser muy** ~ to be a coffee addict

cafishio [ka'fiʃjo] (CS) nm pimp

cagar [ka'ɣar] (fam!) vt to bungle, mess up ♦ vi to have a shit (!)

caída [ka'iða] nf fall; (*declive*) slope; (*disminución*) fall, drop

caído, -a [ka'iðo, a] adj drooping

caiga etc [kaiɣa] vb ver **caer**

caimán [kai'man] nm alligator

caja ['kaxa] nf box; (*para reloj*) case; (de ascensor) shaft; (COM) cashbox; (*donde se hacen los pagos*) cashdesk; (: *en supermercado*) checkout, till ► **caja de ahorros** savings bank ► **caja de cambios** gearbox ► **caja de fusibles** fuse box ► **caja fuerte** o **de caudales** safe, strongbox

cajero, -a [ka'xero, a] nm/f cashier ► **cajero automático** cash dispenser

cajetilla [kaxe'tiʎa] nf (*de cigarrillos*) packet

cajón [ka'xon] nm big box; (*de mueble*) drawer

cajuela (MÉX) nf (AUTO) boot (BRIT), trunk (US)

cal [kal] nf lime

cala ['kala] nf (GEO) cove, inlet; (*de barco*) hold

calabacín [kalaβa'θin] nm (BOT) baby marrow; (: *más pequeño*) courgette (BRIT), zucchini (US)

calabacita (MÉX) [kalaβa'θita] nf courgette (BRIT), zucchini (US)

calabaza [kala'βaθa] nf (BOT) pumpkin

calabozo [kala'βoθo] nm (*cárcel*) prison; (*celda*) cell

calada (ESP) nf (*de cigarrillo*) puff

calado, -a [ka'laðo, a] adj (*prenda*) lace cpd ♦ nm (NÁUT) draught

calamar [kala'mar] nm squid no pl

calambre [ka'lambre] nm (ELEC) shock

calar [ka'lar] vt to soak, drench; (penetrar) to pierce, penetrate; (comprender) to see through; (vela) to lower; **calarse** vr (AUTO) to stall; **calarse las gafas** to stick one's glasses on

calavera [kala'βera] nf skull

calcar [kal'kar] vt (reproducir) to trace; (imitar) to copy

calcetín [kalθe'tin] nm sock

calcio ['kalθjo] nm calcium

calcomanía [kalkoma'nia] nf transfer

calculador, a [kalkula'ðor, a] adj (persona) calculating ❑ **calculadora** [kalkula'ðora] nf calculator

calcular [kalku'lar] vt (MAT) to calculate, compute; **~ que ...** to reckon that ...

caldera [kal'dera] nf boiler

calderilla [kalde'riʎa] nf (moneda) small change

caldo ['kaldo] nm stock; (consomé) consommé

calefacción [kalefak'θjon] nf heating ► **calefacción central** central heating

calefón (RPI) nm boiler

calendario [kalen'darjo] nm calendar

calentador [kalenta'ðor] nm heater

calentamiento [kalenta'mjento] nm (DEPORTE) warm-up

calentar [kalen'tar] vt to heat (up); **calentarse** vr to heat up, warm up; (fig: discusión etc) to get heated

calentón (RPI: fam) adj (sexualmente) horny, randy (BRIT)

calentura [kalen'tura] nf (MED) fever, (high) temperature

calesita (RPI) nf merry-go-round, carousel

calibre [ka'liβre] nm (de cañón) calibre, bore; (diámetro) diameter; (fig) calibre

calidad [kali'ðað] nf quality; **de ~** quality cpd; **en ~ de** in the capacity of, as

cálido, -a ['kaliðo, a] adj hot; (fig) warm

caliente etc [ka'ljente] vb ver **calentar** ♦ adj hot; (fig) fiery; (disputa) heated; (fam: cachondo) randy

calificación [kalifika'θjon] nf qualification; (de alumno) grade, mark

calificado, -a (LAm) adj (competente) qualified; (obrero) skilled

calificar [kalifi'kar] vt to qualify; (alumno) to grade, mark; **~ de** to describe as

calima [ka'lima] nf (cerca del mar) mist

cáliz ['kaliθ] nm chalice

caliza [ka'liθa] nf limestone

callado, -a [ka'ʎaðo, a] adj quiet

callar [ka'ʎar] vt (asunto delicado) to keep quiet about, say nothing about; (persona, opinión) to silence ♦ vi to keep quiet, be silent; **callarse** vr to keep quiet, be silent; **¡cállate!** be quiet!, shut up!

calle ['kaʎe] nf street; (DEPORTE) lane; **~ arriba/abajo** up/down the street ► **calle de sentido único** one-way street ► **calle mayor** (ESP) high (BRIT) o main (US) street ► **calle peatonal** pedestrianized o pedestrian street ► **calle principal** (LAm) high (BRIT) o main (US) street ❑ **callejear** vi to wander (about) the streets ❑ **callejero, -a** adj street cpd ♦ nm street map ❑ **callejón** nm alley, passage ► **callejón sin salida** cul-de-sac ❑ **callejuela** nf side-street, alley

callista [ka'ʎista] nmf chiropodist

callo [ka'ʎo] nm callus; (en el pie) corn; **callos** nmpl (CULIN) tripe sg

calma ['kalma] nf calm

calmante [kal'mante] nm sedative, tranquillizer

calmar [kal'mar] vt to calm, calm down ♦ vi (tempestad) to abate; (mente etc) to become calm

calor [ka'lor] nm heat; (agradable) warmth; **hace ~** it's hot; **tener ~** to be hot

caloría [kalo'ria] nf calorie

calumnia [ka'lumnja] nf calumny, slander

caluroso, -a [kalu'roso, a] adj hot; (sin exceso) warm; (fig) enthusiastic

calva ['kalβa] nf bald patch; (en bosque) clearing

calvario [kal'βarjo] nm stations pl of the cross

calvicie [kal'βiθje] nf baldness

calvo, -a ['kalβo, a] adj bald; (terreno) bare, barren; (tejido) threadbare

calza ['kalθa] nf wedge, chock

calzada [kal'θaða] nf roadway, highway

calzado, -a [kal'θaðo, a] adj shod ♦ nm footwear

calzador [kalθa'ðor] nm shoehorn

calzar [kal'θar] vt (zapatos etc) to wear; (mueble) to put a wedge under; **calzarse** vr: **calzarse los zapatos** to put on one's shoes; **¿qué (número) calza?** what size do you take?

calzón [kal'θon] nm, nm (ESP: pantalón corto) shorts; (LAm: ropa interior: de hombre) underpants, pants, shorts (BRIT), (: de mujer) panties, knickers (BRIT)

calzoncillos [kalθon'θiʎos] nmpl underpants

cama ['kama] nf bed; **hacer la ~** to make the bed ▶ **cama individual/de matrimonio** single/double bed

camaleón [kamale'on] nm chameleon

cámara ['kamara] nf chamber; (habitación) room; (sala) hall; (CINE) cine camera; (fotográfica) camera ▶ **cámara de aire** (ESP) inner tube ▶ **cámara de comercio** chamber of commerce ▶ **cámara de gas** gas chamber ▶ **cámara digital** camera ▶ **cámara frigorífica** cold-storage room

camarada [kama'raða] nm comrade, companion

camarera [kama'rera] nf (en restaurante) waitress; (en casa, hotel) maid

camarero [kama'rero] nm waiter

camarógrafo, -a (LAm) nm/f cameraman/camerawoman

camarón [kama'ron] nm shrimp

camarote [kama'rote] nm cabin

cambiable [kam'bjaβle] adj (variable) changeable, variable; (intercambiable) interchangeable

cambiante [kam'bjante] adj variable

cambiar [kam'bjar] vt to change; (dinero) to exchange ♦ vi to change; **cambiarse** vr (mudarse) to move; (de ropa) to change; **~ de idea** u **opinión** to change one's mind; **cambiarse de ropa** to change (one's clothes)

cambio ['kambjo] nm change; (trueque) exchange; (COM) rate of exchange; (oficina) bureau de change; (dinero menudo) small change; **a ~ de** in return o exchange for; **en ~** on the other hand; (en lugar de) instead ▶ **cambio de divisas** foreign exchange ▶ **cambio de marchas** o **velocidades** gear lever

camelar [kame'lar] vt to sweet-talk

camello [ka'meʎo] nm camel; (fam: traficante) pusher

camerino [kame'rino] nm dressing room

camilla [ka'miʎa] nf (MED) stretcher

caminar [kami'nar] vi (marchar) to walk, go ♦ vt (recorrer) to cover, travel

caminata [kami'nata] nf long walk; (por el campo) hike

camino [ka'mino] nm way, road; (sendero) track; **a medio ~** halfway (there); **en el ~** on the way, en route; **~ de** on the way to ▶ **Camino de**

Santiago Way of St James ► **camino particular** private road

CAMINO DE SANTIAGO

The **Camino de Santiago** is a medieval pilgrim route stretching from the Pyrenees to Santiago de Compostela in north-west Spain, where tradition has it the body of the Apostle James is buried. Nowadays it is a popular tourist route as well as a religious one.

camión [ka'mjon] *nm* lorry (BRIT), truck (US); (MÉX: autobús) bus ► **camión cisterna** tanker ► **camión de la basura** dustcart, refuse lorry ► **camión de mudanzas** removal (BRIT) o moving (US) van ❏ **camionero, -a** *nm/f* lorry o truck driver

camioneta [kamjo'neta] *nf* van, light truck

camisa [ka'misa] *nf* shirt; (BOT) skin ► **camisa de fuerza** straitjacket

camiseta [kami'seta] *nf* (prenda) tee-shirt; (: ropa interior) vest; (de deportista) top

camisón [kami'son] *nm* nightdress, nightgown

camorra [ka'morra] *nf*: buscar ~ to look for trouble

camote *nm* (MÉX, CS: batata) sweet potato, yam; (MÉX: bulbo) tuber, bulb; (CS: fam: enamoramiento) crush

campamento [kampa'mento] *nm* camp

campana [kam'pana] *nf* bell ❏ **campanada** *nf* peal ❏ **campanario** *nm* belfry

campanilla [kampa'niʎa] *nf* small bell

campaña [kam'paɲa] *nf* (MIL, POL) campaign ► **campaña electoral** election campaign

campechano, -a [kampe'tʃano, a] *adj* (franco) open

campeón, -ona [kampe'on, ona] *nm/f* champion ❏ **campeonato** *nm* championship

cámper (LAm) *nm* o *f* caravan (BRIT), trailer (US)

campera (RPI) *nf* anorak

campesino, -a [kampe'sino, a] *adj* country *cpd*, rural; (gente) peasant *cpd* ♦ *nm/f* countryman/woman; (agricultor) farmer

campestre [kam'pestre] *adj* country *cpd*, rural

camping ['kampin] (*pl* **campings**) *nm* camping; (lugar) campsite; **ir** o **estar de ~** to go camping

campo ['kampo] *nm* (fuera de la ciudad) country, countryside; (AGR, ELEC) field; (de fútbol) pitch; (de golf) course; (MIL) camp ► **campo de batalla** battlefield ► **campo de concentración** concentration camp ► **campo de deportes** sports ground, playing field ► **campo visual** field of vision, visual field

camuflaje [kamu'flaxe] *nm* camouflage

cana ['kana] *nf* white o grey hair; **tener canas** to be going grey

Canadá [kana'ða] *nm* Canada ❏ **canadiense** *adj, nm/f* Canadian ♦ *nf* fur-lined jacket

canal [ka'nal] *nm* canal; (GEO) channel, strait; (de televisión) channel; (de tejado) gutter ► **canal de Panamá** Panama Canal

canaleta (LAm) *nf* (de tejado) gutter

canalizar [kanali'θar] *vt* to channel

canalla [ka'naʎa] *nf* rabble, mob ♦ *nm* swine

canapé [kana'pe] (*pl* **~s**) *nm* sofa, settee; (CULIN) canapé

Canarias [ka'narjas] *nfpl* (*tb*: **las Islas ~**) the Canary Islands, the Canaries

canario, -a [ka'narjo, a] *adj, nm/f* (native) of the Canary Isles ♦ *nm* (ZOOL) canary

canasta [ka'nasta] nf (round) basket

canasto [ka'nasto] nm large basket

cancela [kan'θela] nf gate

cancelación [kanθela'θjon] nf cancellation

cancelar [kanθe'lar] vt to cancel; (una deuda) to write off

cáncer ['kanθer] nm (MED) cancer; **C~** (ASTROLOGÍA) Cancer

cancha ['kantʃa] nf (de baloncesto) court; (LAm: campo) field ♦ **cancha de tenis** (LAm) tennis court

canciller [kanθi'ʎer] nm chancellor

canción [kan'θjon] nf song ♦ **canción de cuna** lullaby

candado [kan'daðo] nm padlock

candente [kan'dente] adj red-hot; (fig: tema) burning

candidato, -a [kandi'ðato, a] nm/f candidate

cándido, -a ['kandiðo, a] adj simple; naive

⚠ No confundir **cándido** con la palabra inglesa candid.

candil [kan'dil] nm oil lamp
❑ **candilejas** nfpl (TEATRO) footlights

canela [ka'nela] nf cinnamon

canelones [kane'lones] nmpl cannelloni

cangrejo [kan'grexo] nm crab

canguro [kan'guro] nm kangaroo; **hacer de ~** to babysit

caníbal [ka'niβal] adj, nmf cannibal

canica [ka'nika] nf marble

canijo, -a [ka'nixo, a] adj frail, sickly

canilla (RPI) [ka'niʎa] nf tap (BRIT), faucet (US)

canjear [kanxe'ar] vt to exchange

canoa [ka'noa] nf canoe

canon ['kanon] nm canon; (pensión) rent; (COM) tax

canonizar [kanoni'θar] vt to canonize

canoso, -a [ka'noso, a] adj grey-haired

cansado, -a [kan'saðo, a] adj tired, weary; (tedioso) tedious, boring

cansancio [kan'sanθjo] nm tiredness, fatigue

cansar [kan'sar] vt (fatigar) to tire, tire out; (aburrir) to bore; (fastidiar) to bother; **cansarse** vr to tire, get tired; (aburrirse) to get bored

cantábrico, -a [kan'taβriko, a] adj Cantabrian; **mar C~** Bay of Biscay

cantante [kan'tante] adj singing ♦ nmf singer

cantar [kan'tar] vt to sing ♦ vi to sing; (insecto) to chirp ♦ nm (acción) singing; (canción) song; (poema) poem

cántaro ['kantaro] nm pitcher, jug; **llover a cántaros** to rain cats and dogs

cante ['kante] nm (MÚS) Andalusian folk song ► **cante jondo** flamenco singing

cantera [kan'tera] nf quarry

cantero (RPI) nm (arriate) border

cantidad [kanti'ðað] nf quantity, amount; **~ de** lots of

cantimplora [kantim'plora] nf (frasco) water bottle, canteen

cantina [kan'tina] nf canteen; (de estación) buffet; (LAm: bar) bar

cantinero, -a (MÉX) nm/f barman/ barmaid, bartender (US)

canto ['kanto] nm singing; (canción) song; (borde) edge, rim; (de cuchillo) back ► **canto rodado** boulder

cantor, a [kan'tor, a] nm/f singer

canturrear [kanturre'ar] vi to sing softly

canuto [ka'nuto] nm (tubo) small tube; (fam: droga) joint

caña ['kaɲa] nf (BOT: tallo) stem, stalk; (carrizo) reed; (vaso) tumbler; (de cerveza) glass of beer; (ANAT) shinbone ► **caña de azúcar** sugar cane ♦ **caña de pescar** fishing rod

cañada [ka'ɲaða] nf (entre dos montañas) gully, ravine; (camino) cattle track

cáñamo ['kaɲamo] nm hemp

cañería [kaɲeˈria] nf (tubo) pipe

caño [ˈkaɲo] nm (tubo) tube, pipe; (de albañal) sewer; (MÚS) pipe; (de fuente) jet

cañón [kaˈɲon] nm (MIL) cannon; (de fusil) barrel; (GEO) canyon, gorge

caoba [kaˈoβa] nf mahogany

caos [ˈkaos] nm chaos

capa [ˈkapa] nf cloak, cape; (GEO) layer, stratum ▸ **capa de ozono** ozone layer

capacidad [kapaθiˈðað] nf (medida) capacity; (aptitud) capacity, ability

caparazón [kaparaˈθon] nm shell

capataz [kapaˈtaθ] nm foreman

capaz [kaˈpaθ] adj able, capable; (amplio) capacious, roomy

capellán [kapeˈʎan] nm chaplain; (sacerdote) priest

capicúa [kapiˈkua] adj inv (número, fecha) reversible

capilla [kaˈpiʎa] nf chapel

capital [kapiˈtal] adj capital ♦ nm (COM) capital ♦ nf (ciudad) capital ▸ **capital social** share o authorized capital

capitalismo [kapitaˈlismo] nm capitalism ❏ **capitalista** adj, nmf capitalist

capitán [kapiˈtan] nm captain

capítulo [kaˈpitulo] nm chapter

capó [kaˈpo] nm (AUTO) bonnet

capón [kaˈpon] nm (gallo) capon

capota [kaˈpota] nf (de mujer) bonnet; (AUTO) hood (BRIT), top (US)

capote [kaˈpote] nm (abrigo: de militar) greatcoat; (de torero) cloak

capricho [kaˈpritʃo] nm whim, caprice ❏ **caprichoso, -a** adj capricious

Capricornio [kapriˈkornjo] nm Capricorn

cápsula [ˈkapsula] nf capsule

captar [kapˈtar] vt (comprender) to understand; (RADIO) to pick up; (atención, apoyo) to attract

captura [kapˈtura] nf capture; (JUR) arrest ❏ **capturar** vt to capture; to arrest

capucha [kaˈputʃa] nf hood, cowl

capuchón [ESP] [kapuˈtʃon] nm (de bolígrafo) cap

capullo [kaˈpuʎo] nm (BOT) bud; (ZOOL) cocoon; (fam) idiot

caqui [ˈkaki] nm khaki

cara [ˈkara] nf (ANAT: de moneda) face; (de disco) side; (descaro) boldness; ~ a facing; **de** ~ opposite, facing; **dar la** ~ to face the consequences; **¿~ o cruz?** heads or tails?; **¡qué ~ (más dura)!** what a nerve!

Caracas [kaˈrakas] n Caracas

caracol [karaˈkol] nm (ZOOL) snail; (concha) (sea) shell

carácter [kaˈrakter] (pl **caracteres**) nm character; **tener buen/mal** ~ to be good natured/bad tempered

característica [karakteˈristika] nf characteristic

característico, -a [karakteˈristiko, a] adj characteristic

caracterizar [karakteriˈθar] vt to characterize, typify

caradura [karaˈðura] nmf: **es un** ~ he's got a nerve

carajillo [karaˈxiʎo] nm coffee with a dash of brandy

carajo [kaˈraxo] (fam!) nm: **¡~!** shit! (!)

caramba [kaˈramba] excl good gracious!

caramelo [karaˈmelo] nm (dulce) sweet; (azúcar fundida) caramel

caravana [karaˈβana] nf caravan; (fig) group; (AUTO) tailback

carbón [karˈβon] nm coal; **papel** ~ carbon paper

carbono [karˈβono] nm carbon

carburador [karβuraˈðor] nm carburettor

carburante [karβuˈrante] nm (para motor) fuel

carcajada [karka'xaða] nf (loud) laugh, guffaw

cárcel ['karθel] nf prison, jail; (TEC) clamp

carcoma [kar'koma] nf woodworm

cardar [kar'ðar] vt (pelo) to backcomb

cardenal [karðe'nal] nm (REL) cardinal; (MED) bruise

cardíaco, -a [kar'ðiako, a] adj cardiac, heart cpd

cardinal [karði'nal] adj cardinal

cardo ['karðo] nm thistle

carecer [kare'θer] vi: ~ **de** to lack, be in need of

carencia [ka'renθja] nf lack; (escasez) shortage; (MED) deficiency

careta [ka'reta] nf mask

carga ['karɣa] nf (peso, ELEC) load; (de barco) cargo, freight; (MIL) charge; (responsabilidad) duty, obligation

cargado, -a [kar'ɣaðo, a] adj loaded; (ELEC) live; (café, té) strong; (cielo) overcast

cargamento [karɣa'mento] nm (acción) loading; (mercancías) load, cargo

cargar [kar'ɣar] vt (barco, arma) to load; (ELEC) to charge; (COM: algo en cuenta) to charge; (INFORM) to load ♦ vi (MIL) to charge; (AUTO) to load (up); ~ **con** to pick up, carry away; (peso: fig) to shoulder, bear; **cargarse** vr (fam: estropear) to break; (matar) to bump off

cargo ['karɣo] nm (puesto) post, office; (responsabilidad) duty, obligation; (JUR) charge; **hacerse ~ de** to take charge of o responsibility for

carguero [kar'ɣero] nm freighter, cargo boat; (avión) freight plane

Caribe [ka'riβe] nm: **el ~** the Caribbean; **del ~** Caribbean ❏ **caribeño, -a** [kari'βeɲo, a] adj Caribbean

caricatura [karika'tura] nf caricature

caricia [ka'riθja] nf caress

caridad [kari'ðað] nf charity

caries ['karjes] nf inv tooth decay

cariño [ka'riɲo] nm affection, love; (caricia) caress; (en carta) love ...; **tener ~ a** to be fond of ❏ **cariñoso, -a** adj affectionate

carisma [ka'risma] nm charisma

caritativo, -a [karita'tiβo, a] adj charitable

cariz [ka'riθ] nm: **tener** o **tomar buen/mal ~** to look good/bad

carmín [kar'min] nm lipstick

carnal [kar'nal] adj carnal; **primo ~** first cousin

carnaval [karna'βal] nm carnival

CARNAVAL

Carnaval is the traditional period of fun, feasting and partying which takes place in the three days before the start of Lent ("Cuaresma"). Although in decline during the Franco years the carnival has grown in popularity recently in Spain. Cádiz and Tenerife are particularly well-known for their flamboyant celebrations with fancy-dress parties, parades and firework displays being the order of the day.

---

carne ['karne] nf flesh; (CULIN) meat; **se me pone la ~ de gallina sólo verlo** I get the creeps just seeing it ▶ **carne de cerdo/cordero/ternera/vaca** pork/lamb/veal/beef ▶ **carne de gallina** (fig) gooseflesh ▶ **carne molida** (LAm) mince (BRIT), ground meat (US) ▶ **carne picada** (ESP, RPl) mince (BRIT), ground meat (US)

carné [kar'ne] (ESP) (pl ~s) nm: **carné de conducir** driving licence (BRIT), driver's license (US); **carné de identidad** identity card; **carné de socio** membership card

carnero [kar'nero] nm sheep, ram; (carne) mutton

carnet [kar'ne] (ESP) (pl carnets) nm = **carné**

carnicería [karniθe'ria] *nf* butcher's (shop); (*fig: matanza*) carnage, slaughter

carnicero, -a [karni'θero, a] *adj* carnivorous ♦ *nm/f* butcher; (*carnívoro*) carnivore

carnívoro, -a [kar'niβoro, a] *adj* carnivorous

caro, -a ['karo, a] *adj* dear; (*COM*) dear, expensive ♦ *adv* dear, dearly

carpa ['karpa] *nf* (*pez*) carp; (*de circo*) big top; (*LAm: tienda de campaña*) tent

carpeta [kar'peta] *nf* folder, file ▶ **carpeta de anillas** ring binder

carpintería [karpinte'ria] *nf* carpentry, joinery ❑ **carpintero** *nm* carpenter

carraspear [karraspe'ar] *vi* to clear one's throat

carraspera [karras'pera] *nf* hoarseness

carrera [ka'rrera] *nf* (*acción*) run(ning); (*espacio recorrido*) run; (*competición*) race; (*trayecto*) course; (*profesión*) career; (*licenciatura*) degree; **a la** ~ at (full) speed ▶ **carrera de obstáculos** (*DEPORTE*) steeplechase

carrete [ka'rrete] *nm* reel, spool; (*TEC*) coil

carretera [karre'tera] *nf* (*main*) road, highway ▶ **carretera de circunvalación** ring road ▶ **carretera nacional** ≈ A road (*BRIT*), ≈ state highway (*US*)

carretilla [karre'tiʎa] *nf* trolley; (*AGR*) (wheel)barrow

carril [ka'rril] *nm* furrow; (*de autopista*) lane; (*FERRO*) rail ▶ **carril-bici** cycle lane

carrito [ka'rrito] *nm* trolley

carro ['karro] *nm* cart, wagon; (*MIL*) tank; (*LAm: coche*) car ▶ **carro patrulla** (*LAm*) patrol o panda (*BRIT*) car

carrocería [karroθe'ria] *nf* bodywork, coachwork

carroña [ka'rroɲa] *nf* carrion *no pl*

carroza [ka'rroθa] *nf* (*carruaje*) coach

carrusel [karru'sel] *nm* merry-go-round, roundabout

carta ['karta] *nf* letter; (*CULIN*) menu; (*naipe*) card; (*mapa*) map; (*documento*) document ▶ **carta certificada/urgente** registered/special-delivery letter

cartabón [karta'βon] *nm* set square

cartel [kar'tel] *nm* (*anuncio*) poster, placard; (*ESCOL*) wall chart; (*COM*) cartel ❑ **cartelera** *nf* hoarding, billboard; (*en periódico etc*) entertainments guide; **"en cartelera"** "showing"

cartera [kar'tera] *nf* (*de bolsillo*) wallet; (*de colegial, cobrador*) satchel; (*de señora*) handbag; (*para documentos*) briefcase; (*COM*) portfolio; **ocupa la ~ de Agricultura** she is Minister of Agriculture

carterista [karte'rista] *nmf* pickpocket

cartero [kar'tero] *nm* postman

cartilla [kar'tiʎa] *nf* primer, first reading book ▶ **cartilla de ahorros** savings book

cartón [kar'ton] *nm* cardboard ▶ **cartón piedra** papier-mâché

cartucho [kar'tutʃo] *nm* (*MIL*) cartridge

cartulina [kartu'lina] *nf* card

casa ['kasa] *nf* house; (*hogar*) home; (*COM*) firm, company; **en** ~ at home ▶ **casa consistorial** town hall ▶ **casa de campo** country house ▶ **casa de huéspedes** boarding house ▶ **casa de socorro** first aid post ▶ **casa rodante** (*CS*) caravan (*BRIT*), trailer (*US*)

casado, -a [ka'saðo, a] *adj* married ♦ *nm/f* married man/woman

casar [ka'sar] *vt* to marry; (*JUR*) to quash, annul; **casarse** *vr* to marry, get married

cascabel [kaska'βel] *nm* (*small*) bell

cascada [kas'kaða] *nf* waterfall

cascanueces [kaska'nweθes] *nm inv* nutcrackers *pl*

cascar [kas'kar] *vt* to crack, split, break (open); **cascarse** *vr* to crack, split, break (open)

cáscara ['kaskara] nf (de huevo, fruta seca) shell; (de fruta) skin; (de limón) peel

casco ['kasko] nm (de bombero, soldado) helmet; (NÁUT: de barco) hull; (ZOOL: de caballo) hoof; (botella) empty bottle; (de ciudad): **el ~ antiguo** the old part; **el ~ urbano** the town centre; **los cascos azules** the UN peace-keeping force, the blue berets

cascote [kas'kote] nm rubble

caserío [kase'rio] (ESP) nm farmhouse; (casa) country mansion

casero, -a [ka'sero, a] adj (pan etc) home-made ♦ nm/f (propietario) landlord/lady; **ser muy ~** to be home-loving; **"comida casera"** "home cooking"

caseta [ka'seta] nf hut; (para bañista) cubicle; (de feria) stall

casete [ka'sete] nm o f casette

casi ['kasi] adv almost, nearly; **~ nada** hardly anything; **~ nunca** hardly ever, almost never; **~ te caes** you almost fell

casilla [ka'siʎa] nf (casita) hut, cabin; (AJEDREZ) square; (para cartas) pigeonhole ▶ **casilla de correo** (CS) P.O. Box ▶ **casillero** nm (para cartas) pigeonholes pl

casino [ka'sino] nm club; (de juego) casino

caso ['kaso] nm case; **en ~ de** in case of; **en ~ de que** in case ...; **el ~ es que** the fact is that ...; **en ese/todo ~** in that/ any case; **hacer ~ a** to pay attention to; **venir al ~** to be relevant

caspa ['kaspa] nf dandruff

cassette [ka'sete] nm o f = **casete**

castaña [kas'taɲa] nf chestnut

castaño, -a [kas'taɲo, a] adj chestnut(-coloured), brown ♦ nm chestnut tree

castañuelas [kasta'ɲwelas] nfpl castanets

castellano, -a [kaste'ʎano, a] adj, nm/f Castilian ♦ nm (LING) Castilian, Spanish

castigar [kasti'ɣar] vt to punish; (DEPORTE) to penalize ▶ **castigo** nm punishment; (DEPORTE) penalty

Castilla [kas'tiʎa] nf Castile

castillo [kas'tiʎo] nm castle

castizo, -a [kas'tiθo, a] adj (LING) pure

casto, -a ['kasto, a] adj chaste, pure

castor [kas'tor] nm beaver

castrar [kas'trar] vt to castrate

casual [ka'swal] adj chance, accidental ▶ **casualidad** nf chance, accident; (combinación de circunstancias) coincidence; **da la casualidad de que ...** it (just) so happens that ...; **¡qué casualidad!** what a coincidence!

> ⚠ No confundir **casual** con la palabra inglesa *casual*.

cataclismo [kata'klismo] nm cataclysm

catador, a [kata'ðor, a] nm/f wine taster

catalán, -ana [kata'lan, ana] adj, nm/f Catalan ♦ nm (LING) Catalan

catalizador [kataliθa'ðor] nm catalyst; (AUTO) catalytic convertor

catalogar [katalo'ɣar] vt to catalogue; **~ a algn (de)** (fig) to categorize sb (as)

catálogo [ka'taloɣo] nm catalogue

Cataluña [kata'luɲa] nf Catalonia

catar [ka'tar] vt to taste, sample

catarata [kata'rata] nf (GEO) waterfall; (MED) cataract

catarro [ka'tarro] nm catarrh; (constipado) cold

catástrofe [ka'tastrofe] nf catastrophe

catear [kate'ar] (fam) vt (examen, alumno) to fail

cátedra ['kateðra] nf (UNIV) chair, professorship

catedral [kate'ðral] nf cathedral

catedrático, -a [kate'ðratiko, a] nm/f professor

categoría

categoría [kateɣo'ria] nf category; (rango) rank, standing; (calidad) quality; **de ~** (hotel) top-class

cateto, -a ['kateto, a] (ESP: pey) nm/f peasant

catolicismo [katoli'θismo] nm Catholicism

católico, -a [ka'toliko, a] adj, nm/f Catholic

catorce [ka'torθe] num fourteen

cauce ['kauθe] nm (de río) riverbed; (fig) channel

caucho ['kautʃo] (ESP) nm rubber

caudal [kau'ðal] nm (de río) volume, flow; (fortuna) wealth; (abundancia) abundance

caudillo [kau'ðiʎo] nm leader, chief

causa ['kausa] nf cause; (razón) reason; (JUR) lawsuit, case; **a ~ de** because of □ **causar** [kau'sar] vt to cause

cautela [kau'tela] nf caution, cautiousness □ **cauteloso, -a** adj cautious, wary

cautivar [kauti'βar] vt to capture; (atraer) to captivate

cautiverio [kauti'βerjo] nm captivity

cautividad [kautiβi'ðað] nf = cautiverio

cautivo, -a [kau'tiβo, a] adj, nm/f captive

cauto, -a ['kauto, a] adj cautious, careful

cava ['kaβa] nm champagne-type wine

cavar [ka'βar] vt to dig

caverna [ka'βerna] nf cave, cavern

cavidad [kaβi'ðað] nf cavity

cavilar [kaβi'lar] vt to ponder

cayendo etc [ka'jendo] vb ver **caer**

caza ['kaθa] nf (acción: gen) hunting; (: con fusil) shooting; (una caza) hunt, chase; (de animales) game ♦ nm (AVIAC) fighter; **ir de ~** to go hunting ▸ **caza mayor** game hunting □ **cazador, a** [kaθa'ðor, a] nm/f hunter ▸ **cazadora**

nf jacket □ **cazar** [ka'θar] vt to hunt; (perseguir) to chase; (prender) to catch

cazo ['kaθo] nm saucepan

cazuela [ka'θwela] nf (vasija) pan; (guisado) casserole

CD nm abr (= compact disc) CD

CD-ROM nm abr CD-ROM

CE nf abr (= Comunidad Europea) EC

cebada [θe'βaða] nf barley

cebar [θe'βar] vt (animal) to fatten (up); (anzuelo) to bait; (MIL, TEC) to prime

cebo ['θeβo] nm (para animales) feed, food; (para peces, fig) bait; (de arma) charge

cebolla [θe'βoʎa] nf onion □ **cebolleta** nf spring onion

cebra ['θeβra] nf zebra

cecear [θeθe'ar] vi to lisp

ceder [θe'ðer] vt to hand over, give up, part with ♦ vi (renunciar) to give in, yield; (disminuir) to diminish, decline; (romperse) to give way

cedro ['θeðro] nm cedar

cédula ['θeðula] nf certificate, document ▸ **cédula de identidad** (LAm) identity card ▸ **cédula electoral** (LAm) ballot

cegar [θe'ɣar] vt to blind; (tubería etc) to block up, stop up ♦ vi to go blind; **cegarse** vr: **cegarse (de)** to be blinded (by)

ceguera [θe'ɣera] nf blindness

ceja ['θexa] nf eyebrow

cejar [θe'xar] vi (fig) to back down

celador, a [θela'ðor, a] nm/f (de edificio) watchman; (de museo etc) attendant

celda ['θelda] nf cell

celebración [θeleβra'θjon] nf celebration

celebrar [θele'βrar] vt to celebrate; (alabar) to praise ♦ vi to be glad; **celebrarse** vr to occur, take place

célebre ['θeleβre] adj famous

celebridad [θeleβri'ðað] nf fame; (persona) celebrity

celeste [θe'leste] adj (azul) sky-blue

celestial [θeles'tjal] adj celestial, heavenly

celo¹ [θelo] nm zeal; (REL) fervour; (ZOOL): **en ~** on heat; **celos** nmpl jealousy sg; **dar celos a algn** to make sb jealous; **tener celos** to be jealous

celo® ² [θelo] nm Sellotape®

celofán [θelo'fan] nf cell

celoso, -a [θe'loso, a] adj jealous; (trabajador) zealous

celta ['θelta] adj Celtic ♦ nmf Celt

célula ['θelula] nf cell

celulitis [θelu'litis] nf cellulite

cementerio [θemen'terjo] nm cemetery, graveyard

cemento [θe'mento] nm cement; (hormigón) concrete; (LAm: cola) glue

cena ['θena] nf evening meal, dinner ❑ **cenar** [θe'nar] vt to have for dinner ♦ vi to have dinner

cenicero [θeni'θero] nm ashtray

ceniza [θe'niθa] nf ash, ashes pl

censo ['θenso] nm census ▶ **censo electoral** electoral roll

censura [θen'sura] nf (POL) censorship ❑ **censurar** [θensu'rar] vt (idea) to censure; (cortar: película) to censor

centella [θen'teʎa] nf spark

centenar [θente'nar] nm hundred

centenario, -a [θente'narjo, a] adj centenary; hundred-year-old ♦ nm centenary

centeno [θen'teno] nm (BOT) rye

centésimo, -a [θen'tesimo, a] adj hundredth

centígrado [θen'tiɣraðo] adj centigrade

centímetro [θen'timetro] nm centimetre (BRIT), centimeter (US)

céntimo [θen'timo] nm cent

centinela [θenti'nela] nm sentry, guard

centollo [θen'toʎo] nm spider crab

central [θen'tral] adj central ♦ nf head office; (TEC) plant; (TEL) exchange ▶ **central eléctrica** power station ▶ **central nuclear** nuclear power station ▶ **central telefónica** telephone exchange

centralita [θentra'lita] nf switchboard

centralizar [θentrali'θar] vt to centralize

centrar [θen'trar] vt to centre

céntrico, -a [θentriko, a] adj central

centrifugar [θentrifu'ɣar] vt to spin-dry

centro [θentro] nm centre ▶ **centro comercial** shopping centre ▶ **centro de atención al cliente** call centre ▶ **centro de salud** health centre ▶ **centro escolar** school ▶ **centro juvenil** youth club ▶ **centro turístico** (lugar muy visitado) tourist centre ▶ **centro urbano** urban area, city

centroamericano, -a [θentroameri'kano, a] adj, nm/f Central American

ceñido, -a [θe'niðo, a] adj (chaqueta, pantalón) tight(-fitting)

ceñir [θe'nir] vt (rodear) to encircle, surround; (ajustar) to fit (tightly)

ceño [θeno] nm frown, scowl; **fruncir el ~** to frown, knit one's brow

cepillar [θepi'ʎar] vt to brush; (madera) to plane (down)

cepillo [θe'piʎo] nm brush; (para madera) plane ▶ **cepillo de dientes** toothbrush

cera ['θera] nf wax

cerámica [θe'ramika] nf pottery; (arte) ceramics

cerca ['θerka] nf fence ♦ adv near, nearby, close; **~ de** near, close to

cercanías [θerka'nias] nfpl (afueras) outskirts, suburbs

cercano, -a [θer'kano, a] adj close, near

cercar [θerˈkar] vt to fence in; (rodear) to surround

cerco [ˈθerko] nm (AGR) enclosure; (LAm: valla) fence; (MIL) siege

cerdo, -a [ˈθerðo, a] nm/f pig/sow

cereal [θereˈal] nm cereal; **cereales** nmpl cereals, grain sg

cerebro [θeˈreβro] nm brain; (fig) brains pl

ceremonia [θereˈmonja] nf ceremony
▪ ceremonioso, -a adj ceremonious

cereza [θeˈreθa] nf cherry

cerilla [θeˈriʎa] nf (fósforo) match

cerillo [MÉX] [θeˈriʎo] nm match

cero [ˈθero] nm nothing, zero

cerquillo [CAm, RPl] nm fringe (BRIT), bangs pl (US)

cerrado, -a [θeˈrraðo, a] adj closed, shut; (con llave) locked; (tiempo) cloudy, overcast; (curva) sharp; (acento) thick, broad

cerradura [θerraˈðura] nf (acción) closing; (mecanismo) lock

cerrajero [θerraˈxero] nm locksmith

cerrar [θeˈrrar] vt to close, shut; (paso, carretera) to close; (grifo) to turn off; (cuenta, negocio) to close ♦ vi to close, shut; (noche) to come down; **cerrarse** vr to close, shut; **~ con llave** to lock; **~ un trato** to strike a bargain

cerro [ˈθerro] nm hill

cerrojo [θeˈrroxo] nm (herramienta) bolt; (de puerta) latch

certamen [θerˈtamen] nm competition, contest

certero, -a [θerˈtero, a] adj (gen) accurate

certeza [θerˈteθa] nf certainty

certidumbre [θertiˈðumbre] nf = **certeza**

certificado, -a [θertifiˈkaðo, a] adj (carta, paquete) registered; (aprobado) certified ♦ nm certificate
▪ certificado médico medical certificate

certificar [θertifiˈkar] vt (asegurar, atestar) to certify

cervatillo [θerβaˈtiʎo] nm fawn

cervecería [θerβeθeˈria] nf (fábrica) brewery; (bar) public house, pub

cerveza [θerˈβeθa] nf beer

cesar [θeˈsar] vi to cease, stop ♦ vt (funcionario) to remove from office

cesárea [θeˈsarea] nf (MED) Caesarean operation o section

cese [ˈθese] nm (de trabajo) dismissal; (de pago) suspension

césped [ˈθespeð] nm grass, lawn

cesta [ˈθesta] nf basket

cesto [ˈθesto] nm (large) basket, hamper

cfr abr (= confróntese) cf.

chabacano, -a [tʃaβaˈkano, a] adj vulgar, coarse

chabola [tʃaˈβola] (ESP) nf shack
▶ barrio de chabolas shanty town

chacal [tʃaˈkal] nm jackal

chacha [ˈtʃatʃa] (fam) nf maid

cháchara [ˈtʃatʃara] nf chatter; **estar de ~** to chatter away

chacra [ˈtʃakra] (CS) nf smallholding

chafa [MÉX: fam] adj useless, dud

chafar [tʃaˈfar] vt (aplastar) to crush; (plan etc) to ruin

chal [tʃal] nm shawl

chalado, -a [tʃaˈlaðo, a] (fam) adj crazy

chalé [tʃaˈle] (pl ~s) nm villa, = detached house

chaleco [tʃaˈleko] nm waistcoat, vest (US) **▶ chaleco salvavidas** life jacket

chalet [tʃaˈle] (pl chalets) nm = **chalé**

chamaco, -a [MÉX] [tʃaˈmako, a] nm/f (niño) kid

chambear [MÉX: fam] vi to earn one's living

champán [tʃamˈpan] nm champagne

champiñón [tʃampiˈɲon] nm mushroom

champú [tʃamˈpu] (pl ~es, ~s) nm shampoo

chamuscar [tʃamus'kar] vt to scorch, sear, singe

chance ['tʃanθe] (LAm) nm chance

chancho, -a ['tʃantʃo, a] (LAm) nm/f pig

chanchullo [tʃan'tʃuʎo] (fam) nm fiddle

chandal [tʃan'dal] nm tracksuit

chantaje [tʃan'taxe] nm blackmail

chapa ['tʃapa] nf (de metal) plate, sheet; (de madera) board, panel; (RPI AUTO) number (BRIT) o license (US) plate ❑ **chapado, -a** adj: **chapado en oro** gold-plated

chaparrón [tʃapa'rron] nm downpour, cloudburst

chaperón (MÉX) nm: **hacer de ~** to play gooseberry ❑ **chaperona** (LAm) nf: **hacer de chaperona** to play gooseberry

chapopote (MÉX) [tʃapo'pote] nm tar

chapulín (MÉX, CAm) [tʃapu'lin] nm grasshopper

chapurrear [tʃapurre'ar] vt (idioma) to speak badly

chapuza [tʃa'puθa] nf botched job

chapuzón [tʃapu'θon] nm: **darse un ~** to go for a dip

chaqueta [tʃa'keta] nf jacket

chaquetón [tʃake'ton] nm long jacket

charca ['tʃarka] nf pond, pool

charco ['tʃarko] nm pool, puddle

charcutería [tʃarkute'ria] nf (tienda) shop selling chiefly pork meat products; (productos) cooked pork meats pl

charla ['tʃarla] nf talk, chat; (conferencia) lecture ❑ **charlar** [tʃar'lar] vi to talk, chat; **charlatán, -ana** [tʃarla'tan, ana] nm/f (hablador) chatterbox; (estafador) trickster

charol [tʃa'rol] nm varnish; (cuero) patent leather

charola (MÉX) [tʃa'rola] nf tray

charro (MÉX) ['tʃarro, a] nm typical Mexican

chasco ['tʃasko] nm (desengaño) disappointment

chasis ['tʃasis] nm inv chassis

chasquido [tʃas'kiðo] nm crack; click

chat nm (INTERNET) chat room

chatarra [tʃa'tarra] nf scrap (metal)

chato, -a ['tʃato, a] adj flat; (nariz) snub

chaucha (RPI) ['tʃautʃa] nf runner (BRIT) o pole (US) bean

chaval, -a [tʃa'βal, a] (ESP) nm/f kid, lad/ lass

chavo, -a (MÉX: fam) ['tʃaβo] nm/f guy/ girl

checar (MÉX) vt: **~ tarjeta** (al entrar) to clock in o on; (al salir) to clock off o out

checo, -a ['tʃeko, a] adj, nm/f Czech ♦ nm (LING) Czech

checoslovaco, -a [tʃekosloβako, a] adj, Czech, Czechoslovak

Checoslovaquia [tʃekosloβakja] nf (HIST) Czechoslovakia

cheque ['tʃeke] nm cheque (BRIT), check (US); **cobrar un ~** to cash a cheque ▶ **cheque al portador** cheque payable to bearer ▶ **cheque de viaje** traveller's cheque (BRIT), traveler's check (US) ▶ **cheque en blanco** blank cheque

chequeo [tʃe'keo] nm (MED) check-up; (AUTO) service

chequera [tʃe'kera] (LAm) nf chequebook (BRIT), checkbook (US)

chévere (LAm: fam) ['tʃeβere] adj great

chícharo [tʃitʃaro] (MÉX, CAm) nm pea

chichón [tʃi'tʃon] nm bump, lump

chicle [tʃikle] nm chewing gum

chico, -a ['tʃiko, a] adj small, little ♦ nm/ f (niño) child; (muchacho) boy/girl

chiflado, -a [tʃi'flaðo, a] adj crazy

chiflar [tʃi'flar] vt to hiss, boo

chilango, -a ['tʃa] (MÉX) adj of o from Mexico City

Chile ['tʃile] nm Chile ❑ **chileno, -a** adj, nm/f Chilean

chile ['tʃile] nm chilli pepper

chillar [tʃiˈʎar] vi (persona) to yell, scream; (animal salvaje) to howl; (cerdo) to squeal

chillido [tʃiˈʎiðo] nm (de persona) yell, scream; (de animal) howl

chimenea [tʃimeˈnea] nf chimney; (hogar) fireplace

China [ˈtʃina] nf (tb: la ~) China

chinche [ˈtʃintʃe] nf (insecto) (bed)bug; (TEC) drawing pin (BRIT), thumbtack (US) ♦ nmf nuisance, pest

chincheta [tʃinˈtʃeta] nf drawing pin (BRIT), thumbtack (US)

chingada [MÉX: fam!] [tʃinˈgaða] nf: hijo de la ~ bastard

chino, -a [ˈtʃino, a] adj, nm/f Chinese ♦ nm (LING) Chinese

chipirón [tʃipiˈron] nm (ZOOL, CULIN) squid

Chipre [ˈtʃipre] nf Cyprus ❑ **chipriota** [tʃipriˈota] adj, nmf Cypriot

chiquillo, -a [tʃiˈkiʎo, a] nm/f (fam) kid

chirimoya [tʃiriˈmoja] nf custard apple

chiringuito [tʃirinˈgito] nm small open-air bar

chiripa [tʃiˈripa] nf fluke

chirriar [tʃiˈrrjar] vi to creak, squeak

chirrido [tʃiˈrriðo] nm creak(ing), squeak(ing)

chisme [ˈtʃisme] nm (habladurías) piece of gossip; (fam: objeto) thingummyjig

chismoso, -a [tʃisˈmoso, a] adj gossiping ♦ nm/f gossip

chispa [ˈtʃispa] nf spark; (fig) sparkle; (ingenio) wit; (fam) drunkenness

chispear [tʃispeˈar] vi (lloviznar) to drizzle

chiste [ˈtʃiste] nm joke, funny story

chistoso, -a [tʃisˈtoso, a] adj funny, amusing

chivo, -a [ˈtʃiβo, a] nm/f (billy-/nanny-) goat ► **chivo expiatorio** scapegoat

chocante [tʃoˈkante] adj startling; (extraño) odd; (ofensivo) shocking

chocar [tʃoˈkar] vi (coches etc) to collide, crash ♦ vt to shock; (sorprender) to startle; ~ **con** to collide with; (fig) to run into, run up against; **¡chócala!** (fam) put it there!

chochear [tʃotʃeˈar] vi to be senile

chocho, -a [ˈtʃotʃo, a] adj doddering, senile; (fig) soft, doting

choclo (CS) [ˈtʃoklo] nm (grano) sweet corn; (mazorca) corn on the cob

chocolate [tʃokoˈlate] adj, nm chocolate ❑ **chocolatina** [tʃokolaˈtina] nf chocolate

chofer [tʃoˈfer] nm = **chófer**

chófer [ˈtʃofer] nm driver

chollo [ˈtʃoʎo] (ESP: fam) nm bargain, snip

choque etc [ˈtʃoke] vb ver **chocar** ♦ nm (impacto) impact; (golpe) jolt; (AUTO) crash; (fig) conflict ► **choque frontal** head-on collision

chorizo [tʃoˈriθo] nm hard pork sausage, (type of) salami

chorrada [tʃoˈrraða] (ESP: fam) nf: **¡es una ~!** that's crap! (!); **decir chorradas** to talk crap (!)

chorrear [tʃorreˈar] vi to gush (out), spout (out); (gotear) to drip, trickle

chorro [ˈtʃorro] nm jet; (fig) stream

choza [ˈtʃoθa] nf hut, shack

chubasco [tʃuˈβasko] nm squall

chubasquero [tʃuβasˈkero] nm lightweight raincoat

chuchería [tʃutʃeˈria] nf trinket

chuleta [tʃuˈleta] nf chop, cutlet

chulo [ˈtʃulo] nm (de prostituta) pimp

chupaleta (MÉX) nf lollipop

chupar [tʃuˈpar] vt to suck; (absorber) to absorb; **chuparse** vr to grow thin

chupete [tʃuˈpete] (ESP, CS) nm dummy (BRIT), pacifier (US)

chupetín (RPI) nf lollipop

chupito [tʃuˈpito] (fam) nm shot

chupón [tʃu'pon] nm (*piruleta*) lollipop; (*LAm*: *chupete*) dummy (*BRIT*), pacifier (*US*)

churro ['tʃurro] nm (type of) fritter

chusma ['tʃusma] nf rabble, mob

chutar [tʃu'tar] vi to shoot (at goal)

Cía abr (= *compañía*) Co.

cianuro [θja'nuro] nm cyanide

cibercafé [θiβerka'fe] nm cybercafé

ciberterrorista nmf cyberterrorist

cicatriz [θika'triθ] nf scar ❑ **cicatrizarse** vr to heal (up), form a scar

ciclismo [θi'klismo] nm cycling

ciclista [θi'klista] adj cycle cpd ♦ nmf cyclist

ciclo ['θiklo] nm cycle ❑ **cicloturismo** nm touring by bicycle

ciclón [θi'klon] nm cyclone

ciego, -a ['θjeɣo, a] adj blind ♦ nm/f blind man/woman

cielo ['θjelo] nm sky; (*REL*) heaven; **¡cielos!** good heavens!

ciempiés [θjem'pjes] nm inv centipede

cien [θjen] num ver **ciento**

ciencia [θjenθja] nf science; **ciencias** nfpl (*ESCOL*) science sg ❑ **ciencia-ficción** nf science fiction

científico, -a [θjen'tifiko, a] adj scientific ♦ nm/f scientist

ciento ['θjento] num hundred; **pagar al 10 por** ~ to pay at 10 per cent; ver tb **cien**

cierre etc ['θjerre] vb ver **cerrar** ♦ nm closing, shutting; (*con llave*) locking; (*LAm*: *cremallera*) zip (fastener)

cierto etc vb ver **cerrar**

cierto, -a ['θjerto, a] adj sure, certain; (*un tal*) a certain; (*correcto*) right, correct; **por** ~ by the way; ~ **hombre** a certain man; **ciertas personas** certain o some people; **sí, es** ~ yes, that's correct

ciervo ['θjerβo] nm deer; (*macho*) stag

cifra ['θifra] nf number; (*secreta*) code ❑ **cifrar** [θi'far] vt to code, write in code

cigala [θi'ɣala] nf Norway lobster

cigarra [θi'ɣarra] nf cicada

cigarrillo [θiɣa'rriʎo] nm cigarette

cigarro [θi'ɣarro] nm cigarette; (*puro*) cigar

cigüeña [θi'ɣweɲa] nf stork

cilíndrico, -a [θi'lindriko, a] adj cylindrical

cilindro [θi'lindro] nm cylinder

cima ['θima] nf (*de montaña*) top, peak; (*de árbol*) top; (*fig*) height

cimentar [θimen'tar] vt to lay the foundations of; (*fig*: *fundar*) to found

cimiento [θi'mjento] nm foundation

cincel [θin'θel] nm chisel

cinco ['θinko] num five

cincuenta [θin'kwenta] num fifty

cine ['θine] nm cinema ❑ **cinematográfico, -a** [θinemato'ɣrafiko, a] adj cine-, film cpd

cínico, -a ['θiniko, a] adj cynical ♦ nm/f cynic

cinismo [θi'nismo] nm cynicism

cinta ['θinta] nf band, strip; (*de tela*) ribbon; (*película*) reel; (*de máquina de escribir*) ribbon ▶ **cinta adhesiva/aislante** sticky/insulating tape ▶ **cinta de vídeo** videotape ▶ **cinta magnetofónica** tape ▶ **cinta métrica** tape measure

cintura [θin'tura] nf waist

cinturón [θintu'ron] nm belt ▶ **cinturón de seguridad** safety belt

ciprés [θi'pres] nm cypress (tree)

circo ['θirko] nm circus

circuito [θir'kwito] nm circuit

circulación [θirkula'θjon] nf circulation; (*AUTO*) traffic

circular [θirku'lar] adj, nf circular ♦ vi, vt to circulate ♦ vi (*AUTO*) to drive; **"circule por la derecha"** "keep (to the) right"

círculo [ˈθirkulo] nm circle ▶ **círculo vicioso** vicious circle

circunferencia [θirkunfeˈrenθja] nf circumference

circunstancia [θirkunsˈtanθja] nf circumstance

cirio [ˈθirjo] nm (wax) candle

ciruela [θiˈrwela] nf plum ▶ **ciruela pasa** prune

cirugía [θiruˈxia] nf surgery ▶ **cirugía estética** o **plástica** plastic surgery

cirujano [θiruˈxano] nm surgeon

cisne [ˈθisne] nm swan

cisterna [θisˈterna] nf cistern, tank

cita [ˈθita] nf appointment, meeting; (de novios) date; (referencia) quotation

citación [θitaˈθjon] nf (JUR) summons sg

citar [θiˈtar] vt (gen) to make an appointment with; (JUR) to summons; (un autor, texto) to quote; **citarse** vr: **se citaron en el cine** they arranged to meet at the cinema

cítricos [ˈθitrikos] nmpl citrus fruit(s)

ciudad [θjuˈðað] nf town; (más grande) city □ **ciudadano, -a** nm/f citizen

cívico, -a [ˈθiβiko, a] adj civic

civil [θiˈβil] adj civil ♦ nm (guardia) policeman ♦ **civilización** [θiβiliθaˈθjon] nf civilization □ **civilizar** [θiβiliˈθar] vt to civilize

cizaña [θiˈθaɲa] nf (fig) discord

cl. abr (= centilitro) cl.

clamor [klaˈmor] nm clamour, protest

clandestino, -a [klandesˈtino, a] adj clandestine; (POL) underground

clara [ˈklara] nf (de huevo) egg white

claraboya [klaraˈβoja] nf skylight

clarear [klareˈar] vi (el día) to dawn; (el cielo) to clear up, brighten up; **clarearse** vr to be transparent

claridad [klariˈðað] nf (de día) brightness; (de estilo) clarity

clarificar [klarifiˈkar] vt to clarify

clarinete [klariˈnete] nm clarinet

claro, -a [ˈklaro, a] adj clear; (luminoso) bright; (color) light; (evidente) clear, evident; (poco espeso) thin ♦ nm (en bosque) clearing ♦ adv clearly ♦ excl: ¡~ que sí! of course!; ¡~ que no! of course not!

clase [ˈklase] nf class; **dar ~(s)** to teach ▶ **clase alta/media/obrera** upper/middle/working class ▶ **clases particulares** private lessons o tuition sg

clásico, -a [ˈklasiko, a] adj classical

clasificación [klasifikaˈθjon] nf classification; (DEPORTE) league (table)

clasificar [klasifiˈkar] vt to classify

claustro [ˈklaustro] nm cloister

cláusula [ˈklausula] nf clause

clausura [klauˈsura] nf closing, closure

clavar [klaˈβar] vt (clavo) to hammer in; (cuchillo) to stick, thrust

clave [ˈklaβe] nf key; (MÚS) clef ▶ **clave de acceso** password ▶ **clave lada** (MÉX) dialling (BRIT) o area (US) code

clavel [klaˈβel] nm carnation

clavícula [klaˈβikula] nf collar bone

clavija [klaˈβixa] nf peg, dowel, pin; (ELEC) plug

clavo [ˈklaβo] nm (de metal) nail; (BOT) clove

claxon [ˈklakson] (pl **claxons**) nm horn

clérigo [ˈkleriyo] nm priest

clero [ˈklero] nm clergy

clicar vi (INTERNET) to click; **~ en el icono** to click on an icon; **~ dos veces** to double-click

cliché [kliˈtʃe] nm cliché; (FOTO) negative

cliente, -a [ˈkljente, a] nm/f client, customer o **clientela** [kljenˈtela] nf clientele, customers pl

clima [ˈklima] nm climate □ **climatizado, -a** [klimatiˈθaðo, a] adj air-conditioned

clímax [ˈklimaks] nm inv climax

clínica ['klinika] nf clinic; (*particular*) private hospital

clip [klip] (*pl* **clips**) nm paper clip

clítoris ['klitoris] nm inv (ANAT) clitoris

cloaca [klo'aka] nf sewer

cloro ['kloro] nm chlorine

clóset (*MEX*) nm cupboard

club [klub] (*pl* **clubs** o **clubes**) nm club ► **club nocturno** night club

cm abr (= *centímetro, centímetros*) cm

coágulo [ko'aɣulo] nm clot

coalición [koali'θjon] nf coalition

coartada [koar'taða] nf alibi

coartar [koar'tar] vt to limit, restrict

coba ['koβa] nf: **dar ~ a algn** (*adular*) to suck up to sb

cobarde [ko'βarðe] adj cowardly ♦ nm coward □ **cobardía** nf cowardice

cobaya [ko'βaja] nf guinea pig

cobertizo [koβer'tiθo] nm shelter

cobertura [koβer'tura] nf cover; **estar fuera de ~** to be out of range; **no tengo ~** I'm out of range

cobija [ko'βixa] nf (*LAm*) blanket □ **cobijar** [koβi'xar] vt (*cubrir*) to cover; (*proteger*) to shelter □ **cobijo** nm shelter

cobra ['koβra] nf cobra

cobrador, a [koβra'ðor, a] nm/f (*de autobús*) conductor/conductress; (*de impuestos, gas*) collector

cobrar [ko'βrar] vt (*cheque*) to cash; (*sueldo*) to collect, draw; (*objeto*) to recover; (*precio*) to charge; (*deuda*) to collect ♦ vi to be paid; **cóbrese al entregar** cash on delivery; **¿me cobra, por favor?** how much do I owe you?, can I have the bill, please?

cobre ['koβre] nm copper; **cobres** nmpl (*MÚS*) brass instruments

cobro ['koβro] nm (*de cheque*) cashing; **presentar al ~** to cash

cocaína [koka'ina] nf cocaine

cocción [kok'θjon] nf (CULIN) cooking; (*en agua*) boiling

cocer [ko'θer] vt, vi to cook; (*en agua*) to boil; (*en horno*) to bake

coche ['kotʃe] nm (AUTO) car (BRIT), automobile (US); (*de tren, de caballos*) coach, carriage; (*para niños*) pram (BRIT), baby carriage (US); **ir en ~** to drive ► **coche celular** prison van ► **coche de bomberos** fire engine ► **coche de carreras** racing car ► **coche fúnebre** hearse □ **cochecama** (*pl* **coches-cama**) nm (FERRO) sleeping car, sleeper

cochera [ko'tʃera] nf garage; (*de autobuses, trenes*) depot

coche restaurante (*pl* **coches restaurante**) nm (FERRO) dining car, diner

cochinillo [kotʃi'niʎo] nm (CULIN) suckling pig, sucking pig

cochino, -a [ko'tʃino, a] adj filthy, dirty ♦ nm/f pig

cocido [ko'θiðo] nm stew

cocina [ko'θina] nf kitchen; (*aparato*) cooker, stove; (*acto*) cookery ► **cocina eléctrica/de gas** electric/gas cooker ► **cocina francesa** French cuisine □ **cocinar** vt, vi to cook

cocinero, -a [koθi'nero, a] nm/f cook

coco ['koko] nm coconut

cocodrilo [koko'ðrilo] nm crocodile

cocotero [koko'tero] nm coconut palm

cóctel ['koktel] nm cocktail ► **cóctel molotov** petrol bomb, Molotov cocktail

codazo [ko'ðaθo] nm: **dar un ~ a algn** to nudge sb

codicia [ko'ðiθja] nf greed □ **codiciar** vt to covet

código [ko'ðiɣo] nm code ► **código civil** common law ► **código de barras** bar code ► **código de circulación** highway code ► **código de la zona** (BRIT) dialling (US) o area code ► **código postal** postcode

codillo [ko'ðiʎo] nm (ZOOL) knee; (TEC) elbow (joint)

codo ['koðo] nm (ANAT, de tubo) elbow; (ZOOL) knee

codorniz [koðor'niθ] nf quail

coexistir [koe(k)sis'tir] vi to coexist

cofradía [kofra'ðia] nf brotherhood, fraternity.

cofre ['kofre] nm (de joyas) case; (de dinero) chest

coger [ko'xer] (ESP) vt to take (hold of); (objeto caído) to pick up; (frutas) to pick, harvest; (resfriado, ladrón, pelota) to catch ♦ vi: **~ por el buen camino** to take the right road; **cogerse** vr (el dedo) to catch; **cogerse a algo** to get hold of sth

cogollo [ko'ɣoʎo] nm (de lechuga) heart

cogote [ko'ɣote] nm back o nape of the neck

cohabitar [koaβi'tar] vi to live together, cohabit

coherente [koe'rente] adj coherent

cohesión [koe'sjon] nm cohesion

cohete [ko'ete] nm rocket

cohibido, -a [koi'βiðo, a] adj (PSICO) inhibited; (tímido) shy

coincidencia [koinθi'ðenθja] nf coincidence

coincidir [koinθi'ðir] vi (en idea) to coincide, agree; (en lugar) to coincide

coito ['koito] nm intercourse, coitus

coja etc vb ver **coger**

cojear [koxe'ar] vi (persona) to limp, hobble; (mueble) to wobble, rock

cojera [ko'xera] nf limp

cojín [ko'xin] nm cushion

cojo, -a etc ['koxo, a] vb ver **coger** ♦ adj (que no puede andar) lame, crippled; (mueble) wobbly ♦ nm/f lame person, cripple

cojón [ko'xon] (fam!) nm: **¡cojones!** shit! (!) ♦ **cojonudo, -a** (fam) adj great, fantastic

col [kol] nf cabbage ► **coles de Bruselas** Brussels sprouts

cola ['kola] nf tail; (de gente) queue; (lugar) end, last place; (para pegar) glue, gum; **hacer ~** to queue (up)

colaborador, a [kolaβora'ðor, a] nm/f collaborator

colaborar [kolaβo'rar] vi to collaborate

colada [ko'laða] (ESP) nf: **hacer la ~** to do the washing

colador [kola'ðor] nm (para líquidos) strainer; (para verduras etc) colander

colapso [ko'lapso] nm collapse

colar [ko'lar] vt (líquido) to strain off; (metal) to cast ♦ vi to ooze, seep (through); **colarse** vr to jump the queue; **colarse en** to get into without paying; (fiesta) to gatecrash

colcha ['koltʃa] nf bedspread

colchón [kol'tʃon] nm mattress ► **colchón inflable** air bed o mattress

colchoneta [koltʃo'neta] nf (en gimnasio) mat; (de playa) air bed

colección [kolek'θjon] nf collection ► **coleccionar** vt to collect ► **coleccionista** nmf collector

colecta [ko'lekta] nf collection

colectivo, -a [kolek'tiβo, a] adj collective, joint ♦ nm (ARG: autobús) (small) bus

colega [ko'leɣa] nmf colleague; (ESP: amigo) mate

colegial, a [kole'xjal, a] nm/f schoolboy(-girl)

colegio [ko'lexjo] nm college; (escuela) school; (de abogados etc) association ► **colegio electoral** polling station ► **colegio mayor** (ESP) hall of residence

---

COLEGIO

A **colegio** is normally a private primary or secondary school. In the state system it means a primary school although these are also called **escuelas**. State secondary schools are called **institutos**.

cólera ['kolera] nf (ira) anger; (MED) cholera

colesterol [koleste'rol] nm cholesterol

coleta [ko'leta] nf pigtail

colgante [kol'ɣante] adj hanging ♦ (joya) pendant

colgar [kol'ɣar] vt to hang (up); (ropa) to hang out ♦ vi to hang; (TEL) to hang up

cólico ['koliko] nm colic

coliflor [koli'flor] nf cauliflower

colilla [ko'liʎa] nf cigarette end, butt

colina [ko'lina] nf hill

colisión [koli'sjon] nf collision
  ▶ **colisión frontal** head-on crash

collar [ko'ʎar] nm necklace; (de perro) collar

colmar [kol'mar] vt to fill to the brim; (fig) to fulfil, realize

colmena [kol'mena] nf beehive

colmillo [kol'miʎo] nm (diente) eye tooth; (de elefante) tusk; (de perro) fang

colmo ['kolmo] nm: ¡es el ~! it's the limit!

colocación [koloka'θjon] nf (acto) placing; (empleo) job, position

colocar [kolo'kar] vt to place, put, position; (dinero) to invest; (poner en empleo) to find a job for; **colocarse** vr to get a job

Colombia [ko'lombja] nf Colombia
  ❏ **colombiano, -a** adj, nm/f Colombian

colonia [ko'lonja] nf colony; (agua de colonia) cologne; (MÉX: de casas) residential area ▶ **colonia proletaria** (MÉX) shantytown

colonización [koloniθa'θjon] nf colonization ❏ **colonizador, a** [koloniθa'ðor, a] adj colonizing ♦ nm/f colonist, settler

colonizar [koloni'θar] vt to colonize

coloquio [ko'lokjo] nm conversation; (congreso) conference

color [ko'lor] nm colour

colorado, -a [kolo'raðo, a] adj (rojo) red; (MÉX: chiste) smutty, rude

colorante [kolo'rante] nm colouring

colorear [kolore'ar] vt to colour

colorete [kolo'rete] nm blusher

colorido [kolo'riðo] nm colouring

columna [ko'lumna] nf column; (pilar) pillar; (apoyo) support; (tb: ~ **vertebral**) spine, spinal column; (fig) backbone

columpiar [kolum'pjar] vt to swing; **columpiarse** vr to swing ❏ **columpio** nm swing

coma ['koma] nf comma ♦ nm (MED) coma

comadre [ko'maðre] nf (madrina) godmother; (chismosa) gossip ❏ **comadrona** nf midwife

comal (MÉX, CAm) nm griddle

comandante [koman'dante] nm commandant

comarca [ko'marka] nf region

comba ['komba] (ESP) nf (cuerda) skipping rope; **saltar a la ~** to skip

combate [kom'bate] nm fight

combatir [komba'tir] vt to fight, combat

combinación [kombina'θjon] nf combination; (QUIM) compound; (prenda) slip

combinar [kombi'nar] vt to combine

combustible [kombus'tiβle] nm fuel

comedia [ko'meðja] nf comedy; (TEATRO) play, drama ❏ **comediante** [kome'ðjante] nmf (comic) actor/actress

comedido, -a [kome'ðiðo, a] adj moderate

comedor, a [kome'ðor, a] nm (habitación) dining room; (cantina) canteen

comensal [komen'sal] nmf fellow guest (o diner)

comentar [komen'tar] vt to comment on ❏ **comentario** [komen'tarjo] nm comment, remark; (*literario*) commentary; **comentarios** nmpl (*chismes*) gossip sg ❑ **comentarista** [komenta'rista] nmf commentator

comenzar [komen'θar] vt, vi to begin, start; **~ a hacer algo** to begin o start doing sth

comer [ko'mer] vt to eat; (*DAMAS, AJEDREZ*) to take, capture ♦ vi to eat; (*ESP, MÉX: almorzar*) to have lunch; **comerse** vr to eat up

comercial [komer'θjal] adj commercial; (*relativo al negocio*) business cpd ❑ **comercializar** vt (*producto*) to market; (*pey*) to commercialize

comerciante [komer'θjante] nmf trader, merchant

comerciar [komer'θjar] vi to trade, do business

comercio [ko'merθjo] nm commerce, trade; (*tienda*) shop, store; (*negocio*) business; (*fig*) dealings pl ❑ **comercio electrónico** e-commerce ► **comercio exterior/interior** foreign/domestic trade

comestible [komes'tiβle] adj eatable, edible ❑ **comestibles** nmpl food sg, foodstuffs

cometa [ko'meta] nm comet ♦ nf kite

cometer [kome'ter] vt to commit

cometido [kome'tiðo] nm task, assignment

cómic ['komik] nm comic

comicios [ko'miθjos] nmpl elections

cómico, -a ['komiko, a] adj comic(al) ♦ nm/f comedian

comida [ko'miða] nf (*alimento*) food; (*almuerzo, cena*) meal; (*de mediodía*) lunch ► **comida basura** junk food ► **comida chatarra** (*MÉX*) junk food

comidilla [komi'ðiʎa] nf: **ser la ~ del barrio** o **pueblo** to be the talk of the town

comienzo etc [ko'mjenθo] vb ver **comenzar** ♦ nm beginning, start

comillas [ko'miʎas] nfpl quotation marks

comilona [komi'lona] nf (*fam*) blow-out

comino [ko'mino] nm: **(no) me importa un ~** I don't give a damn

comisaría [komisa'ria] nf (*de policía*) police station; (*MIL*) commissariat

comisario [komi'sarjo] nm (*MIL etc*) commissary; (*POL*) commissioner

comisión [komi'sjon] nf commission ► **Comisiones Obreras** (*ESP*) Communist trade union

comité [komi'te] (pl **~s**) nm committee

comitiva [komi'tiβa] nf retinue

como ['komo] adv as; (*tal*): **~** like; (*aproximadamente*) about, approximately ♦ conj (*ya que, puesto que*) as, since; **¡~ no!** of course!; **~ no lo haga hoy** unless he does it today; **~ si** as if; **es tan alto ~ ancho** it is as high as it is wide

cómo ['komo] adv how?, why? ♦ excl what?, I beg your pardon? ♦ nm: **el ~ y el porqué** the whys and wherefores

cómoda [ko'moða] nf chest of drawers

comodidad [komoði'ðað] nf comfort

comodín [komo'ðin] nm joker

cómodo, -a ['komoðo, a] adj comfortable; (*práctico, de fácil uso*) convenient

compact (pl **compacts**) nm (tb: **~ disc**) compact disk player

compacto, -a [kom'pakto, a] adj compact

compadecer [kompaðe'θer] vt to pity, be sorry for; **compadecerse de** to pity, be o feel sorry for

compadre [kom'paðre] nm (*padrino*) godfather; (*amigo*) friend, pal

compañero, -a [kompa'ɲero, a] nm/f companion; (*novio*) boy/girlfriend ► **compañero de clase** classmate

compañía [kompa'ɲia] nf company; **hacer ~ a algn** to keep sb company

comparación [kompara'θjon] nf comparison; **en ~ con** in comparison with

comparar [kompa'rar] vt to compare

comparecer [kompare'θer] vi to appear (in court)

comparsa [kom'parsa] nmf (TEATRO) extra

compartimiento [komparti'mjento] nm (FERRO) compartment

compartir [kompar'tir] vt to share; (dinero, comida etc) to divide (up), share (out)

compás [kom'pas] nm (MÚS) beat, rhythm; (MAT) compasses pl; (NÁUT etc) compass

compasión [kompa'sjon] nf compassion, pity

compasivo, -a [kompa'siβo, a] adj compassionate

compatible [kompa'tiβle] adj compatible

compatriota [kompa'trjota] nmf compatriot, fellow countryman/ woman

compenetrarse [kompene'trarse] vr to be in tune

compensación [kompensa'θjon] nf compensation

compensar [kompen'sar] vt to compensate

competencia [kompe'tenθja] nf (incumbencia) domain, field; (JUR, habilidad) competence; (rivalidad) competition

competente [kompe'tente] adj competent

competición [kompeti'θjon] nf competition

competir [kompe'tir] vi to compete

compinche [kom'pintʃe] nmf (LAm) mate, buddy (US)

complacer [kompla'θer] vt to please; **complacerse** vr to be pleased

complaciente [kompla'θjente] adj kind, obliging, helpful

complejo, -a [kom'plexo, a] adj, nm complex

complementario, -a [komplemen'tarjo, a] adj complementary

completar [komple'tar] vt to complete

completo, -a [kom'pleto, a] adj complete; (perfecto) perfect; (lleno) full ♦ nm full complement

complicado, -a [kompli'kaðo, a] adj complicated; **estar ~ en** to be mixed up in

cómplice ['kompliθe] nmf accomplice

complot [kom'plo(t)] (pl **complots**) nm plot

componer [kompo'ner] vt (MÚS, LITERATURA, IMPRENTA) to compose; (algo roto) to mend, repair; (arreglar) to arrange; **componerse** vr: **componerse de** to consist of

comportamiento [komporta'mjento] nm behaviour, conduct

comportarse [kompor'tarse] vr to behave

composición [komposi'θjon] nf composition

compositor, a [komposi'tor, a] nm/f composer

compostura [kompos'tura] nf (actitud) composure

compra ['kompra] nf purchase; **hacer la ~** to do the shopping; **ir de compras** to go shopping □ **comprador, a** nm/f buyer, purchaser □ **comprar** [kom'prar] vt to buy, purchase

comprender [kompren'der] vt to understand; (incluir) to comprise, include

comprensión [kompren'sjon] nf understanding □ **comprensivo, -a** adj (actitud) understanding

compresa [kom'presa] nf (para mujer) sanitary towel (BRIT) o napkin (US)

comprimido, -a [kompri'miðo, a] adj compressed ♦ nm (MED) pill, tablet

comprimir [kompri'mir] vt to compress

comprobante [kompro'βante] nm proof; (COM) voucher ▶ **comprobante de compra** proof of purchase

comprobar [kompro'βar] vt to check; (probar) to prove; (TEC) to check, test

comprometer [komprome'ter] vt to compromise; (poner en peligro) to endanger; **comprometerse** vr (involucrarse) to get involved

compromiso [kompro'miso] nm (obligación) obligation; (cometido) commitment; (convenio) agreement; (apuro) awkward situation

compuesto, -a [kom'pwesto, a] adj: ~ **de** composed of, made up of ♦ nm compound

computadora [komputa'ðora] nf computer ▶ **computadora central** mainframe (computer) ▶ **computadora personal** personal computer

cómputo ['komputo] nm calculation

comulgar [komul'ɣar] vi to receive communion

común [ko'mun] adj common ♦ nm: **el ~** the community

comunicación [komunika'θjon] nf communication; (informe) report

comunicado [komuni'kaðo] nm announcement ▶ **comunicado de prensa** press release

comunicar [komuni'kar] vt, vi to communicate; **comunicarse** vr to communicate; **está comunicando** (TEL) the line's engaged (BRIT) o busy (US) ❑ **comunicativo, -a** adj communicative

comunidad [komuni'ðað] nf community ▶ **comunidad autónoma** (ESP) autonomous region ▶ **Comunidad (Económica) Europea** European (Economic) Community ▶ **comunidad de vecinos** residents' association

comunión [komu'njon] nf communion

comunismo [komu'nismo] nm communism ❑ **comunista** adj, nmf communist

con

PALABRA CLAVE

[kon] prep

1 (medio, compañía) with; **comer con cuchara** to eat with a spoon; **pasear con algn** to go for a walk with sb

2 (a pesar de): **con todo, merece nuestros respetos** all the same, he deserves our respect

3 (para con): **es muy bueno para con los niños** he's very good with (the) children

4 (+ infin): **con llegar a las seis estará bien** if you come by six it will be fine

♦ conj: **con que: será suficiente con que le escribas** it will be sufficient for you to write to her

concebir [konθe'βir] vt, vi to conceive

conceder [konθe'ðer] vt to concede

concejal, a [konθe'xal, a] nm/f town councillor

concentración [konθentra'θjon] nf concentration

concentrar [konθen'trar] vt to concentrate; **concentrarse** vr to concentrate

concepto [kon'θepto] nm concept

concernir [konθer'nir] vi to concern; **en lo que concierne a ...** as far as ... is concerned; **en lo que a mí concierne** as far as I'm concerned

concertar [konθer'tar] vt (MÚS) to harmonize; (acordar: precio) to agree; (: tratado) to conclude; (trato) to arrange, fix up; (combinar: esfuerzos) to coordinate ♦ vi to harmonize, be in tune

concesión [konθe'sjon] nf concession

concesionario [konθesjoˈnarjo] *nm* (licensed) dealer, agent

concha [ˈkontʃa] *nf* shell

conciencia [konˈθjenθja] *nf* conscience; **tomar ~ de** to become aware of; **tener la ~ tranquila** to have a clear conscience

concienciar [konθjenˈθjar] *vt* to make aware; **concienciarse** *vr* to become aware

concienzudo, -a [konθjenˈθuðo, a] *adj* conscientious

concierto *etc* [konˈθjerto] *vb ver* **concertar** ♦ *nm* concert; (*obra*) concerto

conciliar [konθiˈljar] *vt* to reconcile; **~ el sueño** to get to sleep

concilio [konˈθiljo] *nm* council

conciso, -a [konˈθiso, a] *adj* concise

concluir [konkluˈir] *vt, vi* to conclude; **concluirse** *vr* to conclude

conclusión [konkluˈsjon] *nf* conclusion

concordar [konkorˈðar] *vt* to reconcile ♦ *vi* to agree, tally

concordia [konˈkorðja] *nf* harmony

concretar [konkreˈtar] *vt* to make concrete, make more specific; **concretarse** *vr* to become more definite

concreto, -a [konˈkreto, a] *adj, nm* (*LAm: hormigón*) concrete; **en ~** (*en resumen*) to sum up; (*especificamente*) specifically; **no hay nada en ~** there's nothing definite

concurrido, -a [konkuˈrriðo, a] *adj* (*calle*) busy; (*local, reunión*) crowded

concursante [konkurˈsante] *nmf* competitor

concurso [konˈkurso] *nm* (*de público*) crowd; (*ESCOL, DEPORTE, competencia*) competition; (*ayuda*) help, cooperation

condal [konˈdal] *adj*: **la Ciudad C~** Barcelona

conde [ˈkonde] *nm* count

condecoración [kondekoraˈθjon] *nf* (*MIL*) medal

condena [konˈdena] *nf* sentence
 ❏ **condenación** [kondenaˈθjon] *nf* condemnation; (*REL*) damnation ❏ **condenar** [kondeˈnar] *vt* to condemn; (*JUR*) to convict; **condenarse** *vr* (*REL*) to be damned

condesa [konˈdesa] *nf* countess

condición [kondiˈθjon] *nf* condition; **a ~ de que ...** on condition that ... ❏ **condicional** *adj* conditional

condimento [kondiˈmento] *nm* seasoning

condominio (*LAm*) [kondoˈminjo] *nm* condominium

condón [konˈdon] *nm* condom

conducir [konduˈθir] *vt* to take, convey; (*AUTO*) to drive ♦ *vi* to drive; (*fig*) to lead; **conducirse** *vi* to behave

conducta [konˈdukta] *nf* conduct, behaviour

conducto [konˈdukto] *nm* pipe, tube; (*fig*) channel

conductor, a [kondukˈtor, a] *adj* leading, guiding ♦ *nm* (*FÍSICA*) conductor; (*de vehículo*) driver

conduje *etc* [konˈduxe] *vb ver* **conducir**

conduzco *etc vb ver* **conducir**

conectado, -a [konekˈtaðo, a] *adj* (*INFORM*) on-line

conectar [konekˈtar] *vt* to connect (up); (*enchufar*) plug in

conejillo [koneˈxiλo] *nm*: **~ de Indias** guinea pig

conejo [koˈnexo] *nm* rabbit

conexión [konekˈsjon] *nf* connection

confección [konfe(k)ˈθjon] *nf* preparation; (*industria*) clothing industry

confeccionar [konfekθjoˈnar] *vt* to make (up)

conferencia [konfeˈrenθja] *nf* conference; (*lección*) lecture; (*ESP TEL*) call ▶ **conferencia de prensa** press conference

conferir [konfe'rir] vt to award

confesar [konfe'sar] vt to confess, admit

confesión [konfe'sjon] nf confession

confesionario [konfesjo'narjo] nm confessional

confeti [kon'feti] nm confetti

confiado, -a [kon'fjaðo, a] adj (crédulo) trusting; (seguro) confident

confianza [kon'fjanθa] nf trust; (seguridad) confidence; (familiaridad) intimacy, familiarity

confiar [kon'fjar] vt to entrust ♦ vi to trust; ~ **en algn** to trust sb; ~ **en que ...** to hope that ...

confidencial [konfiðen'θjal] adj confidential

confidente [konfi'ðente] nmf confidant/e; (policial) informer

configurar [konfiyu'rar] vt to shape, form

confín [kon'fin] nm limit; **confines** nmpl confines, limits

confirmar [konfir'mar] vt to confirm

confiscar [konfis'kar] vt to confiscate

confite [kon'fite] nm sweet (BRIT), candy (US) ☐ **confitería** [konfite'ria] nf (tienda) confectioner's shop

confitura [konfi'tura] nf jam

conflictivo, -a [konflik'tiβo, a] adj (asunto, propuesta) controversial; (país, situación) troubled

conflicto [kon'flikto] nm conflict; (fig) clash

confluir [kon'flwir] vi (ríos) to meet; (gente) to gather

conformar [konfor'mar] vt to shape, fashion ♦ vi to agree; **conformarse** vr to conform; (resignarse) to resign o.s.; **conformarse con algo** to be happy with sth

conforme [kon'forme] adj (correspondiente) ▶ ~ **con** in line with; (de acuerdo) **estar conformes (con algo)**

to be in agreement (with sth) ♦ adv as ♦ excl agreed! ♦ prep: ~ **a** in accordance with; **quedarse ~ (con algo)** to be satisfied (with sth)

confortable [konfor'taβle] adj comfortable

confortar [konfor'tar] vt to comfort

confrontar [konfron'tar] vt to confront; (dos personas) to bring face to face; (cotejar) to compare

confundir [konfun'dir] vt (equivocar) to mistake, confuse; (turbar) to confuse; **confundirse** vr (turbarse) to get confused; (equivocarse) to make a mistake; (mezclarse) to mix

confusión [konfu'sjon] nf confusion

confuso, -a [kon'fuso, a] adj confused

congelado, -a [konxe'laðo, a] adj frozen ☐ **congelados** nmpl frozen food(s) ☐ **congelador** nm (aparato) freezer, deep freeze

congelar [konxe'lar] vt to freeze; **congelarse** vr (sangre, grasa) to congeal

congeniar [konxe'njar] vi to get on (BRIT) o along (US) well

congestión [konxes'tjon] nf congestion

congestionar [konxestjo'nar] vt to congest

congraciarse [kongra'θjarse] vr to ingratiate o.s.

congratular [kongratu'lar] vt to congratulate

congregar [kongre'yar] vt to gather together; **congregarse** vr to gather together

congresista [kongre'sista] nmf delegate, congressman/woman

congreso [kon'greso] nm congress

conjetura [konxe'tura] nf guess ☐ **conjeturar** vt to guess

conjugar [konxu'yar] vt to combine, fit together; (LING) to conjugate

conjunción [konxun'θjon] nf conjunction

conjunto, -a [kon'xunto, a] *adj* joint, united ♦ *nm* whole; (*MÚS*) band; **en ~** as a whole

conmemoración [konmemora'θjon] *nf* commemoration

conmemorar [konmemo'rar] *vt* to commemorate

conmigo [kon'miɣo] *pron* with me

conmoción [konmo'θjon] *nf* shock; (*fig*) upheaval ► **conmoción cerebral** (*MED*) concussion

conmovedor, a [konmoβe'ðor, a] *adj* touching, moving; (*emocionante*) exciting

conmover [konmo'βer] *vt* to shake, disturb; (*fig*) to move

conmutador [konmuta'ðor] *nm* switch; (*LAm: centralita*) switchboard; (: *central*) telephone exchange

cono ['kono] *nm* cone ► **Cono Sur** Southern Cone

conocedor, a [konoθe'ðor, a] *adj* expert, knowledgeable ♦ *nm/f* expert

conocer [kono'θer] *vt* to know; (*por primera vez*) to meet, get to know; (*entender*) to know about; (*reconocer*) to recognize; **conocerse** *vr* (*una persona*) to know o.s.; (*dos personas*) to (get to) know each other; **~ a algn de vista** to know sb by sight

conocido, -a [kono'θiðo, a] *adj* (well-)known ♦ *nm/f* acquaintance

conocimiento [konoθi'mjento] *nm* knowledge; (*MED*) consciousness; **conocimientos** *nmpl* (*saber*) knowledge *sg*

conozco *etc vb ver* **conocer**

conque ['koŋke] *conj* and so, then

conquista [kon'kista] *nf* conquest
❑ **conquistador, a** *adj* conquering ♦ *nm* conqueror ❑ **conquistar** [konkis'tar] *vt* to conquer

consagrar [konsa'ɣrar] *vt* (*REL*) to consecrate; (*fig*) to devote

consciente [kons'θjente] *adj* conscious

consecución [konseku'θjon] *nf* acquisition; (*de fin*) attainment

consecuencia [konse'kwenθja] *nf* consequence, outcome; (*coherencia*) consistency

consecuente [konse'kwente] *adj* consistent

consecutivo, -a [konseku'tiβo, a] *adj* consecutive

conseguir [konse'ɣir] *vt* to get, obtain; (*objetivo*) to attain

consejero, -a [konse'xero, a] *nm/f* adviser, consultant; (*POL*) councillor

consejo [kon'sexo] *nm* advice; (*POL*) council ► **consejo de administración** (*COM*) board of directors ► **consejo de guerra** court martial ► **consejo de ministros** cabinet meeting

consenso [kon'senso] *nm* consensus

consentimiento [konsenti'mjento] *nm* consent

consentir [konsen'tir] *vt* (*permitir, tolerar*) to consent to; (*mimar*) to pamper, spoil; (*aguantar*) to put up with ♦ *vi* to agree, consent; **~ que algn haga algo** to allow sb to do sth

conserje [kon'serxe] *nm* caretaker; (*portero*) porter

conservación [konserβa'θjon] *nf* conservation; (*de alimentos, vida*) preservation

conservador, a [konserβa'ðor, a] *adj* (*POL*) conservative ♦ *nm/f* conservative

conservante [konser'βante] *nm* preservative

conservar [konser'βar] *vt* to conserve, keep; (*alimentos, vida*) to preserve; **conservarse** *vr* to survive

conservas [kon'serβas] *nfpl* canned food(s) *pl*

conservatorio [konserβa'torjo] *nm* (*MÚS*) conservatoire, conservatory

considerable [konsiðe'raβle] *adj* considerable

consideración [konsiðera'θjon] nf consideration; (*estimación*) respect

considerado, -a [konsiðe'raðo, a] adj (*atento*) considerate; (*respetado*) respected

considerar [konsiðe'rar] vt to consider

consigna [kon'siɣna] nf (*orden*) order, instruction; (*para equipajes*) left-luggage office

consigo etc [kon'siɣo] vb ver **conseguir** ♦ pron (m) with him; (f) with her; (Vd) with you; (*reflexivo*) with o.s.

consiguiendo etc [konsi'ɣjendo] vb ver **conseguir**

consiguiente [konsi'ɣjente] adj consequent; **por ~** and so, therefore, consequently

consistente [konsis'tente] adj consistent; (*sólido*) solid, firm; (*válido*) sound

consistir [konsis'tir] vi: **~ en** (*componerse de*) to consist of

consola [kon'sola] nf (*mueble*) console table; (*de videojuegos*) console

consolación [konsola'θjon] nf consolation

consolar [konso'lar] vt to console

consolidar [konsoli'ðar] vt to consolidate

consomé [konso'me] (pl **~s**) nm consommé, clear soup

consonante [konso'nante] adj consonant, harmonious ♦ nf consonant

consorcio [kon'sorθjo] nm consortium

conspiración [konspira'θjon] nf conspiracy

conspirar [konspi'rar] vi to conspire

constancia [kon'stanθja] nf constancy; **dejar ~ de** to put on record

constante [kon'stante] adj, nf constant

constar [kon'star] vi (*evidenciarse*) to be clear o evident; **~ de** to consist of

constipado, -a [konsti'paðo, a] adj: **estar ~** to have a cold ♦ nm cold

⚠ No confundir **constipado** con la palabra inglesa *constipated*.

constitución [konstitu'θjon] nf constitution

constituir [konsti'tuir] vt (*formar, componer*) to constitute, make up; (*fundar, erigir, ordenar*) to constitute, establish

construcción [konstruk'θjon] nf construction, building

constructor, a [konstruk'tor, a] nm/f builder

construir [kon'struir] vt to build, construct

construyendo etc [konstru'jendo] vb ver **construir**

consuelo [kon'swelo] nm consolation, solace

cónsul ['konsul] nm consul
□ **consulado** nm consulate

consulta [kon'sulta] nf consultation; (*MED*): **horas de ~** surgery hours □ **consultar** [konsul'tar] vt to consult; **consultar algo con algn** to discuss sth with sb □ **consultorio** [konsul'torjo] nm (*MED*) surgery

consumición [konsumi'θjon] nf consumption; (*bebida*) drink; (*comida*) food ▶ **consumición mínima** cover charge

consumidor, a [konsumi'ðor, a] nm/f consumer

consumir [konsu'mir] vt to consume; **consumirse** vr to be consumed; (*persona*) to waste away

consumismo [konsu'mismo] nm consumerism

consumo [kon'sumo] nm consumption

contabilidad [kontaβili'ðað] nf accounting, book-keeping; (*profesión*) accountancy □ **contable** nmf accountant

contacto [kon'takto] nm contact; (AUTO) ignition; **estar/ponerse en ~ con algn** to be/to get in touch with sb

contado, -a [kon'taðo, a] adj: **contados** (escasos) numbered, scarce, few ♦ nm: **pagar al ~** to pay (in) cash

contador [konta'ðor] nm (ESP: aparato) meter ♦ nmf (LAm COM) accountant

contagiar [konta'xjar] vt (enfermedad) to pass on, transmit; (persona) to infect; **contagiarse** vr to become infected

contagio [kon'taxjo] nm infection ❏ **contagioso, -a** adj infectious; (fig) catching

contaminación [kontamina'θjon] nf contamination; (polución) pollution

contaminar [kontami'nar] vt to contaminate; (aire, agua) to pollute

contante [kon'tante] adj: **dinero ~ (y sonante)** cash

contar [kon'tar] vt (páginas, dinero) to count; (anécdota, chiste etc) to tell ♦ vi to count; **~ con** to rely on, count on

contemplar [kontem'plar] vt to contemplate; (mirar) to look at

contemporáneo, -a [kontempo'raneo, a] adj, nm/f contemporary

contenedor [kontene'ðor] nm container

contener [konte'ner] vt to contain, hold; (retener) to hold back, contain; **contenerse** vr to control o restrain o.s.

contenido, -a [konte'niðo, a] adj (moderado) restrained; (risa etc) suppressed ♦ nm contents pl, content

contentar [konten'tar] vt (satisfacer) to satisfy; (complacer) to please; **contentarse** vr to be satisfied

contento, -a [kon'tento, a] adj (alegre) pleased; (feliz) happy

contestación [kontesta'θjon] nf answer, reply

contestador [kontesta'ðor] nm (tb: ~ **automático**) answering machine

contestar [kontes'tar] vt to answer, reply; (JUR) to corroborate, confirm

⚠ No confundir **contestar** con la palabra inglesa contest.

contexto [kon'te(k)sto] nm context

contigo [kon'tiɣo] pron with you

contiguo, -a [kon'tiɣwo, a] adj adjacent, adjoining

continente [konti'nente] adj, nm continent

continuación [kontinwa'θjon] nf continuation; **a ~** then, next

continuar [konti'nwar] vt to continue, go on with ♦ vi to continue, go on; **~ hablando** to continue talking o to talk

continuidad [kontinwi'ðað] nf continuity

continuo, -a [kon'tinwo, a] adj (sin interrupción) continuous; (acción perseverante) continual

contorno [kon'torno] nm outline; (GEO) contour; **contornos** nmpl neighbourhood sg, surrounding area sg

contra ['kontra] prep, adv against ♦ nm inv con ♦ nf: **la C~** (de Nicaragua) the Contras pl

contraataque [kontraa'take] nm counter-attack

contrabajo [kontra'βaxo] nm double bass

contrabandista [kontraβan'dista] nmf smuggler

contrabando [kontra'βando] nm (acción) smuggling; (mercancías) contraband

contracción [kontrak'θjon] nf contraction

contracorriente [kontrako'rrjente] nf cross-current

contradecir [kontraðe'θir] vt to contradict

contradicción [kontraðik'θjon] nf contradiction

contradictorio, -a [kontraðik'torjo, a] adj contradictory

contraer [kontra'er] vt to contract; (limitar) to restrict; **contraerse** vr to contract; (limitarse) to limit o.s.

contraluz [kontra'luθ] nm view against the light

contrapartida [kontrapar'tiða] nf: **como ~ (de)** in return (for)

contrapelo [kontra'pelo]: **a ~** adv the wrong way

contrapeso [kontra'peso] nm counterweight

contraportada [kontrapor'taða] nf (de revista) back cover

contraproducente [kontraproðu'θente] adj counterproductive

contrario, -a [kon'trarjo, a] adj contrary; (persona) opposed; (sentido, lado) opposite ♦ nm/f enemy, adversary; (DEPORTE) opponent; **al o por el ~** on the contrary; **de lo ~** otherwise

contrarreloj [kontarre'lo] nf (tb: **prueba ~**) time trial

contrarrestar [kontarres'tar] vt to counteract

contrasentido [kontrasen'tiðo] nm (contradicción) contradiction

contraseña [kontra'seɲa] nf (INFORM) password

contrastar [kontras'tar] vt, vi to contrast

contraste [kon'traste] nm contrast

contratar [kontra'tar] vt (firmar un acuerdo para) to contract for; (empleados, obreros) to hire, engage

contratiempo [kontra'tjempo] nm setback

contratista [kontra'tista] nmf contractor

contrato [kon'trato] nm contract

contraventana [kontraβen'tana] nf shutter

contribución [kontriβu'θjon] nf (municipal etc) tax; (ayuda) contribution

contribuir [kontriβu'ir] vt, vi to contribute; (COM) to pay (in taxes)

contribuyente [kontriβu'jente] nmf (COM) taxpayer; (que ayuda) contributor

contrincante [kontrin'kante] nmf opponent

control [kon'trol] nm control; (inspección) inspection, check ► **control de pasaportes** passport inspection ❑ **controlador, -a** nm/f controller ► **controlador aéreo** air-traffic controller ❑ **controlar** [kontro'lar] vt to control; (inspeccionar) to inspect, check

contundente [kontun'dente] adj (instrumento) blunt; (argumento, derrota) overwhelming

contusión [kontu'sjon] nf bruise

convalecencia [kombale'θenθja] nf convalescence

convalecer [kombale'θer] vi to convalesce, get better

convalidar [kombali'ðar] vt (título) to recognize

convencer [komben'θer] vt to convince; **~ a algn (de o para hacer algo)** to persuade sb (to do sth)

convención [komben'θjon] nf convention

conveniente [kombe'njente] adj suitable; (útil) useful

convenio [kom'benjo] nm agreement, treaty

convenir [kombe'nir] vi (estar de acuerdo) to agree; (venir bien) to suit, be suitable

⚠ No confundir **convenir** con la palabra inglesa **convene**.

convento [kom'bento] nm convent

convenza etc [kom'benθa] vb ver **convencer**

converger [komber'xer], **convergir** [komber'xir] vi to converge

conversación [kombersa'θjon] nf conversation

conversar [komber'sar] vi to talk, converse

conversión [komber'sjon] nf conversion

convertir [komber'tir] vt to convert

convidar [kombi'ðar] vt to invite; ~ a algn a una cerveza to buy sb a beer

convincente [kombin'θente] adj convincing

convite [kom'bite] nm invitation; (banquete) banquet

convivencia [kombi'βenθja] nf coexistence, living together

convivir [kombi'βir] vi to live together

convocar [kombo'kar] vt to summon, call (together)

convocatoria [komboka'torja] nf (de oposiciones, elecciones) notice; (de huelga) call

cónyuge ['konxuxe] nmf spouse

coñac [ko'na(k)] (pl coñacs) nm cognac, brandy

coño ['kono] (fam!) excl (enfado) shit! (!); (sorpresa) bloody hell! (!)

cool [kul] adj (fam) cool

cooperación [koopera'θjon] nf cooperation

cooperar [koope'rar] vi to cooperate

cooperativa [koopera'tiβa] nf cooperative

coordinadora [koorðina'ðora] nf (comité) coordinating committee

coordinar [koorði'nar] vt to coordinate

copa ['kopa] nf cup; (vaso) glass; (bebida): tomar una ~ (to have a) drink; (de árbol) top; (de sombrero) crown; copas nfpl (NAIPES) = hearts

copia ['kopja] nf copy ▶ **copia de respaldo** o **seguridad** (INFORM) back-up copy ▢ **copiar** vt to copy

copla ['kopla] nf verse; (canción) (popular) song

copo ['kopo] nm: ~ **de nieve** snowflake; **copos de maíz** cornflakes

coqueta [ko'keta] adj flirtatious, coquettish ▢ **coquetear** vi to flirt

coraje [ko'raxe] nm courage; (ánimo) spirit; (ira) anger

coral [ko'ral] adj choral ◆ nf (MÚS) choir ◆ nm (ZOOL) coral

coraza [ko'raθa] nf (armadura) armour; (blindaje) armour-plating

corazón [kora'θon] nm heart

corazonada [koraθo'naða] nf impulse; (presentimiento) hunch

corbata [kor'βata] nf tie

corchete [kor'tʃete] nm catch, clasp

corcho [kor'tʃo] nm cork; (PESCA) float

cordel [kor'ðel] nm cord, line

cordero [kor'ðero] nm lamb

cordial [kor'ðjal] adj cordial

cordillera [korði'ʎera] nf range (of mountains)

Córdoba ['korðoβa] n Cordova

cordón [kor'ðon] nm (cuerda) cord, string; (de zapatos) lace; (MIL etc) cordon ▶ **cordón umbilical** umbilical cord

cordura [kor'ðura] nf: **con ~** (obrar, hablar) sensibly

corneta [kor'neta] nf bugle

cornisa [kor'nisa] nf (ARQ) cornice

coro ['koro] nm chorus; (conjunto de cantores) choir

corona [ko'rona] nf crown; (de flores) garland

coronel [koro'nel] nm colonel

coronilla [koro'niʎa] nf (ANAT) crown (of the head)

corporal [korpo'ral] adj corporal, bodily

corpulento, -a [korpu'lento, a] adj (persona) heavily-built

corral [ko'rral] nm farmyard

correa [ko'rrea] nf strap; (cinturón) belt; (de perro) lead, leash ▶ **correa del ventilador** (AUTO) fan belt

corrección [korrek'θjon] nf correction; (represión) rebuke ❏ **correccional** nm reformatory

correcto, -a [ko'rrekto, a] adj correct; (persona) well-mannered

corredizo, -a [korre'ðiθo, a] adj (puerta etc) sliding

corredor, a [korre'ðor, a] nm (pasillo) corridor; (balcón corredizo) gallery; (COM) agent, broker ♦ nm/f (DEPORTE) runner

corregir [korre'xir] vt (error) to correct; **corregirse** vr to reform

correo [ko'rreo] nm post, mail; (persona) courier; **Correos** nmpl (ESP) Post Office sg ▶ **correo aéreo** airmail ▶ **correo basura** (INFORM) spam ▶ **correo electrónico** e-mail, electronic mail ▶ **correo web** webmail

correr [ko'rrer] vt to run; (cortinas) to draw; (cerrojo) to shoot ♦ vi to run; (líquido) to run, flow; **correrse** vr to slide, move; (colores) to run

correspondencia [korrespon'denθja] nf correspondence; (FERRO) connection

corresponder [korrespon'der] vi to correspond; (convenir) to be suitable; (pertenecer) to belong; (concernir) to concern; **corresponderse** vr (por escrito) to correspond; (amarse) to love one another

correspondiente [korrespon'djente] adj corresponding

corresponsal [korrespon'sal] nmf correspondent

corrida [ko'rriða] nf (de toros) bullfight

corrido, -a [ko'rriðo, a] adj (avergonzado) abashed; **un kilo ~ a** good kilo

corriente [ko'rrjente] adj (agua) running; (dinero etc) current; (común) ordinary, normal ♦ nf current ♦ nm current month; **estar al ~ de** to be informed about ▶ **corriente eléctrica** electric current

corrija etc [ko'rrixa] vb ver **corregir**

corro ['korro] nm ring, circle of people)

corromper [korrom'per] vt (madera) to rot; (fig) to corrupt

corrosivo, -a [korro'siβo, a] adj corrosive

corrupción [korrup'θjon] nf rot, decay; (fig) corruption

corsé [kor'se] nm corset

cortacésped [korta'θespeð] nm lawn mower

cortado, -a [kor'taðo, a] adj (gen) cut; (leche) sour; (tímido) shy; (avergonzado) embarrassed ♦ nm coffee (with a little milk)

cortar [kor'tar] vt to cut; (suministro) to cut off; (un pasaje) to cut out ♦ vi to cut; **cortarse** vr (avergonzarse) to become embarrassed; (leche) to turn, curdle; **cortarse el pelo** to have one's hair cut

cortaúñas [korta'uɲas] nm inv nail clippers pl

corte ['korte] nm cut, cutting; (de tela) piece, length ♦ nf: **las Cortes** the Spanish Parliament ▶ **corte de luz** power cut ▶ **corte y confección** dressmaking

cortejo [kor'texo] nm entourage ▶ **cortejo fúnebre** funeral procession

cortés [kor'tes] adj courteous, polite

cortesía [korte'sia] nf courtesy

corteza [kor'teθa] nf (de árbol) bark; (de pan) crust

cortijo [kor'tixo] (ESP) nm farm, farmhouse

cortina [kor'tina] nf curtain

corto, -a ['korto, a] adj (breve) short; (tímido) bashful; **~ de luces** not very bright; **~ de vista** short-sighted; **estar ~ de fondos** to be short of funds ❏ **cortocircuito** nm short circuit ❏ **cortometraje** nm (CINE) short

cosa ['kosa] nf thing; ~ **de** about; **eso es ~ mía** that's my business

coscorrón [kosko'rron] nm bump on the head

cosecha [ko'setʃa] nf (AGR) harvest; (de vino) vintage □ **cosechar** [kose'tʃar] vt to harvest, gather (in)

coser [ko'ser] vt to sew

cosmético, a [kos'metiko, a] adj, nm cosmetic

cosquillas [kos'kiʎas] nfpl: **hacer ~** to tickle; **tener ~** to be ticklish

costa ['kosta] nf (GEO) coast; **a toda ~** at all costs ▶ **Costa Brava** Costa Brava ▶ **Costa Cantábrica** Cantabrian Coast ▶ **Costa del Sol** Costa del Sol

costado [kos'taðo] nm side

costanera (CS) [kosta'nera] nf promenade, sea front

costar [kos'tar] vt (valer) to cost; **me cuesta hablarle** I find it hard to talk to him

Costa Rica [kosta'rika] nf Costa Rica □ **costarricense** (a), nmf Costa Rican □ **costarriqueño, -a**, nm/f Costa Rican

coste ['koste] nm = **costo**

costear [koste'ar] vt to pay for

costero, -a [kos'tero, a] adj (pueblecito, camino) coastal

costilla [kos'tiʎa] nf rib; (CULIN) cutlet

costo ['kosto] nm cost, price ▶ **costo de (la) vida** cost of living □ **costoso, -a** adj costly, expensive

costra ['kostra] nf (corteza) crust; (MED) scab

costumbre [kos'tumbre] nf custom, habit

costura [kos'tura] nf sewing, needlework; (zurcido) seam

costurera [kostu'rera] nf dressmaker

costurero [kostu'rero] nm sewing box o case

cotidiano, -a [koti'ðjano, a] adj daily, day to day

cotilla [ko'tiʎa] (ESP: fam) nmf gossip □ **cotillear** (ESP) vi to gossip □ **cotilleo** (ESP) nm gossip(ing)

cotizar [koti'θar] vt (COM) to quote, price; **cotizarse** vr: **cotizarse a** to sell at, fetch; (BOLSA) to stand at, be quoted at

coto ['koto] nm (terreno cercado) enclosure; (de caza) reserve

cotorra [ko'torra] nf parrot

coyote [ko'jote] nm coyote, prairie wolf

coz [koθ] nf kick

crack (droga) crack

cráneo ['kraneo] nm skull, cranium

cráter ['krater] nm crater

crayón (MÉX, RPI) nm crayon, chalk

creación [krea'θjon] nf creation

creador, a [krea'ðor, a] adj creative ♦ nm/f creator

crear [kre'ar] vt to create, make

crecer [kre'θer] vi to grow; (precio) to rise

creces ['kreθes]: **con ~** adv amply, fully

crecido, -a [kre'θiðo, a] adj (persona, planta) full-grown; (cantidad) large

crecimiento [kreθi'mjento] nm growth; (aumento) increase

credencial [kreðen'θjal] nf (LAm: tarjeta) card; **credenciales** nfpl: credentials ▶ **credencial de socio** (LAm) membership card

crédito ['kreðito] nm credit

credo ['kreðo] nm creed

creencia [kre'enθja] nf belief

creer [kre'er] vt, vi to think, believe; **creerse** vr to believe o.s. (to be); ~ **en** to believe in; **creo que sí/no** I think/don't think so; **¡ya lo creo!** I should think so!

creído, -a [kre'iðo, a] adj (engreído) conceited

crema ['krema] nf cream ▶ **crema batida** (LAm) whipped cream ▶ **crema pastelera** (confectioner's) custard

cremallera [krema'ʎera] nf zip (fastener)

crepe (ESP) nf pancake

cresta ['kresta] nf (GEO, ZOOL) crest

creyendo etc [kre'jendo] vb ver **creer**

creyente [kre'jente] nmf believer

creyó etc [kre'jo] vb ver **creer**

crezco etc vb ver **crecer**

cría etc ['kria] vb ver **criar** ♦ nf (de animales) rearing, breeding; (animal) young; ver tb **crío**

criadero [kria'ðero] nm (ZOOL) breeding place

criado, -a [kri'aðo, a] nm servant ♦ nf servant, maid

criador [kria'ðor] nm breeder

crianza [kri'anθa] nf rearing, breeding; (fig) breeding

criar [kri'ar] vt (educar) to bring up; (producir) to grow, produce; (animales) to breed

criatura [kria'tura] nf creature; (niño) baby, (small) child

cribar [kri'βar] vt to sieve

crimen ['krimen] nm crime

criminal [krimi'nal] adj, nmf criminal

crines nfpl ver **crin**

crío, -a ['krio, a] (fam) nm/f (niño) kid

crisis ['krisis] nf inv crisis ▶ **crisis nerviosa** nervous breakdown

crismas (ESP) nm inv Christmas card

cristal [kris'tal] nm crystal; (de ventana) glass, pane; (lente) lens □ **cristalino, -a** [krista'lino, a] adj crystalline; (fig) clear ♦ nm lens (of the eye)

cristianismo [kristja'nismo] nm Christianity

cristiano, -a [kris'tjano, a] adj, nm/f Christian

Cristo ['kristo] nm Christ; (crucifijo) crucifix

criterio [kri'terjo] nm criterion; (juicio) judgement

crítica ['kritika] nf criticism; ver tb **crítico**

criticar [kriti'kar] vt to criticize

crítico, -a ['kritiko, a] adj critical ♦ nm/f critic

Croacia [kro'aθja] nf Croatia

cromo ['kromo] nm chrome

crónica ['kronika] nf chronicle, account

crónico, -a ['kroniko, a] adj chronic

cronómetro [kro'nometro] nm stopwatch

croqueta [kro'keta] nf croquette

cruce etc ['kruθe] vb ver **cruzar** ♦ nm (para peatones) crossing; (de carreteras) crossroads

crucero [kru'θero] nm (viaje) cruise

crucificar [kruθifi'kar] vt to crucify

crucifijo [kruθi'fixo] nm crucifix

crucigrama [kruθi'ɣrama] nm crossword (puzzle)

cruda (MÉX, CAm: fam) nf hangover

crudo, -a ['kruðo, a] adj raw; (no maduro) unripe; (petróleo) crude; (rudo, cruel) cruel ♦ nm crude (oil)

cruel [krwel] adj cruel □ **crueldad** nf cruelty

crujiente [kru'xjente] adj (galleta etc) crunchy

crujir [kru'xir] vi (madera etc) to creak; (dedos) to crack; (dientes) to grind; (nieve, arena) to crunch

cruz [kruθ] nf cross; (de moneda) tails sg ▶ **cruz gamada** swastika

cruzada [kru'θaða] nf crusade

cruzado, -a [kru'θaðo, a] adj crossed ♦ nm crusader

cruzar [kru'θar] vt to cross; **cruzarse** vr (líneas etc) to cross; (personas) to pass each other

Cruz Roja nf Red Cross

cuaderno [kwa'ðerno] nm notebook; (de escuela) exercise book; (NÁUT) logbook

cuadra ['kwaðra] nf (caballeriza) stable; (LAm: entre calles) block

cuadrado, -a [kwa'ðraðo, a] adj square ♦ nm (MAT) square

cuadrar [kwa'ðrar] vt to square ♦ vi: ~ **con** to square with, tally with; **cuadrarse** vr (soldado) to stand to attention

cuadrilátero [kwaðri'latero] nm (DEPORTE) boxing ring; (GEOM) quadrilateral

cuadrilla [kwa'ðriʎa] nf party, group

cuadro ['kwaðro] nm square; (ARTE) painting; (TEATRO) scene; (diagrama) chart; (DEPORTE, MED) team; **tela a cuadros** checked (BRIT) o chequered (US) material

cuajar [kwa'xar] vt (leche) to curdle; (sangre) to congeal; (CULIN) to set; **cuajarse** vr to curdle; to congeal; to set; (llenarse) to fill up

cuajo ['kwaxo] nm: **de ~** (arrancar) by the roots; (cortar) completely

cual [kwal] adv like, as ♦ pron: **el** etc ~ which; (persona sujeto) who; (: objeto) whom ♦ adj such as; **cada ~** each one; **déjalo tal ~** leave it just as it is

cuál [kwal] pron interr which (one)

cualesquier, a [kwales'kjer(a)] pl de **cualquier(a)**

cualidad [kwali'ðað] nf quality

cualquier [kwal'kjer] adj ver **cualquiera**

cualquiera [kwal'kjera] (pl **cualesquiera**) adj (delante de nm y f **cualquier**) any ♦ pron anybody; **un coche ~ servirá** any car will do; **no es un hombre ~** he isn't just anybody; **cualquier día/libro** any day/book; **eso ~ lo sabe hacer** anybody can do that; **es un ~** he's a nobody

cuando ['kwando] adv when; (aún si) if, even if ♦ conj (puesto que) since ♦ prep: **yo, ~ niño ...** when I was a child ...; **~ no sea así** even if it is not so; **~ más** at (the) most; **~ menos** at least; **~ no** if not, otherwise; **de ~ en ~** from time to time

cuándo ['kwando] adv when; **¿desde ~?** since when?

cuantía [kwan'tia] nf (importe: de pérdidas, deuda, daños) extent

cuanto, -a

PALABRA CLAVE

['kwanto, a] adj

1 (todo): **tiene todo cuanto desea** he's got everything he wants; **le daremos cuantos ejemplares necesite** we'll give him as many copies as o all the copies he needs; **cuantos hombres la ven** all the men who see her

2: **unos cuantos: había unos cuantos periodistas** there were a few journalists

3 (+ más): **cuanto más vino bebes peor te sentirás** the more wine you drink the worse you'll feel

♦ pron: **tiene cuanto desea** he has everything he wants; **tome cuanto/ cuantos quiera** take as much/many as you want

♦ adv: **en cuanto: en cuanto profesor** as a teacher; **en cuanto a mí** as for me; ver tb **antes**

♦ conj

1: **cuanto más gana menos gasta** the more he earns the less he spends; **cuanto más joven más confiado** the younger you are the more trusting you are

2: **en cuanto: en cuanto llegue/ llegué** as soon as I arrive/arrived

cuánto, -a ['kwanto, a] adj (exclamación) what a lot of; (interr: sg) how much?; (: pl) how many? ♦ pron, adv how; (: interr: sg) how much?; (: pl) how many?; **¡cuánta gente!** what a lot of people!; **¿~ cuesta?** how much does it cost?; **¿a cuántos estamos?** what's the date?

cuarenta [kwa'renta] num forty

cuarentena [kwaren'tena] nf quarantine

cuaresma [kwa'resma] nf Lent

cuarta ['kwarta] nf (MAT) quarter, fourth; (palmo) span

cuartel [kwar'tel] nm (MIL) barracks pl ► **cuartel de bomberos** (RPI) fire station ► **cuartel general** headquarters pl

cuarteto [kwar'teto] nm quartet

cuarto, -a ['kwarto, a] adj fourth ♦ nm (MAT) quarter, fourth; (habitación) room ► **cuarto de baño** bathroom ► **cuarto de estar** living room ► **cuarto de hora** quarter (of an) hour ► **cuarto de kilo** quarter kilo ► **cuartos de final** quarter finals

cuatro ['kwatro] num four

Cuba ['kuβa] nf Cuba

cuba ['kuβa] nf cask, barrel

cubano, -a [ku'βano, a] adj, nm/f Cuban

cubata [ku'βata] nm (fam) large drink (of rum and coke etc)

cubeta (ESP, MÉX) [ku'βeta] nf (balde) bucket, tub

cúbico, -a ['kuβiko, a] adj cubic

cubierta [ku'βjerta] nf cover, covering; (neumático) tyre; (NÁUT) deck

cubierto, -a [ku'βjerto, a] pp de **cubrir** ♦ adj covered ♦ nm cover; (lugar en la mesa) place; **cubiertos** nmpl cutlery sg; **a ~** under cover

cubilete [kuβi'lete] nm (en juegos) cup

cubito [ku'βito] nm (tb: **~ de hielo**) ice-cube

cubo ['kuβo] nm (MAT) cube; (ESP: balde) bucket, tub; (TEC) drum ► **cubo de (la) basura** dustbin (BRIT), trash can (US)

cubrir [ku'βrir] vt to cover; **cubrirse** vr (cielo) to become overcast

cucaracha [kuka'ratʃa] nf cockroach

cuchara [ku'tʃara] nf spoon; (TEC) scoop ❏ **cucharada** nf spoonful ► **cucharadita** nf teaspoonful

cucharilla [kutʃa'riʎa] nf teaspoon

cucharón [kutʃa'ron] nm ladle

cuchilla [ku'tʃiʎa] nf (large) knife; (de arma blanca) blade ► **cuchilla de afeitar** razor blade

cuchillo [ku'tʃiʎo] nm knife

cuchitril [kutʃi'tril] nm hovel

cuclillas [ku'kliʎas] nfpl: **en ~** squatting

cuco, -a ['kuko, a] adj pretty; (astuto) sharp ♦ nm cuckoo

cucurucho [kuku'rutʃo] nm cornet

cueca nf Chilean national dance

cuello ['kweʎo] nm (ANAT) neck; (de vestido, camisa) collar

cuenca ['kwenka] nf (ANAT) eye socket; (GEO) bowl, deep valley

cuenco ['kwenko] nm bowl

cuenta etc ['kwenta] vb ver **contar** ♦ nf (cálculo) count, counting; (en café, restaurante) bill (BRIT), check (US); (COM) account; (de collar) bead; **a fin de cuentas** in the end; **caer en la ~** to catch on; **darse ~ de** to realize; **tener en ~** to bear in mind; **echar cuentas to** take stock ► **cuenta atrás** countdown ► **cuenta corriente/de ahorros** current/savings account ► **cuenta de correo (electrónica)** (INFORM) email account ❏ **cuentakilómetros** nm inv = milometer; (de velocidad) speedometer

cuento etc ['kwento] vb ver **contar** ♦ nm story ► **cuento chino** tall story ► **cuento de hadas** a fairy tale

cuerda ['kwerða] nf rope; (fina) string; (de reloj) spring; **dar ~ a un reloj** to wind up a clock ► **cuerda floja** tightrope ► **cuerdas vocales** vocal cords

cuerdo, -a ['kwerðo, a] adj sane; (prudente) wise, sensible

cuerno ['kwerno] nm horn

cuero ['kwero] nm leather; **en cueros** stark naked ► **cuero cabelludo** scalp

cuerpo ['kwerpo] nm body

cuervo ['kwerβo] nm crow

cuesta etc ['kwesta] vb ver **costar** ♦ nf slope; (en camino etc) hill; **~ arriba/abajo** uphill/downhill; **a cuestas** on one's back

cueste etc vb ver **costar**

cuestión [kwes'tjon] nf matter, question, issue

cuete adj (MÉX: fam) drunk ♦ nm (LAm: cohete) rocket; (MÉX, RPl: fam: embriaguez) drunkenness; (MÉX CULIN) steak

cueva ['kweβa] nf cave

cuidado [kwi'ðaðo] nm care, carefulness; (preocupación) worry ♦ excl carefull, look out!; **eso me tiene sin ~** I'm not worried about that

cuidadoso, -a [kwiða'ðoso, a] adj careful; (preocupado) anxious

cuidar [kwi'ðar] vt (MED) to care for; (ocuparse de) to take care of, look after ♦ vi: **~ de** to take care of, look after; **cuidarse** vr to look after o.s.; **cuidarse de hacer algo** to take care to do sth

culata [ku'lata] nf (de fusil) butt

culebra [ku'leβra] nf snake

culebrón [kule'βron] (fam) nm (TV) soap(-opera)

culo ['kulo] nm bottom, backside; (de vaso, botella) bottom

culpa ['kulpa] nf fault; (JUR) guilt; **por ~ de** because of; **echar la ~ a algn** to blame sb for sth; **tener la ~ (de)** to be to blame (for) ❑ **culpable** adj guilty ♦ nmf culprit ♦ **culpar** [kul'par] vt to blame; (acusar) to accuse

cultivar [kulti'βar] vt to cultivate

cultivo [kul'tiβo] nm (acto) cultivation; (plantas) crop

culto, -a ['kulto, a] adj (que tiene cultura) cultured, educated ♦ nm (homenaje) worship; (religión) cult

cultura [kul'tura] nf culture

culturismo [kultu'rismo] nm body-building

cumbia nf popular Colombian dance

cumbre ['kumbre] nf summit, top

cumpleaños [kumple'aɲos] nm inv birthday

cumplido, -a [kum'pliðo, a] adj (abundante) plentiful; (cortés) courteous ♦ nm compliment; **visita de ~** courtesy call

cumplidor, a [kumpli'ðor, a] adj reliable

cumplimiento [kumpli'mjento] nm (de un deber) fulfilment; (acabamiento) completion

cumplir [kum'plir] vt (orden) to carry out, obey; (promesa) to carry out, fulfil; (condena) to serve ♦ vi: **~ con** (deber) to carry out, fulfil; **cumplirse** vr (plazo) to expire; **hoy cumple dieciocho años** he is eighteen today

cuna ['kuna] nf cradle, cot

cundir [kun'dir] vi (noticia, rumor, pánico) to spread; (rendir) to go a long way

cuneta [ku'neta] nf ditch

cuña ['kuɲa] nf wedge

cuñado, -a [ku'ɲaðo, a] nm/f brother-/sister-in-law

cuota ['kwota] nf (parte proporcional) share; (cotización) fee, dues pl

cupe etc vb ver **caber**

cupiera etc [ku'pjera] vb ver **caber**

cupo ['kupo] vb ver **caber** ♦ nm quota

cupón [ku'pon] nm coupon

cúpula ['kupula] nf dome

cura ['kura] nf (curación) cure; (método curativo) treatment ♦ nm priest

curación [kura'θjon] nf cure; (acción) curing

curandero, -a [kuran'dero, a] nm/f quack

curar [ku'rar] vt (MED: herida) to treat, dress; (: enfermo) to cure; (CULIN) to cure, salt; (cuero) to tan; **curarse** vr to get well, recover

curiosear [kurjose'ar] vt to glance at, look over ♦ vi to look round, wander round; (explorar) to poke about

curiosidad [kurjosi'ðað] nf curiosity

curioso, -a [ku'rjoso, a] adj curious
♦ nm/f bystander, onlooker

curita (LAm) nf (sticking) plaster (BRIT), Bandaid® (US)

currante [ku'rrante] (ESP: fam) nmf worker

currar [ku'rrar] (ESP: fam) vi to work

currículo [ku'rrikulo] = **curriculum**

curriculum [ku'rrikulum] nm curriculum vitae

cursi ['kursi] (fam) adj affected

cursillo [kur'siʎo] nm short course

cursiva [kur'siβa] nf italics pl

curso ['kurso] nm course; **en** ~ (año) current; (proceso) going on, under way

cursor [kur'sor] nm (INFORM) cursor

curul (MÉX) nm (escaño) seat

curva ['kurβa] nf curve, bend

custodia [kus'toðja] nf safekeeping; custody

cutis ['kutis] nm inv skin, complexion

cutre ['kutre] (ESP: fam) adj (lugar) grotty

cuyo, -a ['kujo, a] pron (de quien) whose; (de que) whose, of which; **en** ~ **caso** in which case

C.V. abr (= caballos de vapor) H.P.

D, d

D. abr (= Don) Esq

dado, -a ['daðo, a] pp de **dar** ♦ nm die; **dados** nmpl dice; ~ **que** given that

daltónico, -a [dal'toniko, a] adj colour-blind

dama ['dama] nf (gen) lady; (AJEDREZ) queen; **damas** nfpl (juego) draughts sg ▶ **dama de honor** bridesmaid

damasco (RPl) [da'masko] nm apricot

danés, -esa [da'nes, esa] adj Danish
♦ nm/f Dane

dañar [da'ɲar] vt (objeto) to damage; (persona) to hurt; **dañarse** vr (objeto) to get damaged

dañino, -a [da'ɲino, a] adj harmful

daño ['daɲo] nm (objeto) damage; (persona) harm, injury; **daños y perjuicios** (JUR) damages; **hacer** ~ **a** to damage; (persona) to hurt, injure; **hacerse** ~ to hurt o.s.

dar

PALABRA CLAVE

[dar] vt

1 (gen) to give; (obra de teatro) to put on; (film) to show; (fiesta) to hold; **dar algo a algn** to give sb sth o sth to sb; **dar de beber a algn** to give sb a drink

2 (producir: intereses) to yield; (fruta) to produce

3 (locuciones + n): **da gusto escucharle** it's a pleasure to listen to him; ver tb **paseo**

4 (+ n: = perífrasis de verbo): **me da asco** it sickens me

5 (considerar): **dar algo por descontado/entendido** to take sth for granted/as read; **dar algo por concluido** to consider sth finished

6 (hora): **el reloj dio las 6** the clock struck 6 (o'clock)

7 **me da lo mismo** it's all the same to me; ver tb **igual**; **más**

♦ vi

1 **dar con**: **dimos con él dos horas más tarde** we came across him two hours later; **al final di con la solución** I eventually came up with the answer

2 **dar en** (blanco, suelo) to hit; **el sol me da en la cara** the sun is shining (right) on my face

3 **dar de sí** (zapatos etc) to stretch, give

♦ **darse** vr

1 (*darse por vencido*) to give up

2 (*ocurrir*): **se han dado muchos casos** there have been a lot of cases

3 **darse a**: **se ha dado a la bebida** he's taken to drinking

4: **se me dan bien/mal las ciencias** I'm good/bad at science

5 **dárselas de**: **se las da de experto** he fancies himself *o* poses as an expert

dardo ['darðo] *nm* dart

dátil ['datil] *nm* date

dato ['dato] *nm* fact, piece of information ▶ **datos personales** personal details

dcha. *abr* (= *derecha*) r.h.

d. de C. *abr* (= *después de Cristo*) A.D.

de

PALABRA CLAVE

[de] (*de* + *el* = *del*) *prep*

1 (*posesión*) of; **la casa de Isabel/mis padres** Isabel's/my parents' house; **es de ellos** it's theirs

2 (*origen, distancia, con números*) from; **soy de Gijón** I'm from Gijón; **de 8 a 20** from 8 to 20; **salir del cine** to go out *o* leave the cinema; **de 2 en 2** 2 by 2, 2 at a time

3 (*valor descriptivo*): **una copa de vino** a glass of wine; **la mesa de la cocina** the kitchen table; **un billete de 10 euros** a 10 euro note; **un niño de tres años** a three-year-old (child); **una máquina de coser** a sewing machine; **ir vestido de gris** to be dressed in grey; **la niña del vestido azul** the girl in the blue dress; **trabaja de profesora** she works as a teacher; **de lado** sideways; **de atrás/delante** rear/front

4 (*hora, tiempo*): **a las 8 de la mañana** at 8 o'clock in the morning; **de día/**

noche by day/night; **de hoy en ocho días** a week from now; **de niño era gordo** as a child he was fat

5 (*comparaciones*): **más/menos de cien personas** more/less than a hundred people; **el más caro de la tienda** the most expensive in the shop; **menos/más de lo pensado** less/more than expected

6 (*causa*): **del calor** from the heat

7 (*tema*) about; **clases de inglés** English classes; **¿sabes algo de él?** do you know anything about him?; **un libro de física** a physics book

8 (*adj* + *de* + *infin*): **fácil de entender** easy to understand

9 (*oraciones pasivas*): **fue respetado de todos** he was loved by all

10 (*condicional* + *infin*) if; **de ser posible** if possible; **de no terminarlo hoy** if I *etc* don't finish it today

dé [de] *vb ver* **dar**

debajo [de'βaxo] *adv* underneath; **~ de** below, under; **por ~ de** beneath

debate [de'βate] *nm* debate □ **debatir** *vt* to debate

deber [de'βer] *nm* duty ♦ *vt* to owe ♦ *vi*: **debe (de)** it must, it should; **deberes** *nmpl* (*ESCOL*) homework; **deberse** *vr*: **deberse a** to be owing *o* due to; **debo hacerlo** I must do it; **debe de ir** he should go

debido, -a [de'βiðo, a] *adj* proper, just; **~ a** due to, because of

débil ['deβil] *adj* (*persona, carácter*) weak; (*luz*) dim □ **debilidad** *nf* weakness; dimness

debilitar [deβili'tar] *vt* to weaken; **debilitarse** *vr* to grow weak

débito ['deβito] *nm* debit ▶ **débito bancario** (*LAm*) direct debit (*BRIT*) billing (*US*)

debutar [deβu'tar] *vi* to make one's debut

década ['dekaða] *nf* decade

decadencia [deka'ðenθja] *nf* (*estado*) decadence; (*proceso*) decline, decay

decaído, -a [deka'iðo, a] *adj*: **estar ~** (*abatido*) to be down

decano, -a [de'kano, a] *nm/f* (*de universidad etc*) dean

decena [de'θena] *nf*: **una ~** ten (or so)

decente [de'θente] *adj* decent

decepción [deθep'θjon] *nf* disappointment

⚠ No confundir **decepción** con la palabra inglesa *deception*.

decepcionar [deθepθjo'nar] *vt* to disappoint

decidir [deθi'ðir] *vt, vi* to decide; **decidirse** *vr*: **decidirse a** to make up one's mind to

décimo, -a ['deθimo, a] *adj* tenth ♦ *nm* tenth

decir [de'θir] *vt* to say; (*contar*) to tell; (*hablar*) to speak ♦ *nm* saying; **decirse** *vr*: **se dice que** it is said that; **es ~** that is (to say); **~ para sí** to say to o.s.; **querer ~** to mean; **¡dígame!** (*TEL*) hello!; (*en tienda*) can I help you?

decisión [deθi'sjon] *nf* (*resolución*) decision; (*firmeza*) decisiveness

decisivo, -a [deθi'siβo, a] *adj* decisive

declaración [deklara'θjon] *nf* (*manifestación*) statement; (*de amor*) declaration ▶ **declaración fiscal** *o* **de la Renta** income-tax return

declarar [dekla'rar] *vt* to declare ♦ *vi* to declare; (*JUR*) to testify; **declararse** *vr* to propose

decoración [dekora'θjon] *nf* decoration

decorado [deko'raðo] *nm* (*CINE, TEATRO*) scenery, set

decorar [deko'rar] *vt* to decorate ❏ **decorativo, -a** *adj* ornamental, decorative

decreto [de'kreto] *nm* decree

dedal [de'ðal] *nm* thimble

dedicación [deðika'θjon] *nf* dedication

dedicar [deði'kar] *vt* (*libro*) to dedicate; (*tiempo, dinero*) to devote; (*palabras*: *decir, consagrar*) to dedicate, devote ❏ **dedicatoria** *nf* (*de libro*) dedication

dedo ['deðo] *nm* finger; **hacer ~** (*fam*) to hitch (a lift) ▶ **dedo anular** ring finger ▶ **dedo corazón** middle finger ▶ **dedo (del pie)** toe ▶ **dedo gordo** (*de la mano*) thumb; (*del pie*) big toe ▶ **dedo índice** index finger ▶ **dedo meñique** little finger ▶ **dedo pulgar** thumb

deducción [deðuk'θjon] *nf* deduction

deducir [deðu'θir] *vt* (*concluir*) to deduce, infer; (*COM*) to deduct

defecto [de'fekto] *nm* defect, flaw ❏ **defectuoso, -a** *adj* defective, faulty

defender [defen'der] *vt* to defend; **defenderse** *vr* (*desenvolverse*) to get by

defensa [de'fensa] *nf* defence ♦ *nm* (*DEPORTE*) defender, back ❏ **defensivo, -a** *adj* defensive; **a la defensiva** on the defensive

defensor, a [defen'sor, a] *adj* defending ♦ *nm/f* (*abogado defensor*) defending counsel; (*protector*) protector

deficiencia [defi'θjenθja] *nf* deficiency

deficiente [defi'θjente] *adj* (*defectuoso*) defective; **~ en** lacking *o* deficient in; **ser un ~ mental** to be mentally handicapped

déficit ['defiθit] (*pl* **déficits**) *nm* deficit

definición [defini'θjon] *nf* definition

definir [defi'nir] *vt* (*determinar*) to determine, establish; (*decidir*) to define; (*aclarar*) to clarify ❏ **definitivo, -a** *adj* definitive; **en definitiva** definitively; (*en resumen*) in short

deformación [deforma'θjon] nf (alteración) deformation; (RADIO etc) distortion

deformar [defor'mar] vt (gen) to deform; **deformarse** vr to become deformed □ **deformado** (informe) deformed; (feo) ugly; (malhecho) misshapen

defraudar [defrau'ðar] vt (decepcionar) to disappoint; (estafar) to defraud

defunción [defun'θjon] nf death, demise

degenerar [dexene'rar] vi to degenerate

degradar [deɣra'ðar] vt to debase, degrade; **degradarse** vr to demean o.s.

degustación [deɣusta'θjon] nf sampling, tasting

dejar [de'xar] vt to leave; (permitir) to allow, let; (abandonar) to abandon, forsake; (beneficios) to produce, yield ♦ vi: ~ **de** (parar) to stop; (no hacer) to fail to; ~ **a un lado** to leave o set aside; ~ **entrar/salir** to let in/out; ~ **pasar** to let through

del [del] (=**de** + **el**) ver **de**

delantal [delan'tal] nm apron

delante [de'lante] adv in front; (enfrente) opposite; (adelante) ahead; ~ **de** in front of, before

delantera [delan'tera] nf (de vestido, casa etc) front part; (DEPORTE) forward line; **llevar la ~ (a algn)** to be ahead of sb

delantero, -a [delan'tero, a] adj front ♦ nm (DEPORTE) forward, striker

delatar [dela'tar] vt to inform on o against, betray □ **delator, a** nm/f informer

delegación [deleɣa'θjon] nf (acción, delegados) delegation; (COM: oficina) office, branch ▶ **delegación de policía** (MÉX) police station

delegado, -a [dele'ɣaðo, a] nm/f delegate; (COM) agent

delegar [dele'ɣar] vt to delegate

deletrear [deletre'ar] vt to spell (out)

delfín [del'fin] nm dolphin

delgado, -a [del'ɣaðo, a] adj thin; (persona) slim, thin; (tela etc) light, delicate

deliberar [deliβe'rar] vt to debate, discuss

delicadeza [delika'ðeθa] nf (gen) delicacy; (refinamiento, sutileza) refinement

delicado, -a [deli'kaðo, a] adj (gen) delicate; (sensible) sensitive; (quisquilloso) touchy

delicia [de'liθja] nf delight

delicioso, -a [deli'θjoso, a] adj (gracioso) delightful; (exquisito) delicious

delimitar [delimi'tar] vt (función, responsabilidades) to define

delincuencia [delin'kwenθja] nf delinquency □ **delincuente** nmf delinquent; (criminal) criminal

delineante [deline'ante] nmf draughtsman/woman

delirante [deli'rante] adj delirious

delirar [deli'rar] vi to be delirious, rave

delirio [de'lirjo] nm (MED) delirium; (palabras insensatas) ravings pl

delito [de'lito] nm (gen) crime; (infracción) offence

delta ['delta] nm delta

demacrado, -a [dema'kraðo, a] adj: **estar ~** to look pale and drawn, be wasted away

demanda [de'manda] nf (pedido, COM) demand; (petición) request; (JUR) action, lawsuit □ **demandar** [deman'dar] vt (gen) to demand; (JUR) to sue, file a lawsuit against

demás [de'mas] adj: **los ~ niños** the other o remaining children ♦ pron: **los/las ~** the others, the rest (of them); **lo ~** the rest (of it)

demasía [dema'sia] nf (exceso) excess, surplus; **comer en ~** to eat to excess

demasiado, -a [dema'sjaðo, a] *adj*: **~ vino** too much wine ♦ *adv (antes de adj, adv)* too; **demasiados libros** too many books; **¡esto es ~!** that's the limit!; **hace ~ calor** it's too hot; **~ despacio** too slowly; **demasiados** too many

demencia [de'menθja] *nf (locura)* madness

democracia [demo'kraθja] *nf* democracy

demócrata [de'mokrata] *nmf* democrat ☐ **democrático, -a** *adj* democratic

demoler [demo'ler] *vt* to demolish ☐ **demolición** *nf* demolition

demonio [de'monjo] *nm* devil, demon; **¡demonios!** hell!, damn!; **¿cómo demonios?** how the hell?

demora [de'mora] *nf* delay

demos ['demos] *vb ver* **dar**

demostración [demostra'θjon] *nf (MAT)* proof; *(de afecto)* show, display

demostrar [demos'trar] *vt (probar)* to prove; *(mostrar)* to show; *(manifestar)* to demonstrate

den [den] *vb ver* **dar**

denegar [dene'ɣar] *vt (rechazar)* to refuse; *(JUR)* to reject

denominación [denomina'θjon] *nf (acto)* naming ▶ **Denominación de Origen** *see note*

DENOMINACIÓN DE ORIGEN

The **Denominación de Origen**, abbreviated to **D.O.**, is a prestigious classification awarded to food products such as wines, cheeses, sausages and hams which meet the stringent quality and production standards of the designated region. **D.O.** labels serve as a guarantee of quality.

---

densidad [densi'ðað] *nf* density; *(fig)* thickness

denso, -a ['denso, a] *adj* dense; *(espeso, pastoso)* thick; *(fig)* heavy

dentadura [denta'ðura] *nf (set of)* teeth ☐ ▶ **dentadura postiza** false teeth *pl*

dentera [den'tera] *nf (grima)*: **dar ~ a algn** to set sb's teeth on edge

dentífrico, -a [den'tifriko, a] *adj* dental ♦ *nm* toothpaste

dentista [den'tista] *nmf* dentist

dentro ['dentro] *adv* inside ♦ *prep*: **~ de** in, inside, within; **por ~** (on the) inside; **mirar por ~** to look inside; **~ de tres meses** within three months

denuncia [de'nunθja] *nf (delación)* denunciation; *(acusación)* accusation; *(de accidente)* report ☐ **denunciar** *vt* to report; *(delatar)* to inform on o against

departamento [departa'mento] *nm* sección administrativa, department, section; *(LAm: apartamento)* flat *(BRIT)*, apartment

depender [depen'der] *vi*: **~ de** to depend on; **depende** it (all) depends

dependienta [depen'djenta] *nf* saleswoman, shop assistant

dependiente [depen'djente] *adj* dependent ♦ *nm* salesman, shop assistant

depilar [depi'lar] *vt (con cera)* to wax; *(cejas)* to pluck

deportar [depor'tar] *vt* to deport

deporte [de'porte] *nm* sport; **hacer ~** to play sports ☐ **deportista** *adj* sports *cpd* ♦ *nmf* sportsman/woman ☐ **deportivo, -a** *adj (club, periódico)* sports *cpd* ♦ *nm* sports car

depositar [deposi'tar] *vt (dinero)* to deposit; *(mercancías)* to put away, store; **depositarse** *vr* to settle

depósito [de'posito] *nm (gen)* deposit; *(almacén)* warehouse, store; *(de agua, gasolina etc)* tank ▶ **depósito de cadáveres** mortuary

depredador, a [depreða'ðor, a] adj predatory ♦ nm predator

depresión [depre'sjon] nf depression
▶ **depresión nerviosa** nervous breakdown

deprimido, -a [depri'miðo, a] adj depressed

deprimir [depri'mir] vt to depress; **deprimirse** vr (persona) to become depressed

deprisa [de'prisa] adv quickly, hurriedly

depurar [depu'rar] vt to purify; (purgar) to purge

derecha [de'retʃa] nf right(-hand) side; (POL) right; **a la ~** (estar) on the right; (torcer etc) to the right

derecho, -a [de'retʃo, a] adj right, right-hand ♦ nm (privilegio) right; (lado) right(-hand) side; (leyes) law ♦ adv straight, directly; **derechos** nmpl (de aduana) duty sg; (de autor) royalties; **tener ~ a** to have a right to ▶ **derechos de autor** royalties

deriva [de'riβa] nf: **ir o estar a la ~** to drift, to be adrift

derivado [deri'βaðo] nm (COM) by-product

derivar [deri'βar] vt to derive; (desviar) to direct ♦ vi to derive, be derived; (NÁUT) to drift; **derivarse** vr to derive, be derived; to drift

derramamiento [derrama'mjento] nm (dispersión) spilling ▶ **derramamiento de sangre** bloodshed

derramar [derra'mar] vt to spill; (verter) to pour out; (esparcir) to scatter; **derramarse** vr to pour out

derrame [de'rrame] nm (de líquido) spilling; (de sangre) shedding; (de tubo etc) overflow; (pérdida) leakage ▶ **derrame cerebral** brain hæmorrhage

derredor [derre'ðor] adv: **al o en ~ de** around, about

derretir [derre'tir] vt (gen) to melt; (nieve) to thaw; **derretirse** vr to melt

derribar [derri'βar] vt to knock down; (construcción) to demolish; (persona, gobierno, político) to bring down

derrocar [derro'kar] vt (gobierno) to bring down, overthrow

derrochar [derro'tʃar] vt to squander ❏ **derroche** nm (despilfarro) waste, squandering

derrota [de'rrota] nf (NÁUT) course; (MIL, DEPORTE etc) defeat, rout ❏ **derrotar** vt (gen) to defeat ❏ **derrotero** nm (rumbo) course

derrumbar [derrum'bar] vt (edificio) to knock down; **derrumbarse** vr to collapse

des etc [des] vb ver **dar**

desabrochar [desaβro'tʃar] vt (botones, broches) to undo, unfasten; **desabrocharse** vr (ropa etc) to come undone

desacato [desa'kato] nm (falta de respeto) disrespect; (JUR) contempt

desacertado, -a [desaθer'taðo, a] adj (equivocado) mistaken; (inoportuno) unwise

desacierto [desa'θjerto] nm mistake, error

desaconsejar [desakonse'xar] vt to advise against

desacreditar [desakreði'tar] vt (desprestigiar) to discredit, bring into disrepute; (denigrar) to run down

desacuerdo [desa'kwerðo] nm disagreement, discord

desafiar [desa'fjar] vt (retar) to challenge; (enfrentarse a) to defy

desafilado, -a [desafi'laðo, a] adj blunt

desafinado, -a [desafi'naðo, a] adj: **estar ~** to be out of tune

desafinar [desafi'nar] vi (al cantar) to be o go out of tune

desafío etc [desa'fio] vb ver **desafiar**
♦ nm (reto) challenge; (combate) duel; (resistencia) defiance

desafortunado, -a [desafortu'naðo, a] adj (desgraciado) unfortunate, unlucky

desagradable [desaɣra'ðaβle] adj (fastidioso, enojoso) unpleasant; (irritante) disagreeable

desagradar [desaɣra'ðar] vt (disgustar) to displease; (molestar) to bother

desagradecido, -a [desaɣraðe'θiðo, a] adj ungrateful

desagrado [desa'ɣraðo] nm (disgusto) displeasure; (contrariedad) dissatisfaction

desagüe [des'aɣwe] nm (de un líquido) drainage; (cañería) drainpipe; (salida) outlet, drain

desahogar [desao'ɣar] vt (aliviar) to ease, relieve; (ira) to vent; **desahogarse** vr (relajarse) to relax; (desfogarse) to let off steam

desahogo [desa'oɣo] nm (alivio) relief; (comodidad) comfort, ease

desahuciar [desau'θiar] vt (enfermo) to give up hope for; (inquilino) to evict

desairar [desai'rar] vt (menospreciar) to slight, snub

desalentador, a [desalenta'ðor, a] adj discouraging

desaliño [desa'liɲo] nm slovenliness

desalmado, -a [desal'maðo, a] adj (cruel) cruel, heartless

desalojar [desalo'xar] vt (expulsar, echar) to eject; (abandonar) to move out of ♦ vi to move out

desamor [desa'mor] nm (frialdad) indifference; (odio) dislike

desamparado, -a [desampa'raðo, a] adj (persona) helpless; (lugar: expuesto) exposed; (desierto) deserted

desangrar [desaŋ'grar] vt to bleed; (fig: persona) to bleed dry; **desangrarse** vr to lose a lot of blood

desanimado, -a [desani'maðo, a] adj (persona) downhearted; (espectáculo, fiesta) dull

desanimar [desani'mar] vt (desalentar) to discourage; (deprimir) to depress; **desanimarse** vr to lose heart

desapacible [desapa'θiβle] adj (gen) unpleasant

desaparecer [desapare'θer] vi (gen) to disappear; (el sol, el luz) to vanish □ **desaparecido, -a** adj missing □ **desaparición** nf disappearance

desapercibido, -a [desaperθi'βiðo, a] adj (desprevenido) unprepared; **pasar ~** to go unnoticed

desaprensivo, -a [desapren'siβo, a] adj unscrupulous

desaprobar [desapro'βar] vt (reprobar) to disapprove of; (condenar) to condemn; (no consentir) to reject

desaprovechado, -a [desaproβe'tʃaðo, a] adj (oportunidad, tiempo) wasted; (estudiante) slack

desaprovechar [desaproβe'tʃar] vt to waste

desarmador (MÉX) [desarma'ðor] nm screwdriver

desarmar [desar'mar] vt (MIL, fig) to disarm; (TEC) to take apart, dismantle □ **desarme** nm disarmament

desarraigar [desarrai'ɣar] vt to uproot □ **desarraigo** nm uprooting

desarreglar [desarre'ɣlar] vt (desordenar) to disarrange; (trastocar) to upset, disturb

desarrollar [desarro'ʎar] vt (gen) to develop; **desarrollarse** vr to develop; (ocurrir) to take place; (FOTO) to develop □ **desarrollo** nm development

desarticular [desartiku'lar] vt (hueso) to dislocate; (objeto) to take apart; (fig) to break up

desasosegar [desasose'ɣar] vt (inquietar) to disturb, make uneasy

desasosiego etc [desaso'sjeɣo] vb ver **desasosegar** ♦ nm (intranquilidad) uneasiness, restlessness; (ansiedad) anxiety

desastre [de'sastre] nm disaster
❑ **desastroso, -a** adj disastrous

desatar [desa'tar] vt (nudo) to untie; (paquete) to undo; (separar) to detach; **desatarse** vr (zapatos) to come untied; (tormenta) to break

desatascar [desatas'kar] vt (cañería) to unblock, clear

desatender [desaten'der] vt (no prestar atención a) to disregard; (abandonar) to neglect

desatino [desa'tino] nm (idiotez) foolishness, folly; (error) blunder

desatornillar [desatorni'ʎar] vt to unscrew

desatrancar [desatran'kar] vt (puerta) to unbolt; (cañería) to clear, unblock

desautorizado, -a [desautori'θaðo, a] adj unauthorized

desautorizar [desautori'θar] vt (oficial) to deprive of authority; (informe) to deny

desayunar [desaju'nar] vi to have breakfast ♦ vt to have for breakfast
❑ **desayuno** nm breakfast

desazón [desa'θon] nf anxiety

desbarajuste [desβara'xuste] nm confusion, disorder

desbaratar [desβara'tar] vt (deshacer, destruir) to ruin

desbloquear [desβloke'ar] vt (negociaciónes, tráfico) to get going again; (COM: cuenta) to unfreeze

desbordar [desβor'ðar] vt (sobrepasar) to go beyond; (exceder) to exceed; **desbordarse** vr (río) to overflow; (entusiasmo) to erupt

descabellado, -a [deskaβe'ʎaðo, a] adj (disparatado) wild, crazy

descafeinado, -a [deskafei'naðo, a] adj decaffeinated ♦ nm decaffeinated coffee

descalabro [deska'laβro] nm blow; (desgracia) misfortune

♦ **descalificar** [deskalifi'kar] vt to disqualify; (desacreditar) to discredit

descalzar [deskal'θar] vt (zapato) to take off ♦ **descalzo, -a** adj barefoot(ed)

descambiar [deskam'bjar] vt to exchange

descaminado, -a [deskami'naðo, a] adj (equivocado) on the wrong road; (fig) misguided

descampado [deskam'paðo] nm open space

descansado, -a [deskan'saðo, a] adj (gen) rested; (que tranquiliza) restful

descansar [deskan'sar] vt (gen) to rest ♦ vi to rest, have a rest; (echarse) to lie down

descansillo [deskan'siʎo] nm (de escalera) landing

descanso [des'kanso] nm (reposo) rest; (alivio) relief; (pausa) break; (DEPORTE) interval, half time

descapotable [deskapo'taβle] nm (tb: coche ~) convertible

descarado, -a [deska'raðo, a] adj shameless; (insolente) cheeky

descarga [des'karɣa] nf (ARQ, ELEC, MIL) discharge; (NAUT) unloading
❑ **descargar** [deskar'ɣar] vt to unload; (golpe) to let fly; **descargarse** vr to unburden o.s.; **descargarse algo de Internet** to download sth from the Internet

descaro [des'karo] nm nerve

descarriar [deska'rrjar] vt (descaminar) to misdirect; (fig) to lead astray; **descarriarse** vr (perderse) to lose one's way; (separarse) to stray; (pervertirse) to err, go astray

descarrilamiento [deskarrila'mjento] nm (de tren) derailment

descarrilar [deskarri'lar] vi to be derailed

descartar [deskar'tar] vt (rechazar) to reject; (eliminar) to rule out; **descartarse** vr (NAIPES) to discard; **descartarse de** to shirk

descendencia [desθen'denθja] nf (origen) origin, descent; (hijos) offspring

descender [desθen'der] vt (bajar: escalera) to go down ♦ vi to descend; (temperatura, nivel) to fall, drop; ~ **de** to be descended from

descendiente [desθen'djente] nmf descendant

descenso [des'θenso] nm descent; (de temperatura) drop

descifrar [desθi'frar] vt to decipher; (mensaje) to decode

descolgar [deskol'ɣar] vt (bajar) to take down; (teléfono) to pick up; **descolgarse** vr to let o.s. down

descolorido, -a [deskolo'riðo, a] adj faded; (pálido) pale

descompasado, -a [deskompa'saðo, a] adj (sin proporción) out of all proportion; (excesivo) excessive

descomponer [deskompo'ner] vt (desordenar) to disarrange, disturb; (TEC) to put out of order; (dividir) to break down (into parts); (fig) to provoke; **descomponerse** vr (corromperse) to rot, decompose; (LAm TEC) to break down

descomposición [deskomposi'θjon] nf (de un objeto) breakdown; (de fruta etc) decomposition
▶ **descomposición de vientre** (ESP) stomach upset, diarrhoea

descompostura [deskompos'tura] nf (MÉX: avería) breakdown, fault; (LAm: diarrea) diarrhoea

descompuesto, -a [deskom'pwesto, a] adj (corrompido) decomposed; (roto) broken

desconcertado, -a [deskonθer'taðo, a] adj disconcerted, bewildered

desconcertar [deskonθer'tar] vt (confundir) to baffle; (incomodar) to upset, put out; **desconcertarse** vr (turbarse) to be upset

desconchado, -a [deskon'tʃaðo, a] adj (pintura) peeling

desconcierto etc [deskon'θjerto] vb ver **desconcertar** ♦ nm (gen) disorder; (desorientación) uncertainty; (inquietud) uneasiness

desconectar [deskonek'tar] vt to disconnect

desconfianza [deskon'fjanθa] nf distrust

desconfiar [deskon'fjar] vi to be distrustful; ~ **de** to distrust, suspect

descongelar [deskonxe'lar] vt to defrost; (COM, POL) to unfreeze

descongestionar [deskonxestjo'nar] vt (cabeza, tráfico) to clear

desconocer [deskono'θer] vt (ignorar) not to know, to be ignorant of

desconocido, -a [deskono'θiðo, a] adj unknown ♦ nm/f stranger

desconocimiento [deskonoθi'mjento] nm falta de conocimientos, ignorance

desconsiderado, -a [deskonsiðe'raðo, a] adj inconsiderate; (insensible) thoughtless

desconsolar [deskonso'lar] vt to distress

desconsuelo etc [deskon'swelo] vb ver **desconsolar** ♦ nm (tristeza) distress; (desesperación) despair

descontado, -a [deskon'taðo, a] adj: **dar por ~ (que)** to take (it) for granted (that)

descontar [deskon'tar] vt (deducir) to take away, deduct; (rebajar) to discount

descontento, -a [deskon'tento, a] adj dissatisfied ♦ nm dissatisfaction, discontent

descorchar [deskor'tʃar] vt to uncork

descorrer [desko'rrer] vt (cortinas, cerrojo) to draw back

descortés [deskor'tes] *adj* (*mal educado*) discourteous; (*grosero*) rude

descoser [desko'ser] *vt* to unstitch; **descoserse** *vr* to come apart (at the seams)

descosido, -a [desko'siðo, a] *adj* (*COSTURA*) unstitched

descreído, -a [deskre'iðo, a] *adj* (*incrédulo*) incredulous; (*falto de fe*) unbelieving

descremado, -a [deskre'maðo, a] *adj* skimmed

describir [deskri'βir] *vt* to describe ◻ **descripción** [deskrip'θjon] *nf* description

descrito [des'krito] *pp de* **describir**

descuartizar [deskwarti'θar] *vt* (*animal*) to cut up

descubierto, -a [desku'βjerto, a] *pp de* **descubrir** ♦ *adj* uncovered, bare; (*persona*) bareheaded ♦ *nm* (*bancario*) overdraft; **al ~** in the open

descubrimiento [deskuβri'mjento] *nm* (*hallazgo*) discovery; (*revelación*) revelation

descubrir [desku'βrir] *vt* to discover, find; (*inaugurar*) to unveil; (*vislumbrar*) to detect; (*revelar*) to reveal, show; (*destapar*) to uncover; **descubrirse** *vr* to reveal o.s.; (*quitarse sombrero*) to take off one's hat; (*confesar*) to confess

descuento *etc* [des'kwento] *vb ver* **descontar** ♦ *nm* discount

descuidado, -a [deskwi'ðaðo, a] *adj* (*sin cuidado*) careless; (*desordenado*) untidy; (*olvidadizo*) forgetful; (*olvidado*) neglected; (*desprevenido*) unprepared

descuidar [deskwi'ðar] *vt* (*dejar*) to neglect; (*olvidar*) to overlook; **descuidarse** *vr* (*distraerse*) to be careless; (*abandonarse*) to let o.s. go; (*desprevenirse*) to drop one's guard; **¡descuida!** don't worry! ◻ **descuido** *nm* (*dejadez*) carelessness; (*olvido*) negligence

desde [des'de]

['desðe] *prep*

1 (*lugar*) from; **desde Burgos hasta mi casa hay 30 km** it's 30 km from Burgos to my house

2 (*posición*): **hablaba desde el balcón** she was speaking from the balcony

3 (*tiempo: + adv, n*): **desde ahora** from now on; **desde la boda** since the wedding; **desde niño** since I *etc* was a child; **desde 3 años atrás** since 3 years ago

4 (*tiempo: + vb, fecha*) since; for; **nos conocemos desde 1992/desde hace 20 años** we've known each other since 1992/for 20 years; **no le veo desde 1997/desde hace 5 años** I haven't seen him since 1997/for 5 years

5 (*gama*): **desde los más lujosos hasta los más económicos** from the most luxurious to the most reasonably priced

6: **desde luego (que no)** of course (not)

♦ *conj*: **desde que: desde que recuerdo** for as long as I can remember; **desde que llegó no ha salido** he hasn't been out since he arrived

desdén [des'ðen] *nm* scorn

desdeñar [desðe'ɲar] *vt* (*despreciar*) to scorn

desdicha [des'ðitʃa] *nf* (*desgracia*) misfortune; (*infelicidad*) unhappiness ◻ **desdichado, -a** *adj* (*sin suerte*) unlucky; (*infeliz*) unhappy

desear [dese'ar] *vt* to want, desire, wish for

desechar [dese'tʃar] *vt* (*basura*) to throw out o away; (*ideas*) to reject, discard □ **desechos** *nmpl* rubbish *sg*, waste *sg*

desembalar [desemba'lar] *vt* to unpack

desembarazar [desembara'θar] *vt* (*desocupar*) to clear; (*desenredar*) to free; **desembarazarse** *vr*: **desembarazarse de** to free o.s. of, get rid of

desembarcar [desembar'kar] *vt* (*mercancías etc*) to unload ♦ *vi* to disembark

desembocadura [desemboka'ðura] *nf* (*de río*) mouth; (*de calle*) opening

desembocar [desembo'kar] *vi* (*río*) to flow into; (*fig*) to result in

desembolso [desem'bolso] *nm* payment

desembrollar [desembro'ʎar] *vt* (*madeja*) to unravel; (*asunto*, *malentendido*) to sort out

desemejanza [deseme'xanθa] *nf* dissimilarity

desempaquetar [desempake'tar] *vt* (*regalo*) to unwrap; (*mercancía*) to unpack

desempate [desem'pate] *nm* (*FÚTBOL*) replay, play-off; (*TENIS*) tie-break(er)

desempeñar [desempe'ɲar] *vt* (*cargo*) to hold; (*papel*) to perform; (*lo empeñado*) to redeem; **~ un papel** (*fig*) to play a role)

desempleado, -a [desemple'aðo, a] *nm/f* unemployed person □ **desempleo** *nm* unemployment

desencadenar [desenkaðe'nar] *vt* to unchain; (*ira*) to unleash; **desencadenarse** *vr* to break loose; (*tormenta*) to burst; (*guerra*) to break out

desencajar [desenka'xar] *vt* (*hueso*) to dislocate; (*mecanismo*, *pieza*) to disconnect, disengage

desencanto [desen'kanto] *nm* disillusionment

desenchufar [desentʃu'far] *vt* to unplug

desenfadado, -a [desenfa'ðaðo, a] *adj* (*desenvuelto*) uninhibited; (*descarado*) forward □ **desenfado** *nm* (*libertad*) freedom; (*comportamiento*) free and easy manner; (*descaro*) forwardness

desenfocado, -a [desenfo'kaðo, a] *adj* (*FOTO*) out of focus

desenfreno [desen'freno] *nm* wildness; (*de las pasiones*) lack of self-control

desenganchar [desengan'tʃar] *vt* (*gen*) to unhook; (*FERRO*) to uncouple

desengañar [desenga'ɲar] *vt* to disillusion; **desengañarse** *vr* to become disillusioned □ **desengaño** *nm* disillusionment; (*decepción*) disappointment

desenlace [desen'laθe] *nm* outcome

desenmascarar [desenmaska'rar] *vt* to unmask

desenredar [desenre'ðar] *vt* (*pelo*) to untangle; (*problema*) to sort out

desenroscar [desenros'kar] *vt* to unscrew

desentenderse [desenten'derse] *vr*: **~ de** to pretend not to know about; (*apartarse*) to have nothing to do with

desenterrar [desente'rrar] *vt* to exhume; (*tesoro*, *fig*) to unearth, dig up

desentonar [desento'nar] *vi* (*MÚS*) to sing o play out of tune; (*color*) to clash

desentrañar [desentra'ɲar] *vt* (*misterio*) to unravel

desenvoltura [desenβol'tura] *nf* ease

desenvolver [desenβol'βer] *vt* (*paquete*) to unwrap; (*fig*) to develop; **desenvolverse** *vr* (*desarrollarse*) to unfold, develop; (*arreglárselas*) to cope

deseo [de'seo] *nm* desire, wish □ **deseoso, -a** *adj*: **estar deseoso de** to be anxious to

desequilibrado, -a [deseki'liβraðo, a] *adj* unbalanced

desertar [deser'tar] *vi* to desert

desértico, -a [de'sertiko, a] *adj* desert *cpd*

desesperación [desespera'θjon] *nf* (*impaciencia*) desperation, despair; (*irritación*) fury

desesperar [desespe'rar] *vt* to drive to despair; (*exasperar*) to drive to distraction ♦ *vi*: **~ de** to despair of; **desesperarse** *vr* to despair, lose hope

desestabilizar [desestaβili'θar] *vt* to destabilize

desestimar [desesti'mar] *vt* (*menospreciar*) to have a low opinion of; (*rechazar*) to reject

desfachatez [desfatʃa'teθ] *nf* (*insolencia*) impudence; (*descaro*) rudeness

desfalco [des'falko] *nm* embezzlement

desfallecer [desfaʎe'θer] *vi* (*perder las fuerzas*) to become weak; (*desvanecerse*) to faint

desfasado, -a [desfa'saðo, a] *adj* (*anticuado*) old-fashioned ♦ **desfase** *nm* (*diferencia*) gap

desfavorable [desfaβo'raβle] *adj* unfavourable

desfigurar [desfiɣu'rar] *vt* (*cara*) to disfigure; (*cuerpo*) to deform

desfiladero [desfila'ðero] *nm* gorge

desfilar [desfi'lar] *vi* to parade ❏ **desfile** *nm* procession ▸ **desfile de modelos** fashion show

desgana [des'ɣana] *nf* (*falta de apetito*) loss of appetite; (*apatía*) unwillingness ❏ **desganado, -a** *adj*: **estar desganado** (*sin apetito*) to have no appetite; (*sin entusiasmo*) to have lost interest

desgarrar [desɣa'rrar] *vt* to tear (up); (*fig*) to shatter ❏ **desgarro** *nm* (*en tela*) tear; (*aflicción*) grief

desgastar [desɣas'tar] *vt* (*deteriorar*) to wear away o down; (*estropear*) to spoil;

desgastarse *vr* to get worn out ❏ **desgaste** *nm* wear (and tear)

desglosar [desɣlo'sar] *vt* (*factura*) to break down

desgracia [des'ɣraθja] *nf* misfortune; (*accidente*) accident; (*vergüenza*) disgrace; (*contratiempo*) setback; **por ~** unfortunately ❏ **desgraciado, -a** [desɣra'θjaðo, a] *adj* (*sin suerte*) unlucky, unfortunate; (*miserable*) wretched; (*infeliz*) miserable

desgravar [desɣra'βar] *vt* (*impuestos*) to reduce the tax o duty on

desguace (*ESP*) [des'ɣwaθe] *nm* junkyard

deshabitado, -a [desaβi'taðo, a] *adj* uninhabited

deshacer [desa'θer] *vt* (*casa*) to break up; (*TEC*) to take apart; (*enemigo*) to defeat; (*diluir*) to melt; (*contrato*) to break; (*intriga*) to solve; **deshacerse** *vr* (*disolverse*) to melt; (*despedazarse*) to come apart o undone; **deshacerse de** to get rid of; **deshacerse en lágrimas** to burst into tears

deshecho, -a [des'etʃo, a] *adj* undone; (*roto*) smashed; (*persona*): **estar ~ to be shattered**

desheredar [desere'ðar] *vt* to disinherit

deshidratar [desiðra'tar] *vt* to dehydrate

deshielo [des'jelo] *nm* thaw

deshonesto, -a [deso'nesto, a] *adj* indecent

deshonra [des'onra] *nf* (*deshonor*) dishonour; (*vergüenza*) shame

deshora [des'ora]: **a ~** *adv* at the wrong time

deshuesadero (*MÉX*) *nm* junkyard

deshuesar [deswe'sar] *vt* (*carne*) to bone; (*fruta*) to stone

desierto, -a [de'sjerto, a] *adj* (*casa, calle, negocio*) deserted ♦ *nm* desert

designar [desiɣ'nar] *vt* (*nombrar*) to designate; (*indicar*) to fix

desigual [desi'ɣwal] *adj* (*terreno*) uneven; (*lucha etc*) unequal

desilusión [desilu'sjon] *nf* disillusionment; (*decepción*) disappointment ❑ **desilusionar** *vt* to disillusion; to disappoint; **desilusionarse** *vr* to become disillusioned

desinfectar [desinfek'tar] *vt* to disinfect

desinflar [desin'flar] *vt* to deflate

desintegración [desinteɣra'θjon] *nf* disintegration

desinterés [desinte'res] *nm* (*desgana*) lack of interest; (*altruismo*) unselfishness

desintoxicarse [desintoksi'karse] *vr* (*drogadicto*) to undergo detoxification

desistir [desis'tir] *vi* (*renunciar*) to stop, desist

desleal [desle'al] *adj* (*infiel*) disloyal; (*COM: competencia*) unfair ❑ **deslealtad** *nf* disloyalty

desligar [desli'ɣar] *vt* (*desatar*) to untie, undo; (*separar*) to separate; **desligarse** *vr* (*de un compromiso*) to extricate o.s.

desliz [des'liθ] *nm* (*fig*) lapse ❑ **deslizar** *vt* to slip, slide

deslumbrar [deslum'brar] *vt* to dazzle

desmadrarse [desma'ðrarse] (*fam*) *vr* (*descontrolarse*) to run wild; (*divertirse*) to let one's hair down ❑ **desmadre** (*fam*) *nm* (*desorganización*) chaos; (*jaleo*) commotion

desmán [des'man] *nm* (*exceso*) outrage; (*abuso de poder*) abuse

desmantelar [desmante'lar] *vt* (*deshacer*) to dismantle; (*casa*) to strip

desmaquillador [desmakiʎa'ðor] *nm* make-up remover

desmayar [desma'jar] *vi* to lose heart; **desmayarse** *vr* (*MED*) to faint ❑ **desmayo** *nm* (*MED: acto*) faint; (*: estado*) unconsciousness

desmemoriado, -a [desmemo'rjaðo, a] *adj* forgetful

desmentir [desmen'tir] *vt* (*contradecir*) to contradict; (*refutar*) to deny

desmenuzar [desmenu'θar] *vt* (*deshacer*) to crumble; (*carne*) to chop; (*examinar*) to examine closely

desmesurado, -a [desmesu'raðo, a] *adj* disproportionate

desmontable [desmon'taβle] *adj* (*que se quita: pieza*) detachable; (*plegable*) collapsible, folding

desmontar [desmon'tar] *vt* (*deshacer*) to dismantle; (*tierra*) to level ♦ *vi* to dismount

desmoralizar [desmorali'θar] *vt* to demoralize

desmoronar [desmoro'nar] *vt* to wear away, erode; **desmoronarse** *vr* (*edificio, dique*) to collapse; (*economía*) to decline

desnatado, -a [desna'taðo, a] *adj* skimmed

desnivel [desni'βel] *nm* (*de terreno*) unevenness

desnudar [desnu'ðar] *vt* (*desvestir*) to undress; (*despojar*) to strip; **desnudarse** *vr* (*desvestirse*) to get undressed ❑ **desnudo, -a** *adj* naked ♦ *nm* nude; (*desposeído*) to be devoid o bereft of

desnutrición [desnutri'θjon] *nf* malnutrition ❑ **desnutrido, -a** *adj* undernourished

desobedecer [desoβeðe'θer] *vt*, *vi* to disobey ❑ **desobediencia** *nf* disobedience

desocupado, -a [desoku'paðo, a] *adj* at leisure; (*desempleado*) unemployed; (*deshabitado*) empty, vacant

desodorante [desoðo'rante] *nm* deodorant

desolación [desola'θjon] *nf* (*de lugar*) desolation; (*fig*) grief

desolar [deso'lar] *vt* to ruin, lay waste

desorbitado, -a [desorβi'taðo, a] *adj* (*excesivo: ambición*) boundless; (*deseos*) excessive; (*: precio*) exorbitant

desorden [desˈorðen] *nm* confusion; (*politico*) disorder, unrest

desorganización [desorɣaniθaˈθjon] *nf* (*de persona*) disorganization; (*en empresa, oficina*) disorder, chaos

desorientar [desorjenˈtar] *vt* (*extraviar*) to mislead; (*confundir, desconcertar*) to confuse; **desorientarse** *vr* (*perderse*) to lose one's way

despabilado, -a [despaβiˈlaðo, a] *adj* (*despierto*) wide-awake; (*fig*) alert, sharp

despabilar [despaβiˈlar] *vt* (*despertar*) to wake up; (*fig*: *despertar*) to liven up; (*trabajo*) to get through quickly

despachar [despaˈtʃar] *vt* (*negocio*) to do, complete; (*enviar*) to send, dispatch; (*vender*) to sell, deal in; (*billete*) to issue; (*mandar ir*) to send away

despacho [desˈpatʃo] *nm* (*oficina*) office; (*de paquetes*) dispatch; (*venta*) sale; (*comunicación*) message

despacio [desˈpaθjo] *adv* slowly

desparpajo [despaˈrpaxo] *nm* self-confidence; (*pey*) nerve

desparramar [desparraˈmar] *vt* (*esparcir*) to scatter; (*líquido*) to spill

despecho [desˈpetʃo] *nm* spite

despectivo, -a [despekˈtiβo, a] *adj* (*despreciativo*) derogatory; (*LING*) pejorative

despedida [despeˈðiða] *nf* (*adiós*) farewell; (*de obrero*) sacking

despedir [despeˈðir] *vt* (*visita*) to see off, show out; (*empleado*) to dismiss; (*inquilino*) to evict; (*objeto*) to hurl; (*olor etc*) to give out o off; **despedirse** *vr*: **despedirse de** to say goodbye to

despegar [despeˈɣar] *vt* to unstick ♦ *vi* (*avión*) to take off; **despegarse** *vr* to come loose, come unstuck
❑ **despego** *nm* detachment

despegue *etc* [desˈpeɣe] *vb ver* **despegar** ♦ *nm* takeoff

despeinado, -a [despeiˈnaðo, a] *adj* dishevelled, unkempt

despejado, -a [despeˈxaðo, a] *adj* (*lugar*) clear, free; (*cielo*) clear; (*persona*) wide-awake, bright

despejar [despeˈxar] *vt* (*gen*) to clear; (*misterio*) to clear up ♦ *vi* (*el tiempo*) to clear; **despejarse** *vr* (*tiempo, cielo*) to clear (up); (*misterio*) to become clearer; (*cabeza*) to clear

despensa [desˈpensa] *nf* larder

despeñarse [despeˈɲarse] *vr* to hurl o.s. down; (*coche*) to tumble over

desperdicio [desperˈðiθjo] *nm* (*despilfarro*) squandering; **desperdicios** *nmpl* (*basura*) rubbish *sg* (*BRIT*), garbage *sg* (*US*); (*residuos*) waste *sg*

desperezarse [despereˈθarse] *vr* to stretch

desperfecto [desperˈfekto] *nm* (*deterioro*) slight damage; (*defecto*) flaw, imperfection

despertador [despertaˈðor] *nm* alarm clock

despertar [desperˈtar] *nm* awakening ♦ *vt* (*persona*) to wake up; (*recuerdos*) to revive; (*sentimiento*) to arouse ♦ *vi* to awaken, wake up; **despertarse** *vr* to awaken, wake up

despido *etc* [desˈpiðo] *vb ver* **despedir** ♦ *nm* dismissal, sacking

despierto, -a *etc* [desˈpjerto, a] *vb ver* **despertar** ♦ *adj* awake; (*fig*) sharp, alert

despilfarro [despilˈfarro] *nm* (*derroche*) squandering; (*lujo desmedido*) extravagance

despistar [despisˈtar] *vt* to throw off the track o scent; (*confundir*) to mislead, confuse; **despistarse** *vr* to take the wrong road; (*confundirse*) to become confused

despiste [desˈpiste] *nm* absent-mindedness; **un ~** a mistake o slip

desplazamiento [desplaθaˈmjento] *nm* displacement

desplazar [despla'θar] vt to move; (NÁUT) to displace; (INFORM) to scroll; (fig) to oust; **desplazarse** vr (persona) to travel

desplegar [desple'ɣar] vt (tela, papel) to unfold, open out; (bandera) to unfurl □ **despliegue** etc [des'pleɣe] vb ver **desplegar** ♦ nm display

desplomarse [desplo'marse] vr (edificio, gobierno, persona) to collapse

desplumar [desplu'mar] vt (ave) to pluck; (fam: estafar) to fleece

despoblado, -a [despo'βlaðo, a] adj (sin habitantes) uninhabited

despojar [despo'xar] vt (alguien: de sus bienes) to divest of, deprive of; (casa) to strip, leave bare; (alguien: de su cargo) to strip of

despojo [des'poxo] nm (acto) plundering; (objetos) plunder, loot; **despojos** nmpl (de ave, res) offal

desposado, -a [despo'saðo, a] adj, nm/f newly-wed

despreciar [despre'θjar] vt (desdeñar) to despise, scorn; (afrentar) to slight □ **desprecio** nm scorn, contempt; slight

desprender [despren'der] vt (broche) to unfasten; (olor) to give off; **desprenderse** vr (botón: caerse) to fall off; (broche) to come unfastened; (olor, perfume) to give off; **desprenderse de algo que ...** to draw from sth that ...

desprendimiento [desprendi'mjento] nm (gen) loosening; (generosidad) disinterestedness; (de tierra, rocas) landslide ▶ **desprendimiento de retina** detachment of the retina

despreocupado, -a [despreoku'paðo, a] adj (sin preocupación) unworried, nonchalant; (negligente) careless

despreocuparse [despreoku'parse] vr not to worry; **~ de** to have no interest in

desprestigiar [despresti'xjar] vt (criticar) to run down; (desacreditar) to discredit

desprevenido, -a [despreβe'niðo, a] adj (no preparado) unprepared, unready

desproporcionado, -a [desproporθjo'naðo, a] adj disproportionate, out of proportion

desprovisto, -a [despro'βisto, a] adj: **~ de** devoid of

después [des'pwes] adv afterwards, later; (próximo paso) next; **~ de comer** after lunch; **un año ~** a year later; **~ se debatió el tema** next the matter was discussed; **~ de corregido el texto** after the text had been corrected; **~ de todo** after all

desquiciado, -a [deski'θjaðo, a] adj deranged

destacar [desta'kar] vt to emphasize, point up; (MIL) to detach, detail ♦ vi (resaltar) to stand out; (persona) to be outstanding o exceptional; **destacarse** vr to stand out; to be outstanding o exceptional

destajo [des'taxo] nm: **trabajar a ~** to do piecework

destapar [desta'par] vt (botella) to open; (cacerola) to take the lid off; (descubrir) to uncover; **destaparse** vr (revelarse) to reveal one's true character

destartalado, -a [destarta'laðo, a] adj (desordenado) untidy; (ruinoso) tumbledown

destello [des'teʎo] nm (de estrella) twinkle; (de faro) signal light

destemplado, -a [destem'plaðo, a] adj (MUS) out of tune; (voz) harsh; (MED) out of sorts; (tiempo) unpleasant, nasty

desteñir [deste'ɲir] vt to fade ♦ vi to fade; **desteñirse** vr to fade; **esta tela no destiñe** this fabric will not run

desternillarse [desterni'ʎarse] vr: **~ de risa** to split one's sides laughing

desterrar [deste'rrar] vt (exiliar) to exile; (fig) to banish, dismiss

destiempo [des'tjempo]: **a ~** adv out of turn

destierro etc [des'tjerro] vb ver **desterrar ♦ nm** exile

destilar [desti'lar] vt to distil
❏ **destilería** nf distillery

destinar [desti'nar] vt (funcionario) to appoint, assign; (fondos): **~ (a)** to set aside (for)

destinatario, -a [destina'tarjo, a] nm/f addressee

destino [des'tino] nm (suerte) destiny; (de avión, viajero) destination; **con ~ a Londres** (barco) (bound) for London; (avión, carta) to London

destituir [destitu'ir] vt to dismiss

destornillador [destorniʎa'ðor] nm screwdriver

destornillar [destorni'ʎar] vt (tornillo) to unscrew; **destornillarse** vr to unscrew

destreza [des'treθa] nf (habilidad) skill; (maña) dexterity

destrozar [destro'θar] vt (romper) to smash, break (up); (estropear) to ruin; (nervios) to shatter

destrozo [des'troθo] nm (acción) destruction; (desastre) smashing; **destrozos** nmpl (pedazos) pieces; (daños) havoc sg

destrucción [destruk'θjon] nf destruction

destruir [destru'ir] vt to destroy

desuso [des'uso] nm disuse; **caer en ~** to become obsolete

desvalijar [desvali'xar] vt (persona) to rob; (casa, tienda) to burgle; (coche) to break into

desván [des'ßan] nm attic

desvanecer [desßane'θer] vt (disipar) to dispel; (borrar) to blur; **desvanecerse** vr (humo etc) to vanish, disappear; (color) to fade; (recuerdo,

sonido) to fade away; (MED) to pass out; (duda) to be dispelled

desvariar [desßa'rjar] vi (enfermo) to be delirious

desvelar [desße'lar] vt to keep awake; **desvelarse** vr (no poder dormir) to stay awake; (preocuparse) to be vigilant o watchful

desventaja [desßen'taxa] nf disadvantage

desvergonzado, -a [desßeryon'θaðo, a] adj shameless

desvestir [desßes'tir] vt to undress; **desvestirse** vr to undress

desviación [desßja'θjon] nf deviation; (AUTO) diversion, detour

desviar [des'ßjar] vt to turn aside; (río) to alter the course of; (navío) to divert, re-route; (conversación) to sidetrack; **desviarse** vr (apartarse del camino) to turn aside; (: barco) to go off course

desvío etc [des'ßio] vb ver **desviar ♦ nm** (desviación) detour, diversion; (fig) indifference

desvivirse [desßi'ßirse] vr: **~ por** (anhelar) to long for, crave for; (hacer lo posible por) to do one's utmost for

detallar [deta'ʎar] vt to detail

detalle [de'taʎe] nm detail; (gesto) gesture, token; **al ~** in detail; (COM) retail

detallista [deta'ʎista] nmf (COM) retailer

detective [detek'tiße] nmf detective ▶ **detective privado** private detective

detener [dete'ner] vt (gen) to stop; (JUR) to arrest; (objeto) to keep; **detenerse** vr to stop; (demorarse): **detenerse en** to delay over, linger over

detenidamente [deteniða'mente] adv (minuciosamente) carefully; (extensamente) at great length

detenido, -a [dete'niðo, a] adj (arrestado) under arrest ♦ nm/f person under arrest, prisoner

detenimiento [deteni'mjento] *nm*: **con ~** thoroughly; (*observar, considerar*) carefully

detergente [deter'xente] *nm* detergent

deteriorar [deterjo'rar] *vt* to spoil, damage; **deteriorarse** *vr* to deteriorate □ **deterioro** *nm* deterioration

determinación [determina'θjon] *nf* (*empeño*) determination; (*decisión*) decision □ **determinado, -a** *adj* specific

determinar [determi'nar] *vt* (*plazo*) to fix; (*precio*) to settle; **determinarse** *vr* to decide

detestar [detes'tar] *vt* to detest

detractor, a [detrak'tor, a] *nm/f* slanderer, libeller

detrás [de'tras] *adv* (*tb*: **por ~**) behind; (*atrás*) at the back; **~ de** behind

detrimento [detri'mento] *nm*: **en ~ de** to the detriment of

deuda [ˈdeuða] *nf* debt ▶ **deuda exterior/pública** foreign/national debt

devaluación [deβalwa'θjon] *nf* devaluation

devastar [deβas'tar] *vt* (*destruir*) to devastate

deveras [de'veras] (*MÉX*) *nf inv*: **un amigo de (a) ~** a true o real friend

devoción [deβo'θjon] *nf* devotion

devolución [deβolu'θjon] *nf* (*reenvío*) return, sending back; (*reembolso*) repayment; (*JUR*) devolution

devolver [deβol'βer] *vt* to return; (*lo extraviado, lo prestado*) to give back; (*carta al correo*) to send back; (*COM*) to repay, refund ♦ *vi* (*vomitar*) to be sick

devorar [deβo'rar] *vt* to devour

devoto, -a [de'βoto, a] *adj* devout ♦ *nm/f* admirer

devuelto [de'βwelto] *pp de* **devolver**

devuelva *etc* [de'βwelβa] *vb ver* **devolver**

di *etc* [di] *vb ver* **dar**; **decir**

día [ˈdia] *nm* day; **¿qué ~ es?** what's the date?; **estar/poner al ~** to be/keep up to date; **el ~ de hoy/de mañana** today/tomorrow; **al ~ siguiente** (on) the following day; **vivir al ~** to live from hand to mouth; **de ~** by day, in daylight; **en pleno ~** in full daylight ▶ **Día de la Independencia** Independence Day ▶ **Día de los Muertos** (*MÉX*) All Souls' Day ▶ **Día de Reyes** Epiphany ▶ **día feriado** (*LAm*) holiday ▶ **día festivo** (*ESP*) holiday ▶ **día lectivo** teaching day ▶ **día libre** day off

diabetes [dja'βetes] *nf* diabetes

diablo [ˈdjaβlo] *nm* devil □ **diablura** *nf* prank

diadema [dja'ðema] *nf* tiara

diafragma [dja'fraɣma] *nm* diaphragm

diagnóstico [djaɣ'nostiko] *nm* diagnosis

diagonal [djaɣo'nal] *adj* diagonal

diagrama [dja'ɣrama] *nm* diagram

dial [djal] *nm* dial

dialecto [dja'lekto] *nm* dialect

dialogar [djalo'ɣar] *vi*: **~ con** (*POL*) to hold talks with

diálogo [ˈdjaloɣo] *nm* dialogue

diamante [dja'mante] *nm* diamond

diana [ˈdjana] *nf* (*MIL*) reveille; (*de blanco*) centre, bull's-eye

diapositiva [djaposi'tiβa] *nf* (*FOTO*) slide, transparency

diario, -a [ˈdjarjo, a] *adj* daily ♦ *nm* newspaper; **a ~** daily; **de ~** everyday

diarrea [dja'rrea] *nf* diarrhoea

dibujar [diβu'xar] *vt* to draw, sketch □ **dibujo** *nm* drawing ▶ **dibujos animados** cartoons

diccionario [dikθjo'narjo] *nm* dictionary

dice *etc vb ver* **decir**

dicho, -a [ˈditʃo, a] *pp de* **decir** ♦ *adj*: **en dichos países** in the aforementioned countries ♦ *nm* saying

dichoso, -a [diˈtʃoso, a] *adj* happy

diciembre [diˈθjembre] *nm* December

dictado [dikˈtaðo] *nm* dictation

dictador [diktaˈðor] *nm* dictator ◻ **dictadura** *nf* dictatorship

dictar [dikˈtar] *vt* (*carta*) to dictate; (*JUR*: *sentencia*) to pronounce; (*decreto*) to issue; (*LAm*: *clase*) to give

didáctico, -a [diˈðaktiko, a] *adj* educational

diecinueve [djeθiˈnweβe] *num* nineteen

dieciocho [djeˈθjotʃo] *num* eighteen

dieciséis [djeˈθjseis] *num* sixteen

diecisiete [djeˈθjsjete] *num* seventeen

diente [ˈdjente] *nm* (*ANAT*, *TEC*) tooth; (*ZOOL*) fang; (: *de elefante*) tusk; (*de ajo*) clove

diera *etc* [ˈdjera] *vb ver* **dar**

diesel [ˈdisel] *adj*: **motor ~** diesel engine

diestro, -a [ˈdjestro, a] *adj* (*derecho*) right; (*hábil*) skilful

dieta [ˈdjeta] *nf* diet; **estar a ~** to be on a diet

diez [djeθ] *num* ten

diferencia [difeˈrenθja] *nf* difference; **a ~ de** unlike ◻ **diferenciar** *vt* to differentiate between ♦ *vi* to differ; **diferenciarse** *vr* to differ, be different; (*distinguirse*) to distinguish o.s.

diferente [difeˈrente] *adj* different

diferido [difeˈriðo] *nm*: **en ~** (*TV etc*) recorded

difícil [diˈfiθil] *adj* difficult

dificultad [difikulˈtað] *nf* difficulty; (*problema*) trouble

dificultar [difikulˈtar] *vt* (*complicar*) to complicate, make difficult; (*estorbar*) to obstruct

difundir [difunˈdir] *vt* (*calor*, *luz*) to diffuse; (*RADIO*, *TV*) to broadcast; **~ una**

noticia to spread a piece of news; **difundirse** *vr* to spread (out)

difunto, -a [diˈfunto, a] *adj* dead, deceased ♦ *nm/f* deceased (person)

difusión [difuˈsjon] *nf* (*RADIO*, *TV*) broadcasting

diga *etc* [ˈdiɣa] *vb ver* **decir**

digerir [dixeˈrir] *vt* to digest; (*fig*) to absorb ◻ **digestión** *nf* digestion ◻ **digestivo, -a** *adj* digestive

digital [dixiˈtal] *adj* digital

dignarse [diɣˈnarse] *vr* to deign to

dignidad [diɣniˈðað] *nf* dignity

digno, -a [ˈdiɣno, a] *adj* worthy

digo *etc* [ˈdiɣo] *vb ver* **decir**

dije *etc* [ˈdixe] *vb ver* **decir**

dilatar [dilaˈtar] *vt* (*cuerpo*) to dilate; (*prolongar*) to prolong

dilema [diˈlema] *nm* dilemma

diluir [diluˈir] *vt* to dilute

diluvio [diˈluβjo] *nm* deluge, flood

dimensión [dimenˈsjon] *nf* dimension

diminuto, -a [dimiˈnuto, a] *adj* tiny, diminutive

dimitir [dimiˈtir] *vi* to resign

dimos [ˈdimos] *vb ver* **dar**

Dinamarca [dinaˈmarka] *nf* Denmark

dinámico, -a [diˈnamiko, a] *adj* dynamic

dinamita [dinaˈmita] *nf* dynamite

dínamo [ˈdinamo] *nm* dynamo

dineral [dineˈral] *nm* large sum of money, fortune

dinero [diˈnero] *nm* money ▸ **dinero en efectivo** o **metálico** cash ▸ **dinero suelto** (loose) change

dio [djo] *vb ver* **dar**

dios [djos] *nm* god; **¡D~ mío!** (oh,) my God!; **¡por D~!** for heaven's sake! ◻ **diosa** *nf* goddess

diploma [diˈploma] *nm* diploma

diplomacia [diploˈmaθja] *nf* diplomacy; (*fig*) tact

diplomado, -a [diploˈmaðo, a] *adj* qualified

diplomático, -a [diplo'matiko, a] *adj* diplomatic ♦ *nm/f* diplomat

diputación [diputa'θjon] *nf* (*tb:* ~ **provincial**) ≈ county council

diputado, -a [dipu'taðo, a] *nm/f* delegate; (*POL*) ≈ member of parliament (*BRIT*), ≈ representative (*US*)

dique ['dike] *nm* dyke

diré *etc* [di're] *vb ver* **decir**

dirección [direk'θjon] *nf* direction; (*señas*) address; (*AUTO*) steering; (*gerencia*) management; (*POL*) leadership ► **dirección única/prohibida** one-way street/no entry

direccional [direkθjo'nal] *nf* (*AUTO*) indicator

directa [di'rekta] *nf* (*AUTO*) top gear

directiva [direk'tiβa] *nf* (*tb:* **junta ~**) board of directors

directo, -a [di'rekto, a] *adj* direct; (*RADIO, TV*) live; **transmitir en ~ to** broadcast live

director, a [direk'tor, a] *adj* leading ♦ *nm/f* director; (*ESCOL*) head(teacher) (*BRIT*), principal (*US*); (*gerente*) manager/ess; (*PRENSA*) editor ► **director de cine** film director ► **director general** managing director

directorio [direk'torjo] *nm* (*MÉX*) (*telefónico*) phone book

dirigente [diri'xente] *nmf* (*POL*) leader

dirigir [diri'xir] *vt* to direct; (*carta*) to address; (*obra de teatro, film*) to direct; (*MÚS*) to conduct; (*negocio*) to manage; **dirigirse** *vr*: **dirigirse a** to go towards, make one's way towards; (*hablar con*) to speak to

dirija *etc* [di'rixa] *vb ver* **dirigir**

disciplina [disθi'plina] *nf* discipline

discípulo, -a [dis'θipulo, a] *nm/f* disciple

Discman® *nm* Discman®

disco ['disko] *nm* disc; (*DEPORTE*) discus; (*TEL*) dial; (*AUTO: semáforo*) light; (*MÚS*) record ► **disco compacto/de larga duración** compact disc/long-playing record ► **disco de freno** brake disc ► **disco flexible/duro o rígido** (*INFORM*) floppy/hard disk

disconforme [diskon'forme] *adj* differing; **estar ~ (con)** to be in disagreement (with)

discordia [dis'korðja] *nf* discord

discoteca [disko'teka] *nf* disco(theque)

discreción [diskre'θjon] *nf* discretion; (*reserva*) prudence; **comer a ~** to eat as much as one wishes

discreto, -a [dis'kreto, a] *adj* discreet

discriminación [diskrimina'θjon] *nf* discrimination

disculpa [dis'kulpa] *nf* excuse; (*pedir perdón*) apology; **pedir disculpas a/por** to apologize to/for □ **disculpar** *vt* to excuse, pardon; **disculparse** *vr* to excuse o.s.; to apologize

discurso [dis'kurso] *nm* speech

discusión [disku'sjon] *nf* (*diálogo*) discussion; (*riña*) argument

discutir [disku'tir] *vt* (*debatir*) to discuss; (*pelear*) to argue about; (*contradecir*) to argue against ♦ *vi* (*debatir*) to discuss; (*pelearse*) to argue

disecar [dise'kar] *vt* (*conservar: animal*) to stuff; (*: planta*) to dry

diseñar [dise'ɲar] *vt, vi* to design

diseño [di'seɲo] *nm* design

disfraz [dis'fraθ] *nm* (*máscara*) disguise; (*excusa*) pretext □ **disfrazar** *vt* to disguise; **disfrazarse** *vr*: **disfrazarse de** to disguise o.s. as

disfrutar [disfru'tar] *vt* to enjoy ♦ *vi* to enjoy o.s.; **~ de** to enjoy, possess

disgustar [disɣus'tar] *vt* (*no gustar*) to displease; (*contrariar, enojar*) to annoy, upset; **disgustarse** *vr* (*enfadarse*) to get upset; (*dos personas*) to fall out

⚠ No confundir **disgustar** con la palabra inglesa *disgust*.

disgusto [dis'ɣusto] nm (contrariedad) annoyance; (tristeza) grief; (riña) quarrel

disimular [disimu'lar] vt (ocultar) to hide, conceal ♦ vi to dissemble

dislocarse [dislo'karse] vr (articulación) to sprain, dislocate

disminución [disminu'θjon] nf decrease, reduction

disminuido, -a [disminu'iðo, a] nm/f: ~ **mental/físico** mentally/physically handicapped person

disminuir [disminu'ir] vt to decrease, diminish

disolver [disol'βer] vt (gen) to dissolve; **disolverse** vr to dissolve; (COM) to go into liquidation

dispar [dis'par] adj different

disparar [dispa'rar] vt, vi to shoot, fire

disparate [dispa'rate] nm (tontería) foolish remark; (error) blunder; **decir disparates** to talk nonsense

disparo [dis'paro] nm shot

dispersar [disper'sar] vt to disperse; **dispersarse** vr to scatter

disponer [dispo'ner] vt (arreglar) to arrange; (ordenar) to put in order; (preparar) to prepare, get ready ♦ vi: ~ **de** to have, own; **disponerse** vr: **disponerse a** o **para hacer** to prepare to do

disponible [dispo'niβle] adj available

disposición [disposi'θjon] nf arrangement, disposition; (voluntad) willingness; (INFORM) layout; **a su ~ at your service**

dispositivo [disposi'tiβo] nm device, mechanism

dispuesto, -a [dis'pwesto, a] pp de **disponer** ♦ adj (arreglado) arranged; (preparado) disposed

disputar [dispu'tar] vt (carrera) to compete in

disquete [dis'kete] nm floppy disk, diskette

distancia [dis'tanθja] nf distance

distanciar [distan'θjar] vt to space out; **distanciarse** vr to become estranged ♦ **distante** [dis'tante] adj distant

diste [diste] vb ver **dar**

disteis [disteis] vb ver **dar**

distinción [distin'θjon] nf distinction; (elegancia) elegance; (honor) honour

distinguido, -a [distin'ɡiðo, a] adj distinguished

distinguir [distin'ɡir] vt to distinguish; (escoger) to single out; **distinguirse** vr to be distinguished

distintivo [distin'tiβo] nm badge; (fig) characteristic

distinto, -a [dis'tinto, a] adj different; (claro) clear

distracción [distrak'θjon] nf distraction; (pasatiempo) hobby, pastime; (olvido) absent-mindedness, distraction

distraer [distra'er] vt (atención) to distract; (divertir) to amuse; (fondos) to embezzle; **distraerse** vr (entretenerse) to amuse o.s.; (perder la concentración) to allow one's attention to wander

distraído, -a [distra'iðo, a] adj (gen) absent-minded; (entretenido) amusing

distribuidor, a [distriβui'ðor, a] nm/f distributor ❑ **distribuidora** nf (COM) dealer, agent; (CINE) distributor

distribuir [distriβu'ir] vt to distribute

distrito [dis'trito] nm (sector, territorio) region; (barrio) district ▶ **Distrito Federal** (MÉX) Federal District ▶ **distrito postal** postal district

disturbio [dis'turβjo] nm disturbance; (desorden) riot

disuadir [diswa'ðir] vt to dissuade

disuelto [di'swelto] pp de **disolver**

DIU nm abr (= dispositivo intrauterino) IUD

diurno, -a [di'jurno, a] adj day cpd

divagar [diβa'ɣar] vi (desviarse) to digress

diván [di'βan] *nm* divan

diversidad [diβersi'ðað] *nf* diversity, variety

diversión [diβer'sjon] *nf* (*gen*) entertainment; (*actividad*) hobby, pastime

diverso, -a [di'βerso, a] *adj* diverse; **diversos libros** several books
❏ **diversos** *nmpl* sundries

divertido, -a [diβer'tiðo, a] *adj* (*chiste*) amusing; (*fiesta etc*) enjoyable

divertir [diβer'tir] *vt* (*entretener, recrear*) to amuse; **divertirse** *vr* (*pasarlo bien*) to have a good time; (*distraerse*) to amuse o.s.

dividendos [diβi'ðendos] *nmpl* (*COM*) dividends

dividir [diβi'ðir] *vt* (*gen*) to divide; (*distribuir*) to distribute, share out

divierta *etc* [di'βjerta] *vb ver* **divertir**

divino, -a [di'βino, a] *adj* divine

divirtiendo *etc* [diβir'tjendo] *vb ver* **divertir**

divisa [di'βisa] *nf* (*emblema*) emblem, badge; **divisas** *nfpl* foreign exchange *sg*

divisar [diβi'sar] *vt* to make out, distinguish

división [diβi'sjon] *nf* (*gen*) division; (*de partido*) split; (*de país*) partition

divorciar [diβor'θjar] *vt* to divorce; **divorciarse** *vr* to get divorced
❏ **divorcio** *nm* divorce

divulgar [diβul'ɣar] *vt* (*ideas*) to spread; (*secreto*) to divulge

DNI (*ESP*) *nm abr* (= *Documento Nacional de Identidad*) national identity card

---

DNI

The **Documento Nacional de Identidad** is a Spanish ID card which must be carried at all times and produced on request for the police. It contains the holder's photo, fingerprints and personal details. It is also known as the **DNI** or "carnet de identidad".

Dña. *abr* (= *doña*) Mrs

do [do] *nm* (*MÚS*) do, C

dobladillo [doβla'ðiλo] *nm* (*de vestido*) hem; (*de pantalón: vuelta*) turn-up (*BRIT*), cuff (*US*)

doblar [do'βlar] *vt* to double; (*papel*) to fold; (*caño*) to bend; (*la esquina*) to turn, go round; (*film*) to dub ♦ *vi* to turn; (*campana*) to toll; **doblarse** *vr* (*plegarse*) to fold (up), crease; (*encorvarse*) to bend; **~ a la derecha/izquierda** to turn right/left

doble [do'βle] *adj* double; (*de dos aspectos*) dual; (*fig*) two-faced ♦ *nm* double ♦ *nmf* (*TEATRO*) double, stand-in; **dobles** *nmpl* (*DEPORTE*) doubles *sg*; **con ~ sentido** with a double meaning

doce [do'θe] *num* twelve ♦ **docena** *nf* dozen

docente [do'θente] *adj*: **centro/personal ~** teaching establishment/staff

dócil [do'θil] *adj* (*pasivo*) docile; (*obediente*) obedient

doctor, a [dok'tor, a] *nm/f* doctor

doctorado [dokto'raðo] *nm* doctorate

doctrina [dok'trina] *nf* doctrine, teaching

documentación [dokumenta'θjon] *nf* documentation, papers *pl*

documental [dokumen'tal] *adj, nm* documentary

documento [doku'mento] *nm* (*certificado*) document ▶ **documento adjunto** (*INFORM*) attachment ♦ **documento nacional de identidad** identity card

dólar [do'lar] *nm* dollar

doler [do'ler] *vt, vi* to hurt; (*fig*) to grieve; **dolerse** *vr* (*de su situación*) to grieve, feel sorry; (*de las desgracias ajenas*) to sympathize; **me duele el brazo** my arm hurts

dolor [do'lor] *nm* pain; (*fig*) grief, sorrow ▶ **dolor de cabeza/**

estómago/muelas headache/
stomachache/toothache
domar [do'mar] *vt* to tame
domesticar [domesti'kar] *vt* = **domar**
doméstico, -a [do'mestiko, a] *adj*
(*vida, servicio*) home; (*tareas*)
household; (*animal*) tame, pet
domicilio [domi'θiljo] *nm* home;
servicio a ~ home delivery service; **sin
~ fijo** of no fixed abode ▶ **domicilio
particular** private residence
dominante [domi'nante] *adj*
dominant; (*persona*) domineering
dominar [domi'nar] *vt* (*gen*) to
dominate; (*idiomas*) to be fluent in ♦ *vi*
to dominate, prevail
domingo [do'miŋgo] *nm* Sunday
▶ **Domingo de Ramos/
Resurrección** Palm/Easter Sunday
dominio [do'minjo] *nm* (*tierras*)
domain; (*autoridad*) power, authority;
(*de las pasiones*) grip, hold; (*de idiomas*)
command
don [don] *nm* (*talento*) gift; **~ Juan
Gómez** Mr Juan Gómez, Juan Gómez
Esq (BRIT)

DON/DOÑA

The term **don/doña** often abbreviated
to **D./Dña** is placed before the first
name as a mark of respect to an older
or more senior person - eg Don Diego,
Doña Inés. Although becoming rarer
in Spain it is still used with names and
surnames on official documents and
formal correspondence - eg "Sr. D.
Pedro Rodríguez Hernández", "Sra.
Dña. Inés Rodríguez Hernández".

dona (MÉX) *nf* doughnut, donut (US)
donar [do'nar] *vt* to donate
donativo [dona'tiβo] *nm* donation
donde ['donde] *adv* where ♦ *prep*: **el
coche está allí ~ el farol** the car is over
there by the lamppost *o* where the
lamppost is; **en ~** where, in which

dónde ['donde] *adv* where?; **¿a ~ vas?**
where are you going (to)?; **¿de ~
vienes?** where have you been?; **¿por
~?** where?, whereabouts?
dondequiera [donde'kjera] *adv*
anywhere; **por ~** everywhere, all over
the place ♦ *conj*: **~ que** wherever
donut® (ESP) *nm* doughnut, donut (US)
doña ['doɲa] *nf*: **~ Alicia** Alicia; **~
Victoria Benito** Mrs Victoria Benito
dorado, -a [do'raðo, a] *adj* (*color*)
golden; (TEC) gilt
dormir [dor'mir] *vt*: **~ la siesta** to have
an afternoon nap ♦ *vi* to sleep;
dormirse *vr* to fall asleep
dormitorio [dormi'torjo] *nm*
bedroom
dorsal [dor'sal] *nm* (DEPORTE) number
dorso ['dorso] *nm* (*de mano*) back; (*de
hoja*) other side
dos [dos] *num* two
dosis ['dosis] *nf inv* dose, dosage
dotado, -a [do'taðo, a] *adj* gifted; **~ de**
endowed with
dotar [do'tar] *vt* to endow ❏ **dote** *nf*
dowry; **dotes** *nfpl* (*talentos*) gifts
doy [doj] *vb ver* **dar**
drama ['drama] *nm* drama
❏ **dramaturgo** [drama'turɣo] *nm*
dramatist, playwright
drástico, -a ['drastiko, a] *adj* drastic
drenaje [dre'naxe] *nm* drainage
droga ['droɣa] *nf* drug ❏ **drogadicto,
-a** [droɣa'ðikto, a] *nm/f* drug addict
droguería [droɣe'ria] *nf* hardware
shop (BRIT) *o* store (US)
ducha ['dutʃa] *nf* (*baño*) shower; (MED)
douche; **ducharse** *vr* to take a shower
duda ['duða] *nf* doubt; **no cabe ~** there
is no doubt about it ❏ **dudar** *vt, vi* to
doubt ❏ **dudoso, -a** [du'ðoso, a] *adj*
(*incierto*) hesitant; (*sospechoso*)
doubtful
duela *etc vb ver* **doler**

duelo ['dwelo] vb ver **doler** ♦ nm (combate) duel; (luto) mourning

duende ['dwende] nm imp, goblin

dueño, -a ['dweɲo, a] nm/f (propietario) owner; (de pensión, taberna) landlord/lady; (empresario) employer

duermo etc vb ver **dormir**

dulce ['dulθe] adj sweet ♦ adv gently, softly ♦ nm sweet

dulcería (LAm) nf confectioner's (shop)

dulzura [dul'θura] nf sweetness; (ternura) gentleness

dúo ['duo] nm duet

duplicar [dupli'kar] vt (hacer el doble de) to duplicate

duque ['duke] nm duke ❏ **duquesa** nf duchess

duración [dura'θjon] nf (de película, disco etc) length; (de pila etc) life; (curso: de acontecimientos etc) duration

duradero, -a [dura'ðero, a] adj (tela etc) hard-wearing; (fe, paz) lasting

durante [du'rante] prep during

durar [du'rar] vi to last; (recuerdo) to remain

durazno [du'raθno] (LAm) nm (fruta) peach; (árbol) peach tree

durex ['dureks] (MÉX, ARG) nm (tira adhesiva) Sellotape® (BRIT), Scotch tape® (US)

dureza [du'reθa] nf (calidad) hardness

duro, -a ['duro, a] adj hard; (carácter) tough ♦ adv hard ♦ nm (moneda) five-peseta coin o piece

DVD nm abr (= disco de vídeo digital) DVD

E, e

E abr (= este) E

e [e] conj and

ébano ['eβano] nm ebony

ebrio, -a ['eβrjo, a] adj drunk

ebullición [eβuʎi'θjon] nf boiling

echar [e'tʃar] vt to throw; (agua, vino) to pour (out); (empleado: despedir) to fire, sack; (hojas) to sprout; (cartas) to post; (humo) to emit, give out ♦ vi: ~ a correr to run off; **echarse** vr te lie down; ~ **llave a** to lock (up); ~ **abajo** (gobierno) to overthrow; (edificio) to demolish; ~ **mano a** to lay hands on; ~ **una mano a algn** (ayudar) to give sb a hand; ~ **de menos** to miss; **echarse atrás** (fig) to back out

eclesiástico, -a [ekle'sjastiko, a] adj ecclesiastical

eco ['eko] nm echo; **tener** ~ to catch on

ecología [ekolo'yia] nf ecology ❏ **ecológico, -a** adj (producto, método) environmentally-friendly; (agricultura) organic ❏ **ecologista** adj ecological, environmental ♦ nmf environmentalist

economía [ekono'mia] nf (sistema) economy; (carrera) economics

económico, -a [eko'nomiko, a] adj (barato) cheap, economical; (ahorrativo) thrifty; (COM: año etc) financial; (: situación) economic

economista [ekono'mista] nmf economist

Ecuador [ekwa'ðor] nm Ecuador ❏ **ecuador** nm (GEO) equator

ecuatoriano, -a [ekwato'rjano, a] adj, nm/f Ecuadorian

ecuestre [e'kwestre] adj equestrian

edad [e'ðað] nf age; **¿qué ~ tienes?** how old are you?; **tiene ocho años de** ~ he's eight (years old); **de ~ mediana/avanzada** middle-aged/advanced in years; **la E~ Media** the Middle Ages

edición [eði'θjon] nf (acto) publication; (ejemplar) edition

edificar [eðifi'kar] vt, vi to build

edificio [eði'fiθjo] nm building; (fig) edifice, structure

Edimburgo [eðim'burɣo] nm Edinburgh

editar [eði'tar] vt (*publicar*) to publish; (*preparar textos*) to edit.

editor, a [eði'tor, a] nm/f (*que publica*) publisher; (*redactor*) editor ♦ *adj* publishing *cpd* ❑ **editorial** *adj* editorial ♦ *nm* leading article, editorial; **casa editorial** publisher

edredón [eðre'ðon] nm duvet

educación [eðuka'θjon] nf education; (*crianza*) upbringing; (*modales*) (good) manners ef

educado, -a [eðu'kaðo, a] *adj*: **bien/mal ~** well/badly behaved

educar [eðu'kar] vt to educate; (*criar*) to bring up; (*voz*) to train

EE. UU. nmpl abr (= *Estados Unidos*) US(A)

efectivamente [efecti'ßa'mente] *adv* (*como respuesta*) exactly, precisely; (*verdaderamente*) really; (*de hecho*) in fact

efectivo, -a [efek'tiβo, a] *adj* effective; (*real*) actual, real ♦ *nm*: **pagar en ~** to pay (in) cash; **hacer ~ un cheque** to cash a cheque

efecto [e'fekto] nm effect, result; **efectos** nmpl (*efectos personales*) effects; (*bienes*) goods; (*COM*) assets; **en ~** in fact; (*respuesta*) exactly, indeed ▸ **efecto invernadero** greenhouse effect ▸ **efectos especiales/secundarios/sonoros** special/side/sound effects

efectuar [efek'twar] vt to carry out; (*viaje*) to make

eficacia [efi'kaθja] nf (*de persona*) efficiency; (*de medicamento etc*) effectiveness

eficaz [efi'kaθ] *adj* (*persona*) efficient; (*acción*) effective

eficiente [efi'θjente] *adj* efficient

egipcio, -a [e'xipθjo, a] *adj, nm/f* Egyptian

Egipto [e'xipto] nm Egypt

egoísmo [eɣo'ismo] nm egoism

egoísta [eɣo'ista] *adj* egoistical, selfish ♦ *nmf* egoist

Eire ['eire] nm Eire

ej. abr (= *ejemplo*) eg

eje ['exe] nm (*GEO, MAT*) axis; (*de rueda*) axle; (*de máquina*) shaft, spindle

ejecución [exeku'θjon] nf execution; (*cumplimiento*) fulfilment; (*MÚS*) performance; (*JUR: embargo de deudor*) attachment

ejecutar [exeku'tar] vt to execute, carry out; (*matar*) to execute; (*cumplir*) to fulfil; (*MÚS*) to perform; (*JUR: embargar*) to attach, distrain (on)

ejecutivo, -a [exeku'tiβo, a] *adj* executive; **el (poder) ~** the executive (power)

ejemplar [exem'plar] *adj* exemplary ♦ *nm* example; (*ZOOL*) specimen; (*de libro*) copy; (*de periódico*) number, issue

ejemplo [e'xemplo] nm example; **por ~** for example

ejercer [exer'θer] vt to exercise; (*influencia*) to exert; (*un oficio*) to practise ♦ *vi* (*practicar*) to practise; **~ (de)** to practise (as)

ejercicio [exer'θiθjo] nm exercise; (*período*) tenure; **hacer ~** to take exercise ▸ **ejercicio comercial** financial year

ejército [e'xerθito] nm army; **entrar en el ~** to join the army, join up ▸ **ejército del aire/de tierra** Air Force/Army

ejote [e'xote] nm (*MÉX*) green bean

PALABRA CLAVE

el [el] (*f* **la**, *pl* **los, las**, *neutro* **lo**) *art def*
1 *la*; **el libro/la mesa/los estudiantes** the book/table/students
2 (*con n abstracto: no se traduce*): **el amor/la juventud** love/youth
3 (*posesión: se traduce a menudo por adj posesivo*): **romperse el brazo** to

break one's arm; **levantó la mano** he put his hand up; **se puso el sombrero** she put her hat on

4 (valor descriptivo): **tener la boca grande/los ojos azules** to have a big mouth/blue eyes

5 (con días) on; **me iré el viernes** I'll leave on Friday; **los domingos suelo ir a nadar** on Sundays I generally go swimming

6 (lo +adj): **lo difícil/caro** what is difficult/expensive; (cuán): **no se da cuenta de lo pesado que es** he doesn't realise how boring he is

♦ pron relativo

1 (indef): **el que: el (los) que quiera(n) que se vaya(n)** anyone who wants to can leave; **llévese el que más le guste** take the one you like best

2 (def): **el que: el que compré ayer** the one I bought yesterday; **los que se van** those who leave

3 (lo que): **lo que pienso yo/más me gusta** what I think/like most

♦ conj: **el que: el que lo diga** the fact that he says so; **el que sea tan vago me molesta** his being so lazy bothers me

♦ excl: **¡el susto que me diste!** what a fright you gave me!

♦ pron personal

1 (persona: m) him; (: f) her; (: pl)

them; **lo/las veo** I can see him/them

2 (animal, cosa: sg) it; (: pl) them; **lo** (o **la**) **veo** I can see it; **los** (o **las**) **veo** I can see them

3 (como sustituto de frase): **lo: no lo sabía** I didn't know; **ya lo entiendo** I understand now

él [el] pron (persona) he; (cosa) it; (después de prep: persona) him; (: cosa) it; **de él** his

elaborar [elaβo'rar] vt (producto) to make, manufacture; (preparar) to prepare; (madera, metal etc) to work; (proyecto etc) to work on o out

elástico, -a [e'lastiko, a] adj elastic; (flexible) flexible ♦ nm elastic; (un elástico) elastic band

elección [elek'θjon] nf election; (selección) choice, selection
▸ **elecciones generales** general election sg

electorado [elekto'raðo] nm electorate, voters pl

electricidad [elektriθi'ðað] nf electricity

electricista [elektri'θista] nmf electrician

eléctrico, -a [e'lektriko, a] adj electric

electro... [elektro] prefijo electro...
❏ **electrocardiograma** nm electrocardiogram o ❏ **electrocutar** to electrocute o ❏ **electrodo** nm electrode o ❏ **electrodomésticos** nmpl (electrical) household appliances

electrónica [elek'tronika] nf electronics sg

electrónico, -a [elek'troniko, a] adj electronic

elefante [ele'fante] nm elephant

elegancia [ele'yanθja] nf elegance, grace; (estilo) stylishness

elegante [ele'yante] adj elegant, graceful; (estiloso) stylish, fashionable

elegir [ele'xir] vt (escoger) to choose, select; (optar) to opt for; (presidente) to elect

elemental [elemen'tal] adj (claro, obvio) elementary; (fundamental) elemental, fundamental

elemento [ele'mento] nm element; (fig) ingredient; **elementos** nmpl elements, rudiments

elepé [ele'pe] (pl ~s) nm L.P.

elevación [eleβa'θjon] nf elevation; (acto) raising, lifting; (de precios) rise; (GEO etc) height, altitude

elevar [ele'βar] vt to raise, lift (up); (precio) to put up; **elevarse** vr (edificio) to rise; (precios) to go up

eligiendo etc [eli'xjendo] vb ver **elegir**

elija etc [e'lixa] vb ver **elegir**

eliminar [elimi'nar] vt to eliminate, remove

eliminatoria [elimina'torja] nf heat, preliminary (round)

élite ['elite] nf elite

ella ['eʎa] pron (persona) she; (cosa) it; (después de prep: persona) her; (: cosa) it; **de ~** hers

ellas ['eʎas] pron (personas y cosas) they; (después de prep) them; **de ~** theirs

ello ['eʎo] pron it

ellos ['eʎos] pron they; (después de prep) them; **de ~** theirs

elogiar [elo'xjar] vt to praise ❏ **elogio** nm praise

elote [e'lote] (MÉX) nm corn on the cob

eludir [elu'ðir] vt to avoid

email [i'mel] nm email; (dirección) email address; **mandar un ~ a algn** to email sb, send sb an email

embajada [emba'xaða] nf embassy

embajador, a [embaxa'ðor, a] nm/f ambassador/ambassadress

embalar [emba'lar] vt to parcel, wrap (up); **embalarse** vr to go fast

embalse [em'balse] nm (presa) dam; (lago) reservoir

embarazada [embara'θaða] adj pregnant ♦ nf pregnant woman

⚠ No confundir **embarazada** con la palabra inglesa *embarrassed*.

embarazo [emba'raθo] nm (de mujer) pregnancy; (impedimento) obstacle, obstruction; (timidez) embarrassment ❏ **embarazoso, -a** adj awkward, embarrassing

embarcación [embarka'θjon] nf (barco) boat, craft; (acto) embarkation, boarding

embarcadero [embarka'ðero] nm pier, landing stage

embarcar [embar'kar] vt (cargamento) to ship, stow; (persona) to embark, put on board; **embarcarse** vr to embark, go on board

embargar [embar'ɣar] vt (JUR) to seize, impound

embargo [em'barɣo] nm (JUR) seizure; (COM, POL) embargo

embargue etc [em'barɣe] vb ver **embargar**

embarque etc [em'barke] vb ver **embarcar** ♦ nm shipment, loading

embellecer [embeʎe'θer] vt to embellish, beautify

embestida [embes'tiða] nf attack, onslaught; (carga) charge

embestir [embes'tir] vt to attack, assault, to charge, attack ♦ vi to attack

emblema [em'blema] nm emblem

embobado, -a [embo'βaðo, a] adj (atontado) stunned, bewildered

embolia [em'bolja] nf (MED) clot

émbolo ['embolo] nm (AUTO) piston

emborrachar [emborra'tʃar] vt to make drunk, intoxicate; **emborracharse** vr to get drunk

emboscada [embos'kaða] nf ambush

embotar [embo'tar] vt to blunt, dull

embotellamiento [emboteʎa'mjento] nm (AUTO) traffic jam

embotellar [embote'ʎar] vt to bottle

embrague [em'braɣe] nm (tb: **pedal de ~**) clutch

embrión [em'brjon] nm embryo

embrollo [em'broʎo] nm (enredo) muddle, confusion; (aprieto) fix, jam

embrujado, -a [embru'xaðo, a] adj bewitched; **casa embrujada** haunted house

embrutecer [embrute'θer] vt (atontar) to stupefy

embudo [em'buðo] nm funnel

embuste [em'buste] nm (mentira) lie □ **embustero, -a** adj lying, deceitful ♦ nm/f (mentiroso) liar

embutido [embu'tiðo] nm (CULIN) sausage; (TEC) inlay

emergencia [emer'xenθja] nf emergency; (surgimiento) emergence

emerger [emer'xer] vi to emerge, appear

emigración [emiɣra'θjon] nf emigration; (de pájaros) migration

emigrar [emi'ɣrar] vi (personas) to emigrate; (pájaros) to migrate

eminente [emi'nente] adj eminent, distinguished; (elevado) high

emisión [emi'sjon] nf (acto) emission; (COM etc) issue; (RADIO, TV: acto) broadcasting; (: programa) broadcast, programme (BRIT), program (US)

emisora [emi'sora] nf radio o broadcasting station

emitir [emi'tir] vt (olor etc) to emit, give off; (moneda etc) to issue; (opinión) to express; (RADIO) to broadcast

emoción [emo'θjon] nf emotion; (excitación) excitement; (sentimiento) feeling

emocionante [emoθjo'nante] adj (excitante) exciting, thrilling

emocionar [emoθjo'nar] vt (excitar) to excite, thrill; (conmover) to move, touch; (impresionar) to impress

emoticón, emoticono nm smiley

emotivo, -a [emo'tiβo, a] adj emotional

empacho [em'patʃo] nm (MED) indigestion; (fig) embarrassment

empalagoso, -a [empala'ɣoso, a] adj cloying; (fig) tiresome

empalmar [empal'mar] vt to join, connect ♦ vi (dos caminos) to meet, join □ **empalme** nm joint, connection; junction; (de trenes) connection

empanada [empa'naða] nf pie, pasty

empañarse [empa'ɲarse] vr (cristales etc) to steam up

empapar [empa'par] vt (mojar) to soak, saturate; (absorber) to soak up, absorb; **empaparse** vr: **empaparse de** to soak up

empapelar [empape'lar] vt (paredes) to paper

empaquetar [empake'tar] vt to pack, parcel up

empastar [empas'tar] vt (embadurnar) to paste; (diente) to fill

empaste [em'paste] nm (de diente) filling

empatar [empa'tar] vi to draw, tie; **empataron a dos** they drew two-all □ **empate** nm draw, tie

empecé etc [empe'θe] vb ver **empezar**

empedernido, -a [empeðer'niðo, a] adj hard, heartless; (fumador) inveterate

empeine [em'peine] nm (de pie, zapato) instep

empeñado, -a [empe'ɲaðo, a] adj (persona) determined; (objeto) pawned

empeñar [empe'ɲar] vt (objeto) to pawn, pledge; (persona) to compel; **empeñarse** vr (obligarse) to bind o.s., get into debt; **empeñarse en** to be set on, be determined to

empeño [em'peɲo] nm (determinación, insistencia) determination, insistence; **casa de empeños** pawnshop

empeorar [empeo'rar] vt to make worse, worsen ♦ vi to get worse, deteriorate

empezar [empe'θar] vt, vi to begin, start

empiece etc [em'pjeθe] vb ver **empezar**

empiezo etc [em'pjeθo] vb ver **empezar**

emplasto [em'plasto] nm (MED) plaster

emplazar [empla'θar] vt (ubicar) to site, place, locate; (JUR) to summons; (convocar) to summon

empleado, -a [emple'aðo, a] nm/f (gen) employee; (de banco etc) clerk

emplear [emple'ar] vt (usar) to use, employ; (dar trabajo a) to employ; **emplearse** vr (conseguir trabajo) to be employed; (ocuparse) to occupy os.

empleo [em'pleo] nm (puesto) job; (puestos: colectivamente) employment; (uso) use, employment

empollar [empo'ʎar] (ESP: fam) vt, vi to swot (up) ❏ **empollón, -ona** (ESP: fam) nm/f swot

emporio [em'porjo] (LAm) nm (gran almacén) department store

empotrado, -a [empo'traðo, a] adj (armario etc) built-in

emprender [empren'der] vt (empezar) to begin, embark on; (acometer) to tackle, take on ❏ **empresa** [em'presa] nf (de espíritu etc) enterprise; (COM) company, firm ❏ **empresariales** nfpl business studies ❏ **empresario, -a** nm/f (COM) businessman(-woman)

empujar [empu'xar] vt to push, shove

empujón [empu'xon] nm push, shove

empuñar [empu'ɲar] vt (asir) to grasp, take (firm) hold of

en

PALABRA CLAVE

[en] prep

1 (posición) in; (: sobre) on; **está en el cajón** it's in the drawer; **en Argentina/La Paz** in Argentina/La Paz; **en la oficina/el colegio** at the office/school; **está en el suelo/quinto piso** it's on the floor/the fifth floor

2 (dirección) into; **entró en el aula** she went into the classroom; **meter algo en el bolso** to put sth into one's bag

3 (tiempo) in; on; **en 1605/3 semanas/invierno** in 1605/3 weeks/winter; **en (el mes de) enero** in (the month of) January; **en aquella ocasión/época** on that occasion/at that time

4 (precio) for; **lo vendió en 20 dólares** he sold it for 20 dollars

5 (diferencia) by; **reducir/aumentar en una tercera parte/un 20 por ciento** to reduce/increase by a third/20 per cent

6 (manera): **en avión/autobús** by plane/bus; **escrito en inglés** written in English

7 (después de vb que indica gastar etc) on; **han cobrado demasiado en dietas** they've charged too much to expenses; **se le va la mitad del sueldo en comida** he spends half his salary on food

8 (tema, ocupación): **experto en la materia** expert on the subject; **trabaja en la construcción** he works in the building industry

9 (adj + en + infin): **lento en reaccionar** slow to react

enaguas [e'naɣwas] nfpl petticoat sg, underskirt sg

enajenación [enaxena'θjon] nf (PSICO: tb: ~ **mental**) mental derangement

enamorado, -a [enamo'raðo, a] adj in love ♦ nm/f lover; **estar ~ (de)** to be in love (with)

enamorar [enamoˈrar] vt to win the love of; **enamorarse** vr: **enamorarse de algn** to fall in love with sb

enano, -a [eˈnano, a] adj tiny ♦ nm/f dwarf

encabezamiento [enkaβeθaˈmjento] nm (de carta) heading; (de periódico) headline

encabezar [enkaβeˈθar] vt (movimiento, revolución) to lead, head; (lista) to head, be at the top of; (carta) to put a heading to

encadenar [enkaðeˈnar] vt to chain (together); (poner grilletes a) to shackle

encajar [enkaˈxar] vt (ajustar): ~ (en) to fit (into); (fam: golpe) to take ♦ vi to fit (well); (fig: corresponder a) to match

encaje [enˈkaxe] nm (labor) lace

encallar [enkaˈʎar] vi (NÁUT) to run aground

encaminar [enkamiˈnar] vt to direct, send

encantado, -a [enkanˈtaðo, a] adj (hechizado) bewitched; (muy contento) delighted; **¡~!** how do you do, pleased to meet you

encantador, a [enkantaˈðor, a] adj charming, lovely ♦ nm/f magician, enchanter/enchantress

encantar [enkanˈtar] vt (agradar) to charm, delight; (hechizar) to bewitch, cast a spell on; **me encanta eso** I love that ▢ **encanto** nm (hechizo) spell, charm; (fig) charm, delight

encarcelar [enkarθeˈlar] vt to imprison, jail

encarecer [enkareˈθer] vt to put up the price of; **encarecerse** vr to get dearer

encargado, -a [enkarˈɣaðo, a] adj in charge ♦ nm/f agent, representative; (responsable) person in charge

encargar [enkarˈɣar] vt to entrust; (recomendar) to urge, recommend; **encargarse** vr: **encargarse de** to look after, take charge of; **~ algo a algn** to

put sb in charge of sth; **~ a algn que haga algo** to ask sb to do sth

encargo [enˈkarɣo] nm (tarea) assignment, job; (responsabilidad) responsibility; (COM) order

encariñarse [enkariˈɲarse] vr: **~ con** to grow fond of, get attached to

encarnación [enkarnaˈθjon] nf incarnation, embodiment

encarrilar [enkarriˈlar] vt (tren) to put back on the rails; (fig) to correct, put on the right track

encasillar [enkasiˈʎar] vt (fig) to pigeonhole; (actor) to typecast

encendedor [enθendeˈðor] nm lighter

encender [enθenˈder] vt (con fuego) to light; (luz, radio) to put on, switch on; (avivar: pasión) to inflame; **encenderse** vr to catch fire; (excitarse) to get excited; (de cólera) to flare up; (el rostro) to blush

encendido [enθenˈdiðo] nm (AUTO) ignition

encerado [enθeˈraðo] nm (ESCOL) blackboard

encerrar [enθeˈrrar] vt (confinar) to shut in, shut up; (comprender, incluir) to include, contain

encharcado, -a [entʃarˈkaðo, a] adj (terreno) flooded

encharcarse [entʃarˈkarse] vr to get flooded

enchufado, -a [entʃuˈfaðo, a] (fam) nm/f well-connected person

enchufar [entʃuˈfar] vt (ELEC) to plug in; (TEC) to connect, fit together ▢ **enchufe** nm (ELEC: clavija) plug; (: toma) socket; (de dos tubos) joint, connection; (fam: influencia) contact, connection; (: puesto) cushy job

encía [enˈθia] nf gum

encienda etc [enˈθjenda] vb ver **encender**

encierro etc [enˈθjerro] vb ver **encerrar**

encerrar ♦ nm shutting in, shutting up; (calabozo) prison

encima [en'θima] adv (sobre) above, over; (además) besides; **~ de** (en) on, on top of; (sobre) above, over; (además de) besides, on top of; **por ~ de** over; **¿llevas dinero ~?** have you (got) any money on you?; **se me vino ~** it took me by surprise

encina [en'θina] nf holm oak

encinta [en'θinta] adj pregnant

enclenque [en'klenke] adj weak, sickly

encoger [enko'xer] vt to shrink, contract; **encogerse** vr to shrink, contract; (fig) to cringe; **encogerse de hombros** to shrug one's shoulders

encomendar [enkomen'dar] vt to entrust, commend; **encomendarse** vr: **encomendarse a** to put one's trust in

encomienda etc [enko'mjenda] vb ver **encomendar ♦** nf (encargo) charge, commission; (elogio) tribute ▶ **encomienda postal** (LAm) package

encontrar [enkon'trar] vt (hallar) to find; (inesperadamente) to meet, run into; **encontrarse** vr to meet (each other); (situarse) to be (situated); **encontrarse con** to meet; **encontrarse bien (de salud)** to feel well

encrucijada [enkruθi'xaða] nf crossroads sg

encuadernación [enkwaðerna'θjon] nf binding

encuadrar [enkwa'ðrar] vt (retrato) to frame; (ajustar) to fit, insert; (contener) to contain

encubrir [enku'βrir] vt (ocultar) to hide, conceal; (criminal) to harbour, shelter

encuentro etc [en'kwentro] vb ver **encontrar ♦** nm (de personas) meeting; (AUTO etc) collision, crash; (DEPORTE) match, game; (MIL) encounter

encuerado, -a (MÉX) [enkwe'raðo, a] adj nude, naked

encuesta [en'kwesta] nf inquiry, investigation; (sondeo) (public) opinion poll

encumbrar [enkum'brar] vt (persona) to exalt

endeble [en'deβle] adj (persona) weak; (argumento, excusa, persona) weak

endemoniado, -a [endemo'njaðo, a] adj possessed (of the devil); (travieso) devilish

enderezar [endere'θar] vt (poner derecho) to straighten (out); (: verticalmente) to set upright; (situación) to straighten o sort out; (dirigir) to direct; **enderezarse** vr (persona sentada) to straighten up

endeudarse [endeu'ðarse] vr to get into debt

endiablado, -a [endja'βlaðo, a] adj devilish, diabolical; (travieso) mischievous

endilgar [endil'yar] (fam) vt: **endilgarle algo a algn** to lumber sb with sth

endiñar [endi'ɲar] (ESP: fam) vt (bofetón) to land, belt

endosar [endo'sar] vt (cheque etc) to endorse

endulzar [endul'θar] vt to sweeten; (suavizar) to soften

endurecer [endure'θer] vt to harden; **endurecerse** vr to harden, grow hard

enema [e'nema] nm (MED) enema

enemigo, -a [ene'miyo, a] adj enemy, hostile ♦ nm/f enemy

enemistad [enemis'tað] nf enmity

enemistar [enemis'tar] vt to make enemies of, cause a rift between; **enemistarse** vr to become enemies; (amigos) to fall out

energía [ener'xia] nf (vigor) energy, drive; (empuje) push; (TEC, ELEC) energy, power ▶ **energía eólica** wind power ▶ **energía solar** solar energy o power

enérgico, -a [e'nerxiko, a] adj (gen) energetic; (voz, modales) forceful

energúmeno, -a [ener'yumeno, a] (fam) nm/f (fig) madman(-woman)

enero [e'nero] nm January

enfadado, -a [enfa'ðaðo, a] adj angry, annoyed

enfadar [enfa'ðar] vt to anger, annoy; **enfadarse** vr to get angry o annoyed

enfado [en'faðo] nm (enojo) anger, annoyance; (disgusto) trouble, bother

énfasis ['enfasis] nm emphasis, stress

enfático, -a [en'fatiko, a] adj emphatic

enfermar [enfer'mar] vt to make ill ♦ vi to fall ill, be taken ill

enfermedad [enferme'ðað] nf illness
► **enfermedad venérea** venereal disease

enfermera [enfer'mera] nf nurse

enfermería [enferme'ria] nf infirmary; (de colegio etc) sick bay

enfermero [enfer'mero] nm (male) nurse

enfermizo, -a [enfer'miθo, a] adj (persona) sickly, unhealthy; (fig) unhealthy

enfermo, -a [en'fermo, a] adj ill, sick ♦ nm/f invalid, sick person; (en hospital) patient; **caer** o **ponerse ~** to fall ill

enfocar [enfo'kar] vt (foto etc) to focus; (problema etc) to approach

enfoque etc [en'foke] vb ver **enfocar** ♦ nm focus

enfrentar [enfren'tar] vt (peligro) to face (up to), confront; (oponer) to bring face to face; **enfrentarse** vr (dos personas) to face o confront each other; (DEPORTE: dos equipos) to meet; **enfrentarse a** o **con** to face up to, confront

enfrente [en'frente] adv opposite; **la casa de ~** the house opposite, the house across the street; **~ de** opposite, facing

enfriamiento [enfria'mjento] nm chilling, refrigeration; (MED) cold, chill

enfriar [enfri'ar] vt (alimentos) to cool, chill; (algo caliente) to cool down;

enfriarse vr to cool down; (MED) to catch a chill; (amistad) to cool

enfurecer [enfure'θer] vt to enrage, madden; **enfurecerse** vr to become furious, fly into a rage; (mar) to get rough

enganchar [engan'tʃar] vt to hook; (dos vagones) to hitch up; (TEC) to couple, connect; (MIL) to recruit; **engancharse** vr (MIL) to enlist, join up

enganche [en'gantʃe] nm hook; (ESP TEC) coupling, connection; (acto) hooking (up); (MIL) recruitment, enlistment; (MÉX: depósito) deposit

engañar [enga'ɲar] vt to deceive; (estafar) to cheat, swindle; **engañarse** vr (equivocarse) to be wrong; (disimular la verdad) to deceive o.s.

engaño [en'gaɲo] nm deceit; (estafa) trick, swindle; (error) mistake, misunderstanding; (ilusión) delusion ▶ **engañoso, -a** adj (tramposo) crooked; (mentiroso) dishonest, deceitful; (aspecto) deceptive; (consejo) misleading

engatusar [engatu'sar] (fam) vt to coax

engendro [en'xendro] nm (BIO) foetus; (fig) monstrosity

englobar [englo'βar] vt to include, comprise

engordar [engor'ðar] vt to fatten ♦ vi to get fat, put on weight

engorroso, -a [engo'rroso, a] adj bothersome, trying

engranaje [engra'naxe] nm (AUTO) gear

engrasar [engra'sar] vt (TEC: poner grasa) to grease; (: lubricar) to lubricate, oil; (manchar) to make greasy

engreído, -a [engre'iðo, a] adj vain, conceited

enhebrar [ene'βrar] vt to thread

enhorabuena [enora'βwena] excl: ¡~! congratulations! ♦ nf: **dar la ~ a** to congratulate

enigma [e'niɣma] nm enigma; (problema) puzzle; (misterio) mystery

enjambre [en'xambre] nm swarm

enjaular [enxau'lar] vt to (put in a) cage; (fam) to jail, lock up

enjuagar [enxwa'ɣar] vt (ropa) to rinse (out)

enjuague etc [en'xwaɣe] vb ver **enjuagar ♦** nm (MED) mouthwash; (de ropa) rinse, rinsing

enlace [en'laθe] nm link, connection; (relación) relationship; (tb: ~ **matrimonial**) marriage; (de carretera, trenes) connection ♦ **enlace sindical** shop steward

enlatado, -a [enla'taðo, a] adj (alimentos, productos) tinned, canned

enlazar [enla'θar] vt (unir con lazos) to bind together; (atar) to tie; (conectar) to link, connect; (LAm: caballo) to lasso

enloquecer [enloke'θer] vt to drive mad ♦ vi to go mad

enmarañar [enmara'ɲar] vt (enredar) to tangle (up), entangle; (complicar) to complicate; (confundir) to confuse

enmarcar [enmar'kar] vt (cuadro) to frame

enmascarar [enmaska'rar] vt to mask; **enmascararse** vr to put on a mask

enmendar [enmen'dar] vt to emend, correct; (constitución etc) to amend; (comportamiento) to reform; **enmendarse** vr to reform, mend one's ways ❏ **enmienda** nf correction; amendment; reform

enmudecer [enmuðe'θer] vi (perder el habla) to fall silent; (guardar silencio) to remain silent

ennoblecer [ennoβle'θer] vt to ennoble

enojado, -a [eno'xaðo, a] adj (LAm) angry

enojar [eno'xar] vt (encolerizar) to anger; (disgustar) to annoy, upset; **enojarse** vr to get angry; to get annoyed

enojo [e'noxo] nm (cólera) anger; (irritación) annoyance

enorme [e'norme] adj enormous, huge; (fig) monstrous

enredadera [enreða'ðera] nf (BOT) creeper, climbing plant

enredar [enre'ðar] vt (cables, hilos etc) to tangle (up), entangle; (situación) to complicate, confuse; (meter cizaña) to sow discord among o between; (implicar) to embroil, implicate; **enredarse** vr to get entangled, get tangled (up); (situación) to get complicated; (persona) to get embroiled; (LAm: fam) to meddle

enredo [en'reðo] nm (maraña) tangle; (confusión) mix-up, confusion; (intriga) intrigue

enriquecer [enrike'θer] vt to redden make rich, enrich; **enriquecerse** vr to get rich

enrojecer [enroxe'θer] vt to redden ♦ vi (persona) to blush; **enrojecerse** vr to blush

enrollar [enro'ʎar] vt to roll (up), wind (up)

ensalada [ensa'laða] nf salad ❏ **ensaladilla (rusa)** nf Russian salad

ensanchar [ensan'tʃar] vt (hacer más ancho) to widen; (agrandar) to enlarge, expand; (COSTURA) to let out; **ensancharse** vr to get wider, expand

ensayar [ensa'jar] vt to test, try (out); (TEATRO) to rehearse

ensayo [en'sajo] nm test, trial; (QUÍM) experiment; (TEATRO) rehearsal; (DEPORTE) try; (ESCOL, LITERATURA) essay

enseguida [ense'ɣiða] adv at once, right away

ensenada [ense'naða] nf inlet, cove

enseñanza [ense'nanθa] nf (educación) education; (acción) teaching; (doctrina) teaching, doctrine ▶ **enseñanza (de) primaria/ secundaria** elementary/secondary education

enseñar [ense'ɲar] vt (educar) to teach; (mostrar, señalar) to show

enseres [en'seres] nmpl belongings

ensuciar [ensu'θjar] vt (manchar) to dirty, soil; (fig) to defile; **ensuciarse** vr to get dirty; (bebé) to dirty one's nappy

entablar [enta'βlar] vt (recubrir) to board (up); (AJEDREZ, DAMAS) to set up; (conversación) to strike up; (JUR) to file ♦ vi to draw

ente ['ente] nm (organización) body, organization; (fam: persona) odd character

entender [enten'der] vt (comprender) to understand; (darse cuenta) to realize ♦ vi to understand; (creer) to think, believe; **entenderse** vr (comprenderse) to be understood; (ponerse de acuerdo) to agree, reach an agreement; ~ **de** to know all about; ~ **algo de** to know a little about; ~ **en** to deal with, have to do with; ~ **mal** to misunderstand; **entenderse con algn** (llevarse bien) to get on o along with sb; **entenderse mal** (dos personas) to get on badly

entendido, -a [enten'diðo, a] adj (comprendido) understood; (hábil) skilled; (inteligente) knowledgeable ♦ nm/f (experto) expert ♦ excl agreed! ❏ **entendimiento** nm (comprensión) understanding; (inteligencia) mind, intellect; (juicio) judgement

enterado, -a [ente'raðo, a] adj well-informed; **estar ~ de** to know about, be aware of

enteramente [entera'mente] adv entirely, completely

enterar [ente'rar] vt (informar) to inform, tell; **enterarse** vr to find out, get to know

enterito (RPI) [ente'rito] nm boiler suit (BRIT), overalls (US)

entero, -a [en'tero, a] adj (total) whole, entire; (fig: honesto) honest; (: firme) firm, resolute ♦ nm (COM: punto) point

enterrar [ente'rrar] vt to bury

entidad [enti'ðað] nf (empresa) firm, company; (organismo) body; (sociedad) society; (FILOSOFÍA) entity

entiendo etc vb ver **entender**

entierro [en'tjerro] nm (acción) burial; (funeral) funeral

entonación [entona'θjon] nf (LING) intonation

entonar [ento'nar] vt (canción) to intone; (colores) to tone; (MED) to tone up ♦ vi to be in tune

entonces [en'tonθes] adv then, at that time; **desde ~** since then; **en aquel ~** at that time; (pues) ~ and so

entornar [entor'nar] vt (puerta, ventana) to half-close, leave ajar; (los ojos) to screw up

entorpecer [entorpe'θer] vt (entendimiento) to dull; (impedir) to obstruct, hinder; (: tránsito) to slow down, delay

entrada [en'traða] nf (acción) entry, access; (sitio) entrance, way in; (INFORM) input; (COM) receipts pl, takings pl; (CULIN) starter; (DEPORTE) innings sg; (TEATRO) house, audience; (billete) ticket; **entradas y salidas** (COM) income and expenditure; **de ~** from the outset ▶ **entrada de aire** (TEC) air intake o inlet

entrado, -a [en'traðo, a] adj: ~ **en años** elderly; **una vez ~ el verano** in the summer(time), when summer comes

entramparse [entram'parse] vr to get into debt

entrante [en'trante] adj next, coming; **mes/año** ~ next month/year ❏ **entrantes** nmpl starters

entraña [en'traɲa] nf (fig: centro) heart, core; (raíz) root; **entrañas** nfpl (ANAT) entrails; (fig) heart sg ❏ **entrañable** adj close, intimate ❏ **entrañar** vt to entail

entrar [en'trar] vt (introducir) to bring in; (INFORM) to input o in ♦ vi (meterse) to go in, come in, enter; (comenzar): ~

diciendo to begin by saying; **hacer ~** to show in; **me entró sed/sueño** I started to feel thirsty/sleepy; **no me entra** I can't get the hang of it

entre ['entre] *prep* (*dos*) between; (*más de dos*) among(st)

entreabrir [entrea'βrir] *vt* to half-open, open halfway

entrecejo [entre'θexo] *nm*: **fruncir el ~** to frown

entredicho [entre'ðitʃo] *nm* (*JUR*) injunction; **poner en ~** to cast doubt on; **estar en ~** to be in doubt

entrega [en'treɣa] *nf* (*de mercancías*) delivery; (*de novela etc*) instalment ❏ **entregar** [entre'ɣar] *vt* (*dar*) to hand (over), deliver; **entregarse** *vr* (*rendirse*) to surrender, give in, submit; (*dedicarse*) to devote o.s.

entremeses [entre'meses] *nmpl* hors d'œuvres

entremeter [entreme'ter] *vt* to insert, put in; **entremeterse** *vr* to meddle, interfere ❏ **entremetido, -a** *adj* meddling, interfering

entremezclar [entremeθ'klar] *vt* to intermingle; **entremezclarse** *vr* to intermingle

entrenador, a [entrena'ðor, a] *nm/f* trainer, coach

entrenarse [entre'narse] *vr* to train

entrepierna [entre'pjerna] *nf* crotch

entresuelo [entre'swelo] *nm* mezzanine

entretanto [entre'tanto] *adv* meanwhile, meantime

entretecho (*CS*) [entre'tetʃo] *nm* attic

entretejer [entrete'xer] *vt* to interweave

entretener [entrete'ner] *vt* (*divertir*) to entertain, amuse; (*detener*) to hold up, delay; **entretenerse** *vr* (*divertirse*) to amuse o.s.; (*retrasarse*) to delay, linger ❏ **entretenido, -a** *adj* entertaining, amusing ❏ **entretenimiento** *nm* entertainment, amusement

entrever [entre'βer] *vt* to glimpse, catch a glimpse of

entrevista [entre'βista] *nf* interview ❏ **entrevistar** *vt* to interview; **entrevistarse** *vr* to have an interview

entristecer [entriste'θer] *vt* to sadden, grieve; **entristecerse** *vr* to grow sad

entrometerse [entrome'terse] *vr*: **~ (en)** to interfere (in o with)

entumecer [entume'θer] *vt* to numb, benumb; **entumecerse** *vr* (*por el frío*) to go o become numb

enturbiar [entur'βjar] *vt* (*el agua*) to make cloudy; (*fig*) to confuse; **enturbiarse** *vr* (*oscurecerse*) to become cloudy; (*fig*) to get confused, become obscure

entusiasmar [entusjas'mar] *vt* to excite, fill with enthusiasm; (*gustar mucho*) to delight; **entusiasmarse** *vr*: **entusiasmarse con o por** to get enthusiastic o excited about

entusiasmo [entu'sjasmo] *nm* enthusiasm; (*excitación*) excitement

entusiasta [entu'sjasta] *adj* enthusiastic ♦ *nm/f* enthusiast

enumerar [enume'rar] *vt* to enumerate

envainar [embai'nar] *vt* to sheathe

envalentonar [embalento'nar] *vt* to give courage to; **envalentonarse** *vr* (*pey: jactarse*) to boast, brag

envasar [emba'sar] *vt* (*empaquetar*) to pack, wrap; (*enfrascar*) to bottle; (*enlatar*) to can; (*embolsar*) to pocket

envase [em'base] *nm* (*en paquete*) packing, wrapping; (*en botella*) bottling; (*en lata*) canning; (*recipiente*) container; (*paquete*) package; (*botella*) bottle; (*lata*) tin (*BRIT*)

envejecer [embexe'θer] *vt* to make old, age ♦ *vi* (*volverse viejo*) to grow old; (*parecer viejo*) to age

envenenar [embene'nar] *vt* to poison; (*fig*) to embitter

envergadura [embɛrɣaˈðura] nf (fig) scope, compass

enviar [emˈbjar] vt to send; **~ un mensaje a algn** (por movil) to send sb a text message

enviciarse [embiˈθjarse] vr: **~ (con)** to get addicted (to)

envidia [emˈbiðja] nf envy; **tener ~ a** to envy, be jealous of ❑ **envidiar** vt to envy

envío [emˈbio] nm (acción) sending; (de mercancías) consignment; (de dinero) remittance

enviudar [embjuˈðar] vi to be widowed

envoltura [embolˈtura] nf (cobertura) cover; (embalaje) wrapper, wrapping ❑ **envoltorio** nm package

envolver [embolˈβer] vt to wrap (up); (cubrir) to cover; (enemigo) to surround; (implicar) to involve, implicate

envuelto [emˈbwelto] pp de **envolver**

enyesar [enjeˈsar] vt (pared) to plaster; (MED) to put in plaster

enzarzarse [enθarˈθarse] vr: **~ en** (pelea) to get mixed up in; (disputa) to get involved in

épica [ˈepika] nf epic

epidemia [epiˈðemja] nf epidemic

epilepsia [epiˈlepsja] nf epilepsy

episodio [epiˈsoðjo] nm episode

época [ˈepoka] nf period, time; (HIST) age, epoch; **hacer época** to be epoch-making

equilibrar [ekiliˈβrar] vt to balance ❑ **equilibrio** nm balance, equilibrium; **mantener/perder el equilibrio** to keep/lose one's balance ❑ **equilibrista** nmf (funámbulo) tightrope walker; (acróbata) acrobat

equipaje [ekiˈpaxe] nm luggage; (avíos): **hacer el ~** to pack ▶ **equipaje de mano** hand luggage

equipar [ekiˈpar] vt (proveer) to equip

equipararse [ekipaˈrarse] vr: **~ con** to be on a level with

equipo [eˈkipo] nm (conjunto de cosas) equipment; (DEPORTE) team; (de obreros) shift

equis [ˈekis] nf inv (the letter) X

equitación [ekitaˈθjon] nf horse riding

equivalente [ekiβaˈlente] adj, nm equivalent

equivaler [ekiβaˈler] vi to be equivalent o equal

equivocación [ekiβokaˈθjon] nf mistake, error

equivocado, -a [ekiβoˈkaðo, a] adj wrong, mistaken

equivocarse [ekiβoˈkarse] vr to be wrong, make a mistake; **~ de camino** to take the wrong road

era [ˈera] vb ver **ser** ♦ nf era, age

erais [eˈrais] vb ver **ser**

éramos [ˈeramos] vb ver **ser**

eran [ˈeran] vb ver **ser**

eras [ˈeras] vb ver **ser**

erección [erekˈθjon] nf erection

eres vb ver **ser**

erigir [eriˈxir] vt to erect, build; **erigirse** vr: **erigirse en** to set o.s. up as

erizo [eˈriθo] nm (ZOOL) hedgehog ▶ **erizo de mar** sea-urchin

ermita [erˈmita] nf hermitage ❑ **ermitaño, -a** [ermiˈtaɲo, a] nm/f hermit

erosión [eroˈsjon] nf erosion

erosionar [erosjoˈnar] vt to erode

erótico, -a [eˈrotiko, a] adj erotic ❑ **erotismo** nm eroticism

errante [eˈrrante] adj wandering, errant

erróneo, -a [eˈrroneo, a] adj (equivocado) wrong, mistaken

error [eˈrror] nm error, mistake; (INFORM) bug ▶ **error de imprenta** misprint

eructar [erukˈtar] vt to belch, burp

erudito, -a [eru'ðito, a] adj erudite, learned

erupción [erup'θjon] nf eruption; (MED) rash

es [es] vb ver **ser**

esa ['esa] (pl **esas**) adj demos ver **ese**

ésa ['esa] (pl **ésas**) pron ver **ése**

esbelto, -a [es'βelto, a] adj slim, slender

esbozo [es'βoθo] nm sketch, outline

escabeche [eska'βetʃe] nm brine; (de aceitunas etc) pickle; **en ~** pickled

escabullirse [eskaβu'ʎirse] vr to slip away, to clear out

escafandra [eska'fandra] nf (buzo) diving suit; (escafandra espacial) space suit

escala [es'kala] nf (proporción, MÚS) scale; (de mano) ladder; (AVIAC) stopover; **hacer ~ en** to stop o call in at

escalafón [eskala'fon] nm (escala de salarios) salary scale, wage scale

escalar [eska'lar] vt to climb, scale

escalera [eska'lera] nf stairs pl, staircase; (escala) ladder; (NAIPES) run
▶ **escalera de caracol** spiral staircase
▶ **escalera de incendios** fire escape
▶ **escalera mecánica** escalator

escalfar [eskal'far] vt (huevos) to poach

escalinata [eskali'nata] nf staircase

escalofriante [eskalo'frjante] adj chilling

escalofrío [eskalo'frio] nm (MED) chill; **escalofríos** nmpl (fig) shivers

escalón [eska'lon] nm step, stair; (de escalera) rung

escalope [eska'lope] nm (CULIN) escalope

escama [es'kama] nf (de pez, serpiente) scale; (de jabón) flake; (fig) resentment

escampar [eskam'par] vb impers to stop raining

escandalizar [eskandali'θar] vt to scandalize, shock; **escandalizarse** vr to be shocked; (ofenderse) to be offended

escándalo [es'kandalo] nm scandal; (alboroto, tumulto) row, uproar
❏ **escandaloso, -a** adj scandalous, shocking

escandinavo, -a [eskandi'naβo, a] adj, nm/f Scandinavian

escaño [es'kaɲo] nm bench; (POL) seat

escapar [eska'par] vi (gen) to escape, run away; (DEPORTE) to break away; **escaparse** vr to escape, get away; (agua, gas) to leak (out)

escaparate [eskapa'rate] nm shop window

escape [es'kape] nm (de agua, gas) leak; (de motor) exhaust

escarabajo [eskara'βaxo] nm beetle

escaramuza [eskara'muθa] nf skirmish

escarbar [eskar'βar] vt (tierra) to scratch

escarceos [eskar'θeos] nmpl: **en mis ~ con la política ...** in my dealings with politics ... ▶ **escarceos amorosos** love affairs

escarcha [es'kartʃa] nf frost
❏ **escarchado, -a** [eskar'tʃaðo, a] adj (CULIN: fruta) crystallized

escarlatina [eskarla'tina] nf scarlet fever

escarmentar [eskarmen'tar] vt to punish severely ♦ vi to learn one's lesson

escarmiento etc [eskar'mjento] vb ver **escarmentar** ♦ nm (ejemplo) lesson; (castigo) punishment

escarola [eska'rola] nf endive

escarpado, -a [eskar'paðo, a] adj (pendiente) sheer, steep; (rocas) craggy

escasear [eskase'ar] vi to be scarce

escasez [eska'seθ] nf (falta) shortage, scarcity; (pobreza) poverty

escaso, -a [es'kaso, a] adj (poco) scarce; (raro) rare; (ralo) thin, sparse; (limitado) limited

escatimar [eskati'mar] vt to skimp (on), to be sparing with

escayola [eska'jola] nf plaster

escena [es'θena] nf scene ❑ **escenario** [esθe'narjo] nm (TEATRO) stage; (CINE) set; (fig) scene ❑ **escenografía** nf set design

⚠ No confundir **escenario** con la palabra inglesa scenery.

escéptico, -a [es'θeptiko, a] adj sceptical ♦ nm/f sceptic

esclarecer [esklare'θer] vt (misterio, problema) to shed light on

esclavitud [esklaβi'tuð] nf slavery

esclavizar [esklaβi'θar] vt to enslave

esclavo, -a [es'klaβo, a] nm/f slave

escoba [es'koβa] nf broom ❑ **escobilla** nf brush

escocer [esko'θer] vi to burn, sting; **escocerse** vr to chafe, get chafed

escocés, -esa [esko'θes, esa] adj Scottish ♦ nm/f Scotsman(-woman), Scot

Escocia [es'koθja] nf Scotland

escoger [esko'xer] vt to choose, pick, select ❑ **escogido, -a** adj chosen, selected

escolar [esko'lar] adj school cpd ♦ nmf schoolboy(-girl), pupil

escollo [es'koλo] nm (obstáculo) pitfall

escolta [es'kolta] nf escort ❑ **escoltar** vt to escort

escombros [es'kombros] nmpl (basura) rubbish sg; (restos) debris sg

esconder [eskon'der] vt to hide, conceal; **esconderse** vr to hide ❑ **escondidas** (LAm) nfpl: **a escondidas** secretly ❑ **escondite** nm hiding place; (ESP: juego) hide-and-seek ❑ **escondrijo** nm hiding place, hideout

escopeta [esko'peta] nf shotgun

escoria [es'korja] nf (de alto horno) slag; (fig) scum, dregs pl

Escorpio [es'korpjo] nm Scorpio

escorpión [eskor'pjon] nm scorpion

escotado, -a [esko'taðo, a] adj low-cut

escote [es'kote] nm (de vestido) low neck; **pagar a ~** to share the expenses

escotilla [esko'tiλa] nf (NÁUT) hatch(way)

escozor [esko'θor] nm (dolor) sting(ing)

escribir [eskri'βir] vt, vi to write; **~ a máquina** to type; **¿cómo se escribe?** how do you spell it?

escrito, -a [es'krito, a] pp de **escribir** ♦ nm (documento) document; (manuscrito) text, manuscript; **por ~** in writing

escritor, a [eskri'tor, a] nm/f writer

escritorio [eskri'torjo] nm desk

escritura [eskri'tura] nf (acción) writing; (caligrafía) (hand)writing; (JUR: documento) deed

escrúpulo [es'krupulo] nm scruple; (minuciosidad) scrupulousness ❑ **escrupuloso, -a** adj scrupulous

escrutinio [eskru'tinjo] nm (examen atento) scrutiny; (POL: recuento de votos) count(ing)

escuadra [es'kwaðra] nf (MIL etc) squad; (NÁUT) squadron; (flota: de coches etc) fleet ❑ **escuadrilla** nf (de aviones) squadron; (LAm: de obreros) gang

escuadrón [eskwa'ðron] nm squadron

escuálido, -a [es'kwaliðo, a] adj skinny, scraggy; (sucio) squalid

escuchar [esku'tʃar] vt to listen to ♦ vi to listen

escudo [es'kuðo] nm shield

escuela [es'kwela] nf school ▸ **escuela de artes y oficios** (ESP) ≈ technical college ▸ **escuela de choferes** (LAm) driving school ▸ **escuela de manejo** (MEX) driving school

escueto, -a [es'kweto, a] adj plain; (estilo) simple

escuincle [es'kwinkle, a] (MEX: fam) nm/f kid

esculpir [eskul'pir] vt to sculpt; (grabar) to engrave; (tallar) to carve ❑ **escultor, a** nm/f sculptor(-tress) ❑ **escultura** nf sculpture

escupidera [eskupiˈðera] nf spittoon

escupir [eskuˈpir] vt, vi to spit (out)

escurreplatos [eskurreˈplatos] (ESP) nm inv draining board (BRIT), drainboard (US)

escurridero [eskurriˈðero] (LAm) nm draining board (BRIT), drainboard (US)

escurridizo, -a [eskurriˈðiθo, a] adj slippery

escurridor [eskurriˈðor] nm colander

escurrir [eskuˈrrir] vt (ropa) to wring out; (verduras, platos) to drain ♦ vi (líquidos) to drip; **escurrirse** vr (secarse) to drain; (resbalarse) to slip, slide; (escaparse) to slip away

ese [ˈese] (f **esa**, pl **esos, esas**) adj demos (sg) that; (pl) those

ése [ˈese] (f **ésa**, pl **ésos, ésas**) pron (sg) that (one); (pl) those (ones); **ése ... éste ...** the former ... the latter ...; **no me vengas con ésas** don't give me any more of that nonsense

esencia [eˈsenθja] nf essence
❑ **esencial** adj essential

esfera [esˈfera] nf sphere; (de reloj) face
❑ **esférico, -a** adj spherical

esforzarse [esforˈθarse] vr to exert o.s., make an effort

esfuerzo etc [esˈfwerθo] vb ver **esforzarse** ♦ nm effort

esfumarse [esfuˈmarse] vr (apoyo, esperanzas) to fade away

esgrima [esˈɣrima] nf fencing

esguince [esˈɣinθe] nm (MED) sprain

eslabón [eslaˈβon] nm link

eslip [ezˈlip] nm pants pl (BRIT), briefs pl

eslovaco, -a [esloˈβako, a] adj, nm/f Slovak, Slovakian ♦ nm (LING) Slovak, Slovakian

Eslovaquia [esloˈβakja] nf Slovakia

esmalte [esˈmalte] nm enamel
► **esmalte de uñas** nail varnish o polish

esmeralda [esmeˈralda] nf emerald

esmerarse [esmeˈrarse] vr (aplicarse) to take great pains, exercise great care; (afanarse) to work hard

esmero [esˈmero] nm (great) care

esnob [esˈnob] (pl **esnobs**) adj (persona) snobbish ♦ nmf snob

eso [ˈeso] pron that, that thing o matter; **~ de su coche** that business about his car; **~ de ir al cine** all that about going to the cinema; **a ~ de las cinco** at about five o'clock; **en ~** thereupon, at that point; **~ es** that's it; **¡~ sí que es vida!** now that is really living!; **por ~ te lo dije** that's why I told you; **y ~ que llovía** in spite of the fact it was raining

esos [ˈesos] adj demos ver **ese**

ésos [ˈesos] pron ver **ése**

espabilar etc [espaβiˈlar] = **despabilar** etc

espacial [espaˈθjal] adj (del espacio) space cpd

espaciar [espaˈθjar] vt to space (out)

espacio [esˈpaθjo] nm space; (MÚS) interval; (RADIO, TV) programme (BRIT), program (US); **el ~** space ► **espacio aéreo/exterior** air/outer space
❑ **espacioso, -a** adj spacious, roomy

espada [esˈpaða] nf sword; **espadas** nfpl (NAIPES) spades

espaguetis [espaˈɣetis] nmpl spaghetti sg

espalda [esˈpalda] nf (gen) back; **espaldas** nfpl (hombros) shoulders; **a espaldas de algn** behind sb's back; **estar de espaldas** to have one's back turned; **tenderse de espaldas** to lie (down) on one's back; **volver la ~ a algn** to cold-shoulder sb

espantajo [espanˈtaxo] nm = **espantapájaros**

espantapájaros [espantaˈpaxaros] nm inv scarecrow

espantar [espanˈtar] vt (asustar) to frighten, scare; (ahuyentar) to frighten off; (asombrar) to horrify, appal;

espantarse *vr* to get frightened *o* scared; to be appalled

espanto [es'panto] *nm* (*susto*) fright; (*terror*) terror; (*asombro*) astonishment ❑ **espantoso, -a** *adj* frightening; terrifying; astonishing

España [es'paɲa] *nf* Spain ❑ **español, a** *adj* Spanish ♦ *nm/f* Spaniard ♦ *nm* (*LING*) Spanish

esparadrapo [espara'ðrapo] *nm* (sticking) plaster (*BRIT*), adhesive tape (*US*)

esparcir [espar'θir] *vt* to spread; (*diseminar*) to scatter; **esparcirse** *vr* to spread (out), to scatter; (*divertirse*) to enjoy o.s.

espárrago [es'parraɣo] *nm* asparagus

esparto [es'parto] *nm* esparto (grass)

espasmo [es'pasmo] *nm* spasm

espátula [es'patula] *nf* spatula

especia [es'peθja] *nf* spice

especial [espe'θjal] *adj* special ❑ **especialidad** *nf* speciality (*BRIT*), specialty (*US*)

especie [es'peθje] *nf* (*BIO*) species; (*clase*) kind, sort; **en ~** in kind

especificar [espeθifi'kar] *vt* to specify ❑ **específico, -a** *adj* specific

espécimen [es'peθimen] (*pl* **especímenes**) *nm* specimen

espectáculo [espek'takulo] *nm* (*gen*) spectacle; (*TEATRO etc*) show

espectador, a [espekta'ðor, a] *nm/f* spectator

especular [espeku'lar] *vt, vi* to speculate

espejismo [espe'xismo] *nm* mirage

espejo [es'pexo] *nm* mirror ▶ **(espejo) retrovisor** rear-view mirror

espeluznante [espeluθ'nante] *adj* horrifying, hair-raising

espera [es'pera] *nf* (*pausa, intervalo*) wait; (*JUR: plazo*) respite; **en ~ de** waiting for; (*con expectativa*) expecting

esperanza [espe'ranθa] *nf* (*confianza*) hope; (*expectativa*) expectation; **hay pocas esperanzas de que venga** there is little prospect of his coming ▶ **esperanza de vida** life expectancy

esperar [espe'rar] *vt* (*aguardar*) to wait for; (*tener expectativa de*) to expect; (*desear*) to hope for ♦ *vi* to wait; to expect; to hope; **hacer ~ a algn** to keep sb waiting; **~ un bebé** to be expecting (a baby)

esperma [es'perma] *nf* sperm

espeso, -a [es'peso, a] *adj* thick ❑ **espesor** *nm* thickness

espía [es'pia] *nmf* spy ❑ **espiar** *vt* (*observar*) to spy on

espiga [es'piɣa] *nf* (*BOT: de trigo etc*) ear

espigón [espi'ɣon] *nm* (*BOT*) ear; (*NÁUT*) breakwater

espina [es'pina] *nf* thorn; (*de pez*) bone ▶ **espina dorsal** (*ANAT*) spine

espinaca [espi'naka] *nf* spinach

espinazo [espi'naθo] *nm* spine, backbone

espinilla [espi'niʎa] *nf* (*ANAT: tibia*) shin(bone); (*grano*) blackhead

espinoso, -a [espi'noso, a] *adj* (*planta*) thorny, prickly; (*asunto*) difficult

espionaje [espjo'naxe] *nm* spying, espionage

espiral [espi'ral] *adj, nf* spiral

espirar [espi'rar] *vt* to breathe out, exhale

espiritista [espiri'tista] *adj, nmf* spiritualist

espíritu [es'piritu] *nm* spirit ▶ **Espíritu Santo** Holy Ghost *o* Spirit ❑ **espiritual** *adj* spiritual

espléndido, -a [es'plendiðo, a] *adj* (*magnífico*) magnificent, splendid; (*generoso*) generous

esplendor [esplen'dor] *nm* splendour

espolvorear [espolβore'ar] *vt* to dust, sprinkle

esponja [es'ponxa] *nf* sponge; (*fig*) sponger ❑ **esponjoso, -a** *adj* spongy

espontaneidad [espontanei'ðað] nf
spontaneity ❏ **espontáneo, -a** adj
spontaneous

esposa [es'posa] nf wife; **esposas** nfpl
handcuffs ❏ **esposar** vt to handcuff

esposo [es'poso] nm husband

espray [es'prai] nm spray

espuela [es'pwela] nf spur

espuma [es'puma] nf foam; (de cerveza)
froth, head; (de jabón) lather
▸ **espuma de afeitar** shaving foam
❏ **espumadera** [espuma'ðera] nf (utensilio) skimmer
❏ **espumoso, -a** adj frothy, foamy;
(vino) sparkling

esqueleto [eske'leto] nm skeleton

esquema [es'kema] nm (diagrama)
diagram; (dibujo) plan; (FILOSOFÍA)
schema

esquí [es'ki] (pl **~s**) nm (objeto) ski;
(DEPORTE) skiing ▸ **esquí acuático**
water-skiing ❏ **esquiar** vi to ski

esquilar [eski'lar] vt to shear

esquimal [eski'mal] adj, nmf Eskimo

esquina [es'kina] nf corner
❏ **esquinazo** [eski'naθo] nm: **dar
esquinazo a algn** to give sb the slip

esquirol [eski'rol] (ESP) nm
strikebreaker, scab

esquivar [eski'βar] vt to avoid

esta [esta] adj demos ver **este²**

está [es'ta] vb ver **estar**

ésta [esta] pron ver **éste**

estabilidad [estaβili'ðað] nf stability
❏ **estable** adj stable

establecer [estaβle'θer] vt to establish;
establecerse vr to establish o.s.; (echar
raíces) to settle (down)
❏ **establecimiento** nm
establishment

establo [es'taβlo] nm (AGR) stable

estaca [es'taka] nf stake, post; (de tienda
de campaña) peg

estacada [esta'kaða] nf (cerca) fence,
fencing; (palenque) stockade

estación [esta'θjon] nf station; (del año)
season ▸ **estación balnearia** seaside
resort ▸ **estación de autobuses** bus
station ▸ **estación de servicio**
service station

estacionamiento
[estaθjona'mjento] nm (AUTO) parking;
(MIL) stationing

estacionar [estaθjo'nar] vt (AUTO) to
park; (MIL) to station

estadía (LAm) [esta'ðia] nf stay

estadio [es'taðjo] nm (fase) stage,
phase; (DEPORTE) stadium

estadista [esta'ðista] nm (POL)
statesman; (MAT) statistician

estadística [esta'ðistika] nf figure,
statistic; (ciencia) statistics sg

estado [es'taðo] nm (POL: condición)
state; **estar en ~** to be pregnant
▸ **estado civil** marital status
▸ **estado de ánimo** state of mind
▸ **estado de cuenta** bank statement
▸ **estado de sitio** state of siege
▸ **estado mayor** staff ▸ **Estados
Unidos** United States (of America)

estadounidense [estaðouni'ðense]
adj United States cpd, American ♦ nmf
American

estafa [es'tafa] nf swindle, trick
❏ **estafar** vt to swindle, defraud

estáis vb ver **estar**

estallar [esta'ʎar] vi to burst; (bomba)
to explode, go off; (epidemia, guerra,
rebelión) to break out; **~ en llanto** to
burst into tears ❏ **estallido** nm
explosion; (fig) outbreak

estampa [es'tampa] nf print,
engraving ❏ **estampado, -a**
[estam'paðo, a] adj printed ♦ nm
(impresión: acción) printing; (: efecto)
print; (marca) stamping ❏ **estampar**
[estam'par] vt (imprimir) to print;
(marcar) to stamp; (metal) to engrave;
(poner sello en) to stamp; (fig) to stamp,
imprint

estampida [estam'piða] nf stampede

estampido [estam'piðo] nm bang, report

estampilla (LAm) [estam'piʎa] nf (postage) stamp

están [es'tan] vb ver **estar**

estancado, -a [estan'kaðo, a] adj stagnant

estancar [estan'kar] vt (aguas) to hold up, hold back; (COM) to monopolize; (fig) to block, hold up; **estancarse** vr to stagnate

estancia [es'tanθja] nf (ESP, MÉX: permanencia) stay; (sala) room; (RPI: de ganado) farm, ranch □ **estanciero** (RPI) nm farmer, rancher

estanco, -a [es'tanko, a] adj watertight ♦ nm tobacconist's (shop), cigar store (US)

estándar [es'tandar] adj, nm standard

estandarte [estan'darte] nm banner, standard

estanque [es'tanke] nm (lago) pool, pond; (AGR) reservoir

estanquero, -a [estan'kero, a] nm/f tobacconist

estante [es'tante] nm (armario) rack, stand; (biblioteca) bookcase; (anaquel) shelf □ **estantería** nf shelving, shelves pl

estar [es'tar] vi

PALABRA CLAVE

1 (posición) to be; **está en la plaza** it's in the square; **¿está Juan?** is Juan in?; **estamos a 30 km de Junín** we're 30 kms from Junín

2 (+ adj: estado) to be; **estar enfermo** to be ill; **está muy elegante** he's looking very smart; **¿cómo estás?** how are you keeping?

3 (+ gerundio) to be; **estoy leyendo** I'm reading

4 (uso pasivo): **está condenado a muerte** he's been condemned to death; **está envasado en ...** it's packed in ...

5 (con fechas): **¿a cuántos estamos?** what's the date today?; **estamos a 5 de mayo** it's the 5th of May

6 (locuciones): **¿estamos?** (¿de acuerdo?) okay?; **¿listo?** ready?

7: **estar de: estar de vacaciones/viaje** to be on holiday/away o on a trip; **está de camarero** he's working as a waiter

8: **estar para: está para salir** he's about to leave; **no estoy para bromas** I'm not in the mood for jokes

9: **estar por** (propuesta etc) to be in favour of; (persona etc) to support, side with; **está por limpiar** it still has to be cleaned

10: **estar sin: estar sin dinero** to have no money; **está sin terminar** it isn't finished yet

♦ **estarse** vr: **se estuvo en la cama toda la tarde** he stayed in bed all afternoon

estas [estas] adj demos ver **este²**

éstas [estas] pron ver **éste**

estatal [esta'tal] adj state cpd

estático, -a [es'tatiko, a] adj static

estatua [es'tatwa] nf statue

estatura [esta'tura] nf stature, height

este¹ [este] nm east

este² [este] (f **esta**, pl **estos, estas**) adj demos (sg) this; (pl) these

esté *etc* [es'te] *vb ver* **estar**

éste [es'te] (*f* **ésta**, *pl* **estós, éstas**) *pron* (*sg*) this (one); (*pl*) these (ones); **ése ... éste ...** the former ... the latter ...

estén *etc* [es'ten] *vb ver* **estar**

estepa [es'tepa] *nf* (GEO) steppe

estera [es'tera] *nf* mat(ting)

estéreo [es'tereo] *adj inv, nm* stereo
❏ **estereotipo** *nm* stereotype

estéril [es'teril] *adj* sterile, barren; (*fig*) vain, futile ❏ **esterilizar** *vt* to sterilize

esterlina [ester'lina] *adj*: **libra ~** pound sterling

estés *etc* [es'tes] *vb ver* **estar**

estética [es'tetika] *nf* aesthetics *sg*

estético, -a [es'tetiko, a] *adj* aesthetic

estiércol [es'tjerkol] *nm* dung, manure

estigma [es'tiγma] *nm* stigma

estilo [es'tilo] *nm* style; (TEC) stylus; (NATACIÓN) stroke; **algo por el ~** something along those lines

estima [es'tima] *nf* esteem, respect ❏ **estimación** [estima'θjon] *nf* (*evaluación*) estimation; (*aprecio, afecto*) esteem, regard ❏ **estimar** [esti'mar] *vt* (*evaluar*) to estimate; (*valorar*) to value; (*apreciar*) to esteem, respect; (*pensar, considerar*) to think, reckon

estimulante [estimu'lante] *adj* stimulating ✦ *nm* stimulant

estimular [estimu'lar] *vt* to stimulate; (*excitar*) to excite

estímulo [es'timulo] *nm* stimulus; (*ánimo*) encouragement

estirar [esti'rar] *vt* to stretch; (*dinero, suma etc*) to stretch out; **estirarse** *vr* to stretch

estirón [esti'ron] *nm* pull, tug; (*crecimiento*) spurt, sudden growth; **dar** o **pegar un ~** (*fam: niño*) to shoot up (*inf*)

estirpe [es'tirpe] *nf* stock, lineage

estival [esti'βal] *adj* summer *cpd*

esto [esto] *pron* this, this thing o matter; **~ de la boda** this business about the wedding

Estocolmo [esto'kolmo] *nm* Stockholm

estofado [esto'faðo] *nm* stew

estómago [es'tomaγo] *nm* stomach; **tener ~** to be thick-skinned

estorbar [estor'βar] *vt* to hinder, obstruct; (*molestar*) to bother, disturb ✦ *vi* to be in the way ❏ **estorbo** *nm* (*molestia*) bother, nuisance; (*obstáculo*) hindrance, obstacle

estornudar [estornu'ðar] *vi* to sneeze

estos [estos] *adj demos ver* **este²**

éstos [estos] *pron ver* **éste**

estoy [es'toi] *vb ver* **estar**

estrado [es'traðo] *nm* platform

estrafalario, -a [estrafa'larjo, a] *adj* odd, eccentric

estrago [es'traγo] *nm* ruin, destruction; **hacer estragos en** to wreak havoc among

estragón [estra'γon] *nm* tarragon

estrambótico, -a [estram'botiko, a] *adj* (*persona*) eccentric; (*peinado, ropa*) outlandish

estrangular [estrangu'lar] *vt* (*persona*) to strangle; (MED) to strangulate

estratagema [estrata'xema] *nf* (MIL) stratagem; (*astucia*) cunning

estrategia [estra'texja] *nf* strategy ❏ **estratégico, -a** *adj* strategic

estrato [es'trato] *nm* stratum, layer

estrechar [estre'tʃar] *vt* (*reducir*) to narrow; (COSTURA) to take in; (*abrazar*) to hug, embrace; **estrecharse** *vr* (*reducirse*) to narrow, grow narrow; (*abrazarse*) to embrace; **~ la mano** to shake hands

estrechez [estre'tʃeθ] *nf* narrowness; (*de ropa*) tightness; **estrecheces** *nfpl* (*dificultades económicas*) financial difficulties

estrecho, -a [es'tretʃo, a] *adj* narrow; (*apretado*) tight; (*íntimo*) close,

intimate; (*miserable*) mean ♦ *nm* strait;
~ **de miras** narrow-minded

estrella [es'treʎa] *nf* star ► **estrella de mar** (ZOOL) starfish ► **estrella fugaz** shooting star

estrellar [estre'ʎar] *vt* (*hacer añicos*) to smash (to pieces); (*huevos*) to fry; **estrellarse** *vr* to smash; (*chocarse*) to crash; (*fracasar*) to fail

estremecer [estreme'θer] *vt* to shake; **estremecerse** *vr* to shake, tremble

estrenar [estre'nar] *vt* (*vestido*) to wear for the first time; (*casa*) to move into; (*película, obra de teatro*) to première; **estrenarse** *vr* (*persona*) to make one's début □ **estreno** *nm* (CINE etc) première

estreñido, -a [estre'ɲiðo, a] *adj* constipated

estreñimiento [estreɲi'mjento] *nm* constipation

estrepitoso, -a [estrepi'toso, a] *adj* noisy; (*fiesta*) rowdy

estría [es'tria] *nf* groove

estribar [estri'βar] *vi*: ~ **en** to lie on

estribillo [estri'βiʎo] *nm* (LITERATURA) refrain; (MÚS) chorus

estribo [es'triβo] *nm* (*de jinete*) stirrup; (*de coche, tren*) step; (*de puente*) support; (GEO) spur; **perder los estribos** to fly off the handle

estribor [estri'βor] *nm* (NÁUT) starboard

estricto, -a [es'trikto, a] *adj* (*riguroso*) strict; (*severo*) severe

estridente [estri'ðente] *adj* (*color*) loud; (*voz*) raucous

estropajo [estro'paxo] *nm* scourer

estropear [estrope'ar] *vt* to spoil; (*dañar*) to damage; **estropearse** *vr* (*objeto*) to get damaged; (*persona, piel*) to be ruined

estructura [estruk'tura] *nf* structure

estrujar [estru'xar] *vt* (*apretar*) to squeeze; (*aplastar*) to crush; (*fig*) to drain, bleed

estuario [es'twarjo] *nm* estuary

estuche [es'tutʃe] *nm* box, case

estudiante [estu'ðjante] *nmf* student □ **estudiantil** *adj* student *cpd*

estudiar [estu'ðjar] *vt* to study

estudio [es'tuðjo] *nm* study; (CINE, ARTE, RADIO) studio; **estudios** *nmpl* studies; (*erudición*) learning *sg* □ **estudioso, -a** *adj* studious

estufa [es'tufa] *nf* heater, fire

estupefaciente [estupefa'θjente] *nm* drug, narcotic

estupefacto, -a [estupe'fakto, a] *adj* speechless, thunderstruck

estupendo, -a [estu'pendo, a] *adj* wonderful, terrific; (*fam*) great; **¡~!** that's great!, fantastic!

estupidez [estupi'ðeθ] *nf* (*torpeza*) stupidity; (*acto*) stupid thing (to do)

estúpido, -a [es'tupiðo, a] *adj* stupid, silly

estuve *etc* [es'tuβe] *vb ver* **estar**

ETA ['eta] (*ESP*) *nf abr* (= *Euskadi ta Askatasuna*) ETA

etapa [e'tapa] *nf* (*de viaje*) stage; (DEPORTE) leg; (*parada*) stopping place; (*fase*) stage, phase

etarra [e'tarra] *nmf* member of ETA

etc. *abr* (= *etcétera*) etc.

etcétera [et'θetera] *adv* etcetera

eternidad [eterni'ðað] *nf* eternity □ **eterno, -a** *adj* eternal, everlasting

ética ['etika] *nf* ethics *pl*

ético, -a ['etiko, a] *adj* ethical

etiqueta [eti'keta] *nf* (*modales*) etiquette; (*rótulo*) label, tag

Eucaristía [eukaris'tia] *nf* Eucharist

euforia [eu'forja] *nf* euphoria

euro ['euro] *nm* (*moneda*) euro

eurodiputado, -a [euroðipu'taðo, a] *nm/f* Euro MP, MEP

Europa [eu'ropa] *nf* Europe □ **europeo, -a** *adj, nm/f* European

Euskadi [eus'kaði] *nm* the Basque Country *o* Provinces *pl*

euskera [eus'kera] *nm* (LING) Basque

evacuación [eβakwa'θjon] *nf* evacuation

evacuar [eβa'kwar] *vt* to evacuate

evadir [eβa'ðir] *vt* to evade, avoid; **evadirse** *vr* to escape

evaluar [eβa'lwar] *vt* to evaluate

evangelio [eβan'xeljo] *nm* gospel

evaporar [eβapo'rar] *vt* to evaporate; **evaporarse** *vr* to vanish

evasión [eβa'sjon] *nf* escape, flight; (*fig*) evasion ► **evasión de capitales** flight of capital

evasiva [eβa'siβa] *nf* (*pretexto*) excuse

evento [e'βento] *nm* event

eventual [eβen'twal] *adj* possible, conditional (upon circumstances); (*trabajador*) casual, temporary

⚠ No confundir **eventual** con la palabra inglesa *eventual*.

evidencia [eβi'ðenθja] *nf* evidence, proof

evidente [eβi'ðente] *adj* obvious, clear, evident

evitar [eβi'tar] *vt* (*evadir*) to avoid; (*impedir*) to prevent; **~ hacer algo** to avoid doing sth

evocar [eβo'kar] *vt* to evoke, call forth

evolución [eβolu'θjon] *nf* (*desarrollo*) evolution, development; (*cambio*) change; (*MIL*) manoeuvre ❏ **evolucionar** *vi* to evolve; to manoeuvre

ex [eks] *adj* ex-; **el ex ministro** the former minister, the ex-minister

exactitud [eksakti'tuð] *nf* exactness; (*precisión*) accuracy; (*puntualidad*) punctuality ❏ **exacto, -a** *adj* exact; accurate; punctual; **¡exacto!** exactly!

exageración [eksaxera'θjon] *nf* exaggeration

exagerar [eksaxe'rar] *vt, vi* to exaggerate

exaltar [eksal'tar] *vt* to exalt, glorify; **exaltarse** *vr* (*excitarse*) to get excited o worked up

examen [ek'samen] *nm* examination ► **examen de conducir** driving test ► **examen de ingreso** entrance examination

examinar [eksami'nar] *vt* to examine; **examinarse** *vr* to be examined, take an examination

excavadora [ekskaβa'ðora] *nf* excavator

excavar [ekska'βar] *vt* to excavate

excedencia [eksθe'ðenθja] *nf*: **estar en ~** to be on leave; **pedir** o **solicitar la ~** to ask for leave

excedente [eksθe'ðente] *adj, nm* excess, surplus

exceder [eksθe'ðer] *vt* to exceed, surpass; **excederse** *vr* (*extralimitarse*) to go too far

excelencia [eksθe'lenθja] *nf* excellence; **su E~** his Excellency ❏ **excelente** *adj* excellent

excéntrico, -a [eks'θentriko, a] *adj, nm/f* eccentric

excepción [eksθep'θjon] *nf* exception; **a ~ de** with the exception of, except for ❏ **excepcional** *adj* exceptional

excepto [eks'θepto] *adv* excepting, except (for)

exceptuar [eksθep'twar] *vt* to except, exclude

excesivo, -a [eksθe'siβo, a] *adj* excessive

exceso [eks'θeso] *nm* (*gen*) excess; (*COM*) surplus ► **exceso de equipaje/peso** excess luggage/weight ► **exceso de velocidad** speeding

excitado, -a [eksθi'taðo, a] *adj* excited; (*emociones*) aroused

excitar [eksθi'tar] *vt* to excite; (*incitar*) to urge; **excitarse** *vr* to get excited

exclamación [eksklama'θjon] *nf* exclamation

exclamar [ekskla'mar] *vi* to exclaim

excluir [eksklu'ir] *vt* to exclude; (*dejar fuera*) to shut out; (*descartar*) to reject

exclusiva [eksklu'siβa] nf (PRENSA) exclusive, scoop; (COM) sole right

exclusivo, -a [eksklu'siβo, a] adj exclusive; **derecho ~** sole o exclusive right

Excmo. abr (= Excelentísimo) courtesy title

excomulgar [ekskomul'ɣar] vt (REL) to excommunicate

excomunión [ekskomu'njon] nf excommunication

excursión [ekskur'sjon] nf excursion, outing ◻ **excursionista** nmf (turista) sightseer

excusa [eks'kusa] nf excuse; (disculpa) apology ◻ **excusar** [eksku'sar] vt to excuse

exhaustivo, -a [eksaus'tiβo, a] adj (análisis) thorough; (estudio) exhaustive

exhausto, -a [ek'sausto, a] adj exhausted

exhibición [eksiβi'θjon] nf exhibition, display, show

exhibir [eksi'βir] vt to exhibit, display, show

exigencia [eksi'xenθja] nf demand, requirement ◻ **exigente** adj demanding

exigir [eksi'xir] vt (gen) to demand, require; **~ el pago** to demand payment

exiliado, -a [eksi'ljaðo, a] adj exiled ♦ nm/f exile

exilio [ek'siljo] nm exile

eximir [eksi'mir] vt to exempt

existencia [eksis'tenθja] nf existence; **existencias** nfpl stock(s) pl

existir [eksis'tir] vi to exist, be

éxito ['eksito] nm (triunfo) success; (MÚS etc) hit; **tener éxito** to be successful

⚠ No confundir **éxito** con la palabra inglesa exit.

exorbitante [eksorβi'tante] adj (precio) exorbitant; (cantidad) excessive

exótico, -a [ek'sotiko, a] adj exotic

expandir [ekspan'dir] vt to expand

expansión [ekspan'sjon] nf expansion

expansivo, -a [ekspan'siβo, a] adj: **onda expansiva** shock wave

expatriarse [ekspa'trjarse] vr to emigrate; (POL) to go into exile

expectativa [ekspekta'tiβa] nf (espera) expectation; (perspectiva) prospect

expedición [ekspeði'θjon] nf (excursión) expedition

expediente [ekspe'ðjente] nm expedient; (JUR: procedimiento) action, proceedings pl; (: papeles) dossier, file, record

expedir [ekspe'ðir] vt (despachar) to send, forward; (pasaporte) to issue

expensas [eks'pensas] nfpl: **a ~ de** at the expense of

experiencia [ekspe'rjenθja] nf experience

experimentado, -a [eksperimen'taðo, a] adj experienced

experimentar [eksperimen'tar] vt (en laboratorio) to experiment with; (probar) to test, try out; (notar, observar) to experience; (deterioro, pérdida) to suffer ◻ **experimento** nm experiment

experto, -a [eks'perto, a] adj expert, skilled ♦ nm/f expert

expirar [ekspi'rar] vi to expire

explanada [ekspla'naða] nf (llano) plain

explayarse [ekspla'jarse] vr (en discurso) to speak at length; **~ con algn** to confide in sb

explicación [eksplika'θjon] nf explanation

explicar [ekspli'kar] vt to explain; **explicarse** vr to explain (o.s.)

explícito, -a [eks'pliθito, a] adj explicit

explique etc [eks'plike] vb ver **explicar**

explorador, a [eksplora'ðor, a] nm/f (pionero) explorer; (MIL) scout ♦ nm (MED) probe; (TEC) (radar) scanner

explorar [eksplo'rar] vt to explore; (MED) to probe; (radar) to scan

explosión [eksplo'sjon] nf explosion ❏ **explosivo, -a** adj explosive

explotación [eksplota'θjon] nf exploitation; (de planta etc) running

explotar [eksplo'tar] vt to exploit to run, operate ♦ vi to explode

exponer [ekspo'ner] vt to expose; (cuadro) to display; (vida) to risk; (idea) to explain; **exponerse** vr: **exponerse a (hacer) algo** to run the risk of (doing) sth

exportación [eksporta'θjon] nf (acción) export; (mercancías) exports pl

exportar [ekspor'tar] vt to export

exposición [eksposi'θjon] nf (gen) exposure; (de arte) show, exhibition; (explicación) explanation; (declaración) account, statement

expresamente [ekspresa'mente] adv (decir) clearly; (a propósito) expressly

expresar [ekspre'sar] vt to express ❏ **expresión** nf expression

expresivo, -a [ekspre'siβo, a] adj (persona, gesto, palabras) expressive; (cariñoso) affectionate

expreso, -a [eks'preso, a] pp de **expresar** ♦ adj (explícito) express; (claro) specific, clear; (tren) fast ♦ adv: **enviar ~** to send by express (delivery)

express [eks'pres] (LAm) adv: **enviar algo ~** to send sth special delivery

exprimidor [eksprimi'ðor] nm squeezer

exprimir [ekspri'mir] vt (fruta) to squeeze; (zumo) to squeeze out

expuesto, -a [eks'pwesto, a] pp de **exponer** ♦ adj exposed; (cuadro etc) on show, on display

expulsar [ekspul'sar] vt (echar) to eject, throw out; (alumno) to expel; (despedir) to sack, fire; (DEPORTE) to send off ❏ **expulsión** nf expulsion; sending-off

exquisito, -a [ekski'sito, a] adj exquisite; (comida) delicious

éxtasis ['ekstasis] nm ecstasy

extender [eksten'der] vt to extend; (los brazos) to stretch out, hold out; (mapa, tela) to spread (out), open (out); (mantequilla) to spread; (certificado) to issue; (cheque, recibo) to make out; (documento) to draw up; **extenderse** vr (gen) to extend; (persona: en el suelo) to stretch out; (epidemia) to spread ❏ **extendido, -a** adj (abierto) spread out, open; (brazos) outstretched; (costumbre) widespread

extensión [eksten'sjon] nf (de terreno, mar) expanse, stretch; (de tiempo) length, duration; (TEL) extension; **en toda la ~ de la palabra** in every sense of the word

extenso, -a [eks'tenso, a] adj extensive

exterior [ekste'rjor] adj (de fuera) external; (afuera) outside, exterior; (apariencia) outward; (deuda, relaciones) foreign ♦ nm (gen) exterior, outside; (aspecto) outward appearance; (DEPORTE) wing(er); (países extranjeros) abroad; **en el ~** abroad; **al ~** outwardly, on the surface

exterminar [ekstermi'nar] vt to exterminate

externo, -a [eks'terno, a] adj (exterior) external, outside; (superficial) outward ♦ nm/f day pupil

extinguir [ekstin'gir] vt (fuego) to extinguish, put out; (raza, población) to wipe out; **extinguirse** vr (fuego) to go out; (BIO) to die out, become extinct

extintor [ekstin'tor] nm (fire) extinguisher

extirpar [ekstir'par] vt (MED) to remove (surgically)

extra ['ekstra] adj inv (tiempo) extra; (chocolate, vino) good-quality ♦ nmf extra ♦ nm extra; (bono) bonus

extracción [ekstrak'θjon] nf extraction; (en lotería) draw

extracto [eks'trakto] nm extract

extradición [ekstraði'θjon] nf
extradition

extraer [ekstra'er] vt to extract, take
out

extraescolar [ekstraesko'lar] adj:
actividad ~ extracurricular activity

extranjero, -a [ekstran'xero, a] adj
foreign ♦ nm/f foreigner ♦ nm foreign
countries pl; **en el ~** abroad

⚠ No confundir **extranjero** con la
palabra inglesa *stranger*.

extrañar [ekstra'nar] vt (*sorprender*) to
find strange o odd; (*echar de menos*) to
miss; **extrañarse** vr (*sorprenderse*) to be
amazed, be surprised; **me extraña** I'm
surprised

extraño, -a [eks'trano, a] adj
(*extranjero*) foreign; (*raro,
sorprendente*) strange, odd

extraordinario, -a [ekstraorði'narjo,
a] adj extraordinary; (*edición, número*)
special ♦ nm (*de periódico*) special
edition; **horas extraordinarias**
overtime sg

extrarradio [ekstra'rraðjo] nm
suburbs

extravagante [ekstraβa'yante] adj
(*excéntrico*) eccentric; (*estrafalario*)
outlandish

extraviado, -a [ekstra'βjaðo, a] adj
lost, missing

extraviar [ekstra'βjar] vt (*persona:
desorientar*) to mislead, misdirect;
(*perder*) to lose, misplace; **extraviarse**
vr to lose one's way, get lost

extremar [ekstre'mar] vt to carry to
extremes

extremaunción [ekstremaun'θjon] nf
extreme unction

extremidad [ekstremi'ðað] nf (*punta*)
extremity; **extremidades** nfpl (ANAT)
extremities

extremo, -a [eks'tremo, a] adj
extreme; (*último*) last ♦ nm end; (*límite,*

grado sumo) extreme; **en último ~** as a
last resort

extrovertido, -a [ekstroβer'tiðo, a]
adj, nm/f extrovert

exuberante [eksuβe'rante] adj
exuberant; (*fig*) luxuriant, lush

eyacular [ejaku'lar] vt, vi to ejaculate

F, f

fa nm (MÚS) fa, F

fabada [fa'βaða] nf bean and sausage
stew

fábrica ['faβrika] nf factory; **marca de ~**
trademark; **precio de ~** factory price

⚠ No confundir **fábrica** con la
palabra inglesa *fabric*.

fabricación [faβrika'θjon] nf
(*manufactura*) manufacture;
(*producción*) production; **de ~ casera**
home-made ▸ **fabricación en serie**
mass production

fabricante [faβri'kante] nmf
manufacturer

fabricar [faβri'kar] vt (*manufacturar*) to
manufacture, make; (*construir*) to
build; (*cuento*) to fabricate, devise

fábula ['faβula] nf (*cuento*) fable;
(*chisme*) rumour; (*mentira*) fib

fabuloso, -a [faβu'loso, a] adj
(*oportunidad, tiempo*) fabulous, great

facción [fak'θjon] nf (POL) faction;
facciones nfpl (*de rostro*) features

faceta [fa'θeta] nf facet

facha ['fatʃa] nf (*fam*) (*aspecto*) look;
(*cara*) face

fachada [fa'tʃaða] nf (ARQ) façade, front

fácil ['faθil] adj (*simple*) easy; (*probable*)
likely

facilidad [faθili'ðað] nf (*capacidad*)
ease; (*sencillez*) simplicity; (*de palabra*)
fluency; **facilidades** nfpl facilities

▶ **facilidades de pago** credit facilities

facilitar [faθili'tar] vt *(hacer fácil)* to make easy; *(proporcionar)* to provide

factor [fak'tor] nm factor

factura [fak'tura] nf *(cuenta)* bill ❏ **facturación** nf *(de equipaje)* check-in ❏ **facturar** vt *(COM)* to invoice, charge for; *(equipaje)* to check in

facultad [fakul'tað] nf *(aptitud, ESCOL etc)* faculty; *(poder)* power

faena [fa'ena] nf *(trabajo)* work; *(quehacer)* task, job

faisán [fai'san] nm pheasant

faja [faxa] nf *(para la cintura)* sash; *(de mujer)* corset; *(de tierra)* strip

fajo [faxo] nm *(de papeles)* bundle; *(de billetes)* wad

falda ['falda] nf *(prenda de vestir)* skirt ▶ **falda pantalón** culottes pl, split skirt

falla ['faʎa] nf *(defecto)* fault, flaw ▶ **falla humana** (LAm) human error

fallar [fa'ʎar] vt *(JUR)* to pronounce sentence on ♦ vi *(memoria)* to fail; *(motor)* to miss

Fallas nfpl Valencian celebration of the feast of St Joseph

fallecer [faʎe'θer] vi to pass away, die ❏ **fallecimiento** nm decease, demise

fallido, -a [fa'ʎiðo, a] adj *(gen)* frustrated, unsuccessful

fallo ['faʎo] nm *(JUR)* verdict, ruling; *(fracaso)* failure ▶ **fallo cardíaco** heart failure ▶ **fallo humano** *(ESP)* human error

falsificar [falsifi'kar] vt *(firma etc)* to forge; *(moneda)* to counterfeit

falso, -a ['falso, a] adj false; *(documento, moneda etc)* fake; **en ~** falsely

falta ['falta] nf *(defecto)* fault, flaw; *(privación)* lack, want; *(ausencia)* absence; *(carencia)* shortage; *(equivocación)* mistake; *(DEPORTE)* foul; **echar en ~** to miss; **hacer ~ hacer algo** to be necessary to do sth; **me hace una pluma** I need a pen ▶ **falta de educación** bad manners pl ▶ **falta de ortografía** spelling mistake

faltar [fal'tar] vi *(escasear)* to be lacking, be wanting; *(ausentarse)* to be absent, be missing; **faltan 2 horas para llegar** there are 2 hours to go till arrival; **~ al respeto a algn** to be disrespectful to sb; **¡no faltaba más!** *(no hay de qué)* don't mention it

fama ['fama] nf *(renombre)* fame; *(reputación)* reputation

familia [fa'milja] nf family ▶ **familia numerosa** large family ▶ **familia política** in-laws pl ❏ **familiar** [fami'ljar] adj *relativo a la familia, family cpd; (conocido, informal)* familiar ♦ nm relative, relation

famoso, -a [fa'moso, a] adj *(renombrado)* famous

fan [fan] (pl **fans**) nmf fan

fanático, -a [fa'natiko, a] adj fanatical ♦ nm/f fanatic; *(CINE, DEPORTE)* fan

fanfarrón, -ona [fanfa'rron, ona] adj boastful

fango ['fango] nm mud

fantasía [fanta'sia] nf fantasy, imagination; **joyas de ~** imitation jewellery sg

fantasma [fan'tasma] *nm* (espectro) ghost, apparition; (fanfarrón) show-off

fantástico, -a [fan'tastiko, a] *adj* fantastic

farmacéutico, -a [farma'θeutiko, a] *adj* pharmaceutical ♦ *nm/f* chemist (BRIT), pharmacist

farmacia [far'maθja] *nf* chemist's (shop) (BRIT), pharmacy ▸ **farmacia de guardia** all-night chemist

fármaco [farmako] *nm* drug

faro ['faro] *nm* (NÁUT: torre) lighthouse; (AUTO) headlamp ▸ **faros antiniebla** fog lamps ▸ **faros delanteros/ traseros** headlights/rear lights

farol [fa'rol] *nm* lantern, lamp

farola [fa'rola] *nf* street lamp (BRIT) o light (US)

farra (LAM: fam) ['farra] *nf* party; **ir de ~** to go on a binge

farsa ['farsa] *nf* (gen) farce ❏ **farsante** [far'sante] *nmf* fraud, fake

fascículo [fas'θikulo] *nm* (de revista) part, instalment

fascinar [fasθi'nar] *vt* (gen) to fascinate

fascismo [fas'θismo] *nm* fascism ❏ **fascista** *adj, nmf* fascist

fase ['fase] *nf* phase

fashion *adj* (fam) trendy

fastidiar [fasti'ðjar] *vt* (molestar) to annoy, bother; (estropear) to spoil; **fastidiarse** *vr*: **¡que se fastidie!** (fam) he'll just have to put up with it!

fastidio [fas'tiðjo] *nm* (molestia) annoyance ❏ **fastidioso, -a** *adj* (molesto) annoying

fatal [fa'tal] *adj* (gen) fatal; (desgraciado) ill-fated; (fam: malo, pésimo) awful ❏ **fatalidad** *nf* (destino) fate; (mala suerte) misfortune

fatiga [fa'tiɣa] *nf* (cansancio) fatigue, weariness ❏ **fatigar** [fati'ɣar] *vt* to tire, weary ❏ **fatigoso, -a** [fati'ɣoso, a] *adj* (cansador) tiring

fauna ['fauna] *nf* fauna

favor [fa'βor] *nm* favour; **estar a ~ de** to be in favour of; **haga el ~ de ...** would you be so good as to ..., kindly ...; **por ~** please ❏ **favorable** *adj* favourable

favorecer [faβore'θer] *vt* to favour; (vestido etc) to become, flatter; **este peinado le favorece** this hairstyle suits you

favorito, -a [faβo'rito, a] *adj, nm/f* favourite

fax [faks] *nm inv* fax; **mandar por ~** to fax

fe [fe] *nf* (REL) faith; (documento) certificate; **actuar con buena/mala fe** to act in good/bad faith

febrero [fe'βrero] *nm* February

fecha ['fetʃa] *nf* date; **con ~ adelantada** postdated; **en ~ próxima** soon; **hasta la ~** to date, so far; **poner ~** to date ▸ **fecha de caducidad** (de producto alimenticio) sell-by date; (de contrato etc) expiry date ▸ **fecha de nacimiento** date of birth ▸ **fecha límite** o **tope** deadline

fecundo, -a [fe'kundo, a] *adj* (fértil) fertile; (fig) prolific; (productivo) productive

federación [feðera'θjon] *nf* federation

felicidad [feliθi'ðað] *nf* happiness; **¡felicidades!** (deseos) best wishes, congratulations!; (en cumpleaños) happy birthday!

felicitación [feliθita'θjon] *nf* (tarjeta) greeting's card

felicitar [feliθi'tar] *vt* to congratulate

feliz [fe'liθ] *adj* happy

felpudo [fel'puðo] *nm* doormat

femenino, -a [feme'nino, a] *adj, nm* feminine

feminista [femi'nista] *adj, nmf* feminist

fenómeno [fe'nomeno] *nm* phenomenon; (fig) freak, accident ♦ *adj* great ♦ *excl* great!, marvellous! ❏ **fenomenal** *adj* = **fenómeno**

feo, -a ['feo, a] *adj* (*gen*) ugly; (*desagradable*) bad, nasty

féretro ['feretro] *nm* (*ataúd*) coffin; (*sarcófago*) bier

feria ['ferja] *nf* (*gen*) fair; (*descanso*) holiday, rest day; (*MÉX: cambio*) small o loose change; (*CS: mercado*) village market

feriado (*LAm*) ['fe'rjaðo] *nm* holiday

fermentar [fermen'tar] *vi* to ferment

feroz [fe'roθ] *adj* (*cruel*) cruel; (*salvaje*) fierce

férreo, -a ['ferreo, a] *adj* iron

ferretería [ferrete'ria] *nf* (*tienda*) ironmonger's (*shop*) (*BRIT*), hardware store (*US*)

ferrocarril [ferroka'rril] *nm* railway

ferroviario, -a [ferro'βjarjo, a] *adj* rail *cpd*

ferry (*pl* ferrys *o* ferries) *nm* ferry

fértil ['fertil] *adj* (*productivo*) fertile; (*rico*) rich ❑ **fertilidad** *nf* (*gen*) fertility; (*productividad*) fruitfulness

fervor [fer'βor] *nm* fervour

festejar [feste'xar] *vt* (*celebrar*) to celebrate

festejo [fes'texo] *nm* celebration; **festejos** *nmpl* (*fiestas*) festivals

festín [fes'tin] *nm* feast, banquet

festival [festi'βal] *nm* festival

festividad [festiβi'ðað] *nf* festivity

festivo, -a [fes'tiβo, a] *adj* (*de fiesta*) festive; (*CINE, LITERATURA*) humorous; **día ~** holiday

feto ['feto] *nm* foetus

fiable ['fjaβle] *adj* (*persona*) trustworthy; (*máquina*) reliable

fiambre ['fjambre] *nm* cold meat

fiambrera [fjam'brera] *nf* (*para almuerzo*) lunch box

fianza ['fjanθa] *nf* surety; (*JUR*): **libertad bajo ~** release on bail

fiar [fi'ar] *vt* (*salir garante de*) to guarantee; (*vender a crédito*) to sell on credit ♦ *vi* to trust; **fiarse** *vr* to trust (in), rely on; **~ a** (*secreto*) to confide (to); **fiarse de algn** to rely on sb

fibra ['fiβra] *nf* fibre ▶ **fibra óptica** optical fibre

ficción [fik'θjon] *nf* fiction

ficha ['fitʃa] *nf* (*TEL*) token; (*en juegos*) counter, marker; (*tarjeta*) (index) card ❑ **fichaje** *nm* (*DEPORTE*) signing ❑ **fichar** *vt* (*archivar*) to file, index; (*DEPORTE*) to sign; **estar fichado** to have a record; **fichero** *nm* box file; (*INFORM*) file

ficticio, -a [fik'tiθjo, a] *adj* (*imaginario*) fictitious; (*falso*) fabricated

fidelidad [fiðeli'ðað] *nf* (*lealtad*) fidelity, loyalty; **alta ~** high fidelity, hi-fi

fideos [fi'ðeos] *nmpl* noodles

fiebre ['fjeβre] *nf* (*MED*) fever; (*fig*) fever, excitement; **tener ~** to have a temperature ▶ **fiebre aftosa** foot-and-mouth disease

fiel [fjel] *adj* (*leal*) faithful, loyal; (*fiable*) reliable; (*exacto*) accurate, faithful ♦ *nm*: **los fieles** the faithful

fieltro ['fjeltro] *nm* felt

fiera ['fjera] *nf* (*animal feroz*) wild animal o beast; (*fig*) dragon; *ver tb* **fiero**

fiero, -a ['fjero, a] *adj* (*cruel*) cruel; (*feroz*) fierce; (*duro*) harsh

fierro (*LAm*) ['fjerro] *nm* (*hierro*) iron

fiesta ['fjesta] *nf* party; (*de pueblo*) festival; (*vacaciones: tb:* **fiestas**) holiday *sg* ▶ **fiesta mayor** annual festival ▶ **fiesta patria** (*LAm*) independence day

---

FIESTAS

Fiestas can be official public holidays or holidays set by each autonomous region, many of which coincide with religious festivals. There are also many **fiestas** all over Spain for a local patron saint or the Virgin Mary. These often last several days and can include religious processions, carnival parades, bullfights and dancing.

figura 132 **flama**

figura [fi'ɣura] nf (gen) figure; (forma, imagen) shape, form; (NAIPES) face card

figurar [fiɣu'rar] vt (representar) to represent; (fingir) to figure ♦ vi to figure; **figurarse** vr (imaginarse) to imagine; (suponer) to suppose

fijador [fixa'ðor] nm (FOTO etc) fixative; (de pelo) gel

fijar [fi'xar] vt (gen) to fix; (estampilla) to affix, stick (on); **fijarse** vr: **fijarse en** to notice

fijo, -a ['fixo, a] adj (gen) fixed; (firme) firm; (permanente) permanent ♦ adv: **mirar ~** to stare

fila ['fila] nf row; (MIL) rank; **ponerse en ~ fila** to line up, get into line ▶ **fila india** single file

filatelia [fila'telja] nf philately, stamp collecting

filete [fi'lete] nm (de carne) fillet steak; (de pescado) fillet

filiación [filja'θjon] nf (POL) affiliation

filial [fi'ljal] adj filial ♦ nf subsidiary

Filipinas [fili'pinas] nfpl: **las (Islas) ~** the Philippines □ **filipino, -a** adj, nm/f Philippine

filmar [fil'mar] vt to film, shoot

filo ['filo] nm (gen) edge; **sacar ~ a** to sharpen; **al ~ del mediodía** at about midday; **de doble ~** double-edged

filología [filolo'ɣia] nf philology ▶ **filología inglesa** (UNIV) English Studies

filón [fi'lon] nm (MINERÍA) vein, lode; (fig) goldmine

filosofía [filoso'fia] nf philosophy □ **filósofo, -a** nm/f philosopher

filtrar [fil'trar] vt, vi to filter, strain; **filtrarse** vr to filter □ **filtro** nm (TEC, utensilio) filter

fin [fin] nm end; (objetivo) aim, purpose; **al ~ y al cabo** when all's said and done; **a ~ de** in order to; **por ~** finally; **en ~** in short ▶ **fin de semana** weekend

final [fi'nal] adj final ♦ nm end, conclusion ♦ nf final; **al ~** in the end; a

finales de at the end of □ **finalidad** nf (propósito) purpose, intention □ **finalista** nmf finalist □ **finalizar** vt to end, finish; (INFORM) to log out o off ♦ vi to end, come to an end

financiar [finan'θjar] vt to finance □ **financiero, -a** adj financial ♦ nm/f financier

finca ['finka] nf (casa de campo) country house; (ESP: bien inmueble) property, land; (LAm: granja) farm

finde nm abr (fam: fin de semana) weekend

fingir [fin'xir] vt (simular) to simulate, feign ♦ vi (aparentar) to pretend

finlandés, -esa [finlan'des, esa] adj Finnish ♦ nm/f Finn ♦ nm (LING) Finnish

Finlandia [fin'landja] nf Finland

fino, -a ['fino, a] adj fine; (delgado) slender; (de buenas maneras) polite, refined; (jerez) fino, dry

firma ['firma] nf signature; (COM) firm, company

firmamento [firma'mento] nm firmament

firmar [fir'mar] vt to sign

firme ['firme] adj firm; (estable) stable; (sólido) solid; (constante) steady; (decidido) resolute ♦ nm road (surface) □ **firmeza** nf firmness; (constancia) steadiness; (solidez) solidity

fiscal [fis'kal] adj fiscal ♦ nmf public prosecutor; **año ~** tax o fiscal year

fisgonear [fisɣone'ar] vt to poke one's nose into ♦ vi to pry, spy

física [fisika] nf physics sg; ver tb **físico**

físico, -a [fisiko, a] adj physical ♦ nm physique ♦ nm/f physicist

fisura [fi'sura] nf crack; (MED) fracture

flác(c)ido, -a [ˈfla(k)θiðo, a] adj flabby

flaco, -a ['flako, a] adj (muy delgado) skinny, thin; (débil) weak, feeble

flagrante [fla'ɣrante] adj flagrant

flama (MÉX) nf flame □ **flamable** (MÉX) adj flammable

flamante [fla'mante] (fam) adj brilliant; (nuevo) brand-new

flamenco, -a [fla'menko, a] adj (de Flandes) Flemish; (baile, música) flamenco ♦ nm (baile, música) flamenco; (ZOOL) flamingo

flamingo (MÉX) nm flamingo

flan [flan] nm creme caramel

⚠ No confundir **flan** con la palabra inglesa flan.

flash [flaʃ] (pl —o **flashes**) nm (FOTO) flash

flauta ['flauta] nf (MÚS) flute

flecha ['fletʃa] nf arrow

flechazo [fle'tʃaθo] nm love at first sight

fleco ['fleko] nm fringe

flema ['flema] nm phlegm

flequillo [fle'kiʎo] nm (pelo) fringe

flexible [flek'siβle] adj flexible

flexión [flek'sjon] nf press-up

flexo ['flekso] nm adjustable table-lamp

flirtear [flirte'ar] vi to flirt

flojera [flo'xera] (LAm: fam) nf: **me da ~** I can't be bothered

flojo, -a ['floxo, a] adj (gen) loose; (sin fuerzas) limp; (débil) weak

flor [flor] nf flower; **a ~ de** on the surface of □ **flora** nf flora □ **florecer** vi (BOT) to flower, bloom; (fig) to flourish □ **florería** (LAm) nf florist's (shop) □ **florero** nm vase □ **floristería** nf florist's (shop)

flota ['flota] nf fleet

flotador [flota'ðor] nm (gen) float; (para nadar) rubber ring

flotar [flo'tar] vi to float □ **flote** nm: **a flote** afloat; **salir a flote** (fig) to get back on one's feet

fluidez [flui'ðeθ] nf fluidity; (fig) fluency

fluido, -a [flu'iðo, a] adj, nm fluid

fluir [flu'ir] vi to flow

flujo ['fluxo] nm flow ▶ **flujo y reflujo** ebb and flow

flúor ['fluor] nm fluoride

fluorescente [flwores'θente] adj fluorescent ♦ nm fluorescent light

fluvial [fluβi'al] adj (navegación, cuenca) fluvial, river cpd

fobia ['foβja] nf phobia ▶ **fobia a las alturas** fear of heights

foca ['foka] nf seal

foco ['foko] nm focus; (ELEC) floodlight; (MÉX: bombilla) (light) bulb

fofo, -a ['fofo, a] adj soft, spongy; (carnes) flabby

fogata [fo'ɣata] nf bonfire

fogón [fo'ɣon] nm (de cocina) ring, burner

folio ['foljo] nm folio, page

follaje [fo'ʎaxe] nm foliage

folleto [fo'ʎeto] nm (POL) pamphlet

follón [fo'ʎon] (ESP: fam) nm (lío) mess; (conmoción) fuss; **armar un ~** to kick up a row

fomentar [fomen'tar] vt (MED) to foment

fonda ['fonda] nf inn

fondo ['fondo] nm (de mar) bottom; (de coche, sala) back; (ARTE etc) background; (reserva) fund; **fondos** nmpl (COM) funds, resources; **una investigación a ~** a thorough investigation; **en el ~** at bottom, deep down

fonobuzón [fonoβu'θon] nm voice mail

fontanería [fontane'ria] nf plumbing □ **fontanero, -a** nm/f plumber

footing ['futin] nm jogging; **hacer ~** to jog, go jogging

forastero, -a [foras'tero, a] nm/f stranger

forcejear [forθexe'ar] vi (luchar) to struggle

forense [fo'rense] nmf pathologist

forma [ˈforma] nf (figura) form, shape; (MED) fitness; (método) way, means; **las formas** the conventions; **estar en ~** to be fit; **de ~ que** so that ...; **de todas formas** in any case

formación [formaˈθjon] nf (gen) formation; (educación) education ► **formación profesional** vocational training

formal [forˈmal] adj (gen) formal; (fig: serio) serious; (: de fiar) reliable □ **formalidad** nf formality; seriousness □ **formalizar** vt (JUR) to formalize; (situación) to put in order, regularize; **formalizarse** vr (situación) to be put in order, be regularized

formar [forˈmar] vt (componer) to form, shape; (constituir) to make up, constitute; (ESCOL) to train, educate; **formarse** vr (ESCOL) to be trained, educated; (cobrar forma) to form, take form; (desarrollarse) to develop

formatear [formateˈar] vt to format

formato [forˈmato] nm format

formidable [formiˈðaβle] adj (temible) formidable; (estupendo) tremendous

fórmula [ˈformula] nf formula

formulario [formuˈlarjo] nm form

fornido, -a [forˈniðo, a] adj well-built

foro [ˈforo] nm (POL, INFORM etc) forum

forrar [foˈrar] vt (abrigo) to line; (libro) to cover □ **forro** nm (de cuaderno) cover; (COSTURA) lining; (de sillón) upholstery; **forro polar** fleece

fortalecer [fortaleˈθer] vt to strengthen

fortaleza [fortaˈleθa] nf (MIL) fortress, stronghold; (fuerza) strength; (determinación) resolution

fortuito, -a [forˈtwito, a] adj accidental

fortuna [forˈtuna] nf (suerte) fortune, (good) luck; (riqueza) fortune, wealth

forzar [forˈθar] vt (puerta) to force (open); (compeler) to compel

forzoso, -a [forˈθoso, a] adj necessary

fosa [ˈfosa] nf (sepultura) grave; (en tierra) pit ► **fosas nasales** nostrils

fósforo [ˈfosforo] nm (QUÍM) phosphorus; (cerilla) match

fósil [ˈfosil] nm fossil

foso [ˈfoso] nm ditch; (TEATRO) pit; (AUTO) inspection pit

foto [ˈfoto] nf photo, snap(shot); **sacar una ~** to take a photo o picture ► **foto (de) carné** passport(-size) photo

fotocopia [fotoˈkopja] nf photocopy □ **fotocopiadora** nf photocopier □ **fotocopiar** vt to photocopy

fotografía [fotoɣraˈfia] nf (ARTE) photography; (una fotografía) photograph □ **fotografiar** vt to photograph

fotógrafo, -a [foˈtoɣrafo, a] nm/f photographer

fotomatón [fotomaˈton] nm photo booth

FP (ESP) nf abr (= Formación Profesional) vocational courses for 14- to 18-year-olds

fracasar [frakaˈsar] vi (gen) to fail

fracaso [fraˈkaso] nm failure

fracción [frakˈθjon] nf fraction

fractura [frakˈtura] nf fracture, break

fragancia [fraˈɣanθja] nf (olor) fragrance, perfume

frágil [ˈfraxil] adj (débil) fragile; (COM) breakable

fragmento [fraɣˈmento] nm (pedazo) fragment

fraile [ˈfraile] nm (REL) friar; (: monje) monk

frambuesa [framˈbwesa] nf raspberry

francés, -esa [franˈθes, esa] adj French ♦ nm/f Frenchman(-woman) ♦ nm (LING) French

Francia [ˈfranθja] nf France

franco, -a [ˈfranko, a] adj (cándido) frank, open; (COM: exento) free ♦ nm (moneda) franc

francotirador, a [frankotiraˈðor, a] nm/f sniper

franela [fra'nela] nf flannel

franja ['franxa] nf fringe

franquear [franke'ar] vt (camino) to clear; (carta, paquete postal) to frank, stamp; (obstáculo) to overcome

franqueo [fran'keo] nm postage

franqueza [fran'keθa] nf (candor) frankness

frasco ['frasko] nm bottle, flask

frase ['frase] nf sentence ▶ **frase hecha** set phrase; (pey) stock phrase

fraterno, -a [fra'terno, a] adj brotherly, fraternal

fraude ['fraude] nm (cualidad) dishonesty; (acto) fraud

frazada [fra'saða] (LAm) nf blanket

frecuencia [fre'kwenθja] nf frequency; **con ~** frequently, often

frecuentar [frekwen'tar] vt to frequent

frecuente [fre'kwente] adj (gen) frequent

fregadero [freɣa'ðero] nm (kitchen) sink

fregar [fre'ɣar] vt (frotar) to scrub; (platos) to wash (up); (LAm: fam: fastidiar) to annoy; (: malograr) to screw up

fregona [fre'ɣona] nf mop

freír [fre'ir] vt to fry

frenar [fre'nar] vt to brake; (fig) to check

frenazo [fre'naθo] nm: **dar un ~** to brake sharply

frenesí [frene'si] nm frenzy

freno ['freno] nm (TEC, AUTO) brake; (de cabalgadura) bit; (fig) check ▶ **freno de mano** handbrake

frente ['frente] nm (ARQ, POL) front; (de objeto) front part ♦ nf forehead, brow; **~ a** in front of; (en situación opuesta de) opposite; **al ~ de** (fig) at the head of; **chocar al ~** to crash head-on; **hacer ~ a** to face up to

fresa ['fresa] (ESP) nf strawberry

fresco, -a ['fresko, a] adj (nuevo) fresh; (frío) cool; (descarado) cheeky ♦ nm (aire) fresh air; (ARTE) fresco; (LAm: jugo) fruit drink ♦ nm/f (fam): **ser un ~** to have a nerve; **tomar el ~** to get some fresh air □ **frescura** nf freshness; (descaro) cheek, nerve

frialdad [frial'dad] nf (gen) coldness; (indiferencia) indifference

frigidez [frixi'ðeθ] nf frigidity

frigorífico [friɣo'rifiko] nm refrigerator

frijol [fri'xol] nm kidney bean

frío, -a etc [frio, a] vb ver **freír** ♦ adj cold; (indiferente) indifferent ♦ nm cold; indifference; **hace ~** it's cold; **tener ~** to be cold

frito, -a ['frito, a] adj fried; **me trae ese hombre** I'm sick and tired of that man □ **fritos** nmpl fried food

frívolo, -a ['friβolo, a] adj frivolous

frontal [fron'tal] adj frontal; **choque ~** head-on collision

frontera [fron'tera] nf frontier □ **fronterizo, -a** adj frontier cpd; (contiguo) bordering

frontón [fron'ton] nm (DEPORTE: cancha) pelota court; (: juego) pelota

frotar [fro'tar] vt to rub; **frotarse** vr: **frotarse las manos** to rub one's hands

fructífero, -a [fruk'tifero, a] adj fruitful

fruncir [frun'θir] vt to pucker; (COSTURA) to pleat; **~ el ceño** to knit one's brow

frustrar [frus'trar] vt to frustrate

fruta ['fruta] nf fruit □ **frutería** nf fruit shop □ **frutero, -a** adj fruit cpd ♦ nm/f fruiterer ♦ nm fruit bowl

frutilla [fru'tiʎa] (CS) nf strawberry

fruto ['fruto] nm fruit; (fig: resultado) result; (: beneficio) benefit ▶ **frutos secos** nuts and dried fruit pl

fucsia ['fuksja] nf fuchsia

fue [fwe] vb ver **ser**; **ir**

fuego ['fweɣo] nm (gen) fire; **a ~ lento** on a low heat; **¿tienes ~?** have you (got) a light? ▸ **fuego amigo** friendly fire ▸ **fuegos artificiales** fireworks

fuente ['fwente] nf fountain; (manantial: fig) spring; (origen) source; (plato) large dish

fuera etc ['fwera] vb ver **ser**; **ir** ♦ adv out(side); (en otra parte) away; (excepto, salvo) except, save ♦ prep: **~ de** outside; (fig) besides; **~ de sí** beside o.s.; **por ~** (on the) outside

fuera-borda [fwera'βorða] nm speedboat

fuerte ['fwerte] adj strong; (golpe) hard; (ruido) loud; (comida) rich; (lluvia) heavy; (dolor) intense ♦ adv strongly; hard; loud(ly)

fuerza etc ['fwerθa] vb ver **forzar** ♦ nf (fortaleza) strength; (TEC, ELEC) power; (coacción) force; (MIL, POL) force; **a ~ de** by dint of; **cobrar fuerzas** to recover one's strength; **tener fuerzas para** to have the strength to; **a la ~** forcibly, by force; **por ~** of necessity ▸ **fuerza de voluntad** willpower ▸ **fuerzas aéreas** air force sg ▸ **fuerzas armadas** armed forces

fuga ['fuɣa] nf (huida) flight, escape; (de gas etc) leak

fugarse [fu'ɣarse] vr to flee, escape

fugaz [fu'ɣaθ] adj fleeting

fugitivo, a [fuxi'tiβo, a] adj, nm/f fugitive

fui [fwi] vb ver **ser**; **ir**

fulano, a [fu'lano, a] nm/f so-and-so, what's-his-name/what's-her-name

fulminante [fulmi'nante] adj (fig: mirada) fierce; (MED: enfermedad, ataque) sudden; (fam: éxito, golpe) sudden

fumador, a [fuma'ðor, a] nm/f smoker

fumar [fu'mar] vi, vi to smoke; **~ en pipa** to smoke a pipe

función [fun'θjon] nf function; (en trabajo) duties pl; (espectáculo) show;

entrar en funciones to take up one's duties

funcionar [funθjo'nar] vi (gen) to function; (máquina) to work; **"no funciona"** "out of order"

funcionario, -a [funθjo'narjo, a] nm/f civil servant

funda ['funda] nf (gen) cover; (de almohada) pillowcase

fundación [funda'θjon] nf foundation

fundamental [fundamen'tal] adj fundamental, basic

fundamento [funda'mento] nm (base) foundation

fundar [fun'dar] vt to found; **fundarse** vr: **fundarse en** to be founded on

fundición [fundi'θjon] nf fusing; (fábrica) foundry

fundir [fun'dir] vt (gen) to fuse; (metal) to smelt, melt down; (nieve etc) to melt; (COM) to merge; (estatua) to cast; **fundirse** vr (colores etc) to merge, blend; (unirse) to fuse together; (ELEC: fusible, lámpara etc) to fuse, blow; (nieve etc) to melt

fúnebre ['funeβre] adj funeral cpd, funeral

funeral [fune'ral] nm funeral ❑ **funeraria** nf undertaker's

funicular [funiku'lar] nm (tren) funicular; (teleférico) cable car

furgón [fur'ɣon] nm wagon ❑ **furgoneta** nf (AUTO, COM) (transit) van (BRIT), pick-up (truck) (US)

furia ['furja] nf (ira) fury; (violencia) violence ❑ **furioso, -a** adj (iracundo) furious; (violento) violent

furtivo, -a [fur'tiβo, a] adj furtive ♦ nm poacher

fusible [fu'siβle] nm fuse

fusil [fu'sil] nm rifle ❑ **fusilar** vt to shoot

fusión [fu'sjon] nf (gen) melting; (unión) fusion; (COM) merger

fútbol ['futβol] nm football (BRIT), soccer (US) ▸ **fútbol americano**

American football (BRIT), football (US)
▶ **fútbol sala** indoor football (BRIT) o
soccer (US) □ **futbolín** nm table
football □ **futbolista** nmf footballer
futuro, -a [fu'turo, a] adj, nm future

G, g

gabardina [gaβar'ðina] nf raincoat,
gabardine
gabinete [gaβi'nete] nm (POL) cabinet;
(estudio) study; (de abogados etc) office
gachas ['gatʃas] nfpl porridge sg
gafas ['gafas] nfpl glasses ▶ **gafas de
sol** sunglasses
gafe ['gafe] (ESP) nmf jinx
gaita ['gaita] nf bagpipes pl
gajes ['gaxes] nmpl: **~ del oficio**
occupational hazards
gajo ['gaxo] nm (de naranja) segment
gala ['gala] nf (traje de etiqueta) full
dress; **galas** nfpl (ropa) finery sg; **estar
de ~** to be in one's best clothes; **hacer
~ de** to display
galápago [ga'lapaɣo] nm (ZOOL) turtle
galardón [galar'ðon] nm award, prize
galaxia [ga'laksja] nf galaxy
galera [ga'lera] nf (nave) galley; (carro)
wagon; (IMPRENTA) galley
galería [gale'ria] nf (gen) gallery;
(balcón) veranda(h); (pasillo) corridor
▶ **galería comercial** shopping mall
Gales ['gales] nm (tb: **País de ~**)
Wales □ **galés, -esa** adj Welsh ♦ nm/f
Welshman(-woman) ♦ nm (LING) Welsh
galgo, -a ['galɣo, a] nm/f greyhound
gallego, -a [ga'ʎeɣo, a] adj, nm/f
Galician
galleta [ga'ʎeta] nf biscuit (BRIT),
cookie (US)
gallina [ga'ʎina] nf hen ♦ nmf (fam:
cobarde) chicken □ **gallinero** nm
henhouse; (TEATRO) top gallery

gallo ['gaʎo] nm cock, rooster
galopar [galo'par] vi to gallop
gama ['gama] nf (fig) range
gamba ['gamba] nf prawn (BRIT),
shrimp (US)
gamberro, -a [gam'berro, a] (ESP) nm/
f hooligan, lout
gamuza [ga'muθa] nf chamois
gana ['gana] nf (deseo) desire, wish;
(apetito) appetite; (voluntad) will;
(añoranza) longing; **de buena ~**
willingly; **de mala ~** reluctantly; **me da
ganas de** I don't feel like it; I want to; **no me da
la ~** I don't feel like it; **tener ganas de**
to feel like
ganadería [ganaðe'ria] nf (ganado)
livestock; (ganado vacuno) cattle pl;
(cría, comercio) cattle raising
ganadero, -a [gana'ðero, a] nm/f
(hacendado) rancher
ganado [ga'naðo] nm livestock
▶ **ganado porcino** pigs pl
ganador, a [gana'ðor, a] adj winning
♦ nm/f winner
ganancia [ga'nanθja] nf (lo ganado)
gain; (aumento) increase; (beneficio)
profit; **ganancias** nfpl (ingresos)
earnings; (beneficios) profit sg,
winnings
ganar [ga'nar] vt (obtener) to get,
obtain; (sacar ventaja) to gain; (salario
etc) to earn; (DEPORTE, premio) to win;
(derrotar a) to beat; (alcanzar) to reach
♦ vi (DEPORTE) to win; **ganarse** vr:
ganarse la vida to earn one's living
ganchillo [gan'tʃiʎo] nm crochet
gancho [gan'tʃo] nm (gen) hook;
(colgador) hanger
gandul, -a [gan'dul, a] adj, nm/f good-
for-nothing, layabout
ganga ['ganga] nf bargain
gangrena [gan'grena] nf gangrene
ganso, -a ['ganso, a] nm/f (ZOOL) goose;
(fam) idiot
ganzúa [gan'θua] nf skeleton key

garabato [gara'βato] nm (escritura) scrawl, scribble

garaje [ga'raxe] nm garage

garantía [garan'tia] nf guarantee

garantizar [garanti'θar] vt to guarantee

garbanzo [gar'βanθo] nm chickpea (BRIT), garbanzo (US)

garfio ['garfjo] nm grappling iron

garganta [gar'yanta] nf (ANAT) throat; (de botella) neck ♦ **gargantilla** nf necklace

gárgaras ['garyaras] nfpl: **hacer ~ to** gargle

gargarear (LAm) vi to gargle

garita [ga'rita] nf cabin, hut; (MIL) sentry box

garra ['garra] nf (de gato, TEC) claw; (de ave) talon; (fam: mano) hand, paw

garrafa [ga'rrafa] nf carafe, decanter

garrapata [garra'pata] nf tick

gas [gas] nm gas ▶ **gases lacrimógenos** tear gas sg

gasa ['gasa] nf gauze

gaseosa [gase'osa] nf lemonade

gaseoso, -a [gase'oso, a] adj gassy, fizzy

gasoil [ga'soil] nm diesel (oil)

gasóleo [ga'soleo] nm = **gasoil**

gasolina [gaso'lina] nf petrol (BRIT), gas(oline) (US) □ **gasolinera** nf petrol (BRIT) o gas (US) station

gastado, -a [gas'taðo, a] adj (dinero) spent; (ropa) worn out; (usado: frase etc) trite

gastar [gas'tar] vt (dinero, tiempo) to spend; (fuerzas) to use up; (desperdiciar) to waste; (llevar) to wear; **gastarse** vr to wear out; (estropearse) to waste; **~ en** to spend on; **~ bromas** to crack jokes; **¿qué número gastas?** what size (shoe) do you take?

gasto ['gasto] nm (desembolso) expenditure, spending; (consumo, uso) use; **gastos** nmpl (desembolsos) expenses; (cargos) charges, costs

gastronomía [gastrono'mia] nf gastronomy

gatear [gate'ar] vi (andar a gatas) to go on all fours

gatillo [ga'tiλo] nm (de arma de fuego) trigger; (de dentista) forceps

gato, -a ['gato, a] nm/f cat ♦ nm (TEC) jack; **andar a gatas** to go on all fours

gaucho ['gautʃo] nm gaucho

GAUCHO

Gauchos are the herdsmen or riders of the Southern Cone plains. Although popularly associated with Argentine folklore, **gauchos** belong equally to the cattle-raising areas of Southern Brazil and Uruguay. **Gauchos'** traditions and clothing reflect their mixed ancestry and cultural roots. Their baggy trousers are Arabic in origin, while the horse and guitar are inherited from the Spanish conquistadors; the poncho, maté and **boleadoras** (strips of leather weighted at either end with stones) form part of the Indian tradition.

gaviota [ga'βjota] nf seagull

gay [ge] adj inv, nm gay, homosexual

gazpacho [gaθ'patʃo] nm gazpacho

gel [xel] nm: **~ de baño/ducha** bath/ shower gel

gelatina [xela'tina] nf jelly; (polvos etc) gelatine

gema ['xema] nf gem

gemelo, -a [xe'melo, a] adj, nm/f twin; **gemelos** nmpl (de camisa) cufflinks; (prismáticos) field glasses, binoculars

gemido [xe'miðo] nm (quejido) moan, groan; (aullido) howl

Géminis ['xeminis] nm Gemini

gemir [xe'mir] vi (quejarse) to moan, groan; (aullar) to howl

generación [xenera'θjon] nf generation

general [xene'ral] adj general ♦ nm general; **por lo** o **en ~** in general
❑ **Generalitat** nf Catalan parliament
❑ **generalizar** vt to generalize;
generalizarse vr to become generalized, spread

generar [xene'rar] vt to generate

género ['xenero] nm (clase) kind, sort; (tipo) type; (BIO) genus; (LING) gender; (COM) material ▶ **género humano** human race

generosidad [xenerosi'ðað] nf generosity ❑ **generoso, -a** adj generous

genial [xe'njal] adj inspired; (idea) brilliant; (estupendo) wonderful

genio ['xenjo] nm (carácter) nature, disposition; (humor) temper; (facultad creadora) genius; **de mal ~** bad-tempered

genital [xeni'tal] adj genital
❑ **genitales** nmpl genitals

gente ['xente] nf (personas) people pl; (parientes) relatives pl

gentil [xen'til] adj (elegante) graceful; (encantador) charming

⚠ No confundir **gentil** con la palabra inglesa **gentle**.

genuino, -a [xe'nwino, a] adj genuine

geografía [xeoɣra'fia] nf geography

geología [xeolo'xia] nf geology

geometría [xeome'tria] nf geometry

gerente [xe'rente] nmf (supervisor) manager; (jefe) director

geriatría [xerja'tria] nf (MED) geriatrics sg

germen ['xermen] nm germ

gesticular [xestiku'lar] vi to gesticulate; (hacer muecas) to grimace
❑ **gesticulación** nf gesticulation; (mueca) grimace

gestión [xes'tjon] nf management; (diligencia, acción) negotiation

gesto ['xesto] nm (mueca) grimace; (ademán) gesture

Gibraltar [xiβral'tar] nm Gibraltar
❑ **gibraltareño, -a** adj, nm/f Gibraltarian

gigante [xi'ɣante] adj, nmf giant
❑ **gigantesco, -a** adj gigantic

gilipollas [xili'poʎas] (fam) adj inv daft
♦ nmf inv wally

gimnasia [xim'nasja] nf gymnastics pl
❑ **gimnasio** nm gymnasium
❑ **gimnasta** nmf gymnast

ginebra [xi'neβra] nf gin

ginecólogo, -a [xine'koloɣo, a] nm/f gynaecologist

gira ['xira] nf tour, trip

girar [xi'rar] vt (dar la vuelta) to turn (around); (: rápidamente) to spin; (COM: giro postal) to draw; (: letra de cambio) to issue ♦ vi to turn (round); (rápido) to spin

girasol [xira'sol] nm sunflower

giratorio, -a [xira'torjo, a] adj revolving

giro ['xiro] nm (movimiento) turn, revolution; (LING) expression; (COM) draft ▶ **giro bancario/postal** bank draft/money order

gis [xis] (MÉX) nm chalk

gitano, -a [xi'tano, a] adj, nm/f gypsy

glacial [gla'θjal] adj icy, freezing

glaciar [gla'θjar] nm glacier

glándula ['glandula] nf gland

global [glo'βal] adj global
❑ **globalización** nf globalization

globo ['gloβo] nm (esfera) globe, sphere; (aerostato, juguete) balloon

glóbulo ['gloβulo] nm globule; (ANAT) corpuscle

gloria ['glorja] nf glory

glorieta [glo'rjeta] nf (de jardín) bower, arbour; (plazoleta) roundabout (BRIT), traffic circle (US)

glorioso, -a [glo'rjoso, a] adj glorious

glotón, -ona [glo'ton, ona] adj gluttonous, greedy ♦ nm/f glutton

glucosa [glu'kosa] nf glucose

gobernador, a [goβerna'ðor, a] adj governing ♦ nm/f governor
□ **gobernante** adj governing

gobernar [goβer'nar] vt (dirigir) to guide, direct; (POL) to rule, govern ♦ vi to govern; (NÁUT) to steer

gobierno etc [go'βjerno] vb ver **gobernar** ♦ nm (POL) government; (dirección) guidance, direction; (NÁUT) steering

goce etc ['goθe] vb ver **gozar** ♦ nm enjoyment

gol [gol] nm goal

golf [golf] nm golf

golfa ['golfa] (fam!) nf (mujer) slut, whore

golfo, -a ['golfo, a] nm (GEO) gulf ♦ nm/f (niño) urchin; (gamberro) lout

golondrina [golon'drina] nf swallow

golosina [golo'sina] nf (dulce) sweet □ **goloso, -a** adj sweet-toothed

golpe ['golpe] nm blow; (de puño) punch; (de mano) smack; (de remo) stroke; (fig: choque) clash; **no dar ~** to be bone idle; **de un ~** with one blow; **de ~** suddenly ♦ **golpe (de estado)** coup (d'état) □ **golpear** vt, vi to strike, knock; (asestar) to beat; (de puño) to punch; (golpetear) to tap

goma ['goma] nf (caucho) rubber; (elástico) elastic; (una goma) elastic band ▶ **goma de borrar** eraser, rubber (BRIT) ▶ **goma espuma** foam rubber

gomina ['gomina] nf hair gel

gomita (RPl) [go'mita] nf rubber band

gordo, -a ['gorðo, a] adj (gen) fat; (fam) enormous; **el (premio) ~** (en lotería) first prize

gorila [go'rila] nm gorilla

gorra ['gorra] nf cap; (de bebé) bonnet; (militar) bearskin; **entrar de ~** (fam) to gatecrash; **ir de ~** to sponge

gorrión [go'rrjon] nm sparrow

gorro ['gorro] nm (gen) cap; (de bebé, mujer) bonnet

gorrón, -ona [go'rron, ona] nm/f scrounger □ **gorronear** (fam) vi to scrounge

gota ['gota] nf (gen) drop; (de sudor) bead; (MED) gout □ **gotear** vi to drip; (lloviznar) to drizzle □ **gotera** nf leak

gozar [go'θar] vi to enjoy o.s.; **~ de** (disfrutar) to enjoy; (poseer) to possess

gr. abr (= gramo, gramos) g

grabación [graβa'θjon] nf recording

grabado [gra'βaðo] nm print, engraving

grabadora [graβa'ðora] nf tape-recorder

grabar [gra'βar] vt to engrave; (discos, cintas) to record

gracia ['graθja] nf (encanto) grace, gracefulness; (humor) humour, wit; **¡(muchas) gracias!** thanks (very much)!; **gracias a** thanks to; **dar las gracias a algn por algo** to thank sb for sth; **tener ~** (chiste etc) to be funny; **no me hace ~** I am not keen □ **gracioso, -a** adj (divertido) funny, amusing; (cómico) comical ♦ nm/f (TEATRO) comic character

grada ['graða] nf (de escalera) step; (de anfiteatro) tier, row; **gradas** nfpl (DEPORTE: de estadio) terraces

grado ['graðo] nm degree; (de aceite, vino) grade; (grada) step; (MIL) rank; **de buen ~** willingly ▶ **grado centígrado/Fahrenheit** degree centigrade/Fahrenheit

graduación [graðwa'θjon] nf (del alcohol) proof, strength; (ESCOL) graduation; (MIL) rank

gradual [gra'ðwal] adj gradual

graduar [gra'ðwar] vt (gen) to graduate; (MIL) to commission; **graduarse** vr to graduate; **graduarse la vista** to have one's eyes tested

gráfica ['grafika] nf graph

gráfico, -a ['grafiko, a] adj graphic
♦ nm diagram; **gráficos** nmpl (INFORM) graphics

grajo ['graxo] nm rook

gramática [gra'matika] nf grammar

gramo ['gramo] nm gramme (BRIT), gram (US)

gran [gran] adj ver **grande**

grana ['grana] nf (color, tela) scarlet

granada [gra'naða] nf pomegranate; (MIL) grenade

granate [gra'nate] adj deep red

Gran Bretaña [-bre'taɲa] nf Great Britain

grande ['grande] (antes de nmsg **gran**) adj (de tamaño) big, large; (alto) tall; (distinguido) great; (impresionante) grand ♦ nm grandee

granel [gra'nel]: **a ~** adv (COM) in bulk

granero [gra'nero] nm granary, barn

granito [gra'nito] nm (AGR) small grain; (roca) granite

granizado [grani'θaðo] nm iced drink

granizar [grani'θar] vi to hail
☐ **granizo** nm hail

granja ['granxa] nf (gen) farm
☐ **granjero, -a** nm/f farmer

grano ['grano] nm grain; (semilla) seed; (de café) bean; (MED) pimple, spot

granuja [gra'nuxa] nm/f rogue; (golfillo) urchin

grapa ['grapa] nf staple; (TEC) clamp
☐ **grapadora** nf stapler

grasa ['grasa] nf (gen) grease; (de cocinar) fat, lard; (sebo) suet; (mugre) filth ☐ **grasiento, -a** adj greasy; (de aceite) oily □ **graso, -a** adj (leche, queso, carne) fatty; (pelo, piel) greasy

gratinar [grati'nar] vt to cook au gratin

gratis ['gratis] adv free

grato, -a ['grato, a] adj (agradable) pleasant, agreeable

gratuito, -a [gra'twito, a] adj (gratis) free; (sin razón) gratuitous

grave ['graβe] adj heavy; (serio) grave, serious ☐ **gravedad** nf gravity

Grecia ['greθja] nf Greece

gremio ['gremjo] nm trade, industry

griego, -a ['grjeɣo, a] adj, nm/f Greek

grieta ['grjeta] nf crack

grifo ['grifo] (ESP) nm tap (BRIT), faucet (US)

grillo ['griʎo] nm (ZOOL) cricket

gripa [MEX] ['gripa] nf flu, influenza

gripe ['gripe] nf flu, influenza

gris [gris] adj (color) grey

gritar [gri'tar] vt, vi to shout, yell
☐ **grito** nm shout, yell; (de horror) scream

grosella [gro'seʎa] nf (red)currant

grosero, -a [gro'sero, a] adj (poco cortés) rude, bad-mannered; (ordinario) vulgar, crude

grosor [gro'sor] nm thickness

grúa ['grua] nf (TEC) crane; (de petróleo) derrick

grueso, -a ['grweso, a] adj thick; (persona) stout ♦ nm bulk; **el ~ de** the bulk of

grulla ['gruʎa] nf crane

grumo ['grumo] nm clot, lump

gruñido [gru'ɲiðo] nm grunt; (de persona) grumble

gruñir [gru'ɲir] vi (animal) to growl; (persona) to grumble

grupo ['grupo] nm group; (TEC) unit, set
► **grupo de presión** pressure group
► **grupo sanguíneo** blood group

gruta ['gruta] nf grotto

guacho, -a [cs] ['gwatʃo, a] nm/f homeless child

guajolote [MEX] [gwaxo'lote] nm turkey

guante ['gwante] nm glove ► **guantes de goma** rubber gloves ☐ **guantera** nf glove compartment

guapo, -a ['gwapo, a] adj good-looking, attractive; (elegante) smart

guarda ['gwarða] nmf (persona) guard, keeper ♦ nf (acto) guarding; (custodia) custody ▶ **guarda jurado** (armed) security guard ◻ **guardabarros** nm inv mudguard (BRIT), fender (US) ◻ **guardabosques** nm inv gamekeeper ◻ **guardacostas** nm inv coastguard vessel ◻ **guardameta** nmf guardian, protector ◻ **guardaespaldas** nmf inv bodyguard ◻ **guardameta** nmf goalkeeper ◻ **guardar** vt (gen) to keep; (vigilar) to guard, watch over; (dinero: ahorrar) to save; **guardarse** vr (preservarse) to protect o.s.; (evitar) to avoid; **guardar cama** to stay in bed ◻ **guardarropa** nm (en armario) wardrobe; (en establecimiento público) cloakroom

guardería [gwarðeˈria] nf nursery

guardia [ˈgwarðja] nf (MIL) guard; (cuidado) care, custody ♦ nmf guard; (policía) policeman(-woman); **estar de ~** to be on guard; **montar ~** to mount guard ▶ **Guardia Civil** Civil Guard

guardián, -ana [gwarˈðjan, ana] nm/f (gen) guardian, keeper

guarida [gwaˈriða] nf (de animal) den, lair; (refugio) refuge

guarnición [gwarniˈθjon] nf (de vestimenta) trimming; (de piedra) mount; (CULIN) garnish; (arneses) harness; (MIL) garrison

guarro, -a [ˈgwarro, a] nm/f pig

guasa [ˈgwasa] nf joke ◻ **guasón, -ona** adj (bromista) joking ♦ nm/f wit; joker

Guatemala [gwateˈmala] nf Guatemala

guay [gwai] (fam) adj super, great

güero, -a (MÉX) [ˈgwero, a] adj blond(e)

guerra [ˈgerra] nf war; **dar ~** to annoy ▶ **guerra civil** civil war ◻ **guerra fría** cold war ◻ **guerrero, -a** adj fighting; (carácter) warlike ♦ nm/f warrior

guerrilla [geˈrriʎa] nf guerrilla warfare; (tropas) guerrilla band o group

guía etc [ˈgia] vb ver **guiar** ♦ nmf (persona) guide; (nf: libro) guidebook ▶ **guía telefónica** telephone directory ▶ **guía turística** tourist guide

guiar [giˈar] vt to guide, direct; (AUTO) to steer; **guiarse** vr: **guiarse por** to be guided by

guinda [ˈginda] nf morello cherry

guindilla [ginˈdiʎa] nf chilli pepper

guiñar [giˈɲar] vt to wink

guión [giˈon] nm (LING) hyphen, dash; (CINE) script ◻ **guionista** nmf scriptwriter

guiri [ˈgiri] (ESP: fam, pey) nmf foreigner

guirnalda [girˈnalda] nf garland

guisado [giˈsaðo] nm stew

guisante [giˈsante] nm pea

guisar [giˈsar] vt, vi to cook ◻ **guiso** nm cooked dish

guitarra [giˈtarra] nf guitar

gula [ˈgula] nf gluttony, greed

gusano [guˈsano] nm worm; (lombriz) earthworm

gustar [gusˈtar] vt to taste, sample ♦ vi to please, be pleasing; **~ de algo** to enjoy sth; **me gustan las uvas** I like grapes; **le gusta nadar** she likes o enjoys swimming

gusto [ˈgusto] nm (sentido, sabor) taste; (placer) pleasure; **tiene ~ a menta** it tastes of mint; **tener buen ~** to have good taste; **coger el o tomar ~ a algo** to take a liking to sth; **sentirse a ~** to feel at ease; **mucho ~ (en conocerle)** pleased to meet you; **el ~ es mío** the pleasure is mine; **con ~** willingly, gladly

H, h

ha [a] vb ver **haber**

haba [ˈaβa] nf bean

Habana [aˈβana] nf: **la ~** Havana

habano [aˈβano] nm Havana cigar

habéis vb ver **haber**

haber

PALABRA CLAVE

[a'βer] vb aux

1 (tiempos compuestos) to have; **había comido** I had eaten; **antes/después de haberlo visto** before seeing/after seeing o having seen it

2: **¡haberlo dicho antes!** you should have said so before!

3: **haber de, he de hacerlo** I have to do it; **ha de llegar mañana** it should arrive tomorrow

♦ vb impers

1 (existencia: sg) there is; (: pl) there are; **hay un hermano/dos hermanos** there is one brother/there are two brothers; **¿cuánto hay de aquí a Sucre?** how far is it from here to Sucre?

2 (obligación): **hay que hacer algo** something must be done; **hay que apuntarlo para acordarse** you have to write it down to remember

3: **¡hay que ver!** well I never!

4: **¡no hay de o por** (LAm) **qué!** don't mention it!, not at all!

5: **¿qué hay?** (¿qué pasa?) what's up?, what's the matter?; (¿qué tal?) how's it going?

♦ vt: **he aquí unas sugerencias** here are some suggestions; **no hay cintas blancas pero sí las hay rojas** there aren't any white ribbons but there are some red ones

♦ nm (en cuenta) credit side; **haberes** nmpl assets; **¿cuánto tengo en el haber?** how much do I have in my account?; **tiene varias novelas en su haber** he has several novels to his credit

haberse vr: **habérselas con algn** to have it out with sb

habichuela [aβi'tʃwela] nf kidney bean

hábil ['aβil] adj (listo) clever, smart; (capaz) fit, capable; (experto) expert; **día** ~ working day ❑ **habilidad** nf skill, ability

habitación [aβita'θjon] nf (cuarto) room; (BIO: morada) habitat
▶ **habitación doble o de matrimonio** double room
▶ **habitación individual o sencilla** single room

habitante [aβi'tante] nmf inhabitant

habitar [aβi'tar] vt (residir en) to inhabit; (ocupar) to occupy ♦ vi to live

hábito ['aβito] nm habit

habitual [aβi'twal] adj usual

habituar [aβi'twar] vt to accustom; **habituarse** vr: **habituarse a** to get used to

habla ['aβla] nf (capacidad de hablar) speech; (idioma) language; (dialecto) dialect; **perder el** ~ to become speechless; **de** ~ **francesa** French-speaking; **estar al** ~ to be in contact; (TEL) to be on the line; **¡González al** ~! (TEL) González speaking!

hablador, a [aβla'ðor, a] adj talkative
♦ nm/f chatterbox

habladuría [aβlaðu'ria] nf rumour; **habladurías** nfpl gossip sg

hablante [a'βlante] adj speaking ♦ nmf speaker

hablar [a'βlar] vt to speak, talk ♦ vi to speak; **hablarse** vr to speak to each other; ~ **con** to speak to; ~ **de** to speak of o about; **¡ni hablar!** it's out of the question!; **"se habla inglés"** "English spoken here"

habré etc [a'βre] vb ver **haber**

hacendado (LAm) [aθen'daðo] nm rancher, farmer

hacendoso, -a [aθen'doso, a] adj industrious

hacer

PALABRA CLAVE

[a'θer] vt

1 (fabricar, producir) to make; (construir) to build; **hacer una película/un ruido** to make a film/noise; **el guisado lo hice yo** I made o cooked the stew

2 (ejecutar: trabajo etc) to do; **hacer la colada** to do the washing; **hacer la comida** to do the cooking; **¿qué haces?** what are you doing?; **hacer el malo** o **el papel del malo** (TEATRO) to play the villain

3 (estudios, algunos deportes) to do; **hacer español/económicas** to do o study Spanish/economics; **hacer yoga/gimnasia** to do yoga/go to gym

4 (transformar, incidir en): **esto lo hará más difícil** this will make it more difficult; **salir te hará sentir mejor** going out will make you feel better

5 (cálculo): **2 y 2 hacen 4** 2 and 2 make 4; **éste hace 100** this one makes 100

6 (+ sub): **esto hará que ganemos** this will make us win; **harás que no quiera venir** you'll stop him wanting to come

7 (como sustituto de vb) to do; **él bebió y yo hice lo mismo** he drank and I did likewise

8 : **no hace más que criticar** all he does is criticize

♦ vb semi-aux (directo): **hacer +infin**: **les hice venir** I made o had them come; **hacer trabajar a los demás** to get others to work

♦ vi

1 : **haz como que no lo sabes** act as if you don't know

2 (ser apropiado): **si os hace** if it's alright with you

3 : **hacer de: hacer de Otelo** to play Othello

♦ vb impers

1 : **hace calor/frío** it's hot/cold; ver tb **bueno; sol; tiempo**

2 (tiempo): **hace 3 años** 3 years ago; **hace un mes que voy/no voy** I've been going/I haven't been for a month

3 : **¿cómo has hecho para llegar tan rápido?** how did you manage to get here so quickly?

♦ **hacerse** vr

1 (volverse) to become; **se hicieron amigos** they became friends

2 (acostumbrarse): **hacerse a** to get used to

3 : **se hace con huevos y leche** it's made out of eggs and milk; **eso no se hace** that's not done

4 (obtener): **hacerse de** o **con algo** to get hold of sth

5 (fingirse): **hacerse el sueco** to turn a deaf ear

hacha ['atʃa] nf axe; (antorcha) torch

hachís [a'tʃis] nm hashish

hacia ['aθja] prep (en dirección de) towards; (cerca de) near; (actitud) towards; **~ adelante/atrás** forwards/backwards; **~ arriba/abajo** up(wards)/down(wards); **~ mediodía/las cinco** about noon/five

hacienda [a'θjenda] nf (propiedad) property; (finca) farm; (LAm: rancho) ranch; (**Ministerio de H~**) Exchequer (BRIT), Treasury Department (US) ► **hacienda pública** public finance

hada ['aða] nf fairy

hago etc vb ver **hacer**

Haití [ai'ti] nm Haiti

halagar [ala'ɣar] vt to flatter

halago [a'laɣo] *nm* flattery

halcón [al'kon] *nm* falcon, hawk

hallar [a'ʎar] *vt* (*gen*) to find; (*descubrir*) to discover; (*toparse con*) to run into; **hallarse** *vr* to be (situated)

halterofilia [altero'filja] *nf* weightlifting

hamaca [a'maka] *nf* hammock

hambre ['ambre] *nf* hunger; (*plaga*) famine; (*deseo*) longing; **tener ~** to be hungry; **¡me muero de ~!** I'm starving! □ **hambriento, -a** *adj* hungry, starving

hamburguesa [ambur'ɣesa] *nf* hamburger □ **hamburguesería** *nf* burger bar

han [an] *vb ver* **haber**

harapos [a'rapos] *nmpl* rags

haré [a're] *vb ver* **hacer**

harina [a'rina] *nf* flour ▶ **harina de maíz** cornflour (BRIT), cornstarch (US) ▶ **harina de trigo** wheat flour

hartar [ar'tar] *vt* to satiate, glut; (*fig*) to tire, sicken; **hartarse** *vr* (*de comida*) to fill o.s., gorge o.s.; (*cansarse*): **hartarse (de)** to get fed up (with) □ **harto, -a** *adj* (*lleno*) full; (*cansado*) fed up ♦ *adv* (*bastante*) enough; (*muy*) very; **estar harto de hacer algo/de algn** to be fed up of doing sth/with sb

has [as] *vb ver* **haber**

hasta ['asta] *adv* even ♦ *prep* (*alcanzando a*) as far as; up to; down to; (*de tiempo: a tal hora*) till, until; (*antes de*) before ♦ *conj*: **~ que ... until; ~ luego/el sábado** see you soon/on Saturday; **~ ahora** (*al despedirse*) see you in a minute; **~ pronto** see you soon

hay [ai] *vb ver* **haber**

Haya ['aja] *nf*: **la ~** The Hague

haya *etc* ['aja] *vb ver* **haber** ♦ *nf* beech tree

haz [aθ] *vb ver* **hacer** ♦ *nm* (*de luz*) beam

hazaña [a'θaɲa] *nf* feat, exploit

hazmerreír [aθmerre'ir] *nm inv* laughing stock

he [e] *vb ver* **haber**

hebilla [e'βiʎa] *nf* buckle, clasp

hebra ['eβra] *nf* thread; (BOT: *fibra*) fibre, grain

hebreo, -a [e'βreo, a] *adj*, *nm/f* Hebrew ♦ *nm* (LING) Hebrew

hechizar [etʃi'θar] *vt* to cast a spell on, bewitch

hechizo [e'tʃiθo] *nm* witchcraft, magic; (*acto de magia*) spell, charm

hecho, -a ['etʃo, a] *pp de* **hacer** ♦ *adj* (*carne*) done; (COSTURA) ready-to-wear ♦ *nm* deed, act; (*dato*) fact; (*cuestión*) matter; (*suceso*) event ♦ *excl* agreed!, done!; **de ~** in fact, as a matter of fact; **el ~ es que ...** the fact is that ...; **¡bien ~!** well done!

hechura [e'tʃura] *nf* (*forma*) form, shape; (*de persona*) build

hectárea [ek'tarea] *nf* hectare

helada [e'laða] *nf* frost

heladera [ela'ðera] *nf* (LAm) (*refrigerador*) refrigerator

helado, -a [e'laðo, a] *adj* frozen; (*glacial*) icy; (*fig*) chilly, cold ♦ *nm* ice cream

helar [e'lar] *vt* to freeze, ice (up); (*dejar atónito*) to amaze; (*desalentar*) to discourage ♦ *vi* to freeze; **helarse** *vr* to freeze

helecho [e'letʃo] *nm* fern

hélice ['eliθe] *nf* (TEC) propeller

helicóptero [eli'koptero] *nm* helicopter

hembra ['embra] *nf* (BOT, ZOOL) female; (*mujer*) woman; (TEC) nut

hemorragia [emo'rraxja] *nf* haemorrhage

hemorroides [emo'rroiðes] *nfpl* haemorrhoids, piles

hemos ['emos] *vb ver* **haber**

heno ['eno] *nm* hay

heredar [ere'ðar] vt to inherit
□ **heredero, -a** nm/f heir(ess)

hereje [e'rexe] nmf heretic

herencia [e'renθja] nf inheritance

herida [e'riða] nf wound, injury; ver tb **herido**

herido, -a [e'riðo, a] adj injured, wounded ♦ nm/f casualty

herir [e'rir] vt to wound, injure; (fig) to offend

hermanastro, -a [erma'nastro, a] nm/f stepbrother/sister

hermandad [erman'daθ] nf brotherhood

hermano, -a [er'mano, a] nm/f brother/sister ► **hermano(-a) gemelo(-a)** twin brother/sister ► **hermano(-a) político(-a)** brother-in-law/sister-in-law

hermético, -a [er'metiko, a] adj hermetic; (fig) watertight

hermoso, -a [er'moso, a] adj beautiful, lovely; (estupendo) splendid; (guapo) handsome ► **hermosura** nf beauty

hernia ['ernja] nf hernia ► **hernia discal** slipped disc

héroe ['eroe] nm hero

heroína [ero'ina] nf (mujer) heroine; (droga) heroin

herradura [erra'ðura] nf horseshoe

herramienta [erra'mjenta] nf tool

herrero [e'rrero] nm blacksmith

hervidero [erβi'ðero] nm (fig) swarm; (POL etc) hotbed

hervir [er'βir] vi to boil; (burbujear) to bubble; ~ **a fuego lento** to simmer □ **hervor** nm boiling; (fig) ardour, fervour

heterosexual [eterosek'swal] adj heterosexual

hice etc ['iθe] vb ver **hacer**

hidratante [iðra'tante] adj: **crema** ~ moisturizing cream, moisturizer □ **hidratar** vt (piel) to moisturize □ **hidrato** nm hydrate ► **hidratos de carbono** carbohydrates

hidráulico, -a [i'ðrauliko, a] adj hydraulic

hidro... [iðro] prefijo hydro-, water-... □ **hidroeléctrico, -a** adj hydroelectric □ **hidrógeno** nm hydrogen

hiedra ['jeðra] nf ivy

hiel [jel] nf gall, bile; (fig) bitterness

hiela etc vb ver **helar**

hielo ['jelo] nm (gen) ice; (escarcha) frost; (fig) coldness, reserve

hiena ['jena] nf hyena

hierba ['jerβa] nf (pasto) grass; (CULIN, MED: planta) herb; **mala** ~ weed; (fig) evil influence □ **hierbabuena** nf mint

hierro ['jerro] nm (metal) iron; (objeto) iron object

hígado ['iɣaðo] nm liver

higiene [i'xjene] nf hygiene □ **higiénico, -a** adj hygienic

higo ['iɣo] nm fig ► **higo seco** dried fig □ **higuera** nf fig tree

hijastro, -a [i'xastro, a] nm/f stepson/daughter

hijo, -a [ˈixo, a] nm/f son/daughter, child; **hijos** nmpl children, sons and daughters ► **hijo adoptivo** adopted child ► **hijo de papá/mamá** daddy's/mummy's boy ► **hijo de puta** (fam!) bastard (!), son of a bitch (!) ► **hijo/a político(-a)** son-in-law/daughter-in-law

hilera [i'lera] nf row, file

hilo ['ilo] nm thread; (BOT) fibre; (metal) wire; (de agua) trickle, thin stream

hilvanar [ilβa'nar] vt (COSTURA) to tack (BRIT), baste (US); (fig) to do hurriedly

himno ['imno] nm hymn ► **himno nacional** national anthem

hincapié [inka'pje] nm: **hacer hincapié en** to emphasize

hincar [in'kar] vt to drive (in), thrust (in)

hincha ['intʃa] (fam) nmf fan

hinchado, -a [in'tʃaðo, a] adj (gen) swollen; (persona) pompous

hinchar [in'tʃar] vt (gen) to swell; (inflar) to blow up, inflate; (fig) to exaggerate; **hincharse** vr (inflarse) to swell up; (fam: de comer) to stuff o.s. ☐ **hinchazón** f (MED) swelling; (altivez) arrogance

hinojo [i'noxo] nm fennel

hipermercado [ipermer'kaðo] nm hypermarket, superstore

hípico, -a [i'piko, a] adj horse cpd

hipnotismo [ipno'tismo] nm hypnotism ☐ **hipnotizar** vt to hypnotize

hipo ['ipo] nm hiccups pl

hipocresía [ipokre'sia] nf hypocrisy ☐ **hipócrita** adj hypocritical ♦ nmf hypocrite

hipódromo [i'poðromo] nm racetrack

hipopótamo [ipo'potamo] nm hippopotamus

hipoteca [ipo'teka] nf mortgage

hipótesis [i'potesis] nf inv hypothesis

hispánico, -a [is'paniko, a] adj Hispanic

hispano, -a [is'pano, a] adj Hispanic, Spanish, Hispano- ♦ nm/f Spaniard ☐ **Hispanoamérica** nf Latin America ☐ **hispanoamericano, -a** adj, nm/f Latin American

histeria [is'terja] nf hysteria

historia [is'torja] nf history; (cuento) story, tale; **historias** nfpl (chismes) gossip sg; **dejarse de historias** to come to the point; **pasar a la ~** to go down in history ☐ **historiador, a** nm/ f historian ☐ **historial** nm (profesional) curriculum vitae, C.V.; (MED) case history ☐ **histórico, -a** adj historical; (memorable) historic

historieta [isto'rjeta] nf tale, anecdote; (dibujos) comic strip

hito ['ito] nm (fig) landmark

hizo ['iθo] vb ver **hacer**

hocico [o'θiko] nm snout

hockey ['xokei] nm hockey ► **hockey sobre hielo/patines** ice/roller hockey

hogar [o'ɣar] nm fireplace, hearth; (casa) home; (vida familiar) home life ► **hogareño, -a** [oɣa'reɲo] adj home cpd; (persona) home-loving

hoguera [o'ɣera] nf bonfire

hoja ['oxa] nf (gen) leaf; (de flor) petal; (de papel) sheet; (página) page ► **hoja de afeitar** (LAm) razor blade ► **hoja electrónica** o **de cálculo** spreadsheet ► **hoja informativa** leaflet, handout

hojalata [oxa'lata] nf tin(plate)

hojaldre [o'xaldre] nm (CULIN) puff pastry

hojear [oxe'ar] vt to leaf through, turn the pages of

hojuela [o'xwela] nf (MEX) flake

hola ['ola] excl hello!

holá (RPl) excl hello!

Holanda [o'landa] nf Holland ☐ **holandés, -esa** adj Dutch ♦ nm/f Dutchman(-woman) ♦ nm (LING) Dutch

holgado, -a [ol'ɣaðo, a] adj (ropa) loose, baggy; (rico) comfortable

holgar [ol'ɣar] vi (descansar) to rest; (sobrar) to be superfluous

holgazán, -ana [olɣa'θan, ana] adj idle, lazy ♦ nm/f loafer

hollín [o'ʎin] nm soot

hombre ['ombre] nm (gen) man; (raza humana): **el ~** man(kind) ♦ excl: **¡sí ~!** (claro) of course!; (para énfasis) man, old boy ► **hombre de negocios** businessman ► **hombre de pro** honest man ► **hombre-rana** frogman

hombrera [om'brera] nf shoulder strap

hombro ['ombro] nm shoulder

homenaje [ome'naxe] nm (gen) homage; (tributo) tribute

homicida [omi'θiða] adj homicidal ♦ nmf murderer ☐ **homicidio** nm murder, homicide

homologar [omolo'ɣar] vt (COM: productos, tamaños) to standardize

homólogo, -a [o'moloɣo, a] *nm/f*: **su etc ~** his *etc* counterpart o opposite number

homosexual [omosek'swal] *adj, nmf* homosexual

honda (CS) ['onda] *nf* catapult

hondo, -a ['ondo, a] *adj* deep; **lo ~** the depth(s) *pl*, the bottom □ **hondonada** *nf* hollow, depression; (*cañón*) ravine

Honduras [on'duras] *nf* Honduras

hondureño, -a [ondu'reɲo, a] *adj, nm/f* Honduran

honestidad [onesti'ðað] *nf* purity, chastity; (*decencia*) decency □ **honesto, -a** *adj* chaste; decent; (*justo*) just

hongo ['ongo] *nm* (BOT: *gen*) fungus; (: *comestible*) mushroom; (: *venenoso*) toadstool

honor [o'nor] *nm* (*gen*) honour; **en ~ a la verdad** to be fair □ **honorable** *adj* honourable

honorario, -a [ono'rarjo, a] *adj* honorary □ **honorarios** *nmpl* fees

honra ['onra] *nf* (*gen*) honour; (*renombre*) good name □ **honradez** *nf* honesty; (*de persona*) integrity □ **honrado, -a** *adj* honest, upright □ **honrar** [on'rar] *vt* to honour

hora ['ora] *nf* (*una hora*) hour; (*tiempo*) time; **¿qué ~ es?** what time is it? **¿a qué ~?** at what time?; **media ~** half an hour; **a la ~ de recreo** at playtime; **a primera ~** first thing (in the morning); **a última ~** at the last moment; **a altas horas** in the small hours; **¡a buena ~!** about time too!; **pedir ~** to make an appointment; **dar la ~** to strike the hour ▸ **horas de oficina/trabajo** office/working hours ▸ **horas de visita** visiting times ▸ **horas extras** o **extraordinarias** overtime *sg* ▸ **horas pico** (LAm) rush o peak hours ▸ **horas punta** (ESP) rush hours

horario, -a [o'rarjo, a] *adj* hourly, hour *cpd* ♦ *nm* timetable ▸ **horario comercial** business hours *pl*

horca ['orka] *nf* gallows *sg*

horcajadas [orka'xaðas]: **a ~** *adv* astride

horchata [or'tʃata] *nf* cold drink made from tiger nuts and water, tiger nut milk

horizontal [oriθon'tal] *adj* horizontal

horizonte [ori'θonte] *nm* horizon

horma ['orma] *nf* mould

hormiga [or'miɣa] *nf* ant; **hormigas** *nfpl* (MED) pins and needles

hormigón [ormi'ɣon] *nm* concrete ▸ **hormigón armado/pretensado** reinforced/prestressed concrete

hormigonera *nf* cement mixer

hormigueo [ormi'ɣeo] *nm* (*comezón*) itch

hormona [or'mona] *nf* hormone

hornillo [or'niʎo] *nm* (*cocina*) portable stove ▸ **hornillo de gas** gas ring

horno ['orno] *nm* (CULIN) oven; (TEC) furnace; **alto ~** blast furnace

horóscopo [o'roskopo] *nm* horoscope

horquilla [or'kiʎa] *nf* hairpin; (AGR) pitchfork

horrendo, -a [o'rrendo, a] *adj* horrendous, frightful

horrible [o'rriβle] *adj* horrible, dreadful

horripilante [orripi'lante] *adj* hair-raising, horrifying

horror [o'rror] *nm* horror, dread; (*atrocidad*) atrocity; **¡qué ~!** (*fam*) how awful! □ **horrorizar** *vt* to horrify, frighten; **horrorizarse** *vr* to be horrified □ **horroroso, -a** *adj* horrifying, ghastly

hortaliza [orta'liθa] *nf* vegetable

hortelano, -a [orte'lano, a] *nm/f* (market) gardener

hortera [or'tera] (*fam*) *adj* tacky

hospedar [ospe'ðar] *vt* to put up; **hospedarse** *vr* to stay, lodge

hospital [ospi'tal] *nm* hospital

hospitalario, -a [ospitaˈlarjo, a] *adj*
(*acogedor*) hospitable
❑ **hospitalidad** *nf* hospitality

hostal [osˈtal] *nm* small hotel

hostelería [osteleˈria] *nf* hotel
business o trade

hostia [ˈostja] *nf* (REL) host, consecrated
wafer; (fam!: *golpe*) whack, punch
♦ *excl* (fam!): **~(s)!** damn!

hostil [osˈtil] *adj* hostile

hotdog (LAm) *nm* hot dog

hotel [oˈtel] *nm* hotel ❑ **hotelero, -a**
adj hotel *cpd* ♦ *nm/f* hotelier

HOTEL

In Spain you can choose from the
following categories of
accommodation, in descending order
of quality and price: **hotel** (from 5
stars to 1), **hostal**, **pensión**, **casa de
huéspedes**, **fonda**. The State also runs
luxury hotels called **paradores**, which
are usually sited in places of particular
historical interest and are often
historic buildings themselves.

---

hoy [oi] *adv* (*este día*) today; (*la
actualidad*) now(adays) ♦ *nm* present
time; **~ (en) día** now(adays)

hoyo [ˈojo] *nm* hole, pit

hoz [oθ] *nf* sickle

hube *etc* [ˈuβe] *vb ver* **haber**

hucha [ˈutʃa] *nf* money box

hueco, -a [ˈweko, a] *adj* (*vacío*) hollow,
empty; (*resonante*) booming ♦ *nm*
hollow, cavity

huelga *etc* [ˈwelɣa] *vb ver* **holgar** ♦ *nf*
strike; **declararse en ~** to go on strike,
come out on strike ▸ **huelga de
hambre** hunger strike ▸ **huelga
general** general strike

huelguista [welˈɣista] *nmf* striker

huella [ˈweʎa] *nf* (*pisada*) track; (*marca
del paso*) footprint, footstep; (: *de
animal, máquina*) track ▸ **huella
dactilar** fingerprint

huelo *etc vb ver* **oler**

huérfano, -a [ˈwerfano, a] *adj*
orphan(ed) ♦ *nm/f* orphan

huerta [ˈwerta] *nf* market garden; (*en
Murcia y Valencia*) irrigated region

huerto [ˈwerto] *nm* kitchen garden; (*de
árboles frutales*) orchard

hueso [ˈweso] *nm* (ANAT) bone; (*de fruta*)
stone

huésped [ˈwespeð] *nmf* guest

hueva [ˈweβa] *nf* roe

huevera [weˈβera] *nf* eggcup

huevo [ˈweβo] *nm* egg ▸ **huevo a la
copa** (CS) soft-boiled egg ▸ **huevo
duro/escalfado** hard-boiled/
poached egg ▸ **huevo estrellado**
(LAm) fried egg ▸ **huevo frito** (SP)
fried egg ▸ **huevo pasado por agua**
soft-boiled egg ▸ **huevos revueltos**
scrambled eggs ▸ **huevo tibio** (MÉX)
soft-boiled egg

huida [uˈiða] *nf* escape, flight

huir [uˈir] *vi* (*escapar*) to flee, escape;
(*evitar*) to avoid

hule [ˈule] *nm* oilskin; (MÉX: *goma*)
rubber

hulera (MÉX) *nf* catapult

humanidad [umaniˈðað] *nf* (*género
humano*) man(kind); (*cualidad*)
humanity

humanitario, -a [umaniˈtarjo, a] *adj*
humanitarian

humano, -a [uˈmano, a] *adj* (*gen*)
human; (*humanitario*) humane ♦ *nm*
human; **ser ~** human being

humareda [umaˈreða] *nf* cloud of
smoke

humedad [umeˈðað] *nf* (*de clima*)
humidity; (*de pared etc*) dampness; **a
prueba de ~** damp-proof
❑ **humedecer** *vt* to moisten, wet;
humedecerse *vr* to get wet

húmedo, -a [ˈumeðo, a] *adj* (*mojado*)
damp, wet; (*tiempo etc*) humid

humilde [uˈmilde] *adj* humble, modest

humillación [umiʎaˈθjon] nf humiliation ❑ **humillante** adj humiliating

humillar [umiˈʎar] vt to humiliate

humo [ˈumo] nm (de fuego) smoke; (gas nocivo) fumes pl; (vapor) steam, vapour; **humos** nmpl (fig) conceit sg

humor [uˈmor] nm (disposición) mood, temper; (lo que divierte) humour; **de buen/mal** ~ in a good/bad mood ❑ **humorista** nmf comic ❑ **humorístico, -a** adj funny, humorous

hundimiento [undiˈmjento] nm (gen) sinking; (colapso) collapse

hundir [unˈdir] vt to sink; (edificio, plan) to ruin, destroy; **hundirse** vr to sink, collapse

húngaro, -a [ˈungaro, a] adj, nm/f Hungarian

Hungría [unˈgria] nf Hungary

huracán [uraˈkan] nm hurricane

huraño, -a [uˈraɲo, a] adj (antisocial) unsociable

hurgar [urˈɣar] vt to poke, jab; (remover) to stir (up); **hurgarse** vr: **hurgarse (las narices)** to pick one's nose

hurón, -ona [uˈron, ona] nm (ZOOL) ferret

hurtadillas [urtaˈðiʎas]: **a ~** adv stealthily, on the sly

hurtar [urˈtar] vt to steal ❑ **hurto** nm theft, stealing

husmear [usmeˈar] vt (oler) to sniff out, scent; (fam) to pry into

huyo etc vb ver **huir**

I, i

iba etc [ˈiβa] vb ver **ir**

ibérico, -a [iˈβeriko, a] adj Iberian

iberoamericano, -a [iβeroameriˈkano, a] adj, nm/f Latin American

Ibiza [iˈβiθa] nf Ibiza

iceberg [iθeˈβer] nm iceberg

icono [iˈkono] nm ikon, icon

ida [ˈiða] nf going, departure; **~ y vuelta** round trip, return

idea [iˈðea] nf idea; **no tengo la menor ~** I haven't a clue

ideal [iðeˈal] adj, nm ideal ❑ **idealista** nmf idealist ❑ **idealizar** vt to idealize

ídem [ˈiðem] pron ditto

idéntico, -a [iˈðentiko, a] adj identical

identidad [iðentiˈðað] nf identity

identificación [iðentifikaˈθjon] nf identification

identificar [iðentifiˈkar] vt to identify; **identificarse** vr: **identificarse con** to identify with

ideología [iðeoloˈxia] nf ideology

idilio [iˈðiljo] nm love-affair

idioma [iˈðjoma] nm (gen) language

⚠ No confundir **idioma** con la palabra inglesa *idiom*.

idiota [iˈðjota] adj idiotic ♦ nmf idiot

ídolo [ˈiðolo] nm (tb fig) idol

idóneo, -a [iˈðoneo, a] adj suitable

iglesia [iˈɣlesja] nf church

ignorante [iɣnoˈrante] adj ignorant, uninformed ♦ nmf ignoramus

ignorar [iɣnoˈrar] vt not to know, be ignorant of; (no hacer caso a) to ignore

igual [iˈɣwal] adj (gen) equal; (similar) like, similar; (mismo) the same; (constante) constant; (temperatura) even ♦ nm equal; **~ que** like, the same as; **me da o es ~** I don't care; **son iguales** they're the same; **al ~ que** (prep, conj) like, just like

igualar [iɣwaˈlar] vt (gen) to equalize, make equal; (allanar, nivelar) to level (off), even (out); **igualarse** vr (platos de balanza) to balance out

igualdad [iɣwal'daθ] nf equality; (*similaridad*) sameness; (*uniformidad*) uniformity

igualmente [iɣwal'mente] adv equally; (*también*) also, likewise ♦ excl the same to you!

ilegal [ile'ɣal] adj illegal

ilegítimo, -a [ile'xitimo, a] adj illegitimate

ileso, -a [i'leso, a] adj unhurt

ilimitado, -a [ilimi'taðo, a] adj unlimited

iluminación [ilumina'θjon] nf illumination; (*alumbrado*) lighting

iluminar [ilumi'nar] vt to illuminate, light (up); (*fig*) to enlighten

ilusión [ilu'sjon] nf illusion; (*quimera*) delusion; (*esperanza*) hope; **hacerse ilusiones** to build up one's hopes □ **ilusionado, -a** adj excited □ **ilusionar** vi: **le ilusiona ir de vacaciones** he's looking forward to going on holiday; **ilusionarse** vr: **ilusionarse (con)** to get excited (about)

iluso, -a [i'luso, a] adj easily deceived ♦ nm/f dreamer

ilustración [ilustra'θjon] nf illustration; (*saber*) learning, erudition; **la I~** the Enlightenment □ **ilustrado, -a** adj illustrated; learned

ilustrar [ilus'trar] vt to illustrate, (*instruir*) to instruct; (*explicar*) to explain, make clear

ilustre [i'lustre] adj famous, illustrious

imagen [i'maxen] nf (*gen*) image; (*dibujo*) picture

imaginación [imaxina'θjon] nf imagination

imaginar [imaxi'nar] vt (*gen*) to imagine; (*idear*) to think up; (*suponer*) to suppose; **imaginarse** vr to imagine □ **imaginario, -a** adj imaginary □ **imaginativo, -a** adj imaginative

imán [i'man] nm magnet

imbécil [im'beθil] nmf imbecile, idiot

imitación [imita'θjon] nf imitation; **de ~ imitation** cpd

imitar [imi'tar] vt to imitate; (*parodiar, remedar*) to mimic, ape

impaciente [impa'θjente] adj impatient; (*nervioso*) anxious

impacto [im'pakto] nm impact

impar [im'par] adj odd

imparcial [impar'θjal] adj impartial, fair

impecable [impe'kaβle] adj impeccable

impedimento [impeði'mento] nm impediment, obstacle

impedir [impe'ðir] vt (*obstruir*) to impede, obstruct; (*estorbar*) to prevent; **~ a algn hacer** o **que algn haga algo** to prevent sb (from) doing sth, stop sb doing sth

imperativo, -a [impera'tiβo, a] adj (*urgente, LING*) imperative

imperdible [imper'ðiβle] nm safety pin

imperdonable [imperðo'naβle] adj unforgivable, inexcusable

imperfecto, -a [imper'fekto, a] adj imperfect

imperio [im'perjo] nm empire; (*autoridad*) rule, authority; (*fig*) pride, haughtiness

impermeable [imperme'aβle] adj waterproof ♦ nm raincoat, mac (*BRIT*)

impersonal [imperso'nal] adj impersonal

impertinente [imperti'nente] adj impertinent

ímpetu ['impetu] nm (*impulso*) impetus, impulse; (*impetuosidad*) impetuosity; (*violencia*) violence

implantar [implan'tar] vt to introduce

implemento [imple'mento] nm (*LAm*) tool, implement

implicar [impli'kar] vt to involve; (*entrañar*) to imply

implícito, -a [im'pliθito, a] adj (*tácito*) implicit; (*sobreentendido*) implied

imponente [impo'nente] *adj* (*impresionante*) impressive, imposing; (*solemne*) grand

imponer [impo'ner] *vt* (*gen*) to impose; (*exigir*) to exact; **imponerse** *vr* to assert o.s.; (*prevalecer*) to prevail □ **imponible** *adj* (COM) taxable

impopular [impopu'lar] *adj* unpopular

importación [importa'θjon] *nf* (*acto*) importing; (*mercancías*) imports *pl*

importancia [impor'tanθja] *nf* importance; (*valor*) value, significance; (*extensión*) size, magnitude; **no tiene ~** it's nothing □ **importante** *adj* important; valuable, significant

importar [impor'tar] *vt* (*del extranjero*) to import; (*costar*) to amount to ♦ *vi* to be important, matter; **me importa un rábano** I couldn't care less; **no importa** it doesn't matter; **¿le importa que fume?** do you mind if I smoke?

importe [im'porte] *nm* (*total*) amount; (*valor*) value

imposible [impo'sißle] *adj* (*gen*) impossible; (*insoportable*) unbearable, intolerable

imposición [imposi'θjon] *nf* (*del extranjero*) imposition; (COM: *impuesto*) tax; (: *inversión*) deposit

impostor, a [impos'tor, a] *nm/f* impostor

impotencia [impo'tenθja] *nf* impotence □ **impotente** *adj* impotent

impreciso, -a [impre'θiso, a] *adj* imprecise, vague

impregnar [impreɣ'nar] *vt* to impregnate; **impregnarse** *vr* to become impregnated

imprenta [im'prenta] *nf* (*acto*) printing; (*aparato*) press; (*casa*) printer's; (*letra*) print

imprescindible [impresθin'dißle] *adj* essential, vital

impresión [impre'sjon] *nf* (*gen*) impression; (IMPRENTA) printing; (*edición*) edition; (FOTO) print; (*marca*) imprint ► **impresión digital** fingerprint

impresionante [impresjo'nante] *adj* impressive; (*tremendo*) tremendous; (*maravilloso*) great, marvellous

impresionar [impresjo'nar] *vt* (*conmover*) to move; (*afectar*) to impress, strike; (*película fotográfica*) to expose; **impresionarse** *vr* to be impressed; (*conmoverse*) to be moved

impreso, -a [im'preso, a] *pp de* **imprimir** ♦ *adj* printed ► **impresos** *nmpl* printed matter □ **impresora** *nf* printer

imprevisto, -a [impre'ßisto, a] *adj* (*gen*) unforeseen; (*inesperado*) unexpected

imprimir [impri'mir] *vt* to imprint, impress, stamp; (*textos*) to print; (INFORM) to output, print out

improbable [impro'ßaßle] *adj* improbable; (*inverosímil*) unlikely

impropio, -a [im'propjo, a] *adj* improper

improvisado, -a [improßi'saðo, a] *adj* improvised

improvisar [improßi'sar] *vt* to improvise

improviso, -a [impro'ßiso, a] *adj*: **de ~** unexpectedly, suddenly

imprudencia [impru'ðenθja] *nf* imprudence; (*indiscreción*) indiscretion; (*descuido*) carelessness □ **imprudente** *adj* unwise, imprudent; (*indiscreto*) indiscreet

impuesto, -a [im'pwesto, a] *adj* imposed ♦ *nm* tax ► **impuesto al valor agregado** *o* **añadido** (*LAm*) value added tax (BRIT), ≈ sales tax (US) ► **impuesto sobre el valor añadido** (*ESP*) value added tax (BRIT), ≈ sales tax (US)

impulsar [impul'sar] vt to drive; (*promover*) to promote, stimulate

impulsivo, -a [impul'siβo, a] adj impulsive □ **impulso** nm impulse; (*fuerza, empuje*) thrust, drive; (*fig: sentimiento*) urge, strength

impureza [impu'reθa] nf impurity □ **impuro, -a** adj impure

inaccesible [inakθe'siβle] adj inaccessible

inaceptable [inaθep'taβle] adj unacceptable

inactivo, -a [inak'tiβo, a] adj inactive

inadecuado, -a [inaðe'kwaðo, a] adj (*insuficiente*) inadequate; (*inapto*) unsuitable

inadvertido, -a [inaðβer'tiðo, a] adj (*no visto*) noticed

inaguantable [inaɣwan'taβle] adj unbearable

inanimado, -a [inani'maðo, a] adj inanimate

inaudito, -a [inau'ðito, a] adj unheard-of

inauguración [inauɣura'θjon] nf inauguration; opening

inaugurar [inauɣu'rar] vt to inaugurate; (*exposición*) to open

inca ['inka] nmf Inca

incalculable [inkalku'laβle] adj incalculable

incandescente [inkandes'θente] adj incandescent

incansable [inkan'saβle] adj tireless, untiring

incapacidad [inkapaθi'ðað] nf incapacity; (*incompetencia*) incompetence ▶ **incapacidad física/mental** physical/mental disability

incapacitar [inkapaθi'tar] vt (*inhabilitar*) to incapacitate, render unfit; (*descalificar*) to disqualify

incapaz [inka'paθ] adj incapable

incautarse [inkau'tarse] vr: ~ **de** to seize, confiscate

incauto, -a [in'kauto, a] adj (*imprudente*) incautious, unwary

incendiar [inθen'djar] vt to set fire to; (*fig*) to inflame; **incendiarse** vr to catch fire □ **incendiario, -a** adj incendiary

incendio [in'θendjo] nm fire

incentivo [inθen'tiβo] nm incentive

incertidumbre [inθerti'ðumbre] nf (*inseguridad*) uncertainty; (*duda*) doubt

incesante [inθe'sante] adj incessant

incesto [in'θesto] nm incest

incidencia [inθi'ðenθja] nf (MAT) incidence

incidente [inθi'ðente] nm incident

incidir [inθi'ðir] vi (*influir*) to influence; (*afectar*) to affect

incienso [in'θjenso] nm incense

incierto, -a [in'θjerto, a] adj uncertain

incineración [inθinera'θjon] nf incineration; (*de cadáveres*) cremation

incinerar [inθine'rar] vt to burn; (*cadáveres*) to cremate

incisión [inθi'sjon] nf incision

incisivo, -a [inθi'siβo, a] adj sharp, cutting; (*fig*) incisive

incitar [inθi'tar] vt to incite, rouse

inclemencia [inkle'menθja] nf (*severidad*) harshness, severity; (*del tiempo*) inclemency

inclinación [inklina'θjon] nf (*gen*) inclination; (*de tierras*) slope, incline; (*de cabeza*) nod, bow; (*fig*) leaning, bent

inclinar [inkli'nar] vt to incline; (*cabeza*) to nod, bow ♦ vi to lean, slope; **inclinarse** vr to lean; (*encorvarse*) to stoop; **inclinarse a** (*parecerse a*) to take after, resemble; **inclinarse ante** to bow down to; **me inclino a pensar que ...** I'm inclined to think that ...

incluir [inklu'ir] vt to include; (*incorporar*) to incorporate; (*meter*) to enclose

inclusive [inklu'siβe] *adv* inclusive
♦ *prep* including
incluso [in'kluso] *adv* even
incógnita [in'koɣnita] *nf* (MAT)
unknown quantity
incógnito [in'koɣnito] *nm*: **de ~**
incognito
incoherente [inkoe'rente] *adj*
incoherent
incoloro, -a [inko'loro, a] *adj*
colourless
incomodar [inkomo'ðar] *vt* to
inconvenience; (*molestar*) to bother,
trouble; (*fastidiar*) to annoy
incomodidad [inkomoði'ðað] *nf*
inconvenience; (*fastidio, enojo*)
annoyance; (*de vivienda*) discomfort
incómodo, -a [in'komoðo, a] *adj*
(*incómfortable*) uncomfortable;
(*molesto*) annoying; (*inconveniente*)
inconvenient
incomparable [inkompa'raβle] *adj*
incomparable
incompatible [inkompa'tiβle] *adj*
incompatible
incompetente [inkompe'tente] *adj*
incompetent
incompleto, -a [inkom'pleto, a] *adj*
incomplete, unfinished
incomprensible [inkompren'siβle]
adj incomprehensible
incomunicado, -a [inkomuni'kaðo,
a] *adj* (*aislado*) cut off, isolated;
(*confinado*) in solitary confinement
incondicional [inkondiθjo'nal] *adj*
unconditional; (*apoyo*) wholehearted;
(*partidario*) staunch
inconfundible [inkonfun'diβle] *adj*
unmistakable
incongruente [inkon'grwente] *adj*
incongruous
inconsciente [inkons'θjente] *adj*
unconscious; thoughtless
inconsecuente [inkonse'kwente] *adj*
inconsistent

inconstante [inkons'tante] *adj*
inconstant
incontable [inkon'taβle] *adj*
countless, innumerable
inconveniencia [inkombe'njenθja] *nf*
unsuitability, inappropriateness;
(*descortesía*) impoliteness
❑ **inconveniente** *adj* unsuitable;
impolite ♦ *nm* obstacle; (*desventaja*)
disadvantage; **el inconveniente es
que ...** the trouble is that ...
incordiar [inkor'ðjar] (*fam*) *vt* to bug,
annoy
incorporar [inkorpo'rar] *vt* to
incorporate; **incorporarse** *vr* to sit up;
incorporarse a to join
incorrecto, -a [inko'rrekto, a] *adj* (*gen*)
incorrect, wrong; (*comportamiento*)
bad-mannered
incorregible [inkorre'xiβle] *adj*
incorrigible
incrédulo, -a [in'kreðulo, a] *adj*
incredulous, unbelieving; sceptical
increíble [inkre'iβle] *adj* incredible
incremento [inkre'mento] *nm*
increment; (*aumento*) rise, increase
increpar [inkre'par] *vt* to reprimand
incruento, -a [in'krwento, a] *adj*
bloodless
incrustar [inkrus'tar] *vt* to incrust;
(*piedras: en joya*) to inlay
incubar [inku'βar] *vt* to incubate
inculcar [inkul'kar] *vt* to inculcate
inculto, -a [in'kulto, a] *adj* (*persona*)
uneducated; (*grosero*) uncouth ♦ *nm/f*
ignoramus
incumplimiento [inkumpli'mjento]
nm non-fulfilment; **~ de contrato**
breach of contract
incurrir [inku'rrir] *vi*: **~ en** to incur;
(*crimen*) to commit
indagar [inda'ɣar] *vt* to investigate; to
search; (*averiguar*) to ascertain
indecente [inde'θente] *adj* indecent,
improper; (*lascivo*) obscene

indeciso, -a [inde'θiso, a] *adj (por decidir)* undecided; *(vacilante)* hesitant

indefenso, -a [inde'fenso, a] *adj* defenceless

indefinido, -a [indefi'niðo, a] *adj* indefinite; *(vago)* vague, undefined

indemne [in'demne] *adj (objeto)* undamaged; *(persona)* unharmed, unhurt

indemnizar [indemni'θar] *vt* to indemnify; *(compensar)* to compensate

independencia [indepen'denθja] *nf* independence

independiente [indepen'djente] *adj (libre)* independent; *(autónomo)* self-sufficient

indeterminado, -a [indetermi'naðo, a] *adj* indefinite; *(desconocido)* indeterminate

India ['indja] *nf*: **la ~** India

indicación [indika'θjon] *nf* indication; *(señal)* sign; *(sugerencia)* suggestion, hint

indicado, -a [indi'kaðo, a] *adj (momento, método)* right; *(tratamiento)* appropriate; *(solución)* likely

indicador [indika'ðor] *nm* indicator; *(TEC)* gauge, meter

indicar [indi'kar] *vt (mostrar)* to indicate, show; *(termómetro etc)* to read, register; *(señalar)* to point to

índice ['indiθe] *nm index; (catálogo)* catalogue; *(ANAT)* index finger, forefinger ▶ **índice de materias** table of contents

indicio [in'diθjo] *nm* indication, sign; *(en pesquisa etc)* clue

indiferencia [indife'renθja] *nf* indifference; *(apatía)* apathy ❑ **indiferente** *adj* indifferent

indígena [in'dixena] *adj* indigenous, native ♦ *nmf* native

indigestión [indixes'tjon] *nf* indigestion

indigesto, -a [indi'xesto, a] *adj (alimento)* indigestible; *(fig)* turgid

indignación [indiɣna'θjon] *nf* indignation

indignar [indiɣ'nar] *vt* to anger, make indignant; **indignarse** *vr*: **indignarse por** to get indignant about

indigno, -a [in'diɣno, a] *adj (despreciable)* low, contemptible; *(inmerecido)* unworthy

indio, -a ['indjo, a] *adj, nm/f* Indian

indirecta [indi'rekta] *nf* insinuation, innuendo; *(sugerencia)* hint

indirecto, -a [indi'rekto, a] *adj* indirect

indiscreción [indiskre'θjon] *nf (imprudencia)* indiscretion; *(irreflexión)* tactlessness; *(acto)* gaffe, faux pas

indiscreto, -a [indis'kreto, a] *adj* indiscreet

indiscutible [indisku'tiβle] *adj* indisputable, unquestionable

indispensable [indispen'saβle] *adj* indispensable, essential

indispuesto, -a [indis'pwesto, a] *adj (enfermo)* unwell, indisposed

indistinto, -a [indis'tinto, a] *adj* indistinct; *(vago)* vague

individual [indiβi'ðwal] *adj* individual; *(habitación)* single ♦ *nm (DEPORTE)* singles *sg*

individuo, -a [indi'βiðwo, a] *adj, nm* individual

índole ['indole] *nf (naturaleza)* nature; *(clase)* sort, kind

inducir [indu'θir] *vt* to induce; *(inferir)* to infer; *(persuadir)* to persuade

indudable [indu'ðaβle] *adj* undoubted; *(incuestionable)* unquestionable

indultar [indul'tar] *vt (perdonar)* to pardon, reprieve; *(librar de pago)* to exempt ❑ **indulto** *nm* pardon; exemption

industria [in'dustrja] *nf* industry; *(habilidad)* skill ❑ **industrial** *adj* industrial ♦ *nm* industrialist

inédito, -a [in'eðito, a] *adj* (*texto*) unpublished; (*nuevo*) new

ineficaz [inefi'kaθ] *adj* (*inútil*) ineffective; (*ineficiente*) inefficient

ineludible [inelu'ðiβle] *adj* inescapable, unavoidable

ineptitud [inepti'tuð] *nf* ineptitude, incompetence □ **inepto, -a** *adj* inept, incompetent

inequívoco, -a [ine'kiβoko, a] *adj* unequivocal; (*inconfundible*) unmistakable

inercia [in'erθja] *nf* inertia; (*pasividad*) passivity

inerte [in'erte] *adj* inert; (*inmóvil*) motionless

inesperado, -a [inespe'raðo, a] *adj* unexpected, unforeseen

inestable [ines'taβle] *adj* unstable

inevitable [ineβi'taβle] *adj* inevitable

inexacto, -a [inek'sakto, a] *adj* inaccurate; (*falso*) untrue

inexperto, -a [inek'sperto, a] *adj* (*novato*) inexperienced

infalible [infa'liβle] *adj* infallible; (*plan*) foolproof

infame [in'fame] *adj* infamous; (*horrible*) dreadful □ **infamia** [in'famja] *nf* infamy; (*deshonra*) disgrace

infancia [in'fanθja] *nf* infancy, childhood

infantería [infante'ria] *nf* infantry

infantil [infan'til] *adj* (*pueril, aniñado*) infantile; (*cándido*) childlike; (*literatura, ropa etc*) children's

infarto [in'farto] *nm* (*tb:* **~ de miocardio**) heart attack

infatigable [infati'γaβle] *adj* tireless, untiring

infección [infek'θjon] *nf* infection □ **infeccioso, -a** *adj* infectious

infectar [infek'tar] *vt* to infect; **infectarse** *vr* to become infected

infeliz [infe'liθ] *adj* unhappy, wretched ♦ *nmf* wretch

inferior [infe'rjor] *adj* inferior; (*situación*) lower ♦ *nmf* inferior, subordinate

inferir [infe'rir] *vt* (*deducir*) to infer, deduce; (*causar*) to cause

infidelidad [infiðeli'ðað] *nf* (*gen*) infidelity, unfaithfulness

infiel [in'fjel] *adj* unfaithful, disloyal; (*erróneo*) inaccurate ♦ *nmf* infidel, unbeliever

infierno [in'fjerno] *nm* hell

infiltrarse [infil'trarse] *vr*: **~ en** to infiltrate in(to); (*persona*) to work one's way in(to)

ínfimo, -a ['infimo, a] *adj* (*más bajo*) lowest; (*despreciable*) vile, mean

infinidad [infini'ðað] *nf* infinity; (*abundancia*) great quantity

infinito, -a [infi'nito, a] *adj, nm* infinite

inflación [infla'θjon] *nf* (*hinchazón*) swelling; (*monetaria*) inflation; (*fig*) conceit

inflamable *adj* flammable

inflamar [infla'mar] *vt* (*MED: fig*) to inflame; **inflamarse** *vr* to catch fire; to become inflamed

inflar [in'flar] *vt* (*hinchar*) to inflate, blow up; (*fig*) to exaggerate; **inflarse** *vr* to swell (up); (*fig*) to get conceited

inflexible [inflek'siβle] *adj* inflexible; (*fig*) unbending

influencia [influ'enθja] *nf* influence

influir [influ'ir] *vt* to influence

influjo [in'fluxo] *nm* influence

influya *etc vb ver* **influir**

influyente [influ'jente] *adj* influential

información [informa'θjon] *nf* information; (*noticias*) news *sg*; (*JUR*) inquiry; **I~** (*oficina*) Information Office; (*mostrador*) Information Desk; (*TEL*) Directory Enquiries

informal [infor'mal] *adj* (*gen*) informal

informar [infor'mar] *vt* (*gen*) to inform; (*revelar*) to reveal, make known ♦ *vi* (*JUR*) to plead; (*denunciar*) to inform; (*dar cuenta de*) to report on;

informarse vr to find out; **informarse de** to inquire into

informática [infor'matika] nf computer science, information technology

informe [in'forme] adj shapeless ♦ nm report

infracción [infrak'θjon] nf infraction, infringement

infravalorar [infrabalo'rar] vt to undervalue, underestimate

infringir [infrin'xir] vt to infringe, contravene

infundado, -a [infun'daðo, a] adj groundless, unfounded

infundir [infun'dir] vt to infuse, instil

infusión [infu'sjon] nf infusion ▶ **infusión de manzanilla** camomile tea

ingeniería [inxenje'ria] nf engineering ▶ **ingeniería genética** genetic engineering ▶ **ingeniero, -a** [inxe'njero, a] nm/f engineer ▶ **ingeniero civil** o **de caminos** civil engineer

ingenio [in'xenjo] nm (talento) talent; (agudeza) wit; (habilidad) ingenuity, inventiveness ▶ **ingenio azucarero** (LAm) sugar refinery ▶ **ingenioso, -a** [inxe'njoso, a] adj ingenious, clever; (divertido) witty ▶ **ingenuo, -a** adj ingenuous

ingerir [inxe'rir] vt to ingest; (tragar) to swallow; (consumir) to consume

Inglaterra [ingla'terra] nf England

ingle ['ingle] nf groin

inglés, -esa [in'gles, esa] adj English ♦ nm/f Englishman(-woman) ♦ nm (LING) English

ingrato, -a [in'grato, a] adj (gen) ungrateful

ingrediente [ingre'ðjente] nm ingredient

ingresar [ingre'sar] vt (dinero) to deposit ♦ vi to come in; ~ **en el hospital** to go into hospital

ingreso [in'greso] nm (entrada) entry; (en hospital etc) admission; **ingresos** nmpl (dinero) income sg; (COM) takings pl

inhabitable [inaβi'taβle] adj uninhabitable

inhalar [ina'lar] vt to inhale

inhibir [ini'βir] vt to inhibit

inhóspito, -a [i'nospito, a] adj (región, paisaje) inhospitable

inhumano, -a [inu'mano, a] adj inhuman

inicial [ini'θjal] adj, nf initial

iniciar [ini'θjar] vt (persona) to initiate; (empezar) to begin, commence; (conversación) to start up

iniciativa [iniθja'tiβa] nf initiative ▶ **iniciativa privada** private enterprise

ininterrumpido, -a [ininterrum'piðo, a] adj uninterrupted

injertar [inxer'tar] vt to graft ❑ **injerto** nm graft

injuria [in'xurja] nf (agravio, ofensa) offence; (insulto) insult

> No confundir **injuria** con la palabra inglesa *injury*.

injusticia [inxus'tiθja] nf injustice

injusto, -a [in'xusto, a] adj unjust, unfair

inmadurez [inmaðu'reθ] nf immaturity

inmediaciones [inmeðja'θjones] nfpl neighbourhood sg, environs

inmediato, -a [inme'ðjato, a] adj immediate; (contiguo) adjoining; (rápido) prompt; (próximo) neighbouring, next; **de ~** immediately

inmejorable [inmexo'raβle] adj unsurpassable; (precio) unbeatable

inmenso, -a [in'menso, a] adj immense, huge

inmigración [inmiɣra'θjon] nf immigration

inmobiliaria [inmoβi'ljarja] nf estate agency

inmolar [inmo'lar] vt to immolate, sacrifice

inmoral [inmo'ral] adj immoral

inmortal [inmor'tal] adj immortal
❑ **inmortalizar** vt to immortalize

inmóvil [in'moβil] adj immobile

inmueble [in'mweβle] adj: **bienes inmuebles** real estate, landed property ♦ nm property

inmundo, -a [in'mundo, a] adj filthy

inmune [in'mune] adj: **~ (a)** (MED) immune (to)

inmunidad [inmuni'ðað] nf immunity

inmutarse [inmu'tarse] vr to turn pale; **no se inmutó** he didn't turn a hair

innato, -a [in'nato, a] adj innate

innecesario, -a [inneθe'sarjo, a] adj unnecessary

innovación [innoβa'θjon] nf innovation

innovar [inno'βar] vt to innovate

inocencia [ino'θenθja] nf innocence

inocentada [inoθen'taða] nf practical joke

inocente [ino'θente] adj (ingenuo) naive, innocent; (inculpable) innocent; (sin malicia) harmless ♦ nmf simpleton; **el día de los (Santos) Inocentes** ≈ April Fools' Day

DÍA DE LOS (SANTOS) INOCENTES

The 28th December, el **día de los (Santos) Inocentes**, is when the Church commemorates the story of Herod's slaughter of the innocent children of Judaea. On this day Spaniards play **inocentadas** (practical jokes) on each other, much like our April Fool's Day pranks.

inodoro [ino'ðoro] nm toilet, lavatory (BRIT)

inofensivo, -a [inofen'siβo, a] adj inoffensive, harmless

inolvidable [inolβi'ðaβle] adj unforgettable

inoportuno, -a [inopor'tuno, a] adj untimely; (molesto) inconvenient

inoxidable [inoksi'ðaβle] adj: **acero ~** stainless steel

inquietar [inkje'tar] vt to worry, trouble; **inquietarse** vr to worry, get upset ❑ **inquieto, -a** adj anxious, worried ❑ **inquietud** nf anxiety, worry

inquilino, -a [inki'lino, a] nm/f tenant

insaciable [insa'θjaβle] adj insatiable

inscribir [inskri'βir] vt to inscribe; **~ a algn en** (lista) to put sb on; (censo) to register sb on

inscripción [inskrip'θjon] nf inscription; (ESCOL etc) enrolment; (en censo) registration

insecticida [insekti'θiða] nm insecticide

insecto [in'sekto] nm insect

inseguridad [inseɣuri'ðað] nf insecurity ▸ **inseguridad ciudadana** lack of safety in the streets

inseguro, -a [inse'ɣuro, a] adj insecure; (inconstante) unsteady; (incierto) uncertain

insensato, -a [insen'sato, a] adj foolish, stupid

insensible [insen'siβle] adj (gen) insensitive; (movimiento) imperceptible; (sin sentido) numb

insertar [inser'tar] vt to insert

inservible [inser'βiβle] adj useless

insignia [in'siɣnja] nf (señal distintiva) badge; (estandarte) flag

insignificante [insiɣnifi'kante] adj insignificant

insinuar [insi'nwar] vt to insinuate, imply

insípido, -a [in'sipiðo, a] adj insipid

insistir [insis'tir] vi to insist; **~ en algo** to insist on sth; (enfatizar) to stress sth

insolación [insola'θjon] nf (MED) sunstroke

insolente [inso'lente] adj insolent

insólito, -a [in'solito, a] adj unusual

insoluble [inso'luβle] adj insoluble

insomnio [in'somnjo] nm insomnia

insonorizado, -a [insonori'θaðo, a] adj (cuarto etc) soundproof

insoportable [insopor'taβle] adj unbearable

inspección [inspek'θjon] nf inspection, check ❑ **inspeccionar** vt (examinar) to inspect, examine; (controlar) to check

inspector, a [inspek'tor, a] nm/f inspector

inspiración [inspira'θjon] nf inspiration

inspirar [inspi'rar] vt to inspire; (MED) to inhale; **inspirarse** vr: **inspirarse en** to be inspired by

instalación [instala'θjon] nf (equipo) fittings pl, equipment ▸ **instalación eléctrica** wiring

instalar [insta'lar] vt (establecer) to instal; (erguir) to set up, erect; **instalarse** vr to establish o.s.; (en una vivienda) to move into

instancia [ins'tanθja] nf (JUR) petition; (ruego) request; **en última ~** as a last resort

instantáneo, -a [instan'taneo, a] adj instantaneous; **café ~** instant coffee

instante [ins'tante] nm instant, moment; **al ~** right now

instar [ins'tar] vt to press, urge

instaurar [instau'rar] vt (costumbre) to establish; (normas, sistema) to bring in, introduce; (gobierno) to instal

instigar [insti'ɣar] vt to instigate

instinto [ins'tinto] nm instinct; **por ~** instinctively

institución [institu'θjon] nf institution, establishment

instituir [institu'ir] vt to establish; (fundar) to found ❑ **instituto** nm (gen) institute; (ESP ESCOL)

≈ comprehensive (BRIT) o high (US) school

institutriz [institu'triθ] nf governess

instrucción [instruk'θjon] nf instruction

instruir [instru'ir] vt (gen) to instruct; (enseñar) to teach, educate

instrumento [instru'mento] nm (gen) instrument; (herramienta) tool, implement

insubordinarse [insuβorði'narse] vr to rebel

insuficiente [insufi'θjente] adj (gen) insufficient; (ESCOL: calificación) unsatisfactory

insular [insu'lar] adj insular

insultar [insul'tar] vt to insult ❑ **insulto** nm insult

insuperable [insupe'raβle] adj (excelente) unsurpassable; (problema etc) insurmountable

insurrección [insurrek'θjon] nf insurrection, rebellion

intachable [inta'tʃaβle] adj irreproachable

intacto, -a [in'takto, a] adj intact

integral [inte'ɣral] adj integral; (completo) complete; **pan ~** wholemeal (BRIT) o wholewheat (US) bread

integrar [inte'ɣrar] vt to make up, compose; (MAT: fig) to integrate

integridad [inteɣri'ðað] nf wholeness; (carácter) integrity ❑ **íntegro, -a** adj whole, entire; (honrado) honest

intelectual [intelek'twal] adj, nmf intellectual

inteligencia [inteli'xenθja] nf intelligence; (ingenio) ability ❑ **inteligente** adj intelligent

intemperie [intem'perje] nf: **a la ~** out in the open, exposed to the elements

intención [inten'θjon] nf (gen) intention, purpose; **con segundas intenciones** maliciously; **con ~** deliberately

intencionado, -a [intenθjo'naðo, a] *adj* deliberate; **mal ~** ill-disposed, hostile

intensidad [intensi'ðað] *nf* (gen) intensity; (ELEC, TEC) strength; **llover con ~** to rain hard

intenso, -a [in'tenso, a] *adj* intense; (sentimiento) profound, deep

intentar [inten'tar] *vt* (tratar) to try, attempt □ **intento** *nm* attempt

interactivo, -a [interak'tiβo, a] *adj* (INFORM) interactive

intercalar [interka'lar] *vt* to insert

intercambio [inter'kambjo] *nm* exchange, swap

interceder [interθe'ðer] *vi* to intercede

interceptar [interθep'tar] *vt* to intercept

interés [inte'res] *nm* (gen) interest; (parte) share, part; (pey) self-interest ► **intereses creados** vested interests

interesado, -a [intere'saðo, a] *adj* interested; (prejuiciado) prejudiced; (pey) mercenary, self-seeking

interesante [intere'sante] *adj* interesting

interesar [intere'sar] *vt, vi* to interest, be of interest to; **interesarse** *vr*: **interesarse en o por** to take an interest in

interferir [interfe'rir] *vt* to interfere with; (TEL) to jam ♦ *vi* to interfere

interfón [MÉX] *nm* entry phone

interino, -a [inte'rino, a] *adj* temporary ♦ *nm/f* temporary holder of a post; (MED) locum; (ESCOL) supply teacher

interior [inte'rjor] *adj* inner, inside; (COM) domestic, internal ♦ *nm* interior, inside; (fig) soul, mind; **Ministerio del I~** ≈ Home Office (BRIT), ≈ Department of the Interior (US) □ **interiorista** (ESP) *nmf* interior designer

interjección [interxek'θjon] *nf* interjection

interlocutor, a [interloku'tor, a] *nm/f* speaker

intermedio, -a [inter'meðjo, a] *adj* intermediate ♦ *nm* interval

interminable [intermi'naβle] *adj* endless

intermitente [intermi'tente] *adj* intermittent ♦ *nm* (AUTO) indicator

internacional [internaθjo'nal] *adj* international

internado [inter'naðo] *nm* boarding school

internar [inter'nar] *vt* to intern; (en un manicomio) to commit; **internarse** *vr* (penetrar) to penetrate

Internet, internet [inter'net] *nm o f* Internet

interno, -a [in'terno, a] *adj* internal, interior; (POL etc) domestic ♦ *nm/f* (alumno) boarder

interponer [interpo'ner] *vt* to interpose, put in; **interponerse** *vr* to intervene

interpretación [interpreta'θjon] *nf* interpretation

interpretar [interpre'tar] *vt* to interpret; (TEATRO, MÚS) to perform, play □ **intérprete** *nmf* (LING) interpreter, translator; (MÚS, TEATRO) performer, artist(e)

interrogación [interroɣa'θjon] *nf* interrogation; (LING: tb: **signo de ~**) question mark

interrogar [interro'ɣar] *vt* to interrogate, question

interrumpir [interrum'pir] *vt* to interrupt

interrupción [interrup'θjon] *nf* interruption

interruptor [interrup'tor] *nm* (ELEC) switch

intersección [intersek'θjon] *nf* intersection

interurbano, -a [interur'βano, a] *adj*: **llamada interurbana** long-distance call

intervalo [inter'βalo] nm interval; (descanso) break

intervenir [interβe'nir] vt (controlar) to control, supervise; (MED) to operate on ♦ vi (participar) to take part, participate; (mediar) to intervene

interventor, a [interβen'tor, a] nm/f inspector; (COM) auditor

intestino [intes'tino] nm (MED) intestine

intimar [inti'mar] vi to become friendly

intimidad [intimi'ðað] nf intimacy; (familiaridad) familiarity; (vida privada) private life; (JUR) privacy

íntimo, -a ['intimo, a] adj intimate

intolerable [intole'raβle] adj intolerable, unbearable

intoxicación [intoksika'θjon] nf poisoning ▶ **intoxicación alimenticia** food poisoning

intranet [intra'net] nf intranet

intranquilo, -a [intran'kilo, a] adj worried

intransitable [intransi'taβle] adj impassable

intrépido, -a [in'trepiðo, a] adj intrepid

intriga [in'triɣa] nf intrigue; (plan) plot □ **intrigar** vt, vi to intrigue

intrínseco, -a [in'trinseko, a] adj intrinsic

introducción [introðuk'θjon] nf introduction

introducir [introðu'θir] vt (gen) to introduce; (moneda etc) to insert; (INFORM) to input, enter

intromisión [intromi'sjon] nf interference, meddling

introvertido, -a [introβer'tiðo, a] adj, nm/f introvert

intruso, -a [in'truso, a] adj intrusive ♦ nm/f intruder

intuición [intwi'θjon] nf intuition

inundación [inunda'θjon] nf flood(ing) □ **inundar** vt to flood; (fig) to swamp, inundate

inusitado, -a [inusi'taðo, a] adj unusual, rare

inútil [in'util] adj useless; (esfuerzo) vain, fruitless

inutilizar [inutili'θar] vt to make o render useless

invadir [imba'ðir] vt to invade

inválido, -a [im'baliðo, a] adj invalid ♦ nm/f invalid

invasión [imba'sjon] nf invasion

invasor, a [imba'sor, a] adj invading ♦ nm/f invader

invención [imben'θjon] nf invention

inventar [imben'tar] vt to invent

inventario [imben'tarjo] nm inventory

invento [im'bento] nm invention

inventor, a [imben'tor, a] nm/f inventor

invernadero [imberna'ðero] nm greenhouse

inverosímil [imbero'simil] adj implausible

inversión [imber'sjon] nf (COM) investment

inverso, -a [im'berso, a] adj inverse, opposite; **en el orden ~** in reverse order; **a la inversa** inversely, the other way round

inversor, a [imber'sor, a] nm/f (COM) investor

invertir [imber'tir] vt (COM) to invest; (volcar) to turn upside down; (tiempo etc) to spend

investigación [imbestiɣa'θjon] nf investigation; (ESCOL) research ▶ **investigación y desarrollo** research and development

investigar [imbesti'ɣar] vt to investigate; (ESCOL) to do research into

invierno [im'bjerno] nm winter

invisible [imbi'siβle] adj invisible

invitado, -a [imbi'taðo, a] nm/f guest

invitar [imbi'tar] *vt* to invite; (*incitar*) to entice; (*pagar*) to buy, pay for

invocar [imbo'kar] *vt* to invoke, call on

involucrar [imbolu'krar] *vt*: ~ **en** to involve in; **involucrarse** *vr* (*persona*): ~ **en** to get mixed up in

involuntario, -a [imbolun'tarjo, a] *adj* (*movimiento, gesto*) involuntary; (*error*) unintentional

inyección [injek'θjon] *nf* injection

inyectar [injek'tar] *vt* to inject

ir

PALABRA CLAVE

[ir] *vi*

1 to go; (*a pie*) to walk; (*viajar*) to travel; **ir caminando** to walk; **fui en tren** I went *o* travelled by train; **¡(ahora) voy!** (I'm just) coming!

2 **ir (a) por**: **ir (a) por el médico** to fetch the doctor

3 (*progresar: persona, cosa*) to go; **el trabajo va muy bien** work is going very well; **¿cómo te va?** how are things going?; **me va muy bien** I'm getting on very well; **le fue fatal** it went awfully badly for him

4 (*funcionar*): **el coche no va muy bien** the car isn't running very well

5: **te va estupendamente ese color** that colour suits you fantastically well

6 (*locuciones*): **¿vino?** — **¡qué va!** did he come? — of course not!; **vamos, no llores** come on, don't cry; **¡vaya coche!** what a car!, that's some car!

7: **no vaya a ser: tienes que correr, no vaya a ser que pierdas el tren** you'll have to run so as not to miss the train

8 (+ *pp*): **iba vestido muy bien** he was very well dressed

9: **ni me** *etc* **va ni me** *etc* **viene** I *etc* don't care

♦ *vb aux*

1: **ir a**: **voy/iba a hacerlo hoy** I am/ was going to do it today

2 (+ *gerundio*): **iba anocheciendo** it was getting dark; **todo se me iba aclarando** everything was gradually becoming clearer to me

3 (+ *pp*: = *pasivo*): **van vendidos 300 ejemplares** 300 copies have been sold so far

♦ **irse** *vr*

1: **¿por dónde se va al zoológico?** which is the way to the zoo?

2 (*marcharse*) to leave; **ya se habrán ido** they must already have left *o* gone

ira ['ira] *nf* anger, rage

Irak [i'rak] *nm* = **Iraq**

Irán [i'ran] *nm* Iran □ **iraní** *adj, nmf* Iranian

Iraq [i'rak] *nm* Iraq □ **iraquí** *adj, nmf* Iraqi

iris ['iris] *nm inv* (*tb*: **arco ~**) rainbow; (ANAT) iris

Irlanda [ir'landa] *nf* Ireland □ **irlandés, -esa** *adj* Irish ♦ *nm/f* Irishman(-woman); **los irlandeses** the Irish

ironía [iro'nia] *nf* irony □ **irónico, -a** *adj* ironic(al)

IRPF *nm abr* (= *Impuesto sobre la Renta de las Personas Físicas*) (personal) income tax

irreal [irre'al] *adj* unreal

irregular [irreɣu'lar] *adj* (*gen*) irregular; (*situación*) abnormal

irremediable [irreme'ðjaβle] *adj* irremediable; (*vicio*) incurable

irreparable [irrepa'raβle] *adj* (*daños*) irreparable; (*pérdida*) irrecoverable

irrespetuoso, -a [irrespe'twoso, a] *adj* disrespectful

irresponsable [irrespon'saβle] *adj* irresponsible

irreversible [irreβer'siβle] *adj* irreversible

irrigar [irri'ɣar] *vt* to irrigate

irrisorio, -a [irri'sorjo, a] *adj* derisory, ridiculous

irritar [irri'tar] *vt* to irritate, annoy

irrupción [irruβ'θjon] *nf* irruption; (*invasión*) invasion

isla ['isla] *nf* island

islandés, -esa [islan'des, esa] *adj* Icelandic ♦ *nm/f* Icelander

Islandia [is'landja] *nf* Iceland

isleño, -a [is'leɲo, a] *adj* island *cpd* ♦ *nm/f* islander

Israel [isra'el] *nm* Israel □ **israelí** *adj, nmf* Israeli

istmo ['istmo] *nm* isthmus

Italia [i'talja] *nf* Italy □ **italiano, -a** *adj, nm/f* Italian

itinerario [itine'rarjo] *nm* itinerary, route

ITV (*ESP*) *nf abr* (= *inspección técnica de vehículos*) roadworthiness test, ≈ MOT (*BRIT*)

IVA ['iβa] *nm abr* (= *impuesto sobre el valor añadido*) VAT

izar [i'θar] *vt* to hoist

izdo, -a *abr* (= *izquierdo, a*) l

izquierda [iθ'kjerða] *nf* left; (*POL*) left (wing); **a ~** (= *estar*) on the left; (*torcer etc*) (to the) left

izquierdo, -a [iθ'kjerðo, a] *adj* left

J, j

jabalí [xaβa'li] *nm* wild boar

jabalina [xaβa'lina] *nf* javelin

jabón [xa'βon] *nm* soap

jaca ['xaka] *nf* pony

jacal (*MÉX*) [xa'kal] *nm* shack

jacinto [xa'θinto] *nm* hyacinth

jactarse [xak'tarse] *vr* to boast, brag

jadear [xaðe'ar] *vi* to pant, gasp for breath

jaguar [xa'ɣwar] *nm* jaguar

jaiba (*LAm*) ['xaiβa] *nf* crab

jalar (*LAm*) [xa'lar] *vt* to pull

jalea [xa'lea] *nf* jelly

jaleo [xa'leo] *nm* racket, uproar; **armar un ~** to kick up a racket

jalón [xa'lon] (*LAm*) *nm* tug

jamás [xa'mas] *adv* never

jamón [xa'mon] *nm* ham ▶ **jamón dulce** o **de York** cooked ham ▶ **jamón serrano** cured ham

Japón [xa'pon] *nm* Japan □ **japonés, -esa** *adj, nm/f* Japanese ♦ *nm* (*LING*) Japanese

jaque ['xake] *nm* (*AJEDREZ*) check ▶ **jaque mate** checkmate

jaqueca [xa'keka] *nf* (very bad) headache, migraine

jarabe [xa'raβe] *nm* syrup

jardín [xar'ðin] *nm* garden ▶ **jardín infantil** o **de infancia** nursery (school) □ **jardinería** *nf* gardening □ **jardinero, -a** *nm/f* gardener

jarra ['xarra] *nf* jar; (*jarro*) jug

jarro ['xarro] *nm* jug

jarrón [xa'rron] *nm* vase

jaula ['xaula] *nf* cage

jauría [xau'ria] *nf* pack of hounds

jazmín [xaθ'min] *nm* jasmine

J.C. *abr* (= *Jesucristo*) J.C.

jeans [jins, dʒins] (*LAm*) *nmpl* jeans, denims; **unos ~** a pair of jeans

jefatura [xefa'tura] *nf* (*tb:* **~ de policía**) police headquarters *sg*

jefe, -a ['xefe, a] *nm/f* (*gen*) chief, head; (*patrón*) boss ▶ **jefe de cocina** chef ▶ **jefe de estación** stationmaster ▶ **jefe de Estado** head of state ▶ **jefe de estudios** (*ESCOL*) director of studies ▶ **jefe de gobierno** head of government

jengibre [xen'xiβre] *nm* ginger

jeque ['xeke] *nm* sheik

jerárquico, -a [xeˈrarkiko, a] *adj* hierarchic(al)

jerez [xeˈreθ] *nm* sherry

jerga [ˈxerɣa] *nf* jargon

jeringa [xeˈriŋga] *nf* syringe; (*LAm: molestia*) annoyance, bother ❑ **jeringuilla** *nf* syringe

jeroglífico [xeroˈɣlifiko] *nm* hieroglyphic

jersey [xerˈsei] (*pl* **jerseys**) *nm* jersey, pullover, jumper

Jerusalén [xerusaˈlen] *n* Jerusalem

Jesucristo [xesuˈkristo] *nm* Jesus Christ

jesuita [xeˈswita] *adj, nm* Jesuit

Jesús [xeˈsus] *nm* Jesus; **¡~!** good heavens!; (*al estornudar*) bless you!

jinete [xiˈnete] *nmf* horseman(-woman), rider

jipijapa [xipiˈxapa] (*LAm*) *nm* straw hat

jirafa [xiˈrafa] *nf* giraffe

jirón [xiˈron] *nm* rag, shred

jitomate (*MÉX*) [xitoˈmate] *nm* tomato

joder [xoˈðer] (*fam!*) *vt, vi* to fuck (!)

jogging [ˈjoyin] (*RPl*) *nm* tracksuit (*BRIT*), sweat suit (*US*)

jornada [xorˈnaða] *nf* (*viaje de un día*) day's journey; (*camino o viaje entero*) journey; (*día de trabajo*) working day

jornal [xorˈnal] *nm* (day's) wage ❑ **jornalero** *nm* (day) labourer

joroba [xoˈroβa] *nf* hump, hunched back ❑ **jorobado, -a** *adj* hunchbacked ♦ *nm/f* hunchback

jota [ˈxota] *nf* (the letter) J; (*danza*) Aragonese dance; **no saber ni ~** to have no idea

joven [ˈxoβen] (*pl* **jóvenes**) *adj* young ♦ *nm* young man, youth ♦ *nf* young woman, girl

joya [ˈxoja] *nf* jewel, gem; (*fig: persona*) gem ▶ **joyas de fantasía** costume *o* imitation jewellery ❑ **joyería** *nf* (*joyas*) jewellery; (*tienda*) jeweller's

(*shop*) ❑ **joyero** *nm* (*persona*) jeweller; (*caja*) jewel case

juanete [xwaˈnete] *nm* (*del pie*) bunion

jubilación [xuβilaˈθjon] *nf* (*retiro*) retirement

jubilado, -a [xuβiˈlaðo, a] *adj* retired ♦ *nm/f* pensioner (*BRIT*), senior citizen

jubilar [xuβiˈlar] *vt* to pension off, retire; (*fam*) to discard; **jubilarse** *vr* to retire

júbilo [ˈxuβilo] *nm* joy, rejoicing ❑ **jubiloso, -a** *adj* jubilant

judía [xuˈðia] (*ESP*) *nf* (*CULIN*) bean ▶ **judía blanca/verde** haricot/French bean; *ver tb* **judío**

judicial [xuðiˈθjal] *adj* judicial

judío, -a [xuˈðio, a] *adj* Jewish ♦ *nm/f* Jew(ess)

judo [ˈjuðo] *nm* judo

juego *etc* [ˈxweɣo] *vb ver* **jugar** ♦ *nm* (*gen*) play; (*pasatiempo, partido*) game; (*en casino*) gambling; (*conjunto*) set; **fuera de ~** (*DEPORTE: persona*) offside; (*: pelota*) out of play ▶ **juego de palabras** pun, play on words ▶ **Juegos Olímpicos** Olympic Games

juerga [ˈxwerɣa] (*ESP: fam*) *nf* binge; (*fiesta*) party; **ir de ~** to go out on a binge

jueves [ˈxweβes] *nm inv* Thursday

juez [xweθ] *nmf* judge ▶ **juez de instrucción** examining magistrate ▶ **juez de línea** linesman ▶ **juez de salida** starter

jugada [xuˈɣaða] *nf* play; **buena ~** good move *o* shot *o* stroke *etc*

jugador, a [xuɣaˈðor, a] *nm/f* player; (*en casino*) gambler

jugar [xuˈɣar] *vt, vi* to play; (*en casino*) to gamble; (*apostar*) to bet; **~ al fútbol** to play football

juglar [xuˈɣlar] *nm* minstrel

jugo [ˈxuɣo] *nm* (*BOT*) juice; (*fig*) essence, substance ▶ **jugo de naranja** (*LAm*) orange juice

jugoso, -a adj juicy; (fig) substantial, important

juguete [xu'ɣete] nm toy ▢ **juguetear** vi to play ▢ **juguetería** nf toyshop

juguetón, -ona [xuɣe'ton, ona] adj playful

juicio ['xwiθjo] nm judgement; (razón) sanity, reason; (opinión) opinion

julio ['xuljo] nm July

jumper ['dʒumper] (LAm) nm pinafore dress (BRIT), jumper (US)

junco ['xunko] nm rush, reed

jungla ['xungla] nf jungle

junio ['xunjo] nm June

junta ['xunta] nf (asamblea) meeting, assembly; (comité, consejo) council, committee; (COM, FINANZAS) board; (TEC) joint ▶ **junta directiva** board of directors

juntar [xun'tar] vt to join, unite; (maquinaria) to assemble, put together; (dinero) to collect; **juntarse** vr to join, meet; (reunirse: personas) to meet, assemble; (arrimarse) to approach, draw closer; **juntarse con algn** to join sb

junto, -a ['xunto, a] adj joined; (unido) united; (anexo) near, close; (contiguo, próximo) next, adjacent ♦ adv: **todo ~** all at once; **juntos** together; **~ a** near (to), next to; **~ con** (together) with

jurado [xu'raðo] nm (JUR: individuo) juror; (: grupo) jury; (de concurso: grupo) panel of judges); (: individuo) member of a panel

juramento [xura'mento] nm oath; (maldición) oath, curse; **prestar ~** to take the oath; **tomar ~ a** to swear in, administer the oath to

jurar [xu'rar] vt, vi to swear; **~ en falso** to commit perjury; **tenérsela jurada a algn** to have it in for sb

jurídico, -a [xu'riðiko, a] adj legal

jurisdicción [xurisðik'θjon] nf (poder, autoridad) jurisdiction; (territorio) district

justamente [xusta'mente] adv justly, fairly; (precisamente) just, exactly

justicia [xus'tiθja] nf (equidad) fairness, justice

justificación [xustifika'θjon] nf justification ▢ **justificar** vt to justify

justo, -a ['xusto, a] adj (equitativo) just, fair, right; (preciso) exact, correct; (ajustado) tight ♦ adv (precisamente) exactly, precisely; (LAm: apenas a tiempo) just in time

juvenil [xuβe'nil] adj youthful

juventud [xuβen'tuð] nf (adolescencia) youth; (jóvenes) young people pl

juzgado [xuθ'ɣaðo] nm tribunal; (JUR) court

juzgar [xuθ'ɣar] vt to judge; **a ~ por ...** to judge by ..., judging by ...

K, k

kárate ['karate] nm karate

kg abr (= kilogramo) kg

kilo ['kilo] nm kilo ▢ **kilogramo** nm kilogramme ▢ **kilometraje** nm distance in kilometres; ≈ mileage ▢ **kilómetro** nm kilometre ▢ **kilovatio** nm kilowatt

kiosco ['kjosko] nm = **quiosco**

kleenex® nm paper handkerchief, tissue

Kosovo [ko'soβo] nm Kosovo

km abr (= kilómetro) km

kv abr (= kilovatio) kw

L, l

l abr (= litro) l

la [la] art def the ♦ pron her; (Ud.) you; (cosa) it ♦ nm (MÚS) la; **la del sombrero rojo** the girl in the red hat; ver tb **el**

laberinto [laβe'rinto] nm labyrinth

labio ['laβjo] nm lip

labor [la'βor] nf labour; (AGR) farm work; (tarea) job, task; (COSTURA) needlework ► **labores domésticas** o **del hogar** household chores ❑ **laborable** adj (AGR) workable; **día laborable** working day ❑ **laboral** adj (accidente) at work; (jornada) working

laboratorio [laβora'torjo] nm laboratory

laborista [laβo'rista] adj: **Partido L~** Labour Party

labrador, a [laβra'ðor, a] adj farming cpd ♦ nm/f farmer

labranza [la'βranθa] nf (AGR) cultivation

labrar [la'βrar] vt (gen) to work; (madera etc) to carve; (fig) to cause, bring about

laca ['laka] nf lacquer

lacio, -a ['laθjo, a] adj (pelo) straight

lacón [la'kon] nm shoulder of pork

lactancia [lak'tanθja] nf lactation

lácteo, -a ['lakteo, a] adj: **productos lácteos** dairy products

ladear [laðe'ar] vt to tip, tilt ♦ vi to tilt; **ladearse** vr to lean

ladera [la'ðera] nf slope

lado ['laðo] nm (gen) side; (fig) protection; (MIL) flank; **al ~ de** beside; **poner de ~** to put on its side; **poner a un ~** to put aside; **por todos lados** on all sides, all round; (BRIT)

ladrar [la'ðrar] vi to bark ❑ **ladrido** nm bark, barking

ladrillo [la'ðriʎo] nm (gen) brick; (azulejo) tile

ladrón, -ona [la'ðron, ona] nm/f thief

lagartija [layar'tixa] nf (ZOOL) (small) lizard

lagarto [la'yarto] nm (ZOOL) lizard

lago ['layo] nm lake

lágrima ['layrima] nf tear

laguna [la'yuna] nf (lago) lagoon; (hueco) gap

lamentable [lamen'taβle] adj lamentable, regrettable; (miserable) pitiful

lamentar [lamen'tar] vt (sentir) to regret; (deplorar) to lament; **lamentarse** vr to lament; **lo lamento mucho** I'm very sorry

lamer [la'mer] vt to lick

lámina ['lamina] nf (plancha delgada) sheet; (para estampar, estampa) plate

lámpara ['lampara] nf lamp ► **lámpara de alcohol/gas** spirit/gas lamp ► **lámpara de pie** standard lamp

lana ['lana] nf wool

lancha ['lantʃa] nf launch ► **lancha motora** motorboat, speedboat

langosta [lan'gosta] nf (crustáceo) lobster; (: de río) crayfish ❑ **langostino** nm Dublin Bay prawn

lanza ['lanθa] nf (arma) lance, spear

lanzamiento [lanθa'mjento] nm (gen) throwing; (NAÚT, COM) launch, launching ► **lanzamiento de peso** putting the shot

lanzar [lan'θar] vt (gen) to throw; (DEPORTE: pelota) to bowl; (NAÚT, COM) to launch; (JUR) to evict; **lanzarse** vr to throw o.s.

lapa ['lapa] nf limpet

lapicero [lapi'θero] nm (CAm) (bolígrafo) ballpoint pen, Biro®

lápida ['lapiða] nf stone ► **lápida mortuoria** headstone

lápiz ['lapiθ] nm pencil ► **lápiz de color** coloured pencil ► **lápiz de labios** lipstick ► **lápiz de ojos** eyebrow pencil

largar [lar'yar] vt (soltar) to release; (aflojar) to loosen; (lanzar) to launch; (fam) to let fly; (velas) to unfurl; (LAm: lanzar) to throw; **largarse** vr (fam) to beat it; **largarse a** (CS: empezar) to start to

largo, -a ['laryo, a] adj (longitud) long; (tiempo) lengthy; (fig) generous ♦ vt

length; (MÚS) largo; **dos años largos** two long years; **tiene 9 metros de ~** it is 9 metres long; **a la larga** in the long run; **a lo ~ de** along; (tiempo) all through, throughout
❏ **largometraje** nm feature film

⚠ No confundir **largo** con la palabra inglesa *large*.

laringe [la'rinxe] nf larynx
❏ **laringitis** nf laryngitis

las [las] art def the ♦ pron them; **~ que cantan** the ones o women o girls who sing; ver tb **el**

lasaña [la'saɲa] nf lasagne, lasagna

láser ['laser] nm laser

lástima ['lastima] nf (pena) pity; **dar ~** to be pitiful; **es una ~ que ...** it's a pity that ...; **¡qué ~!** what a pity!; **está hecha una ~** she looks pitiful

lastimar [lasti'mar] vt (herir) to wound; (ofender) to offend; **lastimarse** vr to hurt o.s.

lata ['lata] nf (metal) tin; (caja) tin (BRIT), can; (fam) nuisance; **en ~** tinned (BRIT), canned; **dar la ~** to be a nuisance

latente [la'tente] adj latent

lateral [late'ral] adj side cpd, lateral ♦ nm (TEATRO) wings

latido [la'tiðo] nm (de corazón) beat

latifundio [lati'fundjo] nm large estate

latigazo [lati'ɣaθo] nm (golpe) lash; (sonido) crack

látigo ['latiɣo] nm whip

latín [la'tin] nm Latin

latino, -a [la'tino, a] adj Latin
❏ **latinoamericano, -a** adj, nm/f Latin-American

latir [la'tir] vi (corazón, pulso) to beat

latitud [lati'tuð] nf (GEO) latitude

latón [la'ton] nm brass

laurel [lau'rel] nm (BOT) laurel; (CULIN) bay

lava ['laβa] nf lava

lavabo [la'βaβo] nm (pila) washbasin; (tb: **lavabos**) toilet

lavado [la'βaðo] nm washing; (de ropa) laundry; (ARTE) wash ▶ **lavado de cerebro** brainwashing ▶ **lavado en seco** dry-cleaning

lavadora [laβa'ðora] nf washing machine

lavanda [la'βanda] nf lavender

lavandería [laβande'ria] nf laundry; (automática) launderette

lavaplatos [laβa'platos] nm inv dishwasher

lavar [la'βar] vt to wash; (borrar) to wash away; **lavarse** vr to wash o.s.; **lavarse las manos** to wash one's hands; **lavarse los dientes** to brush one's teeth; **y marcar** (pelo) to shampoo and set; **en seco** to dry-clean; **los platos** to wash the dishes

lavarropas [la'βaropas] (RPI) nm inv washing machine

lavavajillas [laβaβa'xiʎas] nm inv dishwasher

laxante [lak'sante] nm laxative

lazarillo [laθa'riʎo] nm (tb: **perro ~**) guide dog

lazo ['laθo] nm knot; (lazada) bow; (para animales) lasso; (trampa) snare; (vínculo) tie

leal [le'al] adj loyal ❏ **lealtad** nf loyalty

lección [lek'θjon] nf lesson

leche ['letʃe] nf milk; **tiene mala ~** (fam!) he's a swine (!) ▶ **leche condensada** condensed milk ▶ **leche desnatada** skimmed milk

lecho ['letʃo] nm (cama: de río) bed; (GEO) layer

lechón [le'tʃon] nm sucking (BRIT) o suckling (US) pig

lechoso, -a [le'tʃoso, a] adj milky

lechuga [le'tʃuɣa] nf lettuce

lechuza [le'tʃuθa] nf owl

lector, a [lek'tor, a] nm/f reader ♦ nm: ~ **de discos compactos** CD player

lectura [lek'tura] nf reading

leer [le'er] vt to read

legado [le'yaðo] nm (don) bequest; (herencia) legacy; (enviado) legate

legajo [le'yaxo] nm file

legal [le'yal] adj (gen) legal; (persona) trustworthy ♦ **legalizar** [leyali'θar] vt to legalize; (documento) to authenticate

legaña [le'yaɲa] nf sleep (in eyes)

legión [le'xjon] nf legion □ **legionario, -a** adj legionary ♦ nm legionnaire

legislación [lexisla'θjon] nf legislation

legislar [lexis'lar] vi to legislate

legislatura [lexisla'tura] nf (POL) period of office

legítimo, -a [le'xitimo, a] adj (genuino) authentic; (legal) legitimate

legua [le'ywa] nf league

legumbres [le'yumbres] nfpl pulses

leído, -a [le'iðo, a] adj well-read

lejanía [lexa'nia] nf distance ▪ **lejano, -a** [le'xano, a] adj far-off; (en el tiempo) distant; (fig) remote

lejía [le'xia] nf bleach

lejos [lexos] adv far, far away; **a lo ~** in the distance; **de o desde ~** from afar; **~ de** far from

lema [lema] nm motto; (POL) slogan

lencería [lenθe'ria] nf linen, drapery

lengua [lengwa] nf tongue; (LING) language; **morderse la ~** to hold one's tongue

lenguado [len'gwaðo] nm sole

lenguaje [len'gwaxe] nm language ▪ **lenguaje de programación** program/ming language

lengüeta [len'gweta] nf (ANAT) epiglottis; (zapatos) tongue; (MÚS) reed

lente [lente] nf lens; (lupa) magnifying glass □ **lentes** nfpl lenses ♦ nmpl (LAm: gafas) glasses ▪ **lentes**

bifocales/de sol (LAm) bifocals/ sunglasses ▪ **lentes de contacto** contact lenses

lenteja [len'texa] nf lentil □ **lentejuela** nf sequin

lentilla [len'tiʎa] nf contact lens

lentitud [lenti'tuð] nf slowness; **con ~** slowly

lento, -a [lento, a] adj slow

leña [leɲa] nf firewood □ **leñador, -a** nm/f woodcutter

leño [leɲo] nm (trozo de árbol) log; (madero) timber; (fig) blockhead

Leo [leo] nm Leo

león [le'on] nm lion ▪ **león marino** sea lion

leopardo [leo'parðo] nm leopard

leotardos [leo'tarðos] nmpl tights

lepra [lepra] nf leprosy ▪ **leproso, -a** nm/f leper

les [les] pron (directo) them; (: ustedes) you; (indirecto) them; (: ustedes) to you

lesbiana [les'bjana] adj, nf lesbian

lesión [le'sjon] nf wound, lesion; (DEPORTE) injury □ **lesionado, -a** adj injured ♦ nm/f injured person

letal [le'tal] adj lethal

letanía [leta'nia] nf litany

letra [letra] nf letter; (escritura) handwriting; (MÚS) lyrics pl ▪ **letra de cambio** bill of exchange ▪ **letra de imprenta** print □ **letrado, -a** adj learned ♦ nm/f lawyer □ **letrero** (cartel) sign; (etiqueta) label

letrina [le'trina] nf latrine

leucemia [leu'θemja] nf leukaemia

levadura [leβa'ðura] nf (para el pan) yeast; (de cerveza) brewer's yeast

levantar [leβan'tar] vt (gen) to raise; (del suelo) to pick up; (hacia arriba) to lift (up); (plan) to make, draw up; (mesa) to clear; (campamento) to strike; (fig) to cheer up, hearten; **levantarse** vr to get up; (enderezarse) to straighten up; (*rebelarse*) to rebel; **~ el ánimo** to cheer up

levante [le'βante] *nm* east coast; **el L~** region of Spain extending from Castellón to Murcia

levar [le'βar] *vt* to weigh

leve ['leβe] *adj* light; (*fig*) trivial

levita [le'βita] *nf* frock coat

léxico ['leksiko] *nm* (*vocabulario*) vocabulary

ley [lei] *nf* (*gen*) law; (*metal*) standard

leyenda [le'jenda] *nf* legend

leyó *etc vb ver* **leer**

liar [li'ar] *vt* to tie (up); (*unir*) to bind; (*envolver*) to wrap (up); (*enredar*) to confuse; (*cigarrillo*) to roll; **liarse** *vr* (*fam*) to get involved; **liarse a palos** to get involved in a fight

Líbano ['liβano] *nm*: **el ~** the Lebanon

libélula [li'βelula] *nf* dragonfly

liberación [liβera'θjon] *nf* liberation; (*de la cárcel*) release

liberal [liβe'ral] *adj, nmf* liberal

liberar [liβe'rar] *vt* to liberate

libertad [liβer'tað] *nf* liberty, freedom
  ▶ **libertad bajo fianza** bail
  ▶ **libertad bajo palabra** parole
  ▶ **libertad condicional** probation
  ▶ **libertad de culto/de prensa/de comercio** freedom of worship/of the press/of trade

libertar [liβer'tar] *vt* (*preso*) to set free; (*de una obligación*) to release; (*eximir*) to exempt

libertino, -a [liβer'tino, a] *adj* permissive ♦ *nm/f* permissive person

libra ['liβra] *nf* pound; **L~** (*ASTROLOGÍA*) Libra ▶ **libra esterlina** pound sterling

libramiento (*MÉX*) [liβra'mjento] *nm* ring road (*BRIT*), beltway (*US*)

librar [li'βrar] *vt* (*de peligro*) to save; (*batalla*) to wage, fight; (*de impuestos*) to exempt; (*cheque*) to make out; (*JUR*) to exempt; **librarse** *vr*: **librarse de** to escape from, free o.s. from

libre ['liβre] *adj* free; (*lugar*) unoccupied; (*asiento*) vacant; (*de deudas*) free of debts; (*de impuestos*) free of tax; **tiro ~** free kick; **los 100 metros libres** the 100 metres freestyle (race); **al aire ~** in the open air

librería [liβre'ria] *nf* (*tienda*) bookshop

librero, -a *nm/f* bookseller

> ⚠ No confundir **librería** con la palabra inglesa *library*.

libreta [li'βreta] *nf* notebook

libro ['liβro] *nm* book ▶ **libro de bolsillo** paperback ▶ **libro de texto** textbook ▶ **libro electrónico** e-book

Lic. *abr* = **licenciado, a**

licencia [li'θenθja] *nf* (*gen*) licence; (*permiso*) permission ▶ **licencia de caza** game licence ▶ **licencia por enfermedad** (*MÉX, RPI*) sick leave ▢ **licenciado, -a** *adj* licensed ♦ *nm/f* graduate ▢ **licenciar** *vt* (*empleado*) to dismiss; (*permitir*) to permit, allow; (*soldado*) to discharge; (*estudiante*) to confer a degree upon; **licenciarse** *vr*: **licenciarse en Derecho** to graduate in law

lícito, -a ['liθito, a] *adj* (*legal*) lawful; (*justo*) fair, just; (*permisible*) permissible

licor [li'kor] *nm* spirits *pl* (*BRIT*), liquor (*US*); (*de frutas etc*) liqueur

licuadora [likwa'ðora] *nf* blender

líder ['liðer] *nmf* leader ▢ **liderato** *nm* leadership ▢ **liderazgo** *nm* leadership

lidia ['liðja] *nf* bullfighting; (*una lidia*) bullfight; **toros de ~** fighting bulls ▢ **lidiar** *vt, vi* to fight

liebre ['ljeβre] *nf* hare

lienzo ['ljenθo] *nm* linen; (*ARTE*) canvas; (*ARQ*) wall

liga ['liɣa] *nf* (*de medias*) garter, suspender; (*LAm: goma*) rubber band; (*confederación*) league

ligadura [liɣa'ðura] *nf* bond, tie; (*MED, MÚS*) ligature

ligamento [liɣa'mento] nm ligament

ligar [li'ɣar] vt (atar) to tie; (unir) to join; (MED) to bind up; (MÚS) to slur ♦ vi to mix, blend; (fam): **(él) liga mucho** he pulls a lot of women; **ligarse** vr to commit o.s.

ligero, -a [li'xero, a] adj (de peso) light; (tela) thin; (rápido) swift, quick; (ágil) agile, nimble; (de importancia) slight; (de carácter) flippant, superficial ♦ adv: **a la ligera** superficially

liguero [li'ɣero] nm suspender (BRIT) o garter (US) belt

lija ['lixa] nf (ZOOL) dogfish; (tb: **papel de ~**) sandpaper

lila ['lila] nf lilac

lima ['lima] nf file; (BOT) lime ▶ **lima de uñas** nailfile ❑ **limar** vt to file

limitación [limita'θjon] nf limitation, limit

limitar [limi'tar] vt to limit; (reducir) to reduce, cut down ♦ vi: **~ con** to border on; **limitarse** vr: **limitarse a** to limit o.s. to

límite ['limite] nm (gen) limit; (fin) end; (frontera) border ▶ **límite de velocidad** speed limit

limítrofe [li'mitrofe] adj neighbouring

limón [li'mon] nm lemon ♦ adj: **amarillo ~** lemon-yellow ❑ **limonada** nf lemonade

limosna [li'mosna] nf alms pl; **vivir de ~** to live on charity

limpiador (MÉX) [limpja'ðor] nm = **limpiaparabrisas**

limpiaparabrisas [limpjapara'βrisas] nm inv windscreen (BRIT) o windshield (US) wiper

limpiar [lim'pjar] vt to clean; (con trapo) to wipe; (quitar) to wipe away; (zapatos) to shine, polish; (fig) to clean up

limpieza [lim'pjeθa] nf (estado) cleanliness; (acto) cleaning; (: de las calles) cleansing; (: de zapatos) polishing; (habilidad) skill; (fig: POLICÍA)

clean-up; (pureza) purity; (MIL): **operación de ~** mopping-up operation ▶ **limpieza en seco** dry cleaning

limpio, -a ['limpjo, a] adj clean; (moralmente) pure; (COM) clear, net; (fam) honest ♦ adv: **jugar ~** to play fair; **pasar a** (LAm) o **en** (ESP) **~** to make a clean copy of

lince [li'nθe] nm lynx

linchar [lin'tʃar] vt to lynch

lindar [lin'dar] vi to adjoin; **~ con** to border on

lindo, -a ['lindo, a] adj pretty, lovely ♦ adv: **nos divertimos de ~** we had a marvellous time; **canta muy ~** (LAm) he sings beautifully

línea ['linea] nf (gen) line; **en ~** (INFORM) on line ▶ **línea aérea** airline ▶ **línea de meta** goal line; (en carrera) finishing line ▶ **línea discontinua** (AUTO) broken line ▶ **línea recta** straight line

lingote [lin'gote] nm ingot

lingüista [lin'gwista] nmf linguist ❑ **lingüística** nf linguistics sg

lino ['lino] nm linen; (BOT) flax

linterna [lin'terna] nf torch (BRIT), flashlight (US)

lío ['lio] nm bundle; (fam) fuss; (desorden) muddle, mess; **armar un ~** to make a fuss

liquen ['liken] nm lichen

liquidación [likiða'θjon] nf liquidation; **venta de ~** clearance sale

liquidar [liki'ðar] vt (mercancías) to liquidate; (deudas) to pay off; (empresa) to wind up

líquido, -a ['likiðo, a] adj liquid; (ganancia) net ♦ nm liquid ▶ **líquido imponible** net taxable income

lira ['lira] nf (MÚS) lyre; (moneda) lira

lírico, -a ['liriko, a] adj lyrical

lirio ['lirjo] nm (BOT) iris

lirón [li'ron] nm (ZOOL) dormouse; (fig) sleepyhead

Lisboa [lis'βoa] n Lisbon

lisiar [li'sjar] vt to maim

liso, -a [ˈliso, a] adj (terreno) flat; (cabello) straight; (superficie) even; (tela) plain

lista [ˈlista] nf list; (de alumnos) school register; (de libros) catalogue; (de platos) menu; (de precios) price list; **pasar ~** to call the roll; **tela de listas** striped material ► **lista de espera** waiting list ► **lista de precios** price list ❏ **listín** nm (tb: **listín telefónico** o **de teléfonos**) telephone directory

listo, -a [ˈlisto, a] adj (perspicaz) smart, clever; (preparado) ready

listón [lisˈton] nm (de madera, metal) strip

litera [liˈtera] nf (en barco, tren) berth; (en dormitorio) bunk, bunk bed

literal [liteˈral] adj literal

literario, -a [liteˈrarjo, a] adj literary

literato, -a [liteˈrato, a] adj literary ♦ nm/f writer

literatura [literaˈtura] nf literature

litigio [liˈtixjo] nm (JUR) lawsuit; (fig): en ~ con in dispute with

litografía [litoɣraˈfia] nf lithography; (una litografía) lithograph

litoral [litoˈral] adj coastal ♦ nm coast, seaboard

litro [ˈlitro] nm litre

lívido, -a [ˈliβiðo, a] adj livid

llaga [ˈʎaɣa] nf wound

llama [ˈʎama] nf flame; (ZOOL) llama

llamada [ʎaˈmaða] nf call ► **llamada a cobro revertido** reverse-charge (BRIT) o collect (US) call ► **llamada al orden** call to order ► **llamada de atención** warning ► **llamada local** (LAm) local call ► **llamada metropolitana** (ESP) local call ► **llamada por cobrar** (MÉX) reverse-charge (BRIT) o collect (US) call

llamamiento [ʎamaˈmjento] nm call

llamar [ʎaˈmar] vt to call; (atención) to attract ♦ vi (por teléfono) to telephone;

(a la puerta) to knock (o ring); (por señas) to beckon; (MIL) to call up; **llamarse** vr to be called, be named; **¿cómo se llama (usted)?** what's your name?

llamativo, -a [ʎamaˈtiβo, a] adj showy; (color) loud

llano, -a [ˈʎano, a] adj (superficie) flat; (persona) straightforward; (estilo) clear ♦ nm plain, flat ground

llanta [ˈʎanta] nf (ESP) (wheel) rim ► **llanta (de goma)** (LAm: neumático) tyre; (: cámara) inner (tube) ► **llanta de repuesto** (LAm) spare tyre

llanto [ˈʎanto] nm weeping

llanura [ʎaˈnura] nf plain

llave [ˈʎaβe] nf key; (del agua) tap; (MECÁNICA) spanner; (de la luz) switch; (MÚS) key; **echar la ~ a** to lock up ► **llave de contacto** (ESP AUTO) ignition key ► **llave de encendido** (LAm AUTO) ignition key ► **llave de paso** stopcock ► **llave inglesa** monkey wrench ► **llave maestra** master key ❏ **llavero** nm keyring

llegada [ʎeˈɣaða] nf arrival

llegar [ʎeˈɣar] vi to arrive; (alcanzar) to reach; (bastar) to be enough; **llegarse** vr: **llegarse a** to approach; **~ a** to manage to, succeed in; **~ a saber** to find out; **~ a ser** to become; **~ a las manos de** to come into the hands of

llenar [ʎeˈnar] vt to fill; (espacio) to cover; (formulario) to fill in o up; (fig) to heap

lleno, -a [ˈʎeno, a] adj full, filled; (repleto) full up ♦ nm (TEATRO) full house; **dar de ~ contra un muro** to hit a wall head-on

llevadero, -a [ʎeβaˈðero, a] adj bearable, tolerable

llevar [ʎeˈβar] vt to take; (ropa) to wear; (cargar) to carry; (quitar) to take away; (en coche) to drive; (transportar) to transport; (traer: dinero) to carry; (conducir) to lead; (MAT) to carry ♦ vi

llorar *(suj: camino etc)*: ~ **a** to lead to; **llevarse** *vt* to carry off, take away; **llevamos dos días aquí** we have been here for two days; **él me lleva 2 años** he's 2 years older than me; ~ **los libros** *(COM)* to keep the books; **llevarse bien** to get on well (together)

llorar [ʎo'rar] *vt, vi* to cry, weep; ~ **de risa** to cry with laughter

llorón, -ona [ʎo'ron, ona] *adj* tearful ♦ *nm/f* cry-baby

lloroso, -a [ʎo'roso, a] *adj (gen)* weeping, tearful; *(triste)* sad, sorrowful

llover [ʎo'βer] *vi* to rain

llovizna [ʎo'βiθna] *nf* drizzle
❑ **lloviznar** *vi* to drizzle

llueve *etc* ['ʎweβe] *vb ver* **llover**

lluvia ['ʎuβja] *nf* rain ► **lluvia radioactiva** (radioactive) fallout
❑ **lluvioso, -a** *adj* rainy

lo [lo] *art def*: **lo bello** the beautiful, what is beautiful, that which is beautiful ♦ *pron (persona)* him; *(cosa)* it; **lo que sea** whatever; *ver tb* **el**

loable [lo'aβle] *adj* praiseworthy

lobo ['loβo] *nm* wolf ► **lobo de mar** *(fig)* sea dog

lóbulo ['loβulo] *nm* lobe

local [lo'kal] *adj* local ♦ *nm* place, site; *(oficinas)* premises *pl* ❑ **localidad** *nf (barrio)* locality; *(lugar)* location; *(TEATRO)* seat, ticket ❑ **localizar** *vt (ubicar)* to locate, find; *(restringir)* to localize; *(situar)* to place

loción [lo'θjon] *nf* lotion

loco, -a ['loko, a] *adj* mad ♦ *nm/f* lunatic, mad person; **estar ~ con** o **por algo/por algn** to be mad about sth/sb

locomotora [lokomo'tora] *nf* engine, locomotive

locuaz [lo'kwaθ] *adj* loquacious

locución [loku'θjon] *nf* expression

locura [lo'kura] *nf* madness; *(acto)* crazy act

locutor, a [loku'tor, a] *nm/f (RADIO)* announcer; *(comentarista)* commentator; *(TV)* newsreader

locutorio [loku'torjo] *nm (en telefónica)* telephone booth

lodo ['loðo] *nm* mud

lógica ['loxika] *nf* logic

lógico, -a ['loxiko, a] *adj* logical

login *nm* login

logística [lo'xistika] *nf* logistics *sg*

logotipo [loðo'tipo] *nm* logo

logrado, -a [lo'ðraðo, a] *adj (interpretación, reproducción)* polished, excellent

lograr [lo'ɣrar] *vt* to achieve; *(obtener)* to get, obtain; ~ **hacer** to manage to do; ~ **que algn venga** to manage to get sb to come

logro ['loɣro] *nm* achievement, success

lóker *(LAm) nm* locker

loma ['loma] *nf* hillock *(BRIT)*, small hill

lombriz [lom'briθ] *nf* worm

lomo ['lomo] *nm (de animal)* back; *(CULIN: de cerdo)* pork loin; *(: de vaca)* rib steak; *(de libro)* spine

lona ['lona] *nf* canvas

loncha ['lontʃa] *nf* = **lonja**

lonchería *(LAm)* [lontʃe'ria] *nf* snack bar, diner *(US)*

Londres ['londres] *n* London

longaniza [longa'niθa] *nf* pork sausage

longitud [lonxi'tuð] *nf* length; *(GEO)* longitude; **tener 3 metros de** ~ to be 3 metres long ► **longitud de onda** wavelength

lonja ['lonxa] *nf* slice; *(de tocino)* rasher ► **lonja de pescado** fish market

loro ['loro] *nm* parrot

los [los] *art def* **the** ♦ *pron* them; *(ustedes)* you; **mis libros y ~ tuyos** my books and yours; *ver tb* **el**

losa ['losa] *nf* stone

lote ['lote] *nm* portion; *(COM)* lot

lotería [lote'ria] nf lottery; (juego) lotto

loza ['loθa] nf crockery

lubina [lu'βina] nf sea bass

lubricante [luβri'kante] nm lubricant

lubricar [luβri'kar] vt to lubricate

lucha ['lutʃa] nf fight, struggle ► **lucha de clases** class struggle ► **lucha libre** wrestling ❑ **luchar** vi to fight

lúcido, -a ['luθiðo, a] adj (persona) lucid; (mente) logical; (idea) crystal-clear

luciérnaga [lu'θjernaɣa] nf glow-worm

lucir [lu'θir] vt to illuminate, light (up); (ostentar) to show off ♦ vi (brillar) to shine; **lucirse** vr (irónico) to make a fool of o.s.

lucro ['lukro] nm profit, gain

lúdico, -a ['luðiko, a] adj (aspecto, actividad) play cpd

luego ['lweɣo] adv (después) next; (más tarde) later, afterwards

lugar [lu'ɣar] nm place; (sitio) spot; **en primer ~** in the first place, firstly; **~ de** instead of; **hacer ~** to make room; **fuera de ~** out of place; **sin ~ a dudas** without doubt, undoubtedly; **dar ~ a** to give rise to; **tener ~** to take place; **yo en su ~** if I were here ► **lugar común** commonplace

lúgubre ['luɣuβre] adj mournful

lujo ['luxo] nm luxury; (fig) profusion, abundance; **de ~** luxury cpd, de luxe ❑ **lujoso, -a** adj luxurious

lujuria [lu'xurja] nf lust

lumbre ['lumbre] nf fire; (para cigarrillo) light

luminoso, -a [lumi'noso, a] adj luminous, shining

luna ['luna] nf moon; (de un espejo) glass; (de gafas) lens; (fig) crescent; **estar en la ~** to have one's head in the clouds ► **luna de miel** honeymoon ► **luna llena/nueva** full/new moon

lunar [lu'nar] adj lunar ♦ nm (ANAT) mole; **tela de lunares** spotted material

lunes ['lunes] nm inv Monday

lupa ['lupa] nf magnifying glass

lustre ['lustre] nm polish; (fig) lustre; **dar ~ a** to polish

luto ['luto] nm mourning; **llevar el o vestirse de ~** to be in mourning

Luxemburgo [luksem'burɣo] nm Luxembourg

luz [luθ] (pl **luces**) nf light; **dar a ~ un niño** to give birth to a child; **sacar a la ~** to bring to light; **dar o encender (LAm) o prender (ESP)/apagar la ~** to switch the light on/off; **tener pocas luces** to be dim o stupid; **traje de luces** bullfighter's costume ► **luces de tráfico** traffic lights ► **luz de freno** brake light ► **luz roja/verde** red/green light

M, m

m abr (= metro) m; (= minuto) m

macana (MÉX) [ma'kana] nf truncheon (BRIT), billy club (US)

macarrones [maka'rrones] nmpl macaroni sg

macedonia [maθe'ðonja] nf (tb: **~ de frutas**) fruit salad

maceta [ma'θeta] nf (de flores) pot of flowers; (para plantas) flowerpot

machacar [matʃa'kar] vt to crush, pound ♦ vi (insistir) to go on, keep on

machete [ma'tʃete] nm machete, (large) knife

machetear (MÉX) vt to swot (BRIT), grind away (US)

machismo [ma'tʃismo] nm male chauvinism □ **machista** (pej) nm sexist

macho ['matʃo] adj male; (fig) virile ♦ nm male; (fig) he-man

macizo, -a [ma'θiθo, a] adj (grande) massive; (fuerte, sólido) solid ♦ nm mass, chunk

madeja [ma'ðexa] nf (de lana) skein, hank; (de pelo) mass, mop

madera [ma'ðera] nf wood; (fig) nature, character; **una ~** a piece of wood

madrastra [ma'ðrastra] nf stepmother

madre ['maðre] adj mother cpd ♦ nf mother; (de vino etc) dregs pl ▶ **madre política/soltera** mother-in-law/ unmarried mother

Madrid [ma'ðrið] n Madrid

madriguera [maðri'ɣera] nf burrow

madrileño, -a [maðri'leɲo, a] adj of o from Madrid ♦ nm/f native of Madrid

madrina [ma'ðrina] nf godmother; (ARQ) prop, shore; (TEC) brace; (de boda) bridesmaid

madrugada [maðru'ɣaða] nf early morning; (alba) dawn, daybreak

madrugador, a [maðruɣa'ðor, a] adj early-rising

madrugar [maðru'ɣar] vi to get up early; (fig) to get ahead

madurar [maðu'rar] vt, vi (fruta) to ripen; (fig) to mature □ **madurez** nf ripeness; maturity □ **maduro, -a** adj ripe; mature

maestra [ma'estra] nf ver **maestro**

maestría [maes'tria] nf mastery; (habilidad) skill, expertise

maestro, -a [ma'estro, a] adj masterly; (principal) main ♦ nm/f master/ mistress; (profesor) teacher ♦ nm (autoridad) authority; (MÚS) maestro; (experto) master ▶ **maestro albañil** master mason

magdalena [maɣða'lena] nf fairy cake

magia ['maxja] nf magic □ **mágico, -a** adj magic(al) ♦ nm/f magician

magisterio [maxis'terjo] nm (enseñanza) teaching; (profesión) teaching profession; (maestros) teachers pl

magistrado [maxis'traðo] nm magistrate

magistral [maxis'tral] adj magisterial; (fig) masterly

magnate [maɣ'nate] nm magnate, tycoon

magnético, -a [maɣ'netiko, a] adj magnetic

magnetofón [maɣneto'fon] nm tape recorder

magnetófono [maɣne'tofono] nm = **magnetofón**

magnífico, -a [maɣ'nifiko, a] adj splendid, magnificent

magnitud [maɣni'tuð] nf magnitude

mago, -a ['maɣo, a] nm/f magician; **los Reyes Magos** the Three Wise Men

magro, -a ['maɣro, a] adj (carne) lean

mahonesa [mao'nesa] nf mayonnaise

maître [metre] nm head waiter

maíz [ma'iθ] nm maize (BRIT), corn (US); sweet corn

majestad [maxes'tað] nf majesty

majo, -a ['maxo, a] adj nice; (guapo) attractive, good-looking; (elegante) smart

mal [mal] adv badly; (equivocadamente) wrongly ♦ adj = **malo** ♦ nm evil; (desgracia) misfortune; (daño) harm, damage; (MED) illness; **~ que bien** rightly or wrongly; **ir de ~ en peor** to get worse and worse

malabarista [malaβa'rista] nmf juggler

malaria [ma'larja] nf malaria

malcriado, -a [mal'krjaðo, a] adj spoiled

maldad [mal'dað] nf evil, wickedness

maldecir [malde'θir] vt to curse

maldición [maldi'θjon] nf curse

maldito, -a [mal'dito, a] adj (condenado) damned; (perverso) wicked; ¡~ **sea!** damn it!

malecón (LAm) [male'kon] nm sea front, promenade

maleducado, -a [maleðu'kaðo, a] adj bad-mannered, rude

malentendido [malenten'diðo] nm misunderstanding

malestar [males'tar] nm (gen) discomfort; (fig: inquietud) uneasiness; (POL) unrest

maleta [ma'leta] nf case, suitcase; (AUTO) boot (BRIT), trunk (US); **hacer las maletas** to pack ❑ **maletero** nm (AUTO) boot (BRIT), trunk (US) ❑ **maletín** nm small case, bag

maleza [ma'leθa] nf (malas hierbas) weeds pl; (arbustos) thicket

malgastar [malɣas'tar] vt (tiempo, dinero) to waste; (salud) to ruin

malhechor, a [male'tʃor, a] nm/f delinquent

malhumorado, -a [malumo'raðo, a] adj bad-tempered

malicia [ma'liθja] nf (maldad) wickedness; (astucia) slyness, guile; (mala intención) malice, spite; (carácter travieso) mischievousness

maligno, -a [ma'liɣno, a] adj evil; (malévolo) malicious; (MED) malignant

malla [maλa] nf mesh; (de baño) swimsuit; (de ballet, gimnasia) leotard; **mallas** nfpl tights ▸ **malla de alambre** wire mesh

Mallorca [ma'λorka] nf Majorca

malo, -a ['malo, a] adj bad, false ♦ nm/f villain; **estar ~** to be ill

malograr [maloɣ'rar] vt to spoil; (plan) to upset; (ocasión) to waste □ **malograrse** vpr (plan) to fail; (persona) to die before one's time

malparado, -a [malpa'raðo, a] adj: **salir ~** to come off badly

malpensado, -a [malpen'saðo, a] adj nasty

malteada [malte'aða] (LAm) nf milkshake

maltratar [maltra'tar] vt to ill-treat, mistreat

malvado, -a [mal'βaðo, a] adj evil, villainous

Malvinas [mal'βinas] nfpl (tb: **Islas ~**) Falklands, Falkland Islands

mama ['mama] nf (de animal) teat; (de mujer) breast

mamá [ma'ma] (pl **~s** (fam)) nf mum, mummy

mamar [ma'mar] vt, vi to suck

mamarracho [mama'ratʃo] nm sight, mess

mameluco (RPl) [mameluko] nm dungarees pl (BRIT), overalls pl (US)

mamífero [ma'mifero] nm mammal

mampara [mam'para] nf (entre habitaciones) partition; (biombo) screen

mampostería [mamposte'ria] nf masonry

manada [ma'naða] nf (ZOOL) herd; (: de leones) pride; (: de lobos) pack

manantial [manan'tjal] nm spring

mancha ['mantʃa] nf stain, mark; (ZOOL) patch □ **manchar** vt (gen) to stain, mark; (ensuciar) to soil, dirty

manchego, -a [man'tʃeɣo, a] adj of o from La Mancha

manco, -a ['manko, a] adj (de un brazo) one-armed; (de una mano) one-handed; (fig) defective, faulty

mancuernas (MEX) [man'kwernas] nfpl cufflinks

mandado (LAm) [man'daðo] nm errand

mandamiento [manda'mjento] nm (orden) order, command; (REL) commandment

mandar [man'dar] vt (ordenar) to order; (dirigir) to lead, command; (enviar) to send; (pedir) to order, ask for ♦ vi to be in charge; (pey) to be bossy; **¿mande?** (MEX: ¿cómo dice?) pardon?, excuse me?; **~ hacer un traje** to have a suit made

mandarina [manda'rina] (ESP) nf tangerine, mandarin (orange)

mandato [man'dato] nm (orden) order; (POL: período) term of office; (: territorio) mandate

mandíbula [man'diβula] nf jaw

mandil [man'dil] nm apron

mando ['mando] nm (MIL) command; (de país) rule; (el primer lugar) lead; (POL) term of office; (TEC) control; **~ a la izquierda** left-hand drive ▶ **mando a distancia** remote control

mandón, -ona [man'don, ona] adj bossy, domineering

manejar [mane'xar] vt to manage; (máquina) to work, operate; (caballo etc) to handle; (casa) to run, manage; (LAm AUTO) to drive; **manejarse** vr (comportarse) to act, behave; (arreglárselas) to manage ❏ **manejo** nm (de bicicleta) handling; (de negocio) management, running; (LAm AUTO) driving; (facilidad de trato) ease, confidence; **manejos** nmpl (intrigas) intrigues

manera [ma'nera] nf way, manner, fashion; **maneras** nfpl (modales) manners; **su ~ de ser** the way he is; (aire) his manner; **de ninguna ~** no way, by no means; **de otra ~** otherwise; **de todas maneras** at any rate; **no hay ~ de persuadirle** there's no way of convincing him

manga ['manga] nf (de camisa) sleeve; (de riego) hose

mango ['mango] nm handle; (BOT) mango

manguera [man'gera] nf hose

maní (LAm) [ma'ni] nm peanut

manía [ma'nia] nf (MED) mania; (fig: moda) rage, craze; (disgusto) dislike; (malicia) spite; **coger ~ a algn** to take a dislike to sb; **tener ~ a algn** to dislike

sb ❏ **maníaco, -a** adj maniac(al) ♦ nm/f maniac

maniático, -a [ma'njatiko, a] adj maniac(al) ♦ nm/f maniac

manicomio [mani'komjo] nm mental hospital (BRIT), insane asylum (US)

manifestación [manifesta'θjon] nf (declaración) statement, declaration; (de emoción) show, display; (POL: desfile) demonstration; (: concentración) mass meeting

manifestar [manifes'tar] vt to show, manifest; (declarar) to state, declare ❏ **manifiesto, -a** adj clear, manifest ♦ nm manifesto

manillar [mani'ʎar] nm handlebars pl

maniobra [ma'njoβra] nf manoeuvre; **maniobras** nfpl (MIL) manoeuvres ❏ **maniobrar** vt to manoeuvre

manipulación [manipula'θjon] nf manipulation

manipular [manipu'lar] vt to manipulate; (manejar) to handle

maniquí [mani'ki] nm dummy ♦ nm/f model

manivela [mani'βela] nf crank

manjar [man'xar] nm (tasty) dish

mano ['mano] nf hand; (ZOOL) foot, paw; (de pintura) coat; (serie) lot, series; **a ~** by hand; **a ~ derecha/izquierda** on the right(-hand side)/left(-hand side); **de primera ~** (at) first hand; **de segunda ~** (at) second hand; **robo a ~ armada** armed robbery; **estrechar la ~ a algn** to shake sb's hand ▶ **mano de obra** labour, manpower

manojo [ma'noxo] nm handful, bunch; (de llaves) bunch

manopla [ma'nopla] nf mitten

manosear [manose'ar] vt (tocar) to handle, touch; (desordenar) to mess up, rumple; (insistir en) to overwork; (LAm: acariciar) to caress, fondle

manotazo [mano'taθo] nm slap, smack

mansalva [man'salβa]: **a ~** adv indiscriminately

mansión [man'sjon] nf mansion

manso, -a [man'so, a] adj gentle, mild; (animal) tame

manta ['manta] (ESP) nf blanket

manteca [man'teka] nf fat; (CS: mantequilla) butter ▶ **manteca de cerdo** lard ❑ **mantecado** [mante'kaðo] (ESP) nm Christmas sweet made from flour, almonds and lard

mantel [man'tel] nm tablecloth

mantendré etc [manten'dre] vb ver **mantener**

mantener [mante'ner] vt to support, maintain; (alimentar) to sustain; (conservar) to keep; (TEC) to maintain, service; **mantenerse** vr (seguir de pie) to be still standing; (no ceder) to hold one's ground; (subsistir) to sustain o.s., keep going ❑ **mantenimiento** nm maintenance; sustenance; (sustento) support

mantequilla [mante'kiʎa] nf butter

mantilla [man'tiʎa] nf mantilla; **mantillas** nfpl (de bebé) baby clothes

manto ['manto] nm (capa) cloak; (de ceremonia) robe, gown

mantuve etc [man'tuβe] vb ver **mantener**

manual [ma'nwal] adj manual ♦ nm manual, handbook

manuscrito, -a [manus'krito, a] adj handwritten ♦ nm manuscript

manutención [manuten'θjon] nf maintenance; (sustento) support

manzana [man'θana] nf apple; (ARQ) block (of houses)

manzanilla [manθa'niʎa] nf (planta) camomile; (infusión) camomile tea

manzano [man'θano] nm apple tree

maña ['maɲa] nf (gen) skill, dexterity; (pey) guile; (destreza) trick, knack

mañana [ma'ɲana] adv tomorrow ♦ nm future ♦ nf morning; **de** o **por la ~** in the morning; **¡hasta ~!** see you

tomorrow!; **~ por la ~** tomorrow morning

mapa ['mapa] nm map

maple (LAm) nm maple

maqueta [ma'keta] nf (scale) model

maquiladora (MÉX) [makila'ðora] nf (COM) bonded assembly plant

maquillaje [maki'ʎaxe] nm make-up; (acto) making up

maquillar [maki'ʎar] vt to make up; **maquillarse** vr to put on (some) make-up

máquina ['makina] nf machine; (de tren) locomotive, engine; (FOTO) camera; (fig) machinery; **escrito a ~** typewritten ▶ **máquina de coser** sewing machine ▶ **máquina de escribir** typewriter ▶ **máquina fotográfica** camera

maquinaria [maki'narja] nf (máquinas) machinery; (mecanismo) mechanism, works pl

maquinilla [maki'niʎa] (ESP) nf (tb: ~ **de afeitar**) razor

maquinista [maki'nista] nmf (de tren) engine driver; (TEC) operator; (NÁUT) engineer

mar [mar] nm o f sea; **~ adentro** out at sea; **en alta ~** on the high seas; **la ~ de** (fam) lots of ▶ **el Mar Negro/Báltico** the Black/Baltic Sea

maraña [ma'raɲa] nf (maleza) thicket; (confusión) tangle

maravilla [mara'βiʎa] nf marvel, wonder; (BOT) marigold ❑ **maravillar** vt to astonish, amaze; **maravillarse** vr to be astonished, be amazed ❑ **maravilloso, -a** adj wonderful, marvellous

marca ['marka] nf (gen) mark; (sello) stamp; (COM) make, brand; **de ~** excellent, outstanding ▶ **marca de fábrica** trademark ▶ **marca registrada** registered trademark

marcado, -a [mar'kaðo, a] adj marked, strong

marcador [marka'ðor] nm (DEPORTE) scoreboard; (: persona) scorer

marcapasos [marka'pasos] nm inv pacemaker

marcar [mar'kar] vt (gen) to mark; (número de teléfono) to dial; (gol) to score; (números) to record, keep a tally of; (pelo) to set ♦ vi (DEPORTE) to score; (TEL) to dial

marcha ['martʃa] nf march; (TEC) running, working; (AUTO) gear; (velocidad) speed; (fig) progress; (dirección) course; **poner en ~** to put into gear; (fig) to set in motion, get going; **dar ~ atrás** to reverse, put into reverse; **estar en ~** to be under way, be in motion ❑ **marchar** [mar'tʃar] vi (ir) to go; (funcionar) to work, go; **marcharse** vr to go away, leave

marchitar [martʃi'tar] vt to wither, dry up; **marchitarse** vr (BOT) to wither; (fig) to fade away ❑ **marchito, -a** adj withered, faded; (fig) in decline

marciano, -a [mar'θjano, a] adj, nm/f Martian

marco ['marko] nm frame; (moneda) mark; (fig) framework

▶ **marea** [ma'rea] nf tide ▶ **marea negra** oil slick

marear [mare'ar] vt (fig) to annoy, upset; (MED): ~ **a algn** to make sb feel sick; **marearse** vr (tener náuseas) to feel sick; (desvanecerse) to feel faint; (aturdirse) to feel dizzy; (fam: emborracharse) to get tipsy

maremoto [mare'moto] nm tidal wave

mareo [ma'reo] nm (náusea) sick feeling; (en viaje) travel sickness; (aturdimiento) dizziness; (fam: lata) nuisance

marfil [mar'fil] nm ivory

margarina [marɣa'rina] nf margarine

margarita [marɣa'rita] nf (BOT) daisy; (TIP) daisywheel

margen ['marxen] nm (borde) edge, border; (fig) margin, space ♦ nf (de río

etc) bank; **dar ~ para** to give an opportunity for; **mantenerse al ~** to keep out (of things)

marginar [marxi'nar] vt (socialmente) to marginalize, ostracize

mariachi [ma'rjatʃi] nm (persona) mariachi musician; (grupo) mariachi band

---

MARIACHI

Mariachi music is the musical style most characteristic of Mexico. From the state of Jalisco in the 19th century, this music spread rapidly throughout the country, until each region had its own particular style of the Mariachi "sound". A Mariachi band can be made up of several singers, up to eight violins, two trumpets, guitars, a "vihuela" (an old form of guitar), and a harp. The dance associated with this music is called the "zapateado".

---

marica [ma'rika] (fam) nm sissy

maricón [mari'kon] (fam) nm queer

marido [ma'riðo] nm husband

marihuana [mari'wana] nf marijuana, cannabis

marina [ma'rina] nf navy ▶ **marina mercante** merchant navy

marinero, -a [mari'nero, a] adj sea cpd ♦ nm sailor, seaman

marino, -a [ma'rino, a] adj sea cpd, marine ♦ nm sailor

marioneta [marjo'neta] nf puppet

mariposa [mari'posa] nf butterfly

mariquita [mari'kita] nf (BRIT) ladybird (BRIT), ladybug (US)

marisco [ma'risko] (ESP) nm shellfish inv, seafood ❑ **mariscos** (LAm) nmpl = **marisco**

marítimo, -a [ma'ritimo, a] adj sea cpd, maritime

mármol ['marmol] nm marble

marqués, -esa [mar'kes, esa] nm/f marquis/marchioness

marrón [ma'rron] *adj* brown

marroquí [marro'ki] *adj, nmf* Moroccan ♦ *nm* Morocco (leather)

Marruecos [ma'rrwekos] *nm* Morocco

martes ['martes] *nm inv* Tuesday; **~ y trece** = Friday 13th

MARTES Y TRECE

According to Spanish superstition Tuesday is an unlucky day, even more so if it falls on the 13th of the month.

martillo [mar'tiʎo] *nm* hammer

mártir ['martir] *nmf* martyr
❏ **martirio** *nm* martyrdom; *(fig)* torture, torment

marxismo [mark'sismo] *nm* Marxism

marzo ['marθo] *nm* March

más

PALABRA CLAVE

[mas] *adj, adv*

1: **más** (**que** o **de**) *(compar)* more (than), ...+ er (than); **más grande/inteligente** bigger/more intelligent; **trabaja más** (**que** yo) he works more (than me); *ver tb* **cada**

2 *(superl):* **el más** the most, ...+ est; **el más grande/inteligente** (**de**) the biggest/most intelligent (in)

3 *(negativo):* **no tengo más dinero** I haven't got any more money; **no viene más por aquí** he doesn't come round here any more

4 *(adicional):* **no le veo más solución que ...** I see no other solution than to ...; **¿quién más?** anybody else?

5 (+ *adj: valor intensivo):* **¡qué perro más sucio!** what a filthy dog!; **¡es más tonto!** he's so stupid!

6 *(locuciones):* **más o menos** more or less; **los más** most people; **es más** furthermore; **más bien** rather; **¡qué más da!** what does it matter!; *ver tb*

no

7: por más: por más que te esfuerces no matter how hard you try; **por más que quisiera ...** much as I should like
to ...

8: de más: veo que aquí estoy de más I can see I'm not needed here; **tenemos uno de más** we've got one extra

♦ *prep:* **2 más 2 son 4** 2 and o plus 2 are 4

♦ *nm inv:* **este trabajo tiene sus más y sus menos** this job's got its good points and its bad points

mas [mas] *conj* but

masa ['masa] *nf (mezcla)* dough; *(volumen)* volume, mass; *(FÍSICA)* mass; **en ~** en masse; **las masas** (POL) the masses

masacre [ma'sakre] *nf* massacre

masaje [ma'saxe] *nm* massage

máscara ['maskara] *nf* mask
▶ **máscara antigás/de oxígeno** gas/oxygen mask ❏ **mascarilla** *nf (de belleza, MED)* mask

masculino, -a [masku'lino, a] *adj* masculine; *(BIO)* male

masía [ma'sia] *nf* farmhouse

masivo, -a [ma'siβo, a] *adj* mass *cpd*

masoquista [maso'kista] *nmf* masochist

máster (*ESP*) ['master] *nm* master

masticar [masti'kar] *vt* to chew

mástil ['mastil] *nm (de navío)* mast; *(de guitarra)* neck

mastín [mas'tin] *nm* mastiff

masturbarse [mastur'βarse] *vr* to masturbate

mata ['mata] *nf (arbusto)* bush, shrub; *(de hierba)* tuft

matadero [mata'ðero] *nm* slaughterhouse, abattoir

matamoscas [mata'moskas] *nm inv* (*pala*) fly swat

matanza [ma'tanθa] *nf* slaughter

matar [ma'tar] *vt, vi* to kill; **matarse** *vr* (*suicidarse*) to kill o.s., commit suicide; (*morir*) to be o get killed; **~ el hambre** to stave off hunger

matasellos [mata'seʎos] *nm inv* postmark

mate ['mate] *adj* matt ◆ *nm* (*en ajedrez*) (check)mate; (*LAm: hierba*) maté; (: *vasija*) gourd

matemáticas [mate'matikas] *nfpl* mathematics □ **matemático, -a** *adj* mathematical ◆ *nm/f* mathematician

materia [ma'terja] *nf* (*gen*) matter; (*TEC*) material; (*ESCOL*) subject; **en ~ de** on the subject of ▶ **materia prima** raw material □ **material** *adj* material ◆ *nm* material; (*TEC*) equipment □ **materialista** *adj* materialist(ic) □ **materialmente** *adv* materially; (*fig*) absolutely

maternal [mater'nal] *adj* motherly, maternal

maternidad [materni'ðað] *nf* motherhood, maternity □ **materno, -a** *adj* maternal; (*lengua*) mother *cpd*

matinal [mati'nal] *adj* morning *cpd*

matiz [ma'tiθ] *nm* shade □ **matizar** *vt* (*variar*) to vary; (*ARTE*) to blend; **matizar de** to tinge with

matón [ma'ton] *nm* bully

matorral [mato'rral] *nm* thicket

matrícula [ma'trikula] *nf* (*registro*) register; (*AUTO*) registration number; (: *placa*) number plate ▶ **matrícula de honor** (*UNIV*) top marks in a subject at university with the right to free registration the following year □ **matricular** *vt* to register, enrol

matrimonio [matri'monjo] *nm* (*pareja*) (married) couple; (*unión*) marriage

matriz [ma'triθ] *nf* (*ANAT*) womb; (*TEC*) mould

matrona [ma'trona] *nf* (*persona de edad*) matron; (*comadrona*) midwife

matufia (*RPl: fam*) *nf* put-up job

maullar [mau'ʎar] *vi* to mew, miaow

maxilar [maksi'lar] *nm* jaw(bone)

máxima ['maksima] *nf* maxim

máximo, -a ['maksimo, a] *adj* maximum; (*más alto*) highest; (*más grande*) greatest ◆ *nm* maximum; **como ~** at most

mayo ['majo] *nm* May

mayonesa [majo'nesa] *nf* mayonnaise

mayor [ma'jor] *adj* main, chief; (*adulto*) adult; (*de edad avanzada*) elderly; (*MÚS*) major; (*comparar: de tamaño*) bigger; (: *de edad*) older; (*superl: de tamaño*) biggest; (: *de edad*) oldest ◆ *nm* (*adulto*) adult; **mayores** *nmpl* (*antepasados*) ancestors; **al por ~** wholesale ▶ **mayor de edad** adult

mayoral [majo'ral] *nm* foreman

mayordomo [major'ðomo] *nm* butler

mayoría [majo'ria] *nf* majority, greater part

mayorista [majo'rista] *nmf* wholesaler

mayoritario, -a [majori'tarjo, a] *adj* majority *cpd*

mayúscula [ma'juskula] *nf* capital letter

mazapán [maθa'pan] *nm* marzipan

mazo ['maθo] *nm* (*martillo*) mallet; (*de flores*) bunch; (*DEPORTE*) bat

me [me] *pron* (*directo*) me; (*indirecto*) (to) me; (*reflexivo*) (to) myself; **¡dámelo!** give it to me!

mear [me'ar] (*fam*) *vi* to pee, piss (*!*)

mecánica [me'kanika] *nf* (*ESCOL*) mechanics *sg*; (*mecanismo*) mechanism; *ver tb* **mecánico, -a** [me'kaniko, a] *adj* mechanical ◆ *nm/f* mechanic

mecanismo [meka'nismo] *nm* mechanism; (*marcha*) gear

mecanografía [mekanoɣraˈfia] nf
typewriting ❑ **mecanógrafo, -a** nm/f
typist

mecate [meˈkate] (MÉX, CAm) nm rope

mecedora [meθeˈðora] nf rocking
chair

mecer [meˈθer] vt (cuna) to rock;
mecerse vr to to rock; (rama) to sway

mecha ['metʃa] nf (de vela) wick; (de
bomba) fuse

mechero [meˈtʃero] nm (cigarette)
lighter

mechón [meˈtʃon] nm (gen) tuft; (de
pelo) lock

medalla [meˈðaʎa] nf medal

media ['meðja] nf stocking; (LAm:
calcetín) sock; (promedio) average

mediado, -a [meˈðjaðo, a] adj half-full;
(trabajo) half-completed; **a mediados
de** in the middle of, halfway through

mediano, -a [meˈðjano, a] adj (regular)
medium, average; (mediocre)
mediocre

medianoche [meðjaˈnotʃe] nf
midnight

mediante [meˈðjante] adv by (means
of), through

mediar [meˈðjar] vi (interceder) to
mediate, intervene

medicamento [meðikaˈmento] nm
medicine, drug

medicina [meðiˈθina] nf medicine

médico, -a [ˈmeðiko, a] adj medical
♦ nm/f doctor

medida [meˈðiða] nf measure;
(medición) measurement; (prudencia)
moderation, prudence; **en cierta/gran
~** up to a point/to a great extent; **un
traje a la ~** a made-to-measure suit; **~
de cuello** collar size; **a ~ de** in
proportion to; (de acuerdo con) in
keeping with; **a ~ que** (conforme) as
❑ **medidor** (LAm) nm meter

medio, -a [ˈmeðjo, a] adj half (a);
(punto) mid, middle; (promedio)
average ♦ adv half ♦ nm (centro)

middle, centre; (promedio) average;
(método) means, way; (ambiente)
environment; **medios** nmpl means,
resources; **~ litro** half a litre; **las tres y
media** half past three; **a ~ terminar**
half finished; **pagar a medias** to share
the cost ▶ **medio ambiente**
environment ▶ **medio de
transporte** means of transport
▶ **Medio Oriente** Middle East
▶ **medios de comunicación** media
❑ **medioambiental** adj (política,
efectos) environmental

mediocre [meˈðjokre] adj mediocre

mediodía [meðjoˈðia] nm midday,
noon

medir [meˈðir] vt, vi (gen) to measure

meditar [meðiˈtar] vt to ponder, think
over, meditate on; (planear) to think
out

mediterráneo, -a [meðiteˈrraneo, a]
adj Mediterranean ♦ nm: **el M~** the
Mediterranean

médula [ˈmeðula] nf (ANAT) marrow
▶ **médula espinal** spinal cord

medusa [meˈðusa] (ESP) nf jellyfish

megáfono [meˈɣafono] nm
megaphone

mejilla [meˈxiʎa] nf cheek

mejillón [mexiˈʎon] nm mussel

mejor [meˈxor] adj, adv (compar) better;
(superl) best; **a lo ~** probably; (quizás)
maybe; **~ dicho** rather; **tanto ~** so
much the better ❑ **mejora** [meˈxora]
nf improvement ❑ **mejorar** vt to
improve, make better ♦ vi to improve,
get better; **mejorarse** vr to improve,
get better

melancólico, -a [melanˈkoliko, a] adj
(triste) sad, melancholy; (soñador)
dreamy

melena [meˈlena] nf (de persona) long
hair; (ZOOL) mane

mellizo, -a [meˈʎiθo, a] adj, nm/f twin

melocotón [melokoˈton] (ESP) nm
peach

melodía [melo'ðia] nf melody, tune

melodrama [melo'ðrama] nm melodrama ▸ **melodramático, -a** adj melodramatic

melón [me'lon] nm melon

membrete [mem'brete] nm letterhead

membrillo [mem'briʎo] nm quince; (**carne de**) ~ quince jelly

memoria [me'morja] nf (gen) memory; **memorias** nfpl (de autor) memoirs ❏ **memorizar** vt to memorize

menaje [me'naxe] nm (tb: **artículos de** ~) household items

mencionar [menθjo'nar] vt to mention

mendigo, -a [men'diɣo, a] nm/f beggar

menear [mene'ar] vt to move; **menearse** vr to shake; (balancearse) to sway; (moverse) to move; (fig) to get a move on

menestra [me'nestra] nf (tb: ~ **de verduras**) vegetable stew

menopausia [meno'pausja] nf menopause

menor [me'nor] adj (más pequeño: compar) smaller; (: superl) smallest; (más joven: compar) younger; (: superl) youngest; (MÚS) minor ▸ nm/f (joven) young person, juvenile; **no tengo la ~ idea** I haven't the faintest idea; **al por** ~ retail ▸ **menor de edad** person under age

Menorca [me'norka] nf Minorca

menos

PALABRA CLAVE

[menos] adj

1: menos (que o de) (compar: cantidad) less (than); (: número) fewer (than); **con menos entusiasmo** with less enthusiasm; **menos gente** fewer people; ver tb **cada**

2 (superl): **es el que menos culpa tiene** he is the least to blame

▸ adv

1 (compar): **menos (que o de)** less (than); **me gusta menos que el otro** I like it less than the other one

2 (superl): **es el menos listo (de su clase)** he's the least bright in his class; **de todas ellas es la que menos me agrada** out of all of them she's the one I like least

3 (locuciones): **no quiero verle y menos visitarle** I don't want to see him, let alone visit him; **tenemos siete de menos** we're seven short; **(por) lo menos** at the (very) least; **¡menos mal!** thank goodness!

◆ prep except; (cifras) minus; **todos menos él** everyone except (for) him; **5 menos 2** 5 minus 2

◆ conj: **a menos que: a menos que venga mañana** unless he comes tomorrow

menospreciar [menospre'θjar] vt to underrate, undervalue; (despreciar) to scorn, despise

mensaje [men'saxe] nm message; **enviar un ~ a algn** (por móvil) to text sb, send sb a text message ▸ **mensaje de texto** text message ❏ **mensajero, -a** nm/f messenger

menso, -a [menso, a] (MÉX: fam) adj stupid

menstruación [menstrua'θjon] nf menstruation

mensual [men'swal] adj monthly; **100 euros mensuales** 100 euros a month ❏ **mensualidad** nf (salario) monthly salary; (COM) monthly payment, monthly instalment

menta ['menta] nf mint

mental [men'tal] adj mental ❏ **mentalidad** nf mentality ❏ **mentalizar** vt (sensibilizar) to make aware; (convencer) to convince; (padres) to prepare (mentally); **mentalizarse** vr (concienciarse) to become aware; **mentalizarse (de) to** get used to the idea (of); **mentalizarse de que ...** (convencerse) to get it into one's head that ...

mente ['mente] nf mind

mentir [men'tir] vi to lie ❏ **mentira** [men'tira] nf (una mentira) lie; (acto) lying; (invención) fiction; **parece mentira que ...** it seems incredible that ..., I can't believe that ...; **-, -a** [menti'roso, a] adj lying ◆ nm/f liar

menú [me'nu] (pl **-s**) nm menu ► **menú del día** set menu ◆ **menú turístico** tourist menu

menudencias (LAm) nfpl giblets

menudo, -a [me'nuðo, a] adj (pequeño) small, tiny; (sin importancia) petty, insignificant; **¡~ negocio!** (fam) some deal!; **a ~** often, frequently

meñique [me'ɲike] nm little finger

mercadillo (ESP) nm flea market

mercado [mer'kaðo] nm market ► **mercado de pulgas** (LAm) flea market

mercancía [merkan'θia] nf commodity; **mercancías** nfpl goods, merchandise sg

mercenario, -a [merθe'narjo, a] adj, nm mercenary

mercería [merθe'ria] nf haberdashery (BRIT), notions pl (US); (tienda) haberdasher's (BRIT), notions store (US)

mercurio [mer'kurjo] nm mercury

merecer [mere'θer] vt to deserve, merit ◆ vi to be deserving, be worthy; **merece la pena** it's worthwhile ❏ **merecido, -a** adj (well) deserved; **llevar su merecido** to get one's deserts

merendar [meren'dar] vt to have for tea ◆ vi to have tea; (en el campo) to have a picnic ❏ **merendero** nm open-air cafe

merengue [me'renge] nm meringue

meridiano [meri'ðjano] nm (GEO) meridian

merienda [me'rjenda] nf (light) tea, afternoon snack; (de campo) picnic

mérito ['merito] nm merit; (valor) worth, value

merluza [mer'luθa] nf hake

mermelada [merme'laða] nf jam

mero, -a ['mero, a] adj mere; (MEX, CAm: fam) very

merodear [meroðe'ar] vi: **~ por** to prowl about

mes [mes] nm month

mesa ['mesa] nf table; (de trabajo) desk; (GEO) plateau; **poner/quitar la ~** to lay/ clear the table ► **mesa electoral** officials in charge of a polling station ► **mesa redonda** (reunión) round table ❏ **mesero, -a** (LAm) nm/f waiter/waitress

meseta [me'seta] nf (GEO) plateau, tableland

mesilla [me'siʎa] nf (tb: **~ de noche**) bedside table

mesón [me'son] nm inn

mestizo, -a [mes'tiθo, a] adj half-caste, of mixed race ◆ nm/f half-caste

meta ['meta] nf goal; (de carrera) finish

metabolismo [metaβo'lismo] nm metabolism

metáfora [me'tafora] nf metaphor

metal [me'tal] nm (materia) metal; (MÚS) brass ❏ **metálico, -a** adj metallic; (de metal) metal ◆ nm (dinero contante) cash

meteorología nf meteorology

meter [me'ter] vt (colocar) to put, place; (introducir) to put in, insert; (involucrar) to involve; (causar) to make, cause; **meterse** vr: **meterse en** to go into, enter; (fig) to interfere in, meddle in; **meterse a** to start; **meterse a escritor** to become a writer; **meterse con uno** to provoke sb, pick a quarrel with sb

meticuloso, -a [metiku'loso, a] adj meticulous, thorough

metódico, -a [me'toðiko, a] adj methodical

método ['metoðo] nm method

metralleta [metra'ʎeta] nf sub-machine-gun

métrico, -a ['metriko, a] adj metric

metro ['metro] nm metre; (tren) underground (BRIT), subway (US)

mexicano, -a [mexi'kano, a] adj, nm/f Mexican

México ['mexiko] nm Mexico; **Ciudad de ~** = Mexico City

mezcla ['meθkla] nf mixture ❑ **mezcladora** [meθkla'ðora] nf (tb: **mezcladora de cemento**) cement mixer ❑ **mezclar** vt to mix (up); **mezclarse** vr to mix, mingle; **mezclarse en** to get mixed up in, get involved in

mezquino, -a [meθ'kino, a] adj mean

mezquita [meθ'kita] nf mosque

mg. abr (= miligramo) mg

mi [mi] adj pos my ♦ nm (MÚS) E

mí [mi] pron me; myself

mía ['mia] pron ver **mío**

michelín [mitʃe'lin] (fam) nm (de grasa) spare tyre

microbio [mi'kroβjo] nm microbe

micrófono [mi'krofono] nm microphone

microondas [mikro'ondas] nm inv (tb: **horno ~**) microwave (oven)

microscopio [mikros'kopjo] nm microscope

miedo ['mjeðo] nm fear; (nerviosismo) apprehension, nervousness; **tener ~** to be afraid; **de ~** wonderful, marvellous; **hace un frío de ~** (fam) it's terribly cold ❑ **miedoso, -a** adj fearful, timid

miel [mjel] nf honey

miembro ['mjembro] nm limb; (socio) member ▶ **miembro viril** penis

mientras ['mjentras] conj while; (duración) as long as ♦ adv meanwhile; **~ tanto** meanwhile

miércoles ['mjerkoles] nm inv Wednesday

mierda ['mjerða] (fam!) nf shit (!)

miga ['miya] nf crumb; (fig: meollo) essence; **hacer buenas migas** (fam) to get on well

mil [mil] num thousand; **dos ~ libras** two thousand pounds

milagro [mi'layro] nm miracle ❑ **milagroso, -a** adj miraculous

milésima [mi'lesima] nf (de segundo) thousandth

mili ['mili] (ESP: fam) nf: **hacer la ~** to do one's military service

milímetro [mi'limetro] nm millimetre

militante [mili'tante] adj militant

militar [mili'tar] adj military ♦ nmf soldier ♦ vi (MIL) to serve; (en un partido) to be a member

milla ['miʎa] nf mile

millar [mi'ʎar] nm thousand

millón [mi'ʎon] num million ❑ **millonario, -a** nm/f millionaire

milusos (MÉX) nm inv odd-job man

mimar [mi'mar] vt to spoil, pamper

mimbre ['mimbre] nm wicker

mímica ['mimika] nf (para comunicarse) sign language; (imitación) mimicry

mimo ['mimo] nm (caricia) caress; (de niño) spoiling; (TEATRO) mime; (: actor) mime artist

mina ['mina] nf mine

mineral [mine'ral] adj mineral ♦ nm (GEO) mineral; (mena) ore

minero, -a [mi'nero, a] adj mining cpd ♦ nm/f miner

miniatura [minja'tura] adj inv, nf miniature

minidisco [mini'disko] nm MiniDisc®

minifalda [mini'falda] nf miniskirt

mínimo, -a ['minimo, a] adj, nm minimum

minino, -a [mi'nino, a] (fam) nm/f puss, pussy

ministerio [minis'terjo] nm Ministry ▶ **Ministerio de Hacienda/de Asuntos Exteriores** Treasury (BRIT),

Treasury Department (US)/Foreign Office (BRIT), State Department (US)

ministro, -a [mi'nistro, a] nm/f minister

minoría [mino'ria] nf minority

minúscula [mi'nuskula] nf small letter

minúsculo, -a [mi'nuskulo, a] adj tiny, minute

minusválido, -a [minus'βaliðo, a] adj (physically) handicapped ♦ nm/f (physically) handicapped person

minuta [mi'nuta] nf (de comida) menu

minutero [minu'tero] nm minute hand

minuto [mi'nuto] nm minute

mío, -a ['mio, a] pron: **el ~/la mía** mine; **un amigo ~** a friend of mine; **lo ~** what is mine

miope [mi'ope] adj short-sighted

mira ['mira] nf (de arma) sight(s (pl); (fig) aim, intention

mirada [mi'raða] nf look, glance; (expresión) look, expression; **clavar la ~ en** to stare at; **echar una ~ a** to glance at

mirado, -a [mi'raðo, a] adj (sensato) sensible; (considerado) considerate; **bien/mal ~** (estimado) well/not well thought of; **bien ~ ...** all things considered ...

mirador [mira'ðor] nm viewpoint, vantage point

mirar [mi'rar] vt to look at; (observar) to watch; (considerar) to consider, think over; (vigilar, cuidar) to watch, look after ♦ vi to look; (ARQ) to face; **mirarse** vr (dos personas) to look at each other; **~ bien/mal** to think highly of/have a poor opinion of; **mirarse al espejo** to look at o.s. in the mirror

mirilla [mi'riʎa] nf spyhole, peephole

mirlo ['mirlo] nm blackbird

misa ['misa] nf mass

miserable [mise'raβle] adj (avaro) mean, stingy; (nimio) miserable, paltry;

(lugar) squalid; (fam) vile, despicable ♦ nmf (malvado) rogue

miseria [mi'serja] nf (pobreza) poverty; (tacañería) meanness, stinginess; (condiciones) squalor; **una ~** a pittance

misericordia [miseri'korðja] nf (compasión) compassion, pity; (piedad) mercy

misil [mi'sil] nm missile

misión [mi'sjon] nf mission
□ **misionero, -a** nm/f missionary

mismo, -a ['mismo, a] adj (semejante) same; (después de pron) -self; (para énfasis) very ♦ adv: **aquí/hoy ~** right here/this very day; **ahora ~** right now ♦ conj: **lo ~ que** just like o as; **el ~ traje** the same suit; **en ese ~ momento** at that very moment; **vino el ~ ministro** the minister himself came; **yo ~ lo vi** I saw it myself; **lo ~** the same (thing); **da lo ~** it's all the same; **quedamos en las mismas** we're no further forward; **por lo ~** for the same reason

misterio [mis'terjo] nm mystery
□ **misterioso, -a** adj mysterious

mitad [mi'tað] nf (medio) half; (centro) middle; **a ~ de precio** (at) half-price; **a ~ del camino** halfway along the road; **cortar por la ~** to cut through the middle

mitin [mi'tin] (pl **mítines**) nm meeting

mito ['mito] nm myth

mixto, -a ['miksto, a] adj mixed

ml. abr (= mililitro) ml

mm. abr = milímetro) mm

mobiliario [moβi'ljarjo] nm furniture

mochila [mo'tʃila] nf rucksack (BRIT), back-pack

moco ['moko] nm mucus; **mocos** nmpl (fam) snot; **limpiarse los mocos de la nariz** (fam) to wipe one's nose

moda ['moða] nf fashion; (estilo) style; **a la ~ o de ~** in fashion, fashionable; **pasado de ~** out of fashion

modales [mo'ðales] nmpl manners

modelar [moðe'lar] vt to model

modelo [mo'ðelo] adj inv, nmf model

módem ['moðem] nm (INFORM) modem

moderado, -a [moðe'raðo, a] adj moderate

moderar [moðe'rar] vt to moderate; (violencia) to restrain, control; (velocidad) to reduce; **moderarse** vr to restrain o.s., control o.s.

modernizar [moðerni'θar] vt to modernize

moderno, -a [mo'ðerno, a] adj modern; (actual) present-day

modestia [mo'ðestja] nf modesty ❏ **modesto, -a** adj modest

modificar [moðifi'kar] vt to modify

modisto, -a [mo'ðisto, a] nm/f (diseñador) couturier, designer; (que confecciona) dressmaker

modo ['moðo] nm way, manner; (MÚS) mode; **modos** nmpl manners; **de ningún ~** in no way; **de todos modos** at any rate ▶ **modo de empleo** directions pl (for use)

mofarse [mo'farse] vr: **~ de** to mock, scoff at

mofle (MÉX, CAm) nm silencer (BRIT), muffler (US)

mogollón [moɣo'ʎon] (ESP: fam) adv a hell of a lot

moho ['moo] nm mould, mildew; (en metal) rust

mojar [mo'xar] vt to wet; (humedecer) to damp(en), moisten; (calar) to soak; **mojarse** vr to get wet

molcajete (MÉX) [molka'xete] nm mortar

molde ['molde] nm mould; (COSTURA) pattern; (fig) model ❏ **moldeado** nm soft perm ❏ **moldear** vt to mould

mole ['mole] nf mass, bulk; (edificio) pile

moler [mo'ler] vt to grind, crush

molestar [moles'tar] vt to bother; (fastidiar) to annoy; (incomodar) to inconvenience, put out ♦ vi to be a nuisance; **molestarse** vr to bother; (incomodarse) to go to trouble;

(ofenderse) to take offence; **¿(no) te molesta si ...?** do you mind if ...?

⚠ No confundir **molestar** con la palabra inglesa **molest**.

molestia [mo'lestja] nf bother, trouble; (incomodidad) inconvenience; (MED) discomfort; **es una ~** it's a nuisance ❏ **molesto, -a** adj (que fastidia) annoying; (incómodo) inconvenient; (inquieto) uncomfortable, ill at ease; (enfadado) annoyed

molido, -a [mo'liðo, a] adj: **estar ~** (fig) to be exhausted o dead beat

molinillo [moli'niʎo] nm hand mill ▶ **molinillo de café** coffee grinder

molino [mo'lino] nm (edificio) mill; (máquina) grinder

momentáneo, -a [momen'taneo, a] adj momentary

momento [mo'mento] nm moment; **de ~** at o for the moment

momia ['momja] nf mummy

monarca [mo'narka] nmf monarch, ruler ❏ **monarquía** nf monarchy

monasterio [monas'terjo] nm monastery

mondar [mon'dar] vt to peel; **mondarse** vr (ESP): **mondarse de risa** (fam) to split one's sides laughing

mondongo (LAm) nm tripe

moneda [mo'neða] nf (tipo de dinero) currency, money; (pieza) coin; **una ~ de 2 euros** a 2 euro piece ❏ **monedero** nm purse

monitor [moni'tor] a nm/f instructor, coach ♦ nm (TV) set; (INFORM) monitor

monja ['monxa] nf nun

monje ['monxe] nm monk

mono, -a ['mono, a] adj (bonito) lovely, pretty; (gracioso) nice, charming ♦ nm/f monkey, ape ♦ nm dungarees pl; (overoles) overalls pl

monopatín [monopa'tin] nm skateboard

monopolio [mono'poljo] nm
monopoly ☐ **monopolizar** vt to
monopolize

monótono, -a [mo'notono, a] adj
monotonous

monstruo ['monstrwo] nm monster
♦ adj inv fantastic ☐ **monstruoso, -a**
adj monstrous

montaje [mon'taxe] nm assembly;
(TEATRO) décor; (CINE) montage

montaña [mon'taɲa] nf (monte)
mountain; (sierra) mountains pl,
mountainous area ▸ **montaña rusa**
roller coaster ☐ **montañero, -a** nm/f
mountaineer ☐ **montañismo** nm
mountaineering

montar [mon'tar] vt (subir a) to mount,
get on; (TEC) to assemble, put together;
(negocio) to set up; (arma) to cock;
(colocar) to lift on to; (CULIN) to beat
♦ vi to mount, get on; (sobresalir) to
overlap; ~ **en bicicleta** to ride a bicycle;
~ **en cólera** to get angry; ~ **a caballo** to
ride, go horseriding

monte ['monte] nm (montaña)
mountain; (bosque) woodland; (área
sin cultivar) wild area, wild country
▸ **monte de piedad** pawnshop

montón [mon'ton] nm heap, pile; (fig):
un ~ de heaps o lots of

monumento [monu'mento] nm
monument

moño ['moɲo] nm bun

moqueta [mo'keta] nf fitted carpet

mora ['mora] nf blackberry; ver tb **moro**

morado, -a [mo'raðo, a] adj purple,
violet ♦ nm bruise

moral [mo'ral] adj moral ♦ nf (ética)
ethics pl; (moralidad) morals pl,
morality; (ánimo) morale

moraleja [mora'lexa] nf moral

morboso, -a [mor'βoso, a] adj morbid

morcilla [mor'θiʎa] nf blood sausage,
≈ black pudding (BRIT)

mordaza [mor'ðaθa] nf (para la boca)
gag; (TEC) clamp

morder [mor'ðer] vt to bite; (fig:
consumir) to eat away, eat into
☐ **mordisco** nm bite

moreno, -a [mo'reno, a] adj (color)
(dark) brown; (de tez) dark; (de pelo
moreno) dark-haired; (negro) black

morfina [mor'fina] nf morphine

moribundo, -a [mori'βundo, a] adj
dying

morir [mo'rir] vi to die; (fuego) to die
down; (luz) to go out; **morirse** vr to die;
(fig) to be dying; **murió en un
accidente** he was killed in an accident;
morirse por algo to be dying for sth

moro, -a ['moro, a] adj Moorish ♦ nm/f
Moor

moroso, -a [mo'roso, a] nm/f bad
debtor, defaulter

morralla [MÉX] nf (cambio) small o
loose change

morro ['morro] nm (ZOOL) snout, nose;
(AUTO, AVIAC) nose

morsa ['morsa] nf walrus

mortadela [morta'ðela] nf mortadela

mortal [mor'tal] adj mortal; (golpe)
deadly ☐ **mortalidad** nf mortality

mortero [mor'tero] nm mortar

mosca ['moska] nf fly

Moscú [mos'ku] n Moscow

mosquearse [moske'arse] vr (fam)
(enojarse) to get cross; (ofenderse) to
take offence

mosquitero [moski'tero] nm
mosquito net

mosquito [mos'kito] nm mosquito

mostaza [mos'taθa] nf mustard

mosto ['mosto] nm (unfermented)
grape juice

mostrador [mostra'ðor] nm (de tienda)
counter; (de café) bar

mostrar [mos'trar] vt to show; (exhibir)
to display, exhibit; (explicar) to explain;
mostrarse vr: **mostrarse amable** to be
kind; to prove to be kind; **no está muy
muestra muy inteligente** he doesn't
seem (to be) very intelligent

mota ['mota] nf speck, tiny piece; (en diseño) dot

mote ['mote] nm nickname

motín [mo'tin] nm (del pueblo) revolt, rising; (del ejército) mutiny

motivar [moti'βar] vt (causar) to cause, motivate; (explicar) to explain, justify ❑ **motivo** nm motive, reason

moto ['moto] (fam) nf = **motocicleta**

motocicleta [motoθi'kleta] nf motorbike (BRIT), motorcycle

motoneta (CS) [moto'neta] nf scooter

motor [mo'tor] nm motor, engine ▶ **motor a chorro** o **de reacción/de explosión** jet engine/internal combustion engine

motora [mo'tora] nf motorboat

movedizo, -a [moβe'ðiθo, a] adj ver **arena**

mover [mo'βer] vt to move; (cabeza) to shake; (accionar) to drive; (fig) to cause, provoke; **moverse** vr to move; (fig) to get a move on

móvil ['moβil] adj mobile; (pieza de máquina) moving; (mueble) movable ♦ nm motive

movimiento [moβi'mjento] nm movement; (TEC) motion; (actividad) activity

mozo, -a ['moθo, a] adj (joven) young ♦ nm/f youth, young man/girl; (CS: mesero) waiter/waitress

MP3 nm MP3; **reproductor (de) ~** MP3 player

mucama (RPI) [mu'kama] nf maid

muchacho, -a [mu'tʃatʃo, a] nm/f (niño) boy/girl; (criado) servant; (criada) maid

muchedumbre [mutʃe'ðumbre] nf crowd

mucho, -a
['mutʃo, a] adj
1 (cantidad) a lot of, much; (número) lots of, a lot of, many; **mucho dinero**

a lot of money; **hace mucho calor** it's very hot; **muchas amigas** lots o a lot of friends

2 (sg: grande): **ésta es mucha casa para él** this house is much too big for him

♦ pron: **tengo mucho que hacer** I've got a lot to do; **muchos dicen que ...** a lot of people say that ...; ver tb **mucho**

♦ adv

1: **me gusta mucho** I like it a lot; **lo siento mucho** I'm very sorry; **come mucho** he eats a lot; **¿te vas a quedar mucho?** are you going to be staying long?

2 (respuesta) very; **¿estás cansado? — ¡mucho!** are you tired? — very!

3 (locuciones): **como mucho** at (the) most; **con mucho: el mejor con mucho** by far the best; **ni mucho menos: no es rico ni mucho menos** he's far from being rich

4: **por mucho que: por mucho que le creas** no matter how o however much you believe her

muda ['muða] nf change of clothes

mudanza [mu'ðanθa] nf (de casa) move

mudar [mu'ðar] vt to change; (ZOOL) to shed ♦ vi to change; **mudarse** vr (ropa) to change; **mudarse de casa** to move house

mudo, -a ['muðo, a] adj dumb; (callado, CINE) silent

mueble ['mweβle] nm piece of furniture; **muebles** nmpl furniture sg

mueca ['mweka] nf face, grimace; **hacer muecas a** to make faces at

muela ['mwela] nf back tooth ▶ **muela del juicio** wisdom tooth

muelle ['mweʎe] nm spring; (NÁUT) wharf; (malecón) pier

muero etc vb ver **morir**

muerte ['mwerte] nf death; (homicidio) murder; **dar ~ a** to kill

muerto, -a ['mwerto, a] pp de **morir** ♦ adj dead ♦ nm/f dead man/woman; (difunto) deceased; (cadáver) corpse; **estar ~ de cansancio** to be dead tired ▶ **Día de los Muertos** (MÉX) All Souls' Day

DÍA DE LOS MUERTOS

All Souls' Day (or "Day of the Dead") in Mexico coincides with All Saints' Day, which is celebrated in the Catholic countries of Latin America on November 1st and 2nd. All Souls' Day is actually a celebration which begins in the evening of October 31st and continues until November 2nd. It is a combination of the Catholic tradition of honouring the Christian saints and martyrs, and the ancient Mexican or Aztec traditions, in which death was not something sinister. For this reason all the dead are honoured by bringing offerings of food, flowers and candles to the cemetery.

muestra ['mwestra] nf (señal) indication, sign; (demostración) demonstration; (prueba) proof; (estadística) sample; (modelo) model, pattern; (testimonio) token

muestro etc vb ver **mostrar**

muevo etc vb ver **mover**

mugir [mu'xir] vi (vaca) to moo

mugre ['muɣre] nf dirt, filth

mujer [mu'xer] nf woman; (esposa) wife ❏ **mujeriego** nm womanizer

mula ['mula] nf mule

muleta [mu'leta] nf (para andar) crutch; (TAUR) stick with red cape attached

multa ['multa] nf fine; **poner una ~ a** to fine ❏ **multar** vt to fine

multicines [multi'θines] nmpl multiscreen cinema sg

multinacional [multinaθjo'nal] nf multinational

múltiple ['multiple] adj multiple; (pl) many, numerous

multiplicar [multipli'kar] vt (MAT) to multiply; (fig) to increase; **multiplicarse** vr (BIO) to multiply; (fig) to be everywhere at once

multitud [multi'tuð] nf (muchedumbre) crowd; **~ de** lots of

mundial [mun'djal] adj world-wide, universal; (guerra, récord) world cpd

mundo ['mundo] nm world; **todo el ~** everybody; **tener ~** to be experienced, know one's way around

munición [muni'θjon] nf ammunition

municipal [muniθi'pal] adj municipal, local

municipio [muni'θipjo] nm (ayuntamiento) town council, corporation; (territorio administrativo) town, municipality

muñeca [mu'neka] nf (ANAT) wrist; (juguete) doll

muñeco [mu'neko] nm (figura) figure; (marioneta) puppet; (fig) puppet, pawn

mural [mu'ral] adj mural, wall cpd ♦ nm mural

muralla [mu'raʎa] nf (city) wall(s) (pl)

murciélago [mur'θjelaɣo] nm bat

murmullo [mur'muʎo] nm murmur(ing); (cuchicheo) whispering

murmurar [murmu'rar] vi to murmur, whisper; (cotillear) to gossip

muro ['muro] nm wall

muscular [musku'lar] adj muscular

músculo ['muskulo] nm muscle

museo [mu'seo] nm museum ▶ **museo de arte** nm art gallery

musgo ['musɣo] nm moss

música ['musika] nf music; ver tb **músico**

músico, -a ['musiko, a] adj musical ♦ nm/f musician

muslo ['muslo] nm thigh

musulmán, -ana [musul'man, ana] nm/f Moslem

mutación [muta'θjon] nf (BIO) mutation; (cambio) (sudden) change

mutilar [muti'lar] vt to mutilate; (a una persona) to maim

mutuo, -a [mutwo, a] adj mutual

muy [mwi] adv very; (demasiado) too; M~ Señor mío Dear Sir; ~ de noche very late at night; eso es ~ de él that's just like him

N, n

N abr (= norte) N

nabo ['naβo] nm turnip

nacer [na'θer] vi to be born; (de huevo) to hatch; (vegetal) to sprout; (río) to rise; **nací en Barcelona** I was born in Barcelona ❑ **nacido, -a** adj born; **recién nacido** newborn ❑ **nacimiento** nm birth; (de Navidad) Nativity; (de río) source

nación [na'θjon] nf nation ❑ **nacional** adj national ❑ **nacionalismo** nm nationalism

nada ['naða] pron nothing ♦ adv not at all, in no way; **no decir ~** to say nothing, not to say anything; **~ más** nothing else; **de ~** don't mention it

nadador, a [naða'ðor, a] nm/f swimmer

nadar [na'ðar] vi to swim

nadie ['naðje] pron nobody, no-one; **~ habló** nobody spoke; **no había ~** there was nobody there, there wasn't anybody there

nado ['naðo]: **a ~** adv: **pasar a ~** to swim across

nafta ['nafta] (RPl) nf petrol (BRIT), gas (US)

naipe ['naipe] nm (playing) card; **naipes** nmpl cards

nalgas ['nalɣas] nfpl buttocks

nalguear (MÉX, CAm) vt to spank

nana ['nana] (ESP) nf lullaby

naranja [na'ranxa] adj inv, nf orange; **media ~** (fam) better half ❑ **naranjada** nf orangeade ❑ **naranjo** nm orange tree

narciso [nar'θiso] nm narcissus

narcótico, -a [nar'kotiko, a] adj, nm narcotic ❑ **narcotizar** vt to drug ❑ **narcotráfico** nm drug trafficking o running

nariz [na'riθ] nf nose ▶ **nariz chata/respingona** snub/turned-up nose

narración [narra'θjon] nf narration

narrar [na'rrar] vt to narrate, recount ❑ **narrativa** nf narrative

nata ['nata] nf cream ▶ **nata montada** whipped cream

natación [nata'θjon] nf swimming

natal [na'tal] adj: **ciudad ~** home town ❑ **natalidad** nf birth rate

natillas [na'tiʎas] nfpl custard sg

nativo, -a [na'tiβo, a] adj, nm/f native

natural [natu'ral] adj natural; (fruta etc) fresh ♦ nmf native ♦ nm (disposición) nature

naturaleza [natura'leθa] nf nature; (género) species, kind ▶ **naturaleza muerta** still life

naturalmente [natural'mente] adv (de modo natural) in a natural way; **¡~!** of course!

naufragar [naufra'ɣar] vi to sink ❑ **naufragio** nm shipwreck

nauseabundo, -a [nausea'βundo, a] adj nauseating, sickening

náuseas ['nauseas] nfpl nausea sg; **me da** ~ it makes me feel sick

náutico, -a ['nautiko, a] adj nautical

navaja [na'βaxa] nf knife; (de barbero, peluquero) razor

naval [na'βal] adj naval

Navarra [na'βarra] n Navarre

nave ['naβe] nf (barco) ship, vessel; (ARQ) nave ▶ **nave espacial** spaceship ▶ **nave industrial** factory premises pl

navegador nm (INFORM) browser

navegante [naβe'ɣante] nmf navigator

navegar [naβe'ɣar] vi (barco) to sail; (avión) to fly; ~ **por Internet** to surf the Net

Navidad [naβi'ðað] nf Christmas; **Navidades** nfpl Christmas time; **¡Feliz ~!** Merry Christmas! ◻ **navideño, -a** adj Christmas cpd

nazca etc vb ver **nacer**

nazi ['naθi] adj, nmf Nazi

NE abr (= nor(d)este) NE

neblina [ne'βlina] nf mist

necesario, -a [neθe'sarjo, a] adj necessary

neceser [neθe'ser] nm toilet bag; (bolsa grande) holdall

necesidad [neθesi'ðað] nf need; (lo inevitable) necessity; (miseria) poverty; **en caso de** ~ in case of need o emergency; **hacer sus necesidades** to relieve o.s.

necesitado, -a [neθesi'taðo, a] adj needy, poor; ~ **de** in need of

necesitar [neθesi'tar] vt to need, require

necio, -a ['neθjo, a] adj foolish

nectarina [nekta'rina] nf nectarine

nefasto, -a [ne'fasto, a] adj ill-fated, unlucky

negación [neɣa'θjon] nf negation; (rechazo) refusal, denial

negar [ne'ɣar] vt (renegar, rechazar) to refuse; (prohibir) to refuse, deny; (desmentir) to deny; **negarse** vr: **negarse a** to refuse to

negativa [neɣa'tiβa] nf negative; (rechazo) refusal, denial

negativo, -a [neɣa'tiβo, a] adj, nm negative

negociante [neɣo'θjante] nmf businessman/woman

negociar [neɣo'θjar] vt, vi to negotiate; ~ **en** to deal o trade in

negocio [ne'ɣoθjo] nm (COM) business; (asunto) affair, business; (operación comercial) deal, transaction; (lugar) place of business; **los negocios** business sg; **hacer** ~ to do business

negra ['neɣra] nf (MÚS) crotchet; ver tb **negro**

negro, -a ['neɣro, a] adj black; (suerte) awful ◆ nm black ◆ nm/f black man/woman

nene, -a ['nene, a] nm/f baby, small child

neón [ne'on] nm: **luces/lámpara de** ~ neon lights/lamp

neoyorquino, -a [neojor'kino, a] adj (of) New York

nervio ['nerβjo] nm nerve ◻ **nerviosismo** nm nervousness, nerves pl ◻ **nervioso, -a** adj nervous

neto, -a ['neto, a] adj net

neumático, -a [neu'matiko, a] adj pneumatic ◆ nm (ESP) tyre (BRIT), tire (US) ▶ **neumático de recambio** spare tyre

neurólogo, -a [neu'roloɣo, a] nm/f neurologist

neurona [neu'rona] nf nerve cell

neutral [neu'tral] adj neutral ◻ **neutralizar** vt to neutralize; (contrarrestar) to counteract

neutro, -a ['neutro, a] adj (BIO, LING) neuter

neutrón [neu'tron] nm neutron

nevada [ne'βaða] nf snowstorm; (caída de nieve) snowfall

nevar [ne'βar] vi to snow

nevera [ne'βera] (ESP) nf refrigerator (BRIT), icebox (US)

nevería [neβe'ria] (MÉX) nf ice-cream parlour

nexo ['nekso] nm link, connection

ni [ni] conj nor, neither; (tb: **ni siquiera**) not ... even; **ni aunque que** not even if;

ni blanco ni negro neither white nor black

Nicaragua [nika'raɣwa] *nf* Nicaragua
❏ **nicaragüense** *adj, nmf* Nicaraguan

nicho ['nitʃo] *nm* niche

nicotina [niko'tina] *nf* nicotine

nido ['niðo] *nm* nest

niebla ['njeβla] *nf* fog; (neblina) mist

niego etc ['njeɣo] *vb ver* **negar**

nieto, -a ['njeto, a] *nm/f* grandson/ daughter; **nietos** *nmpl* grandchildren

nieve ['njeβe] *vb ver* **nevar** ♦ *nf* snow; (MÉX: helado) icecream

NIF *nm abr* (= Número de Identificación Fiscal) personal identification number used for financial and tax purposes

ninfa ['ninfa] *nf* nymph

ningún [nin'gun] *adj ver* **ninguno**

ninguno, -a [nin'guno, a] (delante de nm **ningún**) *adj* no ♦ *pron* (nadie) nobody; (ni uno) none, not one; (ni uno ni otro) neither; **de ninguna manera** by no means, not at all

niña ['niɲa] *nf* (ANAT) pupil; ver tb **niño**

niñera [ni'ɲera] *nf* nursemaid, nanny

niñez [ni'ɲeθ] *nf* childhood; (infancia) infancy

niño, -a ['niɲo, a] *adj* (joven) young; (inmaduro) immature ♦ *nm/f* child, boy/girl

nipón, -ona [ni'pon, ona] *adj, nm/f* Japanese

níquel ['nikel] *nm* nickel

níspero ['nispero] *nm* medlar

nítido, -a ['nitiðo, a] *adj* clear; sharp

nitrato [ni'trato] *nm* nitrate

nitrógeno [ni'troxeno] *nm* nitrogen

nivel [ni'βel] *nm* (GEO) level; (norma) level, standard; (altura) height ▶ **nivel de aceite** oil level ▶ **nivel de aire** spirit level ▶ **nivel de vida** standard of living ▶ **nivelar** *vt* to level out; (fig) to even up; (COM) to balance

no [no] *adv* no; not; (con verbo) not ♦ *excl* no!; **no tengo nada** I don't have

anything, I have nothing; **no es el mío** it's not mine; **ahora no** not now; **¿no lo sabes?** don't you know?; **no mucho** not much; **no bien termine, lo entregaré** as soon as I finish, I'll hand it over; **no más, ayer no más** just yesterday; **¡pase no más!** come in!; **¡a que no lo sabes!** I bet you don't know!; **¡cómo no!** of course!; **la no intervención** non-intervention

noble ['noβle] *adj, nmf* noble
❏ **nobleza** *nf* nobility

noche ['notʃe] *nf* night, night-time; (la tarde) evening; **de ~, por la ~** at night; **es de ~** it's dark ▶ **Noche de San Juan** see note

nochebuena [notʃe'βwena] *nf* Christmas Eve

nochevieja [notʃe'βjexa] *nf* New Year's Eve

nocivo, -a [no'θiβo, a] *adj* harmful

noctámbulo, -a [nok'tambulo, a] *nm/f* sleepwalker

nocturno, -a [nok'turno, a] *adj (de la noche)* nocturnal, night *cpd; (de la tarde)* evening *cpd* ♦ *nm* nocturne

nogal [no'ɣal] *nm* walnut tree

nómada ['nomaða] *adj* nomadic ♦ *nmf* nomad

nombrar [nom'brar] *vt (designar)* to name; *(mencionar)* to mention; *(dar puesto a)* to appoint

nombre ['nombre] *nm* name; *(sustantivo)* noun; **~ y apellidos** name in full; **poner ~ a** to call, name ▶ **nombre común/propio** common/ proper noun ▶ **nombre de pila/de soltera** Christian/maiden name

nómina ['nomina] *nf (lista)* payroll; *(hoja)* payslip

nominal [nomi'nal] *adj* nominal

nominar [nomi'nar] *vt* to nominate

nominativo, -a [nomina'tiβo, a] *adj (COM): cheque ~ a X* cheque made out to X

nordeste [nor'ðeste] *adj* north-east, north-eastern, north-easterly ♦ *nm* north-east

nórdico, -a ['norðiko, a] *adj* Nordic

noreste [no'reste] *adj, nm* = **nordeste**

noria ['norja] *nf (AGR)* waterwheel; *(de carnaval)* big *(BRIT)* o Ferris *(US)* wheel

norma ['norma] *nf* rule of thumb

normal [nor'mal] *adj (corriente)* normal; *(habitual)* usual, natural ❏ **normalizarse** *vr* to return to normal ❏ **normalmente** *adv* normally

normativa [norma'tiβa] *nf (set of) rules pl,* regulations *pl*

noroeste [noro'este] *adj* north-west, north-western, north-westerly ♦ *nm* north-west

norte ['norte] *adj* north, northerly ♦ *nm* north; *(fig)* guide

norteamericano, -a [norteameri'kano, a] *adj, nm/f* (North) American

Noruega [no'rweɣa] *nf* Norway

noruego, -a [no'rweɣo, a] *adj, nm/f* Norwegian

nos [nos] *pron (directo)* us; *(indirecto)* to us; for us; from us; *(reflexivo)* (to) ourselves; *(recíproco)* (to) each other; **~ levantamos a las 7** we get up at 7

nosotros, -as [no'sotros, as] *pron (sujeto)* we; *(después de prep)* us

nostalgia [nos'talxja] *nf* nostalgia

nota ['nota] *nf* note; *(ESCOL)* mark

notable [no'taβle] *adj* notable; *(ESCOL)* outstanding

notar [no'tar] *vt* to notice, note; **notarse** *vr* to be obvious; **se nota que ...** one observes that ...

notario [no'tarjo] *nm* notary

noticia [no'tiθja] *nf (información)* piece of news; **las noticias** the news *sg;* **tener noticias de algn** to hear from sb

⚠ No confundir **noticia** con la palabra inglesa *notice*.

noticiero [noti'θjero] *(LAm) nm* news bulletin

notificar [notifi'kar] *vt* to notify, inform

notorio, -a [no'torjo, a] *adj (público)* well-known; *(evidente)* obvious

novato, -a [no'βato, a] *adj* inexperienced ♦ *nm/f* beginner, novice

novecientos, -as [noβe'θjentos, as] *num* nine hundred

novedad [noβe'ðað] *nf (calidad de nuevo)* newness; *(noticia)* piece of news; *(cambio)* change, (new) development

novel [no'βel] *adj* new; *(inexperto)* inexperienced ♦ *nmf* beginner

novela [no'βela] *nf* novel

noveno, -a [no'βeno, a] *adj* ninth

noventa [no'βenta] *num* ninety

novia [ˈnoβja] nf ver **novio**

novicio, -a [noˈβiθjo, a] nm/f novice

noviembre [noˈβjembre] nm November

novillada [noβiˈʎaða] nf (TAUR) bullfight with young bulls ❑ **novillero** nm novice bullfighter ❑ **novillo** nm young bull, bullock; **hacer novillos** (fam) to play truant

novio, -a [ˈnoβjo, a] nm/f boyfriend/girlfriend; (prometido) fiancé/fiancée; (recién casado) bridegroom/bride; **los novios** the newly-weds

nube [ˈnuβe] nf cloud

nublado, -a [nuˈβlaðo, a] adj cloudy; **nublarse** vr to grow dark

nubosidad [nuβosiˈðað] nf cloudiness; **había mucha ~** it was very cloudy

nuca [ˈnuka] nf nape of the neck

nuclear [nukleˈar] adj nuclear

núcleo [ˈnukleo] nm (centro) core; (FÍSICA) nucleus ▶ **núcleo urbano** city centre

nudillo [nuˈðiʎo] nm knuckle

nudista [nuˈðista] adj/f nudist

nudo [ˈnuðo] nm knot; (de carreteras) junction

nuera [ˈnwera] nf daughter-in-law

nuestro, -a [ˈnwestro, a] adj pos our ♦ pron ours; **~ padre** our father; **un amigo ~** a friend of ours; **es el ~** it's ours

Nueva York [-ˈjɔrk] n New York

Nueva Zelanda [-θeˈlanda] nf New Zealand

nueve [ˈnweβe] num nine

nuevo, -a [ˈnweβo, a] adj (gen) new; **de ~** again

nuez [nweθ] nf walnut; (ANAT) Adam's apple ▶ **nuez moscada** nutmeg

nulo, -a [ˈnulo, a] adj (inepto, torpe) useless; (inválido) (null and) void; (DEPORTE) drawn, tied

núm. abr (= número) no.

numerar [numeˈrar] vt to number

número [ˈnumero] nm (gen) number; (tamaño: de zapato) size; (ejemplar: de diario) number, issue; **sin ~** numberless, unnumbered ▶ **número atrasado** back number ▶ **número de matrícula/teléfono** registration/telephone number ▶ **número impar/par** odd/even number ▶ **número romano** Roman numeral

numeroso, -a [numeˈroso, a] adj numerous

nunca [ˈnunka] adv (jamás) never; **~ lo pensé** I never thought it; **no viene ~** he never comes; **~ más** never again; **más que ~** more than ever

nupcias [ˈnupθjas] nfpl wedding sg, nuptials

nutria [ˈnutrja] nf otter

nutrición [nutriˈθjon] nf nutrition

nutrir [nuˈtrir] vt (alimentar) to nourish; (dar de comer) to feed; (fig) to strengthen ❑ **nutritivo, -a** adj nourishing, nutritious

nylon [niˈlon] nm nylon

Ñ, ñ

ñango, -a (MÉX) adj puny

ñapa (LAm) [ˈɲapa] nf extra

ñata (LAm: fam) nf nose; ver tb **ñato**

ñato, -a [ˈɲato, a] (LAm) adj snub-nosed

ñoñería [ɲoɲeˈria] nf insipidness

ñoño, -a [ˈɲoɲo, a] adj (fam: tonto) silly, stupid; (soso) insipid; (persona) spineless; (ESP: película, novela) sentimental

O, o

O abr (= oeste) W

o [o] conj or

oasis [oˈasis] nm inv oasis

obcecarse [oβθe'karse] *vr* to get o become stubborn

obedecer [oβeðe'θer] *vt* to obey ❑ **obediente** *adj* obedient

obertura [oβer'tura] *nf* overture

obeso, -a [o'βeso, a] *adj* obese

obispo [o'βispo] *nm* bishop

obituario (*LAm*) *nm* obituary

objetar [oβxe'tar] *vt, vi* to object

objetivo, -a [oβxe'tiβo, a] *adj, nm* objective

objeto [oβ'xeto] *nm* (*cosa*) object; (*fin*) aim

objetor, a [oβxe'tor, a] *nm/f* objector

obligación [oβliɣa'θjon] *nf* obligation; (*COM*) bond

obligar [oβli'ɣar] *vt* to force; **obligarse** *vr* to bind o.s. ❑ **obligatorio, -a** *adj* compulsory, obligatory

oboe [o'βoe] *nm* oboe

obra [o'βra] *nf* work; (*ARQ*) construction, building; (*TEATRO*) play; **por ~ de** thanks to (the efforts of) ▸ **obra maestra** masterpiece ▸ **obras públicas** public works ❑ **obrar** *vt* to work; (*tener efecto*) to have an effect on ♦ *vi* to act, behave; (*tener efecto*) to have an effect; **la carta obra en su poder** the letter is in his/her possession

obrero, -a [o'βrero, a] *adj* (*clase*) working; (*movimiento*) labour *cpd* ♦ *nm/f* (*gen*) worker; (*sin oficio*) labourer

obsceno, -a [oβs'θeno, a] *adj* obscene

obscu... = oscu...

obsequiar [oβsek'sjar] *vt* (*ofrecer*) to present with; (*agasajar*) to make a fuss of, lavish attention on ❑ **obsequio** *nm* (*regalo*) gift; (*cortesía*) courtesy, attention

observación [oβserβa'θjon] *nf* observation; (*reflexión*) remark

observador, a [oβserβa'ðor, a] *nm/f* observer

observar [oβser'βar] *vt* to observe; (*anotar*) to notice; **observarse** *vr* to keep to, observe

obsesión [oβse'sjon] *nf* obsession ❑ **obsesivo, -a** *adj* obsessive

obstáculo [oβs'takulo] *nm* obstacle; (*impedimento*) hindrance, drawback

obstante [oβs'tante]: **no ~** *adv* nevertheless

obstinado, -a [oβsti'naðo, a] *adj* obstinate, stubborn

obstinarse [oβsti'narse] *vr* to be obstinate; **~ en** to persist in

obstruir [oβstru'ir] *vt* to obstruct

obtener [oβte'ner] *vt* (*gen*) to obtain; (*premio*) to win

obturador [oβtura'ðor] *nm* (*FOTO*) shutter

obvio, -a [o'βbjo, a] *adj* obvious

oca [o'ka] *nf* (*animal*) goose; (*juego*) = snakes and ladders

ocasión [oka'sjon] *nf* (*oportunidad*) opportunity, chance; (*momento*) occasion, time; (*causa*) cause; **de ~** secondhand ❑ **ocasionar** *vt* to cause

ocaso [o'kaso] *nm* (*fig*) decline

occidente [okθi'ðente] *nm* west

OCDE *nf abr* (= *Organización de Cooperación y Desarrollo Económico*) OECD

océano [o'θeano] *nm* ocean ▸ **Océano Índico** Indian Ocean

ochenta [o't͡ʃenta] *num* eighty

ocho [o't͡ʃo] *num* eight; **dentro de ~ días** within a week

ocio [o'θjo] *nm* (*tiempo*) leisure; (*pey*) idleness

octavilla [okta'viʎa] *nf* leaflet, pamphlet

octavo, -a [ok'taβo, a] *adj* eighth

octubre [ok'tuβre] *nm* October

oculista [oku'lista] *nmf* oculist

ocultar [okul'tar] *vt* (*esconder*) to hide; (*callar*) to conceal ❑ **oculto, -a** *adj* hidden; (*fig*) secret

ocupación [okupa'θjon] nf occupation

ocupado, -a [oku'paðo, a] adj (persona) busy; (plaza) occupied, taken; (teléfono) engaged ❑ **ocupar** vt (gen) to occupy; **ocuparse** vr: **ocuparse de o en** (gen) to concern o.s. with; (cuidar) to look after

ocurrencia [oku'rrenθja] nf (idea) bright idea

ocurrir [oku'rrir] vi to happen; **ocurrirse** vr: **se me ocurrió que ...** it occurred to me that ...

odiar [o'ðjar] vt to hate ❑ **odio** nm hate, hatred ❑ **odioso, -a** adj (gen) hateful; (malo) nasty

odontólogo, -a [oðon'toloɣo, a] nm/f dentist, dental surgeon

oeste [o'este] nm west; **una película del ~** a western

ofender [ofen'der] vt (agraviar) to offend; (insultar) to insult; **ofenderse** vr to take offence ❑ **ofensa** nf offence ❑ **ofensivo, -a** adj offensive

oferta [o'ferta] nf offer; (propuesta) proposal; **la ~ y la demanda** supply and demand; **artículos en ~** goods on O.K.

oficial [ofi'θjal] adj official ♦ nm (MIL) officer

oficina [ofi'θina] nf office ▶ **oficina de correos** post office ▶ **oficina de información** information bureau ▶ **oficina de turismo** tourist office ❑ **oficinista** nmf clerk

oficio [o'fiθjo] nm (profesión) profession; (puesto) post; (REL) service; **ser del ~** to be an old hand; **tener mucho ~** to have a lot of experience ▶ **oficio de difuntos** funeral service

ofimática [ofi'matika] nf office automation

ofrecer [ofre'θer] vt (dar) to offer; (proponer) to propose; **ofrecerse** vr (persona) to offer o.s., volunteer; (situación) to present itself; **¿qué se le**

ofrece?, ¿se le ofrece algo? what can I do for you?, can I get you anything?

ofrecimiento [ofreθi'mjento] nm offer

oftalmólogo, -a [oftal'moloɣo, a] nm/f ophthalmologist

oída [o'iða] nf: **de oídas** by hearsay

oído [o'iðo] nm (ANAT) ear; (sentido) hearing

oigo etc vb ver **oír**

oír [o'ir] vt (gen) to hear; (atender a) to listen to; **¡oiga!** listen!; **~ misa** to attend mass

OIT nf abr (= Organización Internacional del Trabajo) ILO

ojal [o'xal] nm buttonhole

ojalá [oxa'la] excl if only (it were so!), some hope! ♦ conj if only ...!, would that ...!; **¡ojalá (que) venga hoy** I hope he comes today

ojeada [oxe'aða] nf glance

ojera [o'xera] nf: **tener ojeras** to have bags under one's eyes

ojo ['oxo] nm eye; (de puente) span; (de cerradura) keyhole ♦ excl careful!; **tener ~ para** to have an eye for ▶ **ojo de buey** porthole

okey [o'kei] (LAm) excl O.K.

okupa [o'kupa] (ESP: fam) nmf squatter

ola ['ola] nf wave

olé [o'le] excl bravo!, olé!

oleada [ole'aða] nf big wave, swell; (fig) wave

oleaje [ole'axe] nm swell

óleo ['oleo] nm oil ❑ **oleoducto** nm (oil) pipeline

oler [o'ler] vt (gen) to smell; (inquirir) to pry into; (fig: sospechar) to sniff out ♦ vi to smell; **~ a** to smell of

olfatear [olfate'ar] vt to smell; (inquirir) to pry into ❑ **olfato** nm sense of smell

olimpiada [olim'pjaða] nf: **las Olimpiadas** the Olympics ❑ **olímpico, -a** adj Olympic

oliva [o'liβa] *nf* (*aceituna*) olive; **aceite de ~** olive oil □ **olivo** *nm* olive tree

olla ['oʎa] *nf* pan; (*comida*) stew ▸ **olla exprés** *o* **a presión** (*ESP*) pressure cooker ▸ **olla podrida** *type of Spanish stew*

olmo ['olmo] *nm* elm (tree)

olor [o'lor] *nm* smell □ **oloroso, -a** *adj* scented

olvidar [olβi'ðar] *vt* to forget; (*omitir*) to omit; **olvidarse** *vr* (*fig*) to forget o.s.; **se me olvidó** I forgot

olvido [ol'βiðo] *nm* oblivion; (*despiste*) forgetfulness

ombligo [om'bliɣo] *nm* navel

omelette (*LAm*) *nm* omelet(te)

omisión [omi'sjon] *nf* (*abstención*) omission; (*descuido*) neglect

omiso, -a [o'miso, a] *adj*: **hacer caso ~ de** to ignore, pass over

omitir [omi'tir] *vt* to omit

omnipotente [omnipo'tente] *adj* omnipotent

omóplato [o'mioplato] *nm* shoulder blade

OMS *nf abr* (= *Organización Mundial de la Salud*) WHO

once ['onθe] *num* eleven □ **onces** (*CS*) *nfpl* tea break *sg*

onda ['onda] *nf* wave ▸ **onda corta/larga/media** short/long/medium wave □ **ondear** *vt, vi* to wave; (*tener ondas*) to be wavy; (*agua*) to ripple

ondulación [ondula'θjon] *nf* undulation □ **ondulado, -a** *adj* wavy

ONG *nf abr* (= *organización no gubernamental*) NGO

ONU ['onu] *nf abr* (= *Organización de las Naciones Unidas*) UNO

opaco, -a [o'pako, a] *adj* opaque

opción [op'θjon] *nf* (*gen*) option; (*derecho*) right, option

OPEP ['opep] *nf abr* (= *Organización de Países Exportadores de Petróleo*) OPEC

ópera ['opera] *nf* opera ▸ **ópera bufa** *o* **cómica** comic opera

operación [opera'θjon] *nf* (*gen*) operation; (*COM*) transaction, deal

operador, a [opera'ðor, a] *nm/f* operator; (*CINE: de proyección*) projectionist; (: *de rodaje*) cameraman

operar [ope'rar] *vt* (*producir*) to produce, bring about; (*MED*) to operate on ♦ *vi* (*COM*) to operate, deal; **operarse** *vr* to occur; (*MED*) to have an operation

opereta [ope'reta] *nf* operetta

opinar [opi'nar] *vt* to think ♦ *vi* to give one's opinion □ **opinión** *nf* (*creencia*) belief; (*criterio*) opinion

opio ['opjo] *nm* opium

oponer [opo'ner] *vt* (*resistencia*) to put up, offer; **oponerse** *vr* (*objetar*) to object; (*estar frente a frente*) to be opposed; (*dos personas*) to oppose each other; **~ A a B** to set A against B; **me opongo a pensar que ...** I refuse to believe o think that ...

oportunidad [oportuni'ðað] *nf* (*ocasión*) opportunity; (*posibilidad*) chance

oportuno, -a [opor'tuno, a] *adj* (*en su tiempo*) opportune, timely; (*respuesta*) suitable; **en el momento ~** at the right moment

oposición [oposi'θjon] *nf* opposition; **oposiciones** *nfpl* (*ESCOL*) public examinations

opositor, a [oposi'tor, a] *nm/f* (*adversario*) opponent; (*candidato*): **~ (a)** candidate (for)

opresión [opre'sjon] *nf* oppression □ **opresor, a** *nm/f* oppressor

oprimir [opri'mir] *vt* to squeeze; (*fig*) to oppress

optar [op'tar] *vi* (*elegir*) to choose; **~ por** to opt for □ **optativo, -a** *adj* optional

óptico, -a [o'ptiko, a] *adj* optic(al) ♦ *nm/f* optician □ **óptica** *nf* optician's (shop); **desde esta óptica** from this point of view

optimismo [opti'mismo] *nm* optimism ❏ **optimista** *nmf* optimist

opuesto, -a [o'pwesto, a] *adj* (*contrario*) opposite; (*antagónico*) opposing

oración [ora'θjon] *nf* (*REL*) prayer; (*LING*) sentence

orador, a [ora'ðor, a] *nm/f* (*conferenciante*) speaker, orator

oral [o'ral] *adj* oral

orangután [orangu'tan] *nm* orangutan

orar [o'rar] *vi* to pray

oratoria [ora'torja] *nf* oratory

órbita ['orβita] *nf* orbit

orden ['orðen] *nm* (*gen*) order ♦ *nf* (*gen*) order; (*INFORM*) command; **en ~ de prioridad** in order of priority ▶ **orden del día** agenda

ordenado, -a [orðe'naðo, a] *adj* (*metódico*) methodical; (*arreglado*) orderly

ordenador [orðena'ðor] *nm* computer ▶ **ordenador central** mainframe computer

ordenar [orðe'nar] *vt* (*mandar*) to order; (*poner orden*) to put in order, arrange; **ordenarse** *vr* (*REL*) to be ordained

ordeñar [orðe'ɲar] *vt* to milk

ordinario, -a [orði'narjo, a] *adj* (*común*) ordinary, usual; (*vulgar*) vulgar, common

orégano [o'reɣano] *nm* oregano

oreja [o'rexa] *nf* ear; (*MECÁNICA*) lug, flange

orfanato [orfa'nato] *nm* orphanage

orfebrería [orfeβre'ria] *nf* gold/silver work

orgánico, -a [or'ɣaniko, a] *adj* organic

organismo [orɣa'nismo] *nm* (*BIO*) organism; (*POL*) organization

organización [orɣaniθa'θjon] *nf* organization ❏ **organizar** *vt* to organize

órgano ['orɣano] *nm* organ

orgasmo [or'ɣasmo] *nm* orgasm

orgía [or'xia] *nf* orgy

orgullo [or'ɣuʎo] *nm* pride ❏ **orgulloso, -a** *adj* (*gen*) proud; (*altanero*) haughty

orientación [orjenta'θjon] *nf* (*posición*) position; (*dirección*) direction

oriental [orjen'tal] *adj* eastern; (*del Lejano Oriente*) oriental

orientar [orjen'tar] *vt* (*situar*) to orientate; (*señalar*) to point; (*dirigir*) to direct; (*guiar*) to guide; **orientarse** *vr* to get one's bearings

oriente [o'rjente] *nm*: **el O~** the East; **el O~ Medio** the Middle East; **el Próximo/Extremo O~** the Near/Far East

origen [o'rixen] *nm* origin

original [orixi'nal] *adj* (*nuevo*) original; (*extraño*) odd, strange ❏ **originalidad** *nf* originality

originar [orixi'nar] *vt* to start, cause; **originarse** *vr* to originate ❏ **originario, -a** *adj* original; **originario de** native of

orilla [o'riʎa] *nf* (*borde*) border; (*de río*) bank; (*de bosque, tela*) edge; (*de mar*) shore

orina [o'rina] *nf* urine ❏ **orinal** *nm* (chamber) pot ❏ **orinar** *vi* to urinate; **orinarse** *vr* to wet o.s.

oro ['oro] *nm* gold; **oros** *nmpl* (*NAIPES*) hearts

orquesta [or'kesta] *nf* orchestra ▶ **orquesta sinfónica** symphony orchestra

orquídea [or'kiðea] *nf* orchid

ortiga [or'tiɣa] *nf* nettle

ortodoxo, -a [orto'ðokso, a] *adj* orthodox

ortografía [ortoɣra'fia] *nf* spelling

ortopedia [orto'peðja] nf orthopaedics sg ❏ **ortopédico, -a** adj orthopaedic

oruga [o'ruɣa] nf caterpillar

orzuelo [or'θwelo] nm stye

os [os] pron (gen) you; (a vosotros) to you

osa ['osa] nf (she-)bear ► **Osa Mayor/Menor** Great/Little Bear

osadía [osa'ðia] nf daring

osar [o'sar] vi to dare

oscilación [osθila'θjon] nf (movimiento) oscillation; (fluctuación) fluctuation

oscilar [osθi'lar] vi to oscillate; to fluctuate

oscurecer [oskure'θer] vt to darken ♦ vi to grow dark; **oscurecerse** vr to grow o get dark

oscuridad [oskuri'ðað] nf obscurity; (tinieblas) darkness

oscuro, -a [os'kuro, a] adj dark; (fig) obscure; **a oscuras** in the dark

óseo, -a ['oseo, a] adj bone cpd

oso ['oso] nm bear ► **oso de peluche** teddy bear ► **oso hormiguero** anteater

ostentar [osten'tar] vt (gen) to show; (pey) to flaunt, show off; (poseer) to have, possess

ostión (MÉX) nm = **ostra**

ostra ['ostra] nf oyster

OTAN ['otan] nf abr (= Organización del Tratado del Atlántico Norte) NATO

otitis [o'titis] nf earache

otoñal [oto'ɲal] adj autumnal

otoño [o'toɲo] nm autumn

otorgar [otor'ɣar] vt (conceder) to concede; (dar) to grant

otorrino, -a [oto'rrino, a], **otorrinolaringólogo, a** [otorrinolarin'ɡoloɣo, a] nm/f ear, nose and throat specialist

otro, -a
PALABRA CLAVE
['otro, a] adj

1 (distinto: sg) another; (: pl) other; **con otros amigos** with other o different friends

2 (adicional): **tráigame otro café (más), por favor** can I have another coffee please; **otros diez días más** another ten days

♦ pron

1: **el otro** the other one; **(los) otros** (the) others; **de otro** somebody else's; **que lo haga otro** let somebody else do it

2 (recíproco): **se odian (la) una a (la) otra** they hate one another o each other

3: **otro tanto**: **comer otro tanto** to eat the same o as much again; **recibí una decena de telegramas y otras tantas llamadas** he got about ten telegrams and as many calls

ovación [oβa'θjon] nf ovation

oval [o'βal] adj oval o **ovalado, -a** adj oval ❏ **óvalo** nm oval

ovario [o'βario] nm ovary

oveja [o'βexa] nf sheep

overol [oβe'rol] (LAm) nm overalls pl

ovillo [o'βiʎo] nm (de lana) ball of wool

OVNI ['oβni] nm abr (= objeto volante no identificado) UFO

ovulación [oβula'θjon] nf ovulation ❏ **óvulo** nm ovum

oxidación [oksiða'θjon] nf rusting

oxidar [oksi'ðar] vt to rust; **oxidarse** vr to go rusty

óxido ['oksiðo] nm oxide

oxigenado, -a [oksixe'naðo, a] adj (QUÍM) oxygenated; (pelo) bleached

oxígeno [ok'sixeno] nm oxygen

oyente [o'jente] nmf listener

oyes etc vb ver **oír**

ozono [o'θono] nm ozone

P, p

pabellón [paβeˈʎon] nm bell tent; (ARQ) pavilion; (de hospital etc) block, section; (bandera) flag

pacer [paˈθer] vi to graze

paciencia [paˈθjenθja] nf patience

paciente [paˈθjente] adj, nmf patient

pacificación [paθifikaˈθjon] nf pacification

pacífico, -a [paˈθifiko, a] adj (persona) peaceable; (existencia) peaceful; **el (Océano) P~** the Pacific (Ocean)

pacifista [paθiˈfista] nmf pacifist

pacotilla [pakoˈtiʎa] nf: **de ~** (actor, escritor) third-rate

pactar [pakˈtar] vt to agree to o.on ♦ vi to come to an agreement

pacto [ˈpakto] nm (tratado) pact; (acuerdo) agreement

padecer [padeˈθer] vt (sufrir) to suffer; (soportar) to endure, put up with
□ **padecimiento** nm suffering

padrastro [paˈðrastro] nm stepfather

padre [ˈpaðre] nm father ♦ adj (fam): **un éxito ~** a tremendous success; **padres** nmpl parents ▸ **padre político** father-in-law

padrino [paˈðrino] nm (REL) godfather; (tb: **~ de boda**) best man; (fig) sponsor, patron; **padrinos** nmpl godparents

padrón [paˈðron] nm (censo) census, roll

padrote (MEX: fam) [paˈðrote] nm pimp

paella [paˈeʎa] nf paella, dish of rice with meat, shellfish etc

paga [ˈpaɣa] nf (pago) payment; (sueldo) pay, wages pl

pagano, -a [paˈɣano, a] adj, nm/f pagan, heathen

pagar [paˈɣar] vt to pay; (las compras, crimen) to pay for; (fig: favor) to repay ♦ vi to pay; **~ al contado/a plazos** to pay (in) cash/in instalments

pagaré [paɣaˈre] nm I.O.U.

página [ˈpaxina] nf page ▸ **página de inicio** (INFORM) home page ▸ **página web** (INFORM) web page

pago [ˈpaɣo] nm (dinero) payment; **en ~ de** in return for ▸ **pago anticipado/a cuenta/contra reembolso/en especie** advance payment/payment on account/cash on delivery/payment in kind

pág(s). abr (= página(s)) p(p).

pague etc [ˈpaɣe] vb ver **pagar**

país [paˈis] nm (gen) country; (región) land; **los Países Bajos** the Low Countries; **el P~ Vasco** the Basque Country

paisaje [paiˈsaxe] nm landscape, scenery

paisano, -a [paiˈsano, a] adj of the same country ♦ nm/f (compatriota) fellow countryman/woman; **vestir de ~** (soldado) to be in civvies; (guardia) to be in plain clothes

paja [ˈpaxa] nf straw; (fig) rubbish (BRIT), trash (US)

pajarita [paxaˈrita] nf (corbata) bow tie

pájaro [ˈpaxaro] nm bird ▸ **pájaro carpintero** woodpecker

pajita [paˈxita] nf (drinking) straw

pala [ˈpala] nf spade, shovel; (raqueta etc) bat; (: de tenis) racquet; (CULIN) slice ▸ **pala mecánica** power shovel

palabra [paˈlaβra] nf word; (facultad) (power of) speech; (derecho de hablar) right to speak; **tomar la ~** (en mitin) to take the floor

palabrota [palaˈβrota] nf swearword

palacio [paˈlaθjo] nm palace; (mansión) mansion, large house ▸ **palacio de justicia** courthouse ▸ **palacio municipal** town o city hall

paladar [palaˈðar] nm palate
□ **paladear** vt to taste

palanca [paˈlanka] nf lever; (fig) pull, influence

palangana [palanˈɡana] nf washbasin

palco ['palko] nm box

Palestina [pales'tina] nf Palestine □ **palestino, -a** adj/nm/f Palestinian

paleta [pa'leta] nf (de pintor) palette; (de albañil) trowel; (de ping-pong) bat; (MÉX: helado) ice lolly (BRIT), Popsicle® (US)

palidecer [paliðe'θer] vi to turn pale □ **palidez** nf paleness □ **pálido, -a** adj pale

palillo [pa'liʎo] nm (mondadientes) toothpick; (para comer) chopstick

palito [RPI] [pa'lito] nm (helado) ice lolly (BRIT), Popsicle® (US)

paliza [pa'liθa] nf beating, thrashing

palma ['palma] nf (ANAT) palm; (árbol) palm tree; batir o dar palmas to clap, applaud □ **palmada** nf slap; **palmadas** nfpl clapping sg, applause sg

palmar [pal'mar] (fam) vi (tb: **palmarla**) to die, kick the bucket

palmear [palme'ar] vi to clap

palmera [pal'mera] nf (BOT) palm tree

palmo ['palmo] nm (medida) span; (fig) small amount; ~ a ~ inch by inch

palo ['palo] nm stick; (poste) post; (de tienda de campaña) pole; (mango) handle, shaft; (golpe) blow, hit; (de béisbol) bat; (NÁUT) mast; (NAIPES) suit

paloma [pa'loma] nf dove, pigeon

palomitas [palo'mitas] nfpl popcorn sg

palpar [pal'par] vt to touch, feel

palpitar [palpi'tar] vi to palpitate; (latir) to beat

palta ['palta] (CS) nf avocado

paludismo [palu'ðismo] nm malaria

pamela [pa'mela] nf picture hat, sun hat

pampa ['pampa] nf pampas, prairie

pan [pan] nm bread; (una barra) loaf ▸ **pan integral** wholemeal (BRIT) o wholewheat (US) bread ▸ **pan rallado** breadcrumbs pl ▸ **pan tostado** (MÉX: tostada) toast

pana ['pana] nf corduroy

panadería [panaðe'ria] nf baker's (shop) □ **panadero, -a** nm/f baker

Panamá [pana'ma] nm Panama □ **panameño, -a** adj Panamanian

pancarta [pan'karta] nf placard, banner

panceta (ESP, RPI) nf bacon

pancho (RPI) ['pantʃo] nm hot dog

pancito (RPI) [pan'θito] nm (bread) roll

panda ['panda] nm (ZOOL) panda

pandereta [pande'reta] nf tambourine

pandilla [pan'diʎa] nf set, group; (de criminales) gang; (pey: camarilla) clique

panecillo [pane'θiʎo] nm (ESP) (bread) roll

panel [pa'nel] nm panel ▸ **panel solar** solar panel

panfleto [pan'fleto] nm pamphlet

pánico ['paniko] nm panic

panorama [pano'rama] nm panorama; (vista) view

panqueque (LAm) nm pancake

pantalla [pan'taʎa] nf (de cine) screen; (de lámpara) lampshade

pantalón [panta'lon] nm trousers; **pantalones** nmpl trousers; **pantalones cortos** shorts

pantano [pan'tano] nm (ciénaga) marsh, swamp; (depósito: de agua) reservoir; (fig) jam, difficulty

panteón [pante'on] nm (monumento) pantheon

pantera [pan'tera] nf panther

pantimedias (MÉX) nfpl = **pantis**

pantis ['pantis] nmpl tights (BRIT), pantyhose (US)

pantomima [panto'mima] nf pantomime

pantorrilla [panto'rriʎa] nf calf (of the leg)

pants (MÉX) nmpl tracksuit (BRIT), sweat suit (US)

pantufla [pan'tufla] nf slipper

panty(s) [ˈpanti(s)] nm(pl) tights (BRIT), pantyhose (US)

panza [ˈpanθa] nf belly, paunch

pañal [paˈɲal] nm nappy (BRIT), diaper (US); **pañales** nmpl (fig) early stages, infancy sg

paño [ˈpaɲo] nm (tela) cloth; (pedazo de tela) (piece of) cloth; (trapo) duster, rag ▶ **paños menores** underclothes

pañuelo [paˈɲwelo] nm handkerchief, hanky; (fam: para la cabeza) (head)scarf

papa [ˈpapa] nm: **el P~** the Pope ♦ nf (LAm: patata) potato ▶ **papas fritas** (LAm) French fries, chips (BRIT); (de bolsa) crisps (BRIT), potato chips (US)

papá [paˈpa] (fam) nm dad(dy), pa (US)

papada [paˈpaða] nf double chin

papagayo [papaˈɣajo] nm parrot

papalote (MEX, CAm) [papaˈlote] nm kite

papanatas [papaˈnatas] (fam) nm inv simpleton

papaya [paˈpaja] nf papaya

papear [papeˈar] (fam) vt, vi to scoff

papel [paˈpel] nm paper; (hoja de papel) sheet of paper; (TEATRO: fig) role ▶ **papel de aluminio** (BRIT) o **aluminum** (US) foil ▶ **papel de arroz/envolver/fumar** rice/wrapping/cigarette paper ▶ **papel de estaño** o **plata** tinfoil ▶ **papel de lija** sandpaper ▶ **papel higiénico** toilet paper ▶ **papel moneda** paper money ▶ **papel secante** blotting paper

papeleo [papeˈleo] nm red tape

papelera [papeˈlera] nf wastepaper basket; (en la calle) litter bin ▶ **papelera de reciclaje** (INFORM) wastebasket

papelería [papeleˈria] nf stationer's (shop)

papeleta [papeˈleta] (ESP) nf (POL) ballot paper

paperas [paˈperas] nfpl mumps sg

papilla [paˈpiʎa] nf (de bebé) baby food

paquete [paˈkete] nm (de cigarrillos etc) packet; (CORREOS etc) parcel

par [par] adj (igual) like, equal; (MAT) even ♦ nm equal; (de guantes) pair; (de veces) couple; (POL) peer; (GOLF, COM) par; **abrir de ~ en ~** to open wide

para [ˈpara] prep for; **no es ~ comer** it's not for eating; **decir ~ sí** to say to o.s.; **¿~ qué lo quieres?** what do you want it for?; **se casaron ~ separarse otra vez** they married only to separate again; **lo tendré ~ mañana** I'll have it (for) tomorrow; **ir ~ casa** to go home, head for home; **~ profesor es muy estúpido** he's very stupid for a teacher; **¿quién es usted ~ gritar así?** who are you to shout like that?; **tengo bastante ~ vivir** I have enough to live on; ver tb **con**

parabién [paraˈβjen] nm congratulations pl

parábola [paˈraβola] nf parable; (MAT) parabola ❏ **parabólica** nf (tb: **antena parabólica**) satellite dish

parabrisas [paraˈβrisas] nm inv windscreen (BRIT), windshield (US)

paracaídas [parakaˈiðas] nm inv parachute ❏ **paracaidista** nmf parachutist; (MIL) paratrooper

parachoques [paraˈtʃokes] nm inv (AUTO) bumper; (MECÁNICA etc) shock absorber

parada [paˈraða] nf stop; (acto) stopping; (de industria) shutdown, stoppage; (lugar) stopping place ▶ **parada de autobús** bus stop ▶ **parada de taxis** taxi stand o rank (BRIT)

paradero [paraˈðero] nm stopping-place; (situación) whereabouts

parado, -a [paˈraðo, a] adj (persona) motionless, standing still; (fábrica) closed, at a standstill; (coche) stopped; (LAm: de pie) standing (up); (ESP: sin empleo) unemployed, idle

paradoja [paraˈðoxa] nf paradox

parador [para'ðor] nm parador, state-run hotel

paragolpes (RPl) nm inv (AUTO) bumper, fender (US)

paraguas [pa'raɣwas] nm inv umbrella

Paraguay [paraɣwai] nm Paraguay
□ **paraguayo, -a** adj, nm/f Paraguayan

paraíso [para'iso] nm paradise, heaven

paraje [pa'raxe] nm place, spot

paralelo, -a [para'lelo, a] adj parallel

parálisis [pa'ralisis] nf inv paralysis
□ **paralítico, -a** adj, nm/f paralytic

paralizar [parali'θar] vt to paralyse; **paralizarse** vr to become paralysed; (fig) to come to a standstill

páramo ['paramo] nm bleak plateau

paranoico, -a [para'noiko, a] adj, nm/f paranoiac

parapente [para'pente] nm (deporte) paragliding; (aparato) paraglider

parapléjico, -a [para'plexiko, a] adj, nm/f paraplegic

parar [pa'rar] vt to stop; (golpe) to ward off ♦ vi to stop; **pararse** vr to stop; (LAm: ponerse de pie) to stand up; **ha parado de llover** it has stopped raining; **van a ir a ~ a comisaría** they're going to end up in the police station; **pararse en** to pay attention to

pararrayos [para'rrajos] nm inv lightning conductor

parásito, -a [pa'rasito, a] nm/f parasite

parcela [par'θela] nf plot, piece of ground

parche [part∫e] nm (gen) patch

parchís [par't∫is] nm ludo

parcial [par'θjal] adj (pago) part-; (eclipse) partial; (JUR) prejudiced, biased; (POL) partisan

parecer [pare'θer] nm (opinión) opinion, view; (aspecto) looks pl ♦ vi (tener apariencia) to seem, look; (asemejarse) to look o seem like; (aparecer, llegar) to appear; **parecerse** vr to look alike, resemble each other; **al**

~ apparently; según parece evidently, apparently; **parecerse a** to look like, resemble; **me parece que** I think (that), it seems to me that

parecido, -a [pare'θiðo, a] adj similar ♦ nm similarity, likeness, resemblance; **bien ~** good-looking, nice-looking

pared [pa'reð] nf wall

pareja [pa'rexa] nf (par) pair; (dos personas) couple; (otro: de un par) other one (of a pair); (persona) partner

parentesco [paren'tesko] nm relationship

paréntesis [pa'rentesis] nm inv parenthesis; (en escrito) bracket

parezco etc vb ver **parecer**

pariente [pa'rjente] nmf relative, relation

⚠ No confundir **pariente** con la palabra *parent*.

parir [pa'rir] vt to give birth to ♦ vi (mujer) to give birth, have a baby

París [pa'ris] n Paris

parka (LAm) nf anorak

parking ['parkin] nm car park (BRIT), parking lot (US)

parlamentar [parlamen'tar] vi to parley

parlamentario, -a [parlamen'tarjo, a] adj parliamentary ♦ nm/f member of parliament

parlamento [parla'mento] nm parliament

parlanchín, -ina [parlan't∫in, ina] adj indiscreet ♦ nm/f chatterbox

parlar [par'lar] vi to chatter (away)

paro ['paro] nm (huelga) stoppage (of work), strike; (ESP: desempleo) unemployment; (: subsidio) unemployment benefit; **estar en ~** (ESP) to be unemployed ▶ **paro cardíaco** cardiac arrest

parodia [pa'roðja] nf parody
□ **parodiar** vt to parody

parpadear [parpaðe'ar] vi (ojos) to
blink; (luz) to flicker

párpado ['parpaðo] nm eyelid

parque ['parke] nm (lugar verde) park;
(MÉX: munición) ammunition ▶ **parque
de atracciones** fairground ▶ **parque
de bomberos** (ESP) fire station
▶ **parque infantil/temático/
zoológico** playground/theme park/
zoo

parqué [par'ke] nm parquet (flooring)

parquímetro [par'kimetro] nm
parking meter

parra ['parra] nf (grape)vine

párrafo ['parrafo] nm paragraph; **echar
un ~** (fam) to have a chat

parranda [pa'rranda] (fam) nf spree,
binge

parrilla [pa'rriʎa] nf (CULIN) grill; (de
coche) grille; (**carne a la**) **~** barbecue
❏ **parrillada** nf barbecue

párroco ['parroko] nm parish priest

parroquia [pa'rrokja] nf (parish;
(iglesia) parish church; (COM) clientele,
customers pl ❏ **parroquiano, -a** nm/f
parishioner; client, customer

parte ['parte] nm message; (informe)
report ♦ nf part; (lado, cara) side; (de
reparto) share; (JUR) party; **en alguna ~
de Europa** somewhere in Europe; **en o
por todas partes** everywhere; **en gran
~** to a large extent; **la mayor ~ de los
españoles** most Spaniards; **de
tiempo a esta ~** for some time past; **de
~ de algn** on sb's behalf; **¿de ~ de
quién?** (TEL) who is speaking?; **por ~ de**
on the part of; **yo por mí ~** I for my part;
por otra ~ on the other hand; **dar ~** to
inform; **tomar ~** to take part ▶ **parte
meteorológico** weather forecast o
report

participación [partiθipa'θjon] nf
(acto) participation, taking part; (parte,
COM) share; (de lotería) shared prize;
(aviso) notice, notification

participante [partiθi'pante] nmf
participant

participar [partiθi'par] vt to notify,
inform ♦ vi to take part, participate

partícipe [par'tiθipe] nmf participant

particular [partiku'lar] adj (especial)
particular, special; (individual, personal)
private, personal ♦ nm (punto, asunto)
particular, point; (individuo) individual;
tiene coche ~ he has a car of his own

partida [par'tiða] nf (salida) departure;
(COM) entry, item; (juego) game; (grupo
de personas) band, group; **mala ~** dirty
trick ▶ **partida de nacimiento/
matrimonio/defunción** (ESP) birth/
marriage/death certificate

partidario, -a [parti'ðarjo, a] adj
partisan ♦ nm/f supporter, follower

partido [par'tiðo] nm (POL) party;
(DEPORTE) game, match; **sacar ~ de** to
profit o benefit from; **tomar ~** to take
sides

partir [par'tir] vt (dividir) to split, divide;
(compartir, distribuir) to share (out),
distribute; (romper) to break open,
split open; (rebanada) to cut (off) ♦ vi
(ponerse en camino) to set off o out;
(comenzar) to start (off o out); **partirse**
vr to crack o split o break (in two etc); **a
~ de** (starting) from

partitura [parti'tura] nf (MÚS) score

parto ['parto] nm birth; (fig) product,
creation; **estar de ~** to be in labour

parvulario (ESP) [parβu'larjo] nm
nursery school, kindergarten

pasa ['pasa] nf raisin ▶ **pasa de
Corinto** currant

pasacintas (LAm) nm cassette player

pasada [pa'saða] nf passing, passage;
de ~ in passing, incidentally; **una mala
~** a dirty trick

pasadizo [pasa'ðiθo] nm (pasillo)
passage, corridor; (callejuela) alley

pasado, -a [pa'saðo, a] adj past; (malo:
comida, fruta) bad; (muy cocido)
overdone; (anticuado) out of date

♦ *nm* past; **~ mañana** the day after tomorrow; **el mes ~** last month

pasador [pasa'ðor] *nm* (*cerrojo*) bolt; (*de pelo*) hair slide; (*horquilla*) grip

pasaje [pa'saxe] *nm* passage; (*pago de viaje*) fare; (*los pasajeros*) passengers *pl*; (*pasillo*) passageway

pasajero, -a [pasa'xero, a] *adj* passing; (*situación, estado*) temporary; (*amor, enfermedad*) *nm/f* passenger

pasamontañas [pasamon'taɲas] *nm inv* balaclava helmet

pasaporte [pasa'porte] *nm* passport

pasar [pa'sar] *vt* to pass; (*tiempo*) to spend; (*desgracias*) to suffer, endure; (*noticia*) to give, pass on; (*río*) to cross; (*barrera*) to pass through; (*falta*) to overlook, tolerate; (*contincante*) to surpass, do better than; (*coche*) to overtake; (*CINE*) to show; (*enfermedad*) to give, infect with ♦ *vi* (*gen*) to pass; (*terminarse*) to be over; (*ocurrir*) to happen; **pasarse** *vr* (*flores*) to fade; (*comida*) to go bad o off; (*fig*) to overdo it, go too far; **~ de** to go beyond, exceed; **~ por** (*LAm*) to fetch; **pasarlo bien/mal** to have a good/bad time; **¡pase!** come in!; **hacer ~** to show in; **lo que pasa es que ...** the thing is ...; **pasarse al enemigo** to go over to the enemy; **se me pasó** I forgot; **no se le pasa nada** he misses nothing; **pase lo que pase** come what may; **¿qué pasa?** what's going on? what's up?; **¿qué te pasa?** what's wrong?

pasarela [pasa'rela] *nf* footbridge; (*en barco*) gangway

pasatiempo [pasa'tjempo] *nm* pastime, hobby

Pascua ['paskwa] *nf* (*en Semana Santa*) Easter; **Pascuas** *nfpl* Christmas (time); **¡felices Pascuas!** Merry Christmas!

pase ['pase] *nm* pass; (*CINE*) performance, showing

pasear [pase'ar] *vt* to take for a walk; (*exhibir*) to parade, show off ♦ *vi* to walk, go for a walk; **pasearse** *vr* to walk,

go for a walk; **~ en coche** to go for a drive ❏ **paseo** *nm* (*avenida*) avenue; (*distancia corta*) walk, (*trecho*) stroll; **dar un o ir de paseo** to go for a walk ► **paseo marítimo** (*ESP*) promenade

pasillo [pa'siʎo] *nm* passage, corridor

pasión [pa'sjon] *nf* passion

pasivo, -a [pa'siβo, a] *adj* passive; (*inactivo*) inactive ♦ *nm* (*COM*) liabilities *pl*, debts *pl*

pasmoso, -a [pas'moso, a] *adj* amazing, astonishing

paso, -a ['paso, a] *adj* dried ♦ *nm* step; (*modo de andar*) walk; (*huella*) footprint; (*rapidez*) speed, pace, rate; (*camino accesible*) way through, passage; (*cruce*) crossing; (*pasaje*) passing, passage; (*GEO*) pass; (*estrecho*) strait; **a ese ~** (*fig*) at that rate; **salir al ~ de o a** to waylay; **estar de ~** to be passing through; **prohibido el ~** no entry; **ceda el ~** give way ► **paso a nivel** (*FERRO*) level-crossing ► **paso (de) cebra** (*ESP*) zebra crossing ► **paso de peatones** pedestrian crossing ► **paso elevado** flyover

pasota [pa'sota] (*ESP: fam*) *adj, nm/f* = dropout; **ser un ~** to be a bit of a dropout; (*ser indiferente*) not to care about anything

pasta ['pasta] *nf* (*gen*) paste; (*CULIN: masa*) dough; (: *de bizcochos etc*) pastry; (*fam*) dough; **pastas** *nfpl* (*bizcochos*) pastries, small cakes; (*fideos, espaguetis etc*) pasta ► **pasta dentífrica** o **de dientes** toothpaste

pastar [pas'tar] *vt, vi* to graze

pastel [pas'tel] *nm* (*dulce*) cake; (*ARTE*) pastel ► **pastel de carne** meat pie ❏ **pastelería** *nf* cake shop

pastilla [pas'tiʎa] *nf* (*de jabón, chocolate*) bar; (*píldora*) tablet, pill

pasto ['pasto] *nm* (*hierba*) grass; (*lugar*) pasture, field ❏ **pastor, a** [pas'tor, a] *nm/f* shepherd/ess ♦ *nm* (*REL*) clergyman, pastor ► **pastor alemán** Alsatian

pata ['pata] nf (pierna) leg; (pie) foot; (de muebles) leg; **patas arriba** upside down; **metadura de ~** (fam) to put one's foot in it; **tener buena/mala ~** (fam) lucky/unlucky ▶ **pata de cabra** (TEC) crowbar ❑ **patada** nf kick; (en el suelo) stamp

patata [pa'tata] nf potato ▶ **patatas fritas** chips, French fries; (de bolsa) crisps

paté [pa'te] nm pâté

patente [pa'tente] adj obvious, evident; (COM) nf patent

paternal [pater'nal] adj fatherly, paternal ❑ **paterno, -a** adj paternal

patético, -a [pa'tetiko, a] adj pathetic, moving

patilla [pa'tiʎa] nf (de gafas) side(piece); **patillas** nfpl sideburns

patín [pa'tin] nm skate; (de trineo) runner ❑ **patinaje** nm skating ❑ **patinar** vi to skate; (resbalarse) to skid; slip; (fam) to slip up, blunder

patines de ruedas nmpl rollerskates

patineta nf (MÉX: patinete) scooter; (CS: monopatín) skateboard

patinete [pati'nete] nm scooter

patio ['patjo] nm (de casa) patio, courtyard ▶ **patio de recreo** playground

pato ['pato] nm duck; **pagar el ~** (fam) to take the blame, carry the can

patoso, -a [pa'toso, a] (fam) adj clumsy

patotero (CS) nm hooligan, lout

patraña [pa'traɲa] nf story, fib

patria ['patrja] nf native land, mother country

patrimonio [patri'monjo] nm inheritance; (fig) heritage

patriota [pa'trjota] nmf patriot

patrocinar [patroθi'nar] vt to sponsor

patrón, -ona [pa'tron, ona] nm/f (jefe) boss, chief, master(mistress); (propietario) landlord/lady; (REL) patron saint ♦ nm (TEC, COSTURA) pattern

patronato [patro'nato] nm sponsorship; (acto) patronage; (fundación benéfica) trust, foundation

patrulla [pa'truʎa] nf patrol

pausa ['pausa] nf pause, break

pauta ['pauta] nf line, guide line

pava (RPl) ['paβa] nf kettle

pavimento [paβi'mento] nm (de losa) pavement, paving

pavo ['paβo] nm turkey ▶ **pavo real** peacock

payaso, -a [pa'jaso, a] nm/f clown

payo, -a [pa'jo, a] nm/f non-gipsy

paz [paθ] nf peace; (tranquilidad) peacefulness, tranquillity; **hacer las paces** to make peace; (fig) to make up; **¡déjame en ~!** leave me alone!

PC nm PC, personal computer

P.D. abr (= posdata) P.S., p.s.

peaje [pe'axe] nm toll

peatón [pea'ton] nm pedestrian

peatonal adj pedestrian

peca ['peka] nf freckle

pecado [pe'kaðo] nm sin ❑ **pecador, a** adj sinful ♦ nm/f sinner

pecaminoso, -a [pekami'noso, a] adj sinful

pecar [pe'kar] vi (REL) to sin; **peca de generoso** he is generous to a fault

pecera [pe'θera] nf fish tank; (redonda) goldfish bowl

pecho ['petʃo] nm (ANAT) chest; (de mujer) breast; **dar el ~ a** to breast-feed; **tomar algo a ~** to take sth to heart

pechuga [pe'tʃuɣa] nf breast

peculiar [peku'ljar] adj special, peculiar; (característico) typical, characteristic

pedal [pe'ðal] nm pedal ❑ **pedalear** vi to pedal

pedante [pe'ðante] adj pedantic ♦ nmf pedant

pedazo [pe'ðaθo] nm piece, bit; **hacerse pedazos** to smash, shatter

pediatra [pe'ðjatra] nmf paediatrician

pedido [pe'ðiðo] nm (COM) order; (petición) request

pedir [pe'ðir] vt to ask for, request; (comida, COM: mandar) to order; (necesitar) to need, demand, require ♦ vi to ask; **me pidió que cerrara la puerta** he asked me to shut the door; **¿cuánto piden por el coche?** how much are they asking for the car?

pedo ['peðo] (fam!) nm fart

pega ['peɣa] nf snag; **poner pegas (a)** to complain (about)

pegadizo, -a [peɣa'ðiθo, a] adj (MÚS) catchy

pegajoso, -a [peɣa'xoso, a] adj sticky, adhesive

pegamento [peɣa'mento] nm gum, glue

pegar [pe'ɣar] vt (papel, sellos) to stick (on); (cartel) to stick up; (coser) to sew (on); (unir: partes) to join, fix together; (COMPUT) to paste; (MED) to give, infect with; (dar: golpe) to give, deal ♦ vi (adherirse) to stick, adhere; (ir juntos: colores) to match, go together; (golpear) to hit; (quemar: el sol) to strike hot, burn; **pegarse** vr (gen) to stick; (dos personas) to hit each other, fight; (fam): **~ un grito** to let out a yell; **~ un salto** to jump (with fright); **~ en** to touch; **pegarse un tiro** to shoot o.s.

pegatina [peɣa'tina] nf sticker

pegote [pe'ɣote] (fam) nm eyesore, sight

peinado [pei'naðo] nm hairstyle

peinar [pei'nar] vt to comb; (hacer estilo) to style; **peinarse** vr to comb one's hair

peine ['peine] nm comb □ **peineta** nf ornamental comb

p.ej. abr (= por ejemplo) e.g.

Pekín [pe'kin] n Pekin(g)

pelado, -a [pe'laðo, a] adj (fruta, patata etc) peeled; (cabeza) shorn; (campo, fig) bare; (fam: sin dinero) broke

pelar [pe'lar] vt (fruta, patatas etc) to peel; (cortar el pelo a) to cut the hair of; (quitar la piel: animal) to skin; **pelarse** vr (la piel) to peel off; **voy a pelarme** I'm going to get my hair cut

peldaño [pel'daɲo] nm step

pelea [pe'lea] nf (lucha) fight; (discusión) quarrel, row □ **peleado, -a** [pele'aðo, a] adj: **estar peleado (con algn)** to have fallen out (with sb) □ **pelear** [pele'ar] vi to fight; **pelearse** vr to fight; (reñirse) to fall out, quarrel

pelela (CS) nf potty

peletería [pelete'ria] nf furrier's, fur shop

pelícano [pe'likano] nm pelican

película [pe'likula] nf film; (cobertura ligera) thin covering; (FOTO: rollo) roll o reel of film □ **película de dibujos (animados)/del oeste** cartoon/ western

peligro [pe'liɣro] nm danger; (riesgo) risk; **correr ~ de** to run the risk of □ **peligroso, -a** adj dangerous; risky

pelirrojo, -a [peli'rroxo, a] adj red-haired, red-headed ♦ nm/f redhead

pellejo [pe'ʎexo] nm (de animal) skin, hide

pellizcar [peʎiθ'kar] vt to pinch, nip

pelma ['pelma] (ESP: fam) nmf pain (in the neck) □ **pelmazo** [pel'maθo] (fam) nm = **pelma**

pelo ['pelo] nm (cabellos) hair; (de barba, bigote) whisker; (de animal: pellejo) hair, fur, coat; **venir al ~** to be exactly what one needs; **un hombre de ~ en pecho** a brave man; **por los pelos** by the skin of one's teeth; **no tener pelos en la lengua** to be outspoken, not to mince one's words; **con pelos y señales** in minute detail; **tomar el ~ a algn** to pull sb's leg

pelota [pe'lota] nf ball; **en ~** stark naked; **hacer la ~ (a algn)** (ESP: fam) to creep (to sb) ▶ **pelota vasca** pelota

pelotón [pelo'ton] nm (MIL) squad, detachment

peluca [pe'luka] nf wig

peluche [pe'lutʃe] nm: **oso/muñeco de ~** teddy bear/soft toy

peludo, -a [pe'luðo, a] adj hairy, shaggy

peluquería [peluke'ria] nf hairdresser's □ **peluquero, -a** nm/f hairdresser

pelusa [pe'lusa] nf (BOT) down; (en tela) fluff

pena ['pena] nf (congoja) grief, sadness; (remordimiento) regret; (dificultad) trouble; (dolor) pain; (JUR) sentence; **merecer** o **valer la ~** to be worthwhile; **a duras penas** with great difficulty; **¡qué ~!** what a shame! ▶ **pena capital** capital punishment ▶ **pena de muerte** death penalty

penal [pe'nal] adj penal ◆ nm (cárcel) prison

penalidad [penali'ðað] nf (problema, dificultad) trouble, hardship; (JUR) penalty, punishment; **penalidades** nfpl trouble sg, hardship sg

penalti [pe'nalti] nm = **penalty**

penalty [pe'nalti] (pl **penaltys** o **penalties**) nm penalty (kick)

pendiente [pen'djente] adj pending, unsettled ◆ nm earring ◆ nf hill, slope

pene ['pene] nm penis

penetrante [pene'trante] adj (herida) deep; (persona, arma) sharp; (sonido) penetrating, piercing; (mirada) searching; (viento, ironía) biting

penetrar [pene'trar] vt to penetrate, pierce; (entender) to grasp ◆ vi to penetrate, go in; (entrar) to enter, go in; (líquido) to soak in; (fig) to pierce

penicilina [peniθi'lina] nf penicillin

península [pe'ninsula] nf peninsula □ **peninsular** adj peninsular

penique [pe'nike] nm penny

penitencia [peni'tenθja] nf penance

penoso, -a [pe'noso, a] adj (lamentable) distressing; (difícil) arduous, difficult

pensador, a [pensa'ðor, a] nm/f thinker

pensamiento [pensa'mjento] nm thought; (mente) mind; (idea) idea

pensar [pen'sar] vt to think; (considerar) to think over, think out; (proponerse) to intend, plan; (imaginarse) to think up, invent ◆ vi to think; **~ en** to aim at, aspire to □ **pensativo, -a** adj thoughtful, pensive

pensión [pen'sjon] nf (casa) boarding o guest house; (dinero) pension; (cama y comida) board and lodging; **media ~** half-board ▶ **pensión completa** full board □ **pensionista** nmf (jubilado) (old-age) pensioner; (huésped) lodger

penúltimo, -a [pe'nultimo, a] adj penultimate, last but one

penumbra [pe'numbra] nf half-light

peña ['pena] nf (roca) rock; (cuesta) cliff, crag; (grupo) group, circle; (LAm: club) folk club

peñasco [pe'nasko] nm large rock, boulder

peñón [pe'non] nm wall of rock; **el P~** the Rock (of Gibraltar)

peón [pe'on] nm labourer; (LAm AGR) farm labourer, farmhand; (AJEDREZ) pawn

peonza [pe'onθa] nf spinning top

peor [pe'or] adj (comparativo) worse; (superlativo) worst ◆ adv worse; worst; **de mal en ~** from bad to worse

pepinillo [pepi'niʎo] nm gherkin

pepino [pe'pino] nm cucumber; **(no) me importa un ~** I don't care one bit

pepita [pe'pita] nf (BOT) pip; (MINERÍA) nugget

pepito [pe'pito] (ESP) nm (tb: ~ de ternera) steak sandwich

pequeño, -a [pe'keɲo, a] *adj* small, little

pera ['pera] *nf* pear ❑ **peral** *nm* pear tree

percance [per'kanθe] *nm* setback, misfortune

percatarse [perka'tarse] *vr*: ~ **de** to notice, take note of

percebe [per'θeβe] *nm* barnacle

percepción [perθep'θjon] *nf* (*vista*) perception; (*idea*) notion, idea

percha ['pertʃa] *nf* (*coat*)hanger; (*ganchos*) coat hooks *pl*; (*de ave*) perch

percibir [perθi'βir] *vt* to perceive, notice; (*COM*) to earn, get

percusión [perku'sjon] *nf* percussion

perdedor, a [perðe'ðor, a] *adj* losing ♦ *nm/f* loser

perder [per'ðer] *vt* to lose; (*tiempo, palabras*) to waste; (*oportunidad*) to lose, miss; (*tren*) to miss ♦ *vi* to lose; **perderse** *vr* (*extraviarse*) to get lost; (*desaparecer*) to disappear, be lost to view; (*arruinarse*) to be ruined; **echar a ~** (*comida*) to spoil, ruin; (*oportunidad*) to waste

pérdida ['perðiða] *nf* (*de tiempo*) waste; **pérdidas** *nfpl* (*COM*) losses

perdido, -a [per'ðiðo, a] *adj* lost

perdiz [per'ðiθ] *nf* partridge

perdón [per'ðon] *nm* (*disculpa*) pardon, forgiveness; (*clemencia*) mercy; ¡~! sorry!, I beg your pardon! ❑ **perdonar** *vt* to pardon, forgive; (*la vida*) to spare; (*excusar*) to exempt, excuse; **¡perdone (usted)!** sorry!, I beg your pardon!

perecedero, -a [pereθe'ðero, a] *adj* perishable

perecer [pere'θer] *vi* to perish, die

peregrinación [pereɣrina'θjon] *nf* (*REL*) pilgrimage

peregrino, -a [pere'ɣrino, a] *adj* (*idea*) strange, absurd ♦ *nm/f* pilgrim

perejil [pere'xil] *nm* parsley

perenne [pe'renne] *adj* everlasting, perennial

pereza [pe'reθa] *nf* laziness, idleness ❑ **perezoso, -a** *adj* lazy, idle

perfección [perfek'θjon] *nf* perfection ❑ **perfeccionar** *vt* to perfect; (*mejorar*) to improve; (*acabar*) to complete, finish

perfecto, -a [per'fekto, a] *adj* perfect; (*total*) complete

perfil [per'fil] *nm* profile; (*contorno*) silhouette, outline; (*ARQ*) (cross) section; **perfiles** *nmpl* features

perforación [perfora'θjon] *nf* perforation; (*con taladro*) drilling ❑ **perforadora** *nf* punch

perforar [perfo'rar] *vt* to perforate; (*agujero*) to drill, bore; (*papel*) to punch a hole in ♦ *vi* to drill, bore

perfume [per'fume] *nm* perfume, scent

periferia [peri'ferja] *nf* periphery; (*de ciudad*) outskirts *pl*

periférico [peri'feriko] (*LAm*) *nm* ring road (*BRIT*), beltway (*US*)

perilla [pe'riʎa] *nf* (*barba*) goatee; (*LAm: de puerta*) doorknob, door handle

perímetro [pe'rimetro] *nm* perimeter

periódico, -a [pe'rjoðiko, a] *adj* periodic(al) ♦ *nm* newspaper

periodismo [perjo'ðismo] *nm* journalism ❑ **periodista** *nmf* journalist

periodo [pe'rjoðo] *nm* period

período [pe'rioðo] *nm* = **periodo**

periquito [peri'kito] *nm* budgerigar, budgie

perito, -a [pe'rito, a] *adj* (*experto*) expert; (*diestro*) skilled, skilful ♦ *nm/f* expert; skilled worker; (*técnico*) technician

perjudicar [perxuði'kar] *vt* (*gen*) to damage, harm ❑ **perjudicial** *adj* damaging, harmful; (*en detrimento*) detrimental ❑ **perjuicio** *nm* damage, harm

perjurar [perxu'rar] vi to commit perjury

perla ['perla] nf pearl; **me viene de perlas** it suits me fine

permanecer [permane'θer] vi (quedarse) to stay, remain; (seguir) to continue to be

permanente [perma'nente] adj permanent, constant ♦ nf perm

permiso [per'miso] nm permission; (licencia) permit, licence; **con ~** excuse me; **estar de ~** (MIL) to be on leave
▶ **permiso de conducir** driving licence (BRIT), driver's license (US)
▶ **permiso por enfermedad** (LAm) sick leave

permitir [permi'tir] vt to permit, allow

pernera [per'nera] nf trouser leg

pero ['pero] conj but; (aún) yet ♦ nm (defecto) flaw, defect; (reparo) objection

perpendicular [perpendiku'lar] adj perpendicular

perpetuo, -a [per'petwo, a] adj perpetual

perplejo, -a [per'plexo, a] adj perplexed, bewildered

perra ['perra] nf (ZOOL) bitch; **estar sin una ~** (ESP: fam) to be flat broke

perrera [pe'rrera] nf kennel

perrito [pe'rrito] nm (tb: ~ **caliente**) hot dog

perro ['perro] nm dog

persa ['persa] adj, nmf Persian

persecución [perseku'θjon] nf pursuit, chase; (REL, POL) persecution

perseguir [perse'ɣir] vt to pursue, hunt; (cortejar) to chase after; (molestar) to pester, annoy; (REL, POL) to persecute

persiana [per'sjana] nf (Venetian) blind

persistente [persis'tente] adj persistent

persistir [persis'tir] vi to persist

persona [per'sona] nf person
▶ **persona mayor** elderly person

personaje [perso'naxe] nm important person, celebrity; (TEATRO etc) character

personal [perso'nal] adj (particular) personal; (para una persona) single, for one person ♦ nm personnel, staff
❏ **personalidad** nf personality

personarse [perso'narse] vr to appear in person

personificar [personifi'kar] vt to personify

perspectiva [perspek'tiβa] nf perspective; (vista, panorama) view, panorama; (posibilidad futura) outlook, prospect

persuadir [perswa'ðir] vt (gen) to persuade; (convencer) to convince; **persuadirse** vr to become convinced
❏ **persuasión** nf persuasion

pertenecer [pertene'θer] vi to belong; (fig) to concern ❏ **perteneciente** adj: **perteneciente a** belonging to
❏ **pertenencia** nf ownership; **pertenencias** nfpl (bienes) possessions, property sg

pertenezca etc [perte'neθka] vb ver **pertenecer**

pértiga ['pertiɣa] nf: **salto de ~** pole vault

pertinente [perti'nente] adj relevant, pertinent; (apropiado) appropriate; **~ a** concerning, relevant to

perturbación [perturβa'θjon] nf (POL) disturbance; (MED) upset, disturbance

Perú [pe'ru] nm Peru ❏ **peruano, -a** adj, nm/f Peruvian

perversión [perβer'sjon] nf perversion ❏ **perverso, -a** adj perverse; (depravado) depraved

pervertido, -a [perβer'tiðo, a] adj perverted ♦ nm/f pervert

pervertir [perβer'tir] vt to pervert, corrupt

pesa ['pesa] nf weight; (DEPORTE) shot

pesadez [pesa'ðeθ] nf (peso) heaviness; (lentitud) slowness; (aburrimiento) tediousness

pesadilla [pesa'ðiʎa] nf nightmare, bad dream

pesado, -a [pe'saðo, a] adj heavy; (lento) slow; (difícil, duro) tough, hard; (aburrido) boring, tedious; (tiempo) sultry

pésame ['pesame] nm expression of condolence, message of sympathy; **dar el ~** to express one's condolences

pesar [pe'sar] vt to weigh ♦ vi to weigh; (ser pesado) to weigh a lot, be heavy; (fig: opinión) to carry weight; **no pesa mucho** it's not very heavy ♦ nm (arrepentimiento) regret; (pena) grief, sorrow; **a ~ de o pese a (que)** in spite of, despite

pesca ['peska] nf (acto) fishing; (lo pescado) catch; **ir de ~** to go fishing

pescadería [peskaðe'ria] nf fish shop, fishmonger's (BRIT)

pescadilla [peska'ðiʎa] nf whiting

pescado [pes'kaðo] nm fish

pescador, a [peska'ðor, a] nm/f fisherman/woman

pescar [pes'kar] vt (tomar) to catch; (intentar tomar) to fish for; (conseguir: trabajo) to manage to get ♦ vi to fish, go fishing

pesebre [pe'seβre] nm manger

peseta [pe'seta] nf (HIST) peseta

pesimista [pesi'mista] adj pessimistic ♦ nmf pessimist

pésimo, -a ['pesimo, a] adj awful, dreadful

peso ['peso] nm weight; (balanza) scales pl; (moneda) peso; **vender al ~** to sell by weight ► **peso bruto/neto** gross/ net weight ► **peso pesado/pluma** heavyweight/featherweight

pesquero, -a [pes'kero, a] adj fishing cpd

pestaña [pes'taɲa] nf (ANAT) eyelash; (borde) rim

peste ['peste] nf plague; (mal olor) stink, stench

pesticida [pesti'θiða] nm pesticide

pestillo [pes'tiʎo] nm (cerrojo) bolt; (picaporte) door handle

petaca [pe'taka] nf (de cigarros) cigarette case; (de pipa) tobacco pouch; (MÉX: maleta) suitcase

pétalo ['petalo] nm petal

petardo [pe'tardo] nm firework, firecracker

petición [peti'θjon] nf (pedido) request, plea; (memorial) petition; (JUR) plea

peto (ESP) ['peto] nm dungarees pl, overalls pl (US)

petróleo [pe'troleo] nm oil, petroleum ❏ **petrolero, -a** adj petroleum cpd ♦ nm (oil) tanker

peyorativo, -a [pejora'tiβo, a] adj pejorative

pez [peθ] nm fish ► **pez espada** swordfish

pezón [pe'θon] nm teat, nipple

pezuña [pe'θuɲa] nf hoof

pianista [pja'nista] nmf pianist

piano ['pjano] nm piano

piar [pjar] vi to cheep

pibe, -a [i'piβe, a] (RPI) nm/f boy/girl

picadero [pika'ðero] nm riding school

picadillo [pika'ðiʎo] nm mince, minced meat

picado, -a [pi'kaðo, a] adj pricked, punctured; (CULIN) minced, chopped; (mar) choppy; (diente) bad; (tabaco) cut; (enfadado) cross

picador [pika'ðor] nm (TAUR) picador; (minero) faceworker

picadura [pika'ðura] nf (pinchazo) puncture; (de abeja) sting; (de mosquito) bite; (tabaco picado) cut tobacco

picante [pi'kante] adj hot; (comentario) racy, spicy

picaporte [pika'porte] nm (manija) doorhandle; (pestillo) latch

picar [pi'kar] vt (agujerear, perforar) to prick, puncture; (abeja) to sting; (mosquito, serpiente) to bite; (CULIN) to mince, chop; (incitar) to incite, goad; (dañar, irritar) to annoy, bother; (quemar: lengua) to burn, sting ♦ vi (pez) to bite, take the bait; (sol) to burn, scorch; (abeja, MED) to sting; (mosquito) to bite; **picarse** vr (agriarse) to turn sour, go off; (ofenderse) to take offence

picardía [pikar'ðia] nf villainy; (astucia) slyness, craftiness; (una picardía) dirty trick; (palabra) rude/bad word or expression

pícaro, -a ['pikaro, a] adj (malicioso) villainous; (travieso) mischievous ♦ nm (astuto) crafty sort; (sinvergüenza) rascal, scoundrel

pichi [ESP] nm pinafore dress (BRIT), jumper (US)

pichón [pi'tʃon] nm young pigeon

pico ['piko] nm (de ave) beak; (punta) sharp point; (TEC) pick, pickaxe; (GEO) peak, summit; **y ~ a bit**; **las seis y ~** six and a bit

picor [pi'kor] nm itch

picoso, -a [MEX] [pi'koso, a] adj (comida) hot

picudo, -a [pi'kuðo, a] adj pointed, with a point

pidió etc vb ver **pedir**

pido etc vb ver **pedir**

pie [pje] (pl **pies**) nm foot; (fig: motivo) motive, basis; (: fundamento) foothold; **ir a ~** to go on foot, walk; **estar de ~** to be standing (up); **ponerse de ~** to stand up; **de pies a cabeza** from top to bottom; **al ~ de la letra** (citar) literally, verbatim; (copiar) exactly, word for word; **en ~ de guerra** on a war footing; **dar ~ a** to give cause for; **hacer ~** (en el agua) to touch (the) bottom

piedad [pje'ðað] nf (lástima) pity, compassion; (clemencia) mercy; (devoción) piety, devotion

piedra ['pjeðra] nf stone; (roca) rock; (de mechero) flint; (METEOROLOGÍA) hailstone ▶ **piedra preciosa** precious stone

piel [pjel] nf (ANAT) skin; (ZOOL) skin, hide, fur; (cuero) leather; (BOT) skin, peel

pienso etc ['pjenso] vb ver **pensar**

pierdo etc vb ver **perder**

pierna ['pjerna] nf leg

pieza ['pjeθa] nf (pieza; habitación) room ▶ **pieza de recambio** o **repuesto** spare (part)

pigmeo, -a [piɣ'meo, a] adj, nm/f pigmy

pijama [pi'xama] nm pyjamas pl (BRIT), pajamas pl (US)

pila ['pila] nf (ELEC) battery; (montón) heap, pile; (lavabo) sink

píldora ['pilðora] nf pill; **la ~ (anticonceptiva)** the (contraceptive) pill

pileta [pi'leta] (RPI) nf (fregadero) (kitchen) sink; (piscina) swimming pool

pillar [pi'ʎar] vt (saquear) to pillage, plunder; (fam: coger) to catch; (: agarrar) to grasp, seize; (: entender) to grasp, catch on to; **pillarse** vr: **pillarse un dedo con la puerta** to catch one's finger in the door

pillo, -a ['piʎo, a] adj villainous; (astuto) sly, crafty ♦ nm/f rascal, rogue, scoundrel

piloto [pi'loto] nm pilot; (de aparato) (pilot) light; (AUTO: luz) tail o rear light; (: conductor) driver ▶ **piloto automático** automatic pilot

pimentón [pimen'ton] nm paprika

pimienta [pi'mjenta] nf pepper

pimiento [pi'mjento] nm pepper, pimiento

pin [pin] (pl **pins**) nm badge

pinacoteca [pinako'teka] nf art gallery

pinar [pi'nar] nm pine forest (BRIT), pine grove (US)

pincel [pin'θel] nm paintbrush

pinchadiscos [pintʃa'ðiskos] (ESP) nm inv disc-jockey, DJ

pinchar [pin'tʃar] vt (perforar) to prick, pierce; (neumático) to puncture; (fig) to prod; (INFORM) to click

pinchazo [pin'tʃaθo] nm (perforación) prick; (de neumático) puncture; (fig) prod

pincho ['pintʃo] nm savoury (snack)
► **pincho de tortilla** small slice of omelette ► **pincho moruno** shish kebab

ping-pong ['pin'pon] nm table tennis

pingüino [pin'gwino] nm penguin

pino ['pino] nm pine (tree)

pinta ['pinta] nf spot; (de líquidos) spot, drop; (aspecto) appearance, look(s) (pl)
❑ **pintado, -a** adj spotted; (de colores) colourful; **pintadas** nfpl graffiti sg

pintalabios [pinta'laβjos] nm inv lipstick

pintar [pin'tar] vt to paint ♦ vi to paint; (fam) to count, be important; **pintarse** vr to put on make-up

pintor, a [pin'tor, a] nm/f painter

pintoresco, -a [pinto'resko, a] adj picturesque

pintura [pin'tura] nf painting
► **pintura al óleo** oil painting

pinza ['pinθa] nf (ZOOL) claw; (para colgar ropa) clothes peg; (TEC) pincers pl; **pinzas** nfpl (para depilar etc) tweezers pl

piña ['piɲa] nf (de pino) pine cone; (fruta) pineapple; (fig) group

piñata nf container hung up at parties to be beaten with sticks until sweets or presents fall out

piñón [pi'ɲon] nm (fruto) pine nut; (TEC) pinion

pío, -a ['pio, a] adj (devoto) pious, devout; (misericordioso) merciful

piojo ['pjoxo] nm louse

pipa ['pipa] nf pipe; **pipas** nfpl (BOT) (edible) sunflower seeds

pipí [pi'pi] (fam) nm: **hacer pipí** to have a wee-(wee) (BRIT), to have to go (wee-wee) (US)

pique ['pike] nm (resentimiento) pique, resentment; (rivalidad) rivalry, competition; **irse a** ~ to sink; (esperanza, familia) to be ruined

piqueta [pi'keta] nf pick(axe)

piquete [pi'kete] nm (MIL) squad, party; (de obreros) picket; (MEX: de insecto) bite ❑ **piquetear** (LAm) vt to picket

pirado, -a [pi'raðo, a] (fam) adj round the bend ♦ nm/f nutter

piragua [pi'raɣwa] nf canoe
❑ **piragüismo** nm canoeing

pirámide [pi'ramiðe] nf pyramid

pirata [pi'rata] adj, nm/f pirate ► **pirata informático** hacker

Pirineo(s) [piri'neo(s)] nm(pl) Pyrenees pl

pirómano, -a [pi'romano, a] nm/f (MED, JUR) arsonist

piropo [pi'ropo] nm compliment, (piece of) flattery

pirueta [pi'rweta] nf pirouette

piruleta (ESP) nf lollipop

pis [pis] (fam) nm pee, piss; **hacer ~** to have a pee; (para niños) to wee-wee

pisada [pi'saða] nf (paso) footstep; (huella) footprint

pisar [pi'sar] vt (caminar sobre) to walk on, tread on; (apretar con el pie) to press; (fig) to trample on, walk all over ♦ vi to tread, step, walk

piscina [pis'θina] nf swimming pool

Piscis ['pisθis] nm Pisces

piso ['piso] nm (suelo, planta) floor; (ESP: apartamento) flat (BRIT), apartment; **primer ~** first floor; (: LAm: planta baja) ground floor

pisotear [pisote'ar] vt to trample (on o underfoot)

pista ['pista] nf track, trail; (indicio) clue ▶ **pista de aterrizaje** runway ▶ **pista de baile** dance floor ▶ **pista de hielo** ice rink ▶ **pista de tenis** (ESP) tennis court

pistola [pis'tola] nf pistol; (TEC) spray-gun

pistón [pis'ton] nm (TEC) piston; (MÚS) key

pitar [pi'tar] vt (silbato) to blow; (rechiflar) to whistle at, boo ♦ vi to whistle; (AUTO) to sound o toot one's horn; (LAm: fumar) to smoke

pitillo [pi'tiʎo] nm cigarette

pito ['pito] nm whistle; (de coche) horn

pitón [pi'ton] nm (ZOOL) python

pitonisa [pito'nisa] nf fortune-teller

pitorreo [pito'reo] nm joke; **estar de ~** to be joking

piyama (LAm) [pi'jama] nm pyjamas pl (BRIT), pajamas pl (US)

pizarra [pi'θarra] nf (piedra) slate; (ESP: encerado) blackboard

pizarrón (LAm) nm blackboard

pizca ['piθka] nf pinch, spot; (fig) spot, speck; **ni ~** not a bit

placa ['plaka] nf plate; (distintivo) badge, insignia ▶ **placa de matrícula** (LAm) number plate

placard (RPl) [pla'kar] nm cupboard

placer [pla'θer] nm pleasure ♦ vt to please

plaga ['playa] nf pest; (MED) plague; (abundancia) abundance

plagio ['plaxjo] nm plagiarism

plan [plan] nm (esquema, proyecto) plan; (idea, intento) idea, intention; **tener un ~** (fam) to have a date; **tener un ~** (fam) to have an affair; **en ~ económico** (fam) on the cheap; **vamos en ~ de turismo** we're going as tourists; **si te pones en ese ~ ...** if that's your attitude ...

plana ['plana] nf sheet (of paper), page; (TEC) trowel; **en primera ~** on the front page

plancha ['plantʃa] nf (para planchar) iron; (rótulo) plate, sheet; (NÁUT) gangway; **a la ~** (CULIN) grilled ❏ **planchar** vt to iron ♦ vi to do the ironing

planear [plane'ar] vt to plan ♦ vi to glide

planeta [pla'neta] nm planet

plano, -a ['plano, a] adj flat, level, even ♦ nm (MAT, TEC) plane; (FOTO) shot; (ARQ) plan; (GEO) map; (de ciudad) map, street plan; **primer ~** close-up

planta ['planta] nf (BOT, TEC) plant; (ANAT) sole of the foot; (piso) floor; (LAm: personal) staff ▶ **planta baja** ground floor

plantar [plan'tar] vt (BOT) to plant; (levantar) to erect, set up; **plantarse** vr to stand firm; **~ a algn en la calle** to throw sb out; **dejar plantado a algn** (fam) to stand sb up

plantear [plante'ar] vt (problema) to pose; (dificultad) to raise

plantilla [plan'tiʎa] nf (de zapato) insole; (ESP: personal) personnel; **ser de ~** (ESP) to be on the staff

plantón [plan'ton] nm (MIL) guard, sentry; (fam) long wait; **dar (un) ~ a algn** to stand sb up

plasta ['plasta] (ESP: fam) adj inv boring ♦ nmf bore

plástico, -a ['plastiko, a] adj plastic ♦ nm plastic

Plastilina® [plasti'lina] nf Plasticine®

plata ['plata] nf (metal) silver; (cosas hechas de plata) silverware; (CS: dinero) cash, dough

plataforma [plata'forma] nf platform ▶ **plataforma de lanzamiento/ perforación** launch(ing) pad/drilling rig

plátano ['platano] nm (fruta) banana; (árbol) plane tree; banana tree

platea [pla'tea] nf (TEATRO) pit

plática ['platika] nf talk, chat ❏ **platicar** vi to talk, chat

platillo [pla'tiʎo] nm saucer; **platillos** nmpl (MÚS) cymbals ▶ **platillo volante** flying saucer

platino [pla'tino] nm platinum; **platinos** nmpl (AUTO) contact points

plato ['plato] nm plate, dish; (parte de comida) course; (comida) dish; **primer ~** first course ▶ **plato combinado** set main course (served on one plate) ▶ **plato fuerte** main course

playa ['plaja] nf beach; (costa) seaside ▶ **playa de estacionamiento** (CS) car park (BRIT), parking lot (US)

playera [pla'jera] nf (MÉX: camiseta) T-shirt; **playeras** nfpl (zapatos) canvas shoes

plaza ['plaθa] nf square; (mercado) market(place); (sitio) room, space; (de vehículo) seat, place; (colocación) post, job ▶ **plaza de toros** bullring

plazo ['plaθo] nm (lapso de tiempo) time, period; (fecha de vencimiento) expiry date; (pago parcial) instalment; **a corto/largo ~** short-/long-term; **comprar algo a plazos** to buy sth on hire purchase (BRIT) o on time (US)

plazoleta [plaθo'leta] nf small square

plebeyo, -a [ple'βejo, a] adj plebeian; (pey) coarse, common

plegable [ple'ɣaβle] adj collapsible; (silla) folding

pleito ['pleito] nm (JUR) lawsuit, case; (fig) dispute, feud

plenitud [pleni'tuð] nf plenitude, fullness; (abundancia) abundance

pleno, -a ['pleno, a] adj full; (completo) complete ♦ nm plenum; **en ~ día** in broad daylight; **en ~ verano** at the height of summer; **en plena cara** full in the face

pliego etc ['pljeɣo] nm (hoja) sheet (of paper); (carta) sealed letter/document ▶ **pliego de condiciones** details pl, specifications pl

pliegue etc ['pljeɣe] nm fold, crease; (de vestido) pleat

plomería (LAm) nf plumbing ❏ **plomero** [plo'mero] (LAm) nm plumber

plomo ['plomo] nm (metal) lead; (ELEC) fuse; **sin ~** unleaded

pluma ['pluma] nf feather; (para escribir) ~; **(estilográfica)** ink pen; **~ fuente** (LAm) fountain pen

plumero [plu'mero] nm (para el polvo) feather duster

plumón [plu'mon] nm (de ave) down

plural [plu'ral] adj plural

pluriempleo [pluriem'pleo] nm having more than one job

plus [plus] nm bonus

población [poβla'θjon] nf population; (pueblo, ciudad) town, city

poblado, -a [po'βlaðo, a] adj inhabited ♦ nm (aldea) village; (pueblo) (small) town; **densamente ~** densely populated

poblador, a [poβla'ðor, a] nm/f settler, colonist

pobre ['poβre] adj poor ♦ nmf poor person ❏ **pobreza** nf poverty

pocilga [po'θilɣa] nf pigsty

poco, -a

PALABRA CLAVE

[ˈpoko, a] *adj*

1 (*sg*) little, not much; **poco tiempo** little *o* not much time; **de poco interés** of little interest, not very interesting; **poca cosa** not much

2 (*pl*) few, not many; **unos pocos** a few, some; **pocos niños comen lo que les conviene** few children eat what they should

♦ *adv*

1 little, not much; **cuesta poco** it doesn't cost much

2 (+ *adj: negativo, antónimo*): **poco amable/inteligente** not very nice/intelligent

3 **por poco me caigo** I almost fell

4 **a poco: a poco de haberse casado** shortly after getting married

5 **poco a poco** little by little

♦ *nm* a little, a bit; **un poco triste/de dinero** a little sad/money

podar [poˈðar] *vt* to prune

poder

PALABRA CLAVE

[poˈðer] *vi*

1 (*tener capacidad*) can, be able to; **no puedo hacerlo** I can't do it, I'm unable to do it

2 (*tener permiso*) can, may, be allowed to; **¿se puede?** may I (o we)?; **puedes irte ahora** you may go now; **no se puede fumar en este hospital** smoking is not allowed in this hospital

3 (*tener posibilidad*) may, might, could; **puede llegar mañana** he may *o* might arrive tomorrow; **pudiste haberte hecho daño** you might *o* could have hurt yourself; **podías**

habérmelo dicho antes! you might have told me before!

4: **puede ser: puede ser** perhaps; **puede ser que lo sepa Tomás** Tomás may *o* might know

5: **¡no puedo más!** I've had enough!; **es tonto a más no poder** he's as stupid as they come

6: **poder con: no puedo con este crío** this kid's too much for me

♦ *nm* power; **detentar** *o* **ocupar** *o* **estar en el poder** to be in power

▶ **poder adquisitivo/ejecutivo/ legislativo** purchasing/executive/ legislative power ▶ **poder judicial** judiciary

poderoso, -a [poðeˈroso, a] *adj* (*político, país*) powerful

podio [ˈpoðjo] *nm* (*DEPORTE*) podium

podium [ˈpoðjum] = **podio**

podrido, -a [poˈðriðo, a] *adj* rotten, bad; (*fig*) rotten, corrupt

podrir [poˈðrir] = **pudrir**

poema [poˈema] *nm* poem

poesía [poeˈsia] *nf* poetry

poeta [poˈeta] *nmf* poet ❑ **poético, -a** *adj* poetic(al)

poetisa [poeˈtisa] *nf* (woman) poet

póker [ˈpoker] *nm* poker

polaco, -a [poˈlako, a] *adj* Polish ♦ *nm/f* Pole

polar [poˈlar] *adj* polar

polea [poˈlea] *nf* pulley

polémica [poˈlemika] *nf* polemics *sg*; (*una polémica*) controversy, polemic

polen [ˈpolen] *nm* pollen

policía [poliˈθia] *nmf* policeman/ woman ♦ *nf* police ❑ **policíaco, -a** *adj* police cpd; **novela policíaca** detective story ❑ **policial** *adj* police cpd

polideportivo [poliðeporˈtiβo] *nm* sports centre *o* complex

polígono [po'liɣono] nm (MAT) polygon ▶ **polígono industrial** (ESP) industrial estate

polilla [po'liʎa] nf moth

polio ['poljo] nf polio

política [po'litika] nf politics sg; (económica, agraria etc) policy; ver tb **político**

político, -a [po'litiko, a] adj political; (discreto) tactful; (de familia) -in-law ♦ nm/f politician; **padre ~** father-in-law

póliza ['poliθa] nf certificate, voucher; (impuesto) tax stamp ▶ **póliza de seguro(s)** insurance policy

polizón [poli'θon] nm stowaway

pollera [po'ʎera] (CS) nf skirt

pollo ['poʎo] nm chicken

polo ['polo] nm (GEO, ELEC) pole; (helado) ice lolly (BRIT), Popsicle® (US); (DEPORTE) polo; (suéter) polo-neck ▶ **polo Norte/Sur** North/South Pole

Polonia [po'lonja] nf Poland

poltrona [pol'trona] nf easy chair

polución [polu'θjon] nf pollution

polvera [pol'βera] nf powder compact

polvo ['polβo] nm dust; (QUÍM, CULIN, MED) powder; **polvos** nmpl (maquillaje) powder sg; **en ~** powdered; **quitar el ~** to dust; **estar hecho ~** (fam) to be worn out o exhausted ▶ **polvos de talco** talcum powder sg

pólvora ['polβora] nf gunpowder

polvoriento, -a [polβo'rjento, a] adj (superficie) dusty; (sustancia) powdery

pomada [po'maða] nf cream, ointment

pomelo [po'melo] nm grapefruit

pómez ['pomeθ] nf: **piedra ~** pumice stone

pomo ['pomo] nm doorknob

pompa ['pompa] nf (burbuja) bubble; (bomba) pump; (esplendor) pomp, splendour

pómulo ['pomulo] nm cheekbone

pon [pon] vb ver **poner**

ponchadura (MÉX) nf puncture (BRIT), flat (US) ❑ **ponchar** (MÉX) vt (llanta) to puncture

ponche ['pontʃe] nm punch

poncho ['pontʃo] nm poncho

pondré etc [pon'dre] vb ver **poner**

poner

PALABRA CLAVE

[po'ner] vt

1 (colocar) to put; (telegrama) to send; (obra de teatro) to put on; (película) to show; **ponlo más fuerte** turn it up; **¿qué ponen en el Excelsior?** what's on at the Excelsior?

2 (tienda) to open; (instalar: gas etc) to put in; (radio, TV) to switch o turn on

3 (suponer): **pongamos que ...** let's suppose that ...

4 (contribuir): **el gobierno ha puesto otro millón** the government has contributed another million

5 (TEL): **póngame con el Sr. López** can you put me through to Mr. López?

6: **poner de: le han puesto de director general** they've appointed him general manager

7 (+ adj) to make; **me estás poniendo nerviosa** you're making me nervous

8 (dar nombre): **al hijo le pusieron Diego** they called their son Diego ♦ vi (gallina) to lay

♦ **ponerse** vr

1 (colocarse): **se puso a mi lado** he came and stood beside me; **tú ponte en esa silla** you go and sit on that chair

2 (vestido, cosméticos) to put on; **¿por qué no te pones el vestido nuevo?** why don't you put on o wear your

new dress?
3 + adj, to turn; to get, become; **se puso muy serio** he got very serious; **después de lavarla la tela se puso azul** after washing it the material turned blue
4: **ponerse a: se puso a llorar** he started to cry; **tienes que ponerte a estudiar** you must get down to studying

pongo etc ['pongo] vb ver **poner**

poniente [po'njente] nm (occidente) west; (viento) west wind

pontífice [pon'tifiθe] nm pope, pontiff

popa ['popa] nf stern

popote (MEX) nm straw

popular [popu'lar] adj popular; (cultura) of the people, folk cpd
❏ **popularidad** nf popularity

por
PALABRA CLAVE

[por] prep
1 (objetivo) for; **luchar por la patria** to fight for one's country
2 (+ infin): **por no llegar tarde** so as not to arrive late; **por citar unos ejemplos** to give a few examples
3 (causa) out of, because of; **por escasez de fondos** through o for lack of funds
4 (tiempo): **por la mañana/noche** in the morning/at night; **se queda por una semana** she's staying (for) a week
5 (lugar): **pasar por Madrid** to pass through Madrid; **ir a Guayaquil por Quito** to go to Guayaquil via Quito; **caminar por la calle** to walk along the street; **ver tb todo**
6 (cambio, precio): **te doy uno nuevo por el que tienes** I'll give you a new one (in return) for the one you've got

7 (valor distributivo): **6 euros por hora/cabeza** 6 euros an o per hour/a o per head
8 (modo, medio) by; **por correo/avión** by post/air; **entrar por la entrada principal** to go in through the main entrance
9: **10 por 10 son 100** 10 times 10 is 100
10 (en lugar de): **vino él por su jefe** he came instead of his boss
11: **por mí que revienten** as far as I'm concerned they can drop dead
12: **¿por qué?** why?; **¿por qué no?** why not?

porcelana [porθe'lana] nf porcelain; (china) china

porcentaje [porθen'taxe] nm percentage

porción [por'θjon] nf (parte) portion, share; (cantidad) quantity, amount

porfiar [por'fjar] vi to persist, insist; (disputar) to argue stubbornly

pormenor [porme'nor] nm detail, particular

pornografía [pornoɣra'fia] nf pornography

poro ['poro] nm pore

pororó (RPI) nm popcorn

poroso, -a [po'roso, a] adj porous

poroto (CS) [po'roto] nm bean

porque ['porke] conj (a causa de) because; (ya que) since; (con el fin de) so that, in order that

porqué [por'ke] nm reason, cause

porquería [porke'ria] nf (suciedad) filth, dirt; (acción) dirty trick; (objeto) small thing, trifle; (fig) rubbish

porra ['porra] (ESP) nf (arma) stick, club

porrazo [po'rraθo] nm blow, bump

porro ['porro] (fam) nm (droga) joint (fam)

porrón [po'rron] nm glass wine jar with a long spout

portaaviones [porta(a)βjones] nm inv aircraft carrier

portada [por'taða] nf (de revista) cover

portador, a [porta'ðor, a] nm/f carrier, bearer; (COM) bearer, payee

portaequipajes [portaeki'paxes] nm inv (AUTO: maletero) boot; (: baca) luggage rack

portafolio (LAm) [porta'foljo] nm briefcase

portal [por'tal] nm (entrada) vestibule, hall; (portada) porch, doorway; (puerta de entrada) main door; (INTERNET) portal; **portales** nmpl (LAm) arcade sg

portamaletas [portama'letas] nm inv (AUTO: maletero) boot; (: baca) roof rack

portarse [por'tarse] vr to behave, conduct o.s.

portátil [por'tatil] adj portable

portavoz [porta'βoθ] nmf spokesman/woman

portazo [por'taθo] nm: **dar un ~** to slam the door

porte ['porte] nm (COM) transport; (precio) transport charges pl

portentoso, -a [porten'toso, a] adj marvellous, extraordinary

porteño, -a [por'teɲo, a] adj of o from Buenos Aires

portería [porte'ria] nf (oficina) porter's office; (DEPORTE) goal

portero, -a [por'tero, a] nm/f porter; (conserje) caretaker; (ujier) doorman; (DEPORTE) goalkeeper ♦ **portero automático** (ESP) entry phone

pórtico ['portiko] nm (patio) portico, porch; (fig) gateway; (arcada) arcade

portorriqueño, -a [portorri'keɲo, a] adj Puerto Rican

Portugal [portu'yal] nm Portugal
❏ **portugués, -esa** adj, nm/f Portuguese ♦ nm (LING) Portuguese

porvenir [porβe'nir] nm future

pos [pos] prep: **en ~ de** after, in pursuit of

posaderas [posa'ðeras] nfpl backside sg, buttocks

posar [po'sar] vt (en el suelo) to lay down, put down; (la mano) to place, put gently ♦ vi (modelo) to sit, pose; **posarse** vr to settle; (pájaro) to perch; (avión) to land, come down

posavasos [posa'βasos] nm inv coaster; (para cerveza) beermat

posdata [pos'ðata] nf postscript

pose ['pose] nf pose

poseedor, a [posee'ðor, a] nm/f owner, possessor; (de récord, puesto) holder

poseer [pose'er] vt to possess, own; (ventaja) to enjoy; (récord, puesto) to hold

posesivo, -a [pose'siβo, a] adj possessive

posgrado [pos'yraðo] nm: **curso de ~** postgraduate course

posibilidad [posiβili'ðað] nf possibility; (oportunidad) chance
❏ **posibilitar** vt to make possible; (hacer realizable) to make feasible

posible [po'siβle] adj possible; (realizable) feasible; **de ser ~** if possible; **en lo ~** as far as possible

posición [posi'θjon] nf position; (rango social) status

positivo, -a [posi'tiβo, a] adj positive

poso ['poso] nm sediment; (heces) dregs pl

posponer [pospo'ner] vt (relegar) to put behind/below; (aplazar) to postpone

posta ['posta] nf: **a ~** deliberately, on purpose

postal [pos'tal] adj postal ♦ nf postcard

poste ['poste] nm (de telégrafos etc) post, pole; (columna) pillar

póster ['poster] (pl **pósteres, pósters**) nm poster

posterior [poste'rjor] adj back, rear; (siguiente) following, subsequent; (más tarde) later

postgrado [pos'tɣraðo] nm = **posgrado**

postizo, -a [pos'tiθo, a] adj false, artificial ♦ nm hairpiece

postre ['postre] nm sweet, dessert

póstumo, -a ['postumo, a] adj posthumous

postura [pos'tura] nf (del cuerpo) posture, position; (fig) attitude, position

potable [po'taβle] adj drinkable; **agua ~** drinking water

potaje [po'taxe] nm thick vegetable soup

potencia [po'tenθja] nf power ❑ **potencial** [poten'θjal] adj, nm potential

potente [po'tente] adj powerful

potro, -a ['potro, a] nm/f (ZOOL) colt/ filly ♦ nm (de gimnasia) vaulting horse

pozo ['poθo] nm well; (de río) deep pool; (de mina) shaft

PP (ESP) nm abr = **Partido Popular**

práctica ['praktika] nf practice; (método) method; (arte, capacidad) skill; **en la ~** in practice

practicable [prakti'kaβle] adj practicable; (camino) passable

practicante [prakti'kante] nmf (MED: ayudante de doctor) medical assistant; (: enfermero) nurse; (quien practica algo) practitioner ♦ adj practising

practicar [prakti'kar] vt to practise; (DEPORTE) to play; (realizar) to carry out, perform

práctico, -a ['praktiko, a] adj practical; (instruido: persona) skilled, expert

practique etc [prak'tike] vb ver **practicar**

pradera [pra'ðera] nf meadow; (US etc) prairie

prado ['praðo] nm (campo) meadow, field; (pastizal) pasture

Praga ['praɣa] n Prague

pragmático, -a [praɣ'matiko, a] adj pragmatic

precario, -a [pre'karjo, a] adj precarious

precaución [prekau'θjon] nf (medida preventiva) preventive measure, precaution; (prudencia) caution, wariness

precedente [preθe'ðente] adj preceding; (anterior) former ♦ nm precedent

preceder [preθe'ðer] vt, vi to precede, go before, come before

precepto [pre'θepto] nm precept

precinto [pre'θinto] nm (tb: ~ de garantía) seal

precio ['preθjo] nm price; (costo) cost; (valor) value, worth; (de viaje) fare
  ▶ **precio al contado/de coste/de oportunidad** cash/cost/bargain price
  ▶ **precio al por menor** retail price
  ▶ **precio de ocasión** bargain price
  ▶ **precio de venta al público** retail price ▶ **precio tope** top price

preciosidad [preθjosi'ðað] nf (valor) (high) value, (great) worth; (encanto) charm; (cosa bonita) beautiful thing; **es una ~** it's lovely, it's really beautiful

precioso, -a [pre'θjoso, a] adj precious; (de mucho valor) valuable; (fam) lovely, beautiful

precipicio [preθi'piθjo] nm cliff, precipice; (fig) abyss

precipitación [preθipita'θjon] nf haste; (lluvia) rainfall

precipitado, -a [preθipi'taðo, a] adj (conducta) hasty, rash; (salida) hasty, sudden

precipitar [preθipi'tar] vt (arrojar) to hurl down, throw; (apresurar) to hasten; (acelerar) to speed up, accelerate; **precipitarse** vr to throw o.s.; (apresurarse) to rush; (actuar sin pensar) to act rashly

precisamente [preθisa'mente] adv precisely; (exactamente) precisely, exactly

precisar [preθi'sar] vt (*necesitar*) to need, require; (*fijar*) to determine exactly, fix; (*especificar*) to specify

precisión [preθi'sjon] nf (*exactitud*) precision

preciso, -a [pre'θiso, a] adj (*exacto*) precise; (*necesario*) necessary, essential

preconcebido, -a [prekonθe'βiðo, a] adj preconceived

precoz [pre'koθ] adj (*persona*) precocious; (*calvicie etc*) premature

predecir [preðe'θir] vt to predict, forecast

predestinado, -a [preðesti'naðo, a] adj predestined

predicar [preði'kar] vt, vi to preach

predicción [preðik'θjon] nf prediction

predilecto, -a [preði'lekto, a] adj favourite

predisposición [preðisposi'θjon] nf inclination; prejudice; bias

predominar [preðomi'nar] vt to dominate ♦ vi to predominate; (*prevalecer*) to prevail ♦ **predominio** nm predominance; prevalence

preescolar [pree(s)ko'lar] adj preschool

prefabricado, -a [prefaβri'kaðo, a] adj prefabricated

prefacio [pre'faθjo] nm preface

preferencia [prefe'renθja] nf preference; **de ~** preferably, for preference

preferible [prefe'riβle] adj preferable

preferir [prefe'rir] vt to prefer

prefiero etc vb ver **preferir**

prefijo [pre'fixo] nm (TEL) (dialling) code

pregunta [pre'ɣunta] nf question; **hacer una ~** to ask a question ▶ **preguntas frecuentes** FAQs, frequently asked questions ❑ **preguntar** [preɣun'tar] vt to ask; (*cuestionar*) to question ♦ vi to ask; **preguntarse** vr to wonder; **preguntar**

por algn to ask for sb ❑ **preguntón, -ona** [preɣun'ton, ona] adj inquisitive

prehistórico, -a [preis'toriko, a] adj prehistoric

prejuicio [pre'xwiθjo] nm (*acto*) prejudgement; (*idea preconcebida*) preconception; (*parcialidad*) prejudice, bias

preludio [pre'luðjo] nm prelude

prematuro, -a [prema'turo, a] adj premature

premeditar [premeði'tar] vt to premeditate

premiar [pre'mjar] vt to reward; (*en un concurso*) to give a prize to

premio ['premjo] nm reward; prize; (COM) premium

prenatal [prena'tal] adj antenatal, prenatal

prenda ['prenda] nf (*ropa*) garment, article of clothing; (*garantía*) pledge; **prendas** nfpl (*talentos*) talents, gifts

prender [pren'der] vt (*captar*) to catch, capture; (*detener*) to arrest; (COSTURA) to pin, attach; (*sujetar*) to fasten ♦ vi to catch; (*arraigar*) to take root; **prenderse** vr (*encenderse*) to catch fire

prendido, -a [pren'diðo, a] (LAm) adj (*luz etc*) on

prensa ['prensa] nf press; **la ~** the press

preñado, -a [pre'ɲaðo, a] adj pregnant; **~ de** pregnant with, full of

preocupación [preokupa'θjon] nf worry, concern; (*ansiedad*) anxiety

preocupado, -a [preoku'paðo, a] adj worried, concerned; (*ansioso*) anxious

preocupar [preoku'par] vt to worry; **preocuparse** vr to worry; **preocuparse de algo** (*hacerse cargo*) to take care of sth

preparación [prepara'θjon] nf (*acto*) preparation; (*estado*) readiness; (*entrenamiento*) training

preparado, -a [prepa'raðo, a] adj (*dispuesto*) prepared; (CULIN) ready (to serve) ♦ nm preparation

preparar [prepa'rar] vt (disponer) to prepare, get ready; (TEC: tratar) to prepare, process; (entrenar) to teach, train; **prepararse** vr: **prepararse a** o **para** to prepare to o for, get ready to o for □ **preparativo, -a** adj preparatory, preliminary □ **preparativos** nmpl preparations □ **preparatoria** (MEX) nf sixth-form college (BRIT), high school (US)

presa ['presa] nf (cosa apresada) catch; (víctima) victim; (de animal) prey; (de agua) dam

presagiar [presa'xjar] vt to presage, forebode □ **presagio** nm omen

prescindir [presθin'dir] vi: **~ de** (privarse de) to do o go without; (descartar) to dispense with

prescribir [preskri'βir] vt to prescribe

presencia [pre'senθja] nf presence □ **presenciar** vt to be present at; (asistir a) to attend; (ver) to see, witness

presentación [presenta'θjon] nf presentation; (introducción) introduction

presentador, a [presenta'ðor, a] nm/f presenter, compère

presentar [presen'tar] vt to present; (ofrecer) to offer; (mostrar) to show, display; (a una persona) to introduce; **presentarse** vr (llegar inesperadamente) to appear, turn up; (ofrecerse: como candidato) to run, stand; (aparecer) to show, appear; (solicitar empleo) to apply

presente [pre'sente] adj present ♦ nm present; **hacer ~** to state, declare; **tener ~** to remember, bear in mind

presentimiento [presenti'mjento] nm premonition, presentiment

presentir [presen'tir] vt to have a premonition of

preservación [preserβa'θjon] nf protection, preservation

preservar [preser'βar] vt to protect, preserve □ **preservativo** nm sheath, condom

presidencia [presi'ðenθja] nf presidency; (de comité) chairmanship

presidente [presi'ðente] nm/f president; (de comité) chairman/ woman

presidir [presi'ðir] vt (dirigir) to preside at, preside over; (: comité) to take the chair at; (dominar) to dominate, rule ♦ vi to preside; to take the chair

presión [pre'sjon] nf pressure ▶ **presión atmosférica** atmospheric o air pressure □ **presionar** vt to press; (fig) to press, put pressure on ♦ vi: **presionar para** to press for

preso, -a ['preso, a] nm/f prisoner; **tomar** o **llevar ~ a algn** to arrest sb, take sb prisoner

prestación [presta'θjon] nf service; (subsidio) benefit □ **prestaciones** nfpl (TEC, AUTO) performance features

prestado, -a [pres'taðo, a] adj on loan; **pedir ~** to borrow

prestamista [presta'mista] nmf moneylender

préstamo ['prestamo] nm loan ▶ **préstamo hipotecario** mortgage

prestar [pres'tar] vt to lend, loan; (atención) to pay; (ayuda) to give

prestigio [pres'tixjo] nm prestige □ **prestigioso, -a** adj (honorable) prestigious; (famoso, renombrado) renowned, famous

presumido, -a [presu'miðo, a] adj (persona) vain

presumir [presu'mir] vt to presume ♦ vi (tener aires) to be conceited □ **presunto, -a** adj (supuesto) supposed, presumed; (así llamado) so-called □ **presuntuoso, -a** adj conceited, presumptuous

presupuesto [presu'pwesto] pp de **presuponer** ♦ nm (FINANZAS) budget; (estimación: de costo) estimate

pretencioso, -a [preten'θjoso, a] adj
pretentious

pretender [preten'der] vt (intentar) to
try to, seek to; (reivindicar) to claim;
(buscar) to seek, try for; (cortejar) to
woo, court; **~ que** to expect that
❑ **pretendiente** nmf (amante) suitor;
(al trono) pretender; **pretensión** nf
(aspiración) aspiration; (reivindicación)
claim; (orgullo) pretension

⚠ No confundir **pretender** con la
palabra inglesa *pretend*.

pretexto [pre'teksto] nm pretext;
(excusa) excuse

prevención [preβen'θjon] nf
prevention; (precaución) precaution

prevenido, -a [preβe'niðo, a] adj
prepared, ready; (cauteloso) cautious

prevenir [preβe'nir] vt (impedir) to
prevent; (predisponer) to prejudice,
bias; (avisar) to warn; (preparar) to
prepare, get ready; **prevenirse** vr to
get ready, prepare; **prevenirse contra**
to take precautions against
❑ **preventivo, -a** adj preventive,
precautionary

prever [pre'βer] vt to foresee

previo, -a ['preβjo, a] adj (anterior)
previous; (preliminar) preliminary
♦ prep: **~ acuerdo de los otros** subject
to the agreement of the others

previsión [preβi'sjon] nf (perspicacia)
foresight; (predicción) forecast
❑ **previsto, -a** adj anticipated,
forecast

prima ['prima] nf (COM) bonus; (de
seguro) premium; ver tb **primo**

primario, -a [pri'marjo, a] adj primary

primavera [prima'βera] nf spring(-
time)

primera [pri'mera] nf (AUTO) first gear;
(FERRO: tb: **~ clase**) first class; **de ~** (fam)
first-class, first-rate

primero, -a [pri'mero, a] (delante de
nmsg **primer**) adj first; (principal) prime

♦ adv first; (más bien) sooner, rather
▶ **primera plana** front page

primitivo, -a [primi'tiβo, a] adj
primitive; (original) original

primo, -a ['primo, a] adj prime ♦ nm/f
cousin; (fam) fool, idiot; **materias
primas** raw materials ▶ **primo
hermano** first cousin

primogénito, -a [primo'xenito, a] adj
first-born

primoroso, -a [primo'roso, a] adj
exquisite, delicate

princesa [prin'θesa] nf princess

principal [prinθi'pal] adj principal,
main ♦ nm (jefe) chief, principal

príncipe ['prinθipe] nm prince

principiante [prinθi'pjante] nmf
beginner

principio [prin'θipjo] nm (comienzo)
beginning, start; (origen) origin;
(primera instancia) rudiment, basic idea;
(moral) principle; **desde el ~** from the
first; **en un ~** at first; **a principios de** at
the beginning of

pringue ['pringe] nm (grasa) grease,
fat, dripping

prioridad [priori'ðað] nf priority

prisa ['prisa] nf (apresuramiento) hurry,
haste; (rapidez) speed; (urgencia)
(sense of) urgency; **a o de ~** quickly;
correr ~ to be urgent; **darse ~** to hurry
up; **tener ~** to be in a hurry

prisión [pri'sjon] nf (cárcel) prison;
(período de cárcel) imprisonment
❑ **prisionero, -a** nm/f prisoner

prismáticos [pris'matikos] nmpl
binoculars

privado, -a [pri'βaðo, a] adj private

privar [pri'βar] vt to deprive
❑ **privativo, -a** adj exclusive

privilegiar [priβile'xjar] vt to grant a
privilege to; (favorecer) to favour

privilegio [priβi'lexjo] nm privilege;
(concesión) concession

pro [pro] nm o f profit, advantage
♦ prep: **asociación ~ ciegos** association

for the blind ♦ *prefijo*: ~ **americano**
pro-American; **en** ~ **de** on behalf of,
for; **los pros y los contras** the pros and
cons

proa ['proa] *nf* bow, prow; **de** ~ bow
cpd, fore

probabilidad [proβaβili'ðað] *nf*
probability, likelihood; (*oportunidad,
posibilidad*) chance, prospect
❏ **probable** *adj* probable, likely

probador [proβa'ðor] *nm* (*en tienda*)
fitting room

probar [pro'βar] *vt* (*demostrar*) to
prove; (*someter a prueba*) to test, try
out; (*ropa*) to try on; (*comida*) to taste
♦ *vi* to try; **probarse un traje** to try on a
suit

probeta [pro'βeta] *nf* test tube

problema [pro'βlema] *nm* problem

procedente [proθe'ðente] *adj*
(*razonable*) reasonable; (*conforme a
derecho*) proper, fitting; ~ **de** coming
from, originating in

proceder [proθe'ðer] *vi* (*avanzar*) to
proceed; (*actuar*) to act; (*ser correcto*)
to be right (and proper), be fitting
♦ *nm* (*comportamiento*) behaviour,
conduct; ~ **de** to come from, originate
in ❏ **procedimiento** *nm* procedure;
(*proceso*) process; (*método*) means *pl*,
method

procesador [proθesa'ðor] *nm*
processor ▶ **procesador de textos**
word processor

procesar [proθe'sar] *vt* to try, put on
trial

procesión [proθe'sjon] *nf* procession

proceso [pro'θeso] *nm* process; (*JUR*)
trial

proclamar [prokla'mar] *vt* to proclaim

procrear [prokre'ar] *vt, vi* to procreate

procurador, a [prokura'ðor, a] *nm/f*
attorney

procurar [proku'rar] *vt* (*intentar*) to try,
endeavour; (*conseguir*) to get, obtain;

(*asegurar*) to secure; (*producir*) to
produce

prodigio [pro'ðixjo] *nm* prodigy;
(*milagro*) wonder, marvel
❏ **prodigioso, -a** *adj* prodigious,
marvellous

pródigo, -a ['proðiyo, a] *adj*: **hijo** ~
prodigal son

producción [proðuk'θjon] *nf* (*gen*)
production; (*producir*) output
▶ **producción en serie** mass
production

producir [proðu'θir] *vt* to produce;
(*causar*) to cause, bring about;
producirse *vr* (*cambio*) to come about;
(*accidente*) to take place; (*problema etc*)
to arise; (*hacerse*) to be produced, be
made; (*estallar*) to break out

productividad [proðuktiβi'ðað] *nf*
productivity ❏ **productivo, -a** *adj*
productive; (*provechoso*) profitable

producto [pro'ðukto] *nm* product

productor, a [proðuk'tor, a] *adj*
productive, producing ♦ *nm/f*
producer

proeza [pro'eθa] *nf* exploit, feat

profano, -a [pro'fano, a] *adj* profane
♦ *nm/f* layman/woman

profecía [profe'θia] *nf* prophecy

profesión [profe'sjon] *nf* profession;
(*en formulario*) occupation
❏ **profesional** *adj* professional

profesor, a [profe'sor, a] *nm/f* teacher
❏ **profesorado** *nm* teaching
profession

profeta [pro'feta] *nmf* prophet

prófugo, -a ['profuyo, a] *nm/f* fugitive;
(*MIL: desertor*) deserter

profundidad [profundi'ðað] *nf* depth
❏ **profundizar** *vi*: **profundizar en** to
go deeply into ❏ **profundo, -a** *adj*
deep; (*misterio, pensador*) profound

progenitor [proxeni'tor] *nm* ancestor;
progenitores *nmpl* (*padres*) parents

programa [pro'yrama] *nm*
programme (*BRIT*), program (*US*);

► **programa de estudios** curriculum, syllabus

❏ **programación** nf programming

❏ **programador, a** nm/f programmer ❏ **programar** vt to program

progresar [proɣreˈsar] vi to progress, make progress ❏ **progresista** adj, nmf progressive ❏ **progresivo, -a** adj progressive; (gradual) gradual; (continuo) continuous ❏ **progreso** nm progress

prohibición [proiβiˈθjon] nf prohibition, ban

prohibir [proiˈβir] vt to prohibit, ban, forbid; **prohibido** o **se prohibe fumar** no smoking; **"prohibido el paso"** "no entry"

prójimo, -a [ˈproximo, a] nm/f fellow man; (vecino) neighbour

prólogo [ˈproloɣo] nm prologue

prolongar [prolonˈɣar] vt to extend; (reunión etc) to prolong; (calle, tubo) to extend

promedio [proˈmeðjo] nm average; (de distancia) middle, mid-point

promesa [proˈmesa] nf promise

prometer [promeˈter] vt to promise ♦ vi to show promise; **prometerse** vr (novios) to get engaged ❏ **prometido, -a** adj promised; engaged ♦ nm/f fiancé/fiancée

prominente [promiˈnente] adj prominent

promoción [promoˈθjon] nf promotion

promotor [promoˈtor] nm promoter; (instigador) instigator

promover [promoˈβer] vt to promote; (causar) to cause; (instigar) to instigate, stir up

promulgar [promulˈɣar] vt to promulgate; (anunciar) to proclaim

pronombre [proˈnombre] nm pronoun

pronosticar [pronostiˈkar] vt to predict, foretell, forecast ❏ **pronóstico** nm prediction, forecast ► **pronóstico del tiempo** weather forecast

pronto, -a [ˈpronto, a] adj (rápido) prompt, quick; (preparado) ready ♦ adv quickly, promptly; (en seguida) at once, right away; (dentro de poco) soon; (temprano) early ♦ nm: **tiene unos prontos muy malos** he gets ratty all of a sudden (inf); **de ~** suddenly; **por lo ~** meanwhile, for the present

pronunciación [pronunθjaˈθjon] nf pronunciation

pronunciar [pronunˈθjar] vt to pronounce; (discurso) to make, deliver; **pronunciarse** vr to revolt, rebel; (declararse) to declare o.s.

propagación [propaɣaˈθjon] nf propagation

propaganda [propaˈɣanda] nf (POL) propaganda; (COM) advertising

propenso, -a [proˈpenso, a] adj inclined to; **ser ~ a** to be inclined to, have a tendency to

propicio, -a [proˈpiθjo, a] adj favourable, propitious

propiedad [propjeˈðað] nf property; (posesión) possession, ownership ► **propiedad particular** private property

propietario, -a [propjeˈtarjo, a] nm/f owner, proprietor

propina [proˈpina] nf tip

propio, -a [ˈpropjo, a] adj own, of one's own; (característico) characteristic, typical; (debido) proper; (mismo) selfsame, very; **el ~ ministro** the minister himself; **¿tienes casa propia?** have you a house of your own?

proponer [proponˈner] vt to propose, put forward; (problema) to pose; **proponerse** vr to propose, intend

proporción [proporˈθjon] nf proportion; (MAT) ratio; **proporciones**

nfpl (*dimensiones*) dimensions; (*fig*) size *sg* ❑ **proporcionado, -a** *adj* proportionate; (*regular*) medium, middling; (*justo*) just right
▶ **proporcionar** *vt* (*dar*) to give, supply; provide

proposición [proposi'θjon] *nf* proposition; (*propuesta*) proposal

propósito [pro'posito] *nm* purpose; (*intento*) aim, intention ♦ *adv*: **a ~** by the way, incidentally; (*a posta*) on purpose, deliberately; **a ~ de** about, with regard to

propuesta [pro'pwesta] *vb ver* **proponer** ♦ *nf* proposal

propulsar [propul'sar] *vt* to drive, propel; (*fig*) to promote, encourage ❑ **propulsión** *nf* propulsion
▶ **propulsión a chorro o por reacción** jet propulsion

prórroga ['prorroɣa] *nf* extension; (*JUR*) stay; (*COM*) deferment; (*DEPORTE*) extra time ❑ **prorrogar** *vt* (*período*) to extend; (*decisión*) to defer, postpone

prosa ['prosa] *nf* prose

proseguir [prose'ɣir] *vt* to continue, carry on ♦ *vi* to continue, go on

prospecto [pros'pekto] *nm* prospectus

prosperar [prospe'rar] *vi* to prosper, thrive, flourish ❑ **prosperidad** *nf* prosperity; (*éxito*) success
❑ **próspero, -a** *adj* prosperous, flourishing; (*que tiene éxito*) successful

prostíbulo [pros'tiβulo] *nm* brothel (*BRIT*), house of prostitution (*US*)

prostitución [prostitu'θjon] *nf* prostitution

prostituir [prosti'twir] *vt* to prostitute; **prostituirse** *vr* to prostitute o.s., become a prostitute

prostituta [prosti'tuta] *nf* prostitute

protagonista [protaɣo'nista] *nmf* protagonist

protección [protek'θjon] *nf* protection

protector, a [protek'tor, a] *adj* protective, protecting ♦ *nm/f* protector

proteger [prote'xer] *vt* to protect ❑ **protegido, -a** *nm/f* protégé/ protégée

proteína [prote'ina] *nf* protein

protesta [pro'testa] *nf* protest; (*declaración*) protestation

protestante [protes'tante] *adj* Protestant

protestar [protes'tar] *vt* to protest, declare ♦ *vi* to protest

protocolo [proto'kolo] *nm* protocol

prototipo [proto'tipo] *nm* prototype

provecho [pro'βetʃo] *nm* advantage, benefit; (*FINANZAS*) profit; **¡buen ~!** bon appétit!; **en ~ de** to the benefit of; **sacar ~ de** to benefit from, profit by

provenir [proβe'nir] *vi*: **~ de** to come o stem from

proverbio [pro'βerβjo] *nm* proverb

providencia [proβi'ðenθja] *nf* providence

provincia [pro'βinθja] *nf* province

provisión [proβi'sjon] *nf* provision; (*abastecimiento*) provision, supply; (*medida*) measure, step

provisional [proβisjo'nal] *adj* provisional

provocar [proβo'kar] *vt* to provoke; (*alentar*) to tempt, invite; (*causar*) to bring about, lead to; (*promover*) to promote; (*estimular*) to rouse, stimulate; **¿te provoca un café?** (*CAm*) would you like a coffee? ❑ **provocativo, -a** *adj* provocative

proxeneta [prokse'neta] *nm* pimp

próximamente [proksima'mente] *adv* shortly, soon

proximidad [proksimi'ðað] *nf* closeness, proximity ❑ **próximo, -a** *adj* near, close; (*vecino*) neighbouring; (*siguiente*) next

proyectar [projek'tar] vt (objeto) to hurl, throw; (luz) to cast, shed; (CINE) to screen, show; (planear) to plan

proyectil [projek'til] nm projectile, missile

proyecto [pro'jekto] nm plan; (estimación de costo) detailed estimate

proyector [projek'tor] nm (CINE) projector

prudencia [pru'ðenθja] nf (sabiduría) wisdom; (cuidado) care ❑ **prudente** adj sensible, wise; (conductor) careful

prueba etc ['prweβa] vb ver **probar ♦** nf proof; (ensayo) test, trial; (degustación) tasting, sampling; (de ropa) fitting; **a ~** on trial; **a ~ de** proof against; **a ~ de agua/fuego** waterproof/fireproof; **someter a ~** to put to the test

psico... [siko] prefijo psycho...
❑ **psicología** nf psychology
❑ **psicológico, -a** adj psychological
❑ **psicólogo, -a** nm/f psychologist
❑ **psicópata** nmf psychopath
❑ **psicosis** nf inv psychosis

psiquiatra [si'kjatra] nmf psychiatrist
❑ **psiquiátrico, -a** adj psychiatric

PSOE [pe'soe] nm abr = **Partido Socialista Obrero Español**

púa ['pua] nf (BOT, ZOOL) prickle, spine; (para guitarra) plectrum (BRIT), pick (US); **alambre de ~** barbed wire

pubertad [puβer'tað] nf puberty

publicación [puβlika'θjon] nf publication

publicar [puβli'kar] vt (editar) to publish; (hacer público) to publicize; (divulgar) to make public, divulge

publicidad [puβliθi'ðað] nf publicity; (COM: propaganda) advertising
❑ **publicitario, -a** adj publicity cpd; advertising cpd

público, -a ['puβliko, a] adj public **♦** nm public; (TEATRO etc) audience

puchero [pu'tʃero] nm (CULIN: guiso) stew; (: olla) cooking pot; **hacer pucheros** to pout

pucho (CS: fam) ['putʃo] nm cigarette, fag (BRIT)

pude etc vb ver **poder**

pudiente [pu'ðjente] adj (rico) wealthy, well-to-do

pudiera etc vb ver **poder**

pudor [pu'ðor] nm modesty

pudrir [pu'ðrir] vt to rot; **pudrirse** vr to rot, decay

pueblo ['pweβlo] nm people; (nación) nation; (aldea) village

puedo etc vb ver **poder**

puente ['pwente] nm bridge; **hacer ~** (fam) to take extra days off work between two public holidays; to take a long weekend **▸ puente aéreo** shuttle service **▸ puente colgante** suspension bridge **▸ puente levadizo** drawbridge

HACER PUENTE

When a public holiday in Spain falls on a Tuesday or Thursday it is common practice for employers to make the Monday or Friday a holiday as well and to give everyone a four-day weekend. This is known as **hacer puente**. When a named public holiday such as the **Día de la Constitución** falls on a Tuesday or Thursday, people refer to the whole holiday period as e.g. the **puente de la Constitución**.

puerco, -a ['pwerko, a] nm/f pig/sow **♦** adj (sucio) dirty, filthy; (obsceno) disgusting **▸ puerco espín** porcupine

pueril [pwe'ril] adj childish

puerro ['pwerro] nm leek

puerta ['pwerta] nf door; (de jardín) gate; (portal) doorway; (fig) gateway; (portería) goal; **a la ~** at the door; **a ~ cerrada** behind closed doors **▸ puerta giratoria** revolving door

puerto ['pwerto] nm port; (paso) pass; (fig) haven, refuge

Puerto Rico [pwerto'riko] nm Puerto Rico ❏ **puertorriqueño, -a** adj, nm/f Puerto Rican

pues [pwes] adv (entonces) then; (bueno) well, well then; (así que) so ♦ conj (ya que) since; **¡~ sí!** yes!, certainly!

puesta [pwesta] nf (apuesta) bet, stake ► **puesta al día** updating ► **puesta a punto** fine tuning ► **puesta de sol** sunset ► **puesta en marcha** starting

puesto, -a ['pwesto, a] pp de **poner** ♦ adj: **tener algo ~** to have sth on, be wearing sth ♦ nm (lugar, posición) place; (trabajo) post, job; (COM) stall ♦ conj: **~ que** since, as

púgil ['puxil] nm boxer

pulga [pulɣa] nf flea

pulgada [pul'ɣaða] nf inch

pulgar [pul'ɣar] nm thumb

pulir [pu'lir] vt to polish; (alisar) to smooth; (fig) to polish up, touch up

pulmón [pul'mon] nm lung ❏ **pulmonía** nf pneumonia

pulpa [pulpa] nf pulp; (de fruta) flesh, soft part

pulpería [pulpe'ria] nf (LAm) (tienda) small grocery store

púlpito ['pulpito] nm pulpit

pulpo ['pulpo] nm octopus

pulque ['pulke] nm pulque

pulsación [pulsa'θjon] nf beat; **pulsaciones** pulse rate

pulsar [pul'sar] vt (tecla) to touch, tap; (MÚS) to play; (botón) to press, push ♦ vi to pulsate; (latir) to beat, throb

pulsera [pul'sera] nf bracelet

pulso ['pulso] nm (ANAT) pulse; (fuerza) strength; (firmeza) steady hand

pulverizador [pulβeriθa'ðor] nm spray, spray gun

pulverizar [pulβeri'θar] vt to pulverize; (líquido) to spray

puna ['puna] nf (CAm) mountain sickness

punta [punta] nf point, tip; (extremo) end; (fig) touch, trace; **horas ~** peak o rush hours; **sacar ~ a** to sharpen

puntada [pun'taða] nf (COSTURA) stitch

puntal [pun'tal] nm prop, support

puntapié [punta'pje] nm kick

puntería [punte'ria] nf (de arma) aim, aiming; (destreza) marksmanship

puntero, a [pun'tero, a] adj leading ♦ nm (palo) pointer

puntiagudo, -a [puntja'ɣuðo, a] adj sharp, pointed

puntilla [pun'tiʎa] nf (encaje) lace edging o trim; **(andar) de puntillas** (to walk) on tiptoe

punto ['punto] nm (gen) point; (señal diminuta) spot, dot; (COSTURA, MED) stitch; (lugar) spot, place; (momento) point, moment; **a ~** ready; **estar a ~ de** to be on the point of o about to; **en ~** on the dot; **hasta cierto ~** to some extent; **hacer ~** (ESP: tejer) to knit; **dos puntos** (LING) colon ► **punto de interrogación** question mark ► **punto de vista** point of view, viewpoint ► **punto final** full stop (BRIT), period (US) ► **punto muerto** dead center; (AUTO) neutral (gear) ► **punto y aparte** (en dictado) full stop, new paragraph ► **punto y coma** semicolon

puntocom, punto.com adj inv, nf inv dotcom, dot.com

puntuación [puntwa'θjon] *nf*
punctuation; (*puntos: en examen*)
mark(s) (*pl*); (*DEPORTE*) score

puntual [pun'twal] *adj* (*a tiempo*)
punctual; (*exacto*) exact, accurate
❏ **puntualidad** *nf* punctuality;
exactness, accuracy

puntuar [pun'twar] *vi* (*DEPORTE*) to
score, count

punzante [pun'θante] *adj* (*dolor*)
shooting, sharp; (*herramienta*) sharp

puñado [pu'naðo] *nm* handful

puñal [pu'nal] *nm* dagger ❏ **puñalada**
nf stab

puñetazo [puɲe'taθo] *nm* punch

puño [puɲo] *nm* (*ANAT*) fist; (*cantidad*)
fistful, handful; (*COSTURA*) cuff; (*de
herramienta*) handle

pupila [pu'pila] *nf* pupil

pupitre [pu'pitre] *nm* desk

puré [pu're] *nm* purée; (*sopa*) (thick)
soup ❏ **puré de papas** (*LAm*) mashed
potatoes ❏ **puré de patatas** (*ESP*)
mashed potatoes

purga ['purɣa] *nf* purge ❏ **purgante**
adj, nm purgative

purgatorio [purɣa'torjo] *nm*
purgatory

purificar [purifi'kar] *vt* to purify;
(*refinar*) to refine

puritano, -a [puri'tano, a] *adj* (*actitud*)
puritanical; (*iglesia, tradición*) puritan
♦ *nm/f* puritan

puro, -a ['puro, a] *adj* pure; (*verdad*)
simple, plain ♦ *nm* cigar

púrpura ['purpura] *nf* purple

pus [pus] *nm* pus

puse *etc* ['puse] *vb ver* **poner**

pusiera *etc vb ver* **poner**

puta ['puta] (*fam!*) *nf* whore, prostitute

putrefacción [putrefak'θjon] *nf*
rotting, putrefaction

PVP *nm abr* (= *precio de venta al público*)
RRP

---

pyme, PYME ['pime] *nf abr* (= *Pequeña
y Mediana Empresa*) SME

Q, q

que
PALABRA CLAVE

[ke] *conj*

1 (*con oración subordinada: muchas
veces no se traduce*) that; **dijo que
vendría** he said (that) he would
come; **espero que lo encuentres** I
hope (that) you find it; *ver tb* **el**

2 (*en oración independiente*): **¡que
entre!** send him in; **¡Que aproveche!**
enjoy your meal!; **¡que se mejore tu
padre!** I hope your father gets better

3 (*enfático*): **¿me quieres? — ¡que sí!**
do you love me? — of course!

4 (*consecutivo: muchas veces no se
traduce*) that; **es tan grande que no lo
puedo levantar** it's so big (that) I
can't lift it

5 (*comparaciones*): **yo que tú/él** if I
were you/him; *ver tb* **más**; **menos**;
mismo

6 (*valor disyuntivo*): **que le guste o no**
whether he likes it or not; **que venga
o que no venga** whether he comes or
not

7 (*porque*): **no puedo, que tengo
que quedarme en casa** I can't, I've
got to stay in

♦ *pron*

1 (*cosa*) that, which; (+ *prep*) which;
el sombrero que te compraste the
hat (that o which) you bought; **la
cama en que me dormí** the bed (that o
which) I slept in

2 (*persona: suj*) that, who; (*: objeto*)

that, whom; **el amigo que me acompañó al museo** the friend that o who went to the museum with me; **la chica que invité** the girl (that o whom) I invited

qué [ke] adj what?, which? ♦ pron what?; **¡qué divertido!** how funny!; **¿qué edad tienes?** how old are you?; **¿de qué me hablas?** what are you saying to me?; **¿qué tal?** how are you?, how are things?; **¿qué hay (de nuevo)?** what's new?

quebrado, -a [ke'βraðo, a] adj (roto) broken ♦ nm/f bankrupt ♦ nm (MAT) fraction

quebrantar [keβran'tar] vt (infringir) to violate, transgress

quebrar [ke'βrar] vt to break, smash ♦ vi to go bankrupt

quedar [ke'ðar] vi to stay, remain; (encontrarse: sitio) to be; (haber aún) to remain, be left; **quedarse** vr to remain, stay (behind); **quedarse (con) algo** to keep sth; ~ **en** (acordar) to agree on; ~ **en nada** to come to nothing; ~ **por hacer** to be still to be done; ~ **ciego/mudo** to be left blind/dumb; **no te queda bien ese vestido** that dress doesn't suit you; **eso queda muy lejos** that's a long way (away); **quedamos a las seis** we agreed to meet at six

quedo, -a [ˈkeðo, a] adj still ♦ adv softly, gently

quehacer [kea'θer] nm task, job; **quehaceres (domésticos)** nmpl household chores

queja [ˈkexa] nf complaint ▢ **quejarse** vr (enfermo) to moan, groan; (protestar) to complain; **quejarse de que** to complain (about the fact) that ▢ **quejido** nm moan

quemado, -a [ke'maðo, a] adj burnt

quemadura [kema'ðura] nf burn, scald

quemar [ke'mar] vt to burn; (fig: malgastar) to burn up, squander ♦ vi to

be burning hot; **quemarse** vr (consumirse) to burn (up); (del sol) to get sunburnt

quemarropa [kema'rropa]: **a ~** adv point-blank

quepo etc [ˈkepo] vb ver **caber**

querella [keˈreʎa] nf (JUR) charge; (disputa) dispute

querer [keˈrer]

PALABRA CLAVE

1 (desear) to want; **quiero más dinero** I want more money; **quisiera o querría un té** I'd like a tea; **sin querer** unintentionally; **quiero ayudar/que vayas** I want to help/you to go

2 (preguntas: para pedir algo): **¿quiere abrir la ventana?** could you open the window?; **¿quieres echarme una mano?** can you give me a hand?

3 (amar) to love; (tener cariño a) to be fond of; **quiere mucho a sus hijos** he's very fond of his children

4: **le pedí que me dejara ir pero no quiso** I asked him to let me go but he refused

querido, -a [keˈriðo, a] adj dear ♦ nm/f darling; (amante) lover

queso [ˈkeso] nm cheese ▶ **queso crema** (LAm) cream cheese ▶ **queso de untar** (ESP) cream cheese ▶ **queso manchego** sheep's milk cheese made in La Mancha ▶ **queso rallado** grated cheese

quicio [ˈkiθjo] nm hinge; **sacar a algn de ~** to get on sb's nerves

quiebra [ˈkjeβra] nf break, split; (COM) bankruptcy; (ECON) slump

quiebro [ˈkjeβro] nm (del cuerpo) swerve

quien [kjen] *pron* who; **hay ~ piensa que** there are those who think that; **no hay ~ lo haga** no-one will do it

quién [kjen] *pron* who, whom; **¿~ es?** who's there?

quienquiera [kjenˈkjera] (*pl* **quienesquiera**) *pron* whoever

quiero *etc vb ver* **querer**

quieto, -a [ˈkjeto, a] *adj* still; (*carácter*) placid □ **quietud** *nf* stillness

⚠ No confundir **quieto** con la palabra inglesa *quiet*.

quilate [kiˈlate] *nm* carat

químico, -a [ˈkimiko, a] *adj* chemical ♦ *nm/f* chemist ♦ *nf* chemistry

quincalla [kinˈkaʎa] *nf* hardware, ironmongery (BRIT)

quince [ˈkinθe] *num* fifteen; **~ días** a fortnight □ **quinceañero, -a** *nm/f* teenager □ **quincena** *nf* fortnight; (*pago*) fortnightly pay □ **quincenal** *adj* fortnightly

quiniela [kiˈnjela] *nf* football pools *pl*; **quinielas** *nfpl* (*impreso*) pools coupon *sg*

quinientos, -as [kiˈnjentos, as] *adj*, *num* five hundred

quinto, -a [ˈkinto, a] *adj* fifth ♦ *nf* country house; (*MIL*) call-up, draft

quiosco [ˈkjosko] *nm* (*de música*) bandstand; (*de periódicos*) news stand

quirófano [kiˈrofano] *nm* operating theatre

quirúrgico, -a [kiˈrurxiko, a] *adj* surgical

quise *etc* [ˈkise] *vb ver* **querer**

quisiera *etc vb ver* **querer**

quisquilloso, -a [kiskiˈʎoso, a] *adj* (*susceptible*) touchy; (*meticuloso*) pernickety

quiste [ˈkiste] *nm* cyst

quitaesmalte [kitaesˈmalte] *nm* nail-polish remover

quitamanchas [kitaˈmantʃas] *nm inv* stain remover

quitanieves [kitaˈnjeβes] *nm inv* snowplough (BRIT), snowplow (US)

quitar [kiˈtar] *vt* to remove, take away; (*ropa*) to take off; (*dolor*) to relieve; **¡quita de ahí!** get away!; **quitarse** *vr* to withdraw; (*ropa*) to take off; **se quitó el sombrero** he took off his hat

Quito [ˈkito] *n* Quito

quizá(s) [kiˈθa(s)] *adv* perhaps, maybe

R, r

rábano [ˈraβano] *nm* radish; **me importa un ~** I don't give a damn

rabia [ˈraβja] *nf* (MED) rabies *sg*; (*ira*) fury, rage □ **rabiar** *vi* to have rabies; to rage, be furious; **rabiar por algo** to long for sth

rabieta [raˈβjeta] *nf* tantrum, fit of temper

rabino [raˈβino] *nm* rabbi

rabioso, -a [raˈβjoso, a] *adj* rabid; (*fig*) furious

rabo [ˈraβo] *nm* tail

racha [ˈratʃa] *nf* gust of wind; **buena/mala ~** spell of good/bad luck

racial [raˈθjal] *adj* racial, race *cpd*

racimo [raˈθimo] *nm* bunch

ración [raˈθjon] *nf* portion; **raciones** *nfpl* rations

racional [raθjoˈnal] *adj* (*razonable*) reasonable; (*lógico*) rational

racionar [raθjoˈnar] *vt* to ration (out)

racismo [raˈθismo] *nm* racism □ **racista** *adj, nm* racist

radar [raˈðar] *nm* radar

radiador [raðjaˈðor] *nm* radiator

radiante [raˈðjante] *adj* radiant

radical [raðiˈkal] *adj, nmf* radical

radicar [raðiˈkar] *vi*: **~ en** (*dificultad, problema*) to lie in; (*solución*) to consist in

radio ['raðjo] nf radio; (*aparato*) radio (set) ♦ nm (MAT) radius; (QUIM) radium
❏ **radioactividad** nf radioactivity
❏ **radioactivo, -a** adj radioactive
❏ **radiografía** nf X-ray
❏ **radioterapia** nf radiotherapy
❏ **radioyente** nmf listener

ráfaga ['rafaɣa] nf gust; (*de luz*) flash; (*de tiros*) burst

raíz [ra'iθ] nf root; **a ~ de** as a result of ▶ **raíz cuadrada** square root

raja ['raxa] nf (*de melón etc*) slice; (*grieta*) crack ❏ **rajar** vt to split; (*fam*) to slash; **rajarse** vr to split, crack; **rajarse de** to back out of

rajatabla [raxa'taβla] **: a ~** adv (*estrictamente*) strictly, to the letter

rallador [raʎa'ðor] nm grater

rallar [ra'ʎar] vt to grate

rama ['rama] nf branch ❏ **ramaje** nm branches pl, foliage ❏ **ramal** nm (*de cuerda*) strand; (FERRO) branch line (BRIT); (AUTO) branch (road) (BRIT)

rambla ['rambla] nf (*avenida*) avenue

ramo ['ramo] nm branch; (*sección*) department, section

rampa ['rampa] nf ramp ▶ **rampa de acceso** entrance ramp

rana ['rana] nf frog; **salto de ~** leapfrog

ranchero [ran'tʃero] (MÉX) nm (*hacendado*) rancher; smallholder

rancho ['rantʃo] nm (*grande*) ranch; (*pequeño*) small farm

rancio, -a ['ranθjo, a] adj (*comestibles*) rancid; (*vino*) aged, mellow; (*fig*) ancient

rango ['rango] nm rank, standing

ranura [ra'nura] nf groove; (*de teléfono etc*) slot

rapar [ra'par] vt to shave; (*los cabellos*) to crop

rapaz [ra'paθ] (nf **rapaza**) nmf young boy/girl ♦ adj (ZOOL) predatory

rape ['rape] nm (*pez*) monkfish; **al ~** cropped

rapé [ra'pe] nm snuff

rapidez [rapi'ðeθ] nf speed, rapidity ❏ **rápido, -a** adj fast, quick ♦ adv quickly ♦ nm (FERRO) express
❏ **rápidos** nmpl rapids

rapiña [ra'piɲa] nf robbery; **ave de ~** bird of prey

raptar [rap'tar] vt to kidnap ❏ **rapto** nm kidnapping; (*impulso*) sudden impulse; (*éxtasis*) ecstasy, rapture

raqueta [ra'keta] nf racquet

raquítico, -a [ra'kitiko, a] adj stunted; (*fig*) poor, inadequate

rareza [ra'reða] nf rarity; (*fig*) eccentricity

raro, -a ['raro, a] adj (*poco común*) rare; (*extraño*) odd, strange; (*excepcional*) remarkable

ras [ras] nm: **a ~ de** level with; **a ~ de tierra** at ground level

rasar [ra'sar] vt (*igualar*) to level

rascacielos [raska'θjelos] nm inv skyscraper

rascar [ras'kar] vt (*con las uñas etc*) to scratch; (*raspar*) to scrape; **rascarse** vr to scratch (o.s.)

rasgar [ras'ɣar] vt to tear, rip (up)

rasgo ['rasɣo] nm (*con pluma*) stroke; **rasgos** nmpl (*facciones*) features, characteristics; **a grandes rasgos** in outline, broadly

rasguño [ras'ɣuɲo] nm scratch

raso, -a ['raso, a] adj (*liso*) flat, level; (*a baja altura*) very low ♦ nm satin; **cielo ~** clear sky

raspadura [raspa'ðura] nf (*acto*) scrape, scraping; (*marca*) scratch; **raspaduras** nfpl (*de papel etc*) scrapings

raspar [ras'par] vt to scrape; (*arañar*) to scratch; (*limar*) to file

rastra ['rastra] nf (AGR) rake; **a rastras** by dragging; (*fig*) unwillingly

rastrear [rastre'ar] vt (*seguir*) to track

rastrero, -a [ras'trero, a] adj (BOT, ZOOL) creeping; (*fig*) despicable, mean

rastrillo [ras'triʎo] nm rake

rastro ['rastro] nm (AGR) rake; (pista) track, trail; (vestigio) trace; **el R~** (ESP) the Madrid fleamarket

rasurado (MÉX) nm shaving ❏ **rasuradora** [rasuraˈðora] (MÉX) nf electric shaver ❏ **rasurar** [rasuˈrar] (MÉX) vt to shave; **rasurarse** vr to shave

rata ['rata] nf rat

ratear [rateˈar] vt (robar) to steal

ratero, -a [raˈtero, a] adj light-fingered ♦ nm/f (carterista) pickpocket; (ladrón) petty thief

rato ['rato] nm while, short time; **a ratos** from time to time; **hay para ~** there's still a long way to go; **al poco ~** soon afterwards; **pasar el ~** to kill time; **pasar un buen/mal ~** to have a good/rough time; **en mis ratos libres** in my spare time

ratón [raˈton] nm mouse ❏ **ratonera** nf mousetrap

raudal [rauˈðal] nm torrent; **a raudales** in abundance

raya ['raja] nf line; (marca) scratch; (en tela) stripe; (de pelo) parting; (límite) boundary; (pez) ray; (puntuación) dash; **a rayas** striped; **pasarse de la ~** to go too far; **tener a ~** to keep in check ❏ **rayar** vt to line; to scratch; (subrayar) to underline ♦ vi: **rayar en** o **con** to border on

rayo ['rajo] nm (del sol) ray, beam; (de luz) shaft; (en una tormenta) (flash of) lightning ▶ **rayos X** X-rays

raza ['raθa] nf race ▶ **raza humana** human race

razón [raˈθon] nf reason; (justicia) right, justice; (razonamiento) reasoning; (motivo) reason, motive; (MAT) ratio; **a ~ de 10 cada día** at the rate of 10 a day; **en ~ de** with regard to; **dar ~ a algn** to agree that sb is right; **tener ~** to be right ▶ **razón de ser** raison d'être ▶ **razón directa/inversa** direct/inverse proportion ❏ **razonable** adj reasonable; (justo, moderado) fair ❏ **razonamiento** nm (juicio)

judg(e)ment; (argumento) reasoning ❏ **razonar** vt, vi to reason, argue

re nm (MÚS) D

reacción [reakˈθjon] nf reaction; **avión a ~** jet plane ▶ **reacción en cadena** chain reaction ❏ **reaccionar** vi to react

reacio, -a [reˈaθjo, a] adj stubborn

reactivar [reaktiˈβar] vt to revitalize

reactor [reakˈtor] nm reactor

real [reˈal] adj real; (del rey, fig) royal

realidad [realiˈðað] nf reality, fact; (verdad) truth

realista [reaˈlista] nmf realist

realización [realiθaˈθjon] nf fulfilment

realizador, a [realiθaˈðor, a] nm/f film-maker

realizar [realiˈθar] vt (objetivo) to achieve; (plan) to carry out; (viaje) to make, undertake; **realizarse** vr to come about, come true

realmente [realˈmente] adv really, actually

realzar [realˈθar] vt to enhance; (acentuar) to highlight

reanimar [reaniˈmar] vt to revive; (alentar) to encourage; **reanimarse** vr to revive

reanudar [reanuˈðar] vt (renovar) to renew; (historia, viaje) to resume

reaparición [reapariˈθjon] nf reappearance

rearme [reˈarme] nm rearmament

rebaja [reˈβaxa] nf (COM) reduction; (: descuento) discount; **rebajas** nfpl (COM) sale ❏ **rebajar** vt (bajar) to lower; (reducir) to reduce; (disminuir) to lessen; (humillar) to humble

rebanada [reβaˈnaða] nf slice

rebañar [reβaˈɲar] vt (comida) to scrape up; (plato) to scrape clean

rebaño [reˈβaɲo] nm herd; (de ovejas) flock

rebatir [reβaˈtir] vt to refute

rebeca [reˈβeka] nf cardigan

rebelarse [reβe'larse] vr to rebel, revolt

rebelde [re'βelde] adj rebellious; (niño) unruly ♦ nmf rebel ◆ **rebeldía** nf rebelliousness; (desobediencia) disobedience

rebelión [reβe'ljon] nf rebellion

reblandecer [reβlande'θer] vt to soften

rebobinar [reβoβi'nar] vt (cinta, película de vídeo) to rewind

rebosante [reβo'sante] adj overflowing

rebosar [reβo'sar] vi (líquido, recipiente) to overflow; (abundar) to abound, be plentiful

rebotar [reβo'tar] vt to bounce; (rechazar) to repel ♦ vi (pelota) to bounce; (bala) to ricochet ◆ **rebote** nm rebound; **de rebote** on the rebound

rebozado, -a [reβo'θaðo, a] adj fried in batter o breadcrumbs

rebozar [reβo'θar] vt to wrap up; (CULIN) to fry in batter o breadcrumbs

rebuscado, -a [reβus'kaðo, a] adj (amanerado) affected; (palabra) recherché; (idea) far-fetched

rebuscar [reβus'kar] vi ~ **en(por)** to search carefully (in/for)

recado [re'kaðo] nm (mensaje) message; (encargo) errand; **tomar un ~** (TEL) to take a message

recaer [reka'er] vi to relapse; ~ **en** to fall o on; (criminal etc) to fall back into, relapse into ◆ **recaída** nf relapse

recalcar [rekal'kar] vt (fig) to stress, emphasize

recalentar [rekalen'tar] vt (volver a calentar) to reheat; (calentar demasiado) to overheat

recámara [re'kamara] (MÉX) nf bedroom

recambio [re'kambjo] nm spare; (de pluma) refill

recapacitar [rekapaθi'tar] vi to reflect

recargado, -a [rekar'gaðo, a] adj overloaded

recargar [rekar'gar] vt to overload; (batería) to recharge ◆ **recargo** nm surcharge; (aumento) increase

recatado, -a [reka'taðo, a] adj (modesto) modest, demure; (prudente) cautious

recaudación [rekauða'θjon] nf (acción) collection; (cantidad) takings pl; (en deporte) gate ◆ **recaudador, a** nm/f tax collector

recelar [reθe'lar] vt: ~ **que ...** (sospechar) to suspect that ...; (temer) to fear that ... ♦ vi: ~ **de** to distrust ◆ **recelo** nm distrust, suspicion

recepción [reθep'θjon] nf reception ◆ **recepcionista** nmf receptionist

receptor, a [reθep'tor, a] nm/f recipient ♦ nm (TEL) receiver

recesión [reθe'sjon] nf (COM) recession

receta [re'θeta] nf (CULIN) recipe; (MED) prescription

⚠ No confundir **receta** con la palabra inglesa receipt.

rechazar [retʃa'θar] vt to reject; (oferta) to turn down; (ataque) to repel

rechazo [re'tʃaθo] nm rejection

rechinar [retʃi'nar] vi to creak; (dientes) to grind

rechistar [retʃis'tar] vi: **sin ~** without a murmur

rechoncho, -a [re'tʃontʃo, a] (fam) adj thickset (BRIT), heavy-set (US)

rechupete [retʃu'pete]: **de ~** (comida) delicious, scrumptious

recibidor [reθiβi'ðor] nm entrance hall

recibimiento [reθiβi'mjento] nm reception, welcome

recibir [reθi'βir] vt to receive; (dar la bienvenida) to welcome ♦ vi to entertain ◆ **recibo** nm receipt

reciclable adj recyclable

reciclar [reθi'klar] vt to recycle

recién [re'θjen] *adv* recently, newly; **los ~ casados** the newly-weds; **el ~ llegado** the newcomer; **el ~ nacido** the newborn child

reciente [re'θjente] *adj* recent; (*fresco*) fresh

recinto [re'θinto] *nm* enclosure; (*área*) area, place

recio, -a ['reθjo, a] *adj* strong, tough; (*voz*) loud ♦ *adv* hard, loud(ly)

recipiente [reθi'pjente] *nm* receptacle

recíproco, -a [re'θiproko, a] *adj* reciprocal

recital [reθi'tal] *nm* (MÚS) recital; (LITERATURA) reading

recitar [reθi'tar] *vt* to recite

reclamación [reklama'θjon] *nf* claim, demand; (*queja*) complaint

reclamar [rekla'mar] *vt* to claim, demand ♦ *vi*: **~ contra** to complain about ❑ **reclamo** *nm* (*anuncio*) advertisement; (*tentación*) attraction

reclinar [rekli'nar] *vt* to recline, lean; **reclinarse** *vr* to lean back

reclusión [reklu'sjon] *nf* (*prisión*) prison; (*refugio*) seclusion

recluta [re'kluta] *nmf* recruit ♦ *nf* recruitment ❑ **reclutar** *vt* (*datos*) to collect; (*dinero*) to collect up ❑ **reclutamiento** *nm* recruitment

recobrar [reko'βrar] *vt* (*salud*) to recover; (*rescatar*) to get back; **recobrarse** *vr* to recover

recodo [re'koðo] *nm* (*de río, camino*) bend

recogedor [rekoxe'ðor] *nm* dustpan

recoger [reko'xer] *vt* to collect; (AGR) to harvest; (*levantar*) to pick up; (*juntar*) to gather; (*pasar a buscar*) to come for, get; (*dar asilo*) to give shelter to; (*faldas*) to gather up; (*pelo*) to put up ❑ **recogerse** *vr* (*retirarse*) to retire ❑ **recogido, -a** *adj* (*lugar*) quiet, secluded; (*pequeño*) small ♦ *nf* (CORREOS) collection; (AGR) harvest

recolección [rekolek'θjon] *nf* (AGR) harvesting; (*colecta*) collection

recomendación [rekomenda'θjon] *nf* (*sugerencia*) suggestion, recommendation; (*referencia*) reference

recomendar [rekomen'dar] *vt* to suggest, recommend; (*confiar*) to entrust

recompensa [rekom'pensa] *nf* reward, recompense ❑ **recompensar** *vt* to reward, recompense

reconciliación [rekonθilja'θjon] *nf* reconciliation

reconciliar [rekonθi'ljar] *vt* to reconcile; **reconciliarse** *vr* to become reconciled

recóndito, -a [re'kondito, a] *adj* (*lugar*) hidden, secret

reconocer [rekono'θer] *vt* to recognize; (*registrar*) to search; (MED) to examine ❑ **reconocido, -a** *adj* recognized; (*agradecido*) grateful ❑ **reconocimiento** *nm* recognition; search; examination; gratitude; (*confesión*) admission

reconquista [rekon'kista] *nf* reconquest; **la R~** the Reconquest (of Spain)

reconstituyente [rekonstitu'jente] *nm* tonic

reconstruir [rekonstru'ir] *vt* to reconstruct

reconversión [rekonβer'sjon] *nf* (*reestructuración*) restructuring ▶ **reconversión industrial** industrial rationalization

recopilación [rekopila'θjon] *nf* (*resumen*) summary; (*compilación*) compilation ❑ **recopilar** *vt* to compile

récord ['rekorð] (*pl* **récords**) *adj inv*, *nm* record

recordar [rekor'ðar] vt (*acordarse de*) to remember; (*acordar a otro*) to remind ♦ vi to remember

 No confundir **recordar** con la palabra inglesa **record**.

recorrer [reko'rrer] vt (*país*) to cross, travel through; (*distancia*) to cover; (*registrar*) to search; (*repasar*) to look over ❏ **recorrido** nm run, journey; **tren de largo recorrido** main-line train

recortar [rekor'tar] vt to cut out ❏ **recorte** nm (*acción, de prensa*) cutting; (*de telas, chapas*) trimming ▶ **recorte presupuestario** budget cut

recostar [rekos'tar] vt to lean; **recostarse** vr to lie down

recoveco [reko'βeko] nm (*de camino, río etc*) bend; (*en casa*) cubby hole

recreación [rekrea'θjon] nf recreation

recrear [rekre'ar] vt (*entretener*) to entertain; (*volver a crear*) to recreate ❏ **recreativo, -a** adj recreational ❏ **recreo** nm recreation; (*ESCOL*) break, playtime

recriminar [rekrimi'nar] vt to reproach ♦ vi to recriminate; **recriminarse** vr to reproach each other

recrudecer [rekruðe'θer] vt, vi to worsen; **recrudecerse** vr to worsen

recta ['rekta] nf straight line

rectángulo, -a [rek'taŋgulo, a] adj rectangular ♦ nm rectangle

rectificar [rektifi'kar] vt to rectify; (*volverse recto*) to straighten ♦ vi to correct o.s.

rectitud [rekti'tuð] nf straightness

recto, -a ['rekto, a] adj straight; (*persona*) honest, upright; **siga todo ~** go straight on ♦ nm rectum

rector, a [rek'tor, a] adj governing

recuadro [re'kwaðro] nm box; (*TIP*) inset

recubrir [reku'βrir] vt: ~ **(con)** (*pintura, crema*) to cover (with)

recuento [re'kwento] nm inventory; **hacer el ~ de** to count o reckon up

recuerdo [re'kwerðo] nm souvenir; **recuerdos** nmpl (*memorias*) memories; **¡recuerdos a tu madre!** give my regards to your mother!

recular [reku'lar] vi to back down

recuperación [rekupera'θjon] nf recovery

recuperar [rekupe'rar] vt to recover; (*tiempo*) to make up; **recuperarse** vr to recuperate

recurrir [reku'rrir] vi (*JUR*) to appeal; ~ **a** to resort to; (*persona*) to turn to ❏ **recurso** nm resort; (*medios*) means pl, resources pl; (*JUR*) appeal

red [reð] nf net, mesh; (*FERRO etc*) network; (*trampa*) trap; **la R~** (*Internet*) the Net

redacción [reðak'θjon] nf (*acción*) editing; (*personal*) editorial staff; (*ESCOL*) essay, composition

redactar [reðak'tar] vt to draw up, draft; (*periódico*) to edit

redactor, a [reðak'tor, a] nm/f editor

redada [re'ðaða] nf (*de policía*) raid, round-up

rededor [reðe'ðor] nm: **al o en ~** around, round about

redoblar [reðo'βlar] vt to redouble ♦ vi (*tambor*) to roll

redonda [re'ðonda] nf: **a la ~** around, round about

redondear [reðonde'ar] vt to round, round off

redondel [reðon'del] nm (*círculo*) circle; (*TAUR*) bullring, arena

redondo, -a [re'ðondo, a] adj (*circular*) round; (*completo*) complete

reducción [reðuk'θjon] nf reduction

reducido, -a [reðu'θiðo, a] adj reduced; (*limitado*) limited; (*pequeño*) small

reducir [reðu'θir] vt to reduce; to limit; **reducirse** vr to diminish

redundancia [reðun'danθja] *nf*
redundancy

reembolsar [re(e)mbol'sar] *vt*
(*persona*) to reimburse; (*dinero*) to
repay, pay back; (*depósito*) to refund
❏ **reembolso** *nm* reimbursement;
refund

reemplazar [re(e)mpla'θar] *vt* to
replace ❏ **reemplazo** *nm*
replacement; **de reemplazo** (*MIL*)
reserve

reencuentro [re(e)n'kwentro] *nm*
reunion

refacción (*MÉX*) [refak'θjon] *nf* spare
(part)

referencia [refe'renθja] *nf* reference;
con ~ a with reference to

referéndum [refe'rendum] (*pl*
referéndums) *nm* referendum

referente [refe'rente] *adj*: **~ a**
concerning, relating to

réferi (*LAm*) *nmf* referee

referir [refe'rir] *vt* (*contar*) to tell,
recount; (*relacionar*) to refer, relate;
referirse *vr*: **referirse a** to refer to

refilón [refi'lon]: **de ~** *adv* obliquely

refinado, -a [refi'naðo, a] *adj* refined

refinar [refi'nar] *vt* to refine
❏ **refinería** *nf* refinery

reflejar [refle'xar] *vt* to reflect
❏ **reflejo, -a** *adj* reflected;
(*movimiento*) reflex ♦ *nm* reflection;
(*ANAT*) reflex

reflexión [reflek'sjon] *nf* reflection
❏ **reflexionar** *vt* to reflect on ♦ *vi* to
reflect; (*detenerse*) to pause (to think)

reflexivo, -a [reflek'siβo, a] *adj*
thoughtful; (*LING*) reflexive

reforma [re'forma] *nf* reform; (*ARQ etc*)
repair ▶ **reforma agraria** agrarian
reform

reformar [refor'mar] *vt* to reform;
(*modificar*) to change, alter; (*ARQ*) to
repair; **reformarse** *vr* to mend one's
ways

reformatorio [reforma'torjo] *nm*
reformatory

reforzar [refor'θar] *vt* to strengthen;
(*ARQ*) to reinforce; (*fig*) to encourage

refractario, -a [refrak'tarjo, a] *adj*
(*TEC*) heat-resistant

refrán [re'fran] *nm* proverb, saying

refregar [refre'ɣar] *vt* to scrub

refrescante [refres'kante] *adj*
refreshing, cooling

refrescar [refres'kar] *vt* to refresh ♦ *vi*
to cool down; **refrescarse** *vr* to get
cooler; (*tomar aire fresco*) to go out for
a breath of fresh air; (*beber*) to have a
drink

refresco [re'fresko] *nm* soft drink, cool
drink; "**refrescos**" "refreshments"

refriega [re'frjeɣa] *nf* scuffle, brawl

refrigeración [refrixera'θjon] *nf*
refrigeration; (*de sala*) air-conditioning

refrigerador [refrixera'ðor] *nm*
refrigerator (*BRIT*), icebox (*US*)

refrigerar [refrixe'rar] *vt* to refrigerate;
(*sala*) to air-condition

refuerzo [re'fwerθo] *nm*
reinforcement; (*TEC*) support

refugiado, -a [refu'xjaðo, a] *nm/f*
refugee

refugiarse [refu'xjarse] *vr* to take
refuge, shelter

refugio [re'fuxjo] *nm* refuge;
(*protección*) shelter

refunfuñar [refunfu'ɲar] *vi* to grunt,
growl; (*quejarse*) to grumble

regadera [reɣa'ðera] *nf* watering can

regadío [reɣa'ðio] *nm* irrigated land

regalado, -a [reɣa'laðo, a] *adj*
comfortable, luxurious; (*gratis*) free, for
nothing

regalar [reɣa'lar] *vt* (*dar*) to give (as a
present); (*entregar*) to give away;
(*mimar*) to pamper, make a fuss of

regaliz [reɣa'liθ] *nm* liquorice

regalo [re'ɣalo] *nm* (*obsequio*) gift,
present; (*gusto*) pleasure

regañadientes [reɣaɲaˈðjentes]: **a ~** adv reluctantly

regañar [reɣaˈɲar] vt to scold ♦ vi to grumble ◻ **regañón, -ona** adj nagging

regar [reˈɣar] vt to water, irrigate; (fig) to scatter, sprinkle

regatear [reɣateˈar] vt (COM) to bargain over; (escatimar) to be mean with ♦ vi to bargain, haggle; (DEPORTE) to dribble ◻ **regateo** nm bargaining, dribbling; (del cuerpo) swerve, dodge

regazo [reˈɣaθo] nm lap

regenerar [rexeneˈrar] vt to regenerate

régimen [ˈreximen] (pl **regímenes**) nm regime; (MED) diet

regimiento [rexiˈmjento] nm regiment

regio, -a [ˈrexjo, a] adj royal, regal; (fig: suntuoso) splendid; (CS: fam) great, terrific

región [reˈxjon] nf region

regir [reˈxir] vt to govern, rule; (dirigir) to manage, run ♦ vi to apply, be in force

registrar [rexisˈtrar] vt (buscar) to search; (: en cajón) to look through; (inspeccionar) to inspect; (anotar) to register, record; (INFORM) to log; **registrarse** vr to register; (ocurrir) to happen

registro [reˈxistro] nm (acto) registration; (MUS, libro) register; (inspección) inspection, search ▸ **registro civil** registry office

regla [ˈreɣla] nf (ley) rule, regulation; (de medir) ruler, rule; (MED: período) period; **en ~** in order

reglamentación [reɣlamentaˈθjon] nf (acto) regulation; (lista) rules pl

reglamentar [reɣlamenˈtar] vt to regulate ◻ **reglamentario, -a** adj statutory ◻ **reglamento** nm rules pl, regulations pl

regocijarse [reɣoθiˈxarse] vr (alegrarse) to rejoice ◻ **regocijo** nm joy, happiness

regresar [reɣreˈsar] vi to come back, go back, return ◻ **regreso** nm return

reguero [reˈɣero] nm (de sangre etc) trickle; (de humo) trail

regulador [reɣulaˈðor] nm regulator; (de radio etc) knob, control

regular [reɣuˈlar] adj regular; (normal) normal, usual; (común) ordinary; (organizado) regular, orderly; (mediano) average; (fam) not bad, so-so ♦ adv so-so, alright ♦ vt (controlar) to control, regulate; (TEC) to adjust; **por lo ~** as a rule ◻ **regularidad** nf regularity ◻ **regularizar** vt to regularize

rehabilitación [reaβilitaˈθjon] nf rehabilitation; (ARQ) restoration

rehabilitar [reaβiliˈtar] vt to rehabilitate; (ARQ) to restore; (reintegrar) to reinstate

rehacer [reaˈθer] vt (reparar) to mend, repair; (volver a hacer) to redo, repeat; **rehacerse** vr (MED) to recover

rehén [reˈen] nm hostage

rehuir [reuˈir] vt to avoid, shun

rehusar [reuˈsar] vt, vi to refuse

reina [ˈreina] nf queen ◻ **reinado** nm reign

reinar [reiˈnar] vi to reign

reincidir [reinθiˈðir] vi to relapse

reincorporarse [reinkorpoˈrarse] vr: **~ a** to rejoin

reino [ˈreino] nm kingdom ▸ **reino animal/vegetal** animal/plant kingdom ▸ **el Reino Unido** the United Kingdom

reintegrar [reinteˈɣrar] vt (reconstituir) to reconstruct; (persona) to reinstate; (dinero) to refund, pay back; **reintegrarse** vr: **reintegrarse a** to return to

reír [reˈir] vi to laugh; **reírse** vr to laugh; **reírse de** to laugh at

reiterar [reite'rar] vt to reiterate

reivindicación [reiβindika'θjon] nf (demanda) claim, demand; (justificación) vindication

reivindicar [reiβindi'kar] vt to claim

reja ['rexa] nf (de ventana) grille, bars pl; (en la calle) grating

rejilla [re'xiʎa] nf grating, grille; (muebles) wickerwork; (de ventilación) vent; (de coche etc) luggage rack

rejonear [rexonea'θor] nm mounted bullfighter

rejuvenecer [rexuβene'θer] vt, vi to rejuvenate

relación [rela'θjon] nf relation, relationship; (MAT) ratio; (narración) report; **con ~ a**, **en ~ con** in relation to ▶ **relaciones públicas** public relations ❑ **relacionar** vt to relate, connect; **relacionarse** vr to be connected, be linked

relajación [relaxa'θjon] nf relaxation

relajar [rela'xar] vt to relax; **relajarse** vr to relax

relamerse [rela'merse] vr to lick one's lips

relámpago [re'lampaɣo] nm flash of lightning; **visita ~** lightning visit

relatar [rela'tar] vt to tell, relate

relativo, -a [rela'tiβo, a] adj relative; **en lo ~ a** concerning

relato [re'lato] nm (narración) story, tale

relegar [rele'ɣar] vt to relegate

relevante [rele'βante] adj eminent, outstanding

relevar [rele'βar] vt (sustituir) to relieve; **relevarse** vr to relay; **~ a algn de un cargo** to relieve sb of his post

relevo [re'leβo] nm relief; **carrera de relevos** relay race

relieve [re'ljeβe] nm (ARTE, TEC) relief; (fig) prominence, importance; **bajo ~** bas-relief

religión [reli'xjon] nf religion ❑ **religioso, -a** adj religious ♦ nm/f monk/nun

relinchar [relin'tʃar] vi to neigh

reliquia [re'likja] nf relic ▶ **reliquia de familia** heirloom

rellano [re'ʎano] nm (ARQ) landing

rellenar [reʎe'nar] vt (llenar) to fill up; (CULIN) to stuff; (COSTURA) to pad ❑ **relleno, -a** adj full up; stuffed ♦ nm stuffing; (de tapicería) padding

reloj [re'lo(x)] nm clock; **poner el ~ (en hora)** to set one's watch (on the clock) ▶ **reloj (de pulsera)** wristwatch ▶ **reloj despertador** alarm (clock) ▶ **reloj digital** digital watch ❑ **relojero, -a** nm/f clockmaker; watchmaker

reluciente [relu'θjente] adj brilliant, shining

relucir [relu'θir] vi to shine; (fig) to excel

remachar [rema'tʃar] vt to rivet; (fig) to hammer home, drive home ❑ **remache** nm rivet

remangar [reman'gar] vt to roll up

remanso [re'manso] nm pool

remar [re'mar] vi to row

rematado, -a [rema'taðo, a] adj complete, utter

rematar [rema'tar] vt to finish off; (COM) to sell off cheap ♦ vi to end, finish off; (DEPORTE) to shoot

remate [re'mate] nm end, finish; (punta) tip; (DEPORTE) shot; (ARQ) top; **de o para ~** to crown it all (BRIT), to top it off

remedar [reme'ðar] vt to imitate

remediar [reme'ðjar] vt to remedy; (subsanar) to make good, repair; (evitar) to avoid

remedio [re'meðjo] nm remedy; (alivio) relief, help; (JUR) recourse; remedy; **poner ~ a** to correct, stop; **no tener más ~** to have no alternative;

¡qué ~! there's no choice!; **sin ~** hopeless

remendar [remen'dar] vt to repair; (con parche) to patch

remiendo [re'mjendo] nm mend; (con parche) patch; (cosido) darn

remilgado, -a [remil'ɣaðo, a] adj prim; (afectado) affected

remiso, -a [re'miso, a] adj slack, slow

remite [re'mite] nm (en sobre) name and address of sender

remitir [remi'tir] vt to remit, send ♦ vi to slacken; (en carta): **remite: X** sender: X □ **remitente** nmf sender

remo ['remo] nm (de barco) oar; (DEPORTE) rowing

remojar [remo'xar] vt to steep, soak; (galleta etc) to dip, dunk

remojo [re'moxo] nm: **dejar la ropa en ~** to leave clothes to soak

remolacha [remo'latʃa] nf beet, beetroot

remolcador [remolka'ðor] nm (NÁUT) tug; (AUTO) breakdown lorry

remolcar [remol'kar] vt to tow

remolino [remo'lino] nm eddy; (de agua) whirlpool; (de viento) whirlwind; (de gente) crowd

remolque [re'molke] nm tow, towing; (cuerda) towrope; **llevar a ~** to tow

remontar [remon'tar] vt to mend; **remontarse** vr to soar; **remontarse a** (COM) to amount to; **~ el vuelo** to soar

remorder [remor'ðer] vt to distress, disturb; **remorderle la conciencia a algn** to have a guilty conscience □ **remordimiento** nm remorse

remoto, -a [re'moto, a] adj remote

remover [remo'ßer] vt to stir; (tierra) to turn over; (objetos) to move round

remuneración [remunera'θjon] nf remuneration

remunerar [remune'rar] vt to remunerate; (premiar) to reward

renacer [rena'θer] vi to be reborn; (fig) to revive □ **renacimiento** nm rebirth; **el Renacimiento** the Renaissance

renacuajo [rena'kwaxo] nm (ZOOL) tadpole

renal [re'nal] adj renal, kidney cpd

rencilla [ren'θiʎa] nf quarrel

rencor [ren'kor] nm rancour, bitterness □ **rencoroso, -a** adj spiteful

rendición [rendi'θjon] nf surrender

rendido, -a [ren'diðo, a] adj (sumiso) submissive; (cansado) worn-out, exhausted

rendija [ren'dixa] nf (hendedura) crack, cleft

rendimiento [rendi'mjento] nm (producción) output; (TEC, COM) efficiency

rendir [ren'dir] vt (vencer) to defeat; (producir) to produce; (dar beneficio) to yield; (agotar) to exhaust ♦ vi to pay; **rendirse** vr (someterse) to surrender; (cansarse) to wear o.s. out; **~ homenaje** o **culto a** to pay homage to

renegar [rene'ɣar] vi (renunciar) to renounce; (blasfemar) to blaspheme; (quejarse) to complain

RENFE ['renfe] nf abr = **Red Nacional de los Ferrocarriles Españoles**

renglón [ren'ɣlon] nm (línea) line; (COM) item, article; **a ~ seguido** immediately after

renombre [re'nombre] nm renown

renovación [renoßa'θjon] nf (de contrato) renewal; (ARQ) renovation

renovar [reno'ßar] vt to renew; (ARQ) to renovate

renta ['renta] nf (ingresos) income; (beneficio) profit; (alquiler) rent ▶ **renta vitalicia** annuity □ **rentable** adj profitable

renuncia [re'nunθja] nf resignation □ **renunciar** [renun'θjar] vt to renounce; (tabaco, alcohol etc) to give up; **renunciar a** to give up; (oferta, *oportunidad)* to turn down; *(puesto)* to resign ♦ *vi* to resign

reñido, -a [re'niðo, a] *adj (batalla)* bitter, hard-fought; **estar ~ con algn** to be on bad terms with sb

reñir [re'nir] *vt (regañar)* to scold ♦ *vi (estar peleado)* to quarrel, fall out; *(combatir)* to fight

reo ['reo] *nmf* culprit, offender; *(acusado)* accused, defendant

reojo [re'oxo]: **de ~** *adv* out of the corner of one's eye

reparación [repara'θjon] *nf (acto)* mending, repairing; *(TEC)* repair; *(fig)* amends *pl*, reparation

reparar [repa'rar] *vt* to repair; *(fig)* to make amends for; *(observar)* to observe ♦ *vi:* **~ en** *(darse cuenta de)* to notice; *(prestar atención a)* to pay attention to

reparo [re'paro] *nm (advertencia)* observation; *(duda)* doubt; *(dificultad)* difficulty; **poner reparos (a)** to raise objections (to)

repartidor, a [reparti'ðor, a] *nm/f* distributor

repartir [repar'tir] *vt* to distribute, share out; *(CORREOS)* to deliver ❏ **reparto** *nm* distribution; delivery; *(TEATRO, CINE)* cast; *(CAm: urbanización)* housing estate *(BRIT)*, real estate development *(US)*

repasar [repa'sar] *vt (ESCOL)* to revise; *(MECÁNICA)* to check, overhaul; *(COSTURA)* to mend ❏ **repaso** *nm* revision; overhaul, checkup; review

repecho [re'petʃo] *nm* steep incline

repelente [repe'lente] *adj* repellent, repulsive

repeler [repe'ler] *vt* to repel

repente [re'pente] *nm:* **de ~** suddenly

repentino, -a [repen'tino, a] *adj* sudden

repercusión [reperku'sjon] *nf* repercussion

repercutir [reperku'tir] *vi (objeto)* to rebound; *(sonido)* to echo; **~ en** *(fig)* to have repercussions on

repertorio [reper'torjo] *nm* list; *(TEATRO)* repertoire

repetición [repeti'θjon] *nf* repetition

repetir [repe'tir] *vt* to repeat; *(plato)* to have a second helping of ♦ *vi* to repeat; *(sabor)* to come back; **repetirse** *vr (volver sobre un tema)* to repeat o.s.

repetitivo, -a [repeti'tiβo, a] *adj* repetitive, repetitious

repique [re'pike] *nm* pealing, ringing ❏ **repiqueteo** *nm* pealing; *(de tambor)* drumming

repisa [re'pisa] *nf* ledge, shelf; *(de ventana)* windowsill; **~ de la chimenea** the mantelpiece

repito *etc vb ver* **repetir**

replantearse [replante'arse] *vr:* **~ un problema** to reconsider a problem

repleto, -a [re'pleto, a] *adj* replete, full up

réplica ['replika] *nf* answer; *(ARTE)* replica

replicar [repli'kar] *vi* to answer; *(objetar)* to argue, answer back

repliegue [re'pljeɣe] *nm (MIL)* withdrawal

repoblación [repoβla'θjon] *nf* repopulation; *(de río)* restocking ▶ **repoblación forestal** reafforestation

repoblar [repo'βlar] *vt* to repopulate; *(con árboles)* to reafforest

repollito *(CS) nm:* **repollitos de Bruselas** (Brussels) sprouts

repollo [re'poʎo] *nm* cabbage

reponer [repo'ner] *vt* to replace, put back; *(TEATRO)* to revive; **reponerse** *vr* to recover; **~ que ...** to reply that ...

reportaje [repor'taxe] *nm* report, article

reportero, -a [repor'tero, a] *nm/f* reporter

reposacabezas [reposaka'βeθas] nm inv headrest

reposar [repo'sar] vi to rest, repose

reposera (RPl) [repo'sera] nf deck chair

reposición [reposi'θjon] nf replacement; (CINE) remake

reposo [re'poso] nm rest

repostar [repos'tar] vt to replenish; (AUTO) to fill up (with petrol (BRIT) o gasoline (US))

repostería [reposte'ria] nf confectioner's (shop)

represa [re'presa] nf dam; (lago artificial) lake, pool

represalia [repre'salja] nf reprisal

representación [representa'θjon] nf representation; (TEATRO) performance □ **representante** nmf representative; performer

representar [represen'tar] vt to represent; (TEATRO) to perform; (edad) to look; **representarse** vr to imagine □ **representativo, -a** adj representative

represión [repre'sjon] nf repression

reprimenda [repri'menda] nf reprimand, rebuke

reprimir [repri'mir] vt to repress

reprobar [repro'βar] vt to censure, reprove

reprochar [repro'tʃar] vt to reproach □ **reproche** nm reproach

reproducción [reproðuk'θjon] nf reproduction

reproducir [reproðu'θir] vt to reproduce; **reproducirse** vr to breed; (situación) to recur

reproductor, a [reproðuk'tor, a] adj reproductive

reptil [rep'til] nm reptile

república [re'puβlika] nf republic ► **República Dominicana** Dominican Republic □ **republicano, -a** adj, nm republican

repudiar [repu'ðjar] vt to repudiate; (fe) to renounce

repuesto [re'pwesto] nm (pieza de recambio) spare (part); (abastecimiento) supply; **rueda de ~** spare wheel

repugnancia [repuɣ'nanθja] nf repugnance □ **repugnante** adj repugnant, repulsive

repugnar [repuɣ'nar] vt to disgust

repulsa [re'pulsa] nf rebuff

repulsión [repul'sjon] nf repulsion, aversion □ **repulsivo, -a** adj repulsive

reputación [reputa'θjon] nf reputation

requerir [reke'rir] vt (pedir) to ask, request; (exigir) to require; (llamar) to send for, summon

requesón [reke'son] nm cottage cheese

requete... [re'kete] prefijo extremely

réquiem [rekjem] (pl **réquiems**) nm requiem

requisito [reki'sito] nm requirement, requisite

res [res] nf beast, animal

resaca [re'saka] nf (de mar) undertow, undercurrent; (fam) hangover

resaltar [resal'tar] vi to project, stick out; (fig) to stand out

resarcir [resar'θir] vt to compensate; **resarcirse** vr to make up for

resbaladero (MEX) nm slide

resbaladizo, -a [resβala'ðiθo, a] adj slippery

resbalar [resβa'lar] vi to slip, slide; (fig) to slip (up); **resbalarse** vr to slip, slide; to slip (up) □ **resbalón** nm (acción) slip

rescatar [reska'tar] vt (salvar) to save, rescue; (objeto) to get back, recover; (cautivos) to ransom

rescate [res'kate] nm rescue; (de objeto) recovery; **pagar un ~** to pay a ransom

rescindir [resθin'dir] vt to rescind

rescisión [resθi'sjon] nf cancellation

resecar [rese'kar] vt to dry thoroughly; (MED) to cut out, remove; **resecarse** vr to dry up

reseco, -a [re'seko, a] adj very dry; (fig) skinny

resentido, -a [resen'tiðo, a] adj resentful

resentimiento [resenti'mjento] nm resentment, bitterness

resentirse [resen'tirse] vr (debilitarse: persona) to suffer; **~ de** (consecuencias) to feel the effects of; **~ de o por) algo** to resent sth, be bitter about sth

reseña [re'seɲa] nf (cuenta) account; (informe) report; (LITERATURA) review □ **reseñar** [rese'ɲar] vt to describe; (LITERATURA) to review

reserva [re'serβa] nf reserve; (reservación) reservation

reservado, -a [reser'βaðo, a] adj reserved; (retraído) cold, distant ♦ nm private room

reservar [reser'βar] vt (guardar) to keep; (habitación, entrada) to reserve; **reservarse** vr to save o.s.; (callar) to keep to o.s.

resfriado [resfri'aðo] nm cold □ **resfriarse** vr to cool; (MED) to catch a cold

resguardar [resɣwar'ðar] vt to protect, shield; **resguardarse** vr: **resguardarse de** o guard against □ **resguardo** nm defence; (vale) voucher; (recibo) receipt, slip

residencia [resi'ðenθja] nf residence
▶ **residencia de ancianos** residential home, old people's home
▶ **residencia universitaria** hall of residence □ **residencial** nf (urbanización) housing estate

residente [resi'ðente] adj, nmf resident

residir [resi'ðir] vi to reside, live; **~ en** to reside in, lie in

residuo [re'siðwo] nm residue

resignación [resiɣna'θjon] nf resignation □ **resignarse** vr:

to resign o.s. to, be resigned to

resina [re'sina] nf resin

resistencia [resis'tenθja] nf (dureza) endurance, strength; (oposición, ELEC) resistance □ **resistente** adj strong, hardy; resistant

resistir [resis'tir] vt (soportar) to bear; (oponerse a) to resist, oppose; (aguantar) to put up with ♦ vi to resist; (aguantar) to last, endure; **resistirse** vr: **resistirse a** to refuse to, resist

resoluto, -a [reso'luto, a] adj resolute

resolver [resol'βer] vt to resolve; (solucionar) to solve, resolve; (decidir) to decide, settle; **resolverse** vr to make up one's mind

resonar [reso'nar] vi to ring, echo

resoplar [reso'plar] vi to snort □ **resoplido** nm heavy breathing

resorte [re'sorte] nm spring; (fig) lever

resortera [resor'tera] nf (MÉX) catapult

respaldar [respal'dar] vt to back (up), support; **respaldarse** vr to lean back; **respaldarse con** o **en** (fig) to take one's stand on □ **respaldo** nm (de sillón) back; (fig) support, backing

respectivo, -a [respek'tiβo, a] adj respective; **en lo ~** with regard to

respecto [res'pekto] nm: **al ~** on this matter; **con ~ a, ~ de** with regard to, in relation to

respetable [respe'taβle] adj respectable

respetar [respe'tar] vt to respect □ **respeto** nm respect; (acatamiento) deference; **respetos** nmpl respects □ **respetuoso, -a** adj respectful

respingo [res'pingo] nm start, jump

respiración [respira'θjon] nf breathing; (MED) respiration; (ventilación) ventilation ▶ **respiración asistida** artificial respiration (by machine)

respirar [respi'rar] vi to breathe □ **respiratorio, -a** adj respiratory

❏ **respiro** nm breathing; (fig: descanso) respite

resplandecer [resplande'θer] vi to shine ❏ **resplandeciente** adj resplendent, shining ❏ **resplandor** nm brilliance, brightness; (de luz, fuego) blaze

responder [respon'der] vt to answer ♦ vi to answer; (fig) to respond; (pey) to answer back; **~ de** o **por** for answer for ❏ **respondón, -ona** adj cheeky

responsabilidad [responsaβili'ðað] nf responsibility

responsabilizarse [responsaβili'θarse] vr to make o.s. responsible, take charge

responsable [respon'saβle] adj responsible

respuesta [res'pwesta] nf answer, reply

resquebrajar [reskeβra'xar] vt to crack, split; **resquebrajarse** vr to crack, split

resquicio [res'kiθjo] nm chink; (hendedura) crack

resta ['resta] nf (MAT) remainder

restablecer [restaβle'θer] vt to re-establish, restore; **restablecerse** vr to recover

restante [res'tante] adj remaining; **lo ~** the remainder

restar [res'tar] vt (MAT) to subtract; (fig) to take away ♦ vi to remain, be left

restauración [restaura'θjon] nf restoration

restaurante [restau'rante] nm restaurant

restaurar [restau'rar] vt to restore

restituir [restitu'ir] vt (devolver) to return, give back; (rehabilitar) to restore

resto ['resto] nm (residuo) rest, remainder; (apuesta) stake; **restos** nmpl remains

restorán nm (LAm) restaurant

restregar [restre'ɣar] vt to scrub, rub

restricción [restrik'θjon] nf restriction

restringir [restrin'xir] vt to restrict, limit

resucitar [resuθi'tar] vt, vi to resuscitate, revive

resuelto, -a [re'swelto, a] pp de **resolver** ♦ adj resolute, determined

resultado [resul'taðo] nm result; (conclusión) outcome ❏ **resultante** adj resulting, resultant

resultar [resul'tar] vi (ser) to be; (llegar a ser) to turn out to be; (salir bien) to turn out well; (COM) to amount to; **~ de** to stem from; **me resulta difícil hacerlo** it's difficult for me to do it

resumen [re'sumen] (pl **resúmenes**) nm summary, résumé; **en ~** in short

resumir [resu'mir] vt to sum up; (cortar) to abridge, cut down; (condensar) to summarize

⚠ No confundir **resumir** con la palabra inglesa **resume**.

resurgir [resur'xir] vi (reaparecer) to reappear

resurrección [resurre(k)'θjon] nf resurrection

retablo [re'taβlo] nm altarpiece

retaguardia [reta'ɣwarðja] nf rearguard

retahíla [reta'ila] nf series, string

retal [re'tal] nm remnant

retar [re'tar] vt to challenge; (desafiar) to defy, dare

retazo [re'taθo] nm snippet (BRIT), fragment

retención [reten'θjon] nf (tráfico) hold-up ▶ **retención fiscal** deduction for tax purposes

retener [rete'ner] vt (intereses) to withhold

reticente [reti'θente] adj (tono) insinuating; (postura) reluctant; **ser ~ a hacer algo** to be reluctant o unwilling to do sth

retina [re'tina] nf retina

retintín [retin'tin] nm jangle, jingle

retirada [reti'raða] nf (MIL, refugio) retreat; (de dinero) withdrawal; (de embajador) recall ▫ **retirado, -a** adj (lugar) remote; (vida) quiet; (jubilado) retired

retirar [reti'rar] vt to withdraw; (quitar) to remove; (jubilar) to retire, pension off; **retirarse** vr to retreat, withdraw; to retire; (acostarse) to retire, go to bed ▫ **retiro** nm retreat; retirement; (pago) pension

reto ['reto] nm dare, challenge

retocar [reto'kar] vt (fotografía) to touch up, retouch

retoño [re'toɲo] nm sprout, shoot; (fig) offspring, child

retoque [re'toke] nm retouching

retorcer [retor'θer] vt to twist; (manos, lavado) to wring; **retorcerse** vr to become twisted; (mover el cuerpo) to writhe

retorcido, -a [retor'θiðo, a] adj (persona) devious

retorcijón (LAm) nm (tb: ~ **de tripas**) stomach cramp

retórica [re'torika] nf rhetoric; (pey) affectedness

retorno [re'torno] nm return

retortijón [retorti'xon] (ESP) nm (tb: ~ **de tripas**) stomach cramp

retozar [reto'θar] vi (juguetear) to frolic, romp; (saltar) to gambol

retracción [retrak'θjon] nf retraction

retraerse [retra'erse] vr to retreat, withdraw ▫ **retraído, -a** adj shy, retiring ▫ **retraimiento** nm retirement; (timidez) shyness

retransmisión [retransmi'sjon] nf repeat (broadcast)

retransmitir [retransmi'tir] vt (mensaje) to relay; (TV etc) to repeat, retransmit; (: en vivo) to broadcast live

retrasado, -a [retra'saðo, a] adj late; (MED) mentally retarded; (país etc) backward, underdeveloped

retrasar [retra'sar] vt (demorar) to postpone, put off; (retardar) to slow down ♦ vi (atrasarse) to be slow; (reloj) to be slow; (producción) to fall (off); (quedarse atrás) to lag behind; **retrasarse** vr to be late; to be slow; to fall (off); to lag behind

retraso [re'traso] nm (demora) delay; (lentitud) slowness; (tardanza) lateness; (atraso) backwardness; **retrasos** nmpl (FINANZAS) arrears; **llegar con ~** to arrive late ► **retraso mental** mental deficiency

retratar [retra'tar] vt (ARTE) to paint the portrait of; (fotografiar) to photograph; (fig) to depict, describe ▫ **retrato** nm portrait; (fig) likeness ▫ **retrato-robot** (ESP) nm Identikit®

retrete [re'trete] nm toilet

retribuir [retriβ'wir] vt (recompensar) to reward; (pagar) to pay

retro... ['retro] prefijo retro...

retroceder [retroθe'ðer] vi (echarse atrás) to move back(wards); (fig) to back down

retroceso [retro'θeso] nm backward movement; (MED) relapse; (fig) backing down

retrospectivo, -a [retrospek'tiβo, a] adj retrospective

retrovisor [retroβi'sor] nm (tb: **espejo** ~) rear-view mirror

retumbar [retum'bar] vi to echo, resound

reúma [re'uma], **reuma** ['reuma] nm rheumatism

reunión [reu'njon] nf (asamblea) meeting; (fiesta) party

reunir [reu'nir] vt (juntar) to reunite, join (together); (recoger) to gather (together); (personas) to get together; (cualidades) to combine; **reunirse** vr (personas: en asamblea) to meet, gather

revalidar [reβali'ðar] vt (ratificar) to confirm, ratify

revalorizar [reβaloɾi'θar] vt to revalue, reassess

revancha [re'βantʃa] nf revenge

revelación [reβela'θjon] nf revelation

revelado [reβe'laðo] nm developing

revelar [reβe'lar] vt to reveal; (FOTO) to develop

reventa [re'βenta] nf (de entradas: para concierto) touting

reventar [reβen'tar] vt to burst, explode

reventón [reβen'ton] nm (AUTO) blow-out (BRIT), flat (US)

reverencia [reβe'renθja] nf reverence
❑ **reverenciar** vt to revere

reverendo, -a [reβe'rendo, a] adj reverend

reverente [reβe'rente] adj reverent

reversa [re'βersa] nf (MÉX, CAm) (reverse) gear

reversible [reβer'siβle] adj (prenda) reversible

reverso [re'βerso] nm back, other side; (de moneda) reverse

revertir [reβer'tir] vi to revert

revés [re'βes] nm back, wrong side; (fig) reverse, setback; (DEPORTE) backhand; **al ~** the wrong way round; (de arriba abajo) upside down; (ropa) inside out; **volver algo del ~** to turn sth round; (ropa) to turn sth inside out

revisar [reβi'sar] vt (examinar) to check; (texto etc) to revise ❑ **revisión** nf revision ▸ **revisión salarial** wage review

revisor, -a [reβi'sor, a] nm/f inspector; (FERRO) ticket collector

revista [re'βista] nf magazine, review; (TEATRO) revue; (inspección) inspection; **pasar ~ a** to review, inspect ▸ **revista del corazón** magazine featuring celebrity gossip and real-life romance stories

revivir [reβi'βir] vi to revive

revolcarse [reβol'karse] vr to roll about

revoltijo [reβol'tixo] nm mess, jumble

revoltoso, -a [reβol'toso, a] adj (travieso) naughty, unruly

revolución [reβolu'θjon] nf revolution ❑ **revolucionario, -a** adj, nm/f revolutionary

revolver [reβol'βer] vt (desordenar) to disturb, mess up; (mover) to move about ♦ vi: **~ en** to go through, rummage (about) in; **revolverse** vr (volver contra) to turn on o against

revólver [re'βolβer] nm revolver

revuelo [re'βwelo] nm fluttering; (fig) commotion

revuelta [re'βwelta] nf (motín) revolt; (agitación) commotion

revuelto, -a [re'βwelto, a] pp de **revolver** ♦ adj (mezclado) mixed-up, in disorder

rey [rei] nm king; **Día de Reyes** Twelfth Night; **los Reyes Magos** the Three Wise Men, the Magi

REYES MAGOS

On the night before the 6th January (the Epiphany), children go to bed expecting **los Reyes Magos** (the Three Wise Men) to bring them presents. Twelfth Night processions, known as **cabalgatas**, take place that evening when 3 people dressed as **los Reyes Magos** arrive in the town by land or sea to the delight of the children.

reyerta [re'jerta] nf quarrel, brawl

rezagado, -a [reθa'ɣaðo, a] nm/f straggler

rezar [re'θar] vi to pray; **~ con** (fam) to concern, have to do with ❑ **rezo** nm prayer

rezumar [reθu'mar] vt to ooze

ría ['ria] nf estuary

riada [ri'aða] nf flood

ribera [ri'βera] nf (de río) bank; (: área) riverside

ribete [ri'βete] nm (de vestido) border; (fig) addition

ricino [ri'θino] nm: **aceite de ~** castor oil

rico, -a ['riko, a] adj rich; (adinerado) wealthy, rich; (lujoso) luxurious; (comida) delicious; (niño) lovely, cute ♦ nm/f rich person

ridiculez [riðiku'leθ] nf absurdity

ridiculizar [riðikuli'θar] vt to ridicule

ridículo, -a [ri'ðikulo, a] adj ridiculous; **hacer el ~** to make a fool of o.s.; **poner a algn en ~** to make a fool of sb

riego ['rjeɣo] nm (aspersión) watering; (irrigación) irrigation ▶ **riego sanguíneo** blood flow o circulation

riel [rjel] nm rail

rienda ['rjenda] nf rein; **dar ~ suelta a** to give free rein to

riesgo ['rjesɣo] nm risk; **correr el ~ de** to run the risk of

rifa ['rifa] nf (lotería) raffle □ **rifar** vt to raffle

rifle ['rifle] nm rifle

rigidez [rixi'ðeθ] nf rigidity, stiffness; (fig) strictness □ **rígido, -a** adj rigid, stiff; strict, inflexible

rigor [ri'ɣor] nm strictness, rigour; (inclemencia) harshness; **de ~** de rigueur, essential □ **riguroso, -a** adj rigorous; harsh; (severo) severe

rimar [ri'mar] vi to rhyme

rimbombante [rimbom'bante] adj pompous

rímel ['rimel] nm mascara

rímmel ['rimel] nm = **rímel**

rin (MEX) nm (wheel) rim

rincón [rin'kon] nm corner (inside)

rinoceronte [rinoθe'ronte] nm rhinoceros

riña ['riɲa] nf (disputa) argument; (pelea) brawl

riñón [ri'ɲon] nm kidney

río etc ['rio] vb ver **reír** ♦ nm river; (fig) torrent, stream ▶ **río abajo/arriba** downstream/upstream ▶ **Río de la Plata** River Plate

rioja [ri'oxa] nm (vino) rioja (wine)

rioplatense [riopla'tense] adj of o from the River Plate region

riqueza [ri'keθa] nf wealth, riches pl; (cualidad) richness

risa ['risa] nf laughter; (una risa) laugh; **¡qué ~!** what a laugh!

risco ['risko] nm crag, cliff

ristra ['ristra] nf string

risueño, -a [ri'sweɲo, a] adj (sonriente) smiling; (contento) cheerful

ritmo ['ritmo] nm rhythm; **a ~ lento** slowly; **trabajar a ~ lento** to go slow ▶ **ritmo cardíaco** heart rate

rito ['rito] nm rite

ritual [ri'twal] adj, nm ritual

rival [ri'βal] adj, nm/f rival □ **rivalidad** nf rivalry □ **rivalizar** vi: rivalizar con to rival, vie with

rizado, -a [ri'θaðo, a] adj curly ♦ nm curls pl

rizar [ri'θar] vt to curl; **rizarse** vr (pelo) to curl; (agua) to ripple □ **rizo** nm curl; ripple

RNE nf abr = **Radio Nacional de España**

robar [ro'βar] vt to rob; (objeto) to steal; (casa etc) to break into; (NAIPES) to draw

roble ['roβle] nm oak □ **robledal** nm oakwood

robo ['roβo] nm robbery, theft

robot [ro'βot] nm robot ▶ **robot (de cocina)** (ESP) food processor

robustecer [roβuste'θer] vt to strengthen

robusto, -a [ro'βusto, a] adj robust, strong

roca ['roka] nf rock

roce ['roθe] nm (caricia) brush; (TEC) friction; (en la piel) graze; **tener ~ con** to be in close contact with

rociar [ro'θjar] vt to spray

rocín [ro'θin] nm nag, hack

rocío [ro'θio] nm dew

rocola (LAm) nf jukebox

rocoso, -a [ro'koso, a] *adj* rocky

rodaballo [roða'βaʎo] *nm* turbot

rodaja [ro'ðaxa] *nf* slice

rodaje [ro'ðaxe] *nm* (CINE) shooting, filming; (AUTO): **en ~** running in

rodar [ro'ðar] *vt* to surround ♦ *vi* to wheel (along); (escalera) to roll down; (viajar por) to travel (over) ♦ *vi* to roll; (coche) to go, run; (CINE) to shoot, film

rodear [roðe'ar] *vt* to surround ♦ *vi* to go round; **rodearse** *vr*: **rodearse de amigos** to surround o.s. with friends

rodeo [ro'ðeo] *nm* (ruta indirecta) detour; (evasión) evasion; (DEPORTE) rodeo; **hablar sin rodeos** to come to the point, speak plainly

rodilla [ro'ðiʎa] *nf* knee; **de rodillas** kneeling; **ponerse de rodillas** to kneel (down)

rodillo [ro'ðiʎo] *nm* roller; (CULIN) rolling-pin

roedor, a [roe'ðor, a] *adj* gnawing ♦ *nm* rodent

roer [ro'er] *vt* (masticar) to gnaw; (corroer, fig) to corrode

rogar [ro'ɣar] *vt, vi* (pedir) to ask for; (suplicar) to beg, plead; **se ruega no fumar** please do not smoke

rojizo, -a [ro'xiθo, a] *adj* reddish

rojo, -a [ˈroxo, a] *adj, nm* red; **al ~ vivo** red-hot

rol [rol] *nm* list, roll; (papel) role

rollito [ro'ʎito] *nm* (tb: **~ de primavera**) spring roll

rollizo, -a [ro'ʎiθo, a] *adj* (objeto) cylindrical; (persona) plump

rollo [ˈroʎo] *nm* roll; (de cuerda) coil; (madera) log; (ESP: fam) bore; **¡qué ~!** (ESP: fam) what a carry-on!

Roma [ˈroma] *n* Rome

romance [ro'manθe] *nm* (amoroso) romance; (LITERATURA) ballad

romano, -a [ro'mano, a] *adj, nm/f* Roman; **a la romana** in batter

romántico, -a [ro'mantiko, a] *adj* romantic

rombo [ˈrombo] *nm* (GEOM) rhombus

romería [rome'ria] *nf* (REL) pilgrimage; (excursión) trip, outing

ROMERÍA

Originally a pilgrimage to a shrine or church to express devotion to the Virgin Mary or a local Saint, the **romería** has also become a rural festival which accompanies the pilgrimage. People come from all over to attend, bringing their own food and drink, and spend the day in celebration.

romero, -a [ro'mero, a] *nm/f* pilgrim ♦ *nm* rosemary

romo, -a [ˈromo, a] *adj* blunt; (fig) dull

rompecabezas [rompeka'βeθas] *nm inv* riddle, puzzle; (juego) jigsaw (puzzle)

rompehuelgas (LAm) [rompe'welɣas] *nm inv* strikebreaker, scab

rompeolas [rompe'olas] *nm inv* breakwater

romper [rom'per] *vt* to break; (hacer pedazos) to smash; (papel, tela etc) to tear, rip ♦ *vi* (olas) to break; (sol, diente) to break through; **romperse** *vr* to break; **~ un contrato** to break a contract; **~a** (empezar a) to start (suddenly) to; **~ a llorar** to burst into tears; **~ con algn** to fall out with sb

ron [ron] *nm* rum

roncar [ron'kar] *vi* to snore

ronco, -a [ˈronko, a] *adj* (afónico) hoarse; (áspero) raucous

ronda [ˈronda] *nf* (gen) round; (patrulla) patrol ♦ **rondar** *vt* to patrol ♦ *vi* to patrol; (fig) to prowl round

ronquido [ron'kiðo] *nm* snore, snoring

ronronear [ronrone'ar] *vi* to purr

roña [ˈroɲa] *nf* (VETERINARIA) mange; (mugre) dirt, grime; (óxido) rust

roñoso, -a [ro'ɲoso, a] adj (mugriento) filthy; (tacaño) mean

ropa ['ropa] nf clothes pl ▶ **ropa blanca** linen ▶ **ropa de cama** bed linen ▶ **ropa de color** coloureds pl ▶ **ropa interior** underwear ▶ **ropa sucia** dirty washing ❑ **ropaje** nm gown, robes pl

ropero [ro'pero] nm linen cupboard; (guardarropa) wardrobe

rosa ['rosa] adj pink ♦ nf rose

rosado, -a [ro'saðo, a] adj pink ♦ nm rosé

rosal [ro'sal] nm rosebush

rosario [ro'sarjo] nm (REL) rosary; **rezar el ~** to say the rosary

rosca ['roska] nf (de tornillo) thread; (de humo) coil, spiral; (pan, postre) ring-shaped roll/pastry

rosetón [rose'ton] nm rosette; (ARQ) rose window

rosquilla [ros'kiʎa] nf doughnut-shaped fritter

rostro ['rostro] nm (cara) face

rotativo, -a [rota'tiβo, a] adj rotary

roto, -a ['roto, a] pp de **romper** ♦ adj broken

rotonda [ro'tonda] nf roundabout

rótula ['rotula] nf kneecap; (TEC) ball-and-socket joint

rotulador [rotula'ðor] nm felt-tip pen

rótulo ['rotulo] nm heading, title; label; (letrero) sign

rotundamente [rotunda'mente] adv (negar) flatly; (responder, afirmar) emphatically ❑ **rotundo, -a** adj round; (enfático) emphatic

rotura [ro'tura] nf (acto) breaking; (MED) fracture

rozadura [roθa'ðura] nf abrasion, graze

rozar [ro'θar] vt (frotar) to rub; (arañar) to scratch; (tocar ligeramente) to shave, touch lightly; **rozarse** vr to rub (together); **rozarse con** (fam) to rub shoulders with

rte. abr (= remite, remitente) sender

RTVE nf abr (TV) = Radiotelevisión Española

rubí [ru'βi] nm ruby; (de reloj) jewel

rubio, -a ['ruβjo, a] adj fair-haired, blond(e) ♦ nm/f blond/blonde; **tabaco ~** Virginia tobacco

rubor [ru'βor] nm (sonrojo) blush; (timidez) bashfulness ❑ **ruborizarse** vr to blush

rúbrica ['ruβrika] nf (de la firma) flourish ❑ **rubricar** vt (firmar) to sign with a flourish; (concluir) to sign and seal

rudimentario, -a [ruðimen'tarjo, a] adj rudimentary

rudo, -a ['ruðo, a] adj (sin pulir) unpolished; (grosero) coarse; (violento) violent; (sencillo) simple

rueda ['rweða] nf wheel; (círculo) ring, circle; (rodaja) slice, round ▶ **rueda de auxilio** (RPl) spare tyre ▶ **rueda delantera/trasera/de repuesto** front/back/spare wheel ▶ **rueda de prensa** press conference ▶ **rueda gigante** (LAm) big (BRIT) o Ferris (US) wheel

ruedo ['rweðo] nm (círculo) circle; (TAUR) arena, bullring

ruego etc ['rweɣo] vb ver **rogar** ♦ nm request

rugby ['ruɣβi] nm rugby

rugido [ru'xiðo] nm roar

rugir [ru'xir] vi to roar

rugoso, -a [ru'ɣoso, a] adj (arrugado) wrinkled; (áspero) rough; (desigual) ridged

ruido ['rwiðo] nm noise; (sonido) sound; (alboroto) racket, row; (escándalo) commotion, rumpus ❑ **ruidoso, -a** adj noisy, loud; (fig) sensational

ruin [rwin] adj contemptible, mean

ruina ['rwina] nf ruin; (colapso) collapse; (de persona) ruin, downfall

ruinoso, -a [rwi'noso, a] *adj* ruinous; *(destartalado)* dilapidated, tumbledown; *(COM)* disastrous

ruiseñor [rwise'ɲor] *nm* nightingale

rulero *(RPl)* *nm* roller

ruleta [ru'leta] *nf* roulette

rulo ['rulo] *nm (para el pelo)* curler

Rumanía [ruma'nia] *nf* Rumania

rumba ['rumba] *nf* rumba

rumbo ['rumbo] *nm (ruta)* route, direction; *(ángulo de dirección)* course, bearing; *(fig)* course of events; **ir con ~ a** to be heading for

rumiante [ru'mjante] *nm* ruminant

rumiar [ru'mjar] *vt* to chew; *(fig)* to chew over ♦ *vi* to chew the cud

rumor [ru'mor] *nm (ruido sordo)* low sound; *(murmuración)* murmur, buzz ❑ **rumorearse** *vr*: **se rumorea que ...** it is rumoured that ...

rupestre [ru'pestre] *adj* rock *cpd*

ruptura [rup'tura] *nf* rupture

rural [ru'ral] *adj* rural

Rusia ['rusja] *nf* Russia ❑ **ruso, -a** *adj, nm/f* Russian

rústico, -a ['rustiko, a] *adj* rustic; *(ordinario)* coarse, uncouth ♦ *nm/f* yokel

ruta ['ruta] *nf* route

rutina [ru'tina] *nf* routine

S, s

S *abr (= santo, a)* St; *(= sur)* S

s. *abr (= siglo)* C.; *(= siguiente)* foll

S.A. *abr (= Sociedad Anónima)* Ltd. (BRIT), Inc. (US)

sábado ['saβaðo] *nm* Saturday

sábana ['saβana] *nf* sheet

sabañón [saβa'ɲon] *nm* chilblain

saber [sa'βer] *vt* to know; *(llegar a conocer)* to find out, learn; *(tener capacidad de)* to know how to ♦ *vi*: **~ a**

to taste of, taste like ♦ *nm* knowledge, learning; **a ~** namely; **¿sabes conducir/ nadar?** can you drive/swim?; **¿sabes francés?** do you speak French?; **~ de memoria** to know by heart; **~ algo a algn** to inform sb of sth, let sb know sth

sabiduría [saβiðu'ria] *nf (conocimientos)* wisdom; *(instrucción)* learning

sabiendas [sa'βjendas] **a ~** *adv* knowingly

sabio, -a ['saβjo,a] *adj (docto)* learned; *(prudente)* wise, sensible

sabor [sa'βor] *nm* taste, flavour ❑ **saborear** *vt* to taste, savour; *(fig)* to relish

sabotaje [saβo'taxe] *nm* sabotage

sabré *etc* [sa'βre] *vb ver* **saber**

sabroso, -a [sa'βroso, a] *adj* tasty; *(fig: fam)* racy, salty

sacacorchos [saka'kortʃos] *nm inv* corkscrew

sacapuntas [saka'puntas] *nm inv* pencil sharpener

sacar [sa'kar] *vt* to take out; *(fig: extraer)* to get (out); *(quitar)* to remove, get out; *(hacer salir)* to bring out; *(conclusión)* to draw; *(novela etc)* to publish, bring out; *(ropa)* to take off; *(obra)* to make; *(premio)* to receive; *(entradas)* to serve; *(TENIS)* to serve; ~ **adelante** *(niño)* to bring up; *(negocio)* to carry on, go on with; ~ **a algn a bailar** to get sb up to dance; ~ **una foto** to take a photo; ~ **la lengua** to stick out one's tongue; ~ **buenas/ malas notas** to get good/bad marks

sacarina [saka'rina] *nf* saccharin(e)

sacerdote [saθer'ðote] *nm* priest

saciar [sa'θjar] *vt (hambre, sed)* to satisfy; **saciarse** *vr (de comida)* to get full up

saco ['sako] *nm* bag; *(grande)* sack; *(su contenido)* bagful; *(LAm: chaqueta)* jacket ▶ **saco de dormir** sleeping bag

sacramento [sakra'mento] *nm* sacrament

sacrificar [sakrifi'kar] *vt* to sacrifice ❑ **sacrificio** *nm* sacrifice

sacristía [sakris'tia] *nf* sacristy

sacudida [saku'ðiða] *nf* (*agitación*) shake, shaking; (*sacudimiento*) jolt, bump ► **sacudida eléctrica** electric shock

sacudir [saku'ðir] *vt* to shake; (*golpear*) to hit

Sagitario [saxi'tarjo] *nm* Sagittarius

sagrado, -a [sa'γraðo, a] *adj* sacred, holy

Sáhara ['saara] *nm* **el ~ the** Sahara (desert)

sal [sal] *vb ver* **salir ♦** *nf* salt ► **sales de baño** bath salts

sala ['sala] *nf* room; (*tb:* **~ de estar**) living room; (TEATRO) house, auditorium; (*de hospital*) ward ► **sala de espera** waiting room ► **sala de estar** living room ► **sala de fiestas** dance hall

salado, -a [sa'laðo, a] *adj* salty; (*fig*) witty, amusing; **agua salada** salt water

salar [sa'lar] *vt* to salt, add salt to

salario [sa'larjo] *nm* wage, pay

salchicha [sal'tʃitʃa] *nf* (pork) sausage ❑ **salchichón** *nm* (salami-type) sausage

saldo ['saldo] *nm* (*pago*) settlement; (*de una cuenta*) balance; (*lo restante*) remnant(s) (*pl*), remainder; (*de móvil*) credit; **saldos** *nmpl* (*en tienda*) sale

saldré *etc* [sal'dre] *vb ver* **salir**

salero [sa'lero] *nm* salt cellar

salgo *etc vb ver* **salir**

salida [sa'liða] *nf* (*puerta etc*) exit, way out; (*acto*) leaving, going out; (*de tren, AVIAC*) departure; (TEC) output, production; (*fig*) way out; (COM) opening; (GEO, *válvula*) outlet; (*de gas*) leak; **calle sin ~** cul-de-sac ► **salida de baño** bathrobe (RPI) ► **salida de**

emergencia/incendios emergency exit/fire escape

salir [sa'lir] *vi*

PALABRA CLAVE

[sa'lir] *vi*

1 (*partir de:* **salir de**) to leave; **Juan ha salido** Juan is out; **salió de la cocina** he came out of the kitchen

2 (*aparecer*) to appear; (*disco, libro*) to come out; **anoche salió en la tele** she appeared *o* was on TV last night; **salió en todos los periódicos** it was in all the papers

3 (*resultar*): **la muchacha nos salió muy trabajadora** the girl turned out to be a very hard worker; **la comida a ha salido exquisita** the food was delicious; **sale muy caro** it's very expensive

4: **salirle a uno algo**: **la entrevista que hice me salió bien/mal** the interview I did went *o* turned out well/badly

5: **salir adelante**: **no sé cómo haré para salir adelante** I don't know how I'll get by

♦ salirse *vr* (*líquido*) to spill; (*animal*) to escape

saliva [sa'liβa] *nf* saliva

salmo ['salmo] *nm* psalm

salmón [sal'mon] *nm* salmon

salmonete [salmo'nete] *nm* red mullet

salón [sa'lon] *nm* (*de casa*) living room, lounge; (*muebles*) lounge suite ► **salón de baile** dance hall ► **salón de belleza** beauty parlour

salpicadera (MÉX) [salpika'ðera] *nf* mudguard (BRIT), fender (US)

salpicadero [salpika'ðero] *nm* (AUTO) dashboard

salpicar [salpi'kar] *vt* (*rociar*) to sprinkle, spatter; (*esparcir*) to scatter

salpicón [salpi'kon] *nm* (*tb:* **~ de marisco**) seafood salad

salsa ['salsa] nf sauce; (con carne asada) gravy; (fig) spice

saltamontes [salta'montes] nm inv grasshopper

saltar [sal'tar] vt to jump (over), leap (over); (dejar de lado) to skip, miss out ♦ vi to jump, leap; (pelota) to bounce; (al aire) to fly up; (quebrarse) to break; (al agua) to dive; (fig) to explode, blow up

salto ['salto] nm jump, leap; (al agua) dive ► **salto de agua** waterfall ► **salto de altura/longitud** high/long jump

salud [sa'luð] nf health; ¡(a su) ~! cheers!, good health! ❑ **saludable** adj (de buena salud) healthy; (provechoso) good, beneficial

saludar [salu'ðar] vt to greet; (MIL) to salute ❑ **saludo** nm greeting; "saludos" (en carta) "best wishes", "regards"

salvación [salβa'θjon] nf salvation; (rescate) rescue

salvado [sal'βaðo] nm bran

salvaje [sal'βaxe] adj wild; (tribu) savage

salvamanteles nm inv table mat

salvamento [salβa'mento] nm rescue

salvapantallas nm inv screen saver

salvar [sal'βar] vt (rescatar) to save, rescue; (resolver) to overcome, resolve; (cubrir distancias) to cover, travel; (hacer excepción) to except, exclude; (barco) to salvage

salvavidas [salβa'βiðas] adj inv: **bote/chaleco ~** lifeboat/life jacket

salvo, -a ['salβo, a] adj safe ♦ adv except (for), save; **a ~** out of danger; **~ que** unless

san [san] adj saint; **S~ Juan** St John

sanar [sa'nar] vt (herida) to heal; (persona) to cure ♦ vi (persona) to get well, recover; (herida) to heal

sanatorio [sana'torjo] nm sanatorium

sanción [san'θjon] nf sanction

sancochado, -a (MÉX) adj (CULIN) underdone, rare

sandalia [san'dalja] nf sandal

sandía [san'dia] nf watermelon

sandwich ['sanwitʃ] (pl **sandwichs**, **sandwiches**) nm sandwich

sanfermines nmpl festivities in celebration of San Fermín (Pamplona)

sangrar [san'grar] vt, vi to bleed ❑ **sangre** nf blood

sangría [san'gria] nf sangria, sweetened drink of red wine with fruit

sangriento, -a [san'grjento, a] adj bloody

sanguíneo, -a [san'gineo, a] adj blood cpd

sanidad [sani'ðað] nf (tb: ~ **pública**) public health

San Isidro nm patron saint of Madrid

sanitario, -a [sani'tarjo, a] adj health cpd ❏ **sanitarios** nmpl toilets (BRIT), washroom (US)

sano, -a ['sano, a] adj healthy; (sin daños) sound; (comida) wholesome; (entero) whole, intact; **~ y salvo** safe and sound

⚠ No confundir **sano** con la palabra inglesa *sane*.

Santiago [san'tjaɣo] nm: **~ (de Chile)** Santiago

santiamén [santja'men] nm: **en un ~** in no time at all

santidad [santi'ðað] nf holiness, sanctity

santiguarse [santi'ɣwarse] vr to make the sign of the cross

santo, -a ['santo, a] adj holy; (fig) wonderful, miraculous ♦ nm/f saint ♦ nm saint's day; **~ y seña** password

santuario [san'twarjo] nm sanctuary, shrine

sapo ['sapo] nm toad

saque ['sake] nm (TENIS) service, serve; (FUTBOL) throw-in ▶ **saque de esquina** corner (kick)

saquear [sake'ar] vt (MIL) to sack; (robar) to loot, plunder; (fig) to ransack

sarampión [saram'pjon] nm measles sg

sarcástico, -a [sar'kastiko, a] adj sarcastic

sardina [sar'ðina] nf sardine

sargento [sar'xento] nm sergeant

sarmiento [sar'mjento] nm (BOT) vine shoot

sarna ['sarna] nf itch; (MED) scabies

sarpullido [sarpu'ʎiðo] nm (MED) rash

sarro ['sarro] nm (en dientes) tartar, plaque

sartén [sar'ten] nf frying pan

sastre ['sastre] nm tailor ❏ **sastrería** nf (arte) tailoring; (tienda) tailor's (shop)

Satanás [sata'nas] nm Satan

satélite [sa'telite] nm satellite

sátira ['satira] nf satire

satisfacción [satisfak'θjon] nf satisfaction

satisfacer [satisfa'θer] vt to satisfy; (gastos) to meet; (pérdida) to make good; **satisfacerse** vr to satisfy o.s., be satisfied; (vengarse) to take revenge ❏ **satisfecho, -a** adj satisfied; (contento) content(ed), happy; (tb: **satisfecho de sí mismo**) self-satisfied, smug

saturar [satu'rar] vt to saturate; **saturarse** vr (mercado, aeropuerto) to reach saturation point

sauce ['sauθe] nm willow ▶ **sauce llorón** weeping willow

sauna ['sauna] nf sauna

savia ['saβja] nf sap

saxofón [sakso'fon] nm saxophone

sazonar [saθo'nar] vt to ripen; (CULIN) to flavour, season

scooter (ESP) nf scooter

Scotch® (LAm) nm Sellotape® (BRIT), Scotch tape® (US)

SE abr (= sudeste) SE

se

PALABRA CLAVE

[se] pron

1 (reflexivo: sg: m) himself; (: f) herself; (: pl) themselves; (: cosa) itself; (: de Vd) yourself; (: de Vds) yourselves; **se está preparando** she's preparing herself

2 (con complemento indirecto) to him; to her; to them; to it; to you; **a usted se lo dije ayer** I told you yesterday; **se compró un sombrero** he bought himself a hat; **se rompió la pierna** he broke his leg

3 (uso recíproco) each other, one another; **se miraron (el uno al otro)** they looked at each other o one another

4 (en oraciones pasivas): **se han vendido muchos libros** a lot of books have been sold

5 (*impers*): **se dice que ...** people say that ..., it is said that ...; **allí se come muy bien** the food there is very good, you can eat very well there

sé *etc* [se] *vb ver* **saber**; **ser**

sea *etc* ['sea] *vb ver* **ser**

sebo ['seβo] *nm* fat, grease

secador [seka'ðor] *nm*: ~ **de pelo** hair-dryer

secadora [seka'ðora] *nf* tumble dryer

secar [se'kar] *vt* to dry; **secarse** *vr* to dry (off); (*río, planta*) to dry up

sección [sek'θjon] *nf* section

seco, -a ['seko, a] *adj* dry; (*carácter*) cold; (*respuesta*) sharp, curt; **parar en** ~ to stop dead; **decir algo a secas** to say sth curtly

secretaría [sekreta'ria] *nf* secretariat

secretario, -a [sekre'tarjo, a] *nm/f* secretary

secreto, -a [se'kreto, a] *adj* secret; (*persona*) secretive ♦ *nm* secret; (*calidad*) secrecy

secta ['sekta] *nf* sect

sector [sek'tor] *nm* sector

secuela [se'kwela] *nf* consequence

secuencia [se'kwenθja] *nf* sequence

secuestrar [sekwes'trar] *vt* to kidnap; (*bienes*) to seize, confiscate
□ **secuestro** *nm* kidnapping; seizure, confiscation

secundario, -a [sekun'darjo, a] *adj* secondary

sed [seð] *nf* thirst; **tener ~** to be thirsty

seda ['seða] *nf* silk

sedal [se'ðal] *nm* fishing line

sedán (*LAm*) [se'ðan] *nm* saloon (*BRIT*), sedan (*US*)

sedante [se'ðante] *nm* sedative

sede ['seðe] *nf* (*de gobierno*) seat; (*de compañía*) headquarters *pl*; **Santa S~** Holy See

sedentario, -a [seðen'tarjo, a] *adj* sedentary

sediento, -a [se'ðjento, a] *adj* thirsty

sedimento [seði'mento] *nm* sediment

seducción [seðuk'θjon] *nf* seduction

seducir [seðu'θir] *vt* to seduce; (*cautivar*) to charm, fascinate; (*atraer*) to attract □ **seductor, a** *adj* seductive; charming, fascinating; attractive ♦ *nm/f* seducer

segar [se'ɣar] *vt* (*mies*) to reap, cut; (*hierba*) to mow, cut

seglar [se'ɣlar] *adj* secular, lay

seguida [se'ɣiða] *nf*: **en ~** at once, right away

seguido, -a [se'ɣiðo, a] *adj* (*continuo*) continuous, unbroken; (*recto*) straight ♦ *adv* (*directo*) straight (on); (*después*) after; (*LAm: a menudo*) often; **seguidos** consecutive, successive; **5 días seguidos** 5 days running, 5 days in a row

seguir [se'ɣir] *vt* to follow; (*venir después*) to follow on, come after; (*proseguir*) to continue; (*perseguir*) to chase, pursue ♦ *vi* (*gen*) to follow; (*continuar*) to continue, carry o go on; **seguirse** *vr* to follow; **sigo sin comprender** I still don't understand; **sigue lloviendo** it's still raining

según [se'ɣun] *prep* according to ♦ *adv*: **¿irás?** — **— are you going?** — it all depends ♦ *conj* as; ~ **caminamos** while we walk

segundo, -a [se'ɣundo, a] *adj* second ♦ *nm* second ♦ *nf* second meaning; **de segunda mano** second-hand; **segunda (clase)** second class; **segunda (marcha)** (*AUTO*) second (gear)

seguramente [seɣura'mente] *adv* surely; (*con certeza*) for sure, with certainty

seguridad [seɣuri'ðað] *nf* safety; (*del estado, de casa etc*) security; (*certidumbre*) certainty; (*confianza*)

confidence; (*estabilidad*) stability
▶ **seguridad social** social security

seguro, -a [se'ɣuro, a] *adj* (*cierto*) sure, certain; (*fiel*) trustworthy; (*libre de peligro*) safe; (*bien defendido, firme*) secure ♦ *adv* for sure, certainly ♦ *nm* (COM) insurance ▶ **seguro contra terceros/a todo riesgo** third party/ comprehensive insurance ▶ **seguros sociales** social security *sg*

seis [seis] *num* six

seísmo [se'ismo] *nm* tremor, earthquake

selección [selek'θjon] *nf* selection ❑ **seleccionar** *vt* to pick, choose, select

selectividad [selektiβi'ðað] (ESP) *nf* university entrance examination

selecto, -a [se'lekto, a] *adj* select, choice; (*escogido*) selected

sellar [se'ʎar] *vt* (*documento oficial*) to seal; (*pasaporte, visado*) to stamp

sello [se'ʎo] *nm* stamp; (*precinto*) seal

selva [selβa] *nf* (*bosque*) forest, woods *pl*; (*jungla*) jungle

semáforo [se'maforo] *nm* (AUTO) traffic lights *pl*; (FERRO) signal

semana [se'mana] *nf* week; **entre ~** during the week ▶ **Semana Santa** Holy Week ❑ **semanal** *adj* weekly ❑ **semanario** *nm* weekly magazine

---

SEMANA SANTA

In Spain celebrations for **Semana Santa** (Holy Week) are often spectacular. "Viernes Santo", "Sábado Santo" and "Domingo de Resurrección" (Good Friday, Holy Saturday, Easter Sunday) are all national public holidays, with additional days being given as local holidays. There are fabulous **procesiones** all over the country, with members of "cofradías" (brotherhoods) dressing in hooded robes and parading their "pasos"

(religious floats and sculptures) through the streets. Seville has the most famous Holy Week processions.

sembrar [sem'brar] *vt* to sow; (*objetos*) to sprinkle, scatter about; (*noticias etc*) to spread

semejante [seme'xante] *adj* (*parecido*) similar ♦ *nm* fellow man, fellow creature; **semejantes** alike, similar; **nunca hizo cosa ~** he never did any such thing ❑ **semejanza** *nf* similarity, resemblance

semejar [seme'xar] *vi* to seem like, resemble; **semejarse** *vr* to look alike, be similar

semen ['semen] *nm* semen

semestral [semes'tral] *adj* half-yearly, bi-annual

semicírculo [semi'θirkulo] *nm* semicircle

semidesnatado, -a [semiðesna'taðo, a] *adj* semi-skimmed

semifinal [semifi'nal] *nf* semifinal

semilla [se'miʎa] *nf* seed

seminario [semi'narjo] *nm* (REL) seminary; (ESCOL) seminar

sémola ['semola] *nf* semolina

senado [se'naðo] *nm* senate ❑ **senador, a** *nm/f* senator

sencillez [senθi'ʎeθ] *nf* simplicity; (*de persona*) naturalness ❑ **sencillo, -a** *adj* simple; natural, unaffected

senda ['senda] *nf* path, track

senderismo [sende'rismo] *nm* hiking

sendero [sen'dero] *nm* path, track

sendos, -as ['sendos, as] *adj pl*: **les dio ~ golpes** he hit both of them

senil [se'nil] *adj* senile

seno ['seno] *nm* (ANAT) bosom, bust; (*fig*) bosom; **senos** breasts

sensación [sensa'θjon] *nf* sensation; (*sentido*) sense; (*sentimiento*) feeling ❑ **sensacional** *adj* sensational

sensato, -a [sen'sato, a] *adj* sensible

sensible [sen'sible] *adj* sensitive; (*apreciable*) perceptible, appreciable; (*pérdida*) considerable ☐ **sensiblero, -a** *adj* sentimental

⚠ No confundir **sensible** con la palabra inglesa *sensible*.

sensitivo, -a [sensi'tiβo, a] *adj* sense *cpd*

sensorial [senso'rjal] *adj* sensory

sensual [sen'swal] *adj* sensual

sentada [sen'taða] *nf* sitting; (*protesta*) sit-in

sentado, -a [sen'taðo, a] *adj*: **estar ~** to sit, be sitting (down); **dar por ~** to take for granted, assume

sentar [sen'tar] *vt* to sit, seat; (*fig*) to establish ♦ *vi* (*vestido*) to suit; (*alimento*): **~ bien/mal a** to agree/disagree with; **sentarse** *vr* (*persona*) to sit, sit down; (*los depósitos*) to settle

sentencia [sen'tenθja] *nf* (*máxima*) maxim, saying; (*JUR*) sentence ☐ **sentenciar** *vt* to sentence

sentido, -a [sen'tiðo, a] *adj* (*pérdida*) regrettable; (*carácter*) sensitive ♦ *nm* sense; (*sentimiento*) feeling; (*significado*) sense, meaning; (*dirección*) direction; **mi más ~ pésame** my deepest sympathy; **tener ~** to make sense ▶ **sentido común** common sense ▶ **sentido del humor** sense of humour ▶ **sentido único** one-way (street)

sentimental [sentimen'tal] *adj* sentimental; **vida ~** love life

sentimiento [senti'mjento] *nm* feeling

sentir [sen'tir] *vt* to feel; (*percibir*) to perceive, sense; (*lamentar*) to regret, be sorry for ♦ *vi* (*tener la sensación*) to feel; (*lamentarse*) to feel sorry ♦ *nm* opinion, judgement; **sentirse bien/mal** to feel well/ill; **lo siento** I'm sorry

seña ['seɲa] *nf* sign; (*MIL*) password; **señas** *nfpl* (*dirección*) address *sg*

▶ **señas personales** personal description *sg*

señal [se'ɲal] *nf* sign; (*síntoma*) symptom; (*FERRO, TEL*) signal; (*marca*) mark; (*COM*) deposit; **en ~ de** as a token o sign of ☐ **señalar** *vt* to mark; (*indicar*) to point out, indicate

señor [se'ɲor] *nm* (*hombre*) man; (*caballero*) gentleman; (*dueño*) owner, master; (*trato: antes de nombre propio*) Mr; (: *hablando directamente*) sir; **muy ~ mío** Dear Sir; **el ~ alcalde/presidente** the mayor/president

señora [se'ɲora] *nf* (*dama*) lady; (*trato: antes de nombre propio*) Mrs; (: *hablando directamente*) madam; (*esposa*) wife; **Nuestra S~** Our Lady

señorita [seɲo'rita] *nf* (*con nombre y/o apellido*) Miss; (*mujer joven*) young lady

señorito [seɲo'rito] *nm* young gentleman; (*pey*) rich kid

sepa *etc* ['sepa] *vb ver* **saber**

separación [separa'θjon] *nf* separation; (*división*) division; (*hueco*) gap

separar [sepa'rar] *vt* to separate; (*dividir*) to divide; **separarse** *vr* (*parte*) to come away; (*partes*) to come apart; (*persona*) to leave, go away; (*matrimonio*) to separate ☐ **separatismo** *nm* separatism

sepia ['sepja] *nf* cuttlefish

septentrional [septentrjo'nal] *adj* northern

septiembre [sep'tjembre] *nm* September

séptimo, -a ['septimo, a] *adj, nm* seventh

sepulcral [sepul'kral] *adj* (*fig: silencio, atmósfera*) deadly ☐ **sepulcro** *nm* tomb, grave

sepultar [sepul'tar] *vt* to bury ☐ **sepultura** *nf* (*acto*) burial; (*tumba*) grave, tomb

sequía [se'kia] *nf* drought

séquito ['sekito] nm (de rey etc) retinue; (seguidores) followers pl

ser
PALABRA CLAVE
[ser] vi
1 (descripción) to be; **es médica/muy alta** she's a doctor/very tall; **la familia es de Cuzco** his (o her etc) family is from Cuzco; **soy Ana** (TEL) Ana speaking o here
2 (propiedad): **es de Joaquín** it's Joaquín's, it belongs to Joaquín
3 (horas, fechas, números): **es la una** it's one o'clock; **son las seis y media** it's half-past six; **es el 1 de junio** it's the first of June; **somos/son seis** there are six of us/them
4 (en oraciones pasivas): **ha sido descubierto ya** it's already been discovered
5: **es de esperar que ...** it is to be hoped o I etc hope that ...
6 (locuciones con sub): **o sea** that is to say; **sea él sea su hermana** either him o his sister
7: **a no ser por él ...** but for him ...
8: **a no ser que: a no ser que tenga uno ya** unless he's got one already
♦ nm being ▶ **ser humano** human being

sereno, -a [se'reno, a] adj (persona) calm, unruffled; (el tiempo) fine, settled; (ambiente) calm, peaceful
♦ nm night watchman

serial [ser'jal] nm serial

serie ['serje] nf series; (cadena) sequence, succession; **fuera de ~** out of order; (fig) special, out of the ordinary; **fabricación en ~** mass production

seriedad [serje'ðað] nf seriousness; (formalidad) reliability ◻ **serio, -a** adj

serious; reliable, dependable; grave, serious; **en serio** adv seriously

serigrafía [seriɣra'fia] nf silk-screen printing

sermón [ser'mon] nm (REL) sermon

seropositivo, -a [seroposi'tiβo] adj HIV positive

serpentear [serpente'ar] vi to wriggle; (camino, río) to wind, snake

serpentina [serpen'tina] nf streamer

serpiente [ser'pjente] nf snake
▶ **serpiente de cascabel** rattlesnake

serranía [serra'nia] nf mountainous area

serrar [se'rrar] vt to saw

serrín [se'rrin] nm sawdust

serrucho [se'rrutʃo] nm saw

service (RPI) nm (AUTO) service

servicio [ser'βiθjo] nm service; (LAm AUTO) service; **servicios** nmpl (ESP) toilet(s) ▶ **servicio incluido** service charge included ▶ **servicio militar** military service

servidumbre [serβi'ðumbre] nf (sujeción) servitude; (criados) servants pl, slaves

servil [ser'βil] adj servile

servilleta [serβi'ʎeta] nf serviette, napkin

servir [ser'βir] vt to serve ♦ vi to serve; (tener utilidad) to be of use, be useful; **servirse** vr to serve o.s.; **servirse de algo** to make use of sth, use sth; **sírvase pasar** please come in

sesenta [se'senta] num sixty

sesión [se'sjon] nf (POL) session, sitting; (CINE) showing

seso ['seso] nm brain ◻ **sesudo, -a** adj sensible, wise

seta ['seta] nf mushroom ▶ **seta venenosa** toadstool

setecientos, -as [sete'θjentos, as] adj, num seven hundred

setenta [se'tenta] num seventy

seto ['seto] nm hedge

severo, -a [se'βero, a] *adj* severe

Sevilla [se'βiʎa] *n* Seville □ **sevillano, -a** *adj* of o from Seville ♦ *nm/f* native o inhabitant of Seville

sexo ['sekso] *nm* sex

sexto, -a ['seksto, a] *adj*, *nm* sixth

sexual [sek'swal] *adj* sexual; **vida ~** sex life

si [si] *conj* if ♦ *nm* (MÚS) B; **me pregunto si ...** I wonder if o whether ...

sí [si] *adv* yes ♦ *nm* consent ♦ *pron* (uso impersonal) oneself; (sg: m) himself; (: f) herself; (: de cosa) itself; (: de usted) yourself; (pl) themselves; (de ustedes) yourselves; (recíproco) each other; **él no quiere pero yo sí** he doesn't want to but I do; **ella sí vendrá** she will certainly come, she is sure to come; **claro que sí** of course; **creo que sí** I think so

siamés, -esa [sja'mes, esa] *adj*, *nm/f* Siamese

SIDA ['siða] *nm abr* (= Síndrome de Inmunodeficiencia Adquirida) AIDS

siderúrgico, -a [siðe'rurxiko, a] *adj* iron and steel *cpd*

sidra ['siðra] *nf* cider

siembra ['sjembra] *nf* sowing

siempre ['sjempre] *adv* always; (todo el tiempo) all the time; **~ que** (cada vez) whenever; (dado que) provided that; **como ~** as usual; **para ~** for ever

sien [sjen] *nf* temple

siento etc ['sjento] *vb ver* **sentar**; **sentir**

sierra ['sjerra] *nf* (TEC) saw; (cadena de montañas) mountain range

siervo, -a ['sjerβo, a] *nm/f* slave

siesta ['sjesta] *nf* siesta, nap; **echar la ~** to have an afternoon nap o a siesta

siete ['sjete] *num* seven

sifón [si'fon] *nm* syphon

sigla ['siɣla] *nf* abbreviation; acronym

siglo ['siɣlo] *nm* century; (fig) age

significado [siɣnifi'kaðo] *nm* (de palabra etc) meaning

significar [siɣnifi'kar] *vt* to mean, signify; (notificar) to make known, express □ **significativo, -a** *adj* significant

signo ['siɣno] *nm* sign ▸ **signo de admiración** o **exclamación** exclamation mark ▸ **signo de interrogación** question mark

sigo etc *vb ver* **seguir**

siguiente [si'ɣjente] *adj* next, following

siguió etc *vb ver* **seguir**

sílaba ['silaβa] *nf* syllable

silbar [sil'βar] *vt*, *vi* to whistle □ **silbato** *nm* whistle □ **silbido** *nm* whistle, whistling

silenciador [silenθja'ðor] *nm* silencer

silenciar [silen'θjar] *vt* (persona) to silence; (escándalo) to hush up □ **silencio** *nm* silence, quiet □ **silencioso, -a** *adj* silent, quiet

silla ['siʎa] *nf* (asiento) chair; (tb: ~ de montar) saddle ▸ **silla de ruedas** wheelchair

sillón [si'ʎon] *nm* armchair, easy chair

silueta [si'lweta] *nf* silhouette; (de edificio) outline; (figura) figure

silvestre [sil'βestre] *adj* wild

simbólico, -a [sim'boliko, a] *adj* symbolic(al)

simbolizar [simboli'θar] *vt* to symbolize

símbolo ['simbolo] *nm* symbol

similar [simi'lar] *adj* similar

simio ['simjo] *nm* ape

simpatía [simpa'tia] *nf* liking; (afecto) affection; (amabilidad) kindness □ **simpático, -a** *adj* nice, pleasant; kind

⚠ No confundir **simpático** con la palabra inglesa *sympathetic*.

simpatizante [simpati'θante] *nf* sympathizer

simpatizar [simpati'θar] vi: **~ con** to get on well with

simple ['simple] adj simple; (elemental) simple, easy; (mero) mere; (puro) pure, sheer ♦ nmf simpletón ❑ **simpleza** nf simpleness; (necedad) silly thing ❑ **simplificar** vt to simplify

simposio [sim'posjo] nm symposium

simular [simu'lar] vt to simulate

simultáneo, -a [simul'taneo, a] adj simultaneous

sin [sin] prep without; **la ropa está ~ lavar** the clothes are unwashed; **~ que** without; **~ embargo** however, still

sinagoga [sina'ɣoɣa] nf synagogue

sinceridad [sinθeri'ðað] nf sincerity ❑ **sincero, -a** adj sincere

sincronizar [sinkroni'θar] vt to synchronize

sindical [sindi'kal] adj union cpd, trade-union cpd ❑ **sindicalista** adj, nmf trade unionist

sindicato [sindi'kato] nm (de trabajadores) trade(s) union; (de negociantes) syndicate

síndrome ['sindrome] nm (MED) syndrome ▶ **síndrome de abstinencia** (MED) withdrawal symptoms ▶ **síndrome de de la clase turista** (MED) economy-class syndrome

sinfín [sin'fin] nm: **un ~ de** a great many, no end of

sinfonía [sinfo'nia] nf symphony

singular [singu'lar] adj singular; (fig) outstanding, exceptional; (raro) peculiar, odd

siniestro, -a [si'njestro, a] adj sinister ♦ nm (accidente) accident

sinnúmero [si'numero] nm = **sinfín**

sino ['sino] nm fate, destiny ♦ conj (pero) but; (salvo) except, save

sinónimo, -a [si'nonimo, a] adj synonymous ♦ nm synonym

síntesis ['sintesis] nf synthesis ❑ **sintético, -a** adj synthetic

sintió vb ver **sentir**

síntoma ['sintoma] nm symptom

sintonía [sinto'nia] nf (RADIO, MÚS: de programa) tuning ❑ **sintonizar** vt (RADIO: emisora) to tune (in)

sinvergüenza [simber'ɣwenθa] nmf rogue, scoundrel; **¡es un ~!** he's got a nerve!

siquiera [si'kjera] conj even if, even though ♦ adv at least; **ni ~** not even

Siria ['sirja] nf Syria

sirviente, -a [sir'βjente, a] nm/f servant

sirvo etc vb ver **servir**

sistema [sis'tema] nm system; (método) method ▶ **sistema educativo** education system ❑ **sistemático, -a** adj systematic

SISTEMA EDUCATIVO

The reform of the Spanish **sistema educativo** (education system) begun in the early 90s has replaced the courses **EGB, BUP** and **COU** with the following: "Primaria" a compulsory 6 years; "Secundaria" a compulsory 4 years and "Bachillerato" an optional 2-year secondary school course, essential for those wishing to go on to higher education.

sitiar [si'tjar] vt to besiege, lay siege to

sitio ['sitjo] nm (lugar) place; (espacio) room, space; (MIL) siege ▶ **sitio de taxis** (MÉX: parada) taxi stand o rank (BRIT) ▶ **sitio Web** (INFORM) website

situación [sitwa'θjon] nf situation, position; (estatus) position, standing

situado, -a [situ'aðo] adj situated, placed

situar [si'twar] vt to place, put; (edificio) to locate, situate

slip [slip] nm pants pl, briefs pl

smoking ['sməʊkɪŋ, es'mɒkɪŋ] (pl **smokings**) nm dinner jacket (BRIT), tuxedo (US)

⚠ No confundir **smoking** con la palabra inglesa *smoking*.

SMS nm (mensaje) text message, SMS message

snob [es'nɒb] = **esnob**

SO abr (= suroeste) SW

sobaco [so'βako] nm armpit

sobar [so'βar] vt (ropa) to rumple; (comida) to play around with

soberanía [soβera'nia] nf sovereignty □ **soberano, -a** adj sovereign; (fig) supreme ♦ nm/f sovereign

soberbia [so'βerβja] nf pride; haughtiness, arrogance; magnificence □ **soberbio, -a** adj (orgulloso) proud; (altivo) arrogant; (estupendo) magnificent, superb

sobornar [soβor'nar] vt to bribe □ **soborno** nm bribe

sobra ['soβra] nf excess, surplus; **sobras** nfpl left-overs, scraps; **de ~** surplus, extra; **tengo de ~** I've more than enough □ **sobrado, -a** adj (más que suficiente) more than enough; (superfluo) excessive □ **sobrante** adj remaining, extra ♦ nm surplus, remainder □ **sobrar** [so'βrar] vt to exceed, surpass ♦ vi (tener de más) to be more than enough; (quedar) to remain, be left (over)

sobrasada [soβra'saða] nf pork sausage spread

sobre ['soβre] prep (gen) on; (encima) on (top of); (por encima de, arriba de) over, above; (más que) more than; (además) in addition to, besides; (alrededor de) about ♦ nm envelope; **~ todo** above all

sobrecama [soβre'kama] nf bedspread

sobrecargar [soβrekar'ɣar] vt (camión) to overload; (COM) to surcharge

sobredosis [soβre'ðosis] nf inv overdose

sobreentender [soβre(e)nten'der] vt to deduce, infer; **sobreentenderse** vr: **se sobreentiende que ...** it is implied that ...

sobrehumano, -a [soβreu'mano, a] adj superhuman

sobrellevar [soβreʎe'βar] vt to bear, endure

sobremesa [soβre'mesa] nf: **durante la ~** after dinner

sobrenatural [soβrenatu'ral] adj supernatural

sobrenombre [soβre'nombre] nm nickname

sobrepasar [soβrepa'sar] vt to exceed, surpass

sobreponerse [soβrepo'nerse] vr: **~ a** to overcome

sobresaliente [soβresa'ljente] adj outstanding, excellent

sobresalir [soβresa'lir] vi (proyectar) to project, jut out; (fig) to stand out, excel

sobresaltar [soβresal'tar] vt (asustar) to scare, frighten; (sobrecoger) to startle □ **sobresalto** nm (movimiento) start; (susto) scare; (turbación) sudden shock

sobretodo [soβre'toðo] nm overcoat

sobrevenir [soβreβe'nir] vi (ocurrir) to happen (unexpectedly); (resultar) to follow, ensue

sobrevivir [soβreβi'βir] vi to survive

sobrevolar [soβreβo'lar] vt to fly over

sobriedad [soβrje'ðað] nf sobriety, soberness; (moderación) moderation, restraint

sobrino, -a [so'βrino, a] nm/f nephew/ niece

sobrio, -a [so'βrjo, a] adj sober; (moderado) moderate, restrained

socarrón, -ona [soka'rron, ona] adj (sardástico) sarcastic, ironic(al)

socavón [soka'βon] nm (hoyo) hole

sociable [so'θjaβle] adj (persona) sociable, friendly; (animal) social

social [so'θjal] *adj* social; (COM) company *cpd*

socialdemócrata [soθjalde'mokrata] *nmf* social democrat

socialista [soθja'lista] *adj, nm* socialist

socializar [soθjali'θar] *vt* to socialize

sociedad [soθje'ðað] *nf* society; (COM) company ► **sociedad anónima** limited company ► **sociedad de consumo** consumer society

socio, -a [so'θjo, a] *nm/f* (miembro) member; (COM) partner

sociología [soθjolo'xia] *nf* sociology ❑ **sociólogo, -a** *nm/f* sociologist

socorrer [soko'rrer] *vt* to help ❑ **socorrista** *nmf* first aider; (en piscina, playa) lifeguard ❑ **socorro** *nm* (ayuda) help, aid; (MIL) relief; **¡socorro!** help!

soda ['soða] *nf* (sosa) soda; (bebida) soda (water)

sofá [so'fa] (pl ~s) *nm* sofa, settee ❑ **sofá-cama** *nm* studio couch; sofa bed

sofocar [sofo'kar] *vt* to suffocate; (apagar) to smother, put out; **sofocarse** *vr* to suffocate; (fig) to blush, feel embarrassed ❑ **sofoco** *nm* suffocation; embarrassment

sofreír [sofre'ir] *vt* (CULIN) to fry lightly

soga ['soya] *nf* rope

sois *etc* [sois] *vb V* **ser**

soja ['soxa] *nf* soya

sol [sol] *nm* sun; (luz) sunshine, sunlight; (MÚS) G; **hace ~** it's sunny

solamente [sola'mente] *adv* only, just

solapa [so'lapa] *nf* (de chaqueta) lapel; (de libro) jacket

solapado, -a [sola'paðo, a] *adj* (intenciónes) underhand; (gestos, movimiento) sly

solar [so'lar] *adj* solar, sun *cpd* ♦ *nm* (terreno) plot of ground

soldado [sol'daðo] *nm* soldier ► **soldado raso** private

soldador [solda'ðor] *nm* soldering iron; (persona) welder

soldar [sol'dar] *vt* to solder, weld

soleado, -a [sole'aðo, a] *adj* sunny

soledad [sole'ðað] *nf* solitude; (estado infeliz) loneliness

solemne [so'lemne] *adj* solemn

soler [so'ler] *vi* to be in the habit of, be accustomed to; **suele salir a las ocho** she usually goes out at eight o'clock

solfeo [sol'feo] *nm* solfa

solicitar [soliθi'tar] *vt* (permiso) to ask for, seek; (puesto) to apply for; (votos) to canvass for; (atención) to attract

solícito, -a [so'liθito, a] *adj* (diligente) diligent; (cuidadoso) careful ❑ **solicitud** *nf* (calidad) great care; (petición) request; (a un puesto) application

solidaridad [soliðari'ðað] *nf* solidarity ❑ **solidario, -a** *adj* (participación) joint, common; (compromiso) mutually binding

sólido, -a [so'liðo, a] *adj* solid

soliloquio [soli'lokjo] *nm* soliloquy

solista [so'lista] *nmf* soloist

solitario, -a [soli'tarjo, a] *adj* (persona) lonely, solitary; (lugar) lonely, desolate ♦ *nm/f* (recluso) recluse; (en la sociedad) loner ♦ *nm* solitaire

sollozar [soλo'θar] *vi* to sob ❑ **sollozo** *nm* sob

solo, -a ['solo, a] *adj* (único) single, sole; (sin compañía) alone; (solitario) lonely; **hay una sola dificultad** there is just one difficulty; **a solas** alone, by oneself

sólo ['solo] *adv* only, just

solomillo [solo'miλo] *nm* sirloin

soltar [sol'tar] *vt* (dejar ir) to let go of; (desprender) to unfasten, loosen; (librar) to release, set free; (risa etc) to let out

soltero, -a [sol'tero, a] *adj* single, unmarried ♦ *nm/f* bachelor/single woman ❑ **solterón, -ona** *nm/f* old bachelor/spinster

soltura [sol'tura] nf looseness, slackness; (de los miembros) agility, ease of movement; (en el hablar) fluency, ease

soluble [so'luβle] adj (QUIM) soluble; (problema) solvable; **~ en agua** soluble in water

solución [solu'θjon] nf solution ◻ **solucionar** vt (problema) to solve; (asunto) to settle, resolve

solventar [solβen'tar] vt (pagar) to settle, pay; (dificultad) to resolve ◻ **solvente** adj (ECON: empresa, persona) solvent

sombra ['sombra] nf shadow; (como protección) shade; **sombras** nfpl (oscuridad) darkness sg, shadows; **tener buena/mala ~** to be lucky/ unlucky

sombrero [som'brero] nm hat

sombrilla [som'briʎa] nf parasol, sunshade

sombrío, -a [som'brio, a] adj (oscuro) dark; (triste) sombre, sad; (persona) gloomy

someter [some'ter] vt (país) to conquer; (persona) to subject to one's will; (informe) to present, submit; **someterse** vr to give in, yield, submit; **~ a** to subject to

somier [so'mjer] (pl **somiers**) n spring mattress

somnífero [som'nifero] nm sleeping pill

somos ['somos] vb ver **ser**

son [son] vb ver **ser** ♦ nm sound

sonaja (MEX) nf = **sonajero**

sonajero [sona'xero] nm (baby's) rattle

sonambulismo [sonambu'lismo] nm sleepwalking ◻ **sonámbulo, -a** nm/f sleepwalker

sonar [so'nar] vt to ring ♦ vi to sound; (hacer ruido) to make a noise; (pronunciarse) to be sounded, be pronounced; (ser conocido) to sound familiar; (campana) to ring; (reloj) to

strike, chime; **sonarse** vr: **sonarse (las narices)** to blow one's nose; **me suena ese nombre** that name rings a bell

sonda ['sonda] nf (NAUT) sounding; (TEC) bore, drill; (MED) probe

sondear [sonde'ar] vt to sound; to bore (into), drill; to probe, sound; (fig) to sound out ◻ **sondeo** nm sounding; boring, drilling; (fig) poll, enquiry

sonido [so'niðo] nm sound

sonoro, -a [so'noro, a] adj sonorous; (resonante) loud, resonant

sonreír [sonre'ir] vi to smile; **sonreírse** vr to smile ◻ **sonriente** adj smiling ◻ **sonrisa** nf smile

sonrojarse [sonro'xarse] vr to blush, go red ◻ **sonrojo** nm blush

soñador, a [sopa'ðor, a] nm/f dreamer

soñar [so'par] vt, vi to dream; **~ con** to dream about o of

soñoliento, -a [sopo'ljento, a] adj sleepy, drowsy

sopa ['sopa] nf soup

soplar [so'plar] vt (polvo) to blow away, blow off; (inflar) to blow up; (vela) to blow out ♦ vi to blow ◻ **soplo** nm blow, puff; (de viento) puff, gust

soplón, -ona [so'plon, ona] (fam) nm/f (niño) telltale; (de policía) grass (fam)

soporífero [sopo'rifero] nm sleeping pill

soportable [sopor'taβle] adj bearable

soportar [sopor'tar] vt to bear, carry; (fig) to bear, put up with ◻ **soporte** nm support; (fig) pillar, support

> ⚠ No confundir **soportar** con la palabra inglesa **support**.

soprano [so'prano] nf soprano

sorber [sor'βer] vt (chupar) to sip; (absorber) to soak up, absorb

sorbete [sor'βete] nm iced fruit drink

sorbo ['sorβo] nm (trago: grande) gulp, swallow; (: pequeño) sip

sordera [sor'ðera] nf deafness

sórdido, -a [ˈsorðiðo, a] adj dirty, squalid

sordo, -a [ˈsorðo, a] adj (persona) deaf ♦ nm/f deaf person ❑ **sordomudo, -a** adj deaf and dumb

sorna [ˈsorna] nf sarcastic tone

soroche [soˈrotʃe] (CAm) nm mountain sickness

sorprendente [sorprenˈdente] adj surprising

sorprender [sorprenˈder] vt to surprise ❑ **sorpresa** nf surprise

sortear [sorteˈar] vt to draw lots for; (rifar) to raffle; (dificultad) to avoid ❑ **sorteo** nm (en lotería) draw; (rifa) raffle

sortija [sorˈtixa] nf ring; (rizo) ringlet, curl

sosegado, -a [soseˈɣaðo, a] adj quiet, calm

sosiego [soˈsjeɣo] nm quiet(ness), calm(ness)

soso, -a [ˈsoso, a] adj (CULIN) tasteless; (aburrido) dull, uninteresting

sospecha [sosˈpetʃa] nf suspicion ❑ **sospechar** vt to suspect ❑ **sospechoso, -a** adj suspicious; (testimonio, opinión) suspect ♦ nm/f suspect

sostén [sosˈten] nm (apoyo) support; (sujetador) bra; (alimentación) sustenance, food

sostener [sosteˈner] vt to support; (mantener) to keep up, maintain; (alimentar) to sustain, keep going; **sostenerse** vr to support o.s.; (seguir) to continue, remain ❑ **sostenido, -a** adj continuous, sustained; (prolongado) prolonged

sotana [soˈtana] nf (REL) cassock

sótano [ˈsotano] nm basement

soy [soi] vb ver **ser**

soya [ˈsoja] (LAm) nf soya (BRIT), soy (US)

Sr. abr (= Señor) Mr

Sra. abr (= Señora) Mrs

Sres. abr (= Señores) Messrs

Srta. abr (= Señorita) Miss

Sta. abr (= Santa) St

Sto. abr (= Santo) St

su [su] pron (de él) his; (de ella) her; (de una cosa) its; (de ellos, ellas) their; (de usted, ustedes) your

suave [ˈswaβe] adj gentle; (superficie) smooth; (trabajo) easy; (música, voz) soft, sweet ❑ **suavidad** nf gentleness; smoothness; softness, sweetness ❑ **suavizante** nm (de ropa) softener; (del pelo) conditioner ❑ **suavizar** vt to soften; (quitar la aspereza) to smooth (out)

subasta [suˈβasta] nf auction ❑ **subastar** vt to auction (off)

subcampeón, -ona [suβkampeˈon, ona] nm/f runner-up

subconsciente [suβkonˈsθjente] adj, nm subconscious

subdesarrollado, -a [suβðesaroˈʎaðo, a] adj underdeveloped

subdesarrollo [suβðesaˈrroʎo] nm underdevelopment

subdirector, -a [suβðirekˈtor, a] nm/f assistant director

súbdito, -a [ˈsuβðito, a] nm/f subject

subestimar [suβestiˈmar] vt to underestimate, underrate

subida [suˈβiða] nf (de montaña etc) ascent, climb; (de precio) rise, increase; (pendiente) slope, hill

subir [suˈβir] vt (objeto) to raise, lift up; (cuesta, calle) to go up; (colina, montaña) to climb; (precio) to raise, put up ♦ vi to go up, come up; (a un coche) to get in; (a un autobús, tren o avión) to get on, board; (precio) to rise, go up; (río, marea) to rise; **subirse** vr to get up, climb

súbito, -a [ˈsuβito, a] adj (repentino) sudden; (imprevisto) unexpected

subjetivo, -a [suβxeˈtiβo, a] adj subjective

sublevar [suβle'βar] vt to rouse to revolt; **sublevarse** vr to revolt, rise

sublime [su'βlime] adj sublime

submarinismo [suβmari'nismo] nm scuba diving

submarino, -a [suβma'rino, a] adj underwater ♦ nm submarine

subnormal [suβnor'mal] adj subnormal ♦ nmf subnormal person

subordinado, -a [suβorði'naðo, a] adj, nm/f subordinate

subrayar [suβra'jar] vt to underline

subsanar [suβsa'nar] vt to rectify

subsidio [suβ'siðjo] nm (ayuda) aid, financial help; (subvención) subsidy, grant; (de enfermedad, paro etc) benefit, allowance

subsistencia [suβsis'tenθja] nf subsistence

subsistir [suβsis'tir] vi to subsist; (sobrevivir) to survive, endure

subte (RPl) nm underground (BRIT), subway (US)

subterráneo, -a [suβte'rraneo, a] adj underground, subterranean ♦ nm underpass, underground passage

subtítulo [suβ'titulo] nm (CINE) subtitle

suburbio [su'βurβjo] nm (barrio) slum quarter

subvención [suββen'θjon] nf (ECON) subsidy, grant ⬜ **subvencionar** vt to subsidize

sucedáneo, -a [suθe'ðaneo, a] adj substitute ♦ nm substitute (food)

suceder [suθe'ðer] vt, vi to happen; (seguir) to succeed, follow; **lo que sucede es que ...** the fact is that ... ⬜ **sucesión** nf succession; (serie) sequence, series

sucesivamente [suθesiβa'mente] adv: **y así ~** and so on

sucesivo, -a [suθe'siβo, a] adj successive, following; **en lo ~** in future, from now on

suceso [su'θeso] nm (hecho) event, happening; (incidente) incident

⚠ No confundir **suceso** con la palabra inglesa success.

suciedad [suθje'ðað] nf (estado) dirtiness; (mugre) dirt, filth

sucio, -a [su'θjo, a] adj dirty

suculento, -a [suku'lento, a] adj succulent

sucumbir [sukum'bir] vi to succumb

sucursal [sukur'sal] nf branch (office)

sudadera [suða'ðera] nf sweatshirt

Sudáfrica [su'ðafrika] nf South Africa

Sudamérica [suða'merika] nf South America ⬜ **sudamericano, -a** adj, nm/f South American

sudar [su'ðar] vt, vi to sweat

sudeste [su'ðeste] nm south-east

sudoeste [suðo'este] nm south-west

sudor [su'ðor] nm sweat ⬜ **sudoroso, -a** adj sweaty, sweating

Suecia [swe'θja] nf Sweden ⬜ **sueco, -a** adj Swedish ♦ nm/f Swede

suegro, -a [swe'yro, a] nm/f father-/mother-in-law

suela ['swela] nf sole

sueldo ['sweldo] nm pay, wage(s) (pl)

suele etc vb ver **soler**

suelo ['swelo] nm (tierra) ground; (de casa) floor

suelto, -a ['swelto, a] adj loose; (libre) free; (separado) detached; (ágil) quick, agile ♦ nm (loose) change, small change

sueñito (LAm) nm nap

sueño etc ['sweno] vb ver **soñar** ♦ nm sleep; (somnolencia) sleepiness, drowsiness; (lo soñado, fig) dream; **tener ~** to be sleepy

suero ['swero] nm (MED) serum; (de leche) whey

suerte ['swerte] nf (fortuna) luck; (azar) chance; (destino) fate, destiny; (especie) sort, kind; **tener ~** to be lucky

suéter ['sweter] nm sweater

suficiente [sufi'θjente] adj enough, sufficient ♦ nm (ESCOL) pass

sufragio [su'fraxjo] nm (voto) vote; (derecho de voto) suffrage

sufrido, -a [su'friðo, a] adj (persona) tough; (paciente) long-suffering, patient

sufrimiento [sufri'mjento] nm (dolor) suffering

sufrir [su'frir] vt (padecer) to suffer; (soportar) to bear, put up with; (apoyar) to hold up, support ♦ vi to suffer

sugerencia [suxe'renθja] nf suggestion

sugerir [suxe'rir] vt to suggest; (sutilmente) to hint

sugestión [suxes'tjon] nf suggestion; (sutil) hint □ **sugestionar** vt to influence

sugestivo, -a [suxes'tiβo, a] adj stimulating; (fascinante) fascinating

suicida [sui'θiða] adj suicidal ♦ nmf suicidal person; (muerto) suicide, person who has committed suicide □ **suicidarse** vr to commit suicide, kill o.s. □ **suicidio** nm suicide

Suiza ['swiθa] nf Switzerland □ **suizo, -a** adj, nm/f Swiss

sujeción [suxe'θjon] nf subjection

sujetador [suxeta'ðor] nm (sostén) bra

sujetar [suxe'tar] vt (fijar) to fasten; (detener) to hold down; **sujetarse** vr to subject o.s. □ **sujeto, -a** adj fastened, secure ♦ nm subject; (individuo) individual; **sujeto a** subject to

suma ['suma] nf (cantidad) total, sum; (de dinero) sum; (acto) adding (up), addition; **en ~** in short

sumamente [suma'mente] adv extremely, exceedingly

sumar [su'mar] vt to add (up) ♦ vi to add up

sumergir [sumer'xir] vt to submerge; (hundir) to sink

suministrar [sumini'strar] vt to supply, provide □ **suministro** nm supply; (acto) supplying, providing

sumir [su'mir] vt to sink, submerge; (fig) to plunge

sumiso, -a [su'miso, a] adj submissive, docile

sumo, -a ['sumo, a] adj great, extreme; (autoridad) highest, supreme

suntuoso, -a [sun'twoso, a] adj sumptuous, magnificent

supe etc ['supe] vb ver **saber**

super... [super] prefijo super..., over...

superbueno [super'bweno] adj great, fantastic

súper ['super] nf (gasolina) four-star (petrol)

superar [supe'rar] vt (sobreponerse a) to overcome; (rebasar) to surpass, do better than; (pasar) to go beyond; **superarse** vr to excel o.s.

superficial [superfi'θjal] adj superficial; (medida) surface cpd, of the surface

superficie [super'fiθje] nf surface; (área) area

superfluo, -a [su'perflwo, a] adj superfluous

superior [supe'rjor] adj (piso, clase) upper; (temperatura, número, nivel) higher; (mejor: calidad, producto) superior, better ♦ nm superior □ **superioridad** nf superiority

supermercado [supermer'kaðo] nm supermarket

superponer [superpo'ner] vt to superimpose

superstición [supersti'θjon] nf superstition □ **supersticioso, -a** adj superstitious

supervisar [superβi'sar] vt to supervise

supervivencia [superβi'βenθja] nf survival

superviviente [superβi'βjente] adj surviving

supiera etc vb ver **saber**

suplantar [suplan'tar] vt to supplant

suplemento [suple'mento] *nm*
supplement

suplente [su'plente] *adj, nm* substitute

supletorio, -a [suple'torjo, a] *adj*
supplementary ♦ *nm* supplement;
teléfono ~ extension

súplica ['suplika] *nf* request; (*JUR*)
petition

suplicar [supli'kar] *vt* (*cosa*) to beg
(for), plead for; (*persona*) to beg, plead
with

suplicio [su'pliθjo] *nm* torture

suplir [su'plir] *vt* (*compensar*) to make
good, make up for; (*reemplazar*) to
replace, substitute ♦ *vi*: **~ a** to take the
place of, substitute for

supo *etc* ['supo] *vb ver* **saber**

suponer [supo'ner] *vt* to suppose
❑ **suposición** *nf* supposition

suprimir [supri'mir] *vt* to suppress;
(*derecho, costumbre*) to abolish;
(*palabra etc*) to delete; (*restricción*) to
cancel, lift

supuesto, -a [su'pwesto, a] *pp de*
suponer ♦ *adj* (*hipotético*) supposed
♦ *nm* assumption, hypothesis; **~ que**
since; **por ~** of course

sur [sur] *nm* south

surcar [sur'kar] *vt* to plough ❑ **surco**
nm (*en metal, disco*) groove; (*AGR*)
furrow

surgir [sur'xir] *vi* to arise, emerge;
(*dificultad*) to come up, crop up

suroeste [suro'este] *nm* south-west

surtido, -a [sur'tiðo, a] *adj* mixed,
assorted ♦ *nm* (*selección*) selection,
assortment; (*abastecimiento*) supply,
stock ❑ **surtidor** *nm* (*tb*: **surtidor de
gasolina**) petrol pump (*BRIT*), gas
pump (*US*)

surtir [sur'tir] *vt* to supply, provide ♦ *vi*
to spout, spurt

susceptible [susθep'tiβle] *adj*
susceptible; (*sensible*) sensitive; **~ de**
capable of

suscitar [susθi'tar] *vt* to cause,
provoke; (*interés, sospechas*) to arouse

suscribir [suskri'βir] *vt* (*firmar*) to sign;
(*respaldar*) to subscribe to, endorse;
suscribirse *vr* to subscribe
❑ **suscripción** *nf* subscription

susodicho, -a [suso'ðitʃo, a] *adj*
above-mentioned

suspender [suspen'der] *vt* (*objeto*) to
hang (up), suspend; (*trabajo*) to stop,
suspend; (*ESCOL*) to fail; (*interrumpir*) to
adjourn; (*atrasar*) to postpone

suspense (*ESP*) [sus'pense] *nm*
suspense; **película/novela de ~** thriller

suspensión [suspen'sjon] *nf*
suspension; (*fig*) stoppage, suspension

suspenso, -a [sus'penso, a] *adj*
hanging, suspended; (*ESP ESCOL*) failed
♦ *nm* (*ESP ESCOL*) fail; **película o novela
de ~** (*LAm*) thriller; **quedar o estar en ~**
to be pending

suspicaz [suspi'kaθ] *adj* suspicious,
distrustful

suspirar [suspi'rar] *vi* to sigh
❑ **suspiro** *nm* sigh

sustancia [sus'tanθja] *nf* substance

sustento [sus'tento] *nm* support;
(*alimento*) sustenance, food

sustituir [sustitu'ir] *vt* to substitute,
replace ❑ **sustituto, -a** *nm/f*
substitute, replacement

susto ['susto] *nm* fright, scare

sustraer [sustra'er] *vt* to remove, take
away; (*MAT*) to subtract

susurrar [susu'rrar] *vi* to whisper
❑ **susurro** *nm* whisper

sutil [su'til] *adj* (*aroma, diferencia*)
subtle; (*tenue*) thin; (*inteligencia,
persona*) sharp

suyo, -a ['sujo, a] *adj* (*con artículo o después
del verbo ser*) (*de él*) his; (*de ella*)
hers; (*de ellos, ellas*) theirs; (*de Ud, Uds*)
yours; **un amigo ~** a friend of his (*o
hers o theirs o yours*)

T, t

Tabacalera [taβakaˈlera] nf Spanish state tobacco monopoly

tabaco [taˈβako] nm tobacco; (ESP: fam) cigarettes pl

tabaquería [taβakeˈria] nf tobacconist's (shop) (BRIT), smoke shop (US) ❑ **tabaquero, -a** (LAm) nm/f tobacconist

taberna [taˈβerna] nf bar, pub (BRIT)

tabique [taˈβike] nm partition (wall)

tabla [ˈtaβla] nf (de madera) plank; (estante) shelf; (de vestido) pleat; (ARTE) panel; **tablas** nfpl: **estar o quedar en tablas** to draw ❑ **tablado** nm (plataforma) platform; (TEATRO) stage

tablao [taˈβlao] nm (tb: ~ **flamenco**) flamenco show

tablero [taˈβlero] nm (de madera) plank, board; (de ajedrez, damas) board ▸ **tablero de mandos** (LAm AUTO) dashboard

tableta [taˈβleta] nf (MED) tablet; (de chocolate) bar

tablón [taˈβlon] nm (de suelo) plank; (de techo) beam ▸ **tablón de anuncios** notice (BRIT) o bulletin (US) board

tabú [taˈβu] nm taboo

taburete [taβuˈrete] nm stool

tacaño, -a [taˈkaɲo] adj mean

tacha [ˈtatʃa] nf flaw; (TEC) stud ❑ **tachar** vt (borrar) to cross out; **tachar de** to accuse of

tacho [ˈtatʃo] nm (CS) bucket ▸ **tacho de la basura** rubbish bin (BRIT), trash can (US)

taco [ˈtako] nm (BILLAR) cue; (de billetes) book; (CS: de zapato) heel; (tarugo) peg; (palabrota) swear word

tacón [taˈkon] nm heel; **de ~ alto** high-heeled

táctica [ˈtaktika] nf tactics pl

táctico, -a [ˈtaktiko, a] adj tactical

tacto [ˈtakto] nm touch; (fig) tact

tajada [taˈxaða] nf slice

tajante [taˈxante] adj sharp

tajo [ˈtaxo] nm (corte) cut; (GEO) cleft

tal [tal] adj such ♦ pron (persona) someone, such a one; (cosa) something, such a thing ♦ adv: ~ **como** (igual) just as; ~ **como** o **de que** provided that; ~ **cual** (como es) just as it is; ~ **vez** perhaps; ~ **como** such as; ~ **para cual** (dos iguales) two of a kind; **¿qué ~?** how are things?; **¿qué ~ te gusta?** how do you like it?

taladrar [talaˈðrar] vt to drill ❑ **taladro** nm drill

talante [taˈlante] nm (humor) mood; (voluntad) will, willingness

talar [taˈlar] vt to fell, cut down; (devastar) to devastate

talco [ˈtalko] nm (polvos) talcum powder

talento [taˈlento] nm talent; (capacidad) ability

TALGO [ˈtalɣo] (ESP) nm abr (= tren articulado ligero Goicoechea-Oriol) = HST (BRIT)

talismán [talisˈman] nm talisman

talla [ˈtaʎa] nf (estatura, fig, MED) height, stature; (palo) measuring rod; (ARTE) carving; (medida) size

tallar [taˈʎar] vt (madera) to carve; (metal etc) to engrave; (medir) to measure

tallarines [taʎaˈrines] nmpl noodles

talle [ˈtaʎe] nm (ANAT) waist; (fig) appearance

taller [taˈʎer] nm (TEC) workshop; (de artista) studio

tallo [ˈtaʎo] nm (de planta) stem; (de hierba) blade; (brote) shoot

talón [taˈlon] nm (ANAT) heel; (COM) counterfoil; (cheque) cheque (BRIT), check (US)

talonario [taloˈnarjo] nm (de cheques) chequebook (BRIT), checkbook (US); (de recibos) receipt book

tamaño, -a [ta'maɲo, a] *adj* (*tan grande*) such a big; (*tan pequeño*) such a small ♦ *nm* size; **de ~ natural** full-size

tamarindo [tama'rindo] *nm* tamarind

tambalearse [tambale'arse] *vr* (*persona*) to stagger; (*vehículo*) to sway

también [tam'bjen] *adv* (*igualmente*) also, too, as well; (*además*) besides

tambor [tam'bor] *nm* drum; (*ANAT*) eardrum ► **tambor del freno** brake drum

tamizar [tami'θar] *vt* to sieve

tampoco [tam'poko] *adv* nor, neither; **yo ~ lo compré** I didn't buy it either

tampón [tam'pon] *nm* tampon

tan [tan] *adv* so; **~ es así que ...** so much so that ...

tanda ['tanda] *nf* (*gen*) series; (*turno*) shift

tangente [tan'xente] *nf* tangent

tangerina (*LAm*) *nf* tangerine

tangible [tan'xiβle] *adj* tangible

tanque ['tanke] *nm* (*cisterna*, *MIL*) tank; (*AUTO*) tanker

tantear [tante'ar] *vt* (*calcular*) to reckon (up); (*medir*) to take the measure of; (*probar*) to test, try out; (*tomar la medida: persona*) to take the measurements of; (*situación*) to weigh up; (*persona: opinión*) to sound out ♦ *vi* (*DEPORTE*) to score ▶ **tanteo** *nm* (*cálculo*) (rough) calculation; (*prueba*) test, trial; (*DEPORTE*) scoring

tanto, -a ['tanto, a] *adj* (*cantidad*) so much, as much ♦ *adv* (*cantidad*) so much, as much; (*tiempo*) so long, as long ♦ *conj*: **en ~ que** while ♦ *nm* (*suma*) certain amount; (*proporción*) so much; (*punto*) point; (*gol*) goal; **un ~ perezoso** somewhat lazy ♦ *pron*: **cada uno paga ~** each one pays so much; **tantos** so many, as many; **20 y tantos** 20-odd; **hasta ~ (que)** until such time as; **~ tú como yo** both you and I; **~ como eso** as much as that; **~ más ... cuanto que** all the more ... because; **~**

mejor/peor so much the better/the worse; **~ si viene como si va** whether he comes or whether he goes; **~ es así que** so much so that; **por (lo) ~** therefore; **entre ~** meanwhile; **estar al ~** to be up to date; **me he vuelto ronco de o con ~ hablar** I have become hoarse with so much talking; **a tantos de agosto** on such and such a day in August

tapa ['tapa] *nf* (*de caja*, *olla*) lid; (*de botella*) top; (*de libro*) cover; (*comida*) snack

tapadera [tapa'ðera] *nf* lid, cover

tapar [ta'par] *vt* (*cubrir*) to cover; (*envolver*) to wrap o cover up; (*la vista*) to obstruct; (*persona*, *falta*) to conceal; (*MÉX: diente*) to fill; **taparse** *vr* (*Cam*) to wrap o.s. up

taparrabo [tapa'rraβo] *nm* loincloth

tapete [ta'pete] *nm* table cover

tapia ['tapja] *nf* (garden) wall

tapicería [tapiθe'ria] *nf* tapestry; (*para muebles*) upholstery; (*tienda*) upholsterer's (shop)

tapiz [ta'piθ] *nm* (*alfombra*) carpet; (*tela tejida*) tapestry ❑ **tapizar** *vt* (*muebles*) to upholster

tapón [ta'pon] *nm* (*de botella*) top; (*de lavabo*) plug ▶ **tapón de rosca** screw-top

taquigrafía [takiɣra'fia] *nf* shorthand ❑ **taquígrafo, -a** *nm/f* shorthand writer, stenographer

taquilla [ta'kiʎa] *nf* (*donde se compra*) booking office; (*suma recogida*) takings *pl*

tarántula [ta'rantula] *nf* tarantula

tararear [tarare'ar] *vt* to hum

tardar [tar'ðar] *vi* (*tomar tiempo*) to take a long time; (*llegar tarde*) to be late; (*demorar*) to delay; **¿tarda mucho el tren?** does the train take (very) long?; **a más ~** at the latest; **no tardes en venir** come soon

tarde ['tarðe] adv late ♦ nf (de día) afternoon; (al anochecer) evening; **de ~ en ~** from time to time to time; **¡buenas tardes!** good afternoon!; **a o por la ~** in the afternoon, in the evening

tardío, -a [tar'ðio, a] adj (retrasado) late; (lento) slow to ripen

tarea [ta'rea] nf task; (faena) chore; (ESCOL) homework

tarifa [ta'rifa] nf (lista de precios) price list; (precio) tariff

tarima [ta'rima] nf (plataforma) platform

tarjeta [tar'xeta] nf card ▸ **tarjeta de crédito/de Navidad/postal/ telefónica** credit card/Christmas card/postcard/phonecard ▸ **tarjeta de embarque** boarding pass

tarro ['taro] nm jar, pot

tarta ['tarta] nf (pastel) cake; (de base dura) tart

tartamudear [tartamuðe'ar] vi to stammer ❑ **tartamudo, -a** adj stammering ♦ nm/f stammerer

tártaro, -a ['tartaro, a] adj: **salsa tártara** tartar(e) sauce

tasa ['tasa] nf (precio) (fixed) price, rate; (valoración) valuation; (medida, norma) measure, standard ▸ **tasa de cambio/interés** exchange/interest rate ▸ **tasas de aeropuerto** airport tax ▸ **tasas universitarias** university fees ❑ **tasar** vt (arreglar el precio) to fix a price for; (valorar) to value, assess

tasca ['taska] (fam) nf pub

tatarabuelo, -a [tatara'βwelo, a] nm/f great-great-grandfather/mother

tatuaje [ta'twaxe] nm (dibujo) tattoo; (acto) tattooing

tatuar [ta'twar] vt to tattoo

taurino, -a [tau'rino, a] adj bullfighting cpd

Tauro ['tauro] nm Taurus

tauromaquia [tauro'makja] nf tauromachy, (art of) bullfighting

taxi ['taksi] nm taxi ❑ **taxista** [tak'sista] nmf taxi driver

taza ['taθa] nf (de retrete) bowl; ~ **para café** coffee cup ▸ **taza de café** cup of coffee ❑ **tazón** nm (taza grande) mug, large cup; (de fuente) basin

te [te] pron (complemento de objeto) you; (complemento indirecto) (to) you; (reflexivo) (to) yourself; **¿te duele mucho el brazo?** does your arm hurt a lot?; **te equivocas** you're wrong; **¡cálmate!** calm down!

té [te] nm tea

teatral [tea'tral] adj theatre cpd; (fig) theatrical

teatro [te'atro] nm theatre; (LITERATURA) plays pl, drama

tebeo [te'βeo] nm comic

techo ['tetʃo] nm (externo) roof; (interno) ceiling ▸ **techo corredizo** sunroof

tecla ['tekla] nf key ❑ **teclado** nm keyboard ❑ **teclear** vi (MÚS) to strum; (con los dedos) to tap ♦ vt (INFORM) to key in

técnica ['teknika] nf technique; (tecnología) technology; ver tb **técnico**

técnico, -a ['tekniko, a] adj technical ♦ nm/f technician; (experto) expert

tecnología [teknolo'xia] nf technology ❑ **tecnológico, -a** adj technological

tecolote (MÉX) [teko'lote] nm owl

tedioso, -a [te'ðjoso, a] adj boring, tedious

teja ['texa] nf tile; (BOT) lime (tree) ❑ **tejado** nm (tiled) roof

tejemaneje [texema'nexe] nm (lío) fuss; (intriga) intrigue

tejer [te'xer] vt to weave; (hacer punto) to knit; (fig) to fabricate ❑ **tejido** nm (tela) material, fabric; (telaraña) web; (ANAT) tissue

tel [tel] abr (= teléfono) tel

tela ['tela] nf (tejido) material; (telaraña) web; (en líquido) skin □ **telar** nm (máquina) loom

telaraña [tela'raɲa] nf cobweb

tele ['tele] (fam) nf telly (BRIT), tube (US)

tele... ['tele] prefijo tele... □ **telecomunicación** f telecommunication □ **telediario** nm television news □ **teledirigido, -a** adj remote-controlled

teleférico [tele'feriko] nm (de esquí) ski-lift

telefonear [telefone'ar] vi to telephone

telefónico, -a [tele'foniko, a] adj telephone cpd

telefonillo [telefo'niʎo] nm (de puerta) intercom

telefonista [telefo'nista] nmf telephonist

teléfono [te'lefono] nm (tele)phone; **estar hablando al ~** to be on the phone; **llamar a algn por ~** to ring sb (up) o phone sb (up) ▶ **teléfono celular** (LAm) mobile phone ▶ **teléfono inalámbrico** cordless phone ▶ **teléfono móvil** (ESP) mobile phone

telégrafo [te'leɣrafo] nm telegraph

telegrama [tele'ɣrama] nm telegram

tele: telenovela nf soap (opera) □ **teleobjetivo** nm telephoto lens □ **telepatía** nf telepathy □ **telepático, -a** adj telepathic □ **telescopio** nm telescope □ **telesilla** nf chairlift □ **telespectador, a** nm/f viewer □ **telesquí** nm ski-lift □ **teletarjeta** nf phonecard □ **teletipo** nm teletype □ **teletrabajador, a** nm/f teleworker □ **teletrabajo** nm teleworking □ **televentas** nfpl telesales

televidente [teleβi'ðente] nmf viewer

televisar [teleβi'sar] vt to televise

televisión [teleβi'sjon] nf television ▶ **televisión digital** digital television

televisor [teleβi'sor] nm television set

télex ['teleks] nm inv telex

telón [te'lon] nm curtain ▶ **telón de acero** (POL) iron curtain ▶ **telón de fondo** backloth, background

tema ['tema] nm (asunto) subject, topic; (MÚS) theme □ **temático, -a** adj thematic

temblar [tem'blar] vi to shake, tremble; (por frío) to shiver □ **temblor** nm trembling; (de tierra) earthquake □ **tembloroso, -a** adj trembling

temer [te'mer] vt to fear ♦ vi to be afraid; **temo que llegue tarde** I am afraid he may be late

temible [te'miβle] adj fearsome

temor [te'mor] nm (miedo) fear; (duda) suspicion

témpano ['tempano] nm (tb: ~ de hielo) ice-floe

temperamento [tempera'mento] nm temperament

temperatura [tempera'tura] nf temperature

tempestad [tempes'taθ] nf storm

templado, -a [tem'plaðo, a] adj (moderado) moderate; (frugal) frugal; (agua) lukewarm; (clima) mild; (MÚS) well-tuned □ **templanza** nf moderation; mildness

templar [tem'plar] vt (moderar) to moderate; (furia) to restrain; (calor) to reduce; (afinar) to tune (up); (acero) to temper; (tuerca) to tighten up □ **temple** nm (ajuste) tempering; (afinación) tuning; (pintura) tempera

templo ['templo] nm (iglesia) church; (pagano etc) temple

temporada [tempo'raða] nf time, period; (estación) season

temporal [tempo'ral] adj (no permanente) temporary ♦ nm storm

temprano, -a [tem'prano, a] adj early; (demasiado pronto) too soon, too early

ten [ten] vb ver **tener**

tenaces [te'naθes] adj pl ver **tenaz**

tenaz [te'naθ] adj (material) tough; (persona) tenacious; (creencia, resistencia) stubborn

tenaza(s) [te'naθa(s)] nf(pl) (MED) forceps; (TEC) pliers; (ZOOL) pincers

tendedero [tende'ðero] nm (para ropa) drying place; (cuerda) clothes line

tendencia [ten'denθja] nf tendency; **tener ~ a** to tend to, have a tendency to

tender [ten'der] vt (extender) to spread out; (colgar) to hang out; (vía férrea, cable) to lay; (estirar) to stretch ♦ vi: **~ a** to tend to, have a tendency towards; **tenderse** vr to lie down; **~ la cama/mesa** (LAm) to make the bed/lay (BRIT) o set (US) the table

tenderete [tende'rete] nm (puesto) stall; (exposición) display of goods

tendero, -a [ten'dero, a] nm/f shopkeeper

tendón [ten'don] nm tendon

tendré etc [ten'dre] vb ver **tener**

tenebroso, -a [tene'βroso, a] adj (oscuro) dark; (fig) gloomy

tenedor [tene'ðor] nm (CULIN) fork

tenencia [te'nenθja] nf (de casa) tenancy; (de oficio) tenure; (de propiedad) possession

tener [te'ner] vt

PALABRA CLAVE

1 (poseer, gen) to have; (en la mano) to hold; **¿tienes un boli?** have you got a pen?; **va a tener un niño** she's going to have a baby; **¡ten** (o **tenga**)!, **¡aquí tienes** (o **tiene**)! here you are!

2 (edad, medidas) to be; **tiene 7 años** she's 7 (years old); **tiene 15 cm de largo** it's 15 cm long; ver **calor**; **hambre** etc

3 (considerar): **lo tengo por brillante** I consider him to be brilliant; **tener en mucho a algn** to think very highly of sb

4 (+ pp: = pretérito): **tengo terminada ya**

la mitad del trabajo I've done half the work already

5: **tener que hacer algo** to have to do sth; **tengo que acabar este trabajo hoy** I have to finish this job today

6: **¿qué tienes, estás enfermo?** what's the matter with you, are you ill?

♦ **tenerse** vr

1: **tenerse en pie** to stand up

2: **tenerse por** to think o.s.

tengo etc vb ver **tener**

tenia ['tenja] nf tapeworm

teniente [te'njente] nm (rango) lieutenant; (ayudante) deputy

tenis ['tenis] nm tennis ▶ **tenis de mesa** table tennis □ **tenista** nmf tennis player

tenor [te'nor] nm (sentido) meaning; (MÚS) tenor; **a ~ de** on the lines of

tensar [ten'sar] vt to tighten; (arco) to draw

tensión [ten'sjon] nf tension; (TEC) stress; **tener la ~ alta** to have high blood pressure ▶ **tensión arterial** blood pressure

tenso, -a ['tenso, a] adj tense

tentación [tenta'θjon] nf temptation

tentáculo [ten'takulo] nm tentacle

tentador, a [tenta'ðor, a] adj tempting

tentar [ten'tar] vt (seducir) to tempt; (atraer) to attract

tentempié [tentem'pje] nm snack

tenue ['tenwe] adj (delgado) thin, slender; (neblina) light; (lazo, vínculo) slight

teñir [te'nir] vt to dye; (fig) to tinge; **teñirse** vr to dye; **teñirse el pelo** to dye one's hair

teología [teolo'xia] nf theology

teoría [teo'ria] nf theory; **en ~** in theory □ **teórico, -a** adj theoretic(al) ♦ nm/f theoretician, theorist □ **teorizar** vi to theorize

terapéutico, -a [tera'peutiko, a] adj therapeutic

terapia [te'rapja] nf therapy

tercer [ter'θer] adj ver **tercero**

tercermundista [terθermun'dista] adj Third World cpd

tercero, -a [ter'θero, a] (delante de nmsg: **tercer**) adj third ♦ nm (JUR) third party

terceto [ter'θeto] nm trio

terciar [ter'θjar] vi (participar) to take part; (hacer de árbitro) to mediate
❑ **terciario, -a** adj tertiary

tercio [ter'θjo] nm third

terciopelo [terθjo'pelo] nm velvet

terco, -a ['terko, a] adj obstinate

tergal® [ter'ɣal] nm type of polyester

tergiversar [terxiβer'sar] vt to distort

termal [ter'mal] adj thermal

termas ['termas] nfpl hot springs

térmico, -a ['termiko, a] adj thermal

terminal [termi'nal] adj, nm, nf terminal

terminante [termi'nante] adj (final) final, definitive; (tajante) categorical
❑ **terminantemente** adv: **terminantemente prohibido** strictly forbidden

terminar [termi'nar] vt (completar) to complete, finish; (concluir) to end ♦ vi (llegar a su fin) to end; (parar) to stop; (acabar) to finish; **terminarse** vr to come to an end; **~ por hacer algo** to end up (by) doing sth

término ['termino] nm end, conclusion; (parada) terminus; (límite) boundary; **en último ~** (a fin de cuentas) in the last analysis; (como último recurso) as a last resort ▶ **término medio** average; (fig) middle way

termómetro [ter'mometro] nm thermometer

termo(s)® ['termo(s)] nm Thermos®

termostato [termo'stato] nm thermostat

ternero, -a [ter'nero, a] nm/f (animal) calf ♦ nf (carne) veal

ternura [ter'nura] nf (trato) tenderness; (palabra) endearment; (cariño) fondness

terrado [te'rraðo] nm terrace

terraplén [terra'plen] nm embankment

terrateniente [terrate'njente] nmf landowner

terraza [te'rraθa] nf (balcón) balcony; (tejado) (flat) roof; (AGR) terrace

terremoto [terre'moto] nm earthquake

terrenal [terre'nal] adj earthly

terreno [te'rreno] nm (tierra) land; (parcela) plot; (suelo) soil; (fig) field; **un ~ a piece of land**

terrestre [te'rrestre] adj terrestrial; (ruta) land cpd

terrible [te'rriβle] adj terrible, awful

territorio [terri'torjo] nm territory

terrón [te'rron] nm (de azúcar) lump; (de tierra) clod, lump

terror [te'rror] nm terror
❑ **terrorífico, -a** adj terrifying
❑ **terrorista** adj, nmf terrorist

terso, -a ['terso, a] adj (liso) smooth; (pulido) polished

tertulia [ter'tulja] nf (reunión informal) social gathering; (grupo) group, circle

tesis ['tesis] nf inv thesis

tesón [te'son] nm (firmeza) firmness; (tenacidad) tenacity

tesorero, -a [teso'rero, a] nm/f treasurer

tesoro [te'soro] nm treasure; (COM, POL) treasury

testamento [testa'mento] nm will

testarudo, -a [testa'ruðo, a] adj stubborn

testículo [tes'tikulo] nm testicle

testificar [testifi'kar] vt to testify; (fig) to attest ♦ vi to give evidence

testigo [tes'tiɣo] nmf witness
▸ **testigo de cargo/descargo**
witness for the prosecution/defence
▸ **testigo ocular** eye witness

testimonio [testi'monjo] nm
testimony

teta ['teta] nf (de biberón) teat; (ANAT:
fam) breast

tétanos ['tetanos] nm tetanus

tetera [te'tera] nf teapot

tétrico, -a ['tetriko, a] adj gloomy,
dismal

textil [teks'til] adj textile

texto ['teksto] nm text ❏ **textual** adj
textual

textura [teks'tura] nf (de tejido) texture

tez [teθ] nf (cutis) complexion

ti [ti] pron you; (reflexivo) yourself

tía ['tia] nf (pariente) aunt; (fam) chick,
bird

tibio, -a ['tiβjo, a] adj lukewarm

tiburón [tiβu'ron] nm shark

tic [tik] nm (ruido) click; (de reloj) tick;
(MED): ~ **nervioso** nervous tic

tictac [tik'tak] nm (de reloj) tick tock

tiempo ['tjempo] nm time; (época,
período) age, period; (METEOROLOGÍA)
weather; (LING) tense; (DEPORTE) half; a
~ **in time; a un o al mismo** = at the
same time; **al poco** = very soon (after);
se quedó poco = he didn't stay very
long; **hace poco** = not long ago;
mucho ~ a long time; **de** = **en** = from
time to time; **hace buen/mal** ~ the
weather is fine/bad; **estar a** ~ to be in
time; **hace** ~ some time ago; **hacer** ~ to
while away the time; **motor de 2
tiempos** two-stroke engine; **primer** ~
first half

tienda ['tjenda] nf shop, store ▸ **tienda
de abarrotes** (MÉX, CAm) grocer's
(BRIT), grocery store (US) ▸ **tienda
de alimentación o comestibles**
grocer's (BRIT), grocery store (US)
▸ **tienda de campaña** tent

tienes etc vb ver **tener**

tienta etc ['tjenta] vb ver **tentar** ♦ nf:
andar a tientas to grope one's way
along

tiento etc ['tjento] vb ver **tentar** ♦ nm
(tacto) touch; (precaución) wariness

tierno, -a ['tjerno, a] adj (blando)
tender; (fresco) fresh; (amable) sweet

tierra ['tjerra] nf earth; (suelo) soil;
(mundo) earth, world; (país) country,
land; ~ **adentro** inland

tieso, -a ['tjeso, a] adj (rígido) rigid;
(duro) stiff; (fam: orgulloso) conceited

tiesto ['tjesto] nm flowerpot

tifón [ti'fon] nm typhoon

tifus ['tifus] nm typhus

tigre ['tiɣre] nm tiger

tijera [ti'xera] nf scissors pl; (ZOOL) claw;
tijeras nfpl scissors; (para plantas)
shears

tila ['tila] nf lime blossom tea

tildar [til'dar] vt: ~ **de** to brand as

tilde ['tilde] nf (TIP) tilde

tilín [ti'lin] nm tinkle

timar [ti'mar] vt (estafar) to swindle

timbal [tim'bal] nm small drum

timbre ['timbre] nm (sello) stamp;
(campanilla) bell; (tono) timbre; (COM)
stamp duty

timidez [timi'ðeθ] nf shyness
❏ **tímido, -a** adj shy

timo ['timo] nm swindle

timón [ti'mon] nm helm, rudder
❏ **timonel** nm helmsman

tímpano ['timpano] nm (ANAT)
eardrum; (MÚS) small drum

tina ['tina] nf tub; (baño) bath(tub)
❏ **tinaja** nf large jar

tinieblas [ti'njeβlas] nfpl darkness sg;
(sombras) shadows

tino ['tino] nm (habilidad) skill; (juicio)
insight

tinta ['tinta] nf ink; (TEC) dye; (ARTE)
colour

tinte ['tinte] nm dye

tintero [tin'tero] nm inkwell

tinto ['tinto] nm red wine

tintorería [tintore'ria] nf dry cleaner's

tío ['tio] nm (pariente) uncle; (fam: individuo) bloke (BRIT), guy

tiovivo [tio'βiβo] nm merry-go-round

típico, -a ['tipiko, a] adj typical

tipo ['tipo] nm (clase) type, kind; (hombre) fellow; (ANAT: de hombre) build; (: de mujer) figure; (IMPRENTA) type ▶ **tipo bancario/de descuento/ de interés/de cambio** bank/ discount/interest/exchange rate

tipografía [tipoɣra'fia] nf printing cpd

tíquet ['tiket] (pl **tíquets**) nm ticket; (en tienda) cash slip

tiquismiquis [tikis'mikis] nm inv fussy person ♦ nmpl (querellas) squabbling sg; (escrúpulos) silly scruples

tira ['tira] nf strip; (fig) abundance ▶ **tira y afloja** give and take

tirabuzón [tiraβu'θon] nm (rizo) curl

tirachinas [tira't∫inas] nm inv catapult

tirada [ti'raða] nf (acto) cast, throw; (serie) series; (TIP) printing, edition; **de una ~** at one go

tirado, -a [ti'raðo, a] adj (barato) dirt-cheap; (fam: fácil) very easy

tirador [tira'ðor] nm (mango) handle

tirano, -a [ti'rano, a] adj tyrannical ♦ nm/f tyrant

tirante [ti'rante] adj (cuerda etc) tight, taut; (relaciones) strained ♦ nm (ARQ) brace; (TEC) stay; **tirantes** nmpl (de pantalón) braces (BRIT), suspenders (US) ▶ **tirantez** nf tightness; (fig) tension

tirar [ti'rar] vt to throw; (dejar caer) to drop; (volcar) to upset; (derribar) to knock down o over; (desechar) to throw out o away; (dinero) to squander; (imprimir) to print ♦ vi (disparar) to shoot; (de la puerta etc) to pull; (fam: andar) to go; (tender a, buscar realizar) to tend to; (DEPORTE) to shoot; **tirarse** vr to throw o.s.; **~ abajo** to bring down, destroy; **tira más a su**

padre he takes more after his father; **ir tirando** to manage

tirita [ti'rita] nf (sticking) plaster (BRIT), Bandaid® (US)

tiritar [tiri'tar] vi to shiver

tiro ['tiro] nm (lanzamiento) throw; (disparo) shot; (DEPORTE) shot; (GOLF, TENIS) drive; (alcance) range; **caballo de ~** cart-horse ▶ **tiro al blanco** target practice

tirón [ti'ron] nm (sacudida) pull, tug; **de un ~** in one go, all at once

tiroteo [tiro'teo] nm exchange of shots, shooting

tisis ['tisis] nf inv consumption, tuberculosis

títere ['titere] nm puppet

titubear [tituβe'ar] vi to stagger; (fig) to hesitate ❏ **titubeo** nm staggering; stammering; hesitation

titulado, -a [titu'laðo, a] adj (libro) entitled; (persona) titled

titular [titu'lar] adj titular ♦ nmf holder ♦ nm headline ♦ vt to title; **titularse** vr to be entitled ❏ **título** nm title; (de diario) headline; (certificado) professional qualification; (universitario) (university) degree; **a título de** in the capacity of

tiza ['tiθa] nf chalk

toalla [to'aλa] nf towel

tobillo [to'βiλo] nm ankle

tobogán [toβo'ɣan] nm (montaña rusa) roller-coaster; (de niños) chute, slide

tocadiscos [toka'ðiskos] nm inv record player

tocado, -a [to'kaðo, a] adj (fam) touched ♦ nm headdress

tocador [toka'ðor] nm (mueble) dressing table; (cuarto) boudoir; (fam) ladies' toilet (BRIT) o room (US)

tocar [to'kar] vt to touch; (MÚS) to play; (referirse a) to allude to; (timbre) to ring ♦ vi (a la puerta) to knock (on o at the door); (ser de turno) to fall to, be the turn of; (*ser hora*) to be due; **tocarse** *vr* (*cubrirse la cabeza*) to cover one's head; (*tener contacto*) to touch (each other); **por lo que a mí me toca** as far as I am concerned; **te toca a ti** it's your turn

tocayo, -a [to'kajo, a] *nm/f* namesake

tocino [to'θino] *nm* bacon

todavía [toða'βia] *adv* (*aun*) even; (*aún*) still, yet; **~ más** yet more; **~ no** not yet

---

todo, -a

PALABRA CLAVE

[ˈtoðo, a] *adj*

1 (*con artículo sg*) all; **toda la carne** all the meat; **toda la noche** all night, the whole night; **todo el libro** the whole book; **toda una botella** a whole bottle; **todo lo contrario** quite the opposite; **está toda sucia** she's all dirty; **por todo el país** throughout the whole country

2 (*con artículo pl*) all; every; **todos los libros** all the books; **todas las noches** every night; **todos los que quieran salir** all those who want to leave

♦ *pron*

1 everything, all; **todos** everyone, everybody; **lo sabemos todo** we know everything; **todos querían más tiempo** everybody *o* everyone wanted more time; **nos marchamos todos** we all left

2: **con todo: con todo él me sigue gustando** even so I still like him

♦ *adv* all; **vaya todo seguido** keep straight on *o* ahead

♦ *nm*: **como un todo** as a whole; **del todo: no me agrada del todo** I don't entirely like it

---

todopoderoso, -a [toðopoðe'roso, a] *adj* all powerful; (*REL*) almighty

toga ['toɣa] *nf* toga, (*ESCOL*) gown

Tokio ['tokjo] *n* Tokyo

toldo ['toldo] *nm* (*para el sol*) sunshade (*BRIT*), parasol; (*tienda*) marquee

tolerancia [tole'ranθja] *nf* tolerance
  ❑ **tolerante** *adj* (*sociedad*) liberal; (*persona*) open-minded

tolerar [tole'rar] *vt* to tolerate; (*resistir*) to endure

toma ['toma] *nf* (*acto*) taking; (*MED*) dose ▶ **toma de corriente** socket ▶ **toma de tierra** earth (wire)
  ❑ **tomacorriente** (*LAm*) *nm* socket

tomar [to'mar] *vt* to take; (*aspecto*) to take on; (*beber*) to drink ♦ *vi* to take; (*LAm: beber*) to drink; **tomarse** *vr* to take; **tomarse por** to consider o.s. to be; **~ a bien/mal** to take well/badly; **~ en serio** to take seriously; **~ el pelo a algn** to pull sb's leg; **tomarla con algn** to pick a quarrel with sb; **¡tome!** here you are!; **~ el sol** to sunbathe

tomate [to'mate] *nm* tomato

tomillo [to'miʎo] *nm* thyme

tomo ['tomo] *nm* (*libro*) volume

ton [ton] *abr* = **tonelada** ♦ *nm*: **sin ~ ni son** without rhyme or reason

tonalidad [tonali'ðað] *nf* tone

tonel [to'nel] *nm* barrel

tonelada [tone'laða] *nf* ton
  ❑ **tonelaje** *nm* tonnage

tónica ['tonika] *nf* (*MÚS*) tonic; (*fig*) keynote

tónico, -a ['toniko, a] *adj* tonic ♦ *nm* (*MED*) tonic

tono ['tono] *nm* tone; **fuera de ~** inappropriate

tontería [tonte'ria] *nf* (*estupidez*) foolishness; (*cosa*) stupid thing; (*acto*) foolish act; **tonterías** *nfpl* (*disparates*) rubbish *sg*, nonsense *sg*

tonto, -a ['tonto, a] *adj* stupid, silly ♦ *nm/f* fool

topar [to'par] *vi*: **~ contra** *o* **en** to run into; **~ con** to run up against

tope ['tope] *adj* maximum ♦ *nm* (*fin*) end; (*límite*) limit; (*FERRO*) buffer; (*AUTO*) bumper; **al ~** end to end

tópico, -a ['topiko, a] adj topical ♦ nm platitude

topo ['topo] nm (ZOOL) mole; (fig) blunderer

toque etc ['toke] vb ver **tocar** ♦ nm touch; (MÚS) beat; (de campana) peal; **dar un ~ a** to warn ► **toque de queda** curfew

toqué etc vb ver **tocar**

toquetear [tokete'ar] vt to finger

toquilla [to'kiʎa] nf (pañuelo) headscarf; (chal) shawl

tórax ['toraks] nm thorax

torbellino [torbe'ʎino] nm whirlwind; (fig) whirl

torcedura [torθe'ðura] nf twist; (MED) sprain

torcer [tor'θer] vt to twist; (la esquina) to turn; (MED) to sprain ♦ vi (desviar) to turn off; **torcerse** vr (ladearse) to bend; (desviarse) to go astray; (fracasar) to go wrong ❑ **torcido, -a** adj twisted; (fig) crooked ♦ nm curl

tordo, -a ['torðo, a] adj dappled ♦ nm thrush

torear [tore'ar] vt (fig: evadir) to avoid; (jugar con) to tease ♦ vi to fight bulls ❑ **toreo** nm bullfighting ❑ **torero, -a** nm/f bullfighter

tormenta [tor'menta] nf storm; (fig: confusión) turmoil

tormento [tor'mento] nm torture; (fig) anguish

tornar [tor'nar] vt (devolver) to return, give back; (transformar) to transform ♦ vi to go back

tornasolado, -a [tornaso'laðo, a] adj (brillante) iridescent; (reluciente) shimmering

torneo [tor'neo] nm tournament

tornillo [tor'niʎo] nm screw

torniquete [torni'kete] nm (MED) tourniquet

torno ['torno] nm (TEC) winch; (tambor) drum; **en ~ (a)** round, about

toro ['toro] nm bull; (fam) he-man; **los toros** bullfighting

toronja [to'ronxa] nf grapefruit

torpe ['torpe] adj (poco hábil) clumsy, awkward; (lento) dim; (lento) slow

torpedo [tor'peðo] nm torpedo

torpeza [tor'peθa] nf (falta de agilidad) clumsiness; (lentitud) slowness; (error) mistake

torre ['torre] nf tower; (de petróleo) derrick

torrefacto, -a [torre'fakto, a] adj roasted

torrente [to'rrente] nm torrent

torrija [to'rrixa] nf French toast

torsión [tor'sjon] nf twisting

torso ['torso] nm torso

torta ['torta] nf cake; (fam) slap

tortícolis [tor'tikolis] nm inv stiff neck

tortilla [tor'tiʎa] nf omelette; (LAm: de maíz) maize pancake ► **tortilla de papas** (LAm) potato omelette ► **tortilla de patatas** (ESP) potato omelette ► **tortilla francesa** (ESP) plain omelette

tórtola ['tortola] nf turtledove

tortuga [tor'tuɣa] nf tortoise

tortuoso, -a [tor'twoso, a] adj winding

tortura [tor'tura] nf torture ❑ **torturar** vt to torture

tos [tos] nf cough ► **tos ferina** whooping cough

toser [to'ser] vi to cough

tostada [tos'taða] nf piece of toast ❑ **tostado, -a** adj toasted; (por el sol) dark brown; (piel) tanned

tostador [tosta'ðor] (ESP) nm toaster ❑ **tostadora** (LAm) nf = **tostador**

tostar [tos'tar] vt (café) to roast; (persona) to tan; **tostarse** vr to get brown

total [to'tal] adj total ♦ adv in short; (al fin y al cabo) when all is said and done ♦ nm total; **en ~** in all; **~ que** ... to cut (BRIT) o make (US) a long story short ...

totalidad [totali'ðað] nf whole

totalitario, -a [totali'tarjo, a] adj totalitarian

tóxico, -a ['toksiko, a] adj toxic ♦ nm poison ☐ **toxicómano, -a** nm/f drug addict

toxina [to'ksina] nf toxin

tozudo, -a [to'θuðo, a] adj obstinate

trabajador, a [traβaxa'ðor, a] adj hard-working ♦ nm/f worker
▶ **trabajador autónomo** o **por cuenta propia** self-employed person

trabajar [traβa'xar] vt to work; (AGR) to till; (empeñarse en) to work at; (convencer) to persuade ♦ vi to work; (esforzarse) to strive ☐ **trabajo** nm work; (tarea) task; (POL) labour; (fig) effort; **tomarse el trabajo de** to take the trouble to ▶ **trabajo a destajo** piecework ▶ **trabajo en equipo** teamwork ▶ **trabajo por turnos** shift work ▶ **trabajos forzados** hard labour sg

trabalenguas [traβa'lengwas] nm inv tongue twister

tracción [trak'θjon] nf traction
▶ **tracción delantera/trasera** front-wheel/rear-wheel drive

tractor [trak'tor] nm tractor

tradición [traði'θjon] nf tradition ☐ **tradicional** adj traditional

traducción [traðuk'θjon] nf translation

traducir [traðu'θir] vt to translate ☐ **traductor, a** nm/f translator

traer [tra'er] vt to bring; (llevar) to carry; (llevar puesto) to wear; (incluir) to include; (causar) to cause; **traerse** vr: **traerse algo** to be up to sth

traficar [trafi'kar] vi to trade

tráfico ['trafiko] nm (COM) trade; (AUTO) traffic

tragaluz [traɣa'luθ] nm skylight

tragamonedas (LAm) [traɣamo'neðas] nf inv slot machine

tragaperras [traɣa'perras] (ESP) nf inv slot machine

tragar [tra'ɣar] vt to swallow; (devorar) to devour, bolt down; **tragarse** vr to swallow

tragedia [tra'xeðja] nf tragedy ☐ **trágico, -a** adj tragic

trago ['traɣo] nm (líquido) drink; (bocado) gulp; (fam: de bebida) swig; (desgracia) blow; **echar un ~** to have a drink

traición [trai'θjon] nf treachery; (JUR) treason; (una traición) act of treachery ☐ **traicionar** vt to betray

traidor, a [trai'ðor, a] adj treacherous ♦ nm/f traitor

traigo etc vb ver **traer**

traje ['traxe] vb ver **traer** ♦ nm (de hombre) suit; (de mujer) dress; (vestido típico) costume ▶ **traje de baño/chaqueta** swimsuit/suit ▶ **traje de etiqueta** dress suit ▶ **traje de luces** bullfighter's costume

trajera etc [tra'xera] vb ver **traer**

trajín [tra'xin] nm (fam: movimiento) bustle ☐ **trajinar** vi (moverse) to bustle about

trama ['trama] nf (intriga) plot; (de tejido) weft (BRIT), woof (US) ☐ **tramar** vt to plot; (TEC) to weave

tramitar [trami'tar] vt (asunto) to transact; (negociar) to negotiate

trámite ['tramite] nm (paso) step; (JUR) transaction; **trámites** nmpl (burocracia) procedure sg; (JUR) proceedings

tramo ['tramo] nm (de tierra) plot; (de escalera) flight; (de vía) section

trampa ['trampa] nf trap; (en el suelo) trapdoor; (truco) trick; (engaño) fiddle ☐ **trampear** vt, vi to cheat

trampolín [trampo'lin] nm (de piscina etc) diving board

tramposo, -a [tram'poso, a] adj crooked, cheating ♦ nm/f crook, cheat

tranca ['traŋka] nf (palo) stick; (de puerta, ventana) bar □ **trancar** vt to bar

trance ['traŋθe] nm (momento difícil) difficult moment o juncture; (estado hipnotizado) trance

tranquilidad [traŋkili'ðað] nf (calma) calmness, stillness; (paz) peacefulness

tranquilizar [traŋkiliθ'ar] vt (calmar) to calm (down); (asegurar) to reassure; **tranquilizarse** vr to calm down □ **tranquilo, -a** adj (calmado) calm; (apacible) peaceful; (mar) calm; (mente) untroubled

transacción [transak'θjon] nf transaction

transbordador [transβorða'ðor] nm ferry

transbordo [trans'βorðo] nm transfer; **hacer ~** to change (trains etc)

transcurrir [transku'rrir] vi (tiempo) to pass; (hecho) to take place

transcurso [trans'kurso] nm: **~ del tiempo** lapse (of time)

transeúnte [transe'unte] nmf passer-by

transferencia [transfe'renθja] nf transference; (COM) transfer

transferir [transfe'rir] vt to transfer

transformador [transforma'ðor] nm (ELEC) transformer

transformar [transfor'mar] vt to transform; (convertir) to convert

transfusión [transfu'sjon] nf transfusion

transgénico, -a [trans'xeniko, a] adj genetically modified, GM

transición [transi'θjon] nf transition

transigir [transi'xir] vi to compromise, make concessions

transitar [transi'tar] vi to go (from place to place) □ **tránsito** nm transit; (AUTO) traffic □ **transitorio, -a** adj transitory

transmisión [transmi'sjon] nf (TEC) transmission; (transferencia) transfer

▶ **transmisión exterior/en directo** outside/live broadcast

transmitir [transmi'tir] vt to transmit; (RADIO, TV) to broadcast

transparencia [transpa'renθja] nf transparency; (claridad) clearness, clarity; (foto) slide

transparentar [transparen'tar] vt to reveal ♦ vi to be transparent □ **transparente** adj transparent; (claro) clear

transpirar [transpi'rar] vi to perspire

transportar [transpor'tar] vt to transport; (llevar) to carry □ **transporte** nm transport; (COM) haulage

transversal [transβer'sal] adj transverse, cross

tranvía [tram'bia] nm tram

trapeador (LAm) nm mop □ **trapear** (LAm) vt to mop

trapecio [tra'peθjo] nm trapeze □ **trapecista** nmf trapeze artist

trapero, -a [tra'pero, a] nm/f ragman

trapicheo [trapi'tʃeo] (fam) nm scheme, fiddle

trapo ['trapo] nm (tela) rag; (de cocina) cloth

tráquea [trakea] nf windpipe

traqueteo [trake'teo] nm rattling

tras [tras] prep (detrás) behind; (después) after

trasatlántico [trasat'lantiko] nm (barco) (cabin) cruiser

trascendencia [trasθen'denθja] nf (importancia) importance; (FILOSOFÍA) transcendence

trascendental [trasθenden'tal] adj important; (FILOSOFÍA) transcendental

trasero, -a [tra'sero, a] adj back, rear ♦ nm (ANAT) bottom

trasfondo [tras'fondo] nm background

trasgredir [trasɣre'ðir] vt to contravene

trashumante [trasu'mante] adj (animales) migrating

trasladar [trasla'ðar] vt to move; (persona) to transfer; (postergar) to postpone; (copiar) to copy; **trasladarse** vr (mudarse) to move ▶ **traslado** nm move, removal

traslucir [traslu'θir] vt to show

traslucir [traslu'θir] nm reflected light; **al ~** against o up to the light

trasnochador, a [trasnotʃa'ðor, a] nm/f night owl

trasnochar [trasno'tʃar] vi (acostarse tarde) to stay up late

traspapelar [traspape'lar] vt (documento, carta) to mislay, misplace

traspasar [traspa'sar] vt (suj: bala etc) to pierce, go through; (propiedad) to sell, transfer; (calle) to cross over; (límites) to go beyond; (ley) to break ▶ **traspaso** nm (venta) transfer, sale

traspatio (LAm) nm backyard

traspié [tras'pje] nm (tropezón) trip; (error) blunder

trasplantar [trasplan'tar] vt to transplant

traste [traste] nm (MÚS) fret; **dar al ~ con algo** to ruin sth

trastero [tras'tero] nm storage room

trastienda [tras'tjenda] nf back of shop

trasto ['trasto] (pey) nm (cosa) piece of junk; (persona) dead loss

trastornado, a [trastor'naðo, a] adj (loco) mad, crazy

trastornar [trastor'nar] vt (fig: planes) to disrupt; (: nervios) to shatter; (: persona) to drive crazy; **trastornarse** vr (volverse loco) to go crazy ▶ **trastorno** nm (acto) overturning; (confusión) confusion

tratable [tra'taβle] adj friendly

tratado [tra'taðo] nm (POL) treaty; (COM) agreement

tratamiento [trata'mjento] nm treatment ▶ **tratamiento de textos** (INFORM) word processing cpd

tratar [tra'tar] vt (ocuparse de) to treat; (manejar, TEC) to handle; (MED) to treat; (dirigirse a: persona) to address ♦ vi: **~ de** (hablar sobre) to deal with, be about; (intentar) to try to; **tratarse** vr to treat each other; **~ con** (COM) to trade in; (negociar) to negotiate with; (tener contactos) to have dealings with; **¿de qué se trata?** what's it about? ▶ **trato** nm dealings pl; (relaciones) relationship; (comportamiento) manner; (COM) agreement

trauma ['trauma] nm trauma

través [tra'βes] nm (fig) reverse; **al ~** across, crossways; **a ~ de** across; (sobre) over; (por) through

travesaño [traβe'saɲo] nm (ARQ) crossbeam; (DEPORTE) crossbar

travesía [traβe'sia] nf (calle) cross-street; (NAUT) crossing

travesura [traβe'sura] nf (broma) prank; (ingenio) wit

travieso, -a [tra'βjeso, a] adj (niño) naughty

trayecto [tra'jekto] nm (ruta) road, way; (viaje) journey; (tramo) stretch ▶ **trayectoria** nf trajectory; (fig) path

traza ['traθa] nf (aspecto) looks pl; (señal) sign ▶ **trazado, -a** adj: **bien trazado** shapely, well-formed ♦ nm (ARQ) plan, design; (fig) outline

trazar [tra'θar] vt (ARQ) to plan; (ARTE) to sketch; (fig) to trace; (plan) to draw up ▶ **trazo** nm (línea) line; (bosquejo) sketch

trébol [treβol] nm (BOT) clover

trece ['treθe] num thirteen

trecho ['tretʃo] nm (distancia) distance; (tiempo) while

tregua ['treɣwa] nf (MIL) truce; (fig) respite

treinta ['treinta] num thirty

tremendo, -a [tre'mendo, a] *adj*
(*terrible*) terrible; (*imponente: cosa*)
imposing; (*fam: fabuloso*) tremendous

tren [tren] *nm* train ▶ **tren de
aterrizaje** undercarriage ▶ **tren de
cercanías** suburban train

trenca ['trenka] *nf* duffel coat

trenza ['trenθa] *nf* (*de pelo*) plait (BRIT),
braid (US)

trepadora [trepa'ðora] *nf* (BOT) climber

trepar [tre'par] *vt, vi* to climb

tres [tres] *num* three

tresillo [tre'siʎo] *nm* three-piece suite;
(MÚS) triplet

treta ['treta] *nf* trick

triángulo [tri'angulo] *nm* triangle

tribu ['triβu] *nf* tribe

tribuna [tri'βuna] *nf* (*plataforma*)
platform; (DEPORTE) (grand)stand

tribunal [triβu'nal] *nm* (JUR) court;
(*comisión, fig*) tribunal; ▶ **popular** jury

tributo [tri'βuto] *nm* (COM) tax

trigal [tri'ɣal] *nm* wheat field

trigo ['triɣo] *nm* wheat

trigueño, -a [tri'ɣeɲo, a] *adj* (*pelo*)
corn-coloured

trillar [tri'ʎar] *vt* (AGR) to thresh

trimestral [trimes'tral] *adj* quarterly;
(ESCOL) termly

trimestre [tri'mestre] *nm* (ESCOL) term

trinar [tri'nar] *vi* (*pájaros*) to sing;
(*rabiar*) to fume, be angry

trinchar [trin'tʃar] *vt* to carve

trinchera [trin'tʃera] *nf* (*fosa*) trench

trineo [tri'neo] *nm* sledge

trinidad [trini'ðað] *nf* trio; (REL): **la T~**
the Trinity

tripa ['tripa] *nf* (ANAT) intestine; (*fam: tb:*
tripas) insides *pl*

triple ['triple] *adj* triple

triplicado, -a [tripli'kaðo, a] *adj*: **por ~**
in triplicate

tripulación [tripula'θjon] *nf* crew

tripulante [tripu'lante] *nmf* crewman/
woman

tripular [tripu'lar] *vt* (*barco*) to man;
(AUTO) to drive

triquiñuela [triki'nwela] *nf* trick

tris [tris] *nm inv* crack

triste ['triste] *adj* sad; (*lamentable*)
sorry, miserable ❑ **tristeza** *nf*
(*aflicción*) sadness; (*melancolía*)
melancholy

triturar [tritu'rar] *vt* (*moler*) to grind;
(*mascar*) to chew

triunfar [trjun'far] *vi* (*tener éxito*) to
triumph; (*ganar*) to win ❑ **triunfo** *nm*
triumph

trivial [tri'βjal] *adj* trivial

triza ['triθa] *nf*: **hacer trizas** to smash to
bits; (*papel*) to tear to shreds

trocear [troθe'ar] *vt* (*carne, manzana*)
to cut up, cut into pieces

trocha ['trotʃa] *nf* short cut

trofeo [tro'feo] *nm* (*premio*) trophy;
(*éxito*) success

tromba ['tromba] *nf* downpour

trombón [trom'bon] *nm* trombone

trombosis [trom'bosis] *nf inv*
thrombosis

trompa ['trompa] *nf* horn; (*trompo*)
humming top; (*hocico*) snout; (*fam*):
cogerse una ~ to get tight

trompazo [trom'paθo] *nm* bump,
bang

trompeta [trom'peta] *nf* trumpet;
(*clarín*) bugle

trompicón [trompi'kon]: **a
trompicones** *adv* in fits and starts

trompo ['trompo] *nm* spinning top

trompón [trom'pon] *nm* bump

tronar [tro'nar] *vt* (MÉX, CAM: *fusilar*) to
shoot; (MÉX: *examen*) to flunk ♦ *vi* to
thunder; (*fig*) to rage

tronchar [tron'tʃar] *vt* (*árbol*) to chop
down; (*fig: vida*) to cut short;
(*: esperanza*) to shatter; (*persona*) to tire
out; **troncharse** *vr* to fall down

tronco ['tronko] *nm* (*de árbol, ANAT*)
trunk

trono ['trono] nm throne

tropa ['tropa] nf (MIL) troop; (soldados) soldiers pl

tropezar [trope'θar] vi to trip, stumble; (errar) to slip up; **~ con** to run into; (topar con) to bump into □ **tropezón** nm trip; (fig) blunder

tropical [tropi'kal] adj tropical

trópico ['tropiko] nm tropic

tropiezo [tro'pjeθo] vb ver **tropezar** ♦ nm (error) slip, blunder; (desgracia) misfortune; (obstáculo) snag

trotamundos [trota'mundos] nm inv globetrotter

trotar [tro'tar] vi to trot □ **trote** nm trot; (fam) travelling; **de mucho trote** hard-wearing

trozar (LAm) vt to cut up, cut into pieces

trozo ['troθo] nm bit, piece

trucha ['trutʃa] nf trout

truco ['truko] nm (habilidad) knack; (engaño) trick

trueno ['trweno] nm thunder; (estampido) bang

trueque etc ['trweke] nm exchange; (COM) barter

trufa ['trufa] nf (BOT) truffle

truhán, -ana [tru'an, ana] nm/f rogue

truncar [trun'kar] vt (cortar) to truncate; (fig: la vida etc) to cut short; (: el desarrollo) to stunt

tu [tu] adj your

tú [tu] pron you

tubérculo [tu'βerkulo] nm (BOT) tuber

tuberculosis [tuβerku'losis] nf inv tuberculosis

tubería [tuβe'ria] nf pipes pl; (conducto) pipeline

tubo ['tuβo] nm tube, pipe ▶ **tubo de ensayo** test tube ▶ **tubo de escape** exhaust (pipe)

tuerca ['twerka] nf nut

tuerto, -a ['twerto, a] adj blind in one eye ♦ nm/f one-eyed person

tuerza etc ['twerθa] vb ver **torcer**

tuétano ['twetano] nm marrow; (BOT) pith

tufo ['tufo] nm (hedor) stench

tul [tul] nm tulle

tulipán [tuli'pan] nm tulip

tullido, -a [tu'ʎiðo, a] adj crippled

tumba ['tumba] nf (sepultura) tomb

tumbar [tum'bar] vt to knock down; **tumbarse** vr (echarse) to lie down; (extenderse) to stretch out

tumbo ['tumbo] nm: **dar tumbos** to stagger

tumbona [tum'bona] nf (butaca) easy chair; (de playa) deckchair (BRIT), beach chair (US)

tumor [tu'mor] nm tumour

tumulto [tu'multo] nm turmoil

tuna ['tuna] nf (MUS) student music group; ver tb **tuno**

tunante [tu'nante] nmf rascal

túnel ['tunel] nm tunnel

Túnez ['tuneθ] nm Tunisia; (ciudad) Tunis

tuno, -a ['tuno, a] nm/f (fam) rogue ♦ nm member of student music group

tupido, -a [tu'piðo, a] adj (denso) dense; (tela) close-woven

turbante [tur'βante] nm turban

turbar [tur'βar] vt (molestar) to disturb; (incomodar) to upset

turbina [tur'βina] nf turbine

turbio, -a ['turβjo, a] *adj* cloudy; (*tema etc*) confused

turbulencia [turβu'lenθja] *nf* turbulence; (*fig*) restlessness □ **turbulento, -a** [turβu'lento, a] *adj* turbulent; (*fig: intranquilo*) restless; (: *ruidoso*) noisy

turco, -a ['turko, a] *adj* Turkish ♦ *nm/f* Turk

turismo [tu'rismo] *nm* tourism; (*coche*) car □ **turista** *nmf* tourist □ **turístico, -a** *adj* tourist *cpd*

turnar [tur'nar] *vi* to take (it in) turns; **turnarse** *vr* to take (it in) turns □ **turno** (*de trabajo*) shift; (*en juegos etc*) turn

turquesa [tur'kesa] *nf* turquoise

Turquía [tur'kia] *nf* Turkey

turrón [tu'rron] *nm* (*dulce*) nougat

tutear [tute'ar] *vt* to address as familiar "tú"; **tutearse** *vr* to be on familiar terms

tutela [tu'tela] *nf* (*legal*) guardianship □ **tutelar** *adj* tutelary ♦ *vt* to protect

tutor, a [tu'tor, a] *nm/f* (*legal*) guardian; (*ESCOL*) tutor

tuve *etc* ['tuβe] *vb ver* **tener**

tuviera *etc vb ver* **tener**

tuyo, -a ['tujo, a] *adj* yours, of yours ♦ *pron* yours; **un amigo ~** a friend of yours; **los tuyos** (*fam*) your relations o family

TV *nf abr* (= *televisión*) TV

TVE *nf abr* = *Televisión Española*

U, u

u [u] *conj* or

ubicar [uβi'kar] *vt* to place, situate; (*LAm: encontrar*) to find; **ubicarse** *vr* (*LAm: encontrarse*) to lie, be located

ubre ['uβre] *nf* udder

UCI *nf abr* (= *Unidad de Cuidados Intensivos*) ICU

Ud(s) *abr* = **usted(es)**

UE *nf abr* (= *Unión Europea*) EU

ufanarse [ufa'narse] *vr* to boast □ **ufano, -a** (*arrogante*) arrogant; (*presumido*) conceited

UGT (*ESP*) *nf abr* = *Unión General de Trabajadores*

úlcera ['ulθera] *nf* ulcer

ulterior [ulte'rjor] *adj* (*más allá*) farther, further; (*subsecuente, siguiente*) subsequent

últimamente ['ultimamente] *adv* (*recientemente*) lately, recently

ultimar [ulti'mar] *vt* to finish; (*finalizar*) to finalize; (*LAm: matar*) to kill

ultimátum [ulti'matum] (*pl* **ultimátums**) *nm* ultimatum

último, -a ['ultimo, a] *adj* last; (*más reciente*) latest, most recent; (*más bajo*) bottom; (*más alto*) top; **en las últimas** on one's last legs; **por último** finally

ultra ['ultra] *adj ultra* ♦ *nmf* extreme right-winger

ultraje [ul'traxe] *nm* outrage; insult

ultramar [ultra'mar] *nm*: **de o en ~** abroad, overseas

ultramarinos [ultrama'rinos] *nmpl* groceries; **tienda de ~** grocer's (shop)

ultranza [ul'tranθa]: **a ~** *adv* (*a todo trance*) at all costs; (*completo*) outright

umbral [um'bral] *nm* (*gen*) threshold

un, una

PALABRA CLAVE

[un, 'una] *art indef* a; (*antes de vocal*) an; **una mujer/naranja** a woman/an orange ♦ *adj*: **unos** (o **unas**), **hay unos regalos para ti** there are some presents for you; **hay unas cervezas en la nevera** there are some beers in the fridge

unánime [u'nanime] *adj* unanimous □ **unanimidad** *nf* unanimity

undécimo, -a [un'deθimo, a] *adj* eleventh

ungir [un'xir] *vt* to anoint

ungüento [un'gwento] *nm* ointment

único, -a ['uniko, a] *adj* only, sole; (*sin par*) unique

unidad [uni'ðað] *nf* unity; (COM, TEC etc) unit

unido, -a [u'niðo, a] *adj* joined, linked; (*fig*) united

unificar [unifi'kar] *vt* to unite, unify

uniformar [unifor'mar] *vt* to make uniform, level up; (*persona*) to put into uniform

uniforme [uni'forme] *adj* uniform, equal; (*superficie*) even ♦ *nm* uniform

unilateral [unilate'ral] *adj* unilateral

unión [u'njon] *nf* union; (*acto*) uniting, joining; (*unidad*) unity; (TEC) joint
▶ **Unión Europea** European Union

unir [u'nir] *vt* (*juntar*) to join, unite; (*atar*) to tie, fasten; (*combinar*) to combine; **unirse** *vr* to join together, unite; (*empresas*) to merge

unísono [u'nisono] *nm*: **al ~ in** unison

universal [uniβer'sal] *adj* universal; (*mundial*) world *cpd*

universidad [uniβersi'ðað] *nf* university

universitario, -a [uniβersi'tarjo, a] *adj* university *cpd* ♦ *nm/f* (*profesor*) lecturer; (*estudiante*) (university) student; (*graduado*) graduate

universo [uni'βerso] *nm* universe

uno, -a

PALABRA CLAVE

['uno, a] *adj* one; **unos pocos** a few; **unos cien** about a hundred
♦ *pron*

1 one; **quiero sólo uno** I only want one; **uno de ellos** one of them

2 (*alguien*) someone, somebody; **conozco a uno que se te parece** I know somebody o someone who looks like you; **uno mismo** oneself; **unos querían quedarse** some (people) wanted to stay

3: (los) **unos ... (los) otros ...** some ... others

♦ *nf* one; **es la una** it's one o'clock
♦ *nm* (number) one

untar [un'tar] *vt* (*mantequilla*) to spread; (*engrasar*) to grease, oil

uña ['uɲa] *nf* (ANAT) nail; (*garra*) claw; (*casco*) hoof; (*arrancaclavos*) claw

uranio [u'ranjo] *nm* uranium

urbanización [urβaniθa'θjon] *nf* (*barrio, colonia*) housing estate

urbanizar [urβani'θar] *vt* (*zona*) to develop, urbanize

urbano, -a [ur'βano, a] *adj* (*de ciudad*) urban; (*cortés*) courteous, polite

urbe ['urβe] *nf* large city

urdir [ur'ðir] *vt* to warp; (*complot*) to plot, contrive

urgencia [ur'xenθja] *nf* urgency; (*prisa*) haste, rush; (*emergencia*) emergency; **servicios de ~** emergency services; **"Urgencias" "Casualty"** ☐ **urgente** *adj* urgent

urgir [ur'xir] *vi* to be urgent; **me urge** I'm in a hurry for it

urinario, -a [uri'narjo, a] *adj* urinary ♦ *nm* urinal

urna ['urna] *nf* urn; (POL) ballot box

urraca [u'rraka] *nf* magpie

URSS [urs] *nf* (HIST): **la ~** the USSR

Uruguay [uru'ɣwai] *nm* (*tb*: **el ~**) Uruguay ♦ **uruguayo, -a** *adj, nm/f* Uruguayan

usado, -a [u'saðo, a] *adj* used; (*de segunda mano*) secondhand

usar [u'sar] *vt* to use; (*ropa*) to wear; (*tener costumbre*) to be in the habit of; **usarse** *vr* to be used ♦ **uso** *nm* use; wear; (*costumbre*) usage, custom; (*moda*) fashion; **al uso** in keeping with custom; **al uso de** in the style of; **de uso externo** (MED) for external use

usted [us'teð] *pron* (*sg*) you *sg*; (*pl*): **ustedes** you *pl*

usual [u'swal] *adj* usual

usuario, -a [usu'arjo, a] *nm/f* user

usura [u'sura] nf usury ❑ **usurero, -a**
nm/f usurer

usurpar [usur'par] vt to usurp

utensilio [uten'siljo] nm tool; (CULIN)
utensil

útero ['utero] nm uterus, womb

útil ['util] adj useful ♦ nm tool
❑ **utilidad** nf usefulness; (COM) profit
❑ **utilizar** vt to use, utilize

utopía [uto'pia] nf Utopia ❑ **utópico,
-a** adj Utopian

uva ['uβa] nf grape

V, v

v abr (= voltio) v

va [ba] vb ver **ir**

vaca ['baka] nf (animal) cow; **carne de ~**
beef

vacaciones [baka'θjones] nfpl holidays

vacante [ba'kante] adj vacant, empty
♦ nf vacancy

vaciar [ba'θjar] vt to empty out;
(ahuecar) to hollow out; (moldear) to
cast; **vaciarse** vr to empty

vacilar [baθi'lar] vi to be unsteady; (al
hablar) to falter; (dudar) to hesitate,
waver; (memoria) to fail

vacío, -a [ba'θio, a] adj empty; (puesto)
vacant; (desocupado) idle; (vano) vain
♦ nm emptiness; (FÍSICA) vacuum; (un
vacío) (empty) space

vacuna [ba'kuna] nf vaccine
❑ **vacunar** vt to vaccinate

vacuno, -a [ba'kuno, a] adj cow cpd;
ganado ~ cattle

vadear [baðe'ar] vt (río) to ford ❑ **vado**
nm ford

vagabundo, -a [baɣa'βundo, a] adj
wandering ♦ nm tramp

vagancia [ba'ɣanθja] nf (pereza)
idleness, laziness

vagar [ba'ɣar] vi to wander; (no hacer
nada) to idle

vagina [ba'xina] nf vagina

vago, -a ['baɣo, a] adj vague; (perezoso)
lazy ♦ nm/f (vagabundo) tramp; (flojo)
lazybones sg, idler

vagón [ba'ɣon] nm (FERRO: de pasajeros)
carriage; (: de mercancías) wagon

vaho ['bao] nm (vapor) vapour, steam;
(respiración) breath

vaina ['baina] nf sheath

vainilla [bai'niʎa] nf vanilla

vais [bais] vb ver **ir**

vaivén [bai'βen] nm to-and-fro
movement; (de tránsito) coming and
going; **vaivenes** nmpl (fig) ups and
downs

vajilla [ba'xiʎa] nf crockery, dishes pl;
(juego) service, set

valdré etc vb ver **valer**

vale ['bale] nm voucher; (recibo) receipt;
(pagaré) IOU

valedero, -a [bale'ðero, a] adj valid

valenciano, -a [balen'θjano, a] adj
Valencian

valentía [balen'tia] nf courage, bravery

valer [ba'ler] vt to be worth; (MAT) to
equal; (costar) to cost ♦ vi (ser útil) to be
useful; (ser válido) to be valid; **valerse**
vr to take care of oneself; **valerse de** to
make use of, take advantage of; **~ la
pena** to be worthwhile; **¿vale?** (ESP)
OK?; **más vale que nos vayamos** we'd
better go; **eso a mí no me vale!** (MÉX:
fam: no importar) I couldn't care less
about that

valeroso, -a [bale'roso, a] adj brave,
valiant

valgo etc vb ver **valer**

valía [ba'lia] nf worth, value

validar [bali'ðar] vt to validate
❑ **validez** nf validity ❑ **válido, -a** adj
valid

valiente [ba'ljente] adj brave, valiant
♦ nm hero

valija (CS) [ba'lixa] nf (suit)case

valioso, -a [ba'ljoso, a] adj valuable

valla ['baʎa] nf fence; (DEPORTE) hurdle
▶ **valla publicitaria** hoarding
❑ **vallar** vt to fence in

valle ['baʎe] nm valley

valor [ba'lor] nm value, worth; (precio) price; (valentía) valour, courage; (importancia) importance; **valores** nmpl (COM) securities ❑ **valorar** vt to value

vals [bals] nm inv waltz

válvula ['balβula] nf valve

vamos ['bamos] vb ver **ir**

vampiro, -resa [bam'piro, 'resa] nm/f vampire

van [ban] vb ver **ir**

vanguardia [ban'gwardja] nf vanguard; (ARTE etc) avant-garde

vanidad [bani'ðað] nf vanity ❑ **vanidoso, -a** adj vain, conceited

vano, -a ['bano, a] adj vain

vapor [ba'por] nm vapour; (vaho) steam; **al ~** (CULIN) steamed ▶ **vapor de agua** water vapour ❑ **vaporizador** nm atomizer ❑ **vaporizar** vt to vaporize ❑ **vaporoso, -a** adj vaporous

vaquero, -a [ba'kero, a] adj cattle cpd ♦ nm cowboy; **vaqueros** nmpl (pantalones) jeans

vaquilla [ba'kiʎa] nf (ZOOL) heifer

vara ['bara] nf stick; (TEC) rod

variable [ba'rjaβle] adj, nf variable

variación [barja'θjon] nf variation

variar [bar'jar] vt to vary; (modificar) to modify; (cambiar de posición) to switch around ♦ vi to vary

varicela [bari'θela] nf chickenpox

varices [ba'riθes] nfpl varicose veins

variedad [barje'ðað] nf variety

varilla [ba'riʎa] nf stick; (BOT) twig; (TEC) rod; (de rueda) spoke

vario, -a ['barjo, a] adj varied; **varios** various, several

varita [ba'rita] nf (tb: ~ **mágica**) magic wand

varón [ba'ron] nm male, man ❑ **varonil** adj manly, virile

Varsovia [bar'soβja] n Warsaw

vas [bas] vb ver **ir**

vasco, -a ['basko, a] adj, nm/f Basque ❑ **vascongado, -a** [baskon'gaðo, a] adj Basque; **las Vascongadas** the Basque Country

vaselina [base'lina] nf Vaseline®

vasija [ba'sixa] nf container, vessel

vaso ['baso] nm glass, tumbler; (ANAT) vessel

> No confundir **vaso** con la palabra inglesa *vase*.

vástago ['bastaɣo] nm (BOT) shoot; (TEC) rod; (fig) offspring

vasto, -a ['basto, a] adj vast, huge

Vaticano [bati'kano] nm: **el ~** the Vatican

vatio ['batjo] nm (ELEC) watt

vaya etc ['baja] vb ver **ir**

Vd(s) abr = **usted(es)**

ve [be] vb ver **ir; ver**

vecindad [beθin'dað] nf neighbourhood; (habitantes) residents pl

vecindario [beθin'darjo] nm neighbourhood; residents pl

vecino, -a [be'θino, a] adj neighbouring ♦ nm/f neighbour; (residente) resident

veda ['beða] nf prohibition ❑ **vedar** [be'ðar] vt (prohibir) to ban, prohibit; (impedir) to stop, prevent

vegetación [bexeta'θjon] nf vegetation

vegetal [bexe'tal] adj, nm vegetable

vegetariano, -a [bexeta'rjano, a] adj, nm/f vegetarian

vehículo [be'ikulo] nm vehicle; (MED) carrier

veía etc vb ver **ver**

veinte ['beinte] num twenty

vejar [be'xar] vt (irritar) to annoy, vex; (humillar) to humiliate

vejez [be'xeθ] nf old age

vejiga [be'xiɣa] nf (ANAT) bladder

vela ['bela] nf (de cera) candle; (NÁUT) sail; (insomnio) sleeplessness; (vigilia) vigil; (MIL) sentry duty; **estar a dos velas** (fam: sin dinero) to be skint

velado, -a [be'laðo, a] adj veiled; (sonido) muffled; (FOTO) blurred ♦ nf soirée

velar [be'lar] vt (vigilar) to keep watch over ♦ vi to stay awake; **~ por** to watch over, look after

velatorio [bela'torjo] nm (funeral) wake

velero [be'lero] nm (NÁUT) sailing ship; (AVIAC) glider

veleta [be'leta] nf weather vane

veliz [be'lis] (MEX) nm (suit)case

vello ['beʎo] nm down, fuzz

velo ['belo] nm veil

velocidad [beloθi'ðað] nf speed; (TEC, AUTO) gear

velocímetro [belo'θimetro] nm speedometer

velorio [be'lorjo] (LAm) nm (funeral) wake

veloz [be'loθ] adj fast

ven [ben] vb ver **venir**

vena ['bena] nf vein

venado [be'naðo] nm deer

vencedor, a [benθe'ðor, a] adj victorious ♦ nm/f victor, winner

vencer [ben'θer] vt (dominar) to defeat, beat; (derrotar) to vanquish; (superar, controlar) to overcome, master ♦ vi (triunfar) to win (through), triumph; (plazo) to expire ♦ **vencido, -a** adj (derrotado) defeated, beaten; (COM) due ♦ adv: **pagar vencido** to pay in arrears

venda ['benda] nf bandage ♦ **vendaje** nm bandage, dressing ♦ **vendar** vt to bandage; **vendar los ojos** to blindfold

vendaval [benda'βal] nm (viento) gale

vendedor, a [bende'ðor, a] nm/f seller

vender [ben'der] vt to sell; **venderse** vr (estar a la venta) to be on sale; **~ al contado/al por mayor/al por menor** to sell for cash/wholesale/retail; **"se vende"** "for sale"

vendimia [ben'dimja] nf grape harvest

vendré etc [ben'dre] vb ver **venir**

veneno [be'neno] nm poison; (de serpiente) venom ♦ **venenoso, -a** adj poisonous; venomous

venerable [bene'raβle] adj venerable ♦ **venerar** vt (respetar) to revere; (adorar) to worship

venéreo, -a [be'nereo, a] adj: **enfermedad venérea** venereal disease

venezolano, -a [beneθo'lano, a] adj Venezuelan

Venezuela [bene'θwela] nf Venezuela

venganza [ben'ganθa] nf vengeance, revenge ♦ **vengar** vt to avenge; **vengarse** vr to take revenge ♦ **vengativo, -a** adj (persona) vindictive

vengo etc vb ver **venir**

venia ['benja] nf (perdón) pardon; (permiso) consent

venial [be'njal] adj venial

venida [be'niða] nf (llegada) arrival; (regreso) return

venidero, -a [beni'ðero, a] adj coming, future

venir [be'nir] vi to come; (llegar) to arrive; (ocurrir) to happen; (fig): **~ de** to stem from; **~ bien/mal** to be suitable/ unsuitable; **el año que viene** next year; **venirse abajo** to collapse

venta ['benta] nf (COM) sale; **"en ~"** "for sale"; **estar a la** o **en ~** to be (up) for sale o on the market ▶ **venta a domicilio** door-to-door selling ▶ **venta a plazos** hire purchase ▶ **venta al contado/al por mayor/al por menor** cash sale/wholesale/retail

ventaja [ben'taxa] nf advantage
  ❏ **ventajoso, -a** adj advantageous

ventana [ben'tana] nf window
  ❏ **ventanilla** nf (de taquilla) window (of booking office etc)

ventilación [bentila'θjon] nf ventilation; (corriente) draught

ventilador [bentila'ðor] nm fan

ventilar [benti'lar] vt to ventilate; (para secar) to put out to dry; (asunto) to air, discuss

ventisca [ben'tiska] nf blizzard

ventrílocuo, -a [ben'trilokwo, a] nm/f ventriloquist

ventura [ben'tura] nf (felicidad) happiness; (buena suerte) luck; (destino) fortune; **a la (buena) ~** at random ❏ **venturoso, -a** adj happy; (afortunado) lucky, fortunate

veo etc vb ver **ver**

ver [ber] vt to see; (mirar) to look at, watch; (entender) to understand; (investigar) to look into ♦ vi to see; to understand; **verse** vr (encontrarse) to meet; (dejarse ver) to be seen; (hallarse: en un apuro) to find o.s. be; (vamos) a ~ let's see; **no tener nada que ~ con** to have nothing to do with; **a mi modo de ~** as I see it; **ya veremos** we'll see

vera ['bera] nf edge, verge; (de río) bank

veranear [berane'ar] vi to spend the summer ❏ **veraneo** nm summer holiday ❏ **veraniego, -a** adj summer cpd

verano [be'rano] nm summer

veras ['beras] nfpl truth sg; **de ~** really, truly

verbal [ber'βal] adj verbal

verbena [ber'βena] nf (baile) open-air dance

verbo ['berβo] nm verb

verdad [ber'ðað] nf truth; (fiabilidad) reliability; **de ~** real, proper; **a decir ~** to tell the truth ❏ **verdadero, -a** adj (veraz) true, truthful; (fiable) reliable; (fig) real

verde ['berðe] adj green; (chiste) blue, dirty ♦ nm green; **viejo ~** dirty old man ❏ **verdear** vi to turn green ❏ **verdor** nm greenness

verdugo [ber'ðuɣo] nm executioner

verdulero, -a [berðu'lero, a] nm/f greengrocer

verduras [ber'ðuras] nfpl (CULIN) greens

vereda [be'reða] nf path; (CS: acera) pavement (BRIT), sidewalk (US)

veredicto [bere'ðikto] nm verdict

vergonzoso, -a [berɣon'θoso, a] adj shameful; (tímido) timid, bashful

vergüenza [ber'ɣwenθa] nf shame, sense of shame; (timidez) bashfulness; (pudor) modesty; **me da ~** I'm ashamed

verídico, -a [be'riðiko, a] adj true, truthful

verificar [berifi'kar] vt to check; (corroborar) to verify; (llevar a cabo) to carry out; **verificarse** vr (predicción) to prove to be true

verja ['berxa] nf (cancela) iron gate; (valla) iron railings pl; (de ventana) grille

vermut [ber'mut] (pl **vermuts**) nm vermouth

verosímil [bero'simil] adj likely, probable; (relato) credible

verruga [be'rruɣa] nf wart

versátil [ber'satil] adj versatile

versión [ber'sjon] nf version

verso ['berso] nm verse; **un ~** a line of poetry

vértebra ['berteβra] nf vertebra

verter [ber'ter] vt (líquido: adrede) to empty, pour (out); (: sin querer) to spill; (basura) to dump ♦ vi to flow

vertical [berti'kal] adj vertical

vértice ['bertiθe] nm vertex, apex

vertidos [ber'tiðos] nmpl waste sg

vertiente [ber'tjente] nf slope; (fig) aspect

vértigo ['bertiɣo] nm vertigo; (mareo) dizziness

vesícula [be'sikula] nf blister

vespino® [bes'pino] nm o nf moped

vestíbulo [bes'tiβulo] nm hall; (de teatro) foyer

vestido [bes'tiðo] nm (ropa) clothes pl, clothing; (de mujer) dress, frock ♦ pp de **vestir**; ~ de azul/marinero dressed in blue/as a sailor

vestidor (MÉX) nm (DEPORTE) changing (BRIT) o locker (US) room

vestimenta [besti'menta] nf clothing

vestir [bes'tir] vt (poner: ropa) to put on; (llevar: ropa) to wear; (proveer de ropa a) to clothe; (sastre) to make clothes for ♦ vi (vestirse) to dress; (verse bien) to look good; **vestirse** vr to get dressed, dress o.s.

vestuario [bes'twarjo] nm clothes pl, wardrobe; (TEATRO: cuarto) dressing room; (DEPORTE) changing (BRIT) o locker (US) room

vetar [be'tar] vt to veto

veterano, -a [bete'rano, a] adj, nm veteran

veterinaria [beteri'narja] nf veterinary science; ver tb **veterinario**

veterinario, -a [beteri'narjo, a] nm/f vet(erinary surgeon)

veto ['beto] nm veto

vez [beθ] nf time; (turno) turn; **a la ~ que** at the same time as; **a su ~** in its turn; **otra ~** again; **una ~** once; **de una ~** in one go; **de una ~ para siempre** once and for all; **en ~ de** instead of; **a algunas veces** sometimes; **una y otra ~** repeatedly; **de ~ en cuando** from time to time; **7 veces 9** 7 times 9; **hacer las veces de** to stand in for; **tal ~** perhaps

vía ['bia] nf track, route; (FERRO) line; (fig) way; (ANAT) passage, tube ♦ prep via, by way of; **por ~ judicial** by legal means; **en vías de** in the process of ▶ **vía aérea** airway ▶ **Vía Láctea**

Milky Way ▶ **vía pública** public road o thoroughfare

viable [bja'βle] adj (solución, plan, alternativa) feasible

viaducto [bja'ðukto] nm viaduct

viajante [bja'xante] nm commercial traveller

viajar [bja'xar] vi to travel □ **viaje** nm journey, trip; (gira) tour; (NÁUT) voyage; **estar de viaje** to be on a trip ▶ **viaje de ida y vuelta** round trip ▶ **viaje de novios** honeymoon □ **viajero, -a** adj travelling; (ZOOL) migratory ♦ nm/f (quien viaja) traveller; (pasajero) passenger

víbora ['biβora] nf (ZOOL) viper; (: MÉX: venenosa) poisonous snake

vibración [biβra'θjon] nf vibration

vibrar [bi'βrar] vt, vi to vibrate

vicepresidente [biθepresi'ðente] nmf vice-president

viceversa [biθe'βersa] adv vice versa

vicio ['biθjo] nm vice; (mala costumbre) bad habit □ **vicioso, -a** adj (muy malo) vicious; (corrompido) depraved ♦ nm/f depraved person

víctima ['biktima] nf victim

victoria [bik'torja] nf victory □ **victorioso, -a** adj victorious

vid [bið] nf vine

vida ['biða] nf (gen) life; (duración) lifetime; **de por ~** for life; **en la o mi ~** never; **estar con ~** to be still alive; **ganarse la ~** to earn one's living

vídeo ['biðeo] nm video ♦ adj inv: **película de ~** video film □ **videocámara** nf camcorder □ **videocasete** nm video cassette, videotape □ **videoclub** nm video club □ **videojuego** nm video game

vidrio ['biðrjo] nm glass

vieira ['bjeira] nf scallop

viejo, -a ['bjexo, a] adj old ♦ nm/f old man/woman; **hacerse ~** to get old

Viena ['bjena] n Vienna

vienes etc vb ver **venir**

vienés, -esa [bje'nes, esa] adj Viennese

viento ['bjento] nm wind; **hacer ~ to be windy**

vientre ['bjentre] nm belly; (matriz) womb

viernes ['bjernes] nm inv Friday ▶ **Viernes Santo** Good Friday

Vietnam [bjet'nam] nm Vietnam ❏ **vietnamita** adj Vietnamese

viga ['biɣa] nf beam, rafter; (de metal) girder

vigencia [bi'xenθja] nf validity; **estar en ~ to be in force** ❏ **vigente** adj valid, in force; (imperante) prevailing

vigésimo, -a [bi'xesimo, a] adj twentieth

vigía [bi'xia] nm look-out

vigilancia [bixi'lanθja] nf: **tener a algn bajo ~ to keep watch on sb**

vigilar [bixi'lar] vt to watch over ♦ vi (gen) to be vigilant; (hacer guardia) to keep watch; **~ por to take care of**

vigilia [vi'xilja] nf wakefulness, being awake; (REL) fast

vigor [bi'ɣor] nm vigour, vitality; **en ~ in force; entrar/poner en ~ to come/put into effect** ❏ **vigoroso, -a** adj vigorous

VIH nm abr (= virus de la inmunodeficiencia humana) HIV ▶ **VIH negativo/positivo** HIV-negative/ -positive

vil [bil] adj vile, low

villa ['biʎa] nf (casa) villa; (pueblo) small town; (municipalidad) municipality

villancico [biʎan'θiko] nm (Christmas) carol

vilo ['bilo]: **en ~** adv in the air, suspended; (fig) on tenterhooks, in suspense

vinagre [bi'naɣre] nm vinegar

vinagreta [bina'ɣreta] nf vinaigrette, French dressing

vinculación [binkula'θjon] nf (lazo) link, bond; (acción) linking

vincular [binku'lar] vt to link, bind ❏ **vínculo** nm link, bond

vine etc vb ver **venir**

vinicultura [binikul'tura] nf wine growing

viniera etc vb ver **venir**

vino ['bino] vb ver **venir** ♦ nm wine ▶ **vino blanco/tinto** white/red wine

viña ['biɲa] nf vineyard ❏ **viñedo** nm vineyard

viola ['bjola] nf viola

violación [bjola'θjon] nf violation; (sexual) rape

violar [bjo'lar] vt to violate; (sexualmente) to rape

violencia [bjo'lenθja] nf violence, force; (incomodidad) embarrassment; (acto injusto) unjust act ❏ **violentar** vt to force; (casa) to break into; (agredir) to assault; (violar) to violate ❏ **violento, -a** adj violent; (furioso) furious; (situación) embarrassing; (acto) forced, unnatural

violeta [bjo'leta] nf violet

violín [bjo'lin] nm violin

violón [bjo'lon] nm double bass

virar [bi'rar] vi to change direction

virgen ['birxen] adj, nf virgin

Virgo ['birɣo] nm Virgo

viril [bi'ril] adj virile ❏ **virilidad** nf virility

virtud [bir'tuð] nf virtue; **en ~ de by virtue of** ❏ **virtuoso, -a** adj virtuous ♦ nm/f virtuoso

viruela [bi'rwela] nf smallpox

virulento, -a [biru'lento, a] adj virulent

virus ['birus] nm inv virus

visa ['bisa] (LAm) nf ▶ **visado**

visado [bi'saðo] (ESP) nm visa

víscera ['bisθera] nf (ANAT, ZOOL) gut, bowel; **vísceras** nfpl entrails

visceral [bisθe'ral] adj (odio) intense; **reacción ~** gut reaction

visera [bi'sera] nf visor

visibilidad [bisiβili'ðað] nf visibility
❑ **visible** adj visible; (fig) obvious

visillos [bi'siʎos] nmpl lace curtains

visión [bi'sjon] nf (ANAT) vision,
(eye)sight; (fantasía) vision, fantasy

visita [bi'sita] nf call, visit; (persona)
visitor; **hacer ~** to pay a visit
❑ **visitar** [bisi'tar] vt to visit, call on

visón [bi'son] nm mink

visor [bi'sor] nm (FOTO) viewfinder

víspera [bispera] nf: **la ~ de ...** the day
before ...

vista ['bista] nf sight, vision; (capacidad
de ver) (eye)sight; (mirada) look(s) (pl);
a primera ~ at first glance; **hacer la ~
gorda** to turn a blind eye; **volver la ~**
to look back; **está a la ~ que** it's
obvious that; **en ~ de** in view of;
en ~ de que in view of the fact that; **¡hasta
la ~!** so long!, see you!; **con vistas a**
with a view to ❑ **vistazo** nm glance;
dar o echar un vistazo a to glance at

visto, -a ['bisto, a] pp de **ver** ♦ vb ver tb
vestir ♦ adj seen; (considerado)
considered ♦ nm: **~ bueno** approval;
por lo ~ apparently; **está ~ que** it's
clear that; **está bien/mal ~** it's
acceptable/unacceptable; **~ que** since,
considering that

vistoso, -a [bis'toso, a] adj colourful

visual [bi'swal] adj visual

vital [bi'tal] adj life cpd, living cpd; (fig)
vital; (persona) lively, vivacious
❑ **vitalicio, -a** adj for life ❑ **vitalidad**
nf (de persona, negocio) energy; (de
ciudad) liveliness

vitamina [bita'mina] nf vitamin

vitorear [bitore'ar] vt to cheer, acclaim

vitrina [bi'trina] nf show case; (LAm:
escaparate) shop window

viudo, -a ['bjuðo, a] nm/f widower/
widow

viva ['biβa] excl hurrah!; **¡~ el rey!** long
live the king!

vivaracho, -a [biβa'ratʃo, a] adj jaunty,
lively; (ojos) bright, twinkling

vivaz [bi'βaθ] adj lively

víveres ['biβeres] nmpl provisions

vivero [bi'βero] nm (para plantas)
nursery; (para peces) fish farm; (fig)
hotbed

viveza [bi'βeθa] nf liveliness; (agudeza:
mental) sharpness

vivienda [bi'βjenda] nf housing; (una
vivienda) house; (piso) flat (BRIT),
apartment (US)

viviente [bi'βjente] adj living

vivir [bi'βir] vt, vi to live ♦ nm life, living

vivo, -a ['biβo, a] adj living, alive; (fig:
descripción) vivid; (persona: astuto)
smart, clever; **en ~** (transmisión etc) live

vocablo [bo'kaβlo] nm (palabra) word;
(término) term

vocabulario [bokaβu'larjo] nm
vocabulary

vocación [boka'θjon] nf vocation
❑ **vocacional** (LAm) nf ≈ technical
college

vocal [bo'kal] adj vocal ♦ nf vowel
❑ **vocalizar** vt to vocalize

vocero [bo'θero] (LAm) nmf
spokesman/woman

voces ['boθes] pl de **voz**

vodka ['boðka] nm o f vodka

vol abr = **volumen**

volado (MÉX) [bo'laðo] adv in a rush,
hastily

volador, a [bola'ðor, a] adj flying

volandas [bo'landas]: **en ~** adv in the
air

volante [bo'lante] adj flying ♦ nm (de
coche) steering wheel; (de reloj)
balance

volar [bo'lar] vt (edificio) to blow up ♦ vi
to fly

volátil [bo'latil] adj volatile

volcán [bol'kan] nm volcano
❑ **volcánico, -a** adj volcanic

volcar [bol'kar] vt to upset, overturn;
(tumbar, derribar) to knock over;

(*vaciar*) to empty out ♦ *vi* to overturn; **volcarse** *vr* to tip over

voleibol [bolei'βol] *nm* volleyball

volqué *etc* [bol'ke] *vb ver* **volcar**

voltaje [bol'taxe] *nm* voltage

voltear [bolte'ar] *vt* to turn over; (*volcar*) to turn upside down

voltereta [bolte'reta] *nf* somersault

voltio ['boltjo] *nm* volt

voluble [bo'luβle] *adj* fickle

volumen [bo'lumen] (*pl* **volúmenes**) *nm* volume ❏ **voluminoso, -a** *adj* voluminous; (*enorme*) massive

voluntad [bolun'tað] *nf* will; (*resolución*) willpower; (*deseo*) desire, wish

voluntario, -a [bolun'tarjo, a] *adj* voluntary ♦ *nm/f* volunteer

volver [bol'βer] *vt* (*gen*) to turn; (*dar vuelta a*) to turn (over); (*voltear*) to turn round, turn upside down; (*poner al revés*) to turn inside out; (*devolver*) to return ♦ *vi* to return, go back, come back; **volverse** *vr* to turn round; ~ **la espalda** to turn one's back; ~ **triste** *etc* **a algn** to make sb sad *etc*; ~ **a hacer** to do again; ~ **en sí** to come to; **volverse insoportable/muy caro** to get o become unbearable/very expensive; **volverse loco** to go mad

vomitar [bomi'tar] *vt, vi* to vomit ❏ **vómito** *nm* vomit

voraz [bo'raθ] *adj* voracious

vos [bos] (*LAm*) *pron* you

vosotros, -as [bo'sotros, as] (*ESP*) *pron* you; (*reflexivo*): **entre/para** ~ among/ for yourselves

votación [bota'θjon] *nf* (*acto*) voting; (*voto*) vote

votar [bo'tar] *vi* to vote ♦ **voto** *nm* vote; (*promesa*) vow; **votos** *nmpl* (*good*) wishes

voy [boi] *vb ver* **ir**

voz [boθ] *nf* voice; (*grito*) shout; (*rumor*) rumour; (*LING*) word; **dar voces** to shout, yell; **de viva** ~ verbally; **en** ~ **alta**

aloud; **en** ~ **baja** in a low voice, in a whisper ► **voz de mando** command

vuelco ['bwelko] *vb ver* **volcar** ♦ *nm* spill, overturning

vuelo ['bwelo] *vb ver* **volar** ♦ *nm* flight; (*encaje*) lace, frill; **coger al** ~ to catch in flight ► **vuelo chárter/regular** charter/scheduled flight ► **vuelo libre** (*DEPORTE*) hang-gliding

vuelque *etc* ['bwelke] *vb ver* **volcar**

vuelta ['bwelta] *nf* (*gen*) turn; (*curva*) bend, curve; (*regreso*) return; (*revolución*) revolution; (*de circuito*) lap; (*de papel, tela*) reverse; (*cambio*) change; **a la** ~ on one's return; **a la** ~ **(de la esquina)** round the corner; **a** ~ **de correo** by return of post; **dar vueltas** (*cabeza*) to spin; (*volverse*) to turn round; **dar vueltas a una idea** to turn over an idea in (one's head); **estar de** ~ to be back; **dar una** ~ to go for a walk; (*en coche*) to go for a drive ► **vuelta ciclista** (*DEPORTE*) (cycle) tour

vuelto ['bwelto] *pp de* **volver**

vuelvo *etc* *vb ver* **volver**

vuestro, -a ['bwestro, a] *adj pos* your; **un amigo** ~ a friend of yours ♦ *pron*: **el** ~/**la vuestra, los vuestros/las vuestras** yours

vulgar [bul'ɣar] *adj* (*ordinario*) vulgar; (*común*) common ❏ **vulgaridad** *nf* commonness; (*acto*) vulgarity; (*expresión*) coarse expression

vulnerable [bulne'raβle] *adj* vulnerable

vulnerar [bulne'rar] *vt* (*ley, acuerdo*) to violate, breach; (*derechos, intimidad*) to violate; (*reputación*) to damage

W, w

walkie-talkie [walki–'talki] (*pl* **walkie-talkies**) *nm* walkie-talkie

Walkman® [walkman] nm Walkman®

wáter ['bater] nm (taza) toilet; (LAm: lugar) toilet (BRIT), rest room (US)

web [web] nf o (página) website; (red) (World Wide) Web ❑ **webcam** nf webcam ❑ **webmaster** nmf webmaster ❑ **website** nm website

western (pl westerns) nm western

whisky ['wiski] nm whisky, whiskey

windsurf ['winsurf] nm windsurfing; **hacer ~** to go windsurfing

X, x

xenofobia [kseno'foβja] nf xenophobia

xilófono [ksi'lofono] nm xylophone

xocoyote, -a (MÉX) nm/f baby of the family, youngest child

Y, y

y [i] conj and

ya [ja] adv (gen) already; (ahora) now; (en seguida) at once; (pronto) soon ♦ excl all right! ♦ conj (ahora que) now that; **ya lo sé** I know; **ya que** ... since; **¡ya está bien!** that's (quite) enough!; **¡ya voy!** coming!

yacaré (CS) [jaka're] nm cayman

yacer [ja'θer] vi to lie

yacimiento [jaθi'mjento] nm (de mineral) deposit; (arqueológico) site

yanqui ['janki] adj, nmf Yankee

yate ['jate] nm yacht

yazco etc vb ver **yacer**

yedra ['jeðra] nf ivy

yegua ['jeɣwa] nf mare

yema ['jema] nf (del huevo) yolk; (BOT) leaf bud; (fig) best part ♦ **yema del dedo** fingertip

yerno ['jerno] nm son-in-law

yeso ['jeso] nm plaster

yo [jo] pron I; **soy yo** it's me

yodo ['joðo] nm iodine

yoga ['joɣa] nm yoga

yogur(t) [jo'ɣur(t)] nm yoghurt

yuca ['juka] nf (alimento) cassava, manioc root

Yugoslavia [juɣos'laβja] nf (HIST) Yugoslavia

yugular [juɣu'lar] adj jugular

yunque ['junke] nm anvil

yuyo (RPl) ['jujo] nm (mala hierba) weed

Z, z

zafar [θa'far] vt (soltar) to untie; (superficie) to clear; **zafarse** vr (escaparse) to escape; (TEC) to slip off

zafiro [θa'firo] nm sapphire

zaga ['θaɣa] nf: **a la ~** behind, in the rear

zaguán [θa'ɣwan] nm hallway

zalamero, -a [θala'mero, a] adj flattering; (cobista) suave

zamarra [θa'marra] nf (chaqueta) sheepskin jacket

zambullirse [θambu'ʎirse] vr to dive

zampar [θam'par] vt to gobble down

zanahoria [θana'orja] nf carrot

zancadilla [θanka'ðiʎa] nf trip

zanco ['θanko] nm stilt

zángano ['θangano] nm drone

zanja ['θanxa] nf ditch ❑ **zanjar** vt (resolver) to resolve

zapata [θa'pata] nf (MECÁNICA) shoe

zapatería [θapate'ria] nf (oficio) shoemaking; (tienda) shoe shop; (fábrica) shoe factory ❑ **zapatero, -a** nm/f shoemaker

zapatilla [θapa'tiʎa] nf slipper ▶ **zapatilla de deporte** training shoe

zapato [θa'pato] nm shoe

zapping ['θapin] nm channel-hopping; **hacer ~** to flick through the channels

zar [θar] nm tsar, czar

zarandear [θaranðe'ar] (fam) vt to shake vigorously

zarpa ['θarpa] nf (garra) claw

zarpar [θar'par] vi to weigh anchor

zarza ['θarθa] nf (BOT) bramble

zarzamora [θarθa'mora] nf blackberry

zarzuela [θar'θwela] nf Spanish light opera

zigzag [θiɣ'θaɣ] nm zigzag

zinc [θink] nm zinc

zíper (MÉX, CAm) ['θiper] nm zip (fastener) (BRIT), zipper (US)

zócalo ['θokalo] nm (ARQ) plinth, base; (de pared) skirting board (BRIT), baseboard (US); (MÉX: plaza) main o public square

zoclo (MÉX) nm skirting board (BRIT), baseboard (US)

zodíaco [θo'ðiako] nm (ASTROLOGÍA) zodiac

zona ['θona] nf zone ▸ **zona fronteriza** border area ▸ **zona roja** (LAm) red-light district

zonzo, -a (LAm: fam) ['θonθo, a] adj silly ♦ nm/f fool

zoo ['θoo] nm zoo

zoología [θoolo'xia] nf zoology ❑ **zoológico, -a** adj zoological ♦ nm (tb: **parque zoológico**) zoo ❑ **zoólogo, -a** nm/f zoologist

zoom [θum] nm zoom lens

zopilote [θopi'lote] (MÉX, CAm) nm buzzard

zoquete [θo'kete] nm (fam) blockhead

zorro, -a ['θorro, a] adj crafty ♦ nm/f fox/vixen

zozobrar [θoθo'βrar] vi (hundirse) to capsize; (fig) to fail

zueco ['θweko] nm clog

zumbar [θum'bar] vt (golpear) to hit ♦ vi to buzz ❑ **zumbido** nm buzzing

zumo ['θumo] nm juice

zurcir [θur'θir] vt (coser) to darn

zurdo, -a ['θurðo, a] adj (persona) left-handed

zurrar [θu'rrar] (fam) vt to wallop

ENGLISH - SPANISH
ESPAÑOL - INGLÉS

Aa

A [eɪ] n (MUS) la m

a

KEYWORD

[ə] (before vowel or silent h: an) indef art

1 un(a); **a book** un libro; **an apple** una manzana; **she's a doctor** (ella) es médica

2 (instead of the number "one") un(a); **a year ago** hace un año; **a hundred/ thousand** etc **pounds** cien/mil etc libras

3 (in expressing ratios, prices etc): **3 a day/week** 3 al día/a la semana; **10 km an hour** 10 km por hora; **£5 a person** £5 por persona; **30p a kilo** 30p el kilo

A.A. n abbr = **Automobile Association**; (BRIT) ≈ RACE m (SP); (= Alcoholics Anonymous) Alcohólicos Anónimos

A.A.A. n (US) n abbr (= American Automobile Association) ≈ RACE m (SP)

aback [əˈbæk] adv: **to be taken ~** quedar desconcertado

abandon [əˈbændən] vt abandonar; (give up) renunciar a

abattoir [ˈæbətwɑːʳ] (BRIT) n matadero

abbey [ˈæbɪ] n abadía

abbreviation [əˌbriːvɪˈeɪʃən] n (short form) abreviatura

abdomen [ˈæbdəmən] n abdomen m

abduct [æbˈdʌkt] vt raptar, secuestrar

abide [əˈbaɪd] vt: **I can't ~ it/him** no lo/ le puedo ver ▶ **abide by** vt fus atenerse a

ability [əˈbɪlɪtɪ] n habilidad n, capacidad f; (talent) talento

able [ˈeɪbl] adj capaz; (skilled) hábil; **to be ~ to do sth** poder hacer algo

abnormal [æbˈnɔːməl] adj anormal

aboard [əˈbɔːd] adv a bordo ♦ prep a bordo de

abolish [əˈbɒlɪʃ] vt suprimir, abolir

abolition [æbəʊˈlɪʃən] n supresión f, abolición f

abort [əˈbɔːt] vt, vi abortar ▢ **abortion** [əˈbɔːʃən] n aborto; **to have an abortion** abortar, hacerse abortar

about

KEYWORD

[əˈbaʊt] adv

1 (approximately) más o menos, aproximadamente; **about a hundred/thousand** etc unos(unas) cien/mil etc; **it takes about 10 hours** se tarda unas o más o menos 10 horas; **at about 2 o'clock** sobre las dos; **I've just about finished** casi he terminado

2 (referring to place) por todas partes; **to leave things lying about** dejar las cosas (tiradas) por ahí; **to run about** correr por todas partes; **to walk about** pasearse, ir y venir

3: **to be about to do sth** estar a punto de hacer algo

♦ prep

1 (relating to) de, sobre, acerca de; **a book about London** un libro sobre or acerca de Londres; **what is it about?** ¿de qué se trata?; **we talked about it** hablamos de eso or ello; **what** or **how about doing this?** ¿qué tal si hacemos esto?

2 (referring to place) por; **to walk about the town** caminar por la ciudad

above [əˈbʌv] adv encima, por encima, arriba ♦ prep encima de; (greater than: in number) más de; (: in rank) superior a; **mentioned ~** susodicho; **~ all** sobre todo

abroad [əˈbrɔːd] adv (to be) en el extranjero; (to go) al extranjero

abrupt [əˈbrʌpt] adj (sudden) brusco; (curt) áspero

abscess [ˈæbsɪs] n absceso

absence [ˈæbsəns] n ausencia

absent [ˈæbsənt] adj ausente
□ **absent-minded** adj distraído

absolute [ˈæbsəluːt] adj absoluto
□ **absolutely** [-ˈluːtlɪ] adv (totally) totalmente; (certainly!) ¡por supuesto (que sí)!

absorb [əbˈzɔːb] vt absorber; **to be absorbed in a book** estar absorto en un libro □ **absorbent cotton** (US) n algodón m hidrófilo □ **absorbing** adj absorbente

abstain [əbˈsteɪn] vi: **to ~ (from)** abstenerse (de)

abstract [ˈæbstrækt] adj abstracto

absurd [əbˈsəːd] adj absurdo

abundance [əˈbʌndəns] n abundancia

abundant [əˈbʌndənt] adj abundante

abuse [n əˈbjuːs, vb əˈbjuːz] n (insults) insultos mpl, injurias fpl; (ill-treatment) malos tratos mpl; (misuse) abuso ♦ vt insultar; maltratar; abusar de
□ **abusive** adj ofensivo

abysmal [əˈbɪzməl] adj pésimo; (failure) garrafal; (ignorance) supino

abyss [əˈbɪs] n abismo

academic [ækəˈdemɪk] adj académico, universitario; (pej: issue) puramente teórico ♦ n estudioso(-a), profesor(a) m/f universitario(-a) □ **academic year** n (UNIV) año m académico; (SCOL) año m escolar

academy [əˈkædəmɪ] n (learned body) academia; (school) instituto, colegio; **~ of music** conservatorio

accelerate [ækˈseləreɪt] vt, vi acelerar
□ **acceleration** [ækseləˈreɪʃən] n aceleración f □ **accelerator** (BRIT) n acelerador m

accent [ˈæksent] n acento; (fig) énfasis m

accept [əkˈsept] vt aceptar; (responsibility, blame) admitir
□ **acceptable** adj aceptable
□ **acceptance** n aceptación f

access [ˈækses] n acceso; **to have ~ to** tener libre acceso a □ **accessible** [-ˈsesəbl] adj (place, person) accesible; (knowledge etc) asequible

accessory [ækˈsesərɪ] n accesorio; (LAW): **~ to** cómplice de

accident [ˈæksɪdənt] n accidente m; (chance event) casualidad f; **by ~** (unintentionally) sin querer; (by chance) por casualidad □ **accidental** [-ˈdentl] adj accidental, fortuito
□ **accidentally** [-ˈdentəlɪ] adv sin querer; por casualidad □ **Accident and Emergency Department** n (BRIT) Urgencias fpl □ **accident insurance** n seguro contra accidentes

acclaim [əˈkleɪm] vt aclamar, aplaudir ♦ n aclamación f, aplausos mpl

accommodate [əˈkɔmədeɪt] vt (person) alojar, hospedar; (: car, hotel etc) tener cabida para; (oblige, help) complacer

accommodation [əkɔməˈdeɪʃən] (US **accommodations**) n alojamiento

accompaniment [əˈkʌmpənɪmənt] n acompañamiento

accompany [əˈkʌmpənɪ] vt acompañar

accomplice [əˈkʌmplɪs] n cómplice mf

accomplish [əˈkʌmplɪʃ] vt (finish) concluir; (achieve) lograr
□ **accomplishment** n (skill: gen pl) talento; (completion) realización f

accord [əˈkɔːd] n acuerdo ♦ vt conceder; **of his own ~** espontáneamente ☐ **accordance** n: **in accordance with** de acuerdo con ☐ **according to** prep según; (in accordance with) conforme a ☐ **accordingly** adv (appropriately) de acuerdo con esto; (as a result) en consecuencia

account [əˈkaunt] n (COMM) cuenta; (report) informe m; **accounts** npl (COMM) cuentas fpl; **of no ~** de ninguna importancia; **on ~** a cuenta; **on no ~** bajo ningún concepto; **on ~ of** a causa de, por motivo de; **to take into ~**, **take ~ of** tener en cuenta ► **account for** vt fus (explain) explicar; (represent) representar ☐ **accountable** adj: **accountable (to)** responsable (ante) ☐ **accountant** n contable m/f, contador(a) m/f ☐ **account number** n (at bank etc) número de cuenta

accumulate [əˈkjuːmjuleɪt] vt acumular ♦ vi acumularse

accuracy [ˈækjurəsɪ] n (of total) exactitud f; (of description etc) precisión f

accurate [ˈækjurɪt] adj (total) exacto; (description) preciso; (person) cuidadoso; (device) de precisión ☐ **accurately** adv con precisión

accusation [ækjuˈzeɪʃən] n acusación f

accuse [əˈkjuːz] vt: **to ~ sb (of sth)** acusar a algn (de algo) ☐ **accused** n (LAW) acusado(-a)

accustomed [əˈkʌstəmd] adj: **~ to** acostumbrado a

ace [eɪs] n as m

ache [eɪk] n dolor m ♦ vi doler; **my head aches** me duele la cabeza

achieve [əˈtʃiːv] vt (aim, result) alcanzar; (success) lograr, conseguir ☐ **achievement** n (completion) realización f; (success) éxito

acid [ˈæsɪd] adj (CHEM) ácido; (taste) agrio ♦ n (CHEM, inf: LSD) ácido

acknowledge [əkˈnɒlɪdʒ] vt (letter: also: **~ receipt of**) acusar recibo de; (fact, situation, person) reconocer ☐ **acknowledgement** n acuse m de recibo

acne [ˈæknɪ] n acné m

acorn [ˈeɪkɔːn] n bellota

acoustic [əˈkuːstɪk] adj acústico

acquaintance [əˈkweɪntəns] n (person) conocido(-a); (with person, subject) conocimiento

acquire [əˈkwaɪə*] vt adquirir ☐ **acquisition** [ækwɪˈzɪʃən] n adquisición f

acquit [əˈkwɪt] vt absolver, exculpar; **to ~ o.s. well** salir con éxito

acre [ˈeɪkə*] n acre m

acronym [ˈækrənɪm] n siglas fpl

across [əˈkrɒs] prep (on the other side) al otro lado de, del otro lado de; (crosswise) a través de ♦ adv de un lado a otro, de una parte a otra; (measurement): **the road is 10m ~** la carretera tiene 10m de ancho; **to run/swim ~** atravesar corriendo/ nadando; **~ from** enfrente de

acrylic [əˈkrɪlɪk] adj acrílico ♦ n acrílica

act [ækt] n acto, acción f; (of play) acto; (in music hall etc) número; (LAW) decreto, ley f ♦ vi (behave) comportarse; (have effect: drug, chemical) hacer efecto; (THEATRE) actuar; (pretend) fingir; (take action) obrar ♦ vt (part) hacer el papel de; **in the ~ of**, **to catch sb in the ~ of** pillar a algn en el momento en que ...; **to ~ as** actuar or hacer de ► **act up** (inf) vi (person) portarse mal ☐ **acting** adj suplente ♦ n (activity) actuación f; (profession) profesión f de actor

action [ˈækʃən] n acción f, acto; (MIL) acción f, batalla; (LAW) proceso, demanda; **out of ~** (person) fuera de combate; (thing) estropeado; **to take ~** tomar medidas ☐ **action replay** n (TV) repetición f

activate ['æktɪveɪt] vt activar

active ['æktɪv] adj activo, enérgico; (volcano) en actividad ❑ **actively** adv (participate) activamente; (discourage, dislike) enérgicamente

activist ['æktɪvɪst] n activista m/f

activity [-'tɪvɪtɪ] n actividad f ❑ **activity holiday** n vacaciones con actividades organizadas

actor ['æktə'] n actor m

actress ['æktrɪs] n actriz f

actual ['æktjuəl] adj verdadero, real; (emphatic use) propiamente dicho

⚠ Be careful not to translate **actual** by the Spanish word actual.

actually ['æktjuəlɪ] adv realmente, en realidad; (even) incluso

⚠ Be careful not to translate **actually** by the Spanish word actualmente.

acupuncture ['ækjupʌŋktʃə'] n acupuntura

acute [ə'kjuːt] adj agudo

ad [æd] n abbr = advertisement

A.D. adv abbr (= anno Domini) DC

adamant ['ædəmənt] adj firme, inflexible

adapt [ə'dæpt] vt adaptar ◆ vi: **to ~ (to)** adaptarse (a), ajustarse (a) ❑ **adapter**, **adaptor** n (ELEC) adaptador m; (for several plugs) ladrón

add [æd] vt añadir, agregar ▶ **add up** vt (figures) sumar ◆ vi (fig): **it doesn't add up** no tiene sentido ▶ **add up to** vt fus (MATH) sumar, ascender a; (fig: mean) querer decir, venir a ser

addict ['ædɪkt] n adicto(-a); (enthusiast) entusiasta mf ❑ **addicted** [ə'dɪktɪd] adj: **to be addicted to** ser adicto a, ser fanático de ❑ **addiction** [ə'dɪkʃən] n (to drugs etc) adicción f ❑ **addictive** [ə'dɪktɪv] adj que causa adicción

addition [ə'dɪʃən] n (adding up) adición f; (thing added) añadidura, añadido; **in ~** además, por añadidura; **in ~ to**

además de ❑ **additional** adj adicional

additive ['ædɪtɪv] n aditivo

address [ə'dres] n dirección f, señas fpl; (speech) discurso ◆ vt (letter) dirigir; (speak to) dirigirse a, dirigir la palabra a; (problem) tratar ❑ **address book** n agenda (de direcciones)

adequate ['ædɪkwət] adj (satisfactory) adecuado; (enough) suficiente

adhere [əd'hɪə'] vi: **to ~ to** (stick to) pegarse a; (fig: abide by) observar; (belief etc) ser partidario de

adhesive [əd'hiːzɪv] n adhesivo ❑ **adhesive tape** n (BRIT) cinta adhesiva; (US MED) esparadrapo

adjacent [ə'dʒeɪsənt] adj: **~ to** contiguo a, inmediato a

adjective ['ædʒektɪv] n adjetivo

adjoining [ə'dʒɔɪnɪŋ] adj contiguo, vecino

adjourn [ə'dʒɜːn] vt aplazar ◆ vi suspenderse

adjust [ə'dʒʌst] vt (change) modificar; (clothing) arreglar; (machine) ajustar ◆ vi: **to ~ (to)** adaptarse (a) ❑ **adjustable** adj ajustable ❑ **adjustment** n adaptación f; (to machine, prices) ajuste m

administer [əd'mɪnɪstə'] vt administrar ❑ **administration** [-'treɪʃən] n (management) administración f; (government) gobierno ❑ **administrative** [-trətɪv] adj administrativo

administrator [əd'mɪnɪstreɪtə'] n administrador(a) m/f

admiral ['ædmərəl] n almirante m

admiration [ædmə'reɪʃən] n admiración f

admire [əd'maɪə'] vt admirar ❑ **admirer** n (fan) admirador(a) m/f

admission [əd'mɪʃən] n (to university, club) ingreso; (entry fee) entrada; (confession) confesión f

admit [əd'mɪt] vt (confess) confesar; (permit to enter) dejar entrar, dar entrada a; (to club, organization) admitir; (accept: defeat) reconocer; **to be admitted to hospital** ingresar en el hospital ▶ **admit to** vt fus confesarse culpable de ❏ **admittance** n entrada f ❏ **admittedly** adv es cierto or verdad que

adolescent [ædəu'lɛsnt] adj, n adolescente mf

adopt [ə'dɒpt] vt adoptar ❏ **adopted** adj adoptivo ❏ **adoption** [ə'dɒpʃən] n adopción f

adore [ə'dɔː'] vt adorar

adorn [ə'dɔːn] vt adornar

Adriatic [eɪdrɪ'ætɪk] n: **the ~ (Sea)** el (Mar) Adriático

adrift [ə'drɪft] adv a la deriva

adult ['ædʌlt] n adulto(-a) ♦ adj (grown-up) adulto; (for adults) para adultos ❏ **adult education** n educación f para adultos

adultery [ə'dʌltərɪ] n adulterio

advance [əd'vɑːns] n (progress) adelanto, progreso; (money) anticipo, préstamo; (MIL) avance m ♦ adj: ~ **booking** venta anticipada; ~ **notice**, ~ **warning** previo aviso ♦ vt (money) anticipar; (theory, idea) proponer para la discusión) ♦ vi avanzar, adelantarse; **to make advances (to sb)** hacer proposiciones (a algn); **in ~** por adelantado ❏ **advanced** adj avanzado; (SCOL: studies) adelantado

advantage [əd'vɑːntɪdʒ] n (also TENNIS) ventaja; **to take ~ of** (person) aprovecharse de; (opportunity) aprovechar

advent ['ædvənt] n advenimiento; **A~** Adviento

adventure [əd'ventʃə'] n aventura ❏ **adventurous** [-tʃərəs] adj atrevido; aventurero

adverb ['ædvəːb] n adverbio

adversary ['ædvəsərɪ] n adversario, contrario

adverse ['ædvəːs] adj adverso, contrario

advert ['ædvəːt] (BRIT) n abbr = **advertisement**

advertise ['ædvətaɪz] vi (in newspaper etc) anunciar, hacer publicidad; **to ~ for** (staff, accommodation etc) buscar por medio de anuncios ♦ vt anunciar ❏ **advertisement** [əd'vəːtɪsmənt] n (COMM) anuncio ❏ **advertiser** n anunciante mf ❏ **advertising** n publicidad f, anuncios mpl; (industry) industria publicitaria

advice [əd'vaɪs] n consejo, consejos mpl; (notification) aviso; **a piece of ~** un consejo; **to take legal ~** consultar con un abogado

advisable [əd'vaɪzəbl] adj aconsejable, conveniente

advise [əd'vaɪz] vt aconsejar; (inform): **to ~ sb of sth** informar a algn de algo; **to ~ sb against sth/doing sth** desaconsejar algo a algn/aconsejar a algn que no haga algo ❏ **adviser**, **advisor** n consejero(-a); (consultant) asesor(a) m/f ❏ **advisory** adj consultivo

advocate [vb 'ædvəkeɪt, n -kɪt] vt abogar por ♦ n (lawyer) abogado(-a); (supporter): ~ **of** defensor(a) m/f de

Aegean [iː'dʒiːən] n: **the ~ (Sea)** el (Mar) Egeo

aerial ['ɛərɪəl] n antena ♦ adj aéreo

aerobics [ɛə'rəubɪks] n aerobic m

aeroplane ['ɛərəpleɪn] (BRIT) n avión m

aerosol ['ɛərəsɒl] n aerosol m

affair [ə'fɛə'] n asunto; (also: **love ~**) aventura (amorosa)

affect [ə'fɛkt] vt (influence) afectar, influir en; (afflict, concern) afectar; (move) conmover ❏ **affected** adj afectado ❏ **affection** n afecto, cariño ❏ **affectionate** adj afectuoso, cariñoso

afflict [ə'flɪkt] vt afligir

affluent ['æfluənt] adj (wealthy) acomodado; **the ~ society** la sociedad opulenta

afford [ə'fɔːd] vt (provide) proporcionar; **can we ~ (to buy) it?** ¿tenemos bastante dinero para comprarlo? ❑ **affordable** adj asequible

Afghanistan [æf'gænɪstæn] n Afganistán m

afraid [ə'freɪd] adj: **to be ~ of** (person) tener miedo a; (thing) tener miedo de; **to be ~ to** tener miedo de, temer; **I am ~ that** me temo que; **I am ~ not/so** lo siento, pero no/es así

Africa ['æfrɪkə] n África ❑ **African** adj, n africano(-a) m/f ❑ **African-American** adj, n afroamericano(-a)

after ['ɑːftə] prep (time) después de; (place, order) detrás de, tras ◆ adv después ◆ conj después (de) que; **what/who are you ~?** ¿qué a quién busca usted?; **~ having done/he left** después de haber hecho/después de que se marchó; **to name sb ~ sb** llamar a algn después de algn; **it's twenty ~ eight** (US) son las ocho y veinte; **to ask ~ sb** preguntar por algn; **~ all** después de todo, al fin y al cabo; **~ you!** ¡pase usted! ❑ **after-effects** npl consecuencias fpl, efectos mpl ❑ **aftermath** n consecuencias fpl, resultados mpl ❑ **afternoon** n tarde f ❑ **after-shave (lotion)** n aftershave m ❑ **aftersun (lotion/cream)** n loción f/crema para después del sol, aftersun m ❑ **afterwards** (US **afterward**) adv después, más tarde

again [ə'gen] adv otra vez, de nuevo; **to do sth ~** volver a hacer algo; **~ and ~** una y otra vez

against [ə'genst] prep (in opposition to) en contra de, contra; (leaning on, touching) contra, junto a

age [eɪdʒ] n edad f; (period) época ◆ vi envejecer(se) ◆ vt envejecer; **she is 20**

years of ~ tiene 20 años; **to come of ~** llegar a la mayoría de edad; **it's been ages since I saw you** hace siglos que no te veo; **aged 10** de 10 años de edad ❑ **age group** n: **to be in the same age group** tener la misma edad ❑ **age limit** n edad f mínima (or máxima)

agency ['eɪdʒənsɪ] n agencia

agenda [ə'dʒendə] n orden m del día

> ⚠ Be careful not to translate **agenda** by the Spanish word *agenda*.

agent ['eɪdʒənt] n agente mf; (COMM: holding concession) representante mf, delegado(-a); (CHEM, fig) agente m

aggravate ['ægrəveɪt] vt (situation) agravar; (person) irritar

aggression [ə'greʃən] n agresión f

aggressive [ə'gresɪv] adj (belligerent) agresivo; (assertive) enérgico

agile ['ædʒaɪl] adj ágil

agitated ['ædʒɪteɪtɪd] adj agitado

AGM n abbr (= annual general meeting) asamblea anual

ago [ə'gəu] adv: **2 days ~** hace 2 días; **not long ~** hace poco; **how long ~?** ¿hace cuánto tiempo?

agony ['ægənɪ] n (pain) dolor m agudo; (distress) angustia; **to be in ~** retorcerse de dolor

agree [ə'griː] vt (price, date) acordar, quedar en ◆ vi (have same opinion): **to ~ (with/that)** estar de acuerdo (con/que); (correspond) coincidir, concordar; (consent) acceder; **to ~ with** (person) estar de acuerdo con, ponerse de acuerdo con; (: food) sentar bien a; (LING) concordar con; **to ~ to sth/to do sth** consentir en algo/aceptar hacer algo; **to ~ that** (admit) estar de acuerdo en que ❑ **agreeable** adj (sensation) agradable; (person) simpático; (willing) de acuerdo, conforme ❑ **agreed** adj (time, place) convenido ❑ **agreement** n acuerdo; (contract) contrato; **in agreement** de acuerdo, conforme

agricultural [ægrɪˈkʌltʃərəl] adj
agrícola

agriculture [ˈægrɪkʌltʃəʳ] n agricultura

ahead [əˈhɛd] adv (in front) delante;
(into the future): **she had no time to
think** ~ no tenía tiempo de hacer
planes para el futuro; ~ **of** delante de;
(in advance of) antes de; ~ **of time**
antes de la hora; **go right** or **straight** ~
(direction) siga adelante; (permission)
hazlo (or hágalo)

aid [eɪd] n ayuda, auxilio; (device)
aparato ♦ vt ayudar, auxiliar; **in** ~ **of** a
beneficio de

aide [eɪd] n (person, also MIL) ayudante
mf

AIDS [eɪdz] n abbr (= acquired immune
deficiency syndrome) SIDA m

ailing [ˈeɪlɪŋ] adj (person, economy)
enfermizo

ailment [ˈeɪlmənt] n enfermedad f,
achaque m

aim [eɪm] vt (gun, camera) apuntar;
(missile, remark) dirigir; (blow) asestar
♦ vi (also: **take** ~) apuntar ♦ n (in
shooting: skill) puntería; (objective)
propósito, meta; **to** ~ **at** (with weapon)
apuntar a; (objective) aspirar a,
pretender; **to** ~ **to do** tener la
intención de hacer

ain't [eɪnt] (inf) = **am not; aren't; isn't**

air [ɛəʳ] n aire m; (appearance) aspecto
♦ vt (room) ventilar; (clothes, ideas)
airear ♦ cpd aéreo; **to throw sth into
the** ~ (ball etc) lanzar algo al aire; **by** ~
(travel) en avión; **to be on the** ~ (RADIO,
TV) estar en antena □ **airbag** n airbag
m inv □ **airbed** (BRIT) n colchón m
neumático □ **airborne** adj (in the air)
en el aire; **as soon as the plane was
airborne** tan pronto como el avión
estuvo en el aire □ **air-conditioned**
adj climatizado □ **air conditioning** n
aire acondicionado □ **aircraft** n inv
avión m □ **airfield** n campo de
aviación □ **Air Force** n fuerzas fpl
aéreas, aviación f □ **air hostess** (BRIT)

n azafata □ **airing cupboard** n (BRIT)
armario m para oreo □ **airlift** n
puente m aéreo □ **airline** n línea
aérea □ **airliner** n avión m de
pasajeros □ **airmail** n: **by airmail** por
avión □ **airplane** (US) n avión m
□ **airport** n aeropuerto □ **air raid** n
ataque m aéreo □ **airsick** adj: **to be
airsick** marearse (en avión)
□ **airspace** n espacio aéreo
□ **airstrip** n pista de aterrizaje □ **air
terminal** n terminal f □ **airtight** adj
hermético □ **air-traffic controller** n
controlador(a) m/f aéreo(-a) □ **airy** adj
(room) bien ventilado; (fig: manner)
desenfadado

aisle [aɪl] n (of church) nave f; (of theatre,
supermarket) pasillo □ **aisle seat** n
(on plane) asiento de pasillo

ajar [əˈdʒaːʳ] adj entreabierto

à la carte [aːlaːˈkaːt] adv a la carta

alarm [əˈlaːm] n (in shop, bank) alarma;
(anxiety) inquietud f ♦ vt asustar,
inquietar □ **alarm call** n (in hotel etc)
alarma □ **alarm clock** n despertador
m □ **alarmed** adj (person) alarmado,
asustado; (house, car etc) con alarma
□ **alarming** adj alarmante

Albania [ælˈbeɪnɪə] n Albania

albeit [ɔːlˈbiːɪt] conj aunque

album [ˈælbəm] n álbum m; (L.P.) elepé
m

alcohol [ˈælkəhɒl] n alcohol m
□ **alcohol-free** adj sin alcohol
□ **alcoholic** [-ˈhɒlɪk] adj, n
alcohólico(-a) m/f

alcove [ˈælkəuv] n nicho, hueco

ale [eɪl] n cerveza

alert [əˈləːt] adj (attentive) atento; (to
danger, opportunity) alerta ♦ n alerta m,
alarma ♦ vt poner sobre aviso; **to be on
the** ~ (also MIL) estar alerta or sobre
aviso

algebra [ˈældʒɪbrə] n álgebra f

Algeria [ælˈdʒɪərɪə] n Argelia

alias ['eɪlɪəs] adv alias, conocido por ♦ n (of criminal) apodo; (of writer) seudónimo

alibi ['ælɪbaɪ] n coartada

alien ['eɪlɪən] n (foreigner) extranjero(-a); (extraterrestrial) extraterrestre mf ♦ adj: ~ to ajeno a □ **alienate** vt enajenar, alejar

alight [ə'laɪt] adj ardiendo; (eyes) brillante ♦ vi (person) apearse, bajar; (bird) posarse

align [ə'laɪn] vt alinear

alike [ə'laɪk] adj semejantes, iguales ♦ adv igualmente, del mismo modo; **to look ~** parecerse

alive [ə'laɪv] adj vivo; (lively) alegre

all

KEYWORD

[ɔːl] adj (sg) todo(-a); (pl) todos(-as); **all day** todo el día; **all night** toda la noche; **all men** todos los hombres; **all five came** vinieron los cinco; **all the books** todos los libros; **all his life** toda su vida

♦ pron

1 todo; **I ate it all, I ate all of it** me lo comí todo; **all of us went** fuimos todos; **all the boys went** fueron todos los chicos; **is that all?** ¿eso es todo?, ¿algo más?; (in shop) ¿algo más?, ¿alguna cosa más?

2 (in phrases): **above all** sobre todo; por encima de todo; **after all** después de todo; **at all, not at all** (in answer to question) en absoluto; (in answer to thanks) ¡de nada!, ¡no hay de qué!; **I'm not at all tired** no estoy nada cansado(-a); **anything at all will do** cualquier cosa viene bien; **all in all** a fin de cuentas

♦ adv: **all alone** completamente solo(-a); **it's not as hard as all that** no es tan difícil como lo pintas; **the**

more/the better tanto más/mejor; **all but** casi; **the score is 2 all** están empatados a 2

Allah ['ælə] n Alá m

allegation [ælɪ'geɪʃən] n alegato

alleged [ə'ledʒd] adj supuesto, presunto □ **allegedly** adv supuestamente, según se afirma

allegiance [ə'liːdʒəns] n lealtad f

allergic [ə'lɜːdʒɪk] adj: ~ **to** alérgico a

allergy ['ælədʒɪ] n alergia

alleviate [ə'liːvɪeɪt] vt aliviar

alley ['ælɪ] n callejuela

alliance [ə'laɪəns] n alianza

allied ['ælaɪd] adj aliado

alligator ['ælɪgeɪtə*] n (ZOOL) caimán m

all-in (BRIT) ['ɔːlɪn] adj, adv (charge) todo incluido

allocate ['æləkeɪt] vt (money etc) asignar

allot [ə'lɒt] vt asignar

all-out ['ɔːlaut] adj (effort etc) supremo

allow [ə'lau] vt permitir, dejar; (a claim) admitir; (sum, time etc) dar, conceder; (concede): **to ~ that** reconocer que; **to ~ sb to do** permitir a algn hacer; **he is allowed to ...** se le permite ... ► **allow for** vt fus tener en cuenta □ **allowance** n subvención f; (welfare payment) subsidio, pensión f; (pocket money) dinero de bolsillo; (tax allowance) desgravación f; **to make allowances for** (person) disculpar a; (thing) tener en cuenta

all right adv bien; (as answer) ¡conforme!, ¡está bien!

ally ['ælaɪ] n aliado(-a) ♦ vt: **to ~ o.s. with** aliarse con

almighty [ɔːl'maɪtɪ] adj todopoderoso; (row etc) imponente

almond ['ɑːmənd] n almendra

almost ['ɔːlməust] adv casi

alone [ə'ləun] adj, adv solo; **to leave sb ~** dejar a algn en paz; **to leave sth ~** no

tocar algo, dejar algo sin tocar; **let ~ ...**
y mucho menos ...

along [ə'lɒŋ] prep a lo largo de, por
♦ adv: **is he coming ~ with us?** ¿viene
con nosotros?; **he was limping ~** iba
cojeando; **~ with** junto con; **all ~** (all
the time) desde el principio
❑ **alongside** prep al lado de ♦ adv al
lado

aloof [ə'luːf] adj reservado ♦ adv: **to
stand ~** mantenerse apartado

aloud [ə'laud] adv en voz alta

alphabet ['ælfəbet] n alfabeto

Alps [ælps] npl: **the ~** los Alpes

already [ɔːl'redɪ] adv ya

alright ['ɔːl'raɪt] (BRIT) adv = **all right**

also ['ɔːlsəu] adv también, además

altar ['ɔːltə] n altar m

alter ['ɔːltə] vt cambiar, modificar ♦ vi
cambiar ❑ **alteration** [ɔːltə'reɪʃən] n
cambio; (to clothes) arreglo; (to
building) arreglos mpl

alternate [adj ɔl'tɜːnɪt, vb 'ɔltə:neɪt]
(actions etc) alternativo; (events)
alterno; (US) = **alternative** ♦ vi: **to ~
(with)** alternar (con); **on ~ days** un día
sí y otro no

alternative [ɔl'tɜːnətɪv] adj
alternativo ♦ n alternativa; **~ medicine**
medicina alternativa ❑ **alternatively**
adv: **alternatively one could ...** por
otra parte se podría ...

although [ɔːl'ðəu] conj aunque

altitude ['æltɪtjuːd] n altura

altogether [ɔːltə'geðə] adv
completamente, del todo; (on the
whole) en total, en conjunto

aluminium [ælju'mɪnɪəm] (BRIT),
aluminum [ə'luːmɪnəm] (US) n
aluminio

always ['ɔːlweɪz] adv siempre

Alzheimer's (disease)
['æltshaɪməz-] n enfermedad f de
Alzheimer

am [æm] vb see **be**

amalgamate [ə'mælgəmeɪt] vi
amalgamarse ♦ vt amalgamar, unir

amass [ə'mæs] vt amontonar, acumular

amateur ['æmətə] n aficionado(-a),
amateur mf

amaze [ə'meɪz] vt asombrar, pasmar; **to
be amazed (at)** quedar pasmado (de)
❑ **amazed** adj asombrado
❑ **amazement** n asombro, sorpresa
❑ **amazing** adj extraordinario;
(fantastic) increíble

Amazon ['æməzən] n (GEO) Amazonas
m

ambassador [æm'bæsədə] n
embajador(a) m/f

amber ['æmbə] n ámbar m; **at ~** (BRIT
AUT) en el amarillo

ambiguous [æm'bɪgjuəs] adj ambiguo

ambition [æm'bɪʃən] n ambición f
❑ **ambitious** [-ʃəs] adj ambicioso

ambulance ['æmbjuləns] n
ambulancia

ambush ['æmbuʃ] n emboscada ♦ vt
tender una emboscada a

amen [ɑː'mɛn] excl amén

amend [ə'mɛnd] vt enmendar; **to make
amends** dar cumplida satisfacción
❑ **amendment** n enmienda

amenities [ə'miːnɪtɪz] npl
comodidades fpl

America [ə'mɛrɪkə] n (USA) Estados mpl
Unidos ❑ **American** adj, n
norteamericano(-a); estadounidense
mf ❑ **American football** n (BRIT)
fútbol m americano

amicable ['æmɪkəbl] adj amistoso,
amigable

amid(st) [ə'mɪd(st)] prep entre, en
medio de

ammunition [æmju'nɪʃən] n
municiones fpl

amnesty ['æmnɪstɪ] n amnistía

among(st) [ə'mʌŋ(st)] prep entre, en
medio de

amount [ə'maunt] n (gen) cantidad f;
(of bill etc) suma, importe m ♦ vi: **to ~ to**

sumar; (be same as) equivaler a, significar

amp(ère) ['æmp(ɛə')] n amperio

ample ['æmpl] adj (large) grande; (abundant) abundante; (enough) bastante, suficiente

amplifier ['æmplıfaıə'] n amplificador m

amputate ['æmpjuteıt] vt amputar

Amtrak ['æmtræk] (US) n empresa nacional de ferrocarriles de los EEUU

amuse [ə'mju:z] vt divertir; (distract) distraer, entretener □ **amusement** n diversión f; (pastime) pasatiempo; (laughter) risa □ **amusement arcade** n salón m de juegos □ **amusement park** n parque m de atracciones

amusing [ə'mju:zıŋ] adj divertido

an [æn] indef art see **a**

anaemia [ə'ni:mıə] (US anemia) n anemia

anaemic [ə'ni:mık] (US anemic) adj anémico; (fig) soso, insípido

anaesthetic [ænıs'θetık] (US anesthetic) n anestesia

analog(ue) ['ænəlɒg] adj (computer, watch) analógico

analogy [ə'nælədʒı] n analogía

analyse ['ænəlaız] (US analyze) vt analizar □ **analysis** [ə'næləsıs] (pl **analyses**) n análisis m inv □ **analyst** [-lıst] n (political analyst, psychoanalyst) analista mf

analyze ['ænəlaız] (US) vt = **analyse**

anarchy ['ænəkı] n anarquía, desorden m

anatomy [ə'nætəmı] n anatomía

ancestor ['ænsıstə'] n antepasado

anchor ['æŋkə'] n ancla, áncora ♦ vi (also: to drop ~) anclar ♦ vt anclar; to weigh ~ levar anclas

anchovy ['æntʃəvı] n anchoa

ancient ['eınʃənt] adj antiguo

and [ænd] conj y; (before i-, hi- + consonant) e; **men ~ women** hombres

y mujeres; **father ~ son** padre e hijo; **trees ~ grass** árboles y hierba; **~ so on** etcétera, y así sucesivamente; **try ~ come** procura venir; **he talked ~ talked** habló sin parar; **better ~ better** cada vez mejor

Andes ['ændi:z] npl: **the ~** los Andes

Andorra [æn'dɔ:rə] n Andorra

anemia etc [ə'ni:mıə] (US) = **anaemia** etc

anesthetic [ænıs'θetık] (US) = **anaesthetic**

angel ['eındʒəl] n ángel m

anger ['æŋgə'] n cólera

angina [æn'dʒaınə] n angina (del pecho)

angle ['æŋgl] n ángulo; **from their ~** desde su punto de vista

angler ['æŋglə'] n pescador(a) m/f (de caña)

Anglican ['æŋglıkən] adj, n anglicano(-a) m/f

angling ['æŋglıŋ] n pesca con caña

angrily ['æŋgrılı] adv coléricamente, airadamente

angry ['æŋgrı] adj enfadado, airado; (wound) inflamado; **to be ~ with sb/at sth** estar enfadado con algn/por algo; **to get ~** enfadarse, enojarse

anguish ['æŋgwıʃ] n (physical) tormentos mpl; (mental) angustia

animal ['ænıməl] n animal m; (pej: person) bestia ♦ adj animal

animated [-meıtıd] adj animado

animation [ænı'meıʃən] n animación f

aniseed ['ænısi:d] n anís m

ankle ['æŋkl] n tobillo

annex [n 'æneks, vb æ'neks] n (BRIT: also: **annexe**: building) edificio anexo ♦ vt (territory) anexionar

anniversary [ænı'vɜ:sərı] n aniversario

announce [ə'nauns] vt anunciar □ **announcement** n anuncio; (official) declaración f □ **announcer** n (RADIO) locutor(a) m/f; (TV) presentador(a) m/f

annoy [ə'nɔɪ] *vt* molestar, fastidiar; **don't get annoyed!** ¡no se enfade! ❏ **annoying** *adj* molesto, fastidioso; (*person*) pesado

annual ['ænjuəl] *adj* anual ♦ *n* (*BOT*) anual *m*; (*book*) anuario *m* ❏ **annually** *adv* anualmente, cada año

annum ['ænəm] *n see* **per**

anonymous [ə'nɒnɪməs] *adj* anónimo

anorak ['ænəræk] *n* anorak *m*

anorexia [ænə'rɛksɪə] *n* (*MED: also:* **~ nervosa**) anorexia

anorexic [ænə'rɛksɪk] *adj, n* anoréxico(-a) *m/f*

another [ə'nʌðə*] *adj* (*one more, a different one*) otro ♦ *pron* otro; *see* **one**

answer ['ɑːnsə*] *n* contestación *f*, respuesta; (*to problem*) solución *f* ♦ *vi* contestar, responder ♦ *vt* (*reply to*) contestar a, responder a; (*problem*) resolver; (*prayer*) escuchar; **in ~ to your letter** contestando o en contestación a su carta; **to ~ the phone** contestar o coger el teléfono; **to ~ the bell** or **the door** acudir a la puerta ► **answer back** *vi* replicar, ser respondón(-ona) ❏ **answerphone** *n* (*esp BRIT*) contestador *m* (automático)

ant [ænt] *n* hormiga

Antarctic [ænt'ɑːktɪk] *n*: **the ~** el Antártico

antelope ['æntɪləup] *n* antílope *m*

antenatal ['æntɪ'neɪtl] *adj* antenatal, prenatal

antenna [æn'tɛnə, *pl* -niː] (*pl* **antennae**) *n* antena

anthem ['ænθəm] *n*: **national ~** himno nacional

anthology [æn'θɒlədʒɪ] *n* antología

anthrax ['ænθræks] *n* ántrax *m*

anthropology [ænθrə'pɒlədʒɪ] *n* antropología

anti [ænti] *prefix* anti ❏ **antibiotic** [-baɪ'ɒtɪk] *n* antibiótico ❏ **antibody** ['æntɪbɒdɪ] *n* anticuerpo

anticipate [æn'tɪsɪpeɪt] *vt* prever; (*expect*) esperar, contar con; (*look forward to*) esperar con ilusión; (*do first*) anticiparse a, adelantarse a ❏ **anticipation** [-'peɪʃən] *n* (*expectation*) previsión *f*; (*eagerness*) ilusión *f*, expectación *f*

anticlimax [æntɪ'klaɪmæks] *n* decepción *f*

anticlockwise [æntɪ'klɒkwaɪz] (*BRIT*) *adv* en dirección contraria a la de las agujas del reloj

antics ['æntɪks] *npl* gracias *fpl*

anti-: antidote ['æntɪdəut] *n* antídoto ❏ **antifreeze** ['æntɪfriːz] *n* anticongelante *m* ❏ **antihistamine** [-'hɪstəmiːn] *n* antihistamínico ❏ **antiperspirant** [æntɪpə'spɪrənt] *n* antitranspirante *m*

antique [æn'tiːk] *n* antigüedad *f* ♦ *adj* antiguo ❏ **antique shop** *n* tienda de antigüedades

antiseptic [æntɪ'sɛptɪk] *adj, n* antiséptico

antisocial [æntɪ'səuʃəl] *adj* antisocial

antlers ['æntləz] *npl* cuernas *fpl*, cornamenta *sg*

anxiety [æŋ'zaɪətɪ] *n* inquietud *f*; (*MED*) ansiedad *f*; **~ to do** deseo de hacer

anxious ['æŋkʃəs] *adj* inquieto, preocupado; (*worrying*) preocupante; (*keen*): **to be ~ to do** tener muchas ganas de hacer

any

KEYWORD

['ɛnɪ] *adj*

1 (*in questions etc*) algún/alguna; **have you any butter/children?** ¿tienes mantequilla/hijos?; **if there are any tickets left** si quedan billetes, si queda algún billete

2 (*with negative*): **I haven't any money/books** no tengo dinero/ libros

3 (*no matter which*) cualquier; **any**

excuse will do valdrá or servirá cualquier excusa; **choose any book you like** escoge el libro que quieras; **any teacher you ask will tell you** cualquier profesor al que preguntes te lo dirá

4 (in phrases): **in any case** de todas formas, en cualquier caso; **any day now** cualquier día (de estos); **at any moment** en cualquier momento, de un momento a otro; **at any rate** en todo caso; **any time, come (at) any time** ven cuando quieras; **he might come (at) any time** podría llegar de un momento a otro

♦ pron

1 (in questions etc): **have you got any?** ¿tienes alguno(s)/a(s)?; **can any of you sing?** ¿sabe cantar alguno de vosotros/ustedes?

2 (with negative): **I haven't any (of them)** no tengo ninguno

3 (no matter which one(s)): **take any of those books (you like)** toma el libro que quieras de ésos

♦ adv

1 (in questions etc): **do you want any more soup/sandwiches?** ¿quieres más sopa/bocadillos?; **are you feeling any better?** ¿te sientes algo mejor?

2 (with negative): **I can't hear him any more** ya no le oigo; **don't wait any longer** no esperes más

any: **anybody** pron cualquiera (in interrogative sentences) alguien; (in negative sentences): **I don't see anybody** no veo a nadie; **if anybody should phone** ... si llama alguien ...
❑ **anyhow** adv (at any rate) de todos modos, de todas formas; (haphazard): **do it anyhow you like** hazlo como

quieras; **she leaves things just anyhow** deja las cosas como quiera or de cualquier modo; **I shall go anyhow** de todos modos iré ❑ **anyone** pron = **anybody** ❑ **anything** pron (in questions etc) algo, alguna cosa; (with negative): **can you see anything?** ¿ves algo?; **if anything happens to me** ... si algo me ocurre ...; (no matter what): **you can say anything you like** puedes decir lo que quieras; **anything will do** vale todo or cualquier cosa; **he'll eat anything** come de todo or lo que sea ❑ **anytime** adv (at any moment) en cualquier momento, de un momento a otro; (whenever): **no importa cuándo, cuando quiera** ❑ **anyway** adv (at any rate) de todos modos, de todas formas; **I shall go anyway** iré de todos modos; (besides): **anyway, I couldn't even if I wanted to** además, no podría venir aunque quisiera; **why are you phoning, anyway?** ¿entonces, por qué llamas?, ¿por qué llamas, pues? ❑ **anywhere** adv (in questions etc): **can you see him anywhere?** ¿le ves por algún lado?; **are you going anywhere?** ¿vas a algún sitio?; (with negative): **I can't see him anywhere** no le veo por ninguna parte; **anywhere in the world** (no matter where) en cualquier parte (del mundo); **put the books down anywhere** deja los libros donde quieras

apart [ə'pɑ:t] adv (aside) aparte; (situation): **~ (from)** separado (de); (movement): **to pull ~** separar; **10 miles ~** separados or apart 10 millas; **to take ~** desmontar; **~ from** prep aparte de

apartment [ə'pɑ:tmənt] n (US) piso (SP), departamento (LAm), apartamento; (room) cuarto ❑ **apartment building** (US) n edificio de apartamentos

apathy ['æpəθɪ] n apatía, indiferencia

ape [eɪp] n mono ♦ vt imitar, remedar

aperitif [ə'perɪtɪf] n aperitivo

any: **anybody** pron cualquiera (in interrogative sentences) alguien; (in negative sentences): **I don't see anybody** no veo a nadie; **if anybody should phone** ... si llama alguien ... ❑ **anyhow** adv (at any rate) de todos modos, de todas formas; (haphazard): **do it anyhow you like** hazlo como

aperture ['æpətʃʊə] n rendija, resquicio; (PHOT) abertura

APEX ['eɪpeks] n abbr (= Advanced Purchase Excursion Fare) tarifa f APEX

apologize [ə'pɒlədʒaɪz] vi: **to ~ (for sth to sb)** disculparse (con algn de algo)

apology [ə'pɒlədʒɪ] n disculpa, excusa

⚠ Be careful not to translate apology by the Spanish word apología.

apostrophe [ə'pɒstrəfɪ] n apóstrofo

appal [ə'pɔːl] (US **appall**) vt horrorizar, espantar ❑ **appalling** adj espantoso; (awful) pésimo

apparatus [æpə'reɪtəs] n (equipment) equipo; (organization) aparato; (in gymnasium) aparatos mpl

apparent [ə'pærənt] adj aparente; (obvious) evidente ❑ **apparently** adv por lo visto, al parecer

appeal [ə'piːl] vi (LAW) apelar ♦ n (LAW) apelación f; (request) llamamiento; (plea) petición f; (charm) atractivo; **to ~ for** reclamar; **to ~ to** (be attractive to) atraer; **it doesn't ~ to me** no me atrae, no me llama la atención ❑ **appealing** adj (attractive) atractivo

appear [ə'pɪə] vi aparecer, presentarse; (LAW) comparecer; (publication) salir (a la luz), publicarse; (seem) parecer; **to ~ on TV/in "Hamlet"** salir en la tele/hacer un papel en "Hamlet"; **it would ~ that** parecería que ❑ **appearance** n aparición f; (look) apariencia, aspecto

appendices [ə'pendɪsiːz] npl of **appendix**

appendicitis [əpendɪ'saɪtɪs] n apendicitis f

appendix [ə'pendɪks] (pl **appendices**) n apéndice m

appetite ['æpɪtaɪt] n apetito; (fig) deseo, anhelo

appetizer ['æpɪtaɪzə'] n (drink) aperitivo; (food) tapas fpl (SP)

applaud [ə'plɔːd] vt, vi aplaudir

applause [ə'plɔːz] n aplausos mpl

apple ['æpl] n manzana ❑ **apple pie** n pastel m de manzana, pay m de manzana (LAm)

appliance [ə'plaɪəns] n aparato

applicable [ə'plɪkəbl] adj (relevant): **to be ~ (to)** referirse (a)

applicant ['æplɪkənt] n candidato(-a); solicitante mf

application [æplɪ'keɪʃən] n aplicación f; (for a job etc) solicitud f, petición f ❑ **application form** n solicitud f

apply [ə'plaɪ] vt (paint etc) poner; (law etc: put into practice) poner en vigor ♦ vi: **to ~ to** (ask) dirigirse a; (be applicable) ser aplicable a; **to ~ for** (permit, grant, job) solicitar; **to ~ o.s. to** aplicarse a, dedicarse a

appoint [ə'pɔɪnt] vt (to post) nombrar ❑ **appointment** n (with client) cita; (act) nombramiento; (post) puesto; (at hairdresser etc) hora; **to have an appointment** tener hora; **to make an appointment (with sb)** citarse con algn)

⚠ Be careful not to translate appoint by the Spanish word apuntar.

appraisal [ə'preɪzl] n valoración f

appreciate [ə'priːʃɪeɪt] vt apreciar, tener en mucho; (be grateful for) agradecer; (be aware) comprender ♦ vi (COMM) aumentar(se) en valor ❑ **appreciation** [-'eɪʃən] n apreciación f; (gratitude) reconocimiento, agradecimiento; (COMM) aumento en valor

apprehension [æprɪ'henʃən] n (fear) aprensión f

apprehensive [æprɪ'hensɪv] adj aprensivo

apprentice [ə'prentɪs] n aprendiz(a) m/f

approach [ə'prəʊtʃ] vi acercarse ♦ vt acercarse a; (ask, apply to) dirigirse a; (situation, problem) abordar ♦ n acercamiento; (access) acceso; (to *problem, situation*): ~ **(to)** actitud f (ante)

appropriate [*adj* ə'prəuprɪɪt, *vb* ə'prəuprɪeɪt] *adj* apropiado, conveniente ♦ *vt* (*take*) apropiarse de

approval [ə'pru:vəl] *n* aprobación f, visto bueno; (*permission*) consentimiento; **on** ~ (COMM) a prueba

approve [ə'pru:v] *vt* aprobar
▶ **approve of** *vt fus* (*thing*) aprobar; (*person*): **they don't approve of her** (ella) no les parece bien

approximate [ə'prɔksɪmɪt] *adj* aproximado ☐ **approximately** *adv* aproximadamente, más o menos

Apr. *abbr* (= *April*) abr

apricot ['eɪprɪkɔt] *n* albaricoque m, chabacano (MEX), damasco (RPI)

April ['eɪprəl] *n* abril m ☐ **April Fools' Day** *n* el primero de abril, ≈ día m de los Inocentes (*28 December*)

apron ['eɪprən] *n* delantal m

apt [æpt] *adj* acertado, apropiado; (*likely*): ~ **to do** propenso a hacer

aquarium [ə'kwɛərɪəm] *n* acuario m

Aquarius [ə'kwɛərɪəs] *n* Acuario

Arab ['ærəb] *adj, n* árabe mf

Arabia [ə'reɪbɪə] *n* Arabia ☐ **Arabian** *adj* árabe ☐ **Arabic** ['ærəbɪk] *adj*; (*numerals*) arábigo ♦ *n* árabe m

arbitrary ['ɑ:bɪtrərɪ] *adj* arbitrario

arbitration [ɑ:bɪ'treɪʃən] *n* arbitraje m

arc [ɑ:k] *n* arco

arcade [ɑ:'keɪd] *n* (*round a square*) soportales mpl; (*shopping mall*) galería comercial

arch [ɑ:tʃ] *n* arco; (*of foot*) arco del pie ♦ *vt* arquear

archaeology [ɑ:kɪ'ɔlədʒɪ] (US **archeology**) *n* arqueología

archbishop [ɑ:tʃ'bɪʃəp] *n* arzobispo

archeology [ɑ:kɪ'ɔlədʒɪ] (US) = **archaeology**

architect ['ɑ:kɪtekt] *n* arquitecto(-a) ☐ **architectural** [ɑ:kɪ'tektʃərəl] *adj*

arquitectónico ☐ **architecture** *n* arquitectura

archive ['ɑ:kaɪv] *n* (*often pl: also* COMPUT) archivo

Arctic ['ɑ:ktɪk] *adj* ártico ♦ *n*: **the** ~ el Ártico

are [ɑ:r] *vb see* **be**

area [ˈɛərɪə] *n* área, región f; (*part of place*) zona; (MATH *etc*) área, superficie f; (*in room: e.g. dining area*) parte f; (*of knowledge, experience*) campo ♦ **area code** *n* (TEL) prefijo

arena [ə'ri:nə] *n* estadio; (*of circus*) pista

aren't [ɑ:nt] = **are not**

Argentina [ɑ:dʒən'ti:nə] *n* Argentina ☐ **Argentinian** [-'tɪnɪən] *adj, n* argentino(-a) *mf*

arguably ['ɑ:gjuəblɪ] *adv* posiblemente

argue ['ɑ:gju:] *vi* (*quarrel*) discutir, pelearse; (*reason*) razonar, argumentar; **to** ~ **that** sostener que

argument ['ɑ:gjumənt] *n* discusión f, pelea; (*reasons*) argumento

Aries ['ɛəri:z] *n* Aries m

arise [ə'raɪz] (*pt* **arose**, *pp* **arisen**) *vi* surgir, presentarse

arithmetic [ə'rɪθmətɪk] *n* aritmética

arm [ɑ:m] *n* brazo ♦ *vt* armar; **arms** npl armas fpl; ~ **in** ~ cogidos del brazo ☐ **armchair** *n* sillón m, butaca

armed [ɑ:md] *adj* armado ☐ **armed robbery** *n* robo a mano armada

armour ['ɑ:mər] (US **armor**) *n* armadura; (MIL: *tanks*) blindaje m

armpit ['ɑ:mpɪt] *n* sobaco, axila

armrest ['ɑ:mrest] *n* apoyabrazos m inv

army ['ɑ:mɪ] *n* ejército; (*fig*) multitud f

A road *n* (BRIT) ≈ carretera f nacional

aroma [ə'rəumə] *n* aroma m, fragancia ☐ **aromatherapy** *n* aromaterapia

arose [ə'rəuz] *pt of* **arise**

around [ə'raund] *adv* alrededor; (*in the area*): **there is no one ~** no hay nadie más por aquí ♦ *prep* alrededor de

arouse [əˈrauz] *vt* despertar; (*anger*) provocar

arrange [əˈreɪndʒ] *vt* arreglar, ordenar; (*organize*) organizar; **to ~ to do sth** quedar en hacer algo ❏ **arrangement** *n* arreglo; (*agreement*) acuerdo; **arrangements** *npl* (*preparations*) preparativos *mpl*

array [əˈreɪ] *n*: **~ of** (*things*) serie *f* de; (*people*) conjunto de

arrears [əˈrɪəz] *npl* atrasos *mpl*; **to be in ~ with one's rent** estar retrasado en el pago del alquiler

arrest [əˈrest] *vt* detener; (*sb's attention*) llamar ♦ *n* detención *f*; **under ~** detenido

arrival [əˈraɪvəl] *n* llegada; **new ~** recién llegado(-a); (*baby*) recién nacido

arrive [əˈraɪv] *vi* llegar; (*baby*) nacer ▶ **arrive at** *vt fus* (*decision, solution*) llegar a

arrogance [ˈærəgəns] *n* arrogancia, prepotencia (*LAm*)

arrogant [ˈærəgənt] *adj* arrogante

arrow [ˈærəu] *n* flecha

arse [ɑːs] (*BRIT: inf!*) *n* culo, trasero

arson [ˈɑːsn] *n* incendio premeditado

art [ɑːt] *n* arte *m*; (*skill*) destreza ❏ **art college** *n* escuela *f* de Bellas Artes

artery [ˈɑːtəri] *n* arteria

art gallery *n* pinacoteca; (*saleroom*) galería de arte

arthritis [ɑːˈθraɪtɪs] *n* artritis *f*

artichoke [ˈɑːtɪtʃəuk] *n* alcachofa; **Jerusalem ~** aguaturma

article [ˈɑːtɪkl] *n* artículo

articulate [*adj* ɑːˈtɪkjulɪt, *vb* ɑːˈtɪkjuleɪt] *adj* claro, bien expresado ♦ *vt* expresar

artificial [ɑːtɪˈfɪʃl] *adj* artificial; (*affected*) afectado

artist [ˈɑːtɪst] *n* artista *mf*; (*MUS*) intérprete *mf* ❏ **artistic** [ɑːˈtɪstɪk] *adj* artístico

art school *n* escuela de bellas artes

as

KEYWORD

[æz] *conj*

1 (*referring to time*) cuando, mientras; a medida que; **as the years went by** con el paso de los años; **he came in as I was leaving** entró cuando me marchaba; **as from tomorrow** desde *or* a partir de mañana

2 (*in comparisons*): **as big as** tan grande como; **twice as big as** el doble de grande que; **as much money/many books as** tanto dinero/ tantos libros como; **as soon as** en cuanto

3 (*since, because*) como, ya que; **he left early as he had to be home by 10** se fue temprano ya que tenía que estar en casa a las 10

4 (*referring to manner, way*): **do as you wish** haz lo que quieras; **as she said** como dijo; **he gave it to me as a present** me lo dio de regalo

5 (*in the capacity of*): **he works as a barman** trabaja de barman; **as chairman of the company, he ...** como presidente de la compañía ...

6 (*concerning*): **as for** *or* **to that** por *or* en lo que respecta a eso

7: **as if** *or* **though** como si; **he looked as if he was ill** parecía como si estuviera enfermo, tenía aspecto de enfermo; *see also* **long**; **such**; **well**

a.s.a.p. *abbr* (= *as soon as possible*) cuanto antes

asbestos [æzˈbestəs] *n* asbesto, amianto

ascent [əˈsent] *n* subida; (*slope*) cuesta, pendiente *f*

ash [æʃ] *n* ceniza; (*tree*) fresno

ashamed [ə'ʃeɪmd] adj avergonzado, apenado; **to be ~ of** avergonzarse de

ashore [ə'ʃɔː'] adv en tierra; (swim etc) a tierra

ashtray ['æʃtreɪ] n cenicero

Ash Wednesday n miércoles m de Ceniza

Asia ['eɪʃə] n Asia ❑ **Asian** adj, n asiático(-a) m/f

aside [ə'saɪd] adv a un lado ♦ n aparte m

ask [ɑːsk] vt (question) preguntar; (invite) invitar; **to ~ sb sth/to do sth** preguntar algo a algn/pedir a algn que haga algo; **to ~ sb about sth** preguntar algo a algn; **to ~ (sb) a question** hacer una pregunta (a algn); **to ~ sb out to dinner** invitar a cenar a algn ► **ask for** vt fus pedir; (trouble) buscar

asleep [ə'sliːp] adj dormido; **to fall ~** dormirse, quedarse dormido

asparagus [əs'pærəgəs] n (plant) espárrago; (food) espárragos mpl

aspect ['æspekt] n aspecto, apariencia; (direction in which a building etc faces) orientación f

aspirations [æspə'reɪʃənz] npl aspiraciones fpl; (ambition) ambición f

aspire [əs'paɪə'] vi: **to ~ to** aspirar a, ambicionar

aspirin ['æsprɪn] n aspirina

ass [æs] n asno, burro; (inf: idiot) imbécil mf; (US: inf!) culo, trasero

assassin [ə'sæsɪn] n asesino(-a) ❑ **assassinate** vt asesinar

assault [ə'sɔːlt] n asalto; (LAW) agresión f ♦ vt asaltar, atacar; (sexually) violar

assemble [ə'sembl] vt reunir, juntar; (TECH) montar ♦ vi reunirse, juntarse

assembly [ə'semblɪ] n reunión f, asamblea; (parliament) parlamento m; (construction) montaje m

assert [ə'sɜːt] vt afirmar; (authority) hacer valer ❑ **assertion** [-ʃən] n afirmación f

assess [ə'ses] vt valorar, calcular; (tax, damages) fijar; (for tax) gravar ❑ **assessment** n valoración f; (for tax) gravamen m

asset ['æset] n ventaja; **assets** npl (COMM) activo; (property, funds) fondos mpl

assign [ə'saɪn] vt: **to ~ (to)** (date) fijar (para); (task) asignar (a); (resources) destinar (a) ❑ **assignment** n tarea

assist [ə'sɪst] vt ayudar ❑ **assistance** n ayuda, auxilio ❑ **assistant** n ayudante m/f; (BRIT: also: **shop assistant**) dependiente(-a) m/f

associate [adj, n ə'səuʃɪt, vb ə'səuʃɪeɪt] adj asociado ♦ n (at work) colega mf ♦ vt asociar; (ideas) relacionar ♦ vi: **to ~ with sb** tratar con algn

association [əsəusɪ'eɪʃən] n asociación f

assorted [ə'sɔːtɪd] adj surtido, variado

assortment [ə'sɔːtmənt] n (of shapes, colours) surtido; (of books) colección f; (of people) mezcla

assume [ə'sjuːm] vt suponer; (responsibilities) asumir; (attitude) adoptar, tomar

assumption [ə'sʌmpʃən] n suposición f, presunción f; (of power etc) toma

assurance [ə'ʃuərəns] n garantía, promesa; (confidence) confianza, aplomo; (insurance) seguro

assure [ə'ʃuə'] vt asegurar

asterisk ['æstərɪsk] n asterisco

asthma ['æsmə] n asma

astonish [ə'stɒnɪʃ] vt asombrar, pasmar ❑ **astonished** adj estupefacto, pasmado; **to be astonished (at)** asombrarse (de) ❑ **astonishing** adj asombroso, pasmoso; **I find it astonishing that ...** me asombra or pasma que ... ❑ **astonishment** n asombro, sorpresa

astound [ə'staʊnd] vt asombrar, pasmar

astray [əˈstreɪ] adv: **to go ~** extraviarse; **to lead ~** (morally) llevar por mal camino

astrology [æsˈtrɒlədʒɪ] n astrología

astronaut [ˈæstrənɔːt] n astronauta m

astronomer [əsˈtrɒnəmər] n astrónomo(-a)

astronomical [æstrəˈnɒmɪkəl] adj astronómico

astronomy [əsˈtrɒnəmɪ] n astronomía

astute [əsˈtjuːt] adj astuto

asylum [əˈsaɪləm] n (refuge) asilo; (mental hospital) manicomio

at

KEYWORD

[æt] prep

1 (referring to position) en; (direction) a; **at the top** en lo alto; **at home/school** en casa/la escuela; **to look at sth/sb** mirar algo/a algn

2 (referring to time): **at 4 o'clock** a las 4; **at night** por la noche; **at Christmas** en Navidad; **at times** a veces

3 (referring to rates, speed etc): **at £1 a kilo** a una libra el kilo; **two at a time** de dos en dos; **at 50 km/h** a 50 km/h

4 (referring to manner): **at a stroke** de un golpe; **at peace** en paz

5 (referring to activity): **to be at work** estar trabajando; (in the office etc) estar en el trabajo; **to play at cowboys** jugar a los vaqueros; **to be good at sth** ser bueno en algo

6 (referring to cause): **shocked/surprised/annoyed at sth** asombrado/sorprendido/fastidiado por algo; **I went at his suggestion** fui a instancias suyas

ate [eɪt] pt of **eat**

atheist [ˈeɪθɪɪst] n ateo(-a)

Athens [ˈæθɪnz] n Atenas

athlete [ˈæθliːt] n atleta mf

athletic [æθˈletɪk] adj atlético ❏ **athletics** n atletismo

Atlantic [ətˈlæntɪk] adj atlántico ♦ n: **the ~ (Ocean)** el (Océano) Atlántico

atlas [ˈætləs] n atlas m

A.T.M. n abbr (= automated telling machine) cajero automático

atmosphere [ˈætməsfɪər] n atmósfera; (of place) ambiente m

atom [ˈætəm] n átomo ❏ **atomic** [əˈtɒmɪk] adj atómico ❏ **atom(ic) bomb** n bomba atómica

A to Z® n (map) callejero

atrocity [əˈtrɒsɪtɪ] n atrocidad f

attach [əˈtætʃ] vt (fasten) atar; (join) unir, sujetar; (document, letter) adjuntar; (importance etc) dar, conceder; **to be attached to sb/sth** (to like) tener cariño a algn/algo ❏ **attachment** n (tool) accesorio; (COMPUT) archivo, documento adjunto; (love): **attachment (to)** apego (a)

attack [əˈtæk] vt (MIL) atacar; (criminal) agredir, asaltar; (criticize) atacar; (task) emprender ♦ n ataque m, asalto; (on sb's life) atentado; (fig: criticism) crítica; (of illness) ataque m; **heart ~** infarto de miocardio ❏ **attacker** n agresor(a) m/f, asaltante mf

attain [əˈteɪn] vt (also: **~ to**) alcanzar; (achieve) lograr, conseguir

attempt [əˈtempt] n tentativa, intento; (attack) atentado ♦ vt intentar

attend [əˈtend] vt asistir a; (patient) atender ▸ **attend to** vt fus ocuparse de; (customer, patient) atender a ❏ **attendance** n asistencia, presencia; (people present) concurrencia ❏ **attendant** n ayudante mf; (in garage etc) encargado(-a) ♦ adj (dangers) concomitante

attention [əˈtenʃən] n atención f; (care) atenciones fpl ♦ excl (MIL) ¡firme(s)!; **for the ~ of ...** (ADMIN) atención ...

attic [ˈætɪk] n desván m

attitude [ˈætɪtjuːd] n actitud f;
(disposition) disposición f

attorney [əˈtɜːnɪ] n (lawyer)
abogado(-a) f **❏ Attorney General** n
(BRIT) ≈ Presidente m del Consejo del
Poder Judicial (SP); (US) ≈ ministro de
Justicia

attract [əˈtrækt] vt atraer; (sb's
attention) llamar **❏ attraction**
[əˈtrækʃən] n encanto; (gen pl:
amusements) diversiones fpl; (PHYSICS)
atracción f **❏ attractive** adj guapo;
(interesting) atrayente

attribute [n ˈætrɪbjuːt, vb əˈtrɪbjuːt] n
atributo **❖** vt: **to ~ sth to** atribuir algo a

aubergine [ˈəʊbəʒiːn] (BRIT) n
berenjena; (colour) morado

auburn [ˈɔːbən] adj color castaño rojizo

auction [ˈɔːkʃən] n (also: **sale by ~**)
subasta **❖** vt subastar

audible [ˈɔːdɪbl] adj audible, que se
puede oír

audience [ˈɔːdɪəns] n público m; (RADIO)
radioescuchas mpl; (TV)
telespectadores mpl; (interview)
audiencia

audit [ˈɔːdɪt] vt revisar, intervenir

audition [ɔːˈdɪʃən] n audición f

auditor [ˈɔːdɪtər] n interventor(a) m/f,
censor(a) m/f de cuentas

auditorium [ɔːdɪˈtɔːrɪəm] n auditorio

Aug. abbr (= August) ag

August [ˈɔːɡəst] n agosto

aunt [ɑːnt] n tía **❏ auntie** n diminutive
of **aunt ❏ aunty** n diminutive of **aunt**

au pair [ˈəʊˈpɛər] n (also: **~ girl**) (chica)
au pair f

aura [ˈɔːrə] n aura; (atmosphere)
ambiente m

austerity [ɔːˈstɛrɪtɪ] n austeridad f

Australia [ɔsˈtreɪlɪə] n Australia
❏ Australian adj, n australiano(-a) m/f

Austria [ˈɔstrɪə] n Austria **❏ Austrian**
adj, n austríaco(-a) m/f

authentic [ɔːˈθɛntɪk] adj auténtico

author [ˈɔːθər] n autor(a) m/f

authority [ɔːˈθɔrɪtɪ] n autoridad f;
(official permission) autorización f; **the
authorities** npl las autoridades

authorize [ˈɔːθəraɪz] vt autorizar

auto [ˈɔːtəu] (US) n coche m (SP), carro
(LAm), automóvil m

auto: autobiography [ɔːtəbaɪˈɔɡrəfɪ] n
autobiografía **❏ autograph**
[ˈɔːtəɡrɑːf] n autógrafo **❖** vt (photo etc)
dedicar; (programme) firmar
❏ automatic [ɔːtəˈmætɪk] adj
automático **❖** n (gun) pistola
automática; (car) coche m automático
❏ automatically adv
automáticamente **❏ automobile**
[ˈɔːtəməbiːl] (US) n coche m (SP), carro
(LAm), automóvil m **❏ autonomous**
[ɔːˈtɔnəməs] adj autónomo
❏ autonomy [ɔːˈtɔnəmɪ] n autonomía

autumn [ˈɔːtəm] n otoño

auxiliary [ɔːɡˈzɪlɪərɪ] adj, n auxiliar mf

avail [əˈveɪl] vt: **to ~ o.s. of**
aprovechar(se) de **❖** n: **to no ~** en vano,
sin resultado

availability [əveɪləˈbɪlɪtɪ] n
disponibilidad f

available [əˈveɪləbl] adj disponible;
(unoccupied) libre; (person: unattached)
soltero y sin compromiso

avalanche [ˈævəlɑːnʃ] n alud m,
avalancha

Ave. abbr = **avenue**

avenue [ˈævənjuː] n avenida f; (fig)
camino

average [ˈævərɪdʒ] n promedio,
término medio **❖** adj medio, de
término medio; (ordinary) regular,
corriente **❖** vt sacar un promedio de;
on ~ por regla general

avert [əˈvɜːt] vt prevenir; (blow) desviar;
(one's eyes) apartar

avid [ˈævɪd] adj ávido

avocado [ævəˈkɑːdəu] n (also: BRIT: also:
~ pear) aguacate m, palta (SC)

avoid [əˈvɔɪd] vt evitar, eludir

await [əˈweɪt] vt esperar, aguardar

awake [əˈweɪk] (pt **awoke**, pp **awoken**
or **awaked**) adj despierto ♦ vt
despertar ♦ vi despertarse; **to be ~**
estar despierto

award [əˈwɔːd] n premio; (LAW:
damages) indemnización f ♦ vt
otorgar, conceder; (LAW: damages)
adjudicar

aware [əˈwɛəˀ] adj: **~ (of)** consciente
(de); **to become ~ of/that** (realize)
darse cuenta de/de que; (learn)
enterarse de/de que □ **awareness** n
conciencia; (knowledge) conocimiento

away [əˈweɪ] adv fuera; (movement): **she
went ~** se marchó; **far ~** lejos; **two
kilometres ~** a dos kilómetros de
distancia; **two hours ~ by car** a dos
horas en coche; **the holiday was two
weeks ~** faltaban dos semanas para las
vacaciones; **he's ~ for a week** estará
ausente una semana; **to take ~ (from)**
quitar (a); (subtract) substraer (de);
to work/pedal ~ seguir trabajando/
pedaleando; **to fade ~** (colour)
desvanecerse; (sound) apagarse

awe [ɔː] n admiración f respetuosa
□ **awesome** [ˈɔːsəm] (US) adj
(excellent) formidable

awful [ˈɔːfəl] adj horroroso; (quantity):
an ~ lot (of) cantidad (de) □ **awfully**
adv (very) terriblemente

awkward [ˈɔːkwəd] adj desmañado,
torpe; (shape) incómodo;
(embarrassing) delicado, difícil

awoke [əˈwəuk] pt of **awake**

awoken [əˈwəukən] pp of **awake**

axe [æks] (US **ax**) n hacha ♦ vt (project)
cortar; (jobs) reducir

axle [ˈæksl] n eje m, árbol m

ay(e) [aɪ] excl sí

azalea [əˈzeɪlɪə] n azalea

B, b

B [biː] n (MUS) si m

B.A. abbr = **Bachelor of Arts**

baby [ˈbeɪbɪ] n bebé mf; (US: inf: darling)
mi amor □ **baby carriage** (US) n
cochecito □ **baby-sit** vi hacer de
canguro □ **baby-sitter** n canguro(-a)
□ **baby wipe** n toallita húmeda (para
bebés)

bachelor [ˈbætʃələˀ] n soltero; **B~ of
Arts/Science** licenciado(-a) en
Filosofía y Letras/Ciencias

back [bæk] n (of person) espalda; (of
animal) lomo; (of hand) dorso; (as
opposed to front) parte f de atrás; (of
chair) respaldo; (of page) reverso; (of
book) final m; (FOOTBALL) defensa m; (of
crowd): **the ones at the ~** los del fondo
♦ vt (candidate: also: **~ up**) respaldar,
apoyar; (horse: at races) apostar a; (car)
dar marcha atrás o con ♦ vi (car etc)
ir (o salir or entrar) marcha atrás ♦ adj
(payment, rent) atrasado; (seats, wheels)
de atrás ♦ adv (not forward) (hacia)
atrás; (returned): **he's ~** está de vuelta,
ha vuelto; **he ran ~** volvió corriendo;
(restitution): **throw the ball ~** devuelve
la pelota; **can I have it ~?** ¿me la
devuelve?; (again): **he called ~** llamó
de nuevo ♦ **back down** vi echarse
atrás ♦ **back out** vi (of promise)
volverse atrás ♦ **back up** vt (person)
apoyar, respaldar; (theory) defender; (
COMPUT) hacer una copia preventiva
or de reserva □ **backache** n dolor m
de espalda □ **backbencher** (BRIT) n
miembro del parlamento sin cargo
relevante □ **backbone** n columna
vertebral □ **back door** n puerta f
trasera □ **backfire** vi (AUT) petardear;
(plans) fallar, salir mal
□ **backgammon** n backgammon m
□ **background** n fondo; (of events)
antecedentes mpl; (basic knowledge)
bases fpl; (experience) conocimientos

mpl, educación f; **family background**
origen m, antecedentes mpl
❏ **backing** n (fig) apoyo, respaldo
❏ **backlog** n: **backlog of work** trabajo
atrasado ❏ **backpack** n mochila
❏ **backpacker** n mochilero(-a)
❏ **backslash** n pleca, barra inversa
❏ **backstage** adv entre bastidores
❏ **backstroke** n espalda ❏ **backup**
adj suplementario, (COMPUT) de
reserva ♦ n (support) apoyo; (also:
backup file) copia preventiva or de
reserva ❏ **backward** adj (person,
country) atrasado ❏ **backwards** adv
hacia atrás; (read a list) al revés; (fall) de
espaldas ❏ **backyard** n traspatio

bacon ['beikən] n tocino, beicon m

bacteria [bæk'tiəriə] npl bacterias fpl

bad [bæd] adj malo; (mistake, accident)
grave; (food) podrido, pasado; **his ~ leg**
su pierna lisiada; **to go ~** (food) pasarse

badge [bædʒ] n insignia; (policeman's)
chapa, placa

badger ['bædʒə'] n tejón m

badly ['bædli] adv mal; **to reflect ~ on**
sb influir negativamente en la
reputación de algn; **~ wounded**
gravemente herido; **he needs it ~** le
hace gran falta; **to be ~ off** (for money)
andar mal de dinero

bad-mannered ['bæd'mænəd] adj mal
educado

badminton ['bædmintən] n
bádminton m

bad-tempered ['bæd'tempəd] adj de
mal genio or carácter; (temporarily) de
mal humor

bag [bæg] n bolsa; (handbag) bolso;
(satchel) mochila; (case) maleta; **bags**
of (inf) un montón de ❏ **baggage** n
equipaje m ❏ **baggage allowance** n
límite m de equipaje ❏ **baggage**
reclaim n recogida de equipajes
❏ **baggy** adj amplio ❏ **bagpipes** npl
gaita

bail [beil] n fianza ♦ vt (prisoner: gen:
grant bail to) poner en libertad bajo

fianza; (boat: also: ~ **out**) achicar; **on ~**
(prisoner) bajo fianza; **to ~ sb out**
obtener la libertad de algn bajo fianza

bait [beit] n cebo ♦ vt poner cebo en;
(tease) tomar el pelo a

bake [beik] vt cocer (al horno) ♦ vi
cocerse ❏ **baked beans** npl judías fpl
en salsa de tomate ❏ **baked potato** n
patata al horno ❏ **baker** n panadero
❏ **bakery** n panadería; (for cakes)
pastelería ❏ **baking** n (act) amasar m;
(batch) hornada ❏ **baking powder** n
levadura (en polvo)

balance ['bæləns] n equilibrio; (COMM:
sum) balance m; (remainder) resto;
(scales) balanza ♦ vt equilibrar;
(budget) nivelar; (account) saldar;
(make equal) equilibrar; **~ of trade/**
payments balanza de comercio/
pagos ❏ **balanced** adj (personality,
diet) equilibrado; (report) objetivo
❏ **balance sheet** n balance m

balcony ['bælkəni] n (open) balcón m;
(closed) galería; (in theatre) anfiteatro

bald [bɔːld] adj calvo; (tyre) liso

Balearics [bælı'ærıks] npl: **the ~** las
Baleares

ball [bɔːl] n pelota; (football) balón m;
(of wool, string) ovillo; (dance) baile m;
to play ~ cooperar

ballerina [bælə'riːnə] n bailarina

ballet ['bælei] n ballet m ❏ **ballet**
dancer n bailarín(-ina) m/f

balloon [bə'luːn] n globo

ballot ['bælət] n votación f

ballpoint (pen) ['bɔːlpɔint-] n
bolígrafo

ballroom ['bɔːlrum] n salón m de baile

Baltic ['bɔːltik] n: **the ~ (Sea)** el (Mar)
Báltico

bamboo [bæm'buː] n bambú m

ban [bæn] n prohibición f, proscripción
f ♦ vt prohibir, proscribir

banana [bə'nɑːnə] n plátano, banana
(LAm), banano (CAm)

band [bænd] n grupo; (strip) faja, tira; (stripe) lista; (MUS: jazz) orquesta; (: rock) grupo; (MIL) banda

bandage ['bændɪdʒ] n venda, vendaje m ♦ vt vendar

Band-Aid® ['bændeɪd] (US) n tirita

bandit ['bændɪt] n bandido

bang [bæŋ] n (of gun, exhaust) estallido, detonación f; (of door) portazo; (blow) golpe m ♦ vt (one's head) golpear ♦ vi estallar; (door) cerrar de golpe

Bangladesh [bɑːŋglə'deʃ] n Bangladesh m

bangle ['bæŋgl] n brazalete m, ajorca

bangs [bæŋz] (US) npl flequillo

banish ['bænɪʃ] vt desterrar

banister(s) ['bænɪstə(z)] n(pl) barandilla, pasamanos m inv

banjo ['bændʒəu] n (pl banjoes o banjos) n banjo

bank [bæŋk] n (COMM) banco; (of river, lake) ribera, orilla; (of earth) terraplén m ♦ vi (AVIAT) ladearse ► bank on vt fus contar con □ **bank account** n cuenta de banco □ **bank balance** n saldo □ **bank card** n tarjeta bancaria □ **bank charges** npl comisión fsg □ **banker** n banquero □ **bank holiday** n (BRIT) día m festivo or de fiesta □ **banking** n banca □ **bank manager** n director(a) m/f (de sucursal) de banco □ **banknote** n billete m de banco

BANK HOLIDAY

El término **bank holiday** se aplica en el Reino Unido a todo día festivo oficial en el que cierran bancos y comercios. Los más importantes son en Navidad, Semana Santa, finales de mayo y finales de agosto y, al contrario que en los países de tradición católica, no coinciden necesariamente con una celebración religiosa.

bankrupt ['bæŋkrʌpt] adj quebrado, insolvente; **to go ~** hacer bancarrota; **to be ~** estar en quiebra □ **bankruptcy** n quiebra

bank statement n balance m or detalle m de cuenta

banner ['bænə'] n pancarta

bannister(s) ['bænɪstə(z)] n(pl) = **banister(s)**

banquet ['bæŋkwɪt] n banquete m

baptism ['bæptɪzəm] n bautismo; (act) bautizo

baptize [bæp'taɪz] vt bautizar

bar [bɑː'] n (pub) bar m; (counter) mostrador m; (rod) barra; (of window, cage) reja; (of soap) pastilla; (of chocolate) tableta; (fig: hindrance) obstáculo; (prohibition) proscripción f; (MUS) barra ♦ vt obstruir; (person) excluir; (activity) prohibir; **the B~** (LAW) la abogacía; **behind bars** entre rejas; **~ none** sin excepción

barbaric [bɑː'bærɪk] adj bárbaro

barbecue ['bɑːbɪkjuː] n barbacoa

barbed wire ['bɑːbd-] n alambre m de púas

barber ['bɑːbə'] n peluquero, barbero □ **barber's (shop)** (US **barber shop**) n peluquería

bar code n código de barras

bare [bɛə'] adj desnudo; (trees) sin hojas; (necessities etc) básico ♦ vt desnudar; (teeth) enseñar □ **barefoot** adj, adv descalzo □ **barely** adv apenas

bargain [bɑːgɪn] n pacto, negocio; (good buy) ganga ♦ vi negociar; (haggle) regatear; **into the ~** además, por añadidura ► **bargain for** vt fus: **he got more than he bargained for** le resultó peor de lo que esperaba

barge [bɑːdʒ] n barcaza ► **barge in** vi irrumpir; (interrupt: conversation) interrumpir

bark [bɑːk] n (of tree) corteza; (of dog) ladrido ♦ vi ladrar

barley ['bɑːlɪ] n cebada

barmaid ['bɑːmeɪd] n camarera

barman ['bɑːmən] (*irreg*) n camarero, barman m

barn [bɑːn] n granero

barometer [bə'rɒmɪtəʳ] n barómetro

baron ['bærən] n barón m; (*press baron etc*) magnate m □ **baroness** n baronesa

barracks ['bærəks] npl cuartel m

barrage ['bærɑːʒ] n (*MIL*) descarga, bombardeo; (*dam*) presa; (*of criticism*) lluvia, aluvión m

barrel ['bærəl] n barril m; (*of gun*) cañón m

barren ['bærən] adj estéril

barrette [bə'ret] n (*US*) pasador m (*LAm, SP*), broche m (*MEX*)

barricade [bærɪ'keɪd] n barricada

barrier ['bærɪəʳ] n barrera

barring ['bɑːrɪŋ] prep excepto, salvo

barrister ['bærɪstəʳ] n (*BRIT*) abogado(-a)

barrow ['bærəʊ] n (*cart*) carretilla (de mano)

bartender ['bɑːtendəʳ] n (*US*) camarero, barman m

base [beɪs] n base f ◆ vt: **to ~ sth on** basar or fundar algo en ◆ adj bajo, infame

baseball ['beɪsbɔːl] n béisbol m □ **baseball cap** n gorra f de béisbol

basement ['beɪsmənt] n sótano

bases[1] ['beɪsiːz] npl of **basis**

bases[2] ['beɪsɪz] npl of **base**

bash [bæʃ] (*inf*) vt golpear

basic ['beɪsɪk] adj básico □ **basically** adv fundamentalmente, en el fondo; (*simply*) sencillamente □ **basics** npl: **the basics** los fundamentos

basil ['bæzl] n albahaca

basin ['beɪsn] n cuenco, tazón m; (*GEO*) cuenca; (*also:* **washbasin**) lavabo

basis ['beɪsɪs] (*pl* **bases**) n base f; **on a part-time/trial ~** a tiempo parcial/a prueba

basket ['bɑːskɪt] n cesta, cesto; canasta □ **basketball** n baloncesto

bass [beɪs] n (*MUS: instrument*) bajo; (*double bass*) contrabajo; (*singer*) bajo

bastard ['bɑːstəd] n bastardo; (*inf!*) hijo de puta m

bat [bæt] n (*ZOOL*) murciélago; (*for ball games*) pala; (*BRIT: for table tennis*) pala ◆ vt: **he didn't ~ an eyelid** ni pestañeó

batch [bætʃ] n (*of bread*) hornada; (*of letters etc*) lote m

bath [bɑːθ, *pl* bɑːðz] n (*action*) baño; (*bathtub*) baño, tina (*LAm*), bañadera (*RPl*) ◆ vt bañar; **to have a ~** bañarse, tomar un baño; *see also* **baths**

bathe [beɪð] vi bañarse ◆ vt (*wound*) lavar

bathing ['beɪðɪŋ] n el bañarse □ **bathing costume** (*US* **bathing suit**) n traje m de baño

bath: bathrobe n (*man's*) batín m; (*woman's*) bata □ **bathroom** n (*cuarto de*) baño □ **baths** [bɑːðz] npl (*also:* **swimming baths**) piscina □ **bath towel** n toalla de baño □ **bathtub** n bañera

baton ['bætən] n (*MUS*) batuta; (*ATHLETICS*) testigo; (*weapon*) porra

batter ['bætəʳ] vt maltratar; (*rain etc*) azotar ◆ n masa (*para rebozar*) □ **battered** adj (*hat, pan*) estropeado

battery ['bætərɪ] n (*AUT*) batería; (*of torch*) pila □ **battery farming** n cría intensiva

battle ['bætl] n batalla; (*fig*) lucha f ◆ vi luchar □ **battlefield** n campo m de batalla

bay [beɪ] n (*GEO*) bahía; **B~ of Biscay** = mar Cantábrico; **to hold sb at ~** mantener a algn a raya

bazaar [bə'zɑːʳ] n bazar m; (*fete*) venta con fines benéficos

B. & B. n abbr = **bed and breakfast**; (*place*) pensión f; (*terms*) cama y desayuno

BBC n abbr (= British Broadcasting Corporation) cadena de radio y televisión estatal británica

B.C. adv abbr (= before Christ) a. de C.

be

KEYWORD

[bi:] (pt was, were, pp been) aux vb

1 (with present participle: forming continuous tenses): **what are you doing?** ¿qué estás haciendo?, ¿qué haces?; **they're coming tomorrow** vienen mañana; **I've been waiting for you for hours** llevo horas esperándote

2 (with pp: forming passives) ser (but often replaced by active or reflexive constructions); **to be murdered** ser asesinado; **the box had been opened** habían abierto la caja; **the thief was nowhere to be seen** no se veía al ladrón por ninguna parte

3 (in tag questions): **it was fun, wasn't it?** fue divertido, ¿no? or ¿verdad?; **he's good-looking, isn't he?** es guapo, ¿no te parece?; **she's back again, is she?** entonces, ¿ha vuelto?

4 (+to +infin): **the house is to be sold** (necessity) hay que vender la casa; (future) van a vender la casa; **he's not to open it** no tiene que abrirlo

♦ vb +complement

1 (with n or num complement, but see also 3, 4, 5 and impers vb below) ser; **he's a doctor** es médico; **2 and 2 are 4** 2 y 2 son 4

2 (with adj complement: expressing permanent or inherent quality) ser; (: expressing state seen as temporary or reversible) estar; **I'm English** soy inglés(-esa); **she's tall/pretty** es alta/bonita; **he's young** es joven; **be careful/good/quiet** ten cuidado/

pórtate bien/cállate; **I'm tired** estoy cansado(-a); **it's dirty** está sucio(-a)

3 (of health) estar; **how are you?** ¿cómo estás?; **he's very ill** está muy enfermo; **I'm better now** ya estoy mejor

4 (of age) tener; **how old are you?** ¿cuántos años tienes?; **I'm sixteen (years old)** tengo dieciséis años

5 (cost) costar; ser; **how much was the meal?** ¿cuánto fue or costó la comida?; **that'll be £5.75, please** son £5.75, por favor; **this shirt is £17** esta camisa cuesta £17

♦ vi

1 (exist, occur etc) existir, haber; **the best singer that ever was** el mejor cantante que existió jamás; **is there a God?** ¿hay un Dios?, ¿existe Dios?; **be that as it may** sea como sea; **so be it** así sea

2 (referring to place) estar; **I won't be here tomorrow** no estaré aquí mañana

3 (referring to movement): **where have you been?** ¿dónde has estado?

♦ impers vb

1 (referring to time): **it's 5 o'clock** son las 5; **it's the 28th of April** estamos a 28 de abril

2 (referring to distance): **it's 10 km to the village** el pueblo está a 10 km

3 (referring to the weather): **it's too hot/cold** hace demasiado calor/frío; **it's windy today** hace viento hoy

4 (emphatic): **it's me** soy yo; **it was Maria who paid the bill** fue María la que pagó la cuenta

beach [bi:tʃ] n playa ♦ vt varar

beacon ['bi:kən] n (lighthouse) faro; (marker) guía

bead [biːd] n cuenta; (of sweat etc) gota; **beads** npl (necklace) collar m

beak [biːk] n pico

beam [biːm] n (ARCH) viga, travesaño; (of light) rayo, haz m de luz ♦ vi brillar; (smile) sonreír

bean [biːn] n judía; **runner/broad ~** habichuela/haba; **coffee ~** grano de café □ **beansprouts** npl brotes mpl de soja

bear [beə^r] (pt bore, pp borne) n oso ♦ vt (weight etc) llevar; (cost) pagar; (responsibility) tener; (endure) soportar, aguantar; (children) parir, tener; (fruit) dar ♦ vi: **to ~ right/left** torcer a la derecha/izquierda

beard [biəd] n barba

bearer [ˈbeərə^r] n portador(a) m/f

bearing [ˈbeərɪŋ] n porte m, comportamiento; (connection) relación f

beast [biːst] n bestia; (inf) bruto, salvaje m

beat [biːt] (pt ~, pp beaten) n (of heart) latido; (MUS) ritmo, compás m; (of policeman) ronda ♦ vt pegar, golpear; (eggs) batir; (defeat: opponent) vencer, derrotar; (: record) sobrepasar ♦ vi (heart) latir; (drum) redoblar; (rain, wind) azotar; **off the beaten track** aislado; **to ~ it** (inf) largarse ♦ **beat up** vt (attack) dar una paliza a □ **beating** n paliza

beautiful [ˈbjuːtɪful] adj precioso, hermoso, bello □ **beautifully** adv maravillosamente

beauty [ˈbjuːtɪ] n belleza □ **beauty parlour** (US beauty parlor) n salón m de belleza □ **beauty salon** n salón m de belleza □ **beauty spot** n (TOURISM) lugar m pintoresco

beaver [ˈbiːvə^r] n castor m

became [bɪˈkeɪm] pt of **become**

because [bɪˈkɒz] conj porque; **~ of** debido a, a causa de

beckon [ˈbekən] vt (also: **~ to**) llamar con señas

become [bɪˈkʌm] (pt became, pp ~) vt (suit) favorecer, sentar bien a ♦ vi (+ n) hacerse, llegar a ser; (+ adj) ponerse, volverse; **to ~ fat** engordar

bed [bed] n cama; (of flowers) macizo; (of coal, clay) capa; (of river) lecho; (of sea) fondo; **to go to ~** acostarse □ **bed and breakfast** n (place) pensión f; (terms) cama y desayuno □ **bedclothes** npl ropa de cama □ **bedding** n ropa de cama □ **bed linen** n (BRIT) ropa f de cama

BED AND BREAKFAST

Se llama **bed and breakfast** a una forma de alojamiento, en el campo o la ciudad, que ofrece cama y desayuno a precios inferiores a los de un hotel. El servicio se suele anunciar con carteles en los que a menudo se usa únicamente la abreviatura **B. & B.**

bed: bedroom n dormitorio □ **bedside** n: **at the bedside of** a la cabecera de □ **bedside lamp** n lámpara de noche □ **bedside table** n mesilla de noche □ **bedsit(ter)** (BRIT) n cuarto de alquiler □ **bedspread** n cubrecama m, colcha □ **bedtime** n hora de acostarse

bee [biː] n abeja

beech [biːtʃ] n haya

beef [biːf] n carne f de vaca; **roast ~** rosbif m □ **beefburger** n hamburguesa □ **Beefeater** n alabardero de la Torre de Londres

been [biːn] pp of **be**

beer [biə^r] n cerveza □ **beer garden** n (BRIT) terraza f de verano, jardín m (de un bar)

beet [biːt] n (US) (also: **red ~**) remolacha

beetle [ˈbiːtl] n escarabajo

beetroot [ˈbiːtruːt] n (BRIT) remolacha

before [bɪˈfɔː^r] prep (of time) antes de; (of space) delante de ♦ conj (time) antes

beg ♦ *adv* antes, anteriormente; delante, adelante; **~ going** antes de marcharse; **~ she goes** antes de que se vaya; **the week ~** la semana anterior; **I've never seen it ~** no lo he visto nunca □ **beforehand** *adv* de antemano, con anticipación

beg [bɛg] *vi* pedir limosna ♦ *vt* pedir, rogar; (*entreat*) suplicar; **to ~ sb to do sth** rogar a algn que haga algo; *see also* **pardon**

began [bɪˈgæn] *pt of* **begin**

beggar [ˈbɛgəʳ] *n* mendigo(-a)

begin [bɪˈgɪn] (*pt* **began**, *pp* **begun**) *vt*, *vi* empezar, comenzar; **to ~ doing** *or* **to do sth** empezar a hacer algo □ **beginner** *n* principiante *m* □ **beginning** *n* principio, comienzo

begun [bɪˈgʌn] *pp of* **begin**

behalf [bɪˈhɑːf] *n*: **on ~ of** en nombre de, por; (*for benefit of*) en beneficio de; **on my/his ~** por mí/él

behave [bɪˈheɪv] *vi* (*person*) portarse, comportarse; (*well: also:* **~ o.s.**) portarse bien □ **behaviour** (*US* **behavior**) *n* comportamiento, conducta

behind [bɪˈhaɪnd] *prep* detrás de; (*supporting*) **to be ~ sb** apoyar a algn ♦ *adv* detrás, por detrás, atrás ♦ *n* trasero; **to be ~ (schedule)** ir retrasado; **~ the scenes** (*fig*) entre bastidores

beige [beɪʒ] *adj* color beige

Beijing [ˈbeɪˈdʒɪŋ] *n* Pekín *m*

being [ˈbiːɪŋ] *n* ser *m*; (*existence*): **in ~** existente; **to come into ~** aparecer

belated [bɪˈleɪtɪd] *adj* atrasado, tardío

belch [bɛltʃ] *vi* eructar ♦ *vt* (*gen:* **belch out:** *smoke etc*) arrojar

Belgian [ˈbɛldʒən] *adj, n* belga *mf*

Belgium [ˈbɛldʒəm] *n* Bélgica *f*

belief [bɪˈliːf] *n* opinión *f*; (*faith*) fe *f*

believe [bɪˈliːv] *vt, vi* creer; **to ~ in** creer en □ **believer** *n* partidario(-a); (*REL*) creyente *mf*, fiel *mf*

bell [bɛl] *n* campana; (*small*) campanilla; (*on door*) timbre *m*

bellboy [ˈbɛlbɔɪ] (*BRIT*) *n* botones *m inv*

bellhop [ˈbɛlhɔp] (*US*) *n* = **bellboy**

bellow [ˈbɛləʊ] *vi* bramar; (*person*) rugir

bell pepper *n* (*esp US*) pimiento, pimentón *m* (*LAm*)

belly [ˈbɛlɪ] *n* barriga, panza □ **belly button** (*inf*) *n* ombligo

belong [bɪˈlɔŋ] *vi*: **to ~ to** pertenecer a; (*club etc*) ser socio de; **this book belongs here** este libro va aquí □ **belongings** *npl* pertenencias *fpl*

beloved [bɪˈlʌvɪd] *adj* querido(-a)

below [bɪˈləʊ] *prep* bajo, debajo de; (*less than*) inferior a ♦ *adv* abajo, (por) debajo; **see ~** véase más abajo

belt [bɛlt] *n* cinturón *m*; (*TECH*) correa, cinta ♦ *vt* (*thrash*) pegar con correa □ **beltway** (*US*) *n* (*AUT*) carretera de circunvalación

bemused [bɪˈmjuːzd] *adj* perplejo

bench [bɛntʃ] *n* banco; (*BRIT POL*): **the Government/Opposition benches** (los asientos de) los miembros del Gobierno/de la Oposición; **the B~** (*LAW: judges*) magistratura

bend [bɛnd] (*pt, pp* **bent**) *vt* doblar ♦ *vi* inclinarse ♦ *n* (*BRIT: in road, river*) curva; (*in pipe*) codo ▸ **bend down** *vi* inclinarse, doblarse ▸ **bend over** *vi* inclinarse

beneath [bɪˈniːθ] *prep* bajo, debajo de; (*unworthy*) indigno de ♦ *adv* abajo, (por) debajo

beneficial [bɛnɪˈfɪʃəl] *adj* beneficioso

benefit [ˈbɛnɪfɪt] *n* beneficio; (*allowance of money*) subsidio ♦ *vt* beneficiar ♦ *vi*: **he'll ~ from it** le sacará provecho

benign [bɪˈnaɪn] *adj* benigno; (*smile*) afable

bent [bɛnt] *pt, pp of* **bend** ♦ *n* inclinación *f* ♦ *adj*: **to be ~ on** estar empeñado en

bereaved [bɪˈriːvd] npl: **the ~** los íntimos de una persona afligidos por su muerte

beret [ˈbereɪ] n boina

Berlin [bɜːˈlɪn] n Berlín

Bermuda [bɜːˈmjuːdə] n las Bermudas

berry [ˈberɪ] n baya

berth [bɜːθ] n (bed) litera; (cabin) camarote m; (for ship) amarradero ♦ vi atracar, amarrar

beside [bɪˈsaɪd] prep junto a, al lado de; **to be ~ o.s. with anger** estar furioso de sí; **that's ~ the point** eso no tiene nada que ver ♦ **besides** adv además ♦ prep además de

best [best] adj (el/la) mejor ♦ adv (lo) mejor; **the ~ part of** (quantity) la mayor parte de; **at ~** en el mejor de los casos; **to make the ~ of sth** sacar el mejor partido de algo; **to do one's ~** hacer todo lo posible; **to the ~ of my knowledge** que yo sepa; **to the ~ of my ability** como mejor puedo ♦ **best-before date** n fecha de consumo preferente ♦ **best man** (irreg) n padrino de boda ♦ **bestseller** n éxito de librería, bestseller m

bet [bet] (pt, pp or **betted**) n apuesta ♦ vt: **to ~ money on** apostar dinero por ♦ vi apostar; **to ~ sb sth** apostar algo a algn

betray [bɪˈtreɪ] vt traicionar; (trust) faltar a

better [ˈbetə] adj, adv mejor ♦ vt superar ♦ n: **to get the ~ of sb** quedar por encima de algn; **you had ~ do it** más vale que lo hagas; **he thought ~ of it** cambió de parecer; **to get ~** (MED) mejorar(se)

betting [ˈbetɪŋ] n juego, el apostar ♦ **betting shop** (BRIT) n agencia de apuestas

between [bɪˈtwiːn] prep entre ♦ adv (time) mientras tanto; (place) en medio

beverage [ˈbevərɪdʒ] n bebida

beware [bɪˈwɛə] vi: **to ~ (of)** tener cuidado (con); **~ of the dog** "perro peligroso"

bewildered [bɪˈwɪldəd] adj aturdido, perplejo

beyond [bɪˈjɒnd] prep más allá de; (past: understanding) fuera de; (after: date) después de; (above) superior a ♦ adv (in space) más allá; (in time) posteriormente; **~ doubt** fuera de toda duda; **~ repair** irreparable

bias [ˈbaɪəs] n (prejudice) prejuicio, pasión f; (preference) predisposición f ♦ **bias(s)ed** adj parcial

bib [bɪb] n babero

Bible [ˈbaɪbl] n Biblia

bicarbonate of soda [baɪˈkɑːbənɪt-] n bicarbonato sódico

biceps [ˈbaɪseps] n bíceps m

bicycle [ˈbaɪsɪkl] n bicicleta ♦ **bicycle pump** n bomba de bicicleta

bid [bɪd] (pt **bade** or ~, pp **bidden** or ~) n oferta, postura; (in tender) licitación f; (attempt) tentativa, conato ♦ vi hacer una oferta ♦ vt (offer) ofrecer; **to ~ sb good day** dar a algn los buenos días ♦ **bidder** n: **the highest bidder** el mejor postor

bidet [ˈbiːdeɪ] n bidet m

big [bɪg] adj grande; (brother, sister) mayor ♦ **bigheaded** adj engreído ♦ **big toe** n dedo gordo (del pie)

bike [baɪk] n bici f ♦ **bike lane** n carril-bici m

bikini [bɪˈkiːnɪ] n bikini m

bilateral [baɪˈlætərəl] adj (agreement) bilateral

bilingual [baɪˈlɪŋgwəl] adj bilingüe

bill [bɪl] n cuenta; (invoice) factura; (POL) proyecto de ley; (US: banknote) billete m; (of bird) pico; (of show) programa m; **"post no bills"** "prohibido fijar carteles"; **to fit** or **fill the ~** (fig) cumplir con los requisitos ♦ **billboard** (US) n cartelera ♦ **billfold** [ˈbɪlfəʊld] (US) n cartera

billiards ['bɪljədz] n billar m

billion ['bɪljən] n (BRIT) billón m (millón de millones); (US) mil millones mpl

bin [bɪn] n (for rubbish) cubo or bote m (MEX) or tacho (SC) de la basura; (container) recipiente m

bind [baɪnd] (pt, pp **bound**) vt atar; (book) encuadernar; (oblige) obligar
♦ n (inf: nuisance) lata

binge [bɪndʒ] (inf) n: **to go on a ~** ir de juerga

bingo ['bɪŋgəʊ] n bingo m

binoculars [bɪ'nɒkjuləz] npl prismáticos mpl

bio... [baɪə] prefix: **biochemistry** n bioquímica ♦ **biodegradable** [baɪəʊdɪ'greɪdəbl] adj biodegradable ♦ **biography** [baɪ'ɒɡrəfɪ] n biografía ♦ **biological** [baɪə'lɒdʒɪkl] adj biológico ♦ **biology** [baɪ'ɒlədʒɪ] n biología

birch [bɜːtʃ] n (tree) abedul m

bird [bɜːd] n ave f, pájaro; (BRIT: inf: girl) chica ❑ **bird of prey** n ave f de presa ❑ **birdwatching** n: **he likes to go birdwatching on Sundays** los domingos le gusta ir a ver pájaros

Biro® ['baɪərəʊ] n boli

birth [bɜːθ] n nacimiento; **to give ~ to** parir, dar a luz ❑ **birth certificate** n partida de nacimiento ❑ **birth control** n (policy) control m de natalidad; (methods) métodos mpl anticonceptivos ❑ **birthday** n cumpleaños m inv ♦ cpd (cake, card etc) de cumpleaños ❑ **birthmark** n antojo, marca de nacimiento ❑ **birthplace** n lugar m de nacimiento

biscuit ['bɪskɪt] n (BRIT) galleta

bishop ['bɪʃəp] n obispo; (CHESS) alfil m

bistro ['biːstrəʊ] n café-bar m

bit [bɪt] pt of **bite** ♦ n trozo, pedazo, pedacito; (COMPUT) bit m, bitio; (for horse) freno, bocado; **a ~** of un poco de; **a ~ mad** un poco loco; **~ by ~** poco a poco

bitch [bɪtʃ] n perra; (inf: woman) zorra (f)

bite [baɪt] (pt **bit**, pp **bitten**) vt, vi morder; (insect etc) picar ♦ n (insect bite) picadura; (mouthful) bocado; **to ~ one's nails** comerse las uñas; **let's have a ~ (to eat)** (inf) vamos a comer algo

bitten ['bɪtn] pp of **bite**

bitter ['bɪtə'] adj amargo; (wind) cortante, penetrante; (battle) encarnizado ♦ n (BRIT: beer) cerveza típica británica a base de lúpulos

bizarre [bɪ'zɑː'] adj raro, extraño

black [blæk] adj negro; (tea, coffee) solo ♦ n color m negro; (person): **B~** negro(-a) ♦ vt (BRIT INDUSTRY) boicotear; **to give sb a ~ eye** ponerle a algn el ojo morado; **~ and blue** (bruised) amoratado; **to be in the ~** (bank account) estar en números negros ❑ **black out** vi (faint) desmayarse ❑ **blackberry** n zarzamora ❑ **blackbird** n mirlo ❑ **blackboard** n pizarra ❑ **black coffee** n café m solo ❑ **blackcurrant** n grosella negra ❑ **black ice** n hielo invisible en la carretera ❑ **blackmail** n chantaje m ♦ vt chantajear ❑ **black market** n mercado negro ❑ **blackout** n (MIL) oscurecimiento; (power cut) apagón m; (TV, RADIO) interrupción f de programas; (fainting) desvanecimiento ❑ **black pepper** n pimienta f negra ❑ **black pudding** n morcilla ❑ **Black Sea** n: **the Black Sea** el Mar Negro

bladder ['blædə'] n vejiga

blade [bleɪd] n hoja; (of propeller) paleta; (of grass) una brizna de hierba

blame [bleɪm] n culpa ♦ vt: **to ~ sb for sth** echar a algn la culpa de algo; **to be to ~ (for)** tener la culpa (de)

bland [blænd] adj (music, taste) soso

blank [blæŋk] adj en blanco; (look) sin expresión ♦ n (of memory): **my mind is**

a ~ no puedo recordar nada; (on form) blanco, espacio en blanco; (cartridge) cartucho sin bala or de fogueo

blanket ['blæŋkɪt] n manta (SP), cobija (LAm); (of snow) capa; (of fog) manto

blast [blɑːst] n (of wind) ráfaga, soplo; (of explosive) explosión f ♦ vt (blow up) volar

blatant ['bleɪtənt] adj descarado

blaze [bleɪz] n (fire) fuego; (fig: of colour) despliegue m; (: of glory) esplendor m ♦ vi arder en llamas; (fig) brillar ♦ vt: to ~ a trail (fig) abrir un camino; in a ~ of publicity con gran publicidad

blazer ['bleɪzə'] n chaqueta de uniforme de colegial o de socio de club

bleach [bliːtʃ] n (also: household ~) lejía ♦ vt blanquear □ **bleachers** (US) npl (SPORT) gradas fpl al sol

bleak [bliːk] adj (countryside) desierto; (prospect) poco prometedor(a); (weather) crudo; (smile) triste

bled [bled] pt, pp of bleed

bleed [bliːd] (pt, pp bled) vt, vi sangrar; **my nose is bleeding** me está sangrando la nariz

blemish ['blemɪʃ] n marca, mancha; (on reputation) tacha

blend [blend] n mezcla ♦ vt mezclar; (colours etc) combinar, mezclar ♦ vi (colours etc: also: ~ **in**) combinarse, mezclarse □ **blender** n (CULIN) batidora

bless [bles] (pt, pp blessed or blest) vt bendecir; ~ **you!** (after sneeze) ¡Jesús! □ **blessing** n (approval) aprobación f; (godsend) don m del cielo, bendición f; (advantage) beneficio, ventaja

blew [bluː] pt of blow

blight [blaɪt] vt (hopes etc) frustrar, arruinar

blind [blaɪnd] adj ciego, (fig): ~ (**to**) ciego (a) ♦ n (for window) persiana ♦ vt cegar; (dazzle) deslumbrar; (deceive): **to** ~ **sb to ...** cegar a algn a ...; **the** ~ npl los ciegos □ **blind alley** n callejón m

sin salida □ **blindfold** n venda ♦ adv con los ojos vendados ♦ vt vendar los ojos a

blink [blɪŋk] vi parpadear, pestañear; (light) oscilar

bliss [blɪs] n felicidad f

blister ['blɪstə'] n ampolla ♦ vi (paint) ampollarse

blizzard ['blɪzəd] n ventisca

bloated ['bləutɪd] adj hinchado; (person: full) ahíto

blob [blɔb] n (drop) gota; (indistinct object) bulto

block [blɔk] n bloque m; (in pipes) obstáculo; (of buildings) manzana (SP), cuadra (LAm) ♦ vt obstruir, cerrar; (progress) estorbar; ~ **of flats** (BRIT) bloque m de pisos; **mental** ~ bloqueo mental ▶ **block up** vt tapar, obstruir; (pipe) atascar □ **blockade** [-'keɪd] n bloqueo ♦ vt bloquear □ **blockage** n estorbo, obstrucción f □ **blockbuster** n (book) bestséller m; (film) éxito de público □ **block capitals** npl mayúsculas fpl □ **block letters** npl mayúsculas fpl

bloke [bləuk] (BRIT: inf) n tipo, tío

blond(e) [blɔnd] adj, n rubio(-a) m/f

blood [blʌd] n sangre f □ **blood donor** n donante m/f de sangre □ **blood group** n grupo sanguíneo □ **blood poisoning** n envenenamiento de la sangre □ **blood pressure** n presión f sanguínea □ **bloodshed** n derramamiento de sangre □ **bloodshot** adj inyectado en sangre □ **bloodstream** n corriente f sanguínea □ **blood test** n análisis m inv de sangre □ **blood transfusion** n transfusión f de sangre □ **blood type** n grupo sanguíneo □ **blood vessel** n vaso sanguíneo □ **bloody** adj sangriento; (nose etc) lleno de sangre; (BRIT: inf!): **this bloody ...** este condenado or puñetero ... (!) ♦ adv:

bloody strong/good (BRIT: inf!) terriblemente fuerte/bueno

bloom [blu:m] n flor f ♦ vi florecer

blossom ['blɔsəm] n flor f ♦ vi florecer

blot [blɔt] n borrón m; (fig) mancha ♦ vt (stain) manchar

blouse [blauz] n blusa

blow [bləu] (pt **blew**, pp **blown**) n golpe m; (with sword) espadazo ♦ vi soplar; (dust, sand etc) volar; (fuse) fundirse ♦ vt (instrument) tocar; **to ~ one's nose** sonarse ▸ **blow down** vt tumbar (al soplar viento) ▸ **blow off** vt arrancar ▸ **blow out** vi apagarse ▸ **blow up** vi estallar ♦ vt volar; (tyre) inflar; (PHOT) ampliar □ **blow-dry** n moldeado (con secador)

blown [bləun] pp of **blow**

blue [blu:] adj azul; (depressed) deprimido; ~ **film/joke** película/chiste m verde; **out of the** ~ (fig) de repente □ **bluebell** n campanilla, campánula azul □ **blueberry** n arándano □ **blue cheese** n queso azul □ **blues** npl: **the blues** (MUS) el blues; **to have the blues** estar triste □ **bluetit** n herrerillo m (común)

bluff [blʌf] vi tirarse un farol, farolear ♦ n farol m; **to call sb's ~** coger a algn la palabra

blunder [blʌndə*] n patinazo, metedura de pata ♦ vi cometer un error, meter la pata

blunt [blʌnt] adj despuntado; (knife) desafilado, romo; (person) franco, directo

blur [blə:*] n (shape): **to become a ~** hacerse borroso ♦ vt (vision) enturbiar; (distinction) borrar □ **blurred** adj borroso

blush [blʌʃ] vi ruborizarse, ponerse colorado ♦ n rubor m; **blusher** n colorete m

board [bɔ:d] n (cardboard) cartón m; (wooden) tabla, tablero; (on wall) tablón m; (for chess etc) tablero;

(committee) junta, consejo; (in firm) mesa or junta directiva; (NAUT, AVIAT): **on ~** a bordo ♦ vt (ship) embarcarse en; (train) subir a; **full ~** (BRIT) pensión completa; **half ~** (BRIT) media pensión; **to go by the ~** (fig) ser abandonado or olvidado □ **board game** n juego de tablero □ **boarding card** (BRIT) n tarjeta de embarque □ **boarding pass** (US) n = **boarding card** □ **boarding school** n internado □ **board room** n sala de juntas

boast [bəust] vi: **to ~ (about or of)** alardear (de)

boat [bəut] n barco, buque m; (small) barca, bote m

bob [bɔb] vi (also: ~ **up and down**) menearse, balancearse

bobby pin (US) n horquilla

body ['bɔdɪ] n cuerpo; (corpse) cadáver m; (of car) caja, carrocería; (fig: group) grupo; (: organization) organismo □ **body-building** n culturismo □ **bodyguard** n guardaespaldas m inv □ **bodywork** n carrocería

bog [bɔg] n pantano, ciénaga ♦ vt: **to get bogged down** (fig) empantanarse, atascarse

bogus ['bəugəs] adj falso, fraudulento

boil [bɔil] vt (water) hervir; (eggs) pasar por agua, cocer ♦ vi hervir; (fig: with anger) estar furioso; (: with heat) asfixiarse ♦ n (MED) furúnculo, divieso; **to come to the ~**, **to come to a ~** (US) comenzar a hervir; **to ~ down to** (fig) reducirse a ▸ **boil over** vi salirse, rebosar; (anger etc) llegar al colmo □ **boiled egg** n (soft) huevo tibio (MEX) or pasado por agua (SP) or a la copa (SC); (hard) huevo duro □ **boiled potatoes** npl patatas fpl (SP) or papas fpl (LAm) cocidas □ **boiler** n caldera □ **boiling** ['bɔiliŋ] adj: **I'm boiling (hot)** (inf) estoy asado □ **boiling point** n punto de ebullición

bold [bəuld] adj valiente, audaz; (pej) descarado; (colour) llamativo

Bolivia [bə'lɪvɪə] n Bolivia ❑ **Bolivian** adj, n boliviano(-a) m/f

bollard ['boləd] (BRIT) n (AUT) poste m

bolt [bəult] n (lock) cerrojo; (with nut) perno, tornillo ♦ adv: ~ **upright** rígido, erguido ♦ vt (door) echar el cerrojo a; (also: ~ **together**) sujetar con tornillos; (food) engullir ♦ vi fugarse; (horse) desbocarse

bomb [bom] n bomba ♦ vt bombardear ❑ **bombard** [bom'bɑːd] vt bombardear; (fig) asediar ❑ **bomber** n (AVIAT) bombardero ❑ **bomb scare** n amenaza de bomba

bond [bond] n (binding promise) fianza; (FINANCE) bono; (link) vínculo, lazo; (COMM): **in ~** en depósito bajo fianza; **bonds** (chains) cadenas fpl

bone [bəun] n hueso; (of fish) espina ♦ vt deshuesar; quitar las espinas a

bonfire ['bonfaɪə'] n hoguera, fogata

bonnet ['bonɪt] n gorra; (BRIT: of car) capó m

bonus ['bəunəs] n (payment) paga extraordinaria, plus m; (fig) bendición f

boo [buː] excl ¡uh! ♦ vt abuchear, rechiflar

book [buk] n libro; (of tickets) taco; (of stamps etc) librito ♦ vt (ticket) sacar; (seat, room) reservar; **books** npl (COMM) cuentas fpl, contabilidad f ❑ **book in** vi (at hotel) registrarse ▶ **book up** vt: **to be booked up** (hotel) estar completo ❑ **bookcase** n librería, estante m para libros ❑ **booking** n reserva ❑ **booking office** n (BRIT RAIL) despacho de billetes (SP) or boletos (LAm); (THEATRE) taquilla (SP), boletería (LAm) ❑ **book-keeping** n contabilidad f ❑ **booklet** n folleto ❑ **bookmaker** n corredor m de apuestas ❑ **bookmark** n (also: COMPUT) marcador ❑ **bookseller** n librero ❑ **bookshelf** n estante m (para libros) ❑ **bookshop, book store** n librería

boom [buːm] n (noise) trueno, estampido; (in prices etc) alza rápida; (ECON, in population) boom m ♦ vi (cannon) hacer gran estruendo, retumbar; (ECON) estar en alza

boost [buːst] n estímulo, empuje m ♦ vt estimular, empujar

boot [buːt] n bota; (BRIT: of car) maleta, maletero ♦ vt (COMPUT) arrancar; **to ~** (in addition) además, por añadidura

booth [buːð] n (telephone booth, voting booth) cabina

booze [buːz] (inf) n bebida

border ['bɔːdə'] n borde m, margen m; (of a country) frontera; (for flowers) arriate m ♦ vt (road) bordear; (another country: also: ~ **on**) lindar con ❑ **borderline** n: **on the borderline** en el límite

bore [bɔː'] pt of **bear** ♦ vt (hole) hacer un agujero en; (well) perforar; (person) aburrir ♦ n (person) pelmazo, pesado; (of gun) calibre m ❑ **bored** adj aburrido; **he's bored to tears** or **to death** or **stiff** está aburrido como una ostra, está muerto de aburrimiento ❑ **boredom** n aburrimiento

boring ['bɔːrɪŋ] adj aburrido

born [bɔːn] adj: **to be ~** nacer; **I was ~ in 1960** nací en 1960

borne [bɔːn] pp of **bear**

borough ['bʌrə] n municipio

borrow ['borəu] vt: **to ~ sth (from sb)** tomar algo prestado (a algn)

Bosnia(-Herzegovina) ['bɔːsnɪə(hɜːzəˈgəuviːnə)] n Bosnia(-Herzegovina) ❑ **Bosnian** ['bɔznɪən] adj, n bosnio(-a)

bosom ['buzəm] n pecho

boss [bos] n jefe m ♦ vt (also: ~ **about** or **around**) mangonear ❑ **bossy** adj mandón(-ona)

both [bəuθ] adj, pron ambos(-as), los dos; ~ **of us went, we** ~ **went** fuimos los dos, ambos fuimos ♦ adv: ~ **A and B** tanto A como B

bother ['bɔðə] vt (worry) preocupar; (disturb) molestar, fastidiar ♦ vi (also: ~ o.s.) molestarse ♦ n (trouble) dificultad f; (nuisance) molestia, lata; to ~ doing tomarse la molestia de hacer

bottle ['bɔtl] n botella; (small) frasco; (baby's) biberón m ♦ vt embotellar □ **bottle bank** n contenedor m de vidrio □ **bottle-opener** n abrebotellas m inv

bottom ['bɔtəm] n (of box, sea) fondo; (buttocks) trasero, culo; (of page) pie m; (of list) final m; (of class) último(-a) ♦ adj (lowest) más bajo; (last) último

bought [bɔːt] pt, pp of **buy**

boulder ['bəuldə] n canto rodado

bounce [bauns] vi (ball) (re)botar; (cheque) ser rechazado ♦ vt hacer (re)botar ♦ n (rebound) (re)bote m □ **bouncer** (inf) n gorila m (que echa a los alborotadores de un bar, club etc)

bound [baund] pt, pp of **bind** ♦ n (leap) salto; (gen pl: limit) límite m ♦ vi (leap) saltar ♦ vt (border) rodear ♦ adj: ~ by rodeado de; to be ~ to do sth (obliged) tener el deber de hacer algo; he's ~ to come es seguro que vendrá; out of bounds prohibido el paso; ~ for con destino a

boundary ['baundri] n límite m

bouquet ['bukeɪ] n (of flowers) ramo

bourbon ['buəbən] (US) n (also: ~ whiskey) whisky m americano, bourbon m

bout [baut] n (of malaria etc) ataque m; (of activity) período; (BOXING etc) combate m, encuentro

boutique [buːˈtiːk] n boutique f, tienda de ropa

bow¹ [bəu] n (knot) lazo; (weapon, MUS) arco

bow² [bau] n (of the head) reverencia; (NAUT: also: bows) proa ♦ vi inclinarse, hacer una reverencia

bowels [bauəlz] npl intestinos mpl, vientre m; (fig) entrañas fpl

bowl [bəul] n tazón m, cuenco; (ball) bola ♦ vi (CRICKET) arrojar la pelota; see also **bowls** □ **bowler** n (CRICKET) lanzador m (de la pelota); (BRIT: also: **bowler hat**) hongo, bombín m □ **bowling** n (game) bochas fpl, bolos mpl □ **bowling alley** n bolera □ **bowling green** n pista para bochas □ **bowls** n juego de las bochas, bolos mpl

bow tie ['bau-] n corbata de lazo, pajarita

box [bɔks] n (also: **cardboard ~**) caja, cajón m; (THEATRE) palco ♦ vi encajonar ♦ vi (SPORT) boxear □ **boxer** ['bɔksə] n (person) boxeador m □ **boxer shorts** ['bɔksəʃɔːts] pl n bóxers; **a pair of boxer shorts** unos bóxers □ **boxing** ['bɔksɪŋ] n (SPORT) boxeo □ **Boxing Day** (BRIT) n día en que se dan los aguinaldos, 26 de diciembre □ **boxing gloves** npl guantes mpl de boxeo □ **boxing ring** n ring m, cuadrilátero □ **box office** n taquilla (SP), boletería (LAm)

boy [bɔi] n (young) niño; (older) muchacho, chico; (son) hijo

boycott ['bɔikɔt] n boicot m ♦ vt boicotear

boyfriend ['bɔifrend] n novio

bra [braː] n sostén m, sujetador m

brace [breis] n (BRIT: also: **braces**: on teeth) corrector m, aparato; (tool) berbiquí m ♦ vt (knees, shoulders) tensionar; **braces** npl (BRIT) tirantes mpl; to ~ o.s. (fig) prepararse

bracelet ['breislit] n pulsera, brazalete m

bracket ['brækit] n (TECH) soporte m, puntal m; (group) clase f, categoría; (also: **brace**) ♦ soporte m, abrazadera; (also: **round ~**) paréntesis m inv; (also: **square ~**) corchete m ♦ vt (word etc) poner entre paréntesis

brag [bræg] vi jactarse

braid [breid] n (trimming) galón m; (of hair) trenza

brain [breɪn] n cerebro; **brains** npl sesos mpl; **she's got brains** es muy lista

braise [breɪz] vt cocer a fuego lento

brake [breɪk] n (on vehicle) freno ♦ vi frenar ❑ **brake light** n luz f de frenado

bran [bræn] n salvado

branch [brɑːntʃ] n rama; (COMM) sucursal ▶ **branch off** vi: **a small road branches off to the right** hay una carretera pequeña que sale hacia la derecha ▶ **branch out** vi (fig) extenderse

brand [brænd] n marca; (fig: type) tipo ♦ vt (cattle) marcar con hierro candente ❑ **brand name** n marca ❑ **brand-new** adj flamante, completamente nuevo

brandy [brændɪ] n coñac m

brash [bræʃ] adj (forward) descarado

brass [brɑːs] n latón m; **the ~** (MUS) los cobres ▶ **brass band** n banda de metal

brat [bræt] n (pej) mocoso(-a)

brave [breɪv] adj valiente, valeroso ♦ vt (face up to) desafiar ❑ **bravery** n valor m, valentía

brawl [brɔːl] n pelea, reyerta

Brazil [brəˈzɪl] n (el) Brasil ❑ **Brazilian** adj, n brasileño(-a) m/f

breach [briːtʃ] vt abrir brecha en ♦ n (gap) brecha; (breaking): **~ of contract** infracción f de contrato; **~ of the peace** perturbación f del orden público

bread [bred] n pan m ❑ **breadbin** n panera ❑ **breadbox** (US) n panera ❑ **breadcrumbs** npl migajas fpl; (CULIN) pan rallado

breadth [bretθ] n anchura; (fig) amplitud f

break [breɪk] (pt **broke**, pp **broken**) vt romper; (promise) faltar a; (law) violar, infringir; (record) batir ♦ vi romperse, quebrarse; (storm) estallar; (weather) cambiar; (dawn) despuntar; (news story) darse a conocer ♦ n (gap) abertura;

(fracture) fractura; (time) intervalo; (: at school) (período de) recreo; (chance) oportunidad f; **to ~ the news to sb** comunicar la noticia a algn ▶ **break down** vt (figures, data) analizar, descomponer ♦ vi (machine) estropearse; (AUT) averiarse; (person) romper a llorar; (talks) fracasar ▶ **break in** vt (horse etc) domar ♦ vi (burglar) forzar una entrada; (interrupt) interrumpir ▶ **break into** vt fus (house) forzar ▶ **break off** vi (speaker) pararse, detenerse; (branch) partir ▶ **break out** vi estallar; (prisoner) escaparse; **to break out in spots** salirle a algn granos ▶ **break up** vi (ship) hacerse pedazos; (crowd, meeting) disolverse; (marriage) deshacerse; (SCOL) terminar (el curso) ♦ vt (rocks etc) partir; (journey) partir; (fight etc) acabar con ❑ **breakdown** n (AUT) avería; (in communications) interrupción f; (MED: also: **nervous breakdown**) colapso, crisis f nerviosa; (of marriage, talks) fracaso; (of statistics) análisis m inv ❑ **breakdown truck, breakdown van** n (camión m) grúa

breakfast [brekfəst] n desayuno

break: **break-in** n robo con allanamiento de morada ❑ **breakthrough** n (also fig) avance m

breast [brest] n (of woman) pecho, seno; (chest) pecho; (of bird) pechuga ❑ **breast-feed** (pt, pp **breast-fed**) vt, vi amamantar, criar a los pechos ❑ **breast-stroke** n braza (de pecho)

breath [breθ] n aliento, respiración f; **to take a deep ~** respirar hondo; **out of ~** sin aliento, sofocado

Breathalyser® [breθəlaɪzəʔ] (BRIT) n alcoholímetro

breathe [briːð] vt, vi respirar ▶ **breathe in** vt, vi aspirar ▶ **breathe out** vt, vi espirar ❑ **breathing** n respiración f

breath: **breathless** adj sin aliento, jadeante ❑ **breathtaking**

imponente, pasmoso ❑ **breath test**
n prueba de la alcoholemia
bred [bred] pt, pp of **breed**
breed [briːd] (pt, pp **bred**) vt criar ♦ vi
reproducirse, procrear ♦ n (ZOOL) raza,
casta; (type) tipo
breeze [briːz] n brisa
breezy ['briːzɪ] adj de mucho viento,
ventoso; (person) despreocupado
brew [bruː] vt (tea) hacer; (beer)
elaborar ♦ vi (fig: trouble) prepararse;
(storm) amenazar ❑ **brewery** n
fábrica de cerveza, cervecería
bribe [braɪb] n soborno ♦ vt sobornar,
cohechar ❑ **bribery** n soborno,
cohecho
bric-a-brac ['brɪkəbræk] n inv baratijas
fpl
brick [brɪk] n ladrillo ❑ **bricklayer** n
albañil m
bride [braɪd] n novia ❑ **bridegroom** n
novio ❑ **bridesmaid** n dama de
honor
bridge [brɪdʒ] n puente m; (NAUT)
puente m de mando; (of nose)
caballete m; (CARDS) bridge m ♦ vt (fig):
to ~ a gap llenar un vacío
bridle ['braɪdl] n brida, freno
brief [briːf] adj breve, corto n (LAW)
escrito; (task) cometido, encargo ♦ vt
informar; **briefs** npl (for men)
calzoncillos mpl; (for women) bragas
fpl ❑ **briefcase** n cartera (SP),
portafolio (LAm) ❑ **briefing** n (PRESS)
informe m ❑ **briefly** adv (glance)
fugazmente; (say) en pocas palabras
brigadier [brɪgə'dɪə] n general m de
brigada
bright [braɪt] adj brillante; (room)
luminoso; (day) de sol; (person: clever)
listo, inteligente; (: lively) alegre;
(colour) vivo; (future) prometedor(a)
brilliant ['brɪljənt] adj brillante; (inf)
fenomenal
brim [brɪm] n borde m; (of hat) ala
brine [braɪn] n (CULIN) salmuera

bring [brɪŋ] (pt, pp **brought**) vt (thing,
person: with you) traer; (: to sb) llevar,
conducir; (trouble, satisfaction) causar
▶ **bring about** vt ocasionar, producir
▶ **bring back** vt volver a traer; (return)
devolver ▶ **bring down** vt
(government, plane) derribar; (price)
rebajar ▶ **bring in** vt (harvest) recoger;
(person) hacer entrar o pasar; (object)
traer; (POL: bill, law) presentar;
(produce: income) producir, rendir
▶ **bring on** vt (illness, attack) producir,
causar; (player, substitute) sacar (de la
reserva), hacer salir ▶ **bring out** vt
sacar; (book etc) publicar; (meaning)
subrayar ▶ **bring up** vt subir; (person)
educar, criar; (question) sacar a
colación; (food: vomit) devolver,
vomitar
brink [brɪŋk] n borde m
brisk [brɪsk] adj (abrupt: tone) brusco;
(person) enérgico, vigoroso; (pace)
rápido; (trade) activo
bristle ['brɪsl] n cerda ♦ vi: **to ~ in
anger** temblar de rabia
Brit [brɪt] n abbr (inf: = British person)
británico(-a)
Britain ['brɪtən] n (also: **Great ~**) Gran
Bretaña
British ['brɪtɪʃ] adj británico ♦ npl: **the ~**
los británicos ❑ **British Isles** npl: **the
British Isles** las Islas Británicas
Briton ['brɪtən] n británico(-a)
brittle ['brɪtl] adj quebradizo, frágil
broad [brɔːd] adj ancho; (range)
amplio; (smile) abierto; (general:
outlines etc) general; (accent) cerrado;
in ~ daylight en pleno día
❑ **broadband** n banda ancha
❑ **broad bean** n haba ❑ **broadcast**
(pt, pp ~) n emisión f ♦ vt (RADIO) emitir;
(TV) transmitir ♦ vi emitir; transmitir
❑ **broaden** vt ampliar ♦ vi
ensancharse; **to broaden one's mind**
hacer más tolerante a algn ❑ **broadly**
adv en general ❑ **broad-minded** adj
tolerante, liberal

broccoli ['brɒkəlɪ] n brécol m

brochure ['brəʊʃjʊəʳ] n folleto

broil [brɔɪl] vt (CULIN) asar a la parrilla

broiler ['brɔɪləʳ] n (grill) parrilla

broke [brəʊk] pt of **break** ♦ adj (inf) pelado, sin blanca

broken ['brəʊkən] pp of **break** ♦ adj roto; (machine: also: **~ down**) averiado; **~ leg** pierna rota; **in ~ English** en un inglés imperfecto

broker ['brəʊkəʳ] n agente m/f, bolsista m/f; (insurance broker) agente de seguros

bronchitis [brɒŋ'kaɪtɪs] n bronquitis f

bronze [brɒnz] n bronce m

brooch [brəʊtʃ] n prendedor m, broche m

brood [bruːd] n camada, cría ♦ vi (person) dejarse obsesionar

broom [brum] n escoba; (BOT) retama

Bros. abbr (= Brothers) Hnos

broth [brɒθ] n caldo

brothel ['brɒθl] n burdel m

brother ['brʌðəʳ] n hermano ❏ **brother-in-law** n cuñado

brought [brɔːt] pt, pp of **bring**

brow [braʊ] n (forehead) frente m; (eyebrow) ceja; (of hill) cumbre f

brown [braʊn] adj (colour) marrón m; (hair) castaño; (tanned) bronceado, moreno ♦ n (colour) color m marrón o pardo ♦ vt (CULIN) dorar ❏ **brown bread** n pan integral

Brownie ['braʊnɪ] n niña exploradora

brown rice n arroz m integral

brown sugar n azúcar m terciado

browse [braʊz] vi (through book) hojear; (in shop) mirar ❏ **browser** n (COMPUT) navegador m

bruise [bruːz] n cardenal m (SP), moretón m ♦ vt magullar

brunette [bruː'nɛt] n morena

brush [brʌʃ] n cepillo; (for painting, shaving etc) brocha; (artist's) pincel m;

(with police etc) roce m ♦ vt (sweep) barrer; (groom) cepillar; (also: **~ against**) rozar al pasar

Brussels ['brʌslz] n Bruselas

Brussels sprout n col f de Bruselas

brutal ['bruːtl] adj brutal

B.Sc. abbr (= Bachelor of Science) licenciado en Ciencias

BSE n abbr (= bovine spongiform encephalopathy) encefalopatía f espongiforme bovina

bubble ['bʌbl] n burbuja ♦ vi burbujear, borbotar ❏ **bubble bath** n espuma para el baño ❏ **bubble gum** n chicle m de globo

buck [bʌk] n (rabbit) conejo macho; (deer) gamo; (US: inf) dólar m ♦ vi corcovear; **to pass the ~ (to sb)** echar (a algn) el muerto

bucket ['bʌkɪt] n cubo, balde m

buckle ['bʌkl] n hebilla ♦ vt abrochar con hebilla ♦ vi combarse

bud [bʌd] n (of plant) brote m, yema; (of flower) capullo ♦ vi brotar, echar brotes

Buddhism ['budɪzm] n Budismo

Buddhist ['budɪst] adj, n budista m/f

buddy ['bʌdɪ] (US) n compañero, compinche m

budge [bʌdʒ] vt mover; (fig) hacer ceder ♦ vi moverse, ceder

budgerigar ['bʌdʒərɪgɑːʳ] n periquito

budget ['bʌdʒɪt] n presupuesto ♦ vi: **to ~ for sth** presupuestar algo

budgie ['bʌdʒɪ] n = **budgerigar**

buff [bʌf] n (colour) color de ante ♦ n (inf: enthusiast) entusiasta m

buffalo ['bʌfələʊ] (pl **~** or **buffaloes**) n (BRIT) búfalo; (US: bison) bisonte m

buffer ['bʌfəʳ] n (COMPUT) memoria intermedia; (RAIL) tope m

buffet¹ ['bʌfɪt] vt golpear

buffet² ['bu:feɪ] n (BRIT: in station) bar m, cafetería; (food) buffet m ❏ **buffet car** n (BRIT) (RAIL) coche-comedor m

bug [bʌg] n (esp US: insect) bicho, sabandija; (COMPUT) error m; (germ) microbio, bacilo; (spy device) micrófono oculto ♦ vt (inf: annoy) fastidiar; (room) poner micrófono oculto en

buggy ['bʌgɪ] n cochecito de niño

build [bɪld] (pt, pp **built**) n (of person) tipo ♦ vt construir, edificar ► **build up** vt (morale, forces, production) acrecentar; (stocks) acumular ❑ **builder** n (contractor) contratista mf ❑ **building** n construcción f; (structure) edificio ❑ **building site** (BRIT) n obra ❑ **building society** (BRIT) n sociedad f inmobiliaria

built [bɪlt] pt, pp of **build** ❑ **built-in** (cupboard) empotrado; (device) interior, incorporado ❑ **built-up** adj (area) urbanizado

bulb [bʌlb] n (BOT) bulbo; (ELEC) bombilla, foco (MEX), bujía (CAm), bombita (RPl)

Bulgaria [bʌl'gearɪə] n Bulgaria ❑ **Bulgarian** adj, n búlgaro(-a) m/f

bulge [bʌldʒ] n bulto, protuberancia ♦ vi bombearse, pandearse; (pocket etc): to ~ (with) rebosar (de)

bulimia [bə'lɪmɪə] n bulimia

bulimic [bjuː'lɪmɪk] adj, n bulímico(-a) m/f

bulk [bʌlk] n masa, mole f; in ~ (COMM) a granel; the ~ of la mayor parte de ❑ **bulky** adj voluminoso, abultado

bull [bul] n toro; (male elephant, whale) macho

bulldozer ['buldəuzə'] n bulldozer m

bullet ['bulɪt] n bala

bulletin ['bulɪtɪn] n anuncio, parte m; (journal) boletín m ❑ **bulletin board** n (US) tablón m de anuncios; (COMPUT) tablero de noticias

bullfight ['bulfaɪt] n corrida de toros ❑ **bullfighter** n torero ❑ **bullfighting** n los toros, el toreo

bully ['bulɪ] n valentón m, matón m ♦ vt intimidar, tiranizar

bum [bʌm] n (inf: backside) culo; (esp US: tramp) vagabundo

bumblebee ['bʌmblbiː] n abejorro

bump [bʌmp] n (blow) tope m, choque m; (jolt) sacudida; (on road etc) bache m; (on head etc) chichón m ♦ vt (strike) chocar contra ► **bump into** vt fus chocar contra, tropezar con; (person) topar con ❑ **bumper** n (AUT) parachoques m inv ♦ adj: **bumper crop** or **harvest** cosecha abundante ❑ **bumpy** adj (road) lleno de baches

bun [bʌn] n (BRIT: cake) pastel m; (US: bread) bollo; (of hair) moño

bunch [bʌntʃ] n (of flowers) ramo; (of keys) manojo; (of bananas) piña; (of people) grupo; (pej) pandilla; **bunches** npl (in hair) coletas fpl

bundle ['bʌndl] n bulto, fardo; (of sticks) haz m; (of papers) legajo ♦ vt (also: ~ up) atar, envolver; to ~ **sth/sb into** meter algo/a algn precipitadamente en

bungalow ['bʌŋgələu] n bungalow m, chalé m

bungee jumping ['bʌndʒiː'dʒʌmpɪŋ] n puenting m, banyi m

bunion ['bʌnjən] n juanete m

bunk [bʌŋk] n litera ❑ **bunk beds** npl literas fpl

bunker ['bʌŋkə'] n (coal store) carbonera; (MIL) refugio; (GOLF) bunker m

bunny ['bʌnɪ] n (inf: also: ~ **rabbit**) conejito

buoy [bɔɪ] n boya ❑ **buoyant** adj (ship) capaz de flotar; (economy) boyante; (person) optimista

burden ['bɜːdn] n carga ♦ vt cargar

bureau [bjuə'rəu] n (pl **bureaux**) (BRIT: writing desk) escritorio, buró m; (US: chest of drawers) cómoda; (office) oficina, agencia

bureaucracy [bjuə'rɔkrəsɪ] n burocracia

bureaucrat ['bjuərəkræt] n burócrata m/f

bureau de change [-də'dʒɑ̃ʒ] (pl **bureaux de change**) n caja f de cambio

bureaux ['bjuərəuz] npl de **bureau**

burger ['bɜːgə*] n hamburguesa

burglar ['bɜːglə*] n ladrón(-ona) m/f
❏ **burglar alarm** n alarma f antirrobo
❏ **burglary** n robo con allanamiento, robo de una casa

burial ['berɪəl] n entierro

burn [bɜːn] (pt, pp **burned** or **burnt**) vt quemar; (house) incendiar ♦ vi quemarse, arder; incendiarse; (sting) escocer ♦ n quemadura ▶ **burn down** vt incendiar ♦ **burn out** vt (writer etc): **to burn o.s. out** agotarse ❏ **burning** adj (building etc) en llamas; (hot: sand etc) abrasador(a); (ambition) ardiente

Burns' Night [bɜːnz-] n see **recuadro**

> **BURNS' NIGHT**
>
> Cada veinticinco de enero los escoceses celebran la llamada **Burns' Night** (noche de Burns), en honor al poeta escocés Robert Burns (1759-1796). Es tradición hacer una cena en la que, al son de la música de la gaita escocesa, se sirve "haggis", plato tradicional de asadura de cordero cocida en el estómago del animal, acompañado de nabos y puré de patatas. Durante la misma se recitan poemas del autor y varios discursos conmemorativos de carácter festivo.

burnt [bɜːnt] pt, pp of **burn**

burp [bɜːp] (inf) n eructo ♦ vi eructar

burrow ['bʌrəu] n madriguera ♦ vi hacer una madriguera; (rummage) hurgar

burst [bɜːst] (pt, pp ~) vt reventar; (river: banks etc) romper ♦ vi reventarse; (tyre) pincharse ♦ n (of gunfire) ráfaga; (also: ~ pipe) reventón m; **a ~ of energy/**speed/enthusiasm una explosión de energía/un ímpetu de velocidad/un arranque de entusiasmo; **to ~ into flames** estallar en llamas; **to ~ into tears** deshacerse en lágrimas; **to ~ out laughing** soltar la carcajada; **to ~ open** abrirse de golpe; **to be bursting with** (container) estar lleno a rebosar de; (: person) reventar por o de ▶ **burst into** vt fus (room etc) irrumpir en

bury ['berɪ] vt enterrar; (body) enterrar, sepultar

bus [bʌs] (pl **buses**) n autobús m ❏ **bus conductor** n cobrador(a) m/f

bush [buʃ] n arbusto; (scrub land) monte m; **to beat about the ~** andar(se) con rodeos

business ['bɪznɪs] n (matter) asunto; (trading) comercio, negocios mpl; (firm) empresa, casa; (occupation) oficio; **to be away on ~** estar en viaje de negocios; **it's my ~ to** ... me toca o corresponde ...; **it's none of my ~** yo no tengo nada que ver; **he means ~** habla en serio ❏ **business class** n (Aer) clase f preferente ❏ **businesslike** adj eficiente ❏ **businessman** (irreg) n hombre m de negocios ❏ **business trip** n viaje m de negocios ❏ **businesswoman** (irreg) n mujer f de negocios

busker ['bʌskə*] n (BRIT) n músico(-a) ambulante

bus: bus pass n bonobús ❏ **bus shelter** n parada cubierta ❏ **bus station** n estación f de autobuses ❏ **bus-stop** n parada de autobús

bust [bʌst] n (ANAT) pecho; (sculpture) busto ♦ adj (inf: broken) roto, estropeado; **to go ~** quebrar

bustling ['bʌslɪŋ] adj (town) animado, bullicioso

busy ['bɪzɪ] adj ocupado, atareado; (shop, street) concurrido; (TEL: line) comunicando ♦ vt: **to ~ o.s. with** ocuparse en ❏ **busy signal** (US) n (TEL) señal f de comunicado

but

KEYWORD

[bʌt] conj

1 pero; **he's not very bright, but he's hard-working** no es muy inteligente, pero es trabajador

2 (in direct contradiction) sino; **he's not English but French** no es inglés sino francés; **he didn't sing but he shouted** no cantó sino que gritó

3 (showing disagreement, surprise etc): **but that's far too expensive!** ¡pero eso es carísimo!; **but it does work!** ¡(pero) sí que funciona!

♦ prep (apart from, except) menos, salvo; **we've had nothing but trouble** no hemos tenido más que problemas; **no-one but him can do it** nadie más que él puede hacerlo; **who but a lunatic would do such a thing?** ¿sólo un loco haría una cosa así?; **but for you/your help** si no fuera por ti/tu ayuda; **anything but that** cualquier cosa menos eso

♦ adv (just, only): **she's but a child** no es más que una niña; **had I but known** si lo hubiera sabido; **I can but try** al menos lo puedo intentar; **it's all but finished** está casi acabado

butcher ['butʃə'] n carnicero ♦ vt hacer una carnicería con; (cattle etc) matar □ **butcher's (shop)** n carnicería

butler ['bʌtlə'] n mayordomo

butt [bʌt] n (barrel) tonel m; (of gun) culata; (of cigarette) colilla; (BRIT: fig: target) blanco ♦ vt dar cabezadas contra, top(et)ar

butter ['bʌtə'] n mantequilla ♦ vt untar con mantequilla □ **buttercup** n botón m de oro

butterfly ['bʌtəflaɪ] n mariposa; (SWIMMING: also: ~ **stroke**) braza de mariposa

buttocks ['bʌtəks] npl nalgas fpl

button ['bʌtn] n botón m; (US) placa, chapa ♦ vt (also: ~ **up**) abotonar, abrochar ♦ vi abrocharse

buy [baɪ] (pt, pp **bought**) vt comprar ♦ n compra; **to ~ sb sth/sth from sb** comprarle algo a algn; **to ~ sb a drink** invitar a algn a tomar algo ► **buy out** vt (partner) comprar la parte de ► **buy up** vt (property) comprar; (stock) comprar todas las existencias de □ **buyer** n comprador(a) m/f

buzz [bʌz] n zumbido; (inf: phone call) llamada (por teléfono) ♦ vi zumbar □ **buzzer** n timbre m

by

KEYWORD

[baɪ] prep

1 (referring to cause, agent) por; de; **killed by lightning** muerto por un relámpago; **a painting by Picasso** un cuadro de Picasso

2 (referring to method, manner, means): **by bus/car/train** en autobús/coche/tren; **to pay by cheque** pagar con un cheque; **by moonlight/candlelight** a la luz de la luna/una vela; **by saving hard he ...** ahorrando ...

3 (via, through) por; **we came by Dover** vinimos por Dover

4 (close to, past): **the house by the river** la casa junto al río; **she rushed by me** pasó a mi lado como una exhalación; **I go by the post office every day** paso por delante de Correos todos los días

5 (time: not later than) para; (: during): **by daylight** de día; **by 4 o'clock** para las cuatro; **by this time tomorrow** mañana a estas horas; **by the time I**

got here it was too late cuando llegué a ya era demasiado tarde
6 (*amount*): **by the metre/kilo** por metro/kilo; **paid by the hour** pagado por hora
7 (*MATH, measure*): **to divide/multiply by 3** dividir/multiplicar por 3; **a room 3 metres by 4** una habitación de 3 metros por 4; **it's broader by a metre** es un metro más ancho
8 (*according to*) según, de acuerdo con; **it's 3 o'clock by my watch** según mi reloj, son las tres; **it's all right by me** por mí, está bien
9: (all) **by oneself** etc todo solo; **he did it (all) by himself** lo hizo él solo; **he was standing (all) by himself in a corner** estaba de pie solo en un rincón
10: by the way a propósito, por cierto; **this wasn't my idea, by the way** pues, no fue idea mía
♦ *adv*
11 see **go, pass** etc
12: by and by finalmente; **they'll come back by and by** acabarán volviendo; **by and large** en líneas generales, en general

bye(-bye) ['baɪ'baɪ] *excl* adiós, hasta luego
by-election (*BRIT*) *n* elección *f* parcial
bypass ['baɪpɑːs] *n* carretera de circunvalación; (*MED*) (operación *f* de) by-pass *m* ♦ *vt* evitar
byte [baɪt] *n* (*COMPUT*) byte *m*, octeto

C, c

C [siː] *n* (*MUS*) do *m*
cab [kæb] *n* taxi *m*; (*of truck*) cabina

cabaret ['kæbəreɪ] *n* cabaret *m*
cabbage ['kæbɪdʒ] *n* col *f*, berza
cabin ['kæbɪn] *n* cabaña *f*; (*on ship*) camarote *m*; (*on plane*) cabina
❑ **cabin crew** *n* tripulación *f* de cabina
cabinet ['kæbɪnɪt] *n* (*POL*) consejo de ministros; (*furniture*) armario; (*also*: **display ~**) vitrina ❑ **cabinet minister** *n* ministro/-a (del gabinete)
cable ['keɪbl] *n* cable *m* ♦ *vt* cablegrafiar ❑ **cable car** *n* teleférico ❑ **cable television** *n* televisión *f* por cable
cactus ['kæktəs] (*pl* **cacti**) *n* cacto
café ['kæfeɪ] *n* café *m*
cafeteria [kæfɪ'tɪərɪə] *n* cafetería
caffein(e) ['kæfiːn] *n* cafeína
cage [keɪdʒ] *n* jaula
cagoule [kə'guːl] *n* chubasquero
cake [keɪk] *n* (*CULIN: large*) tarta; (: *small*) pastel *m*; (*of soap*) pastilla
calcium ['kælsɪəm] *n* calcio
calculate ['kælkjuleɪt] *vt* calcular ❑ **calculation** [-'leɪʃən] *n* cálculo, cómputo ❑ **calculator** *n* calculadora
calendar ['kæləndə'] *n* calendario
calf [kɑːf] (*pl* **calves**) *n* (*of cow*) ternero, becerro; (*of other animals*) cría; (*also*: **calfskin**) piel *f* de becerro; (*ANAT*) pantorrilla
calibre ['kælɪbə'] (*US* **caliber**) *n* calibre *m*
call [kɔːl] *vt* llamar; (*meeting*) convocar ♦ *vi* (*shout*) llamar; (*TEL*) llamar (por teléfono); (*visit: also*: **~ in**, **~ round**) hacer una visita ♦ *n* llamada; (*of bird*) canto; **to be called** llamarse; **on ~** (*on duty*) de guardia ▶ **call back** *vi* (*return*) volver; (*TEL*) volver a llamar ▶ **call for** *vt fus* (*demand*) pedir, exigir; (*fetch*) pasar a recoger ▶ **call in** *vt* (*doctor, expert, police*) llamar ▶ **call off** *vt* (*cancel: meeting, race*) cancelar; (: *deal*) anular; (: *strike*) desconvocar ▶ **call on** *vt fus* visitar; (*turn to*) acudir a

▶ **call out** *vi* gritar ▶ **call up** *vt* (MIL) llamar al servicio militar; (TEL) llamar ❑ **callbox** (BRIT) *n* cabina telefónica ❑ **call centre** (US **call center**) *n* centro de atención al cliente ❑ **caller** *n* visita; (TEL) usuario(-a)

callous ['kæləs] *adj* insensible, cruel

calm [kɑːm] *adj* tranquilo; (sea) liso, en calma ♦ *n* calma, tranquilidad *f* ♦ *vt* calmar, tranquilizar ▶ **calm down** *vi* calmarse, tranquilizarse ♦ *vt* calmar, tranquilizar ❑ **calmly** ['kɑːmlɪ] *adv* tranquilamente, con calma

Calor gas® ['kælə'-] *n* butano

calorie ['kælərɪ] *n* caloría

calves [kɑːvz] *npl of* **calf**

camcorder ['kæmkɔːdə'] *n* videocámara

came [keɪm] *pt of* **come**

camel ['kæməl] *n* camello

camera ['kæmərə] *n* máquina fotográfica; (CINEMA, TV) cámara; **in** ~ (LAW) a puerta cerrada ❑ **cameraman** (*irreg*) *n* cámara *m*

camouflage ['kæməflɑːʒ] *n* camuflaje *m* ♦ *vt* camuflar

camp [kæmp] *n* campamento, camping *m*; (MIL) campamento; (for prisoners) campo; (fig: faction) bando ♦ *vi* acampar ♦ *adj* afectado, afeminado

campaign [kæm'peɪn] *n* (MIL, POL etc) campaña ♦ *vi* hacer campaña ❑ **campaigner** *n*: **campaigner for** defensor(a) *m/f* de

camp: campbed (BRIT) *n* cama de campaña ❑ **camper** *n* campista *mf*; (vehicle) caravana ❑ **campground** (US) *n* camping *m*, campamento ❑ **camping** *n* camping *m*; **to go camping** hacer camping ❑ **campsite** *n* camping *m*

campus ['kæmpəs] *n* ciudad *f* universitaria

can¹ [kæn] *n* (of oil, water) bidón *m*; (tin) lata, bote *m* ♦ *vt* enlatar

can²

[kæn] (negative **cannot, can't**, conditional and pt **could**) aux vb

1 (be able to) poder; **you can do it if you try** puedes hacerlo si lo intentas; **I can't see you** no te veo

2 (know how to) saber; **I can swim/ play tennis/drive** sé nadar/jugar al tenis/conducir; **can you speak French?** ¿hablas or sabes hablar francés?

3 (may) poder; **can I use your phone?** ¿me dejas or puedo usar tu teléfono?

4 (expressing disbelief, puzzlement etc): **it can't be true!** ¡no puede ser (verdad)!; **what CAN he want?** ¿qué querrá?

5 (expressing possibility, suggestion etc): **he could be in the library** podría estar en la biblioteca; **she could have been delayed** pudo haberse retrasado

Canada ['kænədə] *n* (el) Canadá ❑ **Canadian** [kə'neɪdɪən] *adj*, *n* canadiense *mf*

canal [kə'næl] *n* canal *m*

canary [kə'nɛərɪ] *n* canario

Canary Islands [kə'nɛərɪ'aɪləndz] *npl*: **the** ~ las (Islas) Canarias

cancel ['kænsəl] *vt* cancelar; (train) suprimir; (cross out) tachar, borrar ❑ **cancellation** [-'leɪʃən] *n* cancelación *f*; supresión *f*

Cancer ['kænsə'] *n* (ASTROLOGY) Cáncer *m*

cancer ['kænsə'] *n* cáncer *m*

candidate ['kændɪdeɪt] *n* candidato(-a)

candle ['kændl] *n* vela; (in church) cirio ❑ **candlestick** *n* (single) candelero; (low) palmatoria; (bigger, ornate) candelabro

candy ['kændɪ] n azúcar m cande; (US) caramelo □ **candy bar** (US) n barrita (dulce) □ **candyfloss** (BRIT) n algodón m (azucarado)

cane [keɪn] n (BOT) caña; (stick) vara, palmeta; (for furniture) mimbre f ♦ vt (BRIT: SCOL) castigar (con vara)

canister ['kænɪstə*] n bote m, lata; (of gas) bombona

cannabis ['kænəbɪs] n marijuana

canned [kænd] adj en lata, de lata

cannon ['kænən] (pl ~ or **cannons**) n cañón m

cannot ['kænɔt] = **can not**

canoe [kə'nu:] n canoa; (SPORT) piragua □ **canoeing** n piragüismo

canon ['kænən] n (clergyman) canónigo; (standard) canon m

can-opener ['kænəupnə*] n abrelatas m inv

can't [kænt] = **can not**

canteen [kæn'ti:n] n (eating place) cantina; (BRIT: of cutlery) juego

canter ['kæntə*] vi ir a medio galope

canvas ['kænvəs] n (material) lona; (painting) lienzo; (NAUT) velas fpl

canvass ['kænvəs] vi (POL): **to ~ for** solicitar votos por ♦ vt (COMM) sondear

canyon ['kænjən] n cañón m

cap [kæp] n (hat) gorra; (of pen) capuchón m; (of bottle) tapa, tapón m; (contraceptive) diafragma m; (for toy gun) cápsula ♦ vt (outdo) superar; (limit) recortar

capability [keɪpə'bɪlɪtɪ] n capacidad f

capable ['keɪpəbl] adj capaz

capacity [kə'pæsɪtɪ] n capacidad f; (position) calidad f

cape [keɪp] n capa; (GEO) cabo

caper ['keɪpə*] n (CULIN: gen pl) alcaparra; (prank) broma

capital ['kæpɪtl] n (also: ~ **city**) capital f; (money) capital m; (also: ~ **letter**) mayúscula □ **capitalism** n capitalismo □ **capitalist** adj, n

capitalista mf □ **capital punishment** n pena de muerte

Capitol ['kæpɪtl] n see recuadro

Capricorn ['kæprɪkɔ:n] n Capricornio

capsize [kæp'saɪz] vt volcar, hacer zozobrar ♦ vi volcarse, zozobrar

capsule ['kæpsju:l] n cápsula

captain ['kæptɪn] n capitán m

caption ['kæpʃən] n (heading) título; (to picture) leyenda

captivity [kæp'tɪvɪtɪ] n cautiverio

capture ['kæptʃə*] vt prender, apresar; (animal, COMPUT) capturar; (place) tomar; (attention) captar, llamar ♦ n apresamiento; captura; toma; (data capture) formulación f de datos

car [kɑ:*] n coche m, carro (LAm), automóvil m; (US RAIL) vagón m

carafe [kə'ræf] n jarra

caramel ['kærəmel] n caramelo

carat ['kærət] n quilate m

caravan ['kærəvæn] n (BRIT) caravana, rulóf f; (in desert) caravana □ **caravan site** (BRIT) n camping m para caravanas

carbohydrate [kɑ:bəu'haɪdreɪt] n hidrato de carbono; (food) fécula

carbon ['kɑ:bən] n carbono □ **carbon dioxide** n dióxido de carbono, anhídrido carbónico □ **carbon monoxide** n monóxido de carbono

car boot sale n mercadillo organizado en un aparcamiento, en el que se exponen las mercancías en el maletero del coche

carburettor ['kɑ:bju'retə'] (US **carburetor**) n carburador m

card [kɑ:d] n (material) cartulina; (index card etc) ficha; (playing card) carta, naipe m; (visiting card, greetings card etc) tarjeta ❑ **cardboard** n cartón m ❑ **card game** n juego de naipes or cartas

cardigan ['kɑ:dıgən] n rebeca

cardinal ['kɑ:dınl] adj cardinal; (importance, principal) esencial ♦ n cardenal m

cardphone ['kɑ:dfəun] n cabina que funciona con tarjetas telefónicas

care [keə'] n cuidado m; (worry) inquietud f; (charge) cargo, custodia ♦ vi: **to ~ about** (person, animal) tener cariño a; (thing, idea) preocuparse por; **~ of** en casa de, al cuidado de; **in sb's ~** a cargo de algn; **to take ~ to** cuidarse de, tener cuidado de; **to take ~ of** cuidar; (problem etc) ocuparse de; **I don't ~** no me importa; **I couldn't ~ less** eso me trae sin cuidado ► **care for** vt fus cuidar a; (like) querer

career [kə'rıə'] n profesión f; (in work, school) carrera ♦ vi (also: **~ along**) correr a toda velocidad

care: carefree adj despreocupado ❑ **careful** adj cuidadoso; (cautious) cauteloso; **(be) careful!** ¡tenga cuidado! ❑ **carefully** adv con cuidado, cuidadosamente; con cautela ❑ **caregiver** (US) n (professional) enfermero(-a) m/f; (unpaid) persona que cuida a un pariente o vecino ❑ **careless** adj descuidado; (heedless) poco atento ❑ **carelessness** n descuido, falta de atención ❑ **carer** ['keərə'] n (professional) enfermero(-a) m/f; (unpaid) persona que cuida a un pariente o vecino ❑ **caretaker** n portero(-a), conserje mf

car-ferry ['kɑ:feri] n transbordador m para coches

cargo ['kɑ:gəu] (pl **cargoes**) n cargamento, carga

car hire (BRIT) n alquiler m de automóviles

Caribbean [kærı'bi:ən] n: **the ~ (Sea)** el (Mar) Caribe

caring ['keərıŋ] adj humanitario; (behaviour) afectuoso

carnation [kɑ:'neıʃən] n clavel m

carnival ['kɑ:nıvəl] n carnaval m; (US: funfair) parque m de atracciones

carol ['kærəl] n: **(Christmas) ~** villancico

carousel [kærə'sel] (US) n tiovivo, caballitos mpl

car park (BRIT) n aparcamiento, parking m

carpenter ['kɑ:pıntə'] n carpintero(-a)

carpet ['kɑ:pıt] n alfombra; (fitted) moqueta ♦ vt alfombrar

car rental (US) n alquiler m de coches

carriage ['kærıdʒ] n (BRIT RAIL) vagón m; (horse-drawn) coche m; (of goods) transporte m; (: cost) porte m, flete m ❑ **carriageway** (BRIT) n (part of road) calzada

carrier ['kærıə'] n (transport company) transportista, empresa de transportes; (MED) portador m ❑ **carrier bag** (BRIT) n bolsa de papel or plástico

carrot ['kærət] n zanahoria

carry ['kærı] vt (person) llevar; (transport) transportar; (involve: responsibilities etc) entrañar, implicar; (MED) ser portador de ♦ vi (sound) oírse; **to get carried away** (fig) entusiasmarse ► **carry on** vi (continue) seguir (adelante), continuar ♦ vt proseguir, continuar ► **carry out** vt (orders) cumplir; (investigation) llevar a cabo, realizar

cart [kɑ:t] n carro, carreta ♦ vt (inf: transport) acarrear

carton ['kɑ:tən] n (box) caja (de cartón); (of milk etc) bote m; (of yogurt) tarrina

cartoon [kɑ:'tu:n] n (PRESS) caricatura; (comic strip) tira cómica; (film) dibujos mpl animados

cartridge ['kɑːtrɪdʒ] n cartucho; (of pen) recambio

carve [kɑːv] vt (meat) trinchar; (wood, stone) cincelar, esculpir; (initials etc) grabar ❑ **carving** n (object) escultura; (design) talla; (art) tallado

car wash n lavado de coches

case [keɪs] n (container) caja; (MED) caso; (for jewels etc) estuche m; (LAW) causa, proceso; (BRIT: also: **suitcase**) maleta; **in ~ of** en caso de; **in any ~** en todo caso; **just in ~** por si acaso

cash [kæʃ] n dinero m en efectivo, dinero contante ♦ vt cobrar, hacer efectivo; **to pay (in) ~** pagar al contado; **~ on delivery** cóbrese al entregar ❑ **cashback** n (discount) devolución f; (at supermarket etc) retirada de dinero en efectivo de un establecimiento donde se ha pagado con tarjeta; también dinero retirado ❑ **cash card** n tarjeta f dinero ❑ **cash desk** (BRIT) n caja ❑ **cash dispenser** n cajero automático

cashew [kæˈʃuː] n (also: ~ **nut**) anacardo

cashier [kæˈʃɪə'] n cajero(-a)

cashmere ['kæʃmɪə'] n cachemira

cash point n cajero automático

cash register n caja

casino [kəˈsiːnəu] n casino

casket ['kɑːskɪt] n cofre m, estuche m; (US: coffin) ataúd m

casserole ['kæsərəul] n (food, pot) cazuela

cassette [kæˈset] n casete f ❑ **cassette player, cassette recorder** n casete m

cast [kɑːst] (pt, pp ~) vt (throw) echar, arrojar, lanzar; (glance, eyes) dirigir; (THEATRE) to ~ **sb as Othello** dar a algn el papel de Otelo ♦ vi (FISHING) lanzar ♦ n (THEATRE) reparto; (also: **plaster ~**) vaciado; **to ~ one's vote** votar; **to ~ doubt on** suscitar dudas acerca de ▸ **cast off** vi (NAUT) desamarrar; (KNITTING) cerrar (los puntos)

castanets [kæstəˈnets] npl castañuelas fpl

caster sugar ['kɑːstə'-] (BRIT) n azúcar m extrafino

Castile [kæsˈtiːl] n Castilla ❑ **Castilian** adj, n castellano(-a) m/f

cast-iron ['kɑːstaɪən] adj (lit) (hecho de hierro fundido; (fig: case) irrebatible

castle ['kɑːsl] n castillo; (CHESS) torre f

casual ['kæʒjul] adj fortuito; (irregular: work etc) eventual, temporero; (unconcerned) despreocupado; (clothes) informal

⚠ Be careful not to translate **casual** by the Spanish word casual.

casualty ['kæʒjultɪ] n víctima, herido; (dead) muerto; (MED: department) urgencias fpl

cat [kæt] n gato; (big cat) felino

Catalan ['kætəlæn] adj, n catalán(-ana) m/f

catalogue ['kætəlɔg] (US **catalog**) n catálogo ♦ vt catalogar

Catalonia [kætəˈləuniə] n Cataluña

catalytic converter [kætəˈlɪtɪkkən'vɜːtə'] n catalizador m

cataract ['kætərækt] n (MED) cataratas fpl

catarrh [kəˈtɑː'] n catarro

catastrophe [kəˈtæstrəfɪ] n catástrofe f

catch [kætʃ] (pt, pp **caught**) vt coger (SP), agarrar (LAm); (arrest) detener; (grasp) asir; (breath) contener; (surprise: person) sorprender; (attract: attention) captar; (hear) oir; (MED) contagiarse de, coger; (also: ~ **up**) alcanzar ♦ vi (fire) encenderse; (in branches etc) enredarse ♦ n (fish etc) pesca; (act of catching) cogida; (hidden problem) dificultad f; (game) pilla-pilla; (of lock) pestillo, cerradura; **to ~ fire** encenderse; **to ~ sight of** divisar ▸ **catch up** vi (fig) ponerse al día ❑ **catching** ['kætʃɪŋ] adj (MED) contagioso

category ['kætɪgərɪ] n categoría, clase f

cater ['keɪtəʳ] vi: **to ~ for** (BRIT) abastecer a; (needs) atender a; (COMM: parties etc) proveer comida a

caterpillar ['kætəpɪləʳ] n oruga, gusano

cathedral [kə'θiːdrəl] n catedral f

Catholic ['kæθəlɪk] adj, n (REL) católico(-a) m/f

Catseye® ['kæts'aɪ] (BRIT) n (AUT) catafoto

cattle ['kætl] npl ganado

catwalk ['kætwɔːk] n pasarela

caught [kɔːt] pt, pp of **catch**

cauliflower ['kɔlɪflaʊəʳ] n coliflor f

cause [kɔːz] n causa, motivo, razón f; (principle: also POL) causa ♦ vt causar

caution ['kɔːʃən] n cautela, prudencia; (warning) advertencia, amonestación f ♦ vt amonestar □ **cautious** adj cauteloso, prudente, precavido

cave [keɪv] n cueva, caverna ♦ **cave in** vi (roof etc) derrumbarse, hundirse

caviar(e) ['kævɪɑːʳ] n caviar m

cavity ['kævɪtɪ] n hueco, cavidad f

cc abbr (= cubic centimetres) c.c.; (= carbon copy) copia hecha con papel del carbón

CCTV n abbr (= closed-circuit television) circuito cerrado de televisión

CD n abbr (= compact disc) DC m; (player) (reproductor m de) disco compacto □ **CD player** n reproductor m de discos compactos □ **CD-ROM** [siːdiːˈrɔm] n abbr CD-ROM m

cease [siːs] vt, vi cesar □ **ceasefire** n alto m el fuego

cedar ['siːdəʳ] n cedro

ceilidh ['keɪlɪ] n baile con música y danzas tradicionales escocesas o irlandesas

ceiling ['siːlɪŋ] n techo; (fig) límite m

celebrate ['sɛlɪbreɪt] vt celebrar ♦ vi divertirse □ **celebration** [-'breɪʃən] n fiesta, celebración f

celebrity [sɪ'lɛbrɪtɪ] n celebridad f

celery ['sɛlərɪ] n apio

cell [sɛl] n celda; (BIOL) célula; (ELEC) elemento

cellar ['sɛləʳ] n sótano; (for wine) bodega

cello ['tʃɛləʊ] n violoncelo

Cellophane® ['sɛləfeɪn] n celofán m

cellphone ['sɛlfəʊn] n teléfono celular

Celsius ['sɛlsɪəs] adj centígrado

Celtic ['kɛltɪk] adj celta

cement [sə'mɛnt] n cemento

cemetery ['sɛmɪtrɪ] n cementerio

censor ['sɛnsəʳ] n censor m ♦ vt (cut) censurar □ **censorship** n censura

census ['sɛnsəs] n censo

cent [sɛnt] n (unit of dollar) centavo, céntimo; (unit of euro) céntimo; see also **per**

centenary [sɛn'tiːnərɪ] n centenario

centennial [sɛn'tɛnɪəl] (US) n centenario

center ['sɛntəʳ] (US) = **centre**

centi... [sɛntɪ] prefix: **centigrade** adj centígrado □ **centimetre** (US **centimeter**) n centímetro □ **centipede** ['sɛntɪpiːd] n ciempiés m inv

central ['sɛntrəl] adj central; (of house etc) céntrico □ **Central America** n Centroamérica □ **central heating** n calefacción f central □ **central reservation** n (BRIT AUT) mediana

centre ['sɛntəʳ] (US **center**) n centro; (fig) núcleo ♦ vt centrar □ **centreforward** n (SPORT) delantero centro □ **centre-half** n (SPORT) medio centro

century ['sɛntjʊrɪ] n siglo; **20th ~** siglo veinte

CEO n abbr = **chief executive officer**

ceramic [sɪ'ræmɪk] adj cerámico

cereal ['siːrɪəl] n cereal m

ceremony ['sɛrɪmənɪ] n ceremonia; **to stand on ~** hacer ceremonias, estar de cumplido

certain ['sɜːtən] adj seguro; (person): a
~ **Mr Smith** un tal Sr Smith; (particular,
some) cierto; **for ~** a ciencia cierta
□ **certainly** adv (undoubtedly)
ciertamente; (of course) desde luego,
por supuesto □ **certainty** n certeza,
certidumbre f, seguridad f;
(inevitability) certeza

certificate [sə'tɪfɪkt] n certificado

certify ['sɜːtɪfaɪ] vt certificar; (award
diploma to) conceder un diploma a;
(declare insane) declarar loco

cf. abbr (= compare) cfr

CFC n abbr (= chlorofluorocarbon) CFC m

chain [tʃeɪn] n cadena; (of mountains)
cordillera; (of events) sucesión f ♦ vt
(also: ~ **up**) encadenar □ **chain-
smoke** vi fumar un cigarrillo tras otro

chair [tʃeə] n silla; (armchair) sillón m,
butaca; (of university) cátedra; (of
meeting etc) presidencia ♦ vt (meeting)
presidir □ **chairlift** n telesilla
□ **chairman** (irreg) n presidente m
□ **chairperson** n presidente(-a) m/f
□ **chairwoman** (irreg) n presidenta

chalet ['ʃæleɪ] n chalet m (de madera)

chalk [tʃɔːk] n (GEO) creta; (for writing)
tiza, gis m (MEX) □ **chalkboard** (US) n
pizarrón (LAm), pizarra (SP)

challenge ['tʃælɪndʒ] n desafío, reto
♦ vt desafiar, retar; (statement, right)
poner en duda; **to ~ sb to do sth** retar
a algn a que haga algo
□ **challenging** adj exigente; (tone) de
desafío

chamber ['tʃeɪmbə] n cámara, sala;
(POL) cámara; (BRIT LAW: gen pl)
despacho; **~ of commerce** cámara de
comercio □ **chambermaid** n
camarera

champagne [ʃæm'peɪn] n champaña
m, champán m

champion ['tʃæmpɪən] n
campeón(-ona) m/f; (of cause)
defensor(a) m/f □ **championship** n
campeonato

chance [tʃɑːns] n (opportunity) ocasión
f, oportunidad f; (likelihood)
posibilidad f; (risk) riesgo ♦ vt arriesgar,
probar ♦ adj fortuito, casual; **to ~ it**
arriesgarse, intentarlo; **to take a ~**
arriesgarse; **by ~** por casualidad

chancellor ['tʃɑːnsələ] n canciller m
□ **Chancellor of the Exchequer**
(BRIT) n Ministro de Hacienda

chandelier [ʃændə'lɪə] n araña (de
luces)

change [tʃeɪndʒ] vt cambiar; (replace)
cambiar, reemplazar; (gear, clothes,
job) cambiar de; (transform)
transformar ♦ vi cambiar(se); (change
trains) hacer transbordo; (traffic lights)
cambiar de color; (be transformed): **to ~
into** transformarse en ♦ n cambio;
(alteration) modificación f;
(transformation) transformación f; (of
clothes) muda; (coins) suelto, sencillo;
(money returned) vuelta; **to ~ gear** (AUT)
cambiar de marcha; **to ~ one's mind**
cambiar de opinión o idea; **for a ~**
para variar ♦ **change over** vi (from sth
to sth) cambiar; (players etc)
cambiar(se) □ **changeable** adj (weather)
cambiable □ **change machine** n
máquina de cambio □ **changing
room** (BRIT) n vestuario

channel ['tʃænl] n (TV) canal m; (of river)
cauce m; (groove) ranura; (fig:
medium) medio ♦ vt (river etc)
encauzar; **the (English) C~** el Canal de
la Mancha; **the C~ Islands** las Islas
Normandas □ **Channel Tunnel** n: **the
Channel Tunnel** el túnel del Canal de
la Mancha, el Eurotúnel

chant [tʃɑːnt] n (of crowd) gritos mpl;
(REL) canto ♦ vt (slogan, word) repetir a
gritos

chaos ['keɪɔs] n caos m

chaotic [keɪ'ɔtɪk] adj caótico

chap [tʃæp] (BRIT: inf) n (man) tío, tipo

chapel ['tʃæpəl] n capilla

chapped [tʃæpt] adj agrietado

chapter ['tʃæptə] n capítulo

character ['kærɪktə] n carácter m, naturaleza, índole f; (moral strength, personality) carácter; (in novel, film) personaje m ❑ **characteristic** [-'rɪstɪk] adj característico ♦ n característica ❑ **characterize** ['kærɪktəraɪz] vt caracterizar

charcoal ['tʃɑːkəʊl] n carbón m vegetal; (ART) carboncillo

charge [tʃɑːdʒ] n (LAW) cargo, acusación f; (cost) precio, coste m; (responsibility) cargo ♦ vt (LAW): **to ~ (with)** acusar (de); (battery) cargar; (price) pedir; (customer) cobrar ♦ vi precipitarse; (MIL) cargar, atacar ❑ **charge card** n tarjeta de cuenta ❑ **charger** n (also: **battery charger**) cargador m (de baterías)

charisma [kə'rɪzmə] n carisma m ❑ **charismatic** [kærɪz'mætɪk] adj carismático

charity ['tʃærɪtɪ] n caridad f; (organization) sociedad f benéfica; (money, gifts) limosnas fpl ❑ **charity shop** n (BRIT) tienda de artículos de segunda mano que dedica su recaudación a causas benéficas

charm [tʃɑːm] n encanto, atractivo; (talisman) hechizo; (on bracelet) dije m ♦ vt encantar ❑ **charming** adj encantador(a)

chart [tʃɑːt] n (diagram) cuadro; (graph) gráfica; (map) carta de navegación ♦ vt (course) trazar; (progress) seguir; **charts** npl (Top 40): **the charts** = los 40 principales (SP)

charter ['tʃɑːtə'] vt (plane) alquilar; (ship) fletar ♦ n (document) carta; (of university, company) estatutos mpl ❑ **chartered accountant** (BRIT) n contable m/f diplomado(-a) ❑ **charter flight** n charter m

chase [tʃeɪs] vt (pursue) perseguir; (also: **~ away**) ahuyentar ♦ n persecución f

chat [tʃæt] vi (also: **have a ~**) charlar ♦ n charla ▶ **chat up** vt (inf: girl) ligar con, enrollarse con ❑ **chat room** n (INTERNET) chat m, canal m de charla ❑ **chat show** (BRIT) n programa m de entrevistas

chatter ['tʃætə'] vi (person) charlar; (teeth) castañetear ♦ n (of birds) parloteo; (of people) charla, cháchara

chauffeur ['ʃəʊfə] n chófer m

chauvinist ['ʃəʊvɪnɪst] n (male chauvinist) machista m; (nationalist) chovinista mf

cheap [tʃiːp] adj barato; (joke) de mal gusto; (poor quality) de mala calidad ♦ adv barato ❑ **cheap day return** n billete de ida y vuelta el mismo día ❑ **cheaply** adv barato, a bajo precio

cheat [tʃiːt] vi hacer trampa ♦ vt: **to ~ sb (out of sth)** estafar (algo) a algn ♦ n (person) tramposo(-a) ▶ **cheat on** vt fus engañar

Chechnya [tʃɪtʃ'njɑː] n Chechenia

check [tʃek] vt (examine) controlar; (facts) comprobar; (halt) parar, detener; (restrain) refrenar, restringir ♦ n (inspection) control m, inspección f; (curb) freno; (US: bill) nota, cuenta; (US) = **cheque**; (pattern: gen pl) cuadro ▶ **check in** vi (at hotel) firmar el registro; (at airport) facturar el equipaje ♦ vt (luggage) facturar ▶ **check off** vt (esp US: tick) comprobar; (cross off) tachar ▶ **check out** vi (of hotel) marcharse ▶ **check up** vi: **to check up on sth** comprobar algo; **to check up on sb** investigar a algn ❑ **checkbook** (US) = **chequebook** ❑ **checked** adj a cuadros ❑ **checkers** (US) n juego de damas ❑ **check-in** n (also: **check-in desk**: at airport) mostrador m de facturación ❑ **checking account** (US) n cuenta corriente ❑ **checklist** n lista (de control) ❑ **checkmate** n jaque m mate ❑ **checkout** n caja ❑ **checkpoint** n (punto de) control m ❑ **checkroom** (US) n consigna ❑ **checkup** n (MED) reconocimiento general

cheddar ['tʃedə'] n (also: ~ **cheese**) queso m cheddar

cheek [tʃiːk] n mejilla; (impudence) descaro; **what a ~!** ¡qué cara! □ **cheekbone** n pómulo □ **cheeky** adj fresco, descarado

cheer [tʃiə'] vt vitorear, aplaudir; (gladden) alegrar, animar ♦ vi dar vivas ♦ n viva m □ **cheer up** vi animarse ♦ vt alegrar, animar □ **cheerful** adj alegre

cheerio ['tʃiəriˈəʊ] excl ¡hasta luego!

cheerleader ['tʃiəliːdə'] n animador(a) m/f

cheese [tʃiːz] n queso □ **cheeseburger** n hamburguesa con queso □ **cheesecake** n pastel de queso

chef [ʃef] n jefe(-a) m/f de cocina

chemical ['kemɪkəl] adj químico ♦ n producto químico

chemist ['kemɪst] n (BRIT: pharmacist) farmacéutico(-a); (scientist) químico(-a) m/f □ **chemistry** n química □ **chemist's (shop)** n (BRIT) farmacia

cheque [tʃek] (US **check**) n cheque m □ **chequebook** n talonario de cheques (SP), chequera (LAm) □ **cheque card** n tarjeta de cheque

cherry ['tʃerɪ] n cereza; (also: ~ **tree**) cerezo

chess [tʃes] n ajedrez m

chest [tʃest] n (ANAT) pecho; (box) cofre m, cajón m

chestnut ['tʃesnʌt] n castaña; (also: ~ **tree**) castaño

chest of drawers n cómoda

chew [tʃuː] vt mascar, masticar □ **chewing gum** n chicle m

chic [ʃiːk] adj elegante

chick [tʃɪk] n pollito, polluelo; (inf: girl) chica

chicken ['tʃɪkɪn] n gallina, pollo; (food) pollo; (inf: coward) gallina m/f ► **chicken out** (inf) vi rajarse □ **chickenpox** n varicela

chickpea ['tʃɪkpiː] n garbanzo

chief [tʃiːf] n jefe(-a) m/f ♦ adj principal □ **chief executive (officer)** n director(a) m/f general □ **chiefly** adv principalmente

child [tʃaɪld] n (pl **children**) niño(-a); (offspring) hijo(-a) □ **child abuse** n (with violence) malos tratos mpl a niños; (sexual) abuso m sexual de niños □ **child benefit** n (BRIT) subsidio por cada hijo pequeño □ **childbirth** n parto □ **child-care** n cuidado de los niños □ **childhood** n niñez f, infancia □ **childish** adj pueril, aniñado □ **child minder** n (BRIT) madre f de día □ **children** ['tʃɪldrən] npl of **child**

Chile ['tʃɪlɪ] n Chile m □ **Chilean** adj, n chileno(-a) m/f

chill [tʃɪl] n frío; (MED) resfriado ♦ vt enfriar; (CULIN) congelar ► **chill out** vi (esp US: inf) tranquilizarse

chil(l)i ['tʃɪlɪ] n (BRIT) n chile m, ají m (SC)

chilly [tʃɪlɪ] adj frío

chimney ['tʃɪmnɪ] n chimenea

chimpanzee [tʃɪmpænˈziː] n chimpancé m

chin [tʃɪn] n mentón m, barbilla

China ['tʃaɪnə] n China

china ['tʃaɪnə] n porcelana; (crockery) loza

Chinese [tʃaɪˈniːz] adj chino ♦ n inv chino(-a) m/f; (LING) chino

chip [tʃɪp] n (gen pl: CULIN: BRIT) patata (SP) or papa (LAm) frita; (: US: also: **potato** ~) patata or papa frita; (of wood) astilla; (of glass, stone) lasca; (at poker) ficha; (COMPUT) chip m ♦ vt (cup, plate) desconchar □ **chip shop** n pescadería (donde se vende principalmente pescado rebozado y patatas fritas)

chiropodist [kɪˈrɒpədɪst] n (BRIT) pedicuro(-a), callista m/f

chisel ['tʃɪzl] n (for wood) escoplo; (for stone) cincel m

chives [tʃaɪvz] npl cebollinos mpl

chlorine [ˈklɔːriːn] n cloro

choc-ice [ˈtʃɒkaɪs] n (BRIT) helado m cubierto de chocolate

chocolate [ˈtʃɒklɪt] n chocolate m; (sweet) bombón m

choice [tʃɔɪs] n elección f, selección f; (option) opción f; (preference) preferencia f ♦ adj escogido

choir [ˈkwaɪə*] n coro

choke [tʃəʊk] vi ahogarse; (on food) atragantarse ♦ vt estrangular, ahogar; (block): **to be choked with** estar atascado de ♦ n (AUT) estárter m

cholesterol [kəˈlestərɒl] n colesterol m

choose [tʃuːz] (pt chose, pp chosen) vt escoger, elegir; (team) seleccionar; **to ~ to do sth** optar por hacer algo

chop [tʃɒp] vt (wood) cortar, tajar; (CULIN: also: **~ up**) picar ♦ n (CULIN) chuleta ▶ **chop down** vt (tree) talar ▶ **chop off** vt cortar (de un tajo) ❑ **chopsticks** [ˈtʃɒpstɪks] npl palillos mpl

chord [kɔːd] n (MUS) acorde m

chore [tʃɔː*] n faena, tarea; (routine task) trabajo rutinario

chorus [ˈkɔːrəs] n coro; (repeated part of song) estribillo

chose [tʃəʊz] pt of **choose**

chosen [ˈtʃəʊzn] pp of **choose**

Christ [kraɪst] n Cristo

christen [ˈkrɪsn] vt bautizar ❑ **christening** n bautizo

Christian [ˈkrɪstɪən] adj, n cristiano(-a) m/f ❑ **Christianity** [-ˈænɪtɪ] n cristianismo ❑ **Christian name** n nombre m de pila

Christmas [ˈkrɪsməs] n Navidad f; **Merry ~!** ¡Felices Pascuas! ❑ **Christmas card** n crismas m inv, tarjeta de Navidad ❑ **Christmas carol** n villancico m ❑ **Christmas Day** n día m de Navidad ❑ **Christmas Eve** n Nochebuena ❑ **Christmas pudding** n (esp BRIT) pudín m de

Navidad ❑ **Christmas tree** n árbol m de Navidad

chrome [krəʊm] n cromo

chronic [ˈkrɒnɪk] adj crónico

chrysanthemum [krɪˈsænθəməm] n crisantemo

chubby [ˈtʃʌbɪ] adj regordete

chuck [tʃʌk] (inf) vt lanzar, arrojar; (BRIT: also: **~ up**) abandonar ▶ **chuck out** vt (person) echar (fuera); (rubbish etc) tirar

chuckle [ˈtʃʌkl] vi reírse entre dientes

chum [tʃʌm] n compañero(-a)

chunk [tʃʌŋk] n pedazo, trozo

church [tʃəːtʃ] n iglesia ❑ **churchyard** n cementerio

churn [tʃəːn] n (for butter) mantequera; (for milk) lechera

chute [ʃuːt] n (also: **rubbish ~**) vertedero; (for coal etc) rampa de caída

chutney [ˈtʃʌtnɪ] n condimento a base de frutas de la India

CIA (US) n abbr (= Central Intelligence Agency) CIA f

CID (BRIT) n abbr (= Criminal Investigation Department) = B.I.C. f (SP)

cider [ˈsaɪdə*] n sidra

cigar [sɪˈgɑː*] n puro

cigarette [sɪgəˈret] n cigarrillo ❑ **cigarette lighter** n mechero

cinema [ˈsɪnəmə] n cine m

cinnamon [ˈsɪnəmən] n canela

circle [ˈsəːkl] n círculo; (in theatre) anfiteatro ♦ vi dar vueltas ♦ vt (surround) rodear, cercar; (move round) dar la vuelta a

circuit [ˈsəːkɪt] n circuito; (tour) gira; (track) pista; (lap) vuelta

circular [ˈsəːkjʊlə*] adj circular ♦ n circular f

circulate [ˈsəːkjʊleɪt] vi circular; (person: at party etc) hablar con los invitados ♦ vt poner en circulación ❑ **circulation** [-ˈleɪʃən] n circulación f; (of newspaper) tirada

circumstances [ˈsəːkəmstənsɪz] npl circunstancias fpl; (financial condition) situación f económica

circus [ˈsəːkəs] n circo m

cite [saɪt] vt citar

citizen [ˈsɪtɪzn] n (POL) ciudadano(-a); (of city) vecino(-a), habitante mf ❑ **citizenship** n ciudadanía

citrus fruits [ˈsɪtrəs-] npl agrios mpl

city [ˈsɪtɪ] n ciudad f; the **C~** centro financiero de Londres ❑ **city centre** (BRIT) n centro de la ciudad ❑ **city technology college** n centro de formación profesional (centro de enseñanza secundaria que da especial importancia a la ciencia y tecnología.)

civic [ˈsɪvɪk] adj cívico; (authorities) municipal

civil [ˈsɪvl] adj civil; (polite) atento, cortés ❑ **civilian** [sɪˈvɪlɪən] adj civil (no militar) ♦ n civil mf, paisano(-a)

civilization [sɪvɪlaɪˈzeɪʃən] n civilización f

civilized [ˈsɪvɪlaɪzd] adj civilizado

civil: civil law n derecho civil ❑ **civil rights** npl derechos mpl civiles ❑ **civil servant** n funcionario(-a) del Estado ❑ **Civil Service** n administración f pública ❑ **civil war** n guerra civil

CJD n abbr (= Creutzfeldt-Jakob disease) enfermedad f de Creutzfeldt-Jakob

claim [kleɪm] vt exigir, reclamar; (rights etc) reivindicar; (assert) pretender ♦ vi (for insurance) reclamar ♦ n reclamación f; pretensión f ❑ **claim form** n solicitud f

clam [klæm] n almeja

clamp [klæmp] n abrazadera, grapa ♦ vt (two things together) cerrar fuertemente; (one thing on another) afianzar (m con abrazadera); (AUT: wheel) poner el cepo a

clan [klæn] n clan m

clap [klæp] vi aplaudir

claret [ˈklærət] n burdeos m inv

clarify [ˈklærɪfaɪ] vt aclarar

clarinet [klærɪˈnet] n clarinete m

clarity [ˈklærɪtɪ] n claridad f

clash [klæʃ] n enfrentamiento; choque m; desacuerdo; estruendo ♦ vi (fight) enfrentarse; (beliefs) chocar; (disagree) estar en desacuerdo; (colours) desentonar; (two events) coincidir

clasp [klɑːsp] n (hold) apretón m; (of necklace, bag) cierre m ♦ vt apretar; abrazar

class [klɑːs] n clase f ♦ vt clasificar

classic [ˈklæsɪk] adj, n clásico ❑ **classical** adj clásico

classification [klæsɪfɪˈkeɪʃən] n clasificación f

classify [ˈklæsɪfaɪ] vt clasificar

classmate [ˈklɑːsmeɪt] n compañero(-a) de clase

classroom [ˈklɑːsrum] n aula

classy [ˈklɑːsɪ] adj (inf) elegante, con estilo

clatter [ˈklætə*] n estrépito ♦ vi hacer ruido or estrépito

clause [klɔːz] n cláusula; (LING) oración f

claustrophobic [klɔːstrəˈfəubɪk] adj claustrofóbico; **I feel ~** me entra claustrofobia

claw [klɔː] n (of cat) uña; (of bird of prey) garra; (of lobster) pinza

clay [kleɪ] n arcilla

clean [kliːn] adj limpio; (record, reputation) bueno, intachable; (joke) decente ♦ vt limpiar; (hands etc) lavar ▶ **clean up** vt limpiar, asear ❑ **cleaner** n (person) asistenta; (substance) producto para la limpieza ❑ **cleaner's** n tintorería ❑ **cleaning** n limpieza

cleanser [ˈklenzə*] n (for face) crema limpiadora

clear [klɪə*] adj claro; (road, way) libre; (conscience) limpio, tranquilo; (skin) terso; (sky) despejado ♦ vt (space) despejar, limpiar; (LAW: suspect) absolver; (obstacle) salvar, saltar por encima de; (cheque) aceptar ♦ vi (fog) *etc)* despejarse ♦ *adv*: **~ of** a distancia de; **to ~ the table** recoger or levantar la mesa ► **clear away** *vt (things, clothes etc)* retirar; *(dishes)* quitar (de en medio); *(dishes)* retirar ► **clear up** *vt* limpiar; *(mystery)* aclarar, resolver □ **clearance** *n (removal)* despeje *m*; *(permission)* acreditación *f* □ **clear-cut** *adj* bien definido, nítido □ **clearing** *n (in wood)* claro *m* □ **clearly** *adv* claramente; *(evidently)* sin duda □ **clearway** *(BRIT)* *n* carretera donde no se puede parar

clench [klɛntʃ] *vt* apretar, cerrar

clergy ['klɜːdʒɪ] *n* clero

clerk [klɑːk, *(US)* klɜːrk] *n (BRIT)* oficinista *mf*; *(US)* dependiente(-a) *m/f*

clever ['klɛvəʳ] *adj (intelligent)* inteligente, listo; *(skilful)* hábil; *(device, arrangement)* ingenioso

cliché ['kliːʃeɪ] *n* cliché *m*, frase *f* hecha

click [klɪk] *vt (tongue)* chasquear; *(heels)* taconear ♦ *vi (COMPUT)* hacer clic; **to ~ on an icon** hacer clic en un icono

client ['klaɪənt] *n* cliente *m/f*

cliff [klɪf] *n* acantilado

climate ['klaɪmɪt] *n* clima *m*

climax ['klaɪmæks] *n (of battle, career)* apogeo; *(of film, book)* punto culminante; *(sexual)* orgasmo

climb [klaɪm] *vi* subir; *(plant)* trepar; *(move with effort)*: **to ~ over a wall/into a car** trepar a una tapia/subir a un coche ♦ *vt (stairs)* subir; *(tree)* trepar a; *(mountain)* escalar ♦ *n* subida ► **climb down** *vi (fig)* volverse atrás □ **climber** *n* alpinista *mf (SP, MEX)*, andinista *mf (LAm)* □ **climbing** *n* alpinismo *(SP, MEX)*, andinismo *(LAm)*

clinch [klɪntʃ] *vt (deal)* cerrar; *(argument)* remachar

cling [klɪŋ] *(pt, pp* clung) *vi*: **to ~ to** agarrarse a; *(clothes)* pegarse a

Clingfilm® ['klɪŋfɪlm] *n* plástico adherente

clinic ['klɪnɪk] *n* clínica

clip [klɪp] *n (for hair)* horquilla; *(also:* **paper ~)** sujetapapeles *m inv*, clip *m*; *(TV, CINEMA)* fragmento ♦ *vt (cut)* cortar; *(also:* **~ together)** unir □ **clipping** *n (newspaper)* recorte *m*

cloak [kləʊk] *n* capa, manto ♦ *vt (fig)* encubrir, disimular □ **cloakroom** *n* guardarropa; *(BRIT: WC)* lavabo *(SP)*, aseos *mpl (SP)*, baño *(LAm)*

clock [klɔk] *n* reloj *m* ► **clock in** or **on** *vi (with card)* fichar, picar; *(start work)* entrar a trabajar ► **clock off** or **out** *vi (with card)* fichar or picar la salida; *(leave work)* salir del trabajo □ **clockwise** *adv* en el sentido de las agujas del reloj □ **clockwork** *n* aparato de relojería ♦ *adj (toy)* de cuerda

clog [klɔg] *n* zueco, chanclo ♦ *vt* atascar ♦ *vi (also:* **~ up)** atascarse

clone [kləʊn] *n* clon *m* ♦ *vt* clonar

close¹ [kləʊs] *adj (near):* **~ (to)** cerca (de); *(friend)* íntimo; *(connection)* estrecho; *(examination)* detallado, minucioso; *(weather)* bochornoso ♦ *adv* cerca; **~ by, ~ at hand** muy cerca; **to have a ~ shave** *(fig)* escaparse por un pelo

close² [kləʊz] *vt (shut)* cerrar; *(end)* concluir, terminar ♦ *vi (shop etc)* cerrarse; *(end)* concluirse, terminarse ♦ *n (end)* fin *m*, final *m*, conclusión *f* ► **close down** *vi* cerrarse definitivamente □ **closed** *adj (shop etc)* cerrado

closely ['kləʊslɪ] *adv (study)* con detalle; *(watch)* de cerca; *(resemble)* estrechamente

closet ['klɔzɪt] *n* armario

close-up ['kləʊsʌp] *n* primer plano

closing time *n* hora de cierre

closure ['kləʊʒəʳ] *n* cierre *m*

clot [klɔt] *n (gen)* coágulo; *(inf: idiot)* imbécil *m/f* ♦ *vi (blood)* coagularse

cloth [klɔθ] *n (material)* tela, paño; *(rag)* trapo

clothes [kləʊðz] npl ropa ❑ **clothes line** n cuerda (para tender la ropa) ❑ **clothes peg** (US **clothes pin**) n pinza

clothing ['kləʊðɪŋ] n = **clothes**

cloud [klaʊd] n nube ♦ **cloud over** vi (also fig) nublarse ❑ **cloudy** adj nublado, nuboso; (liquid) turbio

clove [kləʊv] n clavo; **~ of garlic** diente m de ajo

clown [klaʊn] n payaso ♦ vi (also: **~ about, ~ around**) hacer el payaso

club [klʌb] n (society) club m; (weapon) porra, cachiporra; (also: **golf ~**) palo m ♦ vt aporrear ♦ vi: **to ~ together** (for gift) comprar entre todos; **clubs** npl (CARDS) tréboles mpl ❑ **club class** n (AVIAT) clase f preferente

clue [kluː] n pista; (in crosswords) indicación f; **I haven't a ~** no tengo ni idea

clump [klʌmp] n (of trees) grupo

clumsy ['klʌmzɪ] adj (person) torpe, desmañado; (tool) difícil de manejar; (movement) desgarbado

clung [klʌŋ] pt, pp of **cling**

cluster ['klʌstə*] n grupo ♦ vi agruparse, apiñarse

clutch [klʌtʃ] n (AUT) embrague m; (grasp): **clutches** garras fpl ♦ vt asir, agarrar

cm abbr (= centimetre) cm

Co. abbr = **county** = **company**

c/o abbr (= care of) c/a, a/c

coach [kəʊtʃ] n autocar m (SP), coche m de línea; (horse-drawn) coche m; (of train) vagón m, coche m; (SPORT) entrenador/a m/f, instructor/a m/f; (tutor) profesor/a m/f particular ♦ vt (SPORT) entrenar; (student) preparar, enseñar ❑ **coach station** n (BRIT) estación f de autobuses etc ❑ **coach trip** n excursión f en autocar

coal [kəʊl] n carbón m

coalition [kəʊə'lɪʃən] n coalición f

coarse [kɔːs] adj basto, burdo; (vulgar) grosero, ordinario

coast [kəʊst] n costa, litoral m ♦ vi (AUT) ir en punto muerto ❑ **coastal** adj costero, costanero ❑ **coastguard** n guardacostas m inv ❑ **coastline** n litoral m

coat [kəʊt] n abrigo; (of animal) pelaje m, lana; (of paint) mano f, capa ♦ vt cubrir, revestir ❑ **coat hanger** n percha (SP), gancho (LAm) ❑ **coating** n capa, baño

coax [kəʊks] vt engatusar

cob [kɔb] n see **corn**

cobbled ['kɔbld] adj: **~ street** calle f empedrada, calle f adoquinada

cobweb ['kɔbweb] n telaraña

cocaine [kə'keɪn] n cocaína

cock [kɔk] n (rooster) gallo; (male bird) macho ♦ vt (gun) amartillar ❑ **cockerel** n gallito

cockney ['kɔknɪ] n habitante m de ciertos barrios de Londres

cockpit ['kɔkpɪt] n cabina

cockroach ['kɔkrəʊtʃ] n cucaracha

cocktail ['kɔkteɪl] n cóctel m, cóctel m

cocoa ['kəʊkəʊ] n cacao; (drink) chocolate m

coconut ['kəʊkənʌt] n coco

cod [kɔd] n bacalao

C.O.D. abbr (= cash on delivery) C.A.E.

code [kəʊd] n código; (cipher) clave f; (dialling code) prefijo; (post code) código postal

coeducational [kəʊedju'keɪʃənl] adj mixto

coffee ['kɔfɪ] n café m ❑ **coffee bar** (BRIT) n cafetería ❑ **coffee bean** n grano de café ❑ **coffee break** n descanso (para tomar café) ❑ **coffee maker** n máquina de hacer café, cafetera ❑ **coffeepot** n cafetera ❑ **coffee shop** n café m ❑ **coffee table** n mesita (para servir el café)

coffin ['kɔfɪn] n ataúd m

cog [kɔg] n (wheel) rueda dentada; (tooth) diente m

cognac ['kɒnjæk] n coñac m

coherent [kəʊ'hɪərənt] adj coherente

coil [kɔɪl] n rollo; (ELEC) bobina, carrete m; (contraceptive) espiral f ♦ vt enrollar

coin [kɔɪn] n moneda ♦ vt (word) inventar, idear

coincide [kəʊɪn'saɪd] vi coincidir; (agree) estar de acuerdo ❑ **coincidence** [kəʊ'ɪnsɪdəns] n casualidad f

Coke® [kəʊk] n Coca-Cola®

coke [kəʊk] n (coal) coque m

colander ['kɒləndə] n colador m, escurridor m

cold [kəʊld] adj frío ♦ n frío; (MED) resfriado; **it's ~** hace frío; **to be ~** (person) tener frío; **to catch (a) ~** resfriarse; **in ~ blood** a sangre fría ❑ **cold sore** n herpes m pl or f pl

coleslaw ['kəʊlslɔː] n especie de ensalada de col

colic ['kɒlɪk] n cólico

collaborate [kə'læbəreɪt] vi colaborar

collapse [kə'læps] vi hundirse, derrumbarse; (MED) sufrir un colapso ♦ n hundimiento, derrumbamiento; (MED) colapso

collar ['kɒlə] n (of coat, shirt) cuello; (of dog etc) collar ❑ **collarbone** n clavícula

colleague ['kɒliːg] n colega mf; (at work) compañero(-a)

collect [kə'lekt] vt (litter, mail etc) recoger; (as a hobby) coleccionar; (BRIT: call and pick up) recoger; (debts, subscriptions etc) recaudar ♦ vi reunirse; (dust) acumularse; **to call ~** (US TEL) llamar a cobro revertido ❑ **collection** [kə'lekʃən] n colección f; (of mail, for charity) recogida ❑ **collective** [kə'lektɪv] adj colectivo ❑ **collector** n coleccionista mf

college ['kɒlɪdʒ] n colegio mayor; (of agriculture, technology) escuela universitaria

collide [kə'laɪd] vi chocar

collision [kə'lɪʒən] n choque m

cologne [kə'ləʊn] n (also: **eau de ~**) (agua de) colonia

Colombia [kə'lɒmbɪə] n Colombia ❑ **Colombian** adj, n colombiano(-a)

colon ['kəʊlən] n (sign) dos puntos; (MED) colon m

colonel ['kɜːnl] n coronel m

colonial [kə'ləʊnɪəl] adj colonial

colony ['kɒlənɪ] n colonia

colour etc ['kʌlə] (US color) n color m ♦ vt color(e)ar; (dye) teñir; (fig: account) adornar; (: judgement) distorsionar ♦ vi (blush) sonrojarse ▶ **colour in** vt colorear ❑ **colour-blind** adj daltónico ❑ **coloured** adj de color; (photo) en color ❑ **colour film** n película en color ❑ **colourful** adj lleno de color; (story) fantástico; (person) excéntrico ❑ **colouring** n (complexion) tez f; (in food) colorante m ❑ **colour television** n televisión f en color

column ['kɒləm] n columna

coma ['kəʊmə] n coma m

comb [kəʊm] n peine m; (ornamental) peineta ♦ vt (hair) peinar; (area) registrar a fondo

combat ['kɒmbæt] n combate m ♦ vt combatir

combination [kɒmbɪ'neɪʃən] n combinación f

combine [vb kəm'baɪn, n 'kɒmbaɪn] vt combinar; (qualities) reunir ♦ vi combinarse ♦ n (ECON) cartel m

come

KEYWORD

[kʌm] (pt **came**, pp **come**) vi

1 (movement towards) venir; **to come running** venir corriendo

2 (arrive) llegar; **he's come here to**

work ha venido aquí para trabajar; **to come home** volver a casa

3 (*reach*): **to come to** llegar a; **the bill came to £40** la cuenta ascendía a cuarenta libras

4 (*occur*): **an idea came to me** se me ocurrió una idea

5 (*be, become*): **to come loose/undone** *etc* aflojarse/desabrocharse/desatarse *etc*; **I've come to like him** por fin ha llegado a gustarme

► **come across** *vt fus* (*person*) topar con; (*thing*) dar con

► **come along** *vi* (*BRIT: progress*) ir

► **come back** *vi* (*return*) volver

► **come down** *vi* (*price*) bajar; (*tree, building*) ser derribado

► **come from** *vt fus* (*place, source*) ser de

► **come in** *vi* (*visitor*) entrar; (*train, report*) llegar; (*fashion*) ponerse de moda; (*on deal etc*) entrar

► **come off** *vi* (*button*) soltarse, desprenderse; (*attempt*) salir bien

► **come on** *vi* (*pupil*) progresar; (*work, project*) desarrollarse; (*lights*) encenderse; (*electricity*) volver; **come on!** ¡vamos!

► **come out** *vi* (*fact*) salir a la luz; (*book, sun*) salir; (*stain*) quitarse

► **come round** *vi* (*after faint, operation*) volver en sí

► **come to** *vi* (*wake*) volver en sí

► **come up** *vi* (*sun*) salir; (*problem*) surgir; (*event*) aproximarse; (*in conversation*) mencionarse

► **come up with** *vt fus* (*idea*) sugerir; (*money*) conseguir

comeback ['kʌmbæk] *n*: **to make a ~** (*THEATRE*) volver a las tablas

comedian [kə'miːdɪən] *n* humorista *mf*

comedy ['kɒmɪdɪ] *n* comedia *f*; (*humour*) comicidad *f*

comet ['kɒmɪt] *n* cometa *m*

comfort ['kʌmfət] *n* bienestar *m*; (*relief*) alivio ♦ *vt* consolar ☐ **comfortable** *adj* cómodo; (*financially*) acomodado; (*easy*) fácil ☐ **comfort station** (*US*) *n* servicios *mpl*

comic ['kɒmɪk] *adj* (*also*: **comical**) cómico ♦ *n* (*comedian*) cómico; (*BRIT: for children*) tebeo; (*BRIT: for adults*) comic *m* ☐ **comic book** (*US*) *n* libro *m* de cómics ☐ **comic strip** *n* tira cómica

comma ['kɒmə] *n* coma *f*

command [kə'mɑːnd] *n* orden *f*, mandato; (*MIL: authority*) mando; (*mastery*) dominio ♦ *vt* (*troops*) mandar; (*give orders to*): **to ~ sb to do** mandar o ordenar a algn hacer ☐ **commander** *n* (*MIL*) comandante *mf*, jefe(-a) *m/f*

commemorate [kə'meməreɪt] *vt* conmemorar

commence [kə'mens] *vt, vi* comenzar, empezar ☐ **commencement** (*US*) *n* (*UNIV*) (ceremonia de) graduación *f*

commend [kə'mend] *vt* elogiar, alabar; (*recommend*) recomendar

comment ['kɒment] *n* comentario ♦ *vi*: **to ~ on** hacer comentarios sobre; **"no ~"** (*written*) "sin comentarios"; (*spoken*) "no tengo nada que decir" ☐ **commentary** ['kɒməntərɪ] *n* comentario ☐ **commentator** ['kɒmənteɪtə] *n* comentarista *mf*

commerce ['kɒmɜːs] *n* comercio

commercial [kə'mɜːʃəl] *adj* comercial ♦ *n* (*TV, RADIO*) anuncio ☐ **commercial break** *n* intermedio para publicidad

commission [kə'mɪʃən] *n* (*committee, fee*) comisión *f*; (*work of art*) encargar; **out of ~** fuera de servicio ☐ **commissioner** *n* (*POLICE*) comisario de policía

commit [kə'mɪt] vt (act) cometer; (resources) dedicar; (to sb's care) entregar; **to ~ o.s. (to do)** comprometerse (a hacer); **to ~ suicide** suicidarse ❑ **commitment** n compromiso; (to ideology etc) entrega

committee [kə'mɪtɪ] n comité m

commodity [kə'mɒdɪtɪ] n mercancía

common ['kɒmən] adj común; (pej) ordinario ♦ n campo común ❑ **commonly** adv comúnmente ❑ **commonplace** adj de lo más común ❑ **Commons** (BRIT) npl (POL): **the Commons** (la Cámara de) los Comunes ❑ **common sense** n sentido común ❑ **Commonwealth** n: **the Commonwealth**

communal ['kɒmju:nl] adj (property) comunal; (kitchen) común

commune [n 'kɒmju:n, vb kə'mju:n] n (group) comuna ♦ vi: **to ~ with** comulgar o conversar con

communicate [kə'mju:nɪkeɪt] vt comunicar ♦ vi: **to ~ (with)** comunicarse (con); (in writing) estar en contacto (con)

communication [kəmju:nɪ'keɪʃən] n comunicación f

communion [kə'mju:nɪən] n (also: **Holy C~**) comunión f

communism ['kɒmjunɪzəm] n comunismo ❑ **communist** adj, n comunista mf

community [kə'mju:nɪtɪ] n comunidad f; (large group) colectividad f ❑ **community centre** (US **community center**) n centro social ❑ **community service** n trabajo m comunitario (prestado en lugar de cumplir una pena de prisión)

commute [kə'mju:t] vi viajar a diario de la casa al trabajo ♦ vt conmutar ❑ **commuter** n persona que viaja a diario de la casa al trabajo

compact [adj kəm'pækt, n 'kɒmpækt] adj compacto ♦ n (also: **powder ~**)

polvera ❑ **compact disc** n compact disc m ❑ **compact disc player** n reproductor m de disco compacto, compact disc m

companion [kəm'pænɪən] n compañero(-a)

company ['kʌmpənɪ] n compañía; (COMM) sociedad f, compañía; **to keep sb ~** acompañar a algn ❑ **company car** n coche m de la empresa ❑ **company director** n director(a) m/f de empresa

comparable ['kɒmpərəbl] adj comparable

comparative [kəm'pærətɪv] adj relativo; (study) comparativo ❑ **comparatively** adv (relatively) relativamente

compare [kəm'peə] vt: **to ~ sth/sb with** or **to** comparar algo/a algn con ♦ vi: **to ~ (with)** compararse (con) ❑ **comparison** [-'pærɪsn] n comparación f

compartment [kəm'pɑ:tmənt] n (also: RAIL) compartim(i)ento

compass ['kʌmpəs] n brújula; **compasses** npl (MATH) compás m

compassion [kəm'pæʃən] n compasión f

compatible [kəm'pætɪbl] adj compatible

compel [kəm'pel] vt obligar ❑ **compelling** adj (fig: argument) convincente

compensate ['kɒmpənseɪt] vt compensar ♦ vi: **to ~ for** compensar ❑ **compensation** [-'seɪʃən] n (for loss) indemnización f

compete [kəm'pi:t] vi (take part) tomar parte, concurrir; (vie with): **to ~ (with)** competir con, hacer competencia a

competent ['kɒmpɪtənt] adj competente, capaz

competition [kɒmpɪ'tɪʃən] n (contest) concurso; (rivalry) competencia

competitive [kəm'petɪtɪv] adj (ECON, SPORT) competitivo

competitor [kəm'petɪtə] n (rival) competidor(a) m/f; (participant) concursante mf

complacent [kəm'pleɪsənt] adj autocomplaciente

complain [kəm'pleɪn] vi quejarse; (COMM) reclamar □ **complaint** n queja; reclamación f; (MED) enfermedad f

complement [n 'kɒmplɪmənt, vb 'kɒmplɪment] n complemento; (esp of ship's crew) dotación f ♦ vt (enhance) complementar □ **complementary** [kɒmplɪ'mentərɪ] adj complementario

complete [kəm'pliːt] adj (full) completo; (finished) acabado ♦ vt (fulfil) completar; (finish) acabar; (a form) llenar □ **completely** adv completamente □ **completion** [-'pliːʃən] n terminación f; (of contract) realización f

complex ['kɒmpleks] adj, n complejo

complexion [kəm'plekʃən] n (of face) tez f, cutis m

compliance [kəm'plaɪəns] n (submission) sumisión f; (agreement) conformidad f; **in ~ with** de acuerdo con

complicate ['kɒmplɪkeɪt] vt complicar □ **complicated** adj complicado □ **complication** [-'keɪʃən] n complicación f

compliment [n 'kɒmplɪmənt] n (formal) cumplido ♦ vt felicitar □ **complimentary** [-'mentərɪ] adj lisonjero; (free) de favor

comply [kəm'plaɪ] vi: **to ~ with** cumplir con

component [kəm'pəʊnənt] adj componente ♦ n (TECH) pieza

compose [kəm'pəʊz] vt: **to be composed of** componerse de; (music etc) componer; **to ~ o.s.** tranquilizarse □ **composer** n (MUS) compositor(a) m/

f □ **composition** [kɒmpə'zɪʃən] n composición f

composure [kəm'pəʊʒə] n serenidad f, calma

compound ['kɒmpaund] n (CHEM) compuesto; (LING) palabra compuesta; (enclosure) recinto ♦ adj compuesto; (fracture) complicado

comprehension [-'henʃən] n comprensión f

comprehensive [kɒmprɪ'hensɪv] adj exhaustivo; (INSURANCE) contra todo riesgo □ **comprehensive (school)** n centro estatal de enseñanza secundaria, ≈ Instituto Nacional de Bachillerato (SP)

compress [vb kəm'pres, n 'kɒmpres] vt comprimir; (information) condensar ♦ n (MED) compresa

comprise [kəm'praɪz] vt (also: **be comprised of**) comprender, constar de; (constitute) constituir

compromise ['kɒmprəmaɪz] n (agreement) arreglo ♦ vt comprometer ♦ vi transigir

compulsive [kəm'pʌlsɪv] adj compulsivo; (viewing, reading) obligado

compulsory [kəm'pʌlsərɪ] adj obligatorio

computer [kəm'pjuːtə] n ordenador m, computador m, computadora f □ **computer game** n juego para ordenador □ **computer-generated** adj realizado por ordenador, creado por ordenador □ **computerize** vt (data) computerizar; (system) informatizar; **we're computerized now** ya nos hemos informatizado □ **computer programmer** n programador(a) m/f □ **computer programming** n programación f □ **computer science** n informática □ **computer studies** npl informática fsg, computación fsg (LAm) □ **computing** [kəm'pjuːtɪŋ] n (activity, science) informática

con [kɒn] vt (deceive) engañar; (cheat) estafar ♦ n estafa

conceal [kən'siːl] vt ocultar

concede [kən'siːd] vt (point, argument) reconocer; (territory) ceder; **to ~** (defeat) darse por vencido; **to ~ that** admitir que

conceited [kən'siːtɪd] adj presumido

conceive [kən'siːv] vt, vi concebir

concentrate ['kɒnsəntreɪt] vi concentrarse ♦ vt concentrar

concentration [kɒnsən'treɪʃən] concentración f

concept ['kɒnsept] n concepto

concern [kən'sɜːn] n (matter) asunto; (COMM) empresa; (anxiety) preocupación f ♦ vt (worry) preocupar; (involve) afectar; (relate to) tener que ver con; **to be concerned (about)** interesarse (por), preocuparse (por) ❑ **concerning** prep sobre, acerca de

concert ['kɒnsət] n concierto ❑ **concert hall** n sala de conciertos

concerto [kən'tʃɜːtəu] n concierto

concession [kən'seʃən] n concesión f; **tax ~** privilegio fiscal

concise [kən'saɪs] adj conciso

conclude [kən'kluːd] vt concluir; (treaty etc) firmar; (agreement) llegar a; (decide) llegar a la conclusión de ❑ **conclusion** [-'kluːʒən] n conclusión f; firma

concrete ['kɒnkriːt] n hormigón m ♦ adj de hormigón; (fig) concreto

concussion [kən'kʌʃən] n conmoción f cerebral

condemn [kən'dem] vt condenar; (building) declarar en ruina

condensation [kɒnden'seɪʃən] n condensación f

condense [kən'dens] vi condensarse ♦ vt condensar, abreviar

condition [kən'dɪʃən] n condición f, estado; (requirement) condición f ♦ vt condicionar; **on ~ that** a condición (de) que ❑ **conditional** [kən'dɪʃənəl] adj

condicional ❑ **conditioner** n suavizante

condo ['kɒndəu] (US) n (inf) = condominium

condom ['kɒndəm] n condón m

condominium [kɒndə'mɪnɪəm] (US) n (building) bloque m de pisos o apartamentos (propiedad de quienes lo habitan), condominio (LAm); (apartment) piso o apartamento (en propiedad), condominio (LAm)

condone [kən'dəun] vt condonar

conduct [n 'kɒndʌkt, vb kən'dʌkt] n conducta, comportamiento ♦ vt (lead) conducir; (manage) llevar a cabo, dirigir; (MUS) dirigir; **to ~ o.s.** comportarse ❑ **conducted tour** (BRIT) n visita acompañada ❑ **conductor** n (of orchestra) director m; (US: on train) revisor/a m/f; (on bus) cobrador m; (ELEC) conductor m

cone [kəun] n cono; (pine cone) piña; (on road) pivote m; (for ice-cream) cucurucho

confectionery [kən'fekʃənrɪ] n dulces mpl

confer [kən'fɜː] vt: **to ~ sth on** otorgar algo a ♦ vi conferenciar

conference ['kɒnfərns] n (meeting) reunión f; (convention) congreso

confess [kən'fes] vt confesar ♦ vi admitir ❑ **confession** [-'feʃən] n confesión f

confide [kən'faɪd] vi: **to ~ in** confiar en

confidence ['kɒnfɪdns] n (also: self-~) confianza; (secret) confidencia; **in ~** (speak, write) en confianza ❑ **confident** adj seguro de sí mismo; (certain) seguro ❑ **confidential** [kɒnfɪ'denʃəl] adj confidencial

confine [kən'faɪn] vt (limit) limitar; (shut up) encerrar ❑ **confined** adj (space) reducido

confirm [kən'fɜːm] vt confirmar ❑ **confirmation** [kɒnfə'meɪʃən] n confirmación f

confiscate ['kɒnfɪskeɪt] vt confiscar

conflict [n 'kɒnflɪkt, vb kən'flɪkt] n conflicto ♦ vi (opinions) chocar

conform [kən'fɔːm] vi conformarse; **to ~ to** ajustarse a

confront [kən'frʌnt] vt (problems) hacer frente a; (enemy, danger) enfrentarse con ♦ **confrontation** [kɒnfrən'teɪʃən] n enfrentamiento

confuse [kən'fjuːz] vt (perplex) aturdir, desconcertar; (mix up) confundir; (complicate) complicar ♦ **confused** adj confuso; (person) perplejo ♦ **confusing** adj confuso ♦ **confusion** [-ʒən] n confusión f

congestion [kən'dʒestʃən] n congestión f

congratulate [kən'grætjuleɪt] vt: **to ~ sb (on)** felicitar a algn (por) ♦ **congratulations** [-'leɪʃənz] npl felicitaciones fpl; **congratulations!** ¡enhorabuena!

congregation [-'geɪʃən] n (of a church) feligreses mpl

congress ['kɒŋgres] n congreso; (US): **C~** Congreso ♦ **congressman** (irreg: US) n miembro del Congreso ♦ **congresswoman** (irreg: US) n diputada, miembro f del Congreso

conifer ['kɒnɪfə*] n conifera

conjugate ['kɒndʒugeɪt] vt conjugar

conjugation [kɒndʒə'geɪʃən] n conjugación f

conjunction [kən'dʒʌŋkʃən] n conjunción f; **in ~ with** junto con

conjure ['kʌndʒə*] vi hacer juegos de manos

connect [kə'nekt] vt juntar, unir; (ELEC) conectar; (TEL: subscriber) poner; (: caller) poner al habla; (fig) relacionar, asociar ♦ vi: **to ~ with** (train) enlazar con; **to be connected with** (associated) estar relacionado con ♦ **connecting flight** n vuelo m de enlace ♦ **connection** [-ʃən] n juntura, unión f;

(ELEC) conexión f; (RAIL) enlace m; (TEL) comunicación f; (fig) relación f

conquer ['kɒŋkə*] vt (territory) conquistar; (enemy, feelings) vencer

conquest ['kɒŋkwest] n conquista

cons [kɒnz] npl see **convenience**; **pro**

conscience ['kɒnʃəns] n conciencia

conscientious [kɒnʃɪ'enʃəs] adj concienzudo; (objection) de conciencia

conscious ['kɒnʃəs] adj (deliberate) deliberado; (awake, aware) consciente ♦ **consciousness** n conciencia; (MED) conocimiento

consecutive [kən'sekjutɪv] adj consecutivo; **on 3 ~ occasions** en 3 ocasiones consecutivas

consensus [kən'sensəs] n consenso

consent [kən'sent] n consentimiento ♦ vi: **to ~ (to)** consentir (en)

consequence ['kɒnsɪkwəns] n consecuencia; (significance) importancia

consequently ['kɒnsɪkwəntlɪ] adv por consiguiente

conservation [kɒnsə'veɪʃən] n conservación f

conservative [kən'sə:vətɪv] adj conservador(a); (estimate etc) cauteloso ♦ **Conservative** (BRIT) adj, n (POL) conservador(a) m/f

conservatory [kən'sə:vətri] n invernadero; (MUS) conservatorio

consider [kən'sɪdə*] vt considerar; (take into account) tener en cuenta; (study) estudiar, examinar; **to ~ doing sth** pensar en (la posibilidad de) hacer algo ♦ **considerable** adj considerable ♦ **considerably** adv notablemente ♦ **considerate** adj considerado ♦ **consideration** [-'reɪʃən] n consideración f; (factor) factor m; **to give sth further consideration** estudiar algo más a fondo ♦ **considering** prep teniendo en cuenta

consignment [kən'saɪnmənt] n envío

consist [kən'sɪst] vi: **to ~ of** consistir en

consistency [kən'sɪstənsɪ] n (of argument etc) coherencia; consecuencia; (thickness) consistencia

consistent [kən'sɪstənt] adj (person) consecuente; (argument etc) coherente

consolation [kɔnsə'leɪʃən] n consuelo

console[1] [kən'səul] vt consolar

console[2] ['kɔnsəul] n consola

consonant ['kɔnsənənt] n consonante f

conspicuous [kən'spɪkjuəs] adj (visible) visible

conspiracy [kən'spɪrəsɪ] n conjura, complot m

constable ['kʌnstəbl] (BRIT) n policía mf; **chief ~** = jefe m de policía

constant ['kɔnstənt] adj constante □ **constantly** adv constantemente

constipated ['kɔnstɪpeɪtɪd] adj estreñido □ **constipation** [kɔnstɪ'peɪʃən] n estreñimiento

⚠ Be careful not to translate **constipated** by the Spanish word constipado.

constituency [kən'stɪtjuənsɪ] n (POL: area) distrito electoral; (: electors) electorado

constitute ['kɔnstɪtjuːt] vt constituir

constitution [kɔnstɪ'tjuːʃən] n constitución f

constraint [kən'streɪnt] n obligación f; (limit) restricción f

construct [kən'strʌkt] vt construir □ **construction** [-ʃən] n construcción f □ **constructive** adj constructivo

consul ['kɔnsl] n cónsul mf □ **consulate** ['kɔnsjulɪt] n consulado

consult [kən'sʌlt] vt consultar □ **consultant** (BRIT MED) especialista mf; (other specialist) asesor(a) m/f □ **consultation** [kɔnsəl'teɪʃən] n consulta □ **consulting room** (BRIT) n consultorio

consume [kən'sjuːm] vt (eat) comerse; (drink) beberse; (fire etc, COMM) consumir □ **consumer** n consumidor(a) m/f

consumption [kən'sʌmpʃən] n consumo

cont. abbr (= continued) sigue

contact ['kɔntækt] n contacto; (: pej) enchufe m ♦ vt ponerse en contacto con □ **contact lenses** npl lentes fpl de contacto

contagious [kən'teɪdʒəs] adj contagioso

contain [kən'teɪn] vt contener; **to ~ o.s.** contenerse □ **container** n recipiente m; (for shipping etc) contenedor m

contaminate [kən'tæmɪneɪt] vt contaminar

cont'd abbr (= continued) sigue

contemplate ['kɔntəmpleɪt] vt contemplar; (reflect upon) considerar

contemporary [kən'tempərərɪ] adj, n contemporáneo(-a) m/f

contempt [kən'tempt] n desprecio; **~ of court** (LAW) desacato a (los tribunales)

contend [kən'tend] vt (argue) afirmar ♦ vi: **to ~ with/for** luchar contra/por

content [adj, vb kən'tent, n 'kɔntent] adj (happy) contento; (satisfied) satisfecho ♦ vt contentar; satisfacer ♦ n contenido; **contents** npl contenido; **(table of) contents** índice m de materias □ **contented** adj contento; satisfecho

contest [n 'kɔntest, vb kən'test] n lucha; (competition) concurso ♦ vt (dispute) impugnar; (POL) presentarse como candidato(-a) m/f □ **contestant** [kən'testənt] n concursante mf; (in fight) contendiente mf

⚠ Be careful not to translate **contest** by the Spanish word contestar.

context ['kɔntekst] n contexto

continent ['kɒntɪnənt] n continente m; **the C~** (BRIT) el continente europeo ❏ **continental** [-'nɛntl] adj continental ❏ **continental breakfast** n desayuno estilo europeo ❏ **continental quilt** n edredón m

continual [kən'tɪnjuəl] adj continuo ❏ **continually** adv constantemente

continue [kən'tɪnjuː] vi, vt seguir, continuar

continuity [kɒntɪ'njuːtɪ] n (also CINE) continuidad f

continuous [kən'tɪnjuəs] adj continuo ❏ **continuous assessment** n (BRIT) evaluación f continua ❏ **continuously** adv continuamente

contour ['kɒntuə] n contorno; (also: ~ line) curva de nivel

contraception [kɒntrə'sɛpʃən] n contracepción f

contraceptive [kɒntrə'sɛptɪv] adj, n anticonceptivo

contract [n 'kɒntrækt, vb kən'trækt] n contrato ♦ vi (COMM): **to ~ to do sth** comprometerse por contrato a hacer algo; (become smaller) contraerse, encogerse ♦ vt contraer ❏ **contractor** n contratista mf

contradict [kɒntrə'dɪkt] vt contradecir ❏ **contradiction** [-ʃən] n contradicción f

contrary¹ ['kɒntrərɪ] adj contrario ♦ n lo contrario; **on the ~** al contrario; **unless you hear to the ~** a no ser que le digan lo contrario

contrary² [kən'trɛərɪ] adj (perverse) terco

contrast [n 'kɒntrɑːst, vt kən'trɑːst] n contraste m ♦ vt comparar; **in ~ to** en contraste con

contribute [kən'trɪbjuːt] vi contribuir ♦ vt: **to ~ £10/an article to** contribuir con 10 libras/un artículo a; **to ~ to** (charity) donar a; (newspaper) escribir para; (discussion) intervenir en

contribution [kɒntrɪ'bjuːʃən] n (donation) donativo; (BRIT: for social security) cotización f; (to debate) intervención f; (to journal) colaboración f ❏ **contributor** n (to newspaper) colaborador(a) m/f

control [kən'trəul] vt controlar; (process etc) dirigir; (machinery) manejar; (temper) dominar; (disease) contener ♦ n control m; **controls** npl (of vehicle) instrumentos mpl de mando; (of radio) controles mpl; (governmental) medidas fpl de control; **under ~** bajo control; **to be in ~ of** tener el mando de; **the car went out of ~** se perdió el control del coche ❏ **control tower** n (AVIAT) torre f de control

controversial [kɒntrə'vɜːʃl] adj polémico

controversy ['kɒntrəvɜːsɪ] n polémica

convenience [kən'viːnɪəns] n (easiness) comodidad f; (suitability) idoneidad f; (advantage) ventaja; **at your ~** cuando le sea conveniente; **all modern conveniences, all mod cons** (BRIT) todo confort

convenient [kən'viːnɪənt] adj (useful) útil; (place, time) conveniente

convent ['kɒnvənt] n convento

convention [kən'vɛnʃən] n convención f; (meeting) asamblea; (agreement) convenio ❏ **conventional** adj convencional

conversation [kɒnvə'seɪʃən] n conversación f

conversely [-'vɜːslɪ] adv a la inversa

conversion [kən'vɜːʃən] n conversión f

convert [vb kən'vɜːt, n 'kɒnvɜːt] vt (REL, COMM) convertir; (alter): **to ~ sth into/to** transformar algo en/convertir algo a ♦ n converso(-a) ❏ **convertible** adj convertible ♦ n descapotable m

convey [kən'veɪ] vt llevar; (thanks) comunicar; (idea) expresar ❏ **conveyor belt** n cinta transportadora

convict [vb kən'vɪkt, n 'kɒnvɪkt] vt (find guilty) declarar culpable a ♦ n presidiario(-a) □ **conviction** [-ʃən] n condena; (belief, certainty) convicción f

convince [kən'vɪns] vt convencer □ **convinced** adj: **convinced of/that** convencido de/de que □ **convincing** adj convincente

convoy ['kɒnvɔɪ] n convoy m

cook [kuk] vt (dinner etc) guisar; (meal) preparar ♦ vi cocer; (person) cocinar ♦ n cocinero(-a) □ **cook book** n libro de cocina □ **cooker** n cocina □ **cookery** n cocina □ **cookery book** (BRIT) n = **cook book** □ **cookie** (US) n galleta □ **cooking** n cocina

cool [ku:l] adj fresco; (not afraid) tranquilo; (unfriendly) frío ♦ vt enfriar ♦ vi enfriarse ► **cool down** vi enfriarse; (fig: person, situation) calmarse ► **cool off** vi (become calmer) calmarse, apaciguarse; (lose enthusiasm) perder (el) interés, enfriarse

cop [kɒp] (inf) n poli mf (SP), tira mf (MEX)

cope [kəup] vi: **to ~ with** (problem) hacer frente a

copper ['kɒpə*] n (metal) cobre m; (BRIT: inf) poli mf, tira mf (MEX)

copy ['kɒpɪ] n copia; (of book etc) ejemplar m ♦ vt copiar □ **copyright** n derechos mpl de autor

coral ['kɒrəl] n coral m

cord [kɔ:d] n cuerda; (ELEC) cable m; (fabric) pana; **cords** npl (trousers) pantalones mpl de pana □ **cordless** adj sin hilos

corduroy ['kɔ:dərɔɪ] n pana

core [kɔ:*] n centro, núcleo; (of fruit) corazón m; (of problem) meollo ♦ vt quitar el corazón de

coriander [kɒrɪ'ændə*] n culantro

cork [kɔ:k] n corcho; (tree) alcornoque m □ **corkscrew** n sacacorchos m inv

corn [kɔ:n] n (BRIT: cereal crop) trigo; (US: maize) maíz m; (on foot) callo; **~ on the**

cob (CULIN) mazorca, elote m (MEX), choclo (SC)

corned beef ['kɔ:nd-] n carne f acecinada (en lata)

corner ['kɔ:nə*] n (outside) esquina; (inside) rincón m; (in road) curva; (FOOTBALL) córner m; (BOXING) esquina ♦ vt (trap) arrinconar; (COMM) acaparar ♦ vi (in car) tomar las curvas □ **corner shop** (BRIT) tienda de la esquina

cornflakes ['kɔ:nfleɪks] npl copos mpl de maíz, cornflakes mpl

cornflour ['kɔ:nflauə*] (BRIT) n harina de maíz

cornstarch ['kɔ:nstɑ:tʃ] (US) n = **cornflour**

Cornwall ['kɔ:nwəl] n Cornualles m

coronary ['kɒrənərɪ] n (also: ~ **thrombosis**) infarto

coronation [kɒrə'neɪʃən] n coronación f

coroner ['kɒrənə*] n juez mf de instrucción

corporal ['kɔ:pərl] n cabo ♦ adj: ~ **punishment** castigo corporal

corporate ['kɔ:pərɪt] adj (action, ownership) colectivo; (finance, image) corporativo

corporation [kɔ:pə'reɪʃən] n (of town) ayuntamiento; (COMM) corporación f

corps [kɔ:, pl kɔ:z] n inv cuerpo; **diplomatic ~** cuerpo diplomático; **press ~** gabinete m de prensa

corpse [kɔ:ps] n cadáver m

correct [kə'rekt] adj justo, exacto; (proper) correcto ♦ vt corregir; (exam) corregir, calificar □ **correction** [-ʃən] n (act) corrección f; (instance) rectificación f

correspond [kɒrɪ'spɒnd] vi (write): **to ~ (with)** escribirse (con); (be equivalent to): **to ~ (to)** corresponder (a); (be in accordance): **to ~ (with)** corresponder (con) □ **correspondence** n correspondencia □ **correspondent** n corresponsal *mf* ◻ **corresponding** *adj* correspondiente

corridor ['kɔrɪdɔː'] *n* pasillo

corrode [kə'rəud] *vt* corroer ♦ *vi* corroerse

corrupt [kə'rʌpt] *adj* (person) corrupto; (COMPUT) corrompido ♦ *vt* corromper; (COMPUT) degradar ♦ **corruption** *n* corrupción *f*; (of data) alteración *f*

Corsica ['kɔːsɪkə] *n* Córcega

cosmetic [kɔz'metɪk] *adj, n* cosmético ◻ **cosmetic surgery** *n* cirugía *f* estética

cosmopolitan [kɔzmə'pɔlɪtn] *adj* cosmopolita

cost [kɔst] (*pt, pp* ~) *n* (price) precio ♦ *vi* costar, valer ♦ *vt* preparar el presupuesto de; **how much does it ~?** ¿cuánto cuesta?; **to ~ sb time/effort** costarle a algn tiempo/esfuerzo; **it ~ him his life** le costó la vida; **at all costs** cueste lo que cueste; **costs** *npl* (COMM) costes *mpl*; (LAW) costas *fpl*

co-star ['kəʊstɑː'] *n* coprotagonista *mf*

Costa Rica ['kɔstə'riːkə] *n* Costa Rica ◻ **Costa Rican** *adj, n* costarriqueño(-a)

costly ['kɔstlɪ] *adj* costoso

cost of living *n* costo *or* coste *m* (Sp) de la vida

costume ['kɔstjuːm] *n* traje *m*; (BRIT: also: **swimming** ~) traje de baño

cosy ['kəʊzɪ] (US **cozy**) *adj* (person) cómodo; (room) acogedor(a)

cot [kɔt] *n* (BRIT: child's) cuna; (US: campbed) cama de campaña

cottage ['kɔtɪdʒ] *n* casita de campo; (rustic) barraca ◻ **cottage cheese** *n* requesón *m*

cotton ['kɔtn] *n* algodón *m*; (thread) hilo ► **cotton on** *vi* (inf): **to cotton on (to sth)** caer en la cuenta (de algo) ◻ **cotton bud** (BRIT) *n* bastoncillo *m* de algodón ◻ **cotton candy** (US) *n* algodón *m* (azucarado) ◻ **cotton wool** (BRIT) *n* algodón *m* (hidrófilo)

couch [kautʃ] *n* sofá *m*; (doctor's etc) diván *m*

cough [kɔf] *vi* toser ♦ *n* tos *f* ◻ **cough mixture** *n* jarabe *m* para la tos

could [kud] *pt of* **can²** ◻ **couldn't** = **could not**

council ['kaunsl] *n* consejo; **city** *or* **town** ~ consejo municipal ◻ **council estate** (BRIT) *n* urbanización de viviendas municipales de alquiler ◻ **council house** (BRIT) *n* vivienda municipal de alquiler ◻ **councillor** (US **councilor**) *n* concejal(a) *m/f* ◻ **council tax** *n* (BRIT) contribución *f* municipal (dependiente del valor de la vivienda)

counsel ['kaunsl] *n* (advice) consejo; (lawyer) abogado(-a) ♦ *vt* aconsejar ◻ **counselling** (US **counseling**) *n* (PSYCH) asistencia *f* psicológica ◻ **counsellor** (US **counselor**) *n* consejero(-a), abogado(-a)

count [kaunt] *vt* contar; (include) incluir ♦ *vi* contar ♦ *n* cuenta; (of votes) escrutinio; (level) nivel *m*; (nobleman) conde *m* ► **count in** (inf) *vt*: **to count sb in on sth** contar con algn para algo ► **count on** *vt fus* contar con ◻ **countdown** *n* cuenta atrás

counter ['kauntə'] *n* (in shop) mostrador *m*; (in games) ficha ♦ *vt* contrarrestar ♦ *adv*: **to run** ~ **to** ser contrario a, ir en contra de ◻ **counter clockwise** (US) *adv* en sentido contrario a las agujas del reloj

counterfeit ['kauntəfɪt] *n* falsificación *f*, simulación *f* ♦ *vt* falsificar ♦ *adj* falso, falsificado

counterpart ['kauntəpɑːt] *n* homólogo(-a)

countess ['kauntɪs] *n* condesa

countless ['kauntlɪs] *adj* innumerable

country ['kʌntrɪ] *n* país *m*; (native land) patria; (as opposed to town) campo; (region) región *f*, tierra ◻ **country and western** (music) *n* música country ◻ **country house** *n* casa de campo ◻ **countryside** *n* campo

county ['kauntɪ] n condado

coup [ku:] n (pl **coups**) n (also: **~ d'état**) golpe m (de estado); (achievement) éxito

couple ['kʌpl] n (of things) par m; (of people) pareja; (married couple) matrimonio; **a ~ of** un par de

coupon ['ku:pɔn] n cupón m; (voucher) valé m

courage ['kʌrɪdʒ] n valor m, valentía ❏ **courageous** [kə'reɪdʒəs] adj valiente

courgette [kuə'ʒɛt] (BRIT) n calabacín m, calabacita (MEX)

courier ['kurɪə'] n mensajero(-a); (for tourists) guía mf (de turismo)

course [kɔ:s] n (direction) dirección f; (of river, SCOL) curso; (process) transcurso; (MED): — **of treatment** tratamiento; (of ship) rumbo; (part of meal) plato; (GOLF) campo; **of ~** desde luego, naturalmente; **of ~!** ¡claro!

court [kɔ:t] n (royal) corte f; (LAW) tribunal m, juzgado; (TENNIS etc) pista, cancha ♦ vt (woman) cortejar a; **to take to ~** demandar

courtesy ['kə:təsɪ] n cortesía; (by) ~ **of** por cortesía de ❏ **courtesy bus**, **courtesy coach** n autobús m gratuito

court: court-house ['kɔ:thaus] (US) n palacio de justicia ❏ **courtroom** ['kɔ:trum] n sala de justicia ❏ **courtyard** ['kɔ:tjɑ:d] n patio

cousin ['kʌzn] n primo(-a); **first ~** primo(-a) carnal, primo(-a) hermano(-a)

cover ['kʌvə'] vt cubrir; (feelings, mistake) ocultar; (with lid) tapar; (book etc) forrar; (distance) recorrer; (include) abarcar; (protect: also: INSURANCE) cubrir; (PRESS) investigar; (discuss) tratar ♦ n cubierta; (lid) tapa; (of chair etc) funda; (envelope) sobre m; (for book) forro; (of magazine) portada; (shelter) abrigo; (INSURANCE) cobertura; (of spy) cobertura; **covers** npl (on bed) sábanas; mantas; **to take ~** (shelter)

protegerse, resguardarse; **under ~** (indoors) bajo techo; **under ~ of darkness** al amparo de la oscuridad; **under separate ~** (COMM) por separado ▶ **cover up** vi: **to cover up for sb** encubrir a algn ❏ **coverage** n (TV, PRESS) cobertura ❏ **cover charge** n precio del cubierto ❏ **cover-up** n encubrimiento

cow [kau] n vaca; (inf: woman) bruja ♦ vt intimidar

coward ['kauəd] n cobarde mf ❏ **cowardly** adj cobarde

cowboy ['kaubɔɪ] n vaquero

cozy ['kauzɪ] (US) adj = **cosy**

crab [kræb] n cangrejo

crack [kræk] n grieta; (noise) crujido; (drug) crack m ♦ vt agrietar, romper; (nut) cascar; (solve: problem) resolver; (: code) descifrar; (whip etc) chasquear; (knuckles) crujir; (joke) contar ♦ adj (expert) de primera ▶ **crack down on** vt fus adoptar fuertes medidas contra ❏ **cracked** adj (cup, window) rajado; (wall) resquebrajado ❏ **cracker** n (biscuit) cráquer m; (Christmas cracker) petardo sorpresa

crackle ['krækl] vi crepitar

cradle ['kreɪdl] n cuna

craft [krɑ:ft] n (skill) arte m; (trade) oficio; (cunning) astucia; (boat: pl inv) barco; (plane: pl inv) avión m ❏ **craftsman** (irreg) n artesano ❏ **craftsmanship** n (quality) destreza

cram [kræm] vt (fill): **to ~ sth with** llenar algo (a reventar) de; (put): **to ~ sth into** meter algo a la fuerza en ♦ vi (for exams) empollar

cramp [kræmp] n (MED) calambre m ❏ **cramped** adj apretado, estrecho

cranberry ['krænbərɪ] n arándano agrio

crane [kreɪn] n (TECH) grúa; (bird) grulla

crap [kræp] n (inf!) mierda (f)

crash [kræʃ] n (noise) estrépito; (of cars etc) choque m; (of plane) accidente de aviación; (COMM) quiebra ♦ vt (car, plane) estrellar ♦ vi (car, plane) estrellarse; (two cars) chocar; (COMM) quebrar ❑ **crash course** n curso acelerado ❑ **crash helmet** n casco (protector)

crate [kreɪt] n cajón m de embalaje; (for bottles) caja

crave [kreɪv] vt, vi: to ~ (for) ansiar, anhelar

crawl [krɔːl] vi (drag o.s.) arrastrarse; (child) andar a gatas, gatear; (vehicle) avanzar (lentamente) ♦ n (SWIMMING) crol m

crayfish [ˈkreɪfɪʃ] n inv (freshwater) cangrejo de río; (saltwater) cigala

crayon [ˈkreɪən] n lápiz m de color

craze [kreɪz] n (fashion) moda

crazy [ˈkreɪzɪ] adj (person) loco; (idea) disparatado; (inf: keen): ~ **about sb/sth** loco por algn/algo

creak [kriːk] vi (floorboard) crujir; (hinge etc) chirriar, rechinar

cream [kriːm] n (of milk) nata, crema; (lotion) crema; (fig) flor f y nata ♦ adj (colour) color crema ❑ **cream cheese** n queso blanco ❑ **creamy** adj cremoso; (colour) color crema

crease [kriːs] n (fold) pliegue m; (in trousers) raya; (wrinkle) arruga ♦ vt (wrinkle) arrugar ♦ vi (wrinkle up) arrugarse

create [kriːˈeɪt] vt crear ❑ **creation** [-ʃən] n creación f ❑ **creative** adj creativo ❑ **creator** n creador(a) m/f

creature [ˈkriːtʃəʳ] n (animal) animal m, bicho; (person) criatura

crèche [krɛʃ] n guardería (infantil)

credentials [krɪˈdɛnʃlz] npl (references) referencias fpl; (identity papers) documentos mpl de identidad

credibility [krɛdɪˈbɪlɪtɪ] n credibilidad f

credible [ˈkrɛdɪbl] adj creíble; (trustworthy) digno de confianza

credit [ˈkrɛdɪt] n crédito; (merit) honor m, mérito ♦ vt (COMM) abonar; (believe:

also: **give ~ to**) creer, prestar fe a ♦ adj crediticio; **credits** npl (CINEMA) fichas fpl técnicas; **to be in ~** (person) tener saldo a favor; **to ~ sb with** (fig) reconocer a algn el mérito de ❑ **credit card** n tarjeta de crédito

creek [kriːk] n cala, ensenada; (US) riachuelo

creep [kriːp] (pt, pp **crept**) vi arrastrarse

cremate [krɪˈmeɪt] vt incinerar

crematorium [krɛməˈtɔːrɪəm] (pl **crematoria**) n crematorio

crept [krɛpt] pt, pp of **creep**

crescent [ˈkrɛsnt] n media luna; (street) calle f (en forma de semicírculo)

cress [krɛs] n berro

crest [krɛst] n (of bird) cresta; (of hill) cima, cumbre f; (of coat of arms) blasón m

crew [kruː] n (of ship etc) tripulación f; (TV, CINEMA) equipo ❑ **crew-neck** n cuello a la caja

crib [krɪb] n cuna ♦ vt (inf) plagiar

cricket [ˈkrɪkɪt] n (insect) grillo; (game) críquet m ❑ **cricketer** n jugador(a) m/ f de críquet

crime [kraɪm] n (no pl: illegal activities) crimen m; (illegal action) delito ❑ **criminal** [ˈkrɪmɪnl] n criminal mf, delincuente m/f ♦ adj criminal; (illegal) delictivo; (law) penal

crimson [ˈkrɪmzn] adj carmesí

cringe [krɪndʒ] vi agacharse, encogerse

cripple [ˈkrɪpl] n lisiado(-a), cojo(-a) ♦ vt lisiar, mutilar

crisis [ˈkraɪsɪs] (pl **crises**) n crisis f inv

crisp [krɪsp] adj fresco; (vegetables etc) crujiente; (manner) seco ❑ **crispy** adj crujiente

criterion [kraɪˈtɪərɪən] (pl **criteria**) n criterio

critic [ˈkrɪtɪk] n crítico(-a) ❑ **critical** adj crítico; (illness) grave ❑ **criticism** [ˈkrɪtɪsɪzm] n crítica ❑ **criticize** [ˈkrɪtɪsaɪz] vt criticar

Croat [ˈkrəʊæt] adj, n = **Croatian**

Croatia [krəʊˈeɪʃə] n Croacia
❑ **Croatian** adj, n croata m/f ♦ n (LING) croata m

crockery [ˈkrɔkəri] n loza, vajilla

crocodile [ˈkrɔkədaɪl] n cocodrilo

crocus [ˈkrəʊkəs] n croco, crocus m

croissant [ˈkrwɑsɑ̃] n croissant m, medialuna (esp LAm)

crook [krʊk] n ladrón(-ona) m/f; (of shepherd) cayado ❑ **crooked** [ˈkrʊkɪd] adj torcido; (dishonest) nada honrado

crop [krɔp] n (produce) cultivo; (amount produced) cosecha; (riding crop) látigo de montar ♦ vt cortar, recortar ▸ **crop up** vi surgir, presentarse

cross [krɔs] n cruz f; (hybrid) cruce m ♦ vt (street etc) cruzar, atravesar ♦ adj de mal humor, enojado ▸ **cross off** or **out** vt tachar ▸ **cross over** vi cruzar ❑ **cross-Channel ferry** n transbordador m que cruza el Canal de la Mancha ❑ **crosscountry (race)** n carrera a campo traviesa, cross m ❑ **crossing** n (sea passage) travesía; (also: **pedestrian crossing**) paso para peatones ❑ **crossing guard** n persona encargada de ayudar a los niños a cruzar la calle ❑ **crossroads** n cruce m, encrucijada ❑ **crosswalk** (US) n paso de peatones ❑ **crossword** n crucigrama m

crotch [krɔtʃ] n (ANAT, of garment) entrepierna

crouch [kraʊtʃ] vi agacharse, acurrucarse

crouton [ˈkruːtɔn] n cubito de pan frito

crow [krəʊ] n (bird) cuervo; (of cock) canto, cacareo ♦ vi (cock) cantar

crowd [kraʊd] n muchedumbre f, multitud f ♦ vt (fill) llenar ♦ vi (gather): **to ~ round** reunirse en torno a; (cram): **to ~ in** entrar en tropel ❑ **crowded** adj (full) atestado; (densely populated) superpoblado

crown [kraʊn] n corona; (of head) coronilla; (for tooth) funda; (of hill)

cumbre f ♦ vt coronar; (fig) completar, rematar ❑ **crown jewels** npl joyas fpl reales

crucial [ˈkruːʃl] adj decisivo

crucifix [ˈkruːsɪfɪks] n crucifijo

crude [kruːd] adj (materials) bruto; (fig: basic) tosco; (: vulgar) ordinario ❑ **crude (oil)** n (petróleo) crudo

cruel [krʊəl] adj cruel ❑ **cruelty** n crueldad f

cruise [kruːz] n crucero ♦ vi (ship) hacer un crucero; (car) ir a velocidad de crucero

crumb [krʌm] n miga, migaja

crumble [ˈkrʌmbl] vt desmenuzar ♦ vi (building, also fig) desmoronarse

crumpet [ˈkrʌmpɪt] n = bollo para tostar

crumple [ˈkrʌmpl] vt (paper) estrujar; (material) arrugar

crunch [krʌntʃ] vt (with teeth) mascar; (underfoot) hacer crujir ♦ n (fig) hora o momento de la verdad ❑ **crunchy** adj crujiente

crush [krʌʃ] n (crowd) aglomeración f; (infatuation): **to have a ~ on sb** estar loco por algn; (drink): **lemon ~** limonada ♦ vt aplastar; (paper) estrujar; (cloth) arrugar; (fruit) exprimir; (opposition) aplastar; (hopes) destruir

crust [krʌst] n corteza; (of snow, ice) costra ❑ **crusty** adj (bread) crujiente

crutch [krʌtʃ] n muleta

cry [kraɪ] vi llorar ♦ n (shriek) chillido; (shout) grito ▸ **cry out** vi (call out, shout) lanzar un grito, echar un grito ♦ vt gritar

crystal [ˈkrɪstl] n cristal m

cub [kʌb] n cachorro; (also: **~ scout**) niño explorador

Cuba [ˈkjuːbə] n Cuba ❑ **Cuban** adj, n cubano(-a) m/f

cube [kjuːb] n cubo ♦ vt (MATH) cubicar

cubicle [ˈkjuːbɪkl] n (at pool) caseta; (for bed) cubículo

cuckoo [ˈkukuː] n cuco

cucumber ['kjuːkʌmbə'] n pepino
cuddle ['kʌdl] vt abrazar ♦ vi abrazarse
cue [kjuː] n (snooker cue) taco; (THEATRE etc) señal f
cuff [kʌf] n (of sleeve) puño; (US: of trousers) vuelta; (blow) bofetada; **off the ~** adv de improviso **cufflinks** npl gemelos mpl
cuisine [kwɪˈziːn] n cocina
cul-de-sac ['kʌldəsæk] n callejón m sin salida
cull [kʌl] vt (idea) sacar ♦ n (of animals) matanza selectiva
culminate ['kʌlmɪneɪt] vi: **to ~ in** terminar en
culprit ['kʌlprɪt] n culpable mf
cult [kʌlt] n culto
cultivate ['kʌltɪveɪt] vt cultivar
cultural ['kʌltʃərəl] adj cultural
culture ['kʌltʃə'] n (also fig) cultura; (BIOL) cultivo
cumin ['kʌmɪn] n (spice) comino
cunning ['kʌnɪŋ] n astucia ♦ adj astuto
cup [kʌp] n taza; (as prize) copa
cupboard ['kʌbəd] n armario; (in kitchen) alacena
cup final n (FOOTBALL) final f de copa
curator [kjuəˈreɪtə'] n director(a) m/f
curb [kɜːb] vt refrenar; (person) reprimir ♦ n freno; (US) bordillo
curdle ['kɜːdl] vi cuajarse
cure [kjuə'] vt curar ♦ n cura, curación f; (fig: solution) remedio
curfew ['kɜːfjuː] n toque m de queda
curiosity [kjuərɪˈɒsɪtɪ] n curiosidad f
curious ['kjuərɪəs] adj curioso; (person: interested): **to be ~** sentir curiosidad
curl [kɜːl] n rizo ♦ vt (hair) rizar ♦ vi rizarse **curler** n rulo **curly** adj rizado
currant ['kʌrnt] n pasa (de Corinto); (blackcurrant, redcurrant) grosella
currency ['kʌrnsɪ] n moneda; **to gain ~** (fig) difundirse
current ['kʌrnt] n corriente f ♦ adj (accepted) corriente; (present) actual

current account (BRIT) n cuenta corriente **current affairs** npl noticias fpl de actualidad **currently** adv actualmente
curriculum [kəˈrɪkjuləm] (pl **curriculums** or **curricula**) n plan m de estudios **curriculum vitae** n currículum m
curry ['kʌrɪ] n curry m ♦ vt: **to ~ favour with** buscar favores con **curry powder** n curry en polvo
curse [kɜːs] vi soltar tacos ♦ vt maldecir ♦ n maldición f; (swearword) palabra, taco
cursor ['kɜːsə'] n (COMPUT) cursor m
curt [kɜːt] adj corto, seco
curtain ['kɜːtn] n cortina; (THEATRE) telón m
curve [kɜːv] n curva ♦ vi (road) hacer una curva; (line etc) curvarse **curved** adj curvo
cushion ['kuʃən] n cojín m; (of air) colchón m ♦ vt (shock) amortiguar
custard ['kʌstəd] n natillas fpl
custody ['kʌstədɪ] n custodia; **to take into ~** detener
custom ['kʌstəm] n costumbre f; (COMM) clientela
customer ['kʌstəmə'] n cliente m/f
customized ['kʌstəmaɪzd] adj (car etc) hecho a encargo
customs ['kʌstəmz] npl aduana **customs officer** n aduanero(-a)
cut [kʌt] (pt, pp **cut**) vt cortar; (price) rebajar; (text, programme) acortar; (reduce) reducir ♦ vi cortar ♦ n (of garment) corte m; (in skin) cortadura; (in salary etc) rebaja; (in spending) reducción f, recorte m; (slice of meat) tajada; **to ~ a tooth** echar un diente; **to ~ and paste** (COMPUT) cortar y pegar ▶ **cut back** vt (plants) podar; (production, expenditure) reducir ▶ **cut down** vt (tree) derribar; (reduce) reducir ▶ **cut off** vt cortar; (person, place) aislar; (TEL) desconectar ▶

cute vt (shape) recortar; (stop: activity etc) dejar; (remove) quitar ▶ **cut up** vt cortar (en pedazos) ❑ **cutback** n reducción f

cute [kju:t] adj mono

cutlery ['kʌtləri] n cubiertos mpl

cutlet ['kʌtlɪt] n chuleta; (nut etc cutlet) plato vegetariano hecho con nueces y verdura en forma de chuleta

cut: cut-price (BRIT) ['kʌt'praɪs] adj a precio reducido

cut-rate (US) ['kʌt'reɪt] adj = **cut-price**

cutting ['kʌtɪŋ] adj (remark) mordaz ♦ n (BRIT: from newspaper) recorte m; (from plant) esqueje m

CV n abbr = **curriculum vitae**

cwt abbr = **hundredweight(s)**

cybercafé ['saɪbəkæfeɪ] n cibercafé m

cyberspace ['saɪbəspeɪs] n ciberespacio

cycle ['saɪkl] n ciclo; (bicycle) bicicleta ♦ vi ir en bicicleta ❑ **cycle hire** n alquiler m de bicicletas ❑ **cycle lane** n carril-bici m ❑ **cycle path** n carril-bici m ❑ **cycling** n ciclismo ❑ **cyclist** n ciclista mf

cyclone ['saɪkləun] n ciclón m

cylinder ['sɪlɪndə'] n cilindro; (of gas) bombona

cymbal ['sɪmbl] n címbalo, platillo

cynical ['sɪnɪkl] adj cínico

Cypriot ['sɪprɪət] adj, n chipriota m/f

Cyprus ['saɪprəs] n Chipre f

cyst [sɪst] n quiste m ❑ **cystitis** [-'taɪtɪs] n cistitis f

czar [zɑː'] n zar m

Czech [tʃek] adj, n checo(-a) m/f ❑ **Czech Republic** n: the Czech Republic la República Checa

D, d

D [diː] n (MUS) re m

dab [dæb] vt (eyes, wound) tocar (ligeramente); (paint, cream) poner un poco de

dad [dæd] n = **daddy**

daddy ['dædɪ] n papá m

daffodil ['dæfədɪl] n narciso

daft [dɑːft] adj tonto

dagger ['dægə'] n puñal m, daga

daily ['deɪlɪ] adj diario, cotidiano ♦ adv todos los días, cada día

dairy ['dɛərɪ] n (shop) lechería; (on farm) vaquería ❑ **dairy produce** n productos mpl lácteos

daisy ['deɪzɪ] n margarita

dam [dæm] n presa ♦ vt construir una presa sobre, represar

damage ['dæmɪdʒ] n lesión f; daño; (dents etc) desperfectos mpl; (fig) perjuicio ♦ vt dañar, perjudicar; (spoil, break) estropear; **damages** npl (LAW) daños mpl y perjuicios

damn [dæm] vt condenar; (curse) maldecir ♦ n (inf): **I don't give a ~** me importa un pito ♦ adj (inf: also: **damned**) maldito; **~ (it)!** ¡maldito sea!

damp [dæmp] adj húmedo, mojado ♦ n humedad f ♦ vt (also: **dampen**: cloth, rag) mojar; (: enthusiasm) enfriar

dance [dɑːns] n baile m ♦ vi bailar ❑ **dance floor** n pista f de baile ❑ **dancer** n bailador/a m/f; (professional) bailarín(-ina) m/f ❑ **dancing** n baile m

dandelion ['dændɪlaɪən] n diente m de león

dandruff ['dændrəf] n caspa

Dane [deɪn] n danés(-esa) m/f

danger ['deɪndʒə'] n peligro; (risk) riesgo; **~!** (on sign) ¡peligro de muerte!; **to be in ~** correr riesgo de ❑ **dangerous** adj peligroso

dangle ['dæŋgl] vt colgar ♦ vi pender, colgar

Danish ['deɪnɪʃ] adj danés(-esa) ♦ n (LING) danés m

dare [dɛə] vt: **to ~ sb to do** desafiar a algn a hacer ♦ vi: **to ~ (to) do sth** atreverse a hacer algo; **I ~ say** (*I suppose*) puede ser (que) □ **daring** adj atrevido, osado ♦ n atrevimiento, osadía

dark [dɑːk] adj oscuro; (*hair, complexion*) moreno ♦ n: **in the ~** en la oscuras; **to be in the ~ about** (*fig*) no saber nada de; **after ~** después del anochecer □ **darken** vt (*colour*) hacer más oscuro ♦ vi oscurecerse □ **darkness** n oscuridad f □ **darkroom** n cuarto oscuro

darling [dɑːlɪŋ] adj, n querido(-a) m/f

dart [dɑːt] n dardo; (*in sewing*) sisa ♦ vi precipitarse □ **dartboard** n diana □ **darts** n (*game*) dardos mpl

dash [dæʃ] n (*small quantity: of liquid*) gota, chorrito; (*sign*) raya ♦ vt (*throw*) tirar; (*hopes*) defraudar ♦ vi precipitarse, ir de prisa

dashboard [dæʃbɔːd] n (AUT) salpicadero

data [deɪtə] npl datos mpl □ **database** n base f de datos □ **data processing** n proceso de datos

date [deɪt] n (*day*) fecha; (*with friend*) cita; (*fruit*) dátil m ♦ vt fechar; (*person*) salir con; **~ of birth** fecha de nacimiento; **to ~** adv hasta la fecha □ **dated** adj anticuado

daughter [dɔːtə] n hija □ **daughter-in-law** n nuera, hija política

daunting [dɔːntɪŋ] adj desalentador(a)

dawn [dɔːn] n alba, amanecer m; (*fig*) nacimiento ♦ vi (*day*) amanecer; (*fig*): **it dawned on him that ...** cayó en la cuenta de que ...

day [deɪ] n día m; (*working day*) jornada; (*heyday*) tiempos mpl, días mpl; **the ~ before/after** el día anterior/siguiente; **the ~ after tomorrow** pasado mañana; **the ~ before yesterday** anteayer; **the following ~** el día siguiente; **by ~** de día □ **day-care centre** [deɪkɛə-] n

centro de día; (*for children*) guardería infantil □ **daydream** vi soñar despierto **a day** n luz f (del día) □ **daylight** n luz f (del día) □ **day return** (BRIT) n billete m de ida y vuelta (en un día) □ **daytime** n día m □ **day-to-day** adj cotidiano □ **day trip** n excursión f (de un día)

dazed [deɪzd] adj aturdido

dazzle [dæzl] vt deslumbrar □ **dazzling** adj (*light, smile*) deslumbrante; (*colour*) fuerte

DC abbr (= *direct current*) corriente f continua

dead [ded] adj muerto; (*limb*) dormido; (*telephone*) cortado; (*battery*) agotado ♦ adv (*completely*) totalmente; (*exactly*) exactamente; **to shoot sb ~** matar a algn a tiros; **~ tired** muerto de (cansancio); **to stop ~** parar en seco □ **dead end** n callejón m sin salida □ **deadline** n fecha (or hora) tope □ **deadly** adj mortal, fatal □ **Dead Sea** n: **the Dead Sea** el Mar Muerto

deaf [def] adj sordo □ **deafen** vt ensordecer □ **deafening** adj ensordecedor(a)

deal [diːl] n (pt, pp **dealt**) n (*agreement*) pacto, convenio; (*business deal*) trato ♦ vt (*card*) repartir; **a great ~ (of)** bastante, mucho ▶ **deal with** vt fus (*people*) tratar con; (*problem*) ocuparse de; (*subject*) tratar de □ **dealer** n comerciante m/f; (CARDS) mano f □ **dealings** npl (COMM) transacciones fpl; (*relations*) relaciones fpl

dealt [delt] pt, pp of **deal**

dean [diːn] n (REL) deán m; (SCOL: BRIT) decano; (US) decano; rector m

dear [dɪə] adj querido; (*expensive*) caro ♦ n: **my ~** mi querido(-a) ♦ excl: **~ me!** ¡Dios mío!; **D~ Sir/Madam** (*in letter*) Muy Señor Mío, Estimado Señor/ Estimada Señora; **D~ Mr/Mrs X** Estimado(-a) Señor(a) X □ **dearly** adv (*love*) mucho; (*pay*) caro

death [deθ] n muerte f ❏ **death penalty** n pena de muerte ❏ **death sentence** n condena a muerte

debate [dɪ'beɪt] n debate m ♦ vt discutir

debit ['debɪt] n debe m; vt: **to ~ a sum to sb** or **to sb's account** cargar una suma en cuenta a algn ❏ **debit card** n tarjeta f de débito

debris ['debriː] n escombros mpl

debt [det] n deuda; **to be in ~** tener deudas

debut ['deɪbjuː] n presentación f

Dec. abbr (= December) dic

decade ['dekeɪd] n decenio, década

decaffeinated [dɪ'kæfɪneɪtɪd] adj descafeinado

decay [dɪ'keɪ] n (of building) desmoronamiento m; (of tooth) caries f inv ♦ vi (rot) pudrirse

deceased [dɪ'siːst] n: **the ~** el (la) difunto(-a)

deceit [dɪ'siːt] n engaño ❏ **deceive** [dɪ'siːv] vt engañar

December [dɪ'sembəʳ] n diciembre m

decency ['diːsənsɪ] n decencia

decent ['diːsənt] adj (proper) decente; (person: kind) amable, bueno

deception [dɪ'sepʃən] n engaño

deceptive [dɪ'septɪv] adj engañoso

⚠ Be careful not to translate **deception** by the Spanish word *decepción*.

decide [dɪ'saɪd] vt (person) decidir; (question, argument) resolver ♦ vi decidir; **to ~ to do/that** decidir hacer/que; **to ~ on sth** decidirse por algo

decimal ['desɪməl] adj decimal ♦ n decimal m

decision [dɪ'sɪʒən] n decisión f

decisive [dɪ'saɪsɪv] adj decisivo; (person) decidido

deck [dek] n (NAUT) cubierta f; (of bus) piso; (record deck) platina f; (of cards) baraja ❏ **deckchair** n tumbona

declaration [deklə'reɪʃən] n declaración f

declare [dɪ'kleəʳ] vt declarar

decline [dɪ'klaɪn] n disminución f (de), descenso ♦ vt rehusar ♦ vi (person, business) decaer; (strength) disminuir

decorate ['dekəreɪt] vt (adorn): **to ~ (with)** adornar (de), decorar (de); (paint) pintar; (paper) empapelar ❏ **decoration** [-'reɪʃən] n adorno; (act) decoración f; (medal) condecoración f ❏ **decorator** n (workman) pintor m (decorador)

decrease [n 'diːkriːs, vb dɪ'kriːs] n: **~ (in)** disminución f (de) ♦ vt disminuir, reducir ♦ vi reducirse

decree [dɪ'kriː] n decreto

dedicate ['dedɪkeɪt] vt dedicar ❏ **dedicated** adj dedicado; (COMPUT) especializado; **dedicated word processor** procesador m de textos especializado or dedicado ❏ **dedication** [-'keɪʃən] n (devotion) dedicación f; (in book) dedicatoria

deduce [dɪ'djuːs] vt deducir

deduct [dɪ'dʌkt] vt restar; descontar ❏ **deduction** [dɪ'dʌkʃən] n (amount deducted) descuento; (conclusion) deducción f, conclusión f

deed [diːd] n hecho, acto; (feat) hazaña f; (LAW) escritura

deem [diːm] vt (formal) juzgar, considerar

deep [diːp] adj profundo; (expressing measurements) de profundidad; (voice) bajo; (breath) profundo; (colour) intenso ♦ adv: **the spectators stood 20 ~** los espectadores se formaron en 20 en fondo; **to be 4 metres ~** tener 4 metros de profundidad ❏ **deep-fry** vt freír en aceite abundante ❏ **deeply** adv (breathe) a pleno pulmón; (interested, moved, grateful) profundamente, hondamente

deer [dɪəʳ] n inv ciervo

default [dɪ'fɔ:lt] n: **by ~** (win) por incomparecencia ♦ adj (COMPUT) por defecto

defeat [dɪ'fi:t] n derrota ♦ vt derrotar, vencer

defect [n 'di:fekt, vb dɪ'fekt] n defecto ♦ vi: **to ~ to the enemy** pasarse al enemigo ❑ **defective** [dɪ'fektɪv] adj defectuoso

defence [dɪ'fens] (US **defense**) n defensa

defend [dɪ'fend] vt defender ❑ **defendant** n acusado(-a); (in civil case) demandado(-a) ❑ **defender** n defensor(a) m/f; (SPORT) defensa mf

defense [dɪ'fens] (US) = **defence**

defensive [dɪ'fensɪv] adj defensivo ♦ n: **on the ~** a la defensiva

defer [dɪ'fə:r] vt aplazar

defiance [dɪ'faɪəns] n desafío; **in ~ of** en contra de ❑ **defiant** [dɪ'faɪənt] adj (challenging) desafiante, retador(a)

deficiency [dɪ'fɪʃənsɪ] n (lack) falta; (defect) defecto ❑ **deficient** [dɪ'fɪʃənt] adj deficiente

deficit ['defɪsɪt] n déficit m

define [dɪ'faɪn] vt (word etc) definir; (limits etc) determinar

definite ['defɪnɪt] adj (fixed) determinado; (obvious) claro; (certain) indudable; **he was ~ about it** no dejó lugar a dudas (sobre ello) ❑ **definitely** adv desde luego, por supuesto

definition [defɪ'nɪʃən] n definición f; (clearness) nitidez f

deflate [di:'fleɪt] vt desinflar

deflect [dɪ'flekt] vt desviar

defraud [dɪ'frɔ:d] vt: **to ~ sb of sth** estafar algo a algn

defrost [di:'frɔst] vt descongelar

defuse [di:'fju:z] vt desactivar; (situation) calmar

defy [dɪ'faɪ] vt (resist) oponerse a; (challenge) desafiar; (fig): **it defies description** resulta imposible describirlo

degree [dɪ'gri:] n grado; (SCOL) título; **to have a ~ in maths** tener una licenciatura en matemáticas; **by degrees** (gradually) poco a poco, por etapas; **to some ~** hasta cierto punto

dehydrated [di:haɪ'dreɪtɪd] adj deshidratado; (milk) en polvo

de-icer [di:'aɪsər] n descongelador m

delay [dɪ'leɪ] vt demorar, aplazar; (person) entretener; (train) retrasar ♦ vi tardar ♦ n demora, retraso; **to be delayed** retrasarse; **without ~** en seguida, sin tardar

delegate [n 'delɪgɪt, vb 'delɪgeɪt] n delegado(-a) ♦ vt (person) delegar en; (task) delegar

delete [dɪ'li:t] vt suprimir, tachar

deli ['delɪ] n = **delicatessen**

deliberate [adj dɪ'lɪbərɪt, vb dɪ'lɪbəreɪt] adj (intentional) intencionado; (slow) pausado, lento ♦ vi deliberar ❑ **deliberately** adv (on purpose) a propósito

delicacy ['delɪkəsɪ] n delicadeza; (choice food) manjar m

delicate ['delɪkɪt] adj delicado; (fragile) frágil

delicatessen [delɪkə'tesn] n ultramarinos mpl finos

delicious [dɪ'lɪʃəs] adj delicioso

delight [dɪ'laɪt] n (feeling) placer m, deleite m; (person, experience etc) encanto, delicia ♦ vt encantar, deleitar; **to take ~ in** deleitarse en ❑ **delighted** adj: **delighted (at or with/to do)** encantado (con/de hacer) ❑ **delightful** adj encantador(a), delicioso

delinquent [dɪ'lɪŋkwənt] adj, n delincuente mf

deliver [dɪ'lɪvər] vt (distribute) repartir; (hand over) entregar; (message) comunicar; (speech) pronunciar; (MED) asistir al parto de ❑ **delivery**

reparto; entrega; (of speaker) modo de expresarse; (MED) parto, alumbramiento; **to take delivery of** recibir

delusion [dɪˈluːʒən] n ilusión f, engaño

de luxe [dəˈlʌks] adj de lujo

delve [delv] vi: **to ~ into** hurgar en

demand [dɪˈmɑːnd] vt (gen) exigir; (rights) reclamar ♦ n exigencia; (claim) reclamación f; (ECON) demanda f; **to be in ~** ser muy solicitado; **on ~** a solicitud □ **demanding** adj (boss) exigente; (work) absorbente

demise [dɪˈmaɪz] n (death) fallecimiento

demo [ˈdɛməʊ] (inf) n abbr (= demonstration) manifestación f

democracy [dɪˈmɒkrəsɪ] n democracia □ **democrat** [ˈdɛməkræt] n demócrata mf □ **democratic** [dɛməˈkrætɪk] adj democrático; (US) demócrata

demolish [dɪˈmɒlɪʃ] vt derribar, demoler; (fig: argument) destruir □ **demolition** [dɛməˈlɪʃən] n derribo, demolición f

demon [ˈdiːmən] n (evil spirit) demonio

demonstrate [ˈdɛmənstreɪt] vt demostrar; (skill, appliance) mostrar ♦ vi manifestarse □ **demonstration** [-ˈstreɪʃən] n (POL) manifestación f; (proof, exhibition) demostración f □ **demonstrator** n (POL) manifestante mf; (COMM) demostrador(a) m/f; vendedor(a) m/f

demote [dɪˈməʊt] vt degradar

den [dɛn] n (of animal) guarida f; (room) habitación f

denial [dɪˈnaɪəl] n (refusal) negativa f; (of report etc) negación f

denim [ˈdɛnɪm] n tela vaquera; **denims** npl vaqueros mpl

Denmark [ˈdɛnmɑːk] n Dinamarca

denomination [dɪnɒmɪˈneɪʃən] n valor m; (REL) confesión f

denounce [dɪˈnaʊns] vt denunciar

dense [dɛns] adj (crowd) denso; espeso; (: foliage etc) tupido; (inf: stupid) torpe

density [ˈdɛnsɪtɪ] n densidad f; **single/double~ disk** n (COMPUT) disco de densidad sencilla/de doble densidad

dent [dɛnt] n abolladura ♦ vt (also: **make a ~ in**) abollar

dental [ˈdɛntl] adj dental □ **dental floss** [-flɒs] n seda dental □ **dental surgery** n clínica f dental, consultorio m dental

dentist [ˈdɛntɪst] n dentista mf

dentures [ˈdɛntʃəz] npl dentadura (postiza)

deny [dɪˈnaɪ] vt negar; (charge) rechazar

deodorant [diːˈəʊdərənt] n desodorante m

depart [dɪˈpɑːt] vi irse, marcharse; (train) salir; **to ~ from** (fig: differ from) apartarse de

department [dɪˈpɑːtmənt] n (COMM) sección f; (SCOL) departamento m; (POL) ministerio □ **department store** n gran almacén m

departure [dɪˈpɑːtʃə*] n partida f, ida; (of train) salida; (of employee) marcha; **a new ~** un nuevo rumbo □ **departure lounge** n (at airport) sala de embarque

depend [dɪˈpend] vi: **to ~ on** depender de; (rely on) contar con; **it depends** depende, según; **depending on the result** según el resultado □ **dependant** n dependiente mf □ **dependant** adj: **to be dependent on** depender de ♦ n = **dependant**

depict [dɪˈpɪkt] vt (in picture) pintar; (describe) representar

deport [dɪˈpɔːt] vt deportar

deposit [dɪˈpɒzɪt] n depósito; (CHEM) sedimento; (of ore, oil) yacimiento ♦ vt (gen) depositar □ **deposit account** (BRIT) n cuenta de ahorros

depot [ˈdɛpəʊ] n (storehouse) depósito; (for vehicles) parque m; (US) estación f

depreciate [dɪ'priːʃieɪt] vi depreciarse, perder valor

depress [dɪ'pres] vt deprimir; (wages etc) hacer bajar; (press down) apretar □ **depressed** adj deprimido □ **depressing** adj deprimente □ **depression** [dɪ'preʃən] n depresión f

deprive [dɪ'praɪv] vt: **to ~ sb of** privar a algn de □ **deprived** adj necesitado

dept. abbr (= department) dto

depth [depθ] n profundidad f; (of cupboard) fondo; **to be in the depths of despair** sentir la mayor desesperación; **to be out of one's ~** (in water) no hacer pie; (fig) sentirse totalmente perdido

deputy ['depjutɪ] adj: **~ head** subdirector(a) m/f ♦ n sustituto(-a), suplente m/f; (US POL) diputado(-a); (US: also: **~ sheriff**) agente m del sheriff

derail [dɪ'reɪl] vt: **to be derailed** descarrilarse

derelict ['derɪlɪkt] adj abandonado

derive [dɪ'raɪv] vt (benefit etc) obtener ♦ vi: **to ~ from** derivarse de

descend [dɪ'send] vt, vi descender, bajar; **to ~ from** descender de; **to ~ to** rebajarse a □ **descendant** n descendiente m/f

descent [dɪ'sent] n descenso; (origin) descendencia

describe [dɪs'kraɪb] vt describir □ **description** [-'krɪpʃən] n descripción f; (sort) clase f, género

desert [n 'dezət, vb dɪ'zɜːt] n desierto ♦ vt abandonar ♦ vi (MIL) desertar □ **deserted** adj desierto

deserve [dɪ'zɜːv] vt merecer, ser digno de

design [dɪ'zaɪn] n (sketch) bosquejo; (layout, shape) diseño; (pattern) dibujo; (intention) intención f ♦ vt diseñar

designate [vb 'dezɪgneɪt, adj 'dezɪgnɪt] vt (appoint) nombrar; (destine) designar ♦ adj designado

designer [dɪ'zaɪnəʳ] n diseñador(a) m/f; (fashion designer) modisto(-a), diseñador(a) m/f de moda

desirable [dɪ'zaɪərəbl] adj (proper) deseable; (attractive) atractivo

desire [dɪ'zaɪəʳ] n deseo ♦ vt desear

desk [desk] n (in office) escritorio; (for pupil) pupitre m; (in hotel, at airport) recepción f; (BRIT: in shop, restaurant) caja □ **desk-top publishing** ['desktɒp-] n autoedición f

despair [dɪs'peəʳ] n desesperación f ♦ vi: **to ~ of** perder la esperanza de

despatch [dɪs'pætʃ] n, vt = **dispatch**

desperate ['despərɪt] adj desesperado; (fugitive) peligroso; **to be ~ for sth/to do** necesitar urgentemente algo/ hacer □ **desperately** adv desesperadamente; (very) terriblemente, gravemente

desperation [despə'reɪʃən] n desesperación f; **in (sheer) ~** (absolutamente) desesperado

despise [dɪs'paɪz] vt despreciar

despite [dɪs'paɪt] prep a pesar de, pese a

dessert [dɪ'zɜːt] n postre m □ **dessertspoon** n cuchara (de postre)

destination [destɪ'neɪʃən] n destino

destined ['destɪnd] adj: **~ for London** con destino a Londres

destiny ['destɪnɪ] n destino

destroy [dɪs'trɔɪ] vt destruir; (animal) sacrificar

destruction [dɪs'trʌkʃən] n destrucción f

destructive [dɪs'trʌktɪv] adj destructivo, destructor(a)

detach [dɪ'tætʃ] vt separar; (unstick) despegar □ **detached** adj (attitude) objetivo, imparcial □ **detached house** n chalé m, chalet m

detail ['diːteɪl] n detalle m; (no pl: in picture etc) detalles mpl; (trifle) pequeñez f ♦ vt detallar; (MIL) destacar;

in ~ detalladamente ❏ **detailed** adj
detallado

detain [dɪ'teɪn] vt retener; (in captivity)
detener

detect [dɪ'tekt] vt descubrir; (MED,
POLICE) identificar; (MIL, RADAR, TECH)
detectar ❏ **detection** [dɪ'tekʃən] n
descubrimiento; identificación f
❏ **detective** n detective mf
❏ **detective story** n novela policíaca

detention [dɪ'tenʃən] n detención f,
arresto; (SCOL) castigo

deter [dɪ'tɜː'] vt (dissuade) disuadir

detergent [dɪ'tɜːdʒənt] n detergente m

deteriorate [dɪ'tɪərɪəreɪt] vi
deteriorarse

determination [dɪtɜːmɪ'neɪʃən] n
resolución f

determine [dɪ'tɜːmɪn] vt determinar
❏ **determined** adj (person) resuelto,
decidido; **determined to do** resuelto a
hacer

deterrent [dɪ'terənt] n (MIL) fuerza de
disuasión

detest [dɪ'test] vt aborrecer

detour ['diːtuə'] n (gen, US AUT)
desviación f

detract [dɪ'trækt] vt: **to ~ from** quitar
mérito a, desvirtuar

detrimental [detrɪ'mentl] adj: **~ (to)**
perjudicial (a)

devastating ['devəsteɪtɪŋ] adj
devastador(a); (fig) arrollador(a)

develop [dɪ'veləp] vt desarrollar; (PHOT)
revelar; (disease) coger; (habit)
adquirir; (fault) empezar a tener ♦ vi
desarrollarse; (advance) progresar;
(facts, symptoms) aparecer
❏ **developing country** n país m en
(vías de) desarrollo ❏ **development**
n desarrollo; (advance) progreso; (of
affair, case) desenvolvimiento; (of land)
urbanización f

device [dɪ'vaɪs] n (apparatus) aparato,
mecanismo

devil ['devl] n diablo, demonio

devious ['diːvɪəs] adj taimado

devise [dɪ'vaɪz] vt idear, inventar

devote [dɪ'vəut] vt: **to ~ sth to** dedicar
algo a ❏ **devoted** adj (loyal) leal, fiel;
to be devoted to sb querer con
devoción a algn; **the book is devoted
to politics** el libro trata de la política
❏ **devotion** n dedicación f; (REL)
devoción f

devour [dɪ'vauə'] vt devorar

devout [dɪ'vaut] adj devoto

dew [djuː] n rocío

diabetes [daɪə'biːtiːz] n diabetes f

diabetic [daɪə'betɪk] adj, n diabético(-a)
m/f

diagnose ['daɪəgnəuz] vt diagnosticar

diagnosis [daɪəg'nəusɪs] (pl -ses) n
diagnóstico

diagonal [daɪ'ægənl] adj, n diagonal f

diagram ['daɪəgræm] n diagrama m,
esquema m

dial ['daɪəl] n esfera (SP), cara (LAm); (on
radio etc) dial m; (of phone) disco ♦ vt
(number) marcar

dialect ['daɪəlekt] n dialecto

dialling code ['daɪəlɪŋ-] n prefijo

dialling tone (US **dial tone**) n (BRIT)
señal f or tono de marcar

dialogue ['daɪəlɔg] (US **dialog**) n
diálogo

diameter [daɪ'æmɪtə'] n diámetro

diamond ['daɪəmənd] n diamante m;
(shape) rombo; **diamonds** npl (CARDS)
diamantes mpl

diaper ['daɪəpə'] (US) n pañal m

diarrhoea [daɪə'riːə] (US **diarrhea**) n
diarrea

diary ['daɪərɪ] n (daily account) diario;
(book) agenda

dice [daɪs] n inv dados mpl ♦ vt (CULIN)
cortar en cuadritos

dictate [dɪk'teɪt] vt dictar; (conditions) imponer ▫ **dictation** [-'teɪʃən] n dictado; (giving of orders) órdenes fpl

dictator [dɪk'teɪtə'] n dictador m

dictionary ['dɪkʃənrɪ] n diccionario m

did [dɪd] pt of **do**

didn't ['dɪdənt] = **did not**

die [daɪ] vi morir; (fig: fade) desvanecerse, desaparecer; **to be dying for sth/to do sth** morirse por algo/de ganas de hacer algo ▸ **die down** vi apagarse; (wind) amainar ▸ **die out** vi desaparecer

diesel ['diːzəl] n vehículo con motor Diesel

diet ['daɪət] n dieta; (restricted food) régimen m ♦ vi (also: **be on a ~**) estar a dieta, hacer régimen

differ ['dɪfə'] vi: **to ~ (from)** (be different) ser distinto (a), diferenciarse (de); (disagree) discrepar (de) ▫ **difference** n diferencia; (disagreement) desacuerdo ▫ **different** adj diferente, distinto ▫ **differentiate** [-'renʃɪeɪt] vi: **to differentiate (between)** distinguir (entre) ▫ **differently** adv de otro modo, en forma distinta

difficult ['dɪfɪkəlt] adj difícil ▫ **difficulty** n dificultad f

dig [dɪg] (pt, pp **dug**) vt (hole, ground) cavar ♦ n (prod) empujón m; (archaeological) excavación f; (remark) indirecta; **to ~ one's nails into** clavar las uñas en ▸ **dig up** vt (information) desenterrar; (plant) desarraigar

digest [vb daɪ'dʒest, n 'daɪdʒest] vt (food) digerir; (facts) asimilar ♦ n resumen m ▫ **digestion** [dɪ'dʒestʃən] n digestión f

digit ['dɪdʒɪt] n (number) dígito; (finger) dedo ▫ **digital** adj digital ▫ **digital camera** n cámara digital ▫ **digital TV** n televisión f digital

dignified ['dɪgnɪfaɪd] adj grave, solemne

dignity ['dɪgnɪtɪ] n dignidad f

digs [dɪgz] (BRIT: inf) npl pensión f, alojamiento

dilemma [daɪ'lemə] n dilema m

dill [dɪl] n eneldo

dilute [daɪ'luːt] vt diluir

dim [dɪm] adj (light) débil; (outline) indistinto; (room) oscuro; (inf: stupid) lerdo ♦ vt (light) bajar

dime [daɪm] n (US) moneda de diez centavos

dimension [dɪ'menʃən] n dimensión f

diminish [dɪ'mɪnɪʃ] vt, vi disminuir

din [dɪn] n estruendo, estrépito

dine [daɪn] vi cenar ▫ **diner** n (person) comensal mf

dinghy ['dɪŋgɪ] n bote m; (also: **rubber ~**) lancha (neumática)

dingy ['dɪndʒɪ] adj (room) sombrío; (colour) sucio

dining car ['daɪnɪŋ-] (BRIT) n (RAIL) coche-comedor m

dining room ['daɪnɪŋ-] n comedor m

dining table n mesa f de comedor

dinner ['dɪnə'] n (evening meal) cena; (lunch) comida; (public) cena, banquete m ▫ **dinner jacket** n smoking m ▫ **dinner party** n cena ▫ **dinner time** n (evening) hora de cenar; (midday) hora de comer

dinosaur ['daɪnəsɔː'] n dinosaurio m

dip [dɪp] n (slope) pendiente m; (in sea) baño; (CULIN) salsa ♦ vt (in water) mojar; (ladle etc) meter; (BRIT AUT) **to ~ one's lights** poner luces de cruce ♦ vi (road etc) descender, bajar

diploma [dɪ'pləumə] n diploma m

diplomacy [dɪ'pləuməsɪ] n diplomacia

diplomat ['dɪpləmæt] n diplomático(-a) ▫ **diplomatic** [dɪplə'mætɪk] adj diplomático

dipstick ['dɪpstɪk] (BRIT) n (AUT) varilla de nivel (del aceite)

dire [daɪə'] adj calamitoso

direct [daɪ'rekt] adj directo; (challenge) claro; (person) franco ♦ vt dirigir;

direction *(order)*: **to ~ sb to do sth** mandar a algn hacer algo ♦ *adv* derecho; **can you ~ me to ...?** ¿puede indicarme dónde está ...? ❑ **direct debit** (BRIT) *n* domiciliación *f* bancaria de recibos

direction [dɪ'rekʃən] *n* dirección *f*; **sense of ~** sentido de la dirección; **directions** *npl* (*instructions*) instrucciones *fpl*; **directions for use** modo de empleo

directly [dɪ'rektlɪ] *adv* (*in straight line*) directamente; (*at once*) en seguida

director [dɪ'rektə] *n* director(a) *m/f*

directory [dɪ'rektərɪ] *n* (TEL) guía (telefónica); (COMPUT) directorio ❑ **directory enquiries** (US **directory assistance**) *n* (servicio de) información *f*

dirt [dɜ:t] *n* suciedad *f*; (*earth*) tierra ❑ **dirty** *adj* sucio; (*joke*) verde, colorado (MEX) ♦ *vt* ensuciar; (*stain*) manchar

disability [dɪsə'bɪlɪtɪ] *n* incapacidad *f*

disabled [dɪs'eɪbld] *adj*: **to be physically ~** ser minusválido(-a); **to be mentally ~** ser deficiente mental

disadvantage [dɪsəd'vɑ:ntɪdʒ] *n* desventaja, inconveniente *m*

disagree [dɪsə'griː] *vi* (*differ*) discrepar; **to ~ (with)** no estar de acuerdo (con) ❑ **disagreeable** *adj* desagradable; (*person*) antipático ❑ **disagreement** *n* desacuerdo

disappear [dɪsə'pɪə] *vi* desaparecer ❑ **disappearance** *n* desaparición *f*

disappoint [dɪsə'pɔɪnt] *vt* decepcionar, defraudar ❑ **disappointed** *adj* decepcionado ❑ **disappointing** *adj* decepcionante ❑ **disappointment** *n* decepción *f*

disapproval [dɪsə'pruːvəl] *n* desaprobación *f*

disapprove [dɪsə'pruːv] *vi*: **to ~ of** ver mal

disarm [dɪs'ɑːm] *vt* desarmar ❑ **disarmament** [dɪs'ɑːməmənt] *n* desarme *m*

disaster [dɪ'zɑːstə] *n* desastre *m*

disastrous [dɪ'zɑːstrəs] *adj* desastroso

disbelief [dɪsbə'liːf] *n* incredulidad *f*

disc [dɪsk] *n* disco; (COMPUT) = **disk**

discard [dɪs'kɑːd] *vt* (*old things*) tirar; (*fig*) descartar

discharge [*vb* dɪs'tʃɑːdʒ, *n* 'dɪstʃɑːdʒ] *vt* (*task*, *duty*) cumplir; (*waste*) verter; (*patient*) dar de alta; (*employee*) despedir; (*soldier*) licenciar; (*defendant*) poner en libertad ♦ *n* (ELEC) descarga; (MED) supuración *f*; (*dismissal*) despedida; (*of duty*) desempeño; (*of debt*) pago, descargo

discipline ['dɪsɪplɪn] *n* disciplina ♦ *vt* disciplinar; (*punish*) castigar

disc jockey *n* pinchadiscos *mf inv*

disclose [dɪs'kləuz] *vt* revelar

disco ['dɪskəu] *n abbr* discoteca

discoloured [dɪs'kʌləd] (US **discolored**) *adj* descolorido

discomfort [dɪs'kʌmfət] *n* incomodidad *f*; (*unease*) inquietud *f*; (*physical*) malestar *m*

disconnect [dɪskə'nekt] *vt* separar; (ELEC *etc*) desconectar

discontent [dɪskən'tent] *n* descontento

discontinue [dɪskən'tɪnjuː] *vt* interrumpir; (*payments*) suspender; **"discontinued"** (COMM) "ya no se fabrica"

discount [*n* 'dɪskaunt, *vb* dɪs'kaunt] *n* descuento ♦ *vt* descontar

discourage [dɪs'kʌrɪdʒ] *vt* desalentar; (*advise against*): **to ~ sb from doing** disuadir a algn de hacer

discover [dɪs'kʌvə] *vt* descubrir; (*error*) darse cuenta de ❑ **discovery** *n* descubrimiento

discredit [dɪs'kredɪt] *vt* desacreditar

discreet [dɪs'kriːt] *adj* (*tactful*) discreto; (*careful*) circunspecto, prudente

discrepancy [dɪs'krepənsɪ] *n* diferencia

discretion [dɪ'skreʃən] n (tact) discreción f; **at the ~ of** a criterio de

discriminate [dɪ'skrɪmɪneɪt] vi: **to ~ between** distinguir entre; **to ~ against** discriminar contra ❑ **discrimination** [-'neɪʃən] n (discernment) perspicacia; (bias) discriminación f

discuss [dɪ'skʌs] vt discutir; (a theme) tratar ❑ **discussion** [dɪ'skʌʃən] n discusión f

disease [dɪ'ziːz] n enfermedad f

disembark [dɪsɪm'bɑːk] vt, vi desembarcar

disgrace [dɪs'ɡreɪs] n ignominia; (shame) vergüenza, escándalo ♦ vt deshonrar ❑ **disgraceful** adj vergonzoso

disgruntled [dɪs'ɡrʌntld] adj disgustado, descontento

disguise [dɪs'ɡaɪz] n disfraz m ♦ vt disfrazar; **in ~** disfrazado

disgust [dɪs'ɡʌst] n repugnancia ♦ vt repugnar, dar asco a

⚠ Be careful not to translate **disgust** by the Spanish word *disgustar*.

disgusted [dɪs'ɡʌstɪd] adj indignado

⚠ Be careful not to translate **disgusted** by *disgustado*.

disgusting [dɪs'ɡʌstɪŋ] adj repugnante, asqueroso; (behaviour etc) vergonzoso

dish [dɪʃ] n (gen) plato; **to do** or **wash the dishes** fregar los platos ❑ **dishcloth** n estropajo

dishonest [dɪs'ɒnɪst] adj (person) poco honrado; (means) fraudulento

dishtowel ['dɪʃtaʊəl] (US) n estropajo

dishwasher ['dɪʃwɒʃəʳ] n lavaplatos m inv

disillusion [dɪsɪ'luːʒən] vt desilusionar

disinfectant [dɪsɪn'fɛktənt] n desinfectante m

disintegrate [dɪs'ɪntɪɡreɪt] vi disgregarse, desintegrarse

disk [dɪsk] n (esp US) = **disc**; (COMPUT) disco, disquete m; **single-sided ~** disco de una cara ❑ **disk drive** n disc drive m ❑ **diskette** n = **disk**

dislike [dɪs'laɪk] n antipatía, aversión f ♦ vt tener antipatía a

dislocate ['dɪsləkeɪt] vt dislocar

disloyal [dɪs'lɔɪəl] adj desleal

dismal ['dɪzml] adj (gloomy) deprimente, triste; (very bad) malísimo, fatal

dismantle [dɪs'mæntl] vt desmontar, desarmar

dismay [dɪs'meɪ] n consternación f ♦ vt consternar

dismiss [dɪs'mɪs] vt (worker) despedir; (pupils) dejar marchar; (soldiers) dar permiso para irse; (idea, LAW) rechazar; (possibility) descartar ❑ **dismissal** n despido

disobedient [dɪsə'biːdɪənt] adj desobediente

disobey [dɪsə'beɪ] vt desobedecer

disorder [dɪs'ɔːdəʳ] n desorden m; (rioting) disturbios mpl; (MED) trastorno

disorganized [dɪs'ɔːɡənaɪzd] adj desorganizado

disown [dɪs'əʊn] vt (action) renegar de; (person) negar cualquier tipo de relación con

dispatch [dɪs'pætʃ] vt enviar ♦ n (sending) envío; (PRESS) informe m; (MIL) parte m

dispel [dɪs'pɛl] vt disipar

dispense [dɪs'pɛns] vt (medicines) preparar ► **dispense with** vt fus prescindir de ❑ **dispenser** n (container) distribuidor m automático

disperse [dɪs'pɜːs] vt dispersar ♦ vi dispersarse

display [dɪs'pleɪ] n (in shop window) escaparate m; (exhibition) exposición f; (COMPUT) visualización f; (of feeling) manifestación f ♦ vt exponer; (ostentatiously) lucir

displease [dɪs'pliːz] vt (offend) ofender; (annoy) fastidiar

disposable [dɪs'pəʊzəbl] adj desechable; (income) disponible

disposal [dɪs'pəʊzl] n (of rubbish) destrucción f; **at one's ~** a su disposición

dispose [dɪs'pəʊz] vi: **to ~ of** (unwanted goods) deshacerse de; (problem etc) resolver ◻ **disposition** [dɪspə'zɪʃən] n (nature) temperamento; (inclination) propensión f

disproportionate [dɪsprə'pɔːʃənət] adj desproporcionado

dispute [dɪs'pjuːt] n disputa; (also: **industrial ~**) conflicto (laboral) ◆ vt (argue) disputar, discutir; (question) cuestionar

disqualify [dɪs'kwɒlɪfaɪ] vt (SPORT) descalificar; **to ~ sb for sth/from doing sth** incapacitar a algn para algo/hacer algo

disregard [dɪsrɪ'gɑːd] vt (ignore) no hacer caso de

disrupt [dɪs'rʌpt] vt (plans) desbaratar, trastornar; (conversation) interrumpir ◻ **disruption** [dɪs'rʌpʃən] n trastorno; desbaratamiento; interrupción f

dissatisfaction [dɪssætɪsfæk'ʃən] n disgusto, descontento

dissatisfied [dɪs'sætɪsfaɪd] adj insatisfecho

dissect [dɪ'sekt] vt disecar

dissent [dɪ'sent] n disensión f

dissertation [dɪsə'teɪʃən] n tesina

dissolve [dɪ'zɒlv] vt disolver ◆ vi disolverse; **to ~ in(to) tears** deshacerse en lágrimas

distance ['dɪstəns] n distancia; **in the ~** a lo lejos

distant ['dɪstənt] adj lejano; (manner) reservado, frío

distil [dɪs'tɪl] (US **distill**) vt destilar ◻ **distillery** n destilería

distinct [dɪs'tɪŋkt] adj (different) distinto; (clear) claro; (unmistakeable)

inequívoco; **as ~ from** a diferencia de ◻ **distinction** [dɪs'tɪŋkʃən] n distinción f; (honour) honor m; (in exam) sobresaliente m ◻ **distinctive** adj distintivo

distinguish [dɪs'tɪŋgwɪʃ] vt distinguir; **to ~ o.s.** destacarse ◻ **distinguished** adj (eminent) distinguido

distort [dɪs'tɔːt] vt distorsionar; (shape, image) deformar

distract [dɪs'trækt] vt distraer ◻ **distracted** adj distraído ◻ **distraction** [dɪs'trækʃən] n distracción f; (confusion) aturdimiento

distraught [dɪs'trɔːt] adj loco de inquietud

distress [dɪs'tres] n (anguish) angustia, aflicción f ◆ vt afligir ◻ **distressing** adj angustioso; doloroso

distribute [dɪs'trɪbjuːt] vt distribuir; (share out) repartir ◻ **distribution** [-'bjuːʃən] n distribución f, reparto ◻ **distributor** n (AUT) distribuidor m; (COMM) distribuidora

district ['dɪstrɪkt] n (of country) zona, región f; (of town) barrio; (ADMIN) distrito ◻ **district attorney** (US) n fiscal mf

distrust [dɪs'trʌst] n desconfianza ◆ vt desconfiar de

disturb [dɪs'tɜːb] vt (person: bother, interrupt) molestar; (: upset) perturbar, inquietar; (disorganize) alterar ◻ **disturbance** n (upheaval) perturbación f; (political etc: gen pl) disturbio; (of mind) trastorno ◻ **disturbed** adj (worried, upset) preocupado, angustiado; **emotionally disturbed** trastornado; (childhood) inseguro ◻ **disturbing** adj inquietante, perturbador(a)

ditch [dɪtʃ] n zanja; (irrigation ditch) acequia ◆ vt (inf: partner) deshacerse de; (: plan, car etc) abandonar

ditto ['dɪtəʊ] adv idem, lo mismo

dive [daɪv] n (from board) salto; (underwater) buceo; (of submarine)

diverse [daɪˈvəːs] *adj* diversos(-as), varios(-as)

diversion [daɪˈvəːʃən] *n* (BRIT AUT) desviación f; (distraction, MIL) diversión f; (of funds) distracción f

diversity [daɪˈvəːsɪtɪ] *n* diversidad f

divert [daɪˈvəːt] *vt* (turn aside) desviar

divide [dɪˈvaɪd] *vt* dividir; (separate) separar ♦ *vi* dividirse; (road) bifurcarse ❑ **divided highway** (US) *n* carretera de doble calzada

divine [dɪˈvaɪn] *adj* (also fig) divino

diving [ˈdaɪvɪŋ] *n* (SPORT) salto; (underwater) buceo ❑ **diving board** *n* trampolín *m*

division [dɪˈvɪʒən] *n* división f; (sharing out) reparto; (disagreement) diferencias *fpl*; (COMM) sección f

divorce [dɪˈvɔːs] *n* divorcio ♦ *vt* divorciarse de ❑ **divorced** *adj* divorciado ❑ **divorcee** [-ˈsiː] *n* divorciado(-a)

D.I.Y. (BRIT) *adj, n abbr* = **do-it-yourself**

dizzy [ˈdɪzɪ] *adj* (spell) de mareo; **to feel ~** marearse

DJ *n abbr* = **disc jockey**

DNA *n abbr* (= deoxyribonucleic acid) ADN *m*

do

KEYWORD

[duː] (*pt* did, *pp* done) *n* (inf: party etc): we're having a little do on Saturday damos una fiestecita el sábado; it was rather a grand do fue un acontecimiento a lo grande
♦ *aux vb*

1 (in negative constructions: not translated): I don't understand no entiendo

2 (to form questions: not translated): didn't you know? ¿no lo sabías?; what do you think? ¿qué opinas?

3 (for emphasis, in polite expressions): people do make mistakes sometimes sí que se cometen errores a veces; she does seem rather late a mí también me parece que se ha retrasado; do sit down/help yourself siéntate/sírvete por favor; do take care! ¡ten cuidado(, te pido)!

4 (used to avoid repeating vb): she sings better than I do canta mejor que yo; do you agree? — yes, I do/no, I don't ¿estás de acuerdo? — sí (lo estoy)/no (lo estoy); she lives in Glasgow — so do I vive en Glasgow — yo también; he didn't like it and neither did we no le gustó y a nosotros tampoco; who made this mess? — I did ¿quién hizo esta chapuza? — yo; he asked me to help him and I did me pidió que le ayudara y lo hice

5 (in question tags): you like him, don't you? te gusta, ¿verdad? or ¿no?; I don't know him, do I? creo que no le conozco
♦ *vt*

1 (gen, carry out, perform etc): what are you doing tonight? ¿qué haces esta noche?; what can I do for you? ¿en qué puedo servirle?; to do the washing-up/cooking fregar los platos/cocinar; to do one's teeth/hair/nails lavarse los dientes/arreglarse el pelo/arreglarse las uñas

2 (AUT etc): the car was doing 100 el coche iba a 100; we've done 200 km already ya hemos hecho 200 km; he can do 100 in that car puede ir a 100

en ese coche
♦ vi

1 (act, behave) hacer; **do as I do** haz como yo

2 (get on, fare): **he's doing well/badly at school** va bien/mal en la escuela; **the firm is doing well** la empresa anda or va bien; **how do you do?** mucho gusto; (less formal) ¿qué tal?

3 (suit): **will it do?** ¿sirve?, ¿está or va bien?

4 (be sufficient) bastar; **will £10 do?** ¿será bastante con £10?; **that'll do** así está bien; **that'll do!** (in annoyance) ¡ya está bien!, ¡basta ya!; **to make do (with)** arreglárselas (con)

▶ **do up** vt (laces) atar; (zip, dress, shirt) abrochar; (renovate: room, house) renovar

▶ **do with** vt fus (need): **I could do with a drink/some help** no me vendría mal un trago/un poco de ayuda; (be connected) tener que ver con; **what has it got to do with you?** ¿qué tiene que ver contigo?

▶ **do without** vi pasar sin; **if you're late for tea then you'll do without** si llegas tarde tendrás que quedarte sin cenar ♦ vt fus pasar sin; **I can do without a car** puedo pasar sin coche

dock [dɔk] n (NAUT) muelle m; (LAW) banquillo (de los acusados) ♦ vi (enter dock) atracar (la) muelle; (SPACE) acoplarse; **docks** npl (NAUT) muelles mpl, puerto sg

doctor ['dɔktə*] n médico(-a); (Ph.D. etc) doctor(a) m/f ♦ vt (drink etc) adulterar
❏ **Doctor of Philosophy** n Doctor en Filosofía y Letras

document ['dɔkjumənt] n documento n
❏ **documentary** [-'mentəri] adj documental ♦ n documental

❏ **documentation** [-men'teɪʃən] n documentación f

dodge [dɔdʒ] n (fig) truco ♦ vt evadir; (blow) esquivar

dodgy ['dɔdʒi] adj (inf: uncertain) dudoso; (suspicious) sospechoso; (risky) arriesgado

does [dʌz] vb see **do**

doesn't ['dʌznt] = **does not**

dog [dɔg] n perro ♦ vt seguir los pasos de; (bad luck) perseguir ❏ **doggy bag** ['dɔgi-] n bolsa para llevarse las sobras de la comida

do-it-yourself [du:ɪtjɔ:'self] n bricolaje n

dole [dəul] (BRIT) n (payment) subsidio de paro; **on the ~** parado

doll [dɔl] n muñeca; (US: inf: woman) muñeca, gachí f

dollar ['dɔlə*] n dólar m

dolphin ['dɔlfin] n delfín m

dome [dəum] n (ARCH) cúpula

domestic [də'mestɪk] adj (animal, duty) doméstico; (flight, policy) nacional
❏ **domestic appliance** n aparato m doméstico, aparato m de uso doméstico

dominant ['dɔmɪnənt] adj dominante

dominate ['dɔmɪneɪt] vt dominar

domino ['dɔmɪnəu] (pl **dominoes**) n ficha de dominó ❏ **dominoes** n (game) dominó

donate [də'neɪt] vt donar ❏ **donation** [də'neɪʃən] n donativo

done [dʌn] pp of **do**

donkey ['dɔŋki] n burro

donor ['dəunə*] n donante mf ❏ **donor card** n carnet m de donante

don't [dəunt] = **do not**

donut ['dəunʌt] (US) n = **doughnut**

doodle ['du:dl] vi hacer dibujitos or garabatos

doom [du:m] n (fate) suerte f ♦ vt: **to be doomed to failure** estar condenado al fracaso

door [dɔ:] n puerta □ **doorbell** n timbre m □ **door handle** n tirador m; (of car) manija □ **doorknob** n pomo m de la puerta, manilla f (LAm) □ **doorstep** n peldaño □ **doorway** n entrada, puerta

dope [dəʊp] n (inf: illegal drug) droga; (: person) imbécil m/f ♦ vt (horse etc) drogar

dormitory [ˈdɔ:mɪtrɪ] n (BRIT) dormitorio; (US) colegio mayor

DOS n abbr (= disk operating system) DOS m

dosage [ˈdəʊsɪdʒ] n dosis f inv

dose [dəʊs] n dósis f inv

dot [dɒt] n punto ♦ vi: **dotted with** salpicado de; **on the ~** en punto □ **dotted line** [ˈdɒtɪd-] n: **to sign on the dotted line**

double [ˈdʌbl] adj doble ♦ adv (twice): **to cost** ~ costar el doble ♦ n doble m ♦ vt doblar ♦ vi doblarse; **on the ~, at the ~** (BRIT) corriendo □ **double back** vi (person) volver sobre sus pasos □ **double bass** n contrabajo □ **double bed** n cama de matrimonio □ **double-check** vt volver a revisar ♦ vi: **I'll double-check** voy a revisarlo otra vez □ **double-click** vi (COMPUT) hacer doble clic □ **double-cross** vt (trick) engañar; (betray) traicionar □ **doubledecker** n autobús m de dos pisos □ **double glazing** (BRIT) n doble acristalamiento □ **double room** n habitación f doble □ **doubles** n (TENNIS) juego de dobles □ **double yellow lines** npl (BRIT: AUT) línea doble amarilla de prohibido aparcar, ~ línea fsg amarilla continua

doubt [daʊt] n duda ♦ vt dudar; (suspect) dudar de; **to** ~ **that** dudar que □ **doubtful** adj dudoso; (person): **to be doubtful about sth** tener dudas sobre algo □ **doubtless** adv sin duda

dough [dəʊ] n masa, pasta □ **doughnut** (US **donut**) n ~ rosquilla

dove [dʌv] n paloma

down [daʊn] n (feathers) plumón m, flojel m ♦ adv (downwards) abajo, hacia abajo; (on the ground) por o en tierra ♦ prep abajo ♦ vt (inf: drink) beberse; ~ **with X!** ¡abajo X! □ **down-and-out** n vagabundo(-a) □ **downfall** n caída, ruina □ **downhill** adv: **to go downhill** (also fig) ir cuesta abajo

down: download vt (COMPUT) bajar □ **downright** adj (nonsense, lie) manifiesto; (refusal) terminante

Down's syndrome [ˈdaʊnz-] n síndrome m de Down

down: downstairs adv (below) (en el piso de) abajo; (downwards) escaleras abajo □ **down-to-earth** adj práctico □ **downtown** n en el centro de la ciudad □ **down under** adv en Australia (or Nueva Zelanda) □ **downward** [-wəd] adj, adv hacia abajo □ **downwards** [-wədz] adv hacia abajo

doz. abbr = **dozen**

doze [dəʊz] vi dormitar

dozen [ˈdʌzn] n docena; **a ~ books** una docena de libros; **dozens of** cantidad de

Dr. abbr = **doctor; drive**

drab [dræb] adj gris, monótono

draft [drɑ:ft] n (first copy) borrador m; (POL: of bill) anteproyecto; (US: call-up) quinta ♦ vt (plan) preparar; (write roughly) hacer un borrador de; see also **draught**

drag [dræg] vt arrastrar; (river) dragar, rastrear ♦ vi (time) pasar despacio; (play, film etc) hacerse pesado ♦ n (inf) lata; (women's clothing): **in ~** = vestido de travestí; **to ~ and drop** (COMPUT) arrastrar y soltar

dragon [ˈdrægən] n dragón m

dragonfly [ˈdrægənflaɪ] n libélula

drain [dreɪn] n desaguadero, sumidero; (source of loss): **to be a ~ on**

consumir, agotar ♦ vt (land, marshes) desaguar; (reservoir) desecar; (vegetables) escurrir ♦ vi escurrirse □ **drainage** n (act) desagüe m; (MED, AGR) drenaje m; (sewage) alcantarillado □ **drainpipe** n tubo de desagüe

drama ['drɑːmə] n (art) teatro m; (play) drama m; (excitement) emoción f □ **dramatic** [drəˈmætɪk] adj dramático; (sudden, marked) espectacular

drank [dræŋk] pt of **drink**

drape [dreɪp] vt (cloth) colocar; (flag) colgar; **drapes** npl (US) cortinas fpl

drastic ['dræstɪk] adj (measure) severo; (change) radical, drástico

draught [drɑːft] (US **draft**) n (of air) corriente f de aire; (NAUT) calado; **on** ~ (beer) de barril □ **draught beer** n cerveza de barril □ **draughts** (BRIT) n (game) juego de damas

draw [drɔː] (pt **drew**, pp **drawn**) vt (picture) dibujar; (cart) tirar de; (curtain) correr; (take out) sacar; (attract) atraer; (money) retirar; (wages) cobrar ♦ vi (SPORT) empatar ♦ n (SPORT) empate m; (lottery) sorteo □ **draw out** vi (lengthen) alargarse ♦ vt sacar □ **draw up** vi (stop) pararse ♦ vt (chair) acercar; (document) redactar □ **drawback** n inconveniente m, desventaja

drawer [drɔːʳ] n cajón m

drawing ['drɔːɪŋ] n dibujo □ **drawing pin** (BRIT) n chincheta □ **drawing room** n salón m

drawn [drɔːn] pp of **draw**

dread [dred] n pavor m, terror m ♦ vt temer, tener miedo or pavor a □ **dreadful** adj horroroso

dream [driːm] (pt, pp **dreamed** or **dreamt**) n sueño ♦ vt, vi soñar □ **dreamer** n soñador(a) m/f

dreamt [dremt] pt, pp of **dream**

dreary ['drɪərɪ] adj monótono

drench [drentʃ] vt empapar

dress [dres] n (vestido); (clothing) ropa ♦ vt vestir; (wound) vendar ♦ vi

vestirse; **to get dressed** vestirse ► **dress up** vi vestirse de etiqueta; (in fancy dress) disfrazarse □ **dress circle** (BRIT) n principal m □ **dresser** n (furniture) aparador m; (: US) cómoda (con espejo) □ **dressing** n (MED) vendaje m; (CULIN) aliño □ **dressing gown** (BRIT) n bata □ **dressing room** n (THEATRE) camarín m; (SPORT) vestuario □ **dressing table** n tocador m □ **dressmaker** n modista, costurera

drew [druː] pt of **draw**

dribble ['drɪbl] vi (baby) babear ♦ vt (ball) regatear

dried [draɪd] adj (fruit) seco; (milk) en polvo

drier ['draɪəʳ] n = **dryer**

drift [drɪft] n (of current etc) flujo; (of snow) ventisquero; (meaning) significado ♦ vi (boat) ir a la deriva; (sand, snow) amontonarse

drill [drɪl] n (drill bit) broca; (tool for DIY etc) taladro; (of dentist) fresa; (for mining etc) perforadora, barrena; (MIL) instrucción f ♦ vt perforar, taladrar; (troops) enseñar la instrucción a ♦ vi (for oil) perforar

drink [drɪŋk] (pt **drank**, pp **drunk**) n bebida; (sip) trago ♦ vt, vi beber; **to have a** ~ tomar algo; tomar una copa or un trago; **a** ~ **of water** un trago de agua □ **drink-driving**: **to be charged with drink-driving** ser acusado de conducir borracho or en estado de embriaguez □ **drinker** n bebedor(a) m/f □ **drinking water** n agua potable

drip [drɪp] n (act) goteo; (one drip) gota; (MED) gota a gota m ♦ vi gotear

drive [draɪv] (pt **drove**, pp **driven**) n (journey) viaje m (en coche); (also: **driveway**) entrada; (energy) energía, vigor m; (COMPUT: also: **disk** ~) drive m ♦ vt (car) conducir (SP), manejar (LAm); (nail) clavar; (push) empujar; (TECH: motor) impulsar ♦ vi (AUT: at controls) conducir; (: travel) pasearse en coche;

left/right-hand ~ conducción f a la izquierda/derecha; **to ~ sb mad** volverle loco a algn ▶ **drive out** vt (force out) expulsar, echar □ **drive-in** adj (esp US): **drive-in cinema** autocine m

driven ['drɪvn] pp of **drive**

driver ['draɪvəʳ] n conductor(a) m/f (SP), chofer mf (LAM); (of taxi, bus) chófer mf (SP), chofer mf (LAM) □ **driver's license** (US) n carnet m de conducir

driveway ['draɪweɪ] n entrada

driving ['draɪvɪŋ] n el conducir (SP), el manejar (LAM) □ **driving instructor** n profesor/a m/f de autoescuela (SP), instructor(a) m/f de manejo (LAM) □ **driving lesson** n clase f de conducir (SP) or manejar (LAM) □ **driving licence** (BRIT) n licencia de manejo (LAM), carnet m de conducir (SP) □ **driving test** n examen m de conducir (SP) or manejar (LAM)

drizzle ['drɪzl] n llovizna

droop [druːp] vi (flower) marchitarse; (shoulders) encorvarse; (head) inclinarse

drop [drɒp] n (of water) gota; (lessening) baja; (fall) caída ♦ vt dejar caer; (voice, eyes, price) bajar; (passenger) dejar; (omit) omitir ♦ vi (object) caer; (wind) amainar ▶ **drop in** n (inf: visit): **to drop in (on)** pasar por casa (de) ▶ **drop off** vi (sleep) dormirse ♦ vt (passenger) dejar ▶ **drop out** vi (withdraw) retirarse

drought [draʊt] n sequía

drove [drəʊv] pt of **drive**

drown [draʊn] vt ahogar ♦ vi ahogarse

drowsy ['draʊzɪ] adj soñoliento; **to be ~** tener sueño

drug [drʌg] n medicamento; (narcotic) droga ♦ vt drogar; **to be on drugs** drogarse □ **drug addict** n drogadicto(-a) □ **drug dealer** n traficante mf de drogas □ **druggist** (US) n farmacéutico ♦ □ **drugstore** (US) n farmacia

drum [drʌm] n tambor m; (for oil, petrol) bidón m; **drums** npl batería □ **drummer** n tambor m

drunk [drʌŋk] pp of **drink** ♦ adj borracho ♦ n (also: **drunkard**) borracho(-a) □ **drunken** adj borracho; (laughter, party) de borrachos

dry [draɪ] adj seco; (day) sin lluvia; (climate) árido, seco ♦ vt secar; (tears) enjugarse ♦ vi secarse ▶ **dry off** vi secarse ♦ vt secar ▶ **dry up** vi (river) secarse □ **dry-cleaner's** n tintorería □ **dry-cleaning** n lavado en seco □ **dryer** n (for hair) secador m; (US: for clothes) secadora

DSS n abbr = **Department of Social Security**

DTP n abbr (= desk-top publishing) autoedición f

dual ['djuːəl] adj doble □ **dual carriageway** (BRIT) n carretera de doble calzada

dubious ['djuːbɪəs] adj indeciso; (reputation, company) sospechoso

duck [dʌk] n pato ♦ vi agacharse

due [djuː] adj (owed): **he is ~ £10** se le deben 10 libras; (expected: event): **the meeting is ~ on Wednesday** la reunión tendrá lugar el miércoles; (: arrival): **the train is ~ at 8am** el tren tiene su llegada para las 8; (proper) debido ♦ n: **to give sb his** (or **her**) **~** ser justo con algn ♦ adv: **~ north** derecho al norte

duel ['djuːəl] n duelo

duet [djuː'et] n dúo

dug [dʌg] pt, pp of **dig**

duke [djuːk] n duque m

dull [dʌl] adj (light) débil; (stupid) torpe; (boring) pesado; (sound, pain) sordo; (weather, day) gris ♦ vt (pain, grief) aliviar; (mind, senses) entorpecer

dumb [dʌm] adj mudo; (pej: stupid) estúpido

dummy ['dʌmɪ] n (tailor's dummy)
maniquí m; (mock-up) maqueta; (BRIT:
for baby) chupete m; (inf: place) postizo

dump [dʌmp] n (also: rubbish ~)
basurero, vertedero; (inf: place) cuchitril
m ♦ vt (put down) dejar; (get rid of)
deshacerse de; (COMPUT: data) transferir

dumpling ['dʌmplɪŋ] n bola de masa
hervida

dune [dju:n] n duna

dungarees [dʌŋgə'ri:z] npl mono

dungeon ['dʌndʒən] n calabozo

duplex ['dju:pleks] n dúplex m

duplicate [n 'dju:plɪkət, vb 'dju:plɪkeɪt]
n duplicado ♦ vt duplicar; (photocopy)
fotocopiar; (repeat) repetir; **in ~** por
duplicado

durable ['djuərəbl] adj duradero

duration [djuə'reɪʃən] n duración f

during ['djuərɪŋ] prep durante

dusk [dʌsk] n crepúsculo, anochecer m

dust [dʌst] n polvo ♦ vt quitar el polvo
a, desempolvar; (cake etc): **to ~ with**
espolvorear de ❏ **dustbin** (BRIT) n
cubo o bote m (MEX) or tacho (SC) de
la basura ❏ **duster** n paño, trapo
❏ **dustman** (BRIT: irreg) n basurero
❏ **dustpan** n cogedor m ❏ **dusty** adj
polvoriento

Dutch [dʌtʃ] adj holandés(-esa) ♦ n
(LING) holandés m; **the ~** npl los
holandeses; **to go ~** (inf) pagar cada
uno lo suyo ❏ **Dutchman** (irreg) n
holandés m ❏ **Dutchwoman** (irreg) n
holandésa

duty ['dju:tɪ] n deber m; (tax) derechos
mpl de aduana; **on ~** de servicio; (at
night etc) de guardia; **off ~** libre de
servicio ❏ **duty-free** adj libre de
impuestos

duvet ['du:veɪ] (BRIT) n edredón m

DVD n abbr (= digital versatile or video
disc) DVD m ❏ **DVD player** n lector m
(de) DVD

dwarf [dwɔ:f] (pl **dwarves**) n enano(-a)
♦ vt empequeñecer

dwell [dwel] (pt, pp **dwelt**) vi morar
▶ **dwell on** vt fus explayarse en

dwelt [dwelt] pt, pp of **dwell**

dwindle ['dwɪndl] vi disminuir

dye [daɪ] n tinte m ♦ vt teñir

dying ['daɪɪŋ] adj moribundo

dynamic [daɪ'næmɪk] adj dinámico

dynamite ['daɪnəmaɪt] n dinamita

dyslexia [dɪs'leksɪə] n dislexia

dyslexic [dɪs'leksɪk] adj, n disléxico(-a)
m/f

E, e

E [i:] n (MUS) mi m

E111 n abbr (= form E111) impreso E111

each [i:tʃ] adj cada inv ♦ pron cada uno;
~ other el uno al otro; **they hate ~
other** se odian (entre ellos or
mutuamente); **they have 2 books ~**
tienen 2 libros por persona

eager ['i:gə'] adj (keen) entusiasmado;
to be ~ to do sth tener muchas ganas
de hacer algo, impacientarse por
hacer algo; **to be ~ for** tener muchas
ganas de

eagle ['i:gl] n águila

ear [ɪə'] n oreja; oído; (of corn) espiga
❏ **earache** n dolor m de oídos
❏ **eardrum** n tímpano

earl [ə:l] n conde m

earlier ['ə:lɪə'] adj anterior ♦ adv antes

early ['ə:lɪ] adv temprano; (before time)
con tiempo, con anticipación ♦ adj
temprano; (settlers etc) primitivo;
(death, departure) prematuro; (reply)
pronto; **to have an ~ night** acostarse
temprano; **in the ~ or ~ in the spring/
19th century** a principios de
primavera/del siglo diecinueve
❏ **early retirement** n jubilación f
anticipada

earmark ['ɪəmɑ:k] vt: **to ~ (for)** reservar
(para), destinar (a)

earn [əːn] vt (salary) percibir; (interest) devengar; (praise) merecerse

earnest [ˈəːnɪst] adj (wish) fervoroso; (person) serio, formal; **in ~** en serio

earnings [ˈəːnɪŋz] npl (personal) sueldo, ingresos mpl; (company) ganancias fpl

ear: earphones npl auriculares mpl ❏ **earplugs** npl tapones mpl para los oídos ❏ **earring** n pendiente m, arete m

earth [əːθ] n tierra; (BRIT ELEC) cable m de toma de tierra ♦ vt (BRIT ELEC) conectar a tierra ❏ **earthquake** n terremoto

ease [iːz] n facilidad f; (comfort) comodidad f ♦ vt (lessen: problem) mitigar; (: pain) aliviar; (: tension) reducir; **to ~ sth in/out** meter/sacar algo con cuidado; **at ~!** (MIL) ¡descansen!

easily [ˈiːzɪlɪ] adv fácilmente

east [iːst] n este m ♦ adj del este, oriental; (wind) este ♦ adv al este, hacia el este; **the E~** el Oriente; (POL) los países del Este ❏ **eastbound** adj en dirección este

Easter [ˈiːstəʳ] n Pascua (de Resurrección) ❏ **Easter egg** n huevo de Pascua

eastern [ˈiːstən] adj del este, oriental; (oriental) oriental

Easter Sunday n Domingo de Resurrección

easy [ˈiːzɪ] adj fácil; (simple) sencillo; (comfortable) holgado, cómodo; (relaxed) tranquilo ♦ adv: **to take it** or **things ~** (not worry) tomarlo con calma; (rest) descansar ❏ **easy-going** adj acomodadizo

eat [iːt] (pt ate, pp eaten) vt comer
▶ **eat out** vi comer fuera

eavesdrop [ˈiːvzdrɔp] vi: **to ~ (on)** escuchar a escondidas

e-book n libro electrónico

e-business [ˈiːbɪznɪs] n (company) negocio electrónico; (commerce) comercio electrónico

EC n abbr (= European Community) CE f

eccentric [ɪkˈsentrɪk] adj, n excéntrico/a f

echo [ˈekəu] (pl **echoes**) n eco ♦ vt (sound) repetir ♦ vi resonar, hacer eco

eclipse [ɪˈklɪps] n eclipse m

eco-friendly [ˈiːkəufrendlɪ] adj ecológico

ecological [iːkəˈlɔdʒɪkl] adj ecológico

ecology [ɪˈkɔlədʒɪ] n ecología

e-commerce n abbr comercio electrónico

economic [iːkəˈnɔmɪk] adj económico; (business etc) rentable ❏ **economical** adj económico; (person) económico ❏ **economics** n (SCOL) economía ♦ npl (of project etc) rentabilidad f

economist [ɪˈkɔnəmɪst] n economista m/f

economize [ɪˈkɔnəmaɪz] vi economizar, ahorrar

economy [ɪˈkɔnəmɪ] n economía ❏ **economy class** (AVIAT) clase f económica ❏ **economy class syndrome** n síndrome m de la clase turista

ecstasy [ˈekstəsɪ] n éxtasis m inv; (drug) éxtasis m inv ❏ **ecstatic** [eksˈtætɪk] adj extático

eczema [ˈeksɪmə] n eczema m

edge [edʒ] n (of knife) filo; (of object) borde m; (of lake) orilla ♦ vt (SEWING) ribetear; **on ~** (fig) = **edgy**; **to ~ away from** alejarse poco a poco de

edgy [ˈedʒɪ] adj nervioso, inquieto

edible [ˈedɪbl] adj comestible

Edinburgh [ˈedɪnbərə] n Edimburgo

edit [ˈedɪt] vt (be editor of) dirigir; (text, report) corregir, preparar ❏ **edition** [ɪˈdɪʃən] n edición f ❏ **editor** n (of newspaper) director(a) m/f; (of column): **foreign/political editor** encargado de la sección de extranjero/política; (of book) redactor(a) m/f ❏ **editorial** [-ˈtɔːrɪəl] adj editorial ♦ n editorial m

educate ['ɛdjukeɪt] vt (gen) educar; (instruct) instruir ❑ **educated** ['ɛdjukeɪtɪd] adj culto

education [ɛdju'keɪʃən] n educación f; (schooling) enseñanza; (SCOL) pedagogía ❑ **educational** adj (policy etc) educativo; (experience) docente; (toy) educativo

eel [iːl] n anguila

eerie ['ɪərɪ] adj misterioso

effect [ɪ'fɛkt] n efecto ♦ vt efectuar, llevar a cabo; **to take ~** (law) entrar en vigor o vigencia; (drug) surtir efecto; **in ~** en realidad; **effects** npl (property) efectos mpl ❑ **effective** adj eficaz; (actual) verdadero ❑ **effectively** adv eficazmente; (in reality) efectivamente

efficiency [ɪ'fɪʃənsɪ] n eficiencia f; rendimiento

efficient [ɪ'fɪʃənt] adj eficiente; (machine) de buen rendimiento ❑ **efficiently** adv eficientemente, de manera eficiente

effort ['ɛfət] n esfuerzo ❑ **effortless** adj sin ningún esfuerzo; (style) natural

e.g. adv abbr (= exempli gratia) p. ej.

egg [ɛg] n huevo; **hard-boiled/soft-boiled ~** huevo duro/pasado por agua ❑ **eggcup** n huevera ❑ **egg plant** (esp US) n berenjena ❑ **eggshell** n cáscara de huevo ❑ **egg white** n clara de huevo ❑ **egg yolk** n yema de huevo

ego ['iːgəu] n ego

Egypt ['iːdʒɪpt] n Egipto ❑ **Egyptian** ['iː'dʒɪpʃən] adj, n egipcio(-a) m/f

eight [eɪt] num ocho ❑ **eighteen** num diez y ocho, dieciocho ❑ **eighteenth** adj decimoctavo; **the eighteenth floor** la planta dieciocho; **the eighteenth of August** el dieciocho de agosto ❑ **eighth** num octavo ❑ **eightieth** ['eɪtɪɪθ] adj octogésimo

eighty ['eɪtɪ] num ochenta

Eire ['ɛərə] n Eire m

either ['aɪðə'] adj cualquiera de los dos; (both, each) cada ♦ pron: **~ (of them)** cualquiera (de los dos) ♦ adv tampoco ♦ conj: **~ yes or no** o sí o no; **on ~ side** en ambos lados; **I don't like ~** no me gusta ninguno(-a) de los (las) dos; **no, I don't ~** no, yo tampoco

eject [ɪ'dʒɛkt] vt echar, expulsar; (tenant) desahuciar

elaborate [adj ɪ'læbərɪt, vb ɪ'læbəreɪt] adj (complex) complejo ♦ vt (expand) ampliar; (refine) refinar ♦ vi explicar con más detalles

elastic [ɪ'læstɪk] n elástico ♦ adj elástico; (fig) flexible ❑ **elastic band** (BRIT) n gomita

elbow ['ɛlbəu] n codo

elder ['ɛldə'] adj mayor ♦ n (tree) saúco; (person) mayor ❑ **elderly** adj de edad, mayor ♦ npl: **the elderly** los mayores

eldest ['ɛldɪst] adj, n el(-la) mayor

elect [ɪ'lɛkt] vt elegir ♦ adj: **the president ~** el presidente electo; **to ~ to do** optar por hacer ❑ **election** n elección f ❑ **electoral** adj electoral ❑ **electorate** n electorado

electric [ɪ'lɛktrɪk] adj eléctrico ❑ **electrical** adj eléctrico ❑ **electric blanket** n manta eléctrica ❑ **electric fire** n estufa eléctrica ❑ **electrician** [ɪlɛk'trɪʃən] n electricista mf ❑ **electricity** [ɪlɛk'trɪsɪtɪ] n electricidad f ❑ **electric shock** n electrochoque m ❑ **electrify** [ɪ'lɛktrɪfaɪ] vt (RAIL) electrificar; (fig: audience) electrizar

electronic [ɪlɛk'trɒnɪk] adj electrónico ❑ **electronic mail** n correo electrónico ❑ **electronics** n electrónica

elegance ['ɛlɪgəns] n elegancia

elegant ['ɛlɪgənt] adj elegante

element ['ɛlɪmənt] n elemento; (of kettle etc) resistencia

elementary [ɛlɪ'mɛntərɪ] adj elemental; (primitive) rudimentario ❑ **elementary school** (US) n escuela de enseñanza primaria

elephant ['ɛlɪfənt] n elefante m

elevate ['ɛlɪveɪt] vt (gen) elevar; (in rank) ascender

elevator ['ɛlɪveɪtə'] (US) n ascensor m; (in warehouse etc) montacargas m inv

eleven [ɪ'lɛvn] num once ❑ **eleventh** num undécimo

eligible ['ɛlɪdʒəbl] adj: an ~ young man/woman un buen partido; to be ~ for sth llenar los requisitos para algo

eliminate [ɪ'lɪmɪneɪt] vt (suspect, possibility) descartar

elm [ɛlm] n olmo

eloquent ['ɛləkwənt] adj elocuente

else [ɛls] adv: **something** ~ otra cosa; **somewhere** ~ en otra parte; **everywhere** ~ en todas partes menos aquí; **where** ~? ¿dónde más?, ¿en qué otra parte?; **there was little** ~ **to do** apenas quedaba otra cosa que hacer; **nobody** ~ **spoke** no habló nadie más ❑ **elsewhere** adv (be) en otra parte; (go) a otra parte

elusive [ɪ'luːsɪv] adj esquivo; (quality) difícil de encontrar

e-mail ['iːmeɪl] n abbr (= electronic mail) correo electrónico, e-mail m ❑ **e-mail address** n dirección f electrónica, email m

embankment [ɪm'bæŋkmənt] n terraplén m

embargo [ɪm'bɑːgəu] (pl **embargoes**) n (COMM, NAUT) embargo; (prohibition) prohibición f; **to put an ~ on sth** poner un embargo en algo

embark [ɪm'bɑːk] vi embarcarse ♦ vt embarcar; **to ~ on** (journey) emprender; (course of action) lanzarse a

embarrass [ɪm'bærəs] vt avergonzar; (government etc) dejar en mal lugar ❑ **embarrassed** adj (laugh, silence) embarazoso ❑ **embarrassing** adj (situation) violento; (question) embarazoso ❑ **embarrassment** n (shame) vergüenza; (problem): **to be an**

embarrassment for sb poner en un aprieto a algn

⚠ Be careful not to translate **embarrassed** by the Spanish word *embarazada*.

embassy ['ɛmbəsɪ] n embajada

embrace [ɪm'breɪs] vt abrazar, dar un abrazo a; (include) abarcar ♦ vi abrazarse ♦ n abrazo

embroider [ɪm'brɔɪdə'] vt bordar ❑ **embroidery** n bordado

embryo ['ɛmbrɪəu] n embrión m

emerald ['ɛmərəld] n esmeralda

emerge [ɪ'mɜːdʒ] vi salir; (arise) surgir

emergency [ɪ'mɜːdʒənsɪ] n crisis f inv; **in an ~** en caso de urgencia; **state of ~** estado de emergencia ❑ **emergency brake** (US) n freno de mano ❑ **emergency exit** n salida de emergencia ❑ **emergency landing** n aterrizaje m forzoso ❑ **emergency room** (US: MED) n sala f de urgencias ❑ **emergency services** npl (fire, police, ambulance) servicios mpl de urgencia o emergencia

emigrate ['ɛmɪgreɪt] vi emigrar ❑ **emigration** [ɛmɪ'greɪʃən] n emigración f

eminent ['ɛmɪnənt] adj eminente

emissions [ɪ'mɪʃənz] npl emisión f

emit [ɪ'mɪt] vt emitir; (smoke) arrojar; (smell) despedir; (sound) producir

emotion [ɪ'məuʃən] n emoción f ❑ **emotional** adj (needs) emocional; (person) sentimental; (scene) conmovedor(a), emocionante; (speech) emocionado

emperor ['ɛmpərə'] n emperador m

emphasis ['ɛmfəsɪs] (pl **-ses**) n énfasis m inv

emphasize ['ɛmfəsaɪz] vt (word, point) subrayar, recalcar; (feature) hacer resaltar

empire ['ɛmpaɪə'] n imperio

employ [ɪm'plɔɪ] vt emplear
□ **employee** [-'iː] n empleado(-a)
□ **employer** n patrón(-ona) m/f;
empresario □ **employment** n (work)
trabajo □ **employment agency** n
agencia de colocaciones

empower [ɪm'pauə'] vt: **to ~ sb to do**
sth autorizar a algn para hacer algo

empress ['emprɪs] n emperatriz f

emptiness ['emptɪnɪs] n vacío; (of life
etc) vaciedad f

empty ['emptɪ] adj vacío; (place)
desierto; (house) desocupado; (threat)
vano ♦ vt vaciar; (place) dejar vacío ♦ vi
vaciarse; (house etc) quedar
desocupado □ **empty-handed** adj
con las manos vacías

EMU n abbr (= European Monetary
Union) UME f

emulsion [ɪ'mʌlʃən] n emulsión f; (also:
~ paint) pintura emulsión

enable [ɪ'neɪbl] vt: **to ~ sb to do sth**
permitir a algn hacer algo

enamel [ɪ'næməl] n esmalte m; (also:
~ paint) pintura esmaltada

enchanting [ɪn'tʃɑːntɪŋ] adj
encantador(a)

encl. abbr (= enclosed) adj

enclose [ɪn'kləʊz] vt (land) cercar;
(letter etc) adjuntar; **please find**
enclosed te mandamos adjunto

enclosure [ɪn'kləʊʒə'] n cercado,
recinto

encore [ɔŋ'kɔː'] excl ¡otra!, ¡bis! ♦ n bis m

encounter [ɪn'kauntə'] n encuentro
♦ vt encontrar, encontrarse con;
(difficulty) tropezar con

encourage [ɪn'kʌrɪdʒ] vt alentar,
animar; (activity) fomentar; (growth)
estimular □ **encouragement** n
estímulo; (of industry) fomento

encouraging [ɪn'kʌrɪdʒɪŋ] adj
alentador(a)

encyclop(a)edia [ensaɪkləʊ'piːdɪə] n
enciclopedia

end [end] n fin m; (of table) extremo; (of
street) final m; (SPORT) lado ♦ vt
terminar, acabar; (also: **bring to an ~**,
put an ~ to) acabar con ♦ vi terminar,
acabar; **in the ~** al fin; on ~ (object) de
punta, de cabeza; **to stand on ~** (hair)
erizarse; **for hours on ~** hora tras hora
▶ **end up** vi: **to end up in** terminar en;
(place) ir a parar en

endanger [ɪn'deɪndʒə'] vt poner en
peligro; **an endangered species** una
especie en peligro de extinción

endearing [ɪn'dɪərɪŋ] adj simpático,
atractivo

endeavour [ɪn'devə'] (US **endeavor**) n
esfuerzo; (attempt) tentativa ♦ vi: **to ~**
to do esforzarse por hacer; (try)
procurar hacer

ending ['endɪŋ] n (of book) desenlace
m; (LING) terminación f

endless ['endlɪs] adj interminable,
inacabable

endorse [ɪn'dɔːs] vt (cheque) endosar;
(approve) aprobar □ **endorsement** n
(on driving licence) nota de
inhabilitación

endurance [ɪn'djuərəns] n resistencia

endure [ɪn'djuə'] vt (bear) aguantar,
soportar ♦ vi (last) durar

enemy ['enəmɪ] adj, n enemigo(-a) m/f

energetic [enə'dʒetɪk] adj enérgico

energy ['enədʒɪ] n energía

enforce [ɪn'fɔːs] vt (LAW) hacer cumplir

engaged [ɪn'geɪdʒd] adj (BRIT: busy, in
use) ocupado; (betrothed) prometido;
to get ~ prometerse □ **engaged**
tone (BRIT) n (TEL) señal f de
comunicado

engagement [ɪn'geɪdʒmənt] n
(appointment) compromiso, cita;
(booking) contratación f; (to marry)
compromiso; (period) noviazgo
□ **engagement ring** n anillo de
prometida

engaging [ɪn'geɪdʒɪŋ] adj atractivo

engine ['endʒɪn] n (AUT) motor m; (RAIL) locomotora

engineer [endʒɪ'nɪə] n ingeniero m; (BRIT: for repairs) mecánico; (on ship, US RAIL) maquinista m ☐ **engineering** n ingeniería

England ['ɪŋɡlənd] n Inglaterra

English ['ɪŋɡlɪʃ] adj inglés(-esa) ♦ n (LING) inglés m; **the ~** npl los ingleses mpl ☐ **English Channel** n: **the English Channel** (el Canal de) la Mancha ☐ **Englishman** (irreg) n inglés m ☐ **Englishwoman** (irreg) n inglesa

engrave [ɪn'ɡreɪv] vt grabar

engraving [ɪn'ɡreɪvɪŋ] n grabado m

enhance [ɪn'hɑːns] vt (gen) aumentar; (beauty) realzar

enjoy [ɪn'dʒɔɪ] vt (health, fortune) disfrutar de, gozar de; (like) gustarle a algn; **to ~ o.s.** divertirse ☐ **enjoyable** adj agradable; (amusing) divertido ☐ **enjoyment** n (joy) placer m; (activity) diversión f

enlarge [ɪn'lɑːdʒ] vt aumentar; (broaden) extender; (PHOT) ampliar ♦ vi: **to ~ on** (subject) tratar con más detalles ☐ **enlargement** n (PHOT) ampliación f

enlist [ɪn'lɪst] vt alistar; (support) conseguir ♦ vi alistarse

enormous [ɪ'nɔːməs] adj enorme

enough [ɪ'nʌf] adj: **~ time/books** bastante tiempo/bastantes libros ♦ pron bastante(s) ♦ adv: **big~** bastante grande; **he has not worked ~** no ha trabajado bastante; **have you got ~?** ¿tiene usted bastante(s)?; **~ to eat** (lo) suficiente or (lo) bastante para comer; **~!** ¡basta ya!; **that's ~, thanks** con eso basta, gracias; **I've had ~ of him** estoy harto de él; **... which, funnily** or **oddly ~ ...** ... lo que, por extraño que parezca ...

enquire [ɪn'kwaɪə] vt, vi = inquire

enquiry [ɪn'kwaɪərɪ] n (official investigation) investigación

enrage [ɪn'reɪdʒ] vt enfurecer

enrich [ɪn'rɪtʃ] vt enriquecer

enrol [ɪn'rəul] (US **enroll**) vt (members) inscribir; (SCOL) matricular ♦ vi inscribirse; matricularse ☐ **enrolment** (US **enrollment**) n inscripción f, matriculación f

en route [ɔn'ruːt] adv durante el viaje

en suite [ɔn'swiːt] adj: **with ~ bathroom** con baño

ensure [ɪn'ʃuə] vt asegurar

entail [ɪn'teɪl] vt suponer

enter ['entə] vt (room) entrar en; (club) hacerse socio de; (army) alistarse en; (sb for a competition) inscribir; (write down) anotar, apuntar; (COMPUT) meter ♦ vi entrar

enterprise ['entəpraɪz] n empresa; (spirit) iniciativa; **free ~** la libre empresa; **private ~** la iniciativa privada ☐ **enterprising** adj emprendedor(a)

entertain [entə'teɪn] vt (amuse) divertir; (invite: guest) invitar (a casa); (idea) abrigar ☐ **entertainer** n artista mf ☐ **entertaining** adj divertido, entretenido ☐ **entertainment** n (amusement) diversión f; (show) espectáculo

enthusiasm [ɪn'θuːzɪæzəm] n entusiasmo

enthusiast [ɪn'θuːzɪæst] n entusiasta mf ☐ **enthusiastic** [-'æstɪk] adj entusiasta; **to be enthusiastic about** entusiasmarse por

entire [ɪn'taɪə] adj entero ☐ **entirely** adv totalmente

entitle [ɪn'taɪtl] vt: **to ~ sb to sth** dar a algn derecho a algo ☐ **entitled** adj (book) titulado; **to be entitled to do** tener derecho a hacer

entrance [n 'entrəns, vb ɪn'trɑːns] n entrada ♦ vt encantar, hechizar; **to gain ~ to** (university etc) ingresar en ☐ **entrance examination** n examen m de ingreso ☐ **entrance fee** n cuota

❏ **entrance ramp** (US) n (AUT) rampa de acceso

entrant ['entrənt] n (in race, competition) participante mf; (in examination) candidato(-a)

entrepreneur [ɔntrəprə'nɜ:] n empresario

entrust [ɪn'trʌst] vt: **to ~ sth to sb** confiar algo a algn

entry ['entrɪ] n (in competition) participación f; (in register) apunte m; (in account) partida; (in reference book) artículo; **"no ~"** "prohibido el paso"; (AUT) "dirección prohibida" ❏ **entry phone** n portero automático

envelope ['envələup] n sobre m

envious ['envɪəs] adj envidioso; (look) de envidia

environment [ɪn'vaɪərnmənt] n (surroundings) entorno; (natural world): **the ~** el medio ambiente ❏ **environmental** ['-'mentl] adj ambiental; medioambiental ❏ **environmentally** ['-'mentlɪ] adv: **environmentally sound/friendly** ecológico

envisage [ɪn'vɪzɪdʒ] vt prever

envoy ['envɔɪ] n enviado

envy ['envɪ] n envidia ♦ vt tener envidia a; **to ~ sb sth** envidiar algo a algn

epic ['epɪk] n épica ♦ adj épico

epidemic [epɪ'demɪk] n epidemia

epilepsy ['epɪlepsɪ] n epilepsia

epileptic [epɪ'leptɪk] adj, n epiléptico(-a) m/f ❏ **epileptic fit** n ataque m de epilepsia, acceso m epiléptico

episode ['epɪsəud] n episodio

equal ['i:kwl] adj igual; (treatment) equitativo ♦ n igual mf ♦ vt ser igual a; (fig) igualar; **to be ~ to** (task) estar a la altura de ❏ **equality** [i:'kwɔlɪtɪ] n igualdad f ❏ **equalize** vi (SPORT) empatar ❏ **equally** adv igualmente; (share etc) a partes iguales

equation [ɪ'kweɪʒən] n (MATH) ecuación f

equator [ɪ'kweɪtə] n ecuador m

equip [ɪ'kwɪp] vt equipar; (person) proveer; **to be well equipped** estar bien equipado ❏ **equipment** n equipo; (tools) avíos mpl

equivalent [ɪ'kwɪvələnt] adj: **~ (to)** equivalente (a) ♦ n equivalente m

ER abbr (BRIT: = Elizabeth Regina) la reina Isabel; (US: Med) = **emergency room**

era ['ɪərə] n era, época

erase [ɪ'reɪz] vt borrar ❏ **eraser** n goma de borrar

erect [ɪ'rekt] adj erguido ♦ vt erigir, levantar; (assemble) montar ❏ **erection** [-ʃən] n construcción f; (assembly) montaje m; (PHYSIOL) erección f

ERM n abbr = Exchange Rate Mechanism) tipo de cambio europeo

erode [ɪ'rəud] vt (GEO) erosionar; (metal) corroer, desgastar; (fig) desgastar

erosion [ɪ'rəuʒən] n erosión f; desgaste m

erotic [ɪ'rɔtɪk] adj erótico

errand ['ernd] n recado (SP), mandado (LAm)

erratic [ɪ'rætɪk] adj desigual, poco uniforme

error ['erə] n error m, equivocación f

erupt [ɪ'rʌpt] vi entrar en erupción; (fig) estallar ❏ **eruption** [ɪ'rʌpʃən] n erupción f; (of war) estallido

escalate ['eskəleɪt] vi extenderse, intensificarse

escalator ['eskəleɪtə] n escalera móvil

escape [ɪ'skeɪp] n fuga ♦ vi escaparse; (flee) huir, evadirse; (leak) fugarse ♦ vt (responsibility etc) evitar, eludir; (consequences) escapar a; (elude): **his name escapes me** no me sale su nombre; **to ~ from** (place) escaparse de; (person) escaparse a

escort [n 'eskɔ:t, vb ɪ'skɔ:t] n acompañante mf; (MIL) escolta mf ♦ vt acompañar

especially [ɪsˈpeʃlɪ] adv (above all) sobre todo; (particularly) en particular, especialmente

espionage [ˈespɪənɑːʒ] n espionaje m

essay [ˈeseɪ] n (LITERATURE) ensayo; (SCOL: short) redacción f; (: long) trabajo

essence [ˈesns] n esencia

essential [ɪˈsenʃl] adj (necessary) imprescindible; (basic) esencial
□ **essentially** adv esencialmente
□ **essentials** npl lo imprescindible, lo esencial

establish [ɪsˈtæblɪʃ] vt establecer; (prove) demostrar; (relations) entablar; (reputation) ganarse
□ **establishment** n establecimiento; **the Establishment** la clase dirigente

estate [ɪsˈteɪt] n (land) finca, hacienda; (inheritance) herencia; (BRIT: also: **housing ~**) urbanización f □ **estate agent** (BRIT) n agente m inmobiliario(-a) □ **estate car** (BRIT) n furgoneta

estimate [n ˈestɪmət, vb ˈestɪmeɪt] n estimación f, apreciación f; (assessment) tasa, cálculo; (COMM) presupuesto ♦ vt estimar, tasar; calcular

etc abbr (= et cetera) etc

eternal [ɪˈtɜːnl] adj eterno

eternity [ɪˈtɜːnɪtɪ] n eternidad f

ethical [ˈeθɪkl] adj ético □ **ethics** [ˈeθɪks] n ética ♦ npl moralidad f

Ethiopia [iːθɪˈəʊpɪə] n Etiopía

ethnic [ˈeθnɪk] adj étnico □ **ethnic minority** n minoría étnica

etiquette [ˈetɪket] n etiqueta

EU n abbr (= European Union) UE f

euro n euro

Europe [ˈjʊərəp] n Europa □ **European** [-ˈpiːən] adj, n europeo(-a) m/f □ **European Community** n Comunidad f Europea □ **European Union** n Unión f Europea

Eurostar® [ˈjʊərəʊstɑː] n Eurostar® m

evacuate [ɪˈvækjueɪt] vt (people) evacuar; (place) desocupar

evade [ɪˈveɪd] vt evadir, eludir

evaluate [ɪˈvæljueɪt] vt evaluar; (value) tasar; (evidence) interpretar

evaporate [ɪˈvæpəreɪt] vi evaporarse; (fig) desvanecerse

eve [iːv] n: **on the ~ of** en vísperas de

even [ˈiːvn] adj (level) llano; (smooth) liso; (speed, temperature) uniforme; (number) par ♦ adv hasta, incluso; (introducing a comparison) aún, todavía; **~ if, ~ though** aunque +subjun; **~ more** aun más; **~ so** aun así; **not ~** ni siquiera; **~ he was there** hasta él estuvo allí; **~ on Sundays** incluso los domingos; **to get ~ with sb** ajustar cuentas con algn

evening [ˈiːvnɪŋ] n tarde f; (late) noche f; **in the ~** por la tarde □ **evening class** n clase f nocturna □ **evening dress** n (no pl: formal clothes) traje m de etiqueta; (woman's) traje m de noche

event [ɪˈvent] n suceso, acontecimiento; (SPORT) prueba; **in the ~ of** en caso de □ **eventful** adj (life) activo; (day) ajetreado

eventual [ɪˈventʃuəl] adj final □ **eventually** adv (finally) finalmente; (in time) con el tiempo

⚠ Be careful not to translate **eventual** by the Spanish word *eventual*.

ever [ˈevə] adv (at any time) nunca, jamás; (at all times) siempre; (in question): **why ~ not?** ¿y por qué no?; **the best ~** lo nunca visto; **have you ~ seen it?** ¿lo ha visto usted alguna vez?; **better than ~** mejor que nunca; **~ since** adv desde entonces ♦ conj después de que □ **evergreen** n árbol m de hoja perenne

every

KEYWORD

[ˈevrɪ] adj

1 (each) cada; **every one of them** (persons) todos ellos(-as); (objects) cada uno de ellos(-as); **every shop in**

the town was closed todas las tiendas de la ciudad estaban cerradas **2** (all possible) todo(-a); **I gave you every assistance** te di toda la ayuda posible; **I have every confidence in him** tiene toda mi confianza; **we wish you every success** te deseamos toda suerte de éxitos

3 (showing recurrence) todo(-a); **every day/week** todos los días/todas las semanas; **every other car had been broken into** habían forzado uno de cada dos coches; **she visits me every other/third day** me visita cada dos/tres días; **every now and then** de vez en cuando

every: **everybody** pron = **everyone** ❑ **everyday** adj (daily) cotidiano, de todos los días; (usual) acostumbrado ❑ **everyone** pron todos(-as), todo el mundo ❑ **everything** pron todo; **this shop sells everything** esta tienda vende de todo ❑ **everywhere** adv: **I've been looking for you everywhere** te he estado buscando por todas partes; **everywhere you go you meet** ... en todas partes encuentras ...

evict [ɪ'vɪkt] vt desahuciar

evidence ['ɛvɪdəns] n (proof) prueba; (of witness) testimonio; (sign) indicios mpl; **to give ~** prestar declaración, dar testimonio

evident ['ɛvɪdənt] adj evidente, manifiesto ❑ **evidently** adv por lo visto

evil ['iːvl] adj malo; (influence) funesto ♦ n mal m

evoke [ɪ'vəʊk] vt evocar

evolution [iːvə'luːʃən] n evolución f

evolve [ɪ'vɒlv] vt desarrollar ♦ vi evolucionar, desarrollarse

ewe [juː] n oveja

ex (inf) [ɛks] n: **my ex** mi ex

ex- [ɛks] prefix ex

exact [ɪg'zækt] adj exacto; (person) meticuloso ♦ vt: **to ~ sth (from)** exigir algo (de) ❑ **exactly** adv exactamente; (indicating agreement) exacto

exaggerate [ɪg'zædʒəreɪt] vt, vi exagerar ❑ **exaggeration** n exageración f

exam [ɪg'zæm] n abbr (SCOL) = **examination**

examination [ɪgzæmɪ'neɪʃən] n examen m; (MED) reconocimiento

examine [ɪg'zæmɪn] vt examinar; (inspect) inspeccionar, escudriñar; (MED) reconocer ❑ **examiner** n examinador m/f

example [ɪg'zɑːmpl] n ejemplo; **for ~** por ejemplo

exasperated [ɪg'zɑːspəreɪtɪd] adj exasperado

excavate ['ɛkskəveɪt] vt excavar

exceed [ɪk'siːd] vt (amount) exceder; (number) pasar de; (speed limit) sobrepasar; (powers) excederse en; (hopes) superar ❑ **exceedingly** adv sumamente, sobremanera

excel [ɪk'sɛl] vi sobresalir; **to ~ o.s** lucirse

excellence ['ɛksələns] n excelencia

excellent ['ɛksələnt] adj excelente

except [ɪk'sɛpt] prep (also: **~ for, excepting**) excepto, salvo ♦ vt exceptuar, excluir; **~ if/when** excepto si/cuando; **~ that** salvo que ❑ **exception** [ɪk'sɛpʃən] n excepción f; **to take exception to** ofenderse por ❑ **exceptional** [ɪk'sɛpʃənl] adj excepcional ❑ **exceptionally** [ɪk'sɛpʃənlɪ] adv excepcionalmente, extraordinariamente

excerpt ['ɛksɜːpt] n extracto

excess [ɪk'sɛs] n exceso ❑ **excess baggage** n exceso de equipaje ❑ **excessive** adj excesivo

exchange [ɪks'tʃeɪndʒ] n intercambio; (conversation) diálogo; (also: **telephone ~**) central f (telefónica) ♦ vt:

to ~ (for) cambiar (por) ❑ **exchange rate** *n* tipo de cambio

excite [ɪkˈsaɪt] *vt* (*stimulate*) estimular; (*arouse*) excitar ❑ **excited** *adj*: **to get excited** emocionarse ❑ **excitement** *n* (*agitation*) excitación *f*; (*exhilaration*) emoción *f* ❑ **exciting** *adj* emocionante

exclaim [ɪkˈskleɪm] *vt* exclamar ❑ **exclamation** [ɛkskləˈmeɪʃən] *n* exclamación *f* ❑ **exclamation mark** (*BRIT*), **exclamation point** (*US*) *n* punto de admiración

exclude [ɪkˈskluːd] *vt* excluir; exceptuar

excluding [ɪksˈkluːdɪŋ] *prep*: **~ VAT** IVA no incluido

exclusion [ɪksˈkluːʒən] *n* exclusión *f*; **to the ~** of con exclusión de

exclusive [ɪksˈkluːsɪv] *adj* exclusivo; (*club, district*) selecto; **~ of tax** excluyendo impuestos ❑ **exclusively** *adv* únicamente

excruciating [ɪksˈkruːʃɪeɪtɪŋ] *adj* (*pain*) agudísimo, atroz; (*noise, embarrassment*) horrible

excursion [ɪksˈkɜːʃən] *n* (*tourist excursion*) excursión *f*

excuse [*n* ɪkˈskjuːs, *vb* ɪkˈskjuːz] *n* disculpa, excusa; (*pretext*) pretexto ♦ *vt* (*justify*) justificar; (*forgive*) disculpar, perdonar; **to ~ sb from doing sth** dispensar a algn de hacer algo; **~ me!** (*attracting attention*) ¡por favor!; (*apologising*) ¡perdón!; **if you will ~ me** con su permiso

ex-directory [ˈɛksdɪˈrɛktərɪ] (*BRIT*) *adj* que no consta en la guía

execute [ˈɛksɪkjuːt] *vt* (*plan*) realizar; (*order*) cumplir; (*person*) ajusticiar, ejecutar ❑ **execution** [-ˈkjuːʃən] *n* realización *f*; cumplimiento; ejecución *f*

executive [ɪgˈzɛkjutɪv] *n* (*person, committee*) ejecutivo; (*POL: committee*) poder *m* ejecutivo ♦ *adj* ejecutivo

exempt [ɪgˈzɛmpt] *adj*: **~ from** exento de ♦ *vt*: **to ~ sb from** eximir a algn de

exercise [ˈɛksəsaɪz] *n* ejercicio ♦ *vt* (*patience*) usar de; (*right*) valerse de; (*dog*) llevar de paseo; (*mind*) preocupar ♦ *vi* (*also*: **to take ~**) hacer ejercicio(s) ❑ **exercise book** *n* cuaderno

exert [ɪgˈzɜːt] *vt* ejercer; **to ~ o.s.** esforzarse ❑ **exertion** [-ʃən] *n* esfuerzo

exhale [ɛksˈheɪl] *vt* despedir ♦ *vi* exhalar

exhaust [ɪgˈzɔːst] *n* (*AUT: also*: **~ pipe**) escape *m*; (*: fumes*) gases *mpl* de escape ♦ *vt* agotar ❑ **exhausted** *adj* agotado ❑ **exhaustion** [ɪgˈzɔːstʃən] *n* agotamiento; **nervous exhaustion** postración *f* nerviosa

exhibit [ɪgˈzɪbɪt] *n* (*ART*) obra expuesta; (*LAW*) objeto expuesto ♦ *vt* (*show: emotions*) manifestar; (*: courage, skill*) demostrar; (*paintings*) exponer ❑ **exhibition** [ɛksɪˈbɪʃən] *n* exposición *f*; (*of talent etc*) demostración *f*

exhilarating [ɪgˈzɪləreɪtɪŋ] *adj* estimulante, tónico

exile [ˈɛksaɪl] *n* exilio; (*person*) exiliado(-a) ♦ *vt* desterrar, exiliar

exist [ɪgˈzɪst] *vi* existir; (*live*) vivir ❑ **existence** *n* existencia ❑ **existing** *adj* existente, actual

exit [ˈɛksɪt] *n* salida ♦ *vi* (*THEATRE*) hacer mutis; (*COMPUT*) salir (del sistema) ❑ **exit ramp** (*US*) *n* (*AUT*) vía de acceso

⚠ Be careful not to translate **exit** by the Spanish word *éxito*.

exotic [ɪgˈzɒtɪk] *adj* exótico

expand [ɪkˈspænd] *vt* ampliar; (*number*) aumentar ♦ *vi* (*population*) aumentar; (*trade etc*) expandirse; (*gas, metal*) dilatarse

expansion [ɪkˈspænʃən] *n* (*of population*) aumento; (*of trade*) expansión *f*

expect [ɪkˈspɛkt] *vt* esperar; (*require*) contar con; (*suppose*) suponer ♦ *vi*: **to be expecting** (*pregnant woman*) estar embarazada ❑ **expectation**

[ekspek'teɪʃən] n (hope) esperanza; (belief) expectativa

expedition [ekspə'dɪʃən] n expedición f

expel [ɪk'spel] vt arrojar; (from place) expulsar

expenditure [ɪks'pendɪtʃə'] n gasto, gastos mpl, desembolso; consumo

expense [ɪk'spens] n gasto, gastos mpl; (high cost) costa; **expenses** npl (COMM) gastos mpl; **at the ~ of** a costa de □ **expense account** n cuenta de gastos

expensive [ɪk'spensɪv] adj caro, costoso

experience [ɪk'spɪərɪəns] n experiencia ♦ vt experimentar; (suffer) sufrir □ **experienced** adj experimentado

experiment [ɪk'sperɪmənt] n experimento ♦ vi hacer experimentos □ **experimental** [-'mentl] adj experimental; **the process is still at the experimental stage** el proceso está todavía en prueba

expert ['ekspə:t] adj experto, perito ♦ n experto(-a), perito(-a); (specialist) especialista mf ♦ **expertise** [-'ti:z] n pericia

expire [ɪk'spaɪə'] vi caducar, vencer □ **expiry** n vencimiento □ **expiry date** n (of medicine, food item) fecha de caducidad

explain [ɪk'spleɪn] vt explicar □ **explanation** [eksplə'neɪʃən] n explicación f

explicit [ɪk'splɪsɪt] adj explícito

explode [ɪk'spləʊd] vi estallar, explotar; (population) crecer rápidamente; (with anger) reventar

exploit [n 'eksplɔɪt, vb ɪk'splɔɪt] n hazaña ♦ vt explotar □ **exploitation** [-'teɪʃən] n explotación f

explore [ɪk'splɔ:'] vt explorar; (fig) examinar; investigar □ **explorer** n explorador(a) m/f

explosion [ɪk'spləʊʒən] n explosión f □ **explosive** [ɪks'pləʊsɪv] adj, n explosivo

export [vb ɪk'spɔ:t, n, cpd 'ekspɔ:t] vt exportar ♦ n (process) exportación f; (product) producto de exportación ♦ cpd de exportación □ **exporter** n exportador m

expose [ɪk'spəʊz] vt exponer; (unmask) desenmascarar □ **exposed** adj expuesto

exposure [ɪk'spəʊʒə'] n exposición f; (publicity) publicidad f; (PHOT: speed) velocidad f de obturación; (: film) fotografía; **to die from ~** (MED) morir de frío

express [ɪk'spres] adj (definite) expreso, explícito; (BRIT: letter etc) urgente ♦ n (train) rápido ♦ vt expresar □ **expression** [ɪk'spreʃən] n expresión f; (of actor etc) sentimiento □ **expressway** (US) n (urban motorway) autopista

exquisite [ek'skwɪzɪt] adj exquisito

extend [ɪk'stend] vt (visit, street) prolongar; (building) ampliar; (invitation) ofrecer ♦ vi (land) extenderse; (period of time) prolongarse

extension [ɪk'stenʃən] n extensión f; (building) ampliación f; (of time) prolongación f; (TEL: in private house) línea derivada; (: in office) extensión f □ **extension lead** n alargador m, alargadera

extensive [ɪk'stensɪv] adj extenso; (damage) importante; (knowledge) amplio

extent [ɪk'stent] n (breadth) extensión f; (scope) alcance m; **to some ~** hasta cierto punto; **to the ~ of ...** hasta el punto de ...; **to such an ~ that ...** hasta tal punto que ...; **to what ~?** ¿hasta qué punto?

exterior [ek'stɪərɪə'] adj exterior, externo ♦ n exterior m

external [ek'stə:nl] adj externo

extinct [ɪkˈstɪŋkt] adj (volcano) extinguido; (race) extinto
□ **extinction** n extinción f

extinguish [ɪkˈstɪŋgwɪʃ] vt extinguir, apagar

extra [ˈekstrə] adj adicional ♦ adv (in addition) de más ♦ n (luxury, addition) extra m; (CINEMA, THEATRE) extra mf, comparsa mf

extract [vb ɪkˈstrækt, n ˈekstrækt] vt sacar; (tooth) extraer; (money, promise) obtener ♦ n extracto

extradite [ˈekstrədaɪt] vt extraditar

extraordinary [ɪkˈstrɔːdnrɪ] adj extraordinario; (odd) raro

extravagance [ɪkˈstrævəgəns] n derroche m, despilfarro; (thing bought) extravagancia

extravagant [ɪkˈstrævəgənt] adj (lavish: person) pródigo; (: gift) (demasiado) caro; (wasteful) despilfarrador(a)

extreme [ɪkˈstriːm] adj extremo, extremado ♦ n extremo □ **extremely** adv sumamente, extremadamente

extremist [ɪkˈstriːmɪst] adj, n extremista m/f

extrovert [ˈekstrəvɜːt] n extrovertido(-a)

eye [aɪ] n ojo ♦ vt mirar de soslayo, ojear; **to keep an ~ on** vigilar □ **eyeball** n globo ocular □ **eyebrow** n ceja □ **eyedrops** npl gotas fpl para los ojos, colino □ **eyelash** n pestaña □ **eyelid** n párpado □ **eyeliner** n delineador m (de ojos) □ **eyeshadow** n sombreador m de ojos □ **eyesight** n vista □ **eye witness** n testigo mf presencial

F, f

F [ef] n (MUS) fa m

fabric [ˈfæbrɪk] n tejido, tela

⚠ Be careful not to translate **fabric** by the Spanish word fábrica.

fabulous [ˈfæbjuləs] adj fabuloso

face [feɪs] n (ANAT) cara, rostro; (of clock) esfera (SP), cara (LAm); (of mountain) cara, ladera; (of building) fachada ♦ vt (direction) estar de cara a; (situation) hacer frente a; (facts) aceptar; ~ **down** (person, card) boca abajo; **to lose** ~ desprestigiarse; **to make** or **pull a** ~ hacer muecas; **in the** ~ **of** (difficulties etc) ante; **on the** ~ **of it** a primera vista; ~ **to** ~ cara a cara ♦ **face up to** vt fus hacer frente a, arrostrar □ **face cloth** n (BRIT) manopla □ **face pack** n (BRIT) mascarilla

facial [ˈfeɪʃəl] adj de la cara ♦ n (also: beauty ~) tratamiento facial, limpieza

facilitate [fəˈsɪlɪteɪt] vt facilitar

facilities [fəˈsɪlɪtɪz] npl (buildings) instalaciones fpl; (equipment) servicios mpl; **credit** ~ facilidades fpl de crédito

fact [fækt] n hecho; **in** ~ en realidad

faction [ˈfækʃən] n facción f

factor [ˈfæktə] n factor m

factory [ˈfæktərɪ] n fábrica

factual [ˈfæktjuəl] adj basado en los hechos

faculty [ˈfækəltɪ] n facultad f; (US: teaching staff) personal m docente

fad [fæd] n novedad f, moda

fade [feɪd] vi desteñirse; (sound, smile) desvanecerse; (light) apagarse; (flower) marchitarse; (hope, memory) perderse ♦ **fade away** vi (sound) apagarse

fag [fæg] n (BRIT: inf) (cigarette) pitillo (SP), cigarro

Fahrenheit [ˈfærənhaɪt] n Fahrenheit m

fail [feɪl] vt (candidate, test) suspender (SP), reprobar (LAm); (memory etc) fallar a ♦ vi suspender (SP), reprobar (LAm); (be unsuccessful) fracasar; (strength, brakes) fallar; (light) acabarse; **to** ~ **to do sth** (neglect) dejar de hacer algo; (be unable) no poder hacer algo; **without**

~ sin falta □ **failing** n falta, defecto
♦ prep a falta de ♦ **failure** ['feɪljə*] n
fracaso; (person) fracasado(-a);
(mechanical etc) fallo

faint [feɪnt] adj débil; (recollection)
vago; (mark) apenas visible ♦ n
desmayo ♦ vi desmayarse; **to feel ~**
estar mareado, marearse □ **faintest**
adj: **I haven't the faintest idea** no
tengo la más remota idea □ **faintly**
adv débilmente; (vaguely) vagamente

fair [feə*] adj justo; (just, person) rubio;
(weather) bueno; (good enough)
regular; (considerable) considerable
♦ adv (play) limpio ♦ n feria; (BRIT:
funfair) parque m de atracciones
□ **fairground** n recinto ferial □ **fair-
haired** adj (person) rubio □ **fairly**
adv (justly) con justicia; (quite) bastante
□ **fairway** n (GOLF) calle f

fairy ['feərɪ] n hada □ **fairy tale** n
cuento de hadas

faith [feɪθ] n fe f; (trust) confianza; (sect)
religión f □ **faithful** adj (loyal: troops
etc) leal; (spouse) fiel; (account) exacto
□ **faithfully** adv fielmente; **yours
faithfully** (BRIT: in letters) le saluda
atentamente

fake [feɪk] n (painting etc) falsificación f;
(person) impostor(a) m/f ♦ adj falso ♦ vt
fingir; (painting etc) falsificar

falcon ['fɔːlkən] n halcón m

fall [fɔːl] (pt fell, pp fallen) n caída; (in
price etc) descenso; (US) otoño ♦ vi
caer(se); (price) bajar, descender; (rain)
npl (waterfall) cascada, salto de agua;
to ~ flat (on one's face) caerse (boca
abajo); (plan) fracasar; (joke, story) no
hacer gracia ► **fall apart** vi
deshacerse ► **fall down** vi (person)
caerse; (building, hopes) derrumbarse
► **fall for** vt fus (trick) dejarse engañar
por; (person) enamorarse de ► **fall off**
vi caerse; (diminish) disminuir ► **fall
out** vi (friends etc) reñir; (hair, teeth)
caerse ► **fall over** vi caer(se) ► **fall
through** vi (plan, project) fracasar

fallen ['fɔːlən] pp of **fall**

fallout ['fɔːlaut] n lluvia radioactiva

false [fɔːls] adj falso; **under ~ pretences**
con engaños □ **false alarm** n falsa
alarma □ **false teeth** (BRIT) npl
dentadura postiza

fame [feɪm] n fama

familiar [fə'mɪlɪə*] adj conocido,
familiar; (tone) de confianza; **to be ~
with** (subject) conocer (bien)
□ **familiarize** [fə'mɪlɪəraɪz] vt: **to
familiarize o.s. with** familiarizarse con

family ['fæmɪlɪ] n familia □ **family
doctor** n médico(-a) de cabecera
□ **family planning** n planificación f
familiar

famine ['fæmɪn] n hambre f, hambruna

famous ['feɪməs] adj famoso, célebre

fan [fæn] n abanico; (ELEC) ventilador m;
(of pop star) fan m/f; (SPORT) hincha m/f
♦ vt abanicar; (fire, quarrel) atizar

fanatic [fə'nætɪk] n fanático(-a)

fan belt n correa del ventilador

fan club n club m de fans

fancy ['fænsɪ] n (whim) capricho,
antojo; (imagination) imaginación f
♦ adj (luxury) lujoso, de lujo ♦ vt (feel
like, want) tener ganas de; (imagine)
imaginarse; (think) creer; **to take a ~ to
sb** tomar cariño a algn; **he fancies her**
(inf) le gusta (ella) mucho □ **fancy
dress** n disfraz m

fan heater n calefactor m de aire

fantasize ['fæntəsaɪz] vi fantasear,
hacerse ilusiones

fantastic [fæn'tæstɪk] adj (enormous)
enorme; (strange, wonderful) fantástico

fantasy ['fæntəsɪ] n (dream) sueño;
(unreality) fantasía

fanzine ['fænziːn] n fanzine m

FAQs abbr (= frequently asked questions)
preguntas frecuentes

far [fɑː*] adj (distant) lejano ♦ adv lejos;
(much, greatly) mucho; **~ away, ~ off** (a
lo) lejos; **~ better** mucho mejor; **~ from**
lejos de; **by ~** con mucho; **go as ~ as**

the farm vaya hasta la granja; **as ~ as I know** que yo sepa; **how ~?** ¿hasta dónde?; (fig) ¿hasta qué punto?

farce [fɑːs] n farsa

fare [feə'] n (on trains, buses) precio (del billete); (in taxi: cost) tarifa; (food) comida; **half ~** medio pasaje m; **full ~** pasaje completo

Far East n: **the ~** el Extremo Oriente

farewell [feə'wel] excl, n adiós m

farm [fɑːm] n cortijo (SP), hacienda (LAm), rancho (MEX), estancia (RPI) ♦ vt cultivar □ **farmer** n granjero, hacendado (LAm), ranchero (MEX), estanciero (RPI) □ **farmhouse** n granja, casa del hacendado (LAm), rancho (MEX), casco de la estancia (RPI) □ **farming** n agricultura, (of crops) cultivo; (of animals) cría □ **farmyard** n corral m

far-reaching [fɑː'riːtʃɪŋ] adj (reform, effect) de gran alcance

fart [fɑːt] (inf!) vi tirarse un pedo (!) ♦ n (!) pedo (!)

farther [fɑːðə'] adv más lejos, más allá ♦ adj más lejano

farthest [fɑːðɪst] superlative of **far**

fascinate [fæsɪneɪt] vt fascinar □ **fascinated** adj fascinado

fascinating [fæsɪneɪtɪŋ] adj fascinante

fascination [-neɪʃən] n fascinación f

fascist [fæʃɪst] adj, n fascista m/f

fashion [fæʃən] n moda; (fashion industry) industria de la moda; (manner) manera ♦ vt formar; **in ~ a la moda; **out of ~** pasado de moda □ **fashionable** adj de moda □ **fashion show** n desfile m de modelos

fast [fɑːst] adj rápido; (dye, colour) resistente; (clock): **to be ~** estar adelantado ♦ adv rápidamente, de prisa; (stuck, held) firmemente ♦ n ayuno ♦ vi ayunar; **~ asleep** profundamente dormido

fasten [fɑːsn] vt atar, sujetar; (coat, belt) abrochar ♦ vi atarse; abrocharse

fast food n comida rápida, platos mpl preparados

fat [fæt] adj gordo; (book) grueso; (profit) grande, pingüe ♦ n grasa; (on person) carnes fpl; (lard) manteca

fatal [feɪtl] adj (mistake) fatal; (injury) mortal □ **fatality** [fə'tælɪtɪ] n (road death etc) víctima f □ **fatally** adv fatalmente; mortalmente

fate [feɪt] n destino; (of person) suerte f

father [fɑːðə'] n padre m □ **Father Christmas** n Papá m Noel □ **father-in-law** n suegro

fatigue [fə'tiːg] n fatiga, cansancio

fattening [fætnɪŋ] adj (food) que hace engordar

fatty [fætɪ] adj (food) graso ♦ n (inf) gordito(-a), gordinflón(-ona) m/f

faucet [fɔːsɪt] n (US) grifo (SP), llave f, canilla (RPI)

fault [fɔːlt] n (blame) culpa; (defect: in person, machine) defecto; (GEO) falla ♦ vt criticar; **it's my ~** es culpa mía; **to find ~ with** criticar, poner peros a; **at ~** culpable □ **faulty** adj defectuoso

fauna [fɔːnə] n fauna

favour etc [feɪvə'] (US favor) n favor m; (approval) aprobación f ♦ vt (proposition) estar a favor de, aprobar; (assist) ser propicio a; **to do sb a ~** hacer un favor a algn; **to find ~ with sb** caer en gracia a algn; **in ~ of** a favor de □ **favourable** adj favorable □ **favourite** [feɪvrɪt] adj, n favorito, preferido

fawn [fɔːn] n cervato m ♦ adj (also: **~-coloured**) color de cervato, leonado ♦ vi: **to ~ (up)on** adular

fax [fæks] n (document) fax m; (machine) telefax m ♦ vt mandar por telefax

FBI (US) n abbr (= Federal Bureau of Investigation) = BIC f (SP)

fear [fɪə'] n miedo, temor m ♦ vt tener miedo a, temer; **for ~ of** por si □ **fearful** adj temeroso, miedoso; (awful) terrible □ **fearless** adj audaz

feasible ['fiːzəbl] *adj* factible

feast [fiːst] *n* banquete *m*; (*REL: also:* ~ **day**) fiesta ♦ *vi* festejar

feat [fiːt] *n* hazaña

feather ['feðəʳ] *n* pluma

feature ['fiːtʃəʳ] *n* característica; (*article*) artículo de fondo ♦ *vt* (*film*) presentar ♦ *vi:* **to ~ in** tener un papel destacado en; **features** *npl* (*of face*) facciones *fpl* ❑ **feature film** *n* largometraje *m*

Feb. *abbr* (= *February*) feb

February ['februəri] *n* febrero

fed [fed] *pt, pp of* **feed**

federal ['fedərəl] *adj* federal

federation [fedə'reɪʃən] *n* federación *f*

fed up [fed'ʌp] *adj:* **to be ~ (with)** estar harto (de)

fee [fiː] *n* pago; (*professional*) derechos *mpl*, honorarios *mpl*; (*of club*) cuota; **school fees** matrícula

feeble ['fiːbl] *adj* débil; (*joke*) flojo

feed [fiːd] (*pt, pp* **fed**) *n* comida; (*of animal*) pienso; (*on printer*) dispositivo de alimentación ♦ *vt* alimentar; (*BRIT: baby: breastfeed*) dar el pecho a; (*animal*) dar de comer a; (*data, information*) **to ~ into** meter en ❑ **feedback** *n* reacción *f*, feedback *m*

feel [fiːl] (*pt, pp* **felt**) *n* (*sensation*) sensación *f*; (*sense of touch*) tacto; (*impression*) **to have the ~ of** parecerse a ♦ *vt* tocar; (*pain etc*) sentir; (*think, believe*) creer; **to ~ hungry/cold** tener hambre/frío; **to ~ lonely/better** sentirse solo/mejor; **I don't ~ well** no me siento bien; **it feels soft** es suave al tacto; **to ~ like** (*want*) tener ganas de ❑ **feeling** *n* (*physical*) sensación *f*; (*foreboding*) presentimiento; (*emotion*) sentimiento

feet [fiːt] *npl of* **foot**

fell [fel] *pt of* **fall** ♦ *vt* (*tree*) talar

fellow ['feləu] *n* tipo, tío (*SP*); (*comrade*) compañero; (*of learned society*) socio(-a)
❑ **fellow citizen** *n* conciudadano(-a)

❑ **fellow countryman** (*irreg*) *n* compatriota ❑ **fellow men** *npl* semejantes *mpl* ❑ **fellowship** *n* compañerismo; (*grant*) beca

felony ['feləni] *n* crimen *m*

felt [felt] *pt, pp of* **feel** ♦ *n* fieltro ❑ **felt-tip** *n* (*also:* **felt-tip pen**) rotulador *m*

female ['fiːmeɪl] *n* (*pej: woman*) mujer *f*, tía; (*ZOOL*) hembra ♦ *adj* femenino; hembra

feminine ['femɪnɪn] *adj* femenino

feminist ['femɪnɪst] *n* feminista

fence [fens] *n* valla, cerca ♦ *vt* (*also:* ~ **in**) cercar ♦ *vi* (*SPORT*) hacer esgrima ❑ **fencing** *n* esgrima

fend [fend] *vi:* **to ~ for o.s.** valerse por sí mismo ▶ **fend off** *vt* (*attack*) rechazar; (*questions*) evadir

fender ['fendəʳ] (*US*) *n* guardafuego; (*AUT*) parachoques *m inv*

fennel ['fenl] *n* hinojo

ferment [*vb* fə'ment, *n* 'fɜːment] *vi* fermentar ♦ *n* (*fig*) agitación *f*

fern [fɜːn] *n* helecho

ferocious [fə'rəuʃəs] *adj* feroz

ferret ['ferɪt] *n* hurón *m*

ferry ['feri] *n* (*small*) barca (de pasaje), balsa; (*large: also:* **ferryboat**) transbordador *m*, ferry *m* ♦ *vt* transportar

fertile ['fɜːtaɪl] *adj* fértil; (*BIOL*) fecundo ❑ **fertilize** ['fɜːtɪlaɪz] *vt* (*BIOL*) fecundar; (*AGR*) abonar ❑ **fertilizer** *n* abono

festival ['festɪvəl] *n* (*REL*) fiesta; (*ART, MUS*) festival *m*

festive ['festɪv] *adj* festivo; **the ~ season** (*BRIT: Christmas*) las Navidades

fetch [fetʃ] *vt* ir a buscar; (*sell for*) venderse por

fête [feɪt] *n* fiesta

fetus ['fiːtəs] (*US*) *n* = **foetus**

feud [fjuːd] *n* (*hostility*) enemistad *f*; (*quarrel*) disputa

fever ['fiːvəʳ] *n* fiebre *f* ❑ **feverish** *adj* febril

few [fju:] *adj (not many)* pocos ♦ *pron* pocos; algunos; **a ~** *adj* unos pocos, algunos ❑ **fewer** *adj* menos ❑ **fewest** *adj* los (las) menos

fiancé [fɪˈɒnseɪ] *n* novio, prometido ❑ **fiancée** *n* novia, prometida

fiasco [fɪˈæskəʊ] *n* fiasco

fib [fɪb] *n* mentirilla

fibre [ˈfaɪbəʳ] *(US* fiber*) n* fibra ❑ **fibreglass** *(US* Fiberglass*) n* fibra de vidrio

fickle [ˈfɪkl] *adj* inconstante

fiction [ˈfɪkʃən] *n* ficción ❑ **fictional** *adj* novelesco

fiddle [ˈfɪdl] *n (MUS)* violín *m; (cheating)* trampa ♦ *vt (BRIT: accounts)* falsificar ♦ **fiddle with** *vt fus* juguetear con

fidelity [fɪˈdelɪtɪ] *n* fidelidad *f*

field [fi:ld] *n* campo; *(fig)* campo, esfera; *(SPORT)* campo *(SP)*, cancha *(LAm)* ❑ **field marshal** *n* mariscal *m*

fierce [fɪəs] *adj* feroz; *(wind, heat)* fuerte; *(fighting, enemy)* encarnizado

fifteen [fɪfˈtiːn] *num* quince ❑ **fifteenth** *adj* decimoquinto; **the fifteenth floor** la planta quince; **the fifteenth of August** el quince de agosto

fifth [fɪfθ] *num* quinto

fiftieth [ˈfɪftɪɪθ] *adj* quincuagésimo

fifty [ˈfɪftɪ] *num* cincuenta ❑ **fifty-fifty** *adj (deal, split)* a medias ♦ *adv* a medias, mitad por mitad

fig [fɪg] *n* higo

fight [faɪt] *(pt, pp* **fought***) n (gen)* pelea; *(MIL)* combate *m; (struggle)* lucha ♦ *vt* luchar contra; *(cancer, alcoholism)* combatir; *(election)* intentar ganar; *(emotion)* resistir ♦ *vi* pelear, luchar ♦ **fight back** *vi* defenderse; *(after illness)* recuperarse ♦ *vt (tears)* contener ♦ **fight off** *vt (attack, attacker)* rechazar; *(disease, sleep, urge)* luchar contra ❑ **fighting** *n* combate *m*, pelea

figure [ˈfɪgəʳ] *n (DRAWING, GEOM)* figura, dibujo; *(number, cipher)* cifra; *(body, outline)* tipo; *(personality)* figura ♦ *vt*

(esp US) imaginar ♦ *vi (appear)* figurar ♦ **figure out** *vt (work out)* resolver

file [faɪl] *n (tool)* lima; *(dossier)* expediente *m; (folder)* carpeta; *(COMPUT)* fichero; *(row)* fila ♦ *vt* limar; *(LAW: claim)* presentar; *(store)* archivar ❑ **filing cabinet** *n* fichero, archivador *m*

Filipino [fɪlɪˈpiːnəʊ] *adj* filipino ♦ *n (person)* filipino(-a) *m/f; (LING)* tagalo

fill [fɪl] *vt (space):* **to ~ (with)** llenar (de); *(vacancy, need)* cubrir ♦ *n:* **to eat one's ~** llenarse ♦ **fill in** *vt* rellenar ♦ **fill out** *vt (form, receipt)* rellenar ♦ **fill up** *vt* llenar (hasta el borde) ♦ *vi (AUT)* poner gasolina

fillet [ˈfɪlɪt] *n* filete *m* ❑ **fillet steak** *n* filete *m* de ternera

filling [ˈfɪlɪŋ] *n (CULIN)* relleno; *(for tooth)* empaste *m* ❑ **filling station** *n* estación *f* de servicio

film [fɪlm] *n* película ♦ *vt (scene)* filmar ♦ *vi* rodar (una película) ❑ **film star** *n* astro, estrella de cine

filter [ˈfɪltəʳ] *n* filtro ♦ *vt* filtrar ❑ **filter lane** *(BRIT) n* carril *m* de selección

filth [fɪlθ] *n* suciedad *f* ❑ **filthy** *adj* sucio; *(language)* obsceno

fin [fɪn] *n (gen)* aleta

final [ˈfaɪnl] *adj (last)* final, último; *(definitive)* definitivo, terminante ♦ *n (BRIT SPORT)* final *f;* **finals** *npl (SCOL)* examen *m* final; *(US SPORT)* final *f*

finale [fɪˈnɑːlɪ] *n* final *m*

finalist [ˈfaɪnəlɪst] *n (SPORT)* finalista *mf* ❑ **finalize** *vt* concluir, completar ❑ **finally** *adv (lastly)* por último, finalmente; *(eventually)* por fin

finance [faɪˈnæns] *n (money)* fondos *mpl* ♦ *vt* financiar; **finances** *npl (personal finances)* finanzas *fpl; (personal finances)* situación *f* económica ❑ **financial** [-ˈnænʃəl] *adj* financiero ❑ **financial year** *n* ejercicio financiero

find [faɪnd] *(pt, pp* **found***) vt* encontrar, hallar; *(come upon)* descubrir ♦ *n* hallazgo; descubrimiento; **to ~ sb**

guilty (*LAW*) declarar culpable a algn
▶ **find out** *vt* averiguar; (*truth, secret*)
descubrir; **to find out about** (*subject*)
informarse sobre; (*by chance*)
enterarse de □ **findings** *npl* (*LAW*)
veredicto, fallo; (*of report*)
recomendaciones *fpl*

fine [faɪn] *adj* excelente; (*thin*) fino
♦ *adv* (*well*) bien ♦ *n* (*LAW*) multa *f* ♦ *vt*
(*LAW*) multar; **to be ~** (*person*) estar
bien; (*weather*) hacer buen tiempo
□ **fine arts** *npl* bellas artes *fpl*

finger [ˈfɪŋɡəʳ] *n* dedo ♦ *vt* (*touch*)
manosear; **little/index ~** (*dedo*)
meñique *m*/índice *m* □ **fingernail** *n*
uña *f* □ **fingerprint** *n* huella dactilar
□ **fingertip** *n* yema del dedo

finish [ˈfɪnɪʃ] *n* (*end*) fin *m*; (*SPORT*) meta *f*;
(*polish etc*) acabado ♦ *vt, vi* terminar; **to
~ doing sth** acabar de hacer algo; **to ~
third** llegar el tercero ♦ **finish off** *vt*
acabar, terminar; (*kill*) acabar con
▶ **finish up** *vt* acabar, terminar ♦ *vi* ir a
parar, terminar

Finland [ˈfɪnlənd] *n* Finlandia

Finn [fɪn] *n* finlandés(-esa) *m/f*
□ **Finnish** *adj* finlandés(-esa) ♦ *n* (*LING*)
finlandés *m*

fir [fɜːʳ] *n* abeto

fire [ˈfaɪəʳ] *n* fuego; (*in hearth*) lumbre *f*;
(*accidental*) incendio; (*heater*) estufa
♦ *vt* (*gun*) disparar; (*interest*) despertar;
(*inf: dismiss*) despedir ♦ *vi* (*shoot*)
disparar; **on ~** ardiendo, en llamas
□ **fire alarm** *n* alarma de incendios
□ **firearm** *n* arma de fuego □ **fire
brigade** (*US* **fire department**) *n*
(*cuerpo de*) bomberos *mpl* □ **fire
engine** (*BRIT*) *n* coche *m* de bomberos
□ **fire escape** *n* escalera de incendios
□ **fire exit** *n* salida de incendios □ **fire
extinguisher** *n* extintor *m* (de
incendios) □ **fireman** (*irreg*) *n*
bombero □ **fireplace** *n* chimenea
□ **fire station** *n* parque *m* de
bomberos □ **firetruck** (*US*) *n* = **fire
engine** □ **firewall** (*INTERNET*) firewall

m □ **firewood** *n* leña □ **fireworks** *npl*
fuegos *mpl* artificiales

firm [fɜːm] *adj* firme; (*look, voice*)
resuelto ♦ *n* firma, empresa □ **firmly**
adv firmemente; resueltamente

first [fɜːst] *adj* primero ♦ *adv* (*before
others*) primero; (*when listing reasons
etc*) en primer lugar, primeramente ♦ *n*
(*person: in race*) primero(-a); (*AUT*)
primera; (*BRIT SCOL*) título de licenciado
con calificación de sobresaliente; **at ~** al
principio; **~ of all** ante todo □ **first
aid** *n* primera ayuda, primeros auxilios
mpl □ **first-aid kit** *n* botiquín *m*
□ **first-class** (*excellent*) de primera
(categoría); (*ticket etc*) de primera
clase □ **first-hand** *adj* de primera
mano □ **first lady** *n* (*esp US*) primera
dama □ **firstly** *adv* en primer lugar
□ **first name** *n* nombre *m* (de pila)
□ **first-rate** *adj* estupendo

fiscal [ˈfɪskəl] *adj* fiscal □ **fiscal year** *n*
año fiscal, ejercicio

fish [fɪʃ] *n inv* pez *m*; (*food*) pescado ♦ *vt,
vi* pescar; **to go fishing** ir de pesca; **~
and chips** pescado frito con patatas
fritas □ **fisherman** (*irreg*) *n* pescador
m □ **fish fingers** (*BRIT*) *npl* croquetas
fpl de pescado □ **fishing** *n* pesca
□ **fishing boat** *n* barca de pesca
□ **fishing line** *n* sedal *m*
□ **fishmonger** *n* (*BRIT*) pescadero(-a)
□ **fishmonger's (shop)** (*BRIT*) *n*
pescadería □ **fish sticks** (*US*) *npl* =
fish fingers □ **fishy** (*inf*) *adj*
sospechoso

fist [fɪst] *n* puño

fit [fɪt] *adj* (*healthy*) en (buena) forma;
(*proper*) adecuado, apropiado ♦ *vt*
(*clothes*) estar o sentar bien a; (*instal*)
poner; (*equip*) proveer, dotar; (*facts*)
cuadrar o corresponder con ♦ *vi*
(*clothes*) sentar bien; (*in space, gap*)
caber; (*facts*) coincidir ♦ *n* (*MED*) ataque
m; **~ to** (*ready*) a punto de; **~ for**
apropiado para; **a ~ of anger/pride** un
arranque de cólera/orgullo; **this dress**

is a good – este vestido me sienta bien; **by fits and starts** a rachas ▸ **fit in** vi (fig: person) llevarse bien (con todos) ❏ **fitness** n (MED) salud f ❏ **fitted** adj (jacket, shirt) entallado; (sheet) de cuatro picos ❏ **fitted carpet** n moqueta ❏ **fitted kitchen** n cocina amueblada ❏ **fitting** adj apropiado ♦ n (of dress) prueba; (of piece of equipment) instalación f ❏ **fitting room** n probador m ❏ **fittings** npl instalaciones fpl

five [faɪv] num cinco ❏ **fiver** (inf) n (BRIT) billete m de cinco libras; (US) billete m de cinco dólares

fix [fɪks] vt (secure) fijar, asegurar; (mend) arreglar; (prepare) preparar ♦ n: **to be in a** – estar en un aprieto ▸ **fix up** vt (meeting) arreglar; **to fix sb up with sth** proveer a algn de algo ❏ **fixed** adj (prices etc) fijo ❏ **fixture** n (SPORT) encuentro

fizzy ['fɪzɪ] adj (drink) gaseoso

flag [flæg] n bandera; (stone) losa ♦ vi decaer ▸ **flag sb down** vt: **to – sb down** hacer señas a algn para que se pare ❏ **flagpole** n asta de bandera

flair [fleə] n aptitud f especial

flak [flæk] n (MIL) fuego antiaéreo; (inf: criticism) lluvia de críticas

flake [fleɪk] n (of rust, paint) escama; (of snow, soap powder) copo ♦ vi (also: – off) desconcharse

flamboyant [flæm'bɔɪənt] adj (dress) vistoso; (person) extravagante

flame [fleɪm] n llama

flamingo [flə'mɪŋgəʊ] n flamenco

flammable [ˈflæməbl] adj inflamable

flan [flæn] n (BRIT) n tarta

⚠ Be careful not to translate **flan** by the Spanish word flan.

flank [flæŋk] n (of animal) ijar m; (of army) flanco ♦ vt flanquear

flannel [ˈflænl] n (BRIT: also: **face –**) manopla; (fabric) franela

flap [flæp] n (of pocket, envelope) solapa ♦ vt (wings, arms) agitar ♦ vi (sail, flag) ondear

flare [fleə] n llamarada; (MIL) bengala; (in skirt etc) vuelo; (flares) (trousers) pantalones mpl de campana ▸ **flare up** vi encenderse; (fig: person) encolerizarse; (: revolt) estallar

flash [flæʃ] n relámpago; (also: **news –**) noticias (fpl) de última hora; (PHOT) flash m ♦ vt (light, headlights) lanzar un destello con; (news, message) transmitir; (smile) lanzar ♦ vi brillar; (hazard light etc) lanzar destellos; **in a –** en un instante; **he flashed by** or **past** pasó como un rayo ❏ **flashback** n (CINEMA) flashback m ❏ **flashbulb** n bombilla fusible ❏ **flashlight** n linterna

flask [flɑ:sk] n frasco; (also: **vacuum –**) termo

flat [flæt] adj llano; (smooth) liso; (tyre) desinflado; (battery) descargado; (beer) muerto; (refusal etc) rotundo; (MUS) desafinado; (rate) fijo ♦ n (BRIT: apartment) piso (SP); departamento (LAm), apartamento (AUT); pinchazo; (MUS) bemol m; **to work – out** trabajar a toda mecha ❏ **flatten** vt (also: **flatten out**) allanar; (smooth out) alisar; (building, plants) arrasar

flatter [ˈflætə] vt adular, halagar ❏ **flattering** adj halagüeño; (dress) que favorece

flaunt [flɔːnt] vt ostentar, lucir

flavour etc [ˈfleɪvə] (US **flavor** etc) n sabor m, gusto ♦ vt sazonar, condimentar; **strawberry-flavoured** con sabor a fresa ❏ **flavouring** n (in product) aromatizante m

flaw [flɔː] n defecto ❏ **flawless** adj impecable

flea [fliː] n pulga ❏ **flea market** n rastro, mercadillo

flee [fliː] n (pt, pp **fled**) vt huir de ♦ vi huir, fugarse

fleece [fliːs] n vellón m; (wool) lana; (top) forro polar ♦ vt (inf) desplumar

fleet [fliːt] n flota; (of lorries etc) escuadra

fleeting [ˈfliːtɪŋ] adj fugaz

Flemish [ˈflemɪʃ] adj flamenco

flesh [fleʃ] n carne f; (skin) piel f; (of fruit) pulpa

flew [fluː] pt of **fly**

flex [fleks] n cordón m ♦ vt (muscles) tensar □ **flexibility** n flexibilidad f □ **flexible** adj flexible □ **flexitime** (US flextime) n horario flexible

flick [flɪk] n capirotazo; chasquido ♦ vt (with hand) dar un capirotazo a; (whip etc) chasquear; (switch) accionar
► **flick through** vt fus hojear

flicker [ˈflɪkə] vi (light) parpadear; (flame) vacilar

flies [flaɪz] npl of **fly**

flight [flaɪt] n vuelo; (escape) huida, fuga; (also: ~ **of steps**) tramo (de escaleras) □ **flight attendant** n auxiliar mf de vuelo

flimsy [ˈflɪmzɪ] adj (thin) muy ligero; (building) endeble; (excuse) flojo

flinch [flɪntʃ] vi encogerse; **to ~ from** retroceder ante

fling [flɪŋ] (pt, pp **flung**) vt arrojar

flint [flɪnt] n pedernal m; (in lighter) piedra

flip [flɪp] vt dar la vuelta a; (switch: turn on) encender; (turn) apagar; (coin) echar a cara o cruz

flip-flops [ˈflɪpflɒps] npl (esp BRIT) chancletas fpl

flipper [ˈflɪpə] n aleta

flirt [flɜːt] vi coquetear, flirtear ♦ n coqueta

float [fləʊt] n flotador m; (in procession) carroza; (money) reserva ♦ vi flotar; (swimmer) hacer la plancha

flock [flɒk] n (of sheep) rebaño; (of birds) bandada ♦ vi: **to ~ to** acudir en tropel a

flood [flʌd] n inundación f; (of letters, imports etc) avalancha ♦ vt inundar ♦ vi

(place) inundarse; (people): **to ~ into** inundar □ **flooding** n inundaciones fpl □ **floodlight** n foco

floor [flɔː] n suelo; (storey) piso; (of sea) fondo ♦ vt (question) dejar sin respuesta; (: blow) derribar; **ground ~**, **first ~** (US) planta baja; **first ~**, **second ~** (US) primer piso □ **floorboard** n tabla □ **flooring** n suelo; (material) solería □ **floor show** n cabaret m

flop [flɒp] n fracaso ♦ vi (fail) fracasar; (fall) derrumbarse □ **floppy** adj flojo ♦ n (COMPUT: also: **floppy disk**) floppy m

flora [ˈflɔːrə] n flora

floral [ˈflɔːrl] adj (pattern) floreado

florist [ˈflɒrɪst] n florista mf □ **florist's (shop)** n floristería

flotation [fləʊˈteɪʃən] n (of shares) emisión f; (of company) lanzamiento

flour [ˈflaʊə] n harina

flourish [ˈflʌrɪʃ] vi florecer ♦ n ademán m, movimiento (ostentoso)

flow [fləʊ] n (movement) flujo; (of traffic) circulación f; (tide) corriente f ♦ vi (river, blood) fluir; (traffic) circular

flower [ˈflaʊə] n flor f ♦ vi florecer □ **flower bed** n macizo □ **flowerpot** n tiesto

flown [fləʊn] pp of **fly**

fl. oz. abbr = **fluid ounce**

flu [fluː] n: **to have ~** tener la gripe

fluctuate [ˈflʌktjʊeɪt] vi fluctuar

fluent [ˈfluːənt] adj (linguist) que habla perfectamente; (speech) elocuente; **he speaks ~ French**, **he's ~ in French** domina el francés

fluff [flʌf] n pelusa □ **fluffy** adj de pelo suave

fluid [ˈfluːɪd] adj (movement) fluido, líquido; (situation) inestable ♦ n fluido, líquido □ **fluid ounce** n onza f líquida

fluke [fluːk] n (inf) chiripa

flung [flʌŋ] pt, pp of **fling**

fluorescent [flʊəˈresnt] adj fluorescente

fluoride [ˈflʊəraɪd] n fluoruro

flurry ['flʌrɪ] n (of snow) temporal m; ~ **of activity** frenesí m de actividad

flush [flʌʃ] n rubor m; (of youth etc) resplandor m ♦ vt limpiar con agua ♦ vi ruborizarse ♦ adj: ~ **with** a ras de; **to ~ the toilet** hacer funcionar la cisterna

flute [fluːt] n flauta

flutter ['flʌtə*] n (of wings) revoloteo, aleteo; (fig): **a ~ of panic/excitement** una oleada de pánico/excitación ♦ vi revolotear

fly [flaɪ] (pt **flew**, pp **flown**) n mosca; (on trousers: also: **flies**) bragueta ♦ vt (plane) pilot(e)ar; (cargo) transportar (en avión) ♦ vi volar; (distances) recorrer (en avión); (passengers) ir en avión; (escape) evadirse; (flag) ondear ► **fly away, fly off** vi emprender el vuelo ► **fly-drive** n: **fly-drive holiday** vacaciones que incluyen vuelo y alquiler de coche ♦ **flying** n (activity) (el) volar; (action) vuelo ♦ adj: **flying visit** visita relámpago; **with flying colours** con lucimiento ♦ **flying saucer** n platillo volante ♦ **flyover** (BRIT) n paso a desnivel or superior

FM abbr (RADIO: = frequency modulation) FM

foal [fəʊl] n potro

foam [fəʊm] n espuma ♦ vi hacer espuma

focus ['fəʊkəs] (pl **focuses**) n foco; (centre) centro ♦ vt (field glasses etc) enfocar ♦ vi: **to ~ (on)** enfocar a; (issue etc) centrarse en; **in/out of ~** enfocado/desenfocado

foetus ['fiːtəs] (US **fetus**) n feto

fog [fɒg] n niebla ♦ **foggy** adj: **it's foggy** hay niebla, está brumoso ♦ **fog lamp** (US **fog light**) n (AUT) faro de niebla

foil [fɔɪl] vt frustrar ♦ n hoja; (kitchen foil) papel m de aluminio; (complement) complemento; (FENCING) florete m

fold [fəʊld] n (bend, crease) pliegue m; (AGR) redil m ♦ vt doblar; (arms) cruzar ► **fold up** vi plegarse, doblarse;

(business) quebrar ♦ vt (map etc) plegar ♦ **folder** n (for papers) carpeta; (COMPUT) directorio ♦ **folding** adj (chair, bed) plegable

foliage ['fəʊlɪɪdʒ] n follaje m

folk [fəʊk] npl gente f ♦ adj popular, folklórico; **folks** npl (family) familia sg, parientes mpl ♦ **folklore** ['fəʊklɔː*] n folklore m ♦ **folk music** n música folk ♦ **folk song** n canción f popular

follow ['fɒləʊ] vt seguir ♦ vi seguir; (result) resultar; **to ~ suit** hacer lo mismo ► **follow up** vt (letter, offer) responder a; (case) investigar ♦ **follower** n (of person, belief) partidario(-a) ♦ **following** adj siguiente ♦ n afición f, partidarios mpl ♦ **follow-up** n continuación f

fond [fɒnd] adj (memory, smile etc) cariñoso; (hopes) ilusorio; **to be ~ of** tener cariño a; (pastime, food) ser aficionado a

food [fuːd] n comida ♦ **food mixer** n batidora ♦ **food poisoning** n intoxicación f alimenticia ♦ **food processor** n robot m de cocina ♦ **food stamp** (US) n vale m para comida

fool [fuːl] n tonto(-a); (CULIN) puré m de frutas con nata ♦ vt engañar ♦ vi (gen) bromear ► **fool about, fool around** vi hacer el tonto ♦ **foolish** adj tonto; (careless) imprudente ♦ **foolproof** adj (plan etc) infalible

foot [fʊt] (pl **feet**) n pie m; (measure) pie m (= 304 mm); (of animal) pata ♦ vt pagar; **on ~** a pie ♦ **footage** n (CINEMA) imágenes fpl ♦ **foot-and-mouth (disease)** n (tʃand'maʊθ) fiebre f aftosa ♦ **football** n balón m; (game: BRIT) fútbol m; (US) fútbol m americano ♦ **footballer** n (BRIT) = **football player** ♦ **football match** n partido de fútbol ♦ **football player** n (BRIT) futbolista mf; (US) jugador m de fútbol americano ♦ **footbridge** n puente m para peatones ♦ **foothills**

npl estribaciones *fpl* ❑ **foothold** *n* pie *m* firme ❑ **footing** *n* (*fig*) posición *f*; **to lose one's footing** perder el pie ❑ **footnote** *n* nota (al pie de la página) ❑ **footpath** *n* sendero ❑ **footprint** *n* huella, pisada ❑ **footstep** *n* paso ❑ **footwear** *n* calzado

for

KEYWORD

[fɔː] *prep*

1 (*indicating destination, intention*) para; **the train for London** el tren con destino a *or* de Londres; **he left for Rome** marchó para Roma; **he went for the paper** fue por el periódico; **is this for me?** ¿es esto para mí?; **it's time for lunch** es la hora de comer

2 (*indicating purpose*) para; **what's it for?** ¿para qué (es)?; **to pray for peace** rezar por la paz

3 (*on behalf of, representing*) **the MP for Hove** el diputado por Hove; **he works for the government/a local firm** trabaja para el gobierno/en una empresa local; **I'll ask him for you** se lo pediré por ti; **G for George** G de Gerona

4 (*because of*) por esta razón; **for fear of being criticized** por temor a ser criticado

5 (*with regard to*) para; **it's cold for July** hace frío para julio; **he has a gift for languages** tiene don de lenguas

6 (*in exchange for*) por; **I sold it for £5** lo vendí por £5; **to pay 50 pence for a ticket** pagar 50 peniques por un billete

7 (*in favour of*) **are you for or against us?** ¿estás con nosotros o contra nosotros?; **I'm all for it** estoy totalmente a favor; **vote for X** vote (a) X

8 (*referring to distance*) **there are roadworks for 5 km** hay obras en 5

km; **we walked for miles** caminamos kilómetros y kilómetros

9 (*referring to time*): **he was away for two years** estuvo fuera (durante) dos años; **it hasn't rained for 3 weeks** no ha llovido durante *or* en 3 semanas; **I have known her for years** la conozco desde hace años; **can you do it for tomorrow?** ¿lo podrás hacer para mañana?

10 (*with infinitive clauses*): **it is not for me to decide** la decisión no es cosa mía; **it would be best for you to leave** sería mejor que te fueras; **there is still time for you to do it** todavía te queda tiempo para hacerlo; **for this to be possible ...** para que esto sea posible ...

11 (*in spite of*) a pesar de; **for all his complaints** a pesar de sus quejas

♦ *conj* (*since, as: rather formal*) puesto que

forbid [fə'bɪd] (*pt* **forbad(e)**, *pp* **forbidden**) *vt* prohibir; **to ~ sb to do sth** prohibir a algn hacer algo ❑ **forbidden** *pt of* **forbid** ♦ *adj* (*food, area*) prohibido; (*word, subject*) tabú

force [fɔːs] *n* fuerza ♦ *vt* forzar; (*push*) meter a la fuerza; **to ~ o.s. to do sth** hacer un esfuerzo por hacer ❑ **forced** *adj* forzado ❑ **forceful** *adj* enérgico

ford [fɔːd] *n* vado

fore [fɔː'] *n*: **to come to the ~** empezar a destacar ❑ **forearm** *n* antebrazo ❑ **forecast** (*pt, pp* **forecast**) *n* pronóstico ♦ *vt* pronosticar ❑ **forecourt** *n* patio ❑ **forefinger** *n* (*dedo*) índice *m* ❑ **forefront** *n*: **in the forefront of** en la vanguardia de ❑ **foreground** *n* primer plano ❑ **forehead** ['fɔrɪd] *n* frente *f*

foreign ['fɔrɪn] *adj* extranjero; (*trade*) exterior; (*object*) extraño ❑ **foreign currency** *n* divisas *fpl* ❑ **foreigner** *n* extranjero(-a) ❑ **foreign exchange** *n*

divisas *fpl* ❏ **Foreign Office** (BRIT) *n*
Ministerio de Asuntos Exteriores
❏ **Foreign Secretary** (BRIT) *n* Ministro
de Asuntos Exteriores

fore: **foreman** (*irreg*) *n* capataz *m*; (*in construction*) maestro de obras
❏ **foremost** *adj* principal ♦ *adv*: **first and foremost** ante todo ❏ **forename**
n nombre *m* (de pila)

forensic [fəˈrɛnsɪk] *adj* forense

foresee [fɔːˈsiː] (*pt* **foresaw**, *pp* **foreseen**) *vt* prever ❏ **foreseeable**
adj previsible

forest [ˈfɒrɪst] *n* bosque *m* ❏ **forestry**
n silvicultura

forever [fəˈrɛvə] *adv* para siempre; (*endlessly*) constantemente

foreword [ˈfɔːwəd] *n* prefacio

forfeit [ˈfɔːfɪt] *vt* perder

forgave [fəˈgeɪv] *pt of* **forgive**

forge [fɔːdʒ] *n* herrería ♦ *vt* (*signature, money*) falsificar; (*metal*) forjar
❏ **forger** *n* falsificador(a) *m/f*
❏ **forgery** *n* falsificación *f*

forget [fəˈgɛt] (*pt* **forgot**, *pp* **forgotten**) *vt* olvidar ♦ *vi* olvidarse ❏ **forgetful**
adj despistado

forgive [fəˈgɪv] (*pt* **forgave**, *pp* **forgiven**) *vt* perdonar; **to ~ sb for sth**
perdonar algo a algn

forgot [fəˈgɒt] *pt of* **forget**

forgotten [fəˈgɒtn] *pp of* **forget**

fork [fɔːk] *n* (*for eating*) tenedor *m*; (*for gardening*) horca; (*of roads*) bifurcación
f ♦ *vi* (*road*) bifurcarse

forlorn [fəˈlɔːn] *adj* (*person*) triste, melancólico; (*place*) abandonado; (*attempt, hope*) desesperado

form [fɔːm] *n* forma; (BRIT SCOL) clase *f*; (*document*) formulario ♦ *vt* formar; (*idea*) concebir; (*habit*) adquirir; **in top ~** en plena forma; **to ~ a queue** hacer cola

formal [ˈfɔːməl] *adj* (*offer, receipt*) por escrito; (*person etc*) correcto; (*occasion, dinner*) de etiqueta; (*dress*) correcto;

(*garden*) (de estilo) clásico
❏ **formality** [-ˈmælɪtɪ] *n* (*procedure*)
trámite *m*; corrección *f*; etiqueta

format [ˈfɔːmæt] *n* formato ♦ *vt* (COMPUT) formatear

formation [fɔːˈmeɪʃən] *n* formación *f*

former [ˈfɔːmə] *adj* anterior; (*earlier*) antiguo; (*ex*) ex; **the ~ ... the latter ...**
aquél ... éste ... ❏ **formerly** *adv* antes

formidable [ˈfɔːmɪdəbl] *adj*
formidable

formula [ˈfɔːmjulə] *n* fórmula

fort [fɔːt] *n* fuerte *m*

forthcoming [fɔːθˈkʌmɪŋ] *adj*
próximo, venidero; (*help, information*)
disponible; (*character*) comunicativo

fortieth [ˈfɔːtɪɪθ] *adj* cuadragésimo

fortify [ˈfɔːtɪfaɪ] *vt* (*city*) fortificar;
(*person*) fortalecer

fortnight [ˈfɔːtnaɪt] (BRIT) *n* quince días
mpl; quincena ❏ **fortnightly** *adj* de
cada quince días, quincenal ♦ *adv* cada
quince días, quincenalmente

fortress [ˈfɔːtrɪs] *n* fortaleza

fortunate [ˈfɔːtʃənɪt] *adj* afortunado; **it is ~ that ...** (es una) suerte que ...
❏ **fortunately** *adv* afortunadamente

fortune [ˈfɔːtʃən] *n* suerte *f*; (*wealth*)
fortuna ❏ **fortune-teller** *n*
adivino(-a)

forty [ˈfɔːtɪ] *num* cuarenta

forum [ˈfɔːrəm] *n* foro

forward [ˈfɔːwəd] *adj* (*movement, position*) avanzado; (*front*) delantero;
(*in time*) adelantado; (*not shy*) atrevido
♦ *n* (SPORT) delantero *m* ♦ *vt* (*letter*)
remitir; (*career*) promocionar; **to move ~** avanzar ❏ **forwarding address** *n*
destinatario ❏ **forward(s)** *adv* (hacia)
adelante

forward slash *n* barra diagonal

fossil [ˈfɒsl] *n* fósil *m*

foster [ˈfɒstə] *vt* (*child*) acoger en una
familia; fomentar ❏ **foster child** *n*
hijo(-a) adoptivo(-a) ❏ **foster
mother** *n* madre *f* adoptiva

fought [fɔːt] *pt, pp of* **fight**

foul [faul] *adj* sucio, puerco; (*weather, smell etc*) asqueroso; (*language*) grosero; (*temper*) malísimo ♦ *n* (SPORT) falta ♦ *vt* (*dirty*) ensuciar ❑ **foul play** *n* (LAW) muerte *f* violenta

found [faund] *pt, pp of* **find** ♦ *vt* fundar ❑ **foundation** [-'deɪʃən] *n* (*act*) fundación *f*; (*basis*) base *f*; (*also:* **foundation cream**) crema base; **foundations** *npl* (*of building*) cimientos *mpl*

founder ['faundə'] *n* fundador(a) *m/f* ♦ *vi* hundirse

fountain ['fauntɪn] *n* fuente *f* ❑ **fountain pen** *n* (*pluma*) estilográfica (SP), pluma-fuente *f* (LAm)

four [fɔː'] *num* cuatro; **on all fours** a gatas ❑ **four-letter word** *n* taco ❑ **four-poster** *n* (*also:* **four-poster bed**) cama de columnas ❑ **fourteen** *num* catorce ❑ **fourteenth** *adj* decimocuarto ❑ **fourth** *num* cuarto ❑ **four-wheel drive** *n* tracción *f* a las cuatro ruedas

fowl [faul] *n* ave *f* (de corral)

fox [fɔks] *n* zorro ♦ *vt* confundir

foyer ['fɔɪeɪ] *n* vestíbulo

fraction ['frækʃən] *n* fracción *f*

fracture ['fræktʃə'] *n* fractura

fragile ['frædʒaɪl] *adj* frágil

fragment ['frægmənt] *n* fragmento

fragrance ['freɪgrəns] *n* fragancia

frail [freɪl] *adj* frágil; (*person*) débil

frame [freɪm] *n* (TECH) armazón *m*; (*of person*) cuerpo; (*of picture, door etc*) marco; (*of spectacles: also:* **frames**) montura ♦ *vt* enmarcar ❑ **framework** *n* marco

France [frɑːns] *n* Francia

franchise ['fræntʃaɪz] *n* (POL) derecho de votar, sufragio; (COMM) licencia, concesión *f*

frank [fræŋk] *adj* franco ♦ *vt* (*letter*) franquear ❑ **frankly** *adv* francamente

frantic ['fræntɪk] *adj* (*distraught*) desesperado; (*hectic*) frenético

fraud [frɔːd] *n* fraude *m*; (*person*) impostor(a) *m/f*

fraught [frɔːt] *adj*: ~ **with** lleno de

fray [freɪ] *vi* deshilacharse

freak [friːk] *n* (*person*) fenómeno; (*event*) suceso anormal

freckle ['frɛkl] *n* peca

free [friː] *adj* libre; (*gratis*) gratuito ♦ *vt* (*prisoner etc*) poner en libertad; (*jammed object*) soltar; ~ **(of charge)**, **for** ~ gratis ❑ **freedom** *n* libertad *f* ❑ **Freefone®** *n* número gratuito ❑ **free gift** *n* prima ❑ **free kick** *n* tiro libre ❑ **freelance** *adj* independiente ♦ *adv* por cuenta propia ❑ **freely** *adv* libremente; (*liberally*) generosamente ❑ **Freepost®** *n* porte *m* pagado ❑ **free-range** *adj* (*hen, eggs*) de granja ❑ **freeway** (US) *n* autopista ❑ **free will** *n* libre albedrío; **of one's own free will** por su propia voluntad

freeze [friːz] (*pt* **froze**, *pp* **frozen**) *vi* (*weather*) helar; (*liquid, pipe, person*) helarse, congelarse ♦ *vt* (*food, prices, salaries*) congelar ♦ *n* helada; (*on arms, wages*) congelación *f* ❑ **freezer** *n* congelador *m*, freezer *m* (SC)

freezing ['friːzɪŋ] *adj* helado; **three degrees below ~** tres grados bajo cero ❑ **freezing point** *n* punto de congelación

freight [freɪt] *n* (*goods*) carga; (*money charged*) flete *m* ❑ **freight train** (US) *n* tren *m* de mercancías

French [frɛntʃ] *adj* francés(-esa) ♦ *n* (LING) francés *m*; **the ~** *npl* los franceses ❑ **French bean** *n* judía verde ❑ **French bread** *n* pan *m* francés ❑ **French dressing** *n* (CULIN) vinagreta ❑ **French fried potatoes**, **French fries** (US) *npl* patatas *fpl* (SP) o papas *fpl* (LAm) fritas ❑ **Frenchman** (*irreg*) *n* francés *m* ❑ **Frenchwoman** (*irreg*) *n* francesa ❑ **French stick** *n*

barra de pan ❑ **French window** n
puerta de cristal
frenzy ['frenzɪ] n frenesí m
frequency ['friːkwənsɪ] n frecuencia f
frequent [adj 'friːkwənt, vb frɪ'kwent]
adj frecuente ♦ vt frecuentar
❑ **frequently** [-əntlɪ] adv
frecuentemente, a menudo
fresh [freʃ] adj fresco; (bread) tierno;
(new) nuevo ❑ **freshen** vi (wind, air)
soplar más recio ▶ **freshen up** vi
(person) arreglarse, lavarse ❑ **fresher**
(BRIT: inf) n (UNIV) estudiante mf de
primer año ❑ **freshly** adv (made,
painted etc) recién ❑ **freshman** (US:
irreg) n = **fresher** ❑ **freshwater** adj
(fish) de agua dulce
fret [fret] vi inquietarse
Fri abbr (= Friday) vier
friction ['frɪkʃən] n fricción f
Friday ['fraɪdɪ] n viernes m inv
fridge [frɪdʒ] (BRIT) n frigorífico (SP),
nevera (SP), refrigerador m (LAm),
heladera (RPl)
fried [fraɪd] adj frito
friend [frend] n amigo(-a) ❑ **friendly**
adj simpático; (government) amigo;
(place) acogedor(a); (match) amistoso
❑ **friendship** n amistad f
fries [fraɪz] (esp US) npl = **French fried
potatoes**
frigate ['frɪgɪt] n fragata f
fright [fraɪt] n (terror) terror m; (scare)
susto; **to take ~** asustarse ❑ **frighten**
vt asustar ❑ **frightened** adj asustado
❑ **frightening** adj espantoso
❑ **frightful** adj espantoso, horrible
frill [frɪl] n volante m
fringe [frɪndʒ] n (BRIT: of hair) flequillo;
(on lampshade etc) flecos mpl; (of forest
etc) borde m, margen m
Frisbee® ['frɪzbɪ] n frisbee® m
fritter ['frɪtə*] n buñuelo
frivolous ['frɪvələs] adj frívolo
fro [frəu] see **to**
frock [frɒk] n vestido

frog [frɒg] n rana f ❑ **frogman** (irreg) n
hombre-rana m

from

KEYWORD

['frɒm] prep
1 (indicating starting place) de,
desde; **where do you come from?**
¿de dónde eres?; **from London to
Glasgow** de Londres a Glasgow; **to
escape from sth/sb** escaparse de
algo/algn
2 (indicating origin etc) de; **a letter/
telephone call from my sister** una
carta/llamada de mi hermana; **tell
him from me that ...** dígale de mi
parte que ...
3 (indicating time): **from one o'clock
to** or **until** or **till two** de(sde) la una a
or hasta las dos; **from January (on)** a
partir de enero
4 (indicating distance) de; **the hotel is
1 km from the beach** el hotel está a 1
km de la playa
5 (indicating price, number etc) de;
prices range from £10 to £50 los
precios van desde £10 a or hasta £50;
**the interest rate was increased from
9% to 10%** el tipo de interés fue
incrementado de un 9% a un 10%
6 (indicating difference) de; **he can't
tell red from green** no sabe
distinguir el rojo del verde; **to be
different from sb/sth** ser diferente a
algn/algo
7 (because of, on the basis of): **from
what he says** por lo que dice; **weak
from hunger** debilitado por el
hambre

front [frʌnt] n (foremost part) parte f
delantera; (of house) fachada; (of dress)
delantero; (promenade: also: **sea ~**)
paseo marítimo; (MIL, POL, METEO)

frente m; (fig: appearances) apariencias
fpl ♦ adj (wheel, leg) delantero; (row, line)
primero; in ~ (of) delante (de) □ **front
door** n puerta principal □ **frontier**
['frʌntɪəʳ] n frontera □ **front page** n
primera plana □ **front-wheel drive** n
tracción f delantera

frost [frɒst] n helada; (also: hoarfrost)
escarcha □ **frostbite** n congelación f
□ **frosting** n (esp US: icing) glaseado
□ **frosty** adj (weather) de helada;
(welcome etc) glacial

froth [frɒθ] n espuma

frown [fraun] vi fruncir el ceño

froze [frəuz] pt of **freeze**

frozen ['frəuzn] pp of **freeze**

fruit [fruːt] n inv fruta; (fig) fruto;
resultados mpl □ **fruit juice** n zumo
(SP) or jugo (LAm) de fruta □ **fruit
machine** n (BRIT) máquina f tragaperras
□ **fruit salad** n macedonia (SP) or
ensalada (LAm) de frutas

frustrate [frʌs'treit] vt frustrar
□ **frustrated** adj frustrado

fry [frai] (pt, pp **fried**) vt freír; **small ~**
n gente f menuda □ **frying pan** n
sartén f

ft. abbr = **foot; feet**

fudge [fʌdʒ] n (CULIN) caramelo blando

fuel [fjuəl] n (for heating) combustible
m; (coal) carbón m; (wood) leña; (for
engine) carburante m □ **fuel tank** n
depósito (de combustible)

fulfil [ful'fil] vt (function) realizar; cumplir con;
(condition) satisfacer; (wish, desire)
realizar

full [ful] adj lleno; (fig) pleno; (complete)
completo; (maximum) máximo;
(information) detallado; (price) íntegro;
(skirt) amplio ♦ adv: **to know ~ well
that** saber perfectamente que; **I'm ~
(up)** no puedo más; **~ employment**
pleno empleo; **a ~ two hours** dos
horas completas; **at ~ speed** a máxima
velocidad; **in ~** (reproduce, quote)
íntegramente □ **full-length** adj

(novel etc) entero; (coat) largo;
(portrait) de cuerpo entero □ **full
moon** n luna llena □ **full-scale** adj
(attack, war) en gran escala; (model) de
tamaño natural □ **full stop** n punto
□ **full-time** adj (work) de tiempo
completo ♦ adv: **to work full-time**
trabajar a tiempo completo □ **fully**
adv completamente; (at least) por lo
menos

fumble ['fʌmbl] vi: **to ~ with** manejar
torpemente

fume [fjuːm] vi (rage) estar furioso
□ **fumes** npl humo, gases mpl

fun [fʌn] n (amusement) diversión f; **to
have ~** divertirse; **for ~** en broma; **to
make ~ of** burlarse de

function ['fʌŋkʃən] n función f ♦ vi
funcionar

fund [fʌnd] n fondo; (reserve) reserva;
funds npl (money) fondos mpl

fundamental [fʌndə'mentl] adj
fundamental

funeral ['fjuːnərəl] n (burial) entierro;
(ceremony) funerales mpl □ **funeral
director** n director(a) m/f de pompas
fúnebres □ **funeral parlour** (BRIT) n
funeraria

funfair ['fʌnfɛəʳ] (BRIT) n parque m de
atracciones

fungus ['fʌŋgəs] (pl **fungi**) n hongo;
(mould) moho

funnel ['fʌnl] n embudo; (of ship)
chimenea

funny ['fʌni] adj gracioso, divertido;
(strange) curioso, raro

fur [fəːʳ] n piel f; (BRIT: in kettle etc) sarro
□ **fur coat** n abrigo de pieles

furious ['fjuəriəs] adj furioso; (effort)
violento

furnish ['fəːniʃ] vt amueblar; (supply)
suministrar; (information) facilitar
□ **furnishings** npl muebles mpl

furniture ['fəːnitʃəʳ] n muebles mpl;
piece of ~ mueble m

furry ['fəːri] adj peludo

further [ˈfɜːðəʳ] adj (new) nuevo, adicional ♦ adv más lejos; (more) más; (moreover) además ♦ vt promover, adelantar **□ further education** n educación f superior **□ furthermore** adv además

furthest [ˈfɜːðɪst] superlative of **far**

fury [ˈfjuərɪ] n furia f

fuse [fjuːz] (US fuze) n fusible m; (for bomb etc) mecha f ♦ vt (metal) fundir; (fig) fusionar ♦ vi fundirse; fusionarse; (BRIT ELEC): **to ~ the lights** fundir los plomos **□ fuse box** n caja de fusibles

fusion [ˈfjuːʒən] n fusión f

fuss [fʌs] n (excitement) conmoción f; (trouble) alboroto; **to make a ~** (fuss) armar un lío or jaleo; **to make a ~ of sb** mimar a algn **□ fussy** adj (person) exigente; (too ornate) recargado

future [ˈfjuːtʃəʳ] adj futuro; (coming) venidero ♦ n futuro; (prospects) porvenir m; **in ~** de ahora en adelante; **futures** npl (COMM) operaciones fpl a término, futuros mpl

fuze [fjuːz] (US) = **fuse**

fuzzy [ˈfʌzɪ] adj (PHOT) borroso

G, g

G [dʒiː] n (MUS) sol m

g. abbr (= gram(s)) gr.

gadget [ˈgædʒɪt] n aparato

Gaelic [ˈgeɪlɪk] adj, n (LING) gaélico

gag [gæg] n (on mouth) mordaza; (joke) chiste m ♦ vt amordazar

gain [geɪn] n ~ **in** aumento (de, profit) ganancia ♦ vt ganar ♦ vi (watch) adelantarse; **to ~ from/by sth** sacar provecho de algo; **to ~ on sb** ganar terreno a algn; **to ~ 3 lbs** (in weight) engordar 3 libras

gal. abbr = **gallon**

gala [ˈgɑːlə] n fiesta

galaxy [ˈgæləksɪ] n galaxia

gale [geɪl] n (wind) vendaval m

gall bladder [ˈgɔːl-] n vesícula biliar

gallery [ˈgælərɪ] n (also: **art~**: public) pinacoteca; (: private) galería de arte; (for spectators) tribuna

gallon [ˈgælən] n galón m (BRIT = 4,546 litros, US = 3,785 litros)

gallop [ˈgæləp] n galope m ♦ vi galopar

gallstone [ˈgɔːlstəun] n cálculo biliario

gamble [ˈgæmbl] n (risk) riesgo ♦ vt jugar, apostar ♦ vi (take a risk) jugárselas; (bet) apostar; **to ~ on** apostar a; (success etc) contar con **□ gambler** n jugador(a) m/f **□ gambling** n juego

game [geɪm] n juego; (match) partido; (of cards) partida; (HUNTING) caza ♦ adj (willing): **to be ~ for anything** atreverse a todo; **big ~** caza mayor; **games** (contest) juegos; (BRIT: SCOL) deportes mpl **□ games console** [geɪmz-] n consola de juegos **□ game show** n programa m concurso inv, concurso

gammon [ˈgæmən] n (bacon) tocino ahumado; (ham) jamón m ahumado

gang [gæŋ] n (of criminals) pandilla; (of friends etc) grupo; (of workmen) brigada

gangster [ˈgæŋstəʳ] n gángster m

gap [gæp] n vacío (SP), hueco (LAm); (in trees, traffic) claro; (in time) intervalo; (difference): ~ **(between)** diferencia (entre)

gape [geɪp] vi mirar boquiabierto; (shirt etc) abrirse (completamente)

gap year n año sabático (antes de empezar a estudiar en la universidad)

garage [ˈgærɑːʒ] n garaje m; (for repairs) taller m **□ garage sale** n venta de objetos usados (en el jardín de una casa)

garbage [ˈgɑːbɪdʒ] (US) n basura; (inf: nonsense) tonterías fpl **□ garbage can** n cubo o bote m (MEX) or tacho (SC) de la basura **□ garbage collector** (US) n basurero(-a)

garden ['gɑ:dn] n jardín m; **gardens** npl
(park) parque m ❑ **garden centre**
(BRIT) n centro de jardinería
❑ **gardener** n jardinero(-a)
❑ **gardening** n jardinería

garlic ['gɑ:lɪk] n ajo

garment ['gɑ:mənt] n prenda (de
vestir)

garnish ['gɑ:nɪʃ] vt (CULIN) aderezar

garrison ['gærɪsn] n guarnición f

gas [gæs] n gas m; (fuel) combustible m;
(US: gasoline) gasolina ♦ vt asfixiar con
gas ❑ **gas cooker** (BRIT) n cocina de
gas ❑ **gas cylinder** n bombona de
gas ❑ **gas fire** n estufa de gas

gasket ['gæskɪt] n (AUT) junta de culata

gasoline ['gæsəli:n] (US) n gasolina

gasp [gɑ:sp] n boqueada f, (of shock etc)
grito sofocado ♦ vi (pant) jadear

gas: gas pedal n (esp US) acelerador m
❑ **gas station** (US) n gasolinera
❑ **gas tank** (US) n (AUT) depósito de
(gasolina)

gate [geɪt] n puerta f; (iron gate) verja

gateau ['gætəʊ] (pl **gateaux**) n tarta

gatecrash ['geɪtkræʃ] (BRIT) vt colarse en

gateway ['geɪtweɪ] n puerta

gather ['gæðə*] vt (flowers, fruit) coger
(SP), recoger; (assemble) reunir; (pick
up) recoger; (SEWING) fruncir;
(understand) entender ♦ vi (assemble)
reunirse; **to ~ speed** ganar velocidad
❑ **gathering** n reunión f, asamblea

gauge [geɪdʒ] n (instrument) indicador
m ♦ vt medir; (fig) juzgar

gave [geɪv] pt of **give**

gay [geɪ] adj (homosexual) gay; (joyful)
alegre; (colour) vivo

gaze [geɪz] n mirada fija ♦ vi: **to ~ at sth**
mirar algo fijamente

GB abbr = **Great Britain**

GCSE (BRIT) n abbr (= General Certificate
of Secondary Education) examen de
reválida que se hace a los 16 años

gear [gɪə*] n equipo, herramientas fpl;
(TECH) engranaje m; (AUT) velocidad f,

marcha ♦ vt (fig: adapt): **to ~ sth to**
adaptar o ajustar algo a; **top** or **high**
(US)/**low** ~ cuarta/primera velocidad;
in ~ en marcha ▶ **gear up** vi
prepararse ❑ **gear box** n caja de
cambios ❑ **gear lever** n palanca de
cambio ❑ **gear shift** (US) n = **gear
lever** ❑ **gear stick** (BRIT) palanca de
cambios

geese [gi:s] npl of **goose**

gel [dʒel] n gel m

gem [dʒem] n piedra preciosa

Gemini ['dʒemɪnaɪ] n Géminis m,
Gemelos mpl

gender ['dʒendə*] n género

gene [dʒi:n] n gen(e) m

general ['dʒenərl] n general m ♦ adj
general; **in** ~ en general ❑ **general
anaesthetic** (US ~ **anesthetic**) n
anestesia general ❑ **general
election** n elecciones fpl generales
❑ **generalize** vi generalizar
❑ **generally** adv generalmente, en
general ❑ **general practitioner** n
médico general ❑ **general store** n
tienda (que vende de todo), almacén m
(SC, SP)

generate ['dʒenəreɪt] vt (ELEC) generar;
(jobs, profits) producir

generation [dʒenə'reɪʃən] n
generación f

generator ['dʒenəreɪtə*] n generador m

generosity [dʒenə'rɒsɪtɪ] n
generosidad f

generous ['dʒenərəs] adj generoso

genetic [dʒɪ'netɪk] adj: ~ **engineering**
ingeniería genética; ~ **fingerprinting**
identificación f genética
❑ **genetically modified** adj
transgénico ❑ **genetics** n genética

genitals ['dʒenɪtlz] npl (órganos mpl)
genitales mpl

genius ['dʒi:nɪəs] n genio

gent [dʒent] n abbr (BRIT) = **gentleman**

gentle ['dʒɛntl] *adj* apacible, dulce; (*animal*) manso; (*breeze, curve etc*) suave

⚠ Be careful not to translate **gentle** by the Spanish word *gentil*.

gentleman ['dʒɛntlmən] (*irreg*) *n* señor *m*; (*well-bred man*) caballero

gently ['dʒɛntlɪ] *adv* dulcemente; suavemente

gents [dʒɛnts] *n* aseos *mpl* (de caballeros)

genuine ['dʒɛnjuɪn] *adj* auténtico; (*person*) sincero ❏ **genuinely** *adv* sinceramente

geographic(al) [dʒɪə'græfɪk(l)] *adj* geográfico

geography [dʒɪ'ɔgrəfɪ] *n* geografía

geology [dʒɪ'ɔlədʒɪ] *n* geología

geometry [dʒɪ'ɔmətrɪ] *n* geometría

geranium [dʒɪ'reɪnjəm] *n* geranio

geriatric [dʒɛrɪ'ætrɪk] *adj, n* geriátrico(-a) *m/f*

germ [dʒəːm] *n* (*microbe*) microbio, bacteria; (*seed, fig*) germen *m*

German ['dʒəːmən] *adj* alemán(-ana)
♦ *n* alemán(-ana) *m/f*; (*LING*) alemán *m*
❏ **German measles** *n* rubéola

Germany ['dʒəːmənɪ] *n* Alemania

gesture ['dʒɛstjə'] *n* gesto; (*symbol*) muestra

KEYWORD

[get] (*pt, pp* **got**, *pp* **gotten** (*US*)) *vi*
1 (*become, be*) ponerse, volverse; **to get old/tired** envejecer/cansarse; **to get drunk** emborracharse; **to get dirty** ensuciarse; **to get married** casarse; **when do I get paid?** ¿cuándo me pagan *or* se me paga?; **it's getting late** se está haciendo tarde

2 (*go*): **to get to/from** llegar a/de; **to get home** llegar a casa

3 (*begin*) empezar a; **to get to know sb** (llegar a) conocer a algn; **I'm**

getting to like him me está empezando a gustar; **let's get going** *or* **started** ¡vamos (a empezar)/¡vamos a empezar)!

4 (*modal aux vb*): **you've got to do it** tienes que hacerlo
♦ *vt*
1: **to get sth done** (*finish*) terminar algo; (*have done*) mandar hacer algo; **to get one's hair cut** cortarse el pelo; **to get the car going** *or* **to go** arrancar el coche; **to get sb to do sth** conseguir *or* hacer que algn haga algo; **to get sth/sb ready** preparar algo/a algn

2 (*obtain: money, permission, results*) conseguir; (*find: job, flat*) encontrar; (*fetch: person, doctor*) buscar; (*object*) ir a buscar, traer; **to get sth for sb** conseguir algo para algn; **get me Mr Jones, please** (*TEL*) póngame *or* comuníqueme (*LAm*) con el Sr. Jones, por favor; **can I get you a drink?** ¿quieres algo de beber?

3 (*receive: present, letter*) recibir; (*acquire: reputation*) alcanzar; (*: prize*) ganar; **what did you get for your birthday?** ¿qué te regalaron por tu cumpleaños?; **how much did you get for the painting?** ¿cuánto sacaste por el cuadro?

4 (*catch*) coger (*SP*), agarrar (*LAm*); (*hit: target etc*) dar en; **to get sb by the arm/throat** coger *or* agarrar a algn por el brazo/cuello; **get him!** ¡cógelo! (*SP*), ¡atrápalo! (*LAm*); **the bullet got him in the leg** la bala le dio en la pierna

5 (*take, move*) llevar; **to get sth to sb** hacer llegar algo a algn; **do you think we'll get it through the door?** ¿crees que lo podremos meter por la puerta?

6 (catch, take: plane, bus etc) coger (SP), tomar (LAm); **where do I get the train for Birmingham?** ¿dónde se coge *or* se toma el tren para Birmingham?
7 (understand) entender; (hear) oír; **I've got it!** ¡ya lo tengo!, ¡eureka!; **I don't get your meaning** no te entiendo; **I'm sorry, I didn't get your name** lo siento, no cogí tu nombre
8 (have, possess): **to have got** tener
▶ **get away** vi marcharse; (escape) escaparse
▶ **get away with** vt fus hacer impunemente
▶ **get back** vi (return) volver ♦ vt recobrar
▶ **get in** vi entrar; (train) llegar; (arrive home) volver a casa, regresar
▶ **get into** vt fus entrar en; (vehicle) subir a; **to get into a rage** enfadarse
▶ **get off** vi (from train etc) bajar; (depart: person, car) marcharse ♦ vt (remove) quitar ♦ vt fus (train, bus) bajar de
▶ **get on** vi (at exam etc): **how are you getting on?** ¿cómo te va?; (agree): **to get on (with)** llevarse bien (con) ♦ vt fus subir a
▶ **get out** vi salir; (of vehicle) bajar ♦ vt sacar
▶ **get out of** vt fus salir de; (duty etc) escaparse de
▶ **get over** vt fus (illness) recobrarse de
▶ **get through** vi (TEL) lograr comunicarse
▶ **get up** vi (rise) levantarse ♦ vt fus subir

getaway ['getəweɪ] n fuga
Ghana ['gɑːnə] n Ghana
ghastly ['gɑːstlɪ] adj horrible
ghetto ['getəʊ] n gueto

ghost [gəʊst] n fantasma m
giant ['dʒaɪənt] n gigante mf ♦ adj gigantesco, gigante
gift [gɪft] n regalo; (ability) talento ❑ **gifted** adj dotado ❑ **gift shop** (US **gift store**) n tienda de regalos ❑ **gift token, gift voucher** n vale m canjeable por un regalo
gig [gɪg] n (inf: concert) actuación f
gigabyte ['dʒɪɡəbaɪt] n gigabyte m
gigantic [dʒaɪˈgæntɪk] adj gigantesco
giggle ['gɪgl] vi reírse tontamente
gills [gɪlz] npl (of fish) branquias fpl, agallas fpl
gilt [gɪlt] adj, n dorado
gimmick ['gɪmɪk] n truco
gin [dʒɪn] n ginebra
ginger ['dʒɪndʒə'] n jengibre m
gipsy ['dʒɪpsɪ] n = **gypsy**
giraffe [dʒɪˈrɑːf] n jirafa
girl [gɜːl] n (small) niña; (young woman) chica, joven f, muchacha; (daughter) hija; **an English** una (chica) inglesa ❑ **girlfriend** n (of girl) amiga; (of boy) novia ❑ **Girl Scout** (US) n = **Girl Guide**
gist [dʒɪst] n lo esencial
give [gɪv] (pt **gave**, pp **given**) vt dar; (deliver) entregar; (as gift) regalar ♦ vi (break) romperse; (stretch: fabric) dar de sí; **to ~ sb sth, ~ sth to sb** dar algo a algn ▶ **give away** vt (give free) regalar; (betray) traicionar; (disclose) revelar ▶ **give back** vt devolver ▶ **give in** vi ceder ♦ vt entregar ▶ **give out** vt distribuir ▶ **give up** vi rendirse, darse por vencido ♦ vt renunciar a; **to give up smoking** dejar de fumar; **to give o.s. up** entregarse
given ['gɪvn] pp of **give** ♦ adj (fixed: time, amount) determinado ♦ conj: **~ (that) ...** dado (que) ...; **~ the circumstances ...** dadas las circunstancias ...
glacier ['glæsɪə'] n glaciar m

glad [glæd] adj contento ❑ **gladly** ['-lɪ] adv con mucho gusto

glamour ['glæmər] (US **glamor**) n encanto, atractivo ❑ **glamorous** adj encantador(a), atractivo

glance [glɑːns] n ojeada, mirada ◆ vi: **to ~ at** echar una ojeada a

gland [glænd] n glándula

glare [gleər] n (of anger) mirada feroz; (of light) deslumbramiento, brillo: **to be in the ~ of publicity** ser el foco de la atención pública ◆ vi deslumbrar; **to ~ at** mirar con odio a ❑ **glaring** adj (mistake) manifiesto

glass [glɑːs] n vidrio, cristal m; (for drinking) vaso; (: with stem) copa; **glasses** npl (spectacles) gafas fpl

glaze [gleɪz] vt (window) poner cristales a; (pottery) vidriar ◆ n vidriado

gleam [gliːm] vi brillar

glen [glɛn] n cañada

glide [glaɪd] vi deslizarse, (AVIAT, birds) planear ❑ **glider** n (AVIAT) planeador m

glimmer ['glɪmər] n luz f tenue; (of interest) muestra; (of hope) rayo

glimpse [glɪmps] n vislumbre ◆ vt vislumbrar, entrever

glint [glɪnt] vi centellear

glisten ['glɪsn] vi relucir, brillar

glitter ['glɪtər] vi relucir, brillar

global ['gləubl] adj mundial ❑ **global warming** n recalentamiento global or de la tierra

globe [gləub] n globo; (model) globo terráqueo

gloom [gluːm] n oscuridad f; (sadness) tristeza ❑ **gloomy** adj (dark) oscuro; (sad) triste; (pessimistic) pesimista

glorious ['glɔːrɪəs] adj glorioso; (weather etc) magnífico

glory ['glɔːrɪ] n gloria

gloss [glɔs] n (shine) brillo; (paint) pintura de aceite

glossary ['glɔsərɪ] n glosario

glossy ['glɔsɪ] adj lustroso; (magazine) de lujo

glove [glʌv] n guante m ❑ **glove compartment** n (AUT) guantera

glow [gləu] vi brillar

glucose ['gluːkəus] n glucosa

glue [gluː] n goma (de pegar), cemento ◆ vt pegar

GM adj abbr (= genetically modified) transgénico

gm abbr (= gram) g

GMO n abbr (= genetically modified organism) organismo transgénico

GMT abbr (= Greenwich Mean Time) GMT

gnaw [nɔː] vt roer

go [gəu] (pt **went**, pp **gone**, pl **goes**) vi ir; (travel) viajar; (depart) irse, marcharse; (work) funcionar, marchar; (be sold) venderse; (time) pasar; (fit, suit): **to go with** hacer juego con; (become) ponerse; (break etc) estropearse, romperse ◆ n: **to have a go (at)** probar suerte (con); **to be on the go** no parar; **whose go is it?** ¿a quién le toca?; **he's going to do it** va a hacerlo; **to go for a walk** ir de paseo; **to go dancing** ir a bailar; **how did it go?** ¿qué tal salió or resultó?; ¿cómo ha ido?; **to go round the back** pasar por detrás ▶ **go ahead** vi seguir adelante ▶ **go away** vi irse, marcharse ▶ **go back** vi volver ▶ **go by** (time) pasar ◆ vt fus guiarse por ▶ **go down** vi bajar; (ship) hundirse; (sun) ponerse ◆ vt fus bajar ▶ **go for** vt fus (fetch) ir por; (like) gustar; (attack) atacar ▶ **go in** vi entrar ▶ **go into** vt fus entrar en; (investigate) investigar; (embark on) dedicarse a ▶ **go off** vi irse, marcharse; (food) pasarse; (explode) estallar; (event) realizarse ◆ vt fus dejar de gustar; **I'm going off him/ the idea** ya no me gusta tanto él/la idea ▶ **go on** vi (continue) seguir, continuar; (happen) pasar, ocurrir; **to go on doing sth** seguir haciendo algo ▶ **go out** vi salir; (fire, light) apagarse ▶ **go over** vi (ship) zozobrar ◆ vt fus (check) revisar ▸ **go past** vi, vt fus pasar ▸ **go round** vi (circulate: news, rumour) correr; (suffice) alcanzar, bastar; (revolve) girar, dar vueltas; (visit): **to go round to sb's** pasar a ver a (algn); **to go round (by)** (make a detour) dar la vuelta (por) ▸ **go through** vt fus (town etc) atravesar ▸ **go up** vi, vt fus subir ▸ **go with** vt fus (accompany) ir con, acompañar a ▸ **go without** vt fus pasarse sin

go-ahead ['gəʊəhɛd] adj (person) dinámico(a); (firm) innovador(a) ♦ n luz f verde

goal [gəʊl] n meta; (score) gol m ❑ **goalkeeper** n portero ❑ **goalpost** n poste m (de la portería)

goat [gəʊt] n cabra

gobble ['gɒbl] vt (also: ~ down, ~ up) tragarse, engullir

god [gɒd] n Dios m ❑ **godchild** n ahijado(-a) ❑ **goddaughter** n ahijada ❑ **goddess** n diosa ❑ **godfather** n padrino ❑ **godmother** n madrina ❑ **godson** n ahijado

goggles ['gɒglz] npl gafas fpl

going ['gəʊɪŋ] n (conditions) estado del terreno ♦ adj: **the ~ rate** la tarifa corriente o en vigor

gold [gəʊld] n oro ♦ adj de oro ❑ **golden** adj (made of gold) de oro; (gold in colour) dorado ❑ **goldfish** n pez m de colores ❑ **goldmine** n (also fig) mina de oro ❑ **gold-plated** adj chapado en oro

gone [gɒn] pp of **go**

gong [gɒŋ] n gong m

good [gʊd] adj bueno; (pleasant) agradable; (kind) bueno, amable; (well-behaved) educado ♦ n bien m, provecho; **goods** npl (COMM) mercancías fpl; **~!** ¡qué bien!; **to be ~ at**

tener aptitud para; **to be ~ for** servir para; **it's ~ for you** te hace bien; **would you be ~ enough to ...?** ¿podría hacerme el favor de ...?; ¿sería tan amable de ...?; **a ~ deal (of)** mucho; **a ~ many** muchos; **to make ~** reparar; **it's no ~ complaining** no vale la pena (de) quejarse; **for ~** para siempre, definitivamente; **~ morning/afternoon!** ¡buenos días/buenas tardes!; **~ evening!** ¡buenas noches!; **~ night!** ¡buenas noches!

goodbye [gʊd'baɪ] excl ¡adiós!; **to say ~ (to)** despedirse (de)

good: **Good Friday** n Viernes m Santo ❑ **good-looking** adj guapo ❑ **good-natured** adj amable, simpático ❑ **goodness** n (of person) bondad f; **for goodness sake!** ¡por Dios!; **goodness gracious!** ¡Dios mío! ❑ **goods train** (BRIT) n tren m de mercancías ❑ **goodwill** n buena voluntad f

goose [guːs] n (pl geese) ganso, oca

gooseberry ['gʊzbəri] n grosella espinosa; **to play ~** hacer de carabina

goose bumps, goose pimples npl carne f de gallina

gorge [gɔːdʒ] n barranco ♦ vr: **to ~ o.s. (on)** atracarse (de)

gorgeous ['gɔːdʒəs] adj (thing) precioso; (weather) espléndido; (person) guapísimo

gorilla [gə'rɪlə] n gorila m

gosh (inf) [gɒʃ] excl ¡cielos!

gospel ['gɒspl] n evangelio

gossip ['gɒsɪp] n (scandal) cotilleo, chismes mpl; (chat) charla; (person) cotilla m/f, chismoso(-a) ♦ vi cotillear ❑ **gossip column** n ecos mpl de sociedad

got [gɒt] pt, pp of **get**

gotten (US) ['gɒtn] pp of **get**

gourmet ['gʊəmeɪ] n gastrónomo(-a) m/f

govern ['gʌvən] vt gobernar; (influence) dominar ❑ **government** n gobierno

❏ **governor** n gobernador(a) m/f; (of school etc) miembro del consejo; (of jail) director(a) m/f

gown [gaun] n traje m; (of teacher, BRIT: of judge) toga

G.P. n abbr = **general practitioner**

grab [græb] vt coger (SP), agarrar (LAm), arrebatar ◆ vi: **to ~ at** intentar agarrar

grace [greɪs] n gracia ◆ vt honrar; (adorn) adornar; **5 days'** ~ un plazo de 5 días ❏ **graceful** adj grácil, ágil; (style, shape) elegante, gracioso ❏ **gracious** ['greɪʃəs] adj amable

grade [greɪd] n (quality) clase f, calidad f; (in hierarchy) grado; (SCOL: mark) nota; (US: school class) curso ◆ vt clasificar ❏ **grade crossing** (US) n paso a nivel ❏ **grade school** (US) n escuela primaria

gradient ['greɪdɪənt] n pendiente f

gradual ['grædjuəl] adj paulatino ❏ **gradually** adv paulatinamente

graduate [n 'grædjuɪt, vb 'grædjueɪt] n (US: of high school) graduado(-a); (of university) licenciado(-a) ◆ vi graduarse; licenciarse ❏ **graduation** [-'eɪʃən] n (ceremony) entrega del título

graffiti [grə'fi:tɪ] n pintadas fpl

graft [grɑ:ft] n (AGR, MED) injerto; (BRIT: inf) trabajo duro ◆ vt injertar

grain [greɪn] n (single particle) grano; (corn) granos mpl, cereales mpl; (of wood) fibra

gram [græm] n gramo

grammar ['græmə*] n gramática ❏ **grammar school** (BRIT) n = instituto de segunda enseñanza, liceo (SP)

gramme [græm] n = **gram**

gran (inf) [græn] n (BRIT) abuelita

grand [grænd] adj magnífico, imponente; (wonderful) estupendo; (gesture etc) grandioso ❏ **grandad** n = **granddad** ❏ **grandchild** (pl **grandchildren**) n nieto(-a) m/f ❏ **granddad** (inf) n yayo, abuelito

❏ **granddaughter** n nieta ❏ **grandfather** n abuelo ❏ **grandma** (inf) n yaya, abuelita ❏ **grandmother** n abuela ❏ **grandpa** (inf) n = **granddad** ❏ **grandparents** npl abuelos mpl ❏ **grand piano** n piano de cola ❏ **Grand Prix** ['grɑ̃:'pri:] n (AUT) gran premio, Grand Prix m ❏ **grandson** n nieto

granite ['grænɪt] n granito

granny ['grænɪ] n (inf) abuelita, yaya

grant [grɑ:nt] vt (concede) conceder; (admit) reconocer ◆ n (SCOL) beca; (ADMIN) subvención f; **to take sth/sb for granted** dar algo por sentado/no hacer ningún caso a algn

grape [greɪp] n uva

grapefruit ['greɪpfru:t] n pomelo (SP, SC), toronja (LAm)

graph [grɑ:f] n gráfica ❏ **graphic** ['græfɪk] adj gráfico ❏ **graphics** n artes fpl gráficas ◆ npl (drawings) dibujos mpl

grasp [grɑ:sp] vt agarrar, asir; (understand) comprender ◆ n (grip) asimiento; (understanding) comprensión f

grass [grɑ:s] n hierba; (lawn) césped m ❏ **grasshopper** n saltamontes m inv

grate [greɪt] n parrilla de chimenea ◆ vi: **to ~ (on)** chirriar (sobre) ◆ vt (CULIN) rallar

grateful ['greɪtful] adj agradecido

grater ['greɪtə*] n rallador m

gratitude ['grætɪtju:d] n agradecimiento

grave [greɪv] n tumba ◆ adj serio, grave

gravel ['grævl] n grava

gravestone ['greɪvstəun] n lápida

graveyard ['greɪvjɑ:d] n cementerio

gravity ['grævɪtɪ] n gravedad f

gravy ['greɪvɪ] n salsa de carne

gray [greɪ] adj = **grey**

graze [greɪz] vi pacer ◆ vt (touch lightly) rozar; (scrape) raspar ◆ n (MED) abrasión f

grease [griːs] n (fat) grasa; (lubricant) lubricante m ♦ vt engrasar; lubrificar ❑ **greasy** adj grasiento

great [greɪt] adj grande; (inf) magnífico, estupendo ❑ **Great Britain** n Gran Bretaña ❑ **great-grandfather** n bisabuelo ❑ **great-grandmother** n bisabuela ❑ **greatly** adv muy; (with verb) mucho

Greece [griːs] n Grecia

greed [griːd] n (also: **greediness**) codicia, avaricia; (for food) gula; (for power etc) avidez f ❑ **greedy** adj avaro; (for food) glotón(-ona)

Greek [griːk] adj griego ♦ n griego(-a); (LING) griego

green [griːn] adj (also POL) verde; (inexperienced) novato ♦ n verde m; (stretch of grass) césped m; (GOLF) green m; **greens** npl (vegetables) verduras fpl ❑ **green card** n (AUT) carta verde; (US: work permit) permiso de trabajo para los extranjeros en EE. UU. ❑ **greengage** n (ciruela) claudia ❑ **greengrocer** (BRIT) n verdulero(-a) ❑ **greenhouse** n invernadero ❑ **greenhouse effect** n efecto invernadero

Greenland [griːnlənd] n Groenlandia

green salad n ensalada f (de lechuga, pepino, pimiento verde, etc)

greet [griːt] vt (welcome) dar la bienvenida; (receive: news) recibir ❑ **greeting** n (welcome) bienvenida ❑ **greeting(s) card** n tarjeta de felicitación

grew [gruː] pt of **grow**

grey [greɪ] (US **gray**) adj gris; (weather) sombrío ❑ **grey-haired** adj canoso ❑ **greyhound** n galgo

grid [grɪd] n reja; (ELEC) red f ❑ **gridlock** n (traffic jam) retención f

grief [griːf] n dolor m, pena

grievance [griːvəns] n motivo de queja, agravio

grieve [griːv] vi afligirse, acongojarse ♦ vt dar pena a; **to ~ for** llorar por

grill [grɪl] n (on cooker) parrilla; (also: **mixed ~**) parrillada ♦ vt (BRIT) asar a la parrilla; (inf: question) interrogar

grille [grɪl] n reja; (AUT) rejilla

grim [grɪm] adj (place) sombrío; (situation) triste; (person) ceñudo

grime [graɪm] n mugre f, suciedad f

grin [grɪn] n sonrisa abierta ♦ vi sonreír abiertamente

grind [graɪnd] (pt, pp **ground**) vt (coffee, pepper etc) moler; (US: meat) picar; (make sharp) afilar ♦ n (in work) rutina

grip [grɪp] n (hold) asimiento; (control) control m, dominio; (of tyre etc): **to have a good/bad ~** agarrarse bien/mal; (handle) asidero; (holdall) maletín m ♦ vt agarrar; (viewer, reader) fascinar; **to get to grips with** enfrentarse con ❑ **gripping** adj absorbente

grit [grɪt] n gravilla; (courage) valor m ♦ vt (road) poner gravilla en; **to ~ one's teeth** apretar los dientes

grits [grɪts] (US) npl maíz msg a medio moler

groan [grəʊn] n gemido; quejido ♦ vi gemir; quejarse

grocer [grəʊsəʳ] n tendero (de ultramarinos (SP)) ❑ **groceries** npl comestibles mpl ❑ **grocer's (shop)** n tienda de comestibles or (MEX, CAm) abarrotes, almacén (SC) ❑ **grocery** n (shop) tienda de ultramarinos

groin [grɔɪn] n ingle f

groom [gruːm] n mozo/a) de cuadra; (also: **bridegroom**) novio ♦ vt (horse) almohazar; (fig): **to ~ sb for** preparar a algn para; **well-groomed** adj de buena presencia

groove [gruːv] n ranura, surco

grope [grəʊp] vi: **to ~ for** buscar a tientas

gross [grəʊs] adj (neglect, injustice) grave; (vulgar: behaviour) grosero; (: appearance) de mal gusto; (COMM) bruto ❏ **grossly** adv (greatly) enormemente

grotesque [grəˈtɛsk] adj grotesco

ground [graund] pt, pp of **grind** ♦ n suelo, tierra; (SPORT) campo, terreno; (reason: gen pl) causa, razón f; (US: also: ~ **wire**) tierra ♦ vt (plane) mantener en tierra; (US ELEC) conectar con tierra; **grounds** npl (of coffee etc) poso; (gardens etc) jardines mpl, parque m; **on the** ~ en el suelo; **to the** ~ al suelo; **to gain/lose** ~ ganar/ceder terreno ❏ **ground floor** n (BRIT) planta baja ❏ **groundsheet** (BRIT) n tela impermeable; suelo ❏ **groundwork** n preparación n

group [gruːp] n grupo; (musical) conjunto ♦ vt (also: ~ **together**) agrupar ♦ vi (also: ~ **together**) agruparse

grouse [graus] n inv (bird) urogallo ♦ vi (complain) quejarse

grovel [ˈgrɒvl] vi (fig): **to** ~ **before** humillarse ante

grow [grəu] (pt **grew**, pp **grown**) vi crecer; (increase) aumentar; (expand) desarrollarse; (become) volverse; **to** ~ **rich/weak** enriquecerse/debilitarse ♦ vt cultivar; (hair) dejar crecer ► **grow on** vt fus: **that painting is growing on me** ese cuadro me gusta cada vez más ► **grow up** vi crecer, hacerse hombre/mujer

growl [graul] vi gruñir

grown [grəun] pp of **grow** ❏ **grown-up** n adulto(-a), mayor mf

growth [grəuθ] n crecimiento, desarrollo; (what has grown) brote m; (MED) tumor m

grub [grʌb] n larva, gusano; (inf: food) comida

grubby [ˈgrʌbɪ] adj sucio, mugriento

grudge [grʌdʒ] n (motivo de) rencor m ♦ vt: **to** ~ **sb sth** dar algo a algn de mala gana; **to bear sb a** ~ guardar rencor a algn

gruelling [ˈgruəlɪŋ] (US **grueling**) adj penoso, duro

gruesome [ˈgruːsəm] adj horrible

grumble [ˈgrʌmbl] vi refunfuñar, quejarse

grumpy [ˈgrʌmpɪ] adj gruñón(-ona)

grunt [grʌnt] vi gruñir

guarantee [gærənˈtiː] n garantía ♦ vt garantizar

guard [gɑːd] n (squad) guardia; (one man) guardia mf; (BRIT RAIL) jefe m de tren; (on machine) dispositivo de seguridad; (also: **fireguard**) rejilla de protección ♦ vt guardar; (prisoner) vigilar; **to be on one's** ~ estar alerta ❏ **guardian** n guardián(-ana) m/f; (of minor) tutor(a) m/f

guerrilla [gəˈrɪlə] n guerrillero(-a)

guess [gɛs] vi adivinar; (US) suponer ♦ vt adivinar; suponer ♦ n suposición f, conjetura f; **to take** o **have a** ~ tratar de adivinar

guest [gɛst] n invitado(-a); (in hotel) huésped mf ❏ **guest house** n casa de huéspedes, pensión f ❏ **guest room** n cuarto de huéspedes

guidance [ˈgaɪdəns] n consejos mpl

guide [gaɪd] n (person) guía mf; (book, fig) guía; (also: **Girl G~**) guía f ♦ vt (round museum etc) guiar; (lead) conducir; (direct) orientar ❏ **guidebook** n guía ❏ **guide dog** n perro m guía ❏ **guided tour** n visita f con guía ❏ **guidelines** npl (advice) directrices fpl

guild [gɪld] n gremio

guilt [gɪlt] n culpabilidad f ❏ **guilty** adj culpable

guinea pig [ˈgɪnɪ-] n cobaya, (fig) conejillo de Indias

guitar [gɪˈtɑːʳ] n guitarra ❏ **guitarist** n guitarrista m/f

gulf [gʌlf] n golfo; (abyss) abismo

gull [gʌl] n gaviota

gulp [gʌlp] vi tragar saliva ♦ vt (also: ~ **down**) tragarse

gum

gum [gʌm] n (ANAT) encía; (glue) goma, cemento; (also: **chewing-~**) chicle m
♦ vt pegar con goma

gun [gʌn] n (small) pistola, revólver m; (shotgun) escopeta; (rifle) fusil m;
□ **gunfire** n disparos mpl □ **gunman** (irreg) n pistolero □ **gunpoint** n: at gunpoint a mano armada
□ **gunpowder** n pólvora □ **gunshot** n escopetazo

gush [gʌʃ] vi salir a raudales; (person) deshacerse en efusiones

gust [gʌst] n (of wind) ráfaga

gut [gʌt] n intestino; **guts** npl (ANAT) tripas fpl; (courage) valor m

gutter ['gʌtə*] n (of roof) canalón m; (in street) cuneta

guy [gaɪ] n (also: **guyrope**) cuerda; (inf: man) tío (SP), tipo; (figure) monigote m

Guy Fawkes' Night [gaɪ'fɔːks-] n ver recuadro

GUY FAWKES' NIGHT

La noche del cinco de noviembre, **Guy Fawkes' Night**, se celebra en el Reino Unido el fracaso de la conspiración de la pólvora ("Gunpowder Plot"), un intento fallido de volar el parlamento de Jaime I en 1605. Esa noche se lanzan fuegos artificiales y se hacen hogueras en las que se queman unos muñecos de trapo que representan a **Guy Fawkes**, uno de los cabecillas de la revuelta. Días antes, los niños tienen por costumbre pedir a los transeúntes "a penny for the guy", dinero que emplean en comprar cohetes y petardos.

---

gym [dʒɪm] n gimnasio
□ **gymnasium** [dʒɪm'neɪzɪəm] n gimnasio mf
□ **gymnast** ['dʒɪmnæst] n gimnasta mf
□ **gymnastics** [dʒɪm'næstɪks] n gimnasia ♦ adj
□ **gym shoes** npl zapatillas fpl (de deporte)

gynaecologist [gaɪnɪ'kɒlədʒɪst] (US **gynecologist**) n ginecólogo(-a)

gypsy ['dʒɪpsɪ] n gitano(-a)

H, h

haberdashery [hæbə'dæʃərɪ] (BRIT) n mercería

habit ['hæbɪt] n hábito, costumbre f; (drug habit) adicción f; (costume) hábito

habitat ['hæbɪtæt] n hábitat m

hack [hæk] vt (cut) cortar; (slice) tajar ♦ n (pej: writer) escritor(a) a sueldo
□ **hacker** n (COMPUT) pirata mf informático(-a)

had [hæd] pt, pp of **have**

haddock ['hædək] (pl ~ or **haddocks**) n especie de merluza

hadn't ['hædnt] = **had not**

haemorrhage ['hemərɪdʒ] (US **hemorrhage**) n hemorragia

haemorrhoids ['hemərɔɪdz] (US **hemorrhoids**) npl hemorroides fpl

haggle ['hægl] vi regatear

Hague [heɪg] n: The ~ La Haya

hail [heɪl] n (weather) granizo; (fig) lluvia ♦ vt saludar; (taxi) llamar a; (acclaim) aclamar ♦ vi granizar □ **hailstone** n (piedra) de granizo

hair [heə*] n pelo, cabellos mpl; (one hair) pelo, cabello; (on legs etc) vello; **to do one's ~** arreglarse el pelo; **to have grey ~** tener canas fpl □ **hairband** n cinta □ **hairbrush** n cepillo (para el pelo) □ **haircut** n corte m (de pelo) □ **hairdo** n peinado □ **hairdresser** n peluquero(-a) □ **hairdresser's** n peluquería □ **hair dryer** n secador m de pelo □ **hair gel** n fijador □ **hair spray** n laca □ **hairstyle** n peinado □ **hairy** adj peludo; velludo; (inf: frightening) espeluznante

hake [heɪk] (pl ~ or **hakes**) n merluza

half [hɑːf] (pl **halves**) n mitad f; (of beer) = caña (SP), media pinta; (RAIL, BUS) billete m de niño ♦ adj medio ♦ adv medio, a medias; **two and a ~** dos y media; **~ a dozen** media docena; **~ a**

pound media libra; **to cut sth in ~** cortar algo por la mitad ❑ **half board** n (BRIT: in hotel) media pensión ❑ **half-brother** n hermanastro ❑ **half day** n medio día m, media jornada ❑ **half fare** n medio pasaje ❑ **half-hearted** adj indiferente, poco entusiasta ❑ **half-hour** n media hora ❑ **half-price** adj, adv a mitad de precio ❑ **half term** (BRIT) n (SCOL) vacaciones de mediados del trimestre ❑ **half-time** n descanso ❑ **halfway** adv a medio camino; **halfway through** a mitad de

hall [hɔ:l] n (for concerts) sala; (entrance way) hall m; vestíbulo

hallmark [ˈhɔːlmɑːk] n sello

hallo [həˈləʊ] excl = **hello**

hall of residence (BRIT) n residencia

Hallowe'en [ˌhæləʊˈiːn] n víspera de Todos los Santos

hallucination [həluːsɪˈneɪʃən] n alucinación f

hallway [ˈhɔːlweɪ] n vestíbulo

halo [ˈheɪləʊ] n (of saint) halo, aureola

halt [hɔːlt] n (stop) alto, parada ♦ vt parar; interrumpir ♦ vi pararse

halve [hɑːv] vt partir por la mitad

halves [hɑːvz] npl of **half**

ham [hæm] n jamón m (cocido)

hamburger [ˈhæmbɜːɡəʳ] n hamburguesa

hamlet [ˈhæmlɪt] n aldea

hammer [ˈhæməʳ] n martillo ♦ vt (nail) clavar; (force): **to ~ an idea into sb/a message home** meter una idea en la cabeza a algn/machacar una idea ♦ vi dar golpes

hammock [ˈhæmək] n hamaca

hamper [ˈhæmpəʳ] vt estorbar ♦ n cesto

hamster [ˈhæmstəʳ] n hámster m

hamstring [ˈhæmstrɪŋ] n (ANAT) tendón m de la corva

hand [hænd] n mano f; (of clock) aguja; (writing) letra; (worker) obrero ♦ vt dar, pasar; **to give** o **lend sb a ~** echar una mano a algn, ayudar a algn; **at ~** a mano; **in ~** (time) libre; (job etc) entre manos; **on ~** (person, services) a mano, al alcance; **to ~** (information etc) a mano; **on the one ~ ..., on the other ~ ...** por una parte ... por otra (parte) ... ▸ **hand down** vt pasar, bajar; (tradition) transmitir; (heirloom) dejar en herencia; (US: sentence, verdict) imponer ▸ **hand in** vt entregar ▸ **hand out** vt distribuir ▸ **hand over** vt (deliver) entregar ❑ **handbag** n bolso (SP), cartera (LAm), bolsa (MEX) ❑ **hand baggage** n = **hand luggage** ❑ **handbook** n manual m ❑ **handbrake** n freno de mano ❑ **handcuffs** npl esposas fpl ❑ **handful** n puñado

handicap [ˈhændɪkæp] n minusvalía; (disadvantage) desventaja; (SPORT) handicap m ♦ vt estorbar; **to be mentally handicapped** ser mentalmente m/f discapacitado; **to be physically handicapped** ser minusválido(-a)

handkerchief [ˈhæŋkətʃiːf] n pañuelo

handle [ˈhændl] n (of door etc) tirador m; (of cup etc) asa; (of knife etc) mango ♦ vt (touch) tocar; (deal with) encargarse de; (treat: people) manejar,

"~ with care" (manéjese) con cuidado"; **to fly off the ~** perder los estribos ❑ **handlebar(s)** n(pl) manillar m

hand: hand luggage n equipaje m de mano ❑ **handmade** adj hecho a mano ❑ **handout** n (money etc) limosna; (leaflet) folleto

handsome ['hænsəm] adj guapo; (building) bello

handwriting ['hændraitɪŋ] n letra

handy ['hændɪ] adj (close at hand) a la mano; (tool etc) práctico; (skilful) hábil, diestro

hang [hæŋ] (pt, pp hung) vt colgar; (criminal: pt, pp hanged) ahorcar ♦ vi (painting, coat etc) colgar; (hair, drapery) caer ♦ n: **to get the ~ of sth** (inf) lograr dominar algo ▸ **hang about** or **around** vi haraganear ▸ **hang down** vi colgar, pender ▸ **hang on** vi (wait) esperar ▸ **hang out** vt (washing) tender, colgar ♦ vi (inf: live) vivir; (spend time) pasar el rato; **to hang out of sth** colgar fuera de algo ▸ **hang round** vi = **hang around** ▸ **hang up** vi (TEL) colgar ♦ vt colgar

hanger ['hæŋə] n percha

hang-gliding [-'glaidɪŋ] n vuelo libre

hangover ['hæŋəʊvə] n (after drinking) resaca

hankie, hanky ['hæŋkɪ] n abbr = **handkerchief**

happen ['hæpən] vi suceder, ocurrir; (chance): **he happened to hear/see** dió la casualidad de que oyó/vió; **as it happens** da la casualidad de que

happily ['hæpɪlɪ] adv (luckily) afortunadamente; (cheerfully) alegremente

happiness ['hæpɪnɪs] n felicidad f; (cheerfulness) alegría

happy ['hæpɪ] adj feliz; (cheerful) alegre; **to be ~ (with)** estar contento (con); **to be ~ to do** estar encantado de hacer; **~ birthday!** ¡feliz cumpleaños!

harass ['hærəs] vt acosar, hostigar ❑ **harassment** n persecución f

harbour ['hɑːbə] (US **harbor**) n puerto ♦ vt (fugitive) dar abrigo a; (hope etc) abrigar

hard [hɑːd] adj duro; (difficult) difícil; (work) arduo; (severe) severo; (fact) innegable ♦ adv (work) mucho, duro; (think) profundamente; **to look ~ at** clavar los ojos en; **to try ~** esforzarse; **no ~ feelings!** ¡sin rencor(es)!; **to be ~ of hearing** ser duro de oído; **to be ~ done by** ser tratado injustamente ❑ **hardback** n libro en cartoné ❑ **hard disk** n (COMPUT) disco duro or rígido ❑ **harden** vt endurecer; (fig) curtir ♦ vi endurecerse; curtirse

hardly ['hɑːdlɪ] adv apenas; **~ ever** casi nunca

hard: hardship n privación f ❑ **hard shoulder** (BRIT) n (AUT) arcén m ❑ **hard-up** adj (inf) sin un duro (SP), pelado, sin un centavo (MEX), pato (SC) ❑ **hardware** n ferretería; (COMPUT) hardware m; (MIL) armamento ❑ **hardware shop** (US **hardware store**) ferretería ❑ **hard-working** adj trabajador(a)

hardy ['hɑːdɪ] adj fuerte; (plant) resistente

hare [hɛə] n liebre f

harm [hɑːm] n daño, mal m ♦ vt (person) hacer daño a; (health, interests) perjudicar; (thing) dañar; **out of ~'s way** a salvo ❑ **harmful** adj dañino ❑ **harmless** adj (person) inofensivo; (joke etc) inocente

harmony ['hɑːmənɪ] n armonía

harness ['hɑːnɪs] n arreos mpl; (for child) arnés m; (safety harness) arneses mpl ♦ vt (horse) enjaezar; (resources) aprovechar

harp [hɑːp] n arpa f ♦ vi: **to ~ on (about)** machacar (con)

harsh [hɑːʃ] adj (cruel) duro, cruel; (severe) severo; (sound) áspero; (light) deslumbrador(a)

harvest ['hɑːvɪst] n (harvest time) siega; (of cereals etc) cosecha; (of grapes) vendimia ♦ vt cosechar

has [hæz] vb see **have**

hasn't ['hæznt] = **has not**

hassle ['hæsl] (inf) n lata

haste [heɪst] n prisa ❏ **hasten** ['heɪsn] vt acelerar ♦ vi darse prisa ❏ **hastily** adv de prisa; precipitadamente ❏ **hasty** adj apresurado; (rash) precipitado

hat [hæt] n sombrero

hatch [hætʃ] n (NAUT: also: **hatchway**) escotilla; (also: **service** = ventanilla ♦ vi (bird) salir del cascarón ♦ vt incubar; (plot) tramar; **5 eggs have hatched** han salido 5 pollos

hatchback ['hætʃbæk] n (AUT) tres or cinco puertas m

hate [heɪt] vt odiar, aborrecer ♦ n odio ❏ **hatred** ['heɪtrɪd] n odio

haul [hɔːl] vt tirar ♦ n (of fish) redada; (of stolen goods etc) botín m

haunt [hɔːnt] vt (ghost) aparecerse en; (obsess) obsesionar ♦ n guarida ❏ **haunted** adj (castle etc) embrujado

have

KEYWORD

['hæv] (pt, pp had) aux vb

1 (gen) haber; **to have arrived/eaten** haber llegado/comido; **having finished** or **when he had finished, he left** cuando hubo acabado, se fue

2 (in tag questions): **you've done it, haven't you?** lo has hecho, ¿verdad? or ¿no?

3 (in short answers and questions): **I haven't** no; **so have I** pues, es verdad; **we haven't paid — yes we have!** no hemos pagado — sí que hemos pagado!; **I've been there before, have you?** he estado allí antes, ¿y tú?

♦ modal aux vb (be obliged): **to have (got) to do sth** tener que hacer algo;

you haven't to tell her no hay que or no debes decírselo

♦ vt

1 (possess): **he has (got) blue eyes/ dark hair** tiene los ojos azules/el pelo negro

2 (referring to meals etc): **to have breakfast/lunch/dinner** desayunar/ comer/cenar; **to have a drink/a cigar** tomar algo/fumar un puro

3 (receive) recibir; (obtain) obtener; **may I have your address?** ¿puedes darme tu dirección?; **you can have it for £5** lo puedes quedar por £5; **I must have it by tomorrow** lo necesito para mañana; **to have a baby** tener un niño or bebé

4 (maintain, allow): **I won't have it/ this nonsense!** ¡no lo permitiré!/¡no permitiré estas tonterías!; **we can't have that** no podemos permitir eso

5: **to have sth done** hacer or mandar hacer algo; **to have one's hair cut** cortarse el pelo; **to have sb do sth** hacer que algn haga algo

6 (experience, suffer): **to have a cold/ flu** tener un resfriado/la gripe; **she had her bag stolen/her arm broken** le robaron el bolso/se rompió un brazo; **to have an operation** operarse

7 (+ noun): **to have a swim/walk/ bath/rest** nadar/dar un paseo/darse un baño/descansar; **let's have a look** vamos a ver; **let's have a meeting/ party** celebrar una reunión/una fiesta; **let me have a try** déjame intentarlo

haven ['heɪvn] n puerto; (fig) refugio

haven't ['hævnt] = **have not**

havoc ['hævək] n estragos mpl

Hawaii [hə'waiiː] n (Islas fpl) Hawai m

hawk [hɔːk] n halcón m

hawthorn ['hɔːθɔːn] n espino

hay [heɪ] n heno ❏ **hay fever** n fiebre f del heno ❏ **haystack** n almiar m

hazard ['hæzəd] n peligro ♦ vt aventurar ❏ **hazardous** adj peligroso ❏ **hazard warning lights** npl (AUT) señales fpl de emergencia

haze [heɪz] n neblina

hazel ['heɪzl] n (tree) avellano ♦ adj (eyes) color m de avellano ❏ **hazelnut** n avellana

hazy ['heɪzɪ] adj brumoso; (idea) vago

he [hiː] pron él; **he who ...** él que ..., quien ...

head [hed] n cabeza; (leader) jefe(-a) m/f; (of school) director(a) m/f ♦ vt (list) encabezar; (group) capitanear; (company) dirigir; **heads (or tails)** cara (o cruz); **~ first** de cabeza; **~ over heels** (in love) perdidamente; **to ~ the ball** cabecear (la pelota) ▸ **head for** vt fus dirigirse a; (disaster) ir camino de ▸ **head off** vt (threat, danger) evitar ❏ **headache** n dolor m de cabeza ❏ **heading** n título ❏ **headlight** n faro ❏ **headline** n titular m ❏ **head office** n oficina central, central f ❏ **headphones** npl auriculares mpl ❏ **headquarters** npl sede f central; (MIL) cuartel m general ❏ **headroom** n (in car) altura interior; (under bridge) (límite m de) altura ❏ **headscarf** n pañuelo ❏ **headset** n cascos mpl ❏ **headteacher** n director ❏ **head waiter** n maître m

heal [hiːl] vt curar ♦ vi cicatrizarse

health [helθ] n salud f ❏ **health care** n asistencia sanitaria ❏ **health centre** (BRIT) n centro médico ❏ **health food** n alimentos mpl orgánicos ❏ **Health Service** (BRIT) n el servicio de salud pública, ≈ el Insalud (SP) ❏ **healthy** adj sano, saludable

heap [hiːp] n montón m ♦ vt: **to ~ (up)** amontonar; **to ~ sth with** llenar algo hasta arriba de; **heaps of** un montón de

hear [hɪə] (pt, pp heard) vt (also LAW) oír; (news) saber ♦ vi oír; **to ~ about** oír hablar de; **to ~ from sb** tener noticias de algn

heard [hɜːd] pt, pp of **hear**

hearing ['hɪərɪŋ] n (sense) oído; (LAW) vista ❏ **hearing aid** n audífono

hearse [hɜːs] n coche m fúnebre

heart [hɑːt] n corazón m; (fig) valor m; (of lettuce) cogollo; **hearts** npl (CARDS) corazones mpl; **to lose/take ~** descorazonarse/cobrar ánimo; **at ~** en el fondo; **by ~** (learn, know) de memoria ❏ **heart attack** n infarto (de miocardio) ❏ **heartbeat** n latido (del corazón) ❏ **heartbroken** adj: **she was heartbroken about it** esto le partió el corazón ❏ **heartburn** n acedía ❏ **heart disease** n enfermedad f cardíaca

hearth [hɑːθ] n (fireplace) chimenea

heartless ['hɑːtlɪs] adj despiadado

hearty ['hɑːtɪ] adj (person) campechano; (laugh) sano; (dislike, support) absoluto

heat [hiːt] n calor m; (SPORT: also: **qualifying ~**) prueba eliminatoria ♦ vt calentar ▸ **heat up** vi calentarse ♦ vt calentar ❏ **heated** adj caliente; (fig) acalorado ❏ **heater** n estufa; (in car) calefacción f

heather ['heðə] n brezo

heating ['hiːtɪŋ] n calefacción f

heatwave ['hiːtweɪv] n ola de calor

heaven ['hevn] n cielo; (fig) una maravilla ❏ **heavenly** adj celestial; (fig) maravilloso

heavily ['hevɪlɪ] adv pesadamente; (drink, smoke) con exceso; (sigh, sigh) profundamente; (depend) mucho

heavy ['hevɪ] adj pesado; (work, blow) duro; (sea, rain, meal) fuerte; (drinker, smoker) grande; (responsibility) grave; (schedule) ocupado; (weather) bochornoso

Hebrew ['hi:bru:] adj, (LING) hebreo

hectare ['hektɑ:ʳ] n (BRIT) hectárea

hectic ['hektɪk] adj agitado

he'd [hi:d] = he would; he had

hedge [hedʒ] n seto ♦ vi contestar con evasivas; **to ~ one's bets** (fig) cubrirse

hedgehog ['hedʒhɔg] n erizo

heed [hi:d] vt (also: **take ~**) hacer caso de

heel [hi:l] n talón m; (of shoe) tacón m ♦ vt (shoe) poner tacón a

hefty ['heftɪ] adj (person) fornido; (parcel, profit) gordo

height [haɪt] n (of person) estatura; (of building) altura; (high ground) cerro; (altitude) altitud f; (fig: of season): **at the ~ of summer** en los días más calurosos del verano; (: of power etc) cúspide f; (: of stupidity etc) colmo □ **heighten** vt elevar; (fig) aumentar

heir [ɛəʳ] n heredero □ **heiress** n heredera

held [held] pt, pp of **hold**

helicopter ['helɪkɔptəʳ] n helicóptero

hell [hel] n infierno; **~!** (inf) ¡demonios!

he'll [hi:l] = he will; he shall

hello [hə'ləu] excl ¡hola!; (to attract attention) ¡oiga!; (surprise) ¡caramba!

helmet ['helmɪt] n casco

help [help] n ayuda; (cleaner etc) criada, asistenta ♦ vt ayudar; **~!** ¡socorro!; **~ yourself** sírvete; **he can't ~ it** no es culpa suya ♦ **help out** vi ayudar, echar una mano ♦ vt: **to help sb out** ayudar a algn, echar una mano a algn □ **helper** n ayudante mf □ **helpful** adj útil; (person) servicial; (advice) útil □ **helping** n ración f □ **helpless** adj (incapable) incapaz; (defenceless) indefenso □ **helpline** n teléfono de asistencia al público

hem [hem] n dobladillo ♦ vt poner or coser el dobladillo de

hemisphere ['hemɪsfɪəʳ] n hemisferio

hemorrhage ['hemərɪdʒ] (US) n = **haemorrhage**

hemorrhoids ['hemərɔɪdz] (US) npl = **haemorrhoids**

hen [hen] n gallina; (female bird) hembra

hence [hens] adv (therefore) por lo tanto; **2 years ~** de aquí a 2 años

hen night, hen party n (inf) despedida de soltera

hepatitis [hepə'taɪtɪs] n hepatitis f

her [hə:ʳ] pron (direct) la; (indirect) le; (stressed, after prep) ella ♦ adj su; see also **me; my**

herb [hə:b] n hierba □ **herbal** adj de hierbas □ **herbal tea** n infusión f de hierbas

herd [hə:d] n rebaño

here [hɪəʳ] adv aquí; (at this point) en este punto; **~!** (present) ¡presente!; **~ is/ are** aquí está/están; **~ she is** aquí está

hereditary [hɪ'redɪtrɪ] adj hereditario

heritage ['herɪtɪdʒ] n patrimonio

hernia ['hə:nɪə] n hernia

hero ['hɪərəu] (pl **heroes**) n héroe m; (in book, film) protagonista m □ **heroic** [hɪ'rəuɪk] adj heroico

heroin ['herəuɪn] n heroína

heroine ['herəuɪn] n heroína; (in book, film) protagonista

heron ['herən] n garza

herring ['herɪŋ] n arenque m

hers [hə:z] pron (el) suyo ((la) suya) etc; see also **mine¹**

herself [hə:'self] pron (reflexive) se; (emphatic) ella misma; (after prep) sí (misma); see also **oneself**

he's [hi:z] = he is; he has

hesitant ['hezɪtənt] adj vacilante

hesitate ['hezɪteɪt] vi vacilar; (in speech) titubear; (be unwilling) resistirse a ❏ **hesitation** [-'teɪʃən] n indecisión f; titubeo; dudas fpl

heterosexual [hetərəu'seksjuəl] adj heterosexual

hexagon ['heksəgən] n hexágono

hey [heɪ] excl ¡oye!, ¡oiga!

heyday ['heɪdeɪ] n: **the ~ of** el apogeo de

HGV n abbr (= heavy goods vehicle) vehículo pesado

hi [haɪ] excl ¡hola!; (to attract attention) ¡oiga!

hibernate ['haɪbəneɪt] vi invernar

hiccough ['hɪkʌp] = **hiccup**

hiccup ['hɪkʌp] vi hipar

hid [hɪd] pt of **hide**

hidden ['hɪdn] pp of **hide** ♦ adj: **~ agenda** plan m encubierto

hide [haɪd] (pt hid, pp hidden) n (skin) piel f ♦ vt esconder, ocultar ♦ vi: **to ~ (from sb)** esconderse or ocultarse (de algn)

hideous ['hɪdɪəs] adj horrible

hiding ['haɪdɪŋ] n (beating) paliza; **to be in ~** (concealed) estar escondido

hi-fi ['haɪfaɪ] n estéreo, hifi m ♦ adj de alta fidelidad

high [haɪ] adj alto; (speed, number) grande; (price) elevado; (wind) fuerte; (voice) agudo ♦ adv alto, a gran altura; **it is 20 m ~** tiene 20 m de altura; **~ in the air** en las alturas ❏ **highchair** n silla alta ❏ **high-class** adj (hotel) de lujo; (person) distinguido, de categoría; (food) de alta categoría ❏ **higher education** n educación f or enseñanza superior ❏ **high heels** npl (heels) tacones mpl altos; (shoes) zapatos mpl de tacón ❏ **high jump** n (SPORT) salto de altura ❏ **highlands** ['haɪləndz] npl tierras fpl altas; **the Highlands** (in Scotland) las Tierras Altas de Escocia ❏ **highlight** n (fig: of event) punto culminante ♦ vt subrayar;

highlights npl (in hair) reflejos mpl ❏ **highlighter** n rotulador ❏ **highly** adv (paid) muy bien; (critical, confidential) sumamente; (a lot): **to speak/think highly of** hablar muy bien de/tener en mucho a ❏ **highness** n altura; **Her/His Highness** Su Alteza ❏ **high-rise** n (also: **high-rise block, high-rise building**) torre f de pisos ❏ **high school** n = Instituto Nacional de Bachillerato (SP) ❏ **high season** (BRIT) n temporada alta ❏ **high street** (BRIT) n calle f mayor ❏ **high-tech** (inf) adj altec (inf), de alta tecnología ❏ **highway** n carretera; (US) carretera nacional; autopista ❏ **Highway Code** (BRIT) n código de la circulación

hijack ['haɪdʒæk] vt secuestrar ❏ **hijacker** n secuestrador(a) m/f

hike [haɪk] vi (go walking) ir de excursión (a pie) ♦ n caminata ❏ **hiker** n excursionista mf ❏ **hiking** n senderismo

hilarious [hɪ'lɛərɪəs] adj divertidísimo

hill [hɪl] n colina; (high) montaña; (slope) cuesta ❏ **hillside** n ladera ❏ **hill walking** n senderismo (de montaña) ❏ **hilly** adj montañoso

him [hɪm] pron (direct) le, lo; (indirect) le; (stressed, after prep) él; see also **me** ❏ **himself** pron (reflexive) se; (emphatic) mismo; (after prep) sí (mismo); see also **oneself**

hind [haɪnd] adj posterior

hinder ['hɪndə*] vt estorbar, impedir

hindsight ['haɪndsaɪt] n: **with ~** en retrospectiva

Hindu ['hɪnduː] n hindú mf ❏ **Hinduism** n (REL) hinduismo

hinge [hɪndʒ] n bisagra, gozne m ♦ vi (fig): **to ~ on** depender de

hint [hɪnt] n indirecta; (advice) consejo; (sign) dejo ♦ vt: **to ~ that** insinuar que ♦ vi: **to ~ at** hacer alusión a

hip [hɪp] n cadera

hippie

hold

hippie ['hɪpɪ] n hippie m/f, jipi m/f

hippo ['hɪpəʊ] (PL hippos) n hipopótamo

hippopotamus [hɪpə'pɒtəməs] (pl **hippopotamuses** or **hippopotami**) n hipopótamo

hippy ['hɪpɪ] n = **hippie**

hire ['haɪə] vt (BRIT: car, equipment) alquilar; (worker) contratar ♦ n alquiler m; **for** ~ se alquila; (taxi) libre ❑ **hire(d) car** (BRIT) n coche m de alquiler ❑ **hire purchase** (BRIT) n compra a plazos

his [hɪz] pron (el) suyo ((la) suya) etc ♦ adj su; see also **mine¹; my**

Hispanic [hɪs'pænɪk] adj hispánico

hiss [hɪs] vi silbar

historian [hɪ'stɔːrɪən] n historiador(a) m/f

historic(al) [hɪ'stɒrɪk(l)] adj histórico

history ['hɪstərɪ] n historia

hit [hɪt] (pt, pp ~) vt (strike) golpear, pegar; (reach: target) alcanzar; (collide with: car) chocar contra; (fig: affect) afectar ♦ n golpe m; (success) éxito m; **to ~ it off with sb** llevarse bien con algn ► **hit back** vi defenderse; (fig) devolver golpe por golpe

hitch [hɪtʃ] vt (fasten) atar, amarrar; (also: ~ **up**) remangar ♦ n (difficulty) dificultad f; **to ~ a lift** hacer autostop

hitch-hike ['hɪtʃhaɪk] vi hacer autostop ❑ **hitch-hiker** n autostopista m/f ❑ **hitch-hiking** n autostop m

hi-tech [haɪ'tek] adj de alta tecnología

hitman ['hɪtmæn] (irreg) n asesino a sueldo

HIV n abbr (= human immunodeficiency virus) VIH m; **~-negative/positive** VIH negativo/positivo

hive [haɪv] n colmena

hoard [hɔːd] n (treasure) tesoro; (stockpile) provisión f ♦ vt acumular; (goods in short supply) acaparar

hoarse [hɔːs] adj ronco

hoax [həʊks] n trampa

hob [hɒb] n quemador m

hobble ['hɒbl] vi cojear

hobby ['hɒbɪ] n pasatiempo, afición f

hobo ['həʊbəʊ] (US) n vagabundo

hockey ['hɒkɪ] n hockey m ❑ **hockey stick** n palo m de hockey

hog [hɒg] n cerdo, puerco ♦ vt acaparar; **to go the whole ~** poner toda la carne en el asador

Hogmanay ['hɒgmə'neɪ] n see recuadro

HOGMANAY

La Nochevieja o "New's Year's Eve" se conoce como **Hogmanay** en Escocia, donde se festeja de forma especial. La familia y los amigos se suelen juntar para oír las campanadas del reloj y luego se hace el "first-footing", costumbre que consiste en visitar a los amigos y vecinos llevando algo de beber (generalmente whisky) y un trozo de carbón que se supone que traerá buena suerte para el año entrante.

hoist [hɔɪst] n (crane) grúa ♦ vt levantar, alzar; (flag, sail) izar

hold [həʊld] (pt, pp **held**) vt sostener; (contain) contener; (have: power, qualification) tener; (keep back) retener; (believe) sostener; (consider) considerar; (keep in position): **to ~ one's head up** mantener la cabeza alta; (meeting) celebrar ♦ vi (withstand pressure) resistir; (be valid) valer ♦ n (grasp) asimiento; (fig) dominio; **~ the line!** (TEL) ¡no cuelgue!; **to ~ one's own** (fig) defenderse; **to catch or get** (a) **~ of** agarrarse or asirse de ► **hold back** vt retener; (secret) ocultar ► **hold on** vi agarrarse bien; (wait) esperar; **hold on!** (TEL) ¡(espere) un momento! ► **hold out** vt ofrecer ♦ vi (resist) resistir ► **hold up** vt (raise) levantar; (support) apoyar; (delay) retrasar; (rob) asaltar

holdall (BRIT) n bolsa ❑ **holder** n (container) receptáculo; (of ticket, record) poseedor(a) m/f; (of office, title etc) titular mf

hole [həul] n agujero

holiday ['hɔlədeɪ] n vacaciones fpl; (public holiday) (día m de) fiesta, día m feriado; **on ~** de vacaciones ❑ **holiday camp** (BRIT: also: **holiday centre**) n centro de vacaciones ❑ **holiday job** n (BRIT) trabajillo extra para las vacaciones ❑ **holiday-maker** (BRIT) n turista mf ❑ **holiday resort** n centro turístico

Holland ['hɔlənd] n Holanda

hollow ['hɔləu] adj hueco, (claim) vacío; (eyes) hundido; (sound) sordo ♦ n hueco; (in ground) hoyo ♦ vt: **to ~ out** excavar

holly ['hɔlɪ] n acebo

Hollywood ['hɔlɪwud] n Hollywood m

holocaust ['hɔləkɔːst] n holocausto

holy ['həulɪ] adj santo, sagrado; (water) bendito

home [həum] n casa; (country) patria; (institution) asilo ♦ cpd (domestic) casero, de casa; (ECON, POL) nacional ♦ adv (direction) a casa; (right in: nail etc) a fondo; **at ~** en casa; (in country) en el país; (fig) como pez en el agua; **to go/come ~** ir/volver a casa; **make yourself at ~** ¡estás en tu casa! ❑ **home address** n domicilio ❑ **homeland** n tierra natal ❑ **homeless** adj sin hogar, sin casa ❑ **homely** adj (simple) sencillo ❑ **home-made** adj casero ❑ **home match** n partido en casa ❑ **Home Office** n (BRIT) Ministerio del Interior ❑ **home owner** n propietario(-a) m/f de una casa ❑ **home page** n página de inicio ❑ **Home Secretary** n (BRIT) Ministro del Interior ❑ **homesick** adj: **to be homesick** tener morriña, sentir nostalgia ❑ **home town** n ciudad y natal ❑ **homework** n deberes mpl

homicide ['hɔmɪsaɪd] n (US) homicidio

homoeopathic [həumɪə'pæθɪk] (US **homeopathic**) adj homeopático

homoeopathy [həumɪ'ɔpəθɪ] (US **homeopathy**) n homeopatía

homosexual [hɔməu'seksjuəl] adj, n homosexual mf

honest ['ɔnɪst] adj honrado; (sincere) franco, sincero ❑ **honestly** adv honradamente; (frankly) francamente ❑ **honesty** n honradez f

honey ['hʌnɪ] n miel f ❑ **honeymoon** n luna de miel ❑ **honeysuckle** n madreselva

Hong Kong ['hɔŋ'kɔŋ] n Hong-Kong m

honorary ['ɔnərərɪ] adj (member, president) de honor; (title) honorífico; ~ **degree** n doctorado honoris causa

honour ['ɔnə] (US **honor**) vt honrar; (commitment, promise) cumplir con ♦ n honor m, honra; **to graduate with honours** = licenciarse con matrícula (de honor) ❑ **honourable** (US **honorable**) adj honorable ❑ **honours degree** n (SCOL) título de licenciado con calificación alta

hood [hud] n capucha; (BRIT AUT) capota; (US AUT) capó m; (of cooker) campana de humos

hoof [huːf] (pl **hooves**) n pezuña

hook [huk] n gancho; (on dress) corchete m, broche m; (for fishing) anzuelo ♦ vt enganchar; (fish) pescar

hooligan ['huːlɪgən] n gamberro

hoop [huːp] n aro

hooray [huː'reɪ] excl = **hurray**

hoot [huːt] (BRIT) vi (AUT) tocar el pito, pitar; (siren) (hacer) sonar; (owl) ulular

Hoover® (BRIT) n aspiradora ♦ vt: **to hoover** pasar la aspiradora por

hooves [huːvz] npl of **hoof**

hop [hɔp] vi saltar, brincar; (on one foot) saltar con un pie

hope [həup] vt, vi esperar ♦ n esperanza; **I ~ so/not** espero que sí/no ❑ **hopeful** adj (person) optimista; (situation) prometedor(a)

hopefully adv con esperanza; (one hopes): **hopefully he will recover** esperamos que se recupere ❏ **hopeless** adj desesperado; (person): **to be hopeless** ser un desastre

hops [hɔps] npl lúpulo

horizon [hə'raɪzn] n horizonte m ❏ **horizontal** [hɔrɪ'zɒntl] adj horizontal

hormone ['hɔ:məʊn] n hormona

horn [hɔ:n] n cuerno; (MUS: also: **French ~**) trompa; (AUT) pito, claxon m

horoscope ['hɒrəskəʊp] n horóscopo

horrendous [hə'rendəs] adj horrendo

horrible ['hɒrɪbl] adj horrible

horrid ['hɒrɪd] adj horrible, horroroso

horrific [hə'rɪfɪk] adj (accident) horroroso; (film) horripilante

horrifying ['hɒrɪfaɪɪŋ] adj horroroso

horror ['hɒrə'] n horror m ❏ **horror film** n película de horror

hors d'œuvre [ɔ:'də:vrə] n entremeses mpl

horse [hɔ:s] n caballo ❏ **horseback** n: **on horseback** a caballo ❏ **horse chestnut** n (tree) castaño de Indias; (nut) castaña de Indias ❏ **horsepower** n caballo (de fuerza) ❏ **horse-racing** n carreras fpl de caballos ❏ **horseradish** n rábano picante ❏ **horse riding** n (BRIT) equitación f

hose [həʊz] n manguera ❏ **hosepipe** n manguera

hospital ['hɒspɪtl] n hospital m

hospitality [hɒspɪ'tælɪtɪ] n hospitalidad f

host [həʊst] n anfitrión m; (TV, RADIO) presentador m; (REL) hostia; (large number): **a ~ of** multitud de

hostage ['hɒstɪdʒ] n rehén m

hostel ['hɒstl] n hostal m; (youth) albergue m juvenil

hostess ['həʊstɪs] n anfitriona f; (BRIT: air hostess) azafata; (TV, RADIO) presentadora

hostile ['hɒstaɪl] adj hostil

hostility [hɒ'stɪlɪtɪ] n hostilidad f

hot [hɒt] adj caliente; (weather) caluroso, de calor; (as opposed to warm) muy caliente; (spicy) picante; **to be ~** (person) tener calor; (object) estar caliente; (weather) hacer calor ❏ **hot dog** n perro caliente

hotel [həʊ'tɛl] n hotel m

hot-water bottle [hɒt'wɔ:tə'-] n bolsa de agua caliente

hound [haʊnd] vt acosar ♦ n perro (de caza)

hour ['aʊə'] n hora ❏ **hourly** adj (de) cada hora

house [n haʊs, pl 'haʊzɪz, vb haʊz] n (gen, firm) casa; (POL) cámara; (THEATRE) sala ♦ vt (person) alojar; (collection) albergar; **on the ~** (fig) la casa invita ❏ **household** n familia; (home) casa ❏ **householder** n propietario(-a); (head of house) cabeza de familia ❏ **housekeeper** n ama de llaves ❏ **housekeeping** n (work) trabajos mpl domésticos ❏ **housewife** (irreg) n ama de casa ❏ **house wine** n vino m de la casa ❏ **housework** n faenas fpl (de la casa)

housing ['haʊzɪŋ] n (act) alojamiento; (houses) viviendas fpl ❏ **housing development** (BRIT), **housing estate** (BRIT) n urbanización f

hover ['hɒvə'] vi flotar (en el aire) ❏ **hovercraft** n aerodeslizador m

how [haʊ] adv (in what way) cómo; **~ are you?** ¿cómo estás?; **~ much milk/ many people?** ¿cuánta leche/gente?; **~ much does it cost?** ¿cuánto cuesta?; **~ long have you been here?** ¿cuánto hace que estás aquí?; **~ old are you?** ¿cuántos años tienes?; **~ tall is he?** ¿cómo es de alto?; **~ is school?** ¿cómo (te) va (en) la escuela?; **~ was the film?** ¿qué tal la película?; **~ lovely/awful!** ¡qué bonito/horror!

however [haʊ'evə'] adv: **~ I do it** lo haga como lo haga; **~ cold it is por**

mucho frío que haga; **~ fast** he runs por muy rápido que corra; **~ did you do it?** ¿cómo lo hiciste? ♦ *conj* sin embargo, no obstante

howl [haul] *n* aullido ♦ *vi* aullar; *(person)* dar alaridos; *(wind)* ulular

H.P. *n, abbr* = **hire purchase**

h.p. *abbr* = **horsepower**

HQ *n, abbr* = **headquarters**

hr(s) *abbr* (= *hour(s)*) h

HTML *n abbr* (= *hypertext markup language*) lenguaje *m* de hipertexto

hubcap ['hʌbkæp] *n* tapacubos *m inv*

huddle ['hʌdl] *vi*: **to ~ together** acurrucarse

huff [hʌf] *n*: **in a ~** enojado

hug [hʌg] *vt* abrazar; *(thing)* apretar con los brazos

huge [hju:dʒ] *adj* enorme

hull [hʌl] *n (of ship)* casco

hum [hʌm] *vt* tararear, canturrear ♦ *vi* tararear, canturrear; *(insect)* zumbar

human ['hju:mən] *adj, n* humano

humane [hju:'meɪn] *adj* humano, humanitario

humanitarian [hju:mænɪ'tɛərɪən] *adj* humanitario

humanity [hju:'mænɪtɪ] *n* humanidad *f*

human rights *npl* derechos *mpl* humanos

humble ['hʌmbl] *adj* humilde

humid ['hju:mɪd] *adj* húmedo
□ **humidity** [-'mɪdɪtɪ] *n* humedad *f*

humiliate [hju:'mɪlɪeɪt] *vt* humillar

humiliating [hju:'mɪlɪeɪtɪŋ] *adj* humillante, vergonzoso

humiliation [hju:mɪlɪ'eɪʃən] *n* humillación *f*

hummus ['huməs] *n* paté de garbanzos

humorous ['hju:mərəs] *adj* gracioso, divertido

humour ['hju:mə'] *(US* **humor**) *n* humorismo, sentido del humor; *(mood)* humor *m* ♦ *vt (person)* complacer

hump [hʌmp] *n (in ground)* montículo; *(camel's)* giba

hunch [hʌntʃ] *n (premonition)* presentimiento

hundred ['hʌndrəd] *num* ciento; *(before n)* cien; **~s of** centenares de
□ **hundredth** [-ɪdθ] *adj* centésimo

hundredweight *n* (BRIT) = 50.8 kg, 112 lb; (US) = 45.3 kg, 100 lb

hung [hʌŋ] *pt, pp of* **hang**

Hungarian [hʌŋ'gɛərɪən] *adj, n* húngaro(-a) *m/f*

Hungary ['hʌŋgərɪ] *n* Hungría

hunger ['hʌŋgə'] *n* hambre *f* ♦ *vi*: **to ~ for** *(fig)* tener hambre de, anhelar

hungry ['hʌŋgrɪ] *adj*: **~ (for)** hambriento (de); **to be ~** tener hambre

hunt [hʌnt] *vt (seek)* buscar; (SPORT) cazar ♦ *vi (search)*: **to ~ (for)** buscar; (SPORT) cazar ♦ *n* búsqueda; caza, cacería □ **hunter** *n* cazador(a) *m/f*
□ **hunting** *n* caza

hurdle ['hɜ:dl] *n* (SPORT) valla; *(fig)* obstáculo

hurl [hɜ:l] *vt* lanzar, arrojar

hurrah [hu'rɑ:], **hurray** [hu'reɪ] *excl* ¡viva!

hurricane ['hʌrɪkən] *n* huracán *m*

hurry ['hʌrɪ] *n* prisa ♦ *vt (also*: ~ **up**: *person)* dar prisa a; (: *work)* apresurar, hacer de prisa; **to be in a ~** tener prisa ► **hurry up** *vi* darse prisa, apurarse (LAm)

hurt [hɜ:t] *(pt, pp* ~) *vt* hacer daño a ♦ *vi* doler ♦ *adj* lastimado

husband ['hʌzbənd] *n* marido

hush [hʌʃ] *n* silencio ♦ *vt* hacer callar; **~!** ¡chitón!, ¡cállate!

husky ['hʌskɪ] *adj* ronco ♦ *n* perro esquimal

hut [hʌt] *n* cabaña; *(shed)* cobertizo

hyacinth ['haɪəsɪnθ] *n* jacinto

hydrangea [haɪ'dreɪndʒə] *n* hortensia

hydrofoil ['haɪdrəfɔɪl] *n* aerodeslizador *m*

hydrogen ['haɪdrədʒən] *n* hidrógeno

hygiene ['haɪdʒiːn] *n* higiene *f*
❏ **hygienic** [-'dʒiːnɪk] *adj* higiénico

hymn [hɪm] *n* himno

hype [haɪp] *(inf) n* bombardeo publicitario

hyphen ['haɪfn] *n* guión *m*

hypnotize ['hɪpnətaɪz] *vt* hipnotizar

hypocrite ['hɪpəkrɪt] *n* hipócrita *mf*

hypocritical [hɪpə'krɪtɪkl] *adj* hipócrita

hypothesis [haɪ'pɒθɪsɪs] *(pl* **hypotheses**) *n* hipótesis *f inv*

hysterical [hɪ'sterɪkl] *adj* histérico; *(funny)* para morirse de risa

hysterics [hɪ'sterɪks] *npl* histeria; **to be in ~** *(fig)* morirse de risa

I, i

I [aɪ] *pron* yo

ice [aɪs] *n* hielo; *(ice cream)* helado ♦ *vt (cake)* alcorzar ♦ *vi (also:* **~ over, ~ up)** helarse ❏ **iceberg** *n* iceberg *m* ❏ **ice cream** *n* helado ❏ **ice cube** *n* cubito de hielo ❏ **ice hockey** *n* hockey *m* sobre hielo

Iceland ['aɪslənd] *n* Islandia ❏ **Icelander** *n* islandés(-esa) *m/f* ❏ **Icelandic** [aɪs'lændɪk] *adj* islandés(-esa) ♦ *n (LING)* islandés *m*

ice: ice lolly *(BRIT) n* polo ❏ **ice rink** *n* pista de hielo ❏ **ice skating** *n* patinaje *m* sobre hielo

icing ['aɪsɪŋ] *n (CULIN)* alcorza ❏ **icing sugar** *(BRIT) n* azúcar *m* glas(eado)

icon ['aɪkɒn] *n* icono

icy ['aɪsɪ] *adj* helado

I'd [aɪd] = **I would**; **I had**

ID card *n (identity card)* DNI *m*

idea [aɪ'dɪə] *n* idea

ideal [aɪ'dɪəl] *n* ideal *m* ♦ *adj* ideal ❏ **ideally** [-dɪəlɪ] *adv* idealmente; **they're ideally suited** hacen una pareja ideal

identical [aɪ'dentɪkl] *adj* idéntico

identification [aɪdentɪfɪ'keɪʃən] *n* identificación *f*; *(means of)* **~** documentos *mpl* personales

identify [aɪ'dentɪfaɪ] *vt* identificar

identity [aɪ'dentɪtɪ] *n* identidad *f* ❏ **identity card** *n* carnet *m* de identidad

ideology [aɪdɪ'ɒlədʒɪ] *n* ideología *f*

idiom ['ɪdɪəm] *n* modismo; *(style of speaking)* lenguaje *m*

⚠ Be careful not to translate **idiom** by the Spanish word *idioma*.

idiot ['ɪdɪət] *n* idiota *mf*

idle ['aɪdl] *adj (inactive)* ocioso; *(lazy)* holgazán(-ana); *(unemployed)* parado, desocupado; *(machinery etc)* parado; *(talk etc)* frívolo ♦ *vi (machine)* marchar en vacío

idol ['aɪdl] *n* ídolo

idyllic [ɪ'dɪlɪk] *adj* idílico

i.e. *abbr (= that is)* esto es

if [ɪf] *conj* si; **if necessary** si fuera necesario, si hiciese falta; **if I were you** yo en tu lugar; **if so/not** de ser así/si no; **if only I could!** ¡ojalá pudiera!; *see also* **as**; **even**

ignite [ɪg'naɪt] *vt (set fire to)* encender ♦ *vi* encenderse

ignition [ɪg'nɪʃən] *n (AUT: process)* ignición *f*; *(: mechanism)* encendido; **to switch on/off the ~** arrancar/apagar el motor

ignorance ['ɪgnərəns] *n* ignorancia

ignorant ['ɪgnərənt] *adj* ignorante; **to be ~ of** ignorar

ignore [ɪg'nɔːr] *vt (person, advice)* no hacer caso de; *(fact)* pasar por alto

I'll [aɪl] = **I will**; **I shall**

ill [ɪl] *adj* enfermo, malo ♦ *n* mal *m* ♦ *adv* mal; **to be taken ~** ponerse enfermo

illegal [ɪ'liːgl] *adj* ilegal

illegible [ɪ'ledʒɪbl] *adj* ilegible

illegitimate [ɪlɪ'dʒɪtɪmət] *adj* ilegítimo

ill health n mala salud f; **to be in ~** estar mal de salud

illiterate [r'lɪtərət] adj analfabeto

illness ['ɪlnɪs] n enfermedad f

illuminate [r'lu:mɪneɪt] vt (room, street) iluminar, alumbrar

illusion [r'lu:ʒən] n ilusión f; (trick) truco

illustrate ['ɪləstreɪt] vt ilustrar

illustration [ɪlə'streɪʃən] n (act of illustrating) ilustración f; (example) ejemplo, ilustración f; (in book) lámina

I'm [aɪm] = **I am**

image ['ɪmɪdʒ] n imagen f

imaginary [r'mædʒɪnərɪ] adj imaginario

imagination [ɪmædʒɪ'neɪʃən] n imaginación f; (inventiveness) inventiva

imaginative [r'mædʒɪnətɪv] adj imaginativo

imagine [r'mædʒɪn] vt imaginarse

imbalance [ɪm'bæləns] n desequilibrio

imitate ['ɪmɪteɪt] vt imitar ❑ **imitation** [ɪmɪ'teɪʃən] n imitación f; (copy) copia

immaculate [r'mækjulət] adj inmaculado

immature [ɪmə'tjuəʳ] adj (person) inmaduro

immediate [r'mi:dɪət] adj inmediato; (pressing) urgente, apremiante; (nearest: family) próximo; (: neighbourhood) inmediato ❑ **immediately** adv (at once) en seguida; (directly) inmediatamente; **immediately next to** muy junto a

immense [r'mɛns] adj inmenso, enorme; (importance) enorme ❑ **immensely** adv enormemente

immerse [r'mə:s] vt (submerge) sumergir; **to be immersed in** (fig) estar absorto en

immigrant ['ɪmɪgrənt] n inmigrante mf ❑ **immigration** [ɪmɪ'greɪʃən] n inmigración f

imminent ['ɪmɪnənt] adj inminente

immoral [r'mɔrl] adj inmoral

immortal [r'mɔ:tl] adj inmortal

immune [r'mju:n] adj: **~ (to)** inmune (a) ❑ **immune system** n sistema m inmunitario

immunize ['ɪmjunaɪz] vt inmunizar

impact ['ɪmpækt] n impacto

impair [ɪm'pɛəʳ] vt perjudicar

impartial [ɪm'pɑ:ʃl] adj imparcial

impatience [ɪm'peɪʃəns] n impaciencia

impatient [ɪm'peɪʃənt] adj impaciente; **to get** or **grow ~** impacientarse

impeccable [ɪm'pɛkəbl] adj impecable

impending [ɪm'pɛndɪŋ] adj inminente

imperative [ɪm'pɛrətɪv] adj (tone) imperioso; (need) imprescindible ♦ n (LING) imperativo

imperfect [ɪm'pə:fɪkt] adj (goods etc) defectuoso ♦ n (LING: also: **~ tense**) imperfecto

imperial [ɪm'pɪərɪəl] adj imperial

impersonal [ɪm'pə:sənl] adj impersonal

impersonate [ɪm'pə:səneɪt] vt hacerse pasar por; (THEATRE) imitar

impetus ['ɪmpətəs] n ímpetu m; (fig) impulso

implant [ɪm'plɑ:nt] vt (MED) injertar, implantar; (fig: idea, principle) inculcar

implement [n 'ɪmplɪmənt, vb 'ɪmplɪment] n herramienta f; (for cooking) utensilio ♦ vt (regulation) hacer efectivo; (plan) realizar

implicate ['ɪmplɪkeɪt] vt (compromise) comprometer; **to ~ sb in sth** comprometer a algn en algo ❑ **implication** [ɪmplɪ'keɪʃən] n consecuencia f; **by ~** indirectamente

implicit [ɪm'plɪsɪt] adj implícito; (belief, trust) absoluto

imply [ɪm'plaɪ] vt (involve) suponer; (hint) dar a entender que

impolite [ɪmpə'laɪt] adj mal educado

import [vb ɪm'pɔ:t, n 'ɪmpɔ:t] vt importar ♦ n (COMM) importación f;

(: *article*) producto importado; (*meaning*) significado, sentido

importance [ɪm'pɔ:təns] *n* importancia

important [ɪm'pɔ:tənt] *adj* importante; **it's not ~** no importa, no tiene importancia

importer [ɪm'pɔ:tə*r*] *n* importador(a) *m/f*

impose [ɪm'pəʊz] *vt* imponer ♦ *vi*: **to ~ on sb** abusar de algn ❏ **imposing** *adj* imponente, impresionante

impossible [ɪm'pɔsɪbl] *adj* imposible; (*person*) insoportable

impotent ['ɪmpətənt] *adj* impotente

impoverished [ɪm'pɔvərɪʃt] *adj* necesitado

impractical [ɪm'præktɪkl] *adj* (*person, plan*) poco práctico

impress [ɪm'prɛs] *vt* impresionar; (*mark*) estampar; **to ~ sth on sb** hacer entender algo a algn

impression [ɪm'prɛʃən] *n* impresión *f*; (*imitation*) imitación *f*; **to be under the ~ that** tener la impresión de que

impressive [ɪm'prɛsɪv] *adj* impresionante

imprison [ɪm'prɪzn] *vt* encarcelar ❏ **imprisonment** *n* encarcelamiento, (*term of imprisonment*) cárcel *f*

improbable [ɪm'prɔbəbl] *adj* improbable, inverosímil

improper [ɪm'prɔpə*r*] *adj* (*unsuitable: conduct etc*) incorrecto; (: *activities*) deshonesto

improve [ɪm'pru:v] *vt* mejorar; (*foreign language*) perfeccionar ♦ *vi* mejorarse ❏ **improvement** *n* mejoramiento; perfección *f*; progreso

improvise ['ɪmprəvaɪz] *vt, vi* improvisar

impulse ['ɪmpʌls] *n* impulso; **to act on ~** obrar sin reflexión ❏ **impulsive** [ɪm'pʌlsɪv] *adj* irreflexivo

---

in

KEYWORD

[ɪn] *prep*

1 (*indicating place, position, with place names*) en; **in the house/garden** en (la) casa/el jardín; **in here/there** aquí/ahí or allí dentro; **in London/ England** en Londres/Inglaterra

2 (*indicating time*) en; **in spring** en (la) primavera; **in the afternoon** por la tarde; **at 4 o'clock in the afternoon** a las 4 de la tarde; **I did it in 3 hours/ days** lo hice en 3 horas/días; **I'll see you in 2 weeks** or **in 2 weeks' time** te veré dentro de 2 semanas

3 (*indicating manner etc*) en; **in a loud/soft voice** en voz alta/baja; **in pencil/ink** a lápiz/bolígrafo; **the boy in the blue shirt** el chico de la camisa azul

4 (*indicating circumstances*): **in the sun/shade/rain** al sol/a la sombra/ bajo la lluvia; **a change in policy** un cambio de política

5 (*indicating mood, state*): **in tears** en lágrimas, llorando; **in anger/despair** enfadado/desesperado; **to live in luxury** vivir lujosamente

6 (*with ratios, numbers*): **1 in 10 households, 1 household in 10** una de cada 10 familias; **20 pence in the pound** 20 peniques por libra; **they lined up in twos** se alinearon de dos en dos

7 (*referring to people, works*) en; entre; **the disease is common in children** la enfermedad es común entre los niños; **in (the works of) Dickens** en (las obras de) Dickens

8 (*indicating profession etc*): **to be in teaching** estar en la enseñanza

9 (*after superlative*) de; **the best pupil**

in the class el (la) mejor alumno(-a) de la clase

10 (with present participle): **in saying this** al decir esto

♦ adv: **to be in** (person: at home) estar en casa; (at work) estar; (train, fashion, plane) haber llegado; (in fashion) estar de moda; **she'll be in later today** llegará más tarde hoy; **to ask sb in** hacer pasar a algn; **to run/limp etc in** entrar corriendo/cojeando etc ♦ n: **the ins and outs** (of proposal, situation etc) los detalles

inability [ɪnəˈbɪlɪtɪ] n: **~ (to do)** incapacidad f (de hacer)

inaccurate [ɪnˈækjʊrət] adj inexacto, incorrecto

inadequate [ɪnˈædɪkwət] adj (income, reply etc) insuficiente; (person) incapaz

inadvertently [ɪnədˈvɜːtntlɪ] adv por descuido

inappropriate [ɪnəˈprəʊprɪət] adj inadecuado; (improper) poco oportuno

inaugurate [ɪˈnɔːgjʊreɪt] vt inaugurar; (president, official) investir

Inc. (US) abbr (= incorporated) S.A.

incapable [ɪnˈkeɪpəbl] adj incapaz

incense [n ˈɪnsens, vb ɪnˈsens] n incienso ♦ vt (anger) indignar, encolerizar

incentive [ɪnˈsentɪv] n incentivo, estímulo

inch [ɪntʃ] n pulgada; **to be within an ~ of** estar a dos dedos de; **he didn't give an ~** no dio concesión alguna

incidence [ˈɪnsɪdns] n (of crime, disease) incidencia

incident [ˈɪnsɪdnt] n incidente m

incidentally [ɪnsɪˈdentəlɪ] adv (by the way) a propósito

inclination [ɪnklɪˈneɪʃən] n (tendency) tendencia, inclinación f; (desire) deseo; (disposition) propensión f

incline [n ˈɪnklaɪn, vb ɪnˈklaɪn] n pendiente m, cuesta ♦ vt (head) poner de lado ♦ vi inclinarse; **to be inclined to** (tend) tener tendencia a hacer algo

include [ɪnˈkluːd] vt (incorporate) incluir; (in letter) adjuntar ❑ **including** prep incluso, inclusa

inclusion [ɪnˈkluːʒən] n inclusión f

inclusive [ɪnˈkluːsɪv] adj inclusivo; **~ of tax** incluidos los impuestos

income [ˈɪnkʌm] n (earned) ingresos mpl; (from property etc) renta; (from investment etc) rédito ❑ **income support** n (BRIT) = ayuda familiar ❑ **income tax** n impuesto sobre la renta

incoming [ˈɪnkʌmɪŋ] adj (flight, government etc) entrante

incompatible [ɪnkəmˈpætɪbl] adj incompatible

incompetence [ɪnˈkɒmpɪtəns] n incompetencia

incompetent [ɪnˈkɒmpɪtənt] adj incompetente

incomplete [ɪnkəmˈpliːt] adj (partial: achievement etc) incompleto; (unfinished: painting etc) inacabado

inconsistent [ɪnkənˈsɪstənt] adj inconsecuente; (contradictory) incongruente; **~ with** (que) no concuerda con

inconvenience [ɪnkənˈviːnjəns] n inconvenientes mpl; (trouble) molestia, incomodidad f ♦ vt incomodar

inconvenient [ɪnkənˈviːnjənt] adj incómodo, poco práctico; (time, place, visitor) inoportuno

incorporate [ɪnˈkɔːpəreɪt] vt incorporar; (contain) comprender; (add) agregar

incorrect [ɪnkəˈrekt] adj incorrecto

increase [n ˈɪnkriːs, vb ɪnˈkriːs] n aumento ♦ vi aumentar; (grow) crecer; (price) subir ♦ vt aumentar; (price) subir ❑ **increasingly** adv cada vez más, más y más

incredible [ɪnˈkrɛdɪbl] adj increíble
❑ **incredibly** adv increíblemente

incur [ɪnˈkə:ˈ] vt (expenditure) incurrir;
(loss) sufrir; (anger, disapproval)
provocar

indecent [ɪnˈdiːsnt] adj indecente

indeed [ɪnˈdiːd] adv efectivamente, en
realidad; (in fact) en efecto;
(furthermore) es más; **yes ~!** claro que
sí!

indefinitely [ɪnˈdɛfɪnɪtlɪ] adv (wait)
indefinidamente

independence [ɪndɪˈpɛndns] n
independencia ❑ **Independence
Day** (US) n Día m de la Independencia

INDEPENDENCE DAY

El cuatro de julio es **Independence
Day**, la fiesta nacional de Estados
Unidos, que se celebra en
conmemoración de la Declaración de
Independencia, escrita por Thomas
Jefferson y aprobada en 1776. En ella
se proclamaba la independencia total
de Gran Bretaña de las trece colonias
americanas que serían el origen de los
Estados Unidos de América.

---

independent [ɪndɪˈpɛndənt] adj
independiente ❑ **independent
school** n (BRIT) escuela f privada,
colegio m privado

index ['ɪndɛks] (pl **indexes**) n (in book)
índice m; (: in library etc) catálogo; (pl
indices: ratio, sign) exponente m

India ['ɪndɪə] n la India ❑ **Indian** adj, n
indio(-a); **Red Indian** piel roja mf

indicate ['ɪndɪkeɪt] vt indicar
❑ **indication** [-'keɪʃən] n indicio, señal
f ❑ **indicative** [ɪnˈdɪkətɪv] adj: **to be ~
indicative of** indicar ❑ **indicator** n
indicador m; (AUT) intermitente m

indices ['ɪndɪsiːz] npl of **index**

indict [ɪnˈdaɪt] vt acusar ❑ **indictment**
n acusación f

indifference [ɪnˈdɪfrəns] n
indiferencia

indifferent [ɪnˈdɪfrənt] adj
indiferente; (mediocre) regular

indigenous [ɪnˈdɪdʒɪnəs] adj indígena

indigestion [ɪndɪˈdʒɛstʃən] n
indigestión f

indignant [ɪnˈdɪɡnənt] adj: **to be ~ at
sth/with sb** indignarse por algo/con
algn

indirect [ɪndɪˈrɛkt] adj indirecto

indispensable [ɪndɪsˈpɛnsəbl] adj
indispensable, imprescindible

individual [ɪndɪˈvɪdjuəl] n individuo
♦ adj individual; (personal) personal;
(particular) particular ❑ **individually**
adv (singly) individualmente

Indonesia [ɪndəˈniːzɪə] n Indonesia

indoor ['ɪndɔ:ˈ] adj (swimming pool)
cubierto; (plant) de interior; (sport)
bajo cubierta ❑ **indoors** [ɪnˈdɔ:z] adv
dentro

induce [ɪnˈdjuːs] vt inducir, persuadir;
(bring about) producir; (labour)
provocar

indulge [ɪnˈdʌldʒ] vt (whim) satisfacer;
(person) complacer; (child) mimar ♦ vi:
to ~ in darse el gusto de ❑ **indulgent**
adj indulgente

industrial [ɪnˈdʌstrɪəl] adj industrial
❑ **industrial estate** (BRIT) n polígono
(SP) or zona (LAm) industrial
❑ **industrialist** n industrial mf
❑ **industrial park** (US) n = **industrial
estate**

industry ['ɪndəstrɪ] n industria;
(diligence) aplicación f

inefficient [ɪnɪˈfɪʃnt] adj ineficaz,
ineficiente

inequality [ɪnɪˈkwɔlɪtɪ] n desigualdad f

inevitable [ɪnˈɛvɪtəbl] adj inevitable
❑ **inevitably** adv inevitablemente

inexpensive [ɪnɪkˈspɛnsɪv] adj
económico

inexperienced [ɪnɪkˈspɪərɪənst] adj
inexperto

inexplicable [ɪnɪkˈsplɪkəbl] adj
inexplicable

infamous ['ɪnfəməs] adj infame

infant ['ɪnfənt] n niño(-a); (baby) niño(-a) pequeño(-a), bebé mf; (pej) aniñado

infantry ['ɪnfəntrɪ] n infantería

infant school (BRIT) n parvulario

infect [ɪn'fekt] vt (wound) infectar; (food) contaminar; (person, animal) contagiar ❏ **infection** [ɪn'fekʃən] n infección f; (fig) contagio ❏ **infectious** [ɪn'fekʃəs] adj (also fig) contagioso

infer [ɪn'fə:'] vt deducir, inferir

inferior [ɪn'fɪərɪə'] adj, n inferior mf

infertile [ɪn'fə:taɪl] adj estéril; (person) infecundo

infertility [ɪnfə:'tɪlɪtɪ] n esterilidad f; infecundidad f

infested [ɪn'festɪd] adj: ~ **with** plagado de

infinite ['ɪnfɪnɪt] adj infinito ❏ **infinitely** adv infinitamente

infirmary [ɪn'fə:mərɪ] n hospital m

inflamed [ɪn'fleɪmd] adj: **to become** ~ inflamarse

inflammation [ɪnflə'meɪʃən] n inflamación f

inflatable [ɪn'fleɪtəbl] adj (ball, boat) inflable

inflate [ɪn'fleɪt] vt (tyre, price etc) inflar; (fig) hinchar ❏ **inflation** [ɪn'fleɪʃən] n (ECON) inflación f

inflexible [ɪn'fleksəbl] adj (rule) rígido; (person) inflexible

inflict [ɪn'flɪkt] vt: **to ~ sth on sb** infligir algo en algn

influence ['ɪnfluəns] n influencia ♦ vt influir en, influenciar; **under the ~ of alcohol** en estado de embriaguez ❏ **influential** [-'enʃl] adj influyente

influx ['ɪnflʌks] n afluencia

info (inf) ['ɪnfəu] n = **information**

inform [ɪn'fɔ:m] vt: **to ~ sb of sth** informar a algn sobre or de algo ♦ vi: **to ~ on sb** delatar a algn

informal [ɪn'fɔ:məl] adj (manner, speech) familiar; (dress, interview, occasion) informal; (visit, meeting) extraoficial

information [ɪnfə'meɪʃən] n información f; (knowledge) conocimientos mpl; **a piece of ~** un dato ❏ **information office** n información f ❏ **information technology** n informática

informative [ɪn'fɔ:mətɪv] adj informativo

infra-red [ɪnfrə'red] adj infrarrojo

infrastructure ['ɪnfrəstrʌktʃə'] n (of system etc) infraestructura

infrequent [ɪn'fri:kwənt] adj infrecuente

infuriate [ɪn'fjuərɪeɪt] vt: **to become infuriated** ponerse furioso

infuriating [ɪn'fjuərɪeɪtɪŋ] adj (habit, noise) enloquecedor(a)

ingenious [ɪn'dʒi:nɪəs] adj ingenioso

ingredient [ɪn'gri:dɪənt] n ingrediente m

inhabit [ɪn'hæbɪt] vt vivir en ❏ **inhabitant** n habitante mf

inhale [ɪn'heɪl] vt inhalar ♦ vi (breathe in) aspirar; (in smoking) tragar ❏ **inhaler** n inhalador m

inherent [ɪn'hɪərənt] adj: ~ **in** or **to** inherente a

inherit [ɪn'herɪt] vt heredar ❏ **inheritance** n herencia; (fig) patrimonio

inhibit [ɪn'hɪbɪt] vt inhibir, impedir ❏ **inhibition** [-'bɪʃən] n cohibición f

initial [ɪ'nɪʃl] adj primero ♦ n inicial f ♦ vt firmar con las iniciales; **initials** npl (as signature) iniciales fpl; (abbreviation) siglas fpl ❏ **initially** adv al principio

initiate [ɪ'nɪʃɪeɪt] vt iniciar; **to ~ proceedings against sb** (LAW) entablar proceso contra algn

initiative [ɪ'nɪʃətɪv] n iniciativa

inject [ɪnˈdʒɛkt] vt inyectar; **to ~ sb with sth** inyectar algo a algn ❑ **injection** [ɪnˈdʒɛkʃən] n inyección f

injure [ˈɪndʒə] vt (hurt) herir, lastimar; (fig: reputation etc) perjudicar ❑ **injured** adj (person, arm) herido, lastimado ❑ **injury** n herida, lesión f; (wrong) perjuicio, daño

> ⚠ Be careful not to translate **injury** by the Spanish word **injuria**.

injustice [ɪnˈdʒʌstɪs] n injusticia

ink [ɪŋk] n tinta ❑ **ink-jet printer** [ˈɪŋkdʒɛt-] n impresora de chorro de tinta

inland [adj ˈɪnlənd, adv ɪnˈlænd] adj (waterway, port etc) interior ♦ adv tierra adentro ❑ **Inland Revenue** (BRIT) n departamento de impuestos, ≈ Hacienda (SP)

in-laws [ˈɪnlɔːz] npl suegros mpl

inmate [ˈɪnmeɪt] n (in prison) preso(-a), presidiario(-a); (in asylum) internado(-a)

inn [ɪn] n posada, mesón m

inner [ˈɪnə] adj (courtyard, calm) interior; (feelings) íntimo ❑ **inner-city** adj (schools, problems) de las zonas céntricas pobres, de los barrios céntricos pobres

inning [ˈɪnɪŋ] n (US: BASEBALL) inning m, entrada; **innings** (CRICKET) entrada, turno

innocence [ˈɪnəsns] n inocencia

innocent [ˈɪnəsnt] adj inocente

innovation [ɪnəʊˈveɪʃən] n novedad f

innovative [ˈɪnəʊveɪtɪv] adj innovador

in-patient [ˈɪnpeɪʃənt] n paciente m/f interno(-a)

input [ˈɪnpʊt] n entrada f; (of resources) inversión f; (COMPUT) entrada de datos

inquest [ˈɪnkwɛst] n (coroner's) encuesta judicial

inquire [ɪnˈkwaɪə] vi preguntar ♦ vt: **to ~ whether** preguntar si; **to ~ about** (person) preguntar por; (fact) informarse de ❑ **inquiry** n pregunta; (investigation) investigación f, pesquisa; **"Inquiries"** "Información"

ins. abbr = **inches**

insane [ɪnˈseɪn] adj loco; (MED) demente

insanity [ɪnˈsænɪtɪ] n demencia, locura

insect [ˈɪnsɛkt] n insecto ❑ **insect repellent** n loción f contra insectos

insecure [ɪnsɪˈkjʊə] adj inseguro

insecurity [ɪnsɪˈkjʊərɪtɪ] n inseguridad f

insensitive [ɪnˈsɛnsɪtɪv] adj insensible

insert [vb ɪnˈsɜːt, n ˈɪnsɜːt] vt (into sth) introducir ♦ n encarte m

inside [ˈɪnˈsaɪd] n interior m ♦ adj interior, interno ♦ adv (be) (por) dentro; (go) hacia dentro ♦ prep dentro de; (of time): **~ 10 minutes** en menos de 10 minutos ❑ **inside lane** n (AUT: in Britain) carril m izquierdo; (: in US, Europe etc) carril m derecho ❑ **inside out** adv (turn) al revés; (know) a fondo

insight [ˈɪnsaɪt] n perspicacia

insignificant [ɪnsɪɡˈnɪfɪkənt] adj insignificante

insincere [ɪnsɪnˈsɪə] adj poco sincero

insist [ɪnˈsɪst] vi insistir; **to ~ on** insistir en; **to ~ that** insistir en que; (claim) exigir que ❑ **insistent** adj insistente; (noise, action) persistente

insomnia [ɪnˈsɒmnɪə] n insomnio

inspect [ɪnˈspɛkt] vt inspeccionar, examinar; (troops) pasar revista a ❑ **inspection** [ɪnˈspɛkʃən] n inspección f, examen m; (of troops) revista ❑ **inspector** n inspector(-a) m/f; (BRIT: on buses, trains) revisor(-a) m/f

inspiration [ɪnspəˈreɪʃən] n inspiración f ❑ **inspire** [ɪnˈspaɪə] vt inspirar ❑ **inspiring** adj inspirador(-a)

instability [ɪnstəˈbɪlɪtɪ] n inestabilidad f

install [ɪnˈstɔːl] (US **instal**) vt instalar; (official) nombrar □ **installation** [ɪnstəˈleɪʃən] n instalación f

instalment [ɪnˈstɔːlmənt] (US **installment**) n plazo; (of story) entrega; (of TV serial etc) capítulo; **in instalments** (pay, receive) a plazos

instance [ˈɪnstəns] n ejemplo, caso; **for ~** por ejemplo; **in the first ~** en primer lugar

instant [ˈɪnstənt] n instante m, momento ♦ adj inmediato; (coffee etc) instantáneo □ **instantly** adv en seguida

instead [ɪnˈsted] adv en cambio; **~ of** en lugar de, en vez de

instinct [ˈɪnstɪŋkt] n instinto □ **instinctive** adj instintivo

institute [ˈɪnstɪtjuːt] n instituto; (professional body) colegio ♦ vt (begin) iniciar, empezar; (proceedings) entablar; (system, rule) establecer

institution [ɪnstɪˈtjuːʃən] n institución f; (MED: home) asilo; (: asylum) manicomio; (of system etc) establecimiento; (of custom) iniciación f

instruct [ɪnˈstrʌkt] vt: **to ~ sb in sth** instruir a algn en o sobre algo; **to ~ sb to do sth** dar instrucciones a algn de hacer algo □ **instruction** n instrucción f; **instructions** npl (orders) órdenes fpl; **instructions (for use)** modo de empleo □ **instructor** n instructor(a) m/f

instrument [ˈɪnstrəmənt] n instrumento □ **instrumental** [-ˈmentl] adj (MUS) instrumental; **to be instrumental in** ser (el) artífice de

insufficient [ɪnsəˈfɪʃənt] adj insuficiente

insulate [ˈɪnsjuleɪt] vt aislar □ **insulation** [-ˈleɪʃən] n aislamiento

insulin [ˈɪnsjulɪn] n insulina

insult [n ˈɪnsʌlt, vb ɪnˈsʌlt] n insulto ♦ vt insultar □ **insulting** adj insultante

insurance [ɪnˈʃuərəns] n seguro; **fire/ life ~** seguro contra incendios/sobre la vida □ **insurance company** n compañía f de seguros □ **insurance policy** n póliza f de seguros

insure [ɪnˈʃuə] vt asegurar

intact [ɪnˈtækt] adj íntegro; (unharmed) intacto

intake [ˈɪnteɪk] n (of food) ingestión f; (of air) consumo; (BRIT SCOL): **an ~ of 200 a year** 200 matriculados al año

integral [ˈɪntɪɡrəl] adj (whole) íntegro; (part) integrante

integrate [ˈɪntɪɡreɪt] vt integrar ♦ vi integrarse

integrity [ɪnˈtɛɡrɪtɪ] n honradez f, rectitud f

intellect [ˈɪntəlekt] n intelecto □ **intellectual** [-ˈlektjuəl] adj, n intelectual mf

intelligence [ɪnˈtelɪdʒəns] n inteligencia

intelligent [ɪnˈtelɪdʒənt] adj inteligente

intend [ɪnˈtend] vt (gift etc): **to ~ sth for** destinar algo a; **to ~ to do sth** tener intención de o pensar hacer algo

intense [ɪnˈtens] adj intenso

intensify [ɪnˈtensɪfaɪ] vt intensificar; (increase) aumentar

intensity [ɪnˈtensɪtɪ] n (gen) intensidad f

intensive [ɪnˈtensɪv] adj intensivo □ **intensive care** n: **to be in intensive care** estar bajo cuidados intensivos □ **intensive care unit** n unidad f de vigilancia intensiva

intent [ɪnˈtent] n propósito; (LAW) premeditación f ♦ adj (absorbed) absorto; (attentive) atento; **to all intents and purposes** prácticamente; **to be ~ on doing sth** estar resuelto a hacer algo

intention [ɪnˈtenʃən] n intención f, propósito □ **intentional** adj deliberado

interact [ɪntər'ækt] *vi* influirse mutuamente □ **interaction** [ɪntər'ækʃən] *n* interacción *f*, acción *f* recíproca ♦ **interactive** *adj* (COMPUT) interactivo

intercept [ɪntə'sept] *vt* interceptar; (*stop*) detener

interchange ['ɪntətʃeɪndʒ] *n* intercambio; (*on motorway*) intersección *f*

intercourse ['ɪntəkɔːs] *n* (*sexual*) relaciones *fpl* sexuales

interest ['ɪntrɪst] *n* (*also* COMM) interés *m* ♦ *vt* interesar □ **interested** *adj* interesado; **to be interested in** interesarse por □ **interesting** *adj* interesante □ **interest rate** *n* tipo or tasa de interés

interface ['ɪntəfeɪs] *n* (COMPUT) junción *f*

interfere [ɪntə'fɪə'] *vi*: **to ~ in** entrometerse en; **to ~ with** (*hinder*) estorbar; (*damage*) estropear □ **interference** [ɪntə'fɪərəns] *n* intromisión *f*; (RADIO, TV) interferencia *f*

interim ['ɪntərɪm] *n*: **in the ~** en el ínterin ♦ *adj* provisional

interior [ɪn'tɪərɪə'] *n* interior *m* ♦ *adj* interior □ **interior design** *n* interiorismo, decoración *f* de interiores

intermediate [ɪntə'miːdɪət] *adj* intermedio

intermission [ɪntə'mɪʃən] *n* intermisión *f*; (THEATRE) descanso

intern [*vb* ɪn'tɜːn, *n* 'ɪntɜːn] (US) *vt* internar ♦ *n* interno(-a)

internal [ɪn'tɜːnl] *adj* (*layout, pipes, security*) interior; (*injury, structure, memo*) interno □ **Internal Revenue Service** (US) *n* departamento de impuestos, = Hacienda (SP)

international [ɪntə'næʃənl] *adj* internacional ♦ *n* (BRIT: *match*) partido internacional

Internet ['ɪntənet] *n*: **the ~** Internet *m* or *f* □ **Internet café** *n* cibercafé *m* □ **Internet Service Provider** *n* proveedor *m* de (acceso a) Internet □ **Internet user** *n* internauta *mf*

interpret [ɪn'tɜːprɪt] *vt* interpretar; (*translate*) traducir; (*understand*) entender ♦ *vi* hacer de intérprete □ **interpretation** [ɪntɜːprɪ'teɪʃən] *n* interpretación *f*; traducción *f* □ **interpreter** *n* intérprete *mf*

interrogate [ɪn'terəugeɪt] *vt* interrogar □ **interrogation** [-'geɪʃən] *n* interrogatorio

interrogative [ɪntə'rɔgətɪv] *adj* interrogativo

interrupt [ɪntə'rʌpt] *vt, vi* interrumpir □ **interruption** [-'rʌpʃən] *n* interrupción *f*

intersection [ɪntə'sekʃən] *n* (*of roads*) cruce *m*

interstate ['ɪntəsteɪt] (US) *n* carretera interestatal

interval ['ɪntəvl] *n* intervalo; (BRIT THEATRE, SPORT) descanso; (SCOL) recreo; **at intervals** a ratos, de vez en cuando

intervene [ɪntə'viːn] *vi* intervenir; (*event*) interponerse; (*time*) transcurrir

interview ['ɪntəvjuː] *n* entrevista ♦ *vt* entrevistarse con □ **interviewer** *n* entrevistador(a) *m/f*

intimate [*adj* 'ɪntɪmət, *vb* 'ɪntɪmeɪt] *adj* íntimo; (*friendship*) estrecho; (*knowledge*) profundo ♦ *vt* dar a entender

intimidate [ɪn'tɪmɪdeɪt] *vt* intimidar, amedrentar

intimidating [ɪn'tɪmɪdeɪtɪŋ] *adj* amedrentador, intimidante

into ['ɪntuː] *prep* en; (*towards*) a; (*inside*) hacia el interior de; **~ 3 pieces/French** en 3 pedazos/al francés

intolerant [ɪn'tɔlərənt] *adj*: **~ (of)** intolerante (con *or* para)

intranet ['ɪntrənet] *n* intranet *f*

intransitive [ɪn'trænsɪtɪv] *adj*
intransitivo

intricate ['ɪntrɪkət] *adj* (design, pattern)
intrincado

intrigue [ɪn'triːg] *n* intriga ♦ *vt* fascinar
❑ **intriguing** *adj* fascinante

introduce [ɪntrə'djuːs] *vt* introducir,
meter; (speaker, TV show etc) presentar;
to ~ sb (to sb) presentar a algn (a algn);
to ~ sb to (pastime, technique)
introducir a algn a ❑ **introduction**
[-'dʌkʃən] *n* introducción *f*; (of person)
presentación *f* ❑ **introductory**
[-'dʌktərɪ] *adj* introductorio; (lesson,
offer) de introducción

intrude [ɪn'truːd] *vi* (person)
entrometerse; to ~ on estorbar
❑ **intruder** *n* intruso(-a)

intuition [ɪntjuː'ɪʃən] *n* intuición *f*

inundate ['ɪnʌndeɪt] *vt*: to ~ with
inundar de

invade [ɪn'veɪd] *vt* invadir

invalid [n 'ɪnvəlɪd, adj ɪn'vælɪd] *n* (MED)
minusválido(-a) ♦ *adj* (not valid)
inválido, nulo

invaluable [ɪn'væljuəbl] *adj*
inestimable

invariably [ɪn'veərɪəblɪ] *adv* sin
excepción, siempre; **she is ~ late**
siempre llega tarde

invasion [ɪn'veɪʒən] *n* invasión *f*

invent [ɪn'vent] *vt* inventar
❑ **invention** [ɪn'venʃən] *n* invento;
(lie) ficción *f*, mentira ❑ **inventor** *n*
inventor(-a) *m/f*

inventory ['ɪnvəntrɪ] *n* inventario

inverted commas [ɪn'vɜːtɪd-] (BRIT)
npl comillas *fpl*

invest [ɪn'vest] *vt* invertir ♦ *vi*: to ~ in
(company etc) invertir dinero en; (fig:
sth useful) comprar

investigate [ɪn'vestɪgeɪt] *vt* investigar
❑ **investigation** [-'geɪʃən] *n*
investigación *f*, pesquisa

investigator [ɪn'vestɪgeɪtə*] *n*
investigador(a) *m/f*; private ~
investigador(a) *m/f* privado(-a)

investment [ɪn'vestmənt] *n* inversión
f

investor [ɪn'vestə*] *n* inversionista *mf*

invisible [ɪn'vɪzɪbl] *adj* invisible

invitation [ɪnvɪ'teɪʃən] *n* invitación *f*

invite [ɪn'vaɪt] *vt* invitar; (opinions etc)
solicitar, pedir ❑ **inviting** *adj*
atractivo; (food) apetitoso

invoice ['ɪnvɔɪs] *n* factura ♦ *vt* facturar

involve [ɪn'vɒlv] *vt* suponer, implicar;
tener que ver con; (concern, affect)
corresponder; to ~ sb (in sth)
comprometer a algn (con algo)
❑ **involved** *adj* complicado; to be
involved in (take part) tomar parte en;
(be engrossed) estar muy metido en
❑ **involvement** *n* participación *f*;
dedicación *f*

inward ['ɪnwəd] *adj* (movement)
interior, interno; (thought, feeling)
íntimo ❑ **inward(s)** *adv* hacia dentro

IQ *n abbr* (= intelligence quotient)
cociente *m* intelectual

IRA *n abbr* (= Irish Republican Army) IRA
m

Iran [ɪ'rɑːn] *n* Irán *m* ❑ **Iranian**
[ɪ'reɪnɪən] *adj, n* iraní *mf*

Iraq [ɪ'rɑːk] *n* Iraq ❑ **Iraqi** *adj, n* iraquí
mf

Ireland ['aɪələnd] *n* Irlanda

iris ['aɪrɪs] (*pl* **irises**) *n* (ANAT) iris *m*; (BOT)
lirio

Irish ['aɪrɪʃ] *adj* irlandés(-esa) ♦ *npl*: the
~ los irlandeses ❑ **Irishman** (irreg) *n*
irlandés *m* ❑ **Irishwoman** (irreg) *n*
irlandésa

iron ['aɪən] *n* hierro; (for clothes)
plancha ♦ *cpd* de hierro ♦ *vt* (clothes)
planchar

ironic(al) [aɪ'rɒnɪk(l)] *adj* irónico
❑ **ironically** *adv* irónicamente

ironing ['aɪənɪŋ] *n* (activity) planchado;
(clothes: ironed) ropa planchada; (: to be

ironed) ropa por planchar ❑ **ironing board** *n* tabla de planchar

irony [ˈaɪrənɪ] *n* ironía

irrational [ɪˈræʃənl] *adj* irracional

irregular [ɪˈregjulə*] *adj* irregular; (*surface*) desigual; (*action, event*) anómalo; (*behaviour*) poco ortodoxo

irrelevant [ɪˈreləvənt] *adj* fuera de lugar, inoportuno

irresistible [ɪrɪˈzɪstɪbl] *adj* irresistible

irresponsible [ɪrɪˈspɔnsɪbl] *adj* (*act*) irresponsable; (*person*) poco serio

irrigation [ɪrɪˈgeɪʃən] *n* riego

irritable [ˈɪrɪtəbl] *adj* (*person*) de mal humor

irritate [ˈɪrɪteɪt] *vt* fastidiar; (*MED*) picar ❑ **irritating** *adj* fastidioso ❑ **irritation** [-ˈteɪʃən] *n* fastidio; enfado; picazón *f*

IRS (*US*) *n abbr* = **Internal Revenue Service**

is [ɪz] *vb* see **be**

ISDN *n abbr* (= *Integrated Services Digital Network*) RDSI *f*

Islam [ˈɪzlɑːm] *n* Islam *m* ❑ **Islamic** [ɪzˈlæmɪk] *adj* islámico

island [ˈaɪlənd] *n* isla ❑ **islander** *n* isleño(-a)

isle [aɪl] *n* isla

isn't [ˈɪznt] = **is not**

isolated [ˈaɪsəleɪtɪd] *adj* aislado

isolation [aɪsəˈleɪʃən] *n* aislamiento

ISP *n abbr* = **Internet Service Provider**

Israel [ˈɪzreɪl] *n* Israel *m* ❑ **Israeli** [ɪzˈreɪlɪ] *adj, n* israelí *mf*

issue [ˈɪsjuː] *n* (*problem, subject*) cuestión *f*; (*outcome*) resultado; (*of banknotes etc*) emisión *f*; (*of newspaper etc*) edición *f* ◆ *vt* (*rations, equipment*) distribuir, repartir; (*orders*) dar; (*certificate, passport*) expedir; (*decree*) promulgar; (*magazine*) publicar; (*cheques*) extender; (*banknotes, stamps*) emitir; **at ~** en cuestión; **to take ~ with sb** (*over*) estar en

desacuerdo con algn (sobre); **to make an ~ of sth** hacer una cuestión de algo

IT *n abbr* = **information technology**

it [ɪt] *pron*

1 (*specific subject: not generally translated*) él (ella); (: *direct object*) lo, la; (: *indirect object*) le; (*after prep*) él (ella); (*abstract concept*) ello; **it's on the table** está en la mesa; **I can't find it** no lo (*o* la) encuentro; **give it to me** dámelo (*o* dámela); **I spoke to him about it** le hablé del asunto; **what did you learn from it?** ¿qué aprendiste de él (*o* ella)?; **did you go to it?** (*party, concert etc*) ¿fuiste?

2 (*impersonal*): **it's raining** llueve, está lloviendo; **it's 6 o'clock/the 10th of August** son las 6/es el 10 de agosto; **how far is it?** — **it's 10 miles/ 2 hours on the train** ¿a qué distancia está? — a 10 millas/2 horas en tren; **who is it?** — **it's me** ¿quién es? — soy yo

Italian [ɪˈtæljən] *adj* italiano ◆ *n* italiano(-a); (*LING*) italiano

italics [ɪˈtælɪks] *npl* cursiva

Italy [ˈɪtəlɪ] *n* Italia

itch [ɪtʃ] *n* picazón *f* ◆ *vi* (*part of body*) picar; **to ~ to do sth** rabiar por hacer algo ❑ **itchy** *adj*: **my hand is itchy** me pica la mano

it'd [ˈɪtd] = **it would; it had**

item [ˈaɪtəm] *n* artículo; (*on agenda*) asunto (a tratar); (*also: news ~*) noticia

itinerary [aɪˈtɪnərərɪ] *n* itinerario

it'll [ˈɪtl] = **it will; it shall**

its [ɪts] *adj* su; sus *pl*

it's [ɪts] = **it is; it has**

itself [ɪtˈself] *pron* (*reflexive*) sí mismo(-a); (*emphatic*) él mismo (ella misma)

ITV n abbr (BRIT: = Independent Television) cadena de televisión comercial independiente del Estado

I've [aɪv] = **I have**

ivory ['aɪvərɪ] n marfil m

ivy ['aɪvɪ] n (BOT) hiedra

J, j

jab [dʒæb] vt: **to ~ sth into sth** clavar algo en algo ♦ n (inf: MED) pinchazo

jack [dʒæk] n (AUT) gato; (CARDS) sota

jacket ['dʒækɪt] n chaqueta, americana (SP), saco (LAm); (of book) sobrecubierta ❑ **jacket potato** n patata asada (con piel)

jackpot ['dʒækpɔt] n premio gordo

Jacuzzi® [dʒə'ku:zɪ] n jacuzzi® m

jagged ['dʒægɪd] adj dentado

jail [dʒeɪl] n cárcel f ♦ vt encarcelar ❑ **jail sentence** n pena f de cárcel

jam [dʒæm] n mermelada; (also: **traffic ~**) embotellamiento; (inf: difficulty) apuro ♦ vt (passage etc) obstruir; (mechanism, drawer etc) atascar; (RADIO) interferir ♦ vi atascarse, trabarse; **to ~ sth into sth** meter algo a la fuerza en algo

Jamaica [dʒə'meɪkə] n Jamaica

jammed [dʒæmd] adj atascado

Jan abbr (= January) ene

janitor ['dʒænɪtə*] n (caretaker) portero, conserje m

January ['dʒænjuərɪ] n enero

Japan [dʒə'pæn] n (el) Japón ❑ **Japanese** [dʒæpə'ni:z] adj japonés(-esa) ♦ n inv japonés(-esa) m/f; (LING) japonés m

jar [dʒɑ:*] n tarro, bote m ♦ vi (sound) chirriar; (colours) desentonar

jargon ['dʒɑ:gən] n jerga

javelin ['dʒævlɪn] n jabalina

jaw [dʒɔ:] n mandíbula

jazz [dʒæz] n jazz m

jealous ['dʒeləs] adj celoso; (envious) envidioso ❑ **jealousy** n celos mpl; envidia

jeans [dʒi:nz] npl vaqueros mpl, tejanos mpl

Jello® ['dʒeləu] (US) n gelatina

jelly ['dʒelɪ] n (jam) jalea; (dessert etc) gelatina ❑ **jellyfish** n inv medusa, aguaviva (RPl)

jeopardize ['dʒepədaɪz] vt arriesgar, poner en peligro

jerk [dʒɜ:k] n (jolt) sacudida; (wrench) tirón m; (inf) imbécil mf ♦ vt tirar bruscamente de ♦ vi (vehicle) traquetear

Jersey ['dʒɜ:zɪ] n Jersey m

jersey ['dʒɜ:zɪ] n jersey m; (fabric) (tejido de) punto

Jesus ['dʒi:zəs] n Jesús m

jet [dʒet] n (of gas, liquid) chorro; (AVIAT) avión m a reacción ❑ **jet lag** n desorientación f después de un largo vuelo ❑ **jet-ski** vi practicar el motociclismo acuático

jetty ['dʒetɪ] n muelle m, embarcadero

Jew [dʒu:] n judío(-a)

jewel ['dʒu:əl] n joya; (in watch) rubí m ❑ **jeweller** (US **jeweler**) n joyero(-a) ❑ **jeweller's (shop)** (US **jewelry store**) n joyería ❑ **jewellery** (US **jewelry**) n joyas fpl, alhajas fpl

Jewish ['dʒu:ɪʃ] adj judío

jigsaw ['dʒɪgsɔ:] n (also: **~ puzzle**) rompecabezas m inv, puzle m

job [dʒɔb] n (task) tarea; (post) empleo; **it's not my ~** no me incumbe a mí; **it's a good ~ that ...** menos mal que ...; **just the ~!** ¡estupendo! ❑ **job centre** (BRIT) n oficina estatal de colocaciones ❑ **jobless** adj sin trabajo

jockey ['dʒɔkɪ] n jockey mf ♦ vi: **to ~ for position** maniobrar para conseguir una posición

jog [dʒɔg] vt empujar (ligeramente) ♦ vi (run) hacer footing; **to ~ sb's memory**

refrescar la memoria a algn ❑ **jogging** n footing m

join [dʒɔɪn] vt (things) juntar, unir; (club) hacerse socio de; (POL: party) afiliarse a; (queue) ponerse en; (meet: people) reunirse con ♦ vi (roads) juntarse; (rivers) confluir ♦ vi n juntura ❑ join in vi tomar parte, participar ♦ vt fus tomar parte or participar en ❑ **join up** vi reunirse; (MIL) alistarse

joiner [ˈdʒɔɪnəʳ] (BRIT) n carpintero(-a)

joint [dʒɔɪnt] n (TECH) junta, unión f; (ANAT) articulación f; (BRIT CULIN) pieza de carne (para asar); (inf: place) tugurio; (: of cannabis) porro ♦ adj (common) común; (combined) combinado ❑ **joint account** n (with bank etc) cuenta común ❑ **jointly** adv (gen) en común; (together) conjuntamente

joke [dʒəʊk] n chiste m; (also: practical ~) broma ♦ vi bromear; **to play a ~** on gastar una broma a ❑ **joker** n (CARDS) comodín m

jolly [ˈdʒɔlɪ] adj (merry) alegre; (enjoyable) divertido ♦ adv (BRIT: inf) muy, terriblemente

jolt [dʒəʊlt] n (jerk) sacudida f; (shock) susto ♦ vt (physically) sacudir; (emotionally) asustar

Jordan [ˈdʒɔːdən] n (country) Jordania; (river) Jordán m

journal [ˈdʒɜːnl] n (magazine) revista; (diary) periódico, diario ❑ **journalism** n periodismo ❑ **journalist** n periodista mf, reportero(-a)

journey [ˈdʒɜːnɪ] n viaje m; (distance covered) trayecto

joy [dʒɔɪ] n alegría ❑ **joyrider** n gamberro que roba un coche para dar una vuelta y luego abandonarlo ❑ **joy stick** n (AVIAT) palanca de mando; (COMPUT) palanca de control

Jr abbr = **junior**

judge [dʒʌdʒ] n juez mf; (fig: expert) perito ♦ vt juzgar; (consider) considerar

judo [ˈdʒuːdəʊ] n judo

jug [dʒʌg] n jarra

juggle [ˈdʒʌgl] vi hacer juegos malabares ❑ **juggler** n malabarista mf

juice [dʒuːs] n zumo (SP), jugo (LAm) ❑ **juicy** adj jugoso

Jul abbr (= July) jul

July [dʒuːˈlaɪ] n julio

jumble [ˈdʒʌmbl] n revoltijo ♦ vt (also: ~ up) revolver ❑ **jumble sale** (BRIT) n venta de objetos usados con fines benéficos

JUMBLE SALE

Los **jumble sales** son unos mercadillos que se organizan con fines benéficos en los locales de un colegio, iglesia u otro centro público. En ellos puede comprarse todo tipo de artículos baratos de segunda mano, sobre todo ropa, juguetes, libros, vajillas o muebles.

jumbo [ˈdʒʌmbəʊ] n (also: ~ jet) jumbo

jump [dʒʌmp] vi saltar, dar saltos; (with fear etc) pegar un bote; (increase) aumentar ♦ vt saltar ♦ n salto; aumento; **to ~ the queue** (BRIT) colarse

jumper [ˈdʒʌmpəʳ] n (BRIT: pullover) suéter m, jersey m; (US: dress) mandil m

jumper cables (US) npl = **jump leads**

jump leads [dʒʌmp liːdz] npl cables mpl puente de batería

Jun. abbr = **junior**

junction [ˈdʒʌŋkʃən] n (BRIT: of roads) cruce m; (RAIL) empalme m

June [dʒuːn] n junio

jungle [ˈdʒʌŋgl] n selva, jungla

junior [ˈdʒuːnɪəʳ] adj (in age) menor, más joven; (brother/sister etc): **seven years her ~** siete años menor que ella; (position) subalterno ♦ n menor mf, joven mf ❑ **junior high school** (US) n centro de educación secundaria; see also **high school** ❑ **junior school** (BRIT) n escuela primaria

junk [dʒʌŋk] n (cheap goods) baratijas fpl; (rubbish) basura □ **junk food** n alimentos preparados y envasados de escaso valor nutritivo

junkie ['dʒʌŋkɪ] n (inf) drogadicto(-a), yonqui mf

junk mail n propaganda de buzón

Jupiter ['dʒu:pɪtə'] n (MYTHOLOGY, ASTROLOGY) Júpiter m

jurisdiction [dʒʊərɪs'dɪkʃən] n jurisdicción f; **it falls** or **comes within/ outside our ~** es/no es de nuestra competencia

jury ['dʒʊərɪ] n jurado

just [dʒʌst] adj justo ♦ adv (exactly) exactamente; (only) sólo, solamente; **he's ~ done it/left** acaba de hacerlo/ irse; **~ right** perfecto; **~ two o'clock** las dos en punto; **she's ~ as clever as you** (ella) es tan lista como tú; **~ as well that ...** menos mal que ...; **~ as he was leaving** en el momento en que se marchaba; **~ before/enough** justo antes/lo suficiente; **~ here** aquí mismo; **he ~ missed** ha fallado por poco; **~ listen to this** escucha esto un momento

justice ['dʒʌstɪs] n justicia; (US: judge) juez mf; **to do ~ to** (fig) hacer justicia a

justification [dʒʌstɪfɪ'keɪʃən] n justificación f

justify ['dʒʌstɪfaɪ] vt justificar; (text) alinear

jut [dʒʌt] vi (also: **~ out**) sobresalir

juvenile ['dʒu:vənaɪl] adj (court) de menores; (humour, mentality) infantil ♦ n menor m de edad

K, k

K abbr (= one thousand) mil; (= kilobyte) kilobyte m, kilooocteto

kangaroo [kæŋɡə'ru:] n canguro

karaoke [kɑ:rə'əʊkɪ] n karaoke

karate [kə'rɑ:tɪ] n karate m

kebab [kə'bæb] n pincho moruno

keel [ki:l] n quilla; **on an even ~** (fig) en equilibrio

keen [ki:n] adj (interest, desire) grande, vivo; (eye, intelligence) agudo; (competition) reñido; (edge) afilado; (eager) entusiasta; **to be ~ to do** or **on doing sth** tener muchas ganas de hacer algo; **to be ~ on sth/sb** interesarse por algo/algn

keep [ki:p] (pt, pp **kept**) vt (preserve, store) guardar; (hold back) quedarse con; (maintain) mantener; (detain) detener; (shop) ser propietario de; (feed: family etc) mantener; (promise) cumplir; (chickens, bees etc) criar; (accounts) llevar; (diary) escribir; (prevent): **to ~ sb from doing sth** impedir a algn hacer algo ♦ vi (food) conservarse; (remain) seguir, continuar ♦ n (of castle) torreón m; (food etc) comida, subsistencia; (inf): **for keeps** para siempre; **to ~ doing sth** seguir haciendo algo; **to ~ sb happy** tener a algn contento; **to ~ a place tidy** mantener un lugar limpio; **to ~ sth to o.s.** guardar algo para sí mismo; **to ~ sth (back) from sb** ocultar algo a algn; **to ~ time** (clock) mantener la hora exacta ► **keep away** vt: **to keep sth/ sb away from sb** mantener algo/a algn apartado de algn ♦ vi: **to keep away (from)** mantenerse apartado (de) ► **keep back** vt (crowd, tears) contener; (money) quedarse con; (conceal: information): **to keep sth back from sb** ocultar algo a algn ♦ vi hacerse a un lado ► **keep off** vt (dog, person) mantener a distancia ♦ vi: **if the rain keeps off** so no lleuve; **keep your hands off!** ¡no toques!; **"keep off the grass"** "prohibido pisar el césped" ► **keep on** vi: **to keep on doing** seguir or continuar haciendo; **to keep on (about sth)** no parar de hablar (de algo) ► **keep out** vi (stay out) permanecer fuera; **"keep out"** "prohibida la entrada" ▸ **keep up** vt mantener, conservar ♦ vi no retrasarse; **to keep up with** (pace) ir al paso de; (level) mantenerse a la altura de ❑ **keeper** n guardián(-ana) m/f ❑ **keeping** n (care) cuidado; **in keeping with** de acuerdo con

kennel ['kɛnl] n perrera; **kennels** npl residencia canina

Kenya ['kɛnjə] n Kenia

kept [kɛpt] pt, pp of **keep**

kerb [kə:b] (BRIT) n bordillo

kerosene ['kɛrəsi:n] n keroseno

ketchup ['kɛtʃəp] n salsa de tomate, catsup M

kettle ['kɛtl] n hervidor m de agua

key [ki:] n llave f; (MUS) tono; (of piano, typewriter) tecla ♦ adj (issue) clave inv ♦ vt (also: ~ in) teclear ❑ **keyboard** n teclado ❑ **keyhole** n ojo (de la cerradura) ❑ **keyring** n llavero

kg abbr (= kilogram) kg

khaki ['kɑ:kɪ] n caqui

kick [kɪk] vt dar una patada or un puntapié a; (inf: habit) quitarse de ♦ vi (horse) dar coces ♦ n patada; puntapié m; (of animal) coz f; (thrill): **he does it for kicks** lo hace por pura diversión ▸ **kick off** vi (SPORT) hacer el saque inicial ❑ **kick-off** n saque inicial; **the kick-off is at 10 o'clock** el partido empieza a las diez

kid [kɪd] n (inf: child) chiquillo(-a); (animal) cabrito; (leather) cabritilla ♦ vi (inf) bromear

kidnap ['kɪdnæp] vt secuestrar ❑ **kidnapping** n secuestro

kidney ['kɪdnɪ] n riñón m ❑ **kidney bean** n judía, alubia

kill [kɪl] vt matar; (murder) asesinar ♦ n matanza; **to ~ time** matar el tiempo ❑ **killer** n asesino(-a) ❑ **killing** n (one) asesinato; (several) matanza; **to make a killing** (fig) hacer su agosto

kiln [kɪln] n horno

kilo ['ki:ləʊ] n kilo ❑ **kilobyte** n (COMPUT) kilobyte m, kiloocteto ❑ **kilogram(me)** n kilo, kilogramo ❑ **kilometre** ['kɪləmi:tə] (US **kilometer**) n kilómetro ❑ **kilowatt** n kilovatio

kilt [kɪlt] n falda escocesa

kin [kɪn] n see **next-of-kin**

kind [kaɪnd] adj amable, atento ♦ n clase f, especie f; (species) género; **in ~** (COMM) en especie; **a ~ of** una especie de; **to be two of a ~** ser tal para cual

kindergarten ['kɪndəgɑ:tn] n jardín m de la infancia

kindly ['kaɪndlɪ] adj bondadoso; cariñoso ♦ adv bondadosamente, amablemente; **will you ~ ...** sea usted tan amable de ...

kindness ['kaɪndnɪs] n (quality) bondad f, amabilidad f; (act) favor m

king [kɪŋ] n rey m ❑ **kingdom** n reino ❑ **kingfisher** n martín m pescador ❑ **king-size(d) bed** n cama de matrimonio extragrande

kiosk ['ki:ɔsk] n quiosco; (BRIT TEL) cabina

kipper ['kɪpə'] n arenque m ahumado

kiss [kɪs] n beso ♦ vt besar; **to ~ (each other)** besarse ❑ **kiss of life** n respiración f boca a boca

kit [kɪt] n (equipment) equipo; (tools etc) (caja de herramientas fpl; (assembly kit) juego de armar

kitchen ['kɪtʃɪn] n cocina

kite [kaɪt] n (toy) cometa

kitten ['kɪtn] n gatito(-a)

kiwi ['ki:wi:-] n (also: ~ fruit) kiwi m

km abbr (= kilometre) km

km/h abbr (= kilometres per hour) km/h

knack [næk] n: **to have the ~ of doing sth** tener el don de hacer algo

knee [ni:] n rodilla ❑ **kneecap** n rótula

kneel [ni:l] (pt, pp **knelt**) vi (also: ~ down) arrodillarse

knelt [nɛlt] pt, pp of **kneel**

knew [nju:] pt of **know**

knickers ['nɪkəz] (BRIT) npl bragas fpl

knife [naɪf] (pl **knives**) n cuchillo ♦ vt acuchillar

knight [naɪt] n caballero; (CHESS) caballo

knit [nɪt] vt tejer, tricotar ♦ vi hacer punto, tricotar; (bones) soldarse; **to ~ one's brows** fruncir el ceño ❏ **knitting** n labor f de punto ❏ **knitting needle** n aguja de hacer punto ❏ **knitwear** n prendas fpl de punto

knives [naɪvz] npl of **knife**

knob [nɔb] n (of door) tirador m; (of stick) puño; (on radio, TV) botón m

knock [nɔk] vt (strike) golpear; (bump into) chocar contra; (inf) criticar ♦ vi (at door etc) **to ~ at/on** llamar a ♦ n golpe m; (on door) llamada ► **knock down** vt atropellar ► **knock off** (inf) vi (finish) salir del trabajo ♦ vt (from price) descontar; (inf: steal) birlar ► **knock out** vt dejar sin sentido; (BOXING) poner fuera de combate, dejar K.O.; (in competition) eliminar ► **knock over** vt (object) tirar; (person) atropellar ❏ **knockout** n (BOXING) K.O. m, knockout m ♦ cpd (competition etc) eliminatorio

knot [nɔt] n nudo m ♦ vt anudar

know [nəu] (pt **knew**, pp **known**) vt (facts) saber; (be acquainted with) conocer; (recognize) reconocer, conocer; **to ~ how to swim** saber nadar; **to ~ about/of sb/sth** saber de algn/algo ❏ **know-all** n sabelotodo mf ❏ **know-how** n conocimientos mpl ❏ **knowing** adj (look) de complicidad ❏ **knowingly** adv (purposely) adrede; (smile, look) con complicidad ❏ **know-it-all** (US) n = **know-all**

knowledge ['nɔlɪdʒ] n conocimiento; (learning) saber m, conocimientos mpl ❏ **knowledgeable** adj entendido

known [nəun] pp of **know** ♦ adj (thief, facts) conocido; (expert) reconocido

knuckle ['nʌkl] n nudillo

koala [kəu'ɑ:lə] n (also: ~ **bear**) koala m

Koran [kɔ'rɑ:n] n Corán m

Korea [kə'rɪə] n Corea ❏ **Korean** adj, n coreano(-a) m/f

kosher ['kəuʃə'] adj autorizado por la ley judía

Kosovar, Kosovan adj kosovar

Kosovo ['kusəvəu] n Kosovo m

Kremlin ['kremlɪn] n: **the ~** el Kremlin

Kuwait [ku'weɪt] n Kuwait m

L, l

L (BRIT) abbr = **learner driver**

l. abbr (= litre) l

lab [læb] n abbr = **laboratory**

label ['leɪbl] n etiqueta ♦ vt poner etiqueta a

labor etc ['leɪbə'] (US) = **labour** etc

laboratory [lə'bɔrətərɪ] n laboratorio

Labor Day (US) n día m de los trabajadores (primer lunes de septiembre)

labor union (US) n sindicato

labour ['leɪbə'] (US **labor**) n (hard work) trabajo; (labour force) mano f de obra; (MED): **to be in ~** estar de parto ♦ vi: **to ~ (at sth)** trabajar (en algo) ♦ vt: **to ~ a point** insistir en un punto; **L~, the L~ party** (BRIT) el partido laborista, los laboristas mpl ❏ **labourer** n peón m; **farm labourer** peón m; (day labourer) jornalero

lace [leɪs] n encaje m; (of shoe etc) cordón m ♦ vt (shoes: also: ~ **up**) atarse (los zapatos)

lack [læk] n (absence) falta ♦ vt faltarle a algn, carecer de; **through** or **for** ~ of por falta de; **to be lacking** faltar, no haber; **to be lacking in sth** faltarle a algn algo

lacquer ['lækə] n laca

lacy ['leɪsɪ] adj (of lace) de encaje; (like lace) como de encaje

lad [læd] n muchacho, chico

ladder ['lædə] n escalera (de mano); (BRIT: in tights) carrera

ladle ['leɪdl] n cucharón m

lady ['leɪdɪ] n señora; (dignified, graceful) dama; **"ladies and gentlemen ..."** "señoras y caballeros ..."; **young ~** señorita; **the ladies' (room)** los servicios de señoras □ **ladybird** (BRIT), **ladybug** n mariquita

lag [læg] n retraso ♦ vi (also: ~ **behind**) retrasarse, quedarse atrás ♦ vt (pipes) revestir

lager ['lɑːgə] n cerveza (rubia)

lagoon [lə'guːn] n laguna

laid [leɪd] pt, pp of **lay** □ **laid back** (inf) adj relajado

lain [leɪn] pp of **lie**

lake [leɪk] n lago

lamb [læm] n cordero; (meat) (carne f de) cordero

lame [leɪm] adj cojo; (excuse) poco convincente

lament [lə'ment] n quejo ♦ vt lamentarse de

lamp [læmp] n lámpara □ **lamppost** (BRIT) n (poste m de) farol □ **lampshade** n pantalla

land [lænd] n tierra; (country) país m; (piece of land) terreno; (estate) tierras fpl, finca ♦ vi (from ship) desembarcar; (AVIAT) aterrizar; (fig: fall) caer, terminar ♦ vt (passengers, goods) desembarcar; **to ~ sb with sth** (inf) hacer cargar a algn con algo □ **landing** n aterrizaje m; (of staircase) rellano □ **landing card** n tarjeta de desembarque □ **landlady** n (of rented house, pub etc) dueña □ **landlord** n propietario; (of pub etc) patrón m □ **landmark** n lugar m conocido; **to be a landmark** (fig) marcar un hito histórico □ **landowner** n terrateniente mf

□ **landscape** n paisaje m □ **landslide** n (GEO) corrimiento de tierras; (fig: POL) victoria arrolladora

lane [leɪn] n (in country) camino; (AUT) carril m; (in race) calle f

language ['læŋgwɪdʒ] n lenguaje m; (national tongue) idioma m, lengua; **bad ~** palabrotas fpl □ **language laboratory** n laboratorio de idiomas

lantern ['læntən] n linterna, farol m

lap [læp] n (of track) vuelta; (of body) regazo ♦ vt (also: ~ **up**) beber a lengüetadas ♦ vi (waves) chapotear; **to sit on sb's ~** sentarse en las rodillas de algn

lapel [lə'pel] n solapa

lapse [læps] n fallo; (moral) desliz m; (of time) intervalo ♦ vi (expire) caducar; (time) pasar, transcurrir; **to ~ into bad habits** caer en malos hábitos

laptop (computer) ['læptɒp-] n (ordenador m) portátil m

lard [lɑːd] n manteca (de cerdo)

larder ['lɑːdə] n despensa

large [lɑːdʒ] adj grande; **at ~** (free) en libertad; (generally) en general □ **largely** adv (mostly) en su mayor parte; (introducing reason) en gran parte □ **large-scale** adj (map) en gran escala; (fig) importante

⚠️ Be careful not to translate **large** by the Spanish word largo.

lark [lɑːk] n (bird) alondra; (joke) broma

laryngitis [lærɪn'dʒaɪtɪs] n laringitis f

lasagne [lə'zænjə] n lasaña

laser ['leɪzə'] n láser m □ **laser printer** n impresora (por) láser

lash [læʃ] n latigazo; (also: **eyelash**) pestaña ♦ vt azotar; (tie): **to ~ to/ together** atar a/atar ▶ **lash out** vi: **to lash out (at sb)** (hit) arremeter (contra algn); **to lash out against sb** lanzar invectivas contra algn

lass [læs] (BRIT) n chica

last ['lɑːst] adj último; (end: of series etc) final ♦ adv (most recently) la última vez; (finally) por último ♦ vi durar; (continue) continuar, seguir; **~ night** anoche; **~ week** la semana pasada; **at ~** por fin; **~ but one** penúltimo □ **lastly** adv por último, finalmente □ **last-minute** adj de última hora

latch [lætʃ] n pestillo ▶ **latch onto** vt fus (person, group) pegarse a; (idea) agarrarse a

late [leɪt] adj (far on: in time, process etc) al final de; (not on time) tarde, atrasado; (dead) fallecido ♦ adv tarde; (behind time, schedule) con retraso; **of ~** últimamente; **at night** a la última hora de la noche; **in ~ May** hacia fines de mayo; **the ~ Mr X** el difunto Sr X □ **latecomer** n recién llegado(-a) □ **lately** adv últimamente □ **later** adj (date etc) posterior; (version etc) más reciente ♦ adv más tarde, después □ **latest** ['leɪtɪst] adj último; **at the latest** a más tardar

lather ['lɑːðə'] n espuma (de jabón) ♦ vt enjabonar

Latin ['lætɪn] n latín m ♦ adj latino □ **Latin America** n América latina □ **Latin American** adj, n latinoamericano(-a) m/f

latitude ['lætɪtjuːd] n latitud f; (fig) libertad f

latter ['lætə'] adj (second) segundo ♦ n: **the ~** el último, éste

laugh [lɑːf] n risa ♦ vi reír(se); (to do sth) **for a ~** (hacer algo) en broma ▶ **laugh at** vt fus reírse de □ **laughter** n risa

launch [lɔːntʃ] n lanzamiento m; (boat) lancha ♦ vt (ship) botar; (rocket etc) lanzar; (fig) comenzar ▶ **launch into** vt fus lanzarse a

launder ['lɔːndə'] vt lavar

Launderette® [lɔːn'drɛt] (BRIT) n lavandería (automática)

Laundromat® ['lɔːndrəmæt] (US) n = **Launderette**

laundry ['lɔːndrɪ] n (dirty) ropa sucia; (clean) colada; (room) lavadero

lava ['lɑːvə] n lava

lavatory ['lævətəri] n wáter m

lavender ['lævəndə'] n lavanda

lavish ['lævɪʃ] adj (amount) abundante; (person): **~ with** pródigo en ♦ vt: **to ~ sth on sb** colmar a algn de algo

law [lɔː] n ley f; (SCOL) derecho; (a rule) regla; (professions connected with law) jurisprudencia □ **lawful** adj legítimo, lícito □ **lawless** adj (action) criminal

lawn [lɔːn] n césped m □ **lawnmower** n cortacésped m

lawsuit ['lɔːsuːt] n pleito

lawyer ['lɔːjə'] n abogado(-a); (for sales, wills etc) notario(-a)

lax [læks] adj laxo

laxative ['læksətɪv] n laxante m

lay [leɪ] (pt, pp **laid**) pt of **lie** ♦ adj laico; (not expert) lego ♦ vt (place) colocar; (eggs, table) poner; (cable) tender; (carpet) extender ▶ **lay down** vt (pen etc) dejar; (rules etc) establecer; **to lay down the law** (pej) imponer las normas ▶ **lay off** vt (workers) despedir ▶ **lay on** vt (meal, facilities) proveer ▶ **lay out** vt (spread out) disponer, exponer □ **lay-by** n (BRIT AUT) área de aparcamiento

layer ['leɪə'] n capa

layman ['leɪmən] (irreg) n lego

layout ['leɪaut] n (design) plan m, trazado; (PRESS) composición f

lazy ['leɪzɪ] adj perezoso, vago; (movement) lento

lb. abbr = **pound** (weight)

lead¹ [liːd] (pt, pp **led**) n (front position) delantera; (clue) pista; (ELEC) cable m; (for dog) correa; (THEATRE) papel m principal ♦ vt (walk etc in front) ir a la cabeza de; (guide): **to ~ sb somewhere** conducir a algn a algún sitio; (be leader) dirigir; (start, guide: activity) protagonizar ♦ vi (road, pipe etc) conducir a; (SPORT) ir primero; **to be in**

the ~ (SPORT) llevar la delantera; (fig) ir a la cabeza; **to ~ the way** llevar la delantera ► **lead up to** vt fus (events) conducir a; (in conversation) preparar el terreno para

lead² [lɛd] n (metal) plomo; (in pencil) mina

leader ['liːdə'] n jefe(-a) m/f, líder mf; (SPORT) líder mf ❏ **leadership** n dirección f; (position) mando; (quality) iniciativa

lead-free ['lɛdfriː] adj sin plomo

leading ['liːdɪŋ] adj (main) principal; (first) primero; (front) delantero

lead singer [liːd-] n cantante mf

leaf [liːf] (pl **leaves**) n hoja ♦ vi: **to ~ through** hojear; **to turn over a new ~** reformarse

leaflet ['liːflɪt] n folleto

league [liːg] n sociedad f; (FOOTBALL) liga; **to be in ~ with** haberse confabulado con

leak [liːk] n (of liquid, gas) escape m, fuga; (in pipe) agujero; (in roof) gotera; (in security) filtración f ♦ vi (shoes, ship) hacer agua; (pipe) tener (un) escape; (roof) gotear; (liquid, gas) escaparse, fugarse; (fig) divulgarse ♦ vt (fig) filtrar

lean [liːn] (pt, pp **leaned** or **leant**) adj (thin) flaco; (meat) magro ♦ vt: **to ~ sth on sth** apoyar algo en algo ♦ vi (slope) inclinarse; **to ~ against** apoyarse contra; **to ~ on** apoyarse en ► **lean forward** vi inclinarse hacia adelante ► **lean over** vi inclinarse ❏ **leaning (towards)** inclinación f (hacia)

leant [lɛnt] pt, pp of **lean**

leap [liːp] (pt, pp **leaped** or **leapt**) n salto ♦ vi saltar

leapt [lɛpt] pt, pp of **leap**

leap year n año bisiesto

learn [lɜːn] (pt, pp **learned** or **learnt**) vt aprender ♦ vi aprender; **to ~ about sth** enterarse de algo; **to ~ to do sth** aprender a hacer algo ❏ **learner** n (BRIT: also: **learner driver**)

mf ❏ **learning** n el saber m, conocimientos mpl

learnt [lɜːnt] pp of **learn**

lease [liːs] n arriendo ♦ vt arrendar

leash [liːʃ] n correa

least [liːst] adj: **the ~** (slightest) el menor, el más pequeño; (smallest amount of) mínimo ♦ adv (+ vb) menos; (+ adj): **the ~ expensive** el (la) menos costoso(-a); **the ~ possible effort** el menor esfuerzo posible; **at ~** por lo menos, al menos; **you could at ~ have written** por lo menos podías haber escrito; **not in the ~** en absoluto

leather ['lɛðə'] n cuero

leave [liːv] (pt, pp **left**) vt dejar; (go away from) abandonar; (place etc: permanently) salir de ♦ vi irse; (train etc) salir ♦ n permiso; **to ~ sth to sb** (money etc) legar algo a algn; (responsibility etc) encargar a algn de algo; **to be left** quedar, sobrar; **there's some milk left over** sobra or queda algo de leche; **on ~** de permiso ► **leave behind** vt (on purpose) dejar; (accidentally) dejarse ► **leave out** vt omitir

leaves [liːvz] npl of **leaf**

Lebanon ['lɛbənən] n: **the ~** el Líbano

lecture ['lɛktʃə'] n conferencia; (SCOL) clase f ♦ vi dar una clase ♦ vt (scold): **to ~ sb on** or **about sth** echar una reprimenda a algn por algo; **to give a ~ on** dar una conferencia sobre ❏ **lecture hall** n sala de conferencias; (UNIV) aula ❏ **lecturer** n conferenciante mf; (BRIT: at university) profesor(a) m/f ❏ **lecture theatre** n = **lecture hall**

led [lɛd] pt, pp of **lead¹**

ledge [lɛdʒ] n repisa; (of window) alféizar m; (of mountain) saliente m

leek [liːk] n puerro

left [lɛft] pt, pp of **leave** ♦ adj izquierdo; (remaining): **there are two ~** quedan dos ♦ n izquierda ♦ adv a la izquierda; **on** or **to the ~** a la izquierda; **the L-**

(POL) la izquierda ❑ **left-hand** adj: **the left-hand side** la izquierda ❑ **left-hand drive** adj: **a left-hand drive** un cochecon el volante a la izquierda ❑ **left-handed** adj zurdo ❑ **left-luggage locker** n (BRIT) consigna f automática ❑ **left-luggage (office)** (BRIT) n consigna f ❑ **left-overs** npl sobras fpl ❑ **left-wing** adj (POL) de izquierdas, izquierdista

legacy ['lɛgəsɪ] n herencia

legal ['li:gl] adj (permitted by law) lícito; (of law) legal ❑ **legal holiday** (US) n fiesta oficial ❑ **legalize** vt legalizar ❑ **legally** adv legalmente

legend ['lɛdʒənd] n (also fig: person) leyenda ❑ **legendary** [-ərɪ] adj legendario

leggings ['lɛgɪŋz] npl mallas fpl, leggins mpl

legible ['lɛdʒəbl] adj legible

legislation [lɛdʒɪs'leɪʃən] n legislación f

legislative ['lɛdʒɪslətɪv] adj legislativo

legitimate [lɪ'dʒɪtɪmət] adj legítimo

leisure ['lɛʒə*] n ocio, tiempo libre m; **at ~** con tranquilidad ❑ **leisure centre** (BRIT) n centro de recreo ❑ **leisurely** adj sin prisa; lento

lemon ['lɛmən] n limón m ❑ **lemonade** n (fizzy) gaseosa ❑ **lemon tea** n té m con limón

lend [lɛnd] (pt, pp **lent**) vt: **to ~ sth to sb** prestar algo a algn

length [lɛŋθ] n (size) largo, longitud f; (distance): **the ~ of** todo lo largo de; (of swimming pool, cloth) largo; (of wood, string) trozo; (amount of time) duración f; **at ~** (at last) por fin, finalmente; (lengthily) largamente ❑ **lengthen** vt alargar ♦ vi alargarse ❑ **lengthways**

adv a lo largo ❑ **lengthy** adj largo, extenso

lens [lɛnz] n (of spectacles) lente f; (of camera) objetivo

Lent [lɛnt] n Cuaresma

lent [lɛnt] pt, pp of **lend**

lentil ['lɛntl] n lenteja

Leo ['li:əu] n Leo

leopard ['lɛpəd] n leopardo

leotard ['li:əta:d] n mallas fpl

leprosy ['lɛprəsɪ] n lepra

lesbian ['lɛzbɪən] n lesbiana

less [lɛs] adj (in size, degree etc) menor; (in quality) menos ♦ pron, adv menos ♦ prep: **~ tax/10% discount** menos impuestos/el 10 por ciento de descuento; **~ than half** menos de la mitad; **~ than ever** menos que nunca; **~ and ~** cada vez menos; **the ~ he works ...** cuanto menos trabaja ... ❑ **lessen** vi disminuir, reducirse ♦ vt disminuir, reducir ❑ **lesser** ['lɛsə*] adj menor; **to a lesser extent** en menor grado

lesson ['lɛsn] n clase f; (warning) lección f

let [lɛt] (pt, pp **let**) vt (allow) dejar, permitir; (BRIT: lease) alquilar; **to ~ sb do sth** dejar que algn haga algo; **to ~ sb know sth** comunicar algo a algn; **~'s go** ¡vamos!; **~ him come** que venga; **"to ~"** "se alquila" ▶ **let down** vt (tyre) desinflar; (disappoint) defraudar ▶ **let in** vt dejar entrar; (visitor etc) hacer pasar ▶ **let off** vt (culprit) dejar escapar; (gun) disparar; (bomb) accionar; (firework) hacer estallar ▶ **let out** vt dejar salir; (sound) soltar

lethal ['li:θl] adj (weapon) mortífero; (poison, wound) mortal

letter ['lɛtə*] n (of alphabet) letra; (correspondence) carta ❑ **letterbox** (BRIT) n buzón m

lettuce ['lɛtɪs] n lechuga

leukaemia [lu:'ki:mɪə] (US **leukemia**) n leucemia

level ['lɛvl] *adj* (*flat*) llano ♦ *adv*: **to draw ~ with** llegar a la altura de ♦ *n* nivel *m*; (*height*) altura ♦ *vt* nivelar; allanar; (*destroy*: *building*) derribar; (*: forest*) arrasar; **to be ~ with** = exámenes *mpl* de bachillerato superior, B.U.P.; **on the ~** (*fig*: *honest*) serio ❑ **level crossing** (*BRIT*) *n* paso a nivel

lever ['liːvəʳ] *n* (*also fig*) palanca ♦ *vt*: **to ~ up** levantar con palanca ❑ **leverage** *n* (*using bar etc*) apalancamiento *m*; (*fig*: *influence*) influencia

levy ['lɛvɪ] *n* impuesto ♦ *vt* exigir, recaudar

liability [laɪə'bɪlɪtɪ] *n* (*pej*: *person, thing*) estorbo, lastre *m*; (*JUR*: *responsibility*) responsabilidad *f*

liable ['laɪəbl] *adj* (*subject*): **~ to** sujeto a; (*responsible*): **~ for** responsable de; (*likely*): **~ to do** propenso a hacer

liaise [lɪ'eɪz] *vi*: **to ~ with** enlazar con

liar ['laɪəʳ] *n* mentiroso(-a)

liberal ['lɪbərəl] *adj* liberal; (*offer, amount etc*) generoso ❑ **Liberal Democrat** *n* (*BRIT*) demócrata *m/f* liberal

liberate ['lɪbəreɪt] *vt* (*people*: *from poverty etc*) librar; (*prisoner*) libertar; (*country*) liberar

liberation [lɪbə'reɪʃən] *n* liberación *f*

liberty ['lɪbətɪ] *n* libertad *f*; **to be at ~** (*criminal*) estar libre; **to be at ~ to do** estar libre para hacer; **to take the ~ of doing sth** tomarse la libertad de hacer algo

Libra ['liːbrə] *n* Libra

librarian [laɪ'brɛərɪən] *n* bibliotecario(-a)

library ['laɪbrərɪ] *n* biblioteca

⚠ Be careful not to translate **library** by the Spanish word *librería*.

Libya ['lɪbɪə] *n* Libia

lice [laɪs] *npl of* **louse**

licence ['laɪsəns] (*US* **license**) *n* licencia; (*permit*) permiso; (*also*: **driving ~**) carnet *m* de conducir (*SP*), licencia de manejo (*LAm*)

license ['laɪsəns] *n* (*US*) = **licence** ♦ *vt* autorizar, dar permiso a ❑ **licensed** *adj* (*for alcohol*) autorizado para vender bebidas alcohólicas; (*car*) matriculado ❑ **license plate** (*US*) *n* placa (de matrícula) ❑ **licensing hours** (*BRIT*) *npl* horas durante las cuales se permite la venta y consumo de alcohol (*en un bar etc*)

lick [lɪk] *vt* lamer; (*inf*: *defeat*) dar una paliza a; **to ~ one's lips** relamerse

lid [lɪd] *n* (*of box, case*) tapa; (*of pan*) tapadera

lie [laɪ] (*pt* **lay**, *pp* **lain**) *vi* (*rest*) estar echado, estar acostado; (*of object*: *be situated*) estar, encontrarse; (*tell lies*: *pt, pp lied*) mentir ♦ *n* mentira; **to ~ low** (*fig*) mantenerse a escondidas ▶ **lie about** *or* **around** *vi* (*things*) estar tirado; (*person*: *people*) estar tumbado ▶ **lie down** *vi* echarse, tumbarse

Liechtenstein ['lɪktənstaɪn] *n* Liechtenstein *m*

lie-in ['laɪɪn] (*BRIT*) *n*: **to have a ~** quedarse en la cama

lieutenant [lɛf'tɛnənt, *US* luː'tɛnənt] *n* (*MIL*) teniente *mf*

life [laɪf] (*pl* **lives**) *n* vida; **to come to ~** animarse ❑ **life assurance** (*BRIT*) *n* seguro de vida ❑ **lifeboat** *n* lancha de socorro ❑ **lifeguard** *n* vigilante *mf*, socorrista *mf* ❑ **life insurance** *n* = **life assurance** ❑ **life jacket** *n* chaleco salvavidas ❑ **lifelike** *adj* (*model etc*) que parece vivo; (*realistic*) realista ❑ **life preserver** (*US*) *n* cinturón *m*/chaleco salvavidas ❑ **life sentence** *n* cadena perpetua ❑ **lifestyle** *n* estilo de vida ❑ **lifetime** *n* (*of person*) vida; (*of thing*) período de vida

lift [lɪft] *vt* levantar; (*end*: *ban, rule*) levantar, suprimir ♦ *vi* (*fog*) disiparse

light [BRIT: *machine*] ascensor *m*; **to give sb a ~** (BRIT) llevar a algn en el coche ♦ **lift up** vt levantar ❑ **lift-off** *n* despegue *m*

light [laɪt] (pt, pp **lighted** or **lit**) *n* luz *f*; (*lamp*) luz *f*, lámpara; (AUT) faro; (for *cigarette etc*) **have you got a ~?** ¿tienes fuego? ♦ vt (*candle, cigarette, fire*) encender (SP), prender (LAm); (*room*) alumbrar ♦ adj (*colour*) claro; (*not heavy, also fig*) ligero; (*room*) con mucha luz; (*gentle, graceful*) ágil; **lights** npl (*traffic lights*) semáforos mpl; **to come to ~** salir a luz; **in the ~ of** (*new evidence etc*) a la luz de ♦ **light up** vi (*smoke*) encender un cigarrillo; (*face*) iluminarse ♦ vt (*illuminate*) iluminar, alumbrar; (*set fire to*) encender ❑ **light bulb** *n* bombilla (SP), foco (MEX), bujía (CAm), bombita (RPl) ❑ **lighten** vt (*make less heavy*) aligerar ❑ **lighter** *n* (*also: cigarette lighter*) encendedor *m*, mechero ❑ **light-hearted** adj (*person*) alegre; (*remark etc*) divertido ❑ **lighthouse** *n* faro ❑ **lighting** *n* (*system*) alumbrado ❑ **lightly** adv ligeramente; (*not seriously*) con poca seriedad; **to get off lightly** ser castigado con poca severidad

lightning [ˈlaɪtnɪŋ] *n* relámpago, rayo

lightweight [ˈlaɪtweɪt] adj (*suit*) ligero ♦ *n* (BOXING) peso ligero

like [laɪk] vt gustarle a algn ♦ prep como ♦ adj parecido, semejante ♦ *n*: **and the ~** y otros por el estilo; **his likes and dislikes** sus gustos y aversiones; **I would ~, I'd ~** me gustaría; (for *purchase*) quisiera; **would you ~ a coffee?** ¿te apetece un café?; **I ~ swimming** me gusta nadar; **she likes apples** le gustan las manzanas; **to be** or **look ~ sb/sth** parecerse a algn/algo; **what does it look/taste/sound ~?** ¿cómo es/a qué sabe/cómo suena?; **that's just ~ him** es muy de él, es característico de él; **do it ~ this** hazlo así; **it is nothing ~ ...** no tiene parecido

alguno con ... ❑ **likeable** adj simpático, agradable

likelihood [ˈlaɪklɪhʊd] *n* probabilidad *f*

likely [ˈlaɪklɪ] adj probable; **he's ~ to leave** es probable que se vaya; **not ~!** ¡ni hablar!

likewise [ˈlaɪkwaɪz] adv igualmente; **to do ~** hacer lo mismo

liking [ˈlaɪkɪŋ] *n*: **~ (for)** (*person*) cariño (a); (*thing*) afición (a); **to be to sb's ~** ser del gusto de algn

lilac [ˈlaɪlək] *n* (*tree*) lilo; (*flower*) lila

Lilo® [ˈlaɪləʊ] *n* colchoneta inflable

lily [ˈlɪlɪ] *n* lirio, azucena; **~ of the valley** *n* lirio de los valles

limb [lɪm] *n* miembro

limbo [ˈlɪmbəʊ] *n*: **to be in ~** (*fig*) quedar a la expectativa

lime [laɪm] *n* (*tree*) limero; (*fruit*) lima; (GEO) cal *f*

limelight [ˈlaɪmlaɪt] *n*: **to be in the ~** (*fig*) ser el centro de atención

limestone [ˈlaɪmstəʊn] *n* piedra caliza

limit [ˈlɪmɪt] *n* límite *m* ♦ vt limitar ❑ **limited** adj limitado; **to be limited to** limitarse a

limousine [ˈlɪməziːn] *n* limusina

limp [lɪmp] *n*: **to have a ~** tener cojera ♦ vi cojear ♦ adj flojo; (*material*) fláccido

line [laɪn] *n* línea; (*rope*) cuerda; (for *fishing*) sedal *m*; (*wire*) hilo; (*row, series*) fila, hilera; (of *writing*) renglón *m*, línea; (of *song*) verso; (on *face*) arruga; (RAIL) vía ♦ vt (*road etc*) llenar; (SEWING) forrar; **to ~ the streets** llenar las aceras; **in ~ with** alineado con; (*according to*) de acuerdo con ♦ **line up** vi hacer cola ♦ vt alinear; (*prepare*) preparar; organizar

linear [ˈlɪnɪəʳ] adj lineal

linen [ˈlɪnɪn] *n* ropa blanca; (*cloth*) lino

liner [ˈlaɪnəʳ] *n* vapor *m* de línea, transatlántico; (for *bin*) bolsa (de basura)

line-up ['laɪnʌp] n (US: queue) cola; (SPORT) alineación f

linger ['lɪŋgə] vi retrasarse, tardar en marcharse; (smell, tradition) persistir

lingerie ['lænʒəri] n lencería

linguist ['lɪŋgwɪst] n lingüista mf □ **linguistic** adj lingüístico

lining ['laɪnɪŋ] n forro; (ANAT) (membrana) mucosa

link [lɪŋk] n (of a chain) eslabón m; (relationship) relación f, vínculo; (INTERNET) link m, enlace m ♦ vt vincular, unir; (associate): **to ~ with** or **to** relacionar con; **links** (GOLF) campo de golf ▶ **link up** vt acoplar ♦ vi unirse

lion [laɪən] n león m □ **lioness** n leona

lip [lɪp] n labio □ **lipread** vi leer los labios □ **lip salve** n crema protectora para labios □ **lipstick** n lápiz m de labios, carmín m

liqueur [lɪ'kjuə] n licor m

liquid ['lɪkwɪd] adj, n líquido □ **liquidizer** [-aɪzə] n licuadora

liquor ['lɪkə] n licor m, bebidas fpl alcohólicas □ **liquor store** (US) n bodega, tienda de vinos y bebidas alcohólicas

Lisbon ['lɪzbən] n Lisboa

lisp [lɪsp] n ceceo ♦ vi cecear

list [lɪst] n lista ♦ vt (mention) enumerar; (put on a list) poner en una lista

listen ['lɪsn] vi escuchar, oír; **to ~ to sb/ sth** escuchar a algn/algo □ **listener** n oyente mf; (RADIO) radioyente mf

lit [lɪt] pt, pp of **light**

liter ['liːtə] (US) n = **litre**

literacy ['lɪtərəsɪ] n capacidad f de leer y escribir

literal ['lɪtərl] adj literal □ **literally** adv literalmente

literary ['lɪtərərɪ] adj literario

literate ['lɪtərət] adj que sabe leer y escribir; (educated) culto

literature ['lɪtərɪtʃə] n literatura; (brochures etc) folletos mpl

litre ['liːtə] (US **liter**) n litro

litter ['lɪtə] n (rubbish) basura; (young animals) camada, cría □ **litter bin** (BRIT) n papelera □ **littered** adj: **littered with** (scattered) lleno de

little ['lɪtl] adj (small) pequeño; (not much) poco ♦ adv poco; **a ~** un poco (de); **~ house/bird** casita/pajarito; **a ~ bit** un poquito; **~ by ~** poco a poco □ **little finger** n dedo meñique

live[1] [laɪv] adj (animal) vivo; (wire) conectado; (broadcast) en directo; (shell) cargado

live[2] [lɪv] vi vivir ▶ **live together** vi vivir juntos ▶ **live up to** vt fus (fulfil) cumplir con

livelihood ['laɪvlɪhud] n sustento

lively ['laɪvlɪ] adj vivo; (interesting: place, book) animado

liven up ['laɪvn-] vt animar ♦ vi animarse

liver ['lɪvə] n hígado

lives [laɪvz] npl of **life**

livestock ['laɪvstɔk] n ganado

living ['lɪvɪŋ] adj (alive) vivo ♦ n: **to earn** or **make a ~** ganarse la vida □ **living room** n sala (de estar)

lizard ['lɪzəd] n lagarto; (small) lagartija

load [ləud] n carga; (weight) peso ♦ vt (COMPUT) cargar; (also: **~ up**): **to ~ (with)** cargar (con or de); **a ~ of rubbish** (inf) tonterías fpl; **a ~ of, loads of** (fig) (gran) cantidad de, montones de □ **loaded** adj (vehicle): **to be loaded with** estar cargado de

loaf [ləuf] (pl **loaves**) n (barra de) pan m

loan [ləun] n préstamo ♦ vt prestar; **on ~** prestado

loathe [ləuð] vt aborrecer; (person) odiar

loaves [ləuvz] npl of **loaf**

lobby ['lɔbɪ] n vestíbulo, sala de espera; (POL: pressure group) grupo de presión ♦ vt presionar

lobster ['lɔbstə] n langosta

local ['ləʊkl] adj local ♦ n (pub) bar m; **the locals** npl los vecinos, los del lugar ❑ **local anaesthetic** n (MED) anestesia local ❑ **local authority** n municipio, ayuntamiento (SP) ❑ **local government** n gobierno municipal ❑ **locally** [-kəli] adv en la vecindad; por aquí

locate [ləʊ'keɪt] vt (find) localizar; (situate): **to be located in** estar situado en

location [ləʊ'keɪʃən] n situación f; **on ~** (CINEMA) en exteriores

loch [lɒx] n lago

lock [lɒk] n (of door, box) cerradura; (of canal) esclusa; (of hair) mechón m ♦ vt (with key) cerrar (con llave) ♦ vi (door etc) cerrarse (con llave); (wheels) trabarse ► **lock in** vt encerrar ► **lock out** vt (person) cerrar la puerta a ► **lock up** vt (criminal) meter en la cárcel; (mental patient) encerrar; (house) cerrar (con llave) ♦ vi echar la llave

locker ['lɒkə'] n casillero ❑ **locker-room** (US) n (SPORT) vestuario

locksmith ['lɒksmɪθ] n cerrajero(-a)

locomotive [ləʊkə'məʊtɪv] n locomotora

lodge [lɒdʒ] n casita (del guarda) ♦ vi (person): **to ~ (with)** alojarse (en casa de); (bullet, bone) incrustarse ♦ vt presentar ❑ **lodger** n huésped mf

lodging ['lɒdʒɪŋ] n alojamiento, hospedaje m

loft [lɒft] n desván m

log [lɒg] n (of wood) leño, tronco; (written account) diario ♦ vt ► **log in**, **log on** vi (COMPUT) entrar en el sistema ► **log off**, **log out** vi (COMPUT) salir del sistema

logic ['lɒdʒɪk] n lógica ❑ **logical** adj lógico

logo ['ləʊgəʊ] n logotipo

lollipop ['lɒlɪpɒp] n pirulí m ❑ **lollipop man/lady** (BRIT: irreg) n persona

encargada de ayudar a los niños a cruzar la calle

lolly ['lɒlɪ] n (inf: ice cream) polo; (: lollipop) piruleta; (: money) guita

London ['lʌndən] n Londres ❑ **Londoner** n londinense mf

lone [ləʊn] adj solitario

loneliness ['ləʊnlɪnɪs] n soledad f; aislamiento

lonely ['ləʊnlɪ] adj (situation) solitario; (person) solo; (place) aislado

long [lɒŋ] adj largo ♦ adv mucho tiempo, largamente ♦ vi: **to ~ for sth** anhelar algo; **so ~ as** mientras, con tal que; **don't be ~!** ¡no tardes!, ¡vuelve pronto!; **how ~ is the street?** ¿cuánto tiene la calle de largo?; **how ~ is the lesson?** ¿cuánto dura la clase?; **6 metres ~** que mide 6 metros, de 6 metros de largo; **6 months ~** que dura 6 meses, de 6 meses de duración; **all night ~** toda la noche; **he no longer comes** ya no viene; **I can't stand it any longer** ya no lo aguanto más; **~ before** mucho antes; **before ~** (+ future) dentro de poco; (+ past) poco tiempo después; **at ~ last** al fin, por fin ❑ **long-distance** adj (race) de larga distancia; (call) interurbano ❑ **long-haul** adj (flight) de larga distancia ❑ **longing** n anhelo, ansia; (nostalgia) nostalgia ♦ adj anhelante

longitude ['lɒŋgɪtjuːd] n longitud f

long: long jump n salto de longitud ❑ **long-life** adj (batteries) de larga duración; (milk) uperizado ❑ **long-sighted** (BRIT) adj présbita ❑ **long-standing** adj de mucho tiempo ❑ **long-term** adj a largo plazo

loo [luː] (BRIT: inf) n váter m

look [lʊk] vi mirar; (seem) parecer; (building etc): **to ~ south/on to the sea** dar al sur/al mar ♦ n (gen): **to have a ~** mirar; (glance) mirada; (appearance) aire m, aspecto; **looks** npl (good looks) belleza; ~ **(here)!** (expressing annoyance etc) ¡oye!; ~! (expressing surprise) ¡mira! ▶ **look after** vt fus (care for) cuidar a; (deal with) encargarse de ▶ **look around** vi echar una mirada alrededor ▶ **look at** vt fus mirar; (read quickly) echar un vistazo a ▶ **look back** vi mirar hacia atrás ▶ **look down on** vt fus (fig) despreciar, mirar con desprecio ▶ **look for** vt fus buscar ▶ **look forward to** vt fus esperar con ilusión; (in letters): **we look forward to hearing from you** quedamos a la espera de sus gratas noticias ▶ **look into** vt investigar ▶ **look out** vi (beware): **to look out (for)** tener cuidado (de) ▶ **look out for** vt fus (seek) buscar; (await) esperar ▶ **look round** vi volver la cabeza ▶ **look through** vt fus (examine) examinar ▶ **look up** vi mirar hacia arriba; (improve) mejorar ♦ vt (word) buscar ▶ **look up to** vt fus admirar

lookout n (tower etc) puesto de observación; (person) vigía mf; **to be on the lookout for sth** estar al acecho de algo

loom [luːm] vi: ~ **(up)** (threaten) surgir, amenazar; (event: approach) aproximarse

loony ['luːnɪ] (inf) n, adj loco(-a) m/f

loop [luːp] n lazo ♦ vt: **to ~ sth round sth** pasar algo alrededor de algo ▫ **loophole** n escapatoria

loose [luːs] adj suelto; (clothes) ancho; (morals, discipline) relajado; **to be on the ~** estar en libertad; **to be at a ~ end** or **at ~ ends** (US) no saber qué hacer ▫ **loosely** adv libremente, aproximadamente ▫ **loosen** vt aflojar

loot [luːt] n botín m ♦ vt saquear

lop-sided ['lɔp'saɪdɪd] adj torcido

lord [lɔːd] n señor m; **L~ Smith** Lord Smith; **the L~** el Señor; **my ~** (to bishop) Ilustrísima; (to noble etc) Señor; **good L~!** ¡Dios mío! ▫ **Lords** npl (BRIT: POL): **the (House of) Lords** la Cámara de los Lores

lorry ['lɔrɪ] (BRIT) n camión m ▫ **lorry driver** (BRIT) n camionero(-a)

lose [luːz] (pt, pp **lost**) vt perder ♦ vi perder, ser vencido; **to ~ (time)** (clock) atrasarse ▶ **lose out** vi salir perdiendo ▫ **loser** n perdedor(a) m/f

loss [lɔs] n pérdida; **heavy losses** (MIL) grandes pérdidas; **to be at a ~** no saber qué hacer; **to make a ~** sufrir pérdidas

lost [lɔst] pt, pp of **lose** ♦ adj perdido ▫ **lost property** (US **lost and found**) n objetos mpl perdidos

lot [lɔt] n (group: of things) grupo; (at auctions) lote m; **the ~** el todo, todos; **a ~** (large number: of books etc) muchos; (a great deal) mucho, bastante; **a ~ of, lots of** mucho(s) (pl); **I read a ~** leo bastante; **to draw lots (for sth)** echar suertes (para decidir algo)

lotion ['ləʊʃən] n loción f

lottery ['lɔtərɪ] n lotería

loud [laʊd] adj (voice, sound) fuerte; (laugh, shout) estrepitoso; (condemnation etc) enérgico; (gaudy) chillón(-ona) ♦ adv (speak etc) fuerte; **out** ~ en voz alta ▫ **loudly** adv (noisily) fuerte; (aloud) en voz alta ▫ **loudspeaker** n altavoz m

lounge [laʊndʒ] n salón m, sala (de estar); (at airport etc) sala; (BRIT: also: ~ **bar**) salón-bar m ♦ vi (also: ~ **about** or **around**) reposar, holgazanear

louse [laʊs] (pl **lice**) n piojo

lousy ['laʊzɪ] (inf) adj (bad quality) malísimo, asqueroso; (ill) fatal

love [lʌv] n (romantic, sexual) amor m; (kind, caring) cariño ♦ vt amar, querer; (thing, activity) encantarle a algn; ~ **from Anne** (on letter) "un abrazo (de) Anne"; **to ~ to do** encantarle a algn hacer; **to be/fall in ~ with** estar enamorado/enamorarse de; **to make ~** hacer el amor; **for the ~ of** por amor de; **"15 ~"** (TENNIS) "15 a cero"; **I ~ paella** me encanta la paella ▫ **love affair** n aventura sentimental ▫ **love life** n vida sentimental

lovely ['lʌvlɪ] *adj* (*delightful*) encantador(a); (*beautiful*) precioso

lover ['lʌvəʳ] *n* amante *m*; (*person in love*) enamorado; (*amateur*): **a ~ of** un(a) aficionado(-a) *or* un(a) amante de

loving ['lʌvɪŋ] *adj* amoroso, cariñoso; (*action*) tierno

low [ləu] *adj, adv* bajo ♦ *n* (METEOROLOGY) área de baja presión; **to be ~ on** (*supplies etc*) andar mal de; **to feel ~** sentirse deprimido; **to turn (down) ~** bajar □ **low-alcohol** *adj* de bajo contenido en alcohol □ **low-calorie** *adj* bajo en calorías

lower ['ləuəʳ] *adj* más bajo; (*less important*) menos importante ♦ *vt* bajar; (*reduce*) reducir ♦ *vr*: **to ~ o.s.** *to* (*fig*) rebajarse a

low-fat *adj* (*milk, yoghurt*) desnatado; (*diet*) bajo en calorías

loyal ['lɔɪəl] *adj* leal □ **loyalty** *n* lealtad *f* □ **loyalty card** *n* tarjeta cliente

L.P. *n abbr* (= *long-playing record*) elepé *m*

L-plates ['el-] (BRIT) *npl* placas *fpl* de aprendiz de conductor

Lt *abbr* (= *lieutenant*) Tte.

Ltd *abbr* (= *limited company*) S.A.

luck [lʌk] *n* suerte *f*; **bad ~** mala suerte; **good ~!** ¡que tengas suerte!, ¡suerte!; **bad** *or* **hard** *or* **tough ~!** ¡qué pena! □ **luckily** *adv* afortunadamente □ **lucky** *adj* afortunado; (*at cards etc*) con suerte; (*object*) que trae suerte

lucrative ['lu:krətɪv] *adj* lucrativo

ludicrous ['lu:dɪkrəs] *adj* absurdo

luggage ['lʌgɪdʒ] *n* equipaje *m* □ **luggage rack** *n* (*on car*) baca, portaequipajes *m inv*

lukewarm ['lu:kwɔ:m] *adj* tibio

lull [lʌl] *n* tregua ♦ *vt*: **to ~ sb to sleep** arrullar a algn; **to ~ sb into a false sense of security** dar a algn una falsa sensación de seguridad

lullaby ['lʌləbaɪ] *n* nana

lumber ['lʌmbəʳ] *n* (*junk*) trastos *mpl* viejos; (*wood*) maderos *mpl*

luminous ['lu:mɪnəs] *adj* luminoso

lump [lʌmp] *n* terrón *m*; (*fragment*) trozo; (*swelling*) bulto ♦ *vt* (*also*: **~ together**) juntar □ **lump sum** *n* suma global □ **lumpy** *adj* (*sauce*) lleno de grumos; (*mattress*) lleno de bultos

lunatic ['lu:nətɪk] *adj* loco

lunch [lʌntʃ] *n* almuerzo, comida ♦ *vi* almorzar □ **lunch break**, **lunch hour** *n* hora del almuerzo □ **lunch time** *n* hora de comer

lung [lʌŋ] *n* pulmón *m*

lure [luəʳ] *n* (*attraction*) atracción *f* ♦ *vt* tentar

lurk [lə:k] *vi* (*person, animal*) estar al acecho; (*fig*) acechar

lush [lʌʃ] *adj* exuberante

lust [lʌst] *n* lujuria; (*greed*) codicia

Luxembourg ['lʌksəmbə:g] *n* Luxemburgo

luxurious [lʌg'zjuərɪəs] *adj* lujoso

luxury ['lʌkʃərɪ] *n* lujo ♦ *cpd* de lujo

Lycra® ['laɪkrə] *n* licra®

lying ['laɪɪŋ] *n* mentiras *fpl* ♦ *adj* mentiroso

lyrics ['lɪrɪks] *npl* (*of song*) letra

M, m

m. *abbr* = **metre; mile; million**

M.A. *abbr* = **Master of Arts**

ma (*inf*) [mɑː] *n* mamá

mac [mæk] (*BRIT*) *n* impermeable *m*

macaroni [mækəˈrəʊnɪ] *n* macarrones *mpl*

Macedonia [mæsɪˈdəʊnɪə] *n* Macedonia □ **Macedonian** [-ˈdəʊnɪən] *adj* macedonio ♦ *n* macedonio(-a); (*LING*) macedonio

machine [məˈʃiːn] *n* máquina ♦ *vt* (*dress etc*) coser a máquina; (*TECH*) hacer a máquina □ **machine gun** *n* ametralladora □ **machinery** *n* maquinaria; (*fig*) mecanismo □ **machine washable** *adj* lavable a la máquina

macho [ˈmætʃəʊ] *adj* machista

mackerel [ˈmækrəl] *n inv* caballa

mackintosh [ˈmækɪntɒʃ] (*BRIT*) *n* impermeable *m*

mad [mæd] *adj* loco; (*idea*) disparatado; (*angry*) furioso; (*keen*): **to be ~ about sth** volverse loco a algn algo

Madagascar [mædəˈgæskə] *n* Madagascar *m*

madam [ˈmædəm] *n* señora

mad cow disease *n* encefalopatía espongiforme bovina

made [meɪd] *pt, pp of* **make** □ **made-to-measure** (*BRIT*) *adj* hecho a la medida □ **made-up** [ˈmeɪdʌp] *adj* (*story*) ficticio

madly [ˈmædlɪ] *adv* locamente

madman [ˈmædmən] (*irreg*) *n* loco

madness [ˈmædnɪs] *n* locura

Madrid [məˈdrɪd] *n* Madrid *m*

Mafia [ˈmæfɪə] *n* Mafia

mag [mæg] *n abbr* (*BRIT inf*) = **magazine**

magazine [mægəˈziːn] *n* revista; (*RADIO, TV*) programa *m* magazina

maggot [ˈmægət] *n* gusano

magic [ˈmædʒɪk] *n* magia ♦ *adj* mágico □ **magical** *adj* mágico □ **magician** [məˈdʒɪʃən] *n* mago(-a); (*conjurer*) prestidigitador(a)

magistrate [ˈmædʒɪstreɪt] *n* juez *mf* (municipal)

magnet [ˈmægnɪt] *n* imán *m* □ **magnetic** [-ˈnetɪk] *adj* magnético; (*personality*) atrayente

magnificent [mægˈnɪfɪsənt] *adj* magnífico

magnify [ˈmægnɪfaɪ] *vt* (*object*) ampliar; (*sound*) aumentar □ **magnifying glass** *n* lupa

magpie [ˈmægpaɪ] *n* urraca

mahogany [məˈhɒgənɪ] *n* caoba

maid [meɪd] *n* criada; **old ~** (*pej*) solterona

maiden name *n* nombre *m* de soltera

mail [meɪl] *n* correo; (*letters*) cartas *fpl* ♦ *vt* echar al correo □ **mailbox** (*US*) *n* buzón *m* □ **mailing list** *n* lista de direcciones □ **mailman** (*US: irreg*) *n* cartero □ **mail-order** *n* pedido postal

main [meɪn] *adj* principal, mayor ♦ *n* (*pipe*) cañería maestra; (*US*) red *f* eléctrica; **the mains** *npl* (*BRIT ELEC*) la red eléctrica; **in the ~** en general □ **main course** *n* (*CULIN*) plato principal □ **mainland** *n* tierra firme □ **mainly** *adv* principalmente □ **main road** *n* carretera □ **mainstream** *n* corriente *f* principal □ **main street** *n* calle *f* mayor

maintain [meɪnˈteɪn] *vt* mantener □ **maintenance** [ˈmeɪntənəns] *n* mantenimiento; (*LAW*) manutención *f*

maisonette [meɪzəˈnet] *n* dúplex *m*

maize [meɪz] (*BRIT*) *n* maíz *m*, choclo (*SC*)

majesty [ˈmædʒɪstɪ] *n* majestad *f*; (*title*): **Your M~** Su Majestad

major [ˈmeɪdʒə] *n* (*MIL*) comandante *mf* ♦ *adj* principal; (*MUS*) mayor

Majorca [məˈjɔːkə] *n* Mallorca

majority [məˈdʒɒrɪtɪ] *n* mayoría

make [meɪk] (*pt, pp* **made**) *vt* hacer; (*manufacture*) fabricar; (*mistake*) cometer; (*speech*) pronunciar; (*cause to be*): **to ~ sb sad** poner triste a algn; (*force*): **to ~ sb do sth** obligar a algn a hacer algo; (*earn*) ganar; (*equal*): **2 and 2 ~ 4** 2 y 2 son 4 ♦ *n* marca; **to ~ the bed** hacer la cama; **to ~ a fool of sb** poner a algn en ridículo; **to ~ a profit/loss** obtener ganancias/sufrir pérdidas; **to ~ it** (*arrive*) llegar; (*achieve sth*) tener éxito; **what time do you ~ it?** ¿qué hora tienes?; **to ~ do with** contentarse con ▸ **make off** *vi* largarse ▸ **make out** *vt* (*decipher*) descifrar; (*understand*) entender; (*see*) distinguir; (*cheque*) extender ▸ **make up** *vt* (*invent*) inventar; (*prepare*) hacer; (*constitute*) constituir ♦ *vi* reconciliarse; (*with cosmetics*) maquillarse ▸ **make up for** *vt fus* compensar ▸ **makeover** ['meɪkəʊvə'] *n* (*by beautician*) sesión *f* de maquillaje y peluquería; (*change of image*) lavado de cara ▯ **maker** *n* fabricante *mf*; (*of film, programme*) autor(a) *m/f* ▯ **makeshift** *adj* improvisado ▯ **make-up** *n* maquillaje *m*

making ['meɪkɪŋ] *n* (*fig*): **in the ~** en vías de formación; **to have the makings of** (*person*) tener madera de

malaria [mə'leərɪə] *n* malaria

Malaysia [mə'leɪzɪə] *n* Malasia, Malaysia

male [meɪl] *n* (*BIOL*) macho ♦ *adj* (*sex, attitude*) masculino; (*child etc*) varón

malicious [mə'lɪʃəs] *adj* malicioso; rencoroso

malignant [mə'lɪɡnənt] *adj* (*MED*) maligno

mall [mɔːl] *n* (*US*) (*also*: **shopping ~**) centro comercial

mallet ['mælɪt] *n* mazo

malnutrition [mælnjuː'trɪʃən] *n* desnutrición *f*

malpractice [mæl'præktɪs] *n* negligencia profesional

malt [mɔːlt] *n* malta; (*whisky*) whisky *m* de malta

Malta ['mɔːltə] *n* Malta ▯ **Maltese** [-'tiːz] *adj, n inv* maltés(-esa) *m/f*

mammal ['mæml] *n* mamífero

mammoth ['mæməθ] *n* mamut *m* ♦ *adj* gigantesco

man [mæn] (*pl* **men**) *n* hombre *m*; (*mankind*) el hombre ♦ *vt* (*NAUT*) tripular; (*MIL*) guarnecer; (*operate: machine*) manejar; **an old ~** un viejo; **~ and wife** marido y mujer

manage ['mænɪdʒ] *vi* arreglárselas, ir tirando ♦ *vt* (*be in charge of*) dirigir; (*control: person*) manejar; (: *ship*) gobernar ▯ **manageable** *adj* manejable ▯ **management** *n* dirección *f* ▯ **manager** *n* director(a) *m/f*; (*of pop star*) mánager *mf*; (*SPORT*) entrenador *m/f* ▯ **manageress** *n* directora; entrenadora ▯ **managerial** [-ə'dʒɪərɪəl] *adj* directivo ▯ **managing director** *n* director(a) *m/f* general

mandarin ['mændərɪn] *n* (*also*: **~ orange**) mandarina; (*person*) mandarín *m*

mandate ['mændeɪt] *n* mandato

mandatory ['mændətərɪ] *adj* obligatorio

mane [meɪn] *n* (*of horse*) crin *f*; (*of lion*) melena

maneuver [mə'nuːvə'] (*US*) = **manoeuvre**

mangetout [mɒnʒ'tuː] *n* tirabeque *m*

mango ['mæŋɡəʊ] (*pl* **mangoes**) *n* mango

man: manhole *n* agujero de acceso ▯ **manhood** *n* edad *f* viril; (*state*) virilidad *f*

mania ['meɪnɪə] *n* manía ▯ **maniac** ['meɪnɪæk] *n* maníaco(-a); (*fig*) maniático

manic ['mænɪk] *adj* frenético

manicure ['mænɪkjʊə'] *n* manicura

manifest ['mænɪfest] vt manifestar, mostrar ♦ adj manifiesto

manifesto [mænɪ'festəʊ] n manifiesto

manipulate [mə'nɪpjʊleɪt] vt manipular

man: mankind [mæn'kaɪnd] n humanidad f, género humano ❑ **manly** adj varonil ❑ **man-made** adj artificial

manner ['mænə'] n manera, modo; (behaviour) conducta, manera de ser; (type): **all ~ of things** toda clase de cosas; **manners** npl (behaviour) modales mpl; **bad manners** mala educación

manoeuvre [mə'nuːvə'] (US **maneuver**) vt, vi maniobrar ♦ n maniobra

manpower ['mænpaʊə'] n mano f de obra

mansion ['mænʃən] n palacio, casa grande

manslaughter ['mænslɔːtə'] n homicidio no premeditado

mantelpiece ['mæntlpiːs] n repisa, chimenea

manual ['mænjʊəl] adj manual ♦ n manual m

manufacture [mænjʊ'fæktʃə'] vt fabricar ♦ n fabricación f ❑ **manufacturer** n fabricante mf

manure [mə'njʊə'] n estiércol m

manuscript ['mænjʊskrɪpt] n manuscrito

many ['menɪ] adj, pron muchos(-as); **a great ~** muchísimos, un buen número de; **~ a time** muchas veces

map [mæp] n mapa m; **to ~ out** vt proyectar

maple ['meɪpl] n arce m, maple m (LAm)

Mar abbr (= March) marzo

mar [mɑː'] vt estropear

marathon ['mærəθən] n maratón m

marble ['mɑːbl] n mármol m; (toy) canica

March [mɑːtʃ] n marzo

march [mɑːtʃ] vi (MIL) marchar; (demonstrators) manifestarse ♦ n marcha; (demonstration) manifestación f

mare [mɛə'] n yegua

margarine [mɑːdʒə'riːn] n margarina

margin ['mɑːdʒɪn] n margen m; (COMM: profit margin) margen m de beneficios ❑ **marginal** adj marginal ❑ **marginally** adv ligeramente

marigold ['mærɪɡəʊld] n caléndula

marijuana [mærɪ'wɑːnə] n marijuana

marina [mə'riːnə] n puerto deportivo

marinade [mærɪ'neɪd] n adobo

marinate ['mærɪneɪt] vt marinar

marine [mə'riːn] adj marino ♦ n soldado de marina

marital ['mærɪtl] adj matrimonial ❑ **marital status** n estado m civil

maritime ['mærɪtaɪm] adj marítimo

marjoram ['mɑːdʒərəm] n mejorana

mark [mɑːk] n marca, señal f; (in snow, mud etc) huella; (stain) mancha; (BRIT SCOL) nota ♦ vt marcar; manchar; (damage: furniture) rayar; (indicate: place etc) señalar; (BRIT SCOL) calificar, corregir; **to ~ time** marcar el paso; (fig) marcar(se) un ritmo ❑ **marked** adj (obvious) marcado, acusado ❑ **marker** n (sign) marcador m; (bookmark) señal f (de libro)

market ['mɑːkɪt] n mercado ♦ vt (COMM) comercializar ❑ **marketing** n márketing m ❑ **marketplace** n mercado ❑ **market research** n análisis m inv de mercados

marmalade ['mɑːməleɪd] n mermelada de naranja

maroon [mə'ruːn] vt: **to be marooned** quedar aislado; (fig) quedar abandonado ♦ n (colour) granate m

marquee [mɑː'kiː] n entoldado

marriage ['mærɪdʒ] n (relationship, institution) matrimonio; (wedding) boda; (act) casamiento ❑ **marriage certificate** n partida de casamiento

married ['mærɪd] adj casado; (life, love) conyugal

marrow ['mærəu] n médula; (vegetable) calabacín m

marry ['mærɪ] vt casarse con; (father, priest etc) casar ♦ vi (also: **get married**) casarse

Mars [maːz] n Marte m

marsh [maːʃ] n pantano; (salt marsh) marisma

marshal ['maːʃl] n (MIL) mariscal m; (at sports meeting etc) oficial m; (US: of police, fire department) jefe(-a) m/f ♦ vt (thoughts etc) ordenar; (soldiers) formar

martyr ['maːtə'] n mártir m/f

marvel ['maːvl] n maravilla, prodigio ♦ vi: to ~ (at) maravillarse (de) □ **marvellous** (US **marvelous**) adj maravilloso

Marxism ['maːksɪzəm] n marxismo

Marxist ['maːksɪst] adj, n marxista m/f

marzipan ['maːzɪpæn] n mazapán m

mascara [mæs'kaːrə] n rímel m

mascot ['mæskət] n mascota

masculine ['mæskjulɪn] adj masculino

mash [mæʃ] vt machacar □ **mashed potato(es)** n(pl) puré m de patatas (SP) or papas (LAm)

mask [maːsk] n máscara ♦ vt (cover): to ~ one's face ocultarse la cara; (hide: feelings) esconder

mason ['meɪsn] n (also: **stonemason**) albañil m; (also: **freemason**) masón m □ **masonry** n (in building) mampostería

mass [mæs] n (people) muchedumbre f; (of air, liquid etc) masa; (of detail, hair etc) gran cantidad f; (REL) misa ♦ cpd masivo ♦ vi reunirse; concentrarse; **the masses** npl las masas; **masses of** (inf) montones de

massacre ['mæsəkə'] n masacre f

massage ['mæsaːʒ] n masaje m ♦ vt dar masaje en

massive ['mæsɪv] adj enorme; (support, changes) masivo

mass media npl medios mpl de comunicación

mass-produce ['mæsprə'djuːs] vt fabricar en serie

mast [maːst] n (NAUT) mástil m; (RADIO etc) torre f

master ['maːstə'] n (of servant) amo; (of situation) dueño, maestro; (in primary school) maestro; (in secondary school) profesor m; (title for boys): **M~ X** Señorito X ♦ vt dominar □ **mastermind** n inteligencia superior ♦ vt dirigir, planear □ **Master of Arts/Science** n licenciado superior en Letras/Ciencias □ **masterpiece** n obra maestra

masturbate ['mæstəbeɪt] vi masturbarse

mat [mæt] n estera; (also: **doormat**) felpudo; (also: **table ~**) salvamanteles m inv, posavasos m inv ♦ adj = **matt**

match [mætʃ] n cerilla, fósforo; (game) partido; (equal) igual m/f ♦ vt (go well with) hacer juego con; (equal) igualar; (correspond to) corresponder con; (pair: also: ~ **up**) casar con ♦ vi hacer juego; **to be a good ~** hacer juego □ **matchbox** n caja de cerillas □ **matching** adj que hace juego

mate [meɪt] n (workmate) colega m/f; (inf: friend) amigo(-a); (animal) macho/ hembra; (in merchant navy) segundo de a bordo ♦ vi acoplarse, aparearse ♦ vt aparear

material [mə'tɪərɪəl] n (substance) materia; (information) material m; (cloth) tela, tejido ♦ adj material; (important) esencial; **materials** npl materiales mpl □ **materialize** [mə'tɪərɪəlaɪz] vi materializarse

maternal [mə'təːnl] adj maternal

maternity [mə'təːnɪtɪ] n maternidad f □ **maternity hospital** n hospital m de maternidad □ **maternity leave** n baja por maternidad

math [mæθ] (US) n = **mathematics**

mathematical [mæθəˈmætɪkl] adj matemático

mathematician [mæθəməˈtɪʃən] n matemático(-a)

mathematics [mæθəˈmætɪks] n matemáticas fpl

maths [mæθs] (BRIT) n = **mathematics**

matinée [ˈmætɪneɪ] n sesión f de tarde

matron [ˈmeɪtrən] n enfermera f jefe; (in school) ama de llaves

matt [mæt] adj mate

matter [ˈmætə*] n cuestión f, asunto; (PHYSICS) sustancia, materia; (reading matter) material m; (MED: pus) pus m ♦ vi importar; **matters** pl (affairs) asuntos mpl, temas mpl; **it doesn't** ~ no importa; **what's the** ~? ¿qué pasa?; **no** ~ **what** pase lo que pase; **as a** ~ **of course** por rutina; **as a** ~ **of fact** de hecho

mattress [ˈmætrɪs] n colchón m

mature [məˈtjuə*] adj maduro ♦ vi madurar ❑ **mature student** n estudiante de más de 21 años ❑ **maturity** n madurez f

maul [mɔːl] vt magullar

mauve [məuv] adj de color malva (SP) or guinda (LAm)

max abbr = **maximum**

maximize [ˈmæksɪmaɪz] vt (profits etc) llevar al máximo; (chances) maximizar

maximum [ˈmæksɪməm] (pl **maxima**) adj máximo ♦ n máximo

May [meɪ] n mayo

may [meɪ] (conditional **might**) vi (indicating possibility): **he** ~ **come** puede que venga; (be allowed to): ~ **I smoke?** ¿puedo fumar?; (wishes): **God bless you!** ¡que Dios le bendiga!; **you** ~ **as well go** bien puedes irte

maybe [ˈmeɪbiː] adv quizá(s)

May Day n el primero de Mayo

mayhem [ˈmeɪhem] n caos m total

mayonnaise [meɪəˈneɪz] n mayonesa

mayor [mɛə*] n alcalde m ❑ **mayoress** n alcaldesa

maze [meɪz] n laberinto

MD n abbr = **managing director**

me [miː] pron (direct) me; (stressed, after pron) mí; **can you hear me?** ¿me oyes?; **he heard ME** ¡me oyó a mí!; **it's me** soy yo; **give them to me** dámelos/las; **with/without me** conmigo/sin mí

meadow [ˈmedəu] n prado, pradera

meagre [ˈmiːgə*] (US **meager**) adj escaso, pobre

meal [miːl] n comida; (flour) harina ❑ **mealtime** n hora de comer

mean [miːn] (pt, pp **meant**) adj (with money) tacaño; (unkind) mezquino, malo; (shabby) humilde; (average) medio ♦ vt (signify) querer decir, significar; (refer to) referirse a; (intend): **to** ~ **to do sth** pensar or pretender hacer algo ♦ n medio, término medio; **means** npl (way) medio, manera; (money) recursos mpl, medios mpl; **by means of** mediante, por medio de; **by all means!** ¡naturalmente!, ¡claro que sí!; **do you** ~ **it?** ¿lo dices en serio?; **what do you** ~? ¿qué quiere decir?; **to be meant for sb/sth** ser para algn/algo

meaning [ˈmiːnɪŋ] n significado, sentido; (purpose) sentido, propósito ❑ **meaningful** adj significativo ❑ **meaningless** adj sin sentido

meant [ment] pt, pp of **mean**

meantime [ˈmiːntaɪm] adv (also: **in the** ~) mientras tanto

meanwhile [ˈmiːnwaɪl] adv = **meantime**

measles [ˈmiːzlz] n sarampión m

measure [ˈmeʒə*] vt, vi medir ♦ n medida; (ruler) regla ❑ **measurement** [ˈmeʒəmənt] n (measure) medida; (act) medición f; **to take sb's measurements** tomar las medidas a algn

meat [miːt] n carne f; **cold** ~ fiambre m ❑ **meatball** n albóndiga

Mecca [ˈmekə] n La Meca

mechanic [mɪˈkænɪk] n mecánico(-a)
❏ **mechanical** adj mecánico

mechanism [ˈmekənɪzəm] n
mecanismo

medal [ˈmedl] n medalla ❏ **medallist**
(US medalist) n (SPORT) medallista mf

meddle [ˈmedl] vi: **to ~ in** entrometerse
en; **to ~ with** sth manosear algo

media [ˈmiːdɪə] npl medios mpl de
comunicación ♦ npl of **medium**

mediaeval [medɪˈiːvl] adj = **medieval**

mediate [ˈmiːdɪeɪt] vi mediar

medical [ˈmedɪkl] adj médico ♦ n
reconocimiento médico ❏ **medical
certificate** n certificado m médico

medicated [ˈmedɪkeɪtɪd] adj medicinal

medication [medɪˈkeɪʃən] n
medicación f

medicine [ˈmedsɪn] n medicina; (drug)
medicamento

medieval [medɪˈiːvl] adj medieval

mediocre [miːdɪˈəʊkə*] adj mediocre

meditate [ˈmedɪteɪt] vi meditar

meditation [medɪˈteɪʃən] n
meditación f

Mediterranean [medɪtəˈreɪnɪən] adj
mediterráneo; **the ~ (Sea)** el (Mar)
Mediterráneo

medium [ˈmiːdɪəm] (pl **media**) adj
mediano, regular ♦ n (means) medio;
(pl **mediums**: person) médium mf
❏ **medium-sized** adj de tamaño
mediano; (clothes) de (la) talla
mediana ❏ **medium wave** n onda
media

meek [miːk] adj manso, sumiso

meet [miːt] (pt, pp **met**) vt encontrar;
(accidentally) encontrarse con,
tropezar con; (by arrangement)
reunirse con; (for the first time) conocer
(go and fetch) ir a buscar; (opponent)
enfrentarse con; (obligations) cumplir;
(encounter: problem) hacer frente a;
(need) satisfacer ♦ vi encontrarse; (in
session) reunirse; (join: objects) unirse;
(for the first time) conocerse ▶ **meet**

up vi: **to meet up with sb** reunirse con
algn ▶ **meet with** vt fus (difficulty)
tropezar con; **to meet with success**
tener éxito ❏ **meeting** n encuentro;
(arranged) cita, compromiso; (business
meeting) reunión f; (POL) mitin m
❏ **meeting place** n lugar m de
reunión or encuentro

megabyte [ˈmegəbaɪt] n (COMPUT)
megabyte m, megaocteto

megaphone [ˈmegəfəʊn] n megáfono

melancholy [ˈmelənkəlɪ] n melancolía
♦ adj melancólico

melody [ˈmelədɪ] n melodía

melon [ˈmelən] n melón m

melt [melt] vi (metal) fundirse; (snow)
derretirse ♦ vt fundir

member [ˈmembə*] n (gen, ANAT)
miembro; (of club) socio(-a)
❏ **Member of Congress** (US) n
miembro mf del Congreso
❏ **Member of Parliament** n (BRIT)
diputado(-a) m/f, parlamentario(-a) m/
f ❏ **Member of the European
Parliament** n diputado(-a) m/f del
Parlamento Europeo,
eurodiputado(-a) m/f ❏ **Member of
the Scottish Parliament** (BRIT)
diputado(-a) del Parlamento escocés
❏ **membership** n (members) número
de miembros; (state) filiación f
❏ **membership card** n carnet m de
socio

memento [məˈmentəʊ] n recuerdo

memo [ˈmeməʊ] n apunte m, nota

memorable [ˈmemərəbl] adj
memorable

memorandum [meməˈrændəm] (pl
memoranda) n apunte m, nota;
(official note) acta

memorial [mɪˈmɔːrɪəl] n monumento
conmemorativo ♦ adj conmemorativo

memorize [ˈmeməraɪz] vt aprender de
memoria

memory ['mɛmərɪ] n (also: COMPUT) memoria; (instance) recuerdo; (of dead person): **in ~ of** a la memoria de

men [mɛn] npl of **man**

menace ['mɛnəs] n amenaza ♦ vt amenazar

mend [mɛnd] vt reparar, arreglar; (darn) zurcir ♦ vi reponerse ♦ n arreglo, reparación f zurcido ♦ n: **to be on the ~** ir mejorando; **to ~ one's ways** enmendarse

meningitis [mɛnɪn'dʒaɪtɪs] n meningitis f

menopause ['mɛnəupɔːz] n menopausia

men's room (US) n: **the ~** el servicio de caballeros

menstruation [mɛnstru'eɪʃən] n menstruación f

menswear ['mɛnzwɛə'] n confección f de caballero

mental ['mɛntl] adj mental ❑ **mental hospital** n (hospital m) psiquiátrico ❑ **mentality** [mɛn'tælɪtɪ] n mentalidad f ❑ **mentally** adv: **to be mentally ill** tener una enfermedad mental

menthol ['mɛnθɒl] n mentol m

mention ['mɛnʃən] n mención f ♦ vt mencionar; (speak) hablar de; **don't ~ it!** ¡de nada!

menu ['mɛnjuː] n (set menu) menú m; (printed) carta; (COMPUT) menú m

MEP n abbr = Member of the European Parliament

mercenary ['mɜːsɪnərɪ] adj, n mercenario(-a)

merchandise ['mɜːtʃəndaɪz] n mercancías fpl

merchant ['mɜːtʃənt] n comerciante mf ❑ **merchant navy** (US **merchant marine**) n marina mercante

merciless ['mɜːsɪlɪs] adj despiadado

mercury ['mɜːkjurɪ] n mercurio

mercy ['mɜːsɪ] n compasión f; (REL) misericordia; **at the ~ of** a la merced de

mere [mɪə'] adj simple, mero ❑ **merely** adv simplemente, sólo

merge [mɜːdʒ] vt (join) unir ♦ vi unirse; (COMM) fusionarse; (colours etc) fundirse ♦ **merger** n (COMM) fusión f

meringue [mə'ræŋ] n merengue m

merit ['mɛrɪt] n mérito ♦ vt merecer

mermaid ['mɜːmeɪd] n sirena

merry ['mɛrɪ] adj alegre; **M~ Christmas!** ¡Felices Pascuas! ❑ **merry-go-round** n tiovivo

mesh [mɛʃ] n malla

mess [mɛs] n (muddle: of situation) confusión f; (: of room) revoltijo; (dirt) porquería; (MIL) comedor m ▶ **mess about** or **around** (inf) vi perder el tiempo; (pass the time) entretenerse ▶ **mess up** vt (spoil) estropear; (dirty) ensuciar ▶ **mess with** (inf) vt fus (challenge, confront) meterse con (inf); (interfere with) interferir con

message ['mɛsɪdʒ] n recado, mensaje m

messenger ['mɛsɪndʒə'] n mensajero(-a)

Messrs abbr (on letters: = Messieurs) Sres

messy ['mɛsɪ] adj (dirty) sucio; (untidy) desordenado

met [mɛt] pt, pp of **meet**

metabolism [mɛ'tæbəlɪzəm] n metabolismo

metal ['mɛtl] n metal m ❑ **metallic** [-'tælɪk] adj metálico

metaphor ['mɛtəfə'] n metáfora

meteor ['miːtɪə'] n meteoro ❑ **meteorite** [-aɪt] n meteorito

meteorology [miːtɪə'rɔlədʒɪ] n meteorología

meter ['miːtə'] n (instrument) contador m; (US: unit) = **metre** ♦ vt (US POST) franquear

method ['mɛθəd] n método ❑ **methodical** [mɪ'θɒdɪkl] adj metódico

meths [mɛθs] n (BRIT) alcohol m metilado or desnaturalizado

meticulous [me'tikjuləs] adj meticuloso

metre ['mi:tə'] (US **meter**) n metro

metric ['mɛtrɪk] adj métrico

metro ['mɛtrəu] n metro

metropolitan [mɛtrə'pɔlɪtən] adj metropolitano; **the M~ Police** (BRIT) la policía londinense

Mexican ['mɛksɪkən] adj, n mejicano(-a), mexicano(-a)

Mexico ['mɛksɪkəu] n Méjico (SP), México (LAm)

mg abbr (= milligram) mg

mice [maɪs] npl of **mouse**

micro... [maɪkrəu] prefix micro...
□ **microchip** n microplaqueta
□ **microphone** n micrófono
□ **microscope** n microscopio
□ **microwave** n (also: **microwave oven**) horno microondas

mid [mɪd] adj: **in ~ May** a mediados de mayo; **in ~ afternoon** a media tarde; **in ~ air** en el aire □ **midday** n mediodía m

middle ['mɪdl] n centro; (half-way point) medio; (waist) cintura ♦ adj de en medio; (course, way) intermedio; **in the ~ of the night** en plena noche □ **middle-aged** adj de mediana edad □ **Middle Ages** npl: **the Middle Ages** la Edad Media □ **middle-class** adj de clase media; **the middle class(es)** la clase media □ **Middle East** n Oriente m Medio □ **middle name** n segundo nombre □ **middle school** n (US) colegio para niños de doce a catorce años; (BRIT) colegio para niños de ocho o nueve a doce o trece años

midge [mɪdʒ] n mosquito

midget ['mɪdʒɪt] n enano(-a)

midnight ['mɪdnaɪt] n medianoche f

midst [mɪdst] n: **in the ~** (crowd) en medio de; (situation, action) en mitad de

midsummer [mɪd'sʌmə'] n: **in ~** en pleno verano

midway [mɪd'weɪ] adj, adv: **~ (between)** a medio camino (entre); **~ through** a la mitad (de)

midweek [mɪd'wiːk] adv entre semana

midwife ['mɪdwaɪf] (irreg) n comadrona, partera

midwinter [mɪd'wɪntə'] n: **in ~** en pleno invierno

might [maɪt] vb see **may** ♦ n fuerza, poder m □ **mighty** adj fuerte, poderoso

migraine ['miːgreɪn] n jaqueca

migrant ['maɪgrənt] n, adj (bird) migratorio; (worker) emigrante

migrate [maɪ'greɪt] vi emigrar

migration [maɪ'greɪʃən] n emigración f

mike [maɪk] n abbr (= microphone) micro

mild [maɪld] adj (person) apacible; (climate) templado; (slight) ligero; (taste) suave; (illness) leve □ **mildly** ['maɪldlɪ] adv ligeramente; suavemente; **to put it mildly** para no decir más

mile [maɪl] n milla □ **mileage** n número de millas, ≈ kilometraje m □ **mileometer** [maɪ'lɔmɪtə'] n = cuentakilómetros m inv □ **milestone** n mojón m

military ['mɪlɪtərɪ] adj militar

militia [mɪ'lɪʃə] n milicia

milk [mɪlk] n leche f ♦ vt (cow) ordeñar; (fig) chupar □ **milk chocolate** n chocolate m con leche □ **milkman** (irreg) n lechero □ **milky** adj lechoso

mill [mɪl] n (windmill etc) molino; (coffee mill) molinillo; (factory) fábrica ♦ vt moler ♦ vi (also: **~ about**) arremolinarse

millennium [mɪ'lɛnɪəm] (pl **millenniums** or **millennia**) n milenio, milenario

milli... ['mɪlɪ] prefix: **milligram(me)** n miligramo □ **millilitre** ['mɪlɪliːtə'] (US

millilete) n mililitro ◆ **millimetre** (US **millimeter)** n milímetro

million ['mɪljən] n millón m; **a ~ times** un millón de veces ❑ **millionaire** [-ʒə'nɛəˡ] n millonario(-a) ◆ **millionth** [-θ] adj millonésimo

milometer [maɪˈlɒmɪtəˡ] (BRIT) n = **mileometer**

mime [maɪm] n mímica; (actor) ◆ mimo(-a) ◆ vt remedar ◆ vi actuar de mimo

mimic ['mɪmɪk] n imitador/a m/f ◆ adj mímico ◆ vt remedar, imitar

min. abbr = **minimum**; **minute(s)**

mince [mɪns] vt picar ◆ n (BRIT CULIN) carne f picada □ **mincemeat** n conserva de fruta picada; (US: meat) carne f picada □ **mince pie** n empandilla rellena de fruta picada

mind [maɪnd] n mente f; (intellect) intelecto; (contrasted with matter) espíritu m ◆ vt (attend to, look after) ocuparse de, cuidar; (be careful) tener cuidado con; (object to): **I don't ~ the noise** no me molesta el ruido; **it is on my ~** me preocupa; **to bear sth in ~** tomar or tener algo en cuenta; **to make up one's ~** decidirse; **I don't ~** me es igual; **~ you …** te advierto que …; **never ~!** ¡es igual!, ¡no importa!; (don't worry) ¡no te preocupes!; **"~ the step"** "cuidado con el escalón" □ **mindless** adj (crime) sin motivo; (work) de autómata

mine¹ [maɪn] pron el mío/la mía etc; **a friend of ~** un(a) amigo(-a) mío/mía ◆ adj: **this book is ~** este libro es mío

mine² [maɪn] n mina ◆ vt (coal) extraer; (bomb: beach etc) minar □ **minefield** n campo de minas □ **miner** n minero(-a)

mineral ['mɪnərəl] adj mineral ◆ n mineral m □ **mineral water** n agua mineral

mingle ['mɪŋgl] vi: **to ~ with** mezclarse con

miniature ['mɪnətʃəˡ] adj (en) miniatura ◆ n miniatura

minibar ['mɪnɪbɑːˡ] n minibar m

minibus ['mɪnɪbʌs] n microbús m

minicab ['mɪnɪkæb] n taxi m (que sólo puede pedirse por teléfono)

minimal ['mɪnɪml] adj mínimo

minimize ['mɪnɪmaɪz] vt minimizar; (play down) empequeñecer

minimum ['mɪnɪməm] (pl **minima**) n, adj mínimo

mining ['maɪnɪŋ] n explotación f minera

miniskirt ['mɪnɪskəːt] n minifalda

minister ['mɪnɪstəˡ] n (BRIT POL) ministro/-a (SP), secretario/-a (LAm); (REL) pastor m ◆ vi: **to ~** atender a

ministry ['mɪnɪstrɪ] n (BRIT POL) ministerio, secretaría (MEX); (REL) sacerdocio

minor ['maɪnəˡ] adj (repairs, injuries) leve; (poet, planet) menor; (MUS) menor ◆ n (LAW) menor m de edad

Minorca [mɪˈnɔːkə] n Menorca

minority [maɪˈnɒrɪtɪ] n minoría

mint [mɪnt] n (plant) menta, hierbabuena; (sweet) caramelo de menta ◆ vt (coins) acuñar; **the (Royal) M~, the** (US) **M~** la Casa de la Moneda; **in ~ condition** en perfecto estado

minus ['maɪnəs] n (also: **~ sign**) signo de menos ◆ prep menos; **12 ~ 6 equals 6** 12 menos 6 son 6; **~ 24˚C** menos 24 grados

minute¹ ['mɪnɪt] n minuto; (fig) momento; **minutes** npl (of meeting) actas fpl; **at the last ~** a última hora

minute² [maɪˈnjuːt] adj diminuto; (search) minucioso

miracle ['mɪrəkl] n milagro

miraculous [mɪˈrækjʊləs] adj milagroso

mirage ['mɪrɑːʒ] n espejismo

mirror ['mɪrəˡ] n espejo; (in car) retrovisor m

misbehave [mɪsbɪ'heɪv] *vi* portarse mal

misc. *abbr* = **miscellaneous**

miscarriage ['mɪskærɪdʒ] *n* (MED) aborto; ~ **of justice** error *m* judicial

miscellaneous [mɪsɪ'leɪnɪəs] *adj* varios(-as), diversos(-as)

mischief ['mɪstʃɪf] *n* travesuras *fpl*, diabluras *fpl*; (maliciousness) malicia ❑ **mischievous** [-tʃɪvəs] *adj* travieso

misconception [mɪskən'sepʃən] *n* idea equivocada

misconduct [mɪs'kɒndʌkt] *n* mala conducta; **professional ~** falta profesional

miser ['maɪzə'] *n* avaro(-a)

miserable ['mɪzərəbl] *adj* (unhappy) triste, desgraciado; (unpleasant, contemptible) miserable

misery ['mɪzəri] *n* tristeza; (wretchedness) miseria, desdicha

misfortune [mɪs'fɔːtʃən] *n* desgracia

misgiving [mɪs'gɪvɪŋ] *n* (apprehension) presentimiento; **to have misgivings about sth** tener dudas acerca de algo

misguided [mɪs'gaɪdɪd] *adj* equivocado

mishap ['mɪshæp] *n* desgracia, contratiempo

misinterpret [mɪsɪn'tɜːprɪt] *vt* interpretar mal

misjudge [mɪs'dʒʌdʒ] *vt* juzgar mal

mislay [mɪs'leɪ] *vt* extraviar, perder

mislead [mɪs'liːd] *vt* llevar a conclusiones erróneas ❑ **misleading** *adj* engañoso

misplace [mɪs'pleɪs] *vt* extraviar

misprint ['mɪsprɪnt] *n* errata, error *m* de imprenta

misrepresent [mɪsreprɪ'zent] *vt* falsificar

Miss [mɪs] *n* Señorita

miss [mɪs] *vt* (train etc) perder; (fail to hit: target) errar; (regret the absence of): **I ~ him** (yo) le echo de menos o ra

faltar; (fail to see): **you can't ~ it** no tiene pérdida ♦ *vi* fallar ♦ *n* (shot) tiro fallido *or* perdido ► **miss out** (BRIT) vt omitir ► **miss out on** *vt fus* (fun, party, opportunity) perderse

missile ['mɪsaɪl] *n* (AVIAT) mísil *m*; (object thrown) proyectil *m*

missing ['mɪsɪŋ] *adj* (pupil) ausente; (thing) perdido; (MIL): **~ in action** desaparecido en combate

mission [mɪʃən] *n* misión *f*; (official representation) delegación *f* ❑ **missionary** *n* misionero(-a)

misspell [mɪs'spel] (*pt, pp* **misspelt** (Brit) *or* **misspelled** (Brit)) *vt* escribir mal

mist [mɪst] *n* (light) neblina; (heavy) niebla; (at sea) bruma ♦ *vi* (eyes: also: **~ over**, **~ up**) llenarse de lágrimas; (BRIT: windows: also: **~ over**, **~ up**) empañarse

mistake [mɪs'teɪk] (*vt: irreg*) *n* error *m* ♦ *vt* entender mal; **by ~** por equivocación; **to make a ~** equivocarse; **to ~ A for B** confundir A con B ❑ **mistaken** *pp of* **mistake** ♦ *adj* equivocado; **to be mistaken** equivocarse, engañarse

mister ['mɪstə'] (*inf*) *n* señor *m*; *see* **Mr**

mistletoe ['mɪsltəʊ] *n* muérdago

mistook [mɪs'tʊk] *pt of* **mistake**

mistress [mɪstrɪs] *n* (lover) amante *f*; (of house) señora (de la casa); (BRIT: in primary school) maestra; (in secondary school) profesora; (of situation) dueña

mistrust [mɪs'trʌst] *vt* desconfiar de

misty [mɪsti] *adj* (day) de niebla; (glasses etc) empañado

misunderstand [mɪsʌndə'stænd] (*irreg*) *vt, vi* entender mal ❑ **misunderstanding** *n* malentendido

misunderstood [mɪsʌndə'stʊd] *pt, pp* of **misunderstand** ♦ *adj* (person) incomprendido

misuse [*n* mɪs'juːs, *vb* mɪs'juːz] *n* mal uso; (of power) abuso; (of funds) malversación f ♦ vt abusar de; malversar

mitt(en) ['mɪt(n)] n manopla

mix [mɪks] vt mezclar; (combine) unir ♦ vi mezclarse; (people) llevarse bien ♦ n mezcla ► **mix up** vt mezclar; (confuse) confundir □ **mixed** adj mixto; (feelings) encontrado □ **mixed grill** n (BRIT) parrillada mixta □ **mixed salad** n ensalada mixta □ **mixed-up** adj (confused) confuso, revuelto □ **mixer** n (for food) licuadora; (for drinks) coctelera; (person): **he's a good mixer** tiene don de gentes □ **mixture** n mezcla; (also: **cough mixture**) jarabe m □ **mix-up** n confusión f

ml abbr (= millilitre(s)) ml

mm abbr (= millimetre) mm

moan [məun] n gemido ♦ vi gemir; (inf: complain): **to ~ (about)** quejarse (de)

moat [məut] n foso

mob [mɔb] n multitud f ♦ vt acosar

mobile ['məubaɪl] adj móvil ♦ n móvil m □ **mobile home** n caravana □ **mobile phone** n teléfono móvil

mobility [məu'bɪlɪti] n movilidad f

mobilize ['məubɪlaɪz] vt movilizar

mock [mɔk] vt (ridicule) ridiculizar; (laugh at) burlarse de ♦ adj fingido; ~ **exam** examen preparatorio antes de los exámenes oficiales; **mocks** (BRIT: SCOL: inf) exámenes mpl de prueba □ **mockery** n burla

mod cons ['mɔd'kɔnz] npl abbr = modern conveniences; see convenience

mode [məud] n modo

model ['mɔdl] n modelo; (fashion model, artist's model) modelo mf ♦ adj modelo ♦ vt (with clay etc) modelar; (copy): **to ~ o.s. on** tomar como modelo a ♦ vi ser modelo; **to ~ clothes** pasar modelos, ser modelo

modem ['məudəm] n modem m

moderate [adj 'mɔdərət, vb 'mɔdəreɪt] adj moderado(-a) ♦ vi moderarse, calmarse ♦ vt moderar

moderation [mɔdə'reɪʃən] n moderación f; **in ~** con moderación

modern ['mɔdən] adj moderno □ **modernize** vt modernizar □ **modern languages** npl lenguas fpl modernas

modest ['mɔdɪst] adj modesto; (small) módico □ **modesty** n modestia

modification [mɔdɪfɪ'keɪʃən] n modificación f

modify ['mɔdɪfaɪ] vt modificar

module ['mɔdjuːl] n (unit, component, SPACE) módulo

mohair ['məuhɛə°] n mohair m

Mohammed [mə'hæmed] n Mahoma m

moist [mɔɪst] adj húmedo □ **moisture** ['mɔɪstʃə°] n humedad f □ **moisturizer** ['mɔɪstʃəraɪzə°] n crema hidratante

mold etc [məuld] (US) = **mould** etc

mole [məul] n (animal, spy) topo; (spot) lunar m

molecule ['mɔlɪkjuːl] n molécula

molest [məu'lest] vt importunar; (assault sexually) abusar sexualmente de

⚠ Be careful not to translate **molest** by the Spanish word **molestar**.

molten ['məultən] adj fundido; (lava) líquido

mom [mɔm] (US) n = **mum**

moment ['məumənt] n momento; **at the ~** de momento, por ahora □ **momentarily** ['məuməntrɪli] adv momentáneamente; (US: very soon) de un momento a otro □ **momentary** adj momentáneo □ **momentous** [-'mentəs] adj trascendental, importante

momentum [məʊ'mentəm] n momento; (fig) ímpetu m; **to gather ~** cobrar velocidad; (fig) ganar fuerza

mommy ['mɒmɪ] (US) n = **mummy**

Mon abbr (= Monday) lun

Monaco ['mɒnəkəʊ] n Mónaco

monarch ['mɒnək] n monarca mf □ **monarchy** n monarquía

monastery ['mɒnəstərɪ] n monasterio

Monday ['mʌndɪ] n lunes m inv

monetary ['mʌnɪtərɪ] adj monetario

money ['mʌnɪ] n dinero; (currency) moneda; **to make ~** ganar dinero □ **money belt** n riñonera □ **money order** n giro

mongrel ['mʌŋɡrəl] n (dog) perro mestizo

monitor ['mɒnɪtə'] n (SCOL) monitor m; (also: **television ~**) receptor m de control; (of computer) monitor m ♦ vt controlar

monk [mʌŋk] n monje m

monkey ['mʌŋkɪ] n mono

monologue ['mɒnəlɒɡ] n monólogo

monopoly [mə'nɒpəlɪ] n monopolio

monosodium glutamate [mɒnə'səʊdɪəm'ɡluːtəmeɪt] n glutamato monosódico

monotonous [mə'nɒtənəs] adj monótono

monsoon [mɒn'suːn] n monzón m

monster ['mɒnstə'] n monstruo

month [mʌnθ] n mes m □ **monthly** adj mensual ♦ adv mensualmente

monument ['mɒnjʊmənt] n monumento

mood [muːd] n humor m; (of crowd, group) clima m; **to be in a good/bad ~** estar de buen/mal humor □ **moody** adj (changeable) de humor variable; (sullen) malhumorado

moon [muːn] n luna □ **moonlight** n luz f de la luna

moor [mʊə'] n páramo ♦ vt (ship) amarrar ♦ vi echar las amarras

moose [muːs] n inv alce m

mop [mɒp] n fregona; (of hair) greña, melena ♦ vt fregar ► **mop up** vt limpiar

mope [məʊp] vi estar or andar deprimido

moped ['məʊped] n ciclomotor m

moral ['mɒrl] adj moral ♦ n moraleja; **morals** npl moralidad f, moral f

morale [mɒ'rɑːl] n moral f

morality [mə'rælɪtɪ] n moralidad f

morbid ['mɔːbɪd] adj (interest) morboso; (MED) mórbido

---

more

KEYWORD

[mɔː'] adj

1 (greater in number etc) más; **more people/work than before** más gente/trabajo que antes

2 (additional) más; **do you want (some) more tea?** ¿quieres más té?; **is there any more wine?** ¿queda vino?; **it'll take a few more weeks** tardará unas semanas más; **it's 2 kms more to the house** faltan 2 kms para la casa; **more time/letters than we expected** más tiempo del que/más cartas de las que esperábamos

♦ pron (greater amount, additional amount) más; **more than 10** más de 10; **it cost more than the other one/ than we expected** costó más que el otro/más de lo que esperábamos; **is there any more?** ¿hay más?; **many/ much more** muchos(as)/mucho(a) más

♦ adv más; **more dangerous/easily (than)** más peligroso/fácilmente (que); **more and more expensive** cada vez más caro; **more or less** más o menos; **more than ever** más que nunca

moreover [mɔː'rəʊvəᵊ] adv además, por otra parte

morgue [mɔːg] n depósito de cadáveres

morning ['mɔːnɪŋ] n mañana; (early morning) madrugada ♦ cpd matutino, de la mañana; **in the ~** por la mañana; **7 o'clock in the ~** las 7 de la mañana ❑ **morning sickness** n náuseas fpl matutinas

Moroccan [mə'rɒkən] adj, n marroquí m/f

Morocco [mə'rɒkəu] n Marruecos m

moron ['mɔːrɒn] (inf) n imbécil m/f

morphine ['mɔːfiːn] n morfina

Morse [mɔːs] n (also: **~ code**) (código) Morse

mortal ['mɔːtl] adj, n mortal m

mortar ['mɔːtəᵊ] n argamasa

mortgage ['mɔːgɪdʒ] n hipoteca ♦ vt hipotecar

mortician [mɔː'tɪʃən] (US) n director(-a) m/f de pompas fúnebres

mortified ['mɔːtɪfaɪd] adj: **I was ~** me dio muchísima vergüenza

mortuary ['mɔːtjuərɪ] n depósito de cadáveres

mosaic [məu'zeɪɪk] n mosaico

Moslem ['mɒzləm] adj, n = **Muslim**

mosque [mɒsk] n mezquita

mosquito [mɒs'kiːtəu] (pl **mosquitoes**) n mosquito (SP), zancudo (LAm)

moss [mɒs] n musgo

most [məust] adj la mayor parte de, la mayoría de ♦ pron la mayor parte, la mayoría ♦ adv el más; (very) muy; **the ~** (also: **+ adj**) el más; **~ of them** la mayor parte de ellos; **I saw the ~** yo vi el que más; **at the (very) ~** a lo sumo, todo lo más; **to make the ~ of** aprovechar (al máximo); **a ~ interesting book** un libro interesantísimo ❑ **mostly** adv en su mayor parte, principalmente

MOT (BRIT) n abbr = **Ministry of Transport**; **the ~ (test)** inspección (anual) obligatoria de coches y camiones

motel [məu'tel] n motel m

moth [mɒθ] n mariposa nocturna; (clothes moth) polilla

mother ['mʌðəᵊ] n madre f ♦ adj materno ♦ vt (care for) cuidar (como una madre) ❑ **motherhood** n maternidad f ❑ **mother-in-law** n suegra ❑ **mother-of-pearl** n nácar m ❑ **Mother's Day** n Día m de la Madre ❑ **mother-to-be** n futura madre f ❑ **mother tongue** n lengua materna

motif [məu'tiːf] n motivo

motion ['məuʃən] n movimiento; (gesture) ademán m, señal f; (at meeting) moción f ♦ vt, vi: **to ~ (to) sb to do sth** hacer señas a algn para que haga algo ❑ **motionless** adj inmóvil ❑ **motion picture** n película

motivate ['məutɪveɪt] vt motivar

motivation [məutɪ'veɪʃən] n motivación f

motive ['məutɪv] n motivo

motor ['məutəᵊ] n motor m; (BRIT: inf: vehicle) coche m (SP), carro (LAm), automóvil m ♦ adj motor (f: motora or motriz) ❑ **motorbike** n moto f ❑ **motorboat** n lancha motora ❑ **motorcar** (BRIT) n coche m, carro, automóvil m ❑ **motorcycle** n motocicleta ❑ **motorcyclist** n motociclista mf ❑ **motoring** (BRIT) n automovilismo ❑ **motorist** n conductor(a) m/f, automovilista f ❑ **motor racing** (BRIT) n carreras fpl de coches, automovilismo ❑ **motorway** (BRIT) n autopista

motto ['mɒtəu] (pl **mottoes**) n lema m, (watchword) consigna

mould [məuld] (US **mold**) n molde m; (mildew) moho ♦ vt moldear; (fig) formar ❑ **mouldy** adj enmohecido

mound [maund] n montón m, montículo

mount [maunt] n monte m ♦ vt montar, subir a; (jewel) engarzar; (picture) enmarcar; (exhibition)

organizar ♦ vi (increase) aumentar
► **mount up** vi aumentar

mountain ['mauntɪn] n montaña
♦ cpd de montaña ❑ **mountain bike**
n bicicleta de montaña
❑ **mountaineer** n alpinista mf (SP,
MEX), andinista mf (LAm)
❑ **mountaineering** n alpinismo (SP,
MEX), andinismo (LAm)
❑ **mountainous** adj montañoso
❑ **mountain range** n sierra

mourn [mɔːn] vt llorar, lamentar ♦ vi:
to ~ **for** llorar la muerte de
❑ **mourner** n doliente mf;
dolorido(-a) ❑ **mourning** n luto; **in
mourning** de luto

mouse [maus] (pl **mice**) n (ZOOL,
COMPUT) ratón m ❑ **mouse mat** n
(COMPUT) alfombrilla

moussaka [muːˈsɑːkə] n musaca

mousse [muːs] n (CULIN) crema batida;
(for hair) espuma (moldeadora)

moustache [məsˈtɑːʃ] (US **mustache**) n
bigote m

mouth [mauθ, pl mauðz] n boca; (of
river) desembocadura ❑ **mouthful** n
bocado ❑ **mouth organ** n armónica
❑ **mouthpiece** n (of musical
instrument) boquilla; (spokesman)
portavoz mf ❑ **mouthwash** n
enjuague m

move [muːv] n (movement)
movimiento; (in game) jugada; (: turn
to play) turno; (change: of house)
mudanza; (: of job) cambio de trabajo
♦ vt mover; (emotionally) conmover;
(POL: resolution etc) proponer ♦ vi
moverse; (traffic) circular; (also: ~
house) trasladarse, mudarse; **to ~ sb
to do sth** mover a algn a hacer algo; **to
get a ~ on** darse prisa ► **move back** vi
retroceder ► **move in** vi (to a house)
instalarse; (police, soldiers) intervenir
► **move off** vi ponerse en camino
► **move on** vi ponerse en camino
► **move out** vi (of house) mudarse
► **move over** vi apartarse, hacer sitio

► **move up** vi (employee) ser
ascendido ❑ **movement** n
movimiento

movie ['muːvɪ] n película; **to go to the
movies** ir al cine ❑ **movie theater**
(US) n cine m

moving ['muːvɪŋ] adj (emotional)
conmovedor(a); (that moves) móvil

mow [məu] (pt **mowed**, pp **mowed** or
mown) vt (grass, corn) cortar, segar
❑ **mower** n (also: **lawnmower**)
cortacéspedes m inv

Mozambique [məuzæmˈbiːk] n
Mozambique m

MP n abbr = **Member of Parliament**

MP3 n MP3 ❑ **MP3 player** n
reproductor m (de) MP3

mpg n abbr = **miles per gallon**

m.p.h. abbr = **miles per hour** (60
m.p.h. = 96 k.p.h.)

Mr ['mɪstə*] (US **Mr.**) n: **Mr Smith** (el) Sr.
Smith

Mrs ['mɪsɪz] (US **Mrs.**) n: ~ **Smith** (la) Sra.
Smith

Ms [mɪz] (US **Ms.**) n = **Miss** or **Mrs**; **Ms
Smith** (la) Sr(t)a. Smith

MSP n abbr = **Member of the
Scottish Parliament**

Mt abbr (GEO: = mount) m

much [mʌtʃ] adj mucho ♦ adv mucho;
(before pp) muy ♦ n or pron mucho;
how ~ is it? ¿cuánto es?, ¿cuánto
cuesta?; **too ~** demasiado; **it's not ~** no
es mucho; **as ~ as** tanto como;
however ~ he tries por mucho que se
esfuerce

muck [mʌk] n suciedad f ► **muck up**
(inf) vt arruinar, estropear ❑ **mucky**
adj (dirty) sucio

mucus ['mjuːkəs] n mucosidad f, moco

mud [mʌd] n barro, lodo

muddle ['mʌdl] n desorden m,
confusión f; (mix-up) embrollo, lío ♦ vt
(also: ~ **up**) embrollar, confundir

muddy ['mʌdɪ] adj fangoso, cubierto
de lodo

mudguard ['mʌdgɑːd] n guardabarros m inv

muesli ['mjuːzlɪ] n muesli m

muffin ['mʌfɪn] n panecillo dulce

muffled ['mʌfld] adj (noise etc) amortiguado, apagado

muffler (US) ['mʌflə*] n (AUT) silenciador m

mug [mʌg] n taza grande (sin platillo); (for beer) jarra; (inf: face) jeta ♦ vt (assault) asaltar ♦ **mugger** ['mʌgə*] n atracador(a) m/f ♦ **mugging** n asalto

muggy ['mʌgɪ] adj bochornoso

mule [mjuːl] n mula

multicoloured ['mʌltɪkʌləd] (US **multicolored**) adj multicolor

multimedia [mʌltɪ'miːdɪə] adj multimedia

multinational [mʌltɪ'næʃənl] n multinacional f ♦ adj multinacional

multiple ['mʌltɪpl] adj múltiple ♦ n múltiplo ♦ **multiple choice (test)** n examen m de tipo test ♦ **multiple sclerosis** n esclerosis f múltiple

multiplex cinema [mʌltɪpleks-] n multicines mpl

multiplication [mʌltɪplɪ'keɪʃən] n multiplicación f

multiply ['mʌltɪplaɪ] vt multiplicar ♦ vi multiplicarse

multistorey [mʌltɪ'stɔːrɪ] (BRIT) adj de muchos pisos

mum [mʌm] (BRIT: inf) n mamá ♦ adj: to keep ~ mantener la boca cerrada

mumble ['mʌmbl] vt, vi hablar entre dientes, refunfuñar

mummy ['mʌmɪ] n (BRIT: mother) mamá; (embalmed) momia

mumps [mʌmps] n paperas fpl

munch [mʌntʃ] vt, vi mascar

municipal [mjuː'nɪsɪpl] adj municipal

mural ['mjuərl] n (pintura) mural m

murder ['mɜːdə*] n asesinato; (in law) homicidio ♦ vt asesinar, matar ♦ **murderer** n asesino

murky ['mɜːkɪ] adj (water) turbio; (street, night) lóbrego

murmur ['mɜːmə*] n murmullo ♦ vt, vi murmurar

muscle ['mʌsl] n músculo; (fig: strength) garra, fuerza ♦ **muscular** ['mʌskjulə*] adj muscular; (person) musculoso

museum [mjuː'zɪəm] n museo

mushroom ['mʌʃrum] n seta, hongo; (CULIN) champiñón m ♦ vi crecer de la noche a la mañana

music ['mjuːzɪk] n música ♦ **musical** adj musical; (sound) melodioso; (person) con talento musical ♦ n (show) comedia musical ♦ **musical instrument** n instrumento musical ♦ **musician** [-'zɪʃən] n músico(-a)

Muslim ['mʌzlɪm] adj, n musulmán(-ana) m/f

muslin ['mʌzlɪn] n muselina

mussel ['mʌsl] n mejillón m

must [mʌst] aux vb (obligation): I ~ do it debo hacerlo, tengo que hacerlo; (probability): he ~ be there by now ya debe de estar allí ♦ n: it's a ~ es imprescindible

mustache ['mʌstæʃ] (US) n = moustache

mustard ['mʌstəd] n mostaza

mustn't ['mʌsnt] = must not

mute [mjuːt] adj, n mudo(-a) m/f

mutilate ['mjuːtɪleɪt] vt mutilar

mutiny ['mjuːtɪnɪ] n motín m ♦ vi amotinarse

mutter ['mʌtə*] vt, vi murmurar

mutton ['mʌtn] n carne f de cordero

mutual ['mjuːtʃuəl] adj mutuo; (interest) común

muzzle ['mʌzl] n hocico; (for dog) bozal m; (of gun) boca ♦ vt (dog) poner un bozal a

my [maɪ] adj mi(s); **my house/brother/sisters** mi casa/mi hermano/mis hermanas; **I've washed my hair/cut my finger** me he lavado el pelo/

cortado un dedo; **is this my pen or yours?** ¿es este bolígrafo mío o tuyo?

myself [maɪˈsɛlf] pron (reflexive) me; (emphatic) yo mismo; (after prep) mí (mismo); see also **oneself**

mysterious [mɪsˈtɪərɪəs] adj misterioso

mystery [ˈmɪstərɪ] n misterio

mystical [ˈmɪstɪkl] adj místico

mystify [ˈmɪstɪfaɪ] vt (perplex) dejar perplejo

myth [mɪθ] n mito ❏ **mythology** [mɪˈθɒlədʒɪ] n mitología

N, n

n/a abbr (= not applicable) no interesa

nag [næɡ] vt (scold) regañar

nail [neɪl] n (human) uña; (metal) clavo ♦ vt clavar; **to ~ sth to sth** clavar algo en algo; **to ~ sb down to doing sth** comprometer a algn a que haga algo ❏ **nailbrush** n cepillo para las uñas ❏ **nailfile** n lima para las uñas ❏ **nail polish** n esmalte m o laca para las uñas ❏ **nail polish remover** n quitaesmalte m ❏ **nail scissors** npl tijeras fpl para las uñas ❏ **nail varnish** (BRIT) n = **nail polish**

naïve [naɪˈiːv] adj ingenuo

naked [ˈneɪkɪd] adj (nude) desnudo; (flame) expuesto al aire

name [neɪm] n nombre m; (surname) apellido; (reputation) fama, renombre m ♦ vt (child) poner nombre a; (criminal) identificar; (price, date etc) fijar; **what's your ~?** ¿cómo se llama?; **by ~** de nombre; **in the ~ of** en nombre de; **to give one's ~ and address** dar sus señas ❏ **namely** adv a saber

nanny [ˈnænɪ] n niñera

nap [næp] n (sleep) sueñecito, siesta

napkin [ˈnæpkɪn] n (also: **table ~**) servilleta

nappy [ˈnæpɪ] (BRIT) n pañal m

narcotics npl (illegal drugs) estupefacientes mpl, narcóticos mpl

narrative [ˈnærətɪv] n narrativa ♦ adj narrativo

narrator [nəˈreɪtə*] n narrador(a) m/f

narrow [ˈnærəu] adj estrecho, angosto; (fig: majority etc) corto; (: ideas etc) estrecho ♦ vi (road) estrecharse; (diminish) reducirse; **to have a ~ escape** escaparse por los pelos ▶ **narrow down** vt (search, investigation, possibilities) restringir, limitar; (list) reducir ❏ **narrowly** adv (miss) por poco ❏ **narrow-minded** adj de miras estrechas

nasal [ˈneɪzl] adj nasal

nasty [ˈnɑːstɪ] adj (remark) feo; (person) antipático; (revolting: taste, smell) asqueroso; (wound, disease etc) peligroso, grave

nation [ˈneɪʃən] n nación f

national [ˈnæʃənl] adj, n nacional m/f ❏ **national anthem** n himno nacional ❏ **national dress** n vestido nacional ❏ **National Health Service** (BRIT) n servicio nacional de salud pública, ≈ Insalud n (SP) ❏ **National Insurance** (BRIT) n seguro social ❏ **nationalist** adj, n nacionalista m/f ❏ **nationality** [næʃəˈnælɪtɪ] n nacionalidad f ❏ **nationalize** vt nacionalizar ❏ **national park** (BRIT) n parque m nacional ❏ **National Trust** n (BRIT) organización encargada de preservar el patrimonio histórico británico

nationwide [ˈneɪʃənwaɪd] adj en escala or a nivel nacional

native [ˈneɪtɪv] n (local inhabitant) natural mf, nacional mf ♦ adj (indigenous) indígena; (country) natal; (innate) natural, innato; **a ~ of Russia** un(a) natural mf de Rusia ❏ **Native American** n americano(-a) indígena, amerindio(-a) ❏ **native speaker** n hablante m nativo(-a)

NATO ['neɪtəʊ] n abbr (= North Atlantic Treaty Organization) OTAN f

natural ['nætʃrəl] adj natural
❏ **natural gas** n gas m natural
❏ **natural history** n historia natural
❏ **naturally** adv naturalmente; (of course) desde luego, por supuesto ❏ **natural resources** npl recursos mpl naturales

nature ['neɪtʃə'] n (also: N~) naturaleza; (group, sort) género, clase f; (character) carácter m, genio; **by ~** por or de naturaleza ❏ **nature reserve** n reserva natural

naughty ['nɔːtɪ] adj (child) travieso

nausea ['nɔːsɪə] n náuseas fpl

naval ['neɪvl] adj naval, de marina

navel ['neɪvl] n ombligo

navigate ['nævɪgeɪt] vt gobernar ♦ vi navegar; (AUT) ir de copiloto ❏ **navigation** [-'geɪʃən] n (action) navegación f; (science) náutica

navy ['neɪvɪ] n marina de guerra; (ships) armada, flota

Nazi ['nɑːtsɪ] n nazi mf

NB abbr (= nota bene) nótese

near [nɪə'] adj (place, relation) cercano; (time) próximo ♦ adv cerca ♦ prep (also: ~ **to**: space) cerca de, junto a; (: time) cerca de ♦ vt acercarse a, aproximarse a ❏ **nearby** [nɪə'baɪ] adj cercano, próximo ♦ adv cerca ❏ **nearly** adv casi, por poco; **I nearly fell** por poco me caigo ❏ **near-sighted** adj miope, corto de vista

neat [niːt] adj (place) ordenado, bien cuidado; (person) pulcro; (plan) ingenioso; (spirits) solo ❏ **neatly** adv (tidily) con esmero; (skilfully) ingeniosamente

necessarily ['nesɪsrɪlɪ] adv necesariamente

necessary ['nesɪsrɪ] adj necesario, preciso

necessity [nɪ'sesɪtɪ] n necesidad f

neck [nek] n (of person, garment, bottle) cuello; (of animal) pescuezo ♦ vi (inf) besuquearse; **~ and ~** parejos ❏ **necklace** ['neklɪs] n collar m ❏ **necktie** ['nektaɪ] n corbata

nectarine ['nektərɪn] n nectarina

need [niːd] n (lack) escasez f, falta; (necessity) necesidad f ♦ vt (require) necesitar; **I ~ to do it** tengo que or debo hacerlo; **you don't ~ to go** no hace falta que (te) vayas

needle ['niːdl] n aguja ♦ vt (fig: inf) picar, fastidiar

needless ['niːdlɪs] adj innecesario; **~ to say** huelga decir que

needlework ['niːdlwəːk] n (activity) costura, labor f de aguja

needn't ['niːdnt] = need not

needy ['niːdɪ] adj necesitado

negative ['negətɪv] n (PHOT) negativo; (LING) negación f ♦ adj negativo

neglect [nɪ'glekt] vt (one's duty) faltar a, no cumplir con; (child) descuidar, desatender ♦ n (of house, garden etc) abandono; (of child) desatención f; (of duty) incumplimiento

negotiate [nɪ'gəʊʃɪeɪt] vt (treaty, loan) negociar; (obstacle) franquear; (bend in road) tomar ♦ vi: **to ~ (with)** negociar (con)

negotiations [nɪgəʊʃɪ'eɪʃənz] pl n negociaciones

negotiator [nɪ'gəʊʃɪeɪtə'] n negociador(a) m/f

neighbour ['neɪbə'] (US **neighbor** etc) n vecino(-a) ❏ **neighbourhood** n (place) vecindad f, barrio; (people) vecindario ❏ **neighbouring** adj vecino

neither ['naɪðə'] adj ni ♦ conj: **I didn't move and – did John** no me he movido, ni Juan tampoco ♦ pron ninguno ♦ adv: **~ good nor bad** ni bueno ni malo; **~ is true** ninguno(-a) de los (las) dos es cierto(-a)

neon ['niːɒn] n neón m

Nepal [nɪˈpɔːl] n Nepal m

nephew [ˈnevjuː] n sobrino

nerve [nɜːv] n (ANAT) nervio; (courage) valor m; (impudence) descaro, frescura; **nerves** (nervousness) nerviosismo msg, nervios mpl; **a fit of nerves** un ataque de nervios

nervous [ˈnɜːvəs] adj (anxious, ANAT) nervioso; (timid) tímido, miedoso ☐ **nervous breakdown** n crisis f nerviosa

nest [nest] n (of bird) nido m; (wasps' nest) avispero ♦ vi anidar

net [net] n (gen) red f; (fabric) tul m ♦ adj (COMM) neto, líquido ♦ vt coger (SP) or agarrar (LAm) con red; (SPORT) marcar ☐ **netball** n básquet m

Netherlands [ˈneðələndz] npl: **the ~** los Países Bajos

nett [net] adj = **net**

nettle [ˈnetl] n ortiga

network [ˈnetwɜːk] n red f

neurotic [njuəˈrɒtɪk] adj neurótico(-a)

neuter [ˈnjuːtər] adj (LING) neutro ♦ vt castrar, capar

neutral [ˈnjuːtrəl] adj (person) neutral; (colour etc, ELEC) neutro ♦ n (AUT) punto muerto

never [ˈnevər] adv nunca, jamás; **I ~ went** no fui nunca; **~ in my life** jamás en la vida; see also **mind** ☐ **never-ending** adj interminable, sin fin ☐ **nevertheless** [nevəðəˈles] adv sin embargo, no obstante

new [njuː] adj nuevo; (brand new) a estrenar; (recent) reciente ☐ **New Age** n Nueva Era ☐ **newborn** adj recién nacido ☐ **newcomer** [ˈnjuːkʌmər] n recién venido(-a) or llegado(-a) ☐ **newly** adv nuevamente, recién

news [njuːz] n noticias fpl; **a piece of ~** una noticia; **the ~** (RADIO, TV) las noticias fpl ☐ **news agency** n agencia de noticias ☐ **newsagent** (BRIT) n vendedor(a) m/f de periódicos ☐ **newscaster** n presentador(a) m/f,

locutor(a) m/f ☐ **news dealer** (US) n = **newsagent** ☐ **newsletter** n hoja informativa, boletín m ☐ **newspaper** n periódico, diario m ☐ **newsreader** n = **newscaster**

newt [njuːt] n tritón m

New Year n Año Nuevo ☐ **New Year's Day** n Día m de Año Nuevo ☐ **New Year's Eve** n Nochevieja

New Zealand [njuːˈziːlənd] n Nueva Zelanda ☐ **New Zealander** n neozelandés(-esa) m/f

next [nekst] adj (house, room) vecino; (bus stop, meeting) próximo; (following: page etc) siguiente ♦ adv después; **the ~ day** el día siguiente; **~ time** la próxima vez; **~ year** el año próximo or que viene; **~ to** junto a, al lado de; **~ to nothing** casi nada; **~ please!** ¡el siguiente! ☐ **next door** adv en la casa de al lado ♦ adj vecino, de al lado ☐ **next-of-kin** n pariente m más cercano

NHS n abbr = **National Health Service**

nibble [ˈnɪbl] vt mordisquear, mordiscar

nice [naɪs] adj (likeable) simpático; (kind) amable; (pleasant) agradable; (attractive) bonito, lindo (LAm) ☐ **nicely** adv amablemente; bien

niche [niːʃ] n (ARCH) nicho, hornacina

nick [nɪk] n (wound) rasguño; (cut, indentation) mella, muesca ♦ vt (inf) birlar, robar; **in the ~ of time** justo a tiempo

nickel [ˈnɪkl] n níquel m; (US) moneda de 5 centavos

nickname [ˈnɪkneɪm] n apodo, mote m ♦ vt apodar

nicotine [ˈnɪkətiːn] n nicotina

niece [niːs] n sobrina

Nigeria [naɪˈdʒɪəriə] n Nigeria

night [naɪt] n noche f; (evening) tarde f; **the ~ before last** anteanoche; **at ~, by ~** de noche, por la noche ☐ **night**

club n cabaret m ◻ **nightdress** (BRIT)
n camisón m ◻ **nightie** ['naɪtɪ] n =
nightdress ◻ **nightlife** n vida
nocturna ◻ **nightly** adj de todas las
noches ♦ adv todas las noches, cada
noche ◻ **nightmare** n pesadilla
◻ **night school** n clase(s) f(pl)
nocturna(s) ◻ **night shift** n turno
nocturno or de noche ◻ **night-time** n
noche f

nil [nɪl] (BRIT) n (SPORT) cero, nada

nine [naɪn] num nueve ◻ **nineteen**
num diecinueve, diez y nueve
◻ **nineteenth** [naɪn'tiːnθ] adj
decimonoveno, decimonono
◻ **ninetieth** ['naɪntɪɪθ] adj
nonagésimo ◻ **ninety** num noventa

ninth [naɪnθ] adj noveno

nip [nɪp] vt (pinch) pellizcar a; (bite)
morder

nipple ['nɪpl] (ANAT) n pezón m

nitrogen ['naɪtrədʒən] n nitrógeno

no

[nəʊ] (pl **noes**) adv (opposite of "yes")
no; **are you coming? — no (I'm not)**
¿vienes? — no; **would you like some
more?** — no thank you ¿quieres
más? — no gracias

♦ adj (not any): **I have no money/
time/books** no tengo dinero/
tiempo/libros; **no other man would
have done it** ningún otro lo hubiera
hecho; **"no entry"** "prohibido el
paso"; **"no smoking"** "prohibido
fumar"

♦ n no m

nobility [nəʊ'bɪlɪtɪ] n nobleza

noble ['nəʊbl] adj noble

nobody ['nəʊbədɪ] pron nadie

nod [nɒd] vi saludar con la cabeza; (in
agreement) decir que sí con la cabeza;
(doze) dar cabezadas ♦ vt: to ~ **one's
head** inclinar la cabeza ♦ n inclinación

f de cabeza ► **nod off** vi dar
cabezadas

noise [nɔɪz] n ruido; (din) escándalo,
estrépito ◻ **noisy** adj ruidoso; (child)
escandaloso

nominal ['nɒmɪnl] adj nominal

nominate ['nɒmɪneɪt] vt (propose)
proponer; (appoint) nombrar
◻ **nomination** [nɒmɪ'neɪʃən] n
propuesta; nombramiento
◻ **nominee** [-'niː] n candidato(-a)

none [nʌn] pron ninguno(-a) ♦ adv de
ninguna manera; **~ of you** ninguno de
vosotros; **I've ~ left** no me queda
ninguno(-a); **he's ~ the worse for it** no
le ha hecho ningún mal

nonetheless [nʌnðə'les] adv sin
embargo, no obstante

non-fiction [nɒn'fɪkʃən] n literatura
no novelesca

nonsense ['nɒnsəns] n tonterías fpl,
disparates fpl; **~!** ¡qué tonterías!

non-: non-smoker n no fumador(a) m/f
◻ **non-smoking** adj (de) no fumador
◻ **non-stick** adj (pan, surface)
antiadherente

noodles ['nuːdlz] npl tallarines mpl

noon [nuːn] n mediodía m

no-one ['nəʊwʌn] pron = nobody

nor [nɔːr] conj = **neither** ♦ adv see
neither

norm [nɔːm] n norma

normal ['nɔːml] adj normal
◻ **normally** adv normalmente

north [nɔːθ] n norte m ♦ adj del norte,
norteño ♦ adv al or hacia el norte
◻ **North America** n América del
Norte ◻ **North American** adj, n
norteamericano(-a) m/f
◻ **northbound** ['nɔːθbaʊnd] adj
(traffic) que se dirige al norte;
(carriageway) de dirección norte
◻ **north-east** n nor(d)este m
◻ **northeastern** adj nor(d)este, del
nor(d)este ◻ **northern** ['nɔːðən] adj
norteño, del norte ◻ **Northern**

Ireland n Irlanda del Norte □ **North Korea** n Corea del Norte □ **North Pole** n Polo Norte □ **North Sea** n Mar m del Norte □ **north-west** n nor(d)oeste m □ **northwestern** ['nɔːθ'westən] adj noroeste, del noroeste

Norway ['nɔːweɪ] n Noruega f □ **Norwegian** [-'wiːdʒən] adj noruego(-a) ♦ n (person) noruego(-a); (LING) noruego

nose [nəʊz] n (ANAT) nariz f; (ZOOL) hocico; (sense of smell) olfato ♦ vi: **to ~ about** curiosear □ **nosebleed** n hemorragia nasal □ **nosey** (inf) adj curioso, fisgón(-ona)

nostalgia [nɔs'tældʒɪə] n nostalgia

nostalgic [nɔs'tældʒɪk] adj nostálgico

nostril ['nɔstrɪl] n ventana de la nariz

nosy ['nəʊzɪ] (inf) adj = **nosey**

not [nɔt] adv no; **~ that ...** no es que ...; **it's too late, isn't it?** es demasiado tarde, ¿verdad or no?; **~ yet/now** todavía/ahora no; **why ~?** ¿por qué no?; see also **all**; **only**

notable ['nəʊtəbl] adj notable □ **notably** adv especialmente

notch [nɔtʃ] n muesca, corte m

note [nəʊt] n (MUS, record, letter) nota; (banknote) billete m; (tone) tono ♦ vt (observe) notar, observar; (write down) apuntar, anotar □ **notebook** n libreta, cuaderno □ **noted** ['nəʊtɪd] adj célebre, conocido □ **notepad** n bloc m □ **notepaper** n papel m para cartas

nothing ['nʌθɪŋ] n nada; (zero) cero; **he does ~** no hace nada; **~ new** nada nuevo; **~ much** no mucho; **for ~** (free) gratis, sin pago; (in vain) en balde

notice ['nəʊtɪs] n (announcement) anuncio; (warning) aviso; (dismissal) despido; (resignation) dimisión f; (period of time) plazo ♦ vt (observe) notar, observar; **to bring sth to sb's ~** (attention) llamar la atención de algn sobre algo; **to take ~ of** tomar nota de,

prestar atención a; **at short ~** con poca anticipación; **until further ~** hasta nuevo aviso; **to hand in one's ~** dimitir □ **noticeable** adj evidente, obvio

⚠ Be careful not to translate **notice** by the Spanish word **noticia**.

notify ['nəʊtɪfaɪ] vt: **to ~ sb (of sth)** comunicar (algo) a algn

notion ['nəʊʃən] n idea; (opinion) opinión f; **notions** npl (US) mercería

notorious [nəʊ'tɔːrɪəs] adj notorio

notwithstanding [nɔtwɪθ'stændɪŋ] adv no obstante, sin embargo; **~ this** a pesar de esto

nought [nɔːt] n cero

noun [naʊn] n nombre m, sustantivo

nourish ['nʌrɪʃ] vt nutrir; (fig) alimentar □ **nourishment** n alimento, sustento

Nov. abbr (= November) nov

novel ['nɔvl] n novela ♦ adj (new) nuevo, original; (unexpected) insólito □ **novelist** n novelista mf □ **novelty** n novedad f

November [nəʊ'vembə] n noviembre m

novice ['nɔvɪs] n (REL) novicio(-a)

now [naʊ] adv (at the present time) ahora; (these days) actualmente, hoy día ♦ conj: **~ (that)** ya que, ahora que; **right ~** ahora mismo; **by ~** ya; **just ~** ahora mismo; **~ and then, ~ and again** de vez en cuando; **from ~ on** de ahora en adelante □ **nowadays** ['naʊədeɪz] adv hoy (en) día, actualmente

nowhere ['nəʊweə] adv (direction) a ninguna parte; (location) en ninguna parte

nozzle ['nɔzl] n boquilla

nr abbr (BRIT) = **near**

nuclear ['njuːklɪə] adj nuclear

nucleus ['njuːklɪəs] (pl nuclei) n núcleo

nude [njuːd] adj, n desnudo(-a) m/f; **in the ~** desnudo

nudge [nʌdʒ] vt dar un codazo a

nudist ['njuːdɪst] n nudista mf

nudity ['nju:dɪtɪ] n desnudez f

nuisance ['nju:sns] n molestia, fastidio; (person) pesado, latoso; **what a ~!** ¡qué lata!

numb [nʌm] adj: **~ with cold/fear** entumecido por el frío/paralizado de miedo

number ['nʌmbə] n número; (quantity) cantidad f ♦ vt (pages etc) numerar, poner número a; (amount to) sumar, ascender a; **to be numbered among** figurar entre; **they were ten in ~** eran diez algunos; □ **number plate** (BRIT) n matrícula, placa □ **Number Ten** n (BRIT: 10 Downing Street) residencia del primer ministro

numerical [nju:'merɪkl] adj numérico

numerous ['nju:mərəs] adj numeroso

nun [nʌn] n monja, religiosa

nurse [nɜːs] n enfermero(-a); (also: **nursemaid**) niñera ♦ vt (patient) cuidar, atender

nursery ['nɜːsərɪ] n (institution) guardería infantil; (room) cuarto de los niños; (for plants) criadero, semillero □ **nursery rhyme** n canción f infantil □ **nursery school** n parvulario, escuela de párvulos □ **nursery slope** (BRIT) n (SKI) cuesta para principiantes

nursing ['nɜːsɪŋ] n (profession) profesión f de enfermera; (care) asistencia, cuidado □ **nursing home** n clínica de reposo

nurture ['nɜːtʃə] vt (child, plant) alimentar, nutrir

nut [nʌt] n (TECH) tuerca; (BOT) nuez f

nutmeg ['nʌtmeg] n nuez f moscada

nutrient ['nju:trɪənt] adj nutritivo ♦ n elemento nutritivo

nutrition [nju:'trɪʃən] n nutrición f, alimentación f

nutritious [nju:'trɪʃəs] adj nutritivo, alimenticio

nuts [nʌts] (inf) adj loco

NVQ n abbr (BRIT) = **National Vocational Qualification**

nylon ['naɪlɔn] n nilón m ♦ adj de nilón

O, o

oak [əuk] n roble m ♦ adj de roble

O.A.P. (BRIT) n, abbr = **old-age pensioner**

oar [ɔː] n remo

oasis [əu'eɪsɪs] (pl **oases**) n oasis m inv

oath [əuθ] n juramento; (swear word) palabrota; **on** (BRIT) **or under ~** bajo juramento

oatmeal ['əutmi:l] n harina de avena

oats [əuts] npl avena

obedience [ə'bi:dɪəns] n obediencia

obedient [ə'bi:dɪənt] adj obediente

obese [əu'bi:s] adj obeso

obesity [əu'bi:sɪtɪ] n obesidad f

obey [ə'beɪ] vt obedecer; (instructions, regulations) cumplir

obituary [ə'bɪtjuərɪ] n necrología

object [n 'ɔbdʒɪkt, vb əb'dʒekt] n objeto; (purpose) objeto, propósito; (LING) complemento ♦ vi: **to ~ to** estar en contra de; (proposal) oponerse a; **to ~ that** objetar que; **expense is no ~** no importa cuánto cuesta; **I ~!** ¡yo protesto! □ **objection** [əb'dʒekʃən] n protesta; **I have no objection to ...** no tengo inconveniente en que ... □ **objective** adj, n objetivo

obligation [ɔblɪ'geɪʃən] n obligación f; (debt) deber m; **without ~** sin compromiso

obligatory [ə'blɪgətərɪ] adj obligatorio

oblige [ə'blaɪdʒ] vt (do a favour for) complacer, hacer un favor a; **to ~ sb to do sth** forzar or obligar a algn a hacer algo; **to be obliged to sb for sth** estarle agradecido a algn por algo

oblique [ə'bli:k] adj oblicuo; (allusion) indirecto

obliterate [əˈblɪtəreɪt] vt borrar

oblivion [əˈblɪvɪən] n olvido m

oblivious [əˈblɪvɪəs] adj: ~ of inconsciente de

oblong [ˈɒblɒŋ] adj rectangular ♦ n rectángulo

obnoxious [əbˈnɒkʃəs] adj odioso, detestable; (smell) nauseabundo

oboe [ˈəʊbəʊ] n oboe m

obscene [əbˈsiːn] adj obsceno

obscure [əbˈskjʊə] adj oscuro ♦ vt oscurecer; (hide: sun) esconder

observant [əbˈzɜːvnt] adj observador(a)

observation [ɒbzəˈveɪʃən] n observación f; (MED) examen m

observatory [əbˈzɜːvətrɪ] n observatorio

observe [əbˈzɜːv] vt observar; (rule) cumplir ☐ **observer** n observador(a) m/f

obsess [əbˈses] vt obsesionar ☐ **obsession** [əbˈseʃən] n obsesión f ☐ **obsessive** adj obsesivo; obsesionante

obsolete [ˈɒbsəliːt] adj: to be ~ estar en desuso

obstacle [ˈɒbstəkl] n obstáculo; (nuisance) estorbo

obstinate [ˈɒbstɪnɪt] adj terco, porfiado; (determined) obstinado

obstruct [əbˈstrʌkt] vt obstruir; (hinder) estorbar, obstaculizar ☐ **obstruction** [əbˈstrʌkʃən] n (action) obstrucción f; (object) estorbo, obstáculo

obtain [əbˈteɪn] vt obtener; (achieve) conseguir

obvious [ˈɒbvɪəs] adj obvio, evidente ☐ **obviously** adv evidentemente, naturalmente; **obviously not** por supuesto que no

occasion [əˈkeɪʒən] n oportunidad f, ocasión f; (event) acontecimiento ☐ **occasional** adj poco frecuente, ocasional ☐ **occasionally** adv de vez en cuando

occult [ɒˈkʌlt] adj (gen) oculto

occupant [ˈɒkjupənt] n (of house) inquilino(-a); (of car) ocupante mf

occupation [ɒkjuˈpeɪʃən] n ocupación f; (job) trabajo; (pastime) ocupaciones fpl

occupy [ˈɒkjupaɪ] vt (seat, post, time) ocupar; (house) habitar; **to ~ o.s. in doing** pasar el tiempo haciendo

occur [əˈkɜː] vi pasar, suceder; **to ~ to sb** ocurrírsele a algn ☐ **occurrence** [əˈkʌrəns] n acontecimiento; (existence) existencia

ocean [ˈəʊʃən] n océano

o'clock [əˈklɒk] adv: **it is 5 ~** son las 5

Oct. abbr (= October) oct

October [ɒkˈtəʊbə] n octubre m

octopus [ˈɒktəpəs] n pulpo

odd [ɒd] adj extraño, raro; (number) impar; (sock, shoe etc) suelto; **60-~** 60 y pico; **at ~ times** de vez en cuando; **to be the ~ one out** estar de más ☐ **oddly** adv curiosamente, extrañamente; see also **enough** ☐ **odds** npl (in betting) puntos mpl de ventaja; **it makes no odds** lo mismo; **at odds** reñidos(-as); **odds and ends** minucias fpl

odometer [ɒˈdɒmɪtə] (US) n cuentakilómetros m inv

odour [ˈəʊdə] (US **odor**) n olor m; (unpleasant) hedor m

---

of

[ɒv, əv] prep

1 (gen) de; **a friend of ours** un amigo nuestro; **a boy of 10** un chico de 10 años; **that was kind of you** eso fue muy amable por or de tu parte

2 (expressing quantity, amount, dates etc) de; **a kilo of flour** un kilo de harina; **there were three of them** había tres; **three of us went** tres de nosotros fuimos; **the 5th of July** el 5 de julio

❸ (from, out of) de; **made of wood** (hecho) de madera

off [ɒf] adj, adv (engine) desconectado; (light) apagado; (tap) cerrado; (BRIT: food: bad) pasado, malo; (: milk) cortado; (cancelled) cancelado ♦ prep (from) de ♦ (to leave) irse, marcharse; **to be ~ sick** estar enfermo o de baja; **a day ~** un día libre or sin trabajar; **to have an ~ day** tener un día malo; **he had his coat ~** se había quitado el abrigo; **10% ~** (COMM) (con el) 10% de descuento; **5 km ~** (the road) a 5 km (de la carretera); **~ the coast** frente a la costa; **I'm ~ meat** (no longer eat/like it) paso de la carne; **on the ~ chance** por si acaso; **~ and on** de vez en cuando

offence [əˈfɛns] (US **offense**) n (crime) delito; **to take ~** at ofenderse por

offend [əˈfɛnd] vt (person) ofender
❏ **offender** n delincuente mf

offense [əˈfɛns] (US) n = **offence**

offensive [əˈfɛnsɪv] adj ofensivo; (smell etc) repugnante ♦ n (MIL) ofensiva

offer [ˈɒfə*] n oferta, ofrecimiento; (proposal) propuesta ♦ vt ofrecer; (opportunity) facilitar; **"on ~"** (COMM) "en oferta"

offhand [ɒfˈhænd] adj informal ♦ adv de improviso

office [ˈɒfɪs] n (place) oficina; (room) despacho; (position) carga, oficio; **doctor's ~** (US) consultorio; **to take ~** entrar en funciones ❏ **office block** (US **office building**) n bloque m de oficinas ❏ **office hours** npl horas fpl de oficina; (US MED) horas fpl de consulta

officer [ˈɒfɪsə*] n (MIL etc) oficial mf; (also: **police ~**) agente mf de policía; (of organization) director(a) m/f

office worker n oficinista mf

official [əˈfɪʃl] adj oficial, autorizado ♦ n funcionario(-a), oficial m/f

off: off-licence (BRIT) n (shop) bodega, tienda de vinos y bebidas alcohólicas

❏ **off-line** adj, adv (COMPUT) fuera de línea ❏ **off-peak** adj (electricity) de banda económica; (ticket) billete de precio reducido por viajar fuera de las horas punta ❏ **off-putting** (BRIT) adj (person) asqueroso; (remark) desalentador(a) ❏ **off-season** adj, adv fuera de temporada

OFF-LICENCE

En el Reino Unido la venta de bebidas alcohólicas está estrictamente regulada y se necesita una licencia especial, con la que cuentan los bares, restaurantes y los establecimientos de **off-licence**, los únicos lugares en donde se pueden adquirir bebidas alcohólicas para su consumo fuera del local, de donde viene su nombre. También venden bebidas no alcohólicas, tabaco, chocolatinas, patatas fritas, etc. y a menudo forman parte de una cadena nacional.

offset [ˈɒfset] vt contrarrestar, compensar

offshore [ɒfˈʃɔː*] adj (breeze, island) costera; (fishing) de bajura

offside [ˈɒfˈsaɪd] adj (SPORT) fuera de juego; (AUT: in UK) del lado derecho; (: in US, Europe etc) del lado izquierdo

offspring [ˈɒfsprɪŋ] n inv descendencia

often [ˈɒfn] adv a menudo, con frecuencia; **how ~ do you go?** ¿cada cuánto vas?

oh [əu] excl ¡ah!

oil [ɔɪl] n aceite m; (petroleum) petróleo; (for heating) aceite m combustible ♦ vt engrasar ❏ **oil filter** n (AUT) filtro de aceite ❏ **oil painting** n pintura al óleo ❏ **oil refinery** n refinería de petróleo ❏ **oil rig** n torre f de perforación ❏ **oil slick** n marea negra ❏ **oil tanker** n petrolero; (truck) camión m cisterna ❏ **oil well** n pozo (de petróleo) ❏ **oily** adj aceitoso; (food) grasiento

ointment ['ɔɪntmənt] n ungüento

O.K., okay ['əu'keɪ] excl O.K., ¡está bien!, ¡vale! (SP) ♦ adj bien ♦ vt dar el visto bueno a

old [əuld] adj viejo; (former) antiguo; **how ~ are you?** ¿cuántos años tienes?, ¿qué edad tienes?; **he's 10 years ~** tiene 10 años; **older brother** hermano mayor ❏ **old age** n vejez f ❏ **old-age pension** n (BRIT) jubilación f, pensión f ❏ **old-age pensioner** (BRIT) n jubilado(-a) ❏ **old-fashioned** adj anticuado, pasado de moda ❏ **old people's home** n (esp BRIT) residencia f de ancianos

olive ['ɔlɪv] n (fruit) aceituna; (tree) olivo ♦ adj (also: **~-green**) verde oliva ❏ **olive oil** n aceite m de oliva

Olympic [əu'lɪmpɪk] adj olímpico; **the ~ Games, the Olympics** las Olimpiadas

omelet(te) ['ɔmlɪt] n tortilla francesa (SP), omelette f (LAm)

omen ['əumən] n presagio

ominous ['ɔmɪnəs] adj de mal agüero, amenazador(a)

omit [əu'mɪt] vt omitir

on
KEYWORD

[ɔn] prep

1 (indicating position) en; sobre; **on the wall** en la pared; **it's on the table** está sobre or en la mesa; **on the left** a la izquierda

2 (indicating means, method, condition etc): **on foot** a pie; **on the train/plane** (go) en tren/avión; (be) en el tren/el avión; **on the radio/ television/telephone** por or en la radio/televisión/al teléfono; **to be on drugs** drogarse; (MED) estar a tratamiento; **to be on holiday/ business** estar de vacaciones/en viaje de negocios

3 (referring to time): **on Friday** el viernes; **on Fridays** los viernes; **on June 20th** el 20 de junio; **a week on Friday** del viernes en una semana; **on arrival** al llegar; **on seeing this** al ver esto

4 (about, concerning) sobre, acerca de; **a book on physics** un libro de or sobre física

♦ adv

1 (referring to dress): **to have one's coat on** tener or llevar el abrigo puesto; **she put her gloves on** se puso los guantes

2 (referring to covering): **"screw the lid on tightly"** "cerrar bien la tapa"

3 (further, continuously): **to walk etc on** seguir caminando etc

♦ adj

1 (functioning, in operation: machine, radio, TV, light) encendido(-a) (SP), prendido(-a) (LAm); (: tap) abierto(-a); (: brakes) echado(-a), puesto(-a); **is the meeting still on?** (in progress) ¿todavía continúa la reunión?; (not cancelled) ¿va a haber reunión al fin?; **there's a good film on at the cinema** ponen una buena película en el cine

2: **that's not on!** (inf: not possible) ¡eso ni hablar!; (: not acceptable) ¡eso no se hace!

once [wʌns] adv una vez; (formerly) antiguamente ♦ conj una vez que; **~ he had left/it was done** una vez que se había marchado/se hizo; **at ~** en seguida, inmediatamente; (simultaneously) a la vez; **~ a week** una vez por semana; **~ more** otra vez; **~ and for all** de una vez por todas; **~ upon a time** érase una vez

oncoming ['ɔnkʌmɪŋ] adj (traffic) que viene de frente

one

KEYWORD

[wʌn] *num* un(o)/una; **one hundred and fifty** ciento cincuenta; **one by one** uno a uno

♦ *adj*

1 (*sole*) único; **the one book which** el único libro que; **the one man who** el único que

2 (*same*) mismo(-a); **they came in the one car** vinieron en un solo coche

♦ *pron*

1: **this one** éste (ésta); **that one** ése (ésa); (*more remote*) aquél (aquella); **I've already got (a red) one** ya tengo uno(-a) rojo(-a); **one by one** uno(-a) por uno(-a)

2: **one another** (*SP*), se (+ *el uno al otro, unos a otros etc*); **do you two ever see one another?** ¿vosotros dos os veis alguna vez? (*SP*), ¿se ven ustedes dos alguna vez?; **the boys didn't dare look at one another** los chicos no se atrevieron a mirarse (el uno al otro); **they all kissed one another** se besaron unos a otros

3 (*impers*): **one never knows** nunca se sabe; **to cut one's finger** cortarse el dedo; **one needs to eat** hay que comer □ **one-off** (*BRIT: inf*) *n* (*event*) acontecimiento único

oneself [wʌn'self] *pron* (*reflexive*) se; (*after prep*) sí; (*emphatic*) uno(-a) mismo(-a); **to hurt ~** hacerse daño; **to keep sth to ~** guardarse algo; **to talk to ~** hablar solo

one: **one-shot** [wʌn'ʃɒt] (*US*) *n* = **one-off** □ **one-sided** *adj* (*argument*) parcial □ **one-to-one** (*relationship*) de dos □ **one-way** *adj* (*street*) de sentido único

ongoing ['ɒngəʊɪŋ] *adj* continuo

onion ['ʌnjən] *n* cebolla

on-line ['ɒnlaɪn] *adj, adv* (*COMPUT*) en línea

onlooker ['ɒnlʊkə'] *n* espectador(a) *m/f*

only ['əʊnlɪ] *adv* solamente, sólo ♦ *adj* único, solo ♦ *conj* solamente que, pero; **an ~ child** un hijo único; **not ~ ... but also ...** no sólo ... sino también ...

on-screen [ɒn'skriːn] *adj* (*COMPUT etc*) en pantalla; (*romance, kiss*) cinematográfico

onset ['ɒnset] *n* comienzo

onto ['ɒntʊ] *prep* = **on to**

onward(s) ['ɒnwəd(z)] *adv* (*move*) (hacia) adelante; **from that time onward(s)** desde entonces en adelante

oops [ups] *excl* (*also:* **~-a-daisy!**) ¡huy!

ooze [uːz] *vi* rezumar

opaque [əʊ'peɪk] *adj* opaco

open ['əʊpn] *adj* abierto; (*car*) descubierto; (*road, view*) despejado; (*meeting*) público; (*admiration*) manifiesto ♦ *vt* abrir ♦ *vi* abrirse; (*book etc: commence*) comenzar; **in the ~** (*air*) al aire libre ► **open up** *vt* abrir; (*blocked road*) despejar ♦ *vi* abrirse, empezar □ **open-air** *adj* al aire libre □ **opening** *n* abertura; (*start*) comienzo; (*opportunity*) oportunidad *f* □ **opening hours** *npl* horario de apertura □ **open learning** *n* enseñanza flexible a tiempo parcial □ **openly** *adv* abiertamente □ **open-minded** *adj* imparcial □ **open-necked** *adj* (*shirt*) desabrochado; sin corbata □ **open-plan** *adj*: **open-plan office** gran oficina sin particiones □ **Open University** *n* (*BRIT*) ≈ Universidad *f* Nacional de Enseñanza a Distancia, UNED *f*

OPEN UNIVERSITY

La **Open University**, fundada en 1969, está especializada en impartir cursos a distancia que no exigen una dedicación exclusiva. Cuenta con sus propios materiales de apoyo, entre ellos programas de radio y televisión emitidos por la **BBC** y para conseguir los créditos de la licenciatura es necesaria la presentación de sus trabajos y la asistencia a los cursos de verano.

opera ['ɔpərə] n ópera ❏ **opera house** n teatro de la ópera ❏ **opera singer** n cantante m/f de ópera

operate ['ɔpəreit] vt (machine) hacer funcionar; (company) dirigir ♦ vi funcionar; **to ~ on sb** (MED) operar a algn

operating room ['ɔpəreitiŋ-] (US) n quirófano, sala de operaciones

operating theatre (BRIT) n sala de operaciones

operation [ɔpə'reiʃən] n operación f; (of machine) funcionamiento; **to be in ~** estar funcionando or en funcionamiento; **to have an ~** (MED) ser operado ❏ **operational** adj operacional, en buen estado

operative ['ɔpərətiv] adj en vigor

operator ['ɔpəreitə'] n (of machine) maquinista mf, operario(-a); (TEL) operador(a) m/f, telefonista mf

opinion [ə'pinjən] n opinión f; **in my ~** en mi opinión, a mi juicio ❏ **opinion poll** n encuesta, sondeo

opponent [ə'pəunənt] n adversario(-a), contrincante mf

opportunity [ɔpə'tju:niti] n oportunidad f; **to take the ~ of doing** aprovechar la ocasión para hacer

oppose [ə'pəuz] vt oponerse a; **to be opposed to sth** oponerse a algo; **as opposed to** a diferencia de

opposite ['ɔpəzit] adj opuesto, contrario a; (house etc) de enfrente ♦ adv en frente ♦ prep en frente de, frente a ♦ n lo contrario

opposition [ɔpə'ziʃən] n oposición f

oppress [ə'pres] vt oprimir

opt [ɔpt] vi: **to ~ for** optar por; **to ~ to do** optar por hacer ♦ **opt out** vi: **to opt out of** optar por no hacer

optician [ɔp'tiʃən] n óptico m/f

optimism ['ɔptimizəm] n optimismo

optimist ['ɔptimist] n optimista mf ❏ **optimistic** [-'mistik] adj optimista

optimum ['ɔptiməm] adj óptimo

option ['ɔpʃən] n opción f ❏ **optional** adj facultativo, discrecional

or [ɔ:'] conj o; (before o, ho) u; (with negative): **he hasn't seen or heard anything** no ha visto ni oído nada; **or else** si no

oral ['ɔ:rəl] adj oral ♦ n examen m oral

orange ['ɔrindʒ] n (fruit) naranja ♦ adj color naranja ❏ **orange juice** n jugo m de naranja, zumo m de naranja (SP) ❏ **orange squash** n naranjada

orbit ['ɔ:bit] n órbita ♦ vt, vi orbitar

orchard ['ɔ:tʃəd] n huerto

orchestra ['ɔ:kistrə] n orquesta; (US: seating) platea

orchid ['ɔ:kid] n orquídea

ordeal [ɔ:'di:l] n experiencia horrorosa

order ['ɔ:də'] n orden m; (command) orden f; (good order) buen estado; (COMM) pedido ♦ vt (also: **put in ~**) arreglar, poner en orden; (COMM) pedir; (command) mandar, ordenar; **in ~ en orden**; (of document) en regla; **in (working) ~** en funcionamiento; **in ~ to do/that** para hacer/que; **on ~** (COMM) pedido; **to be out of ~** estar desordenado; (not working) no funcionar; **to ~ sb to do sth** mandar a algn hacer algo ❏ **order form** n hoja de pedido ❏ **orderly** n (MIL) ordenanza m; (MED) enfermero(-a) (auxiliar) ♦ adj ordenado

ordinary ['ɔːdnri] adj corriente,
normal; (pej) común y corriente; **out of
the ~** fuera de lo común

ore [ɔː*] n mineral m

oregano [ɒri'gɑːnəu] n orégano

organ ['ɔːgən] n órgano □ **organic**
[ɔː'gænɪk] adj orgánico □ **organism** n
organismo

organization [ɔːgənaɪ'zeɪʃən] n
organización f

organize ['ɔːgənaɪz] vt organizar
□ **organized** ['ɔːgənaɪzd] adj
organizado □ **organizer** n
organizador(a) m/f

orgasm ['ɔːgæzəm] n orgasmo

orgy ['ɔːdʒɪ] n orgía

oriental [ɔːrɪ'entl] adj oriental

orientation [ɔːrɪen'teɪʃən] n
orientación f

origin ['ɒrɪdʒɪn] n origen m

original [ə'rɪdʒɪnl] adj original; (first)
primero; (earlier) primitivo ♦ n original
m □ **originally** adv al principio

originate [ə'rɪdʒɪneɪt] vi: **to ~ from, to
~ in** surgir de, tener su origen en

Orkneys ['ɔːknɪz] npl: **the ~** (also: **the
Orkney Islands**) las Orcadas

ornament ['ɔːnəmənt] n adorno;
(trinket) chuchería □ **ornamental**
['mentl] adj decorativo, de adorno

ornate [ɔː'neɪt] adj muy ornado,
vistoso

orphan ['ɔːfn] n huérfano(-a)

orthodox ['ɔːθədɒks] adj ortodoxo
□ **orthodoxy** n ortodoxia

orthopaedic [ɔːθə'piːdɪk] (US
orthopedic) adj ortopédico

osteopath ['ɒstɪəpæθ] n osteópata mf

ostrich ['ɒstrɪtʃ] n avestruz m

other ['ʌðə*] adj otro ♦ pron: **the ~(one)**
el (la) otro(-a) ♦ adv: ~ **than** aparte de
□ **otherwise** adv de otra manera
♦ conj (if not) si no

otter ['ɒtə*] n nutria

ouch [autʃ] excl ¡ay!

ought [ɔːt] (pt ~) aux vb: **I ~ to do it**
debería hacerlo; **this ~ to have been
corrected** esto debiera haberse
corregido; **he ~ to win** (probability)
debe or debiera ganar

ounce [auns] n onza (28.35g)

our ['auə*] adj nuestro; see also **my**
□ **ours** pron (el) nuestro/(la) nuestra
etc; see also **mine**[1] □ **ourselves** pron
pl (reflexive, after prep) nosotros;
(emphatic) nosotros mismos; see also
oneself

oust [aust] vt desalojar

out [aut] adv fuera, afuera; (not at home)
fuera (de casa); (light, fire) apagado; **~
there allí** (fuera); **he's ~** (absent) no
está, ha salido; **to be ~ in one's
calculations** equivocarse (en sus
cálculos); **to run ~** salir corriendo; **~
loud** en alta voz; **~ of** (outside) fuera de;
(because of: anger etc) por; **~ of petrol**
sin gasolina; **"~ of order"** "no
funciona" □ **outback** n interior m
□ **outbound** adj (flight): de salida;
(flight: not return) de ida □ **outbreak** n
(of war) comienzo; (of disease)
epidemia; (of violence etc) ola
□ **outburst** n explosión f, arranque m
□ **outcast** n paria mf □ **outcome** n
resultado □ **outcry** n protestas fpl
□ **outdated** adj anticuado, fuera de
moda □ **outdoor** adj exterior, de aire
libre; (clothes) de calle □ **outdoors**
adv al aire libre

outer ['autə*] adj exterior, externo
□ **outer space** n espacio exterior

outfit ['autfɪt] n (clothes) conjunto

out: outgoing adj (character)
extrovertido; (retiring: president etc)
saliente □ **outgoings** (BRIT) npl gastos
mpl □ **outhouse** n dependencia

outing ['autɪŋ] n excursión f, paseo

out: outlaw n proscrito ♦ vt proscribir
□ **outlay** n inversión f □ **outlet** n
salida; (of pipe) desagüe m; (US ELEC)
toma de corriente; (also: **retail outlet**)
punto de venta □ **outline** n (shape)

contorno, perfil m; (sketch, plan) esbozo ♦ vt (plan etc) esbozar; **in outline** (fig) a grandes rasgos □ **outlook** n (fig: prospects) perspectivas fpl; (: for weather) pronóstico □ **outnumber** vt superar en número □ **out-of-date** adj (passport) caducado; (clothes) pasado de moda □ **out-of-doors** adv al aire libre □ **out-of-the-way** adj apartado □ **out-of-town** adj (shopping centre etc) en las afueras □ **outpatient** n paciente mf externo(-a) □ **outpost** n puesto avanzado □ **output** n (volumen m de) producción f, rendimiento; (COMPUT) salida

outrage ['autreɪdʒ] n escándalo; (atrocity) atrocidad f ♦ vt ultrajar □ **outrageous** [-'reɪdʒəs] adj monstruoso

outright [adv aut'raɪt, adj 'autraɪt] adv (ask, deny) francamente; (refuse) rotundamente; (win) de manera absoluta; (be killed) en el acto ♦ adj franco; rotundo

outset ['autset] n principio

outside [aut'saɪd] n exterior m ♦ adj exterior, externo ♦ adv fuera ♦ prep fuera de; (beyond) más allá de; (fig) a lo sumo □ **outside lane** n (AUT: in Britain) carril m de la derecha; (: in US, Europe etc) carril m de la izquierda □ **outside line** n (TEL) línea (exterior) □ **outsider** n (stranger) extraño, forastero

out: outsize adj (clothes) de talla grande □ **outskirts** npl alrededores mpl, afueras fpl □ **outspoken** adj muy franco □ **outstanding** adj excepcional, destacado; (remaining) pendiente

outward ['autwad] adj externo; (journey) de ida □ **outwards** adv (esp BRIT) = **outward**

outweigh [aut'weɪ] vt pesar más que

oval ['ouvl] adj ovalado ♦ n óvalo

ovary ['ouvari] n ovario

oven ['ʌvn] n horno □ **oven glove** n guante m para el horno, manopla para el horno □ **ovenproof** adj resistente al horno □ **oven-ready** adj listo para el horno

over ['ouvar] adv encima, por encima ♦ adj or adv (finished) terminado; (surplus) de sobra ♦ prep (por) encima de; (above) sobre; (on the other side of) al otro lado de; (more than) más de; (during) durante; ~ **here** (por) aquí; ~ **there** (por) allí or allá; **all** ~ (everywhere) por todas partes; ~ **and** ~ (**again**) una y otra vez; ~ **and above** además de; **to ask sb** ~ invitar a algn a casa; **to bend** ~ inclinarse

overall [adj, n 'ouvaro:l, adv ouvar'o:l] adj (length etc) total; (study) de conjunto ♦ adv en conjunto ♦ n (BRIT) guardapolvo; **overalls** npl (boiler suit) mono (SP) or overol m (LAm) (de trabajo)

overboard adv (NAUT) por la borda

overcame [ouva'keɪm] pt of **overcome**

overcast ['ouvaka:st] adj encapotado

overcharge [ouva'tʃa:dʒ] vt: **to** ~ **sb** cobrar un precio excesivo a algn

overcoat ['ouvakaut] n abrigo, sobretodo

overcome [ouva'kʌm] vt vencer; (difficulty) superar

over: overcrowded adj atestado de gente; (city, country) superpoblado □ **overdo** (irreg) vt exagerar; (overcook) cocer demasiado; **to overdo it** (work etc) pasarse □ **overdone** [ouva'dʌn] adj (vegetables) recocido; (steak) demasiado hecho □ **overdose** n sobredosis f inv □ **overdraft** n saldo deudor □ **overdrawn** adj (account) en descubierto □ **overdue** adj retrasado □ **overestimate** vt sobreestimar

overflow [vb əuvə'fləu, n 'əuvəfləu] vi desbordarse ♦ n (also: ~ **pipe**) (cañería de) desagüe m

overgrown [əuvə'grəun] adj (garden) invadido por la vegetación

overhaul [vb əuvə'hɔ:l, n 'əuvəhɔ:l] vt revisar, repasar ♦ n revisión f

overhead [adv əuvə'hɛd, adj, n 'əuvəhɛd] adv por arriba o encima ♦ adj (cable) aéreo ♦ n (US =): **overheads** ❏ **overhead projector** n retroproyector ❏ **overheads** npl (expenses) gastos mpl generales

over: **overhear** (irreg) vt oír por casualidad ❏ **overheat** (engine) recalentarse ❏ **overland** adj, adv por tierra ❏ **overlap** [əuvə'læp] vi traslaparse ❏ **overleaf** adv al dorso ❏ **overload** vt sobrecargar ❏ **overlook** vt (have view of) dar a, tener vistas a; (miss: by mistake) pasar por alto; (excuse) perdonar

overnight [əuvə'naɪt] adv durante la noche; (fig) de la noche a la mañana ♦ adj de noche; **to stay** ~ pasar la noche ❏ **overnight bag** n fin m de semana, neceser m de viaje

overpass (US) ['əuvəpɑ:s] n paso superior

overpower [əuvə'pauə] vt dominar; (fig) embargar ❏ **overpowering** adj (heat) agobiante; (smell) penetrante

over: **overreact** [əuvəri'ækt] vi reaccionar de manera exagerada ❏ **overrule** vt (decision) anular; (claim) denegar ❏ **overrun** (irreg) vt (country) invadir; (time limit) rebasar, exceder

overseas [əuvə'si:z] adv (abroad: live) en el extranjero; (travel) al extranjero ♦ adj (trade) exterior; (visitor) extranjero

oversee [əuvə'si:] (irreg) vt supervisar

overshadow ['əuvə'ʃædəu] vt: **to be overshadowed by** estar a la sombra de

oversight ['əuvəsaɪt] n descuido

oversleep [əuvə'sli:p] (irreg) vi quedarse dormido

overspend [əuvə'spɛnd] (irreg) vi gastar más de la cuenta; **we have overspent by 5 pounds** hemos excedido el presupuesto en 5 libras

overt [əu'vɜ:t] adj abierto

overtake [əuvə'teɪk] (irreg) vt sobrepasar; (BRIT AUT) adelantar

over: **overthrow** (irreg) vt (government) derrocar ❏ **overtime** n horas fpl extraordinarias

overtook [əuvə'tuk] pt of **overtake**

over: **overturn** vt volcar; (fig: plan) desbaratar; (: government) derrocar ♦ vi volcar ❏ **overweight** adj demasiado gordo o pesado ❏ **overwhelm** vt aplastar; (emotion) sobrecoger ❏ **overwhelming** adj (victory, defeat) arrollador(a); (feeling) irresistible

ow [au] excl ¡ay!

owe [əu] vt: **to ~ sth sb, to ~ sth to sb** deber algo a algn ❏ **owing to** prep debido a, por causa de

owl [aul] n búho, lechuza

own [əun] vt tener, poseer ♦ adj propio; **a room of my** ~ una habitación propia; **to get one's ~ back** tomar revancha; **on one's** ~ solo, a solas ▶ **own up** vi confesar ❏ **owner** n dueño(-a) ❏ **ownership** n posesión f

ox [ɔks] (pl **oxen**) n buey m

Oxbridge ['ɔksbrɪdʒ] n universidades de Oxford y Cambridge

oxen ['ɔksən] npl of **ox**

oxygen ['ɔksɪdʒən] n oxígeno

oyster ['ɔɪstə'] n ostra

oz. abbr = **ounce(s)**

ozone ['auzaun] n ozono ❏ **ozone friendly** adj que no daña la capa de ozono ❏ **ozone layer** n capa f de ozono

P, p

p [piː] abbr = **penny**; **pence**

P.A. n abbr = **personal assistant**;
public address system

p.a. abbr = **per annum**

pace [peɪs] n paso m ◆ vi: **to ~ up and
down** pasearse de un lado a otro; **to
keep ~ with** llevar el mismo paso que
❑ **pacemaker** n (MED) regulador m
cardíaco, marcapasos m inv; (SPORT:
also: **pacesetter**) liebre f

Pacific [pəˈsɪfɪk] n: **the ~ (Ocean)** el
(Océano) Pacífico

pacifier [ˈpæsɪfaɪəʳ] (US) n (dummy)
chupete m

pack [pæk] n (packet) paquete m; (of
hounds) jauría; (of people) manada,
bando; (of cards) baraja; (bundle) fardo;
(US: of cigarettes) paquete m; (back
pack) mochila ◆ vt (fill) llenar; (in
suitcase etc) meter, poner; (cram)
llenar, atestar; **to ~ (one's bags)**
hacerse la maleta; **to ~ sb off**
despachar a algn ▶ **pack in** (BRIT) vi (watch,
car) estropearse ◆ vt (inf) dejar; **pack it
in!** ¡para!, ¡basta ya! ▶ **pack up** vi (inf:
machine) estropearse; (person) irse ◆ vt
(belongings, clothes) recoger; (goods,
presents) empaquetar, envolver

package [ˈpækɪdʒ] n paquete m; (bulky)
bulto; (also: **~ deal**) acuerdo global
❑ **package holiday** n vacaciones fpl
organizadas ❑ **package tour** n viaje
m organizado

packaging [ˈpækɪdʒɪŋ] n envase m

packed [pækt] adj abarrotado
❑ **packed lunch** n almuerzo frío

packet [ˈpækɪt] n paquete m

packing [ˈpækɪŋ] n embalaje m

pact [pækt] n pacto m

pad [pæd] n (of paper) bloc m; (cushion)
cojinete m; (inf: home) casa ◆ vt
rellenar ❑ **padded** adj (jacket)
acolchado; (bra) reforzado

paddle [ˈpædl] n (oar) canalete m; (US:
for table tennis) paleta ◆ vt impulsar
con canalete ◆ vi (with feet) chapotear
❑ **paddling pool** (BRIT) n estanque m
de juegos

paddock [ˈpædək] n corral m

padlock [ˈpædlɔk] n candado m

paedophile [ˈpiːdəʊfaɪl] (US
pedophile) adj de pedófilos ◆ n
pedófilo(-a)

page [peɪdʒ] n (of book) página; (of
newspaper) plana; (also: **~ boy**) paje m
◆ vt (in hotel etc) llamar por altavoz a

pager [ˈpeɪdʒəʳ] n (TEL) busca m

paid [peɪd] pt, pp of **pay** ◆ adj (work)
remunerado; (holiday) pagado; (official
etc) a sueldo; **to put ~ to** (BRIT) acabar
con

pain [peɪn] n dolor m; **to be in ~** sufrir;
to take pains to do sth tomarse
grandes molestias en hacer algo
❑ **painful** adj doloroso; (difficult)
penoso; (disagreeable) desagradable
❑ **painkiller** n analgésico
❑ **painstaking** [ˈpeɪnzteɪkɪŋ] adj
(person) concienzudo, esmerado

paint [peɪnt] n pintura ◆ vt pintar; **to ~
the door blue** pintar la puerta de azul
❑ **paintbrush** n (of artist) pincel m; (of
decorator) brocha ❑ **painter** n
pintor(a) m/f ❑ **painting** n pintura

pair [pɛəʳ] n (of shoes, gloves etc) par m;
(of people) pareja; **a ~ of scissors** unas
tijeras; **a ~ of trousers** unos
pantalones, un pantalón

pajamas [pəˈdʒɑːməz] (US) npl pijama m

Pakistan [pɑːkɪˈstɑːn] n Paquistán m
❑ **Pakistani** adj, n paquistaní mf

pal [pæl] (inf) n compinche mf,
compañero(-a)

palace [ˈpæləs] n palacio m

pale [peɪl] adj (gen) pálido; (colour)
claro ◆ n: **to be beyond the ~** pasarse
de la raya

Palestine [ˈpælɪstaɪn] n Palestina
□ **Palestinian** [-ˈtɪnɪən] adj, n
palestino(-a) m/f

palm [pɑːm] n (ANAT) palma; (also: ~
tree) palmera, palma ♦ vt: **to ~ sth off
on sb** (inf) encajar algo a algn

pamper [ˈpæmpə] vt mimar

pamphlet [ˈpæmflət] n folleto

pan [pæn] n (also: **saucepan**) cacerola,
cazuela, olla; (also: **frying** ~) sartén f

pancake [ˈpænkeɪk] n crepe f

panda [ˈpændə] n panda m

pane [peɪn] n cristal m

panel [ˈpænl] n (of wood etc) panel m;
(RADIO, TV) panel m de invitados

panhandler [ˈpænhændlə] (US) n (inf)
mendigo(-a)

panic [ˈpænɪk] n terror m pánico ♦ vi
dejarse llevar por el pánico

panorama [pænəˈrɑːmə] n panorama m

pansy [ˈpænzɪ] n (BOT) pensamiento;
(inf, pej) maricón m

pant [pænt] vi jadear

panther [ˈpænθə*] n pantera

panties [ˈpæntɪz] npl bragas fpl, pantis
mpl

pantomime [ˈpæntəmaɪm] (BRIT) n
revista musical representada en Navidad,
basada en cuentos de hadas

PANTOMIME

En época navideña se ponen en escena
en los teatros británicos las llamadas
pantomimes, que son versiones libres
de cuentos tradicionales como Aladino
o El gato con botas. En ella nunca faltan
personajes como la dama ("dame"),
papel que siempre interpreta un actor,
el protagonista joven ("principal boy"),
normalmente interpretado por una
actriz, y el malvado ("villain"). Es un
espectáculo familiar en el que se anima
al público a participar y aunque va
dirigido principalmente a los niños,
cuenta con grandes dosis de humor
para adultos

pants [pænts] n (BRIT: underwear:
woman's) bragas fpl, (: man's)
calzoncillos mpl; (US: trousers)
pantalones mpl

paper [ˈpeɪpə*] n papel m; (also:
newspaper) periódico, diario;
(academic essay) ensayo; (exam)
examen m ♦ adj de papel ♦ vt
empapelar, tapizar (MEX); **papers** npl
(also: **identity papers**) papeles mpl,
documentos mpl □ **paperback** n libro
en rústica □ **paper bag** n bolsa de
papel □ **paper clip** n clip m □ **paper
shop** n tienda de periódicos
□ **paperwork** n trabajo
administrativo

paprika [ˈpæprɪkə] n pimentón m

par [pɑː*] n par f; (GOLF) par m; **to be on
a ~ with** estar a la par con

paracetamol [pærəˈsiːtəmɒl] (BRIT) n
paracetamol m

parachute [ˈpærəʃuːt] n paracaídas m
inv

parade [pəˈreɪd] n desfile m ♦ vt (show)
hacer alarde de ♦ vi desfilar; (MIL) pasar
revista

paradise [ˈpærədaɪs] n paraíso

paradox [ˈpærədɒks] n paradoja

paraffin [ˈpærəfɪn] (BRIT) n (also: ~ **oil**)
parafina

paragraph [ˈpærəgrɑːf] n párrafo

parallel [ˈpærəlɛl] adj en paralelo; (fig)
semejante ♦ n (line) paralela; (fig, GEO)
paralelo

paralysed [ˈpærəlaɪzd] adj paralizado

paralysis [pəˈrælɪsɪs] n parálisis f inv

paramedic [pærəˈmɛdɪk] n auxiliar m/f
sanitario(-a)

paranoid [ˈpærənɔɪd] adj (person,
feeling) paranoico

parasite [ˈpærəsaɪt] n parásito(-a)

parcel [ˈpɑːsl] n paquete m ♦ vt (also: ~
up) empaquetar, embalar

pardon [ˈpɑːdn] n (LAW) indulto ♦ vt
perdonar; ~ **me!, I beg your ~!** (I'm

sorry! ¡perdone usted!; (**I beg your**) ~?, ~ **me?** (US: *what did you say?*) ¿cómo?

parent ['peərənt] n (*mother*) madre f; (*father*) padre m; **parents** npl padres mpl ❑ **parental** [pə'rentl] adj paternal/maternal

⚠ Be careful not to translate **parent** by the Spanish word *pariente*.

Paris ['pærɪs] n París

parish ['pærɪʃ] n parroquia

Parisian [pə'rɪzɪən] adj parisiense mf

park [pɑːk] n parque m ♦ vt aparcar, estacionar ♦ vi aparcar, estacionarse

parking ['pɑːkɪŋ] n aparcamiento, estacionamiento; "**no ~**" "prohibido estacionarse" ❑ **parking lot** (US) n parking m ❑ **parking meter** n parquímetro ❑ **parking ticket** n multa de aparcamiento

parkway ['pɑːkweɪ] (US) n alameda

parliament ['pɑːləmənt] n parlamento; (*Spanish*) Cortes fpl ❑ **parliamentary** [-'mentərɪ] adj parlamentario

PARLIAMENT

El Parlamento británico (**Parliament**) tiene como sede el palacio de Westminster, también llamado "Houses of Parliament" y consta de dos cámaras. La Cámara de los Comunes ("House of Commons"), compuesta por 650 diputados (**Members of Parliament**) elegidos por sufragio universal en su respectiva circunscripción electoral (constituency), se reúne 175 días al año y sus sesiones son moderadas por el Presidente de la Cámara (**Speaker**). La cámara alta es la Cámara de los Lores ("House of Lords") y está formada por miembros que han sido nombrados por el monarca o que han heredado su escaño. Su poder es limitado, aunque actúa como tribunal supremo de apelación, excepto en Escocia.

Parmesan [pɑːmɪ'zæn] n (*also*: ~ **cheese**) queso parmesano

parole [pə'rəul] n: **on ~** libre bajo palabra

parrot ['pærət] n loro, papagayo

parsley ['pɑːslɪ] n perejil m

parsnip ['pɑːsnɪp] n chirivía

parson ['pɑːsn] n cura m

part [pɑːt] n (*gen*, MUS) parte f; (*bit*) trozo; (*of machine*) pieza; (THEATRE *etc*) papel m; (*of serial*) entrega; (US: *in hair*) raya ♦ adv = **partly** ♦ vt separar ♦ vi (*people*) separarse; (*crowd*) apartarse; **to take ~ in** tomar parte or participar en; **to take sth in good** tomar algo en buena parte; **to take sb's** ~ defender a algn; **for my ~** por mi parte; **for the most ~** en su mayor parte; **to ~ one's hair** hacerse la raya ▸ **part with** vt fus ceder, entregar; (*money*) pagar ❑ **part of speech** n parte f de la oración, categoría f gramatical

partial ['pɑːʃl] adj parcial; **to be ~ to** ser aficionado a

participant [pɑː'tɪsɪpənt] n (*in competition*) concursante mf; (*in campaign etc*) participante mf

participate [pɑː'tɪsɪpeɪt] vi: **to ~ in** participar en

particle ['pɑːtɪkl] n partícula; (*of dust*) grano

particular [pə'tɪkjulə*] adj (*special*) particular; (*concrete*) concreto; (*given*) determinado; (*fussy*) quisquilloso; (*demanding*) exigente; **in ~** en particular ❑ **particularly** adv (*in particular*) sobre todo; (*difficult, good etc*) especialmente ❑ **particulars** npl (*information*) datos mpl; (*details*) pormenores mpl

parting ['pɑːtɪŋ] n (*act*) separación f; (*farewell*) despedida; (BRIT: *in hair*) raya ♦ adj de despedida

partition [pɑː'tɪʃən] n (POL) división f; (*wall*) tabique m

partly ['pɑːtlɪ] adv en parte

partner ['pɑːtnə] n (COMM) socio(-a); (SPORT, at dance) pareja; (spouse) cónyuge mf; (lover) compañero(-a) ❑ **partnership** n asociación f; (COMM) sociedad f

partridge ['pɑːtrɪdʒ] n perdiz f

part-time ['pɑːt'taɪm] adj, adv a tiempo parcial

party ['pɑːtɪ] n (POL) partido; (celebration) fiesta; (group) grupo; (LAW) parte f interesada ♦ cpd (POL) de partido

pass [pɑːs] vt (time, object) pasar; (place) pasar por; (overtake) rebasar; (exam) aprobar; (approve) aprobar ♦ vi pasar; (SCOL) aprobar, ser aprobado ♦ n (permit) permiso; (membership card) carnet m; (in mountains) puerto, desfiladero; (SPORT) pase m; (SCOL: also: ~ mark): **to get a ~ in** aprobar en; **to ~ sth through sth** pasar algo por algo; **to make a ~ at sb** (inf) hacer proposiciones a algn ▶ **pass away** vi fallecer ▶ **pass by** vi pasar ♦ vt (ignore) pasar por alto ▶ **pass on** vt transmitir ▶ **pass out** vi desmayarse ▶ **pass over** vi, vt omitir, pasar por alto ▶ **pass up** vt (opportunity) renunciar a ❑ **passable** adj (road) transitable; (tolerable) pasable

passage ['pæsɪdʒ] n (also: **passageway**) pasillo; (act of passing) tránsito; (fare, in book) pasaje m; (by boat) travesía f; (ANAT) tubo

passenger ['pæsɪndʒə] n pasajero(-a), viajero(-a)

passer-by [pɑːsə'baɪ] n transeúnte mf

passing place n (AUT) apartadero

passion ['pæʃən] n pasión f ❑ **passionate** adj apasionado ❑ **passion fruit** n fruta de la pasión, granadilla

passive ['pæsɪv] adj (gen, also LING) pasivo

passport ['pɑːspɔːt] n pasaporte m ❑ **passport control** n control m de pasaporte ❑ **passport office** n oficina de pasaportes

password ['pɑːswɜːd] n contraseña

past [pɑːst] prep (in front of) por delante de; (further than) más allá de; (later than) después de ♦ adj pasado; (president etc) antiguo ♦ n (time) pasado; (of person) antecedentes mpl; **he's ~ forty** tiene más de cuarenta años; **ten/quarter ~ eight** las ocho y diez/cuarto; **for the ~ few/3 days** durante los últimos días/últimos 3 días; **to run ~ sb** pasar a algn corriendo

pasta ['pæstə] n pasta

paste [peɪst] n pasta; (glue) engrudo ♦ vt pegar

pastel ['pæstl] adj pastel; (painting) al pastel

pasteurized ['pæstəraɪzd] adj pasteurizado

pastime ['pɑːstaɪm] n pasatiempo

pastor ['pɑːstə] n pastor m

past participle [-'pɑːtɪsɪpl] n (LING) participio m (de) pasado or (de) pretérito o pasivo

pastry ['peɪstrɪ] n (dough) pasta; (cake) pastel m

pasture ['pɑːstʃə] n pasto

pasty¹ ['pæstɪ] n empanada

pasty² ['peɪstɪ] adj (complexion) pálido

pat [pæt] vt dar una palmadita a; (dog etc) acariciar

patch [pætʃ] n (of material, eye patch) parche m; (mended part) remiendo; (of land) terreno ♦ vt remendar; (to go through) **a bad ~** (pasar por) una mala racha ❑ **patchy** adj desigual

pâté ['pæteɪ] n paté m

patent ['peɪtnt] n patente f ♦ vt patentar ♦ adj patente, evidente

paternal [pə'tɜːnl] adj paternal; (relation) paterno

paternity leave [pə'tɜːnɪtɪ-] n permiso m por paternidad, licencia por paternidad

path [pɑːθ] n camino, sendero; (trail, track) pista; (of missile) trayectoria

pathetic [pə'θetɪk] adj patético, lastimoso; (very bad) malísimo

pathway ['pɑːθweɪ] n sendero, vereda

patience ['peɪʃns] n paciencia; (BRIT CARDS) solitario

patient ['peɪʃnt] n paciente mf ♦ adj paciente, sufrido

patio ['pætɪəʊ] n patio

patriotic [pætrɪ'ɒtɪk] adj patriótico

patrol [pə'trəʊl] n patrulla ♦ vt patrullar por ❏ **patrol car** n coche m patrulla

patron ['peɪtrən] n (in shop) cliente mf; (of charity) patrocinador(a) m/f; **~ of the arts** mecenas m

patronizing ['pætrənaɪzɪŋ] adj condescendiente

pattern ['pætən] n (SEWING) patrón m; (design) dibujo ❏ **patterned** adj (material) estampado

pause [pɔːz] n pausa ♦ vi hacer una pausa

pave [peɪv] vt pavimentar; **to ~ the way for** preparar el terreno para

pavement ['peɪvmənt] (BRIT) n acera, banqueta (MEX), andén m (CAm), vereda (SC)

pavilion [pə'vɪlɪən] n (SPORT) caseta

paving ['peɪvɪŋ] n pavimento, enlosado

paw [pɔː] n pata

pawn [pɔːn] n (CHESS) peón m; (fig) instrumento ♦ vt empeñar ❏ **pawn broker** n prestamista mf

pay [peɪ] (pt, pp **paid**) n (wage etc) sueldo, salario ♦ vt pagar ♦ vi (be profitable) rendir; **to ~ attention** (to) prestar atención (a); **to ~ a visit** hacer una visita a algn; **to ~ one's respects to sb** presentar sus respetos a algn ▶ **pay back** vt (money) reembolsar; (person) pagar ▶ **pay for** vt fus pagar ▶ **pay in** vt ingresar ▶ **pay off** vt saldar ♦ vi (scheme, decision) dar resultado ▶ **pay out** vt (money) gastar,

desembolsar ▶ **pay up** vt pagar (de mala gana) ❏ **payable** adj: **payable to** pagadero a ❏ **pay day** n día m de paga ❏ **pay envelope** (US) n = **pay packet** ❏ **payment** n pago; **monthly payment** mensualidad f ❏ **payout** n pago; (in competition) premio en metálico ❏ **pay packet** (BRIT) n sobre m (de paga) ❏ **pay phone** n teléfono público ❏ **payroll** n nómina ❏ **pay slip** n recibo de sueldo ❏ **pay television** n televisión f de pago

PC n abbr = **personal computer**; (BRIT: = police constable) policía mf ♦ adv abbr = **politically correct**

p.c. abbr = **per cent**

PDA n abbr (= personal digital assistant) agenda electrónica

PE n abbr (= physical education) ed. física

pea [piː] n guisante m (SP), arveja (LAm), chícharo (MEX, CAm)

peace [piːs] n paz f; (calm) paz f, tranquilidad f ❏ **peaceful** adj (gentle) pacífico; (calm) tranquilo, sosegado

peach [piːtʃ] n melocotón m (SP), durazno (LAm)

peacock ['piːkɒk] n pavo real

peak [piːk] n (of mountain) cumbre f, cima; (of cap) visera; (fig) cumbre f ❏ **peak hours** npl horas fpl punta

peanut ['piːnʌt] n cacahuete m (SP), maní m (LAm), cacahuate m (MEX) ❏ **peanut butter** n manteca de cacahuete o maní

pear [peə'] n pera

pearl [pɜːl] n perla

peasant ['peznt] n campesino(-a)

peat [piːt] n turba

pebble ['pebl] n guijarro

peck [pek] vt (also: **~ at**) picotear ♦ vt picotazo; (kiss) besito ❏ **peckish** (BRIT: inf) adj: **I feel peckish** tengo ganas de picar algo

peculiar [pɪ'kjuːlɪə'] adj (odd) extraño, raro; (typical) propio, característico; **~ to** propio de

pedal ['pɛdl] *n* pedal *m* ♦ *vi* pedalear

pedalo ['pɛdələʊ] *n* patín *m* a pedal

pedestal ['pɛdəstl] *n* pedestal *m*

pedestrian [pɪ'dɛstrɪən] *n* peatón(-ona) *m/f* ♦ *adj* pedestre ❑ **pedestrian crossing** (BRIT) *n* paso de peatones ❑ **pedestrianized** *adj*: **a pedestrianized street** una calle peatonal ❑ **pedestrian precinct** (US **pedestrian zone**) *n* zona peatonal

pedigree ['pɛdɪgriː] *n* genealogía, (of animal) raza, pedigrí *m* ♦ *cpd* (animal) de raza, de casta

pedophile ['piːdəʊfaɪl] (US) *n* = **paedophile**

pee [piː] (inf) *vi* mear

peek [piːk] *vi* mirar a hurtadillas

peel [piːl] *n* piel *f*; (of orange, lemon) cáscara; (: removed) peladuras *fpl* ♦ *vt* pelar ♦ *vi* (paint etc) desconcharse; (wallpaper) despegarse, desprenderse; (skin) pelar

peep [piːp] *n* (BRIT: look) mirada furtiva; (sound) pío ♦ *vi* (BRIT: look) mirar furtivamente

peer [pɪə*] *vi*: **to ~ at** esudriñar ♦ *n* (noble) par *m*; (equal) igual *m*; (contemporary) contemporáneo(-a)

peg [pɛg] *n* (for coat etc) gancho, colgadero; (BRIT: also: **clothes ~**) pinza

pelican ['pɛlɪkən] *n* pelícano ❑ **pelican crossing** (BRIT) *n* (AUT) paso de peatones señalizado

pelt [pɛlt] *vt*: **to ~ sb with sth** arrojarle algo a algn ♦ *vi* (rain) llover a cántaros; (inf: run) correr ♦ *n* pellejo

pelvis ['pɛlvɪs] *n* pelvis *f*

pen [pɛn] *n* (fountain pen) pluma; (ballpoint pen) bolígrafo; (for sheep) redil *m*

penalty ['pɛnltɪ] *n* (gen) pena; (fine) multa

pence [pɛns] *npl* of **penny**

pencil ['pɛnsl] *n* lápiz *m* ▶ **pencil in** *vt* (appointment) apuntar con carácter provisional ❑ **pencil case** *n* estuche *m* ❑ **pencil sharpener** *n* sacapuntas *m inv*

pendant ['pɛndnt] *n* pendiente *m*

pending ['pɛndɪŋ] *prep* antes de ♦ *adj* pendiente

penetrate ['pɛnɪtreɪt] *vt* penetrar

penfriend ['pɛnfrɛnd] (BRIT) *n* amigo(-a) por carta

penguin ['pɛngwɪn] *n* pingüino

penicillin [pɛnɪ'sɪlɪn] *n* penicilina

peninsula [pə'nɪnsjʊlə] *n* península

penis ['piːnɪs] *n* pene *m*

penitentiary [pɛnɪ'tɛnʃərɪ] (US) *n* cárcel *f*, presidio

penknife ['pɛnnaɪf] *n* navaja

penniless ['pɛnɪlɪs] *adj* sin dinero

penny ['pɛnɪ] (pl **pennies** or **pence** (BRIT)) *n* penique *m*; (US) centavo

penpal ['pɛnpæl] *n* amigo(-a) por carta

pension ['pɛnʃən] *n* (state benefit) jubilación *f* ❑ **pensioner** (BRIT) *n* jubilado(-a)

pentagon ['pɛntəgən] (US) *n*: **the P~** (POL) el Pentágono

PENTAGON

Se conoce como **Pentagon** al edificio de planta pentagonal que acoge las dependencias del Ministerio de Defensa estadounidense ("Department of Defense") en Arlington, Virginia. En lenguaje periodístico se aplica también a la dirección militar del país.

penthouse ['pɛnthaʊs] *n* ático de lujo

penultimate [pɛ'nʌltɪmət] *adj* penúltimo

people ['piːpl] *npl* gente *f*; (citizens) pueblo, ciudadanos *mpl*; (POL): **the ~** el pueblo ♦ *n* (nation, race) pueblo, nación *f*; **several ~ came** vinieron varias personas; **~ say that ...** dice la gente que ...

pepper ['pɛpə*] *n* (spice) pimienta; (vegetable) pimiento ♦ *vt*: **to ~ with**

(fig) salpicar de ❑ **peppermint** *n (sweet)* pastilla de menta

per [pə:ʳ] *prep* por; **~ day/person** por día/persona; **~ annum** al año

perceive [pəˈsiːv] *vt* percibir; *(realize)* darse cuenta de

per cent *n* por ciento

percentage [pəˈsɛntɪdʒ] *n* porcentaje *m*

perception [pəˈsɛpʃən] *n* percepción f; *(insight)* perspicacia; *(opinion etc)* opinión f

perch [pəːtʃ] *n (fish)* perca; *(for bird)* percha ♦ *vi* **to ~ (on)** *(bird)* posarse (en); *(person)* encaramarse en)

percussion [pəˈkʌʃən] *n* percusión f

perfect [*adj, n* ˈpəːfɪkt, *vb* pəˈfɛkt] *adj* perfecto ♦ *n (also:* **~ tense)** perfecto ♦ *vt* perfeccionar ❑ **perfection** [pəˈfɛkʃən] *n* perfección f ❑ **perfectly** [ˈpəːfɪktlɪ] *adv* perfectamente

perform [pəˈfɔːm] *vt (carry out)* realizar, llevar a cabo; *(THEATRE)* representar; *(piece of music)* interpretar ♦ *vi (well, badly)* funcionar ❑ **performance** *n (of a play)* representación f; *(of actor, athlete etc)* actuación f; *(of car, engine, company)* rendimiento m; *(of economy)* resultados mpl ❑ **performer** *n (actor)* actor m, actriz f

perfume [ˈpəːfjuːm] *n* perfume m

perhaps [pəˈhæps] *adv* quizá(s), tal vez

perimeter [pəˈrɪmɪtəʳ] *n* perímetro

period [ˈpɪərɪəd] *n* periodo; *(SCOL)* clase f; *(full stop)* punto; *(MED)* regla ♦ *adj (costume, furniture)* de época ❑ **periodical** [pɪərɪˈɔdɪkl] *n* periódico ❑ **periodically** *adv* de vez en cuando, cada cierto tiempo

perish [ˈpɛrɪʃ] *vi* perecer; *(decay)* echarse a perder

perjury [ˈpəːdʒərɪ] *n (LAW)* perjurio

perk [pəːk] *n* extra m

perm [pəːm] *n* permanente f

permanent [ˈpəːmənənt] *adj* permanente ❑ **permanently** *adv*

(lastingly) para siempre, de modo definitivo; *(all the time)* permanentemente

permission [pəˈmɪʃən] *n* permiso

permit [*n* ˈpəːmɪt, *vt* pəˈmɪt] *n* permiso, licencia ♦ *vt* permitir

perplex [pəˈplɛks] *vt* dejar perplejo

persecute [ˈpəːsɪkjuːt] *vt* perseguir

persecution [pəːsɪˈkjuːʃən] *n* persecución f

persevere [pəːsɪˈvɪəʳ] *vi* persistir

Persian [ˈpəːʃən] *adj, n* persa mf; **the ~ Gulf** el Golfo Pérsico

persist [pəˈsɪst] *vi:* **to ~ (in doing sth)** persistir (en hacer algo) ❑ **persistent** *adj* persistente; *(determined)* porfiado

person [ˈpəːsn] *n* persona; **in ~** en persona ❑ **personal** *adj* personal, individual; *(visit)* en persona ❑ **personal assistant** *n* ayudante mf personal ❑ **personal computer** *n* ordenador m personal ❑ **personality** [ˈnælɪtɪ] *n* personalidad f ❑ **personally** *adv* personalmente; *(in person)* en persona; **to take sth personally** tomarse algo a mal ❑ **personal organizer** *n* agenda ❑ **personal stereo** *n* Walkman® m

personnel [pəːsəˈnɛl] *n* personal m

perspective [pəˈspɛktɪv] *n* perspectiva

perspiration [pəːspɪˈreɪʃən] *n* transpiración f

persuade [pəˈsweɪd] *vt:* **to ~ sb to do sth** persuadir a algn para que haga algo

persuasion [pəˈsweɪʒən] *n* persuasión f; *(persuasiveness)* persuasiva

persuasive [pəˈsweɪsɪv] *adj* persuasivo

perverse [pəˈvəːs] *adj* perverso; *(wayward)* travieso

pervert [*n* pəˈvəːt, *vb* pəˈvəːt] *n* pervertido(-a) ♦ *vt* pervertir; *(truth, sb's words)* tergiversar

pessimism [ˈpɛsɪmɪzəm] *n* pesimismo

pessimist [ˈpɛsɪmɪst] *n* pesimista mf ❑ **pessimistic** [ˈmɪstɪk] *adj* pesimista

pest [pest] n (insect) insecto nocivo; (fig) lata, molestia

pester ['pestə'] vt molestar, acosar

pesticide ['pestisaid] n pesticida m

pet [pet] n animal m doméstico ♦ cpd favorito ♦ vt acariciar; **teacher's ~** favorito(-a) (del profesor); **~ hate** manía

petal ['petl] n pétalo

petite [pə'ti:t] adj chiquita

petition [pə'tɪʃən] n petición f

petrified ['petrɪfaɪd] adj horrorizado

petrol ['petrəl] (BRIT) n gasolina

petroleum [pə'trəuliəm] n petróleo

petrol: petrol pump (BRIT) n (in garage) surtidor m de gasolina ❑ **petrol station** (BRIT) n gasolinera ❑ **petrol tank** (BRIT) n depósito m (de gasolina)

petticoat ['petikəut] n enaguas fpl

petty ['peti] adj (mean) mezquino; (unimportant) insignificante

pew [pju:] n banco

pewter ['pju:tə'] n peltre m

phantom ['fæntəm] n fantasma m

pharmacist ['fɑ:məsist] n farmacéutico(-a)

pharmacy ['fɑ:məsi] n farmacia

phase [feiz] n fase f ▸ **phase in** vt introducir progresivamente ▸ **phase out** vt (machinery, product) retirar progresivamente; (job, subsidy) eliminar por etapas

Ph.D. abbr = **Doctor of Philosophy**

pheasant ['feznt] n faisán m

phenomena [fə'nɔminə] npl of **phenomenon**

phenomenal [fɪ'nɔminl] adj fenomenal, extraordinario

phenomenon [fə'nɔminən] (pl **phenomena**) n fenómeno

Philippines [filipi:nz] npl: **the ~** las Filipinas

philosopher [fɪ'lɔsəfə'] n filósofo(-a)

philosophical [filə'sɔfikl] adj filosófico

philosophy [fɪ'lɔsəfi] n filosofía

phlegm [flem] n flema

phobia ['fəubjə] n fobia

phone [fəun] n teléfono ♦ vt telefonear, llamar por teléfono; **to be on the ~** tener teléfono; (be calling) estar hablando por teléfono ▸ **phone back** ♦ vt, vi volver a llamar ▸ **phone up** vt, vi llamar por teléfono ❑ **phone book** n guía telefónica ❑ **phone booth** n cabina telefónica ❑ **phone box** n = **phone booth** ❑ **phone call** n llamada (telefónica) ❑ **phonecard** n teletarjeta ❑ **phone number** n número de teléfono

phonetics [fə'netiks] n fonética

phoney ['fəuni] adj falso

photo ['fəutəu] n foto f ❑ **photo album** n álbum m de fotos ❑ **photocopier** n fotocopiadora ❑ **photocopy** n fotocopia ♦ vt fotocopiar

photograph ['fəutəgrɑ:f] n fotografía ♦ vt fotografiar ❑ **photographer** [fə'tɔgrəfə'] n fotógrafo ❑ **photography** [fə'tɔgrəfi] n fotografía

phrase [freiz] n frase f ♦ vt expresar ❑ **phrase book** n libro de frases

physical ['fizikl] adj físico ❑ **physical education** n educación f física ❑ **physically** adv físicamente

physician [fɪ'zɪʃən] n médico(-a)

physicist ['fizisist] n físico(-a)

physics ['fiziks] n física

physiotherapist [fiziəu'θerəpist] n fisioterapeuta

physiotherapy [fiziəu'θerəpi] n fisioterapia

physique [fɪ'zi:k] n físico

pianist ['pi:ənist] n pianista mf

piano [pi'ænəu] n piano

pick [pik] n (tool: also: **~-axe**) pico, piqueta ♦ vt (select) elegir, escoger;

(gather) coger *(SP)*, recoger; *(remove, take out)* sacar, quitar; *(lock)* abrir con ganzúa; **take your ~** escoja lo que quiera; **the ~ of** lo mejor de; **to ~ one's nose/teeth** hurgarse las narices/limpiarse los dientes; **to ~ a quarrel with sb** meterse con algn ► **pick on** *vt fus (person)* escoger ► **pick out** *vt (choose)* escoger; *(distinguish)* identificar ► **pick up** *vi (improve: sales)* mejorar; *(: patient)* reponerse; *(FINANCE)* recobrarse* ♦ *vt (learn)* aprender; *(POLICE: arrest)* detener; *(person: for sex)* ligar; *(RADIO)* captar; **to pick up speed** acelerarse; **to pick o.s. up** levantarse

pickle ['pɪkl] *n (also: **pickles**: as condiment)* escabeche *m*; *(fig: mess)* apuro* ♦ *vt* encurtir

pickpocket ['pɪkpɔkɪt] *n* carterista *mf*

pick-up ['pɪkʌp] *n (also: ~ truck)* furgoneta, camioneta

picnic ['pɪknɪk] *n* merienda* ♦ *vi* ir de merienda □ **picnic area** *n* zona de picnic; *(AUT)* área de descanso

picture ['pɪktʃə'] *n* cuadro; *(painting)* pintura; *(photograph)* fotografía; *(TV)* imagen *f*; *(film)* película; *(fig: description)* descripción *f*; *(: situation)* situación *f* ♦ *vt (imagine)* imaginar; **pictures** *npl*: **the pictures** *(BRIT)* el cine □ **picture frame** *n* marco □ **picture messaging** *n (*envío de) mensajes con imágenes

picturesque [pɪktʃə'resk] *adj* pintoresco

pie [paɪ] *n* pastel *m*; *(open)* tarta; *(small: of meat)* empanada

pie chart *n* gráfico de sectores *or* tarta

piece [pi:s] *n* pedazo, trozo; *(of cake)* trozo; *(item)*: **a ~ of clothing/furniture/ advice** una prenda *(de vestir)/un mueble/un consejo ♦ *vt*: **to ~ together** juntar; *(TECH)* armar; **to take to pieces** desmontar

pier [pɪə'] *n* muelle *m*, embarcadero

pierce [pɪəs] *vt* perforar □ **pierced** *adj*: **I've got pierced ears** tengo los agujeros hechos en las orejas

pig [pɪg] *n* cerdo, chancho *(LAm)*; *(pej: unkind person)* asqueroso; *(: greedy person)* glotón(-ona) *m/f*

pigeon ['pɪdʒən] *n* paloma; *(as food)* pichón *m*

pig: **piggy bank** ['pɪgɪ-] *n* hucha *(en forma de cerdito)* □ **pigsty** ['pɪgstaɪ] *n* pocilga □ **pigtail** *n (girl's)* trenza

pike [paɪk] *n (fish)* lucio

pilchard ['pɪltʃəd] *n* sardina

pile [paɪl] *n* montón *m*; *(of carpet, cloth)* pelo □ **pile up** *vi +adv (accumulate: work)* amontonarse, acumularse ♦ *vt +adv (put in a heap: books, clothes)* apilar, amontonar; *(accumulate)* acumular □ **piles** *npl (MED)* almorranas *fpl*, hemorroides *mpl* □ **pile-up** *n (AUT)* accidente *m* múltiple

pilgrimage ['pɪlgrɪmɪdʒ] *n* peregrinación *f*, romería

pill [pɪl] *n* píldora; **the ~** la píldora

pillar ['pɪlə'] *n* pilar *m*

pillow ['pɪləʊ] *n* almohada □ **pillowcase** *n* funda

pilot ['paɪlət] *n* piloto ♦ *cpd (scheme etc)* piloto ♦ *vt* pilotar □ **pilot light** *n* piloto

pimple ['pɪmpl] *n* grano

PIN *n abbr (= personal identification number)* número personal

pin [pɪn] *n* alfiler *m* ♦ *vt* prender *(con alfiler)*; **pins and needles** hormigueo; **to ~ sb down** *(fig)* hacer que algn concrete; **to ~ sth on sb** *(fig)* colgarle a algn el sambenito de algo

pinafore ['pɪnəfɔ:'] *n* delantal *m*

pinch [pɪntʃ] *n (of salt etc)* pizca ♦ *vt* pellizcar; *(inf: steal)* birlar; **at a ~** en caso de apuro

pine [paɪn] *n (also: ~ tree)* pino ♦ *vi*: **to ~ for** suspirar por

pineapple ['paɪnæpl] *n* piña, ananás *m*

ping [pɪŋ] n (noise) sonido agudo
❏ **ping-pong®** n pingpong® m

pink [pɪŋk] adj rosado, (color de) rosa
♦ n (colour) rosa; (BOT) clavel m,
clavellina

pinpoint ['pɪnpɔɪnt] vt precisar

pint [paɪnt] n pinta (BRIT = 568cc, US =
473cc); (BRIT: inf: of beer) pinta de
cerveza, = jarra (SP)

pioneer [paɪə'nɪə] n pionero(-a)

pious ['paɪəs] adj piadoso, devoto

pip [pɪp] n (seed) pepita; **the pips** (BRIT)
la señal

pipe [paɪp] n tubo, caño; (for smoking)
pipa ♦ vt conducir en cañerías
❏ **pipeline** n (for oil) oleoducto; (for
gas) gasoducto ❏ **piper** n gaitero(-a)

pirate ['paɪərət] n pirata mf ♦ vt
(cassette, book) piratear

Pisces ['paɪsi:z] n Piscis m

piss [pɪs] (inf!) vi mear ❏ **pissed** (inf!)
adj (drunk) borracho

pistol ['pɪstl] n pistola

piston ['pɪstən] n pistón m, émbolo

pit [pɪt] n hoyo; (also: **coal** ~) mina; (in
garage) foso de inspección; (also:
orchestra ~) platea ♦ vt: **to** ~ **one's
wits against sb** medir fuerzas con algn

pitch [pɪtʃ] n (MUS) tono; (BRIT SPORT)
campo, terreno; (fig) punto; (tar) brea
♦ vt (throw) arrojar, lanzar ♦ vi (fall)
caer(se); **to** ~ **a tent** montar una tienda
(de campaña) ❏ **pitch-black** adj
negro como boca de lobo

pitfall ['pɪtfɔ:l] n riesgo

pith [pɪθ] n (of orange) médula

pitiful ['pɪtɪful] adj (touching)
lastimoso, conmovedor(a)

pity ['pɪtɪ] n compasión f, piedad f ♦ vt
compadecer(se de); **what a** ~! ¡qué
pena!

pizza ['pi:tsə] n pizza

placard ['plækɑ:d] n letrero; (in march
etc) pancarta

place [pleɪs] n lugar m, sitio; (seat)
plaza, asiento; (post) puesto; (home):

at/to his ~ en/a su casa; (role: in society
etc) papel m ♦ vt (object) poner,
colocar; (identify) reconocer; **to take** ~
tener lugar; **to be placed** (in race,
exam) colocarse; **out of** ~ (not suitable)
fuera de lugar; **in the first** ~ en primer
lugar; **to change places with sb**
cambiarse de sitio con algn; ~ **of birth**
lugar m de nacimiento ❏ **place mat** n
(wooden etc) salvamanteles m inv;
(linen etc) mantel m individual
❏ **placement** n (positioning)
colocación f; (at work) emplazamiento

placid ['plæsɪd] adj apacible

plague [pleɪg] n plaga; (MED) peste f
♦ vt (fig) acosar, atormentar

plaice [pleɪs] n inv platija

plain [pleɪn] adj (unpatterned) liso;
(clear) claro, evidente; (simple) sencillo;
(not handsome) poco atractivo ♦ adv
claramente ♦ n llano, llanura ❏ **plain
chocolate** n chocolate m amargo
❏ **plainly** adv claramente

plaintiff ['pleɪntɪf] n demandante mf

plait [plæt] n trenza

plan [plæn] n (drawing) plano; (scheme)
plan m, proyecto ♦ vt proyectar,
planificar ♦ vi hacer proyectos; **to** ~ **to
do** pensar hacer

plane [pleɪn] n (AVIAT) avión m; (MATH,
fig) plano; (also: ~ **tree**) plátano; (tool)
cepillo

planet ['plænɪt] n planeta m

plank [plæŋk] n tabla

planning ['plænɪŋ] n planificación f;
family ~ planificación familiar

plant [plɑ:nt] n planta; (machinery)
maquinaria; (factory) fábrica ♦ vt
plantar; (field) sembrar; (bomb) colocar

plantation [plæn'teɪʃən] n plantación
f; (estate) hacienda

plaque [plæk] n placa

plaster ['plɑ:stə] n (for walls) yeso;
(also: ~ **of Paris**) yeso mate, escayola
(SP); (BRIT: also: **sticking** ~) tirita (SP),
curita (LAm) ♦ vt enyesar; (cover): **to** ~

with llenar or cubrir □ **plaster cast** n (MED) escayola; (model, statue) vaciado de yeso

plastic ['plæstɪk] n plástico ♦ adj de plástico □ **plastic bag** n bolsa de plástico □ **plastic surgery** n cirujía f

plate [pleɪt] n (dish) plato; (metal, in book) lámina; (dental plate) placa de dentadura postiza

plateau ['plætəʊ] (pl **plateaus** or **plateaux**) n meseta, altiplanicie f

platform ['plætfɔːm] n (RAIL) andén m; (stage, BRIT: on bus) plataforma; (at meeting) tribuna; (POL) programa m (electoral)

platinum ['plætɪnəm] adj, n platino

platoon [plə'tuːn] n pelotón m

platter ['plætə'] n fuente f

plausible ['plɔːzɪbl] adj verosímil; (person) convincente

play [pleɪ] n (THEATRE) obra, comedia ♦ vt (game) jugar; (compete against) jugar contra; (instrument) tocar; (part: in play etc) hacer el papel de; (tape, record) poner ♦ vi jugar; (band) tocar; (tape, record) sonar; **to ~ safe** ir a lo seguro ▶ **play back** vt (tape) poner ▶ **play up** vi (cause trouble to) dar guerra □ **player** n jugador(a) m/f; (THEATRE) actor (actriz) m/f; (MUS) músico(-a) □ **playful** adj juguetón(-ona) □ **playground** n (in school) patio de recreo; (in park) parque m infantil □ **playgroup** n jardín m de niños □ **playing card** n naipe m, carta □ **playing field** n campo de deportes □ **playschool** n = **playgroup** □ **playtime** n (SCOL) recreo □ **playwright** n dramaturgo(-a)

plc abbr (= public limited company) = S.A.

plea [pliː] n súplica, petición f; (LAW) alegato, defensa

plead [pliːd] vt (LAW): **to ~ sb's case** defender a algn; (give as excuse) poner como pretexto ♦ vi (LAW) declararse; (beg): **to ~ with sb** suplicar or rogar a algn

pleasant ['plɛznt] adj agradable

please [pliːz] excl ¡por favor! ♦ vt (give pleasure to) dar gusto a, agradar ♦ vi (think fit): **do as you ~** haz lo que quieras; (inf) ¡haz lo que quieras!, ¡como quieras! □ **pleased** adj (happy) alegre, contento; **pleased (with)** satisfecho (de); **pleased to meet you** ¡encantado!, ¡tanto gusto!

pleasure ['plɛʒə'] n placer m, gusto; **"it's a ~"** "el gusto es mío"

pleat [pliːt] n pliegue m

pledge [plɛdʒ] n (promise) promesa, voto ♦ vt prometer

plentiful ['plɛntɪful] adj copioso, abundante

plenty ['plɛntɪ] n: **~ of** mucho(s)/a(s)

pliers ['plaɪəz] npl alicates mpl, tenazas fpl

plight [plaɪt] n situación f difícil

plod [plɔd] vi caminar con paso pesado; (fig) trabajar laboriosamente

plonk [plɔŋk] (inf) n (BRIT: wine) vino peleón ♦ vt: **to ~ sth down** dejar caer algo

plot [plɔt] n (scheme) complot m, conjura; (of story, play) argumento; (of land) terreno ♦ vt (mark out) trazar; (conspire) tramar, urdir ♦ vi conspirar

plough [plaʊ] (US **plow**) n arado ♦ vt (earth) arar; **to ~ money into** invertir dinero en □ **ploughman's lunch** (BRIT) n almuerzo de pub a base de pan, queso y encurtidos

plow [plaʊ] (US) = **plough**

ploy [plɔɪ] n truco, estratagema

pluck [plʌk] vt (fruit) coger (SP), recoger (LAm); (musical instrument) puntear; (bird) desplumar; (eyebrows) depilar; **to ~ up courage** hacer de tripas corazón

plug [plʌg] n tapón m; (ELEC) enchufe m, clavija; (AUT: also: **spark(ing) ~**) bujía ♦ vt (hole) tapar; (inf: advertise) dar publicidad a ► **plug in** vt (ELEC) enchufar □ **plughole** n desagüe m

plum [plʌm] n (fruit) ciruela

plumber ['plʌmə*] n fontanero(-a) (SP, CAm), plomero(-a) (LAm)

plumbing ['plʌmɪŋ] n (trade) fontanería, plomería; (piping) cañería

plummet ['plʌmɪt] vi: to ~ (down) caer a plomo

plump [plʌmp] adj rechoncho, rollizo ♦ vi: to ~ for (inf: choose) optar por

plunge [plʌndʒ] n zambullida ♦ vt sumergir, hundir ♦ vi (fall) caer; (dive) saltar; (person) arrojarse; to take the ~ lanzarse

plural ['pluərl] adj plural ♦ n plural m

plus [plʌs] n (also: ~ **sign**) signo más ♦ prep más, y, además de; **ten/twenty ~** más de diez/veinte

ply [plaɪ] vt (a trade) ejercer ♦ vi (ship) ir y venir ♦ n (of wool, rope) cabo; to ~ **sb with drink** insistir en ofrecer a algn muchas copas □ **plywood** n madera contrachapada

P.M. n abbr = **Prime Minister**

p.m. adv abbr (= post meridiem) de la tarde or noche

PMS n abbr (= premenstrual syndrome) SPM m

PMT n abbr (= premenstrual tension) SPM m

pneumatic drill [njuːˈmætɪk-] n martillo neumático

pneumonia [njuːˈməunɪə] n pulmonía

poach [pəutʃ] vt (cook) escalfar; (steal) cazar (or pescar) en vedado ♦ vi cazar (or pescar) en vedado □ **poached** adj escalfado

P.O. Box n abbr (= Post Office Box) apdo., aptdo.

pocket ['pɒkɪt] n bolsillo; (fig: small area) bolsa ♦ vt meter en el bolsillo; (steal) embolsar; to be out of ~ (BRIT) salir perdiendo □ **pocketbook** (US) n cartera □ **pocket money** n asignación f

pod [pɒd] n vaina

podiatrist [pɒˈdiːətrɪst] (US) n pedicuro(-a)

podium ['pəudɪəm] n podio

poem ['pəuɪm] n poema m

poet ['pəuɪt] n poeta m/f □ **poetic** [-'etɪk] adj poético □ **poetry** n poesía

poignant ['pɔɪnjənt] adj conmovedor(a)

point [pɔɪnt] n punto; (tip) punta; (purpose) fin m, propósito; (use) utilidad f; (significant part) lo significativo; (moment) momento; (ELEC) toma (de corriente); (also: **decimal ~**): **2 ~ 3 (2.3)** dos coma tres (2,3) ♦ vt señalar; (gun etc): to ~ **sth at sb** apuntar algo a algn ♦ vi: to ~ **at** señalar; **points** npl (AUT) contactos mpl; (RAIL) agujas fpl; **to be on the ~ of doing sth** estar a punto de hacer algo; **to make a ~ of** poner empeño en; **to get/miss the ~** comprender/no comprender; **to come to the ~** ir al meollo; **there's no ~ (in doing)** no tiene sentido (hacer) ► **point out** vt señalar □ **point-blank** adv (say, refuse) sin más hablar; (also: **at point-blank range**) a quemarropa □ **pointed** adj (shape) puntiagudo, afilado; (remark) intencionado □ **pointer** n (needle) aguja, indicador m □ **pointless** adj sin sentido □ **point of view** n punto de vista

poison ['pɔɪzn] n veneno ♦ vt envenenar □ **poisonous** adj venenoso; (fumes etc) tóxico

poke [pəuk] vt (jab with finger, stick etc) empujar; (put): to ~ **sth in(to)** introducir algo en ► **poke about** or **around** vi fisgonear ► **poke out** vi (stick out) salir

poker ['pəukə*] n atizador m; (CARDS) póker m

Poland ['pəulənd] n Polonia

polar ['pəulə*] adj polar □ **polar bea** n oso polar

Pole [pəul] n polaco(-a)

pole [paul] n palo m; (fixed) poste m; (GEO) polo m □ **pole bean** (US) n ≈ judía verde □ **pole vault** n salto con pértiga

police [pə'li:s] npl policía ♦ vt vigilar □ **police car** n coche-patrulla m □ **police constable** (BRIT) n policía m, guardia m □ **police force** n cuerpo de policía □ **policeman** (irreg) n policía m, guardia m □ **police officer** n guardia m, policía m □ **police station** n comisaría f □ **policewoman** (irreg) n mujer f policía

policy ['pɔlɪsɪ] n política; (also: insurance ~) póliza

polio ['pəulɪəu] n polio f

Polish ['pəulɪʃ] adj polaco ♦ n (LING) polaco

polish ['pɔlɪʃ] n (for shoes) betún m; (for floor) cera (de lustrar); (shine) brillo, lustre m; (fig: refinement) educación f ♦ vt (shoes) limpiar; (make shiny) pulir, sacar brillo a ▸ **polish off** vt (food) despachar □ **polished** adj (fig: person) elegante

polite [pə'laɪt] adj cortés, atento □ **politeness** n cortesía

political [pə'lɪtɪkl] adj político □ **politically** adv políticamente □ **politically correct** políticamente correcto

politician [pɔlɪ'tɪʃən] n político(-a)

politics ['pɔlɪtɪks] n política

poll [pəul] n (election) votación f; (also: opinion ~) sondeo, encuesta ♦ vt encuestar; (votes) obtener

pollen ['pɔlən] n polen m

polling station ['pəulɪŋ-] n centro electoral

pollute [pə'lu:t] vt contaminar

pollution [pə'lu:ʃən] n polución f, contaminación f del medio ambiente

polo ['pəuləu] n (sport) polo □ **polo-neck** adj de cuello vuelto ♦ n (sweater) suéter m de cuello vuelto □ **polo shirt** n polo, niqui m

polyester [pɔlɪ'estə'] n poliéster m

polystyrene [pɔlɪ'staɪri:n] n poliestireno

polythene ['pɔlɪθi:n] n (BRIT) politeno □ **polythene bag** n bolsa de plástico

pomegranate ['pɔmɪgrænɪt] n granada

pompous ['pɔmpəs] adj pomposo

pond [pɔnd] n (natural) charca; (artificial) estanque m

ponder ['pɔndə'] vt meditar

pony ['pəunɪ] n poni m □ **ponytail** n coleta □ **pony trekking** (BRIT) n excursión f a caballo

poodle ['pu:dl] n caniche m

pool [pu:l] n (natural) charca; (also: swimming ~) piscina, alberca (MEX), pileta (RPl); (fig: of light etc) charco; (SPORT) chapolín m ♦ vt juntar; **pools** npl quinielas fpl

poor [puə'] adj pobre; (bad) de mala calidad ♦ npl: **the** ~ los pobres □ **poorly** adj mal, enfermo ♦ adv mal

pop [pɔp] n (sound) ruido seco; (MUS) (música) pop m; (inf: father) papá m; (drink) gaseosa ♦ vt (put quickly) meter (de prisa) ♦ vi reventar; (cork) saltar ▸ **pop in** vi entrar un momento ▸ **pop out** vi salir un momento □ **popcorn** n palomitas fpl

poplar ['pɔplə'] n álamo

popper ['pɔpə'] (BRIT) n automático

poppy ['pɔpɪ] n amapola

Popsicle® ['pɔpsɪkl] (US) n polo

pop star n estrella del pop

popular ['pɔpjulə'] adj popular □ **popularity** [pɔpju'lærɪtɪ] n popularidad f

population [pɔpju'leɪʃən] n población f

porcelain ['pɔ:slɪn] n porcelana

porch [pɔ:tʃ] n pórtico, entrada; (US) veranda

pore [pɔ:'] n poro ♦ vi: **to ~ over** engolfarse en

pork [pɔːk] n carne f de cerdo or (LAm) chancho □ **pork chop** n chuleta de cerdo □ **pork pie** n (BRIT: CULIN) empanada de carne de cerdo

porn [pɔːn] adj (inf) porno inv ♦ n porno □ **pornographic** [pɔːnəˈgræfɪk] adj pornográfico □ **pornography** [pɔːˈnɒgrəfɪ] n pornografía

porridge [ˈpɒrɪdʒ] n gachas fpl de avena

port [pɔːt] n puerto m; (NAUT: left side) babor m; (wine) vino de Oporto; ~ of call puerto de escala

portable [ˈpɔːtəbl] adj portátil

porter [ˈpɔːtə*] n (for luggage) maletero; (doorkeeper) portero(-a), conserje m/f

portfolio [pɔːtˈfəʊlɪəʊ] n cartera

portion [ˈpɔːʃən] n porción f; (of food) ración f

portrait [ˈpɔːtreɪt] n retrato

portray [pɔːˈtreɪ] vt retratar; (actor) representar

Portugal [ˈpɔːtjʊgl] n Portugal m

Portuguese [pɔːtjʊˈgiːz] adj portugués(-esa) ♦ n inv portugués(-esa) m/f; (LING) portugués m

pose [pəʊz] n postura, actitud f ♦ vi (pretend): to ~ as hacerse pasar por ♦ vt (question) plantear; to ~ for posar para

posh [pɒʃ] (inf) adj elegante, de lujo

position [pəˈzɪʃən] n posición f; (job) puesto; (situation) situación f ♦ vt colocar

positive [ˈpɒzɪtɪv] adj positivo; (certain) seguro; (definite) definitivo □ **positively** adv (affirmatively, enthusiastically) de forma positiva; (inf: really) absolutamente

possess [pəˈzes] vt poseer □ **possession** [pəˈzeʃən] n posesión f; **possessions** npl (belongings) pertenencias fpl □ **possessive** adj posesivo

possibility [pɒsɪˈbɪlɪtɪ] n posibilidad f

possible [ˈpɒsɪbl] adj posible; as big as ~ lo más grande posible □ **possibly** adv posiblemente; **I cannot possibly come** me es imposible venir

post [pəʊst] n (BRIT: system) correos mpl; (BRIT: letters, delivery) correo; (job, situation) puesto; (pole) poste m ♦ vt (BRIT: send by post) echar al correo; (BRIT: appoint): to ~ to enviar a □ **postage** n porte m, franqueo □ **postal** adj postal, de correos □ **postal order** n giro postal □ **postbox** (BRIT) n buzón m □ **postcard** n tarjeta postal □ **postcode** (BRIT) n código postal

poster [ˈpəʊstə*] n cartel m

postgraduate [pəʊstˈgrædjuət] n posgraduado(-a)

postman [ˈpəʊstmən] (BRIT: irreg) n cartero

postmark [ˈpəʊstmɑːk] n matasellos m inv

post-mortem [-ˈmɔːtəm] n autopsia

post office n (building) oficina de correos m; (organization): **the Post Office** Correos m inv (SP), Dirección f General de Correos (LAm)

postpone [pəsˈpəʊn] vt aplazar

posture [ˈpɒstʃə*] n postura, actitud f

postwoman [ˈpəʊstwʊmən] (BRIT: irreg) n cartera

pot [pɒt] n (for cooking) olla; (teapot) tetera; (coffeepot) cafetera; (for flowers) maceta; (for jam) tarro, pote m; (inf: marijuana) chocolate m ♦ vt (plant) poner en tiesto; to go to ~ (inf) irse al traste

potato [pəˈteɪtəʊ] (pl potatoes) n patata (SP), papa (LAm) □ **potato peeler** n pelapatatas m inv

potent [ˈpəʊtnt] adj potente, poderoso; (drink) fuerte

potential [pəˈtenʃl] adj potencial, posible ♦ n potencial m

pothole [ˈpɒthəʊl] n (in road) bache m; (BRIT: underground) gruta

pot plant ['pɒtplɑːnt] n planta de interior

potter ['pɒtə'] n alfarero(-a) ♦ vi: **to ~ around** or **about** (BRIT) hacer trabajitos ❑ **pottery** n cerámica; (factory) alfarería

potty ['pɒtɪ] n orinal m de niño

pouch [pautʃ] n (ZOOL) bolsa; (for tobacco) petaca

poultry ['pəʊltrɪ] n aves fpl de corral; (meat) pollo

pounce [pauns] vi: **to ~ on** precipitarse sobre

pound [paund] n libra (weight = 453g or 16oz; money = 100 pence) ♦ vt (beat) golpear; (crush) machacar ♦ vi (heart) latir ❑ **pound sterling** n libra esterlina

pour [pɔː'] vt echar; (tea etc) servir ♦ vi correr, fluir; **to ~ sb a drink** servirle a algn una copa ▶ **pour in** vi (people) entrar en tropel ▶ **pour out** vi salir en tropel ♦ vt (drink) echar, servir; (fig): **to pour out one's feelings** desahogarse ❑ **pouring** adj: **pouring rain** lluvia torrencial

pout [paut] vi hacer pucheros

poverty ['pɒvətɪ] n pobreza, miseria

powder ['paudə'] n polvo; (also: **face ~**) polvos mpl ♦ vt polvorear; **to ~ one's face** empolvarse la cara ❑ **powdered milk** n leche f en polvo

power ['pauə'] n poder m; (strength) fuerza; (nation, TECH) potencia; (drive) empuje m; (ELEC) fuerza, energía ♦ vt impulsar; **to be in ~** (POL) estar en el poder ❑ **power cut** (BRIT) n apagón m ❑ **power failure** n = **power cut** ❑ **powerful** adj poderoso; (engine) potente; (speech etc) convincente ❑ **powerless** adj: **powerless (to do)** incapaz (de hacer) ❑ **power point** (BRIT) n enchufe m ❑ **power station** n central f eléctrica

p.p. abbr = **per procurationem**; **p.p. J. Smith** p.p. (por poder de) J. Smith; (= pages) págs

PR n abbr = **public relations**

practical ['præktɪkl] adj práctico ❑ **practical joke** n broma pesada ❑ **practically** adv (almost) casi

practice ['præktɪs] n (habit) costumbre f; (exercise) práctica, ejercicio; (training) adiestramiento; (MED: of profession) práctica, ejercicio; (MED, LAW: business) consulta ♦ vt, vi (US) = **practise**; **in ~** (in reality) en la práctica; **out of ~** desentrenado

practise ['præktɪs] (US **practice**) vt (carry out) practicar; (profession) ejercer; (train at) practicar ♦ vi ejercer; (train) practicar ❑ **practising** adj (Christian etc) practicante; (lawyer) en ejercicio

practitioner [præk'tɪʃənə'] n (MED) médico(-a)

pragmatic [præg'mætɪk] adj pragmático

prairie ['prɛərɪ] n pampa

praise [preɪz] n alabanza(s) f(pl), elogio(s) m(pl) ♦ vt alabar, elogiar

pram [præm] (BRIT) n cochecito de niño

prank [præŋk] n travesura

prawn [prɔːn] n gamba ❑ **prawn cocktail** n cóctel m de gambas

pray [preɪ] vi rezar ❑ **prayer** [prɛə'] n oración f, rezo; (entreaty) ruego, súplica

preach [priːtʃ] vi predicar ❑ **preacher** n predicador(a) m/f

precarious [prɪ'kɛərɪəs] adj precario

precaution [prɪ'kɔːʃən] n precaución f

precede [prɪ'siːd] vt, vi preceder ❑ **precedent** ['prɛsɪdənt] n precedente m ❑ **preceding** [prɪ'siːdɪŋ] adj anterior

precinct ['priːsɪŋkt] n recinto

precious ['prɛʃəs] adj precioso

precise [prɪ'saɪs] adj preciso, exacto ❑ **precisely** adv precisamente, exactamente

precision [prɪ'sɪʒən] n precisión f

predator ['prɛdətə'] n depredador m

predecessor ['pri:dɪsesə'] n antecesor(a) m/f

predicament [prɪ'dɪkəmənt] n apuro

predict [prɪ'dɪkt] vt pronosticar
❏ **predictable** adj previsible ❏ **prediction** [-'dɪkʃən] n predicción f

predominantly [prɪ'dɒmɪnəntlɪ] adv en su mayoría

preface ['prefəs] n prefacio

prefect ['pri:fekt] (BRIT) n (in school) monitor(a) m/f

prefer [prɪ'fɜ:'] vt preferir; **to ~ doing** or **to do** preferir hacer ❏ **preferable** ['prefrəbl] adj preferible ❏ **preferably** ['prefrəblɪ] adv de preferencia ❏ **preference** ['prefrəns] n preferencia; (priority) prioridad f

prefix ['pri:fɪks] n prefijo

pregnancy ['pregnənsɪ] n (of woman) embarazo; (of animal) preñez f

pregnant ['pregnənt] adj (woman) embarazada; (animal) preñada

prehistoric ['pri:hɪs'tɒrɪk] adj prehistórico

prejudice ['predʒudɪs] n prejuicio ❏ **prejudiced** adj (person) predispuesto

preliminary [prɪ'lɪmɪnərɪ] adj preliminar

prelude ['prelju:d] n preludio

premature ['premətʃuə'] adj prematuro

premier ['premɪə'] adj primero, principal ♦ n (POL) primer(a) ministro(-a)

première ['premɪeə'] n estreno

Premier League ['premɪə-] n primera división

premises ['premɪsɪz] npl (of business etc) local m; **on the ~** en el lugar mismo

premium ['pri:mɪəm] n premio; (insurance) prima; **to be at a ~** ser muy solicitado

premonition [premə'nɪʃən] n presentimiento

preoccupied [pri:'ɒkjupaɪd] adj ensimismado

prepaid [pri:'peɪd] adj porte pagado

preparation [prepə'reɪʃən] n preparación f; **preparations** npl preparativos mpl

preparatory school [prɪ'pærətərɪ-] n escuela preparatoria

prepare [prɪ'peə'] vt preparar, disponer; (CULIN) preparar ♦ vi: **to ~ for** (action) prepararse or disponerse para; (event) hacer preparativos para; **prepared to** dispuesto a; **prepared for** listo para

preposition [prepə'zɪʃən] n preposición f

prep school [prep-] n = **preparatory school**

prerequisite [pri:'rekwɪzɪt] n requisito

preschool ['pri:'sku:l] adj preescolar

prescribe [prɪ'skraɪb] vt (MED) recetar

prescription [prɪ'skrɪpʃən] n (MED) receta

presence ['prezns] n presencia; **in sb's ~** en presencia de algn; **~ of mind** aplomo

present [adj, n 'preznt, vb prɪ'zent] adj (in attendance) presente; (current) actual ♦ n (gift) regalo; (actuality): **the ~** la actualidad, el presente ♦ vt (introduce, describe) presentar; (expound) exponer; (give) presentar, dar, ofrecer; (THEATRE) representar; **to give sb a ~** regalar algo a algn; **at ~** actualmente ❏ **presentable** [prɪ'zentəbl] adj: **to make o.s. presentable** arreglarse ❏ **presentation** [-'teɪʃən] n presentación f; (of report etc) exposición f; (formal ceremony) entrega de un regalo ❏ **present-day** adj actual ❏ **presenter** [prɪ'zentə'] n (RADIO, TV) locutor(a) m/f ❏ **presently** adv (soon) dentro de poco; (now) ahora ❏ **present participle** n participio (de) presente

preservation [prezə'veɪʃən] n conservación f

preservative [prɪ'zɜːvətɪv] n conservante m

preserve [prɪ'zɜːv] vt (keep safe) preservar, proteger; (maintain) mantener; (food) conservar ♦ n (for game) coto, vedado; (often pl: jam) conserva, confitura

preside [prɪ'zaɪd] vi presidir

president ['prezɪdənt] n presidente m/f ☐ **presidential** [-'denʃl] adj presidencial

press [pres] n (newspapers): **the P~** la prensa; (printer's) imprenta; (of button) pulsación f ♦ vt empujar; (button etc) apretar; (clothes: iron) planchar; (put pressure on: person) presionar; (insist): **to ~ sth on sb** insistir en que algn acepte algo ♦ vi (squeeze) apretar; (pressurize): **to ~ for** presionar por; **we are pressed for time/money** estamos apurados de tiempo/dinero ☐ **press conference** n rueda de prensa ☐ **pressing** adj apremiante ☐ **press stud** n (BRIT) botón m de presión ☐ **press-up** n (BRIT) plancha

pressure ['preʃə] n presión f; **to put ~ on sb** presionar a algn ☐ **pressure cooker** n olla a presión ☐ **pressure group** n grupo de presión

prestige [pres'tiːʒ] n prestigio

prestigious [pres'tɪdʒəs] adj prestigioso

presumably [prɪ'zjuːməblɪ] adv es de suponer que, cabe presumir que

presume [prɪ'zjuːm] vt: **to ~ (that)** presumir (que), suponer (que)

pretence [prɪ'tens] (US **pretense**) n fingimiento; **under false pretences** con engaños

pretend [prɪ'tend] vt, vi (feign) fingir

⚠ Be careful not to translate **pretend** by the Spanish word **pretender**.

pretense [prɪ'tens] (US) n = **pretence**

pretentious [prɪ'tenʃəs] adj presumido; (ostentatious) ostentoso, aparatoso

pretext ['priːtekst] n pretexto

pretty ['prɪtɪ] adj bonito, lindo (LAm) ♦ adv bastante

prevail [prɪ'veɪl] vi (gain mastery) prevalecer; (be current) predominar ☐ **prevailing** adj (dominant) predominante

prevalent ['prevələnt] adj (widespread) extendido

prevent [prɪ'vent] vt: **to ~ sb from doing sth** impedir a algn hacer algo; **to ~ sth from happening** evitar que ocurra algo ☐ **prevention** [prɪ'venʃən] n prevención f ☐ **preventive** adj preventivo

preview ['priːvjuː] n (of film) preestreno

previous ['priːvɪəs] adj previo, anterior ☐ **previously** adv antes

prey [preɪ] n presa ♦ vi: **to ~ on** (feed on) alimentarse de; **it was preying on his mind** le preocupaba, le obsesionaba

price [praɪs] n precio ♦ vt (goods) fijar el precio de ☐ **priceless** adj que no tiene precio ☐ **price list** n tarifa

prick [prɪk] n (sting) picadura ♦ vt pinchar; (hurt) picar; **to ~ up one's ears** aguzar el oído

prickly ['prɪklɪ] adj espinoso; (fig: person) enojadizo

pride [praɪd] n orgullo; (pej) soberbia ♦ vt: **to ~ o.s. on** enorgullecerse de

priest [priːst] n sacerdote m

primarily ['praɪmərɪlɪ] adv ante todo

primary ['praɪmərɪ] adj (first in importance) principal ♦ n (US POL) elección f primaria ☐ **primary school** (BRIT) n escuela primaria

prime [praɪm] adj primero, principal; (excellent) selecto, de primera clase ♦ n: **in the ~ of life** en la flor de la vida ♦ vt (wood: fig) preparar; **~ example**

ejemplo típico ❑ **Prime Minister** *n* primer(a) ministro(-a)

primitive ['prɪmɪtɪv] *adj* primitivo; (*crude*) rudimentario

primrose ['prɪmrəʊz] *n* primavera, prímula

prince [prɪns] *n* príncipe *m*

princess [prɪn'ses] *n* princesa

principal ['prɪnsɪpl] *adj* principal, mayor ♦ *n* director(a) *m/f* ❑ **principally** *adv* principalmente

principle ['prɪnsɪpl] *n* principio; **in ~** en principio; **on ~** por principio

print [prɪnt] *n* (*footprint*) huella; (*fingerprint*) huella dactilar; (*letters*) letra de molde; (*fabric*) estampado; (*ART*) grabado; (*PHOT*) impresión *f* ♦ *vt* imprimir; (*cloth*) estampar; (*write in capitals*) escribir en letras de molde; **out of ~** agotado ► **print out** *vt* (*COMPUT*) imprimir ❑ **printer** *n* (*person*) impresor(a) *m/f*; (*machine*) impresora ❑ **printout** *n* (*COMPUT*) impresión *f*

prior ['praɪə] *adj* anterior, previo; (*more important*) más importante; **~ to** antes de

priority [praɪ'ɒrɪtɪ] *n* prioridad *f*; **to have ~ (over)** tener prioridad (sobre)

prison ['prɪzn] *n* cárcel *f*, prisión *f* ♦ *cpd* carcelario ❑ **prisoner** *n* (*in prison*) preso(-a); (*captured person*) prisionero ❑ **prisoner-of-war** *n* prisionero de guerra

pristine ['prɪstiːn] *adj* prístino

privacy ['prɪvəsɪ] *n* intimidad *f*

private ['praɪvɪt] *adj* (*personal*) particular, privado; (*property, industry, discussion etc*) privado; (*person*) reservado; (*place*) tranquilo ♦ *n* soldado raso; "**~**" (*on envelope*) "confidencial"; (*on door*) "prohibido el paso"; **in ~** en privado ❑ **privately** *adv* en privado; (*in o.s.*) en secreto ❑ **private property** *n* propiedad *f*

privada ❑ **private school** *n* colegio particular

privatize ['praɪvətaɪz] *vt* privatizar

privilege ['prɪvɪlɪdʒ] *n* privilegio; (*prerogative*) prerrogativa

prize [praɪz] *n* premio ♦ *adj* de primera clase ♦ *vt* apreciar, estimar ❑ **prize-giving** *n* distribución *f* de premios ❑ **prizewinner** *n* premiado(-a)

pro [prəʊ] *n* (*SPORT*) profesional *mf* ♦ *prep* a favor de; **the pros and cons** los pros y los contras

probability [prɒbə'bɪlɪtɪ] *n* probabilidad *f*; **in all ~** con toda probabilidad

probable ['prɒbəbl] *adj* probable

probably ['prɒbəblɪ] *adv* probablemente

probation [prə'beɪʃən] *n*: **on ~** (*employee*) a prueba; (*LAW*) en libertad condicional

probe [prəʊb] *n* (*MED, SPACE*) sonda; (*enquiry*) encuesta, investigación *f* ♦ *vt* sondar; (*investigate*) investigar

problem ['prɒbləm] *n* problema *m*

procedure [prə'siːdʒə] *n* procedimiento; (*bureaucratic*) trámites *mpl*

proceed [prə'siːd] *vi* (*do afterwards*): **to ~ to do sth** proceder a hacer algo; (*continue*): **to ~ (with)** continuar or seguir (con) ❑ **proceedings** *npl* acto(s) (*pl*); (*LAW*) proceso ❑ **proceeds** ['prəʊsiːdz] *npl* (*money*) ganancias *fpl*, ingresos *mpl*

process ['prəʊses] *n* proceso ♦ *vt* tratar, elaborar

procession [prə'seʃən] *n* desfile *m*; **funeral ~** cortejo fúnebre

proclaim [prə'kleɪm] *vt* (*announce*) anunciar

prod [prɒd] *vt* empujar ♦ *n* empujón *m*

produce [*n* 'prɒdjuːs, *vt* prə'djuːs] *n* (*AGR*) productos *mpl* agrícolas ♦ *vt* producir; (*play, film, programme*) presentar ❑ **producer** *n* productor(a) m/f; (of film, programme) director(a) m/f; (of record) productor(a) m/f

roduct ['prɒdʌkt] n producto

production [prə'dʌkʃən] n producción f; (THEATRE) presentación f □ **productive** [prə'dʌktɪv] adj productivo □ **productivity** [prɒdʌk'tɪvɪtɪ] n productividad f

rof. [prɒf] abbr (= professor) Prof

rofession [prə'feʃən] n profesión f □ **professional** adj profesional ♦ n profesional mf; (skilled person) perito

professor [prə'fesə*] n (BRIT) catedrático(-a); (US, Canada) profesor(a) m/f

rofile ['prəʊfaɪl] n perfil m

rofit ['prɒfɪt] n (COMM) ganancia ♦ vi: **to ~ by** or **from** aprovechar or sacar provecho de □ **profitable** adj (ECON) rentable

rofound [prə'faʊnd] adj profundo

rogramme ['prəʊgræm] (US **program**) n programa m ♦ vt programar □ **programmer** n programador(a) m/f □ **programming** (US **programing**) n programación f

rogress [n 'prəʊgres, vi prə'gres] n progreso; (development) desarrollo ♦ vi progresar, avanzar; **in ~** en curso □ **progressive** [-'gresɪv] adj progresivo; (person) progresista

rohibit [prə'hɪbɪt] vt prohibir; **to ~ sb from doing sth** prohibir a algn hacer algo

roject [n 'prɒdʒekt, vb prə'dʒekt] n proyecto ♦ vt proyectar ♦ vi (stick out) salir, sobresalir □ **projection** [prə'dʒekʃən] n proyección f; (overhang) saliente m □ **projector** [prə'dʒektə*] n proyector m

rolific [prə'lɪfɪk] adj prolífico

rolong [prə'lɒŋ] vt prolongar, extender

prom [prɒm] n abbr = **promenade**; (US: ball) baile m de gala; **the Proms** ver recuadro

PROM

El ciclo de conciertos de música clásica más conocido de Londres es el llamado **the Proms** (promenade concerts), que se celebra anualmente en el Royal Albert Hall. Su nombre se debe a que originalmente el público paseaba durante las actuaciones, costumbre que en la actualidad se mantiene de forma simbólica, permitiendo que parte de los asistentes permanezcan de pie. En Estados Unidos se llama **prom** a un baile de gala en un centro de educación secundaria o universitaria.

promenade [prɒmə'nɑːd] n (by sea) paseo marítimo

prominent ['prɒmɪnənt] adj (standing out) saliente; (important) eminente, importante

promiscuous [prə'mɪskjuəs] adj (sexually) promiscuo

promise ['prɒmɪs] n promesa ♦ vt, vi prometer □ **promising** adj prometedor(a)

promote [prə'məʊt] vt (employee) ascender; (product, pop star) hacer propaganda por; (ideas) fomentar □ **promotion** [-'məʊʃən] n (advertising campaign) campaña f de promoción; (in rank) ascenso

prompt [prɒmpt] adj rápido ♦ adv: **at 6 o'clock ~** a las seis en punto ♦ n (COMPUT) aviso ♦ vt (urge) mover, incitar; (when talking) instar; (THEATRE) apuntar; **~ sb to do sth** instar a algn a hacer algo □ **promptly** adv rápidamente; (exactly) puntualmente

prone [prəʊn] adj (lying) postrado; **~ to** propenso a

prong [prɒŋ] n diente m, punta

pronoun ['prəʊnaʊn] n pronombre m

pronounce [prə'nauns] vt pronunciar
pronunciation [prənʌnsɪ'eɪʃən] n pronunciación f
proof [pruːf] n prueba ♦ adj: ~ **against** a prueba de
prop [prɒp] n apoyo; (fig) sostén m; **props** accesorios mpl, at(t)rezzo msg ▶ **prop up** vt (roof, structure) apuntalar; (economy) respaldar
propaganda [prɒpə'gændə] n propaganda
propeller [prə'pelə'] n hélice f
proper ['prɒpə'] adj (suited, right) propio; (exact) justo; (seemly) correcto, decente; (authentic) verdadero; (referring to place): **the village** ~ el pueblo mismo □ **properly** adv (adequately) correctamente; (decently) decentemente □ **proper noun** n nombre m propio
property ['prɒpətɪ] n propiedad f; (personal) bienes mpl muebles
prophecy ['prɒfɪsɪ] n profecía f
prophet ['prɒfɪt] n profeta m
proportion [prə'pɔːʃən] n proporción f; (share) parte f; **proportions** npl (size) dimensiones fpl □ **proportional** adj: **proportional (to)** en proporción (a)
proposal [prə'pəuzl] n (offer of marriage) oferta de matrimonio; (plan) proyecto
propose [prə'pəuz] vt proponer ♦ vi declararse; **to** ~ **to do** tener intención de hacer
proposition [prɒpə'zɪʃən] n propuesta
proprietor [prə'praɪətə'] n propietario(-a), dueño(-a)
prose [prəuz] n prosa
prosecute ['prɒsɪkjuːt] vt (LAW) procesar □ **prosecution** [-'kjuːʃən] n proceso, causa; (accusing side) acusación f □ **prosecutor** n acusador(a) m/f; (also: **public prosecutor**) fiscal mf
prospect [n 'prɒspekt, vb prə'spekt] n (possibility) posibilidad f; (outlook)

perspectiva ♦ vi: **to** ~ **for** buscar; **prospects** npl (for work etc) perspectivas fpl □ **prospective** [prə'spektɪv] adj futuro
prospectus [prə'spektəs] n prospecto
prosper ['prɒspə'] vi prosperar □ **prosperity** [-'sperɪtɪ] n prosperidad f □ **prosperous** adj próspero
prostitute ['prɒstɪtjuːt] n prostituta; (male) hombre que se dedica a la prostitución
protect [prə'tekt] vt proteger □ **protection** [-'tekʃən] n protección □ **protective** adj protector(a)
protein ['prəutiːn] n proteína
protest [n 'prəutest, vb prə'test] n protesta ♦ vi: **to** ~ **about** or **at/against** protestar de/contra ♦ vt (insist): **to** ~ **(that)** insistir en (que)
Protestant ['prɒtɪstənt] adj, n protestante mf
protester [prə'testə'] n manifestante mf
protractor [prə'træktə'] n (GEOM) transportador m
proud [praud] adj orgulloso; (pej) soberbio, altanero
prove [pruːv] vt probar; (show) demostrar ♦ vi: **to** ~ **(to be) correct** resultar correcto; **to** ~ **o.s.** probar su valía
proverb ['prɒvəːb] n refrán m
provide [prə'vaɪd] vt proporcionar, dar; **to** ~ **sb with sth** proveer a algn de algo ▶ **provide for** vt fus (person) mantener a; (problem etc) tener en cuenta □ **provided (that)** conj: **provided (that)**, a condición de que □ **providing** [prə'vaɪdɪŋ] conj: **providing (that)** a condición de que con tal de que
province ['prɒvɪns] n provincia; (fig) esfera f □ **provincial** [prə'vɪnʃəl] adj provincial; (pej) provinciano
provision [prə'vɪʒən] n (supplying) suministro, abastecimiento; (of

contract etc) disposición f; **provisions** npl (food) comestibles mpl
□ **provisional** adj provisional
□ **provocative** [prə'vɒkətɪv] adj provocativo

provoke [prə'vəuk] vt (cause) provocar, incitar; (anger) enojar

prowl [praul] vi (also: ~ about, ~ around) merodear ♦ n: on the ~ de merodeo

proximity [prɒk'sɪmɪtɪ] n proximidad f

proxy ['prɒksɪ] n: by ~ por poderes

prudent ['pru:dənt] adj prudente

prune [pru:n] n ciruela pasa ♦ vt podar

pry [praɪ] vi: to ~ (into) entrometerse (en)

P.S n abbr (= postscript) P.D.

pseudonym ['sju:dənɪm] n seudónimo

psychiatric [saɪkɪ'ætrɪk] adj psiquiátrico

psychiatrist [saɪ'kaɪətrɪst] n psiquiatra mf

psychic ['saɪkɪk] adj (also: **psychical**) psíquico

psychoanalysis [saɪkəuə'nælɪsɪs] n psicoanálisis m inv

psychological [saɪkə'lɒdʒɪkl] adj psicológico

psychologist [saɪ'kɒlədʒɪst] n psicólogo(-a)

psychology [saɪ'kɒlədʒɪ] n psicología f

psychotherapy [saɪkəu'θerəpɪ] n psicoterapia

pt abbr (= pint(s); point(s)

PTO abbr (= please turn over) sigue

pub [pʌb] n abbr (= public house) pub m, bar m

puberty ['pju:bətɪ] n pubertad f

public ['pʌblɪk] adj público ♦ n: the ~ el público; **in** ~ en público; **to make** ~ hacer público

□ **publication** [pʌblɪ'keɪʃən] n publicación f

public: **public company** n sociedad f anónima □ **public convenience** (BRIT) n aseos mpl públicos (SP), sanitarios mpl (LAm) □ **public holiday** n (día m de) fiesta (SP), (día m) feriado (LAm) □ **public house** n (BRIT) bar m, pub m

publicity [pʌb'lɪsɪtɪ] n publicidad f

publicize ['pʌblɪsaɪz] vt publicitar

public: **public limited company** n sociedad f anónima (S.A.) □ **publicly** adv públicamente, en público □ **public opinion** n opinión f pública □ **public relations** fpl relaciones fpl públicas □ **public school** n (BRIT) escuela privada; (US) instituto □ **public transport** n transporte m público

publish ['pʌblɪʃ] vt publicar □ **publisher** n (person) editor(a) m/f; (firm) editorial f □ **publishing** n (industry) industria del libro

pub lunch n almuerzo que se sirve en un pub; **to go for a** ~ almorzar o comer en un pub

pudding ['pudɪŋ] n pudín m; (BRIT: dessert) postre m; **black** ~ morcilla

puddle ['pʌdl] n charco

Puerto Rico [pwɛː'tɔu'riːkəu] n Puerto Rico

puff [pʌf] n soplo; (of smoke, air) bocanada; (of breathing) resoplido ♦ vt: to ~ one's pipe chupar la pipa ♦ vi (pant) jadear □ **puff pastry** n hojaldre m

pull [pul] n (tug): **to give sth a** ~ dar un tirón a algo ♦ vt tirar de; (press: trigger) apretar; (haul) tirar, arrastrar; (close: curtain) echar o vt tirar; **to** ~ **to pieces** hacer pedazos; **not to** ~ **one's punches** no andarse con bromas; **to** ~ **one's weight** hacer su parte; **to** ~ **o.s. together** sobreponerse; **to** ~ **sb's leg** tomar el pelo a algn ► **pull apart** vt (break) romper ► **pull away** vi (vehicle: move off) salir, arrancar; (draw back) apartarse bruscamente ► **pull**

back vt (lever etc) tirar hacia sí; (curtains) descorrer ♦ vi (refrain) contenerse; (MIL: withdraw) retirarse
▶ **pull down** vt (building) derribar
▶ **pull in** vi (car) parar (junto a la acera); (train) llegar a la estación
▶ **pull off** vt (deal etc) cerrar ▶ **pull out** vi (car, train etc) salir ♦ vt sacar, arrancar ▶ **pull over** vi (AUT) hacerse a un lado ▶ **pull up** vi (stop) parar ♦ vt (raise) levantar; (uproot) arrancar, desarraigar

pulley ['puli] n polea

pullover ['puləʊvə'] n jersey m, suéter m

pulp [pʌlp] n (of fruit) pulpa

pulpit ['pulpit] n púlpito

pulse [pʌls] n (ANAT) pulso; (rhythm) pulsación f; (BOT) legumbre f; **pulses** pl n legumbres

puma ['pju:mə] n puma m

pump [pʌmp] n bomba; (shoe) zapatilla ♦ vt sacar con una bomba ▶ **pump up** vt inflar

pumpkin ['pʌmpkɪn] n calabaza

pun [pʌn] n juego de palabras

punch [pʌntʃ] n (blow) golpe m, puñetazo; (tool) punzón m; (drink) ponche m ♦ vt (hit): **to ~ sb/sth** dar un puñetazo or golpear a algn/algo
□ **punch-up** (BRIT: inf) n riña

punctual ['pʌŋktjuəl] adj puntual

punctuation [pʌŋktju'eɪʃən] n puntuación f

puncture ['pʌŋktʃə'] (BRIT) n pinchazo ♦ vt pinchar

punish ['pʌnɪʃ] vt castigar
□ **punishment** n castigo

punk [pʌŋk] n (also: ~ rocker) punki mf; (also: ~ rock) música punk; (US: inf: hoodlum) rufián m

pup [pʌp] n cachorro

pupil ['pju:pl] n alumno(-a); (of eye) pupila

puppet ['pʌpɪt] n títere m

puppy ['pʌpɪ] n cachorro, perrito

purchase ['pə:tʃɪs] n compra ♦ vt comprar

pure [pjuə'] adj puro □ **purely** adv puramente

purify ['pjuərɪfaɪ] vt purificar, depurar

purity ['pjuərɪtɪ] n pureza

purple ['pə:pl] adj purpúreo; morado

purpose ['pə:pəs] n propósito; **on ~** a propósito, adrede

purr [pə:'] vi ronronear

purse [pə:s] n monedero; (US: handbag) bolso (SP), cartera (LAm), bolsa (MEX) ♦ vt fruncir

pursue [pə'sju:] vt seguir

pursuit [pə'sju:t] n (chase) caza; (occupation) actividad f

pus [pʌs] n pus m

push [puʃ] n empuje m, empujón m; (of button) presión f; (drive) empuje m ♦ vt empujar; (button) apretar; (promote) promover ♦ vi empujar; (demand): **to for** luchar por ▶ **push in** vi colarse
▶ **push off** (inf) vi largarse ▶ **push o** vi seguir adelante ▶ **push over** vt (cause to fall) hacer caer, derribar; (knock over) volcar ▶ **push through** (crowd) abrirse paso a empujones ♦ vt (measure) despachar □ **pushchair** (BRIT) n sillita de ruedas □ **pusher** n (drug pusher) traficante mf de drogas
□ **push-up** (US) n plancha

pussy(-cat) ['pusɪ-] (inf) n minino (inf

put [put] (pt, pp ~) vt (place) poner, colocar; (put into) meter; (say) expresa (a question) hacer; (estimate) estimar
▶ **put aside** vt (lay down: book etc) dejar or poner a un lado; (save) ahorra (in shop) guardar ▶ **put away** vt (stor guardar ▶ **put back** vt (replace) devolver a su lugar; (postpone) aplaza
▶ **put by** vt (money) guardar ▶ **put down** vt (on ground) poner en el suel (animal) sacrificar; (in writing) apunta (revolt etc) sofocar; (attribute): **to put sth down to** atribuir algo a ▶ **put forward** vt (ideas) presentar,

proponer ► **put in** vt (*complaint*) presentar; (*time*) dedicar ► **put off** vt (*postpone*) aplazar; (*discourage*) desanimar ► **put on** vt ponerse; (*light etc*) encender; (*play etc*) presentar; (*gain*): **to put on weight** engordar; (*brake*) echar; (*record, kettle etc*) poner; (*assume*) adoptar ► **put out** vt (*fire, light*) apagar; (*rubbish etc*) sacar; (*cat etc*) echar; (*one's hand*) alargar; (*inf: person*): **to be put out** alterarse ► **put through** vt (*TEL*) poner; (*plan etc*) hacer aprobar ► **put together** vt unir, reunir; (*assemble: furniture*) armar, montar; (*meal*) preparar ► **put up** vt (*raise*) levantar, alzar; (*hang*) colgar; (*build*) construir; (*increase*) aumentar; (*accommodate*) alojar ► **put up with** vt fus aguantar

putt [pʌt] n putt m, golpe m corto ❑ **putting green** n green m; minigolf m

puzzle [pʌzl] n rompecabezas m inv; (*also: crossword ~*) crucigrama m; (*mystery*) misterio ♦ vt dejar perplejo, confundir ♦ vi: **to ~ over sth** devanarse los sesos con algo ❑ **puzzled** adj perplejo ❑ **puzzling** adj misterioso, extraño

pyjamas [pɪˈdʒɑːməz] (*BRIT*) npl pijama m

pylon [ˈpaɪlən] n torre f de conducción eléctrica

pyramid [ˈpɪrəmɪd] n pirámide f

Q, q

quack [kwæk] n graznido; (*pej: doctor*) curandero(-a)

quadruple [kwɒˈdruːpl] vt, vi cuadruplicar

quail [kweɪl] n codorniz f ♦ vi: **to ~ at** or **before** amedrentarse ante

quaint [kweɪnt] adj extraño; (*picturesque*) pintoresco

quake [kweɪk] vi temblar ♦ n abbr = **earthquake**

qualification [kwɒlɪfɪˈkeɪʃən] n (*ability*) capacidad f; (*often pl: diploma etc*) título; (*reservation*) salvedad f

qualified [ˈkwɒlɪfaɪd] adj capacitado; (*professionally*) titulado; (*limited*) limitado

qualify [ˈkwɒlɪfaɪ] vt (*make competent*) capacitar; (*modify*) modificar ♦ vi (*in competition*): **to ~ (for)** calificarse (para); (*pass examination(s)*): **to ~ (as)** calificarse (de), graduarse (en); (*be eligible*): **to ~ (for)** reunir los requisitos (para)

quality [ˈkwɒlɪtɪ] n calidad f; (*of person*) cualidad f

qualm [kwɑːm] n escrúpulo

quantify [ˈkwɒntɪfaɪ] vt cuantificar

quantity [ˈkwɒntɪtɪ] n cantidad f; **in ~** en grandes cantidades

quarantine [ˈkwɒrəntiːn] n cuarentena

quarrel [ˈkwɒrəl] n riña, pelea ♦ vi reñir, pelearse

quarry [ˈkwɒrɪ] n cantera

quart [kwɔːt] n = litro

quarter [ˈkwɔːtə*] n cuarto, cuarta parte f; (*US: coin*) moneda de 25 centavos; (*of year*) trimestre m; (*district*) barrio ♦ vt dividir en cuartos; (*MIL: lodge*) alojar; **quarters** npl (*barracks*) cuartel m; (*living quarters*) alojamiento; **a ~ of an hour** un cuarto de hora ❑ **quarter final** n cuarto de final ❑ **quarterly** adj trimestral ♦ adv cada 3 meses, trimestralmente

quartet(te) [kwɔːˈtet] n cuarteto

quartz [kwɔːts] n cuarzo

quay [kiː] n (*also: quayside*) muelle m

queasy [ˈkwiːzɪ] adj: **to feel ~** tener náuseas

queen [kwiːn] n reina; (*CARDS etc*) dama

queer [kwɪə*] adj raro, extraño ♦ n (*inf: highly offensive*) maricón m

quench [kwentʃ] vt: **to ~ one's thirst** apagar la sed

query ['kwɪərɪ] n (question) pregunta ♦ vt dudar de

quest [kwɛst] n busca, búsqueda

question ['kwɛstʃən] n pregunta; (doubt) duda; (matter) asunto, cuestión f ♦ vt (doubt) dudar de; (interrogate) interrogar, hacer preguntas a; **out of the ~** imposible; ni hablar ❑ **questionable** adj dudoso ❑ **question mark** n punto de interrogación ❑ **questionnaire** [-'neə] n cuestionario

queue [kjuː] (BRIT) n cola ♦ vi (also: ~ up) hacer cola

quick [kwɪk] adj rápido, (agile) ágil; (mind) listo ♦ n: **cut to the ~** (fig) herido en lo vivo; **be ~!** ¡date prisa! ❑ **quickly** adv rápidamente, de prisa

quid [kwɪd] (BRIT: inf) n inv libra

quiet ['kwaɪət] adj (voice, music etc) bajo; (person, place) tranquilo; (ceremony) íntimo; (calm) tranquilidad f ♦ vt, vi (US) = **quieten; quieten** (also: **quieten down**) vi calmarse; callarse ❑ **quietly** adv tranquilamente; (silently) silenciosamente

⚠ Be careful not to translate **quiet** by the Spanish word quieto.

quilt [kwɪlt] n edredón m

quirky ['kwɜːkɪ] adj raro, estrafalario

quit [kwɪt] (pt, pp = ~ or quitted) vt dejar, abandonar; (premises) desocupar ♦ vi (give up) renunciar; (resign) dimitir

quite [kwaɪt] adv (rather) bastante; (entirely) completamente; **that's not ~ big enough** no acaba de ser lo bastante grande; **~ a few of them** un buen número de ellos; **~ (so)!** ¡así es!, ¡exactamente!

quits [kwɪts] adj: **~ (with)** en paz (con); **let's call it ~** dejémoslo en tablas

quiver ['kwɪvə'] vi estremecerse

quiz [kwɪz] n concurso ♦ vt interrogar

quota ['kwəʊtə] n cuota

quotation [kwəʊ'teɪʃən] n cita; (estimate) presupuesto ❑ **quotation marks** npl comillas fpl

quote [kwəʊt] n cita; (estimate) presupuesto ♦ vt citar; (price) cotizar ♦ vi: **to ~ from** citar de; **quotes** npl (inverted commas) comillas fpl

R, r

rabbi ['ræbaɪ] n rabino

rabbit ['ræbɪt] n conejo

rabies ['reɪbiːz] n rabia

RAC (BRIT) n abbr (= Royal Automobile Club) = RACE m

rac(c)oon [rə'kuːn] n mapache m

race [reɪs] n carrera; (species) raza ♦ vt (horse) hacer correr; (engine) acelerar ♦ vi (compete) competir; (run) correr; (pulse) latir a ritmo acelerado ❑ **race car** (US) n = **racing car** ❑ **racecourse** n hipódromo ❑ **racehorse** n caballo de carreras ❑ **racetrack** n pista; (for cars) autódromo

racial ['reɪʃl] adj racial

racing ['reɪsɪŋ] n carreras fpl ❑ **racing car** (BRIT) n coche m de carreras ❑ **racing driver** (BRIT) n piloto mf de carreras

racism ['reɪsɪzəm] n racismo ❑ **racist** [-sɪst] adj, n racista mf

rack [ræk] n (also: **luggage ~**) rejilla; (shelf) estante m; (also: **roof ~**) baca, portaequipajes m inv; (dish rack) escurreplatos m inv; (clothes rack) percha ♦ vt atormentar; **to ~ one's brains** devanarse los sesos

racket ['rækɪt] n (for tennis) raqueta; (noise) ruido, estrépito; (swindle) estafa, timo

racquet ['rækɪt] n raqueta

radar ['reɪdɑː'] n radar m

radiation [reɪdɪ'eɪʃən] n radiación f

radiator ['reɪdɪeɪtə'] n radiador m

radical ['rædɪkl] *adj* radical

radio ['reɪdɪəʊ] *n* radio *f*; **on the ~** por radio ❏ **radioactive** *adj* radioactivo ❏ **radio station** *n* emisora

radish ['rædɪʃ] *n* rábano

RAF *n abbr* (= *Royal Air Force*) las Fuerzas Aéreas Británicas

raffle ['ræfl] *n* rifa, sorteo

raft [rɑːft] *n* balsa; (*also*: **life ~**) balsa salvavidas

rag [ræg] *n* (*piece of cloth*) trapo; (*torn cloth*) harapo; (*pej: newspaper*) periodicucho; (*for charity*) actividades estudiantiles benéficas; **rags** *npl* (*torn clothes*) harapos *mpl*

rage [reɪdʒ] *n* rabia, furor *m* ♦ *vi* rabiar, estar furioso; (*storm*) bramar; **it's all the ~** (*very fashionable*) está muy de moda

ragged ['rægɪd] *adj* (*edge*) desigual, mellado; (*appearance*) andrajoso, harapiento

raid [reɪd] *n* (MIL) incursión *f*; (*criminal*) asalto; (*by police*) redada ♦ *vt* invadir, asaltar

rail [reɪl] *n* (*on stair*) barandilla, pasamanos *m inv*; (*on bridge, balcony*) pretil *m*; (*of ship*) barandilla; (*also*: **towel ~**) toallero ❏ **railcard** *n* (BRIT) tarjeta para obtener descuentos en el tren ❏ **railing(s)** *n(pl)* vallado ❏ **railroad** (US) *n* = **railway** ❏ **railway** (BRIT) *n* ferrocarril *m*, vía férrea ❏ **railway line** (BRIT) *n* línea (de ferrocarril) ❏ **railway station** (BRIT) *n* estación *f* de ferrocarril

rain [reɪn] *n* lluvia ♦ *vi* llover; **in the ~** bajo la lluvia; **it's raining** llueve, está lloviendo ❏ **rainbow** *n* arco iris ❏ **raincoat** *n* impermeable *m* ❏ **raindrop** *n* gota de lluvia ❏ **rainfall** *n* lluvia ❏ **rainforest** *n* selvas *fpl* tropicales ❏ **rainy** *adj* lluvioso

raise [reɪz] *n* aumento ♦ *vt* levantar; (*increase*) aumentar; (*improve: morale*) subir; (: *standards*) mejorar; (*doubts*)

suscitar; (*a question*) plantear; (*cattle, family*) criar; (*crop*) cultivar; (*army*) reclutar; (*loan*) obtener; **to ~ one's voice** alzar la voz

raisin ['reɪzn] *n* pasa de Corinto

rake [reɪk] *n* (*tool*) rastrillo; (*person*) libertino ♦ *vt* (*garden*) rastrillar

rally ['rælɪ] *n* (POL *etc*) reunión *f*, mitin *m*; (AUT) rallye *m*; (TENNIS) peloteo ♦ *vt* reunir ♦ *vi* recuperarse

RAM [ræm] *n abbr* (= *random access memory*) RAM *f*

ram [ræm] *n* carnero; (*also*: **battering ~**) ariete *m* ♦ *vt* (*crash into*) dar contra, chocar con; (*push: fist etc*) empujar con fuerza

Ramadan [ræməˈdæn] *n* ramadán *m*

ramble ['ræmbl] *n* caminata, excursión *f* en el campo ♦ *vi* (*pej: also*: **~ on**) divagar ❏ **rambler** *n* excursionista *mf*; (BOT) trepadora ❏ **rambling** *adj* (*speech*) inconexo; (*house*) laberíntico; (BOT) trepador(a)

ramp [ræmp] *n* rampa; **on/off~** (US AUT) vía de acceso/salida

rampage [ræmˈpeɪdʒ] *n*: **to be on the ~** desmandarse ♦ *vi*: **they went rampaging through the town** recorrieron la ciudad armando alboroto

ran [ræn] *pt of* **run**

ranch [rɑːntʃ] *n* hacienda, estancia

random ['rændəm] *adj* fortuito, sin orden; (COMPUT, MATH) aleatorio ♦ *n*: **at ~** al azar

rang [ræŋ] *pt of* **ring**

range [reɪndʒ] *n* (*of mountains*) cadena de montañas, cordillera; (*of missile*) alcance *m*; (*of voice*) registro; (*series*) serie *f*; (*of products*) surtido; (MIL: *also*: **shooting ~**) campo de tiro; (*also*: **kitchen ~**) fogón *m* ♦ *vt* (*place*) colocar; (*arrange*) arreglar ♦ *vi*: **to ~ over** (*extend*) extenderse por; **to ~ from ... to ...** oscilar entre ... y ...

ranger [reɪndʒəʳ] n guardabosques mf inv

rank [ræŋk] n (row) fila; (MIL) rango; (status) categoría; (BRIT: also: **taxi ~**) parada de taxis ♦ vi: **to ~ among** figurar entre ♦ adj fétido, rancio; **the ~ and file** (fig) la base

ransom [rænsəm] n rescate m; **to hold to ~** (fig) hacer chantaje a

rant [rænt] vi divagar, desvariar

rap [ræp] vt golpear, dar un golpecito en ♦ n (music) rap m

rape [reɪp] n violación f; (BOT) colza ♦ vt violar

rapid [ræpɪd] adj rápido ❑ **rapidly** adv rápidamente ❑ **rapids** npl (GEO) rápidos mpl

rapist [reɪpɪst] n violador m

rapport [ræpɔ:ʳ] n simpatía

rare [reəʳ] adj raro, poco común; (CULIN: steak) poco hecho ❑ **rarely** adv pocas veces

rash [ræʃ] adj imprudente, precipitado ♦ n (MED) sarpullido, erupción f (cutánea); (of events) serie f

rasher [ræʃəʳ] n lonja

raspberry [rɑ:zbərɪ] n frambuesa

rat [ræt] n rata

rate [reɪt] n (ratio) razón f; (price) precio; (: of hotel etc) tarifa; (of interest) tipo; (speed) velocidad f ♦ vt (value) tasar; (estimate) estimar; **rates** npl (BRIT: property tax) impuesto municipal; (fees) tarifa; **to ~ sth/sb as** considerar algo/a algn como

rather [rɑ:ðəʳ] adv: **it's ~ expensive** es algo caro; (too much) es demasiado caro; (to some extent) más bien; **there's ~ a lot** hay bastante; **I would** or **I'd ~ go** preferiría ir; **or ~** mejor dicho

rating [reɪtɪŋ] n tasación f; (score) índice m; (of ship) clase f **ratings** npl (RADIO, TV) niveles mpl de audiencia

ratio [reɪʃɪəu] n razón f; **in the ~ of 100 to 1** a razón de 100 a 1

ration [ræʃən] n ración f ♦ vt racionar; **rations** npl víveres mpl

rational [ræʃənl] (solution, reasoning) lógico, razonable; (person) cuerdo, sensato

rattle [rætl] n golpeteo; (of train etc) traqueteo; (for baby) sonaja, sonajero ♦ vi castañetear; (car, bus): **to ~ along** traquetear ♦ vt hacer sonar agitando

rave [reɪv] vi (in anger) encolerizarse; (with enthusiasm) entusiasmarse; (MED) delirar, desvariar ♦ n (inf: party) rave m

raven [reɪvən] n cuervo

ravine [rəvi:n] n barranco

raw [rɔ:] adj crudo; (not processed) bruto; (sore) vivo; (inexperienced) novato, inexperto; **~ materials** materias primas

ray [reɪ] n rayo; **~ of hope** (rayo de) esperanza

razor [reɪzəʳ] n (open) navaja; (safety razor) máquina de afeitar; (electric razor) máquina (eléctrica) de afeitar ❑ **razor blade** n hoja de afeitar

Rd abbr = **road**

RE n abbr (BRIT) = **religious education**

re [ri:] prep con referencia a

reach [ri:tʃ] n alcance m; (of river etc) extensión f entre dos recodos ♦ vt alcanzar, llegar a; (achieve) lograr ♦ vi extenderse; **within ~** al alcance (de la mano); **out of ~** fuera del alcance ▶ **reach out** vt (hand) tender ♦ vi: **to reach out for sth** alargar or tender la mano para tomar algo

react [ri:ækt] vi reaccionar ❑ **reaction** [-ækʃən] n reacción f ❑ **reactor** [ri:æktəʳ] n (also: **nuclear reactor**) reactor m (nuclear)

read [ri:d, pt, pp red] (pt, pp ~) vi leer ♦ vt leer; (understand) entender; (study) estudiar ▶ **read out** vt leer en alta voz ❑ **reader** n lector(a) m/f; (BRIT: at university) profesor(a) m/f adjunto(-a)

eadily ['redɪlɪ] adv (willingly) de buena gana; (easily) fácilmente; (quickly) en seguida

eading ['riːdɪŋ] n lectura; (on instrument) indicación f

eady ['redɪ] adj listo, preparado; (willing) dispuesto; (available) disponible ♦ adv: ~-**cooked** listo para comer ♦ n: **at the** ~ (MIL) listo para tirar; **to get** ~ vi prepararse ♦ vt preparar □ **ready-made** adj confeccionado

eal [rɪəl] adj verdadero, auténtico; **in ~ terms** en términos reales □ **real ale** n cerveza elaborada tradicionalmente □ **real estate** n bienes mpl raíces □ **realistic** [-'lɪstɪk] adj realista □ **reality** [riː'ælɪtɪ] n realidad f

realization [rɪəlaɪ'zeɪʃən] n comprensión f; (fulfilment, COMM) realización f

ealize ['rɪəlaɪz] vt (understand) darse cuenta de

eally ['rɪəlɪ] adv realmente; (for emphasis) verdaderamente; (actually): **what ~ happened** lo que pasó en realidad; **~?** ¿de veras?; **~!** (annoyance) ¡vamos!, ¡por favor!

ealm [relm] n reino; (fig) esfera

ealtor ['rɪəltɔːʳ] (US) n agente m inmobiliario(-a)

eappear [riːə'pɪəʳ] vi reaparecer

ear [rɪəʳ] adj trasero ♦ n parte f trasera ♦ vt (cattle, family) criar ♦ vi (also: ~ **up**: animal) encabritarse

earrange [riːə'reɪndʒ] vt ordenar or arreglar de nuevo

ear: rear-view mirror n (AUT) (espejo) retrovisor m □ **rear-wheel drive** n tracción f trasera

eason ['riːzn] n razón f ♦ vi: **to ~ with sb** tratar de que algn entre en razón; **it stands to ~ that ...** es lógico que ... □ **reasonable** adj razonable; (sensible) sensato □ **reasonably** adv razonablemente □ **reasoning** n razonamiento, argumentos mpl

reassurance [riːə'ʃʊərəns] n consuelo

reassure [riːə'ʃʊəʳ] vt tranquilizar, alentar; **to ~ sb that ...** tranquilizar a algn asegurando que ...

rebate ['riːbeɪt] n (on tax etc) desgravación f

rebel [n 'rebl, vi rɪ'bel] n rebelde mf ♦ vi rebelarse, sublevarse □ **rebellion** [rɪ'beljən] n rebelión f, sublevación f □ **rebellious** [rɪ'beljəs] adj rebelde; (child) revoltoso

rebuild [riː'bɪld] vt reconstruir

recall [vb rɪ'kɔːl, n rɪ'kɔːl] vt (remember) recordar; (ambassador etc) retirar ♦ n recuerdo; retirada

rec'd abbr (= received) rbdo

receipt [rɪ'siːt] n (document) recibo; (for parcel etc) acuse m de recibo; (act of receiving) recepción f; **receipts** npl (COMM) ingresos mpl

⚠ Be careful not to translate **receipt** by the Spanish word *receta*.

receive [rɪ'siːv] vt recibir; (guest) acoger; (wound) sufrir □ **receiver** n (TEL) auricular m; (RADIO) receptor m; (of stolen goods) perista mf; (COMM) administrador m jurídico

recent ['riːsnt] adj reciente □ **recently** adv recientemente; **recently arrived** recién llegado

reception [rɪ'sepʃən] n recepción f; (welcome) acogida □ **reception desk** n recepción f □ **receptionist** n recepcionista mf

recession [rɪ'seʃən] n recesión f

recharge [riː'tʃɑːdʒ] vt (battery) recargar

recipe ['resɪpɪ] n receta; (for disaster, success) fórmula

recipient [rɪ'sɪpɪənt] n recibidor(a) m/f; (of letter) destinatario(-a)

recital [rɪ'saɪtl] n recital m

recite [rɪ'saɪt] vt (poem) recitar

reckless ['rekləs] adj temerario, imprudente; (driving, driver) peligroso

reckon ['rekən] vt calcular; (consider) considerar; (think): I ~ that ... me parece que ...

reclaim [rɪ'kleɪm] vt (land, waste) recuperar; (land: from sea) rescatar; (demand back) reclamar

recline [rɪ'klaɪn] vi reclinarse

recognition [rekəg'nɪʃən] n reconocimiento; **transformed beyond ~** irreconocible

recognize ['rekəgnaɪz] vt: **to ~ (by/as)** reconocer (por/como)

recollection [rekə'lekʃən] n recuerdo

recommend [rekə'mend] vt recomendar □ **recommendation** [rekəmen'deɪʃən] n recomendación f

reconcile ['rekənsaɪl] vt (two people) reconciliar; (two facts) compaginar; **to ~ o.s. to sth** conformarse a algo

reconsider [ri:kən'sɪdə] vt repensar

reconstruct [ri:kən'strʌkt] vt reconstruir

record [n, adj 'rekɔ:d, vt rɪ'kɔ:d] n (MUS) disco; (of meeting etc) acta; (register) registro, partida; (file) archivo; (also: **criminal** ~) antecedentes mpl; (written) expediente m; (SPORT, COMPUT) récord, sin precedentes ♦ vt registrar; (MUS: song etc) grabar; **in ~ time** en un tiempo récord; **off the ~** adj no oficial ♦ adv confidencialmente □ **recorded delivery** (BRIT) n (POST) entrega con acuse de recibo □ **recorder** n (MUS) flauta de pico □ **recording** n (MUS) grabación f □ **record player** n tocadiscos m inv

recount [rɪ'kaʊnt] vt contar

recover [rɪ'kʌvə] vt recuperar ♦ vi (from illness, shock) recuperarse □ **recovery** n recuperación f

recreate [ri:krɪ'eɪt] vt recrear

recreation [rekrɪ'eɪʃən] n recreo □ **recreational vehicle** (US) n caravan o rulota pequeña; **recreational drug** droga recreativa

recruit [rɪ'kru:t] n recluta mf ♦ vt reclutar; (staff) contratar □ **recruitment** n reclutamiento

rectangle ['rektæŋgl] n rectángulo □ **rectangular** [-'tæŋgjulə] adj rectangular

rectify ['rektɪfaɪ] vt rectificar

rector ['rektə] n (REL) párroco

recur [rɪ'kə:] vi repetirse; (pain, illness) producirse de nuevo □ **recurring** adj (problem) repetido, constante

recyclable [ri:'saɪkləbl] adj reciclable

recycle [ri:'saɪkl] vt reciclar

recycling [ri:'saɪklɪŋ] n reciclaje

red [red] n rojo ♦ adj rojo; (hair) pelirrojo; (wine) tinto; **to be in the ~** (account) estar en números rojos; (business) tener un saldo negativo; **to give sb the ~ carpet treatment** recibir a algn con todos los honores □ **Red Cross** n Cruz f Roja □ **redcurrant** n grosella roja

redeem [rɪ'di:m] vt redimir; (promises) cumplir; (sth in pawn) desempeñar; (fig, also REL) rescatar

red: **red-haired** adj pelirrojo □ **redhead** n pelirrojo(-a) □ **red-hot** adj candente □ **red light** n: **to go through a red light** (AUT) pasar la luz roja □ **red-light district** n barrio chino

red meat n carne f roja

reduce [rɪ'dju:s] vt reducir; **to ~ sb to tears** hacer llorar a algn; **"~ speed now"** (AUT) "reduzca la velocidad" □ **reduced** adj (decreased) reducido, rebajado; **at a reduced price** con rebaja or descuento; **"greatly reduced prices"** "grandes rebajas" □ **reduction** [rɪ'dʌkʃən] n reducción f (of price) rebaja; (discount) descuento; (smaller-scale copy) copia reducida

redundancy [rɪ'dʌndənsɪ] n (dismissal) despido; (unemployment) desempleo

redundant [rɪ'dʌndnt] adj (BRIT: worker) parado, sin trabajo; (detail,

reed [riːd] n (BOT) junco, caña; (MUS) lengüeta

reef [riːf] n (at sea) arrecife m

reel [riːl] n carrete m, bobina; (of film) rollo; (dance) baile escocés ♦ vt (also: ~ up) devanar; (also: ~ in) sacar ♦ vi (sway) tambalear(se)

ref [ref] (inf) n abbr = **referee**

refectory [rɪˈfɛktərɪ] n comedor m

refer [rɪˈfəː] vt (send: patient) referir; (: matter) remitir ♦ vi: to ~ to (allude to) referirse a, aludir a; (apply to) relacionarse con; (consult) consultar

referee [rɛfəˈriː] n árbitro; (BRIT: for job application): to be a ~ for sb proporcionar referencias a algn ♦ vt (match) arbitrar en

reference [ˈrɛfrəns] n referencia; (for job application: letter) carta de recomendación; with ~ to (COMM: in letter) me remito a ❏ **reference number** n número de referencia

refill [vt riːˈfɪl, n ˈriːfɪl] vt rellenar ♦ n repuesto, recambio

refine [rɪˈfaɪn] vt refinar ❏ **refined** adj (person) fino ❏ **refinery** n refinería

reflect [rɪˈflɛkt] vt reflejar ♦ vi (think) reflexionar, pensar; **it reflects badly/well on him** le perjudica/le hace honor ❏ **reflection** [-ˈflɛkʃən] n (act) reflexión f; (image) reflejo; (criticism) crítica; **on reflection** pensándolo bien

reflex [ˈriːflɛks] adj, n reflejo

reform [rɪˈfɔːm] n reforma ♦ vt reformar

refrain [rɪˈfreɪn] vi: to ~ from doing abstenerse de hacer ♦ n estribillo

refresh [rɪˈfrɛʃ] vt refrescar ❏ **refreshing** adj refrescante ❏ **refreshments** npl refrescos mpl

refrigerator [rɪˈfrɪdʒəreɪtə] n frigorífico (SP), nevera (SP), refrigerador m (LAm), heladera (RPl)

object) superfluo; **to be made ~** quedar(se) sin trabajo

refuel [riːˈfjuəl] vi repostar (combustible)

refuge [ˈrɛfjuːdʒ] n refugio, asilo; **to take ~ in** refugiarse en ❏ **refugee** [rɛfjuˈdʒiː] n refugiado(-a)

refund [n ˈriːfʌnd, vb rɪˈfʌnd] n reembolso ♦ vt devolver, reembolsar

refurbish [riːˈfəːbɪʃ] vt restaurar, renovar

refusal [rɪˈfjuːzəl] n negativa; **to have first ~ on** tener la primera opción a

refuse¹ [ˈrɛfjuːs] n basura

refuse² [rɪˈfjuːz] vt rechazar; (invitation) declinar; (permission) denegar ♦ vi: **to ~ to do sth** negarse a hacer algo; (horse) rehusar

regain [rɪˈgeɪn] vt recobrar, recuperar

regard [rɪˈgɑːd] n mirada; (esteem) respeto; (attention) consideración f ♦ vt (consider) considerar; **to give one's regards to** saludar de su parte a; **"with kindest regards"** "con muchos recuerdos"; **as regards, with ~ to** con respecto a, en cuanto a ❏ **regarding** prep con respecto a, en cuanto a ❏ **regardless** adv a pesar de todo; **regardless of** sin reparar en

regenerate [rɪˈdʒɛnəreɪt] vt regenerar

reggae [ˈrɛgeɪ] n reggae m

regiment [ˈrɛdʒɪmənt] n regimiento

region [ˈriːdʒən] n región f; **in the ~ of** (fig) alrededor de ❏ **regional** adj regional

register [ˈrɛdʒɪstə] n registro ♦ vt registrar; (birth) declarar; (car) matricular; (letter) certificar; (instrument) marcar, indicar ♦ vi (at hotel) registrarse; (as student) matricularse; (make impression) producir impresión ❏ **registered** adj (letter, parcel) certificado

registrar [ˈrɛdʒɪstrɑː] n secretario(-a) (del registro civil)

registration [rɛdʒɪsˈtreɪʃən] n (act) declaración f; (AUT: also: ~ number) matrícula

registry office ['redʒɪstrɪ-] (BRIT) n registro civil; **to get married in a ~** casarse por lo civil

regret [rɪ'gret] n sentimiento, pesar m ♦ vt sentir, lamentar ◻ **regrettable** adj lamentable

regular ['regjulə*] adj regular; (soldier) profesional; (usual) habitual; (: doctor) de cabecera ♦ n (client etc) cliente(-a) m/f habitual ◻ **regularly** adv con regularidad; (often) repetidas veces

regulate ['regjuleɪt] vt controlar ◻ **regulation** [-'leɪʃən] n (rule) regla, reglamento

rehabilitation [ri:əbɪlɪ'teɪʃən] n rehabilitación f

rehearsal [rɪ'hə:səl] n ensayo

rehearse [rɪ'hə:s] vt ensayar

reign [reɪn] n reinado; (fig) predominio ♦ vi reinar; (fig) imperar

reimburse [ri:ɪm'bə:s] vt reembolsar

rein [reɪn] n (for horse) rienda

reincarnation [ri:ɪnkɑ:'neɪʃən] n reencarnación f

reindeer ['reɪndɪə*] n inv reno

reinforce [ri:ɪn'fɔ:s] vt reforzar ◻ **reinforcements** npl (MIL) refuerzos mpl

reinstate [ri:ɪn'steɪt] vt reintegrar; (tax, law) reinstaurar

reject [n 'ri:dʒekt, vb rɪ'dʒekt] n (thing) desecho ♦ vt rechazar; (suggestion) descartar; (coin) expulsar ◻ **rejection** [rɪ'dʒekʃən] n rechazo

rejoice [rɪ'dʒɔɪs] vi: **to ~ at or over** regocijarse o alegrarse de

relate [rɪ'leɪt] vt (tell) contar, relatar; (connect) relacionar ♦ vi relacionarse ◻ **related** adj afín; (person) emparentado; **related to** (subject) relacionado con ◻ **relating to** prep referente a

relation [rɪ'leɪʃən] n (person) familiar mf, pariente mf; (link) relación f; **relations** npl (relatives) familiares mpl ◻ **relationship** n relación f; (personal

relaciones fpl; (also: **family relationship**) parentesco

relative [relatɪv] n pariente mf, familiar mf ♦ adj relativo ◻ **relatively** adv (comparatively) relativamente

relax [rɪ'læks] vi descansar; (unwind) relajarse ♦ vt (one's grip) soltar, aflojar; (control) relajar; (mind, person) descansar ◻ **relaxation** [ri:læk'seɪʃən] n descanso; (of rule, control) relajamiento; (entertainment) diversión f ◻ **relaxed** adj relajado; (tranquil) tranquilo ◻ **relaxing** adj relajante

relay ['ri:leɪ] n (race) carrera de relevos ♦ vt (RADIO, TV) retransmitir

release [rɪ'li:s] n (liberation) liberación f; (from prison) puesta en libertad; (of gas etc) escape m; (of film etc) estreno; (of record) lanzamiento ♦ vt (prisoner) poner en libertad; (gas) despedir, arrojar; (from wreckage) soltar; (catch, spring etc) desenganchar; (film) estrenar; (book) publicar; (news) difundir

relegate ['relɪgeɪt] vt relegar; (BRIT SPORT): **to be relegated to** bajar a

relent [rɪ'lent] vi ablandarse ◻ **relentless** adj implacable

relevant ['relavant] adj (fact) pertinente; **~ to** relacionado con

reliable [rɪ'laɪəbl] adj (person, firm) de confianza, de fiar; (method, machine) seguro; (source) fidedigno

relic ['relɪk] n (REL) reliquia; (of the past) vestigio

relief [rɪ'li:f] n (from pain, anxiety) alivio; (help, supplies) socorro, ayuda; (ART, GEO) relieve m

relieve [rɪ'li:v] vt (pain) aliviar; (bring help to) ayudar, socorrer; (take over from) sustituir; (: guard) relevar; **to ~ sb of sth** quitar algo a algn; **to ~ o.s.** hacer sus necesidades ◻ **relieved** adj: **to be relieved** sentir un gran alivio

religion [rɪ'lɪdʒən] n religión f

religious [rɪ'lɪdʒəs] adj religioso
□ **religious education** n educación f religiosa

relish ['relɪʃ] n (CULIN) salsa; (enjoyment) entusiasmo ♦ vt (food etc) saborear; (enjoy): to ~ sth hacerle mucha ilusión a algn algo

relocate [ri:ləu'keɪt] vt cambiar de lugar, mudar ♦ vi mudarse

reluctance [rɪ'lʌktəns] n renuencia

reluctant [rɪ'lʌktənt] adj renuente □ **reluctantly** adv de mala gana

rely on [rɪ'laɪ-] vt fus depender de; (trust) contar con

remain [rɪ'meɪn] vi (survive) quedar; (be left) sobrar; (continue) quedar(se), permanecer □ **remainder** n resto □ **remaining** adj que queda(n); (surviving) restante(s) □ **remains** npl restos mpl

remand [rɪ'mɑ:nd] n: **on** ~ detenido (bajo custodia) ♦ vt: **to be remanded in custody** quedar detenido bajo custodia

remark [rɪ'mɑ:k] n comentario ♦ vt comentar □ **remarkable** adj (outstanding) extraordinario

remarry [ri:'mærɪ] vi volver a casarse

remedy ['remədɪ] n remedio ♦ vt remediar, curar

remember [rɪ'membə'] vt recordar, acordarse de; (bear in mind) tener presente; (send greetings to): ~ **me to him** dale recuerdos de mi parte □ **Remembrance Day** n = día en el que se recuerda a los caídos en las dos guerras mundiales

REMEMBRANCE DAY

En el Reino Unido el domingo más próximo al 11 de noviembre se conoce como **Remembrance Sunday** o **Remembrance Day**, aniversario de la firma del armisticio de 1918 que puso fin a la Primera Guerra Mundial. Ese día, a las once de la mañana (hora

en que se firmó el armisticio), se recuerda a los que murieron en las guerras mundiales con dos minutos de silencio ante los monumentos a los caídos. Allí se colocan coronas de amapolas, flor que también se suele llevar prendida en el pecho tras pagar un donativo destinado a los inválidos de guerra.

remind [rɪ'maɪnd] vt: **to ~ sb to do sth** recordar a algn que haga algo; **to ~ sb of sth** (of fact) recordar algo a algn; **she reminds me of her mother** me recuerda a su madre □ **reminder** n notificación f; (memento) recuerdo

reminiscent [remɪ'nɪsnt] adj: **to be ~ of sth** recordar algo

remnant ['remnənt] n resto; (of cloth) retal m

remorse [rɪ'mɔ:s] n remordimientos mpl

remote [rɪ'məut] adj (distant) lejano; (person) distante □ **remote control** n telecontrol m □ **remotely** adv remotamente; (slightly) levemente

removal [rɪ'mu:vəl] n (taking away) el quitar; (BRIT: from house) mudanza; (from office: dismissal) destitución f; (MED) extirpación f □ **removal man** (irreg) n (BRIT) mozo de mudanzas □ **removal van** (BRIT) n camión m de mudanzas

remove [rɪ'mu:v] vt quitar; (employee) destituir; (name: from list) tachar, borrar; (doubt) disipar; (abuse) suprimir, acabar con; (MED) extirpar

Renaissance [rɪ'neɪsəns] n: **the ~** el Renacimiento

rename [ri:'neɪm] vt poner nuevo nombre a

render ['rendə'] vt (thanks) dar; (aid) proporcionar, prestar; (make): **to ~ sth useless** hacer algo inútil

rendezvous ['rɒndɪvu:] n cita

renew [rɪ'nju:] vt renovar; (resume) reanudar; (loan etc) prorrogar

renovate ['renəveit] vt renovar

renowned [rɪ'naʊnd] adj renombrado

rent [rent] n (for house) arriendo, renta f ♦ vt alquilar □ **rental** n (for television, car) alquiler m

reorganize [riː'ɔːɡənaɪz] vt reorganizar

rep [rep] n abbr = **representative**

repair [rɪ'peə'] n reparación f, compostura ♦ vt reparar, componer; (shoes) remendar; **in good/bad** ~ en buen/mal estado □ **repair kit** n caja de herramientas

repay [riː'peɪ] vt (money) devolver, reembolsar; (sb's efforts) pagar; (debt) liquidar; (sb's efforts) devolver, corresponder a □ **repayment** n reembolso, devolución f; (sum of money) recompensa

repeat [rɪ'piːt] n (RADIO, TV) reposición f ♦ vt repetir ♦ vi repetirse □ **repeatedly** adv repetidas veces □ **repeat prescription** n (BRIT) receta renovada

repellent [rɪ'pelənt] adj repugnante ♦ n: **insect** ~ crema o loción f antiinsectos

repercussions [riːpə'kʌʃənz] npl consecuencias fpl

repetition [repɪ'tɪʃən] n repetición f

repetitive [rɪ'petɪtɪv] adj repetitivo

replace [rɪ'pleɪs] vt (put back) devolver a su sitio; (take the place) reemplazar, sustituir □ **replacement** n (act) reposición f; (thing) recambio; (person) suplente mf

replay [riː'pleɪ] n (SPORT) desempate m; (of tape, film) repetición f

replica ['replɪkə] n copia, reproducción f (exacta)

reply [rɪ'plaɪ] n respuesta, contestación f ♦ vi contestar, responder

report [rɪ'pɔːt] n informe m; (PRESS etc) reportaje m; (BRIT: also: **school** ~) boletín m escolar; (of gun) estallido ♦ vt informar de; (PRESS etc) hacer un

reportaje sobre; (notify: accident, culprit) denunciar ♦ vi (make a report) presentar un informe; (present o.s.): **to ~ (to sb)** presentarse (ante algn) □ **report card** n (US, Scottish) cartilla escolar □ **reportedly** adv según se dice □ **reporter** n periodista mf

represent [reprɪ'zent] vt representar; (COMM) ser agente de; (describe): **to ~ sth as** describir algo como □ **representation** [-'teɪʃən] n representación f □ **representative** n representante mf; (US POL) diputado(-a) m/f ♦ adj representativo

repress [rɪ'pres] vt reprimir □ **repression** [-'preʃən] n represión f

reprimand ['reprɪmɑːnd] n reprimenda ♦ vt reprender

reproduce [riːprə'djuːs] vt reproducir ♦ vi reproducirse □ **reproduction** [-'dʌkʃən] n reproducción f

reptile ['reptaɪl] n reptil m

republic [rɪ'pʌblɪk] n república □ **republican** adj, n republicano(-a) m/f

reputable ['repjutəbl] adj (make etc) de renombre

reputation [repju'teɪʃən] n reputación f

request [rɪ'kwest] n petición f; (formal) solicitud f ♦ vt: **to ~ sth of or from sb** solicitar algo a algn □ **request stop** n (BRIT) parada discrecional

require [rɪ'kwaɪə'] vt (need: person) necesitar, tener necesidad de; (: thing, situation) exigir; (want) pedir; **to ~ sb to do sth** pedir a algn que haga algo □ **requirement** n requisito; (need) necesidad f

resat [riː'sæt] pt, pp of **resit**

rescue ['reskjuː] n rescate m ♦ vt rescatar

research [rɪ'sɜːtʃ] n investigaciones fpl ♦ vt investigar

resemblance [rɪ'zembləns] n parecido

resemble [rɪ'zembl] vt parecerse a

resent [rɪ'zent] vt tomar a mal
❑ **resentful** adj resentido
❑ **resentment** n resentimiento

reservation [rezə'veɪʃən] n reserva
❑ **reservation desk** (US) n (in hotel)
recepción f

reserve [rɪ'zɜːv] n reserva, (SPORT)
suplente mf ♦ vt (seats etc) reservar
❑ **reserved** adj reservado

reservoir ['rezəvwɑː'] n (artificial lake)
embalse m, tank; (small) depósito

residence ['rezɪdəns] n (formal: home)
domicilio; (length of stay) permanencia
❑ **residence permit** (BRIT) n permiso
de permanencia

resident ['rezɪdənt] n (of area)
vecino(-a); (in hotel) huésped mf ♦ adj
(population) permanente; (doctor)
residente ❑ **residential** [-'denʃəl] adj
residencial

residue ['rezɪdjuː] n resto

resign [rɪ'zaɪn] vt renunciar a ♦ vi
dimitir; to ~ o.s. to (situation)
resignarse a ❑ **resignation**
[rezɪg'neɪʃən] n dimisión f; (state of
mind) resignación f

resin ['rezɪn] n resina

resist [rɪ'zɪst] vt resistir, oponerse a
❑ **resistance** n resistencia

resit [riː'sɪt] (BRIT) (pt, pp resat) vt (exam)
volver a presentarse a; (subject)
recuperar, volver a examinarse de (SP)

resolution [rezə'luːʃən] n resolución f

resolve [rɪ'zɒlv] n resolución f ♦ vt
resolver ♦ vi: to ~ to do resolver hacer

resort [rɪ'zɔːt] n (town) centro turístico;
(recourse) recurso ♦ vi: to ~ to recurrir
a; in the last ~ como último recurso

resource [rɪ'sɔːs] n recurso
❑ **resourceful** adj despabilado,
ingenioso

respect [rɪs'pekt] n respeto ♦ vt
respetar ❑ **respectable** adj
respetable; (large: amount) apreciable;
(passable) tolerable ❑ **respectful** adj
respetuoso ❑ **respective** adj

respectivo ❑ **respectively** adv
respectivamente

respite ['respaɪt] n respiro

respond [rɪs'pɒnd] vi responder; (react)
reaccionar ❑ **response** [-'pɒns] n
respuesta; reacción f

responsibility [rɪspɒnsɪ'bɪlɪtɪ] n
responsabilidad f

responsible [rɪs'pɒnsɪbl] adj
(character) serio, formal; (job) de
confianza; (liable): ~ (for) responsable
(de) ❑ **responsibly** adv con seriedad

responsive [rɪs'pɒnsɪv] adj sensible

rest [rest] n descanso, reposo; (MUS,
pause) pausa, silencio; (support) apoyo;
(remainder) resto ♦ vi descansar; (be
supported) apoyarse sobre
♦ vt: to ~ sth on/against apoyar algo
en or sobre/contra; the ~ of them
(people, objects) los demás; it rests
with him to ... depende de él el que ...

restaurant ['restərɒn] n restaurante m
❑ **restaurant car** (BRIT) n (RAIL) coche-
comedor m

restless ['restlɪs] adj inquieto

restoration [restə'reɪʃən] n
restauración f; devolución f

restore [rɪ'stɔː'] vt (building) restaurar;
(sth stolen) devolver; (health)
restablecer; (to power) volver a poner a

restrain [rɪs'treɪn] vt (feeling) contener,
refrenar; (person): to ~ (from doing)
disuadir (de hacer) ❑ **restraint** n
(restriction) restricción f; (moderation)
moderación f; (of manner) reserva

restrict [rɪs'trɪkt] vt restringir, limitar
❑ **restriction** [-kʃən] n restricción f,
limitación f

rest room (US) n aseos mpl

restructure [riː'strʌktʃə'] vt
reestructurar

result [rɪ'zʌlt] n resultado ♦ vi: to ~ in
terminar en, tener por resultado; as a ~
of a consecuencia

resume [rɪ'zju:m] vt reanudar ♦ vi comenzar de nuevo

⚠ Be careful not to translate **resume** by the Spanish word *resumir*.

résumé ['reɪzju:meɪ] n resumen m; (US) currículum m

resuscitate [rɪ'sʌsɪteɪt] vt (MED) resucitar

retail ['ri:teɪl] adj, adv al por menor

retailer n detallista mf

retain [rɪ'teɪn] vt (keep) retener, conservar

retaliation [rɪtælɪ'eɪʃən] n represalias fpl

retarded [rɪ'tɑ:dɪd] adj retrasado

retire [rɪ'taɪə*] vi (give up work) jubilarse; (withdraw) retirarse; (go to bed) acostarse □ **retired** adj (person) jubilado □ **retirement** n (giving up work: state) retiro; (: act) jubilación f

retort [rɪ'tɔ:t] vi contestar

retreat [rɪ'tri:t] n (place) retiro; (MIL) retirada ♦ vi retirarse

retrieve [rɪ'tri:v] vt recobrar; (situation, honour) salvar; (COMPUT) recuperar; (error) reparar

retrospect ['retrəspekt] n: in ~ retrospectivamente □ **retrospective** ['-'spektɪv] adj retrospectivo; (law) retroactivo

return [rɪ'tɜ:n] n (going or coming back) vuelta, regreso; (of sth stolen etc) devolución f; (FINANCE: from land, shares) ganancia, ingresos mpl ♦ cpd (journey) de regreso; (BRIT: ticket) de ida y vuelta; (match) de vuelta ♦ vi (person etc: come or go back) volver, regresar; (symptoms etc) reaparecer; (regain): to ~ to recuperar ♦ vt (decision, AUT) dar marcha atrás a; (position, favour) invertir ♦ vi (BRIT AUT) dar marcha atrás □ **reverse-charge call** (BRIT) n llamada a cobro revertido □ **reversing lights** (BRIT) npl (AUT) luces fpl de retroceso

revert [rɪ'vɜ:t] vi: to ~ to volver a

review [rɪ'vju:] n (magazine, MIL) revista; (of book, film) reseña; (US: examination) repaso, examen m ♦ vt repasar, examinar; (MIL) pasar revista a; (book, film) reseñar

revise [rɪ'vaɪz] vt (manuscript) corregir; (opinion) modificar; (price, procedure) revisar ♦ vi (study) repasar □ **revision**

(SP) or boleto m (LAm) de ida y vuelta, billete m redondo (MEX)

reunion [ri:'ju:nɪən] n (of family) reunión f; (of two people, school) reencuentro

reunite [ri:ju:'naɪt] vt reunir; (reconcile) reconciliar

revamp [ri:'væmp] vt renovar

reveal [rɪ'vi:l] vt revelar □ **revealing** adj revelador(a)

revel ['revl] vi: to ~ in sth/in doing sth gozar de algo/con hacer algo

revelation [revə'leɪʃən] n revelación f

revenge [rɪ'vendʒ] n venganza; to take ~ on vengarse de

revenue ['revənju:] n ingresos mpl, rentas fpl

Reverend ['revərənd] adj (in titles): the ~ John Smith (Anglican) el Reverendo John Smith; (Catholic) el Padre John Smith; (Protestant) el Pastor John Smith

reversal [rɪ'vɜ:sl] n (of order) inversión f; (of direction, policy) cambio; (of decision) revocación f

reverse [rɪ'vɜ:s] n (opposite) contrario; (back: of cloth) revés m; (: of coin) reverso; (: of paper) dorso; (AUT: also: ~ **gear**) marcha atrás, revés m ♦ adj (order) inverso; (direction) contrario; (process) opuesto ♦ vt (decision, AUT) dar marcha atrás a; (position, favour) invertir ♦ vi (BRIT AUT) dar marcha atrás

returns npl (COMM) ingresos mpl; **in ~ (for)** a cambio (de); **by ~ of post** a vuelta de correo; **many happy returns (of the day)!** ¡feliz cumpleaños! □ **return ticket** n (esp BRIT) billete m

[rɪ'vɪʒən] n corrección f; modificación f; (for exam) repaso

revival [rɪ'vaɪvəl] n (recovery) reanimación f; (of interest) renacimiento; (THEATRE) reestreno (of faith) despertar m

revive [rɪ'vaɪv] vt resucitar; (custom) restablecer; (hope) despertar; (play) reestrenar ♦ vi (person) volver en sí; (business) reactivarse

revolt [rɪ'vəult] n rebelión f ♦ vi rebelarse, sublevarse ♦ vt dar asco a, repugnar ▫ **revolting** adj asqueroso, repugnante

revolution [revə'lu:ʃən] n revolución f ▫ **revolutionary** adj, n revolucionario(-a) m/f

revolve [rɪ'vɔlv] vi dar vueltas, girar; (life, discussion): **to ~ (a)round** girar en torno a

revolver [rɪ'vɔlvə'] n revólver m

reward [rɪ'wɔːd] n premio, recompensa f ♦ vt: **to ~ (for)** recompensar o premiar (por) ▫ **rewarding** adj (fig) valioso

rewind [ri:'waɪnd] vt rebobinar

rewrite [ri:'raɪt] (pt **rewrote**, pp **rewritten**) vt reescribir

rheumatism ['ru:mətɪzəm] n reumatismo, reúma m

rhinoceros [raɪ'nɔsərəs] n rinoceronte m

rhubarb ['ru:bɑːb] n ruibarbo

rhyme [raɪm] n rima; (verse) poesía

rhythm ['rɪðm] n ritmo

rib [rɪb] n (ANAT) costilla ♦ vt (mock) tomar el pelo a

ribbon ['rɪbən] n cinta; **in ribbons** (torn) hecho trizas

rice [raɪs] n arroz m ▫ **rice pudding** n arroz con leche

rich [rɪtʃ] adj rico; (soil) fértil; (food) pesado; (: sweet) empalagoso; (abundant): **~ in** (minerals etc) rico en

rid [rɪd] (pt, pp **rid**) vt: **to ~ sb of sth** librar a algn de algo; **to get ~ of** deshacerse or desembarazarse de

riddle ['rɪdl] n (puzzle) acertijo; (mystery) enigma m, misterio ♦ vt: **to be riddled with** ser lleno o plagado de

ride [raɪd] (pt **rode**, pp **ridden**) n paseo; (distance covered) viaje m, recorrido ♦ vi (as sport) montar; (go somewhere: on horse, bicycle) dar un paseo, pasearse; (travel: on bicycle, motorcycle, bus) viajar ♦ vt (a horse) montar a; (a bicycle, motorcycle) andar en; (distance) recorrer; **to take sb for a ~** (fig) engañar a algn ▫ **rider** n (on horse) jinete m/f; (on bicycle) ciclista m/f; (on motorcycle) motociclista m/f

ridge [rɪdʒ] n (of hill) cresta; (of roof) caballete m; (wrinkle) arruga

ridicule ['rɪdɪkjuːl] n irrisión f, burla ♦ vt poner en ridículo, burlarse de ▫ **ridiculous** [-'dɪkjuləs] adj ridículo

riding ['raɪdɪŋ] n equitación f; **I like ~** me gusta montar a caballo ▫ **riding school** n escuela de equitación

rife [raɪf] adj: **to be ~** ser muy común; **to be ~ with** abundar en

rifle ['raɪfl] n rifle m, fusil m ♦ vt saquear

rift [rɪft] n (in clouds) claro; (fig: disagreement) desavenencia

rig [rɪg] n (also: **oil ~** etc) plataforma petrolera ♦ vt (election etc) amañar

right [raɪt] adj (correct) correcto, exacto; (suitable) indicado, debido; (proper) apropiado; (just) justo; (morally good) bueno; (not left) derecho ♦ n (not left) derecha; (title, claim) derecho; (not left) derecha ♦ adv bien, correctamente; (not left) a la derecha; (exactly): **~ now** ahora mismo ♦ vt (correct) corregir ♦ excl ¡bueno!, ¡está bien!; **to be ~** (person) tener razón; (answer) ser correcto; **is that the ~ time?** (of clock) ¿es esa la hora buena?; **by rights** en justicia; **on the ~** a la derecha; **to be in the ~** tener razón; **~ away** en seguida; **~ in the middle** exactamente en el

centro ❑ **right angle** n ángulo recto
❑ **rightful** adj legítimo ❑ **right-hand**
adj: **right-hand drive** conducción f por
la derecha; **the right-hand side**
derecha ❑ **right-handed** adj diestro
❑ **rightly** adv correctamente,
debidamente; (with reason) con razón
❑ **right of way** n (on path etc)
derecho de paso; (AUT) prioridad f
❑ **right-wing** adj (POL) derechista

rigid ['rɪdʒɪd] adj rígido; (person, ideas)
inflexible

rigorous ['rɪɡərəs] adj riguroso

rim [rɪm] n borde m; (of spectacles) aro;
(of wheel) llanta

rind [raɪnd] n (of bacon) corteza; (of
lemon etc) cáscara; (of cheese) costra

ring [rɪŋ] (pt **rang**, pp **rung**) n (of metal)
aro; (on finger) anillo; (of people) corro;
(of objects) círculo; (gang) banda; (for
boxing) cuadrilátero; (of circus) pista;
(bull ring) ruedo, plaza; (sound of bell)
toque m ♦ vi (on telephone) llamar por
teléfono; (bell) repicar; (doorbell,
phone) sonar; (also: ~ **out**) sonar ♦ vt
(BRIT TEL) llamar, telefonear;
(doorbell) tocar; **to give sb a** ~ (BRIT TEL)
llamar or telefonear a algn ► **ring
back** (BRIT) vt, vi (TEL) devolver la
llamada ► **ring off** (BRIT) vi (TEL)
colgar, cortar la comunicación ► **ring
up** (BRIT) vt (TEL) llamar, telefonear
❑ **ringing tone** n (TEL) tono de
llamada ► **ringleader** n (of gang)
cabecilla m ❑ **ring road** (BRIT) n
carretera periférica or de
circunvalación

rink [rɪŋk] n (also: **ice** ~) pista de hielo

rinse [rɪns] n aclarado; (dye) tinte m ♦ vt
aclarar; (mouth) enjuagar

riot [raɪət] n motín m, disturbio ♦ vi
amotinarse; **to run** ~ desmandarse

rip [rɪp] n rasgón m, rasgadura ♦ vt
rasgar, desgarrar ♦ vi rasgarse,
desgarrarse ► **rip off** vt (inf: cheat)
estafar ► **rip up** vt hacer pedazos

ripe [raɪp] adj maduro

rip-off ['rɪpɔf] n (inf): **it's a** ~! ¡es una
estafa!, ¡es un timo!

ripple ['rɪpl] n onda, rizo; (sound)
murmullo ♦ vi

rise [raɪz] (pt **rose**, pp **risen**) n (slope)
cuesta, pendiente f; (hill) altura; (BRIT: in
wages) aumento; (in prices,
temperature) subida; (fig: to power etc)
ascenso ♦ vi subir; (waters) crecer; (sun,
moon) salir; (person: from bed etc)
levantarse; (also: ~ **up**: rebel)
sublevarse; (in rank) ascender; **to rise to
the** ~ **to** dar lugar or origen a; **to** ~ **to the
occasion** ponerse a la altura de las
circunstancias ❑ **risen** ['rɪzn] pp of
rise ❑ **rising** adj (increasing: number)
creciente; (: prices) en aumento or alza;
(tide) creciente; (sun, moon) naciente

risk [rɪsk] n riesgo, peligro ♦ vt
arriesgar; (run the risk of) exponerse a;
to take or **run the** ~ **of doing** correr el
riesgo de hacer; **at** ~ en peligro; **at
one's own** ~ bajo su propia
responsabilidad ❑ **risky** adj
arriesgado, peligroso

rite [raɪt] n rito; **last rites** exequias fpl

ritual ['rɪtjuəl] adj ritual ♦ n ritual m, rite

rival ['raɪvl] n rival mf; (in business)
competidor(a) m/f ♦ adj rival, opuesto
♦ vt competir con ❑ **rivalry** n
competencia

river ['rɪvə] n río ♦ cpd (port) de río;
(traffic) fluvial; **up/down** ~ río arriba/
abajo ❑ **riverbank** n orilla (del río)

rivet ['rɪvɪt] n roblón m, remache m ♦ vt
(fig) captar

road [rəud] n camino; (motorway etc)
carretera; (in town) calle f ♦ cpd
(accident) de tráfico; **major/minor** ~
carretera principal/secundaria
❑ **roadblock** n barricada ❑ **road
map** n mapa m de carreteras ❑ **road
rage** n agresividad en la carretera
❑ **road safety** n seguridad f vial
❑ **roadside** n borde m (del camino)
❑ **roadsign** n señal f de tráfico

road tax n (BRIT) impuesto de rodaje □ **roadworks** npl obras fpl

roam [rəʊm] vi vagar

roar [rɔː] n rugido; (of vehicle, storm) estruendo; (of laughter) carcajada ♦ vi rugir; hacer estruendo; **to ~ with laughter** reírse a carcajadas; **to do a roaring trade** hacer buen negocio

roast [rəʊst] n carne f asada, asado ♦ vt asar; (coffee) tostar □ **roast beef** n rosbif m

rob [rɒb] vt robar; **to ~ sb of sth** robar algo a algn; (fig: deprive) quitar algo a algn □ **robber** n ladrón(-ona) m/f □ **robbery** n robo

robe [rəʊb] n (for ceremony etc) toga; (also: **bathrobe**) albornoz m

robin ['rɒbɪn] n petirrojo

robot ['rəʊbɒt] n robot m

robust [rəʊˈbʌst] adj robusto, fuerte

rock [rɒk] n roca; (boulder) peña, peñasco; (US: small stone) piedrecita; (BRIT: sweet) = pirulí ♦ vt (swing gently: cradle) balancear, mecer; (: child) arrullar; (shake) sacudir ♦ vi mecerse, balancearse; sacudirse; **on the rocks** (drink) con hielo; (marriage etc) en ruinas □ **rock and roll** n rocanrol m □ **rock climbing** n (SPORT) escalada

rocket ['rɒkɪt] n cohete m

rocking chair ['rɒkɪŋ-] n mecedora

rocky ['rɒkɪ] adj rocoso

rod [rɒd] n vara, varilla; (also: **fishing ~**) caña

rode [rəʊd] pt of **ride**

rodent ['rəʊdənt] n roedor m

rogue [rəʊg] n pícaro, pillo

role [rəʊl] n papel m □ **role-model** n modelo a imitar

roll [rəʊl] n rollo; (of bank notes) fajo; (also: **bread ~**) panecillo; (register, list) lista, nómina; (sound of drums etc) redoble m ♦ vt hacer rodar; (also: **~ up**: string) enrollar; (cigarette) liar; (also: **~ out**: pastry) aplanar; (flatten: road, lawn) apisonar ♦ vi rodar; (drum) redoblar; (ship) balancearse ► **roll over** vi dar una vuelta ► **roll up** (inf: arrive) aparecer ♦ vt (carpet) arrollar; (: sleeves) arremangar □ **roller** n rodillo; (wheel) rueda; (for road) apisonadora; (for hair) rulo □ **Rollerblades®** npl patines mpl en línea □ **roller coaster** n montaña rusa □ **roller skates** npl patines mpl de rueda □ **roller-skating** n patinaje sobre ruedas; **to go roller-skating** (sobre ruedas) ir a patinar □ **rolling pin** n rodillo (de cocina)

ROM [rɒm] n abbr (COMPUT: = read only memory) ROM f

Roman ['rəʊmən] adj romano(-a) □ **Roman Catholic** adj, n católico(-a) m/f (romano(-a))

romance [rəˈmæns] n (love affair) amor m; (charm) lo romántico; (novel) novela de amor

Romania etc [ruːˈmeɪnɪə] n = **Rumania** etc

Roman numeral n número romano

romantic [rəˈmæntɪk] adj romántico

Rome [rəʊm] n Roma

roof [ruːf] n (pl **roofs**) n techo; (of house) techo, tejado ♦ vt techar, poner techo a; **the ~ of the mouth** el paladar □ **roof rack** n (AUT) baca, portaequipajes m inv

rook [rʊk] n (bird) graja; (CHESS) torre f

room [ruːm] n cuarto, habitación f; (also: **bedroom**) dormitorio, recámara (MEX), pieza (SC); (in school etc) sala; (space, scope) sitio, cabida □ **roommate** n compañero(-a) de cuarto □ **room service** n servicio de habitaciones □ **roomy** adj espacioso; (garment) amplio

rooster ['ruːstə] n gallo

root [ruːt] n raíz f ♦ vi arraigarse

rope [rəʊp] n cuerda; (NAUT) cable m ♦ vt (tie) atar o amarrar con (una) cuerda; (climbers: also: **~ together**) encordarse; (an area: also: **~ off**) acordonar; **to know the ropes** (*fig*) conocer los trucos (del oficio)

rose [rəuz] *pt of* **rise** ♦ *n* rosa; (*shrub*) rosal *m*; (*on watering can*) roseta

rosé [ˈrəuzeɪ] *n* vino rosado

rosemary [ˈrəuzməri] *n* romero

rosy [ˈrəuzɪ] *adj* rosado, sonrosado; **a ~ future** un futuro prometedor

rot [rɒt] *n* podredumbre *f*; (*fig: pej*) tonterías *fpl* ♦ *vt* pudrir ♦ *vi* pudrirse

rota [ˈrəutə] *n* (*sistema m de*) turnos *mpl*

rotate [rəuˈteɪt] *vt* (*revolve*) hacer girar, dar vueltas a; (*jobs*) alternar ♦ *vi* girar, dar vueltas

rotten [ˈrɒtn] *adj* podrido; (*dishonest*) corrompido; (*inf: bad*) pocho; **to feel ~** (*ill*) sentirse fatal

rough [rʌf] *adj* (*skin, surface*) áspero; (*terrain*) quebrado; (*road*) desigual; (*voice*) bronco; (*person, manner*) tosco, grosero; (*weather*) borrascoso; (*treatment*) brutal; (*sea*) picado; (*town, area*) peligroso; (*cloth*) basto; (*plan*) preliminar; (*guess*) aproximado ♦ *n* (*GOLF*): **in the ~** en las hierbas altas; **to ~ it** vivir sin comodidades; **to sleep ~** (*BRIT*) pasar la noche al raso □ **roughly** *adv* (*handle*) torpemente; (*make*) toscamente; (*speak*) groseramente; (*approximately*) aproximadamente

roulette [ruːˈlet] *n* ruleta

round [raund] *adj* redondo ♦ *n* círculo; (*BRIT: of toast*) rebanada; (*of policeman*) ronda; (*of milkman*) recorrido; (*of doctor*) visitas *fpl*; (*game: of cards, in competition*) partida; (*of ammunition*) cartucho; (*BOXING*) asalto; (*of talks*) ronda ♦ *vt* (*corner*) doblar ♦ *prep* alrededor de; (*surrounding*): **~ his neck/the table** en su cuello/alrededor de la mesa; (*in a circular movement*): **to move ~ the room/sail the world** dar una vuelta a la habitación/circunnavigar el mundo; (*in various directions*): **to move ~ a room/house** moverse por toda la habitación/casa;

(*approximately*) alrededor de ♦ *adv*: **all ~** por todos lados; **the long way ~** por el camino menos directo; **all (the) year ~** durante todo el año; **it's just ~ the corner** (*fig*) está a la vuelta de la esquina; **~ the clock** *adv* las 24 horas; **to go ~ to sb's (house)** ir a casa de algn; **to go ~ the back** pasar por atrás; **enough to go ~** bastante (para todos); **a ~ of applause** una salva de aplausos; **a ~ of drinks/sandwiches** una ronda de bebidas/bocadillos ▸ **round off** *vt* (*speech etc*) acabar, poner término a ▸ **round up** *vt* (*cattle*) acorralar; (*people*) reunir; (*price*) redondear □ **roundabout** (*BRIT*) *n* (*AUT*) isleta; (*at fair*) tiovivo ♦ *adj* (*route, means*) indirecto □ **round trip** *n* viaje *m* de ida y vuelta □ **roundup** *n* rodeo; (*of news*) resumen *m*

rouse [rauz] *vt* (*wake up*) despertar; (*stir up*) suscitar

route [ruːt] *n* ruta, camino; (*of bus*) recorrido; (*of shipping*) derrota

routine [ruːˈtiːn] *adj* rutinario ♦ *n* rutina; (*THEAT*) número

row¹ [rau] *n* (*line*) fila, hilera; (*KNITTING*) pasada ♦ *vi* (*in boat*) remar ♦ *vt* conducir remando; **4 days in a ~** 4 días seguidos

row² [rau] *n* (*racket*) escándalo; (*dispute*) bronca, pelea; (*scolding*) regaño ♦ *vi* pelear(se)

rowboat [ˈrəubəut] (*US*) = **rowing boat**

rowing [ˈrəuɪŋ] *n* remo □ **rowing boat** (*BRIT*) *n* bote *m* de remos

royal [ˈrɔɪəl] *adj* real □ **royalty** *n* (*royal persons*) familia real; (*payment to author*) derechos *mpl* de autor

rpm *abbr* (= *revs per minute*) r.p.m.

R.S.V.P. *abbr* (= *répondez s'il vous plaît*) SRC

Rt. Hon. *abbr* (*BRIT*: = *Right Honourable*) título honorífico de diputado

rub [rʌb] *vt* frotar; (*scrub*) restregar ♦ *vt*: **to give sth a ~** frotar algo; **to ~ sb up or**

~ **sb** (US) **the wrong way** entrarle algn por mal ojo ► **rub in** vt (ointment) aplicar frotando ► **rub off** vi borrarse ► **rub out** vt borrar

rubber ['rʌbə'] n caucho, goma; (BRIT: eraser) goma de borrar ❑ **rubber band** n goma, gomita ❑ **rubber gloves** npl guantes mpl de goma

rubbish ['rʌbɪʃ] (BRIT) n basura; (waste) desperdicios mpl; (fig: pej) tonterías fpl; (junk) pacotilla ❑ **rubbish bin** (BRIT) n cubo o bote m (MEX) o tacho (SC) de la basura ❑ **rubbish dump** n vertedero, basurero

rubble ['rʌbl] n escombros mpl

ruby ['ru:bɪ] n rubí m

rucksack ['rʌksæk] n mochila

rudder ['rʌdə'] n timón m

rude [ru:d] adj (impolite: person) mal educado; (: word, manners) grosero; (crude) crudo; (indecent) indecente

ruffle ['rʌfl] vt (hair) despeinar; (clothes) arrugar; **to get ruffled** (fig: person) alterarse

rug [rʌg] n alfombra; (BRIT: blanket) manta

rugby ['rʌgbɪ] n rugby m

rugged ['rʌgɪd] adj (landscape) accidentado; (features) robusto

ruin ['ru:ɪn] n ruina ♦ vt arruinar; (spoil) estropear; **ruins** npl ruinas fpl, restos mpl

rule [ru:l] n (norm) norma, costumbre f; (regulation, ruler) regla; (government) dominio f; (country, person) gobernar ♦ vt (country) gobernar ♦ vi gobernar; (LAW) fallar; **as a ~** por regla general ► **rule out** vt excluir ❑ **ruler** n (sovereign) soberano; (for measuring) regla ❑ **ruling** adj (party) gobernante; (class) dirigente ♦ n (LAW) fallo, decisión f

rum [rʌm] n ron m

Rumania [ru:'meɪnɪə] n Rumanía ❑ **Rumanian** adj rumano(-a) ♦ n rumano(-a) m/f; (LING) rumano

rumble ['rʌmbl] n (noise) ruido sordo ♦ vi retumbar, hacer un ruido sordo; (stomach, pipe) sonar

rumour ['ru:mə'] (US **rumor**) n rumor m ♦ vt: **it is rumoured that ...** se rumorea que ...

rump steak n filete m de lomo

run [rʌn] (pt **ran**, pp ~) n (fast pace): **at a ~** corriendo; (SPORT, in tights) carrera; (outing) paseo, excursión f; (distance travelled) trayecto; (series) serie f; (THEATRE) temporada; (SKI) pista ♦ vt correr; (operate: business) dirigir; (: competition, course) organizar; (: hotel, house) administrar, llevar; (COMPUT) ejecutar; (pass: hand) pasar; (PRESS: feature) publicar ♦ vi correr; (work: machine) funcionar, marchar; (bus, train: operate) circular, ir; (: travel) ir; (continue: play) seguir; (contract) ser válido; (flow: river) fluir; (colours, washing) desteñirse; (in election) ser candidato; **there was a ~ on** (meat, tickets) hubo mucha demanda de; **in the long ~** a la larga; **on the ~** en fuga; **I'll ~ you to the station** te llevaré a la estación (en coche); **to ~ a risk** correr un riesgo; **to ~ a bath** llenar la bañera ► **run after** vt (to catch up) correr tras; (chase) perseguir ► **run away** vi huir ► **run down** vt (production) ir reduciendo; (factory) ir restringiendo la producción en; (car) atropellar; (criticize) criticar; **to be run down** (person: tired) estar debilitado ► **run into** vt fus (meet: person, trouble) tropezar con; (collide with) chocar con ► **run off** vt (water) dejar correr; (copies) sacar ♦ vi huir corriendo ► **run out** vi (person: will start running) irse; (lease) caducar, vencer; (money etc) acabarse ► **run out of** vt fus quedar sin ► **run over** vt (AUT) atropellar ♦ vt fus (revise) repasar ► **run through** vt fus (instructions) repasar ► **run up** vt (debt) contraer; **to run up against** (difficulties) tropezar con ■ **runaway** adj (horse) desbocado; (truck) sin frenos; (child) escapado de casa

rung [rʌŋ] pp of **ring** ♦ n (of ladder) escalón m, peldaño

runner ['rʌnəʳ] n (in race: person) corredor(a) m/f; (: horse) caballo; (on sledge) patín m ■ **runner bean** (BRIT) n = judía verde ■ **runner-up** n subcampeón(-ona) m/f

running ['rʌnɪŋ] n (sport) atletismo; (of business) administración f ♦ adj (water, costs) corriente; (commentary) continuo; **to be in/out of the ~ for sth** tener/no tener posibilidades de ganar algo; **6 days ~** 6 días seguidos

runny ['rʌnɪ] adj fluido; (nose, eyes) gastante

run-up ['rʌnʌp] n: **~ to** (election etc) período previo a

runway ['rʌnweɪ] n (AVIAT) pista de aterrizaje

rupture ['rʌptʃəʳ] n (MED) hernia ♦ vt: **to ~ o.s** causarse una hernia

rural ['ruərl] adj rural

rush [rʌʃ] n ímpetu m; (hurry) prisa; (COMM) demanda repentina; (current) corriente f fuerte; (of feeling) torrente m; (BOT) junco ♦ vt apresurar; (work) hacer de prisa ♦ vi correr, precipitarse ■ **rush hour** n horas fpl punta

Russia ['rʌʃə] n Rusia ■ **Russian** adj ruso(-a) ♦ n ruso(-a) m/f; (LING) ruso

rust [rʌst] n herrumbre f, moho ♦ vi oxidarse

rusty ['rʌstɪ] adj oxidado

ruthless ['ru:θlɪs] adj despiadado

RV (US) n abbr = **recreational vehicle**

rye [raɪ] n centeno

S, s

Sabbath ['sæbəθ] n domingo; (Jewish) sábado

sabotage ['sæbətɑ:ʒ] n sabotaje m ♦ vt sabotear

saccharin(e) ['sækərɪn] n sacarina

sachet ['sæʃeɪ] n sobrecito

sack [sæk] n (bag) saco, costal m ♦ vt (dismiss) despedir; (plunder) saquear; **to get the ~** ser despedido

sacred ['seɪkrɪd] adj sagrado, santo

sacrifice ['sækrɪfaɪs] n sacrificio ♦ vt sacrificar

sad [sæd] adj (unhappy) triste; (deplorable) lamentable

saddle ['sædl] n silla (de montar); (of cycle) sillín m ♦ vt (horse) ensillar; **to be saddled with sth** (inf) quedar cargado con algo

sadistic [sə'dɪstɪk] adj sádico

sadly ['sædlɪ] adv lamentablemente; **to be ~ lacking in** estar por desgracia carente de

sadness ['sædnɪs] n tristeza

s.a.e. abbr (= stamped addressed envelope) sobre con las propias señas de uno y con sello

safari [sə'fɑ:rɪ] n safari m

safe [seɪf] adj (out of danger) fuera de peligro; (not dangerous, sure) seguro; (unharmed) ileso ♦ n caja de caudales, caja fuerte; **~ and sound** sano y salvo; **(just) to be on the ~ side** para mayor seguridad ■ **safely** adv seguramente, con seguridad; **to arrive safely** llegar bien ■ **safe sex** n sexo seguro o sin riesgo

safety ['seɪftɪ] n seguridad f ■ **safety belt** n cinturón m (de seguridad) ■ **safety pin** n imperdible m, seguro (MEX), alfiler m de gancho (SC)

saffron ['sæfrən] n azafrán m

sag [sæg] vi aflojarse

sage [seɪdʒ] n (herb) salvia; (man) sabio

Sagittarius [sædʒɪ'teərɪəs] n Sagitario

Sahara [sə'hɑ:rə] n: **the ~ (Desert)** el (desierto del) Sáhara

said [sed] pt, pp of **say**

sail [seɪl] n (on boat) vela; (trip): **to go for a ~** dar un paseo en barco ♦ vt (boat) gobernar ♦ vi (travel: ship) navegar; (SPORT) hacer vela; (begin voyage) salir; **they sailed into Copenhagen** arribaron a Copenhague □ **sailboat** (US) n = **sailing boat** □ **sailing** n (SPORT) vela; **to go sailing** hacer vela □ **sailing boat** n barco de vela □ **sailor** n marinero, marino

saint [seɪnt] n santo

sake [seɪk] n: **for the ~ of** por

salad ['sæləd] n ensalada □ **salad cream** (BRIT) n (especie f de) mayonesa □ **salad dressing** n aliño

salami [sə'lɑːmɪ] n salami m, salchichón m

salary ['sælərɪ] n sueldo

sale [seɪl] n venta; (at reduced prices) liquidación f, saldo; (auction) subasta; **sales** npl (total amount sold) ventas fpl, facturación f; **"for ~"** "se vende"; **on ~** en venta; **on ~ or return** (goods) venta por reposición □ **sales assistant** (US **sales clerk**) n dependiente/a m/f □ **salesman/woman** (irreg) n (in shop) dependiente(-a) m/f □ **salesperson** (irreg) n vendedor(a) m/f, dependiente(-a) m/f; **sales rep** n representante mf, agente mf comercial

saline ['seɪlaɪn] adj salino

saliva [sə'laɪvə] n saliva

salmon ['sæmən] n inv salmón m

salon ['sælɒn] n (hairdressing salon) peluquería f; (beauty salon) salón m de belleza

saloon [sə'luːn] n (US) bar m, taberna; (BRIT AUT) coche m (de) turismo; (ship's lounge) cámara, salón m

salt [sɔːlt] n sal f ♦ vt salar; (put salt on) poner sal en □ **saltwater** adj de agua salada □ **salty** adj salado

salute [sə'luːt] n saludo m; (of guns) salva ♦ vt saludar

salvage ['sælvɪdʒ] n (saving) salvamento, recuperación f; (things saved) objetos mpl salvados ♦ vt salvar

Salvation Army [sæl'veɪʃən-] n Ejército de Salvación

same [seɪm] adj mismo ♦ pron: **the ~** el (la) mismo(-a), los (las) mismos(-as); **the ~ book as** el mismo libro que; **at the ~ time** (at the same moment) al mismo tiempo; (yet) sin embargo; **all or just the ~** sin embargo, aun así; **to do the ~** (as sb) hacer lo mismo (que algn); **the ~ to you!** ¡igualmente!

sample ['sɑːmpl] n muestra ♦ vt (food) probar; (wine) catar

sanction ['sæŋkʃən] n aprobación f ♦ vt sancionar; aprobar; **sanctions** npl (POL) sanciones fpl

sanctuary ['sæŋktjuərɪ] n santuario; (refuge) asilo, refugio; (for wildlife) reserva

sand [sænd] n arena; (beach) playa ♦ vt (also: **~ down**) lijar

sandal ['sændl] n sandalia

sand: sandbox (US) n = **sandpit** □ **sandcastle** n castillo de arena □ **sand dune** n duna □ **sandpaper** n papel m de lija □ **sandpit** n (for children) cajón m de arena □ **sands** npl playa sg de arena □ **sandstone** ['sændstəun] n piedra arenisca

sandwich ['sændwɪtʃ] n sandwich m ♦ vt intercalar; **sandwiched between** apretujado entre; **cheese/ham ~** sandwich de queso/jamón

sandy ['sændɪ] adj arenoso; (colour) rojizo

sane [seɪn] adj cuerdo; (sensible) sensato

⚠ Be careful not to translate **sane** by the Spanish word *sano*.

sang [sæŋ] pt of **sing**

sanitary towel (US **sanitary napkin**) n paño higiénico, compresa

sanity ['sæniti] n cordura; (of judgment) sensatez f

sank [sæŋk] pt of **sink**

Santa Claus [sæntə'klɔːz] n San Nicolás, Papá Noel

sap [sæp] n (of plants) savia ♦ vt (strength) minar, agotar

sapphire ['sæfaiə*] n zafiro

sarcasm ['sɑːkæzm] n sarcasmo

sarcastic [sɑː'kæstik] adj sarcástico

sardine [sɑː'diːn] n sardina

SASE (US) n abbr (= self-addressed stamped envelope) sobre con las propias señas de uno y con sello

Sat. abbr (= Saturday) sáb

sat [sæt] pt, pp of **sit**

satchel ['sætʃl] n (child's) mochila, cartera (SP)

satellite ['sætəlait] n satélite m □ **satellite dish** n antena de televisión por satélite □ **satellite television** n televisión f vía satélite

satin ['sætin] n raso ♦ adj de raso

satire ['sætaiə*] n sátira

satisfaction [sætis'fækʃən] n satisfacción f

satisfactory [sætis'fæktəri] adj satisfactorio

satisfied ['sætisfaid] adj satisfecho; **to be ~ (with sth)** estar satisfecho (de algo)

satisfy ['sætisfai] vt satisfacer; (convince) convencer

Saturday ['sætədi] n sábado

sauce [sɔːs] n salsa; (sweet) crema; jarabe m □ **saucepan** n cacerola, olla

saucer ['sɔːsə*] n platillo

Saudi Arabia n Arabia Saudí or Saudita

sauna ['sɔːnə] n sauna

sausage ['sɔsidʒ] n salchicha □ **sausage roll** n empanadita de salchicha

sautéed ['səuteid] adj salteado

savage ['sævidʒ] adj (cruel, fierce) feroz, furioso; (primitive) salvaje ♦ n salvaje mf ♦ vt (attack) embestir

save [seiv] vt (rescue) salvar, rescatar; (money, time) ahorrar; (put by, keep: seat) guardar; (COMPUT) salvar (y guardar); (avoid: trouble) evitar; (SPORT) parar ♦ vi (also: ~ **up**) ahorrar ♦ n (SPORT) parada ♦ prep salvo, excepto

savings ['seiviŋz] npl ahorros mpl □ **savings account** n cuenta de ahorros □ **savings and loan association** (US) n sociedad f de ahorro y préstamo

savoury ['seivəri] (US **savory**) adj sabroso; (dish: not sweet) salado

saw [sɔː] (pt sawed, pp sawed or sawn) pt of **see** ♦ n (tool) sierra ♦ vt serrar □ **sawdust** n (a)serrín m

sawn [sɔːn] pp of **saw**

saxophone ['sæksəfəun] n saxófono

say [sei] (pt, pp said) n: **to have one's ~** expresar su opinión ♦ vt decir; **to have a** or **some ~ in sth** tener voz or tener que ver en algo; **to ~ yes/no** decir que sí/no; **could you ~ that again?** ¿podría repetir eso?; **that is to ~** es decir; **that goes without saying** ni que decir tiene □ **saying** n dicho, refrán m

scab [skæb] n costra; (pej) esquirol m

scaffolding ['skæfəldiŋ] n andamio, andamiaje m

scald [skɔːld] n escaldadura ♦ vt escaldar

scale [skeil] n (gen, MUS) escala; (of fish) escama; (of salaries, fees etc) escalafón m ♦ vt (mountain) escalar; (tree) trepar; **scales** npl (for weighing: small) balanza; (: large) báscula; **on a large ~** en gran escala; **~ of charges** tarifa, lista de precios

scallion ['skæljən] (US) n cebolleta

scallop ['skɔləp] n (ZOOL) venera; (SEWING) festón m

scalp [skælp] n cabellera ♦ vt escalpar

scalpel ['skælpl] n bisturí m

scam [skæm] n (inf) estafa, timo

scampi ['skæmpɪ] npl gambas fpl

scan [skæn] vt (examine) escudriñar; (glance at quickly) dar un vistazo a; (TV, RADAR) explorar, registrar ♦ n (MED): **to have a ~** pasar por el escáner

scandal ['skændl] n escándalo; (gossip) chismes mpl

Scandinavia [skændɪ'neɪvɪə] n Escandinavia ♦ **Scandinavian** adj, n escandinavo(-a) m/f

scanner ['skænə'] n (RADAR, MED) escáner m

scapegoat ['skeɪpgəut] n cabeza de turco, chivo expiatorio

scar [skɑ:] n cicatriz f; (fig) señal f ♦ vt dejar señales en

scarce [skɛəs] adj escaso; **to make o.s. ~** (inf) esfumarse ♦ **scarcely** adv apenas

scare [skɛə'] n susto, sobresalto; (panic) pánico ♦ vt asustar, espantar; **to ~ sb stiff** dar a algn un susto de muerte; **bomb ~** amenaza de bomba ♦ **scarecrow** n espantapájaros m inv ♦ **scared** adj: **to be scared** estar asustado

scarf [skɑ:f] n (pl scarfs or scarves) n (long) bufanda; (square) pañuelo

scarlet ['skɑ:lɪt] adj escarlata

scarves [skɑ:vz] npl of **scarf**

scary ['skɛərɪ] (inf) adj espeluznante

scatter ['skætə'] vt (spread) esparcir, desparramar; (put to flight) dispersar ♦ vi desparramarse; dispersarse

scenario [sɪ'nɑ:rɪəu] n (THEATRE) argumento; (CINEMA) guión m; (fig) escenario

scene [si:n] n (THEATRE, fig etc) escena; (of crime etc) escenario; (view) panorama m; (fuss) escándalo ♦ **scenery** n (THEATRE) decorado; (landscape) paisaje m ♦ **scenic** adj pintoresco

⚠ Be careful not to translate **scenery** by the Spanish word *escenario*.

scent [sɛnt] n perfume m, olor m; (fig: track) rastro, pista

sceptical ['skɛptɪkl] adj escéptico

schedule ['ʃɛdju:l, (US) 'skɛdju:l] n (timetable) horario; (of events) programa m; (list) lista ♦ vt (visit) fijar la hora de; **to arrive on ~** llegar a la hora debida; **to be ahead of/behind ~** estar adelantado/en retraso ♦ **scheduled flight** n vuelo regular

scheme [ski:m] n (plan) plan m, proyecto; (plot) intriga; (arrangement) disposición f; (pension scheme etc) sistema m ♦ vi (intrigue) intrigar

schizophrenic [skɪtzə'frɛnɪk] adj esquizofrénico

scholar ['skɔlə'] n (pupil) alumno(-a); (learned person) sabio(-a), erudito(-a) ♦ **scholarship** n erudición f; (grant) beca

school [sku:l] n escuela, colegio; (in university) facultad f ♦ cpd escolar ♦ **schoolbook** n libro de texto ♦ **schoolboy** n alumno ♦ **school children** npl alumnos mpl ♦ **schoolgirl** n alumna ♦ **schooling** n enseñanza ♦ **schoolteacher** n (primary) maestro(-a); (secondary) profesor(a) m/f

science ['saɪəns] n ciencia ♦ **science fiction** n ciencia-ficción f ♦ **scientific** ['-tɪfɪk] adj científico ♦ **scientist** n científico(-a)

sci-fi ['saɪfaɪ] n abbr (inf) = **science fiction**

scissors ['sɪzəz] npl tijeras fpl; **a pair of ~** unas tijeras

scold [skəuld] vt regañar

scone [skɔn] n pastel de pan

scoop [sku:p] n (for flour etc) pala; (PRESS) exclusiva

scooter ['sku:tə'] n moto f; (toy) patinete m

scope [skəup] n (of plan) ámbito; (of person) competencia; (opportunity) libertad f (de acción)

scorching ['skɔːtʃɪŋ] adj (heat, sun) abrasador(a)

score [skɔː'] n (points etc) puntuación f; (MUS) partitura f; (twenty) veintena ♦ vt (goal, point) ganar; (mark) rayar; (achieve: success) conseguir ♦ vi marcar un tanto; (FOOTBALL) marcar (un) gol; (keep score) llevar el tanteo; **scores of** (lots of) decenas de; **on that ~** en lo que se refiere a eso; **~ 6 out of 10** obtener una puntuación de 6 sobre 10 ▶ **score out** vt tachar □ **scoreboard** n marcador m □ **scorer** n marcador m; (keeping score) encargado(-a) del marcador

scorn [skɔːn] n desprecio

Scorpio ['skɔːpɪəu] n Escorpión m

scorpion ['skɔːpɪən] n alacrán m

Scot [skɔt] n escocés(-esa) m/f

Scotch tape® (US) n cinta adhesiva, celo, scotch® m

Scotland ['skɔtlənd] n Escocia

Scots [skɔts] adj escocés(-esa) □ **Scotsman** (irreg) n escocés □ **Scotswoman** (irreg) n escocesa □ **Scottish** ['skɔtɪʃ] adj escocés(-esa) □ **Scottish Parliament** n Parlamento escocés

scout [skaut] n (MIL: also: **boy ~**) explorador m; **girl ~** = (US) niña exploradora

scowl [skaul] vi fruncir el ceño; **to ~ at sb** mirar con ceño a algn

scramble ['skræmbl] n (climb) subida (difícil); (struggle) pelea ♦ vi: **to ~ through/out** abrirse paso/salir con dificultad; **to ~ for** pelear por □ **scrambled eggs** npl huevos mpl revueltos

scrap [skræp] n (bit) pedacito m; (fig) pizca f; (fight) riña, bronca; (also: **~ iron**) chatarra, hierro viejo ♦ vt (discard) desechar, descartar ♦ vi reñir, armar una bronca; **scraps** npl (waste) sobras fpl, desperdicios mpl □ **scrapbook** n álbum m de recortes

scrape [skreip] n: **to get into a ~** meterse en un lío ♦ vt raspar; (skin etc) rasguñar; (scrape against) rozar ♦ vi: **to ~ through** (exam) aprobar por los pelos

scrap paper n pedazos mpl de papel

scratch [skrætʃ] n rasguño; (from claw) arañazo ♦ vt (paint, car) rayar; (with claw, nail) rasguñar, arañar; (rub: nose etc) rascarse ♦ vi rascarse; **to start from ~** partir de cero; **to be up to ~** cumplir con los requisitos □ **scratch card** n (BRIT) tarjeta f de "rasque y gane"

scream [skriːm] n chillido ♦ vi chillar

screen [skriːn] n (CINEMA, TV) pantalla; (movable barrier) biombo ♦ vt (conceal) tapar; (from the wind etc) proteger; (film) proyectar; (candidates etc) investigar a □ **screening** n (MED) investigación f médica □ **screenplay** n guión m □ **screen saver** n (COMPUT) protector m de pantalla

screw [skruː] n tornillo ♦ vt (also: **~ in**) atornillar ▶ **screw up** vt (paper etc) arrugar; **to screw up one's eyes** arrugar el entrecejo □ **screwdriver** n destornillador m

scribble ['skrɪbl] n garabatos mpl ♦ vt, vi garabatear

script [skrɪpt] n (CINEMA etc) guión m; (writing) escritura, letra

scroll [skrəul] n rollo

scrub [skrʌb] n (land) maleza ♦ vt fregar, restregar; (inf: reject) cancelar, anular

scruffy ['skrʌfɪ] adj desaliñado, piojoso

scrum(mage) ['skrʌm(mɪdʒ)] n (RUGBY) melée f

scrutiny ['skruːtɪnɪ] n escrutinio, examen m

scuba diving ['skuːbə'daɪvɪŋ] n submarinismo

sculptor ['skʌlptə'] n escultor(a) m/f

sculpture ['skʌlptʃə'] n escultura

scum [skʌm] n (on liquid) espuma; (pej: people) escoria

scurry ['skʌrɪ] vi correr; **to ~ off** escabullirse

sea [si:] n mar m ♦ cpd de mar, marítimo; **by ~** (travel) en barco; **on the ~** (boat) en el mar; (town) junto al mar; **to be all at ~** (fig) estar despistado; **out to ~**, **at ~** en alta mar ❏ **seafood** n mariscos mpl ❏ **sea front** n paseo marítimo ❏ **seagull** n gaviota

seal [si:l] n (animal) foca; (stamp) sello ♦ vt (close) cerrar ▶ **seal off** vt (area) acordonar

sea level n nivel m del mar

seam [si:m] n (costura); (of metal) juntura; (of coal) veta, filón m

search [sɔ:tʃ] n (for person, thing) busca, búsqueda; (COMPUT) búsqueda; (inspection: of sb's home) registro ♦ vt (look in) buscar en; (examine) examinar; (person, place) registrar ♦ vi: **to ~** for buscar; **in ~** of en busca de ❏ **search engine** n (COMPUT) buscador m ❏ **search party** n pelotón m de salvamento

sea: seashore n playa, orilla del mar ❏ **seasick** adj mareado ❏ **seaside** n playa, orilla del mar ❏ **seaside resort** n centro turístico costero

season ['si:zn] n (of year) estación f; (sporting etc) temporada; (of films etc) ciclo ♦ vt (food) sazonar; **in/out of ~** en sazón/fuera de temporada ❏ **seasonal** adj estacional ❏ **seasoning** n condimento, aderezo ❏ **season ticket** n abono

seat [si:t] n (in bus, train) asiento; (chair) silla; (PARLIAMENT) escaño; (buttocks) culo, trasero; (of trousers) culera ♦ vt sentar; (have room for) tener cabida para; **to be seated** sentarse ❏ **seat belt** n cinturón m de seguridad ❏ **seating** n asientos mpl

sea: sea water n agua del mar ❏ **seaweed** n alga marina

sec. abbr = **second(s)**

secluded [sɪ'klu:dɪd] adj retirado

second ['sɛkənd] adj segundo ♦ adv en segundo lugar ♦ n segundo; (AUT: also: **~ gear**) segunda; (COMM) artículo con algún desperfecto; (BRIT SCOL: degree) título de licenciado con calificación de notable ♦ vt (motion) apoyar ❏ **secondary** adj secundario ❏ **secondary school** n escuela secundaria ❏ **second-class** adj de segunda clase ♦ adv (RAIL) en segunda ❏ **secondhand** adj de segunda mano, usado ❏ **secondly** adv en segundo lugar ❏ **second-rate** adj de segunda categoría ❏ **second thoughts:** **to have second thoughts** cambiar de opinión; **on second thoughts** or **thought** (US) pensándolo bien

secrecy ['si:krəsɪ] n secreto

secret ['si:krɪt] adj, n secreto; **in ~** en secreto

secretary ['sɛkrətərɪ] n secretario(-a); **S~ of State (for)** (BRIT POL) Ministro (de)

secretive ['si:krətɪv] adj reservado, sigiloso

secret service n servicio secreto

sect [sɛkt] n secta

section ['sɛkʃən] n sección f; (part) parte f; (of document) artículo; (of opinion) sector m; (cross-section) corte m transversal

sector ['sɛktə] n sector m

secular ['sɛkjulə] adj secular, seglar

secure [sɪ'kjuə] adj seguro; (firmly fixed) firme, fijo ♦ vt (fix) asegurar, afianzar; (get) conseguir

security [sɪ'kjuərɪtɪ] n seguridad f; (for loan) fianza; (: object) prenda; **securities** npl (COMM) valores mpl, títulos mpl ❏ **security guard** n guardia m/f de seguridad

sedan [sɪ'dæn] (US) n (AUT) sedán m

sedate [sɪ'deɪt] adj tranquilo ♦ vt tratar con sedantes

sedative ['sɛdɪtɪv] n sedante m, sedativo

seduce [sɪ'dju:s] *vt* seducir □ **seductive** [-'dʌktɪv] *adj* seductor(a)

see [si:] (*pt* **saw**, *pp* **seen**) *vt* ver; (*accompany*) acompañar; **to ~ sb to the door** acompañar a algn a la puerta; (*understand*) ver, comprender ♦ *vi* ver ♦ *n* (*arz*)obispado; **to ~ that** (*ensure*) asegurar que; **~ you soon!** ¡hasta pronto! ► **see off** *vt* despedir ► **see out** *vt* (*take to the door*) acompañar hasta la puerta ► **see through** *vt fus* (*fig*) calar ♦ *vt* (*plan*) llevar a cabo ► **see to** *vt fus* atender a, encargarse de

seed [si:d] *n* semilla; (*in fruit*) pepita; (*fig*: *gen pl*) germen *pl*; (*TENNIS etc*) preseleccionado(-a); **to go to ~** (*plant*) granar; (*fig*) descuidarse

seeing ['si:ɪŋ] *conj*: **~ (that)** visto que, en vista de que

seek [si:k] (*pt, pp* **sought**) *vt* buscar; (*post*) solicitar

seem [si:m] *vi* parecer; **there seems to be ...** parece que hay ... □ **seemingly** *adv* aparentemente, según parece

seen [si:n] *pp of* **see**

seesaw ['si:sɔ:] *n* subibaja

segment ['segmənt] *n* (*part*) sección *f*; (*of orange*) gajo

segregate ['segrɪgeɪt] *vt* segregar

seize [si:z] *vt* (*grasp*) agarrar, asir; (*take possession of*) secuestrar; (*: territory*) apoderarse de; (*opportunity*) aprovechar

seizure ['si:ʒə'] *n* (*MED*) ataque *m*; (*LAW, of power*) incautación *f*

seldom ['seldəm] *adv* rara vez

select [sɪ'lekt] *adj* selecto, escogido ♦ *vt* escoger, elegir; (*SPORT*) seleccionar □ **selection** *n* selección *f*, elección *f*; (*COMM*) surtido □ **selective** *adj* selectivo

self [self] (*pl* **selves**) *n* uno mismo; **the ~** el yo ♦ *prefix* auto... □ **self-assured** *adj* seguro de sí mismo □ **self-catering** (*BRIT*) *adj* (*flat etc*) con cocina

egocéntrico □ **self-confidence** *n* confianza en sí mismo □ **self-confident** *adj* seguro de sí (mismo), lleno de confianza en sí mismo □ **self-conscious** *adj* cohibido □ **self-contained** (*BRIT*) *adj* (*flat*) con entrada particular □ **self-control** *n* autodominio □ **self-defence** (*US* **self-defense**) *n* defensa propia □ **self-drive** *adj* (*BRIT*) sin chofer *or* (*SP*) chófer □ **self-employed** *adj* que trabaja por cuenta propia □ **self-esteem** *n* amor *m* propio □ **self-indulgent** *adj* autocomplaciente □ **self-interest** *n* egoísmo □ **selfish** *adj* egoísta □ **self-pity** *n* lástima de sí mismo □ **self-raising** [self'reɪzɪŋ] (*US* **self-rising**) *adj*: **self-raising flour** harina con levadura □ **self-respect** *n* amor *m* propio □ **self-service** *adj* de autoservicio

sell [sel] (*pt, pp* **sold**) *vt* vender ♦ *vi* venderse; **to ~ at** *or* **for £10** venderse a 10 libras □ **sell off** *vt* liquidar ► **sell out** *vi*: **to sell out of tickets/milk** vender todas las entradas/toda la leche □ **sell-by date** *n* fecha de caducidad □ **seller** *n* vendedor(a) *m/f*

Sellotape® ['seləʊteɪp] (*BRIT*) *n* celo (*SP*), cinta Scotch® (*LAm*) *or* Dúrex® (*MEX, ARG*)

selves [selvz] *npl of* **self**

semester [sɪ'mestə'] (*US*) *n* semestre *m*

semi... [semɪ] *prefix* semi..., medio... □ **semicircle** *n* semicírculo □ **semidetached (house)** *n* (*casa*) semiseparada □ **semi-final** *n* semifinal *m*

seminar ['semɪnɑ:'] *n* seminario

semi-skimmed [semɪ'skɪmd] *adj* semidesnatado □ **semi-skimmed (milk)** *n* leche semidesnatada

senate ['senɪt] *n* senado; **the S~** (*US*) el Senado □ **senator** *n* senador(a) *m/f*

send [send] (*pt, pp* **sent**) *vt* mandar, enviar; (*signal*) transmitir ► **send back** *vt* devolver ► **send for** *vt fus* mandar traer ► **send in** vt (report, application, resignation) mandar ► **send off** vt (goods) despachar; (BRIT SPORT: player) expulsar ► **send on** vt (letter, luggage) remitir; (person) mandar ► **send out** vt (invitation) mandar; (signal) emitir ► **send up** vt (person, price) hacer subir; (BRIT: parody) parodiar ❑ **sender** n remitente mf ❑ **send-off** n: **a good send-off** una buena despedida

senile ['si:naɪl] adj senil

senior ['si:nɪə'] adj (older) mayor, más viejo; (: on staff) de más antigüedad; (of higher rank) superior ❑ **senior citizen** n persona de la tercera edad ❑ **senior high school** (US) n ~ instituto de enseñanza media; see also **high school**

sensation [sen'seɪʃən] n sensación f ❑ **sensational** adj sensacional

sense [sens] n (faculty, meaning) sentido; (feeling) sensación f; (good sense) sentido común, juicio ♦ vt sentir, percibir; **it makes ~** tiene sentido ❑ **senseless** adj estúpido, insensato; (unconscious) sin conocimiento ❑ **sense of humour** (BRIT) n sentido del humor

sensible ['sensɪbl] adj sensato; (reasonable) razonable, lógico

⚠ Be careful not to translate **sensible** by the Spanish word **sensible**.

sensitive ['sensɪtɪv] adj sensible; (touchy) susceptible

sensual ['sensjuəl] adj sensual

sensuous ['sensjuəs] adj sensual

sent [sent] pt, pp of **send**

sentence ['sentns] n (LING) oración f; (LAW) sentencia, fallo ♦ vt: **to ~ sb to death/to 5 years (in prison)** condenar a algn a muerte/a 5 años de cárcel

sentiment ['sentɪmənt] n sentimiento; (opinion) opinión f ❑ **sentimental** [-'mentl] adj sentimental

Sep. abbr (= September) sep., set.

separate [adj 'seprɪt, vb 'sepəreɪt] adj separado; (distinct) distinto ♦ vt separar; (part) dividir ♦ vi separarse ❑ **separately** adv por separado ❑ **separates** npl (clothes) coordinados mpl ❑ **separation** [-'reɪʃən] n separación f

September [sep'tembə'] n se(p)tiembre m

septic ['septɪk] adj séptico ❑ **septic tank** n fosa séptica

sequel ['si:kwl] n consecuencia, resultado; (of story) continuación f

sequence ['si:kwəns] n sucesión f, serie f; (CINEMA) secuencia

sequin ['si:kwɪn] n lentejuela

Serb [sə:b] adj, n = **Serbian**

Serbian ['sə:bɪən] adj serbio ♦ n serbio(-a); (LING) serbio

sergeant ['sɑ:dʒənt] n sargento

serial ['sɪərɪəl] n (TV) telenovela, serie f televisiva; (BOOK) serie f ❑ **serial killer** n asesino(-a) múltiple ❑ **serial number** n número de serie

series ['sɪəri:z] n inv serie f

serious ['sɪərɪəs] adj (grave) grave ❑ **seriously** adv en serio; (ill, wounded etc) gravemente

sermon ['sə:mən] n sermón m

servant ['sə:vənt] n servidor(a) m/f; (house servant) criado(-a)

serve [sə:v] vt servir; (customer) atender; (train) pasar por; (apprenticeship) hacer; (prison term) cumplir ♦ vi (at table) servir; (TENNIS) sacar; **to ~ as/for/to do** servir de/para/para hacer ♦ n (TENNIS) saque m; **it serves him right** se lo tiene merecido ❑ **server** n (COMPUT) servidor m

service ['sə:vɪs] n servicio; (REL) misa; (AUT) mantenimiento; (dishes etc) juego ♦ vt (car etc) revisar; (: repair) reparar; **to be of ~ to sb** ser útil a algn; **~ included/not included** servicio incluido/no incluido; **services** (ECON: tertiary sector) sector m terciario or (de)

serviette servicios; (BRIT: on motorway) área de servicio; (MIL): **the Services** las fuerzas armadas □ **service area** n (on motorway) área de servicio □ **service charge** (BRIT) n servicio □ **serviceman** (irreg) n militar m □ **service station** n estación f de servicio

serviette [sə:vɪ'et] (BRIT) n servilleta

session ['sefən] n sesión f; **to be in** ~ estar en sesión

set [set] (pt, pp ~) n (collection) juego m; (RADIO) aparato; (TV) televisor m; (of utensils) batería; (of cutlery) cubierto; (of books) colección f; (group of people) grupo; (CINEMA) plató m; (THEATRE) decorado; (HAIRDRESSING) marcado ♦ adj (fixed) fijo; (ready) listo ♦ vt (place) poner, colocar; (fix) fijar; (adjust) ajustar, arreglar; (decide: rules etc) establecer, decidir ♦ vi (sun) ponerse; (jam, jelly) cuajarse; (concrete) fraguar; (bone) componerse; **to be** ~ **on doing sth** estar empeñado en hacer algo; **to** ~ **to music** poner música a; **to** ~ **on fire** incendiar, poner fuego a; **to** ~ **free** poner en libertad; **to** ~ **going** poner algo en marcha; **to** ~ **sail** zarpar, hacerse a la vela ▶ **set aside** vt poner aparte, dejar de lado; (money, time) reservar ▶ **set back** vt (in time): **to** ~ **back (by)** retrasar (en); (cost): **it** ~ **me back £5** me costó £5 ▶ **set off** vi partir ♦ vt (bomb) hacer estallar; (events) poner en marcha; (show up well) hacer resaltar ▶ **set out** vi partir ♦ vt (arrange) disponer; (state) exponer; **to** ~ **out to do sth** proponerse hacer algo ▶ **set up** vt establecer □ **setback** n revés m, contratiempo □ **set menu** n menú m

settee [se'ti:] n sofá m

setting ['setɪŋ] n (scenery) marco; (position) disposición f; (of sun) puesta; (of jewel) engaste m, montadura

settle ['setl] vt (argument) resolver; (accounts) ajustar, liquidar; (MED: calm) calmar, sosegar ♦ vi (dust etc) depositarse; (weather) serenarse; **to** ~ **for sth** convenir en aceptar algo; **to** ~ **on sth** decidirse por algo ▶ **settle down** vi (get comfortable) ponerse cómodo, acomodarse; (calm down) calmarse, tranquilizarse; (live quietly) echar raíces ▶ **settle in** vi instalarse ▶ **settle up** vi: **to** ~ **up with sb** ajustar cuentas con algn □ **settlement** n (payment) liquidación f; (agreement) acuerdo, convenio; (village etc) pueblo

setup ['setʌp] n sistema m; (situation) situación f

seven ['sevn] num siete □ **seventeen** num diez y siete, diecisiete □ **seventeenth** [sevn'ti:nθ] adj decimoséptimo □ **seventh** num séptimo □ **seventieth** ['sevntɪθ] adj septuagésimo □ **seventy** num setenta

sever ['sevə] vt cortar; (relations) romper

several ['sevrəl] adj, pron varios(-as) m/ fpl, algunos(-as) m/fpl; ~ **of us** varios de nosotros

severe [sɪ'vɪə] adj severo; (serious) grave; (hard) duro; (pain) intenso

sew [səu] (pt **sewed**, pp **sewn**) vt, vi coser

sewage ['su:idʒ] n aguas fpl residuales

sewer ['su:ə] n alcantarilla, cloaca

sewing ['səuɪŋ] n costura □ **sewing machine** n máquina de coser

sewn [səun] pp of **sew**

sex [seks] n sexo; (lovemaking): **to have** ~ hacer el amor □ **sexism** ['seksɪzəm] n sexismo □ **sexist** adj, n sexista mf □ **sexual** ['seksjuəl] adj sexual □ **sexual intercourse** n relaciones fp sexuales □ **sexuality** [seksju'ælɪtɪ] n sexualidad f □ **sexy** adj sexy

shabby ['ʃæbɪ] adj (person) desharrapado; (clothes) raído, gastado; (behaviour) ruin inv

shack [ʃæk] n choza, chabola

shade [ʃeɪd] n sombra; (for lamp) pantalla; (for eyes) visera; (of colour) matiz m, tonalidad f; (small quantity): a ~ (too big/more) un poquitín (grande/más) ♦ vt dar sombra a; (eyes) proteger del sol; **in the** ~ en la sombra; **shades** npl (sunglasses) gafas fpl de sol

shadow ['ʃædəu] n sombra ♦ vt (follow) seguir y vigilar □ **shadow cabinet** (BRIT) n (POL) gabinete paralelo formado por el partido de oposición

shady ['ʃeɪdɪ] adj sombreado; (fig: dishonest) sospechoso; (: deal) turbio

shaft [ʃɑ:ft] n (of arrow, spear) astil m; (AUT, TECH) eje m, árbol m; (of mine) pozo; (of lift) hueco, caja; (of light) rayo

shake [ʃeɪk] (pt **shook**, pp **shaken**) vt sacudir; (building) hacer temblar; (bottle, cocktail) agitar ♦ vi (tremble) temblar; **to** ~ **one's head** (in refusal) negar con la cabeza; (in dismay) mover or menear la cabeza, incrédulo; **to** ~ **hands with sb** estrechar la mano a algn ► **shake off** vt sacudirse; (fig) deshacerse de ► **shake up** vt agitar; (fig) reorganizar □ **shaky** adj (hand, voice) trémulo; (building) inestable

shall [ʃæl] aux vb: **~ I help you?** ¿quieres que te ayude?; **I'll buy three, ~ I?** compro tres, ¿no te parece?

shallow ['ʃæləu] adj poco profundo; (fig) superficial

sham [ʃæm] n fraude m, engaño

shambles ['ʃæmblz] n confusión f

shame [ʃeɪm] n vergüenza ♦ vt avergonzar; **it is a** ~ **that/to do** es una lástima que/hacer; **what a ~!** ¡qué lástima! □ **shameful** adj vergonzoso □ **shameless** adj desvergonzado

shampoo [ʃæm'pu:] n champú m ♦ vt lavar con champú

shandy ['ʃændɪ] n mezcla de cerveza con gaseosa

shan't [ʃɑ:nt] = **shall not**

shape [ʃeɪp] n forma ♦ vt formar, dar forma a; (sb's ideas) formar; (sb's life) determinar; **to take** ~ tomar forma

share [ʃeə'] n (part) parte f, porción f; (contribution) cuota; (COMM) acción f ♦ vt dividir; (have in common) compartir; **to ~ out** (among or between) repartir (entre) □ **shareholder** (BRIT) n accionista mf

shark [ʃɑ:k] n tiburón m

sharp [ʃɑ:p] adj (blade, nose) afilado; (point) puntiagudo; (outline) definido; (pain) intenso; (MUS) desafinado; (contrast) marcado; (voice) agudo; (person: quick-witted) astuto; (: dishonest) poco escrupuloso ♦ n (MUS) sostenido ♦ adv: **at 2 o'clock** ~ a las 2 en punto □ **sharpen** vt afilar; (pencil) sacar punta a; (fig) agudizar □ **sharpener** n (also: **pencil sharpener**) sacapuntas m inv □ **sharply** adv (turn, stop) bruscamente; (stand out, contrast) claramente; (criticize, retort) severamente

shatter ['ʃætə'] vt hacer añicos or pedazos; (fig: ruin) destruir, acabar con ♦ vi hacerse añicos □ **shattered** adj (grief-stricken) destrozado, deshecho; (exhausted) agotado, hecho polvo

shave [ʃeɪv] vt afeitar, rasurar ♦ vi afeitarse, rasurarse ♦ n: **to have a ~** afeitarse □ **shaver** n (also: **electric shaver**) máquina de afeitar (eléctrica)

shavings ['ʃeɪvɪŋz] npl (of wood etc) virutas fpl

shaving cream ['ʃeɪvɪŋ-] n crema de afeitar

shaving foam n espuma de afeitar

shawl [ʃɔ:l] n chal m

she [ʃi:] pron ella

sheath [ʃi:θ] n vaina f; (contraceptive) preservativo

shed [ʃed] (pt, pp **shed**) n cobertizo ♦ vt (skin) mudar; (tears, blood) derramar; (load) derramar; (workers) despedir

she'd [ʃiːd] = **she had; she would**

sheep [ʃiːp] n inv oveja ❑ **sheepdog** n perro pastor ❑ **sheepskin** n piel f de carnero

sheer [ʃɪə] adj (utter) puro, completo; (steep) escarpado; (material) diáfano ♦ adv verticalmente

sheet [ʃiːt] n (on bed) sábana; (of paper) hoja; (of glass, metal) lámina; (of ice) capa

sheik(h) [ʃeɪk] n jeque m

shelf [ʃelf] (pl **shelves**) n estante m

shell [ʃel] n (on beach) concha; (of egg, nut etc) cáscara; (explosive) proyectil m, obús m; (of building) armazón f ♦ vt (peas) desenvainar; (MIL) bombardear

she'll [ʃiːl] = **she will; she shall**

shellfish [ʃelfɪʃ] n inv crustáceo; (as food) mariscos mpl

shelter [ʃeltə] n abrigo, refugio ♦ vt (aid) amparar, proteger; (give lodging to) abrigar ♦ vi abrigarse, refugiarse ❑ **sheltered** adj (life) protegido; (spot) abrigado

shelves [ʃelvz] npl of **shelf**

shelving [ʃelvɪŋ] n estantería

shepherd [ʃepəd] n pastor m ♦ vt (guide) guiar, conducir ❑ **shepherd's pie** (BRIT) n pastel de carne y patatas

sheriff [ʃerɪf] (US) n sheriff m

sherry [ʃerɪ] n jerez m

she's [ʃiːz] = **she is; she has**

Shetland [ʃetlənd] n (also: **the Shetlands, the ~ Isles**) las Islas de Zetlandia

shield [ʃiːld] n escudo; (protection) blindaje m ♦ vt: **to ~ (from)** proteger (de)

shift [ʃɪft] n (change) cambio; (at work) turno ♦ vt trasladar; (remove) quitar ♦ vi moverse

shin [ʃɪn] n espinilla

shine [ʃaɪn] (pt, pp **shone**) n brillo, lustre m ♦ vi brillar, relucir ♦ vt (shoes) lustrar, sacar brillo a; **to ~ a torch on sth** dirigir una linterna hacia algo

shingles [ʃɪŋglz] n (MED) herpes mpl or fpl

shiny [ʃaɪnɪ] adj brillante, lustroso

ship [ʃɪp] n buque m, barco ♦ vt (goods) embarcar; (send) transportar or enviar por vía marítima ❑ **shipment** n (goods) envío ❑ **shipping** n (act) embarque m; (traffic) buques mpl ❑ **shipwreck** n naufragio ♦ vt: **to be shipwrecked** naufragar ❑ **shipyard** n astillero

shirt [ʃəːt] n camisa; **in (one's) sleeves** en mangas de camisa

shit [ʃɪt] (inf!) excl ¡mierda! (!)

shiver [ʃɪvə] n escalofrío ♦ vi temblar, estremecerse; (with cold) tiritar

shock [ʃɔk] n (impact) choque m; (ELEC) descarga (eléctrica); (emotional) conmoción f; (start) sobresalto, susto; (MED) postración f nerviosa ♦ vt dar un susto a; (offend) escandalizar ❑ **shocking** adj (awful) espantoso; (outrageous) escandaloso

shoe [ʃuː] n zapato; (for horse) herradura ♦ vt (horse) herrar ❑ **shoelace** n cordón m ❑ **shoe polish** n betún m ❑ **shoeshop** n zapatería

shone [ʃɔn] pt, pp of **shine**

shook [ʃuk] pt of **shake**

shoot [ʃuːt] (pt, pp **shot**) n (on branch, seedling) retoño, vástago ♦ vt disparar; (kill) matar a tiros; (wound) pegar un tiro; (execute) fusilar; (film) rodar, filmar ♦ vi (FOOTBALL) chutar ▸ **shoot down** vt (plane) derribar ▸ **shoot up** vi (prices) dispararse ❑ **shooting** n (shots) tiros mpl; (HUNTING) caza con escopeta

shop [ʃɔp] n tienda; (workshop) taller m ♦ vt (also: **go shopping**) ir de compras ❑ **shop assistant** (BRIT) n dependiente(-a) m/f ❑ **shopkeeper** n tendero(-a) ❑ **shoplifting** n mechería ❑ **shopping** n (goods) compras fpl ❑ **shopping bag** n bolsa (de compras) ❑ **shopping centre** (US

shopping center n centro comercial
□ **shopping mall** n centro comercial
□ **shopping trolley** n (BRIT) carrito de la compra □ **shop window** n escaparate m (SP), vidriera (LAm)

shore [[ʃɔː] n orilla ♦ vt: **to ~ (up)** reforzar; **on ~** en tierra

short [[ʃɔːt] adj corto; (in time) breve, de corta duración; (person) bajo; (curt) brusco, seco; (insufficient) insuficiente; **(a pair of) shorts** (unos) pantalones mpl cortos; **to be ~ of** sth estar falto de algo; **in ~** en pocas palabras; **~ of doing ...** fuera de hacer ...; **it is ~ for** es la forma abreviada de; **to cut ~** (speech, visit) interrumpir, terminar inesperadamente; **everything ~ of ...** todo menos ...; **to fall ~ of** no alcanzar; **to run ~ of** quedarle a algn poco; **to stop ~** parar en seco; **to stop ~ of** detenerse antes de □ **shortage** n: **a shortage of** una falta de □ **shortbread** n especie de mantecada □ **shortcoming** n defecto, deficiencia □ **short(crust) pastry** (BRIT) n pasta quebradiza □ **shortcut** n atajo □ **shorten** vt acortar; (visit) interrumpir □ **shortfall** n déficit m □ **shorthand** (BRIT) n taquigrafía □ **short-lived** adj efímero □ **shortly** adv en breve, dentro de poco □ **shorts** npl pantalones mpl cortos; (US) calzoncillos mpl □ **short-sighted** (BRIT) adj miope; (fig) imprudente □ **short story** n cuento □ **short-tempered** adj enojadizo □ **short-term** adj (effect) a corto plazo

shot [[ʃɔt] pt, pp of **shoot** ♦ n (sound) tiro, disparo; (try) tentativa; (injection) inyección f; (PHOT) toma, fotografía; **to be a good/poor ~** (person) tener buena/mala puntería; **like a ~** (without any delay) como un rayo □ **shotgun** n escopeta

should [[ʃud] aux vb: **I ~ go now** debo irme ahora; **he ~ be there now** debe de

haber llegado (ya); **I ~ go** if I were you yo en tu lugar me iría; **I ~ like to** me gustaría

shoulder [[ʃəuldə] n hombro ♦ vt (fig) cargar con □ **shoulder blade** n omóplato

shouldn't [[ʃudnt] = **should not**

shout [[ʃaut] n grito ♦ vt gritar, dar voces ♦ vi gritar

shove [[ʃʌv] n empujón m ♦ vt empujar; (inf: put): **to ~ sth in** meter algo a empollones

shovel [[ʃʌvl] n pala; (mechanical) excavadora ♦ vt mover con pala

show [[ʃəu] (pt **showed**, pp **shown**) n (of emotion) demostración f; (semblance) apariencia; (exhibition) exposición f; (THEATRE) función f, espectáculo; (TV) show m ♦ vt mostrar, enseñar; (courage etc) mostrar, manifestar; (exhibit) exponer; (film) proyectar ♦ vi mostrarse; (appear) aparecer; **for ~** para impresionar; **on ~** (exhibits etc) expuesto ► **show in** vt (person) hacer pasar ► **show off** (pej) vi presumir ♦ vt (display) lucir ► **show out** vt: **to show sb out** acompañar a algn a la puerta ► **show up** vi (stand out) destacar; (inf: turn up) aparecer ♦ vt (unmask) desenmascarar □ **show business** n mundo del espectáculo

shower [[ʃauə] n (rain) chaparrón m, chubasco; (of stones etc) lluvia; (for bathing) ducha, regadera (MEX) ♦ vi llover ♦ vt (fig): **to ~ sb with sth** colmar a algn de algo; **to have a ~** ducharse □ **shower cap** n gorro de baño □ **shower gel** n gel m de ducha

showing [[ʃəuɪŋ] n (of film) proyección f

show jumping n hípica

shown [[ʃəun] pp of **show**

show: **show-off** (inf) n (person) presumido(-a) □ **showroom** n sala de muestras

shrank [[ʃræŋk] pt of **shrink**

shred [ʃred] n (gen pl) triza, jirón m ♦ vt hacer trizas; (CULIN) desmenuzar

shrewd [ʃruːd] adj astuto

shriek [ʃriːk] n chillido ♦ vi chillar

shrimp [ʃrɪmp] n camarón m

shrine [ʃraɪn] n santuario, sepulcro

shrink [ʃrɪŋk] (pt **shrank**, pp **shrunk**) vi encogerse; (be reduced) reducirse; (also: ~ **away**) retroceder ♦ vt encoger ♦ n (inf, pej) loquero(-a); **to ~ from (doing) sth** no atreverse a hacer algo

shrivel [ʃrɪvl] (also: ~ **up**) vt (dry) secar ♦ vi secarse

shroud [ʃraud] n sudario ♦ vt: **shrouded in mystery** envuelto en el misterio

Shrove Tuesday [ʃrəuv-] n martes m de carnaval

shrub [ʃrʌb] n arbusto

shrug [ʃrʌg] n encogimiento de hombros ♦ vt, vi: **to ~ (one's shoulders)** encogerse de hombros ► **shrug off** vt negar importancia a

shrunk [ʃrʌŋk] pp of **shrink**

shudder [ʃʌdə*] n estremecimiento, escalofrío ♦ vi estremecerse

shuffle [ʃʌfl] vt (cards) barajar ♦ vi: **to ~ (one's feet)** arrastrar los pies

shun [ʃʌn] vt rehuir, esquivar

shut [ʃʌt] (pt, pp ~) vt cerrar ♦ vi cerrarse ► **shut down** vt, vi cerrar ► **shut up** vi (inf: keep quiet) callarse ♦ vt (close) cerrar; (silence) hacer callar ► **shutter** n contraventana; (PHOT) obturador m

shuttle [ʃʌtl] n lanzadera; (also: ~ **service**) servicio rápido y continuo entre dos puntos; (AVIAT) puente m aéreo ► **shuttlecock** n volante m

shy [ʃaɪ] adj tímido

sibling [sɪblɪŋ] n (formal) hermano(-a)

Sicily [sɪsɪlɪ] n Sicilia

sick [sɪk] adj (ill) enfermo; (nauseated) mareado; (humour) negro; (vomiting): **to be ~** (BRIT) vomitar; **to feel ~** tener náuseas; **to be ~ of** (fig) estar harto de ► **sickening** adj (fig) asqueroso

❑ **sick leave** n baja por enfermedad

❑ **sickly** adj enfermizo; (smell) nauseabundo ❑ **sickness** n enfermedad f, mal m; (vomiting) náuseas fpl

side [saɪd] n (gen) lado; (of body) costado; (of lake) orilla; (of hill) ladera; (team) equipo ♦ adj (door, entrance) lateral ♦ vi: **to ~ with sb** tomar el partido de algn; **by the ~ of** al lado de; **~ by ~** juntos(-as); **from ~ to ~** de un lado para otro; **from all sides** de todos lados; **to take sides (with)** tomar partido (con) ❑ **sideboard** n aparador m ❑ **sideboards** (BRIT) npl = **sideburns** ❑ **sideburns** npl patillas fpl ❑ **sidelight** n (AUT) luz f lateral ❑ **sideline** n (SPORT) línea de banda; (fig) empleo suplementario ❑ **side order** n plato de acompañamiento ❑ **side road** n (BRIT) calle f lateral ❑ **side street** n calle f lateral ❑ **sidetrack** vt (fig) desviar (de su propósito) ❑ **sidewalk** (US) n acera ❑ **sideways** adv de lado

siege [siːdʒ] n cerco, sitio

sieve [sɪv] n colador m, cribar

sift [sɪft] vt cribar; (fig: information) escudriñar

sigh [saɪ] n suspiro ♦ vi suspirar

sight [saɪt] n (faculty) vista; (spectacle) espectáculo; (on gun) mira, alza ♦ vt divisar; **in ~** a la vista; **out of ~** fuera de (la) vista; **on ~** (shoot) sin previo aviso ❑ **sightseeing** n excursionismo, turismo; **to go sightseeing** hacer turismo

sign [saɪn] n (with hand) señal f, seña; (trace) huella, rastro; (notice) letrero; (written) signo ♦ vt firmar; (SPORT) fichar; **to ~ sth over to sb** firmar el traspaso de algo a algn ► **sign for** vt fus (item) firmar el recibo de ► **sign in** vi firmar el registro (al entrar) ► **sign on** vi (BRIT: as unemployed) registrarse como desempleado; (for course) inscribirse ♦ vt (MIL) alistar; (employee)

signal contratar ▶ **sign up** vi (MIL) alistarse; (for course) inscribirse ♦ vt (player) fichar

signal ['sɪgnl] n señal f ♦ vi señalizar ♦ vt (person) hacer señas a; (message) comunicar por señales

signature ['sɪgnətʃəʳ] n firma

significance [sɪg'nɪfɪkəns] n (importance) trascendencia

significant [sɪg'nɪfɪkənt] adj significativo; (important) trascendente

signify ['sɪgnɪfaɪ] vt significar

sign language n lenguaje m para sordomudos

signpost ['saɪnpəust] n indicador m

Sikh [siːk] adj, n sij mf

silence ['saɪlns] n silencio ♦ vt acallar; (guns) reducir al silencio

silent ['saɪlnt] adj silencioso; (not speaking) callado; (film) mudo; **to remain ~** guardar silencio

silhouette [sɪluː'et] n silueta

silicon chip n ['sɪlɪkən-] n plaqueta de silicio

silk [sɪlk] n seda ♦ adj de seda

silly ['sɪlɪ] adj (person) tonto; (idea) absurdo

silver ['sɪlvəʳ] n plata; (money) moneda suelta ♦ adj de plata; (colour) plateado ❑ **silver-plated** adj plateado

similar ['sɪmɪləʳ] adj: **~ (to)** parecido or semejante (a) ❑ **similarity** [-'lærɪtɪ] n semejanza ❑ **similarly** adv del mismo modo

simmer ['sɪməʳ] vi hervir a fuego lento

simple ['sɪmpl] adj (easy) sencillo; (foolish, COMM: interest) simple ❑ **simplicity** [-'plɪsɪtɪ] n sencillez f ❑ **simplify** ['sɪmplɪfaɪ] vt simplificar ❑ **simply** adv (live, talk) sencillamente; (just, merely) sólo

simulate ['sɪmjuːleɪt] vt fingir, simular

simultaneous [sɪməl'teɪnɪəs] adj simultáneo ❑ **simultaneously** adv simultáneamente

sin [sɪn] n pecado ♦ vi pecar

since [sɪns] adv desde entonces, después ♦ prep desde ♦ conj (time) desde que; (because) ya que, puesto que; **~ then, ever ~** desde entonces

sincere [sɪn'sɪəʳ] adj sincero ❑ **sincerely** adv: **yours sincerely** (in letters) le saluda atentamente

sing [sɪŋ] (pt **sang**, pp **sung**) vt, vi cantar

Singapore [sɪŋə'pɔː'] n Singapur m

singer ['sɪŋəʳ] n cantante mf

singing ['sɪŋɪŋ] n canto

single ['sɪŋgl] adj único, solo; (unmarried) soltero; (not double) simple, sencillo ♦ n (BRIT: also: **~ ticket**) billete m sencillo; (record) sencillo, single m; **singles** npl (TENNIS) individual m ▶ **single out** vt (choose) escoger ❑ **single bed** n cama individual ❑ **single file** n: **in single file** en fila de uno ❑ **single-handed** adv sin ayuda ❑ **single-minded** adj resuelto, firme ❑ **single parent** n padre m soltero, madre f soltera (o divorciado etc); **single parent family** familia monoparental ❑ **single room** n cuarto individual

singular ['sɪŋgjuləʳ] adj (odd) raro, extraño; (outstanding) excepcional ♦ n (LING) singular m

sinister ['sɪnɪstəʳ] adj siniestro

sink [sɪŋk] (pt **sank**, pp **sunk**) n fregadero ♦ vt (ship) hundir, echar a pique; (foundations) excavar ♦ vi hundirse; **to ~ sth into** hundir algo en ▶ **sink in** vi (fig) penetrar, calar

sinus ['saɪnəs] n (ANAT) seno

sip [sɪp] n sorbo ♦ vt sorber, beber a sorbitos

sir [səʳ] n señor m; **S~ John Smith** Sir John Smith; **yes ~**, sí, señor

siren ['saɪərn] n sirena

sirloin ['səːlɔɪn] n (also: **~ steak**) solomillo

sister ['sɪstəʳ] n hermana; (BRIT: nurse) enfermera jefe ❑ **sister-in-law** n cuñada

sit [sɪt] (pt, pp **sat**) vi sentarse; (be sitting) estar sentado; (assembly) reunirse; (for painter) posar ◆ vt (exam) presentarse a ▶ **sit back** vi (in seat) recostarse ▶ **sit down** vi sentarse ▶ **sit on** vt fus (jury, committee) ser miembro de, formar parte de ▶ **sit up** vi incorporarse; (not go to bed) velar

sitcom ['sɪtkɔm] n abbr (= situation comedy) comedia de situación

site [saɪt] n sitio; (also: **building ~**) solar m ◆ vt situar

sitting ['sɪtɪŋ] n (of assembly etc) sesión f; (in canteen) turno □ **sitting room** n sala de estar

situated ['sɪtjueɪtɪd] adj situado

situation [sɪtju'eɪʃən] n situación f; "**situations vacant**" (BRIT) "ofrecen trabajo"

six [sɪks] num seis □ **sixteen** num diez y seis, dieciséis □ **sixteenth** [sɪks'tiːnθ] adj decimosexto □ **sixth** [sɪksθ] num sexto □ **sixth form** n (BRIT) clase f de alumnos del sexto año (de 16 a 18 años de edad) □ **sixth-form college** n instituto m para alumnos de 16 a 18 años □ **sixtieth** [sɪkstɪθ] adj sexagésimo □ **sixty** num sesenta

size [saɪz] n tamaño; (extent) extensión f; (of clothing) talla; (of shoes) número □ **sizeable** adj importante, considerable

sizzle [sɪzl] vi crepitar

skate [skeɪt] n patín m; (fish: pl inv) raya ◆ vi patinar □ **skateboard** n monopatín m □ **skateboarding** n monopatín m □ **skater** n patinador(a) m/f □ **skating** n patinaje m □ **skating rink** n pista de patinaje

skeleton ['skelɪtn] n esqueleto; (TECH) armazón f; (outline) esquema m

skeptical ['skeptɪkl] (US) = **sceptical**

sketch [sketʃ] n (drawing) dibujo; (outline) esbozo, bosquejo; (THEATRE) sketch m ◆ vt dibujar; (plan etc: also: ~ **out**) esbozar

skewer ['skjuːə'] n broqueta

ski [skiː] n esquí m ◆ vi esquiar □ **ski boot** n bota de esquí

ski: skier n esquiador(a) m/f □ **skiing** n esquí m

skilful ['skɪlful] (US **skillful**) adj diestro, experto

ski lift n telesilla m, telesquí m

skill [skɪl] n destreza, pericia; técnica □ **skilled** adj hábil, diestro; (worker) cualificado

skim [skɪm] vt (milk) desnatar; (glide over) rozar, rasar ◆ vi: **to ~ through** (book) hojear □ **skimmed milk** (US **skim milk**) n leche f desnatada

skin [skɪn] n piel f; (complexion) cutis m ◆ vt (fruit etc) pelar; (animal) despellejar □ **skinhead** n cabeza m/f rapada, skin(head) m/f □ **skinny** adj flaco

skip [skɪp] n brinco, salto; (BRIT: container) contenedor m ◆ vi brincar; (with rope) saltar a la comba ◆ vt saltarse

ski: ski pass n forfait m (de esquí) □ **ski pole** n bastón m de esquiar

skipper ['skɪpə'] n (NAUT, SPORT) capitán m

skipping rope ['skɪpɪŋ-] (US **skip rope**) n comba

skirt [skəːt] n falda, pollera (SC) ◆ vt (go round) ladear

skirting board ['skəːtɪŋ-] (BRIT) n rodapié m

ski slope n pista de esquí

ski suit n traje m de esquiar

skull [skʌl] n calavera; (ANAT) cráneo

skunk [skʌŋk] n mofeta

sky [skaɪ] n cielo □ **skyscraper** n rascacielos m inv

slab [slæb] n (stone) bloque m; (flat) losa; (of cake) trozo

slack [slæk] adj (loose) flojo; (slow) de poca actividad; (careless) descuidado □ **slacks** npl pantalones mpl

slain [sleɪn] pp of **slay**

slam [slæm] vt (throw) arrojar (violentamente); (criticize) criticar duramente ♦ vi (door) cerrarse de golpe; **to ~ the door** dar un portazo

slander ['slɑːndə'] n calumnia, difamación f

slang [slæŋ] n argot m; (jargon) jerga

slant [slɑːnt] n sesgo, inclinación f; (fig) interpretación f

slap [slæp] n palmada; (in face) bofetada ♦ vt dar una palmada o bofetada a; (paint etc) to ~ sth on sth embadurnar algo con algo ♦ adv (directly) exactamente, directamente

slash [slæʃ] vt acuchillar; (fig: prices) fulminar

slate [sleɪt] n pizarra ♦ vt (fig: criticize) criticar duramente

slaughter ['slɔːtə'] n (of animals) matanza; (of people) carnicería ♦ vt matar □ **slaughterhouse** n matadero

Slav [slɑːv] adj eslavo

slave [sleɪv] n esclavo(-a) ♦ vi (also: ~ away) sudar tinta □ **slavery** n esclavitud f

slay [sleɪ] (pt slew, pp slain) vt matar

sleazy ['sliːzɪ] adj de mala fama

sled [sled] (US) = **sledge**

sledge [sledʒ] n trineo

sleek [sliːk] adj (shiny) lustroso; (car etc) elegante

sleep [sliːp] (pt, pp slept) n sueño ♦ vi dormir; **to go to ~** quedarse dormido ► **sleep in** vi (oversleep) quedarse dormido ► **sleep together** vi (have sex) acostarse juntos □ **sleeper** n (person) durmiente m; (BRIT RAIL: on track) traviesa; (: train) coche-cama m □ **sleeping bag** n saco de dormir □ **sleeping car** n coche-cama m □ **sleeping pill** n somnífero □ **sleepover** n: **we're having a sleepover at Jo's** nos vamos a quedar a dormir en casa de Jo □ **sleepwalk** vi

caminar dormido; (habitually) ser sonámbulo □ **sleepy** adj soñoliento; (place) soporífero

sleet [sliːt] n aguanieve f

sleeve [sliːv] n manga; (TECH) manguito; (of record) portada □ **sleeveless** adj sin mangas

sleigh [sleɪ] n trineo

slender ['slendə'] adj delgado; (means) escaso

slept [slept] pt, pp of **sleep**

slew [sluː] pt of **slay** ♦ vi (BRIT: veer) torcerse

slice [slaɪs] n (of meat) tajada; (of bread) rebanada; (of lemon) rodaja; (utensil) pala ♦ vt cortar (en tajos), rebanar

slick [slɪk] adj (skilful) hábil, diestro; (clever) astuto ♦ n (also: **oil ~**) marea negra

slide [slaɪd] (pt, pp slid) n (movement) descenso, desprendimiento; (in playground) tobogán m; (PHOT) diapositiva; (BRIT: also: **hair ~**) pasador m ♦ vt correr, deslizar ♦ vi (slip) resbalarse; (glide) deslizarse □ **sliding** adj (door) corredizo

slight [slaɪt] adj (slim) delgado; (frail) delicado; (pain etc) leve; (trivial) insignificante; (small) pequeño ♦ n desaire m ♦ vt (insult) ofender, desairar; **not in the slightest** en absoluto □ **slightly** adv ligeramente, un poco

slim [slɪm] adj (slim) delgado, esbelto; (fig: chance) remoto ♦ vi adelgazar □ **slimming** n adelgazamiento

slimy ['slaɪmɪ] adj cenagoso

sling [slɪŋ] (pt, pp slung) n (MED) cabestrillo; (weapon) honda ♦ vt tirar, arrojar

slip [slɪp] n (slide) resbalón m; (mistake) descuido; (underskirt) combinación f; (of paper) papelito ♦ vt (slide) deslizar ♦ vi deslizarse; (stumble) resbalar(se); (decline) decaer; (move smoothly): **to ~ into/out of** (room etc) introducirse en/

salirse con; **to give sb the ~** eludir a algn; **a ~ of the tongue** un lapsus; **to ~ sth on/off** ponerse/quitarse algo
▶ **slip up** vi (make mistake) equivocarse; meter la pata

slipper ['slɪpə'] n zapatilla, pantufla

slippery ['slɪpərɪ] adj resbaladizo

slip road (BRIT) n carretera de acceso

slit [slɪt] (pt, pp ~) n raja; (cut) corte m ♦ vt rajar; cortar

slog [slɒg] (BRIT) vi sudar tinta; **it was a ~** costó trabajo (hacerlo)

slogan ['sləugən] n eslogan m, lema m

slope [sləup] n (up) cuesta, pendiente f; (down) declive m; (side of mountain) falda, vertiente m ♦ vi: **to ~ down** estar en declive; **to ~ up** inclinarse
❑ **sloping** adj en pendiente; en declive; (writing) inclinado

sloppy ['slɒpɪ] adj (work) descuidado; (appearance) desaliñado

slot [slɒt] n ranura ♦ vt: **to ~ into** encajar en ❑ **slot machine** (BRIT: vending machine) distribuidor m automático; (for gambling) tragaperras f inv

Slovakia [sləu'vækɪə] n Eslovaquia

Slovene [sləu'vi:n] adj esloveno ♦ n esloveno(-a); (LING) esloveno

Slovenia [sləu'vi:nɪə] n Eslovenia
❑ **Slovenian** adj = **Slovene**

slow [sləu] adj lento; (not clever) lerdo; (watch): **to be ~** atrasar ♦ adv lentamente, despacio ♦ vt, vi retardar; **"~"** (road sign) "disminuir velocidad"
▶ **slow down** vi reducir la marcha
❑ **slowly** adv lentamente, despacio
❑ **slow motion** n: **in slow motion** a cámara lenta

slug [slʌg] n babosa; (bullet) posta
❑ **sluggish** adj lento; (person) perezoso

slum [slʌm] n casucha

slump [slʌmp] n (economic) depresión f ♦ vi hundirse; (prices) caer en picado

slung [slʌŋ] pt, pp of **sling**

slur [slə:'] n: **to cast a ~ on** insultar ♦ vt (speech) pronunciar mal

sly [slaɪ] adj astuto; (smile) taimado

smack [smæk] n bofetada ♦ vt dar con la mano a; (child, on face) abofetear ♦ vi: **to ~ of** saber a, oler a

small [smɔ:l] adj pequeño ❑ **small ads** (BRIT) npl anuncios mpl por palabras ❑ **small change** n suelto, cambio

smart [sma:t] adj elegante; (clever) listo, inteligente; (quick) rápido, vivo ♦ vi escocer, picar ❑ **smartcard** n tarjeta inteligente

smash [smæʃ] n (also: **~-up**) choque m; (MUS) exitazo ♦ vt (break) hacer pedazos; (car etc) estrellar; (SPORT: record) batir ♦ vi hacerse pedazos; (against wall etc) estrellarse
❑ **smashing** (inf) adj estupendo

smear [smɪə'] n mancha; (MED) frotis m inv ♦ vt untar ❑ **smear test** n (MED) citología, frotis m inv (cervical)

smell [smɛl] (pt, pp **smelt** or **smelled**) n olor m; (sense) olfato ♦ vt, vi oler
❑ **smelly** adj maloliente

smelt [smɛlt] pt, pp of **smell**

smile [smaɪl] n sonrisa ♦ vi sonreír

smirk [smə:k] n sonrisa falsa or afectada

smog [smɒg] n esmog m

smoke [sməuk] n humo ♦ vi fumar; (chimney) echar humo ♦ vt (cigarettes) fumar ❑ **smoke alarm** n detector m de humo, alarma contra incendios
❑ **smoked** adj (bacon, glass) ahumado ❑ **smoker** n fumador(a) m/f; (RAIL) coche m fumador ❑ **smoking** n: **"no smoking"** "prohibido fumar"
❑ **smoky** adj (room) lleno de humo; (taste) ahumado

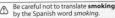 Be careful not to translate **smoking** by the Spanish word *smoking*.

smooth [smu:ð] adj liso; (sea) tranquilo; (flavour, movement) suave;

smother ['smʌðə'] vt sofocar; (repress) contener

SMS n abbr (= short message service) (servicio) SMS m ❑ **SMS message** n (mensaje m) SMS

smudge [smʌdʒ] n mancha ♦ vt manchar

smug [smʌg] adj presumido; orondo

smuggle ['smʌgl] vt pasar de contrabando ❑ **smuggling** n contrabando

snack [snæk] n bocado ❑ **snack bar** n cafetería

snag [snæg] n problema m

snail [sneil] n caracol m

snake [sneik] n serpiente f

snap [snæp] n (sound) chasquido; (photograph) foto f ♦ adj (decision) instantáneo ♦ vt (break) quebrar; (fingers) castañetear ♦ vi quebrarse; (fig: speak sharply) contestar bruscamente; **to ~ shut** cerrarse de golpe ▶ **snap at** vt fus (dog) intentar morder ▶ **snap up** vt agarrar ❑ **snapshot** n foto f (instantánea)

snarl [snɑːl] vi gruñir

snatch [snætʃ] n (small piece) fragmento ♦ vt (snatch away) arrebatar; (fig) agarrar; **to ~ some sleep** encontrar tiempo para dormir

sneak [sniːk] (US) (pt snuck) vi: **to ~ in/ out** entrar/salir a hurtadillas ♦ n (inf) soplón(-ona) m/f; **to ~ up on sb** aparecérsele de improviso a algn ❑ **sneakers** npl zapatos mpl de lona

sneer [snɪə'] vi reír con sarcasmo; (mock): **to ~** at burlarse de

sneeze [sniːz] vi estornudar

sniff [snif] vi sollozar ♦ vt husmear, oler; (drugs) esnifar

snigger ['snɪgə'] vi reírse con disimulo

snip [snip] n tijeretazo; (BRIT: inf: bargain) ganga ♦ vt tijeretear

sniper ['snaipə'] n francotirador(a) m/f

snob [snɔb] n (e)snob mf

snooker ['snuːkə'] n especie de billar

snoop [snuːp] vi: **to ~ about** fisgonear

snooze [snuːz] n siesta ♦ vi echar una siesta

snore [snɔː'] n ronquido ♦ vi roncar

snorkel ['snɔːkl] n (tubo) respirador m

snort [snɔːt] n bufido ♦ vi bufar

snow [snəu] n nieve f ♦ vi nevar ❑ **snowball** n bola de nieve ♦ vi (fig) agrandirse, ampliarse ❑ **snowstorm** n nevada, nevasca

snub [snʌb] vt (person) desairar ♦ n desaire m, repulsa

snug [snʌg] adj (cosy) cómodo; (fitted) ajustado

so

KEYWORD

[sau] adv

1 (thus, likewise) así, de este modo; **if so** de ser así; **I like swimming — so do I** a mí me gusta nadar — a mí también; **I've got work to do — so has Paul** tengo trabajo que hacer — Paul también; **it's 5 o'clock — so it is!** son las cinco — ¡pues es verdad!; **I hope/think so** espero/creo que sí; **so far** hasta ahora; (in past) hasta este momento

2 (in comparisons etc: to such a degree) tan; **so quickly (that)** tan rápido (que); **so big (that)** tan grande (que); **she's not so clever as her brother** no es tan lista como su hermano; **we were so worried** estábamos tan preocupados

3 **so much** adj, adv tanto; **so many** tantos(-as)

4 (phrases): **10 or so** unos 10, 10 o así; **so long!** (inf: goodbye) ¡hasta luego!

♦ conj

1 (expressing purpose): **so as to do**

para hacer; **so (that)** para que +*subjun*

2 (*expressing result*) así que; **so you see, I could have gone** así que ya ves, (yo) podría haber ido

soak [səuk] *vt* (*drench*) empapar; (*steep in water*) remojar; (*steep in water*) remojar, estar a remojo ▶ **soak up** *vt* absorber ❏ **soaking** *adj* (*also:* **soaking wet**) calado *or* empapado (hasta los huesos or el tuétano)

so-and-so ['səuənsəu] *n* (*somebody*) fulano(-a) de tal

soap [səup] *n* jabón *m* ❏ **soap opera** *n* telenovela ❏ **soap powder** *n* jabón *m* en polvo

soar [sɔːʳ] *vi* (*on wings*) remontarse; (*rocket: prices*) dispararse; (*building etc*) elevarse

sob [sɒb] *n* sollozo ♦ *vi* sollozar

sober ['səubəʳ] *adj* (*serious*) serio; (*not drunk*) sobrio; (*colour, style*) discreto ▶ **sober up** *vt* quitar la borrachera

so-called ['səuˈkɔːld] *adj* así llamado

soccer ['sɒkəʳ] *n* fútbol *m*

sociable ['səuʃəbl] *adj* sociable

social ['səuʃl] *adj* social ♦ *n* velada, fiesta ❏ **socialism** *n* socialismo ❏ **socialist** *adj*, *n* socialista *mf* ❏ **socialize** *vi*: **to socialize (with)** alternar (con) ❏ **social life** *n* vida social ❏ **socially** *adv* socialmente ❏ **social security** *n* seguridad *f* social ❏ **social services** *npl* servicios *mpl* sociales ❏ **social work** *n* asistencia social ❏ **social worker** *n* asistente(-a) *m/f* social

society [sə'saɪətɪ] *n* sociedad *f*; (*club*) asociación *f*; (*also:* **high ~**) alta sociedad

sociology [səusɪ'ɒlədʒɪ] *n* sociología

sock [sɒk] *n* calcetín *m*

socket ['sɒkɪt] *n* cavidad *f*; (*BRIT ELEC*) enchufe *m*

soda ['səudə] *n* (*CHEM*) sosa; (*also:* **~ water**) soda; (*US: also:* **~ pop**) gaseosa

sodium ['səudɪəm] *n* sodio

sofa ['səufə] *n* sofá *m* ❏ **sofa bed** *n* sofá-cama *m*

soft [sɒft] *adj* (*lenient, not hard*) blando; (*gentle, not bright*) suave ❏ **soft drink** *n* bebida no alcohólica ❏ **soft drugs** *npl* drogas *fpl* blandas ❏ **soften** ['sɒfn] *vt* ablandar; suavizar; (*effect*) amortiguar ♦ *vi* ablandarse; suavizarse ❏ **softly** *adv* suavemente; (*gently*) delicadamente, con delicadeza ❏ **software** *n* (*COMPUT*) software *m*

soggy ['sɒgɪ] *adj* empapado

soil [sɔɪl] *n* (*earth*) tierra, suelo ♦ *vt* ensuciar

solar ['səuləʳ] *adj* solar ❏ **solar power** *n* energía solar ❏ **solar system** *n* sistema *m* solar

sold [səuld] *pt, pp of* **sell**

soldier ['səuldʒəʳ] *n* soldado; (*army man*) militar *m*

sold out *adj* (*COMM*) agotado

sole [səul] *n* (*of foot*) planta; (*of shoe*) suela; (*fish: pl inv*) lenguado ♦ *adj* único ❏ **solely** *adv* únicamente, sólo, solamente; **I will hold you solely responsible** le consideraré el único responsable

solemn ['sɒləm] *adj* solemne

solicitor [sə'lɪsɪtəʳ] (*BRIT*) *n* (*for wills etc*) ≈ notario(-a); (*in court*) ≈ abogado(-a)

solid ['sɒlɪd] *adj* sólido; (*gold etc*) macizo ♦ *n* sólido

solitary ['sɒlɪtərɪ] *adj* solitario, solo

solitude ['sɒlɪtjuːd] *n* soledad *f*

solo ['səuləu] *n* solo ♦ *adv* (*fly*) en solitario ❏ **soloist** *n* solista *m/f*

soluble ['sɒljubl] *adj* soluble

solution [sə'luːʃən] *n* solución *f*

solve [sɒlv] *vt* resolver, solucionar

solvent ['sɒlvənt] *adj* (*COMM*) solvente ♦ *n* (*CHEM*) solvente *m*

sombre ['sɒmbəʳ] (*US* **somber**) *adj* sombrío

some

KEYWORD

[sʌm] *adj*

1 (*a certain amount or number*): **some tea/water/biscuits** té/agua/(unas) galletas; **there's some milk in the fridge** hay leche en el frigo; **there were some people outside** había algunas personas fuera; **I've got some money, but not much** tengo algo de dinero, pero no mucho

2 (*certain: in contrasts*) algunos(-as); **some people say that ...** hay quien dice que ...; **some films were excellent, but most were mediocre** hubo películas excelentes, pero la mayoría fueron mediocres

3 (*unspecified*): **some woman was asking for you** una mujer estuvo preguntando por ti; **he was asking for some book (or other)** pedía un libro; **some day** algún día; **some day next week** un día de la semana que viene

♦ *pron*

1 (*a certain number*): **I've got some** (*books etc*) tengo algunos(-as)

2 (*a certain amount*): **I've got some** (*money, milk*) tengo algo; **could I have some of that cheese?** ¿me puede dar un poco de ese queso?; **I've read some of the book** he leído parte del libro

♦ *adv*: **some 10 people** unas 10 personas, una decena de personas

some: somebody ['sʌmbədɪ] *pron* = **someone** ❏ **somehow** *adv* de alguna manera; (*for some reason*) por una u otra razón ❏ **someone** *pron* alguien ❏ **someplace** (*US*) *adv* = **somewhere** ❏ **something** *pron* algo; **would you like something to**

eat/drink? ¿te gustaría cenar/tomar algo? ❏ **sometime** *adv* (*in future*) algún día, en algún momento; (*in past*): **sometime last month** durante el mes pasado ❏ **sometimes** *adv* a veces ❏ **somewhat** *adv* algo ❏ **somewhere** *adv* (*be*) en alguna parte; (*go*) a alguna parte; **somewhere else** (*be*) en otra parte; (*go*) a otra parte

son [sʌn] *n* hijo

song [sɒŋ] *n* canción *f*

son-in-law ['sʌnɪnlɔː] *n* yerno

soon [suːn] *adv* pronto, dentro de poco; **~ afterwards** poco después; *see also* **~ sooner** *adv* (*time*) antes, más temprano; (*preference: rather*): **I would sooner do that** preferiría hacer eso; **sooner or later** tarde o temprano

soothe [suːð] *vt* tranquilizar; (*pain*) aliviar

sophisticated [sə'fɪstɪkeɪtɪd] *adj* sofisticado

sophomore ['sɒfəmɔːʳ] (*US*) *n* estudiante *mf* de segundo año

soprano [sə'prɑːnəu] *n* soprano *f*

sorbet ['sɔːbeɪ] *n* sorbete *m*

sordid ['sɔːdɪd] *adj* (*place etc*) sórdido; (*motive etc*) mezquino

sore [sɔːʳ] *adj* (*painful*) doloroso, que duele ♦ *n* llaga

sorrow ['sɒrəu] *n* pena, dolor *m*

sorry ['sɒrɪ] *adj* (*regretful*) arrepentido; (*condition, excuse*) lastimoso; **~!** ¡perdón!, ¡perdone!; **~?** ¿cómo?; **to feel ~ for sb** tener lástima a algn; **I feel ~ for him** me da lástima

sort [sɔːt] *n* clase *f*, género, tipo ▶ **sort out** *vt +adv* (*papers*) clasificar; (*organize*) ordenar, organizar; (*resolve: problem, situation etc*) arreglar, solucionar

SOS *n* SOS *m*

so-so ['səusəu] *adv* regular, así así

sought [sɔːt] *pt, pp of* **seek**

soul [səul] *n* alma

sound [saund] n (noise) sonido, ruido; (volume: on TV etc) volumen m; (GEO) estrecho ♦ adj (healthy) sano; (safe, not damaged) en buen estado; (reliable: person) digno de confianza; (sensible) sensato, razonable; (secure: investment) seguro ♦ adv: **~ asleep** profundamente dormido ♦ vt (alarm) sonar ♦ vi sonar, resonar; (fig: seem) parecer; **to ~ like** sonar a
❑ **soundtrack** n (of film) banda sonora

soup [su:p] n (thick) sopa; (thin) caldo

sour ['sauə'] adj agrio; (milk) cortado; **it's ~ grapes** (fig) están verdes

source [sɔ:s] n fuente f

south [sauθ] n sur m ♦ adj del sur, sureño ♦ adv al sur, hacia el sur
❑ **South Africa** n África del Sur
❑ **South African** adj, n sudafricano(-a) m/f ❑ **South America** n América del Sur, Sudamérica ❑ **South American** adj, n sudamericano(-a) m/f
❑ **southbound** adj (con) rumbo al sur
❑ **southeastern** [sauθi:'stən] n sureste, del sureste ❑ **southern** ['sʌðən] adj del sur, meridional
❑ **South Korea** n Corea del Sur
❑ **South Pole** n Polo Sur
❑ **southward(s)** adv hacia el sur
❑ **south-west** n suroeste m
❑ **southwestern** [sauθ'westən] adj suroeste

souvenir [su:və'nɪə'] n recuerdo

sovereign ['sɔvrɪn] adj, n soberano(-a) m/f

sow[1] [sau] (pt **sowed**, pp **sown**) vt sembrar

sow[2] [sau] n cerda, puerca

soya ['sɔɪə] (BRIT) n soja

spa [spɑ:] n balneario

space [speɪs] n (gen; room) sitio ♦ cpd espacial ♦ vt (also: **~ out**) espaciar ❑ **spacecraft** n nave f espacial ❑ **spaceship** n = **spacecraft**

spacious ['speɪʃəs] adj amplio

spade [speɪd] n (tool) pala, laya; **spades** npl (CARDS: British) picas fpl; (: Spanish) espadas fpl

spaghetti [spə'ɡetɪ] n espaguetis mpl, fideos mpl

Spain [speɪn] n España

spam [spæm] n (junk e-mail) spam m

span [spæn] n (of bird, plane) envergadura; (of arch) luz f; (in time) lapso ♦ vt extenderse sobre, cruzar; (fig) abarcar

Spaniard ['spænjəd] n español(a) m/f

Spanish ['spænɪʃ] adj español(a) ♦ n (LING) español m, castellano; **the ~** npl los españoles

spank [spæŋk] vt zurrar

spanner ['spænə'] (BRIT) n llave f (inglesa)

spare [speə'] adj de reserva; (surplus) sobrante, de más ♦ n = **spare part** ♦ vt (do without) pasarse sin; (refrain from hurting) perdonar; **to ~** (surplus) sobrante, de sobra ❑ **spare part** n pieza de repuesto ❑ **spare room** n cuarto de los invitados ❑ **spare time** n tiempo libre ❑ **spare tyre** (US **spare tire**) n (AUT) neumático (LAm) llanta (LAm) de recambio ❑ **spare wheel** n (AUT) rueda de recambio

spark [spɑ:k] n chispa; (fig) chispazo ❑ **spark(ing) plug** n bujía

sparkle ['spɑ:kl] n centelleo, destello ♦ vi (shine) relucir, brillar

sparrow ['spærəu] n gorrión m

sparse [spɑ:s] adj esparcido, escaso

spasm ['spæzəm] n (MED) espasmo

spat [spæt] pt, pp of **spit**

spate [speɪt] n (fig): **a ~ of** un torrente de

spatula ['spætjulə] n espátula

speak [spi:k] (pt **spoke**, pp **spoken**) vt (language) hablar; (truth) decir ♦ vi hablar; (make a speech) intervenir; **to ~ to sb/of or about sth** hablar con algn/ de or sobre algo; **~ up!** ¡habla fuerte! ❑ **speaker** n (in public) orador(a) m/f (also: **loudspeaker**) altavoz m; (for stereo etc) bafle m; (POL): **the Speaker** (BRIT) el Presidente de la Cámara de los Comunes; (US) el Presidente del Congreso

spear [spɪə'] n lanza ♦ vt alancear

special ['speʃl] adj especial; (edition etc) extraordinario; (delivery) urgente ❑ **special delivery** n (POST): **by special delivery** por entrega urgente ❑ **special effects** npl (CINE) efectos mpl especiales ❑ **specialist** n especialista mf ❑ **speciality** [speʃɪ'ælɪtɪ] (BRIT) n especialidad f ❑ **specialize** vi: **to specialize (in)** especializarse (en) ❑ **specially** adv sobre todo, en particular ❑ **special needs** npl (BRIT): **children with special needs** niños que requieren una atención diferenciada ❑ **special offer** n (COMM) oferta especial ❑ **special school** n (BRIT) colegio m de educación especial ❑ **specialty** (US) n = **speciality**

species ['spi:ʃi:z] n inv especie f

specific [spə'sɪfɪk] adj específico ❑ **specifically** adv específicamente

specify ['spesɪfaɪ] vt, vi especificar, precisar

specimen ['spesɪmən] n ejemplar m; (MED: of urine) espécimen m; (: of blood) muestra

speck [spek] n grano, mota

spectacle ['spektəkl] n espectáculo; **spectacles** npl (BRIT: glasses) gafas fpl (SP), anteojos mpl ❑ **spectacular** [-'tækjulə'] adj espectacular; (success) impresionante

spectator [spek'teɪtə'] n espectador(a) m/f

spectrum ['spektrəm] (pl **spectra**) n espectro

speculate ['spekjuleɪt] vi: **to ~ (on)** especular (en)

sped [sped] pt, pp of **speed**

speech [spi:tʃ] n (faculty) habla; (formal talk) discurso; (spoken language)

lenguaje m ❑ **speechless** adj mudo, estupefacto

speed [spi:d] n velocidad f; (haste) prisa; (promptness) rapidez f; **at full** or **top ~** a máxima velocidad ▸ **speed up** vi acelerarse ♦ vt acelerar ❑ **speedboat** n lancha motora ❑ **speeding** n (AUT) exceso m de velocidad ❑ **speed limit** n límite m de velocidad, velocidad f máxima ❑ **speedometer** [spɪ'dɒmɪtə'] n velocímetro ❑ **speedy** adj (fast) veloz, rápido; (prompt) pronto

spell [spel] (pt, pp **spelt** (BRIT) or **spelled**) n (also: **magic ~**) encanto, hechizo; (period of time) rato, período ♦ vt deletrear; (fig) anunciar, presagiar; **to cast a ~ on sb** hechizar a algn; **he can't ~** pone faltas de ortografía ▸ **spell out** vt (explain): **to spell sth out for sb** explicar algo a algn en detalle ❑ **spellchecker** ['speltʃekə'] n corrector m ortográfico ❑ **spelling** n ortografía

spelt [spelt] pt, pp of **spell**

spend [spend] (pt, pp **spent**) vt (money) gastar; (time) pasar; (life) dedicar ❑ **spending** n: **government spending** gastos mpl del gobierno

spent [spent] pt, pp of **spend** ♦ adj (cartridge, bullets, match) usado

sperm [spə:m] n esperma

sphere [sfɪə'] n esfera

spice [spaɪs] n especia ♦ vt condimentar

spicy ['spaɪsɪ] adj picante

spider ['spaɪdə'] n araña

spike [spaɪk] n (point) punta; (BOT) espiga

spill [spɪl] (pt, pp **spilt** or **spilled**) vt derramar, verter ♦ vi derramarse; **to ~ over** desbordarse

spin [spɪn] (pt, pp **spun**) n (AVIAT) barrena; (trip in car) paseo (en coche); (on ball) efecto ♦ vt (wool etc) hilar; (ball etc) hacer girar ♦ vi girar, dar vueltas

spinach ['spinitʃ] n espinaca; (as food) espinacas fpl

spinal ['spaɪnl] adj espinal

spin doctor n informador(a) parcial al servicio de un partido político etc

spin-dryer (BRIT) n secador m centrífugo

spine [spaɪn] n espinazo, columna vertebral; (thorn) espina

spiral ['spaɪərl] n espiral f ♦ vi (fig: prices) subir desorbitadamente

spire [spaɪəʳ] n aguja, chapitel m

spirit ['spɪrɪt] n (soul) alma; (ghost) fantasma m; (attitude, sense) espíritu m; (courage) valor m, ánimo; **spirits** npl (drink) licor(es) m(pl); **in good spirits** alegre, de buen ánimo

spiritual ['spɪrɪtjuəl] adj espiritual ♦ n espiritual m

spit [spɪt] (pt, pp spat) n (for roasting) asador m, espetón m; (saliva) saliva ♦ vi escupir; (sound) chisporrotear; (rain) lloviznar

spite [spaɪt] n rencor m, ojeriza ♦ vt causar pena a, mortificar; **in ~ of** a pesar de, pese a □ **spiteful** adj rencoroso, malévolo

splash [splæʃ] n (sound) chapoteo; (of colour) mancha ♦ vt salpicar ♦ vi (also: ~ about) chapotear ▶ **splash out** (inf) vi (BRIT) derrochar dinero

splendid ['splendid] adj espléndido

splinter ['splɪntəʳ] n (of wood etc) astilla, (in finger) espigón m ♦ vi astillarse, hacer astillas

split [splɪt] (pt, pp ~) n hendedura, raja; (fig) división f; (POL) escisión f ♦ vt partir, rajar; (party) dividir; (share) repartir ♦ vi dividirse, escindirse ▶ **split up** vi (couple) separarse; (meeting) acabarse

spoil [spɔɪl] (pt, pp spoilt or spoiled) vt (damage) dañar; (mar) estropear; (child) mimar, consentir

spoilt [spɔɪlt] pt, pp of **spoil** ♦ adj (child) mimado, consentido; (ballot paper) invalidado

spoke [spəʊk] pt of **speak** ♦ n rayo, radio

spoken ['spəʊkn] pp of **speak**

spokesman ['spəʊksmən] (irreg) n portavoz m

spokesperson ['spəʊkspɜːsn] (irreg) n portavoz m/f, vocero(-a) (LAm)

spokeswoman ['spəʊkswʊmən] (irreg) n portavoz f

sponge [spʌndʒ] n esponja; (also: ~ cake) bizcocho ♦ vt (wash) lavar con esponja ♦ vi: **to ~ off** or **on sb** vivir a costa de algn □ **sponge bag** (BRIT) n esponjera

sponsor ['spɒnsəʳ] n patrocinador(a) m/f ♦ vt (applicant, proposal etc) proponer □ **sponsorship** n patrocinio

spontaneous [spɒn'teɪnɪəs] adj espontáneo

spooky ['spuːkɪ] (inf) adj espeluznante, horripilante

spoon [spuːn] n cuchara □ **spoonful** n cucharada

sport [spɔːt] n deporte m; (person): **to be a good ~** ser muy majo ♦ vt (wear) lucir, ostentar □ **sport jacket** (US) n = **sports jacket** □ **sports car** n coche m deportivo □ **sports centre** (BRIT) n polideportivo □ **sports jacket** (BRIT) n chaqueta deportiva □ **sportsman** (irreg) n deportista m □ **sportswear** n trajes mpl de deporte or sport □ **sportswoman** (irreg) n deportista f □ **sporty** adj deportista

spot [spɒt] n sitio, lugar m; (dot: on pattern) punto, mancha; (pimple) grano; (RADIO) cuña publicitaria; (TV) espacio publicitario; (small amount): **a ~ of** un poquito de ♦ vt (notice) notar, observar; **on the ~** allí mismo □ **spotless** adj perfectamente limpio □ **spotlight** n foco, reflector m; (AUT) faro auxiliar

spouse [spauz] n cónyuge mf

sprain [spreɪn] n torcedura ♦ vt: **to ~ one's ankle/wrist** torcerse el tobillo/la muñeca

sprang [spræŋ] pt of **spring**

sprawl [sprɔ:l] vi tumbarse

spray [spreɪ] n rociada; (of sea) espuma; (container) atomizador m; (for paint etc) pistola rociadora; (of flowers) ramita ♦ vt rociar; (crops) regar

spread [spred] (pt, pp ~) n extensión f; (for bread etc) pasta para untar; (inf: food) comilona ♦ vt extender; (butter) untar; (wings, sails) desplegar; (work, wealth) repartir; (scatter) esparcir ♦ vi (also: ~ out: stain) extenderse; (news) diseminarse ▸ **spread out** vi (move apart) separarse ❏ **spreadsheet** n hoja electrónica o de cálculo

spree [spri:] n: **to go on a ~** ir de juerga

spring [sprɪŋ] (pt **sprang**, pp **sprung**) n (season) primavera; (leap) salto, brinco; (coiled metal) resorte m; (of water) fuente f, manantial m ♦ vi saltar, brincar ▸ **spring up** vi (thing: appear) aparecer; (problem) surgir ❏ **spring onion** n cebolleta

sprinkle ['sprɪŋkl] vt (pour: liquid) rociar; (: salt, sugar) espolvorear; **to ~ water etc on, ~ with water etc** rociar o salpicar de agua etc

sprint [sprɪnt] n esprint m ♦ vi esprintar

sprung [sprʌŋ] pp of **spring**

spun [spʌn] pt, pp of **spin**

spur [spə:'] n espuela; (fig) estímulo, aguijón m ♦ vt (also: ~ **on**) estimular, incitar; **on the ~ of the moment** de improviso

spurt [spə:t] n chorro; (of energy) arrebato ♦ vi chorrear

spy [spaɪ] n espía mf ♦ vi: **to ~ on** espiar a ♦ vt (see) divisar, lograr ver

sq. abbr = **square**

squabble ['skwɔbl] vi reñir, pelear

squad [skwɔd] n (MIL) pelotón m; (POLICE) brigada; (SPORT) equipo

squadron ['skwɔdrən] n (MIL) escuadrón m; (AVIAT, NAUT) escuadra

squander ['skwɔndə'] vt (money) derrochar, despilfarrar; (chances) desperdiciar

square [skweə'] n cuadro; (in town) plaza; (inf: person) carca mf ♦ adj cuadrado; (inf: ideas, tastes) trasnochado ♦ vt (arrange) arreglar; (reconcile) compaginar; **all** = igual(es); **to have a ~ meal** comer caliente; **2 metres ~** 2 metros en cuadro; **2 ~ metres** 2 metros cuadrados ❏ **square root** n raíz f cuadrada

squash [skwɔʃ] n (BRIT: drink): **lemon/orange ~** zumo (SP) or jugo (LAm) de limón/naranja; (US BOT) calabacín m; (SPORT) squash m ♦ vt aplastar

squat [skwɔt] adj achaparrado ♦ vi (also: ~ **down**) agacharse, sentarse en cuclillas ❏ **squatter** n okupa mf (SP)

squeak [skwi:k] vi (hinge) chirriar, rechinar; (mouse) chillar

squeal [skwi:l] vi chillar, dar gritos agudos

squeeze [skwi:z] n presión f; (of hand) apretón m; (COMM) restricción f ♦ vt (hand, arm) apretar

squid [skwɪd] n inv calamar m; (CULIN) calamares mpl

squint [skwɪnt] vi bizquear, ser bizco ♦ n (MED) estrabismo

squirm [skwə:m] vi retorcerse, revolverse

squirrel ['skwɪrəl] n ardilla

squirt [skwə:t] vi salir a chorros ♦ vt chiscar

Sr abbr = **senior**

Sri Lanka [srɪˈlæŋkə] n Sri Lanka m

St abbr = **saint**; **street**

stab [stæb] n (with knife) puñalada, (of pain) pinchazo; (inf: try): **to have a ~ at (doing) sth** intentar (hacer) algo ♦ vt apuñalar

stability [stə'bɪlɪtɪ] n estabilidad f

stable ['steɪbl] adj estable ♦ n cuadra, caballeriza

stack [stæk] n montón m, pila ♦ vt amontonar, apilar

stadium ['steɪdɪəm] n estadio

staff [stɑːf] n (work force) personal m, plantilla; (BRIT SCOL) cuerpo docente ♦ vt proveer de personal

stag [stæg] n ciervo, venado

stage [steɪdʒ] n escena; (point) etapa; (platform) plataforma; (profession): **the ~** el teatro ♦ vt (play) poner en escena, representar; (organize) montar, organizar; **in stages** por etapas

stagger ['stægə] vi tambalearse ♦ vt (amaze) asombrar; (hours, holidays) escalonar ❏ **staggering** adj asombroso

stagnant ['stægnənt] adj estancado

stag night, stag party n despedida de soltero

stain [steɪn] n mancha; (colouring) tintura ♦ vt manchar; (wood) teñir ❏ **stained glass** n vidrio m de color ❏ **stainless steel** n acero inoxidable

staircase ['steəkeɪs] n = **stairway**

stairs [steəz] npl escaleras fpl

stairway ['steəweɪ] n escalera

stake [steɪk] n estaca, poste m; (COMM) interés m; (BETTING) apuesta ♦ vt (money) apostar; (life) arriesgar; (reputation) poner en juego; (claim) presentar una reclamación; **to be at ~** estar en juego

stale [steɪl] adj (bread) duro; (food) pasado; (smell) rancio; (beer) agrio

stalk [stɔːk] n tallo, caña ♦ vt acechar, cazar al acecho

stall [stɔːl] n (in market) puesto; (in stable) casilla (de establo) ♦ vt (AUT) calar; (fig) dar largas a ♦ vi (AUT) calarse; (fig) andarse con rodeos

stamina ['stæmɪnə] n resistencia

stammer ['stæmə] n tartamudeo ♦ vi tartamudear

stamp [stæmp] n sello (SP), estampilla (LAm), timbre m (MEX); (mark) marca, huella; (also: ~ **one's foot**) patear ♦ vt (mark) marcar; (letter) franquear; (with rubber stamp) sellar ► **stamp out** vt (fire) apagar con el pie; (crime, opposition) acabar con ❏ **stamped addressed envelope** n (BRIT) sobre m sellado con las señas propias

stampede [stæm'piːd] n estampida

stance [stæns] n postura

stand [stænd] (pt, pp stood) n (position) posición f, postura; (for taxis) parada; (hall stand) perchero; (music stand) atril m; (SPORT) tribuna; (at exhibition) stand m ♦ vi (be) estar, encontrarse; (be on foot) estar de pie; (rise) levantarse; (remain) quedar en pie; (in election) presentar candidatura ♦ vt (place) poner, colocar; (withstand) aguantar, soportar; (invite to) invitar; **to make a ~** (fig) mantener una postura firme; **to ~ for parliament** (BRIT) presentarse (como candidato) a las elecciones ► **stand back** vi retirarse ► **stand by** vi (be ready) estar listo ♦ vt fus (opinion) aferrarse a; (person) apoyar ► **stand down** vi (withdraw) ceder el puesto ► **stand for** vt fus (signify) significar; (tolerate) aguantar, permitir ► **stand in for** vt fus suplir a ► **stand out** vi destacarse ► **stand up** vi levantarse, ponerse de pie ► **stand up for** vt fus defender ► **stand up to** vt fus hacer frente a

standard ['stændəd] n patrón m, norma; (level) nivel m; (flag) estandarte m ♦ adj (size etc) normal, corriente; (text) básico; **standards** npl (morals) valores mpl morales ❏ **standard of living** n nivel m de vida

standing ['stændɪŋ] adj (on foot) de pie, en pie; (permanent) permanente ♦ n reputación f; **of many years' ~** que lleva muchos años ❏ **standing order**

stand (BRIT) n (at bank) orden f de pago permanente

stand: standpoint n punto de vista ❏ **standstill** n: **at a standstill** (industry, traffic) paralizado; (car) parado; **to come to a standstill** quedar paralizado; pararse

stank [stæŋk] pt of **stink**

staple [ˈsteɪpl] n (for papers) grapa ◆ adj (food etc) básico ◆ vt grapar

star [stɑː] n estrella; (celebrity) estrella, astro ◆ vt (THEATRE, CINEMA) ser el/la protagonista de; **the stars** npl (ASTROLOGY) el horóscopo

starboard [ˈstɑːbəd] n estribor m

starch [stɑːtʃ] n almidón m

stardom [ˈstɑːdəm] n estrellato m

stare [steə] n mirada fija ◆ vi: **to ~ at** mirar fijo

stark [stɑːk] adj (bleak) severo, escueto ◆ adv: **~ naked** en cueros

start [stɑːt] n principio, comienzo; (departure) salida; (sudden movement) salto, sobresalto; (advantage) ventaja ◆ vt empezar, comenzar; (cause) causar; (found) fundar; (engine) poner en marcha ◆ vi comenzar, empezar; (with fright) asustarse, sobresaltarse; (train etc) salir; **to ~ doing or to do sth** empezar a hacer algo ▶ **start off** vi empezar, comenzar; (leave) salir, ponerse en camino ▶ **start out** vi (begin) empezar; (set out) partir, salir ▶ **start up** vi comenzar; (car) ponerse en marcha ◆ vt comenzar; poner en marcha ❏ **starter** n (AUT) botón m de arranque; (SPORT: official) juez mf de salida; (BRIT CULIN) entrante m ❏ **starting point** n punto de partida

startle [ˈstɑːtl] vt asustar, sobrecoger ❏ **startling** adj alarmante

starvation [stɑːˈveɪʃən] n hambre f

starve [stɑːv] vi tener mucha hambre; (to death) morir de hambre ◆ vt hacer pasar hambre

state [steɪt] n estado ◆ vt (say, declare) afirmar; **the States** los Estados Unidos; **to be in a ~** estar agitado ❏ **statement** n afirmación f ❏ **state school** n escuela or colegio estatal ❏ **statesman** (irreg) n estadista m

static [ˈstætɪk] n (RADIO) parásitos mpl ◆ adj estático

station [ˈsteɪʃən] n estación f; (RADIO) emisora; (rank) posición f social ◆ vt colocar, situar; (MIL) apostar

stationary [ˈsteɪʃnərɪ] adj estacionario, fijo

stationer's (shop) (BRIT) n papelería

stationery [-nərɪ] n papel m de escribir, artículos mpl de escritorio

station wagon (US) n ranchera

statistic [stəˈtɪstɪk] n estadística ❏ **statistics** n (science) estadística

statue [ˈstætjuː] n estatua

stature [ˈstætʃə] n estatura; (fig) talla

status [ˈsteɪtəs] n estado; (reputation) estatus m ❏ **status quo** n (e)statu quo m

statutory [ˈstætjutrɪ] adj estatutario

staunch [stɔːntʃ] adj leal, incondicional

stay [steɪ] n estancia ◆ vi quedar(se); (as guest) hospedarse; **to ~ put** seguir en el mismo sitio; **to ~ the night/5 days** pasar la noche/estar 5 días ▶ **stay away** vi (from person, building) no acercarse; (from event) no acudir ▶ **stay behind** vi quedar atrás ▶ **stay in** vi quedarse en casa ▶ **stay on** vi quedarse ▶ **stay out** vi (of house) no volver a casa; (on strike) permanecer en huelga ▶ **stay up** vi (at night) velar, no acostarse

steadily [ˈstedɪlɪ] adv constantemente; (firmly) firmemente; (work, walk) sin parar; (gaze) fijamente

steady [ˈstedɪ] adj (firm) firme; (regular) regular; (person, character) sensato, juicioso; (boyfriend) formal; (look, voice) tranquilo ◆ vt (stabilize) estabilizar; (nerves) calmar

steak [steɪk] n filete m; (beef) bistec m

steal [stiːl] (pt **stole**, pp **stolen**) vt robar ♦ vi robar; (move secretly) andar a hurtadillas

steam [stiːm] n vapor m; (mist) vaho, humo ♦ vt (CULIN) cocer al vapor ♦ vi echar vapor ► **steam up** vi (window) empañarse; **to get steamed up about sth** (fig) ponerse negro por algo □ **steamy** adj (room) lleno de vapor; (window) empañado; (heat, atmosphere) bochornoso

steel [stiːl] n acero ♦ adj de acero

steep [stiːp] adj escarpado, abrupto; (stair) empinado; (price) exorbitante, excesivo ♦ vt empapar, remojar

steeple [stiːpl] n aguja

steer [stɪə*] vt (car) conducir (SP), manejar (LAm); (person) dirigir ♦ vi conducir, manejar □ **steering** n (AUT) dirección f □ **steering wheel** n volante m

stem [stem] n (of plant) tallo; (of glass) pie m ♦ vt detener; (blood) restañar

step [step] n paso; (on stair) peldaño, escalón m; **to ~ forward/back** dar un paso adelante/hacia atrás; **steps** npl (BRIT) = **stepladder**; **in/out of ~** (with) acorde/en disonancia (con) ► **step down** vi (fig) retirarse ► **step in** vi entrar; (fig) intervenir ► **step up** vt (increase) aumentar □ **stepbrother** n hermanastro □ **stepchild** (pl **stepchildren**) n hijastro(-a) m/f □ **stepdaughter** n hijastra □ **stepfather** n padrastro □ **stepladder** n escalera doble or de tijera □ **stepmother** n madrastra □ **stepsister** n hermanastra □ **stepson** n hijastro

stereo [ˈsterɪəʊ] n estéreo ♦ adj (also: **stereophonic**) estéreo, estereofónico

stereotype [ˈstɪərɪətaɪp] n estereotipo ♦ vt estereotipar

sterile [ˈsteraɪl] adj estéril □ **sterilize** [ˈsterɪlaɪz] vt esterilizar

sterling [ˈstɜːlɪŋ] adj (silver) de ley ♦ n (ECON) libras fpl esterlinas fpl; **one pound ~** una libra esterlina

stern [stɜːn] adj severo, austero ♦ n (NAUT) popa

steroid [ˈstɪərɔɪd] n esteroide m

stew [stjuː] n estofado, guiso ♦ vt estofar, guisar; (fruit) cocer

steward [ˈstjuːəd] n camarero □ **stewardess** n (esp on plane) azafata

stick [stɪk] (pt, pp **stuck**) n palo; (of dynamite) barreno; (as weapon) porra; (also: **walking ~**) bastón m ♦ vt (glue) pegar; (inf: put) meter; (: tolerate) aguantar, soportar; (thrust): **to ~ sth into** clavar or hincar algo en ♦ vi pegarse; (be unmoveable) quedarse parado; (in mind) quedarse grabado ► **stick out** vi sobresalir ► **stick up** vi sobresalir ► **stick up for** vt fus defender □ **sticker** n (label) etiqueta engomada; (with slogan) pegatina □ **sticking plaster** n esparadrapo □ **stick shift** (US) n (AUT) palanca de cambios

sticky [ˈstɪkɪ] adj pegajoso; (label) engomado; (fig) difícil

stiff [stɪf] adj rígido, tieso; (hard) duro; (manner) estirado; (difficult) difícil; (person) inflexible; (price) exorbitante ♦ adv: **scared/bored ~** muerto de miedo/aburrimiento

stifling [ˈstaɪflɪŋ] adj (heat) sofocante, bochornoso

stigma [ˈstɪɡmə] n (fig) estigma m

stiletto [stɪˈletəʊ] (BRIT) n (also: **~ heel**) tacón m de aguja

still [stɪl] adj inmóvil, quieto ♦ adv todavía; (even) aún; (nonetheless) sin embargo, aún así

stimulate [ˈstɪmjʊleɪt] vt estimular

stimulus [ˈstɪmjʊləs] (pl **stimuli**) n estímulo, incentivo

sting [stɪŋ] (pt, pp **stung**) n picadura; (pain) escozor m, picazón f; (organ) aguijón m ♦ vt, vi picar

stink [stɪŋk] (pt **stank**, pp **stunk**) n hedor m, tufo ♦ vi heder, apestar

stir [stə:ʳ] n (fig: agitation) conmoción f ♦ vt (tea etc) remover; (fig: emotions) provocar ♦ vi moverse ▸ **stir up** vt (trouble) fomentar ♦ **stir-fry** vt sofreír removiendo ♦ n plato preparado sofriendo y removiendo los ingredientes

stitch [stɪtʃ] n (SEWING) puntada; (KNITTING) punto; (MED) punto (de sutura); (pain) punzada ♦ vt coser; (MED) suturar

stock [stɔk] n (COMM: reserves) existencias fpl, stock m; (: selection) surtido; (AGR) ganado, ganadería; (CULIN) caldo; (descent) raza, estirpe f; (FINANCE) capital m ♦ adj (fig: reply etc) clásico ♦ vt (have in stock) tener existencias de; **stocks and shares** acciones y valores; **in ~** en existencia or almacén; **out of ~** agotado; **to take ~ of** (fig) asesorar, examinar ❑ **stockbroker** ['stɔkbrəukəʳ] n agente mf or corredor(a) m/f de bolsa ❑ **stock cube** (BRIT) n pastilla de caldo ❑ **stock exchange** n bolsa ❑ **stockholder** ['stɔkhəuldəʳ] (US) n accionista m/f

stocking ['stɔkɪŋ] n media

stock market n bolsa (de valores)

stole [stəul] pt of **steal** ♦ n estola

stolen ['stəuln] pp of **steal**

stomach ['stʌmək] n (ANAT) estómago; (belly) vientre m ♦ vt tragar, aguantar ❑ **stomachache** n dolor m de estómago

stone [stəun] n piedra; (in fruit) hueso (= 6.348 kg; 14 libras) ♦ adj de piedra ♦ vt apedrear; (fruit) deshuesar

stood [stud] pt, pp of **stand**

stool [stu:l] n taburete m

stoop [stu:p] vi (also: ~ **down**) doblarse, agacharse; (also: **have a ~**) ser cargado de espaldas

stop [stɔp] n parada; (in punctuation) punto ♦ vt parar, detener; (break) suspender; (block: pay) suspender; (:

cheque) invalidar; (also: **put a ~ to**) poner término a ♦ vi pararse, detenerse; (end) acabarse; **to ~ doing sth** dejar de hacer algo ▸ **stop by** vi pasar por ▸ **stop off** vi interrumpir el viaje ❑ **stoppage** (strike) paro; (blockage) obstrucción f

storage ['stɔ:rɪdʒ] n almacenaje m

store [stɔ:ʳ] n provisión f; (depot: BRIT: large shop) almacén m; (US) tienda; (reserve) reserva, repuesto ♦ vt almacenar; **stores** npl víveres mpl; **to be in ~ for sb** (fig) esperarle a algn ❑ **storekeeper** (US) n tendero(-a)

storey ['stɔ:rɪ] (US **story**) n piso

storm [stɔ:m] n tormenta; (fig: of applause) salva; (: of criticism) nube f ♦ vi (fig) rabiar ♦ vt tomar por asalto ❑ **stormy** adj tempestuoso

story ['stɔ:rɪ] n historia; (lie) mentira; (US) = **storey**

stout [staut] adj (strong) sólido; (fat) gordo, corpulento; (resolute) resuelto ♦ n cerveza negra

stove [stəuv] n (for cooking) cocina; (for heating) estufa

straight [streɪt] adj recto, derecho; (frank) franco, directo; (simple) sencillo ♦ adv derecho, directamente; (drink) sin mezcla; **to put** or **get sth ~** dejar algo en claro; **~ away, ~ off** en seguida ❑ **straighten** vt (also: **straighten out**) enderezar, poner derecho ♦ vi (also: **straighten up**) enderezarse, ponerse derecho ❑ **straightforward** adj (simple) sencillo; (honest) honrado, franco

strain [streɪn] n tensión f; (TECH) presión f; (MED) torcedura; (breed) tipo, variedad f ♦ vt (back etc) torcerse; (resources) agotar; (stretch) estirar; (food, tea) colar ❑ **strained** adj (muscle) torcido; (laugh) forzado; (relations) tenso ❑ **strainer** n colador m

strait [streɪt] n (GEO) estrecho; **straits** (fig): **to be in dire straits** estar en un gran apuro

strand [strænd] n (of thread) hebra; (of hair) trenza; (of rope) ramal m ❑ **stranded** adj: without money) desamparado; (: without transport) colgado

strange [streɪndʒ] adj (not known) desconocido; (odd) extraño, raro ❑ **strangely** adv de un modo raro; see also **enough** ❑ **stranger** n desconocido(-a); (from another area) forastero(-a)

⚠ Be careful not to translate **stranger** by the Spanish word extranjero.

strangle [ˈstræŋgl] vt estrangular

strap [stræp] n correa; (of slip, dress) tirante m

strategic [strəˈtiːdʒɪk] adj estratégico

strategy [ˈstrætɪdʒɪ] n estrategia

straw [strɔː] n paja; (drinking) caña, pajita; **that's the last ~!** ¡eso es el colmo!

strawberry [ˈstrɔːbərɪ] n fresa, frutilla (SC)

stray [streɪ] adj (animal) extraviado; (bullet) perdido; (scattered) disperso ♦ vi extraviarse, perderse

streak [striːk] n (in hair) raya ♦ vi: **to ~ past** pasar como un rayo

stream [striːm] n riachuelo, arroyo; (of people, vehicles) riada, caravana; (of smoke, insults etc) chorro ♦ vt (SCOL) dividir en grupos por habilidad ♦ vi correr, fluir; **to ~ in/out** (people) entrar/salir en tropel

street [striːt] n calle f ❑ **streetcar** (US) n tranvía m ❑ **street light** n farol m (LAm), farola (SP) ❑ **street map** n plano (de la ciudad) ❑ **street plan** n plano

strength [streŋθ] n fuerza; (of girder, knot etc) resistencia; (fig: power) poder m ❑ **strengthen** vt fortalecer, reforzar

strenuous [ˈstrenjuəs] adj (energetic, determined) enérgico

stress [stres] n presión f; (mental strain) estrés m; (accent) acento ♦ vt subrayar, recalcar; (syllable) acentuar ❑ **stressed** adj (tense) estresado, agobiado; (syllable) acentuado ❑ **stressful** adj (job) estresante

stretch [stretʃ] n (of sand etc) trecho ♦ vi estirarse; (extend): **to ~ to** or **as far as** extenderse hasta ♦ vt extender, estirar; (make demands) exigir el máximo esfuerzo a ▶ **stretch out** vi tenderse ♦ vt (arm etc) extender; (spread) estirar

stretcher [ˈstretʃəʳ] n camilla

strict [strɪkt] adj severo; (exact) estricto ❑ **strictly** adv severamente; estrictamente

stride [straɪd] (pt **strode**, pp **stridden**) n zancada, tranco ♦ vi dar zancadas, andar a trancos

strike [straɪk] (pt, pp **struck**) n huelga; (of oil etc) descubrimiento; (attack) ataque m ♦ vt golpear, pegar; (oil etc) descubrir; (bargain, deal) cerrar ♦ vi declarar la huelga; (attack) atacar; (clock) dar la hora; **on ~** (workers) en huelga; **to ~ a match** encender un fósforo ❑ **striker** n huelguista mf; (SPORT) delantero ❑ **striking** adj llamativo

string [strɪŋ] (pt, pp **strung**) n cuerda; (row) hilera ♦ vt: **to ~ together** ensartar; **to ~ out** extenderse; **the strings** npl (MUS) los instrumentos de cuerda; **to pull strings** (fig) mover palancas

strip [strɪp] n tira; (of land) franja; (of metal) cinta, lámina ♦ vt desnudar; (paint) quitar; (also: ~ **down**: machine) desmontar ♦ vi desnudarse ▶ **strip off** vt (paint etc) quitar ♦ vi (person) desnudarse

stripe [straɪp] n raya; (MIL) galón m ❑ **striped** adj a rayas, rayado

stripper ['strɪpəʳ] n artista mf de striptease

strip-search ['strɪpsə:tʃ] vt: **to ~ sb** desnudar y registrar a algn

strive [straɪv] (pt **strove**, pp **striven**) vi: **to ~ for sth/to do sth** luchar por conseguir/hacer algo

strode [strəud] pt of **stride**

stroke [strəuk] n (blow) golpe m; (SWIMMING) brazada f; (MED) apoplejía; (of paintbrush) toque m ♦ vt acariciar; **at a ~** de un solo golpe

stroll [strəul] n paseo, vuelta ♦ vi dar un paseo or una vuelta □ **stroller** (US) n (for child) sillita de ruedas

strong [strɔŋ] adj fuerte; **they are 50 ~** son 50 □ **stronghold** n fortaleza, (fig) baluarte m □ **strongly** adv fuertemente, con fuerza; (believe) firmemente

strove [strəuv] pt of **strive**

struck [strʌk] pt, pp of **strike**

structure ['strʌktʃəʳ] n estructura; (building) construcción f

struggle ['strʌgl] n lucha ♦ vi luchar

strung [strʌŋ] pt, pp of **string**

stub [stʌb] n (of ticket etc) talón m; (of cigarette) colilla; **to ~ one's toe on sth** dar con el dedo (del pie) contra algo ► **stub out** vt apagar

stubble ['stʌbl] n rastrojo; (on chin) barba (incipiente)

stubborn ['stʌbən] adj terco, testarudo

stuck [stʌk] pt, pp of **stick** ♦ adj (jammed) atascado

stud [stʌd] n (shirt stud) corchete m; (of boot) taco; (earring) pendiente m (de bolita); (also: ~ **farm**) caballeriza; (also: ~ **horse**) caballo semental ♦ vt (fig): **studded with** salpicado de

student ['stju:dənt] n estudiante mf ♦ adj estudiantil □ **student driver** (US) n conductor(a) mf en prácticas □ **students' union** n (building) centro de estudiantes; (BRIT: association) federación f de estudiantes

studio ['stju:diəu] n estudio; (artist's) taller m □ **studio flat** n estudio

study ['stʌdi] n estudio ♦ vt estudiar; (examine) examinar, investigar ♦ vi estudiar

stuff [stʌf] n materia; (substance) material m, sustancia; (things) cosas fpl ♦ vt llenar; (CULIN) rellenar; (animals) disecar; (inf: push) meter □ **stuffing** n relleno □ **stuffy** adj (room) mal ventilado; (person) de miras estrechas

stumble ['stʌmbl] vi tropezar, dar un traspié; **to ~ across, ~ on** (fig) tropezar con

stump [stʌmp] n (of tree) tocón m; (of limb) muñón m ♦ vt: **to be stumped for an answer** no saber qué contestar

stun [stʌn] vt dejar sin sentido

stung [stʌŋ] pt, pp of **sting**

stunk [stʌŋk] pp of **stink**

stunned [stʌnd] vi (dazed) aturdido, atontado; (amazed) pasmado; (shocked) anonadado

stunning ['stʌnɪŋ] adj (fig: news) pasmoso; (: outfit etc) sensacional

stunt [stʌnt] n (in film) escena peligrosa; (publicity stunt) truco publicitario

stupid ['stju:pɪd] adj estúpido, tonto □ **stupidity** [-'pɪdɪtɪ] n estupidez f

sturdy ['stə:dɪ] adj robusto, fuerte

stutter ['stʌtəʳ] n tartamudeo ♦ vi tartamudear

style [staɪl] n estilo; **stylish** adj elegante, a la moda □ **stylist** n (hair stylist) peluquero(-a)

sub... [sʌb] prefix sub... □ **subconscious** adj subconsciente

subdued [səb'dju:d] adj (light) tenue; (person) sumiso, manso

subject [n 'sʌbdʒɪkt, vb səb'dʒɛkt] n súbdito; (SCOL) asignatura; (matter) tema m; (GRAMMAR) sujeto ♦ vt: **to ~ sb to sth** someter a algn a algo; **to be ~ to** (law) estar sujeto a; (person) ser propenso a □ **subjective** [-'dʒɛktɪv]

subjunctive *adj* subjetivo ❏ **subject matter** (*content*) contenido

subjunctive [səbˈdʒʌŋktɪv] *adj, n* subjuntivo

submarine [sʌbməˈriːn] *n* submarino

submission [səbˈmɪʃən] *n* sumisión *f*

submit [səbˈmɪt] *vt* someter ♦ *vi*: **to ~ to sth** someterse a algo

subordinate [səˈbɔːdɪnət] *adj, n* subordinado(-a) *m/f*

subscribe [səbˈskraɪb] *vi* suscribir; **to ~ to** (*opinion, fund*) suscribir, aprobar; (*newspaper*) suscribirse a

subscription [səbˈskrɪpʃən] *n* abono; (*to magazine*) subscripción *f*

subsequent [ˈsʌbsɪkwənt] *adj* subsiguiente, posterior ❏ **subsequently** *adv* posteriormente, más tarde

subside [səbˈsaɪd] *vi* hundirse; (*flood*) bajar; (*wind*) amainar

subsidiary [səbˈsɪdɪərɪ] *adj* secundario ♦ *n* sucursal *f*, filial *f*

subsidize [ˈsʌbsɪdaɪz] *vt* subvencionar

subsidy [ˈsʌbsɪdɪ] *n* subvención *f*

substance [ˈsʌbstəns] *n* sustancia

substantial [səbˈstænʃl] *adj* sustancial, sustancioso; (*fig*) importante

substitute [ˈsʌbstɪtjuːt] *n* (*person*) suplente *mf*; (*thing*) sustituto ♦ *vt*: **to ~ A for B** sustituir A por B, reemplazar B por A ❏ **substitution** *n* sustitución *f*

subtle [ˈsʌtl] *adj* sutil

subtract [səbˈtrækt] *vt* restar, sustraer

suburb [ˈsʌbəːb] *n* barrio residencial; **the suburbs** las afueras (de la ciudad) ❏ **suburban** [səˈbəːbən] *adj* suburbano; (*train etc*) de cercanías

subway [ˈsʌbweɪ] *n* (*BRIT*) paso subterráneo or inferior; (*US*) metro

succeed [səkˈsiːd] *vi* (*person*) tener éxito; (*plan*) salir bien ♦ *vt* suceder a; **to ~ in doing** lograr hacer

success [səkˈses] *n* éxito *m*; **successful** *adj* exitoso, próspero; (*business*) próspero; **to be**

successful (in doing) lograr (hacer) ❏ **successfully** *adv* con éxito

⚠ Be careful not to translate **success** by the Spanish word éxito.

succession [səkˈseʃən] *n* sucesión *f*, serie *f*

successive [səkˈsesɪv] *adj* sucesivo, consecutivo

successor [səkˈsesə] *n* sucesor(a) *m/f*

succumb [səˈkʌm] *vi* sucumbir

such [sʌtʃ] *adj* tal, semejante; (*of that kind*): **~ a book** tal libro; (*so much*): **~ courage** tanto valor ♦ *adv* tan; **~ a long trip** un viaje tan largo; **~ a lot of** tanto(s)/a(s); **~ as** (*like*) tal como; **as ~** como tal ❏ **such-and-such** *adj* tal o cual

suck [sʌk] *vt* chupar; (*bottle*) sorber; (*breast*) mamar

Sudan [suˈdæn] *n* Sudán *m*

sudden [ˈsʌdn] *adj* (*rapid*) repentino, súbito; (*unexpected*) imprevisto; **all of a ~** de repente ❏ **suddenly** *adv* de repente

sue [suː] *vt* demandar

suede [sweɪd] *n* ante *m*, gamuza

suffer [ˈsʌfə] *vt* sufrir, padecer; (*tolerate*) aguantar, soportar ♦ *vi* sufrir; **to ~ from** (*illness etc*) padecer ❏ **suffering** *n* sufrimiento

suffice [səˈfaɪs] *vi* bastar, ser suficiente

sufficient [səˈfɪʃənt] *adj* suficiente, bastante

suffocate [ˈsʌfəkeɪt] *vi* ahogarse, asfixiarse

sugar [ˈʃʊgə] *n* azúcar *m* ♦ *vt* echar azúcar a, azucarar

suggest [səˈdʒest] *vt* sugerir ❏ **suggestion** [-ˈdʒestʃən] *n* sugerencia

suicide [ˈsuːɪsaɪd] *n* suicidio; (*person*) suicida *mf*; *see also* **commit**; **~ bombing** atentado suicida

suit [suːt] *n* (*man's*) traje *m*; (*woman's*) conjunto; (*LAW*) pleito; (*CARDS*) palo

suite [swiːt] n (of rooms, MUS) suite f; (furniture): **bedroom/dining room ~** (juego de) dormitorio/comedor; see also **three-piece suite**

sulfur ['sʌlfər] (US) n = **sulphur**

sulk [sʌlk] vi estar de mal humor

sulphur ['sʌlfər] (US n **sulfur**) n azufre m

sultana [sʌl'tɑːnə] n (fruit) pasa de Esmirna

sum [sʌm] n suma; (total) total m
▶ **sum up** vt resumir ♦ vi hacer un resumen

summarize ['sʌməraɪz] vt resumir

summary ['sʌmərɪ] n resumen m ♦ adj (justice) sumario

summer ['sʌmər] n verano ♦ cpd de verano; **in ~** en verano ❑ **summer holidays** npl vacaciones fpl de verano ❑ **summertime** n (season) verano

summit ['sʌmɪt] n cima, cumbre f; (also: **~ conference, ~ meeting**) (conferencia) cumbre f

summon ['sʌmən] vt (person) llamar; (meeting) convocar; (LAW) citar

Sun. abbr (= Sunday) dom

sun [sʌn] n sol m ❑ **sunbathe** vi tomar el sol ❑ **sunbed** n cama solar ❑ **sunblock** n filtro solar ❑ **sunburn** n (painful) quemadura; (tan) bronceado ❑ **sunburned, sunburnt** adj (painfully) quemado por el sol; (tanned) bronceado

Sunday ['sʌndɪ] n domingo

sunflower ['sʌnflaʊər] n girasol m

sung [sʌŋ] pp of **sing**

sunglasses ['sʌŋglɑːsɪz] npl gafas fpl (SP) or anteojos mpl (LAm) de sol

sunk [sʌŋk] pp of **sink**

sun: sunlight n luz f del sol ❑ **sun lounger** n tumbona, perezosa (LAm) ❑ **sunny** adj soleado; (day) de sol; (fig) alegre ❑ **sunrise** n salida del sol ❑ **sun roof** n (AUT) techo corredizo ❑ **sunscreen** n protector m solar ❑ **sunset** n puesta del sol ❑ **sunshade** n (over table) sombrilla ❑ **sunshine** n sol m ❑ **sunstroke** n insolación f ❑ **suntan** n bronceado ❑ **suntan lotion** n bronceador m ❑ **suntan oil** n aceite m bronceador

super ['suːpər] (inf) adj genial

superb [suː'pɜːb] adj magnífico, espléndido

superficial [suːpə'fɪʃəl] adj superficial

superintendent [suːpərɪn'tendənt] n director(a) m/f; (POLICE) subjefe(-a) m/f

superior [su'pɪərɪər] adj superior; (smug) desdeñoso ♦ n superior m

superlative [su'pɜːlətɪv] adj superlativo

supermarket ['suːpəmɑːkɪt] n supermercado

supernatural [suːpə'nætʃərəl] adj sobrenatural ♦ n: **the ~** lo sobrenatural

superpower ['suːpəpaʊər] n (POL) superpotencia

superstition [suːpə'stɪʃən] n superstición f

superstitious [suːpə'stɪʃəs] adj supersticioso

superstore ['suːpəstɔːr] n (BRIT) hipermercado

supervise ['suːpəvaɪz] vt supervisar ❑ **supervision** [-'vɪʒən] n supervisión f ❑ **supervisor** n supervisor(a) m/f

supper ['sʌpər] n cena

supple ['sʌpl] adj flexible

supplement [n 'sʌplɪmənt, vb sʌplɪ'ment] n suplemento ♦ vt suplir

supplier [sə'plaɪər] n (COMM) distribuidor(a) m/f

supply [sə'plaɪ] vt (provide) suministrar; (equip): **to ~ (with)** proveer (de) ♦ n provisión f; (of gas, water etc) suministro; **supplies** npl (food) víveres mpl; (MIL) pertrechos mpl

support [sə'pɔ:t] n apoyo; (TECH) soporte m ♦ vt apoyar; (financially) mantener; (uphold, TECH) sostener □ **supporter** n (POL etc) partidario(-a); (SPORT) aficionado(-a)

⚠ Be careful not to translate **support** by the Spanish word **soportar**.

suppose [sə'pəuz] vt suponer; (imagine) imaginarse; (duty): **to be supposed to do sth** deber hacer algo □ **supposedly** [sə'pəuzidli] adv según cabe suponer □ **supposing** conj en caso de que

suppress [sə'pres] vt suprimir; (yawn) ahogar

supreme [su'pri:m] adj supremo

surcharge ['sə:tʃɑ:dʒ] n sobretasa, recargo

sure [ʃuə] adj seguro; (definite, convinced) cierto; (to make (= of sth/that) asegurarse de algo/asegurar que; ~! (of course) ¡claro!, ¡por supuesto!; ~ **enough** efectivamente □ **surely** adv (certainly) seguramente

surf [sə:f] n olas fpl ♦ vt: **to ~ the Net** navegar por Internet

surface ['sə:fis] n superficie f ♦ vt (road) revestir ♦ vi salir a la superficie; **by ~ mail** por vía terrestre

surfboard ['sə:fbɔ:d] n tabla (de surf)

surfing ['sə:fiŋ] n surf m

surge [sə:dʒ] n oleada, oleaje m ♦ vi (wave) romper; (people) avanzar en tropel

surgeon ['sə:dʒən] n cirujano(-a)

surgery ['sə:dʒəri] n cirugía; (BRIT: room) consultorio

surname ['sə:neim] n apellido

surpass [sə:'pɑ:s] vt superar, exceder

surplus ['sə:pləs] n excedente m; (COMM) superávit m ♦ adj excedente, sobrante

surprise [sə'praiz] n sorpresa ♦ vt sorprender □ **surprised** adj (look, smile) de sorpresa; **to be surprised** sorprenderse □ **surprising** adj sorprendente □ **surprisingly** adv: **it was surprisingly easy** me etc sorprendió lo fácil que fue

surrender [sə'rendə*] n rendición f, entrega ♦ vi rendirse, entregarse

surround [sə'raund] vt rodear, circundar; (MIL etc) cercar □ **surrounding** adj circundante □ **surroundings** npl alrededores mpl, cercanías fpl

surveillance [sə:'veiləns] n vigilancia

survey [n sə'vei, vb sə'vei] n inspección f, reconocimiento m; (inquiry) encuesta ♦ vt examinar, inspeccionar; (look at) mirar, contemplar □ **surveyor** n agrimensor(a) m/f

survival [sə'vaivl] n supervivencia

survive [sə'vaiv] vi sobrevivir; (custom etc) perdurar ♦ vt sobrevivir a □ **survivor** n superviviente mf

suspect [adj, n sə'spekt, vb sə'spekt] adj, n sospechoso(-a) m/f ♦ vt (person) sospechar de; (think) sospechar

suspend [sə'spend] vt suspender □ **suspended sentence** (LAW) libertad f condicional □ **suspenders** npl (BRIT) ligas fpl; (US) tirantes mpl

suspense [sə'spens] n incertidumbre f, duda; (in film etc) suspense m; **to keep sb in ~** mantener a algn en suspense

suspension [sə'spenʃən] n (gen, AUT) suspensión f; (of driving licence) privación f □ **suspension bridge** n puente m colgante

suspicion [sə'spiʃən] n sospecha; (distrust) recelo □ **suspicious** adj receloso; (causing suspicion) sospechoso

sustain [sə'stein] vt sostener, apoyar; (suffer) sufrir, padecer

swallow ['swɔləu] n (bird) golondrina ♦ vt tragar; (fig, pride) tragarse

swam [swæm] *pt of* **swim**

swamp [swɔmp] *n* pantano, ciénaga
♦ *vt* (*with water etc*) inundar; (*fig*)
abrumar, agobiar

swan [swɔn] *n* cisne *m*

swap [swɔp] *n* canje *m*, intercambio
♦ *vt*: **to ~ (for)** cambiar (por)

swarm [swɔːm] *n* (*of bees*) enjambre *m*;
(*fig*) multitud *f* ♦ *vi* (*bees*) formar un
enjambre; (*people*) pulular; **to be
swarming with** ser un hervidero de

sway [sweɪ] *vi* mecerse, balancearse
♦ *vt* (*influence*) mover, influir en

swear [sweə*] (*pt* **swore**, *pp* **sworn**) *vi*
(*curse*) maldecir; (*promise*) jurar ♦ *vt*
jurar ► **swear in** *vt*: **to be sworn in**
prestar juramento ❏ **swearword** *n*
taco, palabrota

sweat [swet] *n* sudor *m* ♦ *vi* sudar

sweater ['swetə*] *n* suéter *m*

sweatshirt ['swetʃəːt] *n* suéter *m*

sweaty ['swetɪ] *adj* sudoroso

Swede [swiːd] *n* sueco(-a)

swede [swiːd] (*BRIT*) *n* nabo

Sweden ['swiːdn] *n* Suecia ❏ **Swedish**
['swiːdɪʃ] *adj* sueco ♦ *n* (*LING*) sueco

sweep [swiːp] (*pt*, *pp* **swept**) *n* (*act*)
barrido; (*also*: **chimney ~**)
deshollinador(a) *m/f* ♦ *vt* barrer; (*with
arm*) empujar; (*current*) arrastrar ♦ *vi*
barrer; (*arm etc*) moverse
rápidamente; (*wind*) soplar con
violencia

sweet [swiːt] *n* (*candy*) dulce *m*,
caramelo; (*BRIT*: *pudding*) postre *m*
♦ *adj* dulce; (*fig*: *kind*) dulce, amable;
(: *attractive*) mono ❏ **sweetcorn** *n*
maíz *m* ❏ **sweetener** ['swiːtnə*] *n*
(*CULIN*) edulcorante *m* ❏ **sweetheart**
n novio(-a) ❏ **sweetshop** (*BRIT*)
confitería, bombonería

swell [swel] (*pt* **swelled**, *pp* **swollen** *or*
swelled) *n* (*of sea*) marejada, oleaje *m*
♦ *adj* (*US*: *inf*: *excellent*) estupendo,
fenomenal ♦ *vt* hinchar, inflar ♦ *vi* (*also*:
~ up) hincharse; (*numbers*) aumentar;

(*sound, feeling*) ir aumentando
❏ **swelling** *n* (*MED*) hinchazón *f*

swept [swept] *pt*, *pp of* **sweep**

swerve [swəːv] *vi* desviarse
bruscamente

swift [swɪft] *n* (*bird*) vencejo ♦ *adj*
rápido, veloz

swim [swɪm] (*pt* **swam**, *pp* **swum**) *n*: **to
go for a ~** ir a nadar *or* a bañarse ♦ *vi*
nadar; (*head, room*) dar vueltas ♦ *vt*
nadar; (*the Channel etc*) cruzar a nado
❏ **swimmer** *n* nadador(a) *m/f*
❏ **swimming** *n* natación *f*
❏ **swimming costume** (*BRIT*) *n*
bañador *m*, traje *m* de baño
❏ **swimming pool** *n* piscina, alberca
(*MEX*), pileta (*RPI*) ❏ **swimming
trunks** *npl* bañador *m* (de hombre)
❏ **swimsuit** *n* = **swimming
costume**

swing [swɪŋ] (*pt*, *pp* **swung**) *n* (*in
playground*) columpio; (*movement*)
balanceo, vaivén *m*; (*change of
direction*) viraje *m*; (*rhythm*) ritmo ♦ *vt*
balancear; (*also*: **~ round**) voltear, girar
♦ *vi* balancearse, columpiarse; (*also*: **~
round**) dar media vuelta; **to be in full ~**
estar en plena marcha

swipe card [swaɪp-] *n* tarjeta
magnética deslizante, tarjeta swipe

swirl [swəːl] *vi* arremolinarse

Swiss [swɪs] *adj*, *n inv* suizo(-a) *m/f*

switch [swɪtʃ] *n* (*for light etc*)
interruptor *m*; (*change*) cambio ♦ *vt*
(*change*) cambiar de ► **switch off** *vt*
apagar; (*engine*) parar ► **switch on** *vt*
encender (*SP*), prender (*LAm*); (*engine,
machine*) arrancar ❏ **switchboard** *n*
(*TEL*) centralita (*SP*), conmutador *m*
(*LAm*)

Switzerland ['swɪtsələnd] *n* Suiza

swivel ['swɪvl] *vi* (*also*: **~ round**) girar

swollen ['swəulən] *pp of* **swell**

swoop [swuːp] *n* (*by police etc*) redada
♦ *vi* (*also*: **~ down**) calarse

swop [swɔp] = **swap**

sword [sɔːd] n espada ❑ **swordfish** n pez m espada

swore [swɔːʳ] pt of **swear**

sworn [swɔːn] pp of **swear** ♦ adj (statement) bajo juramento; (enemy) implacable

swum [swʌm] pp of **swim**

swung [swʌŋ] pt, pp of **swing**

syllable ['sɪləbl] n sílaba

syllabus ['sɪləbəs] n programa m de estudios

symbol ['sɪmbl] n símbolo ❑ **symbolic(al)** [sɪm'bɒlɪk(l)] adj simbólico; **to be symbolic(al) of sth** simbolizar algo

symmetrical [sɪ'metrɪkl] adj simétrico

symmetry ['sɪmɪtrɪ] n simetría

sympathetic [sɪmpə'θetɪk] adj (understanding) comprensivo; (showing support): ~ **to(wards)** bien dispuesto hacia

⚠ Be careful not to translate **sympathetic** by the Spanish word simpático.

sympathize ['sɪmpəθaɪz] vi: **to ~ with** (person) compadecerse de; (feelings) comprender; (cause) apoyar

sympathy ['sɪmpəθɪ] n (pity) compasión f

symphony ['sɪmfənɪ] n sinfonía

symptom ['sɪmptəm] n síntoma m, indicio

synagogue ['sɪnəgɒg] n sinagoga

syndicate ['sɪndɪkɪt] n sindicato; (of newspapers) agencia (de noticias)

syndrome ['sɪndrəʊm] n síndrome m

synonym ['sɪnənɪm] n sinónimo

synthetic [sɪn'θetɪk] adj sintético

Syria ['sɪrɪə] n Siria

syringe [sɪ'rɪndʒ] n jeringa

syrup ['sɪrəp] n jarabe m; (also: **golden ~**) almíbar m

system ['sɪstəm] n sistema m; (ANAT) organismo ❑ **systematic** [-'mætɪk]

adj sistemático, metódico ❑ **systems analyst** n analista mf de sistemas

T, t

ta [tɑː] (BRIT: inf) excl ¡gracias!

tab [tæb] n lengüeta; (label) etiqueta; **to keep tabs on** (fig) vigilar

table ['teɪbl] n mesa; (of statistics etc) cuadro, tabla ♦ vt (BRIT: motion etc) presentar; **to lay** or **set the ~** poner la mesa ❑ **tablecloth** n mantel m ❑ **table d'hôte** [tɑːbl'dəʊt] adj (of menú ❑ **table lamp** n lámpara de mesa ❑ **tablemat** n (for plate) posaplatos m inv; (for hot dish) salvamantel m ❑ **tablespoon** n cuchara de servir; (also: **tablespoonful**: as measurement) cucharada

tablet ['tæblɪt] n (MED) pastilla, comprimido; (of stone) lápida

table tennis n ping-pong m, tenis m de mesa

tabloid ['tæblɔɪd] n periódico popular sensacionalista

TABLOID PRESS

El término **tabloid press** o **tabloids** se usa para referirse a la prensa popular británica, por el tamaño más pequeño de los periódicos. A diferencia de los de la llamada **quality press**, estas publicaciones se caracterizan por un lenguaje sencillo, una presentación llamativa y un contenido sensacionalista, centrado a veces en los escándalos financieros y sexuales de los famosos, por lo que también reciben el nombre peyorativo de "gutter press".

taboo [tə'buː] adj, n tabú m

tack [tæk] n (nail) tachuela; (fig) rumbo ♦ vt (nail) clavar con tachuelas; (stitch) hilvanar ♦ vi virar

tackle [ˈtækl] n (fishing tackle) aparejo (de pescar); (for lifting) aparejo ♦ vt (difficulty) enfrentarse con; (challenge: person) hacer frente a; (grapple with) agarrar; (FOOTBALL) cargar; (RUGBY) placar

tacky [ˈtæki] adj pegajoso; (pej) cutre

tact [tækt] n tacto, discreción f □ **tactful** adj discreto, diplomático

tactics [ˈtæktɪks] npl táctica

tactless [ˈtæktlɪs] adj indiscreto

tadpole [ˈtædpəʊl] n renacuajo

taffy [ˈtæfɪ] (US) n melcocha

tag [tæg] n (label) etiqueta

tail [teɪl] n cola; (of shirt, coat) faldón m ♦ vt (follow) vigilar a; **tails** npl (formal suit) levita

tailor [ˈteɪlə] n sastre m

Taiwan [taɪˈwɑːn] n Taiwán m □ **Taiwanese** [taɪwɑːˈniːz] adj, n taiwanés(-esa) m/f

take [teɪk] (pt **took**, pp **taken**) vt tomar; (grab) coger (SP), agarrar (LAm); (gain: prize) ganar; (require: effort, courage) exigir; (tolerate: pain etc) aguantar; (hold: passengers etc) tener cabida para; (accompany, bring, carry) llevar; (exam) presentarse a; **to ~ sth from** (drawer etc) sacar algo de; (person) quitar algo a; **I ~ it that ...** supongo que ...; ► **take after** vt fus parecerse a ► **take apart** vt desmontar ► **take away** vt (remove) quitar; (carry) llevar; (MATH) restar ► **take back** vt (return) devolver; (one's words) retractarse de ► **take down** vt (building) derribar; (letter etc) apuntar ► **take in** vt (deceive) engañar; (understand) entender; (include) abarcar; (lodger) acoger, recibir ► **take off** vi (AVIAT) despegar ♦ vt (remove) quitar ► **take on** vt (work) aceptar; (employee) contratar; (opponent) desafiar ► **take out** vt sacar ► **take over** vt (business)

tomar posesión de; (country) tomar el poder ♦ vi: **to take over from sb** reemplazar a algn ► **take up** vt (a dress) acortar; (occupy: time, space) ocupar; (engage in: hobby etc) dedicarse a; (accept): **to take sb up on** aceptar algo de algn □ **takeaway** (BRIT) adj (food) para llevar ♦ n tienda or restaurante m de comida para llevar □ **taken** pp of **take** □ **takeoff** n (AVIAT) despegue m ► **takeout** (US) n = **takeaway** □ **takeover** n (COMM) absorción f □ **takings** npl (COMM) ingresos mpl

talc [tælk] n (also: **talcum powder**) (polvos de) talco

tale [teɪl] n (story) cuento; (account) relación f; **to tell tales** (fig) chivarse

talent [ˈtælnt] n talento □ **talented** adj de talento

talk [tɔːk] n charla; (conversation) conversación f; (gossip) habladurías fpl, chismes mpl ♦ vi hablar; **talks** npl (POL etc) conversaciones fpl ♦ vi: **to ~ about** hablar de; **to ~ sb into doing sth** convencer a algn para que haga algo; **to ~ sb out of doing sth** disuadir a algn de que haga algo; **to ~ shop** hablar del trabajo ► **talk over** vt discutir □ **talk show** n programa m de entrevistas

tall [tɔːl] adj alto; (object) grande; **to be 6 feet ~** (person) → medir 1 metro 80

tambourine [tæmbəˈriːn] n pandereta

tame [teɪm] adj domesticado; (fig) mediocre

tamper [ˈtæmpə] vi: **to ~ with** tocar, andar con

tampon [ˈtæmpən] n tampón m

tan [tæn] n (also: **suntan**) bronceado ♦ vi ponerse moreno ♦ adj (colour) marrón

tandem [ˈtændəm] n tándem m

tangerine [tændʒəˈriːn] n mandarina

tangle [ˈtæŋgl] n enredo; **to get in(to) a ~** enredarse

tank [tæŋk] n (water tank) depósito, tanque m; (for fish) acuario; (MIL) tanque m

tanker ['tæŋkə*] n (ship) buque m, cisterna; (truck) camión m cisterna

tanned [tænd] adj (skin) moreno

tantrum ['tæntrəm] n rabieta

Tanzania [tænzə'nɪə] n Tanzania

tap [tæp] n (BRIT: on sink etc) grifo (SP), llave f, canilla (RPl); (gas tap) llave f; (gentle blow) golpecito ♦ vt (hit gently) dar golpecitos en; (resources) utilizar, explotar; (telephone) intervenir; **on ~** (fig: resources) a mano □ **tap dancing** n claqué n

tape [teɪp] n (also: **magnetic ~**) cinta magnética; (cassette) cassette f, cinta; (sticky tape) cinta adhesiva; (for tying) cinta ♦ vt (record) grabar (en cinta); (stick with tape) pegar con cinta adhesiva □ **tape measure** n cinta métrica, metro □ **tape recorder** n grabadora

tapestry ['tæpɪstrɪ] n (object) tapiz m; (art) tapicería

tar [tɑ:*] n alquitrán m, brea

target ['tɑ:gɪt] n blanco

tariff ['tærɪf] n (on goods) arancel m; (BRIT: in hotels etc) tarifa

tarmac ['tɑ:mæk] n (BRIT: on road) asfaltado m; (AVIAT) pista (de aterrizaje)

tarpaulin [tɑ:'pɔ:lɪn] n lona impermeabilizada

tarragon ['tærəgən] n estragón m

tart [tɑ:t] n (CULIN) tarta; (BRIT: inf: prostitute) puta ♦ adj agrio, ácido

tartan ['tɑ:tn] n tejido escocés

tartar(e) sauce ['tɑ:tə-] n salsa tártara

task [tɑ:sk] n tarea; **to take to ~** reprender

taste [teɪst] n (sense) gusto; (flavour) sabor m; (sample): **have a ~** ¡prueba un poquito!; (fig) muestra, idea ♦ vt probar ♦ vi: **to ~ of** or **like** (fish, garlic etc) saber a; **you can ~ the garlic (in it)** se nota el sabor a ajo; **in good/bad ~**

de buen/mal gusto □ **tasteful** adj de buen gusto □ **tasteless** adj (food) soso; (remark etc) de mal gusto □ **tasty** adj sabroso, rico

tatters ['tætəz] npl: **in ~** = hecho jirones

tattoo [tə'tu:] n tatuaje m; (spectacle) espectáculo militar ♦ vt tatuar

taught [tɔ:t] pt, pp of **teach**

taunt [tɔ:nt] n burla ♦ vt burlarse de

Taurus ['tɔ:rəs] n Tauro

taut [tɔ:t] adj tirante, tenso

tax [tæks] n impuesto ♦ vt gravar (con un impuesto); (fig: memory) poner a prueba; (: patience) agotar □ **tax-free** adj libre de impuestos

taxi ['tæksɪ] n taxi m ♦ vi (AVIAT) rodar por la pista □ **taxi driver** n taxista mf □ **taxi rank** (BRIT) n = **taxi stand** □ **taxi stand** n parada de taxis

tax payer n contribuyente mf

TB n abbr = **tuberculosis**

tea [ti:] n té m; (BRIT: meal) = merienda (SP); cena; **high ~** (BRIT) merienda-cena (SP) □ **tea bag** n bolsita de té □ **tea break** (BRIT) n descanso para el té

teach [ti:tʃ] (pt, pp taught) vt: **to ~ sb sth,~ sth to sb** enseñar algo a algn ♦ vi (be a teacher) ser profesor(a), enseñar □ **teacher** n (in secondary school) profesor(a) m/f; (in primary school) maestro(-a), profesor(a) de EGB □ **teaching** n enseñanza

tea: tea cloth n (BRIT) paño de cocina, trapo de cocina (LAm) □ **teacup** n taza para el té

tea leaves npl hojas de té

team [ti:m] n equipo; (of horses) tiro ► **team up** vi asociarse

teapot ['ti:pɒt] n tetera

tear¹ [tɪə*] n lágrima; **in tears** llorando

tear² [tɛə*] (pt tore, pp torn) n rasgón m, desgarrón m ♦ vt romper, rasgar ♦ vi rasgarse ► **tear apart** vt (also fig) hacer pedazos ► **tear down** vt +adv (building, statue) derribar; (poster, flag) arrancar ► **tear off** vt (sheet of paper etc) arrancar; (one's clothes) quitarse a tirones ► **tear up** vt (sheet of paper etc) romper

:earful ['tɪəfəl] adj lloroso

:ear gas ['tɪə-] n gas m lacrimógeno

:earoom ['tiːruːm] n salón m de té

:ease [tiːz] vt tomar el pelo a

:ea: teaspoon n cucharita; (also: **teaspoonful**: as measurement) cucharadita □ **teatime** n hora del té □ **tea towel** (BRIT) n paño de cocina

:echnical ['tɛknɪkl] adj técnico

:echnician [tɛk'nɪʃn] n técnico(-a)

:echnique [tɛk'niːk] n técnica

:echnology [tɛk'nɔlədʒɪ] n tecnología

:eddy (bear) ['tɛdɪ-] n osito de felpa

:edious ['tiːdɪəs] adj pesado, aburrido

:ee [tiː] n (GOLF) tee m

:een [tiːn] adj (US) = **teenage** ♦ n (US) = **teenager**

:eenage ['tiːneɪdʒ] adj (fashions etc) juvenil; (children) quinceañero □ **teenager** n adolescente mf

:eens [tiːnz] npl: **to be in one's ~** ser adolescente

:eeth [tiːθ] npl of **tooth**

:eetotal ['tiːˈtəutl] adj abstemio

:elecommunications [tɛlɪkəmjuːnɪˈkeɪʃənz] n telecomunicaciones fpl

:elegram ['tɛlɪgræm] n telegrama m

:elegraph pole ['tɛlɪgrɑːf-] n poste m telegráfico

:elephone ['tɛlɪfəun] n teléfono ♦ vt llamar por teléfono, telefonear; (message) dar por teléfono; **to be on the ~** (talking) hablar por teléfono; (possessing telephone) tener teléfono □ **telephone book** n guía f telefónica □ **telephone booth**, **telephone box** (BRIT) n cabina telefónica □ **telephone call** n llamada (telefónica) □ **telephone directory** n guía (telefónica) □ **telephone number** n número de teléfono

telesales ['tɛlɪseɪlz] npl televenta(s) (f(pl))

telescope ['tɛlɪskəup] n telescopio

televise ['tɛlɪvaɪz] vt televisar

television ['tɛlɪvɪʒən] n televisión f; **on ~** en la televisión □ **television programme** n programa m de televisión

tell [tɛl] (pt, pp told) vt decir; (relate: story) contar; (distinguish): **to ~ sth from** distinguir algo de ♦ vi (talk): **to ~ (of)** contar; (have effect) tener efecto; **to ~ sb to do sth** mandar a algn hacer algo ► **tell off** vt: **to tell sb off** regañar a algn □ **teller** n (in bank) cajero(-a)

telly ['tɛlɪ] (BRIT: inf) n abbr (= television) tele f

temp [tɛmp] n abbr (BRIT: = temporary) temporero(-a)

temper ['tɛmpə*] n (nature) carácter m; (mood) humor m; (bad temper) (mal) genio; (fit of anger) acceso de ira ♦ vt (moderate) moderar; **to be in a ~** estar furioso; **to lose one's ~** enfadarse, enojarse

temperament ['tɛmprəmənt] n (nature) temperamento □ **temperamental** [tɛmprəˈmɛntl] adj temperamental

temperature ['tɛmprətʃə*] n temperatura; **to have** or **run a ~** tener fiebre

temple ['tɛmpl] n (building) templo; (ANAT) sien f

temporary ['tɛmpərərɪ] adj provisional; (passing) transitorio; (worker) temporero; (job) temporal

tempt [tɛmpt] vt tentar; **to ~ sb into doing sth** tentar o inducir a algn a hacer algo □ **temptation** n tentación f □ **tempting** adj tentador(a); (food) apetitoso(-a)

ten [tɛn] num diez

tenant ['tɛnənt] n inquilino(-a)

tend [tend] vt cuidar ♦ vi: **to ~ to do sth**
tener tendencia a hacer algo
❑ **tendency** ['tendənsi] n tendencia

tender ['tendə'] adj (person, care)
tierno, cariñoso; (meat) tierno; (sore)
sensible ♦ n (COMM: offer) oferta;
(money): **legal ~** moneda de curso
legal ♦ vt ofrecer

tendon ['tendən] n tendón m

tenner ['tenə'] n (inf) (billete m de) diez
libras fpl

tennis ['tenɪs] n tenis m ❑ **tennis ball**
n pelota de tenis ❑ **tennis court** n
cancha de tenis ❑ **tennis match** n
partido de tenis ❑ **tennis player** n
tenista mf ❑ **tennis racket** n raqueta
de tenis

tenor ['tenə'] n (MUS) tenor m

tenpin bowling ['tenpɪn-] n (juego
de los) bolos

tense [tens] adj (person) nervioso;
(moment, atmosphere) tenso; (muscle)
tenso, en tensión ♦ n (LING) tiempo

tension ['tenʃən] n tensión f

tent [tent] n tienda (de campaña) (SP),
carpa (LAm)

tentative ['tentətɪv] adj (person, smile)
indeciso; (conclusion, plans)
provisional

tenth [tenθ] num décimo

tent: tent peg n clavija, estaca ❑ **tent
pole** n mástil m

tepid ['tepɪd] adj tibio

term [tɜːm] n (word) término; (period)
período; (SCOL) trimestre m ♦ vt llamar;
terms npl (conditions, COMM)
condiciones fpl; **in the short/long ~** a
corto/largo plazo; **to be on good
terms with sb** llevarse bien con algn;
to come to terms with (problem)
aceptar

terminal ['tɜːmɪnl] adj (disease) mortal;
(patient) terminal ♦ n (ELEC) borne m;
(COMPUT) terminal m; (also: **air ~**)
terminal f; (BRIT: also: **coach ~**) estación
f terminal f

terminate ['tɜːmɪneɪt] vt terminar

termini ['tɜːmɪnaɪ] npl of **terminus**

terminology [tɜːmɪˈnɒlədʒɪ] n
terminología

terminus ['tɜːmɪnəs] (pl **termini**) n
término, (estación f) terminal f

terrace ['terəs] n terraza; (BRIT: row of
houses) hilera de casas adosadas; **the
terraces** (BRIT SPORT) las gradas fpl
❑ **terraced** adj (garden) en terrazas;
(house) adosado

terrain [te'reɪn] n terreno

terrestrial [tɪ'restrɪəl] adj (life)
terrestre; (BRIT: channel) de transmisión
(por) vía terrestre

terrible ['terɪbl] adj terrible, horrible;
(inf) atroz ❑ **terribly** adv
terriblemente; (very badly)
malísimamente

terrier ['terɪə'] n terrier m

terrific [tə'rɪfɪk] adj (very great)
tremendo; (wonderful) fantástico,
fenomenal

terrified ['terɪfaɪd] adj aterrorizado

terrify ['terɪfaɪ] vt aterrorizar
❑ **terrifying** adj aterrador(a)

territorial [terɪ'tɔːrɪəl] adj territorial

territory ['terɪtərɪ] n territorio

terror ['terə'] n terror m ❑ **terrorism** n
terrorismo ❑ **terrorist** n terrorista mf

test [test] n (gen, CHEM) prueba; (MED)
examen m; (SCOL) examen m, test m;
(also: **driving ~**) examen m de
conducir ♦ vt probar, poner a prueba;
(MED, SCOL) examinar

testicle ['testɪkl] n testículo

testify ['testɪfaɪ] vi (LAW) prestar
declaración; **to ~ to sth** atestiguar algo

testimony ['testɪmənɪ] n (LAW)
testimonio

test: test match n (CRICKET, RUGBY)
partido internacional ❑ **test tube** n
probeta

tetanus ['tetənəs] n tétano

text [tekst] n texto; (on mobile phone)
mensaje m de texto ♦ vt: **to ~ sb** (inf)

enviar un mensaje (de texto) *or* un SMS
a algn ❑ **textbook** *n* libro de texto

textile ['tekstaɪl] *n* textil *m*, tejido

text message *n* mensaje *m* de texto

text messaging [-'mesɪdʒɪŋ] *n* (envío
de) mensajes *mpl* de texto

texture ['tekstʃə'] *n* textura

Thai [taɪ] *adj*, *n* tailandés(-esa) *m/f*

Thailand ['taɪlænd] *n* Tailandia

than [ðæn] *conj* (*in comparisons*): **more
~ 10/once** más de 10/una vez; **I have
more/less ~ you/Paul** tengo más/
menos que tú/Paul; **she is older ~ you
think** es mayor de lo que piensas

thank [θæŋk] *vt* dar las gracias a,
agradecer; **~ you (very much)** muchas
gracias; **~ God!** ¡gracias a Dios! ♦ *excl*
¡gracias!; **thanks to** *prep* gracias a;
thanks *npl* gracias *fpl* ❑ **thankfully**
adv (*fortunately*) afortunadamente
❑ **Thanksgiving (Day)** *n* día *m* de
Acción de Gracias

THANKSGIVING (DAY)

En Estados Unidos el cuarto jueves de
noviembre es **Thanksgiving Day**,
fiesta oficial en la que se recuerda la
celebración que hicieron los primeros
colonos norteamericanos ("Pilgrims"
o "Pilgrim Fathers") tras la estupenda
cosecha de 1621, por la que se dan
gracias a Dios. En Canadá se celebra
una fiesta semejante el segundo lunes
de octubre, aunque no está
relacionada con dicha fecha histórica.

that

KEYWORD

[ðæt] (*pl* **those**) *adj* (*demonstrative*)
ese(-a); (*pl*) esos(-as); (*more remote*)
aquel (aquella); (*pl*) aquellos(-as);
leave those books on the table deja
esos libros sobre la mesa; **that one**
ése (ésa); (*more remote*) aquél

(aquélla); **that one over there** ése
(ésa) de ahí; aquél (aquélla) de allí
♦ *pron*

1 (*demonstrative*) ése(-a); (*pl*)
ésos(-as); (*neuter*) eso; (*more remote*)
aquél (aquélla); (*pl*) aquéllos(-as);
(*neuter*) aquello; **what's that?** ¿qué es
eso (*or* aquello)?; **who's that?** ¿quién
es ése(-a) (*or* aquél (aquélla))?; **is that
you?** ¿eres tú?; **will you eat all that?**
¿vas a comer todo eso?; **that's my
house** ésa es mi casa; **that's what he
said** eso es lo que dijo; **that is (to say)**
es decir

2 (*relative: subject, object*) que; (*with
preposition*) el ((la)) que *etc*, el (la)
cual *etc*; **the book (that) I read** el libro
que leí; **the books that are in the
library** los libros que están en la
biblioteca; **all (that) I have** todo lo
que tengo; **the box (that) I put it in** la
caja en la que *or* donde lo puse; **the
people (that) I spoke to** la gente con
la que hablé

3 (*relative: of time*) que; **the day
(that) he came** el día (en) que vino
♦ *conj* que; **he thought that I was ill**
creyó que yo estaba enfermo
♦ *adv* (*demonstrative*): **I can't work
that much** no puedo trabajar tanto; **I
didn't realise it was that bad** no creí
que fuera tan malo; **that high** así de
alto

thatched [θætʃt] *adj* (*roof*) de paja;
(*cottage*) con tejado de paja

thaw [θɔ:] *n* deshielo ♦ *vi* (*ice*)
derretirse; (*food*) descongelarse ♦ *vt*
(*food*) descongelar

the

KEYWORD

[ði:, ðə] *def art*
1 (*gen*) el *f*, la *pl*, los *fpl*, las (*NB* 'el'

immediately before f n beginning with stressed (h)a; a+ el = al; de+ el = del; **the boy/girl** el chico/la chica; **the books/flowers** los libros/las flores; **to the postman/from the drawer** al cartero/del cajón; **I haven't the time/money** no tengo tiempo/dinero

2 (*+adj to form n*) los; lo; **the rich and the poor** los ricos y los pobres; **to attempt the impossible** intentar lo imposible

3 (*in titles*): **Elizabeth the First** Isabel primera; **Peter the Great** Pedro el Grande

4 (*in comparisons*): **the more he works the more he earns** cuanto más trabaja más gana

theatre [ˈθɪətə] (*US* **theater**) *n* teatro; (*also:* **lecture ~**) aula; (*MED: also:* **operating ~**) quirófano

theft [θɛft] *n* robo

their [ðɛə] *adj* su ❑ **theirs** *pron* (el) suyo ((la) suya *etc*); see also **my**; **mine**[1]

them [ðɛm, ðəm] *pron* (*direct*) los/las; (*indirect*) les; lo; (*stressed, after prep*) ellos (ellas); see also **me**

theme [θiːm] *n* tema *m* ❑ **theme park** *n* parque de atracciones (*en torno a un tema central*)

themselves [ðəmˈsɛlvz] *pl pron* (*subject*) ellos mismos (ellas mismas); (*complement*) se; (*after prep*) sí mismos (as)); see also **oneself**

then [ðɛn] *adv* (*at that time*) entonces; (*next*) después; (*later*) luego, después; (*and also*) además ♦ *conj* (*therefore*) en ese caso, entonces ♦ *adj*: **the ~ president** el entonces presidente; **by ~** para entonces; **from ~** desde entonces

theology [θɪˈɒlədʒɪ] *n* teología

theory [ˈθɪərɪ] *n* teoría

therapist [ˈθɛrəpɪst] *n* terapeuta *mf*

therapy [ˈθɛrəpɪ] *n* terapia

---

there

[ðɛə] *adv*

1: **there is, there are** hay; **there is no-one here/no bread left** no hay nadie aquí/no queda pan; **there has been an accident** ha habido un accidente

2 (*referring to place*) ahí; (*distant*) allí; **it's there** está ahí; **put it in/on/up/down there** ponlo ahí dentro/encima/arriba/abajo; **I want that book there** quiero ese libro de ahí; **there he is!** ¡ahí está!

3: **there, there** (*esp to child*) ea, ea

---

there: thereabouts *adv* por ahí
❑ **thereafter** *adv* después
❑ **thereby** *adv* así, de ese modo
❑ **therefore** *adv* por lo tanto
❑ **there's** = **there is**; **there has**

thermal [ˈθəːml] *adj* termal; (*paper*) térmico

thermometer [θəˈmɒmɪtə] *n* termómetro

thermostat [ˈθəːməustæt] *n* termostato

these [ðiːz] *pl adj* estos(-as) ♦ *pl pron* éstos(-as)

thesis [ˈθiːsɪs] (*pl* **theses**) *n* tesis *f inv*

they [ðeɪ] *pl pron* ellos (ellas); (*stressed*) ellos (mismos) (ellas (mismas)); **~ say that ...** (*it is said that*) se dice que ...
❑ **they'd** = **they had**; **they would**
❑ **they'll** = **they shall**; **they will**
❑ **they're** = **they are** ❑ **they've** = **they have**

thick [θɪk] *adj* (*in consistency*) espeso; (*in size*) grueso; (*stupid*) torpe ♦ *n*: **in the ~ of the battle** en lo más reñido de la batalla; **it's 20 cm ~** tiene 20 cm de espesor ❑ **thicken** *vi* espesarse ♦ *vt* (*sauce etc*) espesar ❑ **thickness** *n* espesor *m*; grueso

thief [θiːf] (pl **thieves**) n ladrón(-ona) m/f

thigh [θaɪ] n muslo

thin [θɪn] adj (person, animal) flaco; (in size) delgado; (in consistency) poco espeso; (hair, crowd) escaso ♦ vt: **to ~ (down)** diluir

thing [θɪŋ] n cosa; (object) objeto, artículo; (matter) asunto; (mania): **to have a ~ about sth/sb** estar obsesionado con algn/algo; **things** npl (belongings) efectos mpl (personales); **the best ~ would be to ...** lo mejor sería ...; **how are things?** ¿qué tal?

think [θɪŋk] (pt, pp **thought**) vi pensar ♦ vt pensar, creer; **what did you ~ of them?** ¿qué te parecieron?; **to ~ about sth/sb** pensar en algo/algn; **I'll ~ about it** lo pensaré; **to ~ of doing sth** pensar en hacer algo; **I ~ so/not** creo que sí/no; **to ~ well of sb** tener buen concepto de algn ► **think over** vt reflexionar sobre, meditar ► **think up** vt (plan etc) idear

third [θəːd] adj (before n) tercer(a); (following n) tercero(-a) ♦ n tercero(-a); (fraction) tercio; (BRIT SCOL: degree) título de licenciado con calificación de aprobado □ **thirdly** adv en tercer lugar □ **third party insurance** (BRIT) n seguro contra terceros □ **Third World** n Tercer Mundo

thirst [θəːst] n sed f □ **thirsty** adj (person, animal) sediento; (work) que da sed; **to be thirsty** tener sed

thirteen ['θəː'tiːn] num trece □ **thirteenth** [-'tiːnθ] adj decimotercero

thirtieth ['θəːtɪəθ] adj trigésimo

thirty ['θəːtɪ] num treinta

this

KEYWORD

[ðɪs] (pl **these**) adj (demonstrative) este(-a) pl; estos(-as); (neuter) esto; **this man/woman** este hombre (esta mujer); **these children/flowers** estos

chicos/estas flores; **this one (here)** éste(-a), esto (de aquí)

♦ pron (demonstrative) éste(-a) pl, estos(-as); (neuter) esto; **who is this?** ¿quién es éste/ésta?; **what is this?** ¿qué es esto?; **this is where I live** aquí vivo; **this is what he said** esto es lo que dijo; **this is Mr Brown** (in introductions) le presento al Sr. Brown; (photo) éste es el Sr. Brown; (on telephone) habla el Sr. Brown

♦ adv (demonstrative): **this high/long etc** así de alto/largo etc; **this far** hasta aquí

thistle ['θɪsl] n cardo

thorn [θɔːn] n espina

thorough ['θʌrə] adj (search) minucioso; (wash) a fondo; (knowledge, research) profundo; (person) meticuloso □ **thoroughly** adv (search) minuciosamente; (study) profundamente; (wash) a fondo; (utterly: bad, wet etc) completamente, totalmente

those [ðəʊz] pl adj esos (esas); (more remote) aquellos(-as)

though [ðəʊ] conj aunque ♦ adv sin embargo

thought [θɔːt] pt, pp of **think** ♦ n pensamiento; (opinion) opinión f □ **thoughtful** adj pensativo; (serious) serio; (considerate) atento □ **thoughtless** adj desconsiderado

thousand ['θaʊzənd] num mil; **two ~** dos mil; **thousands of** miles de □ **thousandth** num milésimo

thrash [θræʃ] vt azotar; (defeat) derrotar

thread [θred] n hilo; (of screw) rosca ♦ vt (needle) enhebrar

threat [θret] n amenaza □ **threaten** vi amenazar ♦ vt: **to threaten sb with/to do** amenazar a algn con/con hacer

three [θriː] *num* tres ❑ **three-dimensional** *adj* tridimensional ❑ **three-piece suite** *n* tresillo ❑ **three-quarters** *npl* tres cuartas partes; **three-quarters full** tres cuartas partes lleno

threshold ['θreʃhəuld] *n* umbral *m*

threw [θruː] *pt of* **throw**

thrill [θrɪl] *n* (*excitement*) emoción *f*; (*shudder*) estremecimiento ♦ *vt* emocionar; **to be thrilled** (*with gift etc*) estar encantado ❑ **thrilled** *adj*: **I was thrilled** estaba emocionada ❑ **thriller** *n* novela (*or obra or película*) de suspense ❑ **thrilling** *adj* emocionante

thriving ['θraɪvɪŋ] *adj* próspero

throat [θrəut] *n* garganta; **to have a sore ~** tener dolor de garganta

throb [θrɔb] *vi* latir; dar puntadas; vibrar

throne [θrəun] *n* trono

through [θruː] *prep* por, a través de; (*time*) durante; (*by means of*) por medio de, (*owing to*) gracias a ♦ *adj* (*ticket, train*) directo ♦ *adv* completamente, de parte a parte; de principio a fin; **to put sb ~ to sb** (*TEL*) poner *or* pasar a algn con algn; **to be ~** (*TEL*) tener comunicación; (*have finished*) haber terminado; **"no ~ road"** (*BRIT*) "calle sin salida" ❑ **throughout** *prep* (*place*) por todas partes de, por todo; (*time*) durante todo ♦ *adv* por *or* en todas partes

throw [θrəu] (*pt* **threw**, *pp* **thrown**) *n* tiro; (*SPORT*) lanzamiento ♦ *vt* tirar, echar; (*SPORT*) lanzar; (*rider*) derribar; (*fig*) desconcertar; **to ~ a party** dar una fiesta ❑ **throw away** *vt* tirar; (*money*) derrochar ❑ **throw in** *vt* (*SPORT: ball*) sacar; (*include*) incluir ❑ **throw off** *vt* deshacerse de ❑ **throw out** *vt* tirar; (*person*) echar; expulsar ❑ **throw up** *vi* vomitar

thru [θruː] (*US*) = **through**

thrush [θrʌʃ] *n* zorzal *m*, tordo

thrust [θrʌst] (*pt, pp* ~) *vt* empujar con fuerza

thud [θʌd] *n* golpe *m* sordo

thug [θʌg] *n* gamberro(-a)

thumb [θʌm] *n* (*ANAT*) pulgar *m*; **to ~ a lift** hacer autostop ❑ **thumbtack** (*US*) *n* chincheta (*SP*)

thump [θʌmp] *n* golpe *m*; (*sound*) ruido seco *or* sordo ♦ *vt* golpear ♦ *vi* (*heart etc*) palpitar

thunder ['θʌndə*] *n* trueno ♦ *vi* tronar; (*train etc*): **to ~** pasar como un trueno ❑ **thunderstorm** *n* tormenta

Thur(s). *abbr* (= *Thursday*) juev

Thursday ['θɜːzdɪ] *n* jueves *m inv*

thus [ðʌs] *adv* así, de este modo

thwart [θwɔːt] *vt* frustrar

thyme [taɪm] *n* tomillo

Tibet [tɪ'bet] *n* el Tíbet

tick [tɪk] *n* (*sound: of clock*) tictac *m*; (*mark*) palomita; (*ZOOL*) garrapata; (*BRIT: inf*): **in a ~** en un instante ♦ *vi* hacer tictac ♦ *vt* marcar ❑ **tick off** *vt* marcar; (*person*) reñir

ticket ['tɪkɪt] *n* billete *m* (*SP*), boleto (*LAm*); (*for cinema etc*) entrada; (*on goods*) etiqueta; (*for raffle*) papeleta; (*for library*) tarjeta; (*parking ticket*) multa de aparcamiento (*SP*) *or* por estacionamiento (indebido) (*LAm*) ❑ **ticket barrier** *n* (*BRIT: RAIL*) barrera más allá de la cual se necesita billete/boleto ❑ **ticket collector** *n* revisor(a) *m/f* ❑ **ticket inspector** *n* revisor(a) *m/f*, inspector(a) *m/f* de boletos (*LAm*) ❑ **ticket machine** *n* máquina de billetes (*SP*) *or* boletos (*LAm*) ❑ **ticket office** *n* (*THEATRE*) taquilla (*SP*), boletería (*LAm*); (*RAIL*) mostrador *m* de billetes (*SP*) *or* boletos (*LAm*)

tickle ['tɪkl] *vt* hacer cosquillas a ♦ *vi* hacer cosquillas ❑ **ticklish** *adj* (*person*) cosquilloso; (*problem*) delicado

de [taɪd] n marea; (fig: of events etc)
curso, marcha

dy ['taɪdɪ] adj (room etc) ordenado; (dress, work) limpio; (person) (bien) arreglado ♦ vt (also: ~ **up**) poner en orden

e [taɪ] n (string etc) atadura; (BRIT: also: **necktie**) corbata; (fig: link) vínculo, lazo); (SPORT etc: draw) empate m ♦ vt atar ♦ vi (SPORT etc) empatar; **to ~ in a bow** atar con un lazo; **to ~ a knot in** hacer un nudo en algo; ► **tie down** vt (fig: person: restrict) atar; (: to price, date etc) obligar a; ► **tie up** vt (dog, person) atar; (arrangements) concluir; **to be tied up** (busy) estar ocupado

er [tɪə'] n grada; (of cake) piso

ger ['taɪgə'] n tigre m

ght [taɪt] adj (rope) tirante; (money) escaso; (clothes) ajustado; (bend) cerrado; (shoes, schedule) apretado; (budget) ajustado; (security) estricto; (inf: drunk) borracho ♦ adv (squeeze) muy fuerte; (shut) bien ► **tighten** vt (rope) estirar; (screw, grip) apretar; (security) reforzar ♦ vi estirarse; apretarse ► **tightly** adv (grasp) muy fuerte ► **tights** (BRIT) npl panti mpl

e [taɪl] n (on roof) teja; (on floor) baldosa; (on wall) azulejo

l [tɪl] n (box: registradora) ♦ vt (land) cultivar ♦ prep, conj = **until**

t [tɪlt] vt inclinar ♦ vi inclinarse

mber [tɪmbə'] n (material) madera

me [taɪm] n tiempo; (epoch: often pl) época; (by clock) hora; (moment) momento; (occasion) vez f; (MUS) compás m ♦ vt calcular o medir el tiempo de; (race) cronometrar; (remark, visit etc) elegir el momento para; **a long ~** mucho tiempo; **4 at a ~** de 4 en 4; 4 a la vez; **for the ~ being** de momento, por ahora; **from ~ to ~** de vez en cuando; **at times** a veces; **in ~** (soon enough) a tiempo; (after some time) con el tiempo; (MUS) al compás; **a week's ~** dentro de una semana; **in**

no ~ en un abrir y cerrar de ojos; **any ~** cuando sea; **on ~** a la hora; **5 times 5** 5 por 5; **what ~ is it?** ¿qué hora es?; **to have a good ~** pasarlo bien, divertirse ❑ **time limit** n plazo ❑ **timely** adj oportuno ❑ **timer** n (in kitchen etc) programador m horario ❑ **time-share** n apartamento (or casa) a tiempo compartido ❑ **timetable** n horario ❑ **time zone** n huso horario

timid ['tɪmɪd] adj tímido

timing n (SPORT) cronometraje m; **the ~ of his resignation** el momento que eligió para dimitir

tin [tɪn] n estaño; (also: ~ **plate**) hojalata; (BRIT: can) lata ❑ **tinfoil** n papel m de estaño

tingle ['tɪŋgl] vi (person): **to ~ (with)** estremecerse (de); (hands etc) hormiguear

tinker ['tɪŋkə']: ~ **with** vt fus jugar con, tocar

tinned [tɪnd] (BRIT) adj (food) en lata, en conserva

tin opener [-əupnə'] (BRIT) n abrelatas m inv

tint [tɪnt] n matiz m; (for hair) tinte m ❑ **tinted** adj (hair) teñido; (glass, spectacles) ahumado

tiny ['taɪnɪ] adj minúsculo, pequeñito

tip [tɪp] n (end) punta; (gratuity) propina; (BRIT: for rubbish) vertedero; (advice) consejo ♦ vt (waiter) dar una propina a; (tilt) inclinar; (empty: also: ~ **out**) vaciar, echar; (overturn: also: ~ **over**) volcar ► **tip off** vt avisar, poner sobreaviso a

tiptoe ['tɪptəʊ] n: **on ~** de puntillas

tire ['taɪə'] n (US) = **tyre** ♦ vt cansar ♦ vi cansarse; (become bored) aburrirse ❑ **tired** adj cansado; **to be tired of sth** estar harto de algo ❑ **tire pressure** (US) = **tyre pressure** ❑ **tiring** adj cansado

tissue ['tɪʃuː] n tejido; (paper handkerchief) pañuelo de papel, kleenex® m ❏ **tissue paper** n papel m de seda

tit [tɪt] n (bird) herrerillo común; **to give ~ for tat** dar ojo por ojo

title ['taɪtl] n título

T-junction ['tiːdʒʌŋkʃən] n cruce m en T

TM abbr = **trademark**

to
KEYWORD

[tuː, tə] prep

1 (direction) a; **to go to France/ London/school/the station** ir a Francia/Londres/al colegio/a la estación; **to go to Claude's/the doctor's** ir a casa de Claude/al médico; **the road to Edinburgh** la carretera de Edimburgo

2 (as far as) hasta, a; **from here to London** de aquí a or hasta Londres; **to count to 10** contar hasta 10; **from 40 to 50 people** entre 40 y 50 personas

3 (with expressions of time): **a quarter/twenty to 5** las 5 menos cuarto/veinte

4 (for, of): **the key to the front door** la llave de la puerta principal; **she is secretary to the director** es la secretaria del director; **a letter to his wife** una carta a or para su mujer

5 (expressing indirect object): **to give sth to sb** darle algo a algn; **to talk to sb** hablar con algn; **to be a danger to sb** ser un peligro para algn; **to carry out repairs to sth** hacer reparaciones en algo

6 (in relation to): **3 goals to 2** 3 goles a 2; **30 miles to the gallon** ≈ 94 litros a los cien (kms)

7 (purpose, result): **to come to sb's aid** venir en auxilio or ayuda de algn; **to sentence sb to death** condenar a algn a muerte; **to my great surprise** con gran sorpresa mía

♦ with vb

1 (simple infin): **to go/eat** ir/comer

2 (following another vb): **to want/try/ start to do** querer/intentar/empezar a hacer

3 (with vb omitted): **I don't want to** no quiero

4 (purpose, result) para; **I did it to help you** lo hice para ayudarte; **he came to see you** vino a verte

5 (equivalent to relative clause): **I have things to do** tengo cosas que hacer; **the main thing is to try** lo principal es intentarlo

6 (after adj etc): **ready to go** listo para irse; **too old to ...** demasiado viejo (como) para ...

♦ adv: **pull/push the door to** tirar de/ empujar la puerta

toad [təʊd] n sapo ❏ **toadstool** n hongo venenoso

toast [təʊst] n (CULIN) tostada; (drink, speech) brindis m ♦ vt (CULIN) tostar; (drink) brindar por ❏ **toaster** n tostador m

tobacco [təˈbækəʊ] n tabaco

toboggan [təˈbɒgən] n tobogán m

today [təˈdeɪ] adv, n (also fig) hoy m

toddler ['tɒdlə] n niño(-a) (que empieza a andar)

toe [təʊ] n dedo (del pie); (of shoe) punta; **to ~ the line** (fig) conformarse ❏ **toenail** n uña del pie

toffee ['tɒfɪ] n toffee m

together [təˈgeðə] adv juntos; (at same time) al mismo tiempo, a la vez; **~ with** junto con

oilet ['tɔɪlət] n inodoro; (BRIT: room) (cuarto de) baño, servicio ♦ cpd (soap etc) de aseo □ **toilet bag** n neceser m, bolsa de aseo □ **toilet paper** n papel m higiénico □ **toiletries** npl artículos mpl de tocador □ **toilet roll** n rollo de papel higiénico

oken ['təukən] n (sign) señal f, muestra; (souvenir) recuerdo; (disc) ficha ♦ adj (strike, payment etc) simbólico; **book/record ~** (BRIT) vale m para comprar libros/discos; **gift ~** (BRIT) vale-regalo

okyo ['təukjəu] n Tokio, Tokío

old [təuld] pt, pp of **tell**

olerant ['tɔlərnt] adj: **~ of** tolerante con

olerate ['tɔləreɪt] vt tolerar

oll [təul] n (of casualties) número de víctimas; (tax, charge) peaje m ♦ vi (bell) doblar □ **toll call** n (US TEL) conferencia, llamada interurbana □ **toll-free** (US) adj, adv gratis

omato [tə'mɑːtəu] (pl **tomatoes**) n tomate m □ **tomato sauce** n salsa de tomate

omb [tuːm] n tumba □ **tombstone** n lápida

omorrow [tə'mɔrəu] adv, n (also: fig) mañana; **the day after ~** pasado mañana; **~ morning** mañana por la mañana

on [tʌn] n tonelada (BRIT = 1016 kg; US = 907 kg); (metric ton) tonelada métrica; **~s of** (inf) montones de

one [təun] n tono ♦ vi (also: **~ in**) armonizar ♦ **tone down** vt (criticism) suavizar; (colour) atenuar

ongs [tɔŋz] npl (for coal) tenazas fpl; (curling tongs) tenacillas fpl

ongue [tʌŋ] n lengua; **~ in cheek** irónicamente

onic ['tɔnɪk] n (MED) tónico; (also: **~ water**) (agua) tónica

onight [tə'naɪt] adv, n esta noche; esta arde

tonne [tʌn] n tonelada (métrica) (1.000kg)

tonsil ['tɔnsl] n amígdala □ **tonsillitis** [-'laɪtɪs] n amigdalitis f

too [tuː] adv (excessively) demasiado; (also) también; **~ much** demasiado; **~ many** demasiados(-as)

took [tuk] pt of **take**

tool [tuːl] n herramienta □ **tool box** n caja de herramientas □ **tool kit** n juego de herramientas

tooth [tuːθ] (pl **teeth**) n (ANAT, TECH) diente m; (molar) muela □ **toothache** n dolor m de muelas □ **toothbrush** n cepillo de dientes □ **toothpaste** n pasta de dientes □ **toothpick** n palillo

top [tɔp] n (of mountain) cumbre f, cima; (of tree) copa; (of head) coronilla; (of ladder, page) lo alto; (of table) superficie f; (of cupboard) parte f de arriba; (lid: of box) tapa; (: of bottle, jar) tapón m; (of list etc) cabeza; (toy) peonza; (garment) blusa; camiseta ♦ adj de arriba; (in rank) principal, primero; (best) mejor ♦ vt (exceed) exceder; (be first in) encabezar; **on ~ of** (above) sobre, encima de; (in addition to) además de; **from ~ to bottom** de pies a cabeza ♦ **top up** vt llenar □ **top floor** n último piso □ **top hat** n sombrero de copa

topic ['tɔpɪk] n tema m □ **topical** adj actual

topless ['tɔplɪs] adj (bather, bikini) topless inv

topping ['tɔpɪŋ] n (CULIN): **with a ~ of cream** con nata por encima

topple ['tɔpl] vt derribar ♦ vi caerse

torch [tɔːtʃ] n antorcha; (BRIT: electric) linterna

tore [tɔː] pt of **tear²**

torment [n 'tɔːment, vt tɔː'ment] n tormento ♦ vt atormentar; (fig: annoy) fastidiar

torn [tɔːn] pp of **tear²**

tornado [tɔːˈneɪdəu] (pl **tornadoes**) n tornado

torpedo [tɔːˈpiːdəu] (pl **torpedoes**) n torpedo

torrent [ˈtɒrnt] n torrente m □ **torrential** [tɒˈrenʃl] adj torrencial

tortoise [ˈtɔːtəs] n tortuga

torture [ˈtɔːtʃə] n tortura ♦ vt torturar; (fig) atormentar

Tory [ˈtɔːrɪ] (BRIT) adj, n (POL) conservador(a) m/f

toss [tɒs] vt tirar, echar; (one's head) sacudir; **to ~ a coin** echar a cara o cruz; **to ~ up for sth** jugar a cara o cruz algo; **to ~ and turn** (in bed) dar vueltas

total [ˈtəutl] adj total, entero; (emphatic: failure etc) completo, total ♦ n total m, suma ♦ vt (add up) sumar; (amount to) ascender a

totalitarian [təutælɪˈtɛərɪən] adj totalitario

totally [ˈtəutəlɪ] adv totalmente

touch [tʌtʃ] n tacto; (contact) contacto ♦ vt tocar; (emotionally) conmover; **a ~ of** (fig) un poquito de; **to get in ~ with sb** ponerse en contacto con algn; **to lose ~** (friends) perder contacto ▶ **touch down** vi (on land) aterrizar □ **touchdown** n aterrizaje m; (on sea) amerizaje m; (US FOOTBALL) ensayo □ **touched** adj (moved) conmovido □ **touching** adj (moving) conmovedor(a) □ **touchline** n (SPORT) línea de banda □ **touch-sensitive** adj sensible al tacto

tough [tʌf] adj (material) resistente; (meat) duro; (problem etc) difícil; (policy, stance) inflexible; (person) fuerte

tour [tuə] n viaje m, vuelta; (also: **package ~**) viaje m todo comprendido; (of town, museum) visita; (by band etc) gira ♦ vt recorrer, visitar □ **tour guide** n guía mf turístico(-a)

tourism [ˈtuərɪzm] n turismo

tourist [ˈtuərɪst] n turista mf ♦ cpd turístico □ **tourist office** n oficina d turismo

tournament [ˈtuənəmənt] n torneo

tour operator n touroperador(a) m/f operador(a) m/f turístico(-a)

tow [təu] vt remolcar; **"on** or **in** (US) **~"** (AUT) "a remolque" ▶ **tow away** vt llevarse a remolque

toward(s) [təˈwɔːd(z)] prep hacia; (attitude) respecto a, con; (purpose) para

towel [ˈtauəl] n toalla □ **towelling** n (fabric) felpa

tower [ˈtauə] n torre f □ **tower bloc** (BRIT) n torre f (de pisos)

town [taun] n ciudad f; **to go to ~** ir a ciudad; (fig) echar la casa por la ventana □ **town centre** n centro de la ciudad □ **town hall** n ayuntamiento

tow truck (US) n camión m grúa

toxic [ˈtɒksɪk] adj tóxico

toy [tɔɪ] n juguete m ▶ **toy with** vt fu jugar con; (idea) acariciar □ **toysho** n juguetería

trace [treɪs] n rastro ♦ vt (draw) trazar delinear; (locate) encontrar; (follow) seguir la pista de

track [træk] n (mark) huella, pista; (pa gen) camino, senda; (: of bullet etc) trayectoria; (: of suspect, animal) pista rastro; (RAIL) vía; (SPORT) pista; (on tap record) canción f ♦ vt seguir la pista de **to keep ~ of** mantenerse al tanto de seguir ▶ **track down** vt (prey) segui el rastro de; (sth lost) encontrar □ **tracksuit** n chándal m

tractor [ˈtræktə] n tractor m

trade [treɪd] n comercio; (skill, job) oficio ♦ vi negociar, comerciar ♦ vt (exchange) **to ~ sth (for sth)** cambia algo (por algo) ▶ **trade in** vt (old ca etc) ofrecer como parte del pago □ **trademark** n marca de fábrica □ **trader** n comerciante mf

❑ **tradesman** (irreg) n (shopkeeper) tendero ❑ **trade union** n sindicato

rading ['treɪdɪŋ] n comercio

radition [trə'dɪʃən] n tradición f ❑ **traditional** adj tradicional

raffic ['træfɪk] n (gen, AUT) tráfico, circulación f ♦ vi: **to ~ in** (pej: liquor, drugs) traficar en ❑ **traffic circle** (US) n isleta ❑ **traffic island** n refugio, isleta ❑ **traffic jam** n embotellamiento ❑ **traffic lights** npl semáforo ❑ **traffic warden** n guardia mf de tráfico

ragedy ['trædʒədɪ] n tragedia

agic ['trædʒɪk] adj trágico

ail [treɪl] n (tracks) rastro, pista; (path) camino, sendero; (dust, smoke) estela ♦ vt (drag) arrastrar; (follow) seguir la pista de ♦ vi seguir, ir perdiendo ❑ **trailer** n (AUT) remolque m; (caravan) caravana; (CINEMA) trailer m, avance m

ain [treɪn] n tren m; (of dress) cola; (series) serie f ♦ vt (educate, teach skills to) formar; (sportsman) entrenar; (dog) adiestrar; (point: gun etc): **to ~ on** apuntar a ♦ vi (SPORT) entrenarse; (learn a skill): **to ~ as a teacher** etc estudiar para profesor etc; **one's ~ of thought** el razonamiento de algn ❑ **trainee** [treɪ'niː] n aprendiz/a m/f ❑ **trainer** n (SPORT: coach) entrenador(a) m/f; (of animals) domador(a) m/f; **trainers** npl (shoes) zapatillas fpl (de deporte) ❑ **training** n formación f; entrenamiento m; **to be in ~ing** (SPORT) estar entrenando ❑ **training course** n curso de formación ❑ **training shoes** npl zapatillas fpl (de deporte)

ait [treɪt] n rasgo

aitor ['treɪtə'] n traidor(a) m/f

am [træm] (BRIT) n (also: **tramcar**) tranvía m

amp [træmp] n (person) vagabundo(-a); (inf: pej: woman) puta

trample ['træmpl] vt: **to ~ (underfoot)** pisotear

trampoline ['træmpəliːn] n trampolín m

tranquil ['træŋkwɪl] adj tranquilo ❑ **tranquillizer** (US **tranquilizer**) n (MED) tranquilizante m

transaction [træn'zækʃən] n transacción f, operación f

transatlantic ['trænzət'læntɪk] adj transatlántico

transcript ['trænskrɪpt] n copia

transfer [n 'trænsfə', vb træns'fə:'] n (of employees) traslado; (of money, power) transferencia; (SPORT) traspaso; (picture, design) calcomanía ♦ vt trasladar; transferir; **to ~ the charges** (BRIT TEL) llamar a cobro revertido

transform [træns'fɔ:m] vt transformar ❑ **transformation** n transformación f

transfusion [træns'fju:ʒən] n transfusión f

transit ['trænzɪt] n: **in ~** en tránsito

transition [træn'zɪʃən] n transición f

transitive ['trænzɪtɪv] adj (LING) transitivo

translate [trænz'leɪt] vt traducir ❑ **translation** [-'leɪʃən] n traducción f ❑ **translator** n traductor(a) m/f

transmission [trænz'mɪʃən] n transmisión f

transmit [trænz'mɪt] vt transmitir ❑ **transmitter** n transmisor m

transparent [træns'pærnt] adj transparente

transplant [træns'plɑ:nt] n (MED) transplante m

transport [n 'trænspɔ:t, vt træns'pɔ:t] n transporte m; (car) coche m (SP), carro (LAm), automóvil m ♦ vt transportar ❑ **transportation** [-'teɪʃən] n transporte m

transvestite [trænz'vestaɪt] n travestí mf

trap [træp] n (snare, trick) trampa; (carriage) cabriolé m ♦ vt coger (SP) or agarrar (*LAm*) (en una trampa); (*trick*) engañar; (*confine*) atrapar

trash [træʃ] n (*rubbish*) basura; (*nonsense*) tonterías *fpl*, (*pej*): **the book/film is ~** el libro/la película no vale nada □ **trash can** (*US*) n cubo o bote m (*MEX*) or tacho (*SC*) de la basura

trauma [ˈtrɔːmə] n trauma m □ **traumatic** [trɔːˈmætɪk] adj traumático

travel [ˈtrævl] n el viajar ♦ vi viajar ♦ vt (*distance*) recorrer □ **travel agency** n agencia de viajes □ **travel agent** n agente *mf* de viajes □ **travel insurance** n seguro de viaje □ **traveller** (*US* **traveler**) n viajero(-a) □ **traveller's cheque** (*US* **traveler's check**) n cheque m de viajero □ **travelling** (*US* **traveling**) n los viajes, el viajar □ **travel-sick** adj: **to get travel-sick** marearse al viajar □ **travel sickness** n mareo

tray [treɪ] n bandeja; (*on desk*) cajón m

treacherous [ˈtrɛtʃərəs] adj traidor, traicionero; (*dangerous*) peligroso

treacle [ˈtriːkl] (*BRIT*) n melaza

tread [trɛd] (*pt* trod, *pp* **trodden**) n (*step*) paso, pisada; (*sound*) ruido de pasos; (*of stair*) escalón m; (*of tyre*) banda de rodadura ♦ vi pisar ▶ **tread on** vt fus pisar

treason [ˈtriːzə] n tesoro ♦ vt (*value: object, friendship*) apreciar; (*: memory*) guardar □ **treasurer** n tesorero(-a)

treasury [ˈtrɛʒərɪ] n: **the T~** el Ministerio de Hacienda

treat [triːt] n (*present*) regalo ♦ vt tratar; **to ~ sb to sth** invitar a algn a algo □ **treatment** n tratamiento

treaty [ˈtriːtɪ] n tratado

treble [ˈtrɛbl] adj triple ♦ vt triplicar ♦ vi triplicarse

tree [triː] n árbol m; **~ trunk** tronco de (árbol)

trek [trɛk] n (*long journey*) viaje m largo y difícil; (*tiring walk*) caminata

tremble [ˈtrɛmbl] vi temblar

tremendous [trɪˈmɛndəs] adj tremendo, enorme; (*excellent*) estupendo

trench [trɛntʃ] n zanja

trend [trɛnd] n (*tendency*) tendencia; (*of events*) curso; (*fashion*) moda □ **trendy** adj de moda

trespass [ˈtrɛspəs] vi: **to ~ on** entrar sin permiso en; **"no trespassing"** "prohibido el paso"

trial [ˈtraɪəl] n (*LAW*) juicio, proceso; (*test: of machine etc*) prueba □ **trial period** n período de prueba

triangle [ˈtraɪæŋgl] n (*MATH, MUS*) triángulo

triangular [traɪˈæŋgjulə] adj triangular

tribe [traɪb] n tribu f

tribunal [traɪˈbjuːnl] n tribunal m

tribute [ˈtrɪbjuːt] n homenaje m, tributo; **to pay ~** to rendir homenaje

trick [trɪk] n (*skill, knack*) tino, truco; (*conjuring trick*) truco; (*joke*) broma; (*CARDS*) baza ♦ vt engañar; **to play a ~ on sb** gastar una broma a algn; **that should do the ~** a ver si funciona así

trickle [ˈtrɪkl] n (*of water etc*) goteo ♦ vi gotear

tricky [ˈtrɪkɪ] adj difícil; delicado

tricycle [ˈtraɪsɪkl] n triciclo

trifle [ˈtraɪfl] n bagatela; (*CULIN*) dulce de bizcocho borracho, gelatina, fruta y natillas ♦ adv: **a ~ long** un poquito largo

trigger [ˈtrɪgə] n (*of gun*) gatillo

trim [trɪm] adj (*house, garden*) en buen estado; (*person, figure*) esbelto ♦ vt (*haircut etc*) recorte m; (*on car*) guarnición f ♦ vt (*neaten*) arreglar; (*cut*) recortar; (*decorate*) adornar; (*NAUT: a sail*) orientar

trio [ˈtriːəu] n trío

trip [trɪp] n viaje m; (*excursion*) excursión f; (*stumble*) traspié m ♦ vi (*stumble*) tropezar; (*go lightly*) andar con paso ligero; **on a ~** de viaje ▶ **trip up**

tropezar, caerse ♦ vt hacer tropezar or caer

riple ['trɪpl] adj triple

riplets ['trɪplɪts] npl trillizos(-as) mpl/fpl

ipod ['traɪpɒd] n trípode m

iumph ['traɪʌmf] n triunfo m ♦ vi: to ~ (over) vencer □ **triumphant** [traɪˈʌmfænt] adj (team etc) triunfal; (wave, return) triunfal

ivial ['trɪvɪəl] adj insignificante; (commonplace) banal

od [trɒd] pt of **tread**

odden ['trɒdn] pp of **tread**

olley ['trɒlɪ] n carrito; (also: ~ **bus**) trolebús m

ombone [trɒmˈbəʊn] n trombón m

oop [tru:p] n grupo, banda; **troops** npl (MIL) tropas fpl

ophy ['trəʊfɪ] n trofeo

opical ['trɒpɪkl] adj tropical

ot [trɒt] n trote m ♦ vi trotar; **on the ~** BRIT: fig) seguidos(-as)

ouble ['trʌbl] n problema m, dificultad f; (worry) preocupación f; (bother, effort) molestia, esfuerzo; (unrest) inquietud f; (MED): **stomach** etc ~ problemas mpl gástricos etc ♦ vt (disturb) molestar; (worry) preocupar, nquietar ♦ vi: **to ~ to do sth** molestarse en hacer algo; **troubles** npl POL etc) conflictos mpl; (personal) problemas mpl; **to be in ~** estar en un puro; **it's no ~!** ¡no es molestia ninguna!; **what's the ~?** (with broken V etc) ¿cuál es el problema?; (doctor to patient) ¿qué pasa? □ **troubled** (adj person) preocupado; (country, epoch, ife) agitado □ **troublemaker** n gitador(a) m/f; (child) alborotador m □ **troublesome** adj molesto

ough [trɒf] n (also: **drinking ~**) brevadero; (also: **feeding ~**) omedero; (depression) depresión f

ousers ['traʊzəz] npl pantalones mpl; **hort ~** pantalones mpl cortos

trout [traʊt] n inv trucha

trowel ['traʊəl] n (of gardener) palita; (of builder) paleta

truant ['truːənt] n: **to play ~** (BRIT) hacer novillos

truce [truːs] n tregua

truck [trʌk] n (lorry) camión m; (RAIL) vagón m □ **truck driver** n camionero

true [truː] adj verdadero; (accurate) exacto; (genuine) auténtico; (faithful) fiel; **to come ~** realizarse

truly ['truːlɪ] adv (really) realmente; (truthfully) verdaderamente; (faithfully): **yours** ~ (in letter) le saluda atentamente

trumpet ['trʌmpɪt] n trompeta

trunk [trʌŋk] n (of tree, person) tronco; (of elephant) trompa; (case) baúl m; (US AUT) maletero; **trunks** npl (also: **swimming trunks**) bañador m (de hombre)

trust [trʌst] n confianza f; (responsibility) responsabilidad f; (LAW) fideicomiso ♦ vt (rely on) tener confianza en; (hope) esperar; (entrust): **to ~ sth to sb** confiar a algn; **to take sth on ~** fiarse de algo □ **trusted** adj de confianza □ **trustworthy** adj digno de confianza

truth [truːθ, pl truːðz] n verdad f □ **truthful** adj veraz

try [traɪ] n tentativa, intento; (RUGBY) ensayo ♦ vt (attempt) intentar; (test: also: ~ **out**) probar, someter a prueba; (LAW) juzgar, procesar; (strain: patience) hacer perder ♦ vi probar; **to have a ~** probar suerte; **to ~ to do sth** intentar hacer algo; ~ **again!** ¡vuelve a probar!; ~ **harder!** ¡esfuérzate más!; **well, I tried** al menos lo intenté □ **try on** vt (clothes) probarse □ **trying** adj (experience) cansado; (person) pesado

T-shirt n camiseta

tub [tʌb] n cubo (SP), cubeta (SP, MEX), balde m (LAm); (bath) bañera (SP), tina (LAm), bañadera (RPl)

tube [tju:b] n tubo; (BRIT: underground) metro; (for tyre) cámara de aire

tuberculosis [tjubə:kju'ləusɪs] n tuberculosis f inv

tube station (BRIT) n estación f de metro

tuck [tʌk] vt (put) poner ▶ **tuck away** vt (money) guardar; (building): **to be tucked away** esconderse, ocultarse ▶ **tuck in** vt meter dentro; (child) arropar ♦ vi (eat) comer con apetito ❏ **tuck shop** n (SCOL) tienda, ≈ bar m (del colegio)

Tue(s). abbr (= Tuesday) mart

Tuesday ['tju:zdɪ] n martes m inv

tug [tʌg] n (ship) remolcador m ♦ vt tirar de

tuition [tju:'ɪʃən] n (BRIT) enseñanza; (: private tuition) clases fpl particulares; (US: school fees) matrícula

tulip ['tju:lɪp] n tulipán m

tumble ['tʌmbl] n (fall) caída ♦ vi caer; **to ~ to sth** (inf) caer en la cuenta de algo ❏ **tumble dryer** (BRIT) n secadora

tumbler ['tʌmblə*] n (glass) vaso

tummy ['tʌmɪ] (inf) n barriga, tripa

tumour ['tju:mə*] (US **tumor**) n tumor m

tuna ['tju:nə] n inv (also: ~ **fish**) atún m

tune [tju:n] n (MUS) melodía ♦ vt (MUS) afinar; (RADIO, TV, AUT) sintonizar; **to be in/out of ~** (instrument) estar afinado/desafinado; (singer) cantar afinadamente/desafinar; **to be in/out of ~ with** (fig) estar de acuerdo/en desacuerdo con ▶ **tune in** vi: **to tune in (to)** (RADIO, TV) sintonizar (con) ▶ **tune up** vi (musician) afinar (su instrumento)

tunic ['tju:nɪk] n túnica

Tunisia [tju:'nɪzɪə] n Túnez m

tunnel ['tʌnl] n túnel m; (in mine) galería ♦ vi construir un túnel/una galería

turbulence ['tə:bjuləns] n (AVIAT) turbulencia

turf [tə:f] n césped m; (clod) tepe m ♦ vt cubrir con césped

Turk [tə:k] n turco(-a)

Turkey ['tə:kɪ] n Turquía

turkey ['tə:kɪ] n pavo

Turkish ['tə:kɪʃ] adj, n turco; (LING) turco

turmoil ['tə:mɔɪl] n: **in ~** revuelto

turn [tə:n] n turno; (in road) curva; (of mind, events) rumbo; (THEATRE) número; (MED) ataque m ♦ vt girar, volver; (collar, steak) dar la vuelta a; (page) pasar; (change): **to ~ sth into** convertir algo en ♦ vi volver; (person: look back) volverse; (reverse direction) dar la vuelta; (milk) cortarse; (become) **to ~ nasty/forty** ponerse feo/cumplir los cuarenta; **a good ~** un favor; **it gave me quite a ~** me dio un susto; **"no left ~"** (AUT) "prohibido girar a la izquierda"; **it's your ~** te toca a ti; **in ~** por turnos; **to take turns (at)** turnarse (en) ▶ **turn around** vi (person) volverse, darse la vuelta ♦ vt (object) dar la vuelta a, voltear (LAm) ▶ **turn away** vi apartar la vista ♦ vt rechazar ▶ **turn back** vi volverse atrás ♦ vt hacer retroceder; (clock) retrasar ▶ **turn down** vt (refuse) rechazar; (reduce) bajar; (fold) doblar ▶ **turn in** vi (inf: go to bed) acostarse ♦ vt (fold) doblar hacia dentro ▶ **turn off** vi (from road) desviarse ♦ vt (light, tap etc) apagar; (tap) cerrar; (engine) para ▶ **turn on** vt (light, radio etc) encender (SP), prender (LAm); (tap) abrir; (engine) poner en marcha ▶ **turn out** vt (light, gas) apagar; (produce) producir ♦ vi (voters) concurrir; **to turn out to be** resultar ser ... ▶ **turn over** vi (person) volverse ♦ vt (object) dar la vuelta a; (page) volver ▶ **turn round** vi volverse; (rotate) girar ▶ **turn to** vt fu: **to turn to sb** acudir a algn ▶ **turn up** vi (person) llegar, presentarse; (lost object) aparecer ♦ vt (gen) subir

□ turning n (in road) vuelta
□ turning point n (fig) momento decisivo

urnip ['tə:nɪp] n nabo

urn: turnout n concurrencia
□ turnover n (COMM: amount of money) volumen m de ventas; (: of goods) movimiento **□ turnstile** n torniquete m **□ turn-up** (BRIT) n (on trousers) vuelta

urquoise ['tə:kwɔɪz] n (stone) turquesa ♦ adj color turquesa

urtle ['tə:tl] n galápago **□ turtleneck (sweater)** n jersey m de cuello vuelto

usk [tʌsk] n colmillo

utor ['tju:tə*] n profesor(a) m/f
□ tutorial [-'tɔ:rɪəl] n (SCOL) seminario

uxedo [tʌk'si:dəu] (US) n smóking m, esmoquin m

V [ti:'vi:] n abbr (= television) tele f

weed [twi:d] n tweed m

weezers ['twi:zəz] npl pinzas fpl (de depilar)

welfth [twelfθ] num duodécimo

welve [twelv] num doce; **at ~ o'clock** (midday) a mediodía; (midnight) a medianoche

wentieth ['twentɪɪθ] adj vigésimo

wenty ['twentɪ] num veinte

vice [twaɪs] adv dos veces; **~ as much** dos veces más

wig [twɪg] n ramita

wilight ['twaɪlaɪt] n crepúsculo

win [twɪn] adj, n gemelo(-a) m/f ♦ vt hermanar **□ twin(-bedded) room** n habitación f doble **□ twin beds** npl camas fpl gemelas

winkle ['twɪŋkl] vi centellear; (eyes) brillar

vist [twɪst] n (action) torsión f; (in road, coil) vuelta; (in wire, flex) doblez f; (in story) giro ♦ vt torcer; (weave) trenzar; (roll around) enrollar; (fig) deformar ♦ vi serpentear

vit [twɪt] (inf) n tonto

twitch [twɪtʃ] n (pull) tirón m; (nervous) tic m ♦ vi crisparse

two [tu:] num dos; **to put ~ and ~ together** (fig) atar cabos

type [taɪp] n (category) tipo, género; (model) tipo; (TYP) tipo, letra ♦ vt (letter etc) escribir a máquina **□ typewriter** n máquina de escribir

typhoid ['taɪfɔɪd] n tifoidea

typhoon [taɪ'fu:n] n tifón m

typical ['tɪpɪkl] adj típico **□ typically** adv típicamente

typing ['taɪpɪŋ] n mecanografía

typist ['taɪpɪst] n mecanógrafo(-a)

tyre ['taɪə*] (US **tire**) n neumático, llanta (LAm) **□ tyre pressure** (BRIT) n presión f de los neumáticos

U, u

UFO ['ju:fəu] n abbr (= unidentified flying object) OVNI m

Uganda [ju:'gændə] n Uganda

ugly ['ʌglɪ] adj feo; (dangerous) peligroso

UHT abbr (= UHT milk) leche f UHT, leche f uperizada

UK n abbr = **United Kingdom**

ulcer ['ʌlsə*] n úlcera; (mouth ulcer) llaga

ultimate ['ʌltɪmət] adj último, final; (greatest) máximo **□ ultimately** adv (in the end) por último, al final; (fundamentally) a or en fin de cuentas

ultimatum [ʌltɪ'meɪtəm] (pl **ultimatums** or **ultimata**) n ultimátum m

ultrasound ['ʌltrəsaund] n (MED) ultrasonido

ultraviolet ['ʌltrə'vaɪəlɪt] adj ultravioleta

umbrella [ʌm'brelə] n paraguas m inv; (for sun) sombrilla

umpire ['ʌmpaɪə*] n árbitro

UN n abbr (= United Nations) NN. UU.

unable [ʌn'eɪbl] adj: to be ~ to do sth no poder hacer algo

unacceptable [ʌnək'septəbl] adj (proposal, behaviour, price) inaceptable; **it's ~ that** no se puede aceptar que

unanimous [juː'nænɪməs] adj unánime

unarmed [ʌn'ɑːmd] adj (defenceless) inerme; (without weapon) desarmado

unattended [ʌnə'tendɪd] adj desatendido

unattractive [ʌnə'træktɪv] adj poco atractivo

unavailable [ʌnə'veɪləbl] adj (article, room, book) no disponible; (person) ocupado

unavoidable [ʌnə'vɔɪdəbl] adj inevitable

unaware [ʌnə'weə'] adj: to be ~ of ignorar □ **unawares** adv: to catch sb unawares pillar a algn desprevenido

unbearable [ʌn'beərəbl] adj insoportable

unbeatable [ʌn'biːtəbl] adj (team) invencible; (price) inmejorable; (quality) insuperable

unbelievable [ʌnbɪ'liːvəbl] adj increíble

unborn [ʌn'bɔːn] adj que va a nacer

unbutton [ʌn'bʌtn] vt desabrochar

uncalled-for [ʌn'kɔːldfɔː'] adj gratuito, inmerecido

uncanny [ʌn'kænɪ] adj extraño

uncertain [ʌn'sɜːtn] adj incierto; (indecisive) indeciso □ **uncertainty** n incertidumbre f

unchanged [ʌn'tʃeɪndʒd] adj igual, sin cambios

uncle [ʌŋkl] n tío

unclear [ʌn'klɪə'] adj poco claro; **I'm still ~ about what I'm supposed to do** todavía no tengo muy claro lo que tengo que hacer

uncomfortable [ʌn'kʌmfətəbl] adj incómodo; (uneasy) inquieto

uncommon [ʌn'kɒmən] adj poco común, raro

unconditional [ʌnkən'dɪʃənl] adj incondicional

unconscious [ʌn'kɒnʃəs] adj sin sentido; (unaware) to be ~ of no darse cuenta de ♦ n: the ~ el inconsciente

uncontrollable [ʌnkən'trəʊləbl] adj (child etc) incontrolable; (temper) indomable; (laughter) incontenible

unconventional [ʌnkən'venʃənl] adj poco convencional

uncover [ʌn'kʌvə'] vt descubrir; (take lid off) destapar

undecided [ʌndɪ'saɪdɪd] adj (character) indeciso; (question) no resuelto

undeniable [ʌndɪ'naɪəbl] adj innegable

under [ˈʌndə'] prep debajo de; (less than) menos de; (according to) según de acuerdo con; (sb's leadership) bajo ♦ adv debajo, abajo; ~ **there** allí abajo; ~ **repair** en reparación □ **undercover** adj clandestino □ **underdone** adj (CULIN) poco hecho □ **underestimate** vt subestimar □ **undergo** (irreg) vt sufrir; (treatment) recibir □ **undergraduate** n estudiante mf □ **underground** n (BRIT: railway) metro; (POL) movimiento clandestino ♦ adj (car park) subterráneo ♦ adv (work) en la clandestinidad □ **undergrowth** n maleza □ **underline** vt subrayar □ **undermine** vt socavar, minar □ **underneath** [ʌndə'niːθ] adv debajo ♦ prep debajo de, bajo □ **underpants** npl calzoncillos mpl □ **underpass** n (BRIT) n paso subterráneo □ **underprivileged** adj desposeído □ **underscore** vt subrayar □ **undershirt** (US) n camiseta □ **underskirt** (BRIT) n enaguas fpl

understand [ʌndə'stænd] vt, vi entender, comprender; (assume) suponer entendido ❑ **understandable** adj comprensible ❑ **understanding** adj comprensivo ♦ n comprensión f, entendimiento; (agreement) acuerdo

understatement [ˈʌndəsteɪtmənt] n modestia (excesiva); **that's an ~!** ¡eso es decir poco!

understood [ʌndəˈstud] pt, pp of **understand** ♦ adj (agreed) acordado; (implied): **it is ~ that** se sobreentiende que

undertake [ʌndəˈteɪk] vt emprender; **to ~ to do sth** comprometerse a hacer algo

undertaker [ˈʌndəteɪkəˈ] n director(a) m/f de pompas fúnebres

undertaking [ˈʌndəteɪkɪŋ] n empresa; (promise) promesa

under: **underwater** adv bajo el agua ♦ adj submarino ❑ **underway** adj: **to be underway** (meeting) estar en marcha; (investigation) estar llevándose a cabo ❑ **underwear** n ropa interior ❑ **underwent** vb see **undergo** ❑ **underworld** n (of crime) hampa, inframundo

undesirable [ʌndɪˈzaɪrəbl] adj (person) indeseable; (thing) poco aconsejable

undisputed [ʌndɪˈspjuːtɪd] adj incontestable

undo [ʌnˈduː] (irreg) vt (laces) desatar; (button etc) desabrochar; (spoil) deshacer

undone [ʌnˈdʌn] pp of **undo** ♦ adj: **to come ~** (clothes) desabrocharse; (parcel) desatarse

undoubtedly [ʌnˈdautɪdlɪ] adv indudablemente, sin duda

undress [ʌnˈdrɛs] vi desnudarse

unearth [ʌnˈəːθ] vt desenterrar

uneasy [ʌnˈiːzɪ] adj intranquilo, preocupado; (feeling) desagradable; (peace) inseguro

unemployed [ʌnɪmˈplɔɪd] adj parado, sin trabajo ♦ npl: **the ~** los parados

unemployment [ʌnɪmˈplɔɪmənt] n paro, desempleo ❑ **unemployment benefit** n (BRIT) subsidio de desempleo or paro

unequal [ʌnˈiːkwəl] adj (unfair) desigual; (size, length) distinto

uneven [ʌnˈiːvn] adj desigual; (road etc) lleno de baches

unexpected [ʌnɪkˈspɛktɪd] adj inesperado ❑ **unexpectedly** adv inesperadamente

unfair [ʌnˈfɛəˈ] adj: **~ (to sb)** injusto (con algn)

unfaithful [ʌnˈfeɪθful] adj infiel

unfamiliar [ʌnfəˈmɪlɪəˈ] adj extraño, desconocido; **to be ~ with** desconocer

unfashionable [ʌnˈfæʃnəbl] adj pasado or fuera de moda

unfasten [ʌnˈfɑːsn] vt (knot) desatar; (dress) desabrochar; (open) abrir

unfavourable [ʌnˈfeɪvərəbl] (US **unfavorable**) adj desfavorable

unfinished [ʌnˈfɪnɪʃt] adj inacabado, sin terminar

unfit [ʌnˈfɪt] adj bajo de forma; (incompetent): **~ (for)** incapaz (de); **~ for work** no apto para trabajar

unfold [ʌnˈfəuld] vt desdoblar ♦ vi abrirse

unforgettable [ʌnfəˈgɛtəbl] adj inolvidable

unfortunate [ʌnˈfɔːtʃnət] adj desgraciado; (event, remark) inoportuno ❑ **unfortunately** adv desgraciadamente

unfriendly [ʌnˈfrɛndlɪ] adj antipático; (behaviour, remark) hostil, poco amigable

unfurnished [ʌnˈfəːnɪʃt] adj sin amueblar

unhappiness [ʌnˈhæpɪnɪs] n tristeza, desdicha

unhappy [ʌnˈhæpɪ] adj (sad) triste; (unfortunate) desgraciado; (childhood) infeliz; **~ about/with** (arrangements *etc*) poco contento con, descontento de

unhealthy [ʌn'hɛlθɪ] *adj* (*place*) malsano; (*person*) enfermizo; (*fig: interest*) morboso

unheard-of [ʌn'hɜːdɔv] *adj* inaudito, sin precedente

unhelpful [ʌn'hɛlpful] *adj* (*person*) poco servicial; (*advice*) inútil

unhurt [ʌn'hɜːt] *adj* ileso

unidentified [ʌnaɪ'dɛntɪfaɪd] *adj* no identificado, sin identificar; *see also* **UFO**

uniform [ˈjuːnɪfɔːm] *n* uniforme *m* ♦ *adj* uniforme

unify [ˈjuːnɪfaɪ] *vt* unificar, unir

unimportant [ʌnɪm'pɔːtənt] *adj* sin importancia

uninhabited [ʌnɪn'hæbɪtɪd] *adj* desierto

unintentional [ʌnɪn'tɛnʃənəl] *adj* involuntario

union [ˈjuːnjən] *n* unión f; (*also:* **trade ~**) sindicato ♦ *cpd* sindical □ **Union Jack** *n* bandera del Reino Unido

unique [juːˈniːk] *adj* único

unisex [ˈjuːnɪsɛks] *adj* unisex

unit [ˈjuːnɪt] *n* unidad f; (*section: of furniture etc*) elemento; (*team*) grupo; **kitchen ~** módulo de cocina

unite [juːˈnaɪt] *vt* unir ♦ *vi* unirse □ **united** *adj* unido; (*effort*) conjunto □ **United Kingdom** *n* Reino Unido □ **United Nations (Organization)** *n* Naciones fpl Unidas □ **United States (of America)** *n* Estados mpl Unidos

unity [ˈjuːnɪtɪ] *n* unidad f

universal [juːnɪˈvɜːsl] *adj* universal

universe [ˈjuːnɪvɜːs] *n* universo

university [juːnɪˈvɜːsɪtɪ] *n* universidad f

unjust [ʌn'dʒʌst] *adj* injusto

unkind [ʌn'kaɪnd] *adj* poco amable; (*behaviour, comment*) cruel

unknown [ʌn'nəun] *adj* desconocido

unlawful [ʌn'lɔːful] *adj* ilegal, ilícito

unleaded [ʌn'lɛdɪd] *adj* (*petrol, fuel*) sin plombo

unleash [ʌn'liːʃ] *vt* desatar

unless [ʌn'lɛs] *conj* a menos que; **~ he comes** a menos que venga; **~ otherwise stated** salvo indicación contraria

unlike [ʌn'laɪk] *adj* (*not alike*) distinto de o *a*; (*not like*) poco propio de ♦ *prep* a diferencia de

unlikely [ʌn'laɪklɪ] *adj* improbable; (*unexpected*) inverosímil

unlimited [ʌn'lɪmɪtɪd] *adj* ilimitado

unlisted [ʌn'lɪstɪd] *adj* (*US*) (*TEL*) que no consta en la guía

unload [ʌn'ləud] *vt* descargar

unlock [ʌn'lɔk] *vt* abrir (con llave)

unlucky [ʌn'lʌkɪ] *adj* desgraciado; (*object, number*) que da mala suerte; **to be ~** tener mala suerte

unmarried [ʌn'mærɪd] *adj* soltero

unmistak(e)able [ʌnmɪs'teɪkəbl] *adj* inconfundible

unnatural [ʌn'nætʃrəl] *adj* (*gen*) antinatural; (*manner*) afectado; (*habit*) perverso

unnecessary [ʌn'nɛsəsərɪ] *adj* innecesario, inútil

UNO [ˈjuːnəu] *n abbr* (= *United Nations Organization*) ONU f

unofficial [ʌnəˈfɪʃl] *adj* no oficial; (*news*) sin confirmar

unpack [ʌn'pæk] *vi* deshacer las maletas ♦ *vt* deshacer

unpaid [ʌn'peɪd] *adj* (*bill, debt*) sin pagar, impagado; (*COMM*) pendiente; (*holiday*) sin sueldo; (*work*) sin pago, voluntario

unpleasant [ʌn'plɛznt] *adj* (*disagreeable*) desagradable; (*person, manner*) antipático

unplug [ʌn'plʌg] *vt* desenchufar, desconectar

unpopular [ʌn'pɔpjulə'] *adj* impopular, poco popular

nprecedented [ʌnˈpresɪdəntɪd] *adj* sin precedentes

npredictable [ʌnprɪˈdɪktəbl] *adj* imprevisible

nprotected [ˈʌnprəˈtektɪd] *adj* (*sex*) sin protección

nqualified [ʌnˈkwɔlɪfaɪd] *adj* sin título, no cualificado; (*success*) total

nravel [ʌnˈrævl] *vt* desenmarañar

nreal [ʌnˈrɪəl] *adj* irreal; (*extraordinary*) increíble

nrealistic [ʌnrɪəˈlɪstɪk] *adj* poco realista

nreasonable [ʌnˈriːznəbl] *adj* irrazonable; (*demand*) excesivo

nrelated [ʌnrɪˈleɪtɪd] *adj* sin relación; (*family*) no emparentado

nreliable [ʌnrɪˈlaɪəbl] *adj* (*person*) informal; (*machine*) poco fiable

nrest [ʌnˈrest] *n* inquietud *f*, malestar *m*; (*POL*) disturbios *mpl*

nroll [ʌnˈrəʊl] *vt* desenrollar

nruly [ʌnˈruːlɪ] *adj* indisciplinado

nsafe [ʌnˈseɪf] *adj* peligroso

nsatisfactory [ˈʌnsætɪsˈfæktərɪ] *adj* poco satisfactorio

nscrew [ʌnˈskruː] *vt* destornillar

nsettled [ʌnˈsetld] *adj* inquieto, intranquilo; (*weather*) variable

nsettling [ʌnˈsetlɪŋ] *adj* perturbador(a), inquietante

nsightly [ʌnˈsaɪtlɪ] *adj* feo

nskilled [ʌnˈskɪld] *adj* (*work*) no especializado; (*worker*) no cualificado

nspoiled [ʌnˈspɔɪld], **unspoilt** [ˈʌnˈspɔɪlt] *adj* (*place*) que no ha perdido su belleza natural

nstable [ʌnˈsteɪbl] *adj* inestable

nsteady [ʌnˈstedɪ] *adj* inestable

nsuccessful [ʌnsəkˈsesful] *adj* (*attempt*) infructuoso; (*writer, proposal*) sin éxito; **to be ~** (*in attempting sth*) no tener éxito, fracasar

nsuitable [ʌnˈsuːtəbl] *adj* inapropiado; (*time*) inoportuno

unsure [ʌnˈʃʊə] *adj* inseguro, poco seguro

untidy [ʌnˈtaɪdɪ] *adj* (*room*) desordenado; (*appearance*) desaliñado

untie [ʌnˈtaɪ] *vt* desatar

until [ənˈtɪl] *prep* hasta ♦ *conj* hasta que; **~ he comes** hasta que venga; **~ now** hasta ahora; **~ then** hasta entonces

untrue [ʌnˈtruː] *adj* (*statement*) falso

unused [ʌnˈjuːzd] *adj* sin usar

unusual [ʌnˈjuːʒʊəl] *adj* insólito, poco común; (*exceptional*) inusitado
  ❑ **unusually** *adv* (*exceptionally*) excepcionalmente; **he arrived unusually early** llegó más temprano que de costumbre

unveil [ʌnˈveɪl] *vt* (*statue*) descubrir

unwanted [ʌnˈwɒntɪd] *adj* (*clothing*) viejo; (*pregnancy*) no deseado

unwell [ʌnˈwel] *adj*: **to be/feel ~** estar indispuesto/sentirse mal

unwilling [ʌnˈwɪlɪŋ] *adj*: **to be ~ to do sth** estar poco dispuesto a hacer algo

unwind [ʌnˈwaɪnd] (*irreg*) *vt* desenvolver ♦ *vi* (*relax*) relajarse

unwise [ʌnˈwaɪz] *adj* imprudente

unwittingly [ʌnˈwɪtɪŋlɪ] *adv* inconscientemente, sin darse cuenta

unwrap [ʌnˈræp] *vt* desenvolver

unzip [ʌnˈzɪp] *vt* abrir la cremallera de

up

KEYWORD

[ʌp] *prep*: **to go/be up sth** subir/estar subido en algo; **he went up the stairs/the hill** subió las escaleras/la colina; **we walked/climbed up the hill** subimos la colina; **they live further up the street** viven más arriba en la calle; **go up that road and turn left** sigue por esa calle y gira a la izquierda

♦ *adv*

1 (upwards, higher) más arriba; **up in the mountains** en lo alto (de la montaña); **put it a bit higher up** ponlo un poco más arriba or alto; **up there** ahí or allí arriba; **up above** en lo alto, por encima, arriba

2: **to be up** (out of bed) estar levantado; (prices, level) haber subido

3: **up to** (as far as) hasta; **up to now** hasta ahora or la fecha

4: **to be up to**: **it's up to you** (depending on) depende de ti; **he's not up to it** (job, task etc) no es capaz de hacerlo; **his work is not up to the required standard** su trabajo no da la talla; (inf: be doing): **what is he up to?** ¿que estará tramando?

♦ n: **ups and downs** altibajos mpl

up-and-coming [ʌpənd'kʌmɪŋ] adj prometedor(a)

upbringing ['ʌpbrɪŋɪŋ] n educación f

update [ʌp'deɪt] vt poner al día

upfront [ʌp'frʌnt] adj claro, directo ♦ adv a las claras; (pay) por adelantado; **to be ~ about sth** admitir algo claramente

upgrade [ʌp'greɪd] vt (house) modernizar; (employee) ascender

upheaval [ʌp'hiːvl] n trastornos mpl; (POL) agitación f

uphill [ʌp'hɪl] adj cuesta arriba; (fig: task) penoso, difícil ♦ adv: **to go ~** ir cuesta arriba

upholstery [ʌp'həʊlstərɪ] n tapicería

upkeep ['ʌpkiːp] n mantenimiento

upmarket [ʌp'mɑːkɪt] adj (product) de categoría

upon [ə'pɒn] prep sobre

upper ['ʌpə*] adj superior, de arriba ♦ n (of shoe: also: **uppers**) empeine m
❏ **upper-class** adj de clase alta

upright ['ʌpraɪt] adj derecho; (vertical) vertical; (fig) honrado

uprising ['ʌpraɪzɪŋ] n sublevación f

uproar ['ʌprɔː*] n escándalo

upset [n 'ʌpset, vb, adj ʌp'set] n (to plan etc) revés m, contratiempo; (MED) trastorno ♦ vt irreg (glass etc) volcar; (plan) alterar; (person) molestar, disgustar ♦ adj molesto, disgustado; (stomach) revuelto

upside-down [ʌpsaɪd'daʊn] adv al revés; **to turn a place ~** (fig) revolverlo todo

upstairs [ʌp'steəz] adv arriba ♦ adj (room) de arriba ♦ n el piso superior

up-to-date [ʌptə'deɪt] adj al día

uptown ['ʌptaʊn] (US) adv hacia las afueras ♦ adj exterior, de las afueras

upward ['ʌpwəd] adj ascendente
❏ **upward(s)** adv hacia arriba; (more than): **upward(s) of** más de

uranium [jʊə'reɪnɪəm] n uranio

Uranus [jʊə'reɪnəs] n Urano

urban ['ɜːbən] adj urbano

urge [ɜːdʒ] n (desire) deseo ♦ vt: **to ~ sb to do sth** animar a algn a hacer algo

urgency ['ɜːdʒənsɪ] n urgencia

urgent ['ɜːdʒənt] adj urgente; (voice) perentorio

urinal ['jʊərɪnl] n (building) urinario; (vessel) orinal m

urinate ['jʊərɪneɪt] vi orinar

urine ['jʊərɪn] n orina, orines mpl

US n abbr (= United States) EE. UU.

us [ʌs] pron nos; (after prep) nosotros(-as); see also **me**

USA n abbr (= United States of America) EE.UU.

use [n juːs, vb juːz] n uso, empleo; (usefulness) utilidad f ♦ vt usar, emplear; **she used to do it** (ella) solía or acostumbraba hacerlo; **in ~** en uso; **out of ~** en desuso; **to be of ~** servir; **it's no ~** (pointless) es inútil; (not useful) no sirve; **to be used to** estar acostumbrado a, acostumbrar ► **use up** vt (food) consumir; (money) gasta
❏ **used** [juːzd] adj (car) usado
❏ **useful** adj útil ❏ **useless** adj

(*unusable*) inservible; (*pointless*) inútil; (*person*) inepto ❑ **user** n usuario(-a) ❑ **user-friendly** adj (*computer*) amistoso

usual ['ju:ʒuəl] adj normal, corriente; **as ~** como de costumbre ❑ **usually** adv normalmente

utensil [ju:'tensl] n utensilio; **kitchen utensils** batería de cocina

utility [ju:'tɪlɪtɪ] n utilidad f; (*public utility*) empresa f de servicio público

utilize ['ju:tɪlaɪz] vt utilizar

utmost ['ʌtməust] adj mayor ♦ n: **to do one's ~** hacer todo lo posible

utter ['ʌtə] adj total, completo ♦ vt pronunciar, proferir ❑ **utterly** adv completamente, totalmente

U-turn ['ju:'tə:n] n viraje m en redondo

V, v

v. abbr = **verse**; **versus**; (= *volt*) v; (= *vide*) véase

vacancy ['veɪkənsɪ] n (*BRIT: job*) vacante f; (*room*) habitación f libre; **"no vacancies"** "completo"

vacant ['veɪkənt] adj desocupado, libre; (*expression*) distraído

vacate [və'keɪt] vt (*house, room*) desocupar; (*job*) dejar (vacante)

vacation [və'keɪʃən] n vacaciones fpl ❑ **vacationer**, **vacationist** (US) n turista m/f

vaccination [væksɪ'neɪʃən] n vacunación f

vaccine ['væksi:n] n vacuna

vacuum ['vækjum] n vacío ❑ **vacuum cleaner** n aspiradora

vagina [və'dʒaɪnə] n vagina

vague [veɪg] adj vago; (*memory*) borroso; (*ambiguous*) impreciso; (*person: absent-minded*) distraído; (: *evasive*): **to be ~** no decir las cosas claramente

vain [veɪn] adj (*conceited*) presumido; (*useless*) vano, inútil; **in ~** en vano

Valentine's Day ['væləntaɪnzdeɪ] n día de los enamorados

valid ['vælɪd] adj válido; (*ticket*) valedero; (*law*) vigente

valley ['vælɪ] n valle m

valuable ['væljuəbl] adj (*jewel*) de valor; (*time*) valioso ❑ **valuables** npl objetos mpl de valor

value ['vælju:] n valor m; (*importance*) importancia ♦ vt (*fix price of*) tasar, valorar; (*esteem*) apreciar; **values** npl (*principles*) principios mpl

valve [vælv] n válvula

vampire ['væmpaɪə] n vampiro

van [væn] n (*AUT*) furgoneta, camioneta

vandal ['vændl] n vándalo(-a) ❑ **vandalism** n vandalismo ❑ **vandalize** vt dañar, destruir

vanilla [və'nɪlə] n vainilla

vanish ['vænɪʃ] vi desaparecer

vanity ['vænɪtɪ] n vanidad f

vapour ['veɪpə] (US **vapor**) n vapor m; (*on breath, window*) vaho

variable ['veərɪəbl] adj variable

variant ['veərɪənt] n variante f

variation [veərɪ'eɪʃən] n variación f

varied ['veərɪd] adj variado

variety [və'raɪətɪ] n (*diversity*) diversidad f; (*type*) variedad f

various ['veərɪəs] adj (*several: people*) varios(-as); (*reasons*) diversos(-as)

varnish ['vɑːnɪʃ] n barniz m; (*nail varnish*) esmalte m ♦ vt barnizar; (*nails*) pintar (con esmalte)

vary ['veərɪ] vt variar; (*change*) cambiar ♦ vi variar

vase [vɑːz] n jarrón m

⚠ Be careful not to translate **vase** by the Spanish word *vaso*.

Vaseline® ['væsɪli:n] n vaselina®

vast [vɑːst] adj enorme

VAT [væt] (*BRIT*) n abbr (= value added tax) IVA m

vault [vɔːlt] n (of roof) bóveda; (*tomb*) panteón m; (*in bank*) cámara acorazada ♦ vt (*also:* ~ **over**) saltar (por encima de)

VCR n abbr = **video cassette recorder**

VDU n abbr (= visual display unit) UPV f

veal [viːl] n ternera

veer [vɪə] vi (*vehicle*) virar; (*wind*) girar

vegan [ˈviːɡən] n vegetariano(-a) estricto(-a), vegetaliano(-a)

vegetable [ˈvedʒtəbl] n (*BOT*) vegetal m; (*edible plant*) legumbre f, hortaliza ♦ adj vegetal

vegetarian [vedʒɪˈtɛərɪən] adj, n vegetariano(-a) m/f

vegetation [vedʒɪˈteɪʃən] n vegetación f

vehicle [ˈviːɪkl] n vehículo; (*fig*) medio

veil [veɪl] n velo ♦ vt velar

vein [veɪn] n vena; (*of ore etc*) veta

Velcro® [ˈvelkrəu] n velcro® m

velvet [ˈvelvɪt] n terciopelo

vending machine [ˈvendɪŋ-] n distribuidor m automático

vendor [ˈvendɔː] n vendedor(a) m/f; **street ~** vendedor(a) m/f callejero(-a)

vengeance [ˈvendʒəns] n venganza; **with a ~** (*fig*) con creces

venison [ˈvenɪsn] n carne f de venado

venom [ˈvenəm] n veneno; (*bitterness*) odio

vent [vent] n (*in jacket*) respiradero; (*in wall*) rejilla (de ventilación) ♦ vt (*fig: feelings*) desahogar

ventilation [ventɪˈleɪʃən] n ventilación f

venture [ˈventʃə] n empresa ♦ vt (*opinion*) ofrecer ♦ vi aventurarse, lanzarse; **business ~** empresa comercial

venue [ˈvenjuː] n lugar m

Venus [ˈviːnəs] n Venus m

verb [vəːb] n verbo ◻ **verbal** adj verbal

verdict [ˈvəːdɪkt] n veredicto, fallo; (*fig*) opinión f, juicio

verge [vəːdʒ] (*BRIT*) n borde m; **"soft verges"** (*AUT*) "arcén m no asfaltado"; **to be on the ~ of doing sth** estar a punto de hacer algo

verify [ˈverɪfaɪ] vt comprobar, verificar

versatile [ˈvəːsətaɪl] adj (*person*) polifacético; (*machine, tool etc*) versátil

verse [vəːs] n poesía; (*stanza*) estrofa; (*in bible*) versículo

version [ˈvəːʃən] n versión f

versus [ˈvəːsəs] prep contra

vertical [ˈvəːtɪkl] adj vertical

very [ˈverɪ] adv muy ♦ adj: **the ~ book which** el mismo libro que; **the ~ last** el último de todos; **at the ~ least** al menos; **~ much** muchísimo

vessel [ˈvesl] n (*ship*) barco; (*container*) vasija; *see* **blood**

vest [vest] n (*BRIT*) camiseta; (*US: waistcoat*) chaleco

vet [vet] n (*candidate*) investigar ♦ n abbr (*BRIT*) = **veterinary surgeon**

veteran [ˈvetərn] n excombatiente m/f veterano(-a)

veterinary surgeon [ˈvetrɪnrɪ] (*US* **veterinarian** n veterinario(-a) m/f

veto [ˈviːtəu] (*pl* **vetoes**) n veto ♦ vt prohibir, poner el veto a

via [ˈvaɪə] prep por, por medio de

viable [ˈvaɪəbl] adj viable

vibrate [vaɪˈbreɪt] vi vibrar

vibration [vaɪˈbreɪʃən] n vibración f

vicar [ˈvɪkə] n párroco (de la Iglesia Anglicana)

vice [vaɪs] n (*evil*) vicio; (*TECH*) torno de banco ◻ **vice-chairman** (*irreg*) n vicepresidente m

vice versa [ˈvaɪsɪˈvəːsə] adv viceversa

vicinity [vɪˈsɪnɪtɪ] n: **in the ~ (of)** cercano (a)

vicious [ˈvɪʃəs] adj (*attack*) violento; (*words*) cruel; (*horse, dog*) resabido

victim [ˈvɪktɪm] n víctima

ictor [ˈvɪktəʳ] n vencedor(a) m/f

ictorian [vɪkˈtɔːrɪən] adj victoriano

ictorious [vɪkˈtɔːrɪəs] adj vencedor(a)

ictory [ˈvɪktərɪ] n victoria

ideo [ˈvɪdɪəu] n vídeo (SP), video (LAm) ❏ **video camera** n videocámara, cámara de vídeo ❏ **video (cassette) recorder** n vídeo (SP), video (LAm) ❏ **video game** n videojuego ❏ **video shop** n videoclub m ❏ **video tape** n cinta de vídeo

ie [vaɪ] vi: to ~ (with sb for sth) competir (con algn por algo)

ienna [vɪˈenə] n Viena

ietnam [ˈvjetˈnæm] n Vietnam m ❏ **Vietnamese** [-nəˈmiːz] n inv, adj vietnamita mf

iew [vjuː] n vista; (outlook) perspectiva; (opinion) opinión f, criterio ♦ vt (look at) mirar; (fig) considerar; **on ~** (in museum etc) expuesto; **in full ~ (of)** en plena vista (de); **in ~ of the weather/the fact that** en vista del tiempo/del hecho de que; **in my ~** en mi opinión ❏ **viewer** n espectador(a) m/f; (TV) telespectador(a) m/f ❏ **viewpoint** n (attitude) punto de vista; (place) mirador m

igilant [ˈvɪdʒɪlənt] adj vigilante

igorous [ˈvɪɡərəs] adj enérgico, vigoroso

ile [vaɪl] adj vil, infame; (smell) asqueroso; (temper) endemoniado

illa [ˈvɪlə] n (country house) casa de campo; (suburban house) chalet m

illage [ˈvɪlɪdʒ] n aldea ❏ **villager** n aldeano(-a)

illain [ˈvɪlən] n (scoundrel) malvado(-a); (in novel) malo; (BRIT: criminal) maleante mf

inaigrette [vɪneɪˈɡret] n vinagreta

ine [vaɪn] n vid f

inegar [ˈvɪnɪɡəʳ] n vinagre m

ineyard [ˈvɪnjɑːd] n viña, viñedo

vintage [ˈvɪntɪdʒ] n (year) vendimia, cosecha ♦ cpd de época

vinyl [ˈvaɪnl] n vinilo

viola [vɪˈəulə] n (MUS) viola

violate [ˈvaɪəleɪt] vt violar

violation [vaɪəˈleɪʃən] n violación f; **in ~ of sth** en violación de algo

violence [ˈvaɪələns] n violencia

violent [ˈvaɪələnt] adj violento; (intense) intenso

violet [ˈvaɪələt] adj violado, violeta ♦ n (plant) violeta

violin [vaɪəˈlɪn] n violín m

VIP n abbr (= very important person) VIP m

virgin [ˈvɜːdʒɪn] n virgen f

Virgo [ˈvɜːɡəu] n Virgo

virtual [ˈvɜːtjuəl] adj virtual ❏ **virtually** adv prácticamente ❏ **virtual reality** n (COMPUT) mundo or realidad f virtual

virtue [ˈvɜːtjuː] n virtud f; (advantage) ventaja; **by ~ of** en virtud de

virus [ˈvaɪərəs] n (also COMPUT) virus m

visa [ˈviːzə] n visado (SP), visa (LAm)

vise [vaɪs] (US) n (TECH) = **vice**

visibility [vɪzɪˈbɪlɪtɪ] n visibilidad f

visible [ˈvɪzəbl] adj visible

vision [ˈvɪʒən] n (sight) vista; (foresight, in dream) visión f

visit [ˈvɪzɪt] n visita ♦ vt (person: US: also: ~ with) visitar, hacer una visita a; (place) ir a, (ira) conocer ❏ **visiting hours** npl (in hospital etc) horas fpl de visita ❏ **visitor** n (in museum) visitante m/f; (invited to house) visita; (tourist) turista mf ❏ **visitor centre** (US visitor center) n centro m de información

visual [ˈvɪzjuəl] adj visual ❏ **visualize** vt imaginarse

vital [ˈvaɪtl] adj (essential) esencial, imprescindible; (dynamic) dinámico; (organ) vital

vitality [vaɪˈtælɪtɪ] n energía, vitalidad f

vitamin ['vɪtəmɪn] n vitamina

vivid ['vɪvɪd] adj (account) gráfico; (light) intenso; (imagination, memory) vivo

V-neck ['viːnɛk] n cuello de pico

vocabulary [vəʊˈkæbjʊlərɪ] n vocabulario

vocal ['vəʊkəl] adj vocal; (articulate) elocuente

vocational [vəʊˈkeɪʃənl] adj profesional

vodka ['vɔdkə] n vodka m

vogue [vəʊg] n: **in ~** en boga

voice [vɔɪs] n voz f ♦ vt expresar ❑ **voice mail** n fonobuzón m

void [vɔɪd] n vacío; (hole) hueco ♦ adj (invalid) nulo, inválido; (empty): **~ of** carente o desprovisto de

volatile ['vɔlətaɪl] adj (situation) inestable; (person) voluble; (liquid) volátil

volcano [vɔlˈkeɪnəʊ] (pl **volcanoes**) n volcán m

volleyball ['vɔlɪbɔːl] n vol(e)ibol m

volt [vəʊlt] n voltio ❑ **voltage** n voltaje m

volume ['vɔljuːm] n (gen) volumen m; (book) tomo

voluntarily ['vɔləntrɪlɪ] adv libremente, voluntariamente

voluntary ['vɔləntərɪ] adj voluntario

volunteer [vɔlənˈtɪəʳ] n voluntario(-a) ♦ vt (information) ofrecer ♦ vi ofrecerse (de voluntario); **to ~ to do** ofrecerse a hacer

vomit ['vɔmɪt] n vómito ♦ vt, vi vomitar

vote [vəʊt] n voto; (votes cast) votación f; (right to vote) derecho de votar; (franchise) sufragio ♦ vt (chairman) elegir; (propose): **to ~ that** proponer que ♦ vi votar, ir a votar; **~ of thanks** voto de gracias ❑ **voter** n votante mf ❑ **voting** n votación f

voucher ['vaʊtʃəʳ] n (for meal, petrol) vale m

vow [vaʊ] n voto ♦ vt: **to ~ to do/that** jurar hacer/que

vowel ['vaʊəl] n vocal f

voyage ['vɔɪdʒ] n viaje m

vulgar ['vʌlgəʳ] adj (rude) ordinario, grosero; (in bad taste) de mal gusto

vulnerable ['vʌlnərəbl] adj vulnerable

vulture ['vʌltʃəʳ] n buitre m

W, w

waddle ['wɔdl] vi anadear

wade [weɪd] vi: **to ~ through** (water) vadear; (fig: book) leer con dificultad

wafer ['weɪfəʳ] n galleta, barquillo

waffle ['wɔfl] n (CULIN) gofre m ♦ vi dar el rollo

wag [wæg] vt menear, agitar ♦ vi moverse, menearse

wage [weɪdʒ] n (also: **wages**) sueldo, salario ♦ vt: **to ~ war** hacer la guerra

wag(g)on ['wægən] n (horse-drawn) carro; (BRIT RAIL) vagón m

wail [weɪl] n gemido ♦ vi gemir

waist [weɪst] n cintura, talle m ❑ **waistcoat** (BRIT) n chaleco

wait [weɪt] n (interval) pausa ♦ vi esperar; **to be in ~ for** acechar a; **I can't ~ to** (fig) estoy deseando; **to ~ for** esperar (a) ► **wait on** vt fus servir a ❑ **waiter** n camarero ❑ **waiting list** n lista de espera ❑ **waiting room** n sala de espera ❑ **waitress** ['weɪtrɪs] n camarera

waive [weɪv] vt suspender

wake [weɪk] (pt **woke** or **waked**, pp **woken** or **waked**) vt (also: **~ up**) despertar ♦ vi (also: **~ up**) despertarse ♦ n (for dead person) vela, velatorio; (NAUT) estela

Wales [weɪlz] n País m de Gales; **the Prince of ~** el príncipe de Gales

walk [wɔːk] n (stroll) paseo; (hike) excursión f a pie, caminata; (gait) paso

andar m; (in park etc) paseo, alameda
♦ vi andar, caminar; (for pleasure,
exercise) pasear ♦ vt (distance) recorrer
a pie, andar; (dog) pasear; **10 minutes'
~ from here** a 10 minutos de aquí
andando; **people from all walks of life**
gente de todas las esferas ▶ **walk out**
vi (audience) salir; (workers) declararse
en huelga ❏ **walker** n (person)
caminante mf, caminante mf ❏ **walkie-
talkie** ['wɔ:kɪ'tɔ:kɪ] n walkie-talkie m
❏ **walking** n el andar ❏ **walking
shoes** npl zapatos mpl para andar
❏ **walking stick** n bastón m
❏ **Walkman** ® n Walkman® m
❏ **walkway** n paseo

wall [wɔ:l] n pared f; (exterior) muro;
(city wall etc) muralla

wallet ['wɔlɪt] n cartera, billetera

wallpaper ['wɔ:lpeɪpə'] n papel m
pintado ♦ vt empapelar

walnut ['wɔ:lnʌt] n nuez f; (tree) nogal
m

walrus ['wɔ:lrəs] n (pl ~ or **walruses**) n
morsa

waltz [wɔ:lts] n vals m ♦ vi bailar el vals

wand [wɔnd] n (also: **magic ~**) varita
(mágica)

wander ['wɔndə'] vi (person) vagar;
deambular; (thoughts) divagar ♦ vt
recorrer, vagar por

want [wɔnt] vt querer, desear; (need)
necesitar ♦ n: **for ~ of** por falta de
❏ **wanted** adj (criminal) buscado;
"wanted" (in advertisements) "se
busca"

war [wɔ:'] n guerra; **to make ~ (on)**
declarar la guerra (a)

ward [wɔ:d] n (in hospital) sala; (POL)
distrito electoral; (LAW: child: also: **~ of
court**) pupilo(-a)

warden ['wɔ:dn] n (BRIT: of institution)
director(a) m/f; (of park, game reserve)
guardián(-ana) m/f; (BRIT: also: **traffic
~**) guardia mf

wardrobe ['wɔ:drəub] n armario,
ropero; (clothes) vestuario

warehouse ['wɛəhaus] n almacén m,
depósito

warfare ['wɔ:fɛə'] n guerra

warhead ['wɔ:hed] n cabeza armada

warm [wɔ:m] adj caliente; (thanks)
efusivo; (clothes etc) abrigado;
(welcome, day) caluroso; **it's ~** hace
calor; **I'm ~** tengo calor ▶ **warm up** vi
(room) calentarse; (person) entrar en
calor; (athlete) hacer ejercicios de
calentamiento ♦ vt calentar
❏ **warmly** adv afectuosamente
❏ **warmth** n calor m

warn [wɔ:n] vt avisar, advertir
❏ **warning** n aviso, advertencia
❏ **warning light** n luz f de
advertencia

warrant ['wɔrnt] n autorización f; (LAW:
to arrest) orden f de detención; (: to
search) mandamiento de registro

warranty ['wɔrəntɪ] n garantía

warrior ['wɔrɪə'] n guerrero(-a)

Warsaw ['wɔ:sɔ:] n Varsovia

warship ['wɔ:ʃɪp] n buque m or barco de
guerra

wart [wɔ:t] n verruga

wartime ['wɔ:taɪm] n: **in ~** en tiempos
de guerra, en la guerra

wary ['wɛərɪ] adj cauteloso

was [wɔz] pt of **be**

wash [wɔʃ] vt lavar ♦ vi lavarse; (sea etc):
to ~ against/over sth llegar hasta/
cubrir algo ♦ n (clothes etc) lavado; (of
ship) estela; **to have a ~** lavarse
▶ **wash up** vi (BRIT) fregar los platos;
(US) lavarse ❏ **washbasin** (US
washbowl) n lavabo ❏ **wash cloth**
(US) n manopla ❏ **washer** n (TECH)
arandela ❏ **washing** n (dirty) ropa sucia; (clean)
colada ❏ **washing line** n cuerda de
(colgar) la ropa ❏ **washing machine**
n lavadora ❏ **washing powder** (BRIT)
n detergente m (en polvo)

Washington [ˈwɒʃɪŋtən] n
Washington m

wash: wash-up (BRIT) n fregado,
platos mpl (para fregar) ❑ **washing-
up liquid** (BRIT) n líquido lavavajillas
❑ **washroom** (US) n servicios mpl

wasn't [ˈwɒznt] = **was not**

wasp [wɒsp] n avispa

waste [weist] n derroche m,
despilfarro; (of time) pérdida; (food)
sobras fpl; (rubbish) basura,
desperdicios mpl ♦ adj (material) de
desecho; (left over) sobrante; (land)
baldío, descampado ♦ vt malgastar,
derrochar; (time) perder; (opportunity)
desperdiciar ❑ **waste ground** (BRIT) n
terreno baldío ❑ **wastepaper
basket** n papelera

watch [wɒtʃ] n (also: **wrist ~**) reloj m;
(MIL: group of guards) centinela m; (act)
vigilancia; (NAUT: spell of duty) guardia
♦ vt (look at) mirar, observar; (: match,
programme) ver; (spy on, guard) vigilar;
(be careful of) cuidarse de, tener
cuidado de ♦ vi ver, mirar; (keep guard)
montar guardia ▶ **watch out** vi
cuidarse, tener cuidado ❑ **watchdog**
n perro guardián; (fig) persona u
organismo encargado de asegurarse de
que las empresas actúan dentro de la
legalidad ❑ **watch strap** n pulsera (de
reloj)

water [ˈwɔːtə] n agua f ♦ vt (plant) regar
♦ vi (eyes) llorar; (mouth) hacerse la
boca agua ▶ **water down** vt (milk etc)
aguar; (fig: story) dulcificar, diluir
❑ **watercolour** (US **watercolor**) n
acuarela ❑ **watercress** n berro
❑ **waterfall** n cascada, salto de agua
❑ **watering can** n regadera
❑ **watermelon** n sandía
❑ **waterproof** adj impermeable
❑ **water-skiing** n esquí m acuático

watt [wɒt] n vatio

wave [weiv] n (of hand) señal f con la
mano; (on water) ola; (RADIO, in hair)
onda; (fig) oleada ♦ vi agitar la mano;

(flag etc) ondear ♦ vt (handkerchief,
gun) agitar ❑ **wavelength** n longitud
f de onda

waver [ˈweivə] vi (voice, love etc)
flaquear; (person) vacilar

wavy [ˈweivi] adj ondulado

wax [wæks] n cera ♦ vt encerar ♦ vi
(moon) crecer

way [wei] n camino; (distance) trayecto,
recorrido; (direction) dirección f,
sentido; (manner) modo, manera;
(habit) costumbre f; **which ~? — this
~** ¿por dónde?, ¿en qué dirección? —
por aquí; **on the ~** en camino; **to be on one's
~** estar en
camino; **to be in the ~** bloquear el
camino; (fig) estorbar; **to go out of
one's ~ to do sth** desvivirse por hacer
algo; **under ~** en marcha; **to lose one's
~** extraviarse; **in a ~** en cierto modo o
sentido; **no ~!** (inf) ¡de eso nada!; **by
the ~ ...** a propósito ...; **"~ in"** (BRIT)
"entrada"; **"~ out"** (BRIT) "salida"; **the ~
back** el camino de vuelta; **"give ~"** (BRIT
AUT) "ceda el paso"

W.C. n (BRIT) wáter m

we [wiː] pl pron nosotros(-as)

weak [wiːk] adj débil, flojo; (tea etc)
claro ❑ **weaken** vi debilitarse; (give
way) ceder ♦ vt debilitar ❑ **weakness**
n debilidad f; (fault) punto débil; **to
have a weakness for** tener debilidad
por

wealth [welθ] n riqueza; (of details)
abundancia ❑ **wealthy** adj rico

weapon [ˈwepən] n arma; **weapons of
mass destruction** armas de
destrucción masiva

wear [weə] (pt **wore**, pp **worn**) n (use)
uso; (deterioration through use)
desgaste m ♦ vt (clothes) llevar; (shoes)
calzar; (damage: through use) gastar,
usar ♦ vi (last) durar; (rub through etc)
desgastarse; **evening ~** ropa de
etiqueta; **sportswear/babywear** ropa
de deportes/de niños ▶ **wear off** vi
(pain etc) pasar, desaparecer ▶ **wear**

...out vt desgastar; (person, strength) agotar

...eary ['wɪərɪ] adj cansado; (dispirited) abatido ♦ vi: **to ~ of** cansarse de

...easel ['wi:zl] n (ZOOL) comadreja

...eather ['weðə*] n tiempo ♦ vt (storm, crisis) hacer frente a; **under the ~** (fig: ill) indispuesto, pachucho ❑ **weather forecast** n boletín m meteorológico

...eave [wi:v] (pt **wove**, pp **woven**) vt (cloth) tejer; (fig) entretejer

...eb [web] n (of spider) telaraña; (of duck's foot) membrana; (network) red f; **the (World Wide) ~** la Red ❑ **web page** n (página) web ❑ **website** n espacio Web

...ed. abbr (= Wednesday) miérc

...ed [wed] (pt, pp **wedded**) vt casar ♦ vi casarse

...e'd [wi:d] = **we had**; **we would**

...edding ['wedɪŋ] n boda, casamiento ❑ **silver/golden ~ (anniversary)** bodas fpl de plata/de oro ❑ **wedding anniversary** n aniversario de boda ❑ **wedding day** n día m de la boda ❑ **wedding dress** n traje m de novia ❑ **wedding ring** n alianza

...edge [wedʒ] n (of wood etc) cuña; (of cake) trozo ♦ vt acuñar; (push) apretar

...ednesday ['wednzdɪ] n miércoles m inv

...ee [wi:] (Scottish) adj pequeñito

...eed [wi:d] n mala hierba, maleza ♦ vt escardar, desherbar ❑ **weedkiller** n herbicida m

...eek [wi:k] n semana; **a ~ today/on Friday** de hoy/del viernes en ocho días ❑ **weekday** n día m laborable ❑ **weekend** n fin m de semana ❑ **weekly** adv semanalmente, cada semana ♦ adj semanal ♦ n semanario

...eep [wi:p] (pt, pp **wept**) vi, vt llorar

...eigh [weɪ] vt, vi pesar; **to ~ anchor** levar anclas ► **weigh up** vt sopesar

...eight [weɪt] n peso; (metal weight) pesa; **to lose/put on ~** adelgazar/

engordar ❑ **weightlifting** n levantamiento de pesas

weir [wɪə*] n presa

weird [wɪəd] adj raro, extraño

welcome ['welkəm] adj bienvenido ♦ vt dar la bienvenida a; (be glad of) alegrarse de; **thank you — you're ~** gracias — de nada

weld [weld] n soldadura ♦ vt soldar

welfare ['welfeə*] n bienestar m; (social aid) asistencia social ❑ **welfare state** n estado del bienestar

well [wel] n fuente f, pozo ♦ adv bien ♦ adj: **to be ~** estar bien (de salud) ♦ excl ¡vaya!, ¡bueno!; **as ~** también; **as ~ as** además de; **~ done!** ¡bien hecho!; **get ~ soon!** ¡que te mejores pronto!; **to do ~** (business) ir bien; (person) tener éxito

we'll [wi:l] = **we will**; **we shall**

well: **well-behaved** adj bueno ❑ **well-built** (person) fornido ❑ **well-dressed** adj bien vestido

wellies (inf) ['welɪz] npl (BRIT) botas de goma

well: **well-known** adj (person) conocido ❑ **well-off** adj acomodado ❑ **well-paid** [wel'peɪd] adj bien pagado, bien retribuido

Welsh [welʃ] adj galés(-esa) ♦ n (LING) galés m ❑ **Welshman** (irreg) n galés m ❑ **Welshwoman** (irreg) n galesa

went [went] pt of **go**

wept [wept] pt, pp of **weep**

were [wə:*] pt of **be**

we're [wɪə*] = **we are**

weren't [wə:nt] = **were not**

west [west] n oeste m ♦ adj occidental, del oeste ♦ adv al or hacia el oeste; **the W~** el Oeste, el Occidente ❑ **westbound** ['westbaund] adj (traffic, carriageway) con rumbo al oeste ❑ **western** adj occidental ♦ n (CINEMA) película del oeste ❑ **West Indian** adj, n antillano(-a) m/f

wet [wet] *adj* (*damp*) húmedo; (*soaked*): **~ through** mojado; (*rainy*) lluvioso ♦ *n* (*BRIT: POL*) conservador(a) *m/f* moderado(-a); **to get ~** mojarse; "**~ paint**" "recién pintado" ❑ **wetsuit** *n* traje *m* térmico

we've [wiːv] = **we have**

whack [wæk] *vt* dar un buen golpe a

whale [weɪl] *n* (*ZOOL*) ballena

wharf [wɔːf] (*pl* **wharves**) *n* muelle *m*

what [wɔt]

[wɔt] *adj*

1 (*in direct/indirect questions*) qué; **what size is he?** ¿qué talla usa?; **what colour/shape is it?** ¿de qué color/forma es?

2 (*in exclamations*): **what a mess!** ¡qué desastre!; **what a fool I am!** ¡qué tonto soy!

♦ *pron*

1 (*interrogative*) qué; **what are you doing?** ¿qué haces or estás haciendo?; **what is happening?** ¿qué pasa or está pasando?; **what is it called?** ¿cómo se llama?; **what about me?** ¿y yo qué?; **what about doing ...?** ¿qué tal si hacemos ...?

2 (*relative*) lo que; **I saw what you did/was on the table** vi lo que hiciste/había en la mesa

♦ *excl* (*disbelieving*) ¡cómo!; **what, no coffee!** ¡que no hay café!

whatever [wɔtˈevə] *adj*: **~ book you choose** cualquier libro que elijas ♦ *pron*: **do ~ is necessary** haga lo que sea necesario; **~ happens** pase lo que pase; **no reason ~** *or* **whatsoever** ninguna razón sea la que sea; **nothing ~** nada en absoluto

whatsoever [wɔtsəuˈevə] *adj see* **whatever**

wheat [wiːt] *n* trigo

wheel [wiːl] *n* rueda; (*AUT: also*: **steering ~**) volante *m*; (*NAUT*) timón *m* ♦ *vt* (*pram etc*) empujar ♦ *vi* (*also*: **~ round**) dar la vuelta, girar ❑ **wheelbarrow** *n* carretilla ❑ **wheelchair** *n* silla de ruedas ❑ **wheel clamp** *n* (*AUT*) cepo

wheeze [wiːz] *vi* resollar

when [wen]

[wen] *adv* cuando; **when did it happen?** ¿cuándo ocurrió?; **I know when it happened** sé cuándo ocurrió

♦ *conj*

1 (*at, during, after the time that*) cuando; **be careful when you cross the road** ten cuidado al cruzar la calle; **that was when I needed you** fue entonces que te necesité

2 (*on, at which*): **on the day when I met him** el día en qué le conocí

3 (*whereas*) cuando

whenever [wenˈevə] *conj* cuando; (*every time that*) cada vez que ♦ *adv* cuando sea

where [wεə] *adv* dónde ♦ *conj* donde; **this is ~** aquí es donde ❑ **whereabouts** *adv* dónde ♦ *n*: **nobody knows his whereabouts** nadie conoce su paradero ❑ **whereas** *conj* visto que, mientras ❑ **whereby** *pron* por lo cual ❑ **wherever** *conj* dondequiera que; (*interrogative*) dónde

whether [ˈwεðə] *conj* si; **I don't know whether to accept or not** no sé si aceptar o no; **~ you go or not** vayas o no vayas

which [wɪtʃ]

[wɪtʃ] *adj*

1 (*interrogative: direct, indirect*) qué; **which picture(s) do you want?** ¿qué cuadro(s) quieres?; **which one?**

¿cuál?

2: in which case en cuyo caso; **we got there at 8 pm, by which time the cinema was full** llegamos allí a las 8, cuando el cine estaba lleno

♦ *pron*

1 (*interrogative*) cual; **I don't mind which** el/la que sea

2 (*relative: replacing noun*) que; (: *replacing clause*) lo que; (: *after preposition*) el(la)) del que el cual etc; **the apple which you ate/which is on the table** la manzana que comiste/que está en la mesa; **the chair on which you are sitting** la silla en la que estás sentado; **he said he knew, which is true/I feared** dijo que lo sabía, lo cual o lo que es cierto/me temía

whichever [wɪtʃˈevəʳ] *adj*: **take ~ book you prefer** coja (*SP*) el libro que prefiera; **~ book you take** cualquier libro que coja

while [waɪl] *n* rato, momento ♦ *conj* mientras; (*although*) aunque; **for a ~** durante algún tiempo

whilst [waɪlst] *conj* = **while**

whim [wɪm] *n* capricho

whine [waɪn] *n* (*of pain*) gemido; (*of engine*) zumbido; (*of siren*) aullido ♦ *vi* gemir; zumbar; (*fig*: *complain*) gimotear

whip [wɪp] *n* látigo; (*POL: person*) *encargado de la disciplina partidaria en el parlamento* ♦ *vt* azotar; (*CULIN*) batir; (*move quickly*): **to ~ sth out/off** sacar/quitar algo de un tirón ❏ **whipped cream** *n* nata o crema montada

whirl [wɜːl] *vt* hacer girar, dar vueltas a ♦ *vi* girar, dar vueltas; (*leaves etc*) arremolinarse

whisk [wɪsk] *n* (*CULIN*) batidor *m* ♦ *vt* (*CULIN*) batir; **to ~ sb away** *o* **off** llevar volando a algn

whiskers [wɪskəz] *npl* (*of animal*) bigotes *mpl*; (*of man*) patillas *fpl*

whiskey [wɪskɪ] (*US, Ireland*) *n* = **whisky**

whisky [wɪskɪ] *n* whisky *m*

whisper [wɪspəʳ] *n* susurro ♦ *vi, vt* susurrar

whistle [wɪsl] *n* (*sound*) silbido; (*object*) silbato ♦ *vt* silbar

white [waɪt] *adj* blanco; (*pale*) pálido ♦ *n* blanco; (*of egg*) clara ❏ **White House** (*US*) *n* Casa Blanca ❏ **whitewash** *n* (*paint*) jalbegue *m*, cal *f* ♦ *vt* blanquear

whiting [waɪtɪŋ] *n inv* (*fish*) pescadilla

Whitsun [wɪtsn] *n* pentecostés *m*

whittle [wɪtl] *vt*: **to ~ away**, **~ down** ir reduciendo

whizz [wɪz] *vi*: **to ~ past** *o* **by** pasar a toda velocidad

who [huː] *pron*

KEYWORD

1 (*interrogative*) quién; **who is it?**, **who's there?** ¿quién es?; **who are you looking for?** ¿a quién buscas?; **I told her who I was** le dije quién era yo

2 (*relative*) que; **the man/woman who spoke to me** el hombre/la mujer que habló conmigo; **those who can swim** los que saben *o* sepan nadar

whoever [huːˈevəʳ] *pron*: **~ finds it** cualquiera *o* quienquiera que lo encuentre; **ask ~ you like** pregunta a quien quieras; **he marries** no importa con quién se case

whole [həʊl] *adj* (*entire*) todo, entero; (*not broken*) intacto ♦ *n* todo; (*all*): **the ~ of the town** toda la ciudad, la ciudad entera *o* (*total*) total *m*; (*sum*) conjunto; **on the ~**, **as a ~** en general ❏ **wholefood(s)** *n(pl)* alimento(s) *m(pl)* integral(es) ❏ **wholeheartedly** [həʊlˈhɑːtɪdlɪ] *adv* con entusiasmo

❏ **wholemeal** adj integral
❏ **wholesale** n venta al por mayor
♦ adj al por mayor; (fig: destruction) sistemático ❏ **wholewheat** adj = **wholemeal** ❏ **wholly** adv totalmente, enteramente

whom

KEYWORD

[hu:m] pron

1 (interrogative): **whom did you see?** ¿a quién viste?; **to whom did you give it?** ¿a quién se lo diste?; **tell me from whom you received it** dígame de quién lo recibió

2 (relative) que; **to whom** a quien(es); **of whom** de quien(es), del/de la que etc; **the man whom I saw/to whom I wrote** el hombre que vi/a quien escribí; **the lady about/with whom I was talking** la señora de (la) que/con quien o (la) que hablaba

whore [hɔːˈ] (inf, pej) n puta

whose

KEYWORD

[hu:z] adj

1 (possessive: interrogative): **whose book is this?, whose is this book?** ¿de quién es este libro?; **whose pencil have you taken?** ¿de quién es el lápiz que has cogido?; **whose daughter are you?** ¿de quién eres hija?

2 (possessive: relative) cuyo(-a), pl cuyos(-as); **the man whose son you rescued** el hombre cuyo hijo rescataste; **those whose passports I have** aquellas personas cuyos pasaportes tengo; **the woman whose car was stolen** la mujer a quien le robaron el coche

♦ pron de quién; **whose is this?** ¿de

quién es esto?; **I know whose it is** sé de quién es

why

KEYWORD

[waɪ] adv por qué; **why not?** ¿por qué no?; **why not do it now?** ¿por qué no lo haces (or hacemos etc) ahora?

♦ conj: **I wonder why he said that** me pregunto por qué dijo eso; **that's not why I'm here** no es por eso (por lo) que estoy aquí; **the reason why** la razón por la que

♦ excl (expressing surprise, shock, annoyance) ¡hombre!, ¡vaya!; (explaining): **why, it's you!** ¡hombre, eres tú!; **why, that's impossible!** ¡pero sí eso es imposible!

wicked [ˈwɪkɪd] adj malvado, cruel

wicket [ˈwɪkɪt] n (CRICKET: stumps) palo mpl; (: grass area) terreno de juego

wide [waɪd] adj ancho; (area, knowledge) vasto, grande; (choice) amplio ♦ adv: **to open ~** abrir de par en par; **to shoot ~** errar el tiro ❏ **widely** adv (travelled) mucho; (spaced) muy; **is widely believed/known that ...** mucha gente piensa/sabe que ... ❏ **widen** vt ensanchar; (experience) ampliar ♦ vi ensancharse ❏ **wide open** adj abierto de par en par ❏ **widespread** adj extendido, genera[l]

widow [ˈwɪdəu] n viuda ❏ **widower** n viudo

width [wɪdθ] n anchura; (of cloth) ancho

wield [wiːld] vt (sword) blandir; (powe[r]) ejercer

wife [waɪf] (pl **wives**) n mujer f, espos[a]

wig [wɪg] n peluca

wild [waɪld] adj (animal) salvaje; (plan[t]) silvestre; (person) furioso, violento; (idea) descabellado; (rough: sea) brav[o] (: land) agreste; (: weather) muy revuelto ❑ **wilderness** ['wɪldənɪs] n desierto ❑ **wildlife** n fauna ❑ **wildly** adv (behave) locamente; (lash out) a diestro y siniestro; (guess) a lo loco; (happy) a más no poder

will

KEYWORD

[wɪl] aux vb

1 (forming future tense): **I will finish it tomorrow** lo terminaré o voy a terminar mañana; **I will have finished it by tomorrow** lo habré terminado para mañana; **will you do it?** ¿lo harás? — yes I **will/no I won't** ¿lo harás? — sí/no

2 (in conjectures, predictions): **he will** or **he'll be there by now** ya estará o debe (de) haber llegado; **that will be the postman** será o debe ser el cartero

3 (in commands, requests, offers): **will you be quiet!** ¡quieres callarte?; **will you help me?** ¡quieres ayudarme?; **will you have a cup of tea?** ¿te apetece un té?; **I won't put up with it!** ¡no lo soporto!

♦ vt (pt, pp **willed**): **to will sb to do sth** desear que algn haga algo; **he willed himself to go on** con gran fuerza de voluntad, continuó

♦ n voluntad f; (testament) testamento

willing ['wɪlɪŋ] adj (with goodwill) de buena voluntad; (enthusiastic) entusiasta; **he's ~ to do it** está dispuesto a hacerlo ❑ **willingly** adv con mucho gusto

willow ['wɪləʊ] n sauce m

willpower ['wɪlpaʊə'] n fuerza de voluntad

wilt [wɪlt] vi marchitarse

win [wɪn] (pt, pp **won**) n victoria, triunfo ♦ vt ganar; (obtain) conseguir, lograr ♦ vi ganar ▸ **win over** vt convencer a

wince [wɪns] vi encogerse

wind[1] [wɪnd] n viento; (MED) gases mpl ♦ vt (take breath away from) dejar sin aliento a

wind[2] [waɪnd] (pt, pp **wound**) vt enrollar; (wrap) envolver; (clock, toy) dar cuerda a ♦ vi (road, river) serpentear ▸ **wind down** vt (car window) bajar; (fig: production, business) disminuir ▸ **wind up** vt (clock) dar cuerda a; (debate, meeting) concluir, terminar

windfall ['wɪndfɔːl] n golpe m de suerte

winding ['waɪndɪŋ] adj (road) tortuoso; (staircase) de caracol

windmill ['wɪndmɪl] n molino de viento

window ['wɪndəʊ] n ventana; (in car, train) ventanilla; (in shop etc) escaparate m (SP), vidriera (LAm) ❑ **window box** n jardinera de ventana ❑ **window cleaner** n (person) limpiacristales mf inv ❑ **window pane** n cristal m ❑ **window seat** n asiento junto a la ventana ❑ **windowsill** n alféizar m, repisa

windscreen ['wɪndskriːn] (US **windshield**) n parabrisas m inv ❑ **windscreen wiper** (US **windshield wiper**) n limpiaparabrisas m inv

windsurfing ['wɪndsɜːfɪŋ] n windsurf m

windy ['wɪndɪ] adj de mucho viento; **it's ~** hace viento

wine [waɪn] n vino ❑ **wine bar** n enoteca ❑ **wine glass** n copa (para vino) ❑ **wine list** n lista de vinos ❑ **wine tasting** n degustación f de vinos

wing [wɪŋ] n ala; (AUT) aleta ❑ **wing mirror** n (espejo) retrovisor m

wink [wɪŋk] n guiño, pestañeo ♦ vi guiñar, pestañear

winner ['wɪnə'] n ganador(a) m/f

winning ['wɪnɪŋ] *adj* (team) ganador(a); (goal) decisivo; (smile) encantador(a)

winter ['wɪntə*] *n* invierno ♦ *vi* invernar ❑ **winter sports** *npl* deportes *mpl* de invierno ❑ **wintertime** *n* invierno

wipe [waɪp] *n*: **to give sth a ~** pasar un trapo sobre algo ♦ *vt* limpiar; (tape) borrar ▸ **wipe out** *vt* (debt) liquidar; (memory) borrar; (destroy) destruir ▸ **wipe up** *vt* limpiar

wire ['waɪə*] *n* alambre *m*; (ELEC) cable *m* (eléctrico); (TEL) telegrama *m* ♦ *vt* (house) poner la instalación eléctrica en; (also: ~ **up**) conectar; (person: telegram) telegrafiar

wiring ['waɪərɪŋ] *n* instalación *f* eléctrica

wisdom ['wɪzdəm] *n* sabiduría, saber *m*; (good sense) cordura ❑ **wisdom tooth** *n* muela del juicio

wise [waɪz] *adj* sabio; (sensible) juicioso

wish [wɪʃ] *n* deseo ♦ *vt* querer; **best wishes** (on birthday etc) felicidades *fpl*; **with best wishes** (in letter) saludos *mpl*, recuerdos *mpl*; **to ~ sb goodbye** despedirse de algn; **he wished me well** me deseó mucha suerte; **to ~ to do/sb to do sth** querer hacer/que algn haga algo; **to ~ for** desear

wistful ['wɪstful] *adj* pensativo

wit [wɪt] *n* ingenio, gracia; (also: **wits**) inteligencia; (person) chistoso(-a)

witch [wɪtʃ] *n* bruja

with

KEYWORD

[wɪð, wɪθ] *prep*

1 (accompanying, in the company of) con (con +*mí*, *ti*, *sí* = conmigo, contigo, consigo); **I was with him** estaba con él; **we stayed with friends** nos quedamos en casa de unos amigos; **I'm (not) with you** (don't understand) (no) te entiendo; **to be with it** (inf: person: up-to-date) estar al tanto; (:

alert) ser despabilado

2 (descriptive, indicating manner etc) con; de; **a room with a view** una habitación con vistas; **the man with the grey hat/blue eyes** el hombre del sombrero gris/de los ojos azules; **red with anger** rojo de ira; **to shake with fear** temblar de miedo; **to fill sth with water** llenar algo de agua

withdraw [wɪθ'drɔː] *vt* retirar, sacar ♦ *vi* retirarse; **to ~ money (from the bank)** retirar fondos (del banco) ❑ **withdrawal** *n* retirada; (of money) reintegro ❑ **withdrawn** *pp of* **withdraw** ♦ *adj* (person) reservado, introvertido

withdrew [wɪθ'druː] *pt of* **withdraw**

wither ['wɪðə*] *vi* marchitarse

withhold [wɪθ'həʊld] *vt* (money) retener; (decision) aplazar; (permission) negar; (information) ocultar

within [wɪð'ɪn] *prep* dentro de ♦ *adv* dentro; **~ reach (of)** al alcance (de); **~ sight (of)** a la vista (de); **~ the week** antes de acabar la semana; **~ a mile (of)** a menos de una milla (de)

without [wɪð'aʊt] *prep* sin; **to go ~ sth** pasar sin algo

withstand [wɪθ'stænd] *vt* resistir a

witness ['wɪtnɪs] *n* testigo *mf* ♦ *vt* (event) presenciar; (document) atestiguar la veracidad de; **to bear ~ to** (fig) ser testimonio de

witty ['wɪtɪ] *adj* ingenioso

wives [waɪvz] *npl of* **wife**

wizard ['wɪzəd] *n* hechicero

wk *abbr* = **week**

wobble ['wɒbl] *vi* temblar; (chair) cojear

woe [wəʊ] *n* desgracia

woke [wəʊk] *pt of* **wake**

woken ['wəʊkən] *pp of* **wake**

wolf [wʊlf] *n* lobo

woman ['wʊmən] (pl **women**) *n* mujer *f*

womb [wuːm] n matriz f, útero

women ['wɪmɪn] npl of **woman**

won [wʌn] pt, pp of **win**

wonder ['wʌndəʳ] n maravilla, prodigio; (feeling) asombro ♦ vi: to ~ **whether/why** preguntarse si/por qué; **to ~ at** asombrarse de; **to ~ about** pensar sobre o en; **it's no ~ (that)** no es de extrañarse (que +subjun) ❑ **wonderful** adj maravilloso

won't [wəunt] = **will not**

wood [wud] n (timber) madera; (forest) bosque m ❑ **wooden** adj de madera; (fig) inexpresivo ❑ **woodwind** n (MUS) instrumentos mpl de viento de madera ❑ **woodwork** n carpintería

wool [wul] n lana; **to pull the ~ over sb's eyes** (fig) engatusar a algn ❑ **woollen** (US **woolen**) adj de lana ❑ **woolly** (US **wooly**) adj lanudo, de lana; (fig: ideas) confuso

word [wəːd] n palabra; (news) noticia; (promise) palabra f (de honor) ♦ vt redactar; **in other words** en otras palabras; **to break/keep one's ~** faltar a la palabra/cumplir la promesa; **to have words with sb** reñir con algn ❑ **wording** n redacción f ❑ **word processing** n proceso de textos ❑ **word processor** n procesador m de textos

wore [wɔːʳ] pt of **wear**

work [wəːk] n (gen); (job) empleo, trabajo; (ART, LITERATURE) obra f ♦ vi trabajar; (mechanism) funcionar, marchar; (medicine) ser eficaz, surtir efecto ♦ vt (shape) trabajar; (stone etc) tallar; (mine etc) explotar; (machine) manejar, hacer funcionar ♦ npl (of clock, machine) mecanismo; **to be out of ~** = estar parado, no tener trabajo; **to ~ loose** (part) desprenderse; (knot) aflojarse; **works** n (BRIT: factory) fábrica ♦ **work out** vi (plans etc) salir bien, funcionar ♦ vt (problem) resolver; (plan) elaborar; **it works out at £100** suma 100 libras ❑ **worker** n

trabajador(a) m/f, obrero(-a) f ❑ **work experience** n: **I'm going to do my work experience in a factory** voy a hacer las prácticas en una fábrica ❑ **workforce** n mano de obra ❑ **working class** n clase f obrera ♦ adj: **working-class** obrero ❑ **working week** n semana laboral ❑ **workman** (irreg) n obrero ❑ **work of art** n obra de arte ❑ **workout** n (SPORT) sesión f de ejercicios ❑ **work permit** n permiso de trabajo ❑ **workplace** n lugar m de trabajo ❑ **workshop** n taller m ❑ **work station** n puesto o estación f de trabajo ❑ **work surface** n encimera ❑ **worktop** n encimera

world [wəːld] n mundo ♦ cpd (champion) del mundo; (power, war) mundial; **to think the ~ of sb** (fig) tener un concepto muy alto de algn ❑ **World Cup** n (FOOTBALL): **the World Cup** el Mundial, los Mundiales ❑ **world-wide** adj mundial, universal ❑ **World-Wide Web** n: **the World-Wide Web** el World Wide Web

worm [wəːm] n (also: **earth~**) lombriz f

worn [wɔːn] pp of **wear** ♦ adj usado ❑ **worn-out** adj (object) gastado; (person) rendido, agotado

worried ['wʌrɪd] adj preocupado

worry ['wʌrɪ] n preocupación f ♦ vt preocupar, inquietar ♦ vi preocuparse ❑ **worrying** adj inquietante

worse [wəːs] adj, adv peor ♦ n lo peor; **a change for the ~** un empeoramiento ❑ **worsen** vt, vi empeorar ❑ **worse off** adj (financially): **to be worse off** tener menos dinero; (fig): **you'll be worse off this way** de esta forma estarás peor que nunca

worship ['wəːʃɪp] n adoración f ♦ vt adorar; **Your W~** (BRIT: to mayor) señor alcalde; (: to judge) señor juez

worst [wəːst] adj, adv peor ♦ n lo peor; **at ~** en lo peor de los casos

worth [wə:θ] *n* valor *m* ♦ *adj*: **to be ~ valer; it's ~ it** vale *or* merece la pena; **to be ~ one's while to** (hacer) merecer la pena; (*cause*) loable **□ worthless** *adj* sin valor; (*useless*) inútil **□ worthwhile** *adj* (*activity*) que merece la pena; (*cause*) loable

worthy [wə:ðɪ] *adj* respetable; (*motive*) honesto; **~ of** digno de

would

KEYWORD

[wud] *aux vb*

1 (*conditional tense*): **if you asked him he would do it** si se lo pidieras, lo haría; **if you had asked him he would have done it** si se lo hubieras pedido, lo habría *or* hubiera hecho

2 (*in offers, invitations, requests*): **would you like a biscuit?** ¿quieres una galleta?; (*formal*) ¿querría una galleta?; **would you ask him to come in?** ¿quiere hacerle pasar?; **would you open the window please?** ¿quiere *or* podría abrir la ventana, por favor?

3 (*in indirect speech*): **I said I would do it** dije que lo haría

4 (*emphatic*): **it would have to snow today!** ¡tenía que nevar precisamente hoy!

5 (*insistence*): **she wouldn't behave** no quiso comportarse bien

6 (*conjecture*): **it would have been midnight** sería medianoche; **it would seem so** parece ser que sí

7 (*indicating habit*): **he would go there on Mondays** iba allí los lunes

wouldn't [wudnt] = **would not**
wound¹ [wu:nd] *n* herida ♦ *vt* herir
wound² [waund] *pt, pp of* **wind²**
wove [wəuv] *pt of* **weave**
woven [wəuvən] *pp of* **weave**

wrap [ræp] *vt* (*also*: **~ up**) envolver; (*gift*) envolver, abrigar ♦ *vi* (*dress warmly*) abrigarse **□ wrapper** *n* (on chocolate) papel *m*; (*BRIT: of book*) sobrecubierta **□ wrapping** *n* envoltura, envase *m* **□ wrapping paper** *n* papel *m* de envolver; (*fancy*) papel *m* de regalo

wreath [ri:θ, *pl* ri:ðz] *n* (*funeral wreath*) corona

wreck [rɛk] *n* (ship: destruction) naufragio; (: remains) restos *mpl* del barco; (pej: person) ruina ♦ *vt* (car etc) destrozar; (chances) arruinar **□ wreckage** *n* restos *mpl*; (of building) escombros *mpl*

wren [rɛn] *n* (ZOOL) reyezuelo

wrench [rɛntʃ] *n* (TECH) llave *f* inglesa; (tug) tirón *m*; (fig) dolor *m* ♦ *vt* arrancar, **to ~ sth from sb** arrebatar algo violentamente a algn

wrestle [rɛsl] *vi*: **to ~ (with sb)** luchar (con *or* contra algn) **□ wrestler** *n* luchador(a) *m/f* (de lucha libre) **□ wrestling** *n* lucha libre

wretched [rɛtʃɪd] *adj* miserable

wriggle [rɪɡl] *vi* (*also*: **~ about**) menearse, retorcerse

wring [rɪŋ] (pt, pp **wrung**) *vt* retorcer; (wet clothes) escurrir; (fig): **to ~ sth out of sb** sacar algo por la fuerza a algn

wrinkle [rɪŋkl] *n* arruga ♦ *vt* arrugar ♦ *vi* arrugarse

wrist [rɪst] *n* muñeca

write [raɪt] (pt **wrote**, pp **written**) *vt* escribir; (cheque) extender ♦ *vi* escribir ▶ **write down** *vt* escribir; (note) apuntar ▶ **write off** *vt* (debt) borrar (como incobrable); (fig) desechar por inútil ▶ **write out** *vt* escribir ▶ **write off** *n* siniestro total **□ writer** *n* escritor(a) *m/f*

writing [raɪtɪŋ] *n* escritura; (handwriting) letra; (of author) obras *fpl*; **in ~** por escrito **□ writing paper** *n* papel *m* de escribir

written [rɪtn] *pp of* **write**

wrong [rɒŋ] adj (wicked) malo; (unfair) injusto; (incorrect) equivocado, incorrecto; (not suitable) inoportuno, inconveniente; (reverse) del revés ♦ adv equivocadamente ♦ vt ser injusto con; **you are ~ to do it** haces mal en hacerlo; **you are ~ about that, you've got it ~** en eso estás equivocado; **to be in the ~** no tener razón, tener la culpa; **what's ~?** ¿qué pasa?; **to go ~** (person) equivocarse; (plan) salir mal; (machine) estropearse □ **wrongly** adv mal, incorrectamente; (by mistake) por error □ **wrong number** n (TEL): **you've got the wrong number** se ha equivocado de número

rote [rəut] pt of **write**

rung [rʌŋ] pt, pp of **wring**

WW n abbr (= World Wide Web) WWW

X, x

L abbr = **extra large**

mas ['eksməs] n abbr = **Christmas**

-ray ['eksreɪ] n radiografía ♦ vt adiografiar, sacar radiografías de

ylophone ['zaɪləfəun] n xilófono

Y, y

acht [jɒt] n yate m □ **yachting** n (sport) balandrismo

ard [jɑːd] n patio; (measure) yarda □ **yard sale** (US) n venta de objetos sados (en el jardín de una casa articular)

arn [jɑːn] n hilo; (tale) cuento, historia

awn [jɔːn] n bostezo ♦ vi bostezar

d. abbr (= yard) yda

eah [jɛə] (inf) adv sí

year [jɪə] n año; **to be 8 years old** tener 8 años; **an eight-~-old child** un niño de ocho años (de edad) □ **yearly** adj anual ♦ adv anualmente, cada año

yearn [jəːn] vi: **to ~ for sth** añorar algo, suspirar por algo

yeast [jiːst] n levadura

yell [jel] n grito, alarido ♦ vi gritar

yellow ['jeləu] adj amarillo □ **Yellow Pages®** npl páginas fpl amarillas

yes [jes] adv sí ♦ n sí m; **to say/answer ~** decir/contestar que sí

yesterday ['jestədɪ] adv ayer ♦ n ayer m; **~ morning/evening** ayer por la mañana/tarde; **all day ~** todo el día de ayer

yet [jet] adv ya; (negative) todavía ♦ conj sin embargo, a pesar de todo; **it is not finished ~** todavía no está acabado; **the best ~** el/la mejor hasta ahora; **as ~** hasta ahora, todavía

yew [juː] n tejo

Yiddish ['jɪdɪʃ] n yiddish m

yield [jiːld] n (AGR) cosecha; (COMM) rendimiento ♦ vt ceder; (results) producir, dar; (profit) rendir ♦ vi rendirse, ceder; (US AUT) ceder el paso

yob(bo) ['jɒb(bəu)] n (BRIT inf) gamberro

yoga ['jəugə] n yoga m

yog(h)ourt ['jəugət] n yogur m

yog(h)urt ['jəugət] n = **yog(h)ourt**

yolk [jəuk] n yema (de huevo)

---

you

KEYWORD

[juː] pron

1 (subject: familiar) tú; (pl) vosotros(-as) (SP), ustedes (LAm); (polite) usted; (pl) ustedes; **you are very kind** eres/es etc muy amable; **you Spanish enjoy your food** a vosotros (or ustedes) los españoles os (or les) gusta la comida; **you and I will go** iremos tú y yo

2 (object: direct: familiar) te; (pl) os

(SP), les (LAm); (polite) le; (pl) les; (f) la; (pl) las; **I know you** te/le etc conozco
3 (object: indirect: familiar) te; (pl) os (SP), les (LAm); (polite) le; (pl) les; **I gave the letter to you yesterday** te/os etc di la carta ayer
4 (stressed): **I told you to do it** te dije a ti que lo hicieras, es a ti a quien dije que lo hicieras; see also **3, 5**
5 (after prep: NB: con +ti = contigo: familiar) ti; (pl) vosotros(-as) (SP), ustedes (LAm); (: polite) usted; (pl) ustedes; **it's for you** es para ti/vosotros etc
6 (comparisons: familiar) tú; (pl) vosotros(-as) (SP), ustedes (LAm); (: polite) usted; (pl) ustedes; **she's younger than you** es más joven que tú/vosotros etc
7 (impersonal one): **fresh air does you good** el aire puro (te) hace bien; **you never know** nunca se sabe; **you can't do that!** ¡eso no se hace!

you'd [ju:d] n = **you had**; **you would**

you'll [ju:l] n = **you will**; **you shall**

young [jʌŋ] adj joven ♦ npl (of animal) cría; (people): **the** ~ los jóvenes, la juventud ❑ **youngster** n joven mf

your [jɔːʳ] adj tu; (pl) vuestro; (formal) su; see also **my**

you're [juaʳ] = **you are**

yours [jɔːz] pron tuyo (pl), vuestro, (formal) suyo; see also **faithfully**; **mine**[1]; **sincerely**

yourself [jɔːˈself] pron tú mismo; (complement) te; (after prep) ti (mismo); (formal) usted mismo; (: complement) se; (: after prep) sí (mismo) ❑ **yourselves** pl pron vosotros

mismos; (after prep) vosotros (mismos); (formal) ustedes (mismos); (: complement) se; (: after prep) sí mismos see also **oneself**

youth [pl ju:ðz] n juventud f; (young man) joven m ❑ **youth club** n club m juvenil ❑ **youthful** adj juvenil ❑ **youth hostel** n albergue m de juventud

you've [ju:v] = **you have**

Z, z

zeal [zi:l] n celo, entusiasmo

zebra [ˈzi:brə] n cebra ❑ **zebra crossing** (BRIT) n paso de peatones

zero [ˈzɪərəu] n cero

zest [zest] n ánimo, vivacidad f; (of orange) piel f

zigzag [ˈzɪɡzæɡ] n zigzag m ♦ vi zigzaguear, hacer eses

Zimbabwe [zɪmˈbɑ:bwɪ] n Zimbabwe

zinc [zɪŋk] n cinc m, zinc m

zip [zɪp] n (also: ~ **fastener, zipper** (US) cremallera (SP), cierre m (LAm), zíper n (MEX, CAm) ♦ vt (also: ~ **up**) cerrar la cremallera de ❑ **zip code** (US) n código postal ❑ **zipper** (US) n cremallera

zit [zɪt] n grano

zodiac [ˈzəudɪæk] n zodíaco

zone [zəun] n zona

zoo [zu:] n (jardín m) zoo m

zoology [zuˈɒlədʒɪ] n zoología

zoom [zu:m] vi: **to ~ past** pasar zumbando ❑ **zoom lens** n zoom m

zucchini [zu:ˈki:nɪ] (US) n(pl) calabacín(ines) m(pl)

Phrasefinder

Guía del viajero

TOPICS

TEMAS

TOPICS
TEMAS

MEETING PEOPLE
CONOCER A GENTE

Hello!	¡Buenos días!
Good evening!	¡Buenas tardes!
Good night!	¡Buenas noches!
Goodbye!	¡Adiós!
What's your name?	¿Cómo se llama usted?
My name is …	Me llamo …
This is …	Le presento a …
my wife.	mi mujer.
my husband.	mi marido.
my partner.	mi pareja.
Where are you from?	¿De dónde es usted?
I come from …	Soy de …
How are you?	¿Cómo está usted?
Fine, thanks.	Bien, gracias.
And you?	¿Y usted?
Do you speak English?	¿Habla usted inglés?
I don't understand Spanish.	No entiendo el español.
Thanks very much!	¡Muchas gracias!

Asking the Way	¿Cómo ir hasta …?
Where is the nearest …?	¿Dónde está el/la … más próximo(-a)?
How do I get there?	¿Cómo voy hasta allí?
How do I get to …?	¿Cómo voy hasta el/la …?
Is it far?	¿Está muy lejos?
How far is it to there?	¿Qué distancia hay hasta allí?
Is this the right way to …?	¿Es éste el camino correcto para ir al/a la/a …?
I'm lost.	Me he perdido.
Can you show me on the map?	¿Me lo puede señalar en el mapa?
Which signs should I follow?	¿Qué indicadores tengo que seguir?
You have to turn round.	Tiene que dar la vuelta.
Go straight on.	Siga todo recto.
Turn left/right.	Tuerza a la izquierda/a la derecha.
Take the second street on the left/right.	Tome la segunda calle a la izquierda/a la derecha.

Car Hire	Alquiler de coches
I want to hire …	Quisiera alquilar …
a car.	un coche.
a moped.	una motocicleta.
a motorbike.	una moto.
A small car, please.	Un coche pequeño, por favor.
An automatic, please.	Un coche con cambio automático, por favor.

GETTING AROUND
TRASLADOS

How much is it for …?	¿Cuánto cuesta por …?
one day	*un día*
a week	*una semana*
I'd like to leave the car in …	Quisiera entregar el coche en …
Is there a kilometre charge?	¿Hay que pagar kilometraje?
How much is the kilometre charge?	¿Cuánto hay que pagar por kilómetro?
What is included in the price?	¿Qué se incluye en el precio?
I'd like to arrange …	Quisiera contratar …
collision damage waiver.	*un seguro con limitación de responsabilidad.*
personal accident insurance.	*un seguro de ocupates.*
I'd like a child seat for a …-year-old child.	Quisiera un asiento infantil para un niño de … años.
Please show me the controls.	¿Puede explicarme las funciones de los interruptores?
What do I do if I have an accident/if I break down?	¿Qué debo hacer en caso de accidente/de avería?

Breakdowns / Averías

My car has broken down.	Tengo una avería.
Call the breakdown service, please.	Por favor, llame al servicio de auxilio en carretera.
I'm a member of a rescue service.	Soy socio(-a) de un club del automóvil.
I'm on my own.	Estoy solo(-a).
I have children in the car.	Llevo niños conmigo.

TRASLADOS

Can you tow me to the next garage, please?	Por favor, remólqueme hasta el taller más próximo.
Where is the next garage?	¿Dónde está el taller más próximo?
... is broken.	... está roto.
The exhaust	El escape
The gearbox	El cambio
The windscreen	El parabrisas
... are not working.	... no funcionan.
The brakes	Los frenos
The headlights	Las luces
The windscreen wipers	Los limpiaparabrisas
The battery is flat.	La batería está descargada.
The car won't start.	El motor no arranca.
The engine is overheating.	El motor se recalienta.
The oil warning light won't go off.	El piloto del aceite no se apaga.
The oil/petrol tank is leaking.	El cárter de aceite/ el depósito de combustible tiene una fuga.
I have a flat tyre.	He tenido un pinchazo.
Can you repair it?	¿Puede repararlo?
When will the car be ready?	¿Cuándo estará listo el coche?
Do you have the parts for ...?	¿Tienen recambios para ...?
The car is still under warranty.	El coche aún tiene garantía.

Parking	Aparcamiento
Can I park here?	¿Puedo aparcar aquí?
How long can I park here?	¿Cuánto tiempo puedo dejar aparcado el coche aquí?

Do I need to buy a (car-parking) ticket?	¿Tengo que sacar un ticket de estacionamiento?
Where is the ticket machine?	¿Dónde está el expendedor de tickets de estacionamiento?
The ticket machine isn't working.	El expendedor de tickets de estacionamiento no funciona.
Where do I pay the fine?	¿Dónde puedo pagar la multa?

Petrol Station — Gasolinera

Where is the nearest petrol station?	¿Dónde está la gasolinera más próxima?
Fill it up, please.	Lleno, por favor.
30 euros' worth of ..., please.	30 euros de ...
diesel	diesel.
(unleaded) economy petrol	gasolina normal.
premium unleaded	súper.
Pump number ... please.	Número ..., por favor.
Please check ...	Por favor, compruebe ...
the tyre pressure.	la presión de los neumáticos.
the oil.	el aceite.
the water.	el agua.
A token for the car wash, please.	Deme una ficha para el túnel de lavado.

Accident — Accidentes

Please call ...	Por favor, llame ...
the police.	a la policía.
the emergency doctor.	al médico de urgencia.
Here are my insurance details.	Éstos son los datos de mi seguro.

TRASLADOS

Give me your insurance details, please.	Por favor, deme los datos de su seguro.
Can you be a witness for me?	¿Puede ser usted mi testigo?
You were driving too fast.	Usted conducía muy rápido.
It wasn't your right of way.	Usted no tenía preferencia.

Travelling by Car

Viajando en coche

What's the best route to …?	¿Cuál es el mejor camino para ir a …?
Where can I pay the toll?	¿Dónde puedo pagar el peaje?
I'd like a motorway tax sticker …	Quisiera un indicativo de pago de peaje …
for a week.	*para una semana.*
for a month.	*para un mes.*
for a year.	*para un año.*
Do you have a road map of this area?	¿Tiene un mapa de carreteras de esta zona?

Cycling

En bicicleta

Is there a cycle map of this area?	¿Hay mapas de esta zona con carril-bici?
Where is the cycle path to …?	¿Dónde está el carril-bici para ir a …?
How far is it now to …?	¿Cuánto queda para llegar a …?
Can I keep my bike here?	¿Puedo dejar aquí mi bicicleta?
Please lock my bike in a secure place.	Por favor, deje la bicicleta con cadena en un lugar seguro.
My bike has been stolen.	Me han robado la bicicleta.
Where is the nearest bike repair shop?	¿Dónde hay por aquí un taller de bicicletas?

GETTING AROUND
TRASLADOS

The frame is twisted.	El cuadro de la bicicleta se ha torcido.
The brake/gears aren't working.	El freno/el cambio de marchas no funciona.
The chain is broken.	La cadena se ha roto.
I've got a flat tyre.	He tenido un pinchazo.
I need a puncture repair kit.	Necesito una caja de parches.

Train | Ferrocarril

A single to …, please.	Un billete sencillo para …, por favor.
I would like to travel first/second class.	Me gustaría viajar en primera/segunda clase.
Two returns to …, please.	Dos billetes de ida y vuelta para …, por favor.
Is there a reduction …?	¿Hay descuento …?
for students	*para estudiantes*
for pensioners	*para pensionistas*
for children	*para niños*
with this pass	*con este carnet*
I'd like to reserve a seat on the train to … please.	Una reserva para el tren que va a …, por favor.
Non smoking/smoking, please.	No fumadores/fumadores, por favor.
Facing the front, please.	Mirando hacia adelante, por favor.
I want to book a couchette/a berth to …	Quisiera reservar una litera/coche-cama para …
When is the next train to …?	¿Cuándo sale el próximo tren para …?

Is there a supplement to pay?	¿Tengo que pagar suplemento?
Do I need to change?	¿Hay que hacer transbordo?
Where do I change?	¿Dónde tengo que hacer transbordo?
Will my connecting train wait?	¿El tren de enlace esperará?
Is this the train for ...?	¿Es éste el tren que va a ...?
Excuse me, that's my seat.	Perdone, éste es mi asiento.
I have a reservation.	Tengo una reserva.
Is this seat free?	¿Está libre este asiento?
Please let me know when we get to ...	¿Por favor, avíseme cuando lleguemos a ...?
Where is the buffet car?	¿Dónde está el coche restaurante?
Where is coach number ...?	¿Cuál es el vagón número ...?

Ferry	Transbordador
Is there a ferry to ...?	¿Sale algún transbordador para ...?
When is the next ferry to ...?	¿Cuándo sale el próximo transbordador para ...?
When is the first/last ferry to ...?	¿Cuándo sale el primer/último transbordador para ...?
How much is ...?	¿Cuánto cuesta ...?
a single	el billete sencillo
a return	el billete de ida y vuelta
How much is it for a car/camper with ... people?	¿Cuánto cuesta transportar el coche/coche caravana con ... personas?

GETTING AROUND
TRASLADOS

Where does the boat leave from?	¿De dónde zarpa el barco?
How long does the crossing take?	¿Cuánto dura la travesía?
Do they serve food on board?	¿Sirven comida en el barco?
Where is ...?	¿Dónde está ...?
the restaurant	el restaurante
the bar	el bar
the duty-free shop	la tienda de duty-free
How do I get to the car deck?	¿Cómo llego a la cubierta donde están los coches?
Where is cabin number ...?	¿Dónde está la cabina número ...?
Do you have anything for seasickness?	¿Tienen algo para el mareo?

Plane
Avión

Where is the luggage for the flight from ...?	¿Dónde está el equipaje procedente de...?
Where can I change some money?	¿Dónde puedo cambiar dinero?
How do I get to ... from here?	¿Cómo se va desde aquí a ...?
Where is ...?	¿Dónde está ...?
the taxi rank	la parada de taxis
the bus stop	la parada del bus
the information office	la oficina de información
I'd like to speak to a representative of British Airways.	Quisiera hablar con un representante de British Airways.
My luggage hasn't arrived.	Mi equipaje no ha llegado.

TRASLADOS

Can you page …?	¿Puede llamar por el altavoz a …?
Where do I check in for the flight to …?	¿Dónde hay que facturar para el vuelo a …?
Which gate for the flight to …?	¿Cuál es la puerta de embarque del vuelo para …?
When is the latest I can check in …?	¿Hasta qué hora como máximo me puede facturar?
When does boarding begin?	¿Cuándo es el embarque?
Window/aisle, please.	Ventanilla/pasillo, por favor.
I've lost my boarding pass/ my ticket.	He perdido la tarjeta de embarque/el billete.
I'd like to change/cancel my flight.	Quisiera cambiar la reserva de vuelo/anular la reserva.

Local Public Transport	Transporte público de cercanías
How do I get to …?	¿Cómo se llega al/a la/hasta …?
Which number goes to …?	¿Qué línea va hasta …?
Where is the nearest …?	¿Dónde está la próxima …?
bus stop	parada del bus
tram stop	parada de tranvía
underground station	estación de metro
suburban railway station	estación de cercanías
Where is the bus station?	¿Dónde está la estación de autobuses?
A ticket, please.	Un billete, por favor.
To …	A …
For … zones.	Para … zonas.
Is there a reduction …?	¿Hay descuento …?
for students	para estudiantes

GETTING AROUND
TRASLADOS

for pensioners	*para pensionistas*
for children	*para niños*
for the unemployed	*para desempleados*
with this card	*con este carnet*
Do you have multi-journey tickets/day tickets?	¿Hay tarjetas multiviaje/ billetes para todo un día?
How does the (ticket) machine work?	¿Cómo funciona la máquina (de billetes)?
Do you have a map of the rail network?	¿Tiene un plano de la red de trenes?
Please tell me when to get off.	¿Puede decirme cuándo tengo que bajar?
What is the next stop?	¿Cuál es la próxima parada?
Can I get past, please?	¿Me deja pasar?

Taxi — Taxi

Where can I get a taxi?	¿Dónde puedo coger un taxi?
Call me a taxi, please.	¿Puede llamar a un taxi?
Please order me a taxi for ... o'clock.	Por favor, pídame un taxi para las ...
To the airport/station, please.	Al aeropuerto/a la estación, por favor.
To the ... hotel, please.	Al hotel ..., por favor.
To this address, please.	A esta dirección, por favor.
I'm in a hurry.	Tengo mucha prisa.
How much is it?	¿Cuánto cuesta el trayecto?
I need a receipt.	Necesito un recibo.
I don't have anything smaller.	No tengo moneda más pequeña.
Keep the change.	Quédese con el cambio.
Stop here, please.	Pare aquí, por favor.

Camping

Camping

Is there a campsite here?	¿Hay un camping por aquí?
We'd like a site for ...	Quisiéramos un lugar para ...
a tent.	una tienda de campaña.
a camper van.	un coche caravana.
a caravan.	una caravana.
We'd like to stay one night/ ... nights.	Queremos quedarnos una noche/... noches.
How much is it per night?	¿Cuánto es por noche?
Where are ...?	¿Dónde están ...?
the toilets	los lavabos
the showers	las duchas
the dustbins	los contenedores de basura
Where is ...?	¿Dónde está ...?
the shop	la tienda
the site office	la oficina de administración
the restaurant	el restaurante
Can we camp here overnight?	¿Podemos acampar aquí esta noche?
Can we park our camper van/caravan here overnight?	¿Podemos aparcar aquí esta noche el coche caravana/la caravana?

Self-Catering

Vivienda para las vacaciones

Where do we get the key for the apartment/house?	¿Dónde nos dan la llave para el piso/la casa?
Which is the key for this door?	¿Qué llave es la de esta puerta?
Do we have to pay extra for electricity/gas?	¿Hay que pagar aparte la luz/el gas?

ACCOMMODATION
ALOJAMIENTO

Where are the fuses?	¿Dónde están los fusibles?
Where is the electricity meter?	¿Dónde está el contador de la luz?
Where is the gas meter?	¿Dónde está el contador del gas?
How does … work?	¿Cómo funciona …?
the washing maching	*la lavadora*
the cooker	*la cocina*
the heating	*la calefacción*
the water heater	*el calentador de agua*
Please show us how this works.	¿Puede mostrar cómo funciona, por favor?
Whom do I contact if there are any problems?	¿Con quién debo hablar si hubiera algún problema?
We need …	Necesitamos …
a second key.	*otra copia de la llave.*
more sheets.	*más sábanas.*
more crockery.	*más vajilla.*
The gas has run out.	Ya no queda gas.
There is no electricity.	No hay corriente.
Where do we hand in the key when we're leaving?	¿Dónde hay que entregar la llave cuando nos vayamos?
Do we have to clean the apartment/the house before we leave?	¿Hay que limpiar el piso/la casa antes de marcharnos?

Hotel

Hotel

Do you have a … for tonight?	¿Tienen una … para esta noche?
single room	*habitación individual*

ALOJAMIENTO

double room	*habitación doble*
room for ... people	*habitación para ... personas*
with bath	con baño
with shower	con ducha
I want to stay for one night/ ... nights.	Quisiera pasar una noche/ ... noches.
I booked a room in the name of ...	Tengo reservada una habitación a nombre de ...
I'd like another room.	Quisiera otra habitación.
What time is breakfast?	¿Cuándo sirven el desayuno?
Where is breakfast served?	¿Dónde sirven el desayuno?
Can I have breakfast in my room?	¿Podrían traerme el desayuno a la habitación?
Where is ...?	¿Dónde está ...?
the restaurant	*el restaurante*
the bar	*el bar*
the gym	*el gimnasio*
the swimming pool	*la piscina*
Put that in the safe, please.	Por favor, póngalo en la caja fuerte.
I'd like an alarm call for tomorrow morning at ...	Por favor, despiértenme mañana a las ...
I'd like to get these things washed/cleaned.	¿Puede lavarme/limpiarme esto?
Please bring me ...	Por favor, tráigame ...
... doesn't work.	... no funciona.
The key, please.	La llave, por favor.
Room number ...	Número de habitación ...
Are there any messages for me?	¿Hay mensajes para mí?
Please prepare the bill.	Por favor, prepare la cuenta.

SHOPPING
DE COMPRAS

I'm looking for ...	Estoy buscando ...
I'd like ...	Quisiera ...
Do you have ...?	¿Tienen ...?
Can you show me ..., please?	¿Podría mostrarme ...?
Where is the nearest shop which sells ...?	¿Dónde hay por aquí una tienda de ...?
photographic equipment	*fotografía*
shoes	*zapatos*
souvenirs	*recuerdos*
Do you have this ...?	¿Lo tiene ...?
in another size	*en otra talla*
in another colour	*en otro color*
I take size ...	Mi talla es la ...
What shoe size are you?	¿Qué número calza?
I'm a size 5½.	Calzo un cuarenta.
I'll take it.	Me lo quedo.
Do you have anything else?	¿Tienen alguna otra cosa distinta?
That's too expensive.	Es demasiado caro.
I'm just looking.	Sólo estaba mirando.
Do you take ...?	¿Aceptan ...?
credit cards	*tarjetas de crédito*
eurocheques	*eurocheques*

Food Shopping
Alimentos

Where is the nearest ...?	¿Dónde hay por aquí cerca ...?
supermarket	*un supermercado*
baker's	*una panadería*
butcher's	*una carnicería*
greengrocer's	*una frutería y verdulería*

SHOPPING
DE COMPRAS

Where can you buy groceries?	¿Dónde se puede comprar comida?
Where is the market?	¿Dónde está el mercado?
When is the market on?	¿Cuándo hay mercado?
a kilo of ...	un kilo de ...
a pound of ...	medio kilo de ...
200 grams of ...	doscientos gramos de ...
... slices of ...	... lonchas de ...
a litre of ...	un litro de ...
a bottle of ...	una botella de ...
a packet of ...	un paquete de ...

Post Office
Correos

Where is the nearest post office?	¿Dónde queda la oficina de Correos más cercana?
When does the post office open?	¿Cuándo abre Correos?
Where can I buy stamps?	¿Dónde puedo comprar sellos?
I'd like ... stamps for postcards/letters to Britain/the United States.	Quisiera ... sellos para postales/cartas a Gran Bretaña/Estados Unidos.
I'd like to post/send ...	Quisiera entregar ...
this letter.	*esta carta.*
this small packet.	*este pequeño paquete.*
this parcel.	*este paquete.*
By airmail/express mail/ registered mail.	Por avión/por correo urgente/ certificado.
I'd like to send a telegram.	Quisiera mandar un telegrama.
Here is the text.	Aquí tiene el texto.

SHOPPING
DE COMPRAS

Is there any mail for me?	¿Tengo correo?
Where is the nearest postbox?	¿Dónde hay un buzón de correos por aquí cerca?

Photos and Videos
Vídeo y fotografía

A colour film/slide film, please.	Un carrete en color/un carrete para diapositivas, por favor.
With twenty-four/thirty-six exposures.	De veinticuatro/treinta y seis fotos.
Can I have a tape for this video camera, please?	Quisiera una cinta para esta cámara.
Can I have batteries for this camera, please?	Quisiera pilas para esta cámara, por favor.
The camera is sticking.	La cámara se atasca.
Can you take the film out, please.	Por favor, saque el carrete.
Can you develop this film, please?	Quisiera revelar este carrete.
I'd like the photos …	Las fotos las quiero …
matt.	*en mate.*
glossy.	*en brillo.*
ten by fifteen centimetres.	*en formato de diez por quince.*
When will the photos be ready?	¿Cuándo puedo pasar a recoger las fotos?
How much do the photos cost?	¿Cuánto cuesta el revelado?
Are you allowed to take photos here?	¿Aquí se pueden sacar fotos?
Could you take a photo of us, please?	¿Podría sacarnos una foto?

Sightseeing

Visitas turísticas

Where is the tourist office?	¿Dónde está la oficina de turismo?
Do you have any leaflets about …?	¿Tienen folletos sobre …?
What sights can you visit here?	¿Qué se puede visitar aquí?
Are there any sightseeing tours of the town?	¿Se organizan visitas por la ciudad?
When is … open?	¿Cuándo está abierto(-a) …?
the museum	*el museo*
the church	*la iglesia*
the castle	*el palacio*
How much does it cost to get in?	¿Cuánto cuesta la entrada?
Are there any reductions …?	¿Hay descuento …?
for students	*para estudiantes*
for children	*para niños*
for pensioners	*para pensionistas*
for the unemployed	*para desempleados*
Is there a guided tour in English?	¿Hay alguna visita guiada en inglés?
I'd like a catalogue.	Quisiera un catálogo.
Can I take photos here?	¿Puedo sacar fotos?
Can I film here?	¿Puedo filmar?

Entertainment

Ocio

What is there to do here?	¿Qué se puede hacer por aquí?
Do you have a list of events?	¿Tiene una guía de ocio?

LEISURE
OCIO

Where can we ...?	¿Dónde se puede ...?
go dancing	*bailar*
hear live music	*escuchar música en directo*
Where is there ...?	¿Dónde hay ... ?
a nice bar	*un buen bar*
a good club	*una buena discoteca*
What's on tonight ...?	¿Qué dan esta noche ...?
at the cinema	*en el cine*
at the theatre	*en el teatro*
at the opera	*en la ópera*
at the concert hall	*en la sala de conciertos*
Where can I buy tickets	¿Dónde puedo comprar
for ...?	entradas para ...?
the theatre	*el teatro*
the concert	*el concierto*
the opera	*la ópera*
the ballet	*el ballet*
How much is it to get in?	¿Cuánto cuesta la entrada?
I'd like a ticket/... tickets	Quisiera una entrada/...
for ...	entradas para ...
Are there any reductions	¿Hay descuento para ...?
for ...?	
children	*niños*
pensioners	*pensionistas*
students	*estudiantes*
the unemployed	*desempleados*

At the Beach	**En la playa**
Can you swim here/in this lake?	¿Se puede uno bañar aquí/en este lago?
Where is the nearest quiet beach?	¿Dónde hay una playa tranquila por aquí cerca?

OCIO

How deep is the water?	¿Qué profundidad tiene el agua?
What is the water temperature?	¿Qué temperatura tiene el agua?
Are there currents?	¿Hay corrientes?
Is it safe to swim here?	¿Se puede nadar aquí sin peligro?
Is there a lifeguard?	¿Hay socorrista?
Where can you ...?	¿Dónde se puede ... por aquí?
go surfing	hacer surf
go waterskiing	practicar esquí acuático
go diving	bucear
go paragliding	hacer parapente
I'd like to hire ...	Quisiera alquilar ...
a beach chair.	un sillón de playa.
a deckchair.	una tumbona.
a sunshade.	una sombrilla.
a surfboard.	una tabla de surf.
a jet-ski.	una moto acuática.
a rowing boat.	un bote de remos.
a pedal boat.	un patín a pedales.

Sport — Deporte

Where can we ...?	¿Dónde se puede ...?
play tennis/golf	jugar a tenis/golf
go swimming	ir a nadar
go riding	montar a caballo
go fishing	ir a pescar
go rowing	hacer remo
How much is it per hour?	¿Cuánto cuesta la hora?
Where can I book a court?	¿Dónde puedo reservar una pista?

LEISURE
OCIO

Where can I hire rackets?	¿Dónde puedo alquilar raquetas de tenis?
Where can I hire a rowing boat/a pedal boat?	¿Dónde puedo alquilar un bote de remos/un patín a pedales?
Do you need a fishing permit?	¿Se necesita un permiso de pesca?
Where will I get a fishing permit?	¿Dónde me pueden dar un permiso de pesca?
Which sporting events can we go to?	¿Qué actividades deportivas se pueden ver por aquí?
I'd like to see …	Quisiera ver …
a football match.	*un partido de fútbol.*
a horse race.	*carreras de caballos.*

Skiing
Esquí

Where can I hire skiing equipment?	¿Dónde puedo alquilar un equipo de esquí?
I'd like to hire …	Quisiera alquilar …
downhill skis.	*unos esquís (de descenso).*
cross-country skis.	*unos esquís de fondo.*
ski boots.	*unas botas de esquí.*
ski poles.	*unos bastones de esquí.*
Can you tighten my bindings, please?	¿Podría ajustarme la fijación, por favor?
Where can I buy a ski pass?	¿Dónde puedo comprar el forfait?
I'd like a ski pass …	¿Quisiera un forfait …
for a day.	*para un día.*

for five days.	*para cinco días.*
for a week.	*para una semana.*
How much is a ski pass?	*¿Cuánto cuesta el forfait?*
When does the first/last chair-lift leave?	*¿Cuándo sale el primer/el último telesilla?*
Do you have a map of the ski runs?	*¿Tiene un mapa de las pistas?*
Where are the beginners' slopes?	*¿Dónde están las pistas para principiantes?*
How difficult is this slope?	*¿Cuál es la dificultad de esta pista?*
Is there a ski school?	*¿Hay una escuela de esquí?*
Where is the nearest mountain rescue service post?	*¿Dónde se encuentra la unidad más próxima de servicio de salvamento?*
Where is the nearest mountain hut?	*¿Dónde se encuentra el refugio más próximo?*
What's the weather forecast?	*¿Cuál es el pronóstico del tiempo?*
What is the snow like?	*¿Cómo es el estado de la nieve?*
Is there a danger of avalanches?	*¿Hay peligro de aludes?*

FOOD AND DRINK
COMIDA Y BEBIDA

A table for … people, please.
Una mesa para … personas, por favor.

The … please.
Por favor, …
menu
    la carta.
wine list
    la carta de vinos.

What do you recommend?
¿Qué me recomienda?

Do you have …?
¿Sirven …?
any vegetarian dishes
    platos vegetarianos
children's portions
    raciones para niños

Does that contain …?
¿Tiene esto …?
peanuts
    cacahuetes
alcohol
    alcohol

Can you bring (more) … please?
Por favor, traiga (más) …

I'll have …
Para mí …

The bill, please.
La cuenta, por favor.

All together, please.
Cóbrelo todo junto.

Separate bills, please.
Haga cuentas separadas, por favor.

Keep the change.
Quédese con el cambio.

I didn't order this.
Yo no he pedido esto.

The bill is wrong.
La cuenta está mal.

The food is cold/too salty.
La comida está fría/demasiado salada.

Where can I make a phone call?	¿Dónde puedo hacer una llamada por aquí cerca?
Where is the nearest card phone?	¿Dónde hay un teléfono de tarjetas cerca de aquí?
Where is the nearest coin box?	¿Dónde hay un teléfono de monedas cerca de aquí?
I'd like a twenty-five euro phone card.	Quisiera una tarjeta de teléfono de veinticinco euros.
I'd like some coins for the phone, please.	Necesito monedas para llamar por teléfono.
I'd like to make a reverse charge call.	Quisiera hacer una llamada a cobro revertido.
Hello.	Hola.
This is …	Soy …
Who's speaking, please?	¿Con quién hablo?
Can I speak to Mr/Ms …, please?	¿Puedo hablar con el señor/la señora …?
Extension …, please.	Por favor, póngame con el número …
I'll phone back later.	Volveré a llamar más tarde.
Can you text me your answer?	¿Puede contestame con mensaje de móvil?
Where can I charge my mobile phone?	¿Dónde puedo cargar la batería del móvil?
I need a new battery.	Necesito una batería nueva.
Where can I buy a top-up card?	¿Dónde venden tarjetas para móviles?
I can't get a network.	No hay cobertura.

PRACTICALITIES
DATOS PRÁCTICOS

Passport/Customs | Pasaporte/Aduana

Here is … — Aquí tiene …
my passport. — *mi pasaporte.*
my identity card. — *mi documento de identidad.*
my driving licence. — *mi permiso de conducir.*
my green card. — *mi carta verde.*
Here are my vehicle documents. — Aquí tiene la documentación de mi vehículo.
The children are on this passport. — Los niños están incluidos en este pasaporte.
Do I have to pay duty on this? — ¿Tengo que declararlo?
This is … — Esto es …
a present. — *un regalo.*
a sample. — *una muestra.*
This is for my own personal use. — Es para consumo propio.
I'm on my way to … — Estoy de paso para ir a …

At the bank | En el banco

Where can I change money? — ¿Dónde puedo cambiar dinero?
Is there a bank/bureau de change here? — ¿Hay por aquí un banco/una casa de cambio?
When is the bank/bureau de change open? — ¿Cuándo está abierto el banco/abierta la casa de cambio?
I'd like … euros. — Quisiera … euros.
I'd like to cash these traveller's cheques/eurocheques. — Quisiera cobrar estos cheques de viaje/eurocheques.

DATOS PRÁCTICOS

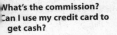

What's the commission?	¿Cuánto cobran de comisión?
Can I use my credit card to get cash?	¿Puedo sacar dinero en efectivo con mi tarjeta de crédito?
Where is the nearest cash machine?	¿Dónde hay por aquí un cajero automático?
The cash machine swallowed my card.	El cajero automático no me ha devuelto la tarjeta.
Can you give me some change, please.	Deme cambio en monedas, por favor.

Repairs / Reparaciones

Where can I get this repaired?	¿Dónde pueden repararme esto?
Can you repair ...?	¿Puede reparar ...?
these shoes	*estos zapatos*
this watch	*este reloj*
this jacket	*esta chaqueta*
Is it worth repairing?	¿Vale la pena repararlo?
How much will the repairs cost?	¿Cuánto cuesta la reparación?
Where can I have my shoes reheeled?	¿Dónde me pueden poner tacones nuevos?
When will it be ready?	¿Cuándo estará listo?
Can you do it straight away?	¿Puede hacerlo ahora mismo?

Emergency Services / Servicios de urgencia

Help!	¡Socorro!
Fire!	¡Fuego!
Please call ...	Por favor, llame a ...
the emergency doctor.	*un médico de urgencia.*

PRACTICALITIES
DATOS PRÁCTICOS

the fire brigade.	los bomberos.
the police.	la policía.
I need to make an urgent phone call.	Tengo que hacer una llamada urgente.
I need an interpreter.	Necesito un intérprete.
Where is the police station?	¿Dónde está la comisaría?
Where is the nearest hospital?	¿Dónde está el hospital más cercano?
I want to report a theft.	Quisiera denunciar un robo.
.... has been stolen.	Han robado …
There's been an accident.	Ha habido un accidente.
There are … people injured.	Hay … heridos.
My location is …	Estoy en …
I've been …	Me han …
robbed.	robado.
attacked.	atracado.
raped.	violado.
I'd like to phone my embassy.	Quisiera hablar con mi embajada.

SALUD

Pharmacy

Farmacia

Where is the nearest pharmacy?
¿Dónde hay por aquí una farmacia?

Which pharmacy provides emergency service?
¿Qué farmacia está de guardia?

I'd like something for …
Quisiera algo para …

  diarrhoea.
  la diarrea.

  a temperature.
  la fiebre.

  travel sickness.
  el mareo.

  a headache.
  el dolor de cabeza.

  a cold.
  el resfriado.

I'd like …
Quisiera …

  plasters.
  tiritas.

  a bandage.
  un vendaje.

  some paracetamol.
  paracetamol.

I can't take …
Soy alérgico(-a) a la …

  aspirin.
  aspirina.

  penicillin.
  penicilina.

Is is safe to give to children?
¿Pueden tomarlo los niños?

How should I take it?
¿Cómo tengo que tomarlo?

At the Doctor's

En la consulta médica

I need a doctor.
Necesito que me atienda un médico.

Where is casualty?
¿Dónde está Urgencias?

I have a pain here.
Me duele aquí.

I feel …
Tengo …

  hot.
  mucho calor.

  cold.
  frío.

I feel sick.
Me siento mal.

I feel dizzy.
Tengo mareos.

HEALTH
SALUD

I'm allergic to ...	Tengo alergia a ...
I am ...	Yo ...
pregnant.	*estoy embarazada.*
diabetic.	*soy diabético(-a).*
HIV-positive.	*soy seropositivo(-a).*
I'm on this medication.	Estoy tomando este medicamento.
My blood group is ...	Mi grupo sanguíneo es ...

At the Hospital — En el hospital

Which ward is ... in?	¿En qué unidad está ...?
When are visiting hours?	¿Cuándo son las horas de visita?
I'd like to speak to ...	Quisiera hablar con ...
a doctor.	*un médico.*
a nurse.	*una enfermera.*
When will I be discharged?	¿Cuándo me van a dar de alta?

At the Dentist's — En el dentista

I need a dentist.	Tengo que ir al dentista.
This tooth hurts.	Me duele este diente.
One of my fillings has fallen out.	Se me ha caído un empaste.
I have an abscess.	Tengo un absceso.
I want/don't want an injection for the pain.	Quiero/no quiero que me ponga una inyección para calmar el dolor.
Can you repair my dentures?	¿Me puede reparar la dentadura?
I need a receipt for the insurance.	Necesito un recibo para mi seguro.

Business Travel

'd like to arrange a meeting with …	Quisiera concertar hora para una reunión con …
have an appointment with Mr/Ms …	Tengo una cita con el señor/la señora …
Here is my card.	Aquí tiene mi tarjeta.
work for …	Trabajo para …
How do I get to your office?	¿Cómo se llega a su despacho?
need an interpreter.	Necesito un intérprete.
Can you copy that for me, please?	Por favor, hágame una copia de eso.
May I use …?	¿Puedo usar …?
your phone	*su teléfono*
your computer	*su ordenador*

Viajes de negocios

Disabled Travellers

Is it possible to visit … with a wheelchair?	¿La visita a … es posible también para personas en silla de ruedas?
Where is the wheelchair-accessible entrance?	¿Por dónde se puede entrar con la silla de ruedas?
Is your hotel accessible to wheelchairs?	¿Tiene su hotel acceso para minusválidos?
I need a room …	Necesito una habitación …
on the ground floor.	*en la planta baja.*
with wheelchair access.	*con acceso para minusuálidos.*
Do you have a lift for wheelchairs?	¿Tienen ascensor para minusválidos?
Do you have wheelchairs?	¿Tienen sillas de ruedas?
Where is the disabled toilet?	¿Dónde está el lavabo para minusválidos?

Minusválidos

TRAVELLERS
VIAJEROS

Can you help me get on/off please?	¿Podría ayudarme a subir/bajar, por favor?
A tyre has burst.	Se ha reventado un neumático
The battery is flat.	La batería está descargada.
The wheels lock.	Las ruedas se bloquean.

Travelling with children — Viajando con niños

Are children allowed in too?	¿Pueden entrar niños?
Is there a reduction for children?	¿Hay descuento para niños?
Do you have children's portions?	¿Sirven raciones para niños?
Do you have …?	¿Tienen …?
a high chair	*una sillita*
a cot	*una cama infantil*
a child's seat	*un asiento infantil*
a baby's changing table	*una mesa para cambiar al bebé*
Where can I change the baby?	¿Dónde puedo cambiar al bebé?
Where can I breast-feed the baby?	¿Dónde puedo dar el pecho al niño?
Can you warm this up, please?	¿Puede calentarlo, por favor?
What is there for children to do?	¿Qué pueden hacer aquí los niños?
Is there a child-minding service?	¿Hay aquí un servicio de guardería?
My son/daughter is ill.	Mi hijo/mi hija está enfermo(-a).